THE YEAR'S WORK IN
MODERN LANGUAGE
STUDIES

THE
YEAR'S WORK IN
MODERN LANGUAGE
STUDIES

GENERAL EDITOR
STEPHEN PARKINSON

ASSISTANT EDITOR
LISA BARBER

SECTION EDITORS

LATIN, ROMANCE LINGUISTICS, FRENCH, OCCITAN, SPANISH, CATALAN, PORTUGUESE, GALICIAN, LATIN AMERICAN, SLAVONIC
STEPHEN PARKINSON, M.A., PH.D.
*Lecturer in
Portuguese Language and Linguistics,
University of Oxford*

ITALIAN, ROMANIAN, RHETO-ROMANCE
JOHN M. A. LINDON, M.A.
*Professor of Italian Studies,
University College London*

CELTIC
DAVID A. THORNE, M.A., PH.D.
*Professor of Welsh,
University of Wales, Lampeter*

GERMANIC
DAVID A. WELLS, M.A., PH.D.
*Professor of German,
Birkbeck College, University of London*

VOLUME 62
2000

MANEY PUBLISHING
for the
MODERN HUMANITIES RESEARCH ASSOCIATION
2001

The Year's Work in Modern Language Studies may be ordered from the Subscriptions Department, Maney Publishing, Hudson Road, Leeds LS9 7DL, UK.

ISBN 1 902653 64 5

ISSN 0084–4152

Produced in Great Britain by
MANEY PUBLISHING
HUDSON ROAD   LEEDS LS9 7DL   UK

CONTENTS

4   GERMANIC LANGUAGES

PREFACE

This volume surveys work, published in 2000, unless otherwise stated, in the fields of Romance, Celtic, Germanic, and Slavonic languages and literatures. An asterisk before the title of a book or article indicates that the item in question has not been seen by the contributor.

The attention of users is drawn to the lists of abbreviations at the end of the volume, which are also available on-line on the MHRA's WWW site (http://www.mhra.org.uk/YWMLS).

Many authors, editors and publishers supply review copies and offprints of their publications. To these we and our contributors are grateful, and we would invite others to follow their example, especially in the case of work issuing from unusual, unexpected, or inaccessible sources of publication. We would ask that, whenever possible, items for review be sent directly to the appropriate contributor; where no obvious recipient can be identified, as in the case of books or journal issues relating to a number of fields, the item should be sent to one of the editors, who will distribute the contents accordingly.

The compilation of a contribution to the volume, especially in the field of the major languages and periods of literature, is a substantial research task requiring wide-ranging and specialized knowledge of the subject besides a huge reading effort accompanied by the constant exercise of critical judgement. We are deeply grateful to the authors who have devoted significant amounts of increasingly precious research time to this enterprise. The measure of their task is indicated by the number of sections for which the editors have failed to find contributors; we encourage approaches from potential contributors or groups of contributors for future volumes.

The completion of this volume would not have been possible without the contribution of Lisa Barber, Assistant Editor and compiler of the Index. Thanks are also due to the other institutions and individuals who have contributed in one way or another to the making of the volume. They include, in particular, Polly Jones, the secretarial and administrative staff of the Faculty of Modern Languages of Oxford University, and our printers, Maney Publishing, particularly Liz Rosindale and Caitlin Meadows, whose expertise and patience have as ever ensured the smooth progress of this complex operation.

15 December 2001   S.R.P., J.M.A.L., D.A.T., D.A.W.

1

LATIN

I. MEDIEVAL LATIN

By Christopher J. McDonough, *Professor of Classics, University of Toronto*

1. General

R. B. C. Huygens, *Ars edendi. A Practical Introduction to Editing Medieval Latin Texts*, Turnhout, Brepols, 80 pp., offers advice to the uninitiated by discussing selected practical problems, illustrated with examples drawn from his own editions. S. Coates, 'Venantius Fortunatus and the image of episcopal authority in late antique and early Merovingian Gaul', *EHR*, 115:1109–37, examines Venantius's treatment in prose and verse of the three elements which shaped his idealized image of the episcopate and suggests that its creation was intended to serve as a model to be imitated. D. Howlett, '*Medius* as "middle" and "mean"', *Peritia*, 13, 1999:93–126, culls from numerous Insular Latin works examples of a tradition of verbal play on the two senses of *medius*. Id., 'Dicuill on the islands of the North', *ib.*, 127–34, offers an edition, translation and analysis of the *Liber de mensura orbis* vii. 6–15, based on Paris, BN, lat. 4806, pointing out the verbal and arithmetical features that help readers to understand why Dicuill corrected the accounts of ancient geographers. Id., 'A Brittonic curriculum: a British child's ABC 123', *CMCS*, 40:21–26, arranges a paragraph from the *Vita Sancti Samsonis*, marked with the clausular and cursus rhythms, in order to illustrate the habit of reckoning letters as numbers. H. McKee, 'Scribes and glosses from Dark Age Wales: the Cambridge Juvencus manuscript', *ib.*, 39:1–22, discusses the paleography of Cambridge, UL, Ff. 4. 42 (1285), and dates the MS to *c.* 900, before she concludes that the Latin glosses are copies and that the exegetical glosses mainly derive from the *Liber questionum de Evangeliis*, a 'Hiberno-Latin' work. P. G. Schmidt, 'Perché tanti anonimi nel medioevo? Il problema della personalità dell'autore nella filologia mediolatina', *FilM*, 6–7:1–8, argues that medieval writers tended towards anonymity because of the limited public for which they wrote and a wish to avoid charges of vanity in a Christian culture that prized the Pauline admonition *scientia inflat*. G. Orlandi, 'Metrica e statistica linguistica come strumenti nel metodo attributivo', *ib.*, 9–31, discusses the merits and limitations of stylometrics as a method for settling questions of disputed attribution, before he applies the chi-squared test to analyse various metrical features of numerous poems, problems in Shakespeare, and the letters of Abelard and Heloise. L. B. Mortensen, 'The diffusion of Roman histories in the Middle Ages. A list of Orosius, Eutropius, Paulus Diaconus, and Landolfus Sagax manuscripts', *ib.*, 101–200, characterizes Orosius's *Historiae* and Eutropius's *Breviarium*, and their continuators, before he sets out the statistical evidence for the diffusion of all four works and a description of the MSS containing full and excerpted texts. F. Cavazza, 'L'elenco, finora conosciuto, dei *Florilegia* medioevali, che comprendono anche *Excerpta Gelliana* o solo *Excerpta Gelliana*', *Maia*, 52:99–126, offers detailed descriptions of MSS containing excerpts from Aulus Gellius alone (Florilegium φ, Florilegium Gallicum, Florilegium Angelicum), and three others in which extracts from the *Noctes Atticae* are combined with other works (Florilegium Valerium-Gellianum, Florilegium morale Oxoniense, and an anonymous patristic collection). G. de Nie, 'Images as "mysteries": the shape of the invisible', *JMLat*, 9, 1999:78–90, investigates Gregory's presentation of events as visual units, in which he presented the meaning of contemporary events as image-patterns of divine action, while J. M. Pizarro, 'Images in texts: the shape of the visible in Gregory of Tours', *ib.*, 91–101, treats the visual component as a textual element and an ideological tool. C. Reinle, 'Exempla weiblicher Stärke? Zu den Ausprägungen des mittelalterlichen Amazonenbildes', *HZ*, 270:1–38, traces the portrayal of the Amazons as sexually aggressive figures, starting from the accounts of Justin and Orosius, before exploring how they became positive models in works such as Boccaccio's *De mulieribus claris*. R. Jakobi, 'Weiteres zu den "Thebais"–Argumenta', *Hermes*, 128:250–52, emends an unmetrical verse (Arg. Stat. *Theb.* III. 3), edits anew the Hexasticha based on Florence, Bibl. Laur., Plut. 91 inf. 10, and prints the Monosticha for *Theb.* V from Paris, BN, lat. 8051. Frank T. Coulson and Bruno Roy, *Incipitarium Ovidianum. A Finding Guide for Texts Related to the Study of Ovid in the Middle Ages and Renaissance*, Turnhout, Brepols, 208 pp., list almost 500 incipits relating to the introductions (*accessus*), lives (*uitae*), and prose summaries (*summae memoriales*) to Ovid's works. C. Brugnoli, 'La *lectura Senecae* dal tardo-antico al XIII secolo', *GIF*, 52:225–47, documents the evidence for knowledge of almost all of Seneca's works, except for the philosophical treatises. M. Stansbury, 'Early-medieval biblical commentaries, their writers and readers', *FmSt*, 33, 1999:49–82, studies the commentaries of Cassiodorus, Gregory the Great, Bede, and Hrabanus Maurus historically, with emphasis on the social context of their production. M. R. Herren, 'The earliest European study of Graeco-Roman mythology (A. D. 600–900)', *Acta Classica*, 34–35, 1999:25–49, identifies the schools, scholars, texts, and learned commentaries that served as the foundation for the expanded interest in pagan mythology in the 11th and 12th centuries.

2. ANGLO-SAXON ENGLAND

B. Ward-Perkins, 'Why did the Anglo-Saxons not become more British?', *EHR*, 115:513–33, argues on the basis of texts from the 6th to the 10th c. that the difference between the two ethnic groups was no mere literary construct, but was a lived reality that was based on cultural and linguistic choices rather than on putative racial differences. J. M. McCulloh, 'Did Cynewulf use a martyrology? Reconsidering the sources of *The Fates of the Apostles*', *ASE*, 29:67–83, rejects as possible sources a pseudo-Bedan compilation and the continental writers Florus, Ado, and Usuard and hypothesizes that a passionary remains the most likely source for most of the details and the treatment of the apostles as a distinct hagiographical group. A. Lutz, 'Aethelweard's *Chronicon* and Old English poetry', *ib.*, 177–214, suggests that the stylistic peculiarities of Aethelweard's Latinity are illuminated when set against subject-matter that recalls OE heroic poetry, especially themes involving fighting, seafaring, loyalty to one's lord, and exile. M. Griffith, 'Aelfric's preface to Genesis: genre, rhetoric and the origins of the *ars dictaminis*', *ib.*, 215–34, argues that the preface is generically mixed, being formed from the conventions of the five-part letter and of the preface.

3. THE CAROLINGIAN AND OTTONIAN PERIOD

G. Cremascoli, 'Das Mittelalter als Erneuerung der Kultur', *MJ*, 35:1–10, discusses the impulses which animated the so-called Carolingian and 12th-c. renaissances, and in the case of the latter emphasizes the expansion of theological consciousness and the desire to restore the contents of the Christian message, while J. Schwind, 'Eine Nachlese zum Thema Dichterreminiszenzen im "Aachener (Paderborner) Karlsepos"', *ib.*, 11–19, discovers new intertexts from classical (Vergil, Ovid, Statius, Lucan, Grattius) and Christian poets (Juvencus, Prudentius, Sedulius, Venantius Fortunatus, Aldhelm, Alcuin). R. McKitterick, 'The illusion of royal power in the Carolingian Annals', *EHR*, 115:1–20, re-assesses the validity of the claims in Frankish narratives, especially the *Annales Regni Francorum* and Einhard's *Vita Karoli*, in relation to the attribution of royal power, and argues that modern understanding of it stems from the creation of the victors, designed to convince contemporaries and posterity of the inevitability of Carolingian and Frankish success. H. F. Petersen, '*The Phoenix*: the art of literary recycling', *NMi*, 101:375–86, examines the use of variation and rhetorical figures to assess the purpose and abilities of the poet. M. Giovìni, 'Gli *inculta poemata* di Paolo Diacono: Prudenzio e Virgilio in una dichiarazione di "poetica del dissidio"', *Maia*, 52:85–97, uncovers contextually significant phrases from Prudentius's *Peristephanon* embedded in the elegy *Angustae vitae fugiunt*, attributed to Paul. F. Bertini, 'Problemi di attribuzione e di datazione del *Waltharius*', *FilM*, 6–7:63–77, isolates the important stages in the debate regarding the poem's authorship, date and provenance, before he discusses three recent editions and translations. F. M. Casaretto, 'Ermenrico di Ellwangen, *Epistola ad Grimaldum abbatem*, MS München, Bayerische Staatsbibliothek, Oefeleana 147: Fisionomia di un "descriptus"', *ib.*, 201–14, sets out the significant errors and other evidence in order to prove that the 16th- or 17th-c. MS is a copy of St. Gall, Stiftsbibliothek MS 265. V. von Büren and J. Meyers, 'Quelques poèmes inédits de Sedulius Scottus dans le *Codex Vaticanus Latinus* 4493', *ALMA*, 57, 1999:53–110, publish from an exemplar copied in the scriptorium of archbishop Hincmar in Reims six moralizing poems that show striking similarities with Sedulian thought and language. O. Szerwiniack, 'Liste provisoire des manuscrits contenant les poèmes "Hanc libam" et "Lumine sidereo" de Jean Scot Érigène', *Scriptorium*, 54:87–91, accounts for the wide diffusion of two poems that John attached to his translation of the works of pseudo-Dionysus. D. Daintree, '*Non omnis moriar*: the re-emergence of the Horatian lyrical tradition in the early Middle Ages', *Latomus*, 59:889–902, argues that poems written in the sapphic metre by Walafrid Strabo, Sedulius Scottus, and Notker were directly influenced by Horace and not by an intermediary. T. Gärtner, 'Der Selbstmord des Judas Iskariot bei Milo von St. Amand', *Eranos*, 98:123–27, points out intertexts from Sedulius and Arator in Milo's *De sobrietate* 1.788–93 and suggests that 1.791 was an alternative composition written by Milo that was later interpolated maladroitly by a copyist. W. Maaz, 'Das Lachen der Frauen vor des Teufels Küche. Ridicula bei Hrotsvit von Gandersheim', pp. 133–54 of *Komische Gegenwelten. Lachen und Literatur in Mittelalter und Früher Neuzeit*, ed. Werner Röcke and Helga Neumann, Paderborn, 1999, 304 pp., uses three hagiographical passages, in which the holy and the sexual intersect in a comic way, in order to exemplify the thesis of Peter L. Berger, a modern theoretician of laughter. F. S. D'Imperio, 'Le glosse ai quattro Vangeli nel ms. St. Gallen, Stiftsbibliothek 50', *SM*, 41:549–90, identifies Jerome, Bede, and Alcuin as the sources of the glosses, examines the glossator's use of them in the episode concerning the blind men of Jericho, and suggests Notker Balbulus as a possible author.

4. THE ELEVENTH CENTURY

C. Bottiglieri, 'Il paradiso perduto del monaco Folcuino. Un poema dell' XI secolo proveniente da Saint-Amand', *SM*, 41:863–89, edits a poetic dialogue in hexameters, entitled *Adam deiecti de deliciis paradisi*, which is uniquely transmitted in Valenciennes, Bibliothèque municipale, MS 298, fols 123–132, with an introduction that discusses the author's identity and dates the poem by analysing its use of rhyme. W. D. McCready, 'Abbot Desiderius, Alberic of Montecassino, and the writing of the *Dialogi de miraculis sancti Benedicti*', *JMLat*, 9, 1999:102–20, concludes after re-examining the paleographical evidence and style that Alberic was not a co-author of the *Dialogues*. L. Lazzari, 'Elementi di un "curriculum" composito in uso ad Abingdon nella prima metà dell' XI secolo (ms. Antwerpen, Museum Plantin-Moretus M. 16. 2 + London, B.L., Add. 32246)', *SM*, 41:85–117, connects the grammatical contents of the MS with two others redacted at Abingdon (Antwerp, Museum Plantin-Moretus M. 16. 8 (olim 190) and Brussels, Bibliothèque Royale 1650 (olim 1520)) before she points out that the texts in the three MSS are arranged to provide its users with a coherent education consistent with the cultural and educational directions introduced by monastic reform. C. Ratkowitsch, 'Der Eupolemius — Ein Epos aus dem Jahre 1096?', *FilM*, 6–7:215–71, discusses improvements to the text, the influence of Prudentius's *Psychomachia* and Avitus, and the priority of the *Sermones* of Sextus Amarcius, in the course of arguing that the poem was composed in early 1096 as propaganda for the First Crusade. Id., 'Der "Liber decem capitulorum" des Marbod von Rennes: ein *simplex et unum*', *MJ*, 34.2, 1999: 85–117 and 35:21–48, uncovers symmetrically paired poems supporting the formal structure of the collection, a feature she attributes to Marbod, not a copyist, before demonstrating that Marbod's programme of Christian instruction is infused with the moral philosophy of Horace's *Epistles* and *Satires*. K. Bate, 'Les normands et la littérature latine au début du nouveau millénium', *CCMe*, 43:233–41, argues that Warner of Rouen's *Moriuht* and the two poems *Jezabel* and *Semiramis* reflect the Scandinavian passion for rhetoric and repartée combined with the indigenous musical culture. D. W. Porter, 'The earliest texts with English and French', *ASE*, 28, 1999:87–110, analyses the *Excerptiones de Prisciano* in two MSS, Antwerp, Plantin-Moretus Museum 16. 2 + London, BL, Add. 32246, and Paris, BN, nouv. acq. lat. 586, from which he reconstructs a picture of a group of Anglo-Saxon scholars producing glosses in several MSS simultaneously. P. Gatti, 'Due favole di Ademaro', *Maia*, 52:505–11, hypothesizes that Ademar inserted two fables of his own invention into a collection of prose paraphrases he made of Phaedrus's fables and compares them with the redaction of two texts found in Frankfurt am Main, Stadt- und Universitätsbibliothek, MS Praed. 60.

5. THE TWELFTH CENTURY

T. Gärtner, 'Textkritische Bemerkungen zur "ars poetica" des Gervasius de Saltu Lacteo', *SM*, 41:849–61, criticizes H. J. Gräb- ener's 1965 edition for relying on a single MS, before he demonstrates that every single variant in all three MSS must be examined if a satisfactory text is to be achieved. B. Roling, 'Der Historiker als Apologet der Weltverachtung. Die "Historia Anglorum" des Hein- rich von Huntingdon', *FmSt*, 33, 1999:125–68, argues that aspects of the history can be illuminated by classifying it within the ascetic tradition of the *De contemptu mundi*, and suggests that Boethius's *De consolatione philosophiae* helped to shape it. M. Giovini, '*Infero vim dubie*: il nichilista Serlone alle prese con uno stupro (e una nota su Pietro di Blois)', *Maia*, 52:513–32, analyses and translates Serlo's comic poem, *Quadam nocte, loco quodam cum virgine quadam*, and suggests that it contains *in nuce* an idea that Peter of Blois developed in his lyric *Grates ago Veneri*. D. R. Howlett, 'Sixes and sevens in Anglo-Latin prologues. 1. Peter of Waltham, "Remediarum conversorum" 11. Fixed forms in "Philobiblon" ', *MJ*, 35:49–70, edits Peter's Prologue from London, BL, MS Royal 7 A VII, arranged by clauses and phrases with the rhythms of the cursus marked and with an analysis of the numerical devices that fixed the text mathematically, before he offers a similar edition of the Prologue and Epilogue of the *Philobiblon* from Oxford, Bodleian Library, Digby 147, which he suggests may be the work of Robert Holcot. T. Gärtner, 'Das Urteil des Alanus ab Insulis über die "Alexandreis" des Walter von Châtillon (*Anticl.* 1 166–170) — ein übersehenes Silvenzitat im "Anticlaudian" ', *ib.*, 71–76, identifies three verbal parallels from Statius, *Silvae* 4. 7. 21–24, a text that he uses to address the problem of the relative chronology of the *Alexandreis* and the *Anticlaudianus*. A. Bisanti, 'Nota a Gualtiero Anglico, "Aesopus" 20, 10.', *ib.*, 77–80, traces the thought in the poem back to Seneca, *Consolatio ad Marciam* 9.2, before he follows its elaboration in the works of Gregory the Great, Bernard of Meung, the *Disticha Catonis*, Andreas Capellanus, and Dante. U. Kühne, 'Deutsch und Latein als Sprachen der Lyrik in den "Carmina Burana" ', *BGDSL*, 122:57–73, underlines the role of poetic transla- tion in the relationship between Latin and the vernacular as he argues in favour of viewing the bilingual poems as German songs with Latin strophes rather than as Latin poems with German insertions. *Hildeberts Prosimetrum De Querimonia und die Gedichte eines Anonymus*, ed. Peter Orth

(Untersuchungen und kritische Editionen, Wiener Studien Beiheft, 26), Vienna, 170 pp., describes and evaluates 25 MSS and previous editions, before he examines the title, dating, and formal aspects of the work. T. H. Bestul, 'The meditation on Mary Magdalene of Alexander Nequam', *JMLat*, 9, 1999:1–40, edits the biblical commentary preserved uniquely in Hereford Cathedral Library, O. 1. 2. T. Hunt, 'Vernacular glossing and clerical instruction', *ib.*, 41–45, prints English and French glosses attached to Peter Comestor's *Historia scolastica* and Honorius of Autun's *Elucidarium* from Oxford, Bodleian Library, Rawlinson C 46. M. Winterbottom, 'Notes on William of Poitiers', *ib.*, 121–30, introduces improvements in punctuation and emends almost 50 passages in the recently-edited *Gesta Guillelmi*. C. Wollin, 'Hero und Leander an der Themse. Ein unbekanntes Epigram Peters von Blois', *Sac*, 39:383–93, augments Peter's canon with a four-line poem from London, BL, Cotton Vespasian B. XIII. T. Gärtner, 'Zum mittelalterlichen Nachleben der spätantiken Genesisversifikation "Alethia" des Claudius Marius Victorius', *ib.*, 99–104, finds evidence of imitation in the *Anticlaudianus* of Alanus ab Insulis, while Id., 'Zu den klassischen und zeitgenössischen Vorbildern im "Liber ad honorem Augusti" des Petrus von Eboli', *DAEM*, 55, 1999:477–98, identifies Vergil, Ovid, Lucan, Statius, Walter of Châtillon's *Alexandreis*, and Alan of Lille's *Anticlaudianus* among the sources of a poem describing the struggle between Henry VI and Count Tancred of Lecce over Sicily. Id., 'Drei Konkjekturen zu hochmittelalterlichen Dramen', *Latomus*, 59:647–51, emends two verses from John of Garland's poem in *Parisiana poetria* ch. 7, and one in Matthew of Vendôme's *Milo*. I. Pagani, 'Il problema dell' attribuzione dell'epistolario di Abelardo ed Eloisa. Status quaestionis', *FilM*, 6–7:79–88, notes that the attempts of recent scholarship to solve the problem of authenticity have failed to generate new hypotheses, while S. R. Kramer, ' "We speak to God with our thoughts": Abelard and the implications of private communication with God', *Church History*, 69:18–40, examines Abelard's ambivalence towards female speech in the *Letters* as part of a wider examination of his theory of intention. R. Jakobi, 'Beiträge zu mittellateinischen Dichtern', *FilM*, 6–7:89–100, emends texts from Bernard Silvestris's *Mathematicus*, the 'Brutus' (a versification of Geoffrey of Monmouth's *Historia regum Britanniae* chap. 1), Brito Metricus, Balduinus Iuvenis's 'Reynardus Vulpes', and the 'Comedia Pamphile' of Dionisius. M. A. Faletra, 'Narrating the matter of Britain: Geoffrey of Monmouth and the Norman colonization of Wales', *ChRev*, 35:60–85, detects a political teleology in the history's linear, genealogical narration which was intended to support the expansion of the Norman imperium over all of Britain. F. Fontana, 'Su alcuni modelli latini di "Historia

Regum Britanniae" 137–138: Ovidio, Plauto e Virgilio', *SM*, 41:809–26, identifies in this Arthurian episode several classical models dealing with the subject of metamorphosis and doubling and argues that Geoffrey had some form of knowledge of Plautus's *Amphitryo*, a text that was known in England at the time. S. Luchitskaja, 'The image of Muhammad in Latin chronography of the twelfth and thirteenth centuries', *JMH*, 26:115–26, finds that direct contact with Islam did not modify the stereotypes of the Prophet and the idea of Islam as evil that were mediated by Byzantine chronicles, Gauthier of Compiègne's *Otia Machometi*, Siegebert of Gembloux, and Tommaso of Tuscany's *Gesta imperatorum et pontificum*. A. Cooper, 'The King's four highways: legal fiction meets fictional law', *ib.*, 351–70, traces the evolution of the English myth of the four roads, which supposedly afforded travellers unique protection, from its invention by Henry of Huntingdon to its elaboration by Geoffrey of Monmouth, and the subsequent adaptation of these ideas in legal and literary texts. T. Gärtner, 'Vier Anmerkungen zum Einleitungsgedicht von *De planctu Nature*', *FilM*, 6–7:273–78, defends, emends, and repunctuates the text. J. Grave, 'Kunsthistorisch motivierte Antikenverehrung im hohen Mittelalter? Die *Narracio de mirabilibus urbis Rome* des Magister Gregorius', *ib.*, 279–93, highlights the problems of the work's intention, its date, the matter of sources and their interrelationship, and the intended audience. A. Bisanti, 'A proposito del *De uxore cerdonis* di Iacopo da Benevento', *ib.*, 295–309, identifies parallels from classical and medieval sources, which include Ovid and Arigo of Settimello's *Elegia de diversitate Fortune*, before he notes its reception in a 15th-c. farce written by Giovan Giorgio Alione. J. P. Pettorelli, 'Vie latine d'Adam et d'Ève. La recension de Paris, BNF, lat. 3832', *ALMA*, 57, 1999:5–52, edits the complete text of a Latin translation of the middle Eastern version of the *Life* but defers the question of why the work was undertaken in Normandy in the 12th century. L. McGuinness, 'Quintilian and medieval pedagogy: the twelfth-century witness Stuttgart, Württembergische Landesbibliothek, Theol. octavo 68', *ib.*, 191–259, edits christianized excerpts from Quintilian, compiled at Zwiefalten, which were directed towards the primary education of a young child and the correct behaviour of the teacher in the classroom. D. Boquet, 'De l'enfant-Dieu à l'homme-enfant: regards sur l'enfance et la psychologie de l'adulte chez Aelred de Rievaulx (1110–1167)', *Médiévales*, 36, 1999:129–43, sifts Aelred's pastoral works for observations on the child Jesus and for autobiographical reminiscences of the author's childhood in order to construct a picture of the medieval child, before he concludes that the affective identity of the adult stems from childhood experiences. D. C. Jackman, 'Abnepos, pronepos', *NQ*, n.s.

47:14–16, mines a passage in William of Malmebury's *Gesta Regum Anglorum* to examine Medieval Latin relationship terminology. B. Munk Olsen, 'Les florilèges et les abrégés de Sénèque au moyen âge', *GIF*, 52:163–83, tracks the important role that excerpts from both the authentic and spurious works of Seneca played in the intellectual life of the period, and their place in the *Florilegium Angelicum*, *Florilegium Gallicum*, and *Florilegium Duacense*. S. Keynes, 'The cult of King Alfred the Great', *ASE*, 28, 1999:225–356, follows the development of the myth of Alfred in poetry, drama, and prose historical writings from Anglo-Saxon times up to the 17th century. C. B. Bouchard, 'The Cistercians and the *Glossa Ordinaria*', *CHR*, 86:183–92, emphasizes the scholarly contribution of the Cistercians in developing and disseminating glossed Bibles in France and England.

6. THE THIRTEENTH CENTURY

A. G. Rigg and P. Binkley, 'Two poetic debates by Henry of Avranches', *MedS*, 62:29–67, edit from London, BL, Cotton Vespasian D.5 the contests which Henry waged against John Bordo and Peter Siler and against William of Laval, while K. Bund, 'Studien zu Magister Heinrich von Avranches I. Zur künftigen Edition seiner Werke', *DAEM*, 56:127–69, includes among the prolegomena to his ambitious editorial project a detailed chronology of Henry's life and works, with sections devoted to his literary formation and social status. W. Maaz, 'Ein alliterierendes Orakel in Hs. Wien, ÖNB lat. 1625 (saec. XIII/XIV). Zu einem unbekannten Detail der Sage vom Vergilius Magus', pp. 1011–20 of *Scrinium Berolinenense*, ed. Peter Jörg Becker et al., Berlin, 1136 pp., discusses the representation of Vergil as a divinely inspired interpreter of oracles. V. Law, 'Why write a verse grammar?', *JMLat*, 9, 1999:46–76, itemizes the various ordering devices, ranging from logical structure to visual representation, which were adopted by grammarians from the 12th to the 15th c. to impose structure on the miscellaneous material. A. Grondeux, 'La révision du *Graecismus* d'Évrard de Béthune par Jean de Garland', *RHTe*, 29, 1999:317–25, documents John's direct interventions into Eberhard's text, demonstrates that the exemplar of the *Graecismus* used by William Brito was a witness that had been influenced by John's revisions, and prints examples of the interpolations from Paris, BN, lat. 14745. T. A.-P. Klein, 'Der *Nouus Esopus* des Alexander Neckam in der Tradition der spätantiken Phaedrus-Paraphrase *Romulus*', *Maia*, 52:127–51, discusses the most important representatives of the 'Romulus' adaptations, including 'Romulus Nilantinus' and the 'Anonymus Neueleti', before he edits and translates three poetic fables by Neckam: *De uulpe et catto*, *De ursa et natis*, and *De mure uxorem petente*. H. Nicholson, 'Following the path of the Lionheart: the *De ortu Walwanii* and the *Itinerarium peregrinorum et gesta regis Ricardi*', *MAe*, 69:21–33, argues that the central points in the description of the relief of Jerusalem in the prose romance, *De ortu Walwanii*, derive from an account of the journey of King Richard the Lionheart to the East contained in the *Itinerarium*, which was compiled by Richard de Templo between 1217 and 1222. K. Ubl, 'Zur Entstehung der Fürstenspiegel Engelberts von Admont (†1331)', *DAEM*, 55, 1999:499–548, addresses three problems surrounding the origin of Englebert's *De regimine principum*, identifies the author with the abbot of St Peter in Salzburg, discusses the attribution and relationships of Admont MS 608, and presents a critical edition of excerpts from the text contained in Admont MS 676. T. B. Payne, '*Aurelianis civitas*: student unrest in medieval France and a conductus by Philip the Chancellor', *Speculum*, 75:589–614, investigates the relationship between a musical work lamenting the consequences of a riot in Orléans, a sermon preached by Philip and the historical accounts, as a basis from which to consider the historical development as well as the social and intellectual settings for the so-called Notre Dame repertory. T. Haye, 'Anonymus: *Satira trenorum*', *MJ*, 34, 1999:57–83, offers a first edition of an anti-clerical poem which survives uniquely in Tours, Bibliothèque municipale 111, with an analysis of its relationship to the biblical *Threni*. M. Lynde-Recchia, 'Deux versions de la *Passio sancti Eustachii* en ancien français: la question de la forme littéraire', *NMi*, 101:5–16, examines the different narrative modalities of a verse and prose translation of an extant Latin text, before noting the former's insistence on the act of the poem's creation and the signs of orality that mark it, and the latter's attempt to appropriate the authority of the Latin original. G. Brunetti and P. Morpurgo, 'Frammenti inediti in volgare meridionale in uno manoscritto delle *Derivationes* di Gualtiero da Adcoli', *MedRom*, 23, 1999:247–76, edit from Laon, Bibliothèque municipale 449, a Latin grammatical treatise with parts in Italian, entitled *Notule* and attributed to Agnello of Gaeta, accompanied by an account of the cultural backround that produced it and an analysis of the phonetics, morphology, and syntax of the vernacular insertions. E. Freeman, 'Wonders, prodigies and marvels: unusual bodies and the fear of heresy in Ralph of Cogges-hall's *Chronicon Anglicanum*', *JMH*, 26:127–43, underlines the metaphorical function of six anecdotes dealing with the irregularities of the human body, and suggests that they serve the theme of the Christian body under assault from external sources. M. C. Miller, 'Religion makes a difference: clerical and lay cultures in the courts of

northern Italy, 1000–1300', *AHR*, 105 : 1095–1130, discusses Salimbene's chronicle as a window into clerical courtly culture, which
valued poetry and song, as part of a wider argument that understanding the differences between the two cultures affords insight into their
different conceptions of authority and assertions of power. G. L.
Potestà, 'Die Genealogia. Ein frühes Werk Joachims von Fiore und
die Anfänge seines Geschichtsbildes', *DAEM*, 56 : 55–101, identifies
and edits an early work that illuminates the genesis and development
of Joachim's conception of history.

7. THE FOURTEENTH AND FIFTEENTH CENTURIES

S. C. Macdougall, 'The surgeon and the saints: Henri de Mondeville
on divine healing', *JMH*, 26 : 253–67, examines Henri's *Chirurgia* for
the attitudes of physicians towards saints, their miracles as recorded
in literature, and the alleged healing powers of St. Eloi. A. Cornish,
'A lady asks: the gender of vulgarization in late medieval Italy', *PMLA*,
115 : 166–80, finds that the translation of classical texts into the
vernacular feminized Latin discourse and as a result complicated the
hierarchy of languages with gender. M.-J. Heijkant, ' "E ti saluto con
amore." Messaggi amorosi epistolari nella letteratura Arturiana in
Italia', *MedRom*, 23, 1999 : 277–98, assesses the influence of the *ars
dictandi* on the letters inserted into writings concerning the 'matter of
Britain', before she investigates their narrative function. A. G. Rigg,
'Propaganda of the Hundred Years War: poems on the battles of
Crecy and Durham (1346): a critical edition', *Traditio*, 54,
1999 : 169–211, edits versions of two polemical poems directed
against the Scots and the French which are contained in Oxford,
Bodleian Library, Bodley 851 and Rawlinson B. 214, and London,
BL, MS Cotton Titus A. XX. C. H. Rawski, 'Petrarch's oration in
Novara: a critical transcription of Vienna, Oesterreichische Nationalbibliothek, MS Pal. 4498, fols. 98r-104v.', *JMLat*, 9, 1999 : 148–93,
prefaces the text with a detailed stylistic analysis of Petrarch's Latin
prose, with sections on *dispositio, elocutio,* and the *cursus*. M. S. Lannutti,
' "Ars" e "scientia", "actio" e "passio". Per l'interpretazione di alcuni
passi del "De vulgari eloquentia" ', *SM*, 41 : 1–38, analyses key terms
in Dante's tract and reveals their Augustinian underpinnings. A. J.
Fletcher, 'The genesis of *The Owl and the Nightingale*: a new hypothesis',
ChRev, 34, 1999 : 1–17, proposes that Robert Holcot's *Moralitates*
reveal knowledge of the vernacular poem. M. Kensak, 'The silences
of pilgrimage: *Manciple's Tale, Paradiso, Anticlaudianus*', *ib.*, 190–206,
points to Alain of Lille's depiction of Phronesis's silence before a
triune god as a source for Chaucer. J. Finlayson, 'Petrarch, Boccaccio,
and Chaucer's *Clerk's Tale*', *SP*, 97 : 255–75, argues that Chaucer's

poem faithfully translates Petrarch's Griselda story as narrated in *Epistolae Seniles* Bk. 17, although he rejects the Petrarchan moral conclusion. P. Chiesa, 'Per un riordino della tradizione manoscritta della Relatio di Odorico da Pordenone', *FilM*, 6–7:311–50, offers a three-fold classification of the MSS as a step towards a critical edition of an important travelogue that survives in different redactions. B. Löfstedt, 'Zur "Lucula noctis" des Giovanni Dominici', *MJ*, 34, 1999:119–24, comments on the text, sources, and language of a polemic against Coluccio Salutati on the issue of the degree to which a Christian was allowed to read pagan literature. L. Wahlgren-Smith, 'Heraldry in Arcadia: the court eclogue of Johannes Opicius', *RenS*, 14:210–34, points out the fusion of classicizing language and allusions with contemporary imagery in a poetic eulogy for Henry VII, before offering a transcription of the autograph work contained in London, BL, Cotton Vespasian B. IV. L. Bernard-Pradelle, 'L'influence de la Seconde Sophistique sur la *Laudatio Florentinae urbis* de Leonardi Bruni', *Rhetorica*, 18:355–87, reveals how Bruni used his rhetorical sources to fashion an image of Florence as a powerful political and cultural city. F. J. Worstbrock, 'Imitatio in Augsburg. Zur Physiognomie des deutschen Frühhumanismus', *ZDA*, 129:187–201, edits a letter of Hermann Schedel to Siegmund Gossembrot celebrating the latter's election as mayor of Augsburg in 1458, contained in Munich, Bayerische Staatsbibliothek, Clm 224. E. Beltran, 'Lettres inédites de Louis XI rédigées par son secrétaire Pierre-Paul Senilis', *BEC*, 157, 1999:607–22, edits from Bâle, Bibliothèque universitaire E. III. 15, correspondence written in the new humanist style and influenced by Cicero which could have served as models for other occasions and other people. E. Séris, 'Galatée chez Ange Politien: une image de mémoire de la poésie antique', *BHR*, 62:591–609, contends that the figure of Galatea functions as a mnemotechnical image intended to evoke three ancient texts: Theocritus, *Idyll* 11, Ovid, *Met.* 3, and Vergil, *Eclogue* 9. J. Solana Pujalte, 'El hexámetro del *Aeneidos Liber XIII* de Maffeo Vegio y sus modelos clásicos (II)', *Latomus*, 59:652–70, enlarges his analysis of selected metrical features of the *Supplementum* to include Lucan, in addition to Vergil and Ovid's *Metamorphoses*, and finds all three to be major inspirations for Maffeo. J.-C. Cassard, 'Clovis [. . .] connais pas! Un absent de marque dans l'historiographie bretonne médiévale', *Médiévales*, 37, 1999:141–50, offers a political reason for the neglect of Clovis in the literature, arguing that historians preferred to highlight the figure of King Arthur, a Breton sovereign and Christian warrior, as a means of emphasizing Breton pre-eminence. D. Canfora, 'Il commento al *Tieste* e l'elogio di Petrarca in un'epistola "Senechiana" di Poggio Bracciolini', *GIF*, 52:249–67, discusses

Poggio's reading of 20 verses from the tragedy *Thyestes*, which led him to meditate on the solitary life and to commend the wisdom of those, including Petrarch, who choose to live lives of quietism. E. Cohen, 'The animated pain of the body', *AHR*, 105:36–68, notes the emergence of a prescriptive vocabulary of physical pain in writers of drama and poetry, and in the visual arts, as she explores expressions of pain and the relationships between theological, medical, and legal theories, prescriptions, and behavioural patterns in western Europe from the 13th to the 15th century. W-W. Ehlers, 'Liebes-, Lebens-, Ehepartner. Pontanos "Amores coniugales"', *MJ*, 35:81–99, surveys three books of elegies, written by a diplomat and prime minister, which are notable for their all-inclusive embrace of themes dealing with love, marriage, and the birth of children, an approach that stands out in the history of Latin love poetry.

NEO-LATIN

POSTPONED

2

ROMANCE LANGUAGES

I. ROMANCE LINGUISTICS

By JOHN N. GREEN, *University of Bradford*

1. ACTA, FESTSCHRIFTEN

Timely and well produced, *CILPR 22* chronicles the 1998 Brussels congress in nine thematic volumes bearing unmistakable signs of vitality and fresh perspectives; most are further discussed below. The annual American Linguistic Symposium on Romance Languages, having outgrown a single volume, now publishes parasessions separately from the main proceedings on the model of *PCLS*. Dworkin, *New Approaches*, assembles 13 papers on historical methodology from the 1999 Ann Arbor meeting, prefaced by D.'s sorrowful remarks on the state of American Romance linguistics: non-comparative, doggedly theoretical, anti-humanistic, and shorn of lexis and derivational morphology (though this collection rather belies his concerns!). *ICHL 12* contains a few Romance items, individually noted below; J. C. Smith's 'Report on the fourteenth International Conference on Historical Linguistics', *Diachronica*, 17:211–19, adumbrates better representation for the future.

La Linguistique, 36.1–2, ed. Colette Feuillard, brings to light 'Les introuvables d'André Martinet', over 30 of M.'s inaccessible writings selected by pupils and colleagues, and prefaced with a nice tribute by Michel Arrivé (9–12). Jean-Claude Chevalier's 75th birthday is marked by an interview with E. Hültenschmidt, ' "Je combinais la tradition encyclopédiste avec un tas d'idées nouvelles" ', *BGS*, 10:157–89. *RRL*, 42.5–6,1997[1999], appears as 'Hommage au Professeur Matilda Caragiu Marioțeanu', with a bibliography of her writings (317–26) and ten articles mainly on Romanian language. A double issue of *ALHisp*, 12–13, 1996–97[2000], ed. César Hernández Alonso et al., is devoted to 'Studia hispanica in honorem Germán de Granda', containing, in addition to a bibliography of G.'s copious writings (xv–xvi), 65 essays mainly on hispanic themes with due recognition for G.'s pioneering work on Afro-Romance contacts and the Spanish-lexicon creoles.

2. GENERAL ROMANCE AND LATIN

Frede Jensen, *A Comparative Study of Romance*, NY, Lang, 1999, xxvi + 446 pp., belies its enticing title, settling — after a shortish essay on sources, classification, and luminaries — into a long treatise on historical phonology which, however rigorous and well exemplified, has not advanced conceptually beyond early Menéndez Pidal. Conversely exceeding the apparent scope of its title, Ángel López García, *Cómo surgió el español. Introducción a la sintaxis histórica del español antiguo*, Madrid, Gredos, 235 pp., seeks to locate the innovatory thrust in 4th-c. syntax (exemplified in the Vulgate), followed by an 11th-c. catastrophic remorphologization, influenced by Cluniac teaching and by Basque, though likely to have happened eventually under its own momentum. Focusing on the same period, but very different in orientation, Roger Wright, *El Tratado de Cabreros (1206): Estudio sociofilológico de una reforma ortográfica* (PMHRS, 19), 130 pp., presents a diplomatic edition of both versions of the Treaty, revealing the slow progress and victory of orthographic reform and reconceptualization in 13th-c. Chancery and *fuero* documents. W. also contributes: 'The assertion of Ibero-Romance', *FMLS*, 36:230–40, an echo of Malkiel induced by anachronistic labelling of Berceo as 'Castilian', which muses on whether the split of Ibero-Romance into separate domains was inevitable or even desirable; and 'Las periodizaciones del romance hispánico (y sus desventajas)', *CILPR 22*, II, 481–84, which divides the written language (demarcated by spelling reforms) from speech, best conceived as a continuous evolutionary flow without raw edges.

So, a modicum of introspection may not be amiss. In a re-launch editorial, A. M. Badia i Margarit, ' "Romania", "Romanitas", "Romanistica" ', *ER*, 22:7–22, taking a long-term view of the discipline and its recent concentration on single-language studies, argues that comparative Romance linguistics can survive current preferences and indeed be enriched by new theoretical models and pluridisciplinarity. But G. Ernst et al., 'Une histoire des langues romanes: pourquoi et comment?', *CILPR 22*, II, 185–89, ask more provocatively what can be meant by the history of the Romance languages when someone who works on a single language can still be conventionally termed a 'Romanist' (see also B. Voigt, 'Romanistik oder romanische Fächer?', *Lusorama*, 36, 1998:78–83). Eclectic to a fault, J. Klausenburger, 'A new view of grammaticalization to replace the "cycle" ', Dworkin, *New Approaches*, 33–44, uses familiar data from the history of the Romance future to argue for unidirectional change within a morphocentric theory; while D. Wanner, 'Beyond parameters', *ib.*, 3–32, stressing the validity of written records and the process of document creation, advocates an 'immanent perspective' that does not force the data and is softer than most theoretical frameworks. Meanwhile heeding Badia's call, Klaus Gabriel, Katja Ide, Dietmar Osthus, and Claudia Polzin, **Rom@nistik im Internet. Eine praktischer Einführung in die Nutzung der neuen Medien im Rahmen der romanischen Linguistik*, Bonn, Romanistischer Vlg, 1999, 119 pp., laud the potential of on-line data, bibliographies and dictionaries.

La preistoria dell'italiano, ed. József Herman and Anna Marinetti, with Luca Mondin, Tübingen, Niemeyer, [viii +] 279 pp., assembles 14 first-rate papers from a 1998 Venice symposium, on both the early history of Latin and its later evolution into Italo-Romance. Refreshed and smoothly translated from the revised Spanish version by Roger Wright, József Herman's *Vulgar Latin*, University Park, PA, Penn State U.P., xiv + 130 pp., remains a succinct and dependable *vademecum* (*YWMLS*, 29:11). *Latín vulgar y tardío. Homenaje a Veikko Väänänen (1905–1997)*, ed. Benjamín García-Hernández, Madrid, Clásicas, xxx + 237 pp., an affectionate tribute from 15 Spanish colleagues, includes a full bibliography of V.'s writings (xix–xxx); J. Elvira on the survival of a two-case system (31–43); and J. de la Villa Polo on word order in the Vulgate (221–37). Philip Burton, *The Old Latin Gospels. A Study of their Texts and Language*, OUP, xii + 232 pp., after an exemplary philological and linguistic commentary on some 30 pre-Vulgate MSS translations of the gospels, concludes that despite the variant readings they do represent a common heritage.

In an extended review of Holtus et al., *Lexikon der romanistischen Linguistik*, II. 1 (*YWMLS*, 58:16), C. Seidl, 'Les études romanes et le latin', *VR*, 59:24–39, complains that the determinedly synchronic perspective understates — indeed denies — the true genealogical relationships. For E. Magni, the snapshot of 'L'ordine delle parole nel latino pompeiano', *AGI*, 85:3–37, owes as much to pragmatic functions like individuation, definiteness and animacy as it does to syntactic word order. H. J. Wolf, 'La romanisation de la Sardaigne', *CILPR 22*, II, 473–80, neatly crystallizes a controversy on which he ultimately declines to take sides: were there really two waves of immigration separated by 300 years resulting in a unique mix of the archaic and truly innovative? R. de Dardel, 'Un double ordre de base en protoroman', *ib.*, 123–28, claims that VSO was the oldest Romance pattern, with an early OVS variant supplanted by the more vigorous SVO. Also according to D., so widespread are the 'Composés rectionnels nominaux nom + nom en protoroman', *Probus*, 11, 1999:177–208, that **BUCCAM-CALLEM > bocacalle* must be reconstructed as a popular template for animals, plants, instruments, and place names (see also *YWMLS*, 61:15). In a partial retraction of his 1958 hypothesis, 'Le parfait fort revisité', *NMi*, 101:429–42, D. now believes that the proto-Romance mixed paradigm (AMAVI, AMASTI / HABUI, HABISTI) directly continues early spoken Latin, co-existing with the analogically levelled, but short-lived, classical perfects. So, back to attested sources, where Hannah Rosén, *Latine loqui. Trends and Directions in the Crystallization of Classical Latin*, Munich, Fink, 1999, 224 pp., pays special attention to morphosyntax and textual cohesion, seeing the evolution of early Latin to classical as a process of loss and stripping down, with expansion and innovation confined to vocabulary.

3. HISTORY OF ROMANCE LINGUISTICS

Auroux, *Geschichte*, 1, impressive in both scholarship and presentation, augurs well for later coverage of Romance; this volume hosts R. Wright, 'The study of Latin as a foreign language in the early Middle Ages' (501–10), ascribing the major roles to Donatus, Priscian and, inevitably, Alcuin. E. Pistolesi, 'L'origine del concetto di "latino volgare" negli studi romanzi', *CILPR 22*, 1, 113–20, examines the 16th-c. treatise on the history of Italian by Celso Cittadini, for whom grammar defined the boundaries of literary expression and unregulated speech, implying symbiotic archaism and continuity. L. Renzi, 'Ancora sugli umanisti italiani e la lingua rumena', *RF*, 112:1–38, concentrates on three important figures: Biondo Flavio (1392–1463), who first recognized the sociolinguistic diversity of Latin, Paolo Pompilio (1455–91), Latinist and teacher in Rome, and Martino Segono (1455–86), Bishop of Montenegro, who all agreed on the continuity of Romanian, identifying 'Vlachs' with the ancient inhabitants of Dacia. R. chides the humanists for their misplaced enthusiasm for 'discovering' new pockets of Romance speech, but is rebuked in turn by A. Varvaro, 'Le notizie di Paolo Pompilio', *ib.*, 495–99, who corroborates the late survival of Afro Romance in mountainous redoubts of Tunisia and Algeria where Christians and Berbers united in their opposition to Islam, while in the Middle East, Pompilio may simply have drawn the wrong inference from the Sephardic diaspora, which began in 1391. To add to their sins, humanists are blamed for confusing language designations by Johannes Kramer, *Die Sprachbezeichnungen 'Latinus' und 'Romanus' im Lateinischen und Romanischen*, Berlin, Schmidt, 1998, 173 pp. (see A. Schönberger in *RF*, 112:301–02).

Raija Vainio, *Latinitas and Barbarisms According to the Roman Grammarians*, Turku, Department of Classics, 1999, 180 pp., examines the effect of language attitudes on the value of terms that might be thought equivalent: correctness (*latinitas* / ἑλληνισμός) was important to both Greek and Roman grammarians, but since Latin words started out with the disadvantage of being barbarisms in Greek, Latin could tolerate no significant internal variation, whereas Greek grammarians accepted metaplasm, dialect shift, as normal (see also *YWMLS*, 61:28). R. Tesi, 'Per la storia del termine *barbarismo*', *LN*, 51:1–25, asks why a word that served sporadically as a technical term for several centuries from the Renaissance became polysemous and eventually fell into disrepute: from the early 19th c. it became too closely associated with ideas of linguistic purity and was shunned when the ideology itself fell from favour.

CILPR 22, 1, 'L'histoire de la linguistique, médiatrice de théories', groups 16 individual studies with a round table on 'La linguistique romane et son passé', presided by P. Swiggers, and a sort of past presidents' corner, in which R. Martin tackles informatics and lexicography (163–66), M. Pfister knocks out etymology (167–68) and B. Pottier umpires a ten-minute guide to semantics (169–74, 197–98). P. Swiggers, 'Les débuts de la linguistique romane comme discipline académique' (183–90), brusquely dispelling the sentimental claims of Raynouard — a literary philologist who 'respirait un comparativisme faussement historique et manquait d'une organisation grammaticale systématique' — awards the palms unhesitatingly to Diez, the true comparatist heir of Bopp, Grimm, and Rask. P. Desmet et al. trace 'Le transfert du "modèle allemand" et les débuts de la dialectologie française' (191–96), while G. Holtus surveys the trajectory of Romance linguistics, non-linear but increasingly rigorous, 'Du *Grundriß* de G. Gröber au *Lexikon der Romanistischen Linguistik*' (207–10), conceding that the *Grundriß* is not yet superseded. Overcompensating, G. Roques urges us to celebrate 'La *Revue de linguistique romane* de 1925 à 1983' (199–205), beneath whose ecru cover beat the purple hearts of scholars of flesh and blood, passions, ambitions, and intellectual vistas [*sic*]. Surely no cultural hegemony here?

E. F. K. Koerner believes that 'Ideology in 19th and 20th century study of language', *IF*, 105:1–26, has been unwisely neglected: a careful study of reactions to the *Urheimat* debate shows that linguistics has never been value-free. A 1992 lecture by Y. Malkiel(†), 'Ein Jahrhundert Amerikanischer Altromanistik', *RF*, 112:159–79 (including a contextual postscript by S. N. Dworkin stressing M.'s abiding interest in the 'first phase'), dates systematic scholarship from the PhD programme founded at Johns Hopkins by A. Marshall Elliott in the early 1880s, though there had been interest throughout the 19th c. from individual precursors, including the poet Henry Longfellow. J. Trabant, 'Geist und Kultur in der Sprachwissenschaft', *BGS*, 10:253–70, reappraises the teachings of Karl Vossler on the 50th anniversary of his death: on creativity and the elegance of language, there are some surprising parallels with Chomsky and Pinker. A.-M. Fryba-Reber, 'Karl Jaberg et la romanistique suisse', *CILPR 22*, 1, 67–73, noting that J. was held in high regard by his contemporaries, dubs him the 'federator' of Swiss linguistics in an exceptionally influential period.

I. Sluiter, 'Seven grammarians on the ablative absolute', *HistL*, 27:379–414, plots the diminishing status of a construction over 18 centuries; originally acknowledged as a seventh part of speech, even before it had an accepted name, it has all but disappeared from lexical functional grammar. Contrary to accepted wisdom, E. Casielles Suárez, 'El tratamiento del orden de palabras', *ib.*, 415–36, finds that Spanish compendious grammars of the 19th and 20th cs do have valuable insights into word order, especially topicalization and dislocation which alter the normal theme/rheme patterns. According to H. Geckeler, 'Observations historiques sur la préhistoire de l'idée du champ lexical', *CILPR 22*, 1, 75–81, G. Ipsen was probably the originator of the term that Trier launched to immediate acclaim in 1931, though as a conscious metaphor and far from precise in its application.

4. PHONOLOGY

Repetti, *Phonological Theory*, celebrating the richness of the Italian domain as a data source, contains several items of wider relevance, notably: A. Calabrese, 'The feature [Advanced Tongue Root] and vowel fronting in Romance' (59–88), positing [ATR], systematic in stressed antepenults, as the explanation for several metaphonies, including the otherwise unmotivated change of /u/ > [y]; M. Loporcaro, 'Stress stability under cliticization' (137–68), boldly claiming, on the basis of dialectal corroboration, that Romance clitics always adjoin to the lexical phonological word and form a postlexical PW with their host; and M. Maiden, 'Phonological dissimilation and clitic morphology' (169–89), distinguishing between dissimilation as a phonological event and the resolution of an unsatisfactory sequence by the substitution of an etymologically unrelated synchronic variant.

Trochees continue to limp, with A. R. Mester's analysis (*YWMLS*, 56:24) twice impugned: H. Jacobs, 'The revenge of the uneven trochee', Lahiri, *Analogy*, 333–52, asserts that a satisfactory optimality treatment of Latin main stress can be achieved by modifying M.'s non-finality constraint (needed in any event to account for Latin syncope) and recognizing uneven trochees as the outcome of interacting constraints; whereas G. Marotta, 'Sulla massimalità dei piedi trocaici', *LS*, 35:387–416, wishes to retain non-finality because it is compatible with both optimal and extrametrical approaches, though Latin feet must be redefined as minimally bimoraic and maximally trimoraic. M. Saltarelli, 'From Latin metre to Romance rhythm', *ICHL 12*, 345–60, shows how, despite the continuity of the locus of stress, systematic violation of the three-syllable window of Classical Latin led to the erosion of quantity-sensitive metre and its replacement by a new system with distinct foot properties but no opposition of heavy and light syllables.

Promising to identify the primitives that drive Romance syncope, D. Hartkemeyer, 'An OT approach to atonic vowel loss patterns in Old French and Old Spanish', Dworkin, *New Approaches*, 65–83, ends up with an almost vacuous process of vowel deletion and a set of output constraints that recall the most abstract phase of generative phonology. A simple taxonomy of changes affecting atonic vowels is offered by D. Uritescu, 'Pour une typologie des processus historiques dans les langues romanes', *CILPR 22*, II, 437–48, while B. Harmegnies and D. Poch-Olivé, 'La descripción de los sistemas fonológicos de las lenguas románicas', *ib.*, III, 193–200, corroborate the intuition that laboratory conditions elicit a very spread vocalic system that is subject to centralization in spontaneous speech. Reviewing an old problem in the light of lexical borrowing from French and Portuguese, C. Paradis and J.-F. Prunet, 'Nasal vowels as two segments', *Language*, 76:324–57, argue that second-language learners have understood the fundamental structure of nasals, which is always a biphonemic V + N sequence.

K. W. Wireback's *Role of Phonological Structure* (*YWMLS*, 59:27, 61:18) receives a long and appreciative review from A. Gather, *RF*, 112:262–73, who nonetheless questions the features used to define the mini natural classes postulated for lenition and degemination, and the adequacy of [length] to explain the propagation of the changes. Also referring to W.'s work, T. D. Cravens, 'Romance lenition', Dworkin, *New Approaches*, 47–64, uses data from Corsican and Sardinian to reconstruct a real-time intermediate stage between Castilian and Italian, where the gradual retreat of *rafforzamento sintattico*, which had originally fed gemination, helped to stabilize [p, t, k] at word boundaries. C. also contributes 'Sociolinguistic subversion of a phonological hierarchy', *Word*, 51:1–19, which draws on the *gorgia toscana* to illustrate how the direction of change predicated on natural classes can be disrupted by extrasystemic factors during a period of synchronic variability. Much earlier influences on Latin /-kt-/ are weighed by M. Mancini, 'Tra dialettologia latina e dialettologia italoromanza', *ZRP*, 116:107–40, who concludes that northern Italic, far from reinforcing gemination through assimilation, may have precipitated weakening to [ht] followed by loss of [h] and compensatory vowel lengthening in a process akin to lenition. In a further Duke-of-York gambit, C. Pensado, 'Sobre la historia del ensordecimiento final', *ER*, 22:29–57, demonstrates how, in almost all of central and western Romance except Portuguese, final consonants that had voiced in the preliterate period regularly devoiced again except before their grammatical head word; preposition + nucleus was the best conservator, other combinations varying by locality and bolstered by frequency.

5. INFLECTIONAL MORPHOLOGY

Jürgen Klausenburger, *Grammaticalization. Studies in Latin and Romance Morphosyntax*, Amsterdam, Benjamins, xiii + 183 pp., heavily influenced by Mayerthaler's iconic morphology, Bauer's right-branching syntax (*YWMLS*, 57:22), and Keller's invisible hands, interprets changes in Romance nominal and verbal inflection as tokens of irreversible grammaticalization. Three linked articles by R. Lazzeroni explore neglected aspects of Latin nominal inflection: 'I neutri latini in -*s*', *SSL*, 37, 1997–99[2000]:63–71, on the competitive productivity that led to the split between older *génus/géneris* and newer *témpus/ témporis*; 'Dall'antroponimo al paradigma', *AGI*, 84, 1999[2000]: 207–14, on the mysterious late declension in -*a/-anis*, probably inspired by Greek proper names and extending to kinship terms; and 'Genere grammaticale e riorganizzazione dei paradigmi', *AGI*, 85:232–37, on the causes and odd residues of the collapse of the fourth declension. Impatient of theoretical naivety, N. La Fauci, 'Strutture funzionali nell'evoluzione della flessione nominale dal latino a varietà romanze', *CILPR 22*, II, 147–56, envisages a centuries-long symbiosis of synthetic and newer analytic forms.

H. Rosén, 'Preclassical and Classical Latin precursors of Romance verb-stem suppletion', *IF*, 105:270–83, throws fascinating new light on *esse/stare*, which maintained a lexical opposition for centuries, and *ire/ambulare*, which from the earliest records had been suppletive by tense and function. D. Embick, 'Features, syntax, and categories in the Latin perfect', *LI*, 31:185–230, proposes a theoretical explanation in 'movement to T' for the alignment of the perfective active with synthetic forms and of the perfect passive and deponent with analytic. Refurbishing older ideas, not least Malkiel's favoured 'lead morpheme', M. Maiden, 'Di un cambiamento intramorfologico', *AGI*, 85:137–71, ascribes stress allomorphy in the strong perfects to a regularizing reanalysis induced from within (for more on mechanisms, see M.'s 'Il "morfema segno" nella storia della morfologia romanza', *CILPR 22*, VI, 337–44). Exercised by the *intaglio*, T. Arnavielle, 'Évolution comparée du "participe gérondif" dans les langues romanes', *ib.*, II, 7–13, wonders whether sheer complexity of functions might lead to morphological invariance. As to the outcome, S. Reinheimer and L. Tasmowski, 'Systématisation de la flexion verbale romane', *ib.*, VI, 437–48, accurately encapsulate the current state of play.

6. MORPHOSYNTAX AND TYPOLOGY

Tense and Aspect in the Languages of Europe, ed. Östen Dahl (Eurotyp 20–6), Berlin, Mouton de Gruyter, xiv + 846 pp., impressive in breadth and clarity, after an opening section on general issues and typology, privileges future time reference, the perfect, and the progressive. Among many valuable contributions, we should single out: O. Dahl, 'The tense-aspect systems of European languages' (3–25), on gram-types, clines, and the five resulting taxonomies; P. M. Bertinetto and D. Delfitto, 'Aspect vs. actionality' (189–225), advocating a three-way distinction into temporal reference, speaker perspective, and type of event (= *Aktionsart*); R. Thieroff, 'On the areal distribution of tense-aspect categories in Europe' (265–305), showing a strong correlation between stable perfects and progressives; M. Squartini and P. M. Bertinetto, 'The simple and compound past in Romance languages' (403–39), on the drift from purely perfectal to aorist functions, revealing a north-south divide from Spanish to the vernaculars of France and north Italy; and P. M. Bertinetto, 'The progressive in Romance' (559–604), elaborating a five-stage gradient from locativity to imperfectivity, noting *en passant* the much greater frequency of 'go' than 'come' as a semiauxiliary, and the general incompatibility of progressive and stative forms.

Confirming verbs of motion and locality as a rich source of grammatical tools, B. Laca, 'Auxiliarisation et copularisation dans les langues romanes', *RLiR*, 64:427–43, still contests the Coseriu-Dik hypothesis of linked processes; there are diverse outcomes and no inevitable link. A. Giacalone Ramat, 'On some grammaticalization patterns for auxiliaries', *ICHL 12*, 125–54, adduces evidence of a cline from full verb to tense-aspect marker, noting that the *Aktionsart* of the full verb does carry forward into its semiauxiliary functions — witness the incompatibility of *andare/venire* with pure states. (More detail can be found in valuable studies by G. Brianti, 'Diacronia delle perifrasi aspettuali dell'italiano', *LN*, 51:35–52, 97–119; and by M. Squartini, 'Voice clashing with aspect: the case of Italian passives', *RivL*, 11, 1999[2000]:341–65.) A. Merlan, 'Sobre as chamadas "perífrases verbais paratácticas" do tipo "pegar e + V₂" nas línguas românicas', *RFLUP*, 16, 1999:159–205, infers from abundant comparative data that the structure is very old and that the auxiliary, though abstractivized, does retain some independence. A. Sorace,

'Gradients in auxiliary selection', *Language*, 76:859–90, proposes that
intransitives choose an auxiliary from a continuum ranging from
polar BE 'telic change of location', to polar HAVE 'non-motional
controlled process'. Applying concepts of control, animacy and
telicity to 'Patterns of "active" syntax in Late Latin pleonastic
reflexives', *ICHL 12*, 35–55, M. Cennamo finds that *sibi* reflexives
associate with change of state and location, while *se* reflexives occur
originally with anticausatives, intransitives and mental processes,
only later extending to verbs denoting other activities.

Paradigm meaning is bravely tackled by E. Almeida, 'L'imparfait
français et l'imperfeito portugais, prétendus "temps du passé"',
CILPR 22, VI, 7–17, making use of valency and actanciality; and by
F. Ferreres Masplá and A. Olivares Pardo, 'Pour un conditionnel
monosémique en français et en espagnol', *ib.*, 175–85.
U. Wandruszka, 'Über die Bedeutung des romanischen Konjunktivs
und die Geburt des Nebensatzes', *ZRP*, 116:56–71, devises ingenious
collocational tests to prove that the Romance indicative-subjunctive
opposition distinguishes usefully between dependent verbs in general
and those subject to specific syntactic government, with the subjunctive exporting superfluous assertivity to the matrix clause. S. Kiss,
'Fonctions et structures du subjonctif: leur évolution du latin tardif
aux langues romanes', *CILPR 22*, II, 235–39, advocates more work
on relative clauses; initial examination of hypotheticals and deontics
reveals parallels in subjunctive usage between subordinate and main
clauses, but the late Latin system was in turmoil and tense relations in
particular were being sorted out. Profiling types of constructions and
types of theoretical explanation, a pellucid diptych by D. Bentley, 'I
costrutti condizionali in siciliano' and 'Semantica e sintassi nello
sviluppo dei costrutti condizionali', *RevR*, 35:3–20 and 163–76,
subdivides hypotheticals into potential and irrealis, which gives a
better account of tense relations, and traces unidirectional and cyclic
patterns of change to the interaction of pragmatic and syntactic
pressures (otherwise known as Traugott and her struggle against the
Penthouse Principle).

Sharp of focus and excellent in presentation, *Le Passif. Actes du
colloque international, Institut d'Études Romanes, Université de Copenhague, du
5 au 7 mars 1998*, ed. Lene Schøsler (ER, 45), Copenhagen, Museum
Tusculanum, 333 pp., assembles a score of papers on morphological,
syntactic and discoursal aspects of the passive, mainly illustrated from
French but with much wider resonance, including: D. Gaatone, 'Pour
une définition restrictive du passif en français' (15–22), M. Manoliu-
Manea, 'Une hypothèse cognitive sur les formes latines en *-r*'
(99–115), B. Lamiroy, 'Sur certains rapports entre le passif pronominal et le datif' (135–54), and M. Wilmet, 'Du passif à la

topicalisation ou pour changer de sujet' (265–75). Well exemplified from the *Peregrinatio, Mulomedicina* and Pompeius, M. Russo, 'Origine protoromanza dell'intransitivizzazione e dell'inversione soggetto-verbo', *ZRP*, 116:377–417, relates word order changes to the subjects of monoargumental verbs; VS was a frequent variant in text types reflecting speech because it favoured topic continuity.

Inspired, unusually, by the potential of interlanguage, B. Moretti, 'Le varietà di apprendimento e il potenziale delle lingue', *RF*, 112:453–69, draws parallels between the prepositional accusative and partitive structures, one of whose functions is to prevent the incorporation of weak objects into the verb. R. Sornicola, 'Processi di convergenza nella formazione di un tipo sintattico: la genesi ibrida dell'oggetto preposizionale', *CILPR 22*, II, 419–27, sees today's relative homogeneity as the product of long struggle among three original types and three phases of propagation. Nonetheless, in 'L'accusatif prépositionnel et l'accusatif non prépositionnel en espagnol', *ib.*, VI, 129–38, N. Delbecque prefers to highlight the range of constructions and idioms with *a* and without, seeking semantic causes of the alternation. Other comparative items from the Brussels congress include: C. Ditvall, '*Tout* français — *tot* roumain: leur place parmi les déterminants', *ib.*, 155–62; and A.-M. Spanoghe, 'L'article indéfini comme marque du blocage de l'inaliénabilité dans quelques langues romanes', *ib.*, 481–90. Reverting, finally, to explanations of change, M. Davies, 'Syntactic diffusion in Spanish and Portuguese infinitival complements', Dworkin, *New Approaches*, 109–27, contrasts the two dominant models of historical linguistics, finding parameter switching ill suited to the complementation structure of *ver, fazer*, and *parecer*, where changes were neither sudden nor simultaneous, and are better treated as grammaticalization and diffusion.

7. FORMAL SYNTAX AND SEMANTICS

Rewarding for its rigour and extensive comparative data, Guido Mensching's minimalist account of *Infinitive Constructions with Specified Subjects. A Syntactic Analysis of the Romance Languages*, OUP, xiv + 267 pp., makes sense of diverse patterns, especially of non-nominative subjects, claiming that 'case properties of functional categories are parametrized with respect to finiteness'. J. Rafel, 'From complementizer to preposition', *Probus*, 12:67–91, has the neat idea that pseudorelatives are small clauses in which the complementizer functions as an aspectual marker, just like the preposition introducing many infinitival expressions. Johan Rooryck, *Configurations of Sentential Complementation. Perspectives from Romance Languages*, London–NY, Routledge, xviii + 265 pp., reworks and supplements his minimalist accounts of raising, control, clitic climbing, and unified marking of relatives, interrogatives, and complementizers.

Documenting the spread and diversity of 'Los predicados impersonales relativos en las lenguas románicas', *RELing*, 29, 1999:317–55, G. Rigau groups together as existential deontics host verbs like *hay que* and apparently impersonal verbs like *urgir* and *tocar*, which nevertheless must mark personal reference with a dative clitic. J. Gutiérrez-Rexach, 'The formal semantics of clitic doubling', *JSem*, 16, 1999[2000]:315–80, after testing for interactions with existentials, negatives, and interrogatives, proposes a daunting treatment within Generalized Quantifier Theory, requiring only a few additional constraints. G. Matos, 'Across-the-board clitic placement in Romance languages', *Probus*, 12:229–59, decides, on the basis of behaviour in parasitic gaps and with due deference to Kayne and others, that ATB is not restricted to proclisis and needs to be defined in relation to the arguments in the conjunct over which the clitic has scope. M. Suñer, 'Object-shift: comparing a Romance language to Germanic', *ib.*, 261–89, explores two types of shift: semantic, when clitic doubling leaves the direct object outside the scope of the VP and hence the lexical tier, and prosodic (Zubizarreta's 'p-movement', which some persist in calling heavy NP shift) which changes the c-command relations so that the salient constituent is relegated to the lowest position in the structure. All true, but does it get us far?

Syntactic and semantic approaches to negation continue to lead to incompatible conclusions (as observed by P. Rowlett in his introduction to a set of conference papers not primarily on Romance, *TPS*, 98:1–13). M. T. Espinal, 'On the semantic status of n-words in Catalan and Spanish', *Lingua*, 110:557–80, believes they are semantically underspecified indefinite expressions incorporated into a null numeral to form weak quantifiers. On the basis of more adventurous data, however, V. Déprez, 'Parallel (a)symmetries and the internal structure of negative expressions', *NLLT*, 18:253–342, seeks to establish a parameter linking the constraints on negatives (*no vi a nadie / nadie (*no) me vio*) with those on bare nominals in preverbal position, since both have a deficient DP and lack quantificational force.

In 'Mismatches: agreement in qualitative constructions', *Probus*, 12:33–65, A. Hulk and C. Tellier ascribe the clashing agreements in *ton phénomène de fille est bien distraite* to the animacy of the head noun and feature percolation during incorporation. B. Schwarze, 'Formale Durchsichtigkeit und semantische Nutzung der Genusklassifikation', *VR*, 59:40–76, claims that the gender opposition has been all but eliminated from French and German, while it flourishes in Spanish, where it is regular, transparent, and possibly productive; but I. M.

Roca, 'On the meaning of gender', *HRJ*, 1:113–28, is less sure, believing that the skewed distribution would support a semantic representation independent of both syntactic structure and real-world pragmatics.

In order to distinguish arguments from circumstantial complements, H. H. Müller, 'Los adjuntos como componentes del sintagma nominal', *RevR*, 35:33–56, proposes 'structural *qualia*' with four categories: form, constituency, function and origin. V. Demonte, 'Semántica composicional y gramática ', *RELing*, 29, 1999:283–316, likewise applies Pustejovsky's proposals for decomposing lexical items into *qualia*, arguing that adjectives are originally underspecified and acquire their full meaning from interaction with associated nouns and verbs. And again in 'Motion events: Romance versus Germanic languages', *RLFRU*, 19: 11–19, F. Melka decomposes the lexemes into [motion], [manner] and [path] as a means of contesting a recent claim by Slobin that Germanic is richer than Romance in the expression of [manner] — an assertion she believes is unprovable.

8. Discourse and Pragmatics

CILPR 22, v, 'Les manuscrits ne brûlent pas', brings together 20 studies mostly on the philology and codicology of individual medieval texts; the title alludes to the article by T. K. Salberg (123–28), on interpreting and reconstructing a half destroyed manuscript. *CILPR 22*, vii, presented by H. Nølke and devoted to the semantics and pragmatics of sense and functions, was something of an innovation at the Brussels congress and, with almost 80 contributions, one of the largest fields represented. The themes of both volumes, generally applied to very recent texts, continue in *CILPR 22*, viii, 'Les effets du sens', ed. A. Jaubert and J.-M. Klinkenberg, closing with a round table at which L. Lundquist, M. Charolles and H. Nølke debate anxiously whether text linguistics is actually linguistics at all (179–204). One item, plucked almost at random, allays their anxieties: K. Ide, 'À propos des stratégies textuelles dans la communication spécialisée de l'économie', *ib.*, vii, 287–96, shows that specialist registers in French and Spanish are just as baffling to non-initiates — perhaps intentionally so.

Dedicated to the memory of S. Fleischman whose ideas inspired its contents, Herring, *Parameters*, assembles 13 papers from a 1993 symposium; the section on text types draws extensively on Romance illustrations, as does F.'s overview, 'Methodologies and ideologies in historical linguistics' (33–58), which attacks the myth of monoglossia and stresses the importance of variationist sociolinguistics for credible reconstruction. Drawing on F.'s claim that the imperfect introduces the character's perspective in a narrative, M. M. Manoliu, 'From *deixis ad oculos* to discourse markers via *deixis ad phantasma*', *ICHL 12*, 243–60, relates the divergent outcomes of temporal adverbials and distal deictics to their functions in relation to the time of uttering and the world view created by the text. M. also researches 'La pragma-sémantique d'un opérateur complexe', *CILPR 22*, VII, 433–43, on Rom. *și* and its near equivalents, deciding that it has become an inclusion operator within a superordinate unity. In similar vein, A. Torrent-Lenzen, 'La negació contextual en català i en les altres llengües romàniques', *ELLC*, 39, 1999:289–311, contrasts *pas*, an explicit negator always diatopically marked, with *no*, serving widely (except in Portuguese) in contextual negation, where it could just as well be classed as a modal particle.

By 'Capitalization', *ICHL 12*, 295–309, C. J. Pountain means the maximal exploitation of a linguistic feature, leading to paradoxical effects of economy and profusion, and capturing a little of the elusive notion *génie de la langue*. P.'s 'Pragmatic factors in the evolution of the Romance reflexive', *HRJ*, 1:5–25, follows up an uncontentious hierarchy of functions and senses with the more hazardous claim that Romance languages can be classified according to their capitalization on reflexive morphology. Comparing ' "Special effects": Stereotype Stileffekte mit Demonstrativa', *RJ*, 50:29–51, in literary French, Spanish, and German, E. Lavric concludes that a subset of demon-stratives and possessives has similar connotative effects in all three languages, though one cannot predict the locus of privilege. Different approaches to direct speech are evident in two commendably thorough studies: M. Suñer, 'The syntax of direct quotes', *NLLT*, 18:525–78, has to abandon the null-subject parameter as the main driver when complex verbs, transitivity relations, and negation are revealed to pattern unpredictably in Spanish, French, and English; while M.-B. Mosegaard Hansen, 'The syntactic and semiotic status of direct quotes', *TPS*, 98:281–322, views citation as a signal of grammaticalized code-switching.

The proof of the proverb, it seems, is in the collecting. Joachim Lengert, *Romanische Phraseologie und Parömiologie. Eine teilkommentierte Bibliographie (von den Anfängen bis 1997)*, 2 vols, Tübingen, Narr, 1999, xl + 1112, xxiv + 1113–2132 pp., an indispensable reference, if a little flaccid in its definitions, bears witness to an extraordinary flowering of interest in the set phrases of what may now be an endangered oral culture. If so, it is very old: J. A. Samper Padilla and D. Munteanu Colán, 'Los refranes románicos: unidad y diferencia-ción', *CILPR 22*, IX, 275–87, present a corpus of Latin proverbs with patent antecedents for many current Romance forms. M. Conenna, having announced a 'Dictionnaire électronique de proverbes français et italiens', *ib.*, III, 137–45, offers a contrastive analysis, 'Structure syntaxique des proverbes français et italiens', *Langages*, 139:27–38, observing that the aphoristic kernel survives minor variations in the surrounding syntax. Complementary is: J. Sevilla Muñoz, 'Les proverbes et phrases proverbiales français, et leurs équivalences en espagnol', *ib.*, 98–109, lamenting the decline of proverbs in urban speech, though they continue to flourish in Spanish rural communities.

9. Lexis

CILPR 22, IV, 'Des mots aux dictionnaires', assembles over 60 contributions, mostly mono-cultural, on novel and traditional themes in lexicology, lexicography, onomastics, and toponymy, culminating in a round table on specialist languages, of which L. Schena gives an informative 'Synthèse de travaux' (611–28), though with no report of discussion. Items with a comparative perspective include: A. Blank et al., 'Onomasiologie, sémasiologie et l'étymologie des langues romanes: esquisse d'un projet' (103–13); O. Felecan, 'Noţiunea "muncă" în latină şi în limbile romanice' (213–22), an onomasiological exploration of 'work'; and V. Popovici, 'L'onomastique: la parente pauvre des dictionnaires étymologiques' (483–91), continuing the theme reported last year (*YWMLS*, 61:27), this time illustrated by PETRŌSUS. Lexical items also feature in other volumes of *CILPR 22*. V. Nyckees, 'La généalogie d'une signification abstraite', *ib.*, VII, 539–48, tracks the Latin exponents of trickery and deception. F. Rainer, 'Syntaxe historique des pourcentages dans les langues romanes', *ib.*, II, 361–69, identifies a 13th-c. innovation by L. Fibonacci blossoming into 16th-c. variants with and without a definite article (*comprar el sesenta por ciento*). E. Lavric, 'Indéfinis pluriels français et espagnols', *ib.*, VII, 377–86, classifies *quelques/algunos* and some common quantifiers by a feature matrix: objective vs subjective, small vs large, concluding that French has a better developed system than Spanish for valuing higher amounts (*bien de, maint(s)*).

Several scholars are exercised by the consequences of lexical borrowing. I. M. Alves, 'Étude contrastive du processus créatif en portugais et en français dans le vocabulaire de l'intelligence artificielle', *La Banque des Mots*, 60:89–102, finds that terms borrowed, calqued, or loan-shifted from English — even in a rapidly evolving field like AI — constrain the diversity and usually respect the patterns of the receiving language. That would not surprise M. Saltarelli, whose 'Lenguas románicas y gramática universal', *CILPR 22*, IX, 269–74, proposes an 'intuitive index of cognitive permeability' to judge degrees of integration. However, challenging received wisdom that a new concept can be incorporated almost without consequence for the semantic field while an alien synonym will either displace the native term or provoke differentiation, E. Buchi, 'Le point de vue onomasiologique en étymologie', *RLiR*, 64:347–78, reflects on Rom. *vreme* and *timp*, which seem to have been synonymous from the earliest records, but whose relative frequency was dramatically reversed in the 19th c., probably as a result of the Latin revival. Much earlier, J. Grzega explores whether 'Le basi *atr*- "nero" e *alb*- "bianco" nella Romania cisalpina (e transalpina)', *VR*, 59:108–15, are Latin or pre-Latin, since there is evidence of homophonous relict forms in the locality; they might even be Celto-Latin lexical 'compromises'. In '*Mystère* "représentation théâtrale"', *RLiR*, 64:321–45, G. A. Runnalls attempts not an etymology, but the dating of a semantic shift, concluding that the narrow sense of a miracle play probably dates from the late 14th c., and the more general sense of any medieval religious play only from the 18th. Tackling another mystery, T. J. Walsh, 'The etymology of Hispano-Romance *tomar* "to take"', *HR*, 68:243–65, dismisses previous explanations, including Malkiel's ingenious *AESTUMĀRE* (*YWMLS*, 52:26), preferring DOMĀRE, via *ADDOMĀRE, which he believes to be semantically plausible and not unprecedented in its aphaeresis, degemination, and devoicing.

I. Pujol Payet, 'Del latín *sex* a los derivados romances' *CILPR 22*, IV, 503–09, is informative even shorn of its derivational productivity. H. Wilkinson, 'Proto-Romance verb formation by suffixation', *Ronshu* (Aoyama Gakuin), 35:159–74, traces the vicissitudes and eventual fusion of the classical inchoatives -ISCERE and -ESCERE, finding interesting areal distributions reinforced by the later innovations -IZARE, -ICARE, -IARE, -ANTARE and -ICIRE. D. Pharies, 'Origin of the Hispano-Romance suffix -*ucho*', *Iberoromania*, 49, 1999:1–25, observes that while many words end in -*ucho* most are not suffixal; the suffix, where it does occur, is best traced to -USCULUS, of ambivalent syllabification, so rehabilitating the proposal first made by J. Leite de Vasconcellos in 1890. Finally, C. Schmitt, 'À propos de l'européisation des langues romanes', *CILPR 22*, VI, 457–65, reflects on the harmonizing (or perhaps insidious) consequences of suffixal borrowing.

10. DIALECTS, CONTACT, AND SOCIOLINGUISTICS

H. Thun gives a masterly overview of 'La géographie linguistique romane à la fin du XXe siècle', *CILPR 22*, III, 367–88, and J. Kabatek surveys 'La variation linguistique dans le domaine des langues romanes: théorie et réalité empirique' (215–24), in a volume that concentrates on dialectology, geolinguistics, and sociolinguistics, and ends with a round table, also organized by H. Thun, on linguistic atlases and variability, in which S. A. M. Cardoso asks 'Que dimensões outras, que não a diatópica, interessam aos atlas lingüísticos?' (411–15), M. D'Agostino sketches 'La nuova generazione di atlanti linguistici' (417–23), H. Goebl reports briefly on analytic techniques (425–27) and N. A. Vigil dares to suggest that sociolinguistic methods may be inherently superior to those of dialectology (429–33). New life is breathed into the maps of the *ALF* and *AIS* by three important works. David Heap, *La variation grammaticale en géolinguistique: les pronoms sujet en roman central*, Munich, LinCom Europa, 230 pp., cleverly computes transitional zones that call into question the sharply binary null-subject parameter of P&P linguistics (see also H.'s 'Contraintes morphosyntaxiques et asymmétries de personne en roman central', *CILPR 22*, VI, 219–25). H. Goebl, applying modern dialectometry to 'Langues standards et dialectes locaux', *IJSL*, 145:181–215, confirms that fragmentation has been hastened at state boundaries as a direct result of nation(alist) policies. R. A. M. Temple, 'Old wine into new wineskins', *TPS*, 98:353–94, finds that the *ALF*'s mapping of voicing in plosives matches closely the findings of recent experimental phonetic and sociolinguistic research. Investigating 'La pertinenza degli eventi catastrofici naturali', *RID*, 23:9–38, J. B. Trumper and G. Chiodo present earthquake maps of the 'Lausberg area' of southern Italy, whose archaic character can be correlated with seismic activity keeping the population confined and cut off from outside stimuli.

In 'Langue et *nation* — une relation périlleuse', *ER*, 22:23–28, G. Kremnitz cautions against the glib assumption that history has been shaped by these concepts, which pre-date by some way the French Revolution; the converse is more probable. In a thoughtful piece drawing extensively on the work of Kremnitz, W. Zwanenburg, 'La Charte européenne des langues régionales ou minoritaires et les langues romanes', *RLFRU*, 19:61–70, asks whether the well-intentioned Charter defines a 'language' rigorously enough, whether it can be applied, and whether it will have the desired effect of supporting Rhaeto-Romance, Sardinian, Occitan, and Catalan against the depredations of their more powerful neighbours; regretfully, he decides that there are grounds for doubting all three. M. J. Bello Rivas, 'Gallego y castellano en conflicto: mecanismos de diferencialismo en la lengua' *CILPR 22*, III, 57–68, reports on what might be called written distanciation. Examining political discourse and attitudinal surveys in Galicia, J. del Valle, 'Monoglossic policies for a heteroglossic culture', *Language and Communication*, 20:105–32, finds an uncomfortable mismatch between monoglossic ideology and the polynomic reality experienced by most speakers. Less conflictual,

J. L. Blas Arroyo and D. Tricker, 'Principles of variationism for disambiguating language contact phenomena', *LVC*, 12:103–40, decide that lone Spanish nouns embedded in Catalan discourse behave on grammatical criteria like Catalan nouns and should therefore be classed as loans rather than code-switches.

Žarko Muljačić, *Das Dalmatische. Studien zu einer untergangenen Sprache*, Vienna, Böhlau, 434 pp., is an elegant and convenient reprint of 34 studies dating from 1956–97. Gustav Ineichen, **Arabisch-orientalische Sprachkontakte in der Romania* (RA, 41), 1997, viii + 109 pp., deemed excellent by R. Kontzi (*RF*, 112:380–83), identifies three types of contact: erudite via translators, natural in multilingual communities, and imposed by Mediterranean trade. J. Cremona, 'Français et italien en Tunisie au XVIIe siècle: la langue des documents en italien du consulat français de Tunis, 1582–1705', *CILPR 22*, III, 135–43, is valuable for its documentation of a neglected area. A. Bartens, 'Vers une typologie socio- et psycholinguistique des produits du contact linguistique: exemples romans', *ib.*, IX, 7–18, consists of a vast schema (which she describes as 'peu scientifique') showing the possible consequences of contact and the complex interactions between a language and the identity of its users; current terminology is woolly and unsatisfactory, but she does not think that brand new terms would succeed. G. A. Lorenzino, 'El rol de la gramaticalización en la formación de nuevas lenguas (criollización)', *ib.*, 163–69, applies the Traugott-Heine model to Haitian, Kriol and Tok Pisin. D. Munteanu Colán, 'La génesis de las lenguas románicas, resultado del contacto lingüístico', *ib.*, 201–15, argues that Romance languages are the product of fusion of inputs among which Latin was by so far the most important that it imposed its own structures on the contact process.

II. FRENCH STUDIES*

LANGUAGE

By GLANVILLE PRICE,
University of Wales Aberystwyth

1. GENERAL AND BIBLIOGRAPHICAL

Adrian Battye, Marie-Anne Hintze, and Paul Rowlett, *The French Language Today. A Linguistic Introduction*, 2nd edn, London, Routledge, xiv + 345 pp., is a revised version of a book first published in 1992 (see my generally favourable comments, *YWMLS*, 54:28); the basic structure remains, though a good deal of rewriting has gone on (some of it in an inappropriate register of English: *there's, aren't, we'll*, etc.); unfortunately some of the errors noted in D. A. Trotter's review (*MLR*, 89:466–67) have not been corrected. **Le Français dans sa variation*, ed. Claudine Bavoux et al., L'Harmattan, 128 pp. Henriette Walter, **Le Français d'ici, de là, de là-bas*, LGF, 480 pp. *Le Français parlé, corpus et résultats: Actes du colloque international Université de Copenhague du 29 au 30 octobre 1998*, ed. Hanne Leth Anderson and Anita Berit Hansen, Copenhagen, Museum Tusculanum, 193 pp., includes: D. Willems, 'Le rapport entre théorie et données. Le cas du passif en français' (13–27); F. Gadet, 'On n'en a pas fini avec les problèmes de recueil de corpus' (29–44); A. B. Hansen and I. Malderez, 'La négation en français parlé — une enquête en région parisienne' (45–63); I. Malderez, 'L'analyse de la variation phonétique de corpus de français parlé: problèmes méthodologiques' (65–87); M.-A. Morel, 'Complémentarité des indices du plan segmental et du plan supra-segmental dans l'oral spontané en français' (89–104); L. Schøsler, 'Le statut de la forme zéro du complément d'objet direct en français moderne' (105–29); B. Defrancq, 'Un aspect de la subordination en français parlé: l'interrogation indirecte' (131–41); H. L. Andersen, 'Discours rapporté en français parlé: rection du verbe de citation et éléments délimitant la citation directe' (143–55); M.-B. Mosegaard Hansen, 'La polysémie de l'adverbe *déjà*'(157–77); and S. Schlyter, 'Acquisition du français parlé. Une comparaison entre apprenants formels et informels' (179–93).

R. Anthony Lodge has compiled, as a special number *hors série* of *CAFLS*, 6, *A Brief Guide to Research in French Language and Linguistics*, 52 pp., consisting of 25 brief but in most cases useful surveys by

---

* The place of publication of books is Paris unless otherwise stated.

various authors, most of them including *inter alia* a statement of 'areas in need of research'. **Tu parles? Le français dans tous ses états*, ed. Bernard Cerquiglini et al., Flammarion, 416 pp. Contributors to *FM*, 68.1, subtitled 'Quels français pour demain?', were invited to answer that question without however attempting to 'jouer les visionnaires'; the resulting articles are: C. Blanche-Benveniste, 'Le français au XXIe siècle. Quelques observations sur la grammaire' (3–15); M. Dominicy, 'La dynamique du système phonologique en français' (17–30); C. Marchello-Nizia, 'Le décumul du "thème" dans l'évolution du français' (31–40); S. Mejri, 'Figement et renouvellement du lexique: quand le processus détermine la dynamique du système' (41–62); L.-J. Calvet, 'Les mutations du français. Une approche écolinguistique' (63–78); G. Boulard, 'Les puristes face au désenchantement linguistique: défection, prise de parole et loyauté' (79–108); and I. Pierozak, 'Les pratiques discursives des internautes' (109–29).

Taking illustrations only from French, B. Pallaud, 'Lapsus et phénomènes voisins dans la langue parlée. Problèmes d'identification', *RFP*, 15, 1999:9–40, seeks to define on the basis of strictly linguistic criteria just what *lapsus linguae* are, and, in so doing, provides useful bibliographical guidance to previous work on the topic.

**Linguistic Identities and Policies in France and the French-speaking World*, ed. Dawn Marley, Marie-Anne Hintze, and Gabrielle Parker, London, AFLS–CILT, 1998, 319 pp. Marie-Josée de Saint Robert, **La Politique de la langue française* ('Que sais-je?', 3572), PUF, 126 pp. Petra Braselmann, **Sprachpolitik und Sprachbewußtsein in Frankreich heute*, Tübingen, Niemeyer, 1999, vi + 162 pp. J. Munro, 'If it isn't clear, it isn't French: language and identity', Kidd and Reynolds, *Contemporary French*, 129–39, considers French attitudes towards the language and what lies behind them.

CILPR 22 includes the following items of relevance to this section of *YWMLS*: I: P. Desmet, P. Lauwers and P. Swiggers, 'Le transfert du "modèle allemand" et les débuts de la dialectologie française' (191–96); II: J. Bonneau and M. Champagne, 'Le rôle de la morphosyntaxe dans le changement linguistique: une approche minimaliste à une analyse diachronique du français' (31–37); M. Champagne, 'Typologie des anaphores réciproques et leur évolution de l'ancien français au français moderne' (105–12); W. De Muller and A. Vanderheyden, 'Vers une sémantique diachronique cognitive? Réflexions sur l'évolution de la préposition *à*' (129–37); A. Anglebert, '*Si, car, et, or* — signes de ponctuation de l'ancien français' (175–84); M. Goyens, 'L'alternance dans les constructions prépositionnelles des verbes français: une étude historique de l'emploi de la préposition *à*' (203–10); U. Jokinen, 'Réflexions sur le syntagme nominal en moyen français: un bilan' (221–33); V. Kojemiakina, 'Les textes non-littéraires dans le système de l'ancien français' (241–45), Y.-C. Liu, 'Mutation du système verbal de l'indicatif en ancien français: le cas de la littérature épistolaire' (269–77); C. Marchello-Nizia, 'Le tragique destin de *moult* en français: changement linguistique et structures sémantico-cognitives' (285–96); A. Mazzola, 'L'analyse à l'encontre de l'analogie: proparoxytons et paroxytons dans l'histoire du français' (319–26); O. Ozolina, 'A propos des doublets étymologiques constitués par un latinisme et sa variante populaire en moyen français' (345–53); R. Sampson, 'La liaison et les voyelles nasales françaises: tendances évolutives plus récentes' (387–92); L. Schøsler, 'Permanence et variation de la valence verbale: réflexions sur la construction des verbes en latin, en ancien français, en moyen français et en français moderne' (407–18); R. Van Deyck, 'Les voyelles nasalisées en diatopie et en diachronie' (449–60); W. Van Hoecke, 'Les répercussions de la perte de la flexion en nombre en français' (461–72); and Y. Yajima, 'L'analogie verbale en protofrançais' (485–88); III: C. Bauvois, 'Des Belges et de l'assourdissement des sonores' (35–43); M. Bento, 'Nature phonologique des assibilées en français québécois' (69–77); T. Bulot, 'Le parler rouennais ou l'appropriation du territoire urbain' (87–94); Z. Fagyal, 'Le retour du *e* final en français parisien: changement phonétique conditionné par la prosodie' (151–60); N. Firsova, 'Le français régional en Normandie' (161–63); S. Golopentia [*sic*] and M.-R. Simoni-Arembou, ' "Les paysans n'ont pas de mots abstraits" ' (173–83); L. Rodriguez, 'Évaluation et évolution lexicométriques d'une langue romane en contexte minoritaire: séries synonymiques en franco-manitobain' (323–29); S. Skorokhodko, 'Facteurs et formes de la variation de la norme syntaxique du français littéraire: en Afrique centrale francophone' (351–55); and J. Walker, 'Les attitudes envers les anglicismes: une étude comparative francophone' (399–404).

2. HISTORY OF GRAMMAR AND OF LINGUISTIC THEORY

Colette Demaizière has published a critical edition of Pierre de la Ramée dit Ramus, **Grammaire (1572)*, Champion, 168 pp. P. Swiggers examines 'Terminologie et description grammaticales dans les *Elemens ou Institutions de la langue Françoise* de Jean Bousquet (1586)', *TLP*, 38:253–73. André Combaz, **Claude Favre de Vaugelas: mousquetaire de la langue française*, Klincksieck, 622 pp. Jeanne Streicher's 1934 edition of Vaugelas's *Remarques* has been reissued, Geneva, Slatkine, li + 624 pp. **Dominique Bouhours: Doutes sur la langue françoise proposez à*

Messieurs de l'Académie Françoise, ed. Giovanni Dotoli and Fulvia Fiorino, Fasano, Schena — Paris, Didier, 1998, 430 pp.

Carol Sanders, 'Linguistic historiography: a survey with particular reference to French linguistics at the turn of the century', *JFLS*, 10 : 273–92, covers multi-volume and one-volume histories, discusses a number of methodological and other general issues, and devotes special attention to Michel Bréal and Gustave Guillaume.

CFS, 53, is largely devoted to publishing papers from a round table, 'Lecture plurielle de W. Von Humboldt' (Lausanne, 1999); these, and most other contributions to this volume, fall outside the scope of *YWMLS*, with the exception of M.-C. Capt-Artaud, 'Des mots pour penser' (141–57), which examines the use made of a number of technical terms by some of Saussure's successors.

3. History of the Language

Thierry Revol, *Introduction à l'ancien français*, Nathan, 256 pp. Nelly Andrieux-Reix et al., *Petit traité de langue française médiévale*, PUF, 170 pp., provides a useful summary of morphology and the main features of syntax, with a commendable abundance of examples. *Histoire de la langue française, 1945–2000*, ed. Gérald Antoine and Bernard Cerquiglini, CNRS, 1028 pp.

W. Ayres-Bennett, 'Voices from the past: sources of seventeenth-century French', *RF*, 112 : 323–48, seeks 'to consider the extent to which it is possible to find sources of spoken French in the 17th c., and to evaluate their reliability'.

4. Phonetics and Phonology

LaFr, 126, 'Où en est la phonologie du français?', ed. Bernard Laks. A. di Cristo concludes his article 'Vers une modélisation de l'accentuation du français', *JFLS*, 10 : 27–44 (see *YWMLS*, 61 : 33). B. Post discusses 'Pitch accent, liaison and the phonological phrase in French', *Probus*, 12 : 127–64. R. A. M. Temple, 'Old wine into new wineskins. A variationist investigation into patterns of voicing in plosives in the *Atlas linguistique de la France*', *TPS*, 98 : 353–94, reveals 'the interaction between linguistic and extra-linguistic factors in conditioning patterns of variability'; more generally, this survey illustrates the continuing serviceability of the *ALF* and 'gives further credit to Edmond Edmont's skill as a fieldworker'. *La Linguistique*, 36, subtitled 'Les introuvables d'André Martinet', usefully reprints in tribute to the memory of A.M. a number of his articles many of which are indeed now virtually *introuvable*, and including 'Remarques sur le système phonologique du français' (329–39), 'La prononciation du français entre 1880 et 1945' (341–65), and 'Les sons é et è en français' (367–70).

5. ORTHOGRAPHY

*Dictionnaire orthographique: comprenant les difficultés de la langue française et une grammaire très détaillée, Auzou, 650 pp.

6. GRAMMAR

OLD AND MIDDLE FRENCH

T. Ponchon, 'Le français médiéval à l'aube du deuxième millénaire', *IG*, 86:4–13, surveys recent work. Claude Buridant, *Grammaire nouvelle de l'ancien français*, Sedes, 800 pp., is excellent. Three general chapters, 'Introduction', 'Éléments de phonologie et de morphonologie', and 'Les paramètres de la description linguistique de l'ancien français', are followed by 14 others devoted to the morphology and syntax of the various parts of speech and 13 on different types of clause, indirect speech, 'Les modalités du discours', and 'L'ordre des constituants', with, by way of conclusion, a brief 'Aperçu typologique'. The grammatical analysis throughout is subtle and far-reaching, and every syntactical statement is backed up with one or more precisely localized examples. There is an extensive bibliography which, in contrast to all too many books or articles by French scholars, reveals commendable familiarity with work published in English or German. This admirable volume will inevitably come to be regarded as an authoritative, standard work on the subject and could, indeed, supersede all others. No one discussing any aspect of Old French grammar can afford to ignore it.

P. van Reenen and L. Schøsler, 'Declension in Old and Middle French: two opposing tendencies', *ICHL 12*, 327–44, partially overlaps with their 1997 article (see *YWMLS*, 59:40) but introduces a substantial amount of new material. L. Schøsler also offers 'Réflexions sur l'optionnalité des compléments d'objet direct en latin, en ancien français, en moyen français et en français moderne', Lund, *Langue*, 9–27. M. Perret offers 'Quelques remarques sur l'anaphore nominale aux XIVe et XVe siècles', *IG*, 87:17–23.

N. Sarré discusses the 'Morphologie des formes en -*ant* en moyen français', *IG*, 86:40–52.

Evelyne Oppermann, *Les Emplois injonctifs du futur en français médiéval* (PRF, 225), 350 pp., is an important work that maintains the high standard one has come to expect of the distinguished series in which it appears; based on a corpus of 80 texts ranging in date from all the earliest French texts to *La Farce du Pauvre Jouhan* (1502) and representing a wide variety of prose and verse genres, it covers the use of the future tense to express 'un ordre, une requête, une interdiction'; defining her theoretical approach, the author acknowledges in particular a debt to C. Kerbrat-Orecchioni's *L'Implicite* (1986).

P. van Reenen and L. Schøsler discuss 'The pragmatic functions of the Old French particles *ainz, apres, donc, lors, or, puis* and *si*', Herring, *Parameters*, 59–105.

S. Marcotte, 'La coordination de relatives incidentes à un antécédent différent: un tour propre au moyen français?', *IG*, 87:10–16, shows that the answer is apparently 'yes', since the construction is 'sinon absent, du moins très rare en ancien français' and prohibited in standard modern French.

Asking 'Les grammaticalisations ont-elles une cause?', C. Marchello-Nizia examines the use of *beaucoup, moult,* and *tres* in Old French, *IG*, 87:3–9. U. Jokinen, '*Pour tout dire* ou *somme toute*: observations sur *tout* adverbial et locutionnel en moyen français', *NMi*, 101:209–16, itemizes eight characteristic features. M.-L. Ollier, '*Or* dans l'énoncé interrogatif', *IG*, 86:31–39, relates to Old French.

MODERN FRENCH

Rodney Ball, *Colloquial French Grammar: A Practical Guide*, Oxford, Blackwell, x + 245 pp., is a much needed work that provides a clear and comprehensive coverage of its subject; an introductory chapter is followed by others dealing with 'three grammatical processes' (negatives, questions, and relative clauses), with noun phrases, verb phrases, conjunctions and prepositions, and sentence structure and organization, and assessment of the 'grammatical effects of an unreformed spelling system'; there are several sets of well-devised exercises, with answers, and appendices explaining grammatical terms and the International Phonetic Alphabet. Maurice Lévy, **Grammaire du français: approche énonciative*, Gap, Ophrys, 248 pp.

Christine Rouget, *Distribution et sémantique des constructions Nom 'de' Nom*, Champion, 256 pp., based on a corpus of 1000 examples drawn from authentic spoken French, identifies eight distinct types, four of which (counting for some 20% of the examples) are considered to be 'formes en marge du système' while four are 'formes de base' (types *la chambre de ses parents, la synthèse d'une protéine, une bouteille de beaujolais, une question de conscience*).

T. Meisenburg, 'Vom Wort zum Flexiv? Zu den französischen Pronominaklitika', *ZFSL*, 110:223–37, argues that French pronominal clitics occupy an intermediate position between words and affixes and should be regarded as constituting an independent and functionally meaningful category. A. Coveney, 'Vestiges of *nous* and the 1st person plural verb in informal spoken French', *LSc*, 22:447–81, concludes that, if one cannot claim that the use of *nous* + 1 plur. verb is disappearing from everyday spoken French, it is nevertheless characteristic only of a relatively formal style.

A. Burgi, 'Le pronom *ça* en français moderne', *VR*, 58, 1999:149–71, is a synchronic study. C. Schnedecker, ' "Ordres" des ordinaux pronominaux', *TrL*, 41:7–34, returns to a topic she has previously written about on various occasions and tells us she has not yet said her last word on it.

Véronique Lagae, *Les Constructions en 'de' + adjectif: typologie et analyse*, Leuven U.P., 1998, vii + 143 pp. R. Veland and S. Whittaker, 'Caractérisants à complément causatif et restructurabilité: *exceptionnel de beauté/ d'une beauté exceptionnelle*', *TrL*, 41:35–58, take issue with, principally but not only, L. Picabia, *Les Constructions adjectivales en français*, 1979 (see *YWMLS*, 40:39).

C. de Cat, 'Towards a unified analysis of French floating quantifiers', *JFLS*, 10:1–25, analyses what she terms 'anaphoric quantifiers' *(tou(te)s, chacun(e))*, and various pronominal and adverbial quantifiers according to the principles of Government and Binding theory.

K. Baschung and M. Desmets, 'On the phrasal vs. clausal syntactic status of French infinitives: causative constructions and subject inversion', *JFLS*, 10:205–28, is strictly for those familiar with Head-driven Phrase Structure Grammar. É. Castaigne, 'Apports des données orales dans l'analyse des valences à l'infinitif des adjectifs recteurs', *RFP*, 15, 1999:113–36, distinguishes between 'tournures avec formule courte' *(une langue difficile (à apprendre))* and 'tournures sans formule courte' *(une affection difficile à combattre)*. *TrL*, 40, ed. Céline Benninger, Anne Carlier, and Véronique Lagae, is devoted to 'Le présent' and contains: G. R. Marschall, 'Le présent prétendu — interpolations, injonctions, reports et cache-cache' (11–30); S. de Vogüé, 'Calcul des valeurs d'un énoncé "au présent" ' (31–54); L. Gosselin, 'Présentation et représentation: les rôles du "présent historique" ' (55–72); A. Carlier, 'La disposition et ses rapports avec l'itération' (73–86); and C. Schapira, 'L'expression de la durée et de l'événement dans la phrase générique: proverbe et maxime' (87–96); it is doubtless not by coincidence that S. Meillet, 'Chronique de linguistique générale et française, XII', *ib.*, 97–111, is also devoted to 'Le présent'. C. Blanche-Benveniste and J.-P. Adam, 'La conjugaison des verbes: virtuelle, attestée, défective', *RFP*, 15, 1999:87–112, demonstrate that (as, indeed, one might have expected), in spoken French only verbs of high frequency have 'une large conjugaison effective', while, for many others, 'la conjugaison effectivement attestée' is 'extrêmement réduite' and, for some, only the past participle, the infinitive and the 3rd person singular of the present indicative are in normal use. While not totally rejecting the notion, R. Salkie, 'Does French have a relative past tense?', *JFLS*, 10:245–71, argues that recent work proposing to distinguish between the imperfect as a relative or anaphoric tense and the *passé simple* and *passé composé* as absolute or deictic tenses, rather than in terms of aspect, is fundamentally incorrect. I. Novakova, 'Le futur antérieur français: temps, aspect, modalités', *ZFSL*, 110:113–35, argues, on the basis of a transcategorial approach, that 'c'est la valeur d'*accompli* et non celle d'*antérieur* qui devrait être retenue comme valeur de base' in explaining the multifarious uses of the tense. H. Portine, 'Le(s) conditionnel(s) et *Le schizo*: de la mise en texte', *TrL*, 41:85–106, is inordinately long and of little interest.

Le Passif: Actes du colloque international, Institut d'études romanes, Université de Copenhague, du 5 au 7 mars 1998, ed. Lene Schøsler, Copenhagen, Museum Tusculanum, 333 pp., includes the following all of which, including those that are more wide-ranging, are of direct relevance to French: D. Gaatone, 'Pour une définition restrictive du passif en français' (15–22); M. Gross, 'Sur quelques extensions possibles de l'appellation passif' (23–37); M. H. Haff, 'Les périphrases passives pronominales — constructions non-prototypiques du passif' (39–48); C. Muller, 'Le passif processif et ses concurrents. Définition et quelques particularités' (49–69); M. Herslund, 'Les deux passifs du français' (71–81); H. P. Helland, 'Le passif verbal et le passif adjectival' (83–97); M. Manoliu-Manea, 'Une hypothèse cognitive sur les formes latines en -*r*. A la recherche d'un invariant' (99–115); A. Rousseau, 'Formation et statut du passif. Comparaison typologique entre langues romanes et langues germaniques' (117–33); B. Lamiroy, 'Sur certains rapports entre le passif pronominal et le datif' (135–54); N. Rivière, 'Le pronominal face à l'actif et au passif: la construction du sens' (155–69); D. Willems, 'Les verbes de perception et le passif' (171–83); B. Defrancq, 'Approche contrastive des (semi-)auxiliaires du passif de l'objet prépositionnel' (185–204); L.-O. Marstrander, 'La proposition infinitive et le passif' (205–12); L. Kupferman, 'Existe-t-il une catégorie du passif nominal?' (213–26); G. Gross, 'Passifs nominaux et verbes intransitifs' (227–36); J.-C. Anscombre, 'Un problème de sémantique lexicale: l'interprétation active/passive des adjectifs verbaux participes en position d'épithète' (237–59); G. Boysen, 'Les adectifs en -*able*/-*ible*: esquisse d'une typologie' (261–64); M. Wilmet, 'Du passif à la topicalisation ou pour changer de sujet' (265–75); C. Vet, 'Formation et sens du passif et de quelques "passivoïdes"' (277–88); A. Brahim, 'Relief actanciel et diathèse verbale' (289–301); C. Blanche-Benveniste, 'Analyse de deux types de passifs dans les productions du français parlé' (303–19); and K. W. Rasmussen, 'Le passif vu à travers le contrat bilatéral: fonction de focalisation' (321–33). Yvette Yannick Mathieu, *Les Verbes de sentiment: de l'analyse linguistique au traitement automatique*, CNRS, 224 pp.

Christian Molinier and Françoise Lévrier, *Grammaire des adverbes: description des formes en -ment*, Geneva, Droz, 527 pp., is the latest addition (no. 33) to the distinguished 'Langue et cultures' series to which we have drawn attention in these pages (most recently, *YWMLS*, 61 : 37); the theoretical framework within which the authors operate is that of Z. S. Harris in the version thereof proposed by M. Gross; some 3000 adverbs, drawn from all the current standard dictionaries and other sources, are classified, according to rigorously defined criteria, in nine principal categories (three categories of 'adverbes de phrase', five types of adverbs of manner, and focalizers), each having a number of subcategories; the semantic and syntactical properties of each subcategory are analysed and illustrated and two substantial appendices summarize the syntactical features of each adverb (pp. 310–425) and itemize them alphabetically (pp. 428–519). Henriette Gezundhajt, *Adverbes en -ment et opérations énonciatives: analyse linguistique et discursive*, Berne, Lang, xii + 353 pp. R. Veland, 'Le détachement en *même* faisant suite à un mot de négation', *SN*, 71 : 206–23, discusses, with extensive exemplification, the distinction between *pas même* and *même pas*. Paul Rowlett, *Sentential Negation in French*, OUP, 1998, xvii + 233 pp.

Taking as his text Hugo's *Un cosaque survint qui prit l'enfant en croupe*, N. Furukawa discusses the 'construction événementielle à prédicat complexe', *TrL*, 41 : 59–74, while D. Van Raemedonck, *ib.*, 75–84, taking as his starting point Nerval's *toi qui m'as consolé*, asks if the type of relative clause in question is always predicative and, following M. Wilmet and in opposition to G. Kleiber and A. Goosse, answers in the negative.

Le Style indirect libre et ses contextes, ed. Sylvie Mellet and Marcel Vuillaume (Cahiers Chronos, 5), Amsterdam, Rodopi, iii + 130 pp., is a relatively unimportant volume, with, on French, articles by A. Jaubert, 'Le discours indirect libre. Dire et montrer: approche pragmatique' (49–69), S. Mellet, 'A propos de deux marqueurs de "bivocalité"' (91–106), and M. Vuillaume, 'La signalisation du style indirect libre' (107–30). It is not clear how this volume meets the stated aim of the series which is to publish 'des recueils d'articles représentatifs de la diversité des approches dans le domaine de la sémantique temporelle'. In this, as in other respects, *Cahier* no. 6, *Passé et parfait*, ed. Anne Carlier, Véronique Lagae, and Céline Benninger, Amsterdam, Rodopi, v + 142 pp., which publishes papers given at a colloquium at Valenciennes, is far more satisfactory; eight of the ten papers relate to French: J. Moeschler, 'L'ordre temporel dans le discours: le modèle des inférences directionnelles' (1–11); C. Vetters and W. De Mulder, 'Passé simple et imparfait: contenus conceptuel et procédural' (13–36); L. de Saussure, 'Quand le temps ne progresse pas avec le passé simple' (37–48); B. Verine, 'Pour une interprétation aspectuelle des tiroirs du passé: deux insertions cotextuelles du zeugme' (49–57); J. Bres, 'Un emploi discursif qui ne manque pas de style: l'imparfait en contexte narratif' (59–77); B. Sthioul, 'Passé simple, imparfait et sujet de conscience' (79–93), M. Vuillaume, 'Heureusement que Pierre n'est pas venu demain!' (107–16); and D. Creissels, 'L'emploi résultatif de *être* + *participe passé* en français' (133–42).

F. Lefeuvre, 'Toutes les phrases sont-elles binaires? Exemples de la phrase averbale existentielle', *FM*, 68:191–201, concludes that 'devant l'absence de la binarité sujet-prédicat, une autre relation [binaire] se met souvent en place' and that 'un seul terme compose rarement une phrase'. Marie-Noëlle Roubaud, *Les Constructions pseudo-clivées en français contemporain*, Champion, 448 pp., provides a thorough treatment of a construction that, though very frequent in both spoken and written contemporary French, has attracted relatively little attention from grammarians. Typically, the construction in question follows the pattern *ce* + relative clause + *c'est* [. . .], e.g. *ce qui m'interésse* (or *ce dont je me souviens*) *c'est (de) la linguistique*, though parallel constructions (in particular adj. + *c'est*, e.g. *l'essentiel c'est les différents instruments*) are also fully covered. A third of the book is devoted to a structural analysis of each of the 1514 examples constituting the corpus. Adeline Nazarenko, **La Cause et son expression en français*, Gap, Ophrys, 160 pp. J. Deulofeu, 'Questions de méthode dans la description morphosyntaxique de l'élément *que* en français contemporain', *RFP*, 15, 1999:163–98, finds previous studies unsatisfactory and seeks a coherent approach to the morphosyntactic description of *que*, taking account of constructions in which it serves as a 'circonstanciel universel', as a 'subordonnant à valeur de coordonnant', and as an element introducing what is in effect a main clause (e.g. *il me le demanderait à genoux que je ne cèderais pas*). S. Vogeleer, 'Intentional relations and suspended reading of "before" clauses: the case of French *avant que*', *Linguistics*, 38:1015–51, seeks to account for sentences in which the clause followed by an *avant que* clause is evaluated as neither true nor false.

P. Cappeau, 'Sujets éloignés. Esquisse d'une caractérisation des sujets lexicaux séparés de leur verbe', *RFP*, 15, 1999:199–231, points out that word-order studies have concentrated on the position of the subject in relation to the verb and have devoted insufficient attention to determining the conditions in which the subject may be separated from a following verb by some intervening element. M. Hobæk Haff, 'Regard sur l'inversion du sujet en français moderne', *RRom*, 35:21–32, takes issue with some of the views of H. Korzen. M. Bilger, 'Coordination: analyses syntaxes et annotations', *RFP*, 15, 1999:255–72, draws attention to problems in the treatment of coordinate clauses, while G. Bès discusses 'La phrase verbale noyau en francais', *ib.*, 273–38. S. Fontvielle and M. Hug, 'Phrases interrogatives partielles. Une enquête d'usage linguistique', *TLP*, 38:51–82, conclude that 'la forme à inversion simple' is more widespread than is generally supposed and that 'les autres formes de l'interrogation partielle ont chacune une zone privilégiée d'emploi'. M.-B. Mosegaard Hansen examines 'The syntactic and semiotic status of direct quotes, with reference to French', *TPS*, 98:281–322.

Asking 'What is "what" in French?', *JL*, 36:511–30, B. Plunkett tackles some of the peculiarities of the restrictions on 'what' questions in French.

7. Lexicography

The *FEW* has reached fasc. 156, constituting vol. 25 ('refonte du tome 1er'), pp. 961–1056, and covering AURELIANUS--AUSCULTARE. Raymond Arveiller's 25 articles, dating from 1969 to 1996, to which attention has often been drawn in these pages (see most recently *YWMLS*, 58:40), are reprinted as **Addenda au FEW XIX (Orientalia)* (*ZRP*, Beiheft 298), ed. Max Pfister, Tübingen, Niemeyer, 1999, xi + 645 pp. The *DEAF* has reached *fasc. H5–H6.

Alan Hindley, Frederick W. Langley, and Brian J. Levy, *Old French – English Dictionary*, CUP, xv + 621 pp., is a derivative of a computerized lexicon and its primary aim is essentially practical ('this is a dictionary of words and is not intended as a primary source of information on Old French morphology, grammar or syntax'; nor are there any examples or etymological indications); it contains some 60,000 entries, very many of them one-liners with sigla indicating grammatical function and a brief definition or definitions, e.g. '**aneille** *sf* crutch', '**enjanglé** *a* voluble, talkative', '**repuier** *vt* climb up; repulse, thrust away' (as in this last example, significantly different definitions are separated by semi-colons); where necessary, however, lists of definitions may run to several lines and a certain number of common locutions are included, e.g., under **cuidier**, '**au mien c.**, in my opinion, to my mind; **sanz nul c.**, without hesitation'; the problem of the vagaries of Old French spelling is solved more or less satisfactorily by (a) normally following the regularized graphies adopted by Tobler-Lommatzsch, (b) listing frequent alternatives either in the introduction (e.g. '**ol**- see **ou**- (*molt/mout*)') or occasionally in the body of the text, and (c) cross-referring extensively (e.g. 'nouveleté see noveleté' - but many of these could have been adequately dealt with under procedure (b), as when, curiously, 'descr- see also discr-' is followed immediately by 'descrecion *sf* see discrecion').

Pierre Enckell, **Le Dictionnaire de façons de parler du XVIe siècle*, CNRS, 448 pp. M. Bierbach studies 'Caractères et fonctions du discours lexicologique dans les dictionnaires de Robert Estienne', *CLe*, 76: 151–66.

Gaston Cayrou, **Dictionnaire du français classique: la langue du XVIIe siècle*, LGF, 765 pp., is a reprint of the 2nd edn of 1924. Laurent Bray, **Matthias Kramer et la lexicographie du français en Allemagne au XVIIIe siècle*, Tübingen, Niemeyer, viii + 519 pp.

**Le Nouveau Petit Robert*, ed. Josette Rey-Debove and Alain Rey, Le Robert, 2841 pp., is a revised and expanded edition. I. Turcain and R. Wooldridge, 'L'informatisation du *Dictionnaire de l'Académie française* (1694–1935)', *CLe*, 75, 1999: 153–72, examines aspects of the first edition (1694) revealed by the on-going computerization of the eight completed editions.

Igor Mel'cug, **Dictionnaire explicatif et combinatoire du français contemporain: recherches lexico-sémantiques*, vol. 4, Montreal U.P., 1999, xix + 347 pp. Dontcho Dontchev, *Dictionnaire du français argotique, populaire et familier*, Monaco, Rocher, 436 pp., falls into two parts; the basic dictionary consists of some 8500 entries, many of them subdivided to take account of different meanings, and the great majority including phrases as well as individual words; this is complemented by a 'répertoire alphabétique de synonymes argotiques, populaires et familiers', listing the synonyms for a given word in the standard language (about 80 of them for 'argent', for example, and about 130 for 'prostituée'); the author makes no claim to exhaustiveness but does aim to be up to date, having excluded, in general, 'les mots obsolètes, les archaïsmes et les termes qui appartiennent aux argots spécialisés'. Fabrice Antoine, *Dictionnaire français-anglais des mots tronqués*, Louvain-la-Neuve, Peeters, lx + 211 pp., arose from an awareness on the part of the author that well established truncations like *gynéco*, *survêt(e)* were often absent from standard dictionaries (monolingual as well as bilingual); the result is this most welcome volume that draws both on existing dictionaries and on a wide range of other written and oral sources; the 911 entries include, in addition to truncations strictly so termed (the great majority), a certain number of other words from slang (e.g. *méduche* = *médaille*) or *verlan* (e.g. *meuf* = *femme*); in addition to English translations or definitions, we are provided with sources and/or illustrative examples, and in most cases dates of earliest attestations; theoretical and methodological matters are dealt with in a substantial introduction.

8. LEXICOLOGY

IG, 86, which is devoted to Old and Middle French, includes C. Buridant, 'Prolégomènes à une étude synthétique de la morphologie dérivationnelle en ancien français' (14–20), R. Martion, 'Où puiser en lexicologie du moyen français?' (53–56), and C. Thomasset, 'Réflexion sur le vocabulaire scientifique du moyen français' (57–60). G. Roques, '*Gresillon* et les dénominations du "grillon" en français médiéval', *TLP*, 38:7–25, argues persuasively that *gresillon* (the term used, *inter alia*, with reference to Frobert the cricket in the *Renart*) was originally a western dialectal form. C. Schmitt, 'Zu den Namen der französischen Wasservögel', *ZRP*, 116:72–106, is well documented but could have been better organized, with alphabetically or thematically ordered subdivisions.

The scope of François Gaudin and Louis Guespin, *Initiation à la lexicologie française: de la néologie aux dictionnaires*, Louvain-la-Neuve, Duculot, 355 pp., is well indicated by its title and subtitle. The first chapter in this excellent volume traces the history of French lexicography from Robert Estienne's *Thesaurus* (1531) to computerized works, and is followed by another surveying a wide range of contemporary dictionaries, with particular attention to their theoretical basis and methodology. A chapter on 'Lexicologie: le point de vue saussurien' leads into others on 'Les relations lexicales' and 'Le problème du mot'. Finally, four chapters cover neologisms (problems and history; derivation, composition, abbreviations, and loan-words; and semantic neologisms).

B. Farrington, 'Words as new as the hills. Concept formation in the field of high altitude topography (1750–1850)', *JFLS*, 10:45–72, discusses the complex process involved in the development of a lexical system to describe 'a set of newly discovered things', viz. mountain features. Annie Mollard-Desfour, **Le Dictionnaire des mots et expressions de couleur du XXe siècle. 2, Le Rouge*, CNRS, 490 pp. Hans-Burkard Krause, **Lexikologische Beschreibungen zum konzeptuell-semantischen Netz 'intelligence' im heutigen Französisch*, Berne, Lang, 1999, 393 pp.

Jean-François Sablayrolles, *La Néologie en français contemporain: examen du concept et analyse de productions néologiques récentes*, Champion, 588 pp., is the latest addition (no. 4) to the distinguished 'Lexica' series; section I, 'L'état de la question', has chapters on the history of the notion of lexical innovation (taking us as far back as the Greeks), on typology, and on the role of the concept of neology in a number of contemporary linguistic models; section II, 'Examen méthodique du

concept et propositions', deals with the nature of the 'unité linguistique néologique', the notion of 'nouveauté', and neological
procedures; and the final three chapters, under the general heading
'Aspects sociolinguistiques et énonciatifs', present the results of S.'s
own research, setting out the bases of the construction of his corpus,
the analysis thereof, and finally asking, and answering at considerable
length, the question 'Pourquoi des néologismes?'. A. Thibault,
'"Grand-maman et grand-papa en costume de bain au petit-
déjeuner!"'. Contribution à l'histoire de quelques lexies complexes',
CLe, 75, 1999:35–54, deals only with French.

C. Schapira, 'Du prototype au stéréotype, et inversement: le cliché
comme + SN', *CLe*, 76:27–40, discusses the semantic features, formation, and linguistic status of the cliché in question. D. Delaplace offers
'Notes pour l'étude linguistique du vocabulaire dit "familier"', *ib.*,
111–31. D. Mayaffre discusses '*Nation* et *patrie* dans le discours de
droite à la veille de la guerre', *ib.*, 133–50, with a view to answering
the question 'Quels signifiants pour signifier quel patriotisme?'.

F. Gaudin, 'Histoires de sens: quelques métaphores de biologistes',
CLe, 75, 1999:91–112, deals with French terms (all of which,
however, have cognates or translation equivalents in other languages).

9. SEMANTICS

Martina Batteux, *Die französische Synonymie im Spannungsfeld zwischen
Paradigmatik und Syntagmatik, Berne, Lang, xii + 390 pp.

10. ONOMASTICS

J.-P. Chambon, 'Pour la chronologie des toponymes gallo(romans)
d'origine délexicale. Étude d'un type tardo-antique aquitain: *Fornols*',
ER, 22:59–82, is methodologically important. M. Dorch, '*Lauben* als
Ortsnamentyp im Deutschen und im Französischen — ein Relikt der
frühmittelarterlichen Waldwirtschaft', *ZRP*, 116:418–37, covers such
forms as French *Loge, Lalobbe, La Vieille-Loye*.

11. DIALECTS AND REGIONAL FRENCH

T. Pooley, 'Sociolinguistics, regional varieties of French and regional
languages in France', *JFLS*, 10:117–57, consists principally of a
review, with an extensive bibliography, of sociolinguistic studies of
the present situation of regional languages in France itself.

Jacques Mercier, *Le Français tel qu'il se parle en Belgique*, Tournai,
Renaissance du Livre, 361 pp., consists of over 300 one-page essays
(originally published in the newspaper *La Libre Belgique*), well written

and often instructive and entertaining, on the origin and use of words and expressions, many of them however not specifically Belgian and some (e.g. 'L'épée de Damoclès') not even specifically French; and, given the title, one might have expected some attention to be paid to other aspects (grammar, pronunciation) of French as spoken in Belgium. Cléante [no initial], *Tours et expressions de Belgique: prononciation, grammaire, vocabulaire*, Louvain-la-Neuve, Duculot, 160 pp., consists of some 400 notes (originally published in *Le Soir*, but some of them here reissued in an expanded form) classified into the categories referred to in the title; this is generally a more informative and more specifically 'Belgian' work than Mercier's. C. Corneau, 'An EPG study of palatalization in French: cross-dialect and inter-subject variation', *LVC*, 12:25–50, studies the phenomenon in standard Belgium (*sic*) French by means of electropalatography.

Jean-Baptiste Martin, *Le Parler du Forez et du Roannais*, Bonneton, 160 pp., is the latest addition to the series 'Dictionnaires du français régional' to which we have frequently drawn attention in these pages (see most recently *YWMLS*, 61:46); it replaces the same author's *Dictionnaire du français régional du Pilat* (1989, see *YWMLS*, 51:48) in the series, from which it differs in including only words and expressions still enjoying 'une certaine vitalité' but also in covering a wider geographical area (the whole of the department of the Loire). Éloi Guitteny, **Le Vieux Langage du pays de Retz: lexique du parler régional*, Laval, Siloë, 302 pp.

J.-P. Chambon, 'Frm. *fayard* "hêtre": étude lexicographique et lexicologique d'un régionalisme', *RLaR*, 103:229–45, and P. Rézeau, 'Gourmandises régionales du français de France: *coque, coustade, pastis* et *tourtière*', *ib.*, 347–61, both reproduce articles from the *Dictionnaire des régionalismes de France (1950–2000)*, in preparation at INLF/CNRS, Nancy. B. Moreux, 'Les syntagmes figés en français du sud-ouest: essai de typologie synchronique et diachronique', *ib.*, 295–315, is of general methodological interest.

G. Price, 'French in the Channel Islands', in Price, *Languages*, 187–96, deals with the historical background and present situation of the traditional dialect in each island. M. C. Jones, 'Swimming against the tide: language planning on Jersey', *LPLP*, 24:167–96, puts into their sociolinguistic context the different agencies of language planning in the island and, by comparing their activity with what has been happening elsewhere, particularly in the Celtic-speaking countries, assesses the chances of a successful outcome to their endeavours to maintain Jèrriais. N. C. W. Spence studies 'L'évolution des voyelles protoniques et atones dans les parlers jersiais', *AnN*, 50:459–64, and 'Nasalisation et dénasalisation dans les parlers jersiais', *ib.*, 569–74. In an article that breaks new ground, given that the syntax of Channel

Islands French in general has been so little studied in the past, M. C. Jones examines the syntax and morphology of 'The subjunctive in Guernsey Norman French', *JFLS*, 10:73–99.

J. Médélice, 'Sur quelques anthropomorphismes liés à l'activité humaine dans les désignations de la faune et la flore sauvages', *Géolinguistique*, 8 , 1999 [2000]:51–81, draws on data from the *ALF*, the atlases of the *Nouvel Atlas Linguistique de la France par régions*, the *Atlas Linguistique de la Wallonie*, and the *Glossaire des Patois de la Suisse Romande*.

Bernard Moreux and Robert Razou, *Les Mots de Toulouse: lexique du français toulousain*, Toulouse, Le Mirail U.P., 671 pp., is the fruit of a collaboration between a native speaker of Toulouse French, R.R. (1902–97), and a trained linguist, B.M.; of the 1285 regionalisms listed, 778 are said to be in addition to those given in J. Séguy's *Le français parlé à Toulouse* (1950); entries give pronunciation (according to the IPA) and definitions or translations, often with examples, together with a linguistic commentary, indications as to geographical spread, and etymological notes (often with reference to such dictionaries as the *FEW*, Mistral's *Tresor dóu Felibrige*, and Simon Palay's Gascon dictionary); there is a 16–page bibliography. A. Valli, 'Remarques sur le français parlé de locuteurs de la région de Marseille. Usage régional du français et "régionalisme"', *RFP*, 15, 1999:59–86, seeks to define the status of 'regional French', taking up a number of features highlighted by A. Brun, *Le français de Marseille* (1930), and drawing on data provided by the corpus being compiled by the Groupe Aixois de Recherches en Syntaxe. Léon Mazzella and Pascale Mazzella, **Si tu meurs avant moi je te tue: une anthologie des expressions pied-noires*, Biarritz, Atlantica, 112 pp.

*Le Petit Dictionnaire suisse romand: particularités lexicales du français contemporain: version condensée du Dictionnaire suisse romand, ed. Pierre Knecht, Carouge, Zoé, 293 pp. M.-T. Vinet and C. Rubattel, 'Propriétés configurationnelles: un *ça* objet déficient', *Lingua*, 110:891–929, is based on the French of the Swiss canton of Vaud.

12. ANGLO-NORMAN

D. A. Trotter, 'Anglo-Norman', in Price, *Languages*, 197–206, achieves his stated three-fold aim of outlining the establishment and subsequent social and spatial distribution of Anglo-Norman, tracing its development in terms of its functional roles, and discussing its impact on the other languages (principally, of course, English) with which it was in contact. W. Rothwell offers 'Glanures lexicologiques dans des documents des 14e et 15e siècles provenant de l'évêché de Durham', *ZRP*, 116:213–36, and comments on 'The trial scene in *Lanval* and the development of the legal register in Anglo-Norman', *NMi*,

101:17–36. D. Trotter, 'L'avenir de la lexicographie anglo-normande: vers une refonte de l'*Anglo-Norman Dictionary?*', *RLiR*, 64:391–405, explains the differences between the first edition (1977–92) of the dictionary and the revision now in preparation.

13. FRENCH IN NORTH AMERICA

E. Khaznadar, 'Masculin et féminin dans la dénomination humaine: linguistique et politique', *FM*, 68:141–70, offers an 'aperçu de la pratique québécoise'. Terry Nadasdi, *Variation grammaticale et langue minoritaire: le cas des pronoms clitiques en français ontarien*, Munich, LINCOM Europa, v + 158 pp. M.-T. Vinet, 'Feature representation and -*tu (pas)* in Quebec French', *SL*, 54:381–411, proposes an analysis of the interogative particle -*tu* (= -*ti*) in terms of its 'formal, semantic and phonological features [...]' within a minimalist approach'. Marcel Béliveau and Sylvie Granger, *Savoureuses expressions québécoises*, Monaco, Rocher, 90 pp. J.-C. Boulanger discusses 'Images de la norme du français québécois. Les perspectives lexicographiques contemporaines', *CLe*, 75, 1999:113–27. Louise Péronnet et al., *Atlas linguistique du vocabulaire maritime acadien*, Quebec, Laval U.P., 1998, xiii + 667 pp. Chantal Naud, *Dictionnaire des régionalismes du français parlé des îles de la Madeleine*, Vignaud, 1998, xxv + 311 pp. M. Russo, 'Linguistic change in endangered dialects: the case of alternation between *avoir* and *être* in Vermont French', *LVC*, 11:1–13, attributes the change to internal linguistic constraints rather than to social factors.

14. FRENCH IN AFRICA AND MADAGASCAR

Fouzia Benzakour, Driss Gaadi, and Ambroise Queffélec, *Le français au Maroc: lexique et contacts de langues*, Louvain-la-Neuve, Duculot, 360 pp., is the first publication to emerge from a wide-ranging research programme on the spoken and written French of the Maghreb. Part 1, 'Le français au Maroc: de l'implantation au contact et à l'intégration', presents not only an informative historical survey but also an account of the role and relative status of French, Arabic, and other languages (in particular, Berber), together with a more in-depth account of the situation of French in Morocco and of the varieties of Moroccan French. The entries (some 780 in all) in Part 2, 'Lexique', which takes up well over half of the volume, are extensively illustrated with examples drawn mainly from the written and spoken media with a few from spontaneous conversation; many, but not all, also include etymological, semantic, and/or sociolinguistic observations. There is also a useful classified bibliography. Paul Zang Zang,

Le Processsus de dialectalisation du français en Afrique. Le cas du Cameroun, Munich, LINCOM Europa, 450 pp.

Claudine Bavoux, *Le Français de Madagascar: contribution à un inventaire des particularités lexicales* ('Champs linguistiques'), Louvain-la-Neuve, Duculot, 212 pp., itemizes over 1000 words and expressions with definitions, examples, etymological (and, in some cases, socio-linguistic) comments, and cross-references to 'lexies associées'.

15. FRENCH CREOLES

Chris Corne, *From French to Creole. The Development of New Vernaculars in the French Colonial World*, London, Univ. of Westminster Press, 1999, x + 263 pp., is a much needed work, providing as it does, in English, a wide-ranging and informative survey of French Creoles. It is organized primarily on geographical lines, with, after a general introduction, chapters on New Caledonia, Réunion, Louisiana, the West Indies and Guyana, and Mauritius, and others on 'Pidgins, the Ivory Coast, and the Red River [in Manitoba]' and 'New vernaculars from old'. The geographically-based chapters include, typically, a survey of the historical background and a selection of texts, with, in some cases, appendices on grammatical or other features of the variety on question. There is also an extensive bibliography.

Under the general heading 'Les créoles français', *IG*, 85, includes: D. Véronique,'Créole, créoles français et théories de la créolisation' (33–38); D. Fattier, 'Genèse de la détermination postnominale en haïtien: l'empreinte africaine' (39–46); D. de Robillard, 'Pluri-fonctionnalité de(s) *la* en créole mauricien' (47–52); and A. Valdman, 'L'évolution du lexique dans les créoles à base lexicale française' (53–60). T. A. Klingler, 'Louisiana creole: the multiple-genesis hypothesis reconsidered', *JPCL*, 15 : 1–35, argues in favour of 'the scenario of a single genesis'.

The rapid growth in the field of Creole studies makes it increasingly difficult to give it adequate coverage within the limited space available here. Much fuller coverage than can be achieved here is provided by the quarterly newsletter, *Gazet sifon ble / Lavwa ka bay*, produced by the Institut d'Études Créoles at the Université d'Aix-en-Provence, which is also displayed on its web site <http://www.lpl.univ-aix.fr/iecf/>. Consequently, this subsection will not figure in future volumes of *YWMLS*.

16. DISCOURSE ANALYSIS AND TEXT LINGUISTICS

The contents of *CLF*, 19, 20, and 21 fall mainly under this heading. *CLF*, 19, 'Problèmes d'analyse du discours', includes: M. Burger,

'Positions d'interaction: une approche modulaire' (11–46); L. Filliettaz, 'Des enjeux actionnels dans les interactions verbales: une définition de la dimension référentielle du discours' (47–82); A. Grobet, 'La ponctuation prosodique dans les dimensions périodique et informationnelle du discours' (83–123); É. Miche, 'L'organisation polyphonique d'un fragment de débat radiophonique' (125–47); E. Roulet, 'L'organisation polyphonique et l'organisation inférentielle d'un dialogue romanesque' (149–79); L. Perrin, 'Force réflexive conventionnelle des énoncés, délocutivité et discours rapporté' (181–203); A. Kuyumcuyan, 'L'invention du lecteur ou la "diaphonie potentielle": quelques remarques sur l'incipit de *Si par une nuit d'hiver un voyageur* d'Italo Calvino' (205–31), which is based on the French translation of the novel; C. Rossari and J. Jayez, 'Connecteurs de conséquence et portée sémantique' (233–65); K. Stroumza and A. Auchlin, 'L'étrange polyphonie du texte de l'apprenti rédacteur' (267–304); R. Yessouroun, 'Le destinataire: qu'en faire?' (305–22); L. de Saussure, 'Passé simple et encapsulation d'événements' (323–44); and M. Kozlowska, 'Bornage et ordre temporel' (345–68). *Ib.*, 20, 'Le discours écrit: qualité(s), spécificités, et acquisitions', publishes the 'Actes du VIIème Colloque de pragmatique de Genève (37–29 mai 1998)', and includes (in addition to some items not relating solely or substantially to French): J.-M. Adam, 'La qualité des productions discursives: réflexions théoriques et étude de cas' (13–29); K. Adamzik, 'Le début du texte. Le titre et les premières phrases dans des textes académiques' (31–64); R. Amacker, 'La servante maîtresse' (65–86), on F. de Saussure and W. von Humboldt; R. Bouchard, M.-M. De Gaulmyn, and R. Sadni-Jallab, '*Impeccable!* Le processus d'amélioration du texte en écriture coopérative' (103–27); J.-L. Chiss, 'Le discours écrit entre modèle(s) et style(s)' (129–38); L. Jenny, 'Bonheur d'expression' (197–208): A. Reboul and J. Moeschler, 'Théorie de l'esprit, rationalité et principe de charité: l'évaluation de la qualité des textes' (209–27); M.-J. Béguelin, 'Le rapport écrit-oral. Tendances dissimilatrices, tendances assimilatrices' (229–53); and K. Stroumza, 'Le style et l'énonciation: quelques ronds dans l'eau' (275–86). *Ib.*, 21, 'Décrire la complexité de l'organisation des discours', falls into two parts; the first, consisting of papers given at the round table, 'Plans d'organisation du discours', on the occasion of the 6th International Pragmatics Congress at Rheims (July, 1998), includes: D. Apotheloz and F. Zay, 'Incidents de la programmation syntagmatique: reformulations micro- et macro-syntaxiques' (11–34); M. Burger, 'Identités de statut, identités de rôle' (35–59); J. Espuny, 'La diaphonie dans l'échange face à face' (61–77); L. Filliettaz, 'La structure actancielle et la structure textuelle des interactions verbales' (79–100); A. Grobet, 'La continuité topicale dans les dialogues radiophoniques: quelques relations de discours' (101–20); K. Kostulski and A. Trognon, 'L'explication logique des aspects cognitifs de la conversation: existe-t-il une isomorphie entre le domaine cognitif et l'architecture d'une conversation?' (121–50); A. Kuyumcuyan, 'Hétérogénéité textuelle: l'exemple de la fable' (151–79); C. Rossari, 'Les relations de discours avec ou sans connecteurs' (181–92); and B. Wetzel-Kranz, 'Ressemblances et différences dans différents types d'entretien' (193–212); in the second section, under the overall heading 'Approche modulaire de l'hétérogénéité compositionnelle de la narration', we find: L. Filliettaz and A. Grobet, 'L'hétérogénéité compositionnelle du discours: quelques remarques préliminaires' (213–60); L. Filliettaz, 'Une approche modulaire de l'hétérogénéité compositionnelle des discours: le cas des récits oraux' (261–327); A. Grobet, 'L'organisation topicale de la narration. Les interrelations de l'organisation topicale et des organisations séquentielle et compositionnelle' (329–68); and A. Kuyumcuyan, 'Prolégomènes à une définition du discours narratif' (369–86). L. Rosier, 'Le moyen français revisité par l'énonciation: "signes et mentions" du discours rapporté', *IG*, 87:24–32, seeks to 'faire le point sur le traitement grammatical et linguistique réservé à ce mécanisme énonciatif courant et complexe'. K. Fløttum, 'Le discours rapporté dans l'éditorial', *TrL*, 41:107–15, is based on leading articles in *Le Monde*, 1995–96.

17. Contrastive Studies

Nigel Turner, *Étude contrastive de l'infinitif en français et en anglais*, Gap, Ophrys, 265 pp. P. Reed, '*Any* and its French equivalents', *JFLS*, 10:101–16, shows that the contrast between existential and universal *any* is less significant in French than in English. M. N'Diaye, 'Les constructions comparatives en *plus/moins* [. . .] *que*', *RFP*, 15, 1999:137–61, contrasts French with a number of other languages ranging from Tahitian to Latin. H. de Swart and A. Molendijk, 'Le passé composé narratif: une analyse discursive de *L'étranger* de Camus', *RLFRU*, 19:45–60, contrast the use of the perfect in French, English, and Dutch. Siméon Grammenidis, *La Deixis dans le passage du grec au français*, Gap, Ophrys, 181 pp.

EARLY MEDIEVAL LITERATURE

By SARA I. JAMES, *Honorary Research Fellow, University of Hull*, and
ADRIAN P. TUDOR, *Department of French, University of Hull*

I. GENERAL

Yasmina Foehr-Janssens, *La Veuve en majesté: deuil et savoir au féminin dans la littérature médiévale*, Geneva, Droz, 301 pp., examines not only widows, but female protagonists in adversity in general in 13th-c. and later literature. The various heroines who suffer persecution invariably use their melancholy situations as a catalyst for a search for knowledge and truth. Jean-Marie Fritz, *Paysages sonores du Moyen Age: Le versant épistémologique* (STCM, 5), Champion, 477 pp., will be of greatest interest to scholars of religious, didactic and philosophical texts, focusing as it does on the role played by sound in the Middle Ages — a subject that to date has been often neglected in favour of the visual. John L. Grigsby, **The Gab as Latent Genre in Medieval French Literature: Drinking and Boasting in the Middle Ages*, Cambridge, MA, Medieval Academy of America, ix + 255 pp. Richard W. Kaeuper, *Chivalry and Violence in Medieval Europe*, OUP, xi + 338 pp., uses a variety of *chansons de geste* and OF Arthurian texts as a means of studying the rules and beliefs underpinning the violence often associated with the Middle Ages. K. distances himself from the modern tendency to ascribe medieval displays of violence purely to alterity, and examines how literature functions both descriptively and prescriptively in an age in which violence and devotion, while coexisting, were not without conflict. Molly Lynde-Recchia, *Prose, Verse and Truth-Telling in the Thirteenth Century: An Essay on Form and Function in Selected Texts, accompanied by an edition of the Prose 'Thèbes' as found in the 'Histoire ancienne jusqu'à César'* (Edward C. Armstrong Memorial Monographs on Medieval Literature, 10), Lexington, French Forum, 206 pp., examines the strategies of authors seeking to invest prose texts with their own narrative authority. The use of prose supported their Christian didacticism and infused their narratives with historical 'truth'. Our understanding of the use and development of prose is enhanced by a study of the influence of philosophical texts, underpinned by considerations of wider cultural context. Donald Maddox, *Fictions of Identity in Medieval France*, CUP, xx + 260 pp., analyses episodes from various OF texts, focusing on what he calls 'specular encounters', in which the hero's purpose and identity are revealed. M. argues that the variety and depth of these exchanges attests to both the authors' versatility and the wealth of hermeneutic possibilities in all genres. Texts studied include the 13th-c. *Vie de saint*

Eustace, the *Lais* of Marie de France, the works of Chrétien de Troyes, *Le Bel inconnu*, the prose *Lancelot*, *La Queste del saint Graal*, *La Châtelaine de Vergi*, the *Tristan* corpus, *La fille du comte de Pontieu*, *Mélusine*, *La Vie de saint Alexis*, and *Le Roman de la Rose*. James R. Simpson, *Fantasy, Identity and Misrecognition in Medieval French Narrative*, Berne, Lang, 290 pp., is a compelling analysis of a diverse range of texts from the 13th c. and later. S. uses psychoanalytic theory to untangle the complex and conflicted creation of medieval identity from the gratuitous violence often associated with the Middle Ages. Far from undermining notions of identity, the misrecogition of the title serves as a foil for the reinforcement of self, which is itself constructed and disseminated by means of fantasy. *Si a parlé par moult ruiste vertu. Mélanges de littérature médiévale offerts à Jean Subrenat*, ed. Jean Dufournet, Champion, 301 pp. *Sommes et cycles (XIIe–XIVe siècles)*, ed. Marie-Étiennette Bély, Jean-René Valette, and Jean-Claude Vallecalle, Univ. Catholique de Lyon. *Zumthor Vol.* will be of general interest to most OF scholars; although it studies Zumthor's contribution to scholarship on various topics rather than any particular work or genre in detail, it nevertheless provides a valuable overview of his research and influence. C. Bouillot, 'Aux antipodes du beau geste: le geste laid et inconvenant dans la littérature des XIIème et XIIIème siècles', *Senefiance*, 43:47–56, rejects the notion that only epic and *fabliau* present non-courtly behaviour. B. posits that the *roman* shows both manners to imitate and those to shun, with the aim of constructing a more refined and elegant society. D. Boutet, 'Royauté et transcendance dans la fiction littéraire au temps de Philippe Auguste', Bély, *Personne*, 35–59, traces the development of the notion that royal personages are a breed apart, semi-human, semi-divine, in a variety of texts, including romance, epic, and chronicle. D. Nicolle, 'The nature and perception of the *besague* in Old French narrative', *NMS*, 44:49–68, examines literary and visual evidence of the weapon known as the *besague*, mentioned most prominently in *Partonopeus de Blois*, but also in other romances, saints' lives, and epic. P. Wackers, 'There are no genres: remarks on the classification of literary texts', *Reinardus*, 13:237–48, is a provocative and refreshing discussion of classification, with particular attention paid to beast epic, fable, and *fabliau*. Historical and modern notions of genres are both useful, but need to be used with care.

2. Epic

GENERAL. K. A. Campbell, 'En haute mer: navire et marin dans la chanson de geste', *Senefiance*, 45:35–49, discusses episodes of sea voyages and associated fantastical events from a variety of epic poems (including *Anseÿs de Mes*, *Les Enfances Guillaume*, *Huon de Bordeaux*, and *Doon de Mayence*). The sea was seen through the eyes of epic heroes who, for all their prowess, are seafaring amateurs; descriptions of terrifying storms, lavish decorations, and divine interventions reflect this. H. Legros, 'Décrire Jérusalem', *ib.*, 153–66, discusses both chronicle and epic, drawing upon Guillaume de Tyr's translation of the *Historia rerum in partibus transmarinis gestarum*, Ernoul's post-1187 chronicle, *La Conquête de Jérusalem*, and *Le Voyage de Charlemagne à Jérusalem et à Constantinople*. All four texts are united in presenting an image of the city that, while grounding itself in 'realistic' description, never loses sight of the religious and crusading vision associated with it. P. Ménard, 'Les noms et qualificatifs des génies et des enchanteurs dans les chansons de geste', *ib.*, 179–91, studies the likely provenance of magicians' names and concludes that many of them were ironic or subtly undermined the impressive talents of the character. J. Raidelet-Galdeano, 'Beauté apparente et laideur inconsciente: reflet des errances de l'âme dans quelques chansons de geste,' *ib.*, 43:437–55, bases much of the argument — a relatively original one — on *Raoul de Cambrai* and *Robert le Diable*. In a volume dedicated to the theme of beauty and ugliness in medieval literature and culture, R.-D. avoids the habitual study of fair Franks vs. demonic Saracens to examine, initially, how aesthetic perceptions of weather, architecture, and nature reflect order or chaos within the plot. R.-D. then goes on to analyse all too briefly some instances in *Girart de Roussillon* in which physical beauty does not equal moral rectitude in the hero. This analysis, like the first part of the article, merits further discussion. M. Houdeville, 'Les Sarrasins, miroir des chrétiens?', *ib.*, 46:77–83, discusses briefly the ways in which the Christian-Saracen binarism works to illuminate both sides, each reflecting the other. D. Hüe, 'La chrétienté au miroir sarrasin', *ib.*, 85–99, analyses the ways in which the Saracen fulfils a critical psychological function within epic, not only in reinforcing a positive Christian identity, but also, according to H., playing a role in what he calls the 'roman familial' of the epic. H. claims that the Saracen does so by invoking both paternal and maternal roles, through being both forbidding and comforting. F. Suard, 'La chrétienté au péril de l'invasion sarrasine', *ib.*, 231–48, bases his observations upon works from all three epic cycles, demonstrating that Christian crusade and Saracen invasion are not mutually exclusive themes. The coexistence of both forms of conflict not only guarantees narrative variety and tension, but also reinforces the ideological message of constant vigilance. J. Subrenat, 'L'esprit de la conversion dans les chansons de geste françaises', *ib.*, 263–76, compares collective with individual baptisms, and the variety of circumstances surrounding the motif of the Saracen converting to

Christianity, whether by force or by choice. *Guerres, voyages et quêtes au Moyen Age: mélanges offerts à Jean-Claude Faucon, ed. Alain Labbé, Daniel W. Lacroix, and Danielle Quéruel, Champion, 467 pp.

ROLAND AND CHARLEMAGNE. Karl Reichl, *Singing the Past: Turkic and Medieval Heroic Poetry*, Ithaca–London, Cornell U.P., xiv + 221 pp., devotes a sub-section (153–63) entitled ' "Nos avum dreit": history and identity in the *Chanson de Roland*' to a review of the various possible links between the poem and the 778 ambush. R. also claims that use of terms such as 'nos' indicates a homogeneous cultural identity at the time of composition. M. Cramer Vos, 'Le paysage montagneux dans l'épopée, *La Chanson de Roland*', *Senefiance*, 45:83–95, posits that the numerous descriptions of rocky terrain in the poem reflect not only the logistical difficulties encountered by Charlemagne's army, but also their spiritual struggle. G. Gouiran, 'Le sarrasin: du fond de l'enfer aux portes de salut', *ib.*, 46:41–50, provides a useful but far too brief overview of the portrayal of Saracens in the Occitan version of the *Chanson de Roland*, the *Ronsasvals*. R. Lafont, 'Le tueur martyr: "saint Roland" ', *PRIS-MA*, 16:101–16, makes a case for the *Chanson de Roland* as hagiography. M. W. Morris, 'The concept of empire and transcendental mission: an Augustinist scheme in the *Chanson de Roland*', *MedP*, 15:82–92, assigns to each actor in the *Roland* a role in establishing God's rule on earth, with Charlemagne burdened by his divine duty. H.-E. Keller, 'Exile and return in the *Chanson de Mainet*', *Senefiance*, 45:113–21, links epic to folklore studies through judicious use of the latter to analyse the theme of the hero who, after being wrongly judged and dismissed, returns in triumph. J.-C. Vallecalle, 'Le héros et l'ermite: sur un passage de *L'Entrée d'Espagne*', *ib.*, 277–87, posits that, although the role of the holy man is a venerated one, the epic sees the hero who fights God's fight as the more accessible spiritual ideal.

GUILLAUME D'ORANGE AND THE GARIN CYCLE. Michael A. Newth provides a new translation of Bertrand de Bar-sur-Aube, *The Song of Girart de Vienne* (MRTS, 196), 1999, xxiv + 200 pp. *Le Siège de Barbastre*, ed. Bernard Guidot (CFMA, 137), 490 pp., provides a much-needed new edition of this Monglane cycle poem.

EPICS OF REVOLT. D. Boutet, 'Le roi Louis et la signification politico-historique de *Raoul de Cambrai*', *Romania*, 118:315–35, examines not only *Raoul de Cambrai* but also *La Chronique de Waubert* and (in passing) *La Vengeance Fromondin*, in order to contest the view that Raoul's rebellion mirrors aristocratic discontent under Philip Augustus. In the latter two texts, Raoul acts as an invader seeking vengeance, whereas in the eponymous work he seeks recognition of his status, which only exists if linked explicitly to a fiefdom. The situation arises from Louis's weakness and his offending all parties through an impossible attempt to offend none. Confusion arises from refusal to see the king as the originator of conflict; B. concludes that there are in fact more links between *Raoul de Cambrai* and the 12th- and 13th-c. monarchy and the Orange cycle, than with Philip Augustus and his reign. J.-C. Herbin, 'Sarrasins et chrétiens dans la *Geste des Loherains*', *Senefiance*, 46:51–76, shows how the poems of this cycle see true evil as emanating from individual human flaws such as greed, ambition, and epic *démesure*, present in many of the Christian characters, rather than from the external pagan. A. Labbé, ' "Li garçonnés petis": l'enfant et le saint dans *Anseÿs de Mes*', *ib.*, 123–39, discusses the rare instance of the true child in epic, emblem of innocence yet witness to violence and criminality, as distinct from the young heroes of epic *enfances*. L. further develops this theme in 'Quand les saints vivaient parmi nous: sainteté, pouvoir et condamnation du siècle dans *Anseÿs de Mes*', *PRIS-MA*, 16:77–100, in which the seemingly contradictory role of the saint-hermit is examined. Although the epic saint often intervenes towards the end, in *Anseÿs de Mes* he plays an ambivalent role throughout, both marking and condemning conflict and bloodshed. V. Naudet, 'La chrétienté au péril sarrasin? (Les Sarrasins dans la geste des Loherens)', *ib.*, 161–82, uses *Garin le Loheren*, *Gerbert de Mes*, and *Anseÿs de Mes* to demonstrate the marginal role played by Saracens in these works, in which the primary conflict occurs between Christian Franks. F. Suard, 'Le *Beuves d'Aigremont* dans la version des incunables et dans les manuscrits en vers', *Senefiance*, 45:253–61, will be of use to scholars specifically interested in the transmission of this text, traditionally seen as the prologue to *Renaut de Montauban*.

OTHER EPICS. *Jourdain de Blaye en alexandrins*, ed. Takeshi Matsumura, 2 vols (TLF, 520), 1999, lxii + 1163, provides a comprehensive critical apparatus to this new edition of a relatively little-known text. M. discusses the age of the text extensively, taking issue with the traditional late 12th- to early 13th-c. dating in favour of placing it in the late 14th century. V. Galent-Fasseur, 'La tentation sarrasine de Beuve de Hantone', *Senefiance*, 46:27–39, examines the way in which the young Beuve, after his initial betrayal at the hands of his Christian family, seeks to find his place among Saracens and other 'others', using deception and betrayal in his turn. R. Wolf-Bonvin, 'Escopart, le géant dépérissant de Beuve de Hantone', *ib.*, 249–65, analyses the physical appearance of this character, as well as his name, to reveal heterogeneous and often inconsistent views of the monstrous other. H. Legros, 'Réalités et imaginaires du péril sarrasin', *ib.*, 125–45, studies the apparent contradiction inherent in the *chansons d'Antioche* and *de Jérusalem*, as well as in the associated chronicles. Although depicting actual Christian-Saracen conflict, they show greater awareness of the complexity and nuances of the *réalité*, distancing themselves from the stark binarism of earlier poems, based almost exclusively on the *imaginaire*. F. Suard, *'L'image du roi dans les chansons de geste du premier cycle de la croisade', *BDBA*, 18 : 153–70. J.-C. Vallecalle, 'Du surnaturel au merveilleux: les apparitions célestes dans les chansons de geste tardives', Bély, *Personne*, 169–86, examines instances of miraculous or divine dreams, apparitions or premonitions in the epic, concluding that what in early epics manifests itself as divine intervention is, by the later epic, assimilated into the *merveilleux* aspects of certain characters. The epic world, V. concludes, remains a closed one.

3. ROMANCE

GENERAL. Peggy McCracken, *The Romance of Adultery: Queenship and Sexual Transgression in Old French Literature*, Philadelphia, Pennsylvania U.P., 1998, xiii + 224 pp., includes discussions of *La Châtelaine de Vergi*, works by Chrétien de Troyes, Gautier d'Arras's *Eracle*, *La fille du comte de Pontieu*, the *Lancelot en prose*, *La mort le roi Artu*, *Le Roman des sept sages*, *Le Roman de Silence*, various *fabliaux*, and other brief narratives. M. examines the theme of adulterous queens in medieval romance not in the context of the traditional courtly love *topos*, but in terms of the broader social and political implications of adultery. She also discusses the role of the texts in charting the changing nature of queenship as an institution. Krueger, *Romance*, intended for students, is an attractive and user-friendly introduction to the genre. Many of the 15 essays deal directly with OF texts, as subjects or sources: M. T. Bruckner, 'The shape of romance in medieval France' (13–28), provides a succinct overview of narrative structures, themes, and motifs in early OF texts; C. Baswell, 'Marvels of translation and crises of transition in the romances of antiquity' (29–44), outlines the notions of *translatio studii* and *translatio imperii* in the *romans d'antiquité*, explores new forms of social order, and examines textual erotic tension; S. Gaunt, 'Romance and other genres' (45–59), concisely highlights the various intertextual relationships between romance and other traditions; S. Huot, 'The manuscript context of medieval romance' (60–77), provides an introduction to manuscript culture, discussing issues of transmission and reception; S. Kay, 'Courts, clerks and courtly love' (81–96), discusses representations of courtliness and courtly love in literary texts, concentrating on clerical and lay attitudes towards the complexities they reflect; R. Kaeuper, 'The societal role of chivalry in romance: northwestern Europe' (97–114), begins his discussion of romance as an active social force with a number of OF examples; J. Rider, 'The other worlds of romance'

(115–31), studies the *merveilleux* as a narrative tool; R. L. Krueger, 'Questions of gender in Old French courtly romance' (132–49), is a provocative account of romance debates on gender roles and identities; N. J. Lacy, 'The evolution and legacy of French prose romance' (167–82), stresses the centrality of OF texts in the development of European romance and offers a brief précis of texts and cycles. *Modern Retellings of Chivalric Texts*, ed. Gloria Allaire, Aldershot, Ashgate, 1999, ix + 186 pp., contains ten essays which identify and examine re-workings and mis- or re-readings of Renaissance and medieval texts (Bédier's 'primitive' *Tristan*, Chrétien, OF prose romances). B. Ceretti-Malinowski, 'Les chercheurs de vérité: l'invention du quotidien par quelques romanciers du XIIIe siècle', *RLaR*, 104 : 37–70, identifies texts (e.g. *L'Escoufle, Galeron de Bretagne*) in which love and marvels are abandoned for 'real-life' adventures. N. Grandperrin, **'Le roi, mari trahi: par sa femme, son imagination ou ses hommes? (Lais et romans arthuriens des XIIe et XIIIe siècles)', *BDBA*, 17 : 143–58. Kathleen C. Kelly, *Performing Virginity and Testing Chastity in the Middle Ages* (Routledge Research in Medieval Studies, 2), London–NY, Routledge, x + 197 pp., is of interest given its focus on romance and hagiography. In a wide-ranging study of both female and male virginity, a number of OF texts are considered alongside medical treatises, and historical and legal documents. K. concludes that the idea of virginity in the Middle Ages was conditional, heteroglossic, and conflicted. R. Dragonetti, 'Les sirènes du roman médiéval', *RLaR*, 104 : 1–22, suggests that the very essence of romance is to be found in its poetry and music. A. Guerreau-Jalabert, 'Des fées et des diables: observations sur le sens des récits mélusiniens au Moyen Âge', Boivin, *Mélusines*, 105–38, is a detailed study of prefigurations of Mélusine in Latin, OF and A-N texts. Michelle Sweeney, *Magic in Medieval Romance from Chrétien de Troyes to Geoffrey Chaucer*, Dublin, Four Courts, 199 pp., discusses the supernatural as a means to explore otherwise prohibited issues. Ch. 1 deals with the origins of the *Matière de Bretagne*, especially Wace; ch. 2 centres on Marie de France and Chrétien, where magic reflects a character's greatest achievements and exposes his worst weaknesses. From these texts magic will develop into an art of science and religion. Jean-Jacques Vincensini, **Motifs et thèmes du roman médiéval*, Nathan, vi + 154 pp.

CHRÉTIEN DE TROYES. Philippe Ménard, *De Chrétien de Troyes au 'Tristan en Prose'* (PRF, 224), 1999, 176 pp., is a collection of 14 previously published essays. D. B. Schwartz, '*Par bel mentir*: Chrétien's hermits and clerkly responsibility', *Uitti Vol.*, 287–310, views Chrétien's hermits as rewritings of Béroul's Ogrin: they are central to Chrétien's implicit defence of Arthurian fiction and so, by extension,

to his taking responsibility for his art. C. W. Carroll, 'The knights of
the round table in the manuscripts of *Erec et Enide*', *Lacy Vol.*, 117–27,
asks whether Chrétien wrote a short list of names to which scribes
added, or a long list which scribes chose to abridge. C. favours the
latter conclusion and suggests that the list found in MS *B* is Chrétien's
original work. M. Houdeville, 'Le beau et le laid: fonction et
signification dans *Erec et Enide* de Chrétien de Troyes', *Senefiance*,
43:231–37, suggests that for Chrétien, unlike other medieval
thinkers, concepts of beauty are relative, depending not only on
physical but also 'socialized' criteria. Chrétien's *Erec* is compared
with Hartmann von Aue's version in two essays from *Fest. Johnson*:
W. Haug, 'Joie de la Curt' (271–90); and M. Jones, '*Durch schoenen
lister sprach*: empathy, pretence and narrative point of view in
Hartmann von Aue's *Erec*' (291–308). J. Ribard, 'L'énigme Calogre-
nant', *Lacy Vol.*, 425–34, suggests that Chrétien, in his deliberately
surprising and perplexing opening to *Yvain*, is inviting the reader to
use his imagination and apply his own interpretations. J.-G. Gouttebroze, 'La laide demoiselle du *Conte du Graal*: le chant de deuil de la
terre', *Senefiance*, 43:179–84, studies *Perceval* as a chain of autonomous
events which contribute to the anonymity of the narrator. G. G.
Heyworth, 'Perceval and the seeds of culture: work, profit and leisure
in the prologue of *Perceval*', *Neophilologus*, 84:19–35, identifies the
relationship between work and reward as central to the prologue; it
informs the subsequent narrative in a subtle and mature way. Barbara
N. Sargent-Baur, *La destre et la senestre: étude sur le 'Conte du Graal' de
Chrétien de Troyes* (Faux Titre, 186), Amsterdam–Atlanta, Rodopi,
222 pp., provides a valuable commentary in the light of Chrétien's
atypical words in the prologue. *Perceval* is different from Chrétien's
earlier romances, a more mature invitation to readers to draw their
own conclusions from a text which opposes charity and vainglory in
a subtle and serious manner.

OTHER ARTHURIAN.   P. Ménard, 'Réflexions sur les coutumes dans
les romans arthuriens', *Lacy Vol.*, 357–70, posits that 'coutumes' give
an appearance of reality to unlikely literary motifs, sometimes even
veiling the irrational: in this way marvels can be justified. Michael
Camille, *The Medieval Art of Love. Objects and Subjects of Desire*, London,
Laurence King, 1999, 176 pp., returns frequently to OF Arthurian
texts to underpin his lavishly illustrated account of how images in
medieval art taught those looking at them 'the art of love'. Sandra
Billington, *Midsummer: A Cultural Sub-Text from Chrétien de Troyes to Jean
Michel* (Medieval Texts and Cultures of Northern Europe, 3),
Turnhout, Brepols, xiv + 249 pp., is of particular interest for chapters
2–5, which study the cultural, literary, political, and theatrical
significance of midsummer, highlighting it as a centre of subversion,

in the OF texts of *Yvain, Erec, Lancelot,* and *Galeran de Bretagne.*
Chrétien's wit and occasional absurdity mirror midsummer madness,
whereas Renaut provides a closer point of contact through his
treatment of psychological complexities.

The Lancelot-Grail Reader, ed. Norris J. Lacy, NY, Garland,
xviii + 430 pp., is a collection of excerpts, connected by narrative
summaries, taken from Garland's complete translation of the Vulgate
and Post-Vulgate cycles. Intended for students, it comprises a very
brief introduction (but no notes), and attractive translations of
sizeable sections from: *L'Estoire del saint Graal, Merlin, Lancelot, La Queste
del saint Graal,* and *La Mort Artu.* C. Chase, 'Whatever happened to
Hector's *amie*? Love, marriage, and land in the Prose *Lancelot*', *Lacy
Vol.,* 129–47, refers to the socio-historical context and folklore
traditions in an examination of women playing secondary or minor
roles. Hector forgets both women who love him since marriage is
indefinitely postponed for all landless youths in this world, a world
which continuously demands courageous and heroic deeds. Micheline
de Combarieu du Grès, *D'aventures en Aventure ('semblances' et 'senefiances'
dans le 'Lancelot en prose')* (*Senefiance,* 45), 551 pp., is a collection of 14
previously published essays and one new essay: 'La fée et les sortilèges
(Magie et illusion dans le *Lancelot Graal*)' (479–544). E. Kennedy, 'The
placing of miniatures in relation to the pattern of interlace in two
manuscripts of the Prose *Lancelot*', *Lacy Vol.,* 269–82, studies narrative
switches (according to place rather than person) and miniatures in
two MSS, both highlighting significantly different narrative and
structural elements. A. Longley, 'The Lady of the Lake: Lancelot's
mirror of self-knowledge', *ib.,* 311–21, explores the Lady of the Lake
as a vital character in terms of narrative direction, one whose
influence extends to the entire romance. D. Maddox, ' "A tombeau
ouvert": memory and mortuary monuments in the Prose *Lancelot*', *ib.,*
323–38, considers the revelatory and empowering aspect of the tomb
as mediator. M. convincingly argues that funerary monuments both
inform the memories of the protagonists and act as a textual aid to
the reader.

E. Schmid, 'Wahrheitsspiele in der *Mort Artu*', *GRM,* 49:373–89,
considers the chain of events that brings about a clean-cut end to the
narrative. F. Bogdanow, 'Un nouvel examen des rapports entre la
Queste Post-Vulgate et la *Queste* incorporée dans la deuxième version du
Tristan en Prose', *Romania,* 118:1–32, finds it probable, in the light of
the textual history of the *Queste Vulgate,* that the *Queste P-V* formed the
basis of the *Queste Tr. II.* P. McCracken, 'Damsels and severed heads:
more on linking in the *Perlesvaus*', *Lacy Vol.,* 339–55, develops Lacy's
work on linking by considering the symbolic and narrative functions
of the many severed heads in the text. A. Williams, 'Perspectives on

the Grail: subjectivity of experience in *La Queste del Saint Graal*, *RMS*, 26:141–53, posits that the reader's understanding of the text's mysteries depends on how much he has learned from the adventures of the protagonists. In 'Looping the loop through a tale of beginnings, middles and ends: from Chrétien to Gerbert in the *Perceval* Continuations', *Lacy Vol.*, 33–51, M. T. Bruckner studies the continuity and discontinuity of the *Perceval* continuations, such as the verbatim repetition of the last 14 lines of the *Second Continuation* at the beginning and end of the *Fourth Continuation*. She suggests that disentangling the 'middle' is of more import to the reader's pleasure than knowing, for example, what the end of the Grail adventure will be. J. Wood, 'The Holy Grail: from romance motif to modern genre', *Folklore*, 111:169–90, traces the interface between literary and popular culture.

F. Dubost, 'Lancelot et Tristan ou la transcendance décalée', Bély, *Personne*, 17–34, is an absorbing study of the emergence of a more laicised image of the 'person'. Stoyan Atanassov, **L'Idole inconnue: le personnage de Gauvain dans quelques romans du XIIIe siècle* (Coll. Medievalia, 31), Paradigme, 142 pp. W. Kibler, 'Sagremor in the Arthurian verse romances', *Lacy Vol.*, 283–92, examines this important name but elusive knight, a foil to Gauvain in verse texts through his *démesure*, and whose unruliness make him a formidable but lesser knight. V. Bubenicek, *'Quelques figures de rois-chevaliers errants dans le roman en prose de Guiron le Courtois', *BDBA*, 17:49–62. J.-G. Gouttebroze, *'De la reine à son fils, du roi à son épouse. Pour une bonne actualisation de la dévolution de la souveraineté en milieu celtique et arthurien', *ib.*, 131–42. A. Saly, 'Roi hermite, roi ascète', *PRIS-MA*, 16:289–301, studies this figure in Gerbert de Montreuil and the *Perlesvaus*, signaling in particular the importance of the Sanskrit *Ramayana of Valmiki* in the tradition of Arthurian legend. J.-R. Valette, 'Personnage, signe et transcendance dans les scènes du Graal (de Chrétien de Troyes à la *Queste del saint Graal*)', Bély, *Personne*, 187–214, examines the *transitus* of the Grail characters and views the hero of the *QSG* as closer to Roland than to his Arthurian companions.

L. J. Walters, 'Resurrecting Gauvain in *L'Atre périlleux* and the Middle Dutch *Walewein*', *Lacy Vol.*, 509–37, believes that the *AP*'s anti-feminism undermines the chivalric ideals supposedly embodied by Gauvain: his name, intertextually, locks Gawain into certain negative character traits, whereas in the MD text a name change is key to the knight's positive portrait. D. Kelly, 'The name topos in the *Chevalier aux deux épées*', *ib.*, 257–68, considers the romance as a partial rewriting of Chrétien's *Perceval*: both authors share similar writing practices, but the early text is much superior. P. V. Rockwell, '*Appellation contrôlée*: motif transfer and the adaptation of names in the

Chevalier as deus espees', *ib.*, 435–52, explores the discontinuity between Gauvain's *non* and *renon* and the questions this thematic gap raises concerning the source of narrative authority. S. Sturm-Maddox, 'Arthurian evasions: the end(s) of fiction in *Floriant et Florete*', *ib.*, 475–89, is a study of the final segment of the text which suggests that more credit should be given for its innovative, if puzzling, Arthurian elements. *Fils sans père: études sur le Merlin de Robert de Boron*, ed. Denis Hüe (Coll. Medievalia, 35), Paradigme, 214 pp. *Merlin, Robert de Boron*, ed. Danielle Quéruel and Christine Ferlampin Archer (Coll. CAPES/Agrégation Lettres), Ellipses-Marketing, 128 pp.

TRISTAN AND ISEUT. J.-M. Pastré, *'Le roi et son champion: Marc et son neveu dans les romans de Tristan', *BDBA*, 18:101–12.

Béroul, *Tristan et Iseut*, ed. and trans. Philippe Walter and Corina Stanesco (Classiques de Poche, 16072), Livre de Poche, 159 pp., is an attractive translation, aimed at *lycéens*, of the text found in B.N. fr. 2171. It includes a brief introduction and an elementary but useful 'dossier'.

In 'Killing giants and translating empires: the Tristan romances of Thomas and Gottfried', *Fest. Johnson*, 409–26, A. Stevens studies the evolution of the symbolic history of love, via narrative interpolation and historical allusion, from Geoffrey of Monmouth and Wace to Thomas and Gottfried. N. Zotz, 'Programmatische Vieldeutigkeit und verschlüsselte Eindeutigkeit', *GRM*, 50:1–19, examines the structure of the confession of love in the Carlisle fragment of Thomas's *Tristan* and in Gottfried's version.

Le Roman de Tristan en Prose, II, ed. Noëlle Laborderie and Thierry Delcourt (CFMA, 133), 1999, 542 pp., and III, ed. Jean-Paul Ponceau (CFMA, 135), 519 pp., follow on from Blanchard and Quéreuil's 1997 vol. I (CFMA, 123). The editions, based on B.N. fr. 757, are carefully established and meticulously documented. Vol. II begins with the feast held by Arthur at Camelot at Pentecost, and includes Lancelot's *folie*, the war between Tristan and Marc, and other episodes of adventure absent in detail from the *Prose* Vulgate. Vol. III covers the period from the lovers' arrival at Joyeuse Garde to the end of the Louveserp tournament, the longest passage present in all the versions of the text. B. Milland-Bove, *'Les aventures de Marc en Logres dans le *Tristan en prose*', *BDBA*, 18:73–84.

ROMANS D'ANTIQUITÉ. P. Logié, 'Fonctions du beau et du laid dans les romans d'antiquité', *Senefiance*, 43:351–67, establishes links between aesthetics and ethics: authors were fully conscious of the ambiguities of physical beauty which, if not necessarily condemned, was implicitly acknowledged as a potential source of danger.

C. Gaullier-Bougassas, 'Alexandre et les brahmanes dans les *Romans d'Alexandre* français, du XIIe au XIVe siècle', *MA*, 106:467–94, follows the appropriation and re-writing of a narrative sequence by successive authors. Id., 'Alexandre le Grand et la conquête de l'ouest dans les *Romans d'Alexandre* du XIIe siècle, leurs mises en prose au XVe siècle, et le *Perceforest*', *Romania*, 118:83–104, 394–430, is a meticulous study of Alexander's will to conquer both east and west as part of a universal empire. S. Friede, 'Alexander und Narcissus — ein Fall direkter Rezeption? Das Lied von Narcissus in der Amazonenepisode des *Romans d'Alexandre*, die Narcissus-Episode bei Ovid und der französische *Narcisse*', Baumbach, *Tradita*, 19–36, examines not only the common theme but also the very close similarities in text between the three versions. U. Mölk, 'Le poème d'Alexandre du chanoine Albéric', *Senefiance*, 45:207–15, considers how this extremely erudite author was inspired by a vast array of Latin, OF, and Provençal sources to produce a text which was ideologically suited to the noble classes.

V. Gontero, 'La chambre de beautés: nouvelle Jérusalem céleste?', *Senefiance*, 43:123–38, examines the motif in the *Roman de Troie* and its biblical antecedent in Revelations. P. Logié, *'Le roi Priam dans Le Roman de Troie de Benoît de Sainte-Maure', BDBA*, 18:57–72. A. Petit, *'Les rois dans le Roman de Thèbes', ib.*, 113–24.

M.-M. Castellani, '*Athis et Prophilias*, roman d'antiquité ou autre roman?' *RLaR*, 104:23–36, is an intriguing study of the short (early) and long (late) versions of a romance that is of contemporary composition but set in antiquity. P. Eley, 'The subversion of meaning in Hue de Rotelande's *Ipomedon*', *RMS*, 26:97–112, views the text as a sophisticated hermeneutic game in which the author deliberately sets out to make it impossible for the reader to construct meaning: this poem, which bears all the hallmarks of a romance, has no *sens*.

OTHER ROMANCES. S. L. Burch, '*Amadas et Ydoine*, *Cligès*, and the impediment of crime', *FMLS*, 36:185–95, concerns the fascinating question of Ydoine's refusal to grant Amadas her love when still married to the Count of Nevers: canon law prohibited the marriage of adulterers to each other, so is Fenice's marriage to Cligès really a happy ending? E. Derrien, *'Blancandin* ou l'apprentissage de la royauté', *BDBA*, 17:91–102. J. Weiss, 'The Anglo-Norman *Boeve de Haumtone:* A fragment of a new manuscript', *MLR*, 95:304–10, edits the 62 line fragment which is common to both MSS *B* and *D*. M. Gally, 'Ouvrages de dames: l'invention romanesque au XIIIe siècle', *RLaR*, 104:91–110, posits that *Galeron de Bretagne* reflects contemporary theoretical debates on the fundamental nature of love. C. Pierreville, *'L'image du roi et de l'empereur dans les romans de Gautier d'Arras', BDBA*, 18:125–38. J. Turnbull and P. Simons, 'The Pear Tree Episode in *Joufroi de Poitiers*', *FSB*, 75:2–4, explore the literary and cultural traditions linked to the pear tree, stressing in particular its sexual associations. K. Busby, '*Mise en texte* and *Mise en image*: *Meraugis de Portlesguez* in Vienna, ÖNB 2599', *Lacy Vol.*, 95–116, is a meticulous examination of a single-text codex which is ambiguous in terms of oral performance: punctuation, painted capitals, and miniatures bring out the basic dynamics between the various characters and both reflect and guide the reading of the narrative. P. Eley and P. Simons, 'Poets, birds and readers in *Partonopeus de Blois*', *FMLS*, 36:1–15, examine two sequences of three birds in the prologue and at the end of MS *A*: both invoke many layers of symbolic and intertextual meaning, the first inviting the reader to take part in the game of subversion, the second challenging that act of subversion. E. Llamas Pombo, 'Beauté, amour et mort dans les *Ovidiana* français du XIIe siècles', *Senefiance*, 43:337–50, finds that in *Piramus et Tisbé*, *Narcisus* and *Philomena*, notions of love and beauty are firmly rooted in traditional rhetoric and Latin literature. C. Lachet, 'La conjointure dans *Jehan et Blonde*: du roman idyllique au roman utopique', *RLaR*, 104:111–28, considers the text's political and social dimensions. S. Lécuyer, 'Un idéal social, politique et religieux transmis de père en fils: du roman de *Jehan et Blonde* aux *Coutumes de Beauvaisis*', *ib.*, 129–42, considers *Jehan et Blonde* a new model of society and a probing parable which will be echoed in the *Coutumes*. B. N. Sargent-Baur, 'Encore sur la datation de *Jehan et Blonde* de Philippe de Rémi', *Romania*, 118:236–48, rejects Claerr's identification of Jean de Trie with the hero of *Jehan et Blonde*: this is an early literary composition by a skilful author who had no need to model his characters on figures from real life. L. M. Rouillard, 'Reading the reader: Jean de Wauquelin's prose adaptation of *La Manekine*', *MedP*, 15:93–103, studies the additional Latin quotations and religious exemplars.

R. Lejeune, 'Jean Renart, pseudonyme littéraire de l'évêque de Liège, Hugues de Pierrepont (1200–1229)', *RBPH*, 77:271–97, is an important and stimulating contribution to the study of R.'s identity: carefully laid out circumstantial evidence is strong enough for Lejeune to put forward a positive identification. F. Le Nan, 'Essai sur la perfection: Liénor ou la pérégrine solitaire dans *Guillaume de Dole* de Jean Renart', *PRIS-MA*, 16:141–56, is surprised to argue that Liénor's journey through the text is hagiographical in every way. Id., 'De quelques "pérégrines" ou la mobilité des dames dans l'oeuvre présumée de Jean Renart', *RLaR*, 104:47–70, finds that here the traditional mobility of men and immobility of women is less marked, hence the subtle psychological depth of R's characters. B. Guidot, 'Le style enjoué de Jean Renart dans *L'Escoufle*', *TLit*, 13:11–27, noting the presence of the author throughout the text, suggests that *L'Escoufle*'s emotion, sensuality and humour is worthy of Chrétien. John W. Baldwin, *Aristocratic Life in Medieval France: The Romances of*

Jean Renart and Gerbert de Montreuil, 1190–1230, Baltimore–London, Johns Hopkins U.P., xix + 359 pp., views vernacular fiction as a vitally important source for historians studying the activities of the laity: these have always been obscured by the solemn *veritas* of Latin clerics. He establishes a dialogue between Latin and vernacular texts, focusing in particular on grey areas for religious writers (tournaments, sex, fighting), and, within his well-defined parameters, puts forward a strong and richly illustrated argument for his material to be admitted to the realm of reliable historical sources. E. Bermejo Larrea, 'La descripción en *L'Escoufle* de Jean Renart', *MLMed*, 11:139–64, discusses the traditional and personal aspects of Renart's romance. L. Lovison, 'Le récit de Jouglet: un pacte de lecture du *Roman de la Rose*', *RLaR*, 104:71–90, does not view Jouglet as Jean Renart's *alter ego* but as the conduit for a brilliant metatextual illusion.

J. Dornbush, ' "Songes et Senefiance": Macrobius and Guillaume de Lorris' *Roman de la Rose*', *Uitti Vol.*, 105–116, illustrates how Lorris exploited Macrobius in keeping his text open to interpretation. Through a careful analysis of Vieillesse's portrait, M. M. Heywood, 'The withered rose: seduction and the poetics of old age in the *Roman de la Rose* of Guillaume de Lorris', *FrF*, 25:2–22, asserts that the passage of time is by no means wholly banished from the *Rose*. The pairing of the old guardian woman and Vieillesse constitutes a message to Guillaume's extradiegetic dedicatee: in the present she must grant him her love, for in the future she will be unlovable. C. Nouvet, 'A reversing mirror: Guillaume de Lorris' *Romance of the Rose*', *Uitti Vol.*, 189–206, focuses on the specular quality of the dream: the lyric 'I' is split into two figures, a vital difference when the myth of Narcissus is recalled by the author. V. Galent-Fasseur, 'Des deux arcs d'Amour à la maison de Fortune: grâces et disgrâces selon *Le Roman de la Rose*', *Senefiance*, 43:105–21, considers the whole *Roman* to be a parallel to the Bible. D. M. Gonzalez Doreste, 'La représentation du beau et du laid dans *Le Roman de la Rose* (manuscrit 387 de la Bibliothèque de l'Université de Valence)', *ib.* 155–75, assesses the medieval illuminator's reading of the text.

A. Martínez Pérez, 'Narratividad y lirismo: tradición y estructuración lírica en el *Roman de Cleomades*', *RPM*, 2:175–94, studies the many and varied lyric borrowings in Adenet le Roi's romance. N. V. Durling, 'Women's visible honor in medieval romance: the example of the Old French *Roman du Comte de Poitiers*', *Uitti Vol.*, 117–32, discovers a rhetoric of visible honour in this and other OF romances: with regard to the female body, 'seeing' is not always 'believing'. M. Demaules, 'L'art de la ruse dans le *Roman de la Violette* de Gerbert de Montreuil', *RLaR*, 104:143–61, is an absorbing study of a text whose author replaces the idealism of the Arthurian world with the often disturbing realities of feudal society.

LAIS. G. M. Armstrong, 'Engendering the text: Marie de France and Dhuoda', *Uitti Vol.*, 27–50, considers the *Lais* (esp. *Le Fresne* and *Milun*) in the light of Dhuoda's *Liber Manualis*: women who generate children and narrative have a hidden power. L. A. Callahan, '"En remembrance e en memoire"': grief, memory and memorialization in the *Lais* of Marie de France', *RoN*, 41 : 259–70, views the building of a tomb as a metaphor for the construction of the *lai*. J. C. Declos, 'A la recherche du chèvrefeuille: réflexions sur un lai de Marie de France', *MA*, 106 : 37–46, uncovers the lay's rigorous structure and poetic secrets. W. Rothwell, 'The trial scene in *Lanval* and the development of the legal register in Anglo-Norman', *NMi*, 101 : 17–36, provides a detailed examination of legal and literary language and a glossary of legal terms. L. Brook, '*Omnia Vincit Rhetorica*: the "Lai du Conseil"', *SFr*, 44 : 69–76, views good sense, an ability to speak well of love, and wisdom to be the qualities necessary to draw the lady's love. There is irony in the author's skill in telling the story yet inability to resolve his own love situation. L. Löfstedt, 'Une nouvelle lecture du *Lai de l'Espine*', *NMi*, 101 : 253–59, studies the lay in the light of Church decretals on incest. In the impressive 'The ambiguous Narcissus figure in *Le Lai de Narcisus* and "Can Vei la Lauzeta Mover"', *FS*, 54 : 427–38, T. Adams asserts that the *Narcisus* poet and Bernart de Ventadorn exploited the myth's ambiguity quite consciously and were the first medieval authors to place it at the centre of explorations into the fundamental problem of love.

4. RELIGIOUS WRITINGS

La Vie de Saint Alexis, ed. Maurizio Perugi (TLF, 529), 319 pp., is an impressively comprehensive edition of the text found in the Hildesheim codex, offering a study of Latin and vernacular sources, a linguistic analysis, and a detailed commentary. P. Damian-Grint, 'Apocalyptic prophecy in Old French: an overview', *RMS*, 26 : 49–76, explains why these popular OF texts are dry, unimaginative, and lacking in commentary: authors strove not to do anything that might distort the word of revelation. C. Jouanno, '*Barlaam et Joasaph*: une aventure spirituelle en forme de roman d'amour', *PRIS-MA*, 26 : 61–76, compares the OF and Greek texts and offers a sustained literary commentary on the former. Jean-Guy Gouttebroze, *Le Précieux Sang de Fécamp: Origine et développement d'un mythe chrétien* (Essais sur le Moyen Âge, 23), Champion, 111 pp., traces an interesting history of the myth via medieval and early modern texts, central to which is the *Histoire de l'Abbaye de Fécamp en vers français du XIIIe siècle*.

J.-L. Benoit, 'La sainteté dans les *Miracles de Nostre Dame* de Gautier de Coinci', *PRIS-MA*, 16:31–46, establishes a typology of plot structures and character types, concluding that all the faithful are potential candidates for sanctity. R. Blumenfeld-Kosinski, 'Sexual and textual violence in the "Femme d'Arras" miracle by Gautier de Coincy', *Uitti Vol.*, 51–64, provides a useful commentary on this intriguing text: it dramatizes the many (violent) obstacles on the road to sainthood and illustrates the difficulties of defining medieval genre. Olivier Collet has published two important works on Gautier de Coinci. His edition of *La Vie de sainte Cristine: Édition critique d'après le manuscrit f. fr. 817 de la Bibliothèque nationale de France* (TLF, 510), 1999, xxiii + 179 pp., gives scholars access to a work which, until now, has remained inaccessible and relatively unknown. For notes and glossary, this edition should be read alongside his *Glossaire et index critiques des oeuvres d'attribution certaine de Gautier de Coinci* (PRF, 227), cx + 589 pp. Here C. provides an introduction of 110 pages, comprising mainly lists of corrections to Koenig's editions of the *Miracles de Nostre Dame*, words whose first attested use is by (or likely to be by) Gautier, and dialectal terms. It also includes a morphological classification of these terms and a useful bibliography. The 500–page glossary is selective but detailed and offers many critical commentaries.

Ulrike Schemmann, *Confessional Literature and Lay Education: The 'Manuel des Pechez' as a Book of Good Conduct and Guide to Personal Religion* (Studia Humaniora, 32), Düsseldorf, Droste, 362 pp., approaches the *Manuel* as a practical handbook of social morality for a lay audience in the reforming climate of the first half of the 13th century. S. studies the religious and cultural context, surveys penitential literature, highlights the text's insistence upon self-determination, suggests that confession post-Lateran IV is, in the light of the *Manuel*, a positive offer of help, and offers a useful discussion of target audience and mode of reception.

J. E. Merceron, 'De l'hagiographie à la chanson d'aventures: l'image de sainte Bathilde reine de France', *Senefiance*, 45:193–206, discusses both Latin and OF writings. L. Evdokimova, 'La version "X" de la *Vie de sainte Marie l'Égyptienne*. Entre la prose et le vers: du style sublime au style moderne', *Romania*, 118:431–48, examines the text's sources and notes that, stylistically, it represents an important landmark at the confluence of a number of traditions. D. Robertson, 'Authority and anonymity: the twelfth-century French Life of St Mary the Egyptian', *Uitti Vol.*, 245–60, applies Uitti and Foulet's 'editorial grid' and discovers a poem that maintains its stylistic identity throughout its MS history, remaining distinctive and authoritative despite *variance* and *mouvance*. Wauchier de Denain, *La Vie mon signeur Seint Nicholas le beneoit confessor*, ed. John Jay Thompson (TLF, 508),

1999, 271 pp., is the first critical edition of this long, and early, vernacular prose text. Thompson confirms Wauchier's authorship of the collection entitled *Li seint confessor* and identifies Latin sources for his translations. D. Boutet, 'Hagiographie et historiographie: la *Vie de saint Thomas Becket* de Guernes de Pont-Saint-Maxence et la *Vie de saint Louis* de Joinville', *MA*, 106: 377–93, shows, through a close comparison of the two texts, how Guernes set out to write a work of hagiography but in fact wrote a work of historiography. Id., *'L'approche des figures royales et de la royauté dans la *Vie de saint Thomas Becket* de Guernes de Pont-Sainte-Maxence', *BDBA*, 17: 35–48.

P. Noble, 'Les Hébreux au péril des Cananéens et d'eux-même dans le *Poème anglo-normand sur l'Ancien Testament*', *Senefiance*, 46: 183–202, studies the embellishments of the author, in particular epic battle scenes. A. Tudor, 'Concevoir et accoucher dans les fabliaux, les miracles et les contes pieux', *Reinardus*, 13: 195–213, argues that sex in the fabliaux is for fun, and that pregnancy and childbirth are no laughing matter; in miracles conception often serves as divine punishment; and in pious tales it can even be a sign of grace. Michel Zink, *Le Jongleur de Notre Dame* (Coll. La Mémoire des Sources), Seuil, 1999, 204 pp., is an attractive retelling in MF of pious tales from the OF *Vie des Pères* and a number of Latin and vernacular miracle collections.

5. OTHER GENRES

LYRIC. Pierre Bec, *La Joute poétique: de la tenson médiévale aux débats chantés traditionnels*, Les Belles Lettres, 521 pp., is a handsome anthology of poetic debates: the *tenson* and *jeu-parti*, representing a Golden Age of such texts, are central to both the introductory essay and the anthology. D. Burrows, 'The *Chastoisement des clers*: a *Dit* concerning the nations of the University of Paris, edited from Paris, B.N. MS F.Fr. 837', *MAe*, 69: 211–26, suggests how the *dit* throws light on the internal conflict of the University of Paris. R. L. Krueger, 'Female voices in convents, courts and households: the French Middle Ages', in Stephens, *Women's Writing*, 10–40, is a rather sweeping view of medieval women writers in France as both victims and victors. *Medieval Lyric: Genres in Historical Context*, ed. William D. Paden, Urbana, Illinois U.P., 371 pp. F. Wolfzettel, 'Le thème du souvenir et la structure temporelle dans le grand chant courtois: Thibaut de Champagne et Gace Brulé', *Lacy Vol.*, 539–52, concludes that, paradoxically, it is the 12th-c. poet who appears the more modern.

ROMAN DE RENART. *Le Roman de Renart (extraits)*, ed. and trad. Daphne Deron et al. (Petits Classiques Larousse, 68), 208 pp. Varty,

Reynard, is a fine volume tracking the course of the legend through time and space. Of particular interest to students of the OF tradition are: J. Subrenat, 'Rape and adultery: reflected facets of feudal justice in the *Roman de Renart*' (37–54), which studies the juridical branches in relation to the administration of justice for the crime of rape in 12th-c. northern France; and J. Goossens, 'The ill-fated consequence of the tom-cat's jump, and its illustration' (113–24), which explores the changing sensibilities of new readers faced with the episode of Tibert and the village priest. Y. Takana, 'La Parodie dans le *Roman de Renart*: une étude de la parodie renardienne des romans d'amour des XIIe et XIIIe siècles dans une perspective comparative et diachronique', *Fukoka University Review of Literature and Humanities*, 31 : 1271–86, 2017–30, posits that the *Renard* puts a burlesque spin on a variety of specific OF texts, including the Tristan corpus, *Le Chevalier à l'épée*, *Le Lai du cor*, and *Le Mantel mautaillé*. A. J. Williams, 'Ritual in branch XVII of the *Roman de Renart (Mort et procession Renart)*: a key to a carnivalesque reading of the texts?', *MLR*, 95:954–63, posits that branch XVII is a microcosm of the whole text and that religious, judicial, inverted, and ludic rituals here offer vital and deliberate intertextual references.

FABLIAUX. Brian J. Levy, *The Comic Text: Patterns and Images in the Old French Fabliaux* (Faux Titre, 186), Amsterdam–Atlanta, Rodopi, viii + 312 pp., is a significant study of a number of key images (animals, gambling, dancing, water, damnation, sickness) as ironic patterns running throughout the corpus. L. identifies these images as a common fund of comic rhetoric, acting on two levels: within the broader tradition of medieval literature; and within the genre itself. He concludes that these rather neglected elements are in fact central to the ludic, adversarial nature of the comic text. C. Revard, 'From French "fabliau manuscripts" and MS Harley 2253 to the *Decameron* and the *Canterbury Tales*', *MAe*, 69 : 261–78, discusses the difference between 'miscellanies' and 'anthologies'. R. J. Pearcy, 'Anglo-Norman fabliaux and Chaucer's *Merchant's Tale*', *ib.*, 227–60, considers the chronological and textual relationships between A-N and OF fabliaux, establishes some characteristic features of insular fabliaux, and suggests that, unlike Chaucer's other fabliaux, the *Merchant's Tale* derived directly from the insular tradition. D. Burrows, '*Constant du Hamel*: textual tradition and ecclesiastical castration', *FSB*, 76:2–4, assesses the variants connected with the scene of the dogs' attack on the priest. A. Corbellari, 'Un fabliau retrouvé: essai d'édition critique du *Chevalier à la poubelle*', *Variations*, 5 : 149–56, is just the sort of skillful spoof that authentic *fableors* would have thoroughly enjoyed. Y. Foehr-Janssens, 'La chevauchée merveilleuse: Le *Vair Palefroi* ou la naissance d'une fée', *Reinardus*, 13 : 79–95, returns to the question of typology, arguing that *VP*'s central figure is an atypical female character and that this sets it apart from other lays and fabliaux. H.-E. Keller, '*Richeut* ou la lutte éternelle entre les sexes', *Lacy Vol.*, 247–55, views the victory of the woman in the *conte* as a one of empiricism over rationalism: the tale is a clear reflection of the teaching of philosophy. In 'A priest's worst (k)nightmare: fabliau justice in *Le Prestre et le chevalier*', *FrF*, 25:137–44, N. J. Lacy offers a commentary on this long and remarkable text. Milles d'Amiens gives unusually detailed descriptions, moving the fabliau towards the genre's borders with romance and the lay. These sections make the more 'typical' fabliau action all the more shocking. In particular, the audience's ignorance of whether or not the knight is prepared to sodomize the priest, and a subtle play on class and manners, add much dramatic tension and comic effect. C. Müller, 'Gourmandise et luxure: le champ de la métaphore dans *Les Perdrix*, *L'Oue au chapelain* et *Cele qui fu foutue et desfoutue*', *Reinardus*, 13:135–48, is an interesting study of those fabliaux where gluttony replaces sex: these stories are amongst the most erotic, an eroticism due not only to the metaphor but to the writing itself. E. W. Poe, '*La Vieille Truande*: a fabliau among the romances of B.N., fr. 375', *Lacy Vol.*, 405–23, points out that, according to codicological evidence, this unsettling piece was one of the most popular fabliaux. P. suggests its appeal to the compiler of a codex dominated by romances is likely to be thematic or personal. P. Romagnoli, 'Amour, argent et sens à la foire de Champagne: *La Bourse pleine de Sens*', *MA*, 106:323–45, places *La BPS* firmly within the group of fabliaux whose central *jeu* is of meaning and language. B. N. Sargent-Baur, 'Philippe de Rémi's "Conte de fole larguesce": a fabliau with a difference', *Lacy Vol.*, 463–74, asks whether the story, although displaying certain characteristic traits of a fabliau, is truly comic: Rémi plays on the expectations of his audience in delivering an atypical and mildly didactic *conte*.

MORAL, DIDACTIC, AND ALLEGORICAL WORKS. C. Gaullier-Bougassas, *'La vie d'Alexandre le Grand dans *Renart le Contrefait* et le *Livre de la Mutacion de Fortune*', *BDBA*, 17:119–30. G. Parussa, 'Les "Livres de fables": Enquête sur les manuscrits médiévaux contenant des fables ésopiques', *Reinardus*, 13:149–67, is a careful textual and intertextual analysis of 37 fable MSS: scribes appear always to be aware of the moralising nature of their work and so the relationship between fables and neighbouring texts in a codex needs to be further explored. D. Boutet, '*Le Roman de Renart* et la fable ésopique aux treizième et quatorzième siècles', *Reinardus*, 13:35–47, studies the *Ispoet de Lyon* and *Isopets I et II de Paris* in the light of their borrowings from the *RdeR*: these hybrids are part myth, part tale, part fable. G. Parussa, 'De l'ancien au moyen français, ou comment transcrire les *Fables* de Marie de France au XVe siècle', *TLP*, 38:27–50, in addition to a detailed linguistic analysis, stresses the importance of later manuscripts as aids to our understanding of the medieval reception of a medieval text. H. R. Runte, 'Marie de France's courtly fables', *Lacy Vol.*, 453–62, argues that Marie's *Fables* are full of home-spun truisms at which a courtly audience would scoff. Most of Marie's bad fables have Alfredian or English roots (the good ones being based on Latin or French models), and Marie's uncharacteristic distance from her text is due to the fact that she wrote only under the duress of a princely commission. In 'Sweet dreams: parody, satire and alimentary allegory in Raoul de Houdenc's *Le Songe d'Enfer*', *Lacy Vol.*, 53–74, M. Burde explores the rich ecclesiastical and political history of the allegory of consumption and challenges conventional defini-tions of parody and satire, arguing that Raoul's text offers important lessons on the nature of medieval ludic textuality. N. Cartlidge, 'Aubrey de Bassingbourn, Ida de Beauchamp, and the context of the *Estrif de deus dames* in Oxford Bodleian Library MS Digby 86', *NQ*, 74:411–14, discusses a text which contrasts marriage and *amour courtois* from a female point of view. T. Hunt edits the A-N text found in MS 101 of the Society of Antiquaries of London in 'A new fragment of Jofroi de Waterford's *Segré de segrez*', *Romania*, 118:289–314. Id., 'Solomon and Marcolf', *Lacy Vol.*, 199–224, is an edition of two versions of the legend, from MS B.N. fr. 837, and roll no. 12692 (Shropshire Records and Research Centre).

DRAMA. Thierry Revol, *Représentations du sacré dans les textes dramatiques des XIe–XIIIe siècles en France* (Nouvelle Bibliothèque du Moyen Âge, 51), Champion, 1999, 577 pp., is an important contribu-tion to the study of the origins of medieval theatre. From liturgical representations to the emergence of the dramatic character, R. studies in parallel OF and Latin texts, providing a sustained, anthropological analysis of an art that is at once sacred and profane. Id., 'Le personnage et le sacré dans la première partie du *Jeu d'Adam*', Bély, *Personne*, 143–67, studies *Adam* as a sacred and dramatic text in which each character represents a particular definition of transcendence. It is even possible to 'play' God through the imminence of theatrical representation.

HISTORIOGRAPHY AND CHRONICLE. C. Croizy-Naquet, 'Ecrire l'histoire: le choix du vers ou de la prose aux XIIe et XIIIe siècles', *BDBA*, 17:71–85, uses the *roman d'antiquité* as a basis for examining the associations between verse and prose, fiction and truth, *romanz* and historiography. M. Ailes, 'Early French chronicle — history or literature?', *JMH*, 26:301–312, mentions a wide range of both verse and prose chronicles (Wace, Benoît de Sainte-Maure, Gaimar, Jordan Fantosme, Ambroise, Villehardouin, Robert de Clari, Henri de

Valenciennes) in an article that traces the history of criticism of these texts, showing that certain aspects of these texts — use of rhetoric, accounts of miracles, versification — have all been used to discredit works that do not conform to modern notions of historically accurate documentation. P. Eley and P. E. Bennett, 'The Battle of Hastings according to Gaimar, Wace and Benoît: rhetoric and politics', *NMS*, 43:47–78, leaves the discussion of chronicle as fact or fiction to other scholars, instead focusing on how three chroniclers recount the same event. E. and B. analyse the significant differences to see how each account was shaped by the political conditions and literary sources of the time. C. Lucken, 'La fin des temps et la fiction des origines. L'historiographie des îles britanniques: du royaume des anges à la terre des Bretons', *Médiévales*, 38:35–70, touches upon *Brut*, *Roman de Rou*, and the *Grandes Chroniques de France*, in an article based primarily upon Latin texts. L. posits that two very different approaches can be seen in medieval historiography: the first emphasizes the emerging nation as a grouping of souls subservient to the Church, while the second sees the same group from a social and political perspective. C. Anderson, 'Wace's *Roman de Rou* and Henry II's court: character and power', *RoQ*, 47:67–83, examines how the progress of Rollo from pagan brute to Christian knight parallels the establishment of order in and by the Norman court after the Conquest. Rollo serves not only as a model in his idealized form, but also as a warning in his previous incarnation.

O. Collet, 'Littérature, histoire, pouvoir et mécénat: la cour de Flandre au XIIIe siècles', *Médiévales*, 38:87–110, studies the conditions under which writers such as Henri de Valenciennes and Philippe Mousket flourished. C. compares the literary production associated with the Flemish court with that of the northern French court, as well as considering the limitations and benefits of patronage. M.-G. Grossel, 'Ces "chroniqueurs à l'oreille épique": remarques sur l'utilisation de la geste chez Philippe Mousket et Aubri des Trois-Fontaines', *Senefiance*, 45:97–112, compares two authors whose works have previously been examined as weaker versions of *chansons de geste* rather than as examples of historiography. For these chroniclers, the age of certain tales and legends is sufficient to confer authority and establish them as reliable sources. G. has also produced *'L'image du roi dans *L'Histoire de la guerre sainte* d'Ambroise (Richard Coeur de Lion et Philippe Auguste)', *BDBA*, 17:159–80. Catherine Croizy-Naquet, *Ecrire l'histoire romaine au début du XIIIe siècle* (Nouvelle Bibliothèque du Moyen Age, 53), Champion, 1999, 344 pp., examines two OF prose texts, *L'Histoire ancienne jusqu'à César* and *Li Fet des Romains*. The study suggests that a major factor in the association of prose and the writing of history was simply that the one needed the other. C. Hanley, 'The siege engine as metaphor in four Old French chronicles', *FSB*, 77 : 2–4, uses the works of Jordan Fantosme, the anonymous continuator of the *Chanson de la croisade albigeoise*, Ambroise, and the Minstrel of Reims, arguing that depictions of various types of siege machinery find parallels in depictions of the French combatants and the larger conflict.

LATE MEDIEVAL LITERATURE
POSTPONED

THE SIXTEENTH CENTURY

By CATHERINE REUBEN, *Kingston University*

1. GENERAL

Table 1 shows the number of mentions in titles of articles and reviews of various 16th-c. literary figures (source: ISI, 1 January 2000–1 April 2001) and books, counted manually, compared with 1999 totals (*YWMLS*, 61:92).

Table 1: 16th-century French authors in titles of 2000 publications (1999 figures in parentheses)

	Articles/Reviews	Books
Montaigne	72 (87)	7 (6)
Rabelais	39 (48)	2 (2)
Ronsard	23 (15)	2 (1)
Marot	19 (14)	1 (2)
d'Aubigné	16 (9)	2 (4)
Marguerite de Navarre	10 (10)	4 (1)
Labé	7 (12)	1
Baïf	7 (5)	(1)
Du Bartas	6 (2)	(2)
La Boétie	6 (4)	(1)
Budé	5 (8)	
Papillon	4	
Sebond	3	
De Crenne	3	1
Scève	2 (3)	
Dorat	2	
Lemaire de Belges	2	
Thenaud	2	
Jean de la Taille	2	
Desportes	2	
Estienne	2	

About the same number of articles appeared as in 1999. D'Aubigné and Du Bartas have improved their positions slightly and there has been a move away from the better-known authors towards 'undiscovered' ones, but, otherwise, the balance of research has remained remarkably constant. This seems a dominant feature of 16th-c. literary research, at any rate in the short term.

2. HUMANISM, THEOLOGY, AND IDEAS

F. Rigolot, 'Tolérance et condescendance dans la littérature française du XVIe siècle', *BHR*, 62:25–47, feels that the links between the notions of tolerance and condescension have been underestimated by students of Renaissance French literature, and wishes to remedy this through the use of historical semantics. The adjective *tolérant* did not exist in the 16th c. when the verb 'to tolerate' was passive, like 'to endure' or 'to suffer'. *Liberté de conscience*, on the other hand, had an active meaning for Protestant theologians such as Luther, Melanchthon, and even Calvin. It meant to be able to liberate oneself by *foi vive* from the strictures of the Catholic Church. Likewise *condescendance* as used at the beginning of the 16th c. in evangelical circles goes back to the Church Fathers, an interest encouraged by Erasmus. It meant being able to put oneself on the same level as an inferior being, as God appearing to man. Not being able to appear in his true form to human eyes, he must '*condescendre* (c'est la traduction littérale du verbe grec *sygkatabainein*), pour s'accomoder (latin *accommodatus* donné par Suidas) aux nécessités de la vision humaine'. R. considers various aspects of *condescendance* with respect to '*caritas* humaniste', Rabelais, Labé, Montaigne, Ronsard, and d'Aubigné. This is an original and important article.

Jean Dorat, *Mythologicum ou interprétation allégorique de l'Odyssée X-XII et de l'Hymne à Aphrodite*, ed. Philip Ford, Geneva, Droz, 169 pp., is an edition of a manuscript dated by F. between 1569 and 1571, consisting of the notes made by an anonymous student on the lectures which Jean Dorat gave on the *Odyssey*, songs X-XII, as well as the opening of the *Hymne homérique à Aphrodite*. The student reproduces the words of the master as if in dictation, rather than the modern idea of a lecture. D. quotes Strabo, Athenaeus, Macrobius, and Cicero, amongst others, and also the Bible. For instance, from the first pages of the *Mythologicum* 'Par "couvre-lit" et "lits sculptés" on peut entendre le ciel, que Dieu a étendu comme un tapis (in the margin: ainsi parlent David et la Sibylle) une peau maculée, semble-t-il, de certains trous, par lesquels les astres, les lumières et les flammes célestes nous apparaissent.' Not only does this illustrate contemporary cosmological beliefs, it also shows, through the quotation from Psalm 104, that classical and biblical studies were considered equally valuable at the time. Moreover, these are the sort of lectures that would have been followed by Ronsard, Baïf, and Du Bellay.

One can scarcely imagine deriving much amusement from volume 22 of anything, but *Correspondence de Théodore de Bèze*, XXII: *(1581)*, ed. Hippolyte Aubert, Geneva, Droz, 282 pp., throws an intriguing light on religious controversies of the time. The minutely annotated letters are in Latin and explained in French. Correspondents in this volume include Gwalther, Henri de Navarre, Ann Bacon, William Cecil, and Lord Burghley. A letter from Gwalther comes in the name of the Pastors of Zurich to the Pastors of Geneva, Zurich, 12 May 1581: 'With reference to the Concord of Wittenberg signed in 1536, the signatories (Bucer, Luther, and Melanchthon) recognise that, in the Last Supper, the body and blood of Christ are really and substantially present, offered and received with the bread and the wine.'

Frank Greiner, *Les Métamorphoses d'Hermès: tradition alchimique et esthétique littéraire dans la France de l'âge baroque (1583–1646)*, Champion, 663 pp., declares in his introduction that alchemy — the science of synthesis and synthesis of science — engendered many writings involving the good, the true, and the useful. There were dissertations, speeches, and treatises in a language designed to conceal the alchemical secrets, but also poems and novels. Their authors had the nice conceit that, instead of transforming base metals into gold, they would break with the laboratory and instead transform base words into verbal gold.

Fantasy fiction became an official literary genre as late as 1830. Marianne Closson, *L'Imaginaire démoniaque en France (1550–1650). Genèse de la littérature fantastique*, Geneva, Droz, 544 pp., describes its darker origins. Both Catholics and Protestants persecuted witches and, between the 14th and 17th cs, an estimated 300,000 harmless women were executed, 400 in Toulouse alone in 1577. It seems that fantasy had not only the sense of the imaginary, but also the diabolical, and thus the abnormal was linked with madness and the devil. This immensely readable book deals with the literary heritage, the metamorphoses of the devil in medieval mysteries and in Rabelais, and also the image of the stranger (gypsy and Jew) as diabolical figures. The bizarre belief structures about witches selling their souls to Satan were exploited by writers of fantasy literature.

Hélène Germa-Romann, *Du 'bel mourir' au 'bien mourir'. Le sentiment de la mort chez les gentilshommes français (1515–1643)*, Geneva, Droz, 352 pp., traces changes in attitudes to death among the French nobility from just before the battle of Pavia until the end of the Thirty Years War. During this period, the wish for a noble death — the *belle mort*, death in battle — evolved into a wish for a good death — the *bonne mort*, death in one's own bed.

The reign of Suleiman the Magnificent was the apogee of the Ottoman Empire. He was sufficiently confident to admit Western visitors, who were fascinated by the zoological curiosities, the topography of Jerusalem, the veiled women, and other aspects of an alien and infidel culture. Their accounts and those of their colleagues travelling to the New World reinforced the change during the

Renaissance from belief in literature (believing what Pliny said) to belief in contemporary travellers' tales (believing what Jean de Léry said)(see p. 96). Frédéric Tinguely, *L'Ecriture du Levant à la Renaissance. Enquête sur les voyageurs français dans l'empire de Soliman le Magnifique*, Geneva, Droz, 304 pp., examines the intertextual and anthropological strategies developed by Western travellers under the protection of the French ambassador from 1546 to 1553, Gabriel d'Aramon. T. focuses on the writings of seven authors: Belon, Chesnau, Gassot, Gilles, Nicolay, Postel, and Thevet. Their views of the mysterious orient are forerunners of the more sympathetic view of Moslem culture developed by Washington Irving and the Romantics in the early 19th century.

3. POETRY AND PROSE

Dominique Millet-Gérard, *Le Chant initiatique: esthétique et spiritualité de la bucolique*, Geneva, Ad Solem, 346 pp., analyses various authors over the centuries, in particular Virgil but also Dante, André Chénier, Maurice de Guérin, Paul Valéry, and Francis Jammes, in order to seek constants in theme, style and, above all, aesthetics in texts that are bucolic or more or less similar. 'Les Bucoliques, écrit Hans Urs von Balthasar, sont l'horizon extrême de la vision poétique du monde.' Apart from Guérin's *poèmes en prose*, they are all concerned with poetry and M.-G. studies how the bucolic develops between paganism and Christianity. For example, the fourth book of Virgil's *Bucolics* foretells the birth of a child, which the early Christians took to be a reference to Jesus and led to the 'Christianization' of Virgil.

I. Pantin, *NRSS*, 18 : 7–8, introduces a special issue of the journal, dealing with an approach to the *arts poétiques* through the vernacular. She questions the definition of the *art poétique*. Is its intention to steer poets in the way of tradition or to encourage them to find new routes? Is it addressing a particular situation or a general or ideal view? 'Est-il enfin un livre à part entière, qui, au delà de son propos didactique, suppose un vrai choix d'écriture, voire exprime un choix éthique?' C. Jomphe, 'Lecture, émotion et économie dans l'*Art poétique* (1555) de Jacques Peletier du Mans', *ib.*, 95–112, stipulates that the Renaissance *arts poétiques* can be read as attempts to define and legitimize the poetic task, to find a proper place for it between the divine gift and the treatise on versification. Under the heading of reading and brevity, she points out that many writers, including Sébillet, Du Bellay, and Ronsard, use P.'s method of ensuring brevity by asking the reader to read texts from other books, such as other *arts poétiques*, Horace, or Aristotle. For P., the conflict between the divine gift and the art of versification is resolved by concentrating on the former and trying to formulate a philosophy and ethic of poetry. But, in the search for a French Virgil, at this time of giving *droit de cité* to the French language, the *art poétique* helps the poetic process by showing what to read and how to read. In T. Mantovani, 'Pierre Fabri et la poétique des puys dans le second livre du *Grand et vrai art de pleine rhétorique*', *ib.*, 41–54, the 'second book' refers to the *seconde rhétorique*, and its author is associated with the cult of Mary and the *Puy de l'Immaculée conception de Rouen*, for whom he wrote the work, published posthumously in 1521. For M., it is a clumsy compromise between a defence of the *Chant royal* and a general consideration of poetic techniques rife at the beginning of the 16th century. F. is hampered by his dual role representing the Puys at the same time as theorising on the second rhetoric. M. Magnien, '"Ordre" et "méthode" dans l'*Art poétique reduit et abregé* de Claude de Boissière (1554)', *ib.*, 113–30, notes that this slim book appeared in a decade which produced many theoretical works including those by Sébillet and Ronsard. De B. also published an *Art d'arithmetique*, and M. suggests that the juxtaposition of the two intends to dignify poetic composition in the vernacular by associating it with the science of numbers or harmonies. Under the probable influence of Ramus, B. has restructured the *art poétique* according to the laws of reason, without reference to the role of inspiration. This may explain its failure. Other articles in this volume are by M. Gally (9–24), D. Hüe (25–40), J.-C. Monferran (55–76), K. Meerhoff (77–94), D. de Courcelles (131–56), and F. Graziani (157–82).

Memory was a popular theme in 1999. Goodden, *Memory*, continues this. Her first chapter, 'Breaking the mould', points out that medieval writers regarded memory 'as the mark of a superior moral character as well as a proof of intellect', whereas the Renaissance 'selectively disapproved of cognitive memory on the grounds that it failed to encourage independance of thought'. The latter, however, still respected the past and relied, if necessary, on the classics for inspiration. G. examines Montaigne's work in the light of this attitude.

4. Architecture and Graphic Arts

In the introduction to Margaret McGowan, *The Vision of Rome in Late Renaissance France*, Newhaven, Yale U.P., 461 pp., the first half deals with records of actual travel to Rome, guide books, the acquisition of goods from Rome by French princes and collectors, and the images of Rome from the pens of four writers who played major roles in introducing 16th-c. French readers to images of Rome. The second half considers the reactions of French writers and artists to received images of Rome, including Du Bellay and Montaigne, but also the figure of Caesar and the Triumph. '[. . .] many Frenchmen, especially Protestants, attacked the notion of building from the past and attempting to re-enact its forms. Some, like Grevin and Garnier, argued against the status which Rome had acquired and turned the vision of a "Rome ruinée" into a more active agent of destruction, "Rome ruineuse" '. The delight of this interdisciplinary book is that it covers writers, artists, and architects and is beautifully illustrated and referenced.

Laurence Grove and Daniel Russell, *The French Emblem: Bibliography of Secondary Sources*, Geneva, Droz, xx + 244 pp., is the second and concluding volume of the bibliography by Alison Adams reviewed in *YWMLS*, 61:96.

5. WOMEN'S STUDIES

Women's Writing in the French Renaissance: Proceedings of the 5th Cambridge French Renaissance Colloquium, 7–9 July 1997, ed. Philip Ford and Gillian Jondorf, Cambridge French Colloquia, 1999, xii + 243 pp., is devoted to expanding the number of women that one would expect to see on a list of French Renaissance writers beyond Marguerite de Navarre, Louise Labé, and Perrette du Guillet. There are nonetheless four papers on Labé. Hélisenne de Crenne was the pseudonym of Marguerite Briet and this is discussed at length by D. S. Wood. She is also one of the foci of J. O'Brien's paper, which criticizes her florid, latinate style (see also p. 97)

Jean de Marconville, *De la bonté et mauvaistié des femmes*, ed. Richard A. Carr, Champion, 235 pp., is a spirited defence of women, published in 1564, and written by a man. He considers the 'querelle des femmes' and reinterprets some of the traditional arguments in the light of his humanist beliefs. Chapters on the positive side include 'De l'excellence des femmes, et ingenieuses inventions d'icelles', 'Des femmes qui ont esté cause de repurger les pays et republiques des Tyrans qui les infestoient et molestoient', and 'De la constance merveilleuse et superhumaine d'aucunes femmes'. M.'s negative chapters bring ambiguous irony to the whole work: 'Des maux et miseres qui ont esté au monde par les mauvaises femmes', 'De la barbare cruauté et horrible tyrannie d'aucunes femmes', and 'Des femmes heretiques, et de quelles heresies elles ont esté occasion'. C. suggests that the views of modern critics, in particular Michel Simonin, who points to the Renaissance vogue for the compilation, defined as 'a creation which rests on translation, plagiarism, [. . .] the rewriting and subverting of texts or familiar genres', is the key to understanding the work.

Stephens, *Women's Writing*, is a clearly written and stimulating book introducing a plethora of women writers who demand further reading. The only 16th-c. contribution is C. M. Bauschatz, 'To choose ink and pen: French Renaissance women's writing' (41–63). B. has selected nine women writers in the 16th c., 'each important for the way in which they modify the genre (or genres) in which they write, and change its definition for subsequent authors, whether male or female'. She points to three major factors that influenced women's literacy at this time — printing, the Reformation insistence on reading in the vernacular, and the influence of Italy and the Italian Renaissance. B. examines Jean de Flore, Hélisenne de Crenne, Marguerite de Navarre, Pernette de Guillet, Louise Labé, Madeleine and Catherine Des Roches, Marguerite de Valois (la reine Margot), and Marie de Gournay, who wrote essays in her own right as well as editing those of Montaigne.

6. Collections, Conferences, and Works of Reference

Trevor Peach, *Catalogue descriptif des éditions françaises, néo-latines et autres (1501–1600) de la bibliothèque municipale de Poitiers*, Geneva, Slatkine, 768 pp., states that his selection criteria covered 'tout ouvrage rédigé en français ou écrit par un auteur d'origine française, et tout ouvrage publié dans les limites actuelles de la France par un auteur étranger, entre 1501–1600 inclus'. Thus editions of classical writers are excluded as are Greek and Latin Bibles, but P. has retained commentaries that shed important light on a particular author. Most of the editions are from Paris, with many also from Lyons, and the South West is represented as is Poitiers itself. This impressive catalogue includes such names as Rabelais, Du Bellay, Montaigne, Jan Bouchet, Salmon Macrin, Jacques Yver, and Jean Imbert. The works themselves are described in detail with provenance and even binding. The catalogue has four indices — publisher and place of publication, names of editors and printers, names of people, and pressmarks.

Frank Lestringant, Josiane Rieu, and Alexandre Tarrête, *Littérature française du XVIe siècle*, PUF, 503 pp., is an authoritative overview placing the century's writing against a historical background. The authors emphasize that the Renaissance and the 16th c. are not synonymous. Apart from sections on the best-known authors, this book covers Maurice Scève, Pernette de Guillet, Louise Labé, and Claude de Taillement. The section on polemical litterature is divided into 'Poursuite des controverses religieuses', 'Polémiques contre la tyrannie', and 'Les pamphlets au temps de la ligue'. There are useful sections on 'Humanisme et réforme' and 'Baroque et littérature religieuse'. This book is a must for anyone seeking to relate 16th-c. poetry, prose, and theatre to the historical events of that troubled century.

Riflessioni teoretiche e trattati die poetica tra Francia e Italia nel cinquecento: atti del convengo internazionale di studio, Castello Malescine, 22–24 Maggio, 1997, ed. Elio Mosele, Brindisi, Schena, 1999, 252 pp., discusses the tension between writing harking back to the Greeks and Romans and the desire to use modern languages and develop them into literary works as a point of national pride. M. claims that the 16th-c. French, in particular Du Bellay, reject their literary past and use classical examples to elevate 'vulgar' language to a literary level. Two generations of theoreticians disagree. Aneau and Sébillet do not reject the 'ancient' and see in Marot, Saint-Gelais, Scève, and Heroët 'divine' poets to aspire towards, referring back to the classics via recent French examples. The poets of the Pléiade, on the other hand, exalt inspiration. Sébillet and Aneau draw on a Christian and moralizing ideal while the Pléiade poets choose ancient and pagan inspiration.

André Tournon is honoured by a *Festschrift, D'une fantastique bigarrure (La texte composite à la Renaissance)*, ed. Jean-Raymond Fanlo, Champion, 314 pp. F. opens his preamble with a quotation from Montaigne, 'Traiter diversement les matières est aussi bien les traiter que conformément', in order to show the breadth of subjects covered, and reflecting Tournon's expertise '[. . .] en interrogeant l'énigme difficile des solutions de continuité et des effets de disparate'. Under the headings 'Recueils: biggarures et projet auctorial, Montaigne et les *Essais'*, and 'Variations, réécritures, hybridations' are articles by numerous authors including M. Jeanneret, J.-C. Arnould, T. Cave, G. Hoffmann, F. Lecercle, and N. Kenny.

The special issue *DFS*, 52, honours Paul Chavy, renowned scholar, *inter alia*, of Renaissance translation. Eva Kushner, 'Trois locutrices du XVIe siècle; deux "miroirs"' (14–21), asks whether the mirrors in question (poetry and dialogue) link Louise Labé, Catherine Des Roches, and Marguerite de Navarre at a time when dialogue was evolving from a debate with fixed positions towards an exchange in which arguments on both sides were more open. All three writers use poetry as mirrors for their quest for poetic identity, as well as their relationship with the Other, and these tendencies are developed in the dialogues, 'fortifiant dans ces échanges leur conscience d'elles-mêmes et créant sans le savoir une intertextualité réflexive'. Another contribution is K. Waterson, ' "Sçait-il du Grec . . .?" or, Ennoblement from Montaigne to La Bruyère' (51–56).

A French Forum: Mélanges de la littérature française offerts à Raymond C. et Virginia A. La Charité, Klincksieck, 341 pp., is a *Festschrift* for the La Charités on their retirement. The presence of so many well-known names among the contributors is a testament to the popularity of this couple, who have done so much to further scholarship respectively in Renaissance and 20th-c. studies and also to encourage the work of others. E. Duval, 'Littérature pédagogique et formes maïeutiques à la Renaissance' (45–57), takes Montaigne as his example of the social and moral aims of Renaissance literature. In the *Essais*, M. is sowing doubt in the minds of readers not only by expressing his own doubts but also by forcing them to question their own views through a series of contradictory arguments designed to lead to the only possible conclusions, the 'What do I know?' of the Pyrrhonians. D. discusses the use of allegory by Jean Lemaire, Clément Marot, and Marguerite de Navarre and suggests that the modern reader might benefit by following the tortuous routes indicated by these writers with a certain amount of 'docility', rather than the 'suspicious' ways we now have of decoding texts. And, who knows, maybe we will then end up 'autres plus sages, meilleurs?'.

Les Fruits de la Saison: Mélanges de littératures des XVIe et XVIIe siècles offerts au professeur André Gendre, ed. Philippe Terrier, Loris Petris, and Marie-Jeanne Liengme Bessire, Geneva, Droz, xx + 510 pp., is a collection dedicated on his retirement to the Professor of French for 30 years at the University of Neuchâtel.

Franco Giacone, *Histoires d'ecritures: la Bible et la théologie, de Marguerite de Navarre à Agrippa d'Aubigné*, CUP, 1999, 400 pp., is a collection of articles written over the past 10 years. G. is interested in how religion becomes literature. He has added some new articles notably on the *Cymbalum Mundi*, the *Cinqiesme Livre*, the translations of the 'mort de Clorinde', the theology of Pontus de Tyard, on the Vaudois according to Christofle de Gamon and Agrippa d'Aubigné. Jean Céard notes in his preface that the death of Clarinde in Tasso's *Jérusalem délivré* has been translated by Pierre Poupo, a Calvinist, and Blaise de Vignère, a Catholic, which adds an extra dimension to their work. G. has found a third manuscript of Marguerite d'Angoulême's *Pater Noster*, which led him to re-read her correspondence (1521–1524) with Guillaume Briçonnet, the Bishop of Meaux, and conclude that the work to which she refers is indeed the *Pater Noster* and not the *Dialogue en forme de vision nocturne*, as has been supposed until now.

L'histoire littéraire: ses méthodes et ses résultats, ed. Luc Fraisse, Geneva, Droz, 872 pp., recognises the enormous contribution of Madeleine Bertaud, the former director of ADIREL, to literary scholarship. It is dedicated to her by 58 contributors including the well-known 16th-c. scholars M. Simonin, J. Balsamo, O. Millet, and G. Schrenk. The collection is divided into 'Méthodes et bilans' and 'Enquêtes historiques'.

7. INDIVIDUAL AUTHORS
MONTAIGNE

PLit, 24, devotes the greater part of an issue to a symposium on Montaigne. D. Quint, 'Letting oneself go: "Of Anger" and Montaigne's ethical reflections' (126–37), deals with M.'s refusal to bottle up his anger because of the toll it took on his nature, preferring to let his passions run their course. This, at any rate, is M.'s view in the so-called B-text of the *Essays*, and Q. traces the changes in M.'s thought from the earlier A-text. 'Go ahead and slap your servant', M. advises, rather than hold a silent grudge [. . .].' This is the opposite of Plutarch's view that merited punishments be carried out once reason has restored its control over anger. M. slaps his servant in anger, while Plutarch dispassionately has his slave flogged. A. Hartle, 'Montaigne's accidental moral philosophy' (138–53), asks if M. is a moral relativist, who holds that there is no way to justify moral standards, or a sceptic, who holds that we cannot know certainly what is good or evil, and that we should therefore adopt a pragmatic attitude governed by custom. She concludes that M. has an 'accidental philosophy', a kind of innocence that knowingly returns to what he learned in the nursery, as he says himself. H. does not consider how M.'s morals, implanted in him by nature, differ from, for example, Rousseau who deduces quite different rules of conduct written 'in the depths of his heart, written by nature in ineffaceable characters'. She does however compare his views with those of Machiavelli and the reaction of both men to contact with pagan religions. This theme is present in Tinguely's book (see above, p. 78) and is raised in a more detailed form by W. Hamlin, 'On continuities between skepticism and early ethnography; or, Montaigne's providential diversity', *SCJ*, 31 : 361–79. H. claims that the observations of travellers were used to *refute* the opinions of atheists and sceptics (although it is difficult to see how this could have been so), and were also used to *describe* or *explain* such attitudes. M., on the one hand, observes native customs with Pyrrhonian scepticism but then makes a leap of faith to reject 'tout autre choix que celuy qui vient de la main expresse de Dieu'.

J. Schwartz, 'Reflections on Montaigne's ethical thinking', *PLit*, 24 : 154–64, places the question, 'What constitutes true freedom?' as the ethical centre of the *Essays*. For the stoic, freedom is the ability to scorn death. The cannibals live under the 'sweet freedom' of nature's laws but their freedom is constituted wholly negatively. M. emerges as a 'skeptical moralist', who realises that absolute individual freedom does not exist and needs to be continually weighed in the balance of the social, cultural, and personal constraints that circumscribe it. P. Henry, 'Getting the message in Montaigne's *Essays*', *ib.*, 165–84, notes that ethics is once more a hot topic in literary studies. He reviews the arguments put forward by A. Hartle, D. Quint, and J. Schwartz in the symposium and Alexander Nehamas elsewhere and emphasizes M.'s rejection of didacticism and the model of heroic virtue as practised by 'the constant Stoic, the honour-bound aristocrat [and] the religious zealot'. M. published his thoughts, which sometimes differed from the orthodox Catholic views of the time. For example, he opposed the burning of witches and his essay *Of Prayers* was censored in 1580 for its 'objectionable' claim that 'We must have our soul clean, at least in that moment in which we pray to [God], and rid of vicious passions'. On the other hand essays containing heterodox ideas were prefaced by formulae of submission to the Church. This lends poignancy to Schwartz's unanswered question as to whether M. would be prepared to sacrifice his physical liberty even for a desirable or just political cause.

Montaigne, *Journal de voyage en Alsace et en Suisse (1580–1581)*, *Actes du Colloque de Mulhouse-Bâle*, ed. Claude Blum, Philippe Derendinger, and Anne Toia, Champion, 254 pp., provides a new aspect of M. studies, with the caveat by Oliver Pot that it was rare in the 16th c. that individuals would admit to travelling as tourists purely for pleasure. At a time when 'l'oisiveté' is still considered as 'une infraction', a serious pretext is required to authorize the 'holidays' that the 'flânerie du voyage' demands. Of particular interest are the illustrations showing 'Maison de bain et de plaisir' and 'Le bain alchimique', which intrigued M. in Switzerland and reminds us that bathing in the 16th c. had little to do with cleanliness. S. Moussa, O. Pot, G. Polizzi, R. Beroulli, F. Garavini, and Z. Samaras contribute to this fascinating book.

Nuccio Ordine, *Le rendez-vous des savoirs*, Klincksieck, 1999, 209 pp., follows logically from 'le bain thérapeutique', even though it has nothing to do with Montaigne. Here are tales of the French embassy in Venice at the time of François 1er. Venice was a hotbed of intrigue but also a meeting place for writers and artists. Laughter, so much a feature of the *Year's Work* in 1999, invades philosophy and medicine as well as literature and poetry, and there, amongst the questions of theory, is 'le rire thérapeutique'. Lucretius recommends laughter for curing the ills of the soul. O. emphasizes that, for Renaissance doctors such as Rabelais, the care of the body has to involve the care of the soul, and therefore includes laughter. Indeed many writers claimed to have cured themselves of illnesses through laughter. The eight

essays in this delightful book provide a glimpse not only into the ways
of the court but into a new world vision. Distinctions are waived
between men of letters, philosophers, doctors, diplomats, and artists.

H. Grady, 'Shakespeare's links to Machiavelli and Montaigne:
constructing intellectual modernity in early modern Europe', *CL*,
52:119–42, considers Shakespeare's *Richard II* and argues that the
'modern' subjectivity therein 'demands a supplementation of Machiavelli with Montaigne, since Shakespeare's concept of Richard's
subjectivity veers from the ideas of *The Prince* into those of M.'s
seminal texts'. G. dwells upon Machiavelli and instrumental reason,
and points out that chapters 5 and 6 of *Essais, Book I*, share
Machiavelli's fascination with the gap between political power and
morality. An analysis of *Richard II* shows that the play before Richard's
abdication displays elements of the Machiavellian approach to
politics. With Richard's subjectivity after the abdication, there is a
move from dissection of Machiavellian power to a look at the
dynamics of Montaignean subjectivity.

At the beginning of the 21st c., when so much literary criticism is
written in barely comprehensible jargon, it is salutary to find that
M. eschewed the traditional forms of philosophical discourse by
writing in French rather than Latin, so as to be understood by a wider
public, including women. E. Limbrick, 'Montaigne et le refus du
discours philosophique traditionnel dans l'*"Apologie de Raimond
Sebond"* ', *DFS*, 52:22–27, maintains that this revolutionized literature
in France, as the Pléiade poets had hoped. By the use of a wider essay
form rather than the more restrictive dialogue, M. acquires total
liberty of both structure and thought. His lack of dogmatism and
originality of mind are expressed in his chapter "Des prières", where
he states 'Je propose des fantaisies informes et irresolues, comme ceux
qui publient des questions doubteuses, à débattre aux écoles: non pas
pour establir la vérité, mais pour la chercher.' L. believes that when
M. says with mock humility, 'Je ne suis pas philosophe', he is refusing
to be bound by the limits such a definition would impose, thus
perhaps showing scorn for the profession, but above all demanding
his freedom of expression. Paul Mathias has edited an extract from
M.'s *Essais* (II,12), *L'Apologie de Raymond Sebond*, Flammarion, 1999,
331 pp. Unlike Limbrick, Mathias sees the 'apology' as a jerky and
uneven text, but one that illustrates M.'s philosophical and metaphysical outlook, which is the result of 'une crise permanente et
salutaire de la pensée abandonnée à elle-même, à ses peines et ses
incertitudes.'

James J. Supple, *Les Essais de Montaigne: méthode(s) et méthodologies*,
Champion, 468 pp., is an unusual book in that it seeks to show all the
diverse critical approaches to the *Essais*, many of them contradictory,

and explains the viewpoints of numerous specialists such as Rigolot, Cave, Defaux, Sayce, and Holyoake. The introduction, for example, shows how views on M.'s religion differ. The first part of the book shows how the results obtained by analysts are a direct reflection of their methods; the second part analyses some of the essays to illustrate the pros and cons of the various critical approaches, and the third part is a call to exclude dogmatic generalisations and respect the *Essais* as a form of dialogue.

Montaigne et la question de l'homme, ed. Marie-Luce Demonet, *PUF*, 1999, 184 pp., is introduced by the editor in 'L'homme en gros' in which she writes of M., 'Loin de lui l'ambition d'examiner les relations entre l'homme et l'être. Pourtant, déduire des *Essais* l'ontologie de M. serait une approche possible de la question de "l'homme."' This thesis is followed by André Tournon, Jean-Yves Pouilloux, M.-L. Demonet, Pierre Magnard, Thierry Gontier, and Emmanuel Faye.

M.'s aim to portray himself '*au vif*' (*Essais* II.8.386a; 278) is usually taken as claiming that the writer works 'from life'. G. Hoffmann, 'Portrayal from life, or to life? The *Essais*'s living effigy', *FF*, 25:145–63, translates it rather as portraits drawn to life, that is to appear life-like. 'From life' could better be expressed as '*après* le vif'. Building a somewhat Talmudic argument on his revised translation, he develops an intriguing argument that, even if M. did not go so far as to substitute a secular ideal of immortality for the promise of Christian salvation, he certainly saw his writings as offering at least a form of eternal life. Given M.'s dominance of the present 16th c. French research scene, his view must be seen to have validity.

Harpagon's motto 'Il faut manger pour vivre et non vivre par manger', brought the quotation from Socrates to a wide public. In his article discussing the intertext relating to food in M.'s final essay, *De l'experience*, J. O'Brien, 'At Montaigne's table', *FS*, 54:1–16, considers the analyses by Jules Brody and Jean Céard. Both see a narrative line between the classical past and the Renaissance present. As far as M.'s food preferences were concerned, O'B. seeks ways of widening the perspectives to include, for example, contemporary medical theories. He argues that the reader, by active intervention,, will determine 'the contingency or necessity of textual details' and refers to Michel Jeanneret's use of the term 'brassage', which involves terms taken from outside as well as inside the literary sphere.

K. Westerwelle, 'Montaignes Kritik an Platos Dichtungstheorie', Baumbach, *Tradita*, 147–63, observes that M. considered poetry to be the highest form of human communication, not in its lyrical form, but in its stylistic effect, the 'force et beauté des propos'. He disagrees with the principle of *furor poeticus* as defined by Plato in *Ion* and in

Phaidros. The dynamic in the *Essais* comes from the challenge to the platonic ideal of poetry as inspiration. M. questions the discrepancy between literature and philosophy, madness and reason, and expresses doubts as to Plato's establishment of a critical authority which is fundamentally independent of *Dichtung*.

M.-A. Wiesmann, 'Intertextual labyrinths: Ariadne's lament in Montaigne's *Sur des vers de Virgile*', *RQ*, 53:792–820, reconstructs the thematic and literary presence of a labyrinth in M.'s essay. The so-called multicursal labyrinth is a literary device to take a reader on a series of detours that prevent penetration to the core of the text but render exit almost impossible. M. is said to have followed this model especially in his essay on Virgil. W. displays impressive breadth of classical and Renaissance scholarship but, in the end (and M. can't be wrong) this paper seems also to share many of the characteristics of the multicursal labyrinth.

Gisèle Mathieu-Castellani, *Montaigne ou la vérité du mensonge*, Geneva, Droz, 160 pp., raises similar issues to Wiesmann. Whilst assuring readers that his *Essais* are written in good faith, M. seeks to mislead, seduce, and trap them. Truth has as many faces as the lie, and M. sometimes chooses to disguise or only partially to reveal it. M.-C. points out that M. was fond of word play and the 'discours oblique' of the oracle and felt that one could not reveal everything; he also knew that some words mean more than they say and others imply what they do not say.

RABELAIS

In Véronique Zaercher, *Le dialogue rabelaisien, le Tiers Livre exemplaire*, Geneva, Droz, 347 pp., Z. points out that, when the *Tiers Livre* appeared in 1546, it must have surprised its readers not only because both Pantagruel and Gargantua (resuscitated in chapter 35) have, without further explanation, shrunk to normal size, and their prodigious feats of the past have disappeared, but also because the *Tiers Livre* is based largely on dialogue, with a particular importance accorded to Lucien de Samostate. Z. compares the *Tiers Livre* with contemporary dialogues such as the *Heptaméron* and *Cymbalum mundi* and says that the important thing is the comparison between the texts and the dialogue.

In his preface to Chaoying Sun, *Rabelais, mythes, images, sociétés*, Desclée de Brouwer, 268 pp., G. Durand points to the author's wide heritage and background, and her constant references to Chinese thought in her analysis of R.'s text. For example, the disappointing brevity of the 'Dive's' reply together with the water of the fantastic fountain changing into wine can be explained both by the *tao* of an oriental *vide* (emptiness) and even further by the *Xijouji* when the pilgrims realise that the fruit of their perilous journey is nothing but empty pages. Sun herself explains the importance of the myth in its widest sense to 16th-c. writers, and her analysis even includes the *Kabbala*. The book is copiously annotated but has no index or bibliography, which is disappointing in a scholarly work.

M. in *De l'amité* proclaims the superiority of his friendship with Etienne de La Boétie over those recorded by Aristotle, Cicero, and Lucian. La B. bequeathed *Voluntary Servitude* to M., who promised it would occupy the centre pages of book 1 of the *Essais*. 17 years later, when the work was published, he omitted it, claiming that he was protecting la B.'s memory by not allowing his name to be embroiled in a revolutionary context. P. Moser, 'Montaigne's literary patrons: the case of La Boétie', *SCJ*, 31:381–97, discusses Richard Regosin's theory that M. felt the need to reject *patrons* whose work might overshadow his own authorial identity and analyses the nature of M.'s friendship with La B. who was at various times both an equal friend and a father figure.

RONSARD

Danièle Duport, *Les Jardins qui sentent le sauvage: Ronsard et la poétique du paysage*, Geneva, Droz, 144 pp., has taken a line from Ronsard, 'J'aime fort les jardins qui sentent le sauvage', as inspiration for her study of how nature and gardens reflect the powers of poetry. 'Le paysage' shows 'les artifices naturels' and the garden the art of the gardener, which Malherbe celebrates as 'l'eternelle structure' which 'Aux miracles de l'art fait céder la nature'.

In the *Amours* (1552–1553), Cassandre is, of course, the main figure, but L.-G. Tin, 'Les *Amours* de Cassandre: un concours poétique', *BHR*, 62:249–57, points out that she shares the stage with numerous poets including Homer, Pindar, Ovid, Petrarch, Baïf, and Pontus de Tyard. In describing this as a poetic contest, of which the *Puys* was one of many examples at the time, Tin examines the figure of the poet within the *Amours* and shows how the poem can be read as a *concours* which will be a monument to the glory of R. To this end, R. classifies the poets in various ways and takes care to define his own image *vis-à-vis* the models that he hopes to equal if not surpass. R. organizes the competition, chooses the winner and, with the title *L'Humble discours de son livre immortel*, launches himself and his reputation for posterity.

In 1572 R. published the fourth edition of his works. Claudine Jomphe, *Les Théories de la disposition et le Grand Œuvre de Ronsard*, Champion, 410 pp., observes that it included the *Franciade*, a promised epic poem intended to dignify the new generation of poets, but it had many structural problems and was not a great success. It was the story of Francus, son of Hector, a Trojan who was to found the French nation after numerous trials and tribulations, and it seemed an odd choice to link the history of France with that of Troy, and present the French as losers. J. feels that the structure of the *Franciade* must be studied through its 'disposition' according to contemporary theories and reassesses the position of this neglected poem in R.'s work.

M. Quainton, 'Unusual births in the poetry of Pierre de Ronsard', *NCo*, 27–28 : 7–21, points not only to R.'s use of mythical figures such as Apollo and Mercury, who have overt links to poetry, but to Pallas Athene and Bacchus who were born without a mother. This is to 'demonstrate how these strange, even monstrous, births are employed by the poet both to voice his constant concerns with poetics and to give expression to processes of divine self-engendering.' R. refers to himself as a mother in the sense of giving birth to poetry, with Plato's distinction between the 'superior and spiritual children born from the head of man' and the normal and necessarily inferior children born of woman. However Athene and Bacchus are also used to illustrate R.'s use of *libre contrainte/paisible contrainte*, according to the rhetorical levels of *inventio, dispositio* and *elocutio*. Q. feels that R.'s use of images of 'self-replication and self-renewal' illustrates a general problem for Renaissance poets of how to be creative oneself rather than recreating the works of others.

DU BELLAY

George H. Tucker, *Les Regrets et autres œuvres poëtiques de Joachim Du Bellay*, Gallimard, 209 pp. is another in a series of useful guides. It provides a dossier and copious notes on Du B.'s contemporaries mentioned in *Les Regrets*, together with a section on 'documents et témoignages'. This contains Du B.'s comments but also those of his contemporaries such as Claude Binet, Thomas Sébillet, and Bar-thélemy Aneau. Another section deals with 'Le travail technique du poète', with further comments by contemporary critics such as Etienne Pasquier, later ones such as Sainte-Beuve, and present-day ones such as Floyd Gray and Josiane Rieu.

MAROT

In a sparse year for Marot studies, it cannot be immodest to say that Catherine Reuben, *La traduction des Psaumes de David par Clément Marot: aspects poétiques et théologiques*, Champion, 288 pp., is the best (indeed the only) book to appear. It aims to show that M. played a major role as a poet of the Reformation, by studying both the poetic and theological aspects of his translation of the Psalms into French poetry. It examines the sources on which he based his interpretations of the Psalms. The Christian hebraists, Olivetan, Bucer, and Campensis are of particular significance, and by *Hebraica veritas* M. meant that he was following the Hebrew Masoretic text rather than the Hebrew Vulgate as favoured by Lefèvre d'Etaples, representing the first generation of 16th-c. biblical translators. The many editions of M.'s translation have been sorted out by previous scholars, so only the variants between the *antérieure* and *définitive* versions are examined. The four remaining chapters show how the metrical form and the use of parallelism, repetition, and imagery have enabled M.'s translation to stand the test of time. In slightly altered form and completed by de Bèze, it is still the basis of the Protestant Psalter in France. Several of these themes are further developed in Id., 'Clément Marot: poet of the Reformation', *RRR*, 3:78–109, dealing especially with the Christian hebraists, and giving a detailed analysis of M.'s translation of Psalm 23.

I. His, ' "Sous lesquels ont esté mises des paroles morales" ': un cas de *contrafactum* de psaumes entre 1598 et 1618', *RMus*, 85:189–225, records that in 1618 twelve of M.'s psalms were rewritten as moral poems in accordance with the spirit of the Edict of Nantes. A *contrafactum* was normally a vulgar reworking, but in this case the Psalms had become disturbing because of their Huguenot associations and were to be made 'more moral' so as to reach 'more devout souls'. For example, in Psalm 23, 'Mon Dieu me paist sous sa puissance haute:/ C'est mon berger, de rien je n'aurai faute:' became 'Mon Dieu combien un seul ventre dévore/ D'or & d'argent, & si ne peut encore'. The music, however, remained that of Claude Le Jeune, so that the Huguenot connotations survived. This is a splendid article illustrating the difficulties faced by religious obscurantists.

M. Bouchard, '*Ethos* et *Eros*: *l'Épistre de Maguelonne à Pierre de Provence* de Clément Marot', *RoN*, 41:45–54, compares Marot's version of the medieval romance, *Pierre de Provence et la belle Maguelonne* with Anne de Graville's (*c.* 1490–*c.* 1540) reworking, *Beau romant de deux amans*. She aims to show that the notion of 'ethos' rather than 'subject' or 'author' allows the identification of both the aims and the vision of the world as implied by the 'instance narrative' and the 'destinataire'. Marot's version is that of a court poet; A. de G.'s version adds a feminine ethos, as also in Marguerite de Navarre's *Heptaméron*, which shows a change in view from masculine to feminine language, positive characteristics becoming vices. The great conqueror in love and war, searching for new victories, becomes a fickle Lothario; the brilliant strategist and fine speaker is reduced to a cunning hypocrite. This provides a new slant on the 'parfait amour'.

Marguerite de Navarre, *L'Heptaméron des nouvelles,* ed. N. Cazauran, Gallimard, 753 pp., is a welcome popular edition of M. de N. According to the cover, M. de N., 'Corps féminin, cœur d'homme et tête d'ange', as Marot described her, is the 16th-c. equivalent of Guy de Maupassant. The book is richly annotated with a chronology, a genealogical table, and many other scholarly aids.

Marguerite de Navarre, *Comédies bibliques,* ed. Barbara Marczuk, Geneva, Droz, 360 pp., is the first critical edition of M. de N.'s four plays, *Comédie de la Nativité, Comédie de l'Adoration des trois Rois, Comédie des Innocents* and *Comédie du Désert.* They were not only a contribution to literature but also a part of the French evangelical movement. The portrait of the Virgin as a reader of the Bible and the mystical soul ('effacée') submissive to the will of God shows M. de N.'s interest in new ideas and the reform of the cult of the Virgin Mary. The *Comédie de l'Adoration,* for example, has two unusual characters in the shape of 'inspiration' and 'intelligence divine'. It is to the latter that God says, 'Or levez vous Parfait Intelligence;/De mes secrets cachez aux Escritures,/Allez là bas, et faites diligence/D'en faire à tous salutaires lectures.' In other words, spread to everyone the evangelical message of the scriptures.

In the 21st story of the *Heptaméron,* Rolandine, a 30-year-old spinster, lacking beauty and worldly skills, has a chaste romance with a courtier, who is socially down-market because of his bastardy. They converse from opposite windows of a castle, he pretending to read a romance of the Round Table, she working on an openwork bedcover in crimson silk. M.-A. Wiesmann, 'Rolandine's *lict de reseul*: An arachnological reading of a tale by Marguerite de Navarre', *SCJ,* 31:433–55, argues an outwardly improbable association between embroidery (Arachne and the weaving contest in Ovid) and feminine resistance to the male-dominated order. In one of many examples, he quotes Marot's 'erudita' Ysabeau, who defends her literary pursuits as developing in her the *prudence* to *gouverner sa maison à poinct. A poinct* is a pun on the *poinct* of needlecraft, indicating the compatibility of textiles and intellectual activity.

A. Allen, 'Barbares et "grands discoureux": autour d'une anecdote italienne dans *l'Heptaméron* (VI,1)', *DFS,* 51:3–11, suggests a reading of the 51st story in M. de N.'s *Heptaméron* in the light of J. Balsamo's call to 'examiner la part indissociable de l'italianisme et de l'anti-italianisme dans une identité française qui existe, se transforme et se confirme, d'éclairer une culture française lorsqu'elle se définit par une référence à l'Italie et contre une Italie pensée et formulée selon ses besoins originaux'. M. de N. wrote her *Heptaméron* (1540–42) at the same time that her secretary, Le Maçon, was translating the *Decaméron* for her, and praising, as did Estienne Roffet, the French nation and its language. The anti-Italian aspect includes some of the vices commonly ascribed to the Italians such as cruelty and sodomy, much as the Italians thought of the French as barbarians. A. feels that the discussion by the protagonists goes beyond the historical and political register to touch the philosophical and theological.

In *The Pleasure of Discernment: Marguerite de Navarre as Theologian*, OUP, 175 pp., Carol Thysell argues that, in order to understand how M. de N. expresses herself in the *Heptaméron*, one must consider the theological and philosophical options available to early 16th-c. thinkers. For instance, T. feels that 'the collection of tales reveals M. de N.'s constructive proposal on evil, which negotiates a third way, as it were, between Calvin's own view and that of the spiritual libertines'. T. fills in the theological background to the *Heptameron*, particularly with reference to Calvin, one of the many evangelicals who sought refuge at M. de N.'s court. She was an advocate of both justification by faith and the priesthood of all believers and 'encouraged all to join her in a conversation that ultimately might draw them into union with each other and with God.'

The words *sage* and *sagement* appear often in the *Heptaméron* and refer to three sorts of wisdom — religious, moral, and practical. I. Morrison, 'Sage et sagement dans l'Heptaméron de Marguerite de Navarre', *NMi*, 101 : 32–44, points out that the book often dwells on the negative aspects of *sagesse*, such as the fact that religious wisdom is based on the worthlessness of man. Other forms of wisdom are more positive but difficult to achieve. Furthermore, practical wisdom may be reduced to deception and thus seem to contradict the religious and moral aspects. This contradiction may be excused by the compromises necessary in order to survive in a world of sin, but it also reflects through the storytellers an appreciation of the practical but undeserved success of certain tricks.

LABÉ

Daniel Martin, *Signe(s) d'Amante. L'agencement des Evvres de Louïze Labé Lionnoize*, Champion, 1999, 526 pp., says that although Labé's work appears heterogeneous — a mythological dialogue in prose, 3 elegies and 24 sonnets in one volume — there are, in fact, links between the texts. M. considers various types of echo in vocabulary, syntax, rhythm, versification, images, and stylistic effects. He examines the disposition and frequency of these effects both in each part and between the various parts, as well as opposition, contrast, and alternation, and compares Louise Labé's organization of her work with that of Marot in *L'Adolescence Clementine*.

AGRIPPA D'AUBIGNÉ

*Agrippa d'Aubigné, *Histoire universelle*, XI: *Index général*, ed. André Thierry, Geneva, Droz, 240 pp., is the final volume of this definitive edition of d'Aubigné's massive work. In *Les Tragiques* (1577–1616) the Protestant poet makes eight references to the Waldensians, a Puritan sect living in the valleys of Piedmont, Dauphiné, and Provence, who were much persecuted in the 16th and 17th centuries. F. Giacone, 'Les Tragiques d'Agrippa d'Aubigné et les vaudois', *RHR*, 217:179–96, believes he can name the 'vieil pasteur d'Angrongne' who encouraged A. d'A. to publish his work; he could be Etienne Noël, author of *L'Histoire des persécutions*. From this book comes the image of the Vaudois as David fighting Goliath as taken up in *Les Tragiques*, which shows the Waldensians as almost ideal yet modest models.

In the *Discours des misères de ce temps*, the Catholic Ronsard exhorts Catherine de' Médicis to mitigate the horrors of the French wars of religion by restoring the authority of the Church and ending the Reform heresy. D'A., the Protestant, in *Les Tragiques* (not published until 1616) blames Catherine for interfering and aggravating the political situation. Z. Zalloua, 'Ronsard et Aubigné, poètes-polémistes rivaux dans *Discours des misères de ce temps* et *Les Tragiques*: objet référentiel et construction poétique', *RoN*, 41:55–67, examines the representation of Catherine in *Les Tragiques* in terms of a dialogue between two poets divided both by religious and poetic convictions. D'A. is writing 10 years after R. and refuses to conform to poetic ideals, particularly after the St. Bartholomew Massacre. His role is not to teach or please but to move the reader. Z. feels that, for d'A., the visionary, Catherine is a historical figure outside the poem and also a poetic device, an allegory. This makes *Les Tragiques* both 'engagé' and 'poétique', and d'A., like Ronsard, a 'poète-créateur'.

8. MINOR WRITERS

PROSE

Alain Cullière, '*La Conversion de sainte Thècle* de Guilaume Reboul (1602)', *Adirel*, 13:81–100, discusses Reboul, a lesser known writer, who converted to Catholicism having served the King of Navarre and was executed in 1611. R. was regarded as a turncoat and disliked by both sides, and then forgotten by posterity. C. has, however, rediscovered *La Conversion*, which develops from a moral story of the life of the Saint into a proper novel. Thècle is supposed to be the first female Christian martyr. It is unusual to have a saint's life as a subject for a novel as opposed to a play and C. praises R.'s use of hyperbole and false modesty, which ensure the success of the work.

David La Guardia, in *The Iconography of Power: the French Nouvelle at the end of the Middle Ages*, Newark, Delaware U.P., 1999, 178 pp. considers the *nouvelle* as a repository of information about everyday life across a wide social spectrum in France in the 15th and 16th centuries. He maintains that the *nouvelle* is not forerunner of the modern, realist novel, but rather it insists upon the definition of characters by means of insignia or icons that situate them with respect to one another on hierarchical social grids, circumscribing the possible roles, actions, and identities of each character, and constituting structures of power.

Gilbert Schrenck, *Nicolas de Harlay, sieur de Sancy (1546–1629): L'antagoniste d'Agrippa d'Aubigné. Étude biographique et contexte pamphlétaire*, Champion, 282 pp., fleshes out a man hitherto known only as the antagonist described by d'Aubigné in his biting pamphlet. 'Il constitue même l'une des apparitions les plus significatives de l'histoire française de l'époque, oeuvrant à l'instauration d'une conception "politique" de l'état moderne.' Nicolas de Harlay, sieur de Sancy, *Discours sur l'occurrence de ses affaires*, ed. G. Schrenck, Champion, 156 pp., follows on from the previous book. These memoirs cover the period from 1589 to 1610, when Sancy, as soldier, diplomat, and politician played an important role at the courts of Henri III and Henri IV. They make fascinating reading as, for example, in the episode in the coach with the King, when Gabrielle d'Estrées, the King's mistress, broached the subject of legitimizing her children. 'J'eus opinion qu'elle ne s'estoit mise sur ce discours que pour faire veoir au Roy que si j'avois la hardiesse de parler à sa majesté franchement sur ce subject en son absence, je n'oserais le faire en sa presence [. . .]. Mais elle se trompa, car je lui respondis sans aucun respect ce que je pensay estre de la raison et de mon devoir, pour l'empescher de penser plus à cela. Elle s'en trouva estonnée [. . .].'

R. Aulotte, 'Cyre Foucault, traducteur (1597) des *Lettres d'amour* d'Aristénète', *DFS*, 52:29–35, describes this lively adaptation by a virtually unknown author for his contemporary audience. At the end of letter I.25, a courtesan accuses her sister of stealing her lover and vows revenge. The traditional Vieillfond translation reads, 'Et bien, nous allons nous faire du trot réciproquement! Je trouverai moi aussi quelque moyen semblable ou un autre tour de Renard (que ce soit bien décidée) ou que le fer soit chassé par le fer. Je ne serais pas embarrassée pour lui enlever, à cette insatiable, trois amants pour un.' F.'s version reads, 'Puisqu'ainsi est faisons à qui pis pis. Je lui baillerai du Bris contre Robert, à mauchat mau-rat, passe sans flux pour ce coup, un clou sert à pousser l'autre, pour un qu'elle m'a osté, je lui en volerai trois'. A. remarks that F.'s translation is not always faithful, and his vocabulary, syntax, and style are marks of his time.

It is currently fashionable to work on early modern travel narratives. Marie-Christine Gomez-Géraud, *Ecrire le voyage au 16e siècle en France*, PUF, 128 pp., seeks to consider works that have not been favoured recently and includes a 'lexique des voyageurs et de leurs ouvrages'. It is divided into 'Approches littéraires' and 'Approches linguistiques'. Under 'Nouveaux mondes, nouveaux mots', the author considers words which have entered the French language in their original form such as 'bazar', and also the Tupi language used by Jean de Léry after his 10-month sojourn among the 'savages'. This book is a useful introduction to further study. (see also above Blum (p. 85), Nuccio Ordine (p. 85), Tinguely (p. 78).

Readers of the memoirs of royal governesses will get a frisson from Louise Boursier, *Récit véritable de la naissance de messeigneurs et dames les enfants de France, Instruction à ma fille et autre textes*, ed. François Rouget and Colette H. Winn, Geneva, Droz, 166 pp. She was a midwife and provides the inside story of many royal births. Indeed she was the first of her ilk to write of her professional experiences. She writes in a dignified way to defend herself against the attacks of the doctors after the death of 'Madame' (Marie de Bourbon Montpensier, duchesse d'Orléans) sister-in-law of the King, on June 5th 1627. Equally touching is her answer to the young prince eagerly awaiting the arrival of a sibling and anxious to find out whether it would be boy or girl. The prince offered her a large reward if she would tell him. Assuring him that it would be sufficient if she had his favour, Louise told him that *she* decided the sex of the child and that it would be a boy. It was!

F. Lestringant, 'Histoires tragiques et vies des hommes illustres : la rencontre des genres. À propos de quelques histoires orientales chez Belleforest et Thevet', *Adirel*, 13:49–67, points out that Belleforest and Thevet were as famous in their time as Laurel and Hardy and the same relative shapes. He posits that the line dividing history and fiction was not as clear for Renaissance writers as it is for us. He follows two stories through Belleforest's *Sixiesme Tome des Histoires tragiques (1583)* and Thevet's *Vrais Pourtraits et Vies des hommes illustres (1584)*, those of 'Cherif (ou Serif) Roy de Fez et de Marroc' et 'Sultan Mustapha, fils de Sultan Solyman'. Belleforest tends to amplify and Thevet to condense, but both have a didactic and moral viewpoint. They were holding up a mirror to their own times.

M. Tetel, 'François de la Noue, conscience de son temps', *Adirel*, 13:69–79, brings out points in common between Montaigne (who mentions La Noue in his *De la praesumption*) and François de la Noue in his *Discours*. Although La Noue was Protestant, both encouraged tolerance and moderation. La Noue tried to reconcile the two camps and played an important role in the conversion of Henry IV. For both writers, the continuity of the monarchy was the most important thing. Among the quotations from the *Discours* is the sad reflection on the political situation: 'Nous avons fait la folie, ne trouvons donc pas estrange si nous la beuvons. Toutefois il y a apparence que le breuvage sera bien amer.'

Les Amadis en France au 16e siècle, ed. Nicole Cazauran, Rue d'Ulm, 220 pp., is a collection of articles about the *Amadis de Gaule*, a series of 15th c. Spanish romances translated by Herberay des Essarts from 1540 onwards. They were a success from the start and translations continued well into the 17th century. C. and her colleagues (S. Roubaud, J.-M. Chatelain, C. de Buzon, A.-M. Capdeboscq, Y. Giraud, V. Duché, R. Gorris, V. Benhaïm, M. Huchon, M. Bideaux) want to explain their success and persuade others to read these forgotten works which, in their time, were 'parfaicte idée de la langue françoise'.

Diane S. Wood, *Hélisenne de Crenne: At the Crossroads of Renaissance Humanism and Feminism*, Madison NJ, Fairleigh Dickinson U.P. — London, Assoc. Univ. Presses, 186 pp., deals with a pioneer feminist and serious scholar in the Humanist tradition. She published eight editions of her best-selling novel, *Les Angoysses douloureuses qui procèdent d'amours*, between 1538 and 1560. She wrote three other works, *Epistres familières et invectives* (1539), *Le Songe* (1540), and *Les Eneydes* (1541), all linked by morality, social interaction, and the role of women. Questions about women — unhappy marriages, women engaging in intellectual affairs, the dangers of passion — are central to her texts. She wrote in the idiom of her time (see O'Brien, p. 87), and used the literary conventions of patriarchal society to undermine the central principle of patriarchy. Her work reflects the complicated contemporary religious turmoil. References to the Bible in French imply Protestant leanings, but her insistence on the Catholic notion of free will helps her to create sentimental and epistolatory novels.

The research of B. Roussel, to whom the following book is dedicated, and that of R. G. Hobbs has uncovered much evidence of the importance of the evangelicals of the Haut Rhin for the Reformation cause. Reinhard Bodenmann, *Wolfgang Musculus (1497–1563): destin d'un autodidacte lorrain au siècle des Réformes*, Geneva, Droz, 724 pp., writes persuasively about Musculus and tells of his life through the biography *Vita Wolfgangi Musculi* by his son, Abraham, which B. has translated into French and annotated. Musculus was incapable of sycophantic behaviour and felt that a true friend should speak his mind. However, he detested all forms of aggression and verbal violence, and B. suggests that he wanted to avoid direct confrontation with Luther or Calvin. Musculus indulged Bucer in his desire for communal unity as long as this did not conflict with his idea of the essential Truths. With the notes from an earlier scholar, B. has succeeded in deciphering Musculus's secret writing, which turns out to be German transliterated into Arabic script, which Musculus used for his notes from the interconfessional meetings at Worms and Ratisbonne (1540–41). This provides a compelling and fascinating read even for non-specialists.

C. La Charité considers 'Le problème de l'attribution de *L'Instruction pour les jeunes dames* (1572) et l'énigmatique cryptonyme M.D.R.', *BHR*, 62 : 119–28, in the light of previous theories that the translation was by Marie de Romieu, as her contemporaries La Croix du Maine and Guillaume Colletet thought; or by Madeleine Des Roches; or by Jacques de Romieu using Marie as a pseudonym; or by another unknown author. La C. points out that the theme of 'mespris de la loy de mariage' in the *Premières œuvres poétiques,* the fact that Marie had a penchant for translation and adaptation and probably knew Latin, the identical signature in the prologue to the *Instruction* and the volume of poems, and the chronology of the compositions combine to prove that Marie de Romieu was indeed the author.

Henri II Estienne, *Hypomneses* (1582), ed. J. Chomorat, Champion, 1999, 510 pp. Henri was the son of Robert Estienne of the famous printing family. Robert was sufficiently a scholar to annotate his Bibles himself. Henri inherited the printing works on the understanding that he would remain true to the Reformed faith. He edited the classics and the *Thesaurus Linguae Graecae* (1572) and was equally renowned for his enthusiasm for the French language. The *Hypomneses* are 'recommandations aux étrangers qui désirent apprendre notre langue, et qui ne seront pas inutiles aux Français eux-mêmes'. Among the points made are that 'le bon usage' is geographically that of Paris and socially that of the *Parlement* and not of the court, but that the language of Paris (as was the case with Greek) can be enriched by the use of dialect. The *Hypomneses* are half way between the 'ordonnance' of Villers-Cotteret (1539) which substituted French for Latin in the courts, and the founding by Richelieu of the *Académie française* in 1635. Bénédicte Boudou, *Mars et les muses dans l'apologie pour Herodote d'Henri Estienne*, Geneva, Droz, 686 pp., examines the history of H.'s *Apologie* and compares his French 'translation' with the Latin. This reveals H.'s evolving critical method, based on experience, sensitivity and rational synthesis. In choosing to defend a historian as controversial as Herodotus, H. is trying to reappraise the relationship that his contemporaries had with the classics, whilst at the same time, as a *réformé*, fighting the present corruption, which he blames on the Catholic Church.

P. Hummel, 'Le détour pindarique de Bonaventura Vulcanius (1592)', *BHR*, 61, 1999:669–67, wonders what prompted Bonaventura Vulcanius (alias de Smet, 1538–1614) to stray from his work on late classical and Byzantine literature in order to lecture on Pindar at Leiden University in 1592. As Vulcanius was also an occasional corrector for Henri Estienne in Geneva (after 1574) and for Froben in Basle, it could be more than coincidence that the 1590 edition of Pindar by F. Van Raphelingen, based on the third edition by Estienne (1586) was published almost at the same time as Vulcanius' *De mundo*, also published by Estienne.

P. M. Smith, 'Une édition de la *Satyre Menippée* et de sa postface, la *Svitte du Catholicon d'Espagne*', *BHR*, 62:363–72, hopes to shed light on the problematic bibliography of the *Satyre Menippée* through an edition bound together with a second foreword from the printer, Jamet Mettayer, to the reader entitled *Svitte du Catholicon d'Espagne* with the sub-title *Avec l'explication du mot de Higuiero d'Infierno, & autres y contenues*, which appears not to have aroused previous critical interest. S. considers this is a postface to the *Satyre* which gives vital information on the history of the work and the metamorphoses it has undergone since its publication. This version of the *Satyre* is dated 1594, but this could just be the date of the *Svitte*, which is not yet fully integrated with the *Satyre*. There are only three copies of this unique edition in two parts, and S. gives a full description of the only complete version at the Bibliothèque Mazarine. She concludes that it is probably the first printing of the postface to the *Satyre* and was printed, like the *Satyre*, by Mettayer, which gives it both authority and interest.

P. M. Smith, 'The reception and influence of Josephus's *Jewish War* in the late French Renaissance with special reference to the *Satyre Menippée*', *RenS*, 13, 1999:173–91, points out that Josephus was even more popular a historical writer than Plutarch and that the number of editions of *The Jewish War* in the period 1450–1700 was exceeded only by the same author's *Jewish Antiquities*. J.'s popularity peaked in the years 1550–1599 especially in French translation. His subject matter was sensational and he was seen as bridging the gap in the Graeco-Judaic synthesis. During the French wars of religion, furthermore, he was enlisted in support of both sides and also in internecine struggles. For example, Louis Dorléans drew an analogy between the Jewish Zealots and the Catholic extremists in his own party who, in his view, threatened to destroy the *Ligue*. This was then seized upon by D.'s *Politique* adversaries, the authors of the *Satyre Menippée*, who in turn exhorted their supporters to read *The Jewish War* for the parallels it afforded to the situation in France.

POETS

The problems of environmental pollution in the late 20th century have led to a myth of an idyllic pastoral and pollution-free past that ignores the problems from coal burning, tanneries, and related industries. E. Vinestock, 'Myth and environmentalism in a Renaissance poem: Jean-Antoine de Baïf's *La Ninfe Bievre*', *NCo*, 27–28:22–33, tries to redress the balance. She describes *La Ninfe Bievre* as a strange and surprising work, because the nymph in question laments both her dishonour and the pollution of the waters of her river. In this hitherto overlooked poem, Baïf, in order to persuade the readers to take action, has the nymph appealing directly for pity by describing her calamitous metamorphosis from a pure rippling stream to a stinking sewer through the discharge of untreated waste products from the Gobelin dye factory. B.'s use of the myth to state his case is evidence that the making or remaking of myths was part of the fabric of Renaissance consciousness.

The relationship between Du Bartas and James VI of Scotland (and future James I of England) is well known (see *YWMLS*, 61:115). G. Banderier, 'Du Bartas et la littérature écossaise: une hypothèse', *BHR*, 62:89–92, investigates a further possible link between the poet and Maitland, author of a poem entitled 'On the Creation and Paradyce lost'. A sonnet by Du B. was found in the possession of Sir Richard Maitland's son John. As Maitland studied law in Paris, he could well have read Du B.'s *Sepmaine* in the original, although it had not yet been translated. B. can find no formal evidence linking the two men; nevertheless, as they were both politicians and poets in the service of the King, who was a fan of Du B., it is certainly a possibility.

Olivier de Magny, *Œuvres poétiques* 1: *Amours-Hymne-Gayetez*, ed. François Rouget, Champion, 1999, 550 pp., is another of the minor poets from the reign of Henri II whose time has come for reappraisal. He is seen as a gallant and adept courtier and a faithful disciple of Ronsard, even though he did not share the latter's poetic genius. His work is often weak and suffers from 'maniérisme'. His efforts to obtain an epideictic or showy register sometimes led to compositions that suffer from sentimentality and exaggerated flattery. R. tries to situate him in the French poetic scene of the 1550s.

Although his poetry is virtually unexplored, François Perrin (1533–1606), Canon of Autun, is of interest to A. Sirvin, 'François Perrin: un parcours immobile (les enseignements du paratexte dans l'œuvre du poète autunois)', *BHR*, 62:303–15, because through his work we can evaluate the 'identité sociale comme poétique' of many other provincial authors of this period. His first volume, 'Le Pourtraict de la vie humaine' (1574), is a zealous imitation of the Pléiade poets. P. had no success at court, although his father was doctor to François Ier, but he dedicates the volume to two people, Bishop Charles Ailleboust and Jean des Caurres, Principal of the College of Amiens, whom he hopes might help him succeed in promoting himself.

As a follow-up to Champion's Joachim Du Bellay concordance, Keith Cameron has produced a *Concordance des œuvres poétiques de Philippe Desportes*, Geneva, Droz, 32 pp. + CD-ROM. It is a sign of the times that the concordance (actually three concordances) is not contained in the miniscule number of pages but on the attached CD-ROM, readable on IBM-compatible computers. D.'s psalm translation is excluded. *Philippe Desportes (1546–1606): un poète presque parfait entre Renaissance et classicisme,* ed. Jean Balsamo, Klincksieck, 569 pp., is the fruit of a conference in Rheims in 1998. B. points out that, although D. published his *Cent psaumes de David* in 1598 and was the favourite poet of Henri III, his anniversaries are not celebrated nationally, and he is misjudged to this day because he was rich, loved, and influential, accused of being a courtier who wrote poetry without really believing in it, as opposed to Ronsard or d'Aubigné. D. enjoyed great success, having, at his death, both a great literary reputation and the revenue from four abbeys! The book is divided into four sections: 'L'homme et ses contemporarains', 'L'oeuvre', 'La Poétique', and 'La Réception'.

THEATRE

The latest addition to the series 'Théâtre français de la Renaissance' is *La Tragédie à l'époque d'Henri III, 2e série, vol. 2 (1579–1582),* ed. Christine Lauvergnat-Gagnière et al., PUF, 520 pp. It contains Anon., *Tragédie nouvelle appelée Pompée*; Robert Garnier, *Antigone ou la pieté*; Adrien D'Amboise, *Holoferne*; Fronton du Duc, *L'Histoire tragique de la pucelle de Dom-Remy*; Thomas Lecoq, *Tragédie de Cain*; and Jean de Beaubreuil, *Regulus.* The notes to *Antigone* mention how often the tragedy has been rewritten, by Anouillh, Brecht, Racine, Rotrou, and Hölderlin among others. Charles Mazouer suggests that there is a double Antigone, the rebel, and the pious Antigone of *Oedipus at Colonus,* and that it is not certain that Garnier has chosen between the two. Garnier also uses the story of Antigone to illustrate to his contemporaries the fate of France torn by the wars of religion.

Pierre Gringore, *Le Jeu du Prince des Sotz et de Mère Sotte,* ed. Alan Hindley, Champion, 224 pp., contains a collection of plays performed 'aux Halles de Paris, le mardy gras, l'an mil cinq cens et unze' to amuse the people but also to show them the anti-papal policy of Louis XII. G. was a Catholic, and the edition contains material showing his role in the propaganda battle between King and Pope. Quite apart from their historical interest and what they reveal of religious polemic and popular culture at the dawn of the Renaissance, these plays still have the power to amuse with their blend of satire and farce.

THE SEVENTEENTH CENTURY

By J. Trethewey, *University of Wales, Aberystwyth*, and J. P. Short, *formerly Senior Lecturer in French at the University of Sheffield*

1. General

M. Alet, 'La mélancolie dans la psycho-physiologie du début du XVIIe siècle', *PFSCL*, 27:447–71, begins with 'un tableau de la physiologie et de la "psychologie"' of the period and concludes with a study of aspects of melancholy and attitudes towards it of contemporary physicians and moralists.

David M. Posner, *The Performance of Nobility in Early Modern European Literature* (Cambridge Studies in Renaissance Literature and Culture, 33), CUP, 1999, 272 pp., surveys English and French idealized literary and dramatic representations of nobility and courtly behaviour. P. takes three plays by Corneille, *Le Cid*, *Cinna*, and *Suréna* (with a brief glance at *Nicomède*) as examples of 'the theatre of aristocratic revolt', and finally turns to La Bruyère whose *Caractères*, he claims, depict 'the end of the theatre of nobility'. *Durand Vol.* contains mainly historical articles, but the following are pertinent: J.-L. Gazzaniga, 'La formation des avocats au XVIIe et XVIIIe siècles' (259–74), cites the opinions of Gabriel Cayron, Bernard de Laroche Flavin, Jérôme Bignon, and Pierre Biarnoy de Merville among others; P. Hurtubise, 'Une grande inconnue: la littérature casuistique des XVIe, XVIIe et XVIIIe siècles' (317–30), offers a 'premier survol' of this post-tridentine material scorned by Pascal; F.-J. Ruggiu, ' "O fortunatos nimium, sua si bona norint, agricolas!" ou le journal d'un gentilhomme campagnard au début du XVIIIe siècle' (471–87), introduces us to François Joseph Le Clerc, seigneur de Bussy, author of this *inédit*; A. Walch, 'Trois traités moraux et spirituels au XVIIe siècle' (529–44), considers three 'normative' treatises on marriage by Grenaille, Fortin de La Hoguette, and Antoine de Courtin. James S. Amelang, *The Flight of Icarus: Artisan Autobiography in Early Modern Europe*, Stanford U.P., 1998, 497 pp., has collected in both North America and Europe a vast quantity of such material — diaries, family and business memoirs, pious and impious musings, religious and political polemic — none of it meant for publication in the normal sense, and covering the 16th-19th cs. There are 14 French 17th-c. contributors — not an impressive figure compared to other countries and periods — of whom one or two, like the midwife Louise Bourgeois, are known to history. *Transmission du savoir dans l'Europe des XVIe–XVIIe siècles, ed. Marie Roig Miranda (Colloques, congrès et conférences sur la Renaissance, 19), Champion, 544 pp., prints conference papers on all aspects of the handing down of practical and technical as well as intellectual and theoretical knowledge.

Nativel, *Femmes savantes*, contains the following: C. Biet, 'Quand la veuve contre-attaque: droit et fiction littéraire sous l'Ancien Régime' (17–26), examines three *factums* concerning a late 17th-c. civil court case, outlines the social and legal circumstances, and indicates the input of fiction in the evidence offered by both plaintiff and defendant to strengthen their cases; C. H. Winn, 'Les femmes et la rhétorique de combat: argumentation et (auto)référentialité' (39–50), looks at aspects of women's use of rhetoric in 'les protestations et revendications féminines' in mid-16th-c. to late 17th-c. works. S. Juratic, 'Marchandes ou savantes? Les veuves de libraires parisiens sous le règne de Louis XIV' (59–68), finds many widows active in the book trade. J. is covering ground also explored by Romeo Arbour (see *YWMLS*, 60:119). Courcelles, *Femmes*, contains papers in French and Spanish, of which two concern the 17th c.: J. Balsamo, 'Abel L'Angelier et ses dames: les Dames Des Roches, Madeleine de L'Aubespine, Marie Le Gendre, Marie de Gournay' (117–36), surveys late 16th-c. and early 17th-c. works published by L'A. and written for female readers, dedicated to women or composed by the above authors; M. Simonin, 'Trois femmes en librairie: Françoise de Louvain, Marie L'Angelier, Françoise Patelé (1571–1645)' (149–73), covers the lives of three generations, from grandmother to granddaughter, in order to 'mieux comprendre ce que furent conditions et comportements féminins dans le milieu des marchands du Palais et de la rue Saint-Jacques'. C. Baxter, 'Repression or liberation? Notions of the body among the nuns of Port-Royal', Meek, *Women*, 153–71, starts from the notion that 'the body is fundamentally shaped by culture' to provide a framework for her study of memoirs left by the nuns and those close to them. S. Reid, 'Writing motherhood in the reign of Louis XIV: some fictional and political representations', *ib.*, 172–84, is concerned with childbirth and avoiding it, with the 'natural' right of men to dominate, with midwifery, and above all the increasing tendency as the century advances to counsel 'confinement, containment and moral virtue' as the duty of women. François de Sales, Moïse Amyrault, and Fénelon are cited as illustrative of the tendency, with Poulain de La Barre as a refreshing dissident. E. Lesne, 'L'écriture des Camisards: de l'histoire au prophétisme', *LitC*, 39:149–73, reviews various accounts of the War of the Cévennes, by Cavalier, Mazel, Bonbonnoux, and Marion, in order to bring out the 'aspects les plus saillants du discours historique informant ces relations ou mémoires'. M.-C. Gomez-Géraud, '*Peregrinus in eremo*: le lieu du désert dans les récits des pèlerins de la Contre-Réforme', *RSH*, 258:149–62, surveys early 17th-c. works by Jean Boucher, Henry

Castela, and Jean Zuallart, and the anonymous *Pèlerin véritable*. H. Bost, 'Le désert des Huguenots: une poétique de l'épreuve', *ib.*, 177–206, finds 17th-c. writers imitating d'Aubigné and evoking a *désert* 'qui symbolise à la fois un lieu de retraite, de secret, de dépouillement du croyant et un lieu de refuge et d'épreuve pour l'Église persécutée'. Works such as the anonymous *Discours contre les révoltéz* (1676), and those of Claude Brousson, Pierre Jurieu, and Elie Benoist are examined.

Robert Rapley, *A Case of Witchcraft: the Trial of Urbain Grandier*, Manchester U.P., 1998, viii + 277 pp., re-examines all the material, MS and published, in this thorough and very readable account. N. Jacques-Chaquin, 'La curiosité sorcière: représentations du désir féminin du savoir chez les démonologues (XVIe–XVIIe siècles)', Nativel, *Femmes savantes*, 107–18, reveals that these misogynistic writers consider that interest in the magic arts is frequently a symptom of a more general (and deplorable) feminine thirst for knowledge. Jean Bodin, Pierre de Lancre, and Jean Wier are the most frequently cited 'démonologues'. S. Houdard, 'Possession et spiritualité: deux modèles de savoir féminin' *ib.*, 119–29, compares accounts of cases of mystic exaltation and demonic possession ('double expérience') from the 16th and 17th cs. See also below under SURIN.

Myriam Maître, *Les Précieuses: naissance des femmes de lettres en France au XVIIe siècle*, Champion, 1999, 799 pp., covers the period from 1643 until the early 18th c. and re-analyses 'ces actes de discours que sont les portraits des précieuses' with a view to 'interroger la place qui leur est faite dans l'histoire par l'ensemble de ces discours tenus sur elles'. An 'annexe' gives brief biographies in note form of some 130 women identified as *précieuses*.

Jean-Claude Ternaux, *Lucain et la littérature de l'âge baroque en France: citation, imitation et création* (BLR, 43), 461 pp., traces, through commentary, translation, imitation, and inspiration, the presence of L. in French culture, education, and scholarship, during the period 1560–1660, a period of violence in France like that of L.'s own day and the time covered by the *Pharsala*. Among 17th-c. authors, Chevreau (*Hermiogène*), Brébeuf (*Lucain travesty*), and Corneille (*Pompée*) particularly attract T.'s attention. Véronique Gély-Ghedira, *La Nostalgie du moi: Écho dans la littérature européenne*, PUF, 422 pp., attempts selectively to 'rassembler, [. . .] confronter le divers: époques, lieux, genres, en exploitant les formes d'une singulière figure', covering the Renaissance to the 20th c. Sorel and La Fontaine are among the many 17th-c. writers named and quoted. Laurence Kerslake, *Essays on the Sublime*, Berne–NY, Lang, 472 pp., presents a chronological series of studies of contributors to the debate, starting with Longinus, and proceeding via Boileau and 29 more authors to La Harpe. K.'s conclusions are cautious: there is no linear progression, only a 'very real complexity and diversity'. Hence, his final overview is of 'aspects' of the sublime, and 'a few observations on the consequences of certain approaches'. S. Hache, 'La rhétorique du sublime au XVIIe siècle: ses enjeux dans la reconnaissance d'une littérature française', Mazouer, *Recherches*, 129–38, starts with Boileau's translation of Longinus and his remarks on it in his 'préface' and 'Réflexions critiques', and goes on to pick out those commentators who saw France as the inheritor of ancient Greece and Rome in its theatre and pulpit oratory. Corneille comes in for most praise in this context, but Fléchier, Bourdaloue, Senault, and Bossuet benefit too. G. Declercq, 'Topique de l'ineffable dans l'esthétique classique: rhétorique et sublime', *DSS*, 52:199–220, also starts from Boileau's version of Longinus and its recognition that the sublime can have both 'une forme langagière' and 'une forme spéculaire', and goes on to study the tensions between 'l'ineffable' (which needs only silence), and classical rhetoric. B. Rubidge, 'Catharsis through admiration: Corneille, Le Moyne, and the social uses of emotion', *MP*, 95, 1998:316–33, compares C.'s views expressed in the *examen* to *Nicomède* with those of European theorists ancient and modern, particularly Le M. in his *Traité du poème héroïque*. J. Emelina, 'Peut-on imaginer un classicisme heureux?' *RHLF*, 100:1481–501, attempts to counter the general tendency by pointing to 'la gloire de Versailles (Le Brun), l'éclat d'un théâtre total (Quinault-Lully), la galanterie (Benserade), le sourire et le rire (La Fontaine et Molière)'.

A Bibliography of French Emblem Books of the Sixteenth and Seventeenth Centuries, *1*, ed. Alison Adams, Stephen Rawles, and Alison Saunders (THR, 331), 1999, xxxii + 672 pp. *The French Emblem: Bibliography of Secondary Sources*, ed. Laurence Grove and Daniel Russell (THR, 342), xx + 244 pp. Alison Saunders, *The Seventeenth-Century French Emblem: a Study in Diversity* (Travaux du Grand Siècle, 18), Geneva, Droz, xiii + 439 pp. A.-E. Spica, 'Une mise en lettres de l'écriture: emblématique et méditation au XVIIe siècle', *LitC*, 39:17–28, notes the vogue in the early to mid-17th c. for collections of 'emblèmes sacrées' in which 'l'Écriture voilée par l'emblème se fait écriture parfaite'. Id, 'Le motif horticole dans la symbolique humaniste et emblématique (1550–1690)', *DSS*, 52:627–44, reviews vocabulary, the notion of 'nature artificialisée' and 'les jardins de l'emblématique sacrée'. D. Denis, 'Du *Parterre* aux *Promenades*: une scène pour la littérature au XVIIe siècle', *ib.*, 655–69, notes a 'réinvestissement remarquable du motif horticole dans les "ouvrages de l'esprit", à compter des années 1640', emerging, significantly, at the same time as a new literary category: *les oeuvres galantes*. D. sets herself the task of finding out how such a setting served to 'faire accréditer cette

littérature moderne de divertissement' and studies the nature of its
readership. H. Campangne, 'Claude-François Ménestrier: des *Histoires prodigieuses* à *L'Art des Emblèmes'*, *ib.*, 691–701, investigates the use
to which M. has put the 52 engravings which he has borrowed
unacknowledged from the *Histoires prodigieuses* (1597, 1598) for his *Art
des emblèmes* (1684), having chosen to interpret the borrowed *vignettes*
'en leur imposant une signification qui n'est pas forcément la leur, ou
en les faisant coïncider avec ses propres démonstrations'. H. Phillips,
'Sacred text and sacred image: France in the seventeenth century',
BJR, 81, 1999: 299–319, surveys problems associated in the Counter-
Reformation with the need to control the content of sacred images so
that they 'should conform to what was considered to be orthodox'.
Florence Vuilleumier-Laurens, **La Raison des figures symboliques à la
Renaissance et à l'âge classique: études sur les fondements philosophiques,
théologiques et rhétoriques de l'image* (THR, 340), 546 pp.

Georges Bonnant, *Le Livre genevois sous l'Ancien Régime* (Travaux
d'histoire éthico-politiques, 58), Geneva, Droz, 1999, 362 pp., collects
eight papers published between 1956 and 1990 in which he studies all
aspects of the relations between the Geneva book trade and the
countries of Western Europe and Latin America from the Renaissance to the end of the 18th c. V. Maigne, 'Le manuscrit comme
absolu', Lebrave, *Genèses*, 17–26, is, as M. points out, a revision of the
article of the same title which appeared in *DSS*, 48, 1996: 591–99 (see
YWMLS, 58: 122). B. Beugnot, 'Pratiques de l'écriture au XVIIe
siècle: du manuscrit à l'imprimé', *ib.*, 27–51, seeks out, and draws
conclusions from, 17th-c. views expressed on the role of writing and
rewriting in the process of literary creation. D. P. Fisk, 'Shakespearean
manuscripts, French Jansenists, and the cultural politics of misprision', *HLQ*, 62: 25–42, is intrigued by an anonymous MS translation
(*c.* 1680, Folger Library, MS V.a.312) of Nicole's *Traité de la comédie*
which, despite its references to Corneille and obvious French
provenance, was taken to be an anonymous attack on the English
Restoration stage, Shakespeare, and Dryden, a misprision which
continued until at least 1929, leading over the centuries to considerably inflated prices being paid for it at sales.

Roger Duchêne, **Mon XVIIe siècle: de la marquise de Sévigné à Marcel
Proust*, Montpellier, Éditions du CMR17, CD-ROM, collects articles
and extracts published by D. between 1961 and 2000, and 'une partie
inédite comportant six cents lettres de femmes du XVIIe siècle avec
une bibliographie de la publication de ces lettres'.

2. POETRY

Jean Serroy, *Poètes français de l'âge baroque. Anthologie (1571–1677)*,
Imprimerie Nationale, 1999, 531 pp., is an anthology of poets of the

âge baroque and not of baroque poets as the editor is careful to emphasize. His presentation of these poets provides an excellent summary of the debate surrounding the word 'baroque' in this context. There are 54 poets represented, the majority of whom belong to the 17th c. either by date of birth or date of publication of their works and each poet is introduced succinctly bringing out the characteristics and value of his work. The poets range from the very well known to the not-so-well known and the variety is therefore very wide but the space allocated to each poet only allows for a few poems to be quoted and these not always completely. For longer poems extracts have to suffice but this is the nature of an anthology and, as a broad view of poetry in this period, this one could hardly be bettered. Dominique Millet-Gérard, *Le Chant initiatique, esthétique et spiritualité de la bucolique,* Geneva, Ad Solem, 348 pp., is a discussion of bucolic and pastoral poetry and traces themes treated by Virgil in his *Eclogues* and makes the point that nature can only be fully comprehended and appreciated through the culture which this work specifically celebrates. G. Bosco, 'La poésie épique au XVIIe siècle et l'élaboration d'un mythe chrétien', *LitC*, 39 : 123–35, discusses the problem of the *merveilleux* in Christian epics of the 17th c. and gives a detailed account of epics dealing with the identity of Mary Magdelene and the elaboration of the myth that she came to Provence. A. Mantero, 'Louange et ineffable: la poésie mystique du XVIIe siècle français', *ib.,* 297–315, analyses the work of a number of 'mystic poets': Claude Hopil, Jean-Joseph Surin, Jean de Labadie, Madame Guyon, François Malaval and shows how they cope with the seeming contradiction of expressing the ineffable in words. M.-N. Casals, 'Nature et fonction de la représentation du poète en poésie et dans les arts poétiques du premier XVIIe siècle français', Mazouer, *Recherches,* 267–77, is basically a discussion of the role of the poet in the creation of poetry by examining what poets themselves say and the theories elaborated in 17th-c. *Traités poétiques.* N. Negroni, 'Poésie et imagination dans le premier XVIIe siècle: relations et interactions', *ib.,* 279–91, searches for a link between concepts of the imagination as expressed in *Arts poétiques* and the way poetry reflects them, but does not think one can be found. The exploration is nevertheless worthwhile as it makes discoveries which illuminate poetic writing. L. Rescia, 'Le mythe de Narcisse dans la littérature française baroque (1580–1630)', *ib.,* 309–20, looks at the myth of Narcissus not only in the poetry of the earlier part of the 17th c. but also in novels and letters and shows the complexity of the myth as expressed in baroque literature. T. Gheeraert, 'La poésie à Port-Royal: le chant de la grâce', *ib.,* 321–31, discusses the paradox which the presence of poetry in the Jansenist Port-Royal would seem to be but shows that there is no inconsistency as those who wrote poetry there considered it a means of expressing religious truths in a way to appeal to hardened sinners. It is a weapon against the arrogance of reason. R. Maber, 'Le véritable champ du sublime? The ode in France in the seventeenth century', *SCen*, 15:244–65, discusses the idea of the sublime in 17th-c. France and the difficulty of defining it. An analysis of the development of the ode shows that attempts to impose a strict structure on the stanza in the ode resulted in a striking failure to achieve the sublime which earlier poets such as Malherbe had achieved in their more irregular structure using the octosyllabic *dizaine*. Poets at the end of the century such as Racine (in his *Cantiques*) and La Fontaine were more successful because they did not follow the 4 + 3 + 3 structure of the stanza imposed earlier.

BOILEAU. F. Briot, 'Boileau ou la voie libre', *Elseneur*, 15–16:137–47, is a discussion of 19th-c. views of Boileau suggesting that those who, like Sainte-Beuve, praised Boileau passed over much that was worthwhile in the 17th c. because of this.

DRELINCOURT. F.-X. Cuche, 'Les correspondances sacrées de Laurent Drelincourt. Géométrie, typologie et théologie dans le second livre des *Sonnets chrétiens*', *LitC*, 39:137–47, looks at the neglected work of Laurent Drelincourt published in 1677. The analysis of these sonnets concentrates on the significance of calling a sonnet *chrétien* and the implication of this, and concludes that here *chrétien* can be said to mean a literary category.

LA FONTAINE. J.-P. Collinet, 'La Fontaine et la poésie de l'intériorité', *Beugnot Vol.*, 195–202, is a subtle voyage into the characters painted by La F. in which C. shows that whereas the inimitable art of the poet in painting his characters makes an immediate and unforgettable impression, what is even more admirable is the skill with which he penetrates into the characters and paints them from the inside out. A. Soare, '*Il* et *elle*: essai d'analyse stylistique de "La Mort et le Bûcheron"', *ib.*, 203–13, is an analysis of the style of the fable in question and is penetrating and remarkable for its dissection of the sounds of the words used, showing the skill with which La F. balances one sound against another thus enhancing the underlying meaning of the fable. J. F. Gaines, 'Molière, La Fontaine and authority', *PFSCL*, 27:405–14, claims that there are three levels of authority in the *Fables*: ethical (corresponding to family and community), political (corresponding to institutions and their monarchical framework) and epistemological (corresponding to the more abstract authority of Truth itself). G. then looks at the presentation of these forms of authority in La F. and M. and shows the difference in approach and conception in both. R. Hong, 'La réécriture de deux contes de La Fontaine et sa signification', *ib.*, 472–88, examines the narrative structure of two contes: *La servante justifiée* and *Le faiseur d'oreilles et le raccommodeur de moules*. The technique used is compared with the sources of the *conte* in the 16th c. and arrives at a definition of the distinction between a *conte* and a *nouvelle*: one is to be spoken and the other read.

LE MOYNE.   Yvan Loskoutoff, *L'Armoriale de Calliope. L'oeuvre du Père Le Moyne, S.J. (1602–1671); littérature, héraldique, spiritualité* (Biblio 17, 125), Tübingen, Narr, 360 pp., is a long promenade through the poetry of Le Moyne using heraldry as a guide to his aims and intentions especially in his epic *Saint-Louis*. A vast display of the importance of heraldry in the earlier part of the 17th c. is used to relate the history of the Jesuits, their founder Saint Ignatius, and their best known French representatives of whom Le M. was one. The equation of heraldry and nobility is very much to the front of Le M.'s mind (himself a member of the nobility) and this emerges in his poetry where the symbolism of heraldry often provides him with metaphors, but in the end the glories which shields and coats of arms flaunt, as shown in *Saint-Louis*, have to bow down to the real glories of religion which finally overcome earthly pride. This is a dense and testing text which opens interesting vistas on the whole of the middle years of the 17th century.

LE PETIT.   R. P. C. Conner, 'Burning desire: Claude Le Petit, libertine poet', *PFSCL*, 27:420–33, discusses homoeroticism in the 17th c. and shows that this was really the reason for the burning at the stake of Claude Le Petit in 1662. C. emphasizes the relationship between homosexuality and *libertinage* in French literature and history and sees Le P. as striking a blow for freedom in this area.

SAINT-AMANT.   G. Peureux, 'Le caprice ou l'esthétique du spectacle chez Saint-Amant', Mazouer, *Recherches*, 293–307, is an examination of the *caprice* with reference to its Italian forbears and the part it plays in S-A.'s poetry. It helps to define his poetic vision and shows him emerging as a poet.

SURIN.   B. Papasogli, 'La parole trouvée au fond de l'abîme: les *Cantiques spirituels* de Jean-Joseph Surin', *LitC*, 39:317–30, discusses this work of the Jesuit S. published in 1655 after a long period in which his mind seemed to lose its bearings possibly because of his involvement with the drama of Loudun which gives these *Cantiques* a special resonance.

THÉOPHILE DE VIAU.   L. Hinds, 'Honni soit qui mal y pense: avowals, accusations and witnessing in the trial of Théophile de Viau', *PFSCL*, 27:434–44, examines the proposition that those accused of sodomy are also accused of heresy, but there is also the question that those who accuse may themselves be guilty and

Théophile exploits this possibility at his trial and so avoids the death sentence.

3. DRAMA

Claude Bourqui, *La Commedia dell'arte*, Sedes, 1999, is extremely useful in that it describes the history and organization of the *Commedia* giving information which is often difficult to find elsewhere. The chapter on the *Commedia dell'arte* in France has an enlightening section on Molière and a relevant bibliography. D. Conroy, 'Tragic ambiguities: gender and sovereignty in French classical drama', Meek, *Women*, 185–204, examines the part played by women sovereigns in plays and interprets the role assigned to them. Can women be the equal of men in this role? It appears that they can and although their frailty sometimes precludes them from warlike heroics they are still the equal of men in their ability to kill themselves to preserve their *gloire*. G. Forestier, 'D'une poétique politique: *La Pratique du théâtre* de l'abbé d'Aubignac ou la rationalité absolue de la représentation classique', *Beugnot Vol.*, 229–46, discusses various aspects of *La Pratique*, especially *vraisemblance*, and corrects some misapprehensions concerning its meaning. He compares d'Aubignac's approach to that of Aristotle and shows that the former has a more perfectionist view of what *vraisemblance* is trying to do. Bruno Garnier, *Pour une poétique de la traduction. L'Hécube d'Euripide en France de la traduction humaniste à la tragédie classique*, L'Harmattan, 1999, 272 pp. Translations of the *Hecuba* of Euripides are used as a guide through 16th-, 17th-, and 18th-c. tragedies. Not only are direct translations of the text considered but also texts which are manifestly based on the *Hecuba*. In the 17th c. *La Mort d'Achille* of Hardy is discussed and then the *Troades* of Sallebray and Pradon and other adaptations of the subject produced by Borée, Benserade, Thomas Corneille, Campistron, and La Fosse. The analyses of these plays throw light on the evolution of tragedy in the period, showing how the outpourings of the Greek text become more logical and rational in the French versions. This approach permits a suggestive and interesting view of the influence, so often debated, of Greek tragedy on 17th-c. tragedy. C. Marchal-Weyl, 'De la *comedia* espagnole au théâtre français: la notion de personnage', Mazouer, *Recherches*, 15–25, discusses the role of the *comedia* in the development of social types in the French theatre between 1630 and 1660 paying particular attention to the portrayal of the aristocracy in the two genres and its importance in the elaboration of the plots, and throws light on the different mental structures of the two societies. H. Phillips, 'Les acteurs et la loi au XVIIe siècle en France', *LitC*, 40:87–101, looks at the status of actors and the attempts which were made to give them hope that they would become socially acceptable and religiously correct, but, because of the influence of Saint Charles Borromée they did not succeed. P. Scott, 'Une femme dramaturge dévoilée: the case of Jean/ne Bisson (de?) la Coudraye', *SCFS*, 22 : 194–204, uses the case of a tragedy written by a man in the middle of the 17th c. and published as the work of a woman at the beginning of the 18th c. to discuss the role of women as dramatists and their place in society in the 17th century. G. Spielmann, 'Le mariage classique, des apories du droit au questionnement comique', *LitC*, 40 : 223–57, describes the history of marriage as an institution and its place in canon and civil law before the 17th c., and then explores its importance in some comedies of the later 17th c. (Dancourt, Dufresny, Fatouville), showing how the interpretation of the rules of marriage constitutes a prime part of the plot as well as throwing light on the institution as part of the social background. Id., 'La "Comédie post-moliéresque" et son double: éléments pour une problématique', *CDs*, 7.2 : 105–20, sets out to prove that comedy written in the last years of the reign of Louis XIV, 1680–1715, was much more than a pale imitation of Molière; it has suffered from having to undergo this comparison, whereas it has its own strength and meaning independent of and different from Molière. L. Thirouin, 'Les dévots contre le théâtre, ou de quelques simplifications fâcheuses', *LitC*, 39 : 105–21, tries to disentangle the attacks against the theatre in the 1660s showing that there were different motives behind the position of different groups like the *Compagnie du Saint-Sacrement* and the Jansenists. They are not coherent groups and these differences must be understood to appreciate fully the meaning of these attacks.

BARON. M.-F. Hilgar, 'Les héroïnes baronesques', *CDs*, 7.2 : 1–12, examines the comedies of Baron with the aim of seeing whether they are mere copies of Molière or can claim to be original and decides that they can.

CORNEILLE. C. Biet, 'Les saints, la prostituée, l'actrice. L'impossible modèle religieux dans *Théodore vierge et martyre* de Corneille', *LitC*, 39 : 81–105, is a long and intricate analysis of the role of religion in the theatre. B. looks at all the problems raised by *Théodore* and, by examining the possible reasons why C. chose to dramatize this martyr story, shows in what ways it differs from traditional martyr tales. Claire Cerasi, *Pierre Corneille à l'image et semblance de François de Sales* (Université catholique de Paris, Cultures et Christianisme, 6), Beauchesne, 165 pp., does not pretend to discover an influence of F. de S. on C., but attempts to prove that the theatre of C. can be better understood and appreciated when the principles underlying the attitudes and beliefs of F. de S. are examined. There are detailed analyses of the work of both authors and there is no doubt that the

ingenious thesis is well sustained; however, the author's understanding of C. seems rather old-fashioned and many of the propositions
which she makes about him have long since been discredited. What
is new is her examination of these attitudes in the light of her analysis
of the works of F. de S. and this does illuminate in a new way some of
C.'s theatre. Cynthia B. Kerr, *Corneille à l'affiche* (Biblio 17, 123),
Tübingen, Narr, is a lively, informative and provocative account of
performances of some of C.'s plays. The plays discussed are *Sertorius,
L'Illusion, Le Cid, Polyeucte, Sophonisbe, La Veuve, La Place Royale,* and *Le
Menteur.* In discussing productions of these plays K. finds some
astonishingly new interpretations of the texts which, in some cases,
overturn accepted views. The discussions show, even more than
usual, the extent to which original theatrical minds (as are those of
the *metteurs en scène* in question) can, in putting the text on the stage,
bring out meanings previously overlooked. A. Rykner, 'Hugo lecteur
de Corneille: jeux de miroirs et jeux de rôles', *Elseneur,* 15–16:35–52,
claims that Hugo, who made a virtue of denouncing 17th-c. drama,
made an exception of Corneille; his admiration for him is revealed in
much of his work and indeed he planned a play to be called *Pierre
Corneille. PFSCL,* 52, is a special issue, introduced by Alain Niderst,
devoted to Corneille and Racine. On Corneille: F. Lasserre, 'Corneille et *l'Alexandre* de Racine' (45–55), suggests that *Alexandre* explains
the genesis of *Attila.* C. disapproved of using a tragedy to flatter Louis
XIV and shows this by choosing the subject of *Attila*; J. Rohou, 'De
Pertharite à *Andromaque*: les enseignements d'une comparaison historique' (57–84), is not a comparison of texts but a comparison of the
ways the dramatists see the human condition. The difference between
C.'s approach which analyses the motives behind heroism and R.'s
which sees heroism as no longer viable is well brought out in these
plays; N. Hepp, 'Perspectives cornélienne et racinienne sur Rome
ennemie: autour de *Nicomède* et de *Mithridate*' (143–52), sees that
Rome is more present in *Nicomède* than in *Mithridate* and is seen as
being much more vicious in the latter than in the former but is
Mithridate any better?; M. Gutleben, 'Faste et pompe, monstres et
sublime dans *Médée* de Corneille et *Phèdre* de Racine' (153–61),
considers that Médée imposes by spectacle and grandeur, Phèdre by
the horror of what she is and what she becomes through passion;
C. Carlin, 'Chimène et Phèdre mélancoliques: la féminisation de la
mélancolie' (162–75), considers that both Chimène and Phèdre are
examples of the way melancholy is seen as a negative attitude, killing
initiative and making action very difficult; J. Grimm, '*Suréna* et *Phèdre*
ou l'abdication du héros' (176–86), examines the political subtext of
these plays and shows that there is no room for Suréna or Phèdre in a
world governed by an absolute monarch or, in Phèdre's case, a world

governed by implacable forces; A. Couprie, 'De l'usage de l'histoire dans les tragédies de Corneille et de Racine: deux visions différentes de la tragédie politique' (224–34), discusses how both R. and C. use history to justify their inventions but do it differently. For C. history provides a new point of departure but R. looks to the past because for him history is repetitive; M.-O. Sweetser, 'Corneille et Racine dramaturges, au-delà de la polémique et de la rivalité' (250–67), stresses what links C. and R. rather than what divides them by demonstrating that they both adapted legend and history to suit 17th-c. France; J. Deprun, 'Les "noms divins" chez Corneille et Racine: le cas des "noms ontologiques"' (268–76), examines different ways of naming God in C. and R. and concludes that, as far as vocabulary is concerned, C. is more metaphysical than R. perhaps because the latter had abandoned 'l'exubérance baroque'; A. Philonenko, 'Réflexion sur le sacré et le profane chez Corneille et Racine' (277–84), is a philosophical discourse examining meanings of sacred and profane in C. and R. and concludes that religion in their plays is more deism than Christianity.

THOMAS CORNEILLE. N. Paige, 'L'affaire des poisons et l'imaginaire de l'enquête: de Molière à Thomas Corneille', *LitC*, 40:195–208, discusses *La Devineresse* of Thomas Corneille and Donneau de Visé as an example of the increasing use in the theatre of crime and disguise.

GOUGENOT. N. Gougenot, *La 'Comédie des comédiens' et le 'Discours à Cliton'*, ed. François Lasserre (Biblio 17, 128), Tübingen, Narr, is a detailed, though somewhat confusing, edition of these two works. Much space is devoted to putting G. in his place in the history of 17th-c. drama and this is a useful summary of the state of the theatre in the early 1630s. The presence of the actors of the Hôtel de Bourgogne in the play gives rise to a discussion of the actors and some interesting details emerge. The arguments for attributing the *Discours à Cliton* to G. seem convincing and this is a useful text to have as it is relevant to the *querelle du Cid*. Although not always easy to follow, this edition provides access to little known texts which are well worth having available.

LONGEPIERRE. *Médée*, ed. Emmanuel Minel, Champion, 204 pp., is a very well documented edition of *Médée* with a long and informative introduction with discussion of different *Médée*s and their relationship with each other. Also included are the *Parallèle de Monsieur Corneille et de Monsieur Racine* and the *Dissertation sur la tragédie de Médée par l'abbé Pellegrin*.

MAIRET. C. Delmas, 'Les *Sophonisbe*s et le renouveau de la tragédie en France', *DSS*, 208:443–64, shows that the subject of *Sophonisbe* was particularly suitable for the development of classical tragedy by its mixture of heroism and passion. D. traces the history of the subject before M. and shows the originality of his treatment compared with his predecessors. This is a penetrating examination of the subject.

MOLIÈRE. Roger Pensom, *Molière l'inventeur. C'est avec du vieux qu'on fait du neuf*, Berne, Lang, 175 pp., sets out to explore the transformation which a text undergoes when it is translated from the page to the stage. By detailed analyses of various scenes in the plays, P. shows the extraordinary denseness of Molière's texts which yield up unexpected meanings when this aspect is explored. It is essential to be aware that the written text itself contains the properties which only become apparent in the performed text. In displaying this, much light is thrown on hidden corners of M. often not perceived by other approaches. Virginia Scott, *Molière, a Theatrical Life*, CUP, 333 pp., is a well-researched biography of Molière written in a readable style using all the known facts. There is, however, a certain amount of speculation used to add to the readability which does nothing for the authenticity of the biography. Written for non-French speakers as well as French speakers, all quotations are translated. The discussion of the plays, admittedly not the primary aim of the book, amounts to little more than accounts of what happens and adds nothing to the corpus of Molière criticism. Readable, sound (up to a point) and informative, the book is nevertheless not a great contribution to Molière studies. A. Albert-Galtier, 'Un comédien en colère: masques et grimaces de Molière dans *La Querelle de l'Ecole des Femmes*', CDs, 7.2:91–104, is a discussion of ways of knowing how Molière acted by considering the plays written concerning *L'École des Femmes*. It teases out the various layers which make up the actor, the role he is playing, and the way he is perceived by others. L. F. Norman, 'Le nom dit: Molière, satire et diffamation', *LitC*, 40:209–21, asks why Molière was not sued more often by those whom he allegedly defamed in his comedies, and makes interesting suggestions about the role of satire and the law. E. Woodrough, 'Parodying the pleasure principle: *Dom Juan*, a festival play for Parisians', *SCFS*, 22:167–79, discusses the staging and circumstances surrounding the first performance of *Dom Juan* and the subsequent history of its suppression, and sets the plays in the context of happenings in 1664 and 1665. J.-P. Van Elslande, 'Molière ou le moraliste à la fête', *PFSCL*, 53:363–74, shows that *La Princesse d'Élide* is an interesting example of a moral lesson being delivered through a court performance in which the king himself is involved. L. Sonderegger, 'Sources of translation: a discussion of Matthew Medbourne's 1670 translation of Molière's *Tartuffe*', *ib.*, 552–72, discusses the changes made by Medbourne in his translation of *Tartuffe*. S. argues that some of these can be attributed to Medbourne using passages from an earlier version of *Tartuffe* which

M. removed in the final published version. R. Racevskis, 'Connaissance de soi et des autres dans *George Dandin*', *ib.*, 375–84, claims that this play is a powerful study of the forces at work in society which isolate individuals, and calls into question the whole social underpinning of the 17th c. and the court of Louis XIV. M. S. Koppisch, 'Dom Juan's equal opportunity rivalry', *ib.*, 385–92, is an examination of Dom Juan showing that he can be seen as forever trying to dominate others, which is the only way he can define himself, and his ultimate failure in this. C. Danielou, 'Constance et inconstance : *Le Misanthrope* et la tradition moraliste', *ib.*, 393–404, points out that while trumpeting his adhesion to the principle of 'constance', Alceste is in fact very inconstant while Célimene is constant, even inflexible. *Le Misanthrope* shows that constancy is only a mask which deceives.

LitC, 38, is a special issue devoted to Molière, presented by Charles Mazouer. J. Serroy, ' "Vous a-t-on point dit comme on le nomme?": Alceste, Dandin, Jourdain, entre titrologie et onomastique' (9–17), is an analysis of the significance of names in M.'s comedies and an examination of these three names and the light they throw on the themes and treatment of the subject of the comedies in which they appear; G. Conesa, '*Le Misanthrope* ou les limites de l'aristotélisme' (19–29), shows that in this play the normal techniques of comedy are exploited to create an impression of linearity in the development of the plot, as is the case in tragedy; F.-X. Cuche, 'Simple note sur la structure dramatique du *Bourgeois gentilhomme*' (31–39), sets out to prove that the *B.g.* is not a miscellany of disparate scenes but a rigorously constructed comedy and *comédie-ballet;* A.-M. Cocula, 'Regards d'historiens sur le temps de Molière' (41–49), is a consideration of the economic, social, and political factors which created the environment in which Molière's comedies were produced. J. Grimm, '*Le Misanthrope* portrait du siècle' (51–61), relates the play to the specific decade in which it was written, that of the first years of the personal reign of Louis XIV, and proposes interpretations of Alceste and Philinte as representatives of the changing values of that period; F. Népote-Desmarres, 'Jeux de parole et jeux de vérité dans *Le Misanthrope, George Dandin* et *Le Bourgeois gentilhomme*' (63–77), analyses the function of 'parole' in the three comedies and attempts to determine the role of 'parole' in expressing 'vérité'; R. McBride, '*Le Misanthrope* ou les mobiles humains mis à nu' (79–89), considers the methods used by M. in portraying the characters in this play to penetrate into the meaning of sincerity in human relationships where what dominates behaviour is human fallibility, even if it assumes the guise of sincerity; M.-C. Canova-Green, 'Je, tu, il ... ou le dédoublement du moi dans le *George Dandin* de Molière' (91–101), examines the use that can be made of this play to explore the meaning of identity and the problems that arise when the individual seeks to understand himself but is unable to do so because of the images of himself reflected by others. George Dandin learns this very hard lesson; J. Emelina, 'Les comiques de Molière' (103–15), is a dense exploration of the different sorts of comedy and comic effects in the plays of M. E. analyses with great skill the contradictions apparent in many interpretations of the comic in M. and reveals aspects of his treatment of comic subjects often overlooked; C. Nédélec, 'Galanteries burlesques, ou burlesque galanterie?' (117–37), is a very detailed examination of various definitions of *galanterie* and *burlesque* with some particularly illuminating comments on *Le Misanthrope*; C. Mazouer, '*Le Misanthrope, George Dandin* et *le Bourgeois gentilhomme*, trois comédies écrites pour la scène' (139–58), sees how by looking at the scenic qualities of these comedies the author throws considerable light on the relationship between character and the exploitation of resources such as place, and sees M.'s talents as director and producer using the particular strengths of his actors to great effect; R. Landy, '*George Dandin* et *le Bourgeois gentilhomme*: le mariage de la comédie et du ballet' (159–77), asks how M. reconciles a sombre story (*George Dandin*) with the tales of young love typical of the pastoral, and finds the answer in the use of ballet and/or music in both comedies.

QUINAULT. S. Cornic, '*Ad limina templis Polymniae*: les fonctions du prologue d'opéra chez Quinault', Mazouer, *Recherches*, 47–62. In the prologues to his *tragédies en musique* Quinault expresses ideas of dramatic structure and dramaturgy which he did not formulate anywhere else. L. Naudeix, 'Par où commencer une tragédie lyrique?', *ib.*, 63–73, discusses the prologue in Quinault's *tragédies lyriques* as the link between the real world and the fictional world which Q. creates. The spectator is led over the bridge of the prologue into the fantasy world of the opera. C. Berrone, 'Du théâtre parlé à la tragédie lyrique: Médée héroïne noire de Quinault', *ib.*, 75–87, is a subtle analysis of the links between Quinault's tragedies and his operas using the figure of Médée in the opera *Thésée* to show that she has the same attitudes as those of some of his other heroines in the tragedies. J. Pesque, '*Renaud et Armide*: opéra des princes, opéra des peuples', *ib.*, 89–97, discusses the popularity of this theme for operas and plays throughout the 17th and early 18th cs and suggests that this is because it reflects some of the standards and preoccupations of the society of the period. B. Norman, 'Opera as drama, opera as theater: Quinault's *Isis* in a Racinocentric world', *CDs*, 7.2:57–71. By examining this opera N. draws conclusions about the relative importance of plot and structure as elements of the dramatic, and shows the importance of the innovative approach of Q. here when compared with his previous opera *Atys*.

RACINE. Jean Rohou, *Avez-vous lu Racine? Mise au point polémique*, L'Harmattan, 407 pp., is a polemical work setting out to demonstrate that those who write about the tragedies of Racine as though they were representations of reality are a long way from the truth. These are great poetic works of fiction which are an allegorical expression of a vision of the human condition. This fascinating romp through Racinian criticism is characterized by a personal approach which adds salt to the subject. R. is critical of many approaches to Racine but is nevertheless fair in his judgments of many and, although he has some doubts about Forestier's recent Pléiade edtion, he finds it praiseworthy as well. This is a stimulating and controversial book which will no doubt give rise to various responses. *PFSCL*, 52, is a special issue devoted to Corneille (see above) and Racine. J. Dubu, 'De Corneille à Racine: *La Thébaïde* de 1664 à 1697' (15–27), is a discussion of the changes which occurred in this play in its three versions showing how Racine reacted poetically to the lines he had written in order to improve them, but also sees a sensitivity to the changing atmosphere of the period as the reign of Louis XIV progressed and became more dictatorial; S. Guellouz, ' "Le chef d'oeuvre" "le plus tragique" "de l'Antiquité" l'*Oedipe* de Corneille et *La Thébaïde* de Racine' (29–43), compares the treatment of the Oedipus theme in the two plays and shows that each author treats it in a way which reflects his concerns as expressed in the rest of his work; A. Soare, 'L'intertexte cornélien d'*Alexandre* à *Bajazet*' (85–113), is a very dense and subtle exploration of resemblances and imitations in situations and language in the tragedies of C. and R.; S. Ackerman, 'Les Bérénices' (114–25), discusses the history of the 'myth' of Bérénice through the ages, considering the different interpretations in different centuries (is it a myth of success or failure?), and is based on the author's 1978 book on the subject; S. Dosmond, 'La troisième *Bérénice*. Un palimpseste de Corneille et de Racine' (126–39), examines the *Reine de Césarée* by Robert Brasillach and demonstrates that B. used both Corneille and Racine but added his own interpretation; E. Minel, 'Trois parallèles de Corneille et Racine dans les années 1680–90: Longepierre (1686), La Bruyère (1688,–89,–91) et Fontenelle (1693)' (189–200), sets out to demonstrate that these three non-contemporary comparisons are interesting as a reflection of the different conceptions of literary history. A. Desprechins, '*L'Astrée* sur les lisses dans les marges de Corneille et de Racine' (217–23), suggests that the creators of tapestries with scenes from the *Astrée* were influenced by R. and C. in their treatment of the subjects; C. Mazouer, 'Corneille et Racine dramaturges comiques' (237–49), says that Racine in *Les Plaideurs* creates characters that are not realistic but fantastic whereas Corneille seeks realism in his comedies. The result is that the spectator is more detached as far as R. is concerned. M.-C. Planche-Touron, 'De Chauveau à Guérin: le théâtre de Racine source d'inspiration pour les arts visuels', Mazouer, *Recherches*, 27–44, analyses representations in painting of scenes in the tragedies of R. in the 17th, 18th and 19th cs pointing out the efforts of the artists to represent the passions described in the text and the methods used. A. Chevalier, '*Phèdre*, lectures en abyme dans *A la recherche du temps perdu*', *Elseneur*, 15–16:343–352, claims that references to *Phèdre* in Proust's novel provide insight into the understanding and appreciation of R. at the end of the 19th and the beginning of the 20th centuries. C. Grisé, 'Fausses espérances dans *Britannicus*', *CDs*, 7.2:57–71, applies theories of frame analysis encompassing the ideas of self-deception and wishful thinking in *Britannicus*, showing that R. was already aware of their power in human relationships. *SCFS*, 22, has a wide range of articles on Racine: J. Dubu, 'Les *Vies* de Racine , de *l'Homme Illustre* de Perrault aux *Hommes Illustres* dans *La République des Lettres*, de Niceron, etc.' (5–19), analyses accounts of R.'s life as recounted in various publications from the end of the 17th c. to the middle of the 18th c. with the aim of getting an historically accurate picture, but acknowledges that the problems of doing this are very great; A. Viala, 'Tendances actuelles de la représentation de Racine' (21–33), shows that R.'s drama can still be performed today and the performances available raise questions about our way of looking at the past; M. Hawcroft, 'Reading Racine: punctuation and capitalization in the first editions of his plays' (35–50), makes many significant observations by comparing the two Pléiade editions of Racine: Picard (1950) and Forestier (1999), based on the changes in punctuation between the first and last editions of the plays; V. Worth-Stylianou, 'Listening to Racine's *Confidents*' (51–62), discusses the importance of listening to *confidents* and points out that their silence can sometimes be as significant as their speech. Burrhus and Narcisse provide good examples of this; M. Reilly, 'Racine and Orwell: classical newspeak?' (63–75), uses a parallel with Orwell's newspeak in *1984* to examine cases in Racine where the manipulation of language to exercise power is evident, showing that in drama where 'word is action' words are often used in a destructive manner; V. Grégoire, 'La difficulté à 's'entendre' dans *Les Plaideurs* ou la folie à l'oeuvre' (77–93), is an analysis of the role played in this play by 'madness' which is carefully defined showing that 'les héros monomanes [. . .] se trompent parce qu'ils sont métaphoriquement aveugles et mentalement monolithiques'; J.-C. Ranger, 'Mémoire et pouvoir chez Racine' (95–106), explores the role of memory in the tragedies of R. showing what a powerful force it is. Unlike in Corneille the future does not play a role, or if it does, as in *Bérénice*, it is only to underline the tragedy;

N. Hammond, 'Educating Joas: the power of memory in *Athalie*' (107–14), traces the theme of memory in the tragedy and shows how important is the link between education and memory and how this determines much of the presentation of Joas; V. Desnain, 'Clytemnestre: mythical harpy or feminist paragon?' (115–23), argues that the traditional view of Clytemnestra has been fashioned by seeing the world from a dominating masculine point of view and ought to be countered by a modern, feminist version; H. T. Barnwell, 'Drama and poetry of the unseen in Racinian tragedy' (125–40), examines the role of the action that is not seen on the stage in R.'s tragedies and argues that 'what is staged is the real, significant action in the causes and consequences and perception of what we do not see'; P. France, 'War and commerce in Racinian tragedy' (141–51), is a study of the contrast between words denoting the values of war and those dealing with commerce in R.'s tragedies and concludes that the latter reveal to how great an extent these values operate in the relationship between characters; H. Phillips, 'L'art de bien mourir: last moments in Racinian tragedy' (153–65), is a discussion of the ways in which different forms of death are portrayed in the tragedies. It questions whether it is possible to establish categories of 'good' or 'bad' deaths and concludes that Racine uses different ways of dying to distance his own tragedies from tragedies of lamentation. G. Boquet and J.-C. Drouot, 'Le parcours racinien de Silvia Montfort', *RHT*, 52 : 147–54, describes and discusses Silvia Montfort's interpretations of the Racinian roles she played from 1950 to 1987. E. Cleynen-Serghiev, 'Fortune et infortune de Racine en Roumanie', *ib.*, 155–65, is an interesting survey of the fortunes of Racine in Romania. R.-L. Barnett, 'Les enjeux du schisme. Essai d'herméneutique racinienne', *ib.*, 166–76, is a discussion of the structure of *Athalie*, arguing that there is a double side to it which produces a paradox in the tragic meaning of the play.

REGNARD. Z. Elmarsafy, 'Regnard and post-classical theatre', *CDs*, 7.2 : 169–84, looks at the significance of Regnard, showing that there is a paradox in that he used the methods of Molière to try and prove that he is not Molière.

ROTROU. A. Riffaud, 'Le réseau des images chez Rotrou: l'exemple d'*Iphigénie*', *PFSCL*, 53 : 509–26, analyses carefully and thoroughly imagery relating to dark and light on the one hand and calm and storm on the other to illustrate themes running through R.'s tragedy which differentiates it from that of Euripides.

4. PROSE

Alain Niderst, *Essai d'histoire littéraire: Guilleragues, Subligny et Challe, des 'Lettres portugaises' aux 'Illustres Françaises'*, Saint-Genouph, Nizet, 1999,

100 pp., links the above three writers, together with the Comtesse de La Suze and Mme de Villedieu, in an investigation into late 17th-c. friendships, influences, collaborations, borrowings, ghostings, and thefts. N. would have us consider returning the authorship of the *Lettres portugaises* to the nun herself, Mariana Alcoforado, and credit Subligny with their translation. He is the central figure in N.'s study, and is preferred to Mme de Villedieu as the author of the *Mémoires d'Henriette Silvie de Molière*. A complex but lively and readable piece of research; a pity about the poor proof-reading.

J. Villeneuve, 'Résistance narrative et utopies: l'art de la "gouverne" au XVIIe siècle', *PFSCL*, 27 : 587–98, points out that narration and plot are not usually to be found in 'l'utopie, définie comme la projection d'un monde idéal, donc sans intrigue', but that Campanella's *Civita Solis* and Cyrano's *Autre monde* allow 'l'élaboration d'un récit'. Unlike traditional utopias, going back to Plato's *Republic*, 17th-c. utopian literature finds in fiction 'un espace où la narrativité déferle à nouveau'.

I. Trivisani-Moreau, 'Romans au jardin: aspects et évolution de quelques stéréotypes', Mazouer, *Recherches*, 219–27, surveys 'la représentation de l'espace' in some 200 works of fiction written between 1660 and 1680. J. Weisgerber, 'Quelques jardins littéraires en France vers 1650', *DFS*, 52 : 36–50, notes how in the mid-17th c. 'l'on voit les jardins envahir l'intrigue des romans'. Mlle de Scudéry provides most of the examples. M.-M. Fragonard, 'Déserts romanesques et dévotion aisée', *RSH*, 258 : 163–76, looks at narrative works by Nervèze, N. Piloust, J.-P. Camus, and H. de Lisdam. N. Grande, 'Faut-il parler? Faut-il se taire? Silence et roman dans *La Princesse de Clèves* et *Les Désordres de l'amour*', *DSS*, 52 : 185–98, compares La F.'s novel with a *nouvelle* in V.'s collection. She views silence from various angles, and concludes that 'les différentes formes du silence que déclinent les situations romanesques [. . .] renvoient toutes le lecteur à sa propre lecture du texte'. G. Hautcoeur, 'La nouvelle espagnole en France au XVIIe siècle: traduction et évolution du roman', *RLC*, 74 : 155–74, shows translations into French following public taste by evolving, as early as the 1630s, from romance to historical veracity and psychological realism. S. Robic-De Baecque, 'Romans et dévotion au XVIIe siècle', *LitC*, 39 : 29–49, finds definitions difficult and change constant, as regards both novels and piety. R. traces the history of this troubled relationship from the beginning of the century to *La Princesse de Clèves* which she regards as 'une mise en abyme de l'impossibilité d'un roman dévot, de l'aporie des relations entre romanesque et dévotion'. F. Briot, 'L'empire des cygnes (poétique du travestissement sexuel au XVIIe siècle)', *RSH*, 252, 1998 : 37–48, gives examples of fictional transvestites who forget they are 'travestis' and 'become' what they appear to be, finding them in La Fontaine's *Songe de Vaux*, d'Urfé's *L'Astrée*, the Abbé de Choisy's *Mémoires*, and elsewhere. Shirley Jones Day, *The Search for Lyonnesse: Women's Fiction in France 1670–1703*, Berne–NY, Lang, 1999, 340 pp., seeks to 'study the works of a small group of women novelists who both consciously followed in the footsteps of Mme de La Fayette and traced out new paths in common'. Besides *La Princesse de Clèves*, J.D. covers the fiction of Villedieu, Bernard, d'Aulnoy, and La Force. N. Grande, 'L'instruction primaire des romancières', Nativel, *Femmes savantes*, 51–57, looks at La Fayette, Montpensier, Villedieu, and Mlle de Scudéry, considers what was the nature of their 'instruction primaire' and how, 'en inventant de nouveaux modes d'appropriation de la culture' they managed to 'pallier les lacunes d'une éducation effectivement primaire dans tous les sens du terme'. *Nouvelles françaises du XVIIe siècle*, ed. Frédéric Charbonneau and Réal Ouellet, Quebec, L'Instant même, 300 pp., prints *nouvelles* and *contes* by 14 authors, some famous, some obscure, one anonymous, each one briefly introduced and annotated. There is a substantial general introduction, and an anthology of the opinions of various contemporary authors on the 'Théorie et critique de la nouvelle au XVIIe siècle'.

F. Charbonneau, 'Ambivalence d'un duc et pair', Mazouer, *Recherches*, 229–39, points out that 'la moitié des Mémoires du XVIIe siècle [. . .] furent écrits entre 1660 et 1685 — acquérant une position originelle, exemplaire, par laquelle ils ont pris, au plan de l'invention, le relais des *Commentaires* de César et de Commynes'. He is particularly impressed by the influence on the others of the memoirs of La Rochefoucauld.

G. Haroche-Bouzinac, 'La lettre féminine dans les secrétaires: l'enfance de l'art', *DSS*, 52:465–84, notes the rarity in 17th-c. letter-writing manuals of examples by women, and asserts that 'l'approbation, sélection, correction par des hommes, tel est le prix que la lettre féminine doit acquitter avant d'accéder à l'impression'. She then surveys examples of the various types of letters written by (or attributed to) women in these manuals.

CPR, 48, 1999, prints colloquium papers on 'Port-Royal et les mémoires': P. Mengotti-Thouvenin, 'Port-Royal, laboratoire de mémoires' (15–55), notes the 'rapport entre écriture individuelle et écriture collective' and goes on to suggest a series de 'jalons chronologiques' to define 'choix narratifs' and 'tendances génériques', and underlines the influence on all these writers of the *Confessions* of St. Augustine; C. Cagnat-Deboeuf, 'Rêveries autour d'un lieu mythique: Port-Royal des Champs dans les mémoires des anciens solitaires (Lancelot, Du Fossé, Fontaine)' (197–213), compares these texts and discerns in them a 'chant polyphonique à la gloire de Port-Royal'; A. Bord, 'Éclairages différents et témoignages neutres' (215–27), looks first to throw light on the personality of Roger du Plessis, Duc de Liancourt, by comparing views and information to be found in contemporary memoirs, letters, etc. relating to Port-Royal 'dont plusieurs auteurs semblent en dehors du conflit', highlighting among these Conrart, Retz, and Mlle de Montpensier; E. Lesne, 'La dialectique de la marginalité et du conformisme dans les *Mémoires* de l'abbé Arnauld et de Brienne le Jeune' (229–43), argues for the value of the testimony of these 'amis du dehors', and considers the circumstances which led them to write about Port-Royal.

Two works of reference are worthy of our attention: *The Oxford Companion to Fairy Tales*, ed. Jack Zipes, OUP, xxxii + 601 pp., is an encyclopedia with entries for authors (late 16th-c. to modern), tales (identified by their usual English titles, including versions in film, theatre, opera, and paintings), countries (European and North-American), and with entries too on all aspects of the telling of tales. The lengthy introduction is largely historical. *Dictionary of Literary Utopias*, ed. Vita Fortunati and Raymond Trousson (Dictionnaires et Références, 5), Champion, 732 pp., also covers Europe and North America, and the period 1516 to 1989. It has a much briefer introduction concerned with method rather than history. The entries appear alphabetically by title (of the utopian text) or by theme (but for 'death' see 'health', and for 'divorce' see 'women' or 'family').

ANGÉLIQUE ARNAULD D'ANDILLY. P. Sellier, 'Élégance rhétorique et évangile: une lettre d'Angélique Arnauld d'Andilly à Antoine Arnauld', *CPR*, 48, 1999:301–09, introduces and reproduces this letter of August, 1666.

ROBERT ARNAULD D'ANDILLY. J. Garapon, 'Fidélité à soi et liberté dans les *Mémoires* d'Arnauld d'Andilly', *CPR*, 48, 1999:183–95, describes, and observes in them 'le fonctionnement d'une mémoire, sélective, passionnée, imaginative', and finally analyses 'la cohérence morale de cette oeuvre roborative'.

D'AUBIGNAC. J. Alexander, *'Utopia inverted: a contemporary German translation of François Hédelin d'Aubignac's *Royaume de la coqueterie* (1654)', *Neophilologus*, 84:87–96.

D'AULNOY. M.-A. Thirard, 'Le Féminisme dans les contes de Mme d'Aulnoy', *DSS*, 52:501–14, finds it manifested 'd'abord à travers la revendication de la prééminence de la femme-écrivain'. Themes which, according to T., reveal feminist preoccupations are forced marriages, the 'fiancé monstrueux', and 'le pouvoir féminin' expressed as an evocation of ideal states in which women have the ascendancy or are completely free of the presence of men. S. Jones Day, 'Madame d'Aulnoy's Julie: a heroine of the 1690s', Jones Day,

Writers and Heroines, 71–88, compares and contrasts the heroine of A.'s *Histoire d'Hypolite, comte de Duglas* with that of *La Princesse de Clèves*, and points to A.'s heroine's rejection of the conception of 'marriage as a socio-economic arrangement', preferring to regard it as a 'union des coeurs', a preference which the tale ultimately justifies. J. D. then goes on to compare A.'s heroine with two other Julies — those of Prévost in his *Mémoires d'un homme de qualité*, and Rousseau in *La Nouvelle Héloïse*.

BARCLAY. *_Euphormion_, trans. Jean Bérault, ed. Alain Cuillière, Klincksieck, xxv + 284 pp., reprints the only 17th-c. French translation (1640) of Barclay's Latin picaresque novel of 1602.

BOSSUET. J.-P. Landry, 'Parole de Dieu et parole des hommes: limites et légitimité de la prédication selon Bossuet', *LitC*, 39 : 221–36, reviews B.'s references to preaching and finds him emphasizing the necessity for humility and simplicity in the preacher who must hope for divine inspiration to turn his words into 'éloquence sacrée'.

J.-P. CAMUS. Sylvie Robic-De Baecque, *Le Salut par l'excès: Jean-Pierre Camus (1584–1652), la poétique d'un évêque romancier* (Lumière classique, 23), Champion, 1999, 453 pp., concentrates on the fifty or so very popular 'Histoires dévotes' written between 1620 and 1644 in which C., an admiring follower of François de Sales, 'affirmant oeuvrer pour la dévotion avec l'arme des séductions romanesques', makes use of 'une complexe distorsion des attentes ordinaires des lecteurs de romans' who are regaled with the 'fondement spirituel [. . .] du conflit entre l'amour-propre et le pur Amour' and are made aware of 'les fondements moral et psychologique d'une conception de la lecture étayée par une forte théorie des passions'. J. Zufferey, 'Fiction et vérité dans les nouvelles de J.-P. Camus', *Poétique*, 124 : 475–84, quotes from C.'s defence of his own works ('des Antiromans') claiming that they are a direct attack on the fictional output of his day.

CHALLE. J. Beale, 'Angel or sylph? The two-faced in *Les Illustres Françaises*', Jones Day, *Writers and Heroines*, 89–103, follows the different fortunes of two of C.'s 'dysphoric' heroines, Angélique de Contamine and Sylvie de Frans, viewing them as 'one woman with two faces' because both are, for different reasons, socially unacceptable. *_Lectures de Robert Challe_, ed. Jacques Cormier (Varia 40), Champion, 1999, 172 pp.

CYRANO DE BERGERAC. P. Harwig Van Ells, 'Alchemical metaphor and Cyrano de Bergerac's apology of the imagination', *CDs*, 7.2 : 13–22, draws our attention to C.'s exploitation of alchemical imagery, particularly in *Les États et Empires du Soleil*. Paul Mourouy, *_Cyrano de Bergerac: illustre mais inconnu_, Monaco, Rocher, 330 pp.

DACIER. E. Bury, 'Madame Dacier', Nativel, *Femmes savantes*, 209–20, discusses her life, including 'le poids d'un père qui fut un savant illustre' (Tanneguy Lefèvre), and finally 'le caractère original de son érudition' in Greek and Latin philology.

DU FOSSÉ. A. Villard, 'Les *Mémoires* du sieur de Pontis (1676) au plus près de la parole', *CPR*, 48, 1999: 57–77, gives biographical detail on Pontis, and on his biographer, and outlines the history of the first two editions of the *Mémoires* (1676 and 1678), and then shows how Du F. has managed to capture the speech and character of Pontis and his 'belle vigueur soldatesque'. S.-A. Vinci-Roussel, 'Écriture autobiographique et humiliation du moi dans les *Mémoires* de Pierre Thomas du Fossé' *ib.*, 79–86, claims that the personal aspect of the work, cut in many editions, is as interesting and valuable as the sections devoted to Pontis and Port-Royal. Of these, V.-R. concentrates on two: 'le culte des exploits familiaux' and the observations on travel, medicine, magic, and alchemy. Louis de Pontis, **Mémoires 1676: avec la totalité des modifications de 1678*, ed. Andrée Villard (Sources classiques, 24), Champion, 816 pp.

DU NOYER. H. Goldwyn, 'Journalisme polémique à la fin du XVIIe siècle: le cas de Mme du Noyer', Nativel, *Femmes savantes*, 247–56, gives us an outline of this protestant writer's life in exile and the nature of her polemical journalism, particularly of the *Lettres historiques et galantes* (1704–17), comparing them in style and effectiveness to Pascal's *Provinciales*.

FÉNELON. *DSS*, 52.1, prints six *actes* from a 'Journée Fénelon': A. Lanavère, 'L'imagination de Fénelon dans ses premiers écrits de fiction' (11–25), examines the *Fables et opuscules pédagogiques*, classifies them, and looks in them for signs of the 'imagination créatrice' that was shortly to compose *Télémaque*; F. Trémolières, 'Fénelon et les beaux-arts' (27–45), notes a scattering of references among F.'s works of which some, in the *Dialogues des morts*, offer *aperçus* and arresting comments on Poussin in particular; E. Bury, 'Fénelon pédagogue' (47–56), begins with the influence of Malebranche and Fleury, and ends with F.'s use of fable to appeal to children and to impress on young adults the need to 'toujours conserver la simplicité de l'enfance'; B. Papásogli, 'Espace intérieur et vie spirituelle chez Fénelon' (57–72), dwells on the notion, exploited by F., of a 'monde intérieur'. F.-X. Cuche, 'Fénelon. Une politique tirée de l'Evangile?' (73–95), contrasts F. who relies on the New Testament with Bossuet who prefers the Old, and notes also the relative rarity in F.'s political texts of direct biblical quotation, though nevertheless, 'l'imaginaire évangélique imprègne d'une façon décisive la politique fénelonienne'; G. Deregnaucourt, 'Fénelon à Cambrai (1695–1715): remarques sur un épiscopat et perspectives de recherches' (97–110), summarizes the papers given at a colloquium on *Fénelon, Évêque et pasteur en son temps*.

FEUILLET. J. Lesaulnier, 'La découverte des *Mémoires* de Nicolas Feuillet, chanoine janséniste de Saint-Cloud', *CPR*, 48, 1999: 145–69, tells of the discovery of the MS, relates it to F.'s life and other known writings, and judges him and his work to be 'un auteur et un ouvrage bien originaux, qui sentent quelque peu le soufre'.

FLÉCHIER. *Fléchier et les Grands Jours d'Auvergne*, ed. Emmanuèle Lesne-Jaffro (Biblio 17, 122), Tübingen, Narr, 137 pp., contains 'actes d'une journée d'étude': P. Charbonnier, 'Coupables ou adversaires? *Les Grands Jours* et les seigneurs d'Auvergne' (13–21), reveals the almost medieval attitude of Auvergnat nobility in the 1660s towards tenants whom they still treat as serfs, and the determination of the 'pouvoirs royaux', represented by F., to exert a modernizing authority — with only partial success; A. Lebigre, '*Les Grands Jours d'Auvergne*, un tournant dans l'histoire de la justice' (23–30), concentrates on two aims of the Grands Jours, 'juger les juges qui ont démérité, réformer les pratiques illégales ou inadaptées aux exigences d'une "bonne justice"'; B. Dompnier, 'Clermont en 1665. Un diocèse à l'écart de la Réforme catholique?' (33–53), casts doubt on F.'s opinion of 'la piètre qualité des gens d'Église — tant séculiers que réguliers', and suggests that he 'aurait surtout recherché l'anecdotique pour satisfaire un lectorat parisien en quête des signes d'un retard provincial'; R. Sauzet, 'Esprit Fléchier évêque de Nîmes (1687–1710) vu par son notaire' (55–63), introduces us to the 'livre de raison' of Étienne Borelly, an enthusiastic supporter of F., and a virulent anti-protestant, particularly during the revolt of the Camisards; J. Garapon, '*Les Mémoires sur les Grands Jours d'Auvergne*, une promenade en littérature' (65–76), provides examples to illustrate his view that this 'livre gigogne' is characterised by 'la recherche de l'agrément, de la grâce enjouée, de la diversité de la conversation'; A. Fontvieille, 'La critique de la rhétorique dans les *Mémoires sur les Grands Jours d'Auvergne* d'Esprit Fléchier' (77–91), contrasts F. with the 'orateurs d'Auvergne' with their fidelity to 'une tradition rhétorique démodée' by his use of a 'langue sobre, claire et agréable', and his 'jeu subtil sur la variété des tons'; F.-X. Cuche, '*Le Panégyrique de saint Louis* de Fléchier' (93–114), examines this work in the light of F.'s views on rhetoric and eloquence revealed in the *Mémoires*, but also contrasts the author of the *Panégyrique*, 'sérieux, abstrait, austère même, théologien augustinien, adepte de la morale sévère', with the younger 'abbé mondain et plein d'esprit'; C. Cagnat-Deboeuf, 'Fléchier, lecteur de Pascal. Ou de l'art du plagiat' (115–25), examines F.'s 1682 Advent sermon and finds him practising an exploitation 'si littérale, et en même temps si déguisée, qu'on hésite à le nommer réécriture', of the *Pensées*; E. Lesne-Jaffro, 'Le mauvais genre des *Mémoires* de Fléchier' (127–37), notes the liberties taken by F. with facts and chronology, and attributes them to 'le plaisir de l'élaboration fictive [. . .] le plaisir du verbe'.

FONTAINE. P. Mengotti-Thouvenin, 'Un coeur augustinien: la sensibilité dans les *Mémoires* de Nicolas Fontaine' *CPR*, 48, 1999:87–107, concentrates on the word *coeur*: 'terme essentiel dans la désignation de la vie intérieure'. F. Charbonneau, 'Le théâtre d'ombres de Nicolas Fontaine: augustinisme, platonisme, mémoire', *ib.*, 171–81, dwells on the neo-Platonism of this extrovert author.

GOMBERVILLE. B. Teyssandier, '*La Doctrine des moeurs*: d'un exercice de l'intuition à une rhétorique de l'intention', Mazouer, *Recherches*, 175–85, explains the *évolution* or *révolution* accomplished by G. with the unacknowledged borrowing in 1646, 'pour les assortir d'un long commentaire moralisé', of a collection of emblems by Otto Van Veen published in 1607.

GUILLERAGUES. G.J. Mallinson, 'Writing wrongs: *Lettres portugaises* and the search for an identity', Jones Day, *Writers and Heroines*, 31–47, analyses the subtle variety of expression in the letters which captures the fictional writer's mood changes, and then outlines the different assumptions and prejudices which caused generations of readers to accept the letters as genuine. M. McAlpin, 'Poststructuralist feminism and the imagining woman writer: the *Lettres portugaises*', *RR*, 90:27–44, examines Mariana Alcoforado's 'full-fledged authorial renaissance in the 1980s as the unlikely heroine of poststructuralist feminism' in 'a celebrated debate between Nancy K. Miller and Peggy Kamuf as to the value of the female signature'. See *YWMLS*, 44:109, and 50:124, and also Alain Niderst, pp. 120–21 above.

LA BRUYÈRE. Marine Ricord, "*Les Caractères*" de La Bruyère ou les exercices de l'esprit, PUF, 243 pp., is concerned with *esprit* — the quality that the 'galerie de sots et de fats' portrayed in this work do not have, but which is that by which La B. measures everything and everybody. K. Waterson, ' "Sçait-il du Grec. . .?" or, ennoblement from Montaigne to La Bruyère', *DFS*, 52:51–63, deals with La B.'s debt to M. when defining 'true worth' among humans. J. Parkin, 'La Bruyère: a study in satire', Parkin, *Humour*, 87–108, is concerned with primary and secondary 'value-systems', with 'clan divisions', and other 'inconsistencies' which La B. resorts to in order to vary and complicate his angle of attack.

MME DE LA FAYETTE. *La Princesse de Clèves*, ed. Bernard Pingaud (Folio classique, 3381), Gallimard, 275 pp. V. P. Brady, '*La Princesse de Clèves* and the refusal of love: heroic denial or pathetic submission?' *Neophilologus*, 84:517–30, in effect favours the latter, applying Eric Berne's method of psychoanalysis to the Princesse's 'case'. J.-P.

Montier, 'Arrêt sur l'image dans *La Princesse de Clèves*', *Littérature*, 119:3–20, notes that the 'dimension visuelle dans cette oeuvre' is able to 'énoncer un discours amoureux relativement indépendant par rapport au discours verbal'. M. Moriarty, 'Decision, desire, and assymmetry in *La Princesse de Clèves*', Jones Day, *Writers and Heroines*, 49–70, dwells at length on the Princess's inner debate about whether or not to marry Nemours, on the social context in which she finds herself (as do Nemours and all the others) which must be taken into account in her deliberations.

LA FORCE.   M.-A. Thirard, 'Les contes de Mlle de La Force: un nouvel art du récit féérique à travers un exemple privilégié', *PFSCL*, 27:573–85, desiring to rescue this author from obscurity, chooses one story, 'Plus Belle que Fée', to serve as example of 'des techniques de composition originales dont la complexité n'aurait rien à envier à l'écriture d'un long roman'.

LANCELOT.   D. Donetzkoff, ' "Mon dessein n'est pas d'écrire sa vie": les *Mémoires* de Lancelot sur l'abbé de Saint-Cyran', *CPR*, 48, 1999:109–32, remarks on the absence of writings on St.-C. before 1666, and then looks for evidence that L. too was a reluctant memorialist.

LE MAISTRE.   J. Lesaulnier, '*La Vie de saint Bernard, premier abbé de Clairvaux et père de l'Église* d'Antoine Le Maistre', *CPR*, 48, 1999:249–76, gives a résumé of Le M.'s life as a *solitaire* and of the circumstances surrounding the composition of the *Vie*.

MONTPENSIER.   *Portraits littéraires*, ed. Christian Bouyer, Séguier, 228 pp. J. Cherbuliez, 'Before and beyond Versailles: the counter-court of the Duchesse de Montpensier, 1652–1660', *NFS*, 39:129–39, evokes la Grande Mademoiselle and her entourage's social and cultural activities during her exile at Saint-Fargeau where she succeeded, according to C., in creating 'a court society beyond Louis XIV's reach'.

PERRAULT.   T. Gheeraert, 'Une allégorie de la civilité: *Cendrillon* ou l'art de plaire à la cour', *DSS*, 52:485–99, examines the 'pièces liminaires et les moralités' of the *Contes*, and then leads us on a 'parcours de *Cendrillon* d'après ses moralités', the most important of which is social advancement.

RACINE.   J. Dubu, 'À propos de l'*Abrégé de l'Histoire de Port-Royal* de Jean Racine', *CPR*, 48, 1999:277–300, brings together what is known about its composition and the circumstances of its posthumous publication, and analyses its contents.

RETZ.   G. Banderier, 'Une lettre inédite du cardinal de Retz', *DSS*, 52:515–18, reproduces and annotates a letter of 1674, and speculates about the addressee whom he believes to be the Maréchal de Turenne. Simone Bertière, *Le Cardinal de Retz* (Bibliographie des Ecrivains Français, 20), Memini, 182 pp.

SAINT-ÉVREMOND. *Entretiens sur toutes choses*, ed. David Bensoussan, Desjonquères, 1998, 206 pp., presents an annotated selection of essays, 'jugements', 'observations', and letters. M. Jaspers, 'Le Moraliste et l'histoire: Saint-Évremond à l'aube des Lumières', Mazouer, *Recherches*, 241–52, looks at St.-É.'s 'modernité', at what he has in common with 'les courants modernistes qui s'imposent lentement entre 1680 et 1715 et préparent le XVIIIe siècle éclairé'.

SAINT-RÉAL. C. Carasco, 'L'imaginaire tacitéen de Saint-Réal dans *Dom Carlos*', Mazouer, *Recherches*, 207–17, surveys in St.-R.'s theoretical works 'la leçon d'histoire fortement imprégnée d'humanisme', and then finds in *Dom Carlos* 'une ambiance antique particulière', and compares Tacitus on the death of Seneca with St.-R. on that of Dom Carlos.

MADELEINE DE SCUDÉRY. Marie-Gabrielle Lallemand, *La Lettre dans le récit: étude de l'oeuvre de Mlle de Scudéry* (Biblio 17, 120), Tübingen, Narr, 446 pp., presents an all-embracing survey of letters, their quantity, length, purpose, frequency, distribution, their relation to other writers' correspondence — real or fictional — and to other forms of ornamentation in fiction. All S.'s letters are listed and located in *annexes*, and many quoted at length. N. Grande, 'Stratégie d'écriture: la carrière de Madeleine de Scudéry' *CDs*, 7.2:189–96, defines the style and structure of S.'s novels and seeks in her life the experiences that shaped them and their development — salon life, literary success, social and professional ambition, the increasing importance of women in literary pursuits. M.-G. Lallemand, 'Deux ornements du récit: lettres et poésies dans l'oeuvre de Mlle de Scudéry', *ib.*, 197–206, summarizes, as far as letters are concerned, the contents of her doctoral thesis (see above). Lyric poetry appears belatedly, as 'l'influence de l'esthétique galante' grows in S.'s fiction from the last part of *Cyrus* onwards. A. Niderst, 'L'enjouée Plotine, Madame de Maintenon, Madeleine de Scudéry et Ninon de Lenclos', *PFSCL*, 27:501–08, wonders who, among the 'cabale affectueuse' surrounding Mme de M., inspired the character Plotine in S.'s *Clélie*, and opts finally for Ninon. C. Morlet Chantalat, 'Parler du savoir, savoir pour parler: Madeleine de Scudéry et la vulgarisation galante', Nativel, *Femmes savantes*, 177–95, shows S.'s ability, in her romances and other works, to render knowledge palatable, using techniques more effective than those of would-be popularizers of the time.

SOREL. Martine Debaisieux, *Le Procès du roman: écriture et contrefaçon chez Charles Sorel* (Références, 18), Orléans, Paradigme, 188 pp., is a second edition of this study first published in 1989 (see *YWMLS*, 52:117). *Histoire comique de Francion: anthologie critique*, ed. Patrick

Dandrey et al. (Parcours critique, 15), Klincksieck, 173 pp., provides a useful analytical bibliography of salient 17th- and 20th-c. commentaries on the novel, followed by a selection of eight of what are considered to be the most important of these published during the last 30 years. The volume ends with a 'sélection de variantes (1623–1626–1633)'. Other similar studies are: *Lectures du 'Francion' de Charles Sorel, ed. Daniel Riou, Rennes U.P., 106 pp.; Michèle Rosellini and Geneviève Salvan, *Le 'Francion' de Charles Sorel, Neuilly-sur-Seine, Atlande, 288 pp.; Frank Greiner and Véronique Sternberg, *L'Histoire comique de Francion: de Charles Sorel, SEDES, 122 pp. H. Tucker, 'Pleasure, seduction, and the authorial identity in Charles Sorel's Le Berger extravagant', Neophilologus, 84:347–358, dwells on the relationship between the Anti-roman and the novels it mocks, and on the author himself and his 'masks'.

TALLEMANT DES RÉAUX. J. F. Gaines, 'Nobility and the sexual economy in the Historiettes', CDs, 7.2:193–206, finds a cohesion in the fragments 'at least in their treatment of the theme of galanterie and its decay among the nobility'.

TRISTAN L'HERMITE. B. Donné, 'Tristan et "Un des plus excellents esprits de ce siècle": note sur le prélude du Page disgracié', CTH, 22:79–84, on the question of whom T. was praising with these words, first reconsiders Montaigne and Théophile, but finally opts for Balzac.

D'URFÉ. A. Zuerner, 'Neoplatonism, gender, and disguise: rereading d'Urfé's l'Astrée', CDs, 7.2:207–209, notes the complexity of the erotic effects sought by U., and claims that 'far from being effeminized by his temporary transvestism, Céladon is virilized through fetishistic cross-dressing and the symbolic fulfilment of the neoplatonic ideal it represents'. L. A. Gregorio, 'Silvandre's symposium: the Platonic and the ambiguous in L'Astrée', PQ, 52, 1999:782–804, points to the ambiguity of gender identity in the novel, reviews the comments of others on it, and proposes a 'strategy of reading' which, he feels, would justify it. A. Desprechins de Gaesebeke, 'L'Astrée sur les lisses dans les marges de Corneille et de Racine', PFSCL, 27:447–71, comments on the popularity of U's romance as a provider of inspiration, not only for C. and R., but also for tapestries throughout the 17th c.

MARGUERITE DE VALOIS. E. Viennot, Écriture et culture chez Marguerite de Valois', Nativel, Femmes savantes, 167–75, considers all the Queen's writings in order to arrive at an 'idée moins simpliste' about her than that encouraged by Dumas père and other popularizers.

VEIRAS. V. Joucla, 'De la fiction romanesque au projet réel, adduction d'eau et réalisations hydrauliques chez Denis Veiras', DSS, 52:329–38, comments on the technical ingenuity in hydraulics displayed by the Sévarambes in V.'s *Histoire*, and compares it to V.'s own plans for canals and irrigation which he proposed to the Etats du Languedoc in 1696.

VILLEDIEU. R. Démoris, 'Écriture féminine en *je* et subversion des savoirs chez Mme de Villedieu (les *Mémoires d'Henriette-Sylvie de Molière*)', Nativel, *Femmes savantes*, 197–208, presents V. as a fiction writer who (like Saint-Réal) embroiders history with her creative imagination. D. takes the *Mémoires* — 'un vrai roman' — as his principal example. But see also A. Niderst, pp. 120–21 above.

5. THOUGHT

M. Bourgeois, 'Bien penser dans la culture mondaine: la *Logique de Port-Royal*', Mazouer, *Recherches*, 117–28, is aware of the varied 'types de discours' which use or comment on the notion of 'bien penser', particularly after Pascal's reference to it in fr. 232 (Sellier), but confines herself to what she has found in the *Logique* and to 'la mesure de l'écart qui s'établit [. . .] entre "ce qu'est bien penser" et ce que fut, dans l'ordre de l'éloquence, bien parler'. D. Descotes, 'Les Anges quadrateurs', *LitC*, 39:179–96, is disappointed with the rare references made by 17th-c. Christian apologists to squaring the circle. P. Laude, 'L'intelligence contemplative et l'expérience du temps et de l'espace dans la mystique de pur amour et de simple regard', *ib.*, 349–61, studies the views of Jeanne Guyon, Malaval, Fénelon, and Bossuet.

R. Dekoninck, 'L'image prise au mot: méditations et rhétorique visuelle jésuites', Mazouer, *Recherches*, 161–74, describes an aspect of the role played by the Jesuits in the Catholic Church's campaign to reassert its monopoly in the Counter Reformation, for which 'l'image, instrument stratégique du consensus, devint aussi l'une des principales armes de la reconquête, dans un premier temps, et du maintien de la croyance obéissante, dans un second temps'. V. Jullien, 'Silences cosmologiques', *DSS*, 52:235–56, compares the reactions of Descartes, Gassendi, Pascal, and Roberval to the Church's condemnation of heliocentrism. Simone Mazauric, *Gassendi, Pascal et la querelle du vide* (Philosophies, 110), PUF, 1998, 128 pp., surveys the whole debate, from Aristotle and Epicurus, via Descartes and Gassendi, Galileo and Torricelli, to Pascal and 'la réussite du Puy de Dôme', and thence to objections raised and answered. M. ends with the claim that the episode is a vital moment in 'la constitution de la science moderne'. See also below under PASCAL.

CPR, 49, prints papers presented at a *journée d'étude* on 'Port-Royal au miroir du XXe siècle', including studies, notably, on Henri

Bremond (by J.-R. Armogathe) and Lucien Goldmann (by G. Ferrey-rolles). It also contains three articles introducing and quoting samples of work in progress on a projected *Dictionnaire de Port-Royal*: A. McKenna, 'Port-Royal électronique: présentation' (171–75); J. Lesaulnier, 'Trois théologiens de Port-Royal: Amable de Bourzeis, Noël de Lalane et Louis Gorin de Saint-Amour' (177–218); D. Descotes, 'CD-ROM PC et Macintosh: Pascal: *Lettres de A. Dettonville*' (219–21).

B. Joly, 'Rhétorique de l'alchimie au XVIIe siècle: cacher l'échec et diffuser la doctrine', *DSS*, 52:221–33, notes the paradox of a 'science' which reserves its secrets for its adepts but which also works hard at self-publicity.

ANTOINE ARNAULD. *Examen du Traité de l'essence du corps contre Descartes*, ed. Emmanuel Faye (Corpus des Oeuvres de Philosophie en Langue Française), Fayard, 1999, 141 pp., reprints the 1780 edition with corrections from the MS of 1680 (Arsenal 2098).

BAYLE. S. L. Jenkinson, 'Nourishing men's anger and inflaming the fires of hatred: Bayle on religious violence and the "Novus Ordo Saeclorum"', *Terrorism and Political Violence*, 10.4, 1998:64–79, comments on B.'s article *Macon* in his *Dictionnaire*, recalling the atrocities perpetrated in that town during the Wars of Religion and proposing political reforms which would prevent such events. An English translation of the article is appended. *Political Writings*, ed. Sally L. Jenkinson (Cambridge Texts in the History of Political Thought), CUP, xiii + 367 pp., translates into English a selection of relevant articles from the *Dictionnaire*, and precedes it with a lengthy introduction summarizing the political ideas which B. supported and opposed. Thomas M. Lennon, *Reading Bayle*, Toronto U.P., 1999, xi + 202 pp., offers a Bakhtinian reading of B.'s views on integrity, authority, toleration, idolatry, and providence. Gianluca Mori, **Études sur la philosophie de Pierre Bayle*, Champion, 1999, 362 pp.

BÉRULLE. C. Belin, 'Le "Discours en forme d'élévation" selon Bérulle', *LitC*, 39:253–64, shows how B. reconciles in one *discours* 'le cheminement rationnel d'une foi qui cherche à comprendre' and 'l'élan cordial d'une foi qui cherche à aimer'. H. Michon, 'L'anéantissement: de l'ontologie à la mystique', *ib.*, 265–82, studies in particular the *Oeuvres de piété* in her consideration of the theme of 'l'anéantissement de la créature' in the light of the variety of B.'s sources and his 'discours complexe, unissant indissociablement la théologie spéculative et la théologie mystique'. A. Ferrari, 'Les formes du silence dans le discours mystique, ou quand dire, c'est taire', *ib.*, 283–96, relates B.'s various techniques for putting into words 'l'expérience de Dieu [. . .] une expérience qui requiert le silence'.

CHALLE. *Difficultés sur la religion proposées au père Malebranche; édition nouvelle d'après le manuscrit complet et fidèle de la Staatsbibliothek de Munich*, ed. Frédéric Deloffre and François Moureau (TLF, 521), 814 pp., firmly establishes C.'s arguments for deism as being truly his, and rescues them from the fate of many clandestine works which have been subject to 'remaniements qui en ont altéré le contenu, le ton, les intentions'.

DESCARTES. Pierre Guenancia, *Lire Descartes* (Folio Essais, 354), Gallimard, 576 pp., is a thorough general introduction presenting firstly the works and secondly Cartesianism, the ramifications of Cartesian thought, and the reactions of other philosophers and movements over the centuries. Roger Ariew, *Descartes and the Last Scholastics*, Ithaca, Cornell U.P., 1999, xi + 230 pp., collects, reworks and expands essays published over ten years dealing with D.'s thought, its relationship to scholasticism, and its reception in the early 18th c. Andrea Nye, *The Princess and the Philosopher: Letters of Elisabeth of the Palatine to René Descartes*, Lanham, MD, Rowman and Littlefield, 1999, xiii + 187 pp., analyses the friendly opposition the letters reveal between these two unlikely correspondents. P.-J. Salazar, 'Elizabeth à Descartes: "être mieux instruite de votre bouche" ', Nativel, *Femmes savantes*, 131–39, studies the same letters, noting in particular her reactions to his teaching and compliments. Zbigniew Janowski, *Cartesian Theodicy: Descartes' Quest for Certitude*, Dordrecht, Kluwer, 181 pp., points to certain problems which D. seemed not to confront, such as those posed by the notion of 'freedom of indifference'. J. also emphasises the need to place D.'s writings in their cultural context. Jorge Secada, *Cartesian Metaphysics: The Late Scholastic Origins of Modern Philosophy*, CUP, xii + 333 pp., seeks to 'offer a unified reading of Descartes's metaphysics against the background of scholastic philosophy', particularly that of Aquinas and Francisco Suarez. F. de Buzon, '*Democritica*: la réfutation cartésienne de l'atomisme', Salen, *L'Atomisme*, 27–41, reveals less a refutation than a cautious questioning of the ideas of Democritus and other ancient philosophers. D. Scott, 'Occasionalism and occasional causation in Descartes' philosophy', *JHP*, 38:503–28, looks first (and in vain) for evidence in D.'s writings of his wishing to advance body-mind occasionalism, and then for evidence for his belief in occasional causation. H. van Ruler, 'Minds, forms, and spirits: the nature of Cartesian disenchantment', *JHI*, 61:381–95. *Descartes*, ed. John Cottingham (Oxford Readings in Philosophy), OUP, 1998, viii + 326 pp., collects 13 previously published articles and essays by eminent anglophone Cartesians (plus G. Rodis-Lewis, translated).

DUVERGIER DE HAURANNE. C. Blanquie, 'Duvergier de Hauranne et l'évêque de Luçon', *CPR*, 49:223–31, reproduces a letter by D. to

Richelieu dated Bayonne, 10 December, 1615, and relates it to the careers of both men.

FÉNELON. F. Trémolières, 'Rhétorique profane, rhétorique sacrée: les *Dialogues sur l'éloquence* de Fénelon', *LitC*, 39:221–36, writes a commentary on this early work. **Nouvel État présent des Travaux sur Fénelon*, ed. Henk Hillenaar (CRIN, 36), Amsterdam–Atlanta, Rodopi, 199 pp.

FONTENELLE. G. M. Adkins, 'When ideas matter: the moral philosophy of Fontenelle', *JHI*, 61:433–52, examines the ideas expressed in F.'s 69 *Éloges* written in honour of recently deceased members of the Académie Royale des Sciences of which he was *secrétaire perpétuel*.

GASSENDI. J. Kany-Turpin, 'Atomisme et molécules dans les *Animadversiones* de Gassendi', Salen, *L'Atomisme*, 59–71, comments on the extensive *Lettre à Hérodote* from the above work. **Libertinage et philosophie au XVIIe siècle. 4. Gassendi et les gassendistes. Les passions libertines*, ed. Antony McKenna and Pierre-François Moreau, Saint-Étienne U.P., 217 pp., prints papers given at a *journée d'études*.

LA MOTHE LE VAYER. Philippe-Joseph Salazar, '*La Divine Sceptique': Éthique et rhétorique au 17e siècle; autour de La Mothe Le Vayer* (ELF, 68), Tübingen, Narr, 131 pp., finds this author ill-served by both editors and academics, and sets about studying all aspects of this 'formidable rhéteur'. A. G. Shelford, 'François de La Mothe Le Vayer and the defence of pagan virtue', *SCen*, 15:67–89, studies *De la vertu des payens*, a reaction to Jansenius's *Augustinus*, in particular 'his theological arguments and their import' and 'his revealing but problematic case studies of individual pagans'.

LE MOYNE. V. Kapp, 'Instruction des femmes et politique chrétienne dans *La Gallerie des femmes fortes* du Père Le Moyne', *LitC*, 39:51–66, approves of this 'ouvrage tout à fait remarquable' and reveals the Jesuit's favourable view of women's innate moral and intellectual qualities, which make them as worthy of education as men.

LÉVESQUE. A. Walch, 'Du singulier à l'universel: *La Perfection de l'amour* selon Catherine Lévesque (1616–1693)', *DSS*, 52:703–18, presents this work of piety published in 1685.

MALEBRANCHE. *The Cambridge Companion to Malebranche*, ed. Steven Nadler, CUP, xi + 319 pp., offers 11 essays which aim to provide a comprehensive introduction to M.'s thought.

PIERRE NICOLE. *Essais de morale*, ed. Laurent Thirouin (Philosophie morale), PUF, 440 pp., provides an annotated selection of ten of the 50 or so essays written by N. The essays have been chosen, either for their 'caractère représentatif', or because they seem to T. to 's'imposer par leur intérêt intrinsèque'.

PASCAL. *Pensées*, ed. Gérard Ferreyrolles (Le Livre de Poche classique), Librairie Générale Française, 736 pp., reproduces the Sellier ordering of the fragments, and provides a presentation, notes, 'dossier', and 'tables de concordance'. Philippe Sellier, *Port-Royal et la littérature. I. Pascal* (Lumière classique, 21), Champion, 1999, 356 pp., collects some of Sellier's impressive contributions to P. studies, reprinting previously published papers and articles dating from 1966 to 1999. There is only one *inédit:* 'Pascal et saint Augustin: théologie et anthropologie' (249–62), which points to P.'s deep knowledge of the works of St. A., and examines it in three stages: the 'théologie pascalienne (et augustinienne) de la Chute', then 'la mise au jour de la théorie anthropologique qui découle de cet "état" corrompu de l'homme', and finally 'la stratégie apologétique, la théologie fonda-mentale de Pascal'. *Pascal. Qu'est-ce que la vérité?*, ed. Martine Péchar-man (Débats philosophiques), PUF, 166 pp., prints seven essays: M. Pécharman, 'Préface. La vérité, de la logique à l'anthropologie' (1–12), distinguishes between the debt to Cartesian philosophy accepted by the authors of the *Logique de Port-Royal*, and that to theology avowed by Pascal in *De l'esprit géométrique;* P. Magnard, ' "On se fait une idole de la vérité même" '(15–28), explores the significance of fragment 926 (Lafuma) and of ones with similar implications; J.-P. Cléro, 'La temporalité du vrai et de la vérité dans les *Pensées*' (29–62), surveys P.'s use of *vrai* and *vérité* and in particular considers what is meant by fr. 776 (Lafuma); H. Bouchillous, 'Vérité phénoménale et vérité essentielle chez Pascal' (63–88), is concerned 'en leurs ordres respectifs' with Pyrrhonism, geometry, and Augustinian theology, and also with how 'cette articulation pascalienne du pyrrhonisme et de la géométrie s'oppose radicalement à l'entreprise cartésienne de fondation métaphysique de la science'; C. Lazzeri, 'Pascal et l'impératif de complémentarité' (89–113), looks at irreconcilable positions taken up up by rival schools of philosophy, and by Molinists opposed to Calvinists, at Pascal's awareness of these positions, seeing in each pair a *rapport de complémentarité* and a *limitation réciproque*, which, when recognised, can lead to reconciliation; B. Sève, 'Vérité au-delà du pyrrhonisme, erreur en deçà? La triple vérité du pyrrhonisme dans les *Pensées* de Pascal' (115–35), defines with P. three such *vérités* and then admits their necessarily unstable nature, hence the imposs-ible need to 'changer de terrain, à passer de l'esprit à la charité'; M. Pécharman, 'La vérité, destination morale de l'homme dans les *Pensées*' (137–64), points to 'la question de l'immortalité de l'âme' as having 'le contenu propre d'une doctrine de la vérité dépassant la philosophie humaine'. M. Bouvier, 'À propos du *Pari* de Pascal', *DSS*, 52:339–42, comments at length on the 'shocking' expression 'et vous abêtira', offering reasons for Nicole's omission of it from the 1670 edition of the *Pensées*. He himself rejects the 'mécanisation' explanation of P.'s choice of words here, preferring to see in them the need for 'humiliation de la raison orgueilleuse'. H. Mazaheri, 'L'apologétique et le mythe du juif dans les *Pensées* of Blaise Pascal', *ib.*, 131–39, shows how P.'s apology for Christianity leads him to attack and denigrate Judaism and Islam. G. Ansart, 'Le concept de figure dans les *Pensées*', *Poétique*, 121 : 49–59, regards the concept as fundamentally important because it is applied 'au domaine anthropologique et social aussi bien qu'au domaine religieux, ces deux domaines constituant les deux grands pôles de la réflexion pascalienne'. A. looks for what links these 'domaines' and also what distinguishes them ('concupiscence' and 'charité'). S. C. Toczyski, 'Performative tension: parabolic resistance in the *Pensées* of Blaise Pascal', *CDs*, 7.2 : 141–48, examines 'a non-coincidence in Pascal's lexicon, a missing link or lack', namely his uninterest in biblical parables, and his avoidance in the *Pensées* of the word *parabole*, despite his mathematical interests and his fondness for mathematical language. G. Magniont, 'La voix de Salomon de Tultie', Mazouer, *Recherches*, 139–47, notes the frequent reference by commentators to 'la voix de Pascal' or 'la voix des *Pensées*', and himself comments, referring to P. and his fr. 618 (Sellier), on 'le rapport qu'entretient le discours avec son énonciateur et avec son destinateur'. J.-V. Blanchard, 'Optique et rhétorique au XVIIe siècle: de l'*ekphrasis* jésuite au fragment pascalien', *ib.*, 149–59, re-examines the rhetorical term *dispositio* in the context of 'l'opposition canonique existant entre la rhétorique des jésuites français de la période Henri IV et Louis XIII et la conception de la persuasion de Pascal'. P. Force, 'Conditions d'efficacité du discours apologétique dans les *Pensées*' *LitC*, 39 : 197–206, argues against the premise proposed by Sara E. Melzer (see *YWMLS*, 48 : 148) that 'la démarche de Pascal [in his *Pensées*] est aporétique' and suggests that such a 'démarche [. . .] est au service de l'intention apologétique et non pas en conflit avec elle'. T. Shiokawa, 'Le "pari" de Pascal: de l'apologétique à la spiritualité', *ib.*, 207–18, argues that the fragment in question has to go beyond apologetics into the domain of the 'spirituel' because its rational argument 'n'a pas d'efficacité pratique'. C. Meurillon, 'Oubli de soi, oubli de Dieu: écriture et oubli chez Pascal', *RSH*, 252, 1998 : 23–36, ponders on P.'s 'expérience mentale de l'oubli' recorded in various *pensées*, which 'rappelle la faiblesse de l'homme' and of our fallen state, abandoned by God. Benoît Denis, *Littérature et engagement de Pascal à Sartre*, devotes a chapter to 'Pascal ou le pathos de l'engagement'.

J. F. Boitano, ' "Horror Vacui" and Pascal's *Expériences nouvelles touchant le vide*', *CDs*, 7.2 : 121–30, examines first the historical framework for the debate on this subject, and then P.'s treatise together with his correspondence with the Jesuit Father Étienne Noël.

A. Le Noxaïc, 'Le "vide" mis en évidence par Pascal est-il exempt d'atomes?', Salen, *L'Atomisme*, 15–25, examines this same correspondence in an attempt to 'rééquilibrer' the debate more in favour of Father Noël. M. A. O'Neil, 'Pascalian reflections in *Les Misérables*', *PQ*, 78, 1999: 335–48, finds a strong influence of P. and of Jansenism throughout Hugo's novel.

André Bord, *La Vie de Blaise Pascal: Une ascension spirituelle; suivie d'un essai, 'Plotin, Montaigne, Pascal'*, Beauchesne, 232 pp., is hagiography. There are two other new biographies: Jacques Attali, *Blaise Pascal ou le génie français, Fayard, 500 pp.; André Le Gall, *Pascal, Flammarion, 516 pp.

PEIRESC.   Peter N. Miller, *Peiresc's Europe: Learning and Virtue in the Seventeenth Century, Yale U.P., 256 pp., studies the man and his vast circle of friends and correspondents.

SURIN.   S. Houdard, 'Expérience et écriture des "choses de l'autre vie" chez Jean-Joseph Surin', *LitC*, 39: 331–47, reviews S.'s *Science expérimentale des choses de l'autre vie*, an autobiographical work recounting his experiences at Loudun with Jeanne des Anges and her devils.

VINCENT DE PAUL.   Jean-Yves Ducourneau, *Vincent de Paul, l'amour à l'infini. . .*, Médiaspaul, 254 pp., is a biography. The select bibliography contains a section on Louise de Marillac.

THE EIGHTEENTH CENTURY

By D. A. DESSERUD, *Professor of Politics,*
University of New Brunswick at Saint John; RUSSELL GOULBOURNE, *Lecturer in French, University of Leeds;* ROBIN HOWELLS, *Reader in French, Birkbeck College, London;* HEATHER LLOYD, *Senior Lecturer in French, University of Glasgow;* and KATE E. TUNSTALL, *Fellow in French, Worcester College, Oxford.*

(This survey covers the years 1998–2000)

1. GENERAL

Jay Caplan, *In the King's Wake: Post-Absolutist Culture in France,* Chicago U.P., 1999, vii + 213 pp., traces the emergence in the 18th c. of post-absolutist (as opposed to pre-Revolutionary) culture, examining images of value and devaluation across a range of works and genres, including Saint-Simon's memoirs, Voltaire's *Œdipe,* and Marivaux's *Le Jeu de l'amour et du hasard* and *Les Fausses Confidences.* Monique Cottret, *Jansénismes et Lumières,* Albin Michel, 1998, 419 pp., contains much information in the text and notes, but diffuse treatment and 'popular' presentation reduce its usefulness. Elisabeth Bourguinat, *Le Siècle du persiflage,* PUF, 1998, 228 pp., is a systematic study of the 18th-c. French mode of mocking verbal play, in society and literature. An impressive lexical basis is used to build a sociological interpretation. Anne Coudreuse, *Le Goût des larmes au XVIIIe siècle,* PUF, 1999, 314 pp., provides a useful and wide-ranging analysis of the cultural phenomenon of tears in the 18th c., based on a careful examination of the place of pathos and 'le pathétique' in 18th-c. aesthetic theory and discussing in some detail a number of novels and plays of the period. Anne C. Vila, *Enlightenment and Pathology. Sensibility in the Literature and Medicine of Eighteenth-Century France,* Johns Hopkins U.P., 1998, xii + 391 pp., is a valuable study of 'body-based meanings' in physiology (chs 1–3) and the novel (chs 4–8). In literature the shift around 1750 'from the morally delicate sensitive soul to the vitally reactive sensible body' is also from aristocratic to more bourgeois thinking. A rigorous account of vitalist scientific thought is offered by Roselyne Rey, *Naissance et développement du vitalisme en France de la deuxième moitié du 18e siècle à la fin du Premier Empire* (*StV,* 381), Oxford, Voltaire Foundation, xii + 472 pp. Silver, *Épistolières,* offers an interesting conspectus of women's correspondence through individual articles on Graffigny, Du Châtelet, d'Epinay, Du Deffand, Lespinasse, Roland, Charrière, Genlis, and others, with a good overview by B. Didier.

2. DIDEROT

GENERAL. *Dictionnaire de Diderot*, ed. Roland Mortier and Raymond Trousson, Champion, 546 pp., is an informative work with useful cross-references. Walter E. Rex, *Diderot's Counterpoints: The Dynamics of Contrariety in his Major Works* (*StV*, 363), Oxford, Voltaire Foundation, 1998, xvi + 318 pp., tackles D.'s tendency to say one thing one minute and the opposite the next. Rex tracks this contrariety with subtlety to produce a stimulating study and a major contribution to D. scholarship. Marie-Hélène Chabut, *Denis Diderot: Extravagance et génialité*, Amsterdam, Rodopi, 1998, 170 pp., consists of five essays exploring images and metaphors of genius ('le disparate' in the *Réfutation d'Helvétius*, 'l'écart' in the *Lettre sur les aveugles*, 'le délire' in *Le Rêve*, 'le déguisement' in the *Supplément au Voyage de Bougainville*, and 'la dissonance' in *Le Neveu de Rameau*). Eliane Martin-Haag, *Un Aspect de la politique de Diderot: savoirs et pouvoirs*, Ellipses, 1999, 192 pp. Fresh analyses of D.'s early works are to be found in Anne Elisabeth Sejten, *Diderot ou le défi esthétique*, Vrin, 1999, 255 pp.

D. and materialism is the theme of *RDE*, 26, 1999, which includes A. Tosel, 'Diderot: un matérialisme entre nominalisme et conjecture' (9–16); M. Skrzypek, 'Les catégories centrales dans la philosophie de Diderot' (27–36); E. Martin-Haag, 'Droit naturel et histoire dans la philosophie de Diderot' (37–48); M. Spallanzani, 'Figures de philosophes dans l'œuvre de Diderot' (49–64); J.-C. Bourdin, 'Matérialisme et scepticisme chez Diderot' (85–98); F. Salaün, 'L'identité personelle selon Diderot' (113–24); A. Ibrahim, 'Matière des métaphores, métaphores de la matière' (125–34); A. Suratteau-Iberraken, 'Diderot et la médecine, un matérialiste vitaliste' (173–96); A. Thomson, 'Diderot, le matérialisme et la division de l'espèce humaine' (197–212); C. T. Wolfe, 'Machine et organisme chez Diderot' (213–32). In chapter four of Goodden, *Memory*, G. explores D.'s notions of memory and the self present in *La Religieuse* and the *Salons* as well as in *Le Rêve*, to show that his adherence to materialist accounts of these phenomena is limited. F. Duchesneau, *Diderot et la physiologie de la sensibilité*, *DhS*, 31, 1999:194–216.

D.'s æsthetics have been the subject of a number of studies, among them Jeannette Geffriaud Rosso, *Diderot et le portrait*, Pisa, Libreria Goliardica, 1998, xii + 236 pp., which explores D. and portraiture 'sous toutes ses faces': portraits of D., portraits in D., D.'s æsthetics and his notion of portraiture. C. Duflo, 'Le système de dégoût. Diderot critique de Boucher', *RDE*, 29:85–101, considers D.'s view of Boucher as a technically able but ultimately corrupt and corrupting artist. P. Quintili, 'Diderot, l'esthétique et le naturalisme. L'autre science de l'interprétation de la nature', *DhS*, 31, 1999:269–82.

Studies on the *Lettre sur les aveugles* include G. Stenger, 'La théorie de la connaissance dans la *Lettre sur les aveugles*', *RDE*, 26, 1999:99–112. *RDE*, 28, is devoted to the *Lettre sur les aveugles* in response to its being set for the *Agrégation*, and contains: C. Duflo, 'Introduction' (7–12); M. Parmentier, 'Le problème de Molyneux de Locke à Diderot' (13–24); V. Le Ru, 'La *Lettre sur les aveugles* et le bâton de la raison' (25–42); A. Charrak, 'Géométrie et métaphysique dans la *Lettre sur les aveugles* de Diderot' (43–54); M. Crampe-Casnabet, 'Qu'appelle-t-on sensibilité?' (55–66); S. Audidière, 'La *Lettre sur les aveugles* et l'éducation des sens' (67–82); J.-C. Bourdin, 'Le matérialisme dans la *Lettre sur les aveugles*' (83–96); A. Ibrahim, 'Une philosophie d'aveugle: la matière fait de l'esprit' (97–106); C. Duflo, 'La fin du finalisme. Les deux natures: Holmes ou Saunderson' (107–31). D.'s presentation of blindness is seen as contradictory, both natural and monstrous, in A. Curran, 'Diderot's revisionism: Enlightenment and blindness in the *Lettre sur les aveugles*' *DS*, 28:75–93.

DS, 28, also includes: G. Ansart, 'Aspects of rationality in Diderot's *Supplément au Voyage de Bougainville*' (11–20); M. Black, 'Lucretius tells Diderot: here's the plan' (39–58); C. Duflo, 'Et pourquoi des dialogues au temps des systèmes?' (95–111); L. Mall, 'Une autobiolecture: l'*Essai sur les règnes de Claude et de Néron* de Diderot' (111–23); K. E. Tunstall, 'Hieroglyph and device in the *Lettre sur les sourds et muets*' (161–72). O. Richard, 'De la lettre à la "rêverie": Diderot randonneur de l'esprit dans les *Lettres à Sophie Volland*', *RDE*, 29:71–83, focuses on the presence of gardens and accounts of 'promenades' in the letters, and relates the 'rêveries' which they often provoke to the work of Rousseau. *RDE*, 27, includes: C. Lannoy, 'La sensibilité épistémologique de Diderot: expression matérialiste d'un désir d'éternité' (59–88); F. A. Kafker, 'Brullé: L' "Ostrogoth" identifié' (105–10); F. Moureau, 'Lumières méditerranéennes: Diderot dans les bibliothèques des chevaliers de Malte' (153–60). *RDE*, 29, includes: R. Hernandez, 'Le dernier voyage de Diderot à Cuba' (9–24); P. Pellerin, 'Naigeon: une certaine image de Diderot sous la révolution' (25–44); E. Martin-Haag, 'Du "rêve" comme condition humaine: poésie et philosophie dans le *Rêve de d'Alembert*' (103–18).

THEATRE. D.'s theatre has been the subject of some exciting studies. *Etudes sur Le Fils naturel et les Entretiens sur Le Fils naturel de Diderot*, ed. Nicholas Cronk, Oxford, Voltaire Foundation, ix + 325 pp., offers a wide-ranging collection of articles, exploring the presence of other writers such as Horace, Voltaire, and Rousseau, the uncertain genre of the text, its wider resonances in 18th-c. æsthetics and its influence outside France. It contains: N. Rizzoni, 'Du *Fils naturel* au fils dramaturge' (1–20); I. C. Demarte, 'A la relecture du *Fils naturel* et des *Entretiens sur Le Fils naturel*: entre théâtre et roman, les transgressions d'une "espèce de roman"' (21–40); M.-E. Plagnol-Diéval, '*Le Fils naturel* ou le fantasme d'un théâtre privé' (41–52); A. Goodden, '*Le Fils naturel*: langage du corps et discours sur le corps' (53–64); G. Stenger, 'Vertu et vérité dans *Le Fils naturel*' (65–78); F. Moureau, 'Les paradoxes de Lampédouse' (79–88); A. Ménil, '*Ut pictura poesis erit*? Théâtre et anti-théâtralité dans la théorie du drame' (89–111); R. Goulbourne, 'Diderot et Horace, ou le paradoxe du théâtre moderne' (112–22); N. Cronk, 'Dorval et le dialogue à trois voix: la présence de Rousseau et de Voltaire dans *Le Fils naturel* et les *Entretiens*' (123–37); M. Hobson, 'Notes pour les *Entretiens sur Le Fils naturel*' (138–49); M. de Rougemont, 'Pallas ou l'orme: notes sur la *Lettre à Mme Riccoboni* de Diderot' (150–58); A. Kahn, '*Le Fils naturel* et la réforme de la comédie russe' (159–70); F. Lamport, 'Lessing traducteur et critique de Diderot' (171–80); R. Goulbourne, 'Essai bibliographique' (181–210); 'Dossier' compiled by K. E. Tunstall (211–324). P. Pellerin, 'La place du théâtre de Diderot sous la Révolution', *RDE*, 27, 1999:89–103, looks at performances of *Le Père de famille* and the adaptation of *Jacques le fataliste* to the revolutionary stage. H. Ida, 'La "pantomime" selon Diderot. Le geste et la démonstration morale', *ib.*, 25–42.

PROSE FICTION. D.'s novels continue to generate interesting debates. J. E. Fowler, *Voicing Desire: Family and Sexuality in Diderot's Narrative*, Oxford, Voltaire Foundation, ix + 169 pp., combines narratology and psychoanalysis to provide new readings of *Les Bijoux indiscrets*, *Le Fils naturel*, *La Religieuse*, *Jacques le fataliste et son maître*, and *Le Neveu de Rameau*. N. Cronk, '*Jacques le Fataliste* et le renouveau du roman carnavalesque', *DhS*, 32:33–49, is a study not only of the carnivalesque as an intertextual phenomenon in *Jacques*, related to Rabelais as well as to *Candide* and *Compère Matthieu*, but also of the presence of carnival culture in the novel. Jean Terrasse, *Le Temps et l'espace dans les romans de Diderot* (*StV*, 379), Oxford, Voltaire Foundation, 1999, xii + 180 pp. D. Lecourt, 'La philosophie de *Jacques le fataliste*', *RDE*, 26, 1999:135–40; A. Deneys-Tunney, 'La critique de la métaphysique dans les *Bijoux Indiscrets* et *Jacques le Fataliste* de Diderot', *ib.*, 141–52; G. Beeharry-Paray, '*Les Bijoux Indiscrets* de Diderot: pastiche, forgerie ou charge du conte crebillonien?', *DS*, 28:21–38. P. Quintili, 'Révolution et praxis dans *Le Neveu de Rameau*, roman du jeu de l'éthique sociale', *RDE*, 26, 1999:153–72. W. E. Rex, '*Le Neveu de Rameau*: musique et structure', *ib.*, 27, 1999:7–23, explores the role of music in the text, linking it to imitation, and the structure of the text itself, focusing on D.'s use of the classical unities. A. J. Singerman, 'Desperately seeking Suzanne: the semiotics of the sound track in Jacques Rivette's *La Religieuse*', *DS*, 28:141–60.

A. Coudreuse, 'Pour un nouveau lecteur: *La Religieuse* de Diderot et ses destinataires', *RDE*, 27:43–58.

THE ENCYCLOPÉDIE. Marie Leca-Tsiomis, *Ecrire l'Encyclopédie. Diderot: de l'usage des dictionnaires à la grammaire philosophique* (*StV*, 375), Oxford, Voltaire Foundation, 1999, xii + 528 pp., is a scholarly exploration of D.'s use of other reference works such as *Trévoux*. L.-T. concentrates on the section 10-JOUISSANCE of volume VIII (1759) to reveal D. in dialogue with his former collaborator, d'Alembert, and his former friend, Rousseau. S. Auroux and B. Colombat, 'L'horizon de rétrospection des grammariens de l'*Encyclopédie*', *RDE*, 27:111–52. L. Young-Mock, 'Diderot et la lutte parlementaire au temps de l'*Encyclopédie* (première partie)', *ib.*, 29:45–72; V. Le Ru, 'L'ambivalence de l'idée de progrès dans le *Discours préliminaire* de l'*Encyclopédie* ou le labyrinthe de la raison', *ib.*, 119–28; J. Hæchler and F. Jouffroy-Gauja, 'L'article CERTITUDE de l'*Encyclopédie* commenté par un souscripteur anonyme', *ib.*, 129–48. V. Le Ru, 'L'aigle à deux têtes de l'*Encyclopédie*: accords et divergences de Diderot et d'Alembert de 1751 à 1759', *ib*, 26, 1999:17–26; S. Lojkine, 'Le décentrement matérialiste du champ des connaissances dans l'*Encyclopédie*', *ib.*, 65–84.

3. MONTESQUIEU
(This section covers the year 2000)

WORKS. More volumes of the critical edition of M.'s works are beginning to see the light of day with the publication of *Oeuvres complètes de Montesquieu*, 2, Oxford, Voltaire Foundation, xix + 382 pp. This volume contains *Considérations sur les causes de la grandeur des Romains et de leur décadence*, ed. Françoise Weil and Cecil Courtney, introd. P. Andrivet and C. Volpilhac-Auger, and *Réflexions sur la monarchie universelle en Europe*, ed. Françoise Weil, introd. C. Larrère and F. Weil. *Réflexions sur la monarchie universelle en Europe*, ed. Michel Porret, Geneva, Droz, 126 pp, is a more affordable edition of the *Réflexions*. Both editions provide valuable introductions and other scholarly apparatus. J. Ehrard, 'Les "Œuvres complètes" de Montesquieu', *StV*, 370, 1999:49–55. With the aid of several correspondents, E. examines over 40 of the largest French libraries for editions of M.'s collected works, eventually identifying over 100 such editions. M. Platania, 'Una recente sfida editoriale: la nuova edizione delle *Œuvres Complètes* di Montesquieu', *RSI*, 111, 1999:947–56, comments on the challenges facing the editors of the *OC*.

THOUGHT AND INTELLECTUAL RELATIONSHIPS. R. Runte, 'Montesquieu et La Fontaine: artifice et vérité', *DFS*, 52:57–63, discusses M.'s attitude towards F. and fables. C. Robin, 'Reflections on fear:

Montesquieu in retrieval', *APSR*, 94:347–60, offers a nuanced reading of M.'s theory of despotism, arguing that M.'s apparently one dimensional portrayal of fear was rhetorical; a more in-depth analysis of M.'s writings reveals the multiple faces of fear, and the complicated strategies employed by those who live under it. S. Krause, 'The spirit of separate powers in Montesquieu', *RPol*, 62:231–65, reviews an old question: did M. consider England, with its separation leading to a balance of powers, as an 'ideal regime'. K. argues that while M. clearly had 'no doubts about the merits of the principle of separate powers', nevertheless he questioned just 'how fully and how securely this general principle [was] realized' in the English case. While M.'s readers have noted his ambivalence toward England and its constitution, M.'s concerns have not been fully elaborated. D. Desserud, 'Commerce and political participation in Montesquieu's "Letter to Domville"', *HEI*, 25, 1999:135–51, examines M.'s reply to an inquiry from Domville in which M. outlines his theory of commerce and politics as it pertains to England.

M. McAlpin, 'Between men for all eternity: feminocentrism in Montesquieu's *Lettres persanes*', *ECL*, 24:45–61, makes an unconvincing argument that M.'s 'misogyny' is merely concealed rather than refuted by his portrayal of women in the *LP*. D. Schaub, 'Of believers and barbarians: Montesquieu's enlightened toleration', pp. 225–48 of *Early Modern Skepticism and the Origins of Toleration*, ed. Alan Levine, Lanham–Oxford, Lexington, 1999, vi + 282 pp., discusses M.'s analysis of why some religions are tolerant and others intolerant.

4. ROUSSEAU

WORKS, BIOGRAPHY. *Dialogues de Rousseau juge de Jean-Jacques, suivis de Le Lévite d'Ephraïm*, ed. Erik Leborgne, GF Flammarion, 1999, 539 pp. The introduction and notes, mainly on the former work, link the two through the psychology of paranoia. *Le Lévite d'Ephraïm*, ed. Frédéric S. Eigeldinger, Champion, 1999, 156 pp., includes a draft version alongside the final text. The introduction suggests that the text of 1762 was revised in 1768, and considers the influence of Gessner and the Bible. Rejecting biographical approaches, it perceives the work in terms of R.'s moral and political philosophy (like Wingrove, below.)

Rousseau visité, Rousseau visiteur: les dernières années (1770–1778). Actes du colloque de Genève (21–22 juin 1996), ed. Jacques Berchtold and Michel Porret (*AsocRous*, 42), Geneva, Droz, 532 pp., is a spacious collection and includes: J.-M. Candaux on R.'s last Genevan visitors (21–32); A. Gür on an alleged plot in 1764 (33–51); M. Porret on the drama with Dusaulx (177–207); R. Barny on Deleyre's attempts to reconcile R. and Diderot (253–79); R. Trousson on the visit of the prince de Ligne (237–50); A. Ngendahimana on R. and Bernardin de Saint-Pierre (327–38); J.-C. Bonnet on Mercier (341–50), and B. Baczko on other pilgrims to the shrine of R. at Ermenonville (351–401); R. Monnier on the apotheosis of R. by the Revolution (403–28). Y. Séité looks at R.'s claims (coquettish and false) to have given up on the written word (209–36); B. Didier centres complementarily on R.'s self-representation in the *Dialogues* as a musician, and ultimately as Orpheus (165–75). Y. Citton, 'M. Jacques chez l'ami des hommes. Visite de Rousseau au coeur de l'économisme' (53–73), considers R.'s short stay with Mirabeau in 1767. He shows very nicely, beneath apparent philosophical similarities, the fundamental opposition between R.'s ethos (autarchy and 'pitié') and that of Physiocracy (productivity and rationality; all too familiar today). G. Incorvati examines the 'bio-ethic' implicit in R., opposing Linnaeus to Buffon (281–326). J. Berchtold explores the implicit dimensions of R.'s chess-playing at the *café de la Régence* (95–145). C. Wacjman considers R.'s habitual recourse to a 'tiers', in relation to paranoia (429–44). J. Starobinski, '*Quia non intelligor illis*' (445–517), closes the volume by examining R.'s self-justifications (he is misunderstood by all but himself), with lengthy detours through classical rhetoric and Augustinian moral theology.

THOUGHT AND RECEPTION. Yves Touchefeu, *L'Antiquité et le christianisme dans la pensée de Jean-Jacques Rousseau* (*StV*, 372), Oxford, Voltaire Foundation, 1999, xi + 704 pp., in effect tackles from this angle the classic problem of 'citoyen' versus 'homme'. The book is well researched, with a definite view (finding the binary unresolved), though its breadth makes it rather diffuse. Laurence D. Cooper, *Rousseau, Nature, and the Problem of the Good Life*, University Park, Pennsylvania U.P., 1999, xvi + 223 pp., carefully locates R. and its account of his thought within moral philosophy. The good life is found chiefly in *Emile* (R.'s middle way between collectivism and personal withdrawal). His modern Naturalism emphasises 'original dispositions', which are to be sublimated through conscience and the love of order. Steven Johnston, *Encountering Tragedy: Rousseau and the Project of Democratic Order*, Ithaca–London, Cornell U.P., 1999, xii + 189 pp., examines 'the paradoxes of things political' in R., giving in effect a Nietzschean spin to the topic of tensions and contradictions in his social thought. Margaret Ogrodnick, *Instinct and Intimacy. Political Philosophy and Autobiography in Rousseau*, Toronto U.P., 238 pp., proposes a progressivist synthesis of the psychological (read more through Jung than Freud) and the political in Rousseau. Elizabeth Rose Wingrove, *Rousseau's Republican Romance*, Princeton U.P., xiii + 255 pp., argues (within a US political-feminist-deconstructive frame) that R.'s political philosophy and sexual politics are not opposed. Both offer a model of 'consensual nonconsensuality', i.e. a submission between partners (albeit unequal) that is chosen and maintained through performative negotiation. Nor is this just R.'s compensatory fantasy, for his corporeal language implies real-world reference, and the presentation collapses R.'s own binaries. A dense, clever, and well-written book. P. Hegarty, 'Doubling legitimacy: reading Rousseau's *Contrat social* after Pateman's *Sexual Contract*', *FS*, 53, 1999:292–306. M. di Palma, 'Rousseau's Enlightenment ethics: the synthesis of materialism and morals', *SVEC 2000:05*, 73–227, valuably elucidates, in its period context, the thinking outlined in the title of R.'s abandoned work *La Morale sensitive, ou Le matérialisme du sage*. It is found to be fully compatible in R. with 'an ethics of freedom'.

Etudes Jean-Jacques Rousseau, 10, 1998, entitled 'Spiritualité de Rousseau', contains 11 articles around this topic. Of particular interest are: A. Pintor-Ramos, 'Une théodicée religieuse' (9–28), linking the significance of the neologism (Leibniz, 1710) and R.'s concern with order; M.-H. Cotoni, 'Le "Christianisme" de Rousseau au temps des *Rêveries*' (57–75), which finds R.'s positions no less personal but more anxiously self-centred than 15 years earlier; T. L'Aminot, 'Satori à Vincennes' (105–20), reading R.'s accounts of his 'illumination' in terms of conversion. Among other articles, useful is N. Ben Saad, 'Rousseau et Machiavel' (229–42). (On religion, see too Coz, below p. 145.) *Etudes Jean-Jacques Rousseau*, 11, 1999, entitled 'Rousseau: Economie politique', has articles around this topic (not just this work) by R. Bach, L. Charles and P. Steiner, Y. Citton, P. Rétat, F. Gauthier, and Y. Vargas. The valuable main theme is R.'s thought and Physiocracy (Mirabeau and others) as nascent social science, related back to Montesquieu and forward to the Revolution. Useful among other articles are G. Forni Rosa, 'L'amour impossible: passion et mariage dans *La Nouvelle Héloïse*' (235–42), and A. Cohen, 'Le mal, funeste hasard ou tragique nécessité?' (257–68).

Raymond Trousson, *Jean-Jacques Rousseau jugé par ses contemporains: du 'Discours sur les sciences et les arts' aux 'Confessions'*, Champion, 635 pp., is a monument of scholarship on the contemporary (francophone) reception of each of R.'s works. Gregory Dart, *Rousseau, Robespierre and English Romanticism*, CUP, 1998, 288 pp., follows R.'s English reception from Wollstonecraft to Hazlitt in relation to his (mis)appropriation by the Revolution. Gilbert Py, *Rousseau et les éducateurs: étude sur la fortune des idées pédagogiques de Jean-Jacques Rousseau en France et en Europe au xviiie siècle* (*StV*, 356), Oxford, Voltaire Foundation, 1997, vi + 624 pp., examines informatively the reception of *Emile*, projects for private and public education, the contribution of medicine (vitalism, 'woman'), and the rise of educational literature for children. (On Reception, see also Still, Grogan, below p. 147)

LITERARY. Michèle Crogiez, *Rousseau et le paradoxe*, Champion, 1997, 725 pp., treats its subject very broadly, and provides more of a review than an argument. The bibliography is remarkably comprehensive. Monique Anne Gyalokay, *Rousseau, Northrop Frye et la Bible. Essai de mythocritique*, Champion, 1999, 208 pp., examines R.'s biblical borrowings within four Frygian archetypal categories (Mountain, Garden, Cave, Furnace), and then more generally. Paola Sosso, *Jean-Jacques Rousseau: Imagination, illusions, chimères*, Champion, 1999, 269 pp., is a disappointing treatment of an important topic. J.-F. Perrin, 'Le récit d'enfance du 17e siècle à Rousseau', *DhS*, 30, 1998:211–20. J. Berchtold, 'Jean-Jacques dans le taureau de Phalaris. Mythologisation du moi-victime et modèles d'identités dans *Rousseau juge de Jean-Jacques*', Fest. Böschenstein, 149–64, is a very good piece on self-images of monstrosity in the *Dialogues*. Id., 'La tentation du désert dans *La Nouvelle Héloïse*', *RSH*, 258:207–31, examines the motif of the 'île'. Id., 'L'impossible virginité du jardin verbal. Les leçons de la nature selon la Lettre IV, 11, de *La Nouvelle Héloïse*', pp. 53–83 of *Le Rousseauisme, Evangile de la Nature*, ed. Peter Söring, Berne, Lang, 1999, questions whether either the garden or the writing can be 'natural'. *DhS*, 29, 1997, on the theme of wine, includes M. Crogiez, 'L'éloge du vin chez Rousseau: entre franchise et salubrité' (185–97), on wine and water; and E. Fougère, 'Le vin dans *La Nouvelle Héloïse*: "in vino veritas"' (199–210), on wine and truth.

Jean-Jacques Rousseau et la lecture (StV, 369), ed. Tanguy L'Aminot, Oxford, Voltaire Foundation, 1999, vii + 360 pp., is in fact a rather heterogeneous collection. G. Johnston, 'Rousseau et la critique moderne' (293–307), nicely reviews the successive critical moments of Burgelin, Starobinski, Derrida, and De Man. F. Bocquentin, 'Comment lire J.-J. Rousseau selon J.-J.Rousseau?' (329–49), is very good on R.'s instructions to his own reader. C. Kelly, 'Taking readers as they are: Rousseau's turn from discourses to novels', *ECS*, 33, 1999:85–101, argues that R. makes a generic shift in the later 1750s from philosophy and theatre (*La Mort de Lucrèce*) to prose fiction, to offer a message that is more modestly reformist and more accessible. L. Mall, 'D'Homère à Fénelon à Rousseau: les problèmes du modèle dans le Livre V d'*Emile*', *SFr*, 127, 1999:30–43, points to the fictional mediations and ideal aspirations within which R. enmeshes himself and Emile in Book V (but neglects to note that 'Sophie' herself begins as the Tutor's prophylactic fiction for Emile, in Book IV). W. Ray, 'Rethinking reading: the novel and cultural stratification', *EcentF*, 10, 1998:151–70, seeks to build a very broad argument on the basis of 'reading paradigms' in the reflexive Second Preface to *Julie* and the visible manipulation of Emile. S. Herbold, 'Rousseau's dance of veils: the *Confessions* and the imagined woman reader', *ECS*, 32, 1999:333–53, ambitiously argues that R.'s theoretical binaries (notably public/private, male/female, prescriptive/experiential) are flirtatiously destabilized in his 'more fictional texts'.

Philippe Lefebvre, *L'Esthétique de Rousseau* (Collection Esthétique), SEDES, 1997, 219 pp., presents R.'s positions on music and literature, in an introduction (100 pp.) and an anthology (100 pp.), with no strong interpretative line. J.-C. Rebejkow, 'Rousseau et l'opéra-comique: les raisons d'un rejet', *RR*, 89, 1998:161–85, frames R.'s *Devin du village* and *Pygmalion* within contemporary philosophies of musical theatre. P. Stewart, 'Traduire le roman du 18e siècle', *DhS*, 30, 1998:221–31, centres on his 1997 translation with Jean Vaché of *Julie*.

SEXUAL POLITICS. (See also Hegarty, Wingrove, above.) Paule Adamy, *Les Corps de Jean-Jacques Rousseau*, Champion, 1997, 672 pp., is actually about R.'s 'imaginaire érotique', which is seen as tending to sado-masochism and homosexuality. It offers remarkable assemblages of quotations from R. and the period, but lacks modern theoretical or critical reference. Michel Coz, *La Cène et l'autre scène: Désir et profession de foi chez Jean-Jacques Rousseau*, Champion, 1998, 318 pp., offers a modified Oedipal reading of faith and desire. R.'s refusal of the Incarnation and of mediation generally leaves him guilty, feminized, and dependent on the Father. However through fiction (*Julie*) he is able to break down the father-figure. B. Weltman-Aron, 'Educating girls: Rousseau's Sophi(e)stry', *StV*, 362:41–53, finds R.'s positions in Book 5 of *Emile* objectionable but also self-contradictory. C. Roulston, 'Separating the inseparables: female friendship and its discontents in Eighteenth-Century France', *ECS*, 32, 1998:215–31, looks at the male treatment of women's friendship (ambivalence, disruption, confinement) in *Julie*, the *Lettre à d'Alembert*, and the *Liaisons dangereuses*, and notes the abuse directed at Marie-Antoinette. Christine Roulston, **Virtue, Gender, and the Authentic Self in Eighteenth-Century Fiction: Richardson, Rousseau, and Laclos*, Gainesville, Florida U.P., 1998, xx + 211 pp. J. Still, 'The re-working of *La Nouvelle Héloïse* in Genlis's *Mademoiselle de Clermont*', *FSB*, 77:7–11, links usefully with her 'Genlis's *Mademoiselle de Clermont*: a textual and intertextual reading', *AJFS*, 37:331–47. C. Grogan, 'The politics of seduction in British fiction of the 1790s: the female reader and *Julie ou La Nouvelle Héloïse*', *EcentF*, 11, 1998–99:459–76, examines four of the many works by British women in the 1790s which incorporate in various ways R.'s novel. Elena Pulcini, *Amour-passion et amour conjugal. Rousseau et l'origine d'un conflit moderne*, Champion, 1998, 260 pp. This study tries to read *Julie* in terms of a conflict between 'passion' and marriage understood as 'autoconservation'; and also to map on to this binary many other dimensions (including R.'s own preference for fantasy, historical changes, Freud and Lacan). Claude Habib, *Le Consentement amoureux. Rousseau, les femmes et la cité*, Hachette, 1998, 296 pp., uses R. (*Emile* Book 5, *Julie*) in support of a modern polemic favouring heterosexuality, love, and a consent to order.

5. VOLTAIRE

WORKS. The new critical edition of V.'s works, now under the general editorship of Haydn Mason, continues apace with the appearance of several volumes, here listed by order of volume number: *Œuvres de 1728–1730* (Œuvres complètes de Voltaire, 5), Oxford, Voltaire Foundation, 1998, xxvi + 638 pp., contains *Brutus, tragédie*, ed. John Renwick, *Eriphyle, tragédie*, ed. Robert Niklaus, *Harangue prononcée le jour de la clôture du théâtre*, ed. Robert Niklaus, *La Mort de mademoiselle Lecouvreur*, ed. Robert Niklaus, *Du suicide ou de l'homicide de soi-même*, ed. Ahmad Gunny, and *Poésies 1728–1730*, ed. Nicole Masson. *Œuvres de 1732–1733* (Œuvres complètes de Voltaire, 9), Oxford, Voltaire Foundation, 1999, xxv + 531 pp., contains *Le Temple de l'amitié*, ed. O. R. Taylor, *Le Temple du goût*, ed. O. R. Taylor, *La Mule du pape*, ed. Sylvain Menant, *Epître sur la calomnie*, ed. D. J. Fletcher, *Lettre à un premier commis*, ed. Pierre Rétat, *La Vie de Molière, avec de petits sommaires de ses pièces*, ed. Samuel S. B. Taylor, and *Poésies de 1732–1733*, ed. Nicole Masson and Sylvain Menant. *Anecdotes sur le czar Pierre le Grand*, ed. Michel Mervaud, and the *Première partie* of *Histoire de l'empire de Russie sous Pierre le Grand*, ed. Michel Mervaud with the collaboration of Ulla Kölving, Christiane Mervaud, and Andrew Brown, along with its continuation volume containing the *Deuxième partie* of *Histoire de l'empire de Russie sous Pierre le Grand* (Œuvres complètes de Voltaire, 46–47), 2 vols, Oxford, Voltaire Foundation, 1999, xxxi + 1–699, 700–1338 pp., represents a monumental editorial enterprise. *Œuvres de 1762 (*II) (Œuvres complètes de Voltaire, 56B), ed. Robert Granderoute, Oxford, Voltaire Foundation, xvi + 384 pp., after a very substantial general introduction entitled 'Voltaire et l'affaire Calas', contains (i) *Pièces originales concernant la mort des sieurs Calas et le jugement rendu à Toulouse*, (ii) *A monseigneur le chancelier. Requête au roi en son conseil*, (iii) *Mémoire de Donat Calas pour son père, sa mère, et son frère*, and (iv) *Histoire d'Elisabeth Canning et de Jean Calas*. The *Traité sur la tolérance* (Œuvres complètes de Voltaire, 56C), ed. John Renwick, Oxford, Voltaire Foundation, xxviii + 365 pp., reflecting the meticulous scholarship and enormous utility of all these volumes, appears at a timely moment, given the great deal of recent interest in this text. *Œuvres de 1768 (*II) (Œuvres complètes de Voltaire, 66),

Oxford, Voltaire Foundation, 1999, xix + 801 pp., contains *La Princesse de Babylone*, ed. Jacqueline Hellegouarc'h, *L'Homme aux quarante écus*, ed. Brenda M. Bloesch, *Avertissement de l'édition du théâtre de 1768*, ed. W. S. Rogers, *Les Guèbres*, ed. John Renwick, *Les Deux tonneaux, esquisse d'opéra comique*, ed. R. J. V. Cotte, *Le Baron d'Otrante, opéra buffa*, ed. R. J. V. Cotte, and *Le Marseillois et le lion*, ed. Sylvain Menant. *Mémoires pour servir à la vie de M. de Voltaire, écrits par lui-même, ed. Jacqueline Hellegouarc'h, Librairie générale française, 1998, 288 pp.

THOUGHT AND INFLUENCE. *Etudes sur le 'Traité sur la tolérance' de Voltaire*, ed. Nicholas Cronk, Oxford, Voltaire Foundation, vi + 324 pp., is a wide-ranging collection of accessible articles. The contents are: R. Pomeau, 'La "Prière à Dieu": théisme et tolérance' (1–6); H. T. Mason, 'La tolérance chez Locke, Bayle et Voltaire: fausses influences?' (7–11); C. Volpilhac-Auger, 'Saint Socrate, ou la tolérance selon les Grecs' (12–22); G. Gargett, 'Voltaire, les protestants et le protestantisme, avant et dans le *Traité sur la tolérance* (23–33); A.-M. Mercier-Faivre, 'Le *Traité sur la tolérance*, tolérance et réécriture' (34–55); R. Granderoute, 'L'affaire Calas, les mémoires voltairiens et le *Traité sur la tolérance*' (56–67); H. Bost and C. Lauriol, 'L'affaire Calas d'après les lettres de La Condamine à La Beaumelle' (68–84); J. Dagen, 'Rousseau, Voltaire et la composition du *Traité sur la tolérance*' (85–101); J.-M. Moureaux, 'D'une lecture préparatoire au *Traité sur la tolérance* . . .' (102–19); N. Cronk, 'Comment lire le *Traité sur la tolérance*?: la présentation typographique de l'édition Cramer' (120–35); S. Menant, 'Le titre et le genre du *Traité sur la tolérance*' (136–49); F. Bessire, ' "Très court, et un peu salé": forme et composition du *Traité sur la tolérance*' (150–58); C. Mervaud, 'Fonction et signification des notes de Voltaire dans le *Traité sur la tolérance*'(159–73); M.-H. Cotoni, 'Ambivalences et ambiguïtés dans le *Traité sur la tolérance*' (174–90); C. Seth, 'Voltaire pragmatique: l'argent dans le *Traité sur la tolérance*' (191–204); J. Vercruysse, 'La leçon hollandaise' (205–13); F. Jacob, 'Mon frère le Chinois? La Chine dans le *Traité sur la tolérance*' (214–23); M. Delon, 'Le Mourant et le Barbare' (224–29). J. Renwick has contributed an 'Essai bibliographique' (230–47), summarising 34 key books and articles, mostly published over the last two or three decades, on the *Traité*, the *affaire Calas* and contemporary debates on tolerance and intolerance. A final *dossier* makes available a number of related writings including extracts on tolerance from the *Dictionnaire philosophique* and *Questions sur l'Encyclopédie*. Valérie van Crugten-André, *Le 'Traité sur la tolérance' de Voltaire: un champion des Lumières contre le fanatisme*, Paris, Champion — Geneva, Slatkine, 1999, 187 pp., provides, in its first half, a concise introduction to issues relevant to the text, including V.'s attitudes to religion and the historical background against which the *affaire Calas* arose, and, in the second half, a commentary on the text itself. François Bessire, *La Bible dans la correspondance de Voltaire* (*StV*, 367), Oxford, Voltaire Foundation, 1999, vii + 346 pp., is an exhaustive cataloguing and analysis of the almost 3,000 biblical quotations, references and allusions (as opposed to the approximately 700 noted by Besterman) in V.'s letters. Discussion focuses on their all-pervasiveness, the wit and irony with which V. manipulates them, his negative attitude to the Bible as literature, and the evidence of his extensive knowledge of biblical criticism. V.'s use of the Bible is not only characterized by a 'refus du sacré', in his hands it becomes a weapon against religion.

Stephen Bird, *Reinventing Voltaire: The Politics of Commemoration in Nineteenth-Century France* (SVEC 2000:09), Oxford, Voltaire Foundation, xii + 224 pp., is a fascinating and detailed account of the politicization of V.'s legacy between 1830 and 1900, with particular reference to the 1867 campaign for the first open-air statue of V. and on the circumstances surrounding various subsequent displays of his effigy; to working-class editions and their readership; and to the uses to which his person and works were put in the classroom. Over the period in question V.'s legacy was tirelessly reinvented in a variety of causes. On the same general theme of commemoration, M.-L. Chastang, 'Voltairiana', *EFL*, 35–36, 1998–99:50–68, documents some of the many pronouncements made on V., and ways in which he has been commemorated, between his death and the 1944 celebration of the 250th anniversary of his birth. *StV*, 358, 1997, includes T. E. D. Braun, 'Voltaire, *Zadig, Candide*, and chaos' (1–20), a discussion of these *contes* in terms of chaos theory, emphasizing among other things their non-linearity and the centrality of questioning in them; S. Ben Messaoud, 'Trois lettres de Voltaire à Lemierre' (21–25), a presentation, with critical apparatus, of three letters from the period 1759–64 from a benevolent V. to the young dramatist; and B. E. Schwarzbach, 'Voltaire et les Juifs: bilan et plaidoyer' (27–91), a wide-ranging exploration of V.'s knowledge of and attitudes towards the Jews and Judaism, concluding that, although he failed to understand them, he explicitly rejected Christian antisemitism. R. Wokler, 'Pistols for two and coffee for one! Rekindling Voltaire's and Rousseau's quarrel in footnotes', *StV*, 362, 1998:1–10, is an entertaining account of the way in which Theodore Besterman and Ralph Leigh, editors respectively of V.'s and Rousseau's correspondence, replicated the quarrels that animated the relationship of their 18th-c. heroes. *StV*, 371, 1999, includes M. S. Rivière, 'Voltaire, reader of women's memoirs: "The difference of value"' (23–52), an examination of V.'s inconsistent and ultimately

biased attitude towards women memorialists whose work he nevertheless incorporated into his own historical writings; and N. Cronk, 'The
epicurean spirit: champagne and the defence of poetry in Voltaire's
Le Mondain' (53–80), in which the author demonstrates that V.'s poem
is not only a defence of secularity and luxury but also, in the context
of the 'querelle des vers', a defence of poetry, itself a form of luxury.
SVEC 2000:05 contains six pieces on Voltaire. J.-J. Robrieux,
'Oppositions d'idées et réfutation dans le *Traité sur la tolérance*. Etude
rhétorico-argumentative' (11–27), studies the rhetoric of the *Traité*
including V.'s use of antithesis and the different types of argument
employed in his refutations of the Bible and Christian tradition; J.-M.
Moureaux, 'Un épisode inconnu de la querelle Voltaire-Needham'
(29–45), argues from the evidence of letters written by Needham that
he was the author of the spirited annotations in a copy of V.'s *Idées
républicaines* believed to have belonged to him. R. Laplace, 'Autour de
la création d'*Irène*' (47–51), some notebook observations of the actor
and writer Jacques-Marie Boutet [Monvel] on changes made to the
text of *Irène* deemed necessary by friends of Voltaire on the occasion
of its *première*. E. M. Langille, 'Allusions to homosexuality in Voltaire's
Candide: a reassessment' (53–63), identifies possible and hitherto
unrecognised allusions, notably 'l'exercice bulgarien', and suggests
that Candide has a 'central place in the tale's homosexual sub-plot'
(57). Links are made between subtle allusions here and more direct
and biting references in V.'s posthumously published *Mémoires*. S. Ben
Massaoud, 'La succession de Voltaire: l'abstention de l'abbé Mignot'
(65–72), presents and reproduces in facsimile the 'acte d'abstention'
whereby l'abbé Mignot, V.'s nephew and one of his legatees,
renounced his right to his inheritance. R. Goulbourne, 'The eighteenth-century "querelle des vers" and Jean Du Castre d'Auvigny's
La Tragédie en prose' (371–410), reconstructs the debate between V. and
La Motte on whether tragedy should be written in prose or verse, and
presents, with an edition of the text, d'Auvigny's one-act comedy
inspired by the debate. Serguë Karp, **Quand Catherine II achetait la
bibliothèque de Voltaire*, Ferney-Voltaire, CIEDS, 1999, 74 pp.
D. Droixhe, 'A la recherche du *Candide* liégeois', *AJFS*, 37:127–64,
constructs an extensive and intricate body of evidence to identify an
early pirated edition of *Candide* as having been printed in Liège. Ling-
Ling Sheu, 'Sur les *Lettres chinoises, indiennes et tartares* de Voltaire',
RHLF, 2:305–09, is a note on the genesis and publication of this
work, appearing pseudonymously in 1776. S. Pierse, 'Limiers and
Voltaire: historical games', *SVEC 2000:08*, 203–09, after considering
some references to games in texts of the late 17th and 18th cs, focuses
on Limiers's references to the war games of Louis XIV, and on V.'s
use of the chess motif in the *Histoire de Charles XII*.

Voltaire en Europe: Hommage à Christiane Mervaud, ed. M. Delon and
C. Seth, Oxford, Voltaire Foundation, xxii + 383 pp., is a splendid
volume on a theme of capital interest, bringing together 32 articles.
G. Barber, 'Voltaire et Oxford. Esquisse rapide d'un intérêt vieux de
deux siècles et demi' (3–11), includes information about the Bodleian
Library's early holdings of works by V. and the appearance of his
works on 19th and early 20th-c. Oxford syllabi. N. Cronk, 'Voltaire
rencontre Monsieur le Spectateur. Addison et la genèse des *Lettres
anglaises*' (13–21), argues convincingly that V. drew inspiration from
Addison and the *Spectator* as regards both source material and the
cultivation of a certain prose style. H. T. Mason, 'Voltaire Européen
naissant et l'Angleterre' (23–31), explores V.'s reasons for going to
England and discusses his friendship with Bolingbroke and Fawkener.
M. Mervaud, 'Voltaire et le tsarévitch immolé' (33–56), examines
V.'s judgements, in the *Anecdotes sur le czar Pierre le Grand* and then in
the *Histoire de l'empire de Russie sous Pierre le Grand*, on the conflict
between the great reforming czar and his son Alexis, which ended in
the latter's death. J. Renwick, 'Voltaire, William Duncombe et la
traduction de *Brutus*' (57–75), advances the hypothesis that Duncombe, in translating V.'s *Brutus*, was directly influenced by V. himself, particularly as concerns the *dénouement*, which, in the English
version, is more violent than V. may have judged acceptable for the
French stage. R. Virolle, 'Voltaire et les "nouveaux Argonautes"
(1769–1772)' (77–92), reviews the correspondence between V. and
Catherine II relating to Russia's naval combats against Turkey.
D. Williams, 'William Mickle et Voltaire. A la recherche de Camões'
(93–103), discusses the hostile critique of V.'s comments on Camões
in *An essay upon the epick poetry* made by Mickle, Camões's 16th-c.
Scottish translator. P. Zaborov, 'Vassili Ipatovitch Polianski, l'ami
oublié de Voltaire' (105–10), traces the fortunes of a Russian protégé
of Catherine to whom V. played host at Ferney. G. Artigas-Menant,
'"D'un bout de l'Europe à l'autre". La circulation clandestine des
"ouvrages hardis"' (113–23), attempts to unravel the complexities
surrounding V.'s use of the names and clandestine works of a host of
minor writers against fanaticism, as part of his campaign to crush
'l'infâme'. M.-H. Cotoni, 'Présence de Voltaire dans la correspondance de Frédéric II avec l'élite intellectuelle européenne' (125–41),
focuses on the three decades following the rupture between Frederick
and V., charting the fluctuations in Frederick's attitude. R. Granderoute, 'L'Europe et le droit pénal à travers le *Prix de la justice et de
l'humanité* (1777)' (143–50), shows how V.'s essay exposed the extent
to which civil and religious laws were intertwined and cruel penalties
available, painting a dark picture against which England stood out
for its more enlightened approach. J. Hellegouarc'h, 'Une clef de

Candide. Cunégonde de Prusse' (151–57), convincingly identifies
Amelia of Prussia, sister of Frederick II, and Frederick as models
respectively for Cunégonde and the baron her brother. G. Laudin,
'De Sélis aux *Mémoires secrets*. L'intertextualité satirique dans la farce
de H. L. Wagner, *Voltaire au soir de son apothéose*' (159–72), presents the
German dramatist H. L. Wagner's one-act play of 1778 in relation to
other contemporary writings also less than flattering to Voltaire.
C. Lauriol, 'La Beaumelle, l'affaire Calas et le *Traité sur la tolérance*'
(173–80), documents the role of the Huguenot lawyer La Beaumelle,
an adversary of V.'s, who nevertheless worked clandestinely in
defence of the Calas family and whose writings may well have left
their mark on the *Traité*. S. Menant, 'Vu de Londres, vu de Hambourg,
le Voltaire de Rivarol' (195–206), discusses Rivarol's appraisal of
V. in his *Pensées diverses* which, written in the last years of the 18th c.,
purport to establish V.'s limitations as well as his greatness. R. Mortier, 'Le capucin indigne et frère Ganganelli, ou Voltaire et le pape
Clément XIV' (207–16), outlines V.'s favourable attitude to Clement
XIV, whom he judged more moderate than his predecessors. U. van
Runset, 'Voltaire et l'Académie. Emulation et instrument socio-
politique' (217–29), outlines V.'s relations with learned societies,
particularly the *Académie française* and the Berlin Academy. C. Volpilhac-Auger, 'Voltaire invente l'Amérique' (231–39), shows how V. in
his *Essai sur les moeurs* provides an arresting account of the discovery
of America through his presentation of Columbus, Cortes, and
Pizarro as emblematic figures. W. Barber, 'Voltaire and natural
science: from apples to fossils' (243–54), discusses, against the
background of V.'s Newtonianism, his attitudes to geological and
biological controversies, the latter stimulated in particular by the
work of Joseph Needham. F. Bessire, 'Entre poètes. La poésie dans la
correspondance entre Voltaire et le prince royal de Prusse
(1736–1740)' (263–71), dubs the 126 letters exchanged between
V. and Frederick during the period in question 'un cours par
correspondance', both practical and theoretical, in poetry; more than
one third of the letters refer to *La Henriade*. J. Dagen, 'De la
contradiction selon Voltaire' (273–81), illustrates V.'s rejection of
dualistic modes of thought. M. Delon, ' "Convulsions de l'inquiétude"
ou "léthargie de l'ennui". Variations autour d'un thème voltairien'
(283–90), discerns in the Revolutionary period and early Romanticism echoes and variations of V.'s formulation in *Candide*, attributed
to Martin, that humankind is caught between 'l'inquiétude' and
'l'ennui'. É. Guitton, 'Une singularité bibliographique et littéraire.
Les *Contes de Guillaume Vadé* (1764) ou Voltaire et l'impact vadéen'
(291–97), sees in the contents of this collection, first published
pseudonymously by V. and later broken up and in some cases

published with other of his works, evidence of an identity crisis on
V.'s part. G. Haroche-Bouzinac, 'Voltaire et ses images dans la
correspondance' (299–306), catalogues the wide range of images that
V. proposes for himself in his correspondence and his attitude to
representations of himself, including his statue by Pigalle. A. Magnan,
'Une lettre oubliée de Beaumarchais sur l'édition de Kehl et sur la
genèse de *Candide*' (307–19), reproduces the text of a letter by
Beaumarchais, published in 1799, and indicates the light that it sheds
on early efforts to assemble V.'s correspondence after his death, as
well as a glimpse that it gives of the existence of a 'correspondance
piquante' between V. and the duc de La Vallière as a backdrop to the
composition of *Candide*. F. Moureau, 'Dans les coulisses de *Samson*.
Voltaire et le nouvelliste' (321–29), draws attention to the reporting
in informal gazettes of incidents in V.'s early career, with particular
reference to the reporting of an early version of *Samson*. J.-M.
Moureaux, 'Voltaire et Saint-Evrémond' (331–43), asserts that, while
V.'s negative appraisal of Saint-Evrémond in the *Temple du goût* was
somewhat tempered in later pronouncements, he steadfastly refused
to recognise him as a worthy precursor of himself in matters of
philosophy. J. Pappas, 'Voltaire et le problème du mal' (345–51), is
the translation from English of an article which first appeared in 1963
in *L'Esprit créateur* and which argues that, long after *Candide*, V. continued to seek a solution to the problem of evil in philosophical
optimism. C. Seth, 'Épaves et trésors cachés. Les Voltaire de la
bibliothèque de Cideville' (353–62), details those volumes of Voltaire's works now available in the Bibliothèque municipale de Rouen.
J. Vercruysse, 'Le prince et le hibou philosophe. A propos d'une lettre
défigurée du prince de Ligne à Voltaire' (363–68), presents, with
variants, the text of a 1776 letter in verse from the Prince de Ligne to
V. and argues that the variants of the version in the *Correspondance
littéraire* are not authentic and distort the intention of the original.
A. McKenna, 'L'abbé de Saint-Pierre et la critique du moralisme
augustinien' (181–94), sees in the anti-augustinianism of the abbé
(whose critique of Pascal, La Rochefoucauld, Bayle, and Mandeville
he reproduces) a utilitarianism that foreshadows that of the *Lettres
philosophiques*.

LITERARY.   (See also above THOUGHT AND INFLUENCE.) *L'Invitation
au voyage: Studies in honour of Peter France*, ed. John Renwick, Oxford,
Voltaire Foundation, xx + 325 pp., includes three articles on Voltaire.
W. H. Barber, 'Voltaire: travel and travellers' tales' (65–74), documents the comparatively limited nature of V.'s own travels and traces
the uses to which he put the theme of travel in his fiction. N. Cronk,
'Voltaire, Lucian, and the philosophical traveller' (75–84), analyses
the influence on V's fiction of two of Lucian's dialogues which

incorporate fantastic journeys, *Icaromenippus* and *A true story*. R. Howells, 'Universal grotesque: Voltaire's *Histoire des voyages de Scarmentado*' (103–10), outlines the pattern and meaning of the barbaric public rituals experienced across three continents by the eponymous hero of V.'s *conte*. N. Masson, 'Voltaire et ses rogatons', *StV*, 370, 1999:41–47, discusses V.'s attitude to his very early poems and defends their inclusion in the canon of his works.

THEATRE. (See also above THOUGHT AND INFLUENCE.) Marvin Carlson, *Voltaire and the Theatre of the Eighteenth Century* (Lives of the Theatre), Westport, Greenwood, 1998, xvii + 186 pp., in a series designed to provide introductions to important periods in the history of world theatre, is a clear, lively and panoramic account organized along biographical lines. R. Goulbourne, 'Gender trouble: identity games in Voltaire's *La Prude*', *SVEC 2000:08*, 195–202, invokes game theory in an analysis of disguise and gender confusion in V.'s play.

6. PROSE FICTION

GENERAL. Thomas A. Beebee, *Epistolary Fiction in Europe 1500–1850*, CUP, 1999, x + 277 pp. makes much reference — not surprisingly — to letter novels from 18th-c. France. Goodden, *Memory*, centres on the 18th c. (the rise of individualism and interiority), with chapters on Marivaux and Prévost, Crébillon, Duclos and Louvet, Diderot, and Rousseau. Shirley Jones Day, *The Search for Lyonesse. Women's Fiction in France 1670–1703*, Berne, Lang, 1999, 340 pp., includes sections on the novels of d'Aulnoy and of her contemporaries Catherine Bernard and Mlle de La Force. E. Zawisza, 'Ces titres qui parlaient femme: l'intitulation au féminin dans les romans des Lumières', *DFS*, 47:61–74, offers statistics from her substantial database of title-pages, and interpretation. Pierre Hartmann, *Le Contrat et la séduction: essai sur la subjectivité amoureuse dans le roman des Lumières*, Champion, 1998, 469 pp., finds in the period's fiction a new form of subjectivity, depicted in interpersonal relations of amorous understanding or deception. Chapters follow on Marivaux, Crébillon, Richardson, Rousseau, Laclos, Sade, and Rétif. This is a curiously laborious book from such an able critic. Jenny Mander, *Circles of Learning: Narratology and the Eighteenth-Century French Novel* (*StV*, 366), Oxford, Voltaire Foundation, 1999, viii + 232 pp., challenges the modern view that the mode of first-person fiction is individualizing and destabilizing, on a variety of grounds: a conceptual and historical critique of biases in narratology; layering in the texts (chiefly of the 1730s); and contemporary instructions for reading.

Le Roman des années trente: la génération de Prévost et de Marivaux, ed. Annie Rivara and Antony McKenna, Saint-Etienne U.P., 1998,

167 pp., includes the following articles: C. Cazenobe, 'La parodie de *Manon* et de *Cleveland* dans les *Aventures du Chevalier de Beauchêne*' (9–25), a careful analysis of Lesage's parodic 1732 novel; M. Gilot, 'L'émotion autobiographique dans deux romans des années 1730' (27–36), a discussion of Prévost's *Cleveland* and Marivaux's *La Vie de Marianne*; C. Labrosse, '*Manon Lescaut*: le désir, la fiction et la fable' (37–47), a re-examination of the representation of love in Prévost's novel; H. Duranton, 'Ce que chuchote une demi-bouteille de vin de Bourgogne: Marivaux moraliste et romancier' (49–62), a discussion of Marivaux the social commentator and the portrayer of 'le réel' (objects, language, the body) in his fiction; G. Goubier, 'Le roman des années trente: les premiers illusionnistes' (63–75), a consideration of how novelists of the 1730s foreshadow the aesthetics of the 19th c.; R. Granderoute, 'Fiction et philosophie dans *Sethos*' (77–86), a sensitive reading of the abbé Terrasson's 1731 pedagogical novel; C. Dornier, 'Préfaces et intentions d'auteur' (87–101), a consideration of how the prefaces to Prévost's *Mémoires d'un homme de qualité* and Crébillon *fils*'s *Les Égarements du cœur et de l'esprit* announce their respective author's aesthetic agendas; J. Herman, 'Manuscrit trouvé et interdiction du roman' (103–18), a wide-ranging and well-informed account of how novelists tried to circumvent official opposition to their work; J. Mander, 'Téléphone arabe: la nature discursive du roman des années trente' (119–30), a subtle examination of the relationship between first-person narrative and the autobiographical form, highlighting the paradoxical status of the prefaces to novels in the 1730s; R. Jomand-Baudry, 'Signification des notes auctoriales dans la fiction orientale du début des années 1730' (131–43), an enlightening analysis of fictional footnotes; N. Ferrand, 'Que lisent les personnages dans le roman des années trente? Un catalogue des bibliothèques romanesques (1728–1740)' (145–60), a fascinating and scholarly examination of the role of real and imaginary books within novels.

Folies romanesques au siècle des Lumières, ed. René Démoris and Henri Lafon, Desjonquères, 1998, 417 pp., notably embraces follies, quix-otic, passionate, and authorial. It contains: R. Démoris and H. Lafon, 'Présentation' (9–15); R. Howells, 'Statut du romanesque: l'opposi-tion *roman/histoire* dans la pratique signifiante de 1635 à 1785' (19–39); G. Hautcoeur, 'De la folie quichottesque à la folie de l'intériorité' (40–57); J.-J. Tatin-Gourier, 'Les mises-en-scène de la folie dans *Le Diable boiteux* de Le Sage' (58–64); F. Rubellin, 'Folie narrative et raison romanesque dans *La Voiture embourbée*' (65–81); J.-P. Sermain, 'Le testament de Don Quichotte' (82–100); M. Cortey, 'Du boudoir aux petites maisons: la courtisane hystérique' (103–15); E. Leborgne, 'Folie et pulsion de mort dans les romans de Prévost: le

cas de *Clèveland* et des *Campagnes philosophiques*' (116–31); Y. Salaün,
'Folie et infanticide dans le roman sensible: Prévost, Baculard,
Fauque' (132–53); M. Bokobza-Kahan, 'De la normalité à la
transgression dans l'*Histoire de Madame la Comtesse de Montglas* de
Carné' (154–64); C. Dornier, 'Raconter la folie: les recueils de *Folies
sentimentales* (1786)' (165–84); P. Hartmann, 'La démence d'Edmond:
folie et communauté dans *Le Paysan et la Paysanne pervertis*' (187–98);
M. Moser-Verrey, 'Tableaux de la folle sagesse dans *Caliste* d'Isabelle
de Charrière' (199–213); D. Masseau, 'Les folles par amour dans le
roman français à la veille de la Révolution' (214–24); K. Bénac,
'Vérité de soi et folie romanesque: *L'Indigent philosophe*, enfant du
baroque?' (227–36); F. Magnot, 'De la folie aveugle à la folie
spectacle: double registre et théâtralité dans les *Mémoires et aventures
d'un homme de qualité* et dans *Clèveland* de l'abbé Prévost' (237–51);
E. Bordas, 'La folie du romanesque dans *Histoire de la jeunesse du
commandeur*' (252–72); A. Gaillard, '*Le Chef-d'oeuvre d'un inconnu* de
Thémiseul de Saint-Hyacinthe (1714): folie raisonnante' (275–93);
J.-F. Perrin, 'Féerie et folie selon Crébillon' (294–304); M. Brunet,
'*Lamekis* de Mouhy ou la tentation de l'illisible' (305–17); M. Nuel,
'Folies paratextuelles dans le roman de la seconde moitié du xviiie
siècle' (318–28); B. Kaech-Toumarkine, '*Châteaux en Espagne*: folie
contagieuse et écriture romanesque de Malebranche à Condillac'
(331–50); A. Rivara, 'Savoir délirant et encyclopédie détraquée:
figures du savant fou dans *Le Prince Rasselas* de Johnson et le *Compère
Matthieu* de Du Laurens' (351–64); C. Martin, 'Belle captive en
enfance: dérives d'un topos littéraire dans les *Mémoires de deux amis* de
Henri-François de La Solle' (365–79); R. Démoris, 'La folie Jean-
Jacques' (380–97); H. Lafon, 'Le délire et la feinte: Fromaget, Dorat,
Loaisel, Louvet, Cottin' (398–407). The collection ends with a
bibliography of criticism, and a descriptive checklist of relevant
primary works from 1674 to 1804.

INDIVIDUAL AUTHORS

GRAFFIGNY. *Correspondance de Mme de Graffigny, vol. 5*, ed. Judith
Curtis, Oxford, Voltaire Foundation, 1997, xix + 578 pp., covers
January-October 1744; *vol. 6*, ed. Pierre Bouillaguet, Judith Curtis,
and J. A. Dainard, Oxford, Voltaire Foundation, xix + 638 pp.,
covers October 1744–September 1745. This is a monumental and
exemplary edition. Vol. 5 includes G.'s only surviving letter to her
great love, Desmarest (a bitter missive); Vol. 6 ends with notable early
references to the drafting and planning of the future *Péruvienne*.
S. Cornand, 'Le corps exhibé: les propos sur la santé dans la
correspondance de Mme. de Graffigny', *StV*, 362, 1999:93–107,

examines the copious material in G.'s letters of 1743 to Devaux. G. Bérubé, 'Mme de Graffigny à Cirey: écrire pour exister "par procuration"', Silver, *Épistolières*, 23–32; V. L. Grayson, 'Ecrire son identité: la genèse des *Lettres d'une Péruvienne*', *ib.*, 33–40. R. L. Mesch, 'Did women have an Enlightenment? Graffigny's Zilia as female philosopher', *RR*, 89, 1998:523–37, finds that 'Zilia is a feminist writer', but is a little more original on the defamiliarization of verbal language. S. Davies, '*Lettres d'une Péruvienne*, 1977–1997: the present state of studies', *SVEC 2000:05*, 295–324, performs a very necessary service by surveying the huge recent critical output on G.'s novel.

LE PRINCE DE BEAUMONT. Jeanne Marie Le Prince de Beaumont, *Contes et autres écrits*, ed. Barbara Kaltz (Vif), Oxford, Voltaire Foundation, xxiii + 192 pp., includes extracts from Le P. de B.'s pioneering works on ladies's education, and provides substantial introductions detailing their European diffusion. Marie-Jeanne Le Prince de Beaumont, **Civan, Roi de Bungo, Histoire japonaise, ou Tableau de l'éducation d'un prince*, ed. Alix Deguise, Slatkine, 1999, 487 pp.

MARIVAUX. Michel Gilot, *L'Esthétique de Marivaux* (Collection Esthétique) SEDES, 1998, 303 pp., offers a lucid account of M.'s ideas on literature and his role in the *Querelle des anciens et des modernes*, combining critical discussion of all aspects of M.'s theory and practice (7–216) with a useful anthology of the most pertinent texts (217–88). Jean-Paul Sermain, *Le Singe de Don Quichotte: Marivaux, Cervantes et le roman postcritique* (*StV*, 368), Oxford, Voltaire Foundation, 1999, vi + 288 pp., considers M.'s three early burlesque prose fictions, *Pharsamon*, *Télémaque travesti*, and *La Voiture embourbée*, as responses to Cervantes and anticipations of Diderot, and as illustrative of an early-18th-c. aesthetic of naïvety, heterogeneity, and imagination.

RMar, 6, 1997[1998], a special number devoted to *Le Paysan parvenu*, contains the following articles: J. Dagen, 'Marivaux Crébillon 1734' (5–21); J. Guilhembert, '*Le Paysan parvenu* au carrefour des genres' (23–41); M. Escola, '*Le Paysan parvenu* ou les romans possibles' (43–54); S. Dervaux, 'La comédie du récit: remarques sur la théâtralité du *Paysan parvenu*' (55–66); P. Stewart, '*Le Paysan parvenu* illustré' (67–84); J.-M. Gouvard, 'Les proverbes dans *Le Paysan parvenu*' (85–109); M. Fernández, 'De l'information à l'argumentation: deux pôles de "l'ambiguité" du discours marivaudien?' (111–25); M. Wauthion, 'Conversations et intentions dans *Le Paysan parvenu*' (127–44); C. Gallouët, 'Jacob, ou la commodité des femmes' (145–58); P. Hartmann, 'Triomphes et déboires d'un paysan parvenant: essai sur le programme narratif du *Paysan parvenu*' (159–74); R. Démoris, 'Inquiétante étrangeté, vœu de mort et dévoration dans *Le Paysan parvenu*' (175–93); R. Howells, 'Le discours burlesque dans *Le Paysan parvenu*' (195–208); J.-P. Sermain, 'Pourquoi riez-vous? La question du *Paysan parvenu'* (209–29); H. Lafon, 'Jacob au regard de l'Ingénu' (231–38).

G. Ansart, ' "Ancien" et "moderne" dans *Manon Lescaut* et *La Vie de Marianne'*, *RHLF*, 99, 1999:989–1006, examines similar scenes from the two novels and uses these as a starting point for a broader discussion of the narrative and ideological differences between the two texts, arguing that *Manon Lescaut* is more forward-looking in its portrayal of social class and mobility. P. Brady, 'Chaos, complexity, catastrophe and control in Marivaux's *La Vie de Marianne'*, Braun, *Disrupted Patterns*, 65–77, is an attempt to apply chaos theory to M.'s novel. F. Gevrey, '*Le Paysan parvenu* et la vérité', *Sicard Vol.*, 49–56, argues that M. is less interested in the truthfulness of his narrative than in the truthfulness of the expression of sentiment in his fiction. C. H. Meiner, 'Aspects onto-sémiotiques de la parole russe dans *La Vie de Marianne'*, Grodek, *Ruse*, 211–26, is an idiosyncratic treatment, based on the theories of Lukacs and Bakhtin, of telling in M.'s novel, claiming that 'the act of telling is the essential element of an onto-semiotics which transforms the arbitrary nature of empiric life'. M. Dobie, 'Violence à l'origine, violence et identité dans *La Vie de Marianne'*, Debaisieux, *Violence*, 303–11, examines the theme of social, not physical, violence in M.'s novel, showing too how the theme is reflected in the linguistic violence of the text. C. Gallouët-Schutter, 'De la séduction à la contrainte: la dégradation d'un topos dans le roman du XVIIIe siècle', *ib.*, 313–25, reviews violence in *Les Effets surprenants de la sympathie* and *La Vie de Marianne*, examining the complex relationship between the novels and the prevailing mode and idioms of contemporary sentimental fiction. P. Roger, 'Plus dure sera la chute: désamour et inachèvement dans *La Vie de Marianne'*, *Mauzi Vol.*, 125–36, explores the movement from delusion to self-insight in the novel, which involves a movement from being in love to not being in love, contrasting therefore with M.'s *comédies d'amour*.

R. Howells, 'Marivaux's *Le Bilboquet* (1714): the game as subversive principle', *SVEC 2000:08*, 175–78, sets M's subversive mock-heroic tale in the context of contemporary rococo aesthetics. E. Nye, 'Bilboquet, calembours, and modernity', *ib.*, 179–86, explores the use of bilboquet as a symbol of modernity in the writings of M. and others.

D. J. Culpin, 'Journalisme et fiction dans *Le Spectateur français* de Marivaux', Cook, *Journalisme*, 113–21, examines the interplay of fact and fiction at the level of both content and form in *Le Spectateur français*, illustrating convincingly the tension between *vraisemblance* and *imagination* that runs throughout the work and suggesting links with M.'s techniques as a novelist. L.-L. Sheu, 'Réalisme et imaginaire dans les *Lettres sur les habitants de Paris*', *ib.*, 123–36, examines M.'s first journalistic publications and stresses their fictionality, showing how M. is a selective and subjective observer. C. Gallouët, 'Ruses de femmes, coquetterie d'auteur: ruses textuelles dans la fiction marivaudienne', Grodek, *Ruse*, 227–39, focuses primarily on the narrator and questions of gender in *Le Spectateur français*, arguing that women's efforts to seduce men can be seen as a symbol of the author's efforts to please his audience.

PRÉVOST. Perhaps the most notable recent contribution is *L'Abbé Prévost au tournant du siècle*, ed. Richard A. Francis and Jean Mainil (*SVEC*, 2000:11), Oxford, Voltaire Foundation, ix + 390 pp. After an attentive and thorough introduction by R. Francis (1–19), articles are grouped into three sections. The first is on 'P. and his milieu' and contains: S. Larkin, 'Prévost, les Néaulme et les femmes' (23–32); A. Principato, 'L'"honnête homme" et les sociétés mondaines autour de 1745' (33–46); P. Berthiaume, 'Furori sacrum' (47–54), on moments of frenzy in the fictions (47–54); P. Stewart, '*Le Philosophe anglais* et le crépuscule de l'Édit de Nantes' (55–64); J. Sgard, 'Le monde familial de Prévost' (65–75), on family patterns in the fictions. P. Pelckmans, 'De la soumission au tabou: la mort dans les *Mémoires d'un Homme de qualité*' (77–89), finds P. exemplifying a profound historical shift in attitudes to death; M. Fujiwara, 'Les figures de l'auteur chez Prévost' (91–102), shows another shift, towards the modern idea of the ownership of a work by an author (and P.'s ambivalence again); J. Walsh, 'Littérature et caractère national d'après Prévost et Grimm' (103–10), has P. on the classical side; M. Calder, 'La résistance langagière de la Grecque moderne' (111–17), is rather at odds with the more ironic reading by P. Tremewan, 'Orient et Occident dans l'*Histoire d'une Grecque moderne*' (119–26).

The second section, 'The search for an aesthetic order', contains: R. Francis, 'Les fins de roman chez l'abbé Prévost' (129–40); J.-P. Sermain 'L'humour de Prévost' (141–56), argues that *sententiae* are ironically undermined by the narrative; F. Galtayries-Capdetrey, 'Formes et enjeux de l'ironie dans trois romans des années 40 de Prévost' (157–68), points to broader and burlesque effects; J. Mander, 'La narration à la première personne et la perspective subjective dans l'écriture de l'abbé Prévost' (169–79), argues against the modern critical emphasis on 'unreliable narration' (as in her book; see above PROSE FICTION, GENERAL), except in the case of the *Grecque moderne*; J. Herman, 'Cleveland et l'invraisemblable vraisemblance' (181–92), examines this paradox of the referential and the literary; E. Leal, '*Cleveland*: les discontinuités d'une voix singulière' (193–97); M. Bernoussi, 'De la métaphysique de la malédiction au roman noir' (199–208); D. Orsini, 'Les enjeux de la narration dans l'*Histoire d'une*

Grecque moderne' (209–18), seems like familiar ground; finally three articles consider different kinds of hypertextuality: S. Charles, 'Prévost et la réécriture: *Manon Lescaut et Oroonoko*' (219–31); E. Lavezzi, 'L'abbé Prévost, plagiaire de C.-A. Coypel dans *Le Pour et contre*' (233–41); E. Moerman, 'Traduire l'image: les portraits de Clarissa chez Richardson et Prévost' (243–58).

The third section, 'P. and literary tradition', contains: F. Létoublon, 'Les *Leçons de Ténèbres*' (261–71), on caverns, and possible Greek romance sources; S. Jones, 'Présences et absences féminines dans les *Mémoires d'un homme de qualité*' (273–81), mainly on d'Aulnoy's *Hippolyte* as an intermediary; F. Deloffre, 'De Fanchon des Îles à Manon Lescaut' (283–90), considers this adventuress's autobiography from Challe's *Journal d'un voyage* as an intertext; H. Coulet, 'Le monde falsifié de Prévost' (291–304), presents several continuations by other writers; R. Frautschi, 'Les *Mémoires d'un honnête homme* et sa suite ou le dédoublement du double registre' (305–17), compares statistically the relation between story and narration in P. and in one of these continuations; M. Cook, 'Une "fiction morale": *Le Nouveau Doyen de Killerine* de Mercier' (319–24), looks at an adaptation for the stage; K. Astbury, 'Les "contes moraux" de Prévost' (325–31), shows how stories from *Le Pour et contre* were anthologized in the wake of Marmontel's success; J. Mainil, 'Ah! Quels contes! Idéologies du conte licencieux au siècle des Lumières' (333–43), sees the lewd tales of the period 1734–54 as evidence of male sexual anxiety; E. Hindie Lemay, '*Histoire générale des voyages*: Démeunier et l'abbé Prévost' (345–53), perceives a debt to P.s vast work in D.'s more philosophical *Esprit des usages des différents peuples* of 1776; V. Altachina, 'L'œuvre de l'abbé Prévost en Russie' (355–60), points to the role of translations from French in the 18th c. in forming a Russian literature; T. Artemieva, ' "Manon russe": la transmutation personnelle' (361–67), presents the fictional autobiography of an adventuress; A. Singerman, '*Manon Lescaut* au cinéma' (369–82) ends the volume nicely with some 20th-c. updating.

7. THEATRE

GENERAL. André Blanc, *Le Théâtre français du XVIIIe siècle*, Ellipses, 1998, 120 pp., gives a useful overview of the main aspects of theatre production in the period. David Trott, *Théâtre du XVIIIe siècle*, Montpellier, Espaces, 304 pp., is a detailed and well-informed account of the diversity of 18th-c. French drama, from the official Parisian theatres to the private world of *théâtres de société*. Jeffrey S. Ravel, *The Contested Parterre: Public Theater and French Political Culture, 1680–1791*, Ithaca–London, Cornell U.P., 1999, xi + 256 pp., is a stimulating history of theatre audiences which engages with notions of the public sphere and which aims to demonstrate that the problems of the public in the tumultuous parterre reflected tensions at the heart of the *Ancien Régime*. Pierre Frantz, *L'Esthétique du tableau dans le théâtre du XVIIIe siècle*, PUF, 1998, 267 pp., is an impressive examination of the aesthetic innovations of the second half of the 18th c., focusing necessarily on Diderot, but also including detailed discussions of Voltaire, Beaumarchais, Mercier, and Rétif de la Bretonne. René Tarin, *Le Théâtre de la Constituante ou l'école du peuple* (Les Dix-huitièmes siècles, 13), Champion, 1998, 302 pp., is a useful introduction to the theatre of the French Revolution which focuses primarily on a small number of published plays and their prefaces. S. Davies, 'Ireland and the French Theatre', Gargett, *Ireland*, 197–212, is a well-researched analysis of the reception of French drama in Ireland, discussing published adaptations as well as theatre performances up to the Revolution.

Sylviane Léoni, *Le Poison et le remède: théâtre, morale et rhétorique en France et en Italie, 1694–1758* (*StV*, 360), Oxford, Voltaire Foundation, 1998, 430 pp., is a thorough and scholarly examination of debates about the legitimacy of the theatre which succeeds in highlighting the many and suggestive parallels between France and Italy. C. Jaëcklé-Plunian, 'A propos des écrits sur le théâtre au dix-huitième siècle', *StV*, 373, 1999:1–231, is a detailed examination of Fontenelle's *Histoire du théâtre français* and Rétif de la Bretonne's *La Mimographe*. S. McMeekin, 'From Beaumarchais to Chénier: the *droits d'auteur* and the fall of the *Comédie-Française*, 1777–1791', *ib.*, 235–371, chronicles the political war waged between a number of élite Parisian playwrights and the *Comédie-Française*.

Maria Ines Aliverti, *La Naissance de l'acteur moderne: l'acteur et son portrait au XVIIIe siècle*, Gallimard, 1998, 256 pp., is an engaging account of how actors in 18th-c. France and England, amidst debates about the morality of their profession, came to be recognized and painted by such respectable artists as De Troy, Vanloo, Gainsborough, and Reynolds. Sylvie Chalaye, *Du noir au nègre: l'image du noir au théâtre (1550–1960)*, L'Harmattan, 1998, 453 pp., includes a useful survey of the dramatic representation of black people in the 18th c., tracing a significant evolution from the *bon sauvage* of the early years to the *bon nègre* of the Revolution (67–142). P. Peyronnet, ' "C'est pour rire . . ." ou la Chine sur le théâtre français au dix-huitième siècle', *DFS*, 43, 1998:119–29, is a wide-ranging account of how dramatists represent the Far East, despite their apparent lack of interest in local colour. I. G. Marasescu, 'Du joueur au dissipateur: une métamorphose sous la Régence', *SVEC 2000:08*, 151–59, is a brisk review of some of the plays dealing with gambling in the early

18th c., setting the plays in the context of changing views of human nature.

Claude Bourqui, *La Commedia dell'arte: introduction au théâtre professionel italien entre le XVIe et le XVIIIe siècle*, SEDES, 1999, 160 pp., examines Italian influences on the aesthetics and performance of French comic drama. Bernard Jolibert, *La Commedia dell'arte et son influence en France du XVIe au XVIIIe siècle*, L'Harmattan, 1999, 126 pp., covers similar ground to Bourqui, though he focuses in more detail on specific authors, including Lesage, Marivaux, and Beaumarchais. *Paradrames: parodies du drame, 1775–1777*, ed. Martine de Rougemont, Saint-Étienne U.P., 1998, 195 pp., is a significant contribution to our understanding of the contemporary reception of the *drame bourgeois*, providing the first modern editions of three little known parodies from the 1770s: Coqueley de Chaussepierre's *Monsieur Cassandre ou les Effets de l'amour et du vert-de-gris*, the anonymous *I.K.L.*, and Marchand and Nougaret's *Le Vidangeur sensible*. M. de Rougemont, 'Le rire et la parodie: Freud ou Bergson?', *DhS*, 32:51–66, explores further the role of theatrical parody as a distinct genre. P. Robinson, 'Reflexions on early eighteenth-century French theatrical parody', Connon, *Drama*, 139–52, is an examination of the vogue for parodies between 1725 and 1745, focusing on how parodies subvert the aesthetics of serious theatre and play a role in the critical exploration of the nature and function of drama in the period. M. Darlow, 'Parody and the *comédie mêlée d'ariettes*, 1752–1789', *ib.*, 185–203, is a wide-ranging analysis of the musical dimension of parody in the second half of the 18th c., exploring in particular parodied melodies in the late works of Favart.

D. Quéro, 'Les éclats de rire du public de théâtre', *DhS*, 32:67–83, examines instances of theatre audiences laughing out loud, either to condemn a complete flop or to confirm the success of a true comedy. P. Frantz, 'Rire et théâtre carnavalesque pendant la Révolution', *ib.*, 291–306, discusses the social meaning and didactic function of revolutionary laughter in a number of carnivalesque plays. Jean Goldzink, *Comique et comédie au siècle des Lumières*, L'Harmattan, 381 pp., explores the vicissitudes of the comic from Marivaux via Diderot to Beaumarchais, highlighting well the various attempts made over the century to make comedy moral or sentimental, or to reconcile it with the concerns of the *philosophes*. Antoine de Baecque, *Les Eclats du rire: la culture des rieurs au XVIIIe siècle*, Calmann-Lévy, 338 pp., offers a wide-ranging and richly documented account of laughter in all its manifestations, from the theatrical to the political, in the supposedly serious 18th century.

K. Astbury, 'Marmontel's theories on comedy and his moral tales: the influence of prose on the theatre in the second half of the eighteenth century', Connon, *Drama*, 171–84, explores the complex organic links between Marmontel's discussion of comedy and the comic in the *Encyclopédie*, his 'theatrical' moral tales, and the dramatic adaptations of those tales. G. S. Brown, 'Dramatic authorship and the honor of men of letters', *SECC*, 27, 1998:259–82, is a well-documented account of the role of the *Comédie-Française* in helping to confer respectability upon dramatists in the 18th century. J. Letzter and R. Adelson, 'Women opera composers face the Parisian *comités de lecture*: where institutional barriers meet social barriers to perform-ance', *SVEC 2000:05*, 355–69, concentrates on the attempts of Julie Candeille, Sophie Bawr, Caroline Wuiet, and Isabelle de Charrière to have their operas accepted by the Parisian theatre committees. D. Steinberger, 'Spectacles of intimacy: a new look at the *comédie larmoyante*', *EsC*, 39.3, 1999:64–75, argues for a more sympathetic assessment of the plays of Destouches and La Chaussée.

INDIVIDUAL AUTHORS

AUTREAU.   *Le Chevalier Bayard*, ed. Richard Waller (Liverpool Online Series, 3), Liverpool U.P., 192 pp., is a careful and scholarly edition of the performance and published versions of A.'s play. R. Waller, 'The theatrical writings of Jacques Autreau and the problems of experimentation', Connon, *Drama*, 99–115, is a detailed and persuas-ive account of A.'s constant experimentation and innovation in his theatre.

BEAUMARCHAIS.   *Théâtre*, ed. Jean-Pierre de Beaumarchais, Librai-rie générale française, 1999, 766 pp., is a richly annotated edition, the fruit of much recent research on B.'s theatre. *Le Barbier de Séville*, ed. Pierre Testud, Larousse, 1999, 231 pp., and *Le Mariage de Figaro*, ed. Elisabeth Lavezzi, Flammarion, 1999, 256 pp., are useful student editions. Maurice Lever, *Pierre-Augustin Caron de Beaumarchais*, I: *L'Irrésistible ascension*, 1732–1774, Fayard, 1999, 587 pp., is the lively and well-informed first part of a projected two-volume biography of Beaumarchais. Violaine Géraud, *Beaumarchais, l'aventure d'une écriture* (Unichamp, 90), Champion, 1999, 208 pp, examines the first two Figaro plays in terms of B.'s attempt to shape his public image through his theatre. Sophie Lecarpentier, *Le Langage dramatique dans la trilogie de Beaumarchais: efficacité, gaieté, musicalité*, Saint-Genouph, Nizet, 1998, 193 pp., is an impressionistic survey which adds little to our understanding of B.'s dramatic language.

B. Didier, 'Figaro barbier et dramaturge', pp. 53–63 of *Le Maître et le valet: figures et ruses du pouvoir*, ed. Béatrice Didier and Gwenhaël Ponnau, SEDES, 1998, 107 pp., is a concise analysis of master-servant relations in *Le Barbier de Séville*, reviewing the play's genesis and its place in the dramatic tradition, and offering a view of Figaro as a dramatist-figure. G. Zaragoza, '*Le Barbier de Séville*, ou comment "faire la barbe à tout le monde"', pp. 81–102 of *Le Triomphe du valet de comédie: Plaute, Goldoni, Beaumarchais, Hofmannsthal*, ed. Daniel Mortier, Champion, 1998, 137 pp., examines Figaro's 'maîtrise absolue du jeu' through a careful analysis of his language and his use of stage space. J.-P. de Beaumarchais, 'Les métamorphoses de Figaro', *SVEC 2000:05*, 1–10, is a neat account of B.'s changing conception of his most famous character. M. Ledbury, 'Beaumarchais's visual vocabulary', Connon, *Drama*, 205–25, examines B.'s use of visual stage vocabulary in relationship to Diderot's conception of stage *tableaux*, the traditional gestural language of fairground theatre, the visual theatricality of contemporary *opéra-comique*, B.'s experience of Spanish theatre, and visual arts of the period. B. Didier, 'Beaumarchais aux origines du mélodrame', pp. 15–26 of *Mélodrames et romans noirs, 1750–1890*, ed. Simone Bernard-Griffiths and Jean Sgard, Toulouse-Le Mirail U.P., 534 pp., considers how B.'s *Tarare*, *Eugénie*, and *La Mère coupable* foreshadow aspects of 19th-c. melodrama, notably in the exploitation of music and gesture.

BOINDIN. J. Dunkley, 'Nicolas Boindin: the presentation and re-presentation of alterity', *RoS*, 31, 1998:83–94, is a study of B.'s personal experience of otherness and his ludic re-presentation of it in four comedies written between 1701 and 1707.

CRÉBILLON *fils*. *Rhadamisthe et Zénobie*, ed. Magali Soulatges, Montpellier, Espaces 34, 1999, 86 pp., is a useful edition of this author's most popular tragedy, offering a brief presentation of the play, but no textual annotation.

DESTOUCHES. J. Dunkley, 'Destouches and moralising comedy: the defining of a genre', Connon, *Drama*, 153–70, demonstrates convincingly that any attempt simplistically to label D.'s dramas is problematic.

DU CASTRE D'AUVIGNY. R. Goulbourne, 'The eighteenth-century "querelle des vers" and Jean Du Castre d'Auvigny's *La Tragédie en prose*', *SVEC 2000:05*, 371–410, presents the first modern edition of D.'s satirical comedy and assesses its polemical significance in the context of the 1730 debate between Voltaire and La Motte about prose tragedy.

LESAGE. *Théâtre de la Foire*, ed. Isabelle Vissière and Jean-Louis Vissière, Desjonquères, 294 pp., and *Turcaret*, ed. Philippe Hourcade, Flammarion, 1998, 192 pp., are both welcome and affordable editions. I. Martin, 'Usage et esthétique du miroir dans une pièce orientale: *La Statue merveilleuse* de Lesage', *EsC*, 39.3, 1999:47–55, is a close reading of L.'s 1719 *opéra-comique* in the context of rococo aesthetics. M. Cardy, 'A trumpet *obbligato*: contextualisation of a passage from Lesage's *Turcaret'*, Connon, *Drama*, 87–98, is a deft explanation of a significant, but hitherto neglected, musical allusion in act IV, scene V of *Turcaret*.

MARIVAUX. *Le Jeu de l'amour et du hasard*, ed. David J. Culpin, London, Bristol Classical Press, xl + 57 pp., reproduces the punctuation of the first edition (1730) and deftly sets the play in its intellectual and theatrical contexts. Other useful editions include: *La Double Inconstance*, ed. Françoise Rubellin, Gallimard, 222 pp.; *La Fausse Suivante*, ed. Pierre Malandain, Librairie générale française, 1999, 127 pp.; *Les Fausses Confidences*, ed. Catherine Naugrette-Christophe, Flammarion, 1999, 192 pp.; *L'Ile des esclaves*, ed. Jean Goulemot, Librairie générale française, 1999, 90 pp.; *L'Ile des esclaves*, ed. Henri Coulet, Gallimard, 137 pp.; *L'Ile des esclaves*, ed. Florence Magnot, Flammarion, 1999, 144 pp.; *Le Jeu de l'amour et du hasard*, ed. Marie Cartier and Hélène Sibelle, Larousse, 1999, 191 pp.; *Le Jeu de l'amour et du hasard*, ed. Emmanuelle Malhappe, Flammarion, 1999, 162 pp.; and *Le Triomphe de l'amour*, ed. Henri Coulet, Gallimard, 1998, 222 pp.

E. Russo, 'Libidinal economy and gender trouble in Marivaux's *La Fausse Suivante*', *MLN*, 115:690–713, examines what she sees as the troubling discourses on gender and sex in this play which revolves around the transvestism of the female protagonist. A. Wyngaard, 'Switching codes: class, clothing, and cultural change in the works of Marivaux and Watteau', *ECS*, 33:523–41, is a careful analysis of the social implications of costume in *L'Ile des esclaves*, *Le Jeu de l'amour et du hasard*, as well as in *Le Paysan parvenu*, which fruitfully compares M.'s technique with Watteau's. P. Marteinson, 'Le topos littéraire: unité de base d'une sémantique intentionnelle et élément idéel d'une grammaire culturelle', Grodek, *Ruse*, 49–59, uses highly technical quantitative pragmatics as the basis for a difficult treatment of ruse and master-servant relations in *Le Jeu de l'amour et du hasard*. R. Sabry, 'Le dialogue au second degré dans le théâtre de Marivaux', *Poétique*, 114, 1998:305–25, is a detailed and fruitful analysis of the different forms and functions of reported speech in M.'s theatre. C. Martin, 'Tentations et "embarras de l'âme" chez Marivaux', *RSH*, 254, 1999:129–38, is a discussion of the quasi-biblical temptation to transgress moral codes as it is represented in *La Double Inconstance* and *Le Prince travesti*, as well as in *La Vie de Marianne*. G. Evans, 'Marivaux's *Arlequin poli par l'amour* and the implications of play-acting', Connon, *Drama*, 117–26, examines how this early comedy foreshadows the comic and moral concerns in the rest of M.'s dramatic output.

MONVEL. Roselyne Laplace, *Monvel, un aventurier du théâtre au siècle des Lumières* (Les Dix-huitièmes siècles, 17), Champion, 1998, 410 pp., is a broad and detailed historical account of the life and works of this actor-dramatist in the second half of the 18th c.

PANNARD. Nathalie Rizzoni, *Charles-François Pannard et l'esthétique du 'petit'* (SVEC 2000:01), Oxford, Voltaire Foundation, x + 526 pp., is a probing and scholarly reassessment of the life and works of P., one of the founders of the *opéra-comique* in the early 18th c., as well as a prolific poet.

PIRON. D. F. Connon, 'Piron's *Arlequin-Deucalion*: fair play, or anti-fair play?', Connon, *Drama*, 127–38, offers a detailed analysis of the play, highlighting its ambiguities and its paradoxical status as one of the most popular fairground plays which nevertheless in many ways departs from, and even parodies, the conventional aesthetics of the fairground.

RUTLIDGE. *Les Comédiens ou le foyer, Le Bureau d'esprit, Le Train de Paris ou les bourgeois du temps* (L'Age des Lumières, 3), ed. Pierre Peyronnet, Champion, 1999, 382 pp., is a sound critical edition of R.'s three satirical comedies which, while perhaps not great drama, nevertheless add to our understanding of the history of ideas towards the end of the 18th c.

SADE. Sylvie Dangeville, *Le Théâtre change et représente: lecture critique des œuvres dramatiques du marquis de Sade* (Les Dix-huitièmes siècles, 29), Champion, 1999, 732 pp., offers a broad and primarily descriptive overview of S.'s theatre in its theatrical and socio-historical context, laying particular emphasis on the genesis and style of his plays. M. Kozul, 'Les fragments inédits du théâtre de Sade: *La Ruse d'amour* et la théâtralité sadienne', *SVEC 2000:05*, 243–79, provides an edition of the manuscript fragments of the first version of *La Ruse d'amour* and demonstrates the importance of self-conscious theatricality in the work.

SEDAINE. Mark Ledbury, *Sedaine, Greuze and the Boundaries of Genre* (*StV*, 380), Oxford, Voltaire Foundation, xi + 355 pp., fills a big gap in S. studies, offering a wide-ranging and systematic analysis of the dramatist's experimentation and his role in contemporary aesthetic debates. *Michel-Jean Sedaine (1719–1797): Theatre, Opera and Art*, ed. David Charlton and Mark Ledbury, Aldershot, Ashgate, xiii + 322 pp., is a valuable edition of conference proceedings, comprising the following articles: M. Ledbury, 'Sedaine and the question of genre' (13–38); S. Rosenfeld, '*Les Philosophes* and *le savoir*: words, gestures and other signs in the era of Sedaine' (39–51); J. Dunkley, 'The representation of the female in the dramas of Sedaine' (52–67); M. Couvreur, '*Aline, reine de Golconde*: une bergère d'opéra-comique à l'Académie Royale de Musique' (71–96); M. Noiray, 'Quatre rois à la chasse: Dodsley, Collé, Sedaine, Goldoni' (97–118); R. Legrand, ' "Risquer un genre nouveau en musique": l'opéra-comique de Sedaine et Monsigny' (119–45); M. de Rougemont, 'Sedaine et les images' (149–72); P. Taïeb, 'Un jugement de François Benoît Hoffman sur Sedaine en 1812' (173–95); D. Charlton, 'Sedaine's prefaces: pretexts for a new musical drama' (196–272); M. Ledbury, 'An iconography of Sedaine and his works' (275–87); and D. Charlton and M. Ledbury, 'A Sedaine bibliography' (288–313).

8. NON-FICTION

DUCLOS. Charles Duclos, *Considérations sur les moeurs de ce siècle*, ed. Carole Dornier, Champion, 267 pp., is a comprehensive and excellent critical edition.

MONCRIF. François-Augustin Paradis de Moncrif, *Essais sur la nécessité et sur les moyens de plaire*, ed. Geneviève Haroche-Bouzinac, Saint-Etienne U.P., 1998, 110 pp., is a welcome edition, based on the first published version of the text (1738), with variants from the second edition, and including a useful introduction which sets the text in the context of contemporary conduct books and discussions of the art of conversation.

THE ROMANTIC ERA

By JOHN WHITTAKER, *University of Hull*

1. GENERAL

J.-Y. Mollier, 'Diffuser les connaissances au 19e siècle, un exercice délicat', *Romantisme*, 108:91–101, considers the restrictions on the publishing world of 1810–70, and the development of the educational system and literacy, concluding that real changes only came with the Third Republic. R. Lloyd, 'The nineteenth century: shaping women', Stephens, *Women's Writing*, 120–46, is an authoritative perspective of the women writers of the century, with an admirable choice of representative individuals. Michel Brix, *Le Romantisme français — Esthétique platonicienne et modernité littéraire, Louvain–Namur, Peeters–Société des Études Classiques, 1999, 304 pp. Peter Brooks, *History Painting and Narrative: Delacroix's 'Moments'* (EHRC Special lecture series, 2), Oxford, Legenda, 1998, 37 pp., shows the cultural influence of particular paintings during our period and beyond. *Romantismes européens et Romantisme français*, ed. Pierre Brunel, Montpellier, Espaces 34, 270 pp., includes: F. Susini-Anastopoulos, 'Romantisme allemand et poétique du fragment' (27–42); D. Chauvin, 'Élie et Ézéchiel: les chars de feu de l'imagination romantique' (43–66); M. Edwards, 'Sur un vers de Wordsworth' (67–81); R. Ellrodt, 'L'imagination romantique et le rêve: le "Khubla Khan" de Coleridge' (83–106); M. Porée, 'Fins Keatsiennes' (107–32); J. Céard, 'La redécouverte de la Pléiade par les Romantiques français' (133–47); B. Didier, 'George Sand et le Romantisme européen' (149–64); R. Stricker, 'Henri Heine critique musical' (165–85); J.-R. Aymes, 'Existe-t-il un Romantisme espagnol' (187–205); M. Maslowski, 'L'aliénation du geste héroïque: *Kordian* et *Lorenzaccio*' (207–26); S. Michaud, 'Mme de Staël et Nietzsche' (227–52). Alison Finch, *Women's Writing in Nineteenth-Century France*, CUP, xvi + 316 pp., is an apt reminder of the very considerable contribution which women made to the literature of the period. A broad chronological survey, extending from Mme de Staël to Rachilde, shows that the 19th c. was a time when women authors prepared the ground for a future when they could be considered equal to men. That they made remarkable progress in the first half of the century is evident from the list of major works of 92 women writers. Alain Lange, *Les grands courants du romantisme littéraire et artistique (1820–1850), Cognac, Lange, 17 pp.

2. CONSULATE WRITERS

CHATEAUBRIAND. F. Bercegol, 'Chateaubriand ou la conversion au progrès', *Romantisme*, 108:23–51, finds that, though C. began by rejecting all ideas related to change or improvement, when he was writing *Le Génie du Christianisme*, he developed a more optimistic view. B. Chaouat, 'À vau-l'eau: l'Amérique désécrite de Chateaubriand', *FrF*, 25:277–89, shows that the *Voyage en Amérique*, though it takes a traditional form and style, marks the point at which C.'s inspiration and technique started to move in new directions. *Chateaubriand Mémorialiste: Colloque du cent cinquantenaire (1848–1998)*, ed. Jean-Claude Berchet and Philippe Berthier, Geneva, Droz, 336 pp., contains the Proceedings of the conference held at the École Normale Supérieure in June 1998 to mark the anniversary of the death of C. and the publication of the *Mémoires d'outre-tombe*. It includes: P. Berthier, 'Avant-propos' (9–10); M. Fumaroli, 'Histoire et mémoires' (11–34), on a well-established genre which was slow to be admitted to the canon, and the great surge of publications after the Revolution, in which C. was eventually to take his place; D. Zanone, 'Les Mémoires et la tentation du roman: l'exception épique des *Mémoires d'outre-tombe*' (35–45), considering the work of C. as a means to establish a literary genre; P. Riberette, 'Mémoires par lettres' (47–57), on letters reproduced in the *Mémoires*; B. Didier, 'Voyages croisés' (59–68), on the integration of travel writing in C.'s work; P. Glaudes, ' "Une idée qui vient du ciel": le sublime dans les *Mémoires d'outre-tombe*' (69–85), on C.'s aristocratic ethos; J.-C. Bonnet, 'Les formes de célébration' (87–92), on his unfavourable view of 18th-c. writers; H. P. Lund, 'Les artistes dans les *Mémoires d'outre-tombe*' (93–107), concluding that their function is the resurrection of a glorious past; F. Orlando, 'Temps de l'histoire, espace des images' (109–18), on temporality; M. Sheringham, 'La mémoire-palimpseste dans les *Mémoires d'outre-tombe*' (119–31), which begins with the famous text twice quoted in *À la recherche du temps perdu*; A. Verlet, 'Épitaphes vagabondes' (133–47), suggesting that they represent a point of access to poetic space; P. Berthier, 'Mémoires pour rire' (149–67), on C.'s metaphysical joke with death; I. Rosi, 'La rhétorique allusive' (169–86), focusing on *La Vie de Rancé*; J.-M. Roulin, 'La clausule dans les *Mémoires d'outre-tombe*' (187–204), on the strategic use thereof in what may be termed an open or unfinished text; F. Bercegol, 'Poétique de l'anecdote' (205–34), on an important element in the construction of C.'s fiction; A. Compagnon, 'Poétique de la citation' (235–49), on his frequent use of quotations; J.-F. Perrin, 'Figures de lecture' (251–59), on C.'s acute awareness of narratological problems; B. Degout, 'Le "Journal" du Sacre' (261–75), on the chapters devoted to the coronation of Charles X; J.-P. Clément, 'La fascination du politique' (277–90), on C.'s visionary politics; J. Lecarme, 'Ministres autobiographes' (291–306), on how C., unlike the majority of political figures, managed to combine the personal and the political in his *Mémoires*; J.-C. Berchet, 'Chateaubriand et le théâtre du monde' (307–20), on the influence of the theatrical canon on his style. Jean-Christophe Cavallin, *Chateaubriand et 'l'homme aux songes': initiation à la poésie dans les 'Mémoires d'outre-tombe'*, PUF, 1999, 247 pp., presents C. as having two lives: man of action and man of dreams. The *Mémoires* are more concerned with the second, and with the author's initiation into the world of poetry. Three stages are identified by means of symbolic scenes, starting beside the lake in Combourg and ending in the American desert. It is suggested that the poetic faculty implies feminization, explaining C.'s description of himself as an 'androgyne bizarre'. Id., *Chateaubriand mythographe: autobiographie et allégorie dans les 'Mémoires d'outre-tombe'*, Champion, 576 pp., concludes that one is mistaken to read them as autobiography. The man of the *Mémoires* is a literary creation deriving from legendary figures, a hybrid, incarnating a myth. The account is detailed, and the argument well delivered, with the aim of restoring the work's literary intention and symbolic unity. *Chateaubriand 98*, ed. Jacques Gury, Rennes, Institut Culturel de Bretagne, 1999, 301 pp., includes: R. Couanau, 'Au Grand-Bé le 4 juillet 1998' (11–13), the mayor of Saint-Malo expressing his appreciation of C.'s decision to be buried there; P. Poupard, '*Le Génie du Christianisme*' (15–19), suggesting that the work was a political act in order to establish the position of the believer in the modern world; J. de la Celle, 'Il revit en nous' (21–25), a descendant of C. on his family and his enduring influence; there follow a number of appreciations of C. by mayors of the Breton towns he frequented and by corporate bodies such as France Télécom Rennes; C. Bazin, 'Le rêve américain de François-René de Chateaubriand' (107–09), on the notes he kept from his American journey; J.-P. Gury, 'Chateaubriand et les monuments indiens: quelques réflexions' (111–16), on earth works in Ohio which attracted C.'s attention; P. Moisan, 'Le Nouveau Monde de Chateaubriand: des alluvions à l'érosion' (117–22), focusing on *Les Natchez*; B. Chevignard, 'Chateaubriand et Crèvecoeur aux Chutes du Niagara' (123–33), comparing the *Voyages* of Michel-Guillaume Jean de Crèvecoeur with *La Vie de Rancé*; M. Blain-Pinel, 'Esthétique et symbolisme de la mer chez Chateaubriand' (135–52), concerning the association at the end of the *Mémoires* of the sea with the sacred; F. Bergot, 'Peinture et poésie chez Chateaubriand' (153–74), on links between C.'s writing and the visual arts; J.-L. Paumier, 'Chateaubriand, Saint François d'Assise et les Franciscains' (175–78), an appreciation of C. from a Franciscan perspective; B. Heudré, 'Chateaubriand, un chrétien dans son siècle' (179–89), showing his influence on 19th-c. religious sensibility; C. de la Cochetière, 'La religion de Chateaubriand et le religieux dans son oeuvre' (191–202), concerned with *Le Génie du Christianisme*; J. Georgel, 'Les femmes de Chateaubriand' (207–16), on his relationships with numerous women; M. Mohrt, 'Chateaubriand et l'émigration' (217–21), with particular reference to the *Mémoires d'outre-tombe*; G. de Diesbach, 'Chateaubriand et la Guerre d'Espagne' (223–36), giving particular attention to his *Congrès de Vérone*; M. Denis, 'Chateaubriand et le légitimisme "Jeune France"' (237–48), on his resolute attachment to his own brand of legitimism and his early recognition of the potential of the young Romantics; J.-P. Clément, 'Chateaubriand: pouvoir et liberté' (249–62), on his position as a partisan of enlightened conservatism, a lover of liberty without being a liberal; G. Bigot and Y.-A. Marc, 'Chateaubriand a-t-il pensé objectivement la Révolution?' (263–77), suggesting that his negative view was linked to his attitude to death; R. Drago, 'Chateaubriand et la naissance du parlementarisme' (279–85), on his political writings from *De la Monarchie selon le charte* to the *Mémoires d'outre-tombe*; E. Guitton, 'Chateaubriand, un écrivain écartelé' (287–93), suggesting a need to relocate C. between the extremes of the 17th c., the Enlightenment, and the future.

CONSTANT. *ABC*, 22, 1999, 146 pp., includes: T. Todorov, 'Benjamin Constant et la pensée humaniste' (7–13), a lecture by the winner of the 1998 Prix Européen de l'Essai, suggesting that C. was a true European; I. Vissière, 'Plaidoyer pour Constant d'Hermenches' (19–44), on C.'s 18th-c. uncle; V. Cossy, '*Caleb Williams* traduit "par des gens de la campagne": Samuel de Constant et ses enfants traducteurs de William Godwin' (45–71), on the translation which was published in Lausanne in 1796; F. Rosset, 'Notice sur Samuel de Constant par sa fille Rosalie' (73–79), concerning a text which may have been written for Philippe-Sirice Bridel's unfinished *Matériaux pour une histoire littéraire du Canton de Vaud*; A. Hofmann and A. Leresche, 'Un inédit de Charles de Constant: le *Journal d'une course à Lausanne et Montreux*' (81–102), on a type of travel writing by C.'s cousin; A.-J. Czouz-Tornare, 'Du 10 août 1792 à la révolution belge de 1830: l'itinéraire royaliste et antilibéral du général Jean-Victor Constant de Rebecque (1773–1850)' (103–15), concerning another of C.'s cousins; F. Rosset, 'Madame de Staël dans les archives polonaises: autographes inédits, portraits et témoignages inconnus' (119–32), presenting a number of letters; P. Delbouille, 'Chronique des *Oeuvres complètes*' (135–36), reviews recent editions of C.'s work. Filomena Vitale, *Benjamin Constant, écriture et culpabilité*, Geneva, Droz, 226 pp., takes an idea first formulated by Jean Starobinski and applies it to the whole of C.'s output. Guilt is shown to be an inescapable part of the national psyche in the years following the Revolution. It is also a universal feature of C.'s writing, though his generally relativist approach causes him to be described as a predecessor of existentialism.

MME DE DURAS.   D. Dimauro, '*Ourika*, or Galatea reverts to stone', *NCFS*, 28:187–211, shows that D. inverts the myth of Pygmalion and Galatea in order to provide a general framework and themes for her text.

MME DE STAËL.   E. Bricco, 'De *Delphine* à *Corinne*: le pacte romanesque chez Mme de Staël', *SFr*, 44:315–32, considers the two texts which seek to define the modern novel, and the structural, stylistic and moral evolution that is evident between the two. F. Lotterie, 'L'année 1800 — perfectibilité, progrès et révolution dans *De la Littérature* de Madame de Staël', *Romantisme*, 108:9–22, shows S. maintaining a dialogue with 18th-c. thought, drawing from it a model for progress in literature, and finding that it enabled a positive view of the Revolution. B. Waggaman, 'Ruses de langage et stratégies de subversion dans *Delphine* de Mme de Staël', *AJFS*, 37:348–58, shows that the novel, for which Napoleon exiled her from Paris, was not as apolitical as she claimed in the preface. *Une Mélodie intellectuelle: Corinne ou l'Italie de Germaine de Staël*, ed. Christine Planté, Christine Pouzoulet, and Alain Vaillant, Montpellier III Paul Valéry U.P., 234 pp., includes: D. Zanone, 'L'esthétique du "tableau philosophique" dans *Corinne ou l'Italie*' (9–29), showing the balance which S. sought between the aesthetic and the philosophical; P. Laforgue, 'Roman, romanesque et imaginaire dans *Corinne*' (31–44), identifying the extent and the limitations of each; A. Vaillant, 'De l'*Essai sur les fictions* à *Corinne ou l'Italie*: théorie et pratique de la sublimité romanesque' (45–60), on the rejection of allegory; C. Planté, 'Sur les improvisations de *Corinne*' (61–79), showing the work to be an experiment in the development of the prose poem; F. Brunet, 'Le jeu de l'acteur selon Madame de Staël: de Corinne à Talma' (81–106), showing S.'s awareness of a need for renewal of the theatrical practice of the time; F. Lotterie, ' "La puissance d'aimer": progrès et sensibilité dans *Corinne ou l'Italie*' (109–25), showing S. as a link between the 18th c. and Stendhal's concept of perfectibility; G. Gengembre, 'L'enthousiasme dans *Corinne*' (127–38), on the application of the concept to fiction; F. Rosset, 'Poétique des nations dans *Corinne*' (139–58), on the different cultures which are brought together; C. Saminadayar-Perrin, 'Autour de Virgile: poétique et politique' (159–80), showing the influence of the Aeneid; C. Seth, 'La part des anges: signes et présages dans *Corinne*' (181–204), on the function of prophecies and portents; C. Pouzoulet, 'Des ambivalences de l'"Improvisation de Corinne au Capitole" ou la recherche d'une nouvelle italianité' (205–32), on the influence of Shakespeare and Dante. *Lectures de Corinne ou l'Italie de Madame de Staël*, ed. Jean-Marie Seillan, Nice Sophia Antipolis U.P., 92 pp., contains: V. Magri-Mourgues, '*Corinne et le voyage*' (11–25), showing to what extent the journey provides the book's structure and governs the narrative and characters, turning Corinne into an allegorical figure representing the Italian nation; J. Domenach, 'Monsieur Maltigues et Lord Nelvil' (27–50), showing that the confrontation between the two represents a philosophical debate between revolutionary principles and sentiment; L. Viglieno, 'Corinne héritière des "âmes sensibles"' (51–72), suggesting that the work represents an 18th-c. sensitivity pursuing the investigation of melancholy; J.-M. Seillan, 'Pathétique et comique involontaire dans *Corinne*' (73–92), dealing with the problem that scenes of the greatest pathos tend to make modern readers laugh, stereotyped gestures and redundant formulae, originally intended to show differences of national character, now appearing ridiculous. Joanne Wilkes, *Lord Byron and Madame de Staël: Born for Opposition*, Aldershot, Ashgate, 1999, ix + 210 pp., is a detailed account of the extent to which the English poet was influenced by S.'s writings. Although he occasionally declared his opposition to her work, he expressed admiration for her, and the two can be seen to have shared a range of affinities.

3. POETRY

R. Sauvé, 'Les *Poésies* de Clotilde de Surville: supercherie littéraire et subversion des genres', *NCFS*, 29:21–34, measures the impact upon the Romantics, and the subsequent reception, of this literary hoax of 1803. E. S. Burt, *Poetry's Appeal: Nineteenth-Century French Lyric and the Political Space*, Stanford U.P., 1999, x + 287 pp., finds that poetry addresses history and the political through a disjunction between its illusory status as a song of private, lyrical intent and its acute state as a material inscription, inevitably public in character. The two chapters on Chénier are particularly interesting, and that on Hugo's 'La Révolution', which lays emphasis on the hallucinatory nature of his poetry.

BARBIER. I. Tournier, 'Le moment Barbier ou la "vérité" de juillet', *Romantisme*, 106:101–15, retraces the origins of the poem 'La Curée', first published in September 1830, which was felt at the time to represent the truth about the Revolution.

BANVILLE. E. Souffrin-Le Breton, 'Banville and his three sonnets on the mythical amazons', *MLR*, 95:72–84, identifies the origin of the image in an exhibit in the 1843 *Salon*, tracing the development of the three from a sonnet first published in 1846.

BERTRAND. *Oeuvres complètes*, ed. Helen Hart Poggenburg, Champion, 1176 pp., contains the complete works of the poet who is chiefly remembered for the prose poem *Gaspard de la nuit*, the MS of which was rediscovered in 1992. The verse is of particular interest, though many genres are included. This will enable a more complete assessment of B.'s output.

GAUTIER. N. E. Smith, 'Parnassian (im)perfection: Gautier's "Contralto"', *RoN*, 40:145–52, considers the poem from *Émaux et camées*, concluding that the oppositions we find in it reinforce the notion of an ideal and very personal conception of beauty. *Correspondance générale 1872 et compléments*, ed. Claudine Lacoste-Veysseyre, Geneva, Droz, 411 pp., is the 12th and last volume of the collection, containing dated letters from 1872, including the funeral invitation. It is a very thorough and fascinating edition. As before, one has not only G.'s letters but also those written to him. More important are the undated letters, numbered in such a way that one can find their place in previous volumes. Some are documents which have been recently found. *Victor Hugo par Théophile Gautier*, ed. Françoise Court-Pérez, Champion, 259 pp., is an anthology of extracts which assists in our undertanding of both writers. The introduction reminds us that G. was rather more than the red waistcoat of *Hernani*, and that he saw it as his duty to explain H. to the public. The selected texts cover the years 1830–70, constituting not only a valuable contemporary view of H.'s work but also an insight into the cultural history of the period.

HUGO. Laurence M. Porter, *Victor Hugo*, NY, Twayne, 1999, xviii + 190 pp., is a sound introduction to H., who is presented as 'an icon of popular culture'. There is a helpful emphasis on the development of his style, and biographical detail is restrained. The reader is given useful starting points in the textual examples which are provided, though one may regret that quotations from prose are given only in English.

GUÉRIN. J. M. Vast, 'New light on Maurice de Guérin's recently recovered lines of "Vous m'avez invité ..."', *NCFS*, 28:212–26, shows that these lines, among a number of fragments and poems recovered since 1980, illuminate a crucial period in G.'s literary career, and point to the need for a reconsideration of him as a poet.

LAMARTINE. *Correspondance d'Alphonse de Lamartine 1830–1867*, ed. Christian Croisille, vol. 1, Champion, 693 pp., is the first part of the collection, dealing with the period 1830–32, from the point at which L. was admitted to the Académie to the death of his daughter Julia. This is a thorough and detailed edition which will be of considerable value to those seeking an insight into the poet's personal life.

4. THE NOVEL

GENERAL

G. Zaragoza, 'Rire de la solitude et solitude du rire chez quelques écrivains romantiques', *NCFS*, 28:242–58, is mainly concerned with Nodier's *La Fée aux miettes* and Hugo's *L'Homme qui rit*. Christophe Lamiot, *Littérature et hôpital en France: Balzac, Sue, Hugo*, Chilly-Mazarin, Sciences en Situation, 1999, 194 pp., compares the representation of hospitals in novels with data on their history. In each novel, the relationship between doctor and patient is crucial, though the reader is warned to be wary of treatment. The authors demonstrate that health care is vital to us all. Anne Teissier-Ensminger, *La Beauté du droit*, Descartes, 1999, 315 pp., considers Balzac's *Le Contrat de mariage*, Hugo's *Les Misérables* and Jules Renard's *Poil de Carotte*. The general theme is that of law in literature, with the first novel being related to resourceful women gaining an inheritance, the second to suicide and the third to maternal power.

BALZAC

A. Michel, 'Balzac et l'idée de progrès en littérature', *Romantisme*, 108:53–64, shows that, though B. believed neither in social nor individual progress, he believed in progress in literature, particularly when a spirit of liberty enabled the reconciliation of differences between opposing viewpoints. A. K. Mortimer, 'Myth and mendacity: Balzac's *Pierrette* and Béatrice Cenci, *DFS*, 51:12–25, examines the bases for B.'s comparison of his story to that of a 16th-c. girl who was beheaded, and shows the modifications he made. S. Pold, 'Panoramic realism: an early and illustrative passage from urban space to media space in Balzac's Paris novels, *Ferragus* and *Le Père Goriot*', *NCFS*, 29:47–63, shows how the emergence of the first visual mass medium was used by B. in his realist technique. K.-F. Yau, 'Spacing and timing: contract and mise-en-scène in fiction by Balzac, Sacher-Masoch and Lu Xun', *TP*, 14.1:81–95, examines space and time as frames of differences in *Le Père Goriot*, *Venus im Peltz*, and the short story 'Revealing (to) the public', with emphasis on B.'s contractual approach to writing.

ABa, n.s., 20, includes: M. Ambrière, 'Lire Balzac en l'an 2000' (5–14), underlining the continuing relevance of B. studies on the bicentenary of his birth; M. Delon, 'Souvenirs balzaciens de "Faublas"' (17–27), on the influence of a novel by Jean-Baptiste Louvet; E. Leborgne, 'Balzac lecteur de *Gil Blas*: essai de mythologie romanesque comparée' (29–46), on a possible model for *La Comédie humaine*; J.-C. Abramovici, 'Cronos écrivain: jeunesse et vieillesse dans les *Contes drolatiques*' (47–58), showing that B. used the stories not only as a vehicle for stylistic innovation, but also as a means to break free from the literary canon of the time; R. Boyer, 'Balzac et l'illuminisme, notamment swedenborgien' (61–74), introducing a complex subject and describing B. and S. as soul mates; A. H. Pasco, '*Les Proscrits* et l'unité du "Livre mystique"' (75–92), suggesting that a more complete understanding may be obtained by reading the novels in their original order; M. Andréoli, 'Balzac philosophe?' (93–104), showing how B. devised his own philosophy; A. Michel, 'Le Dieu de Balzac' (105–16), on his distinctive theology; M. Lichtlé, 'Balzac et le Code civil' (119–40), concluding that his admiration for this body of legislation was comparatively restrained, and that he saw ways of improving it; R.-A. Courteix, 'Balzac et les droits de l'homme' (141–52), suggesting that he cared less for human rights than for human problems; O. Heathcote, 'Nécessité et gratuité de la violence chez Balzac: *Z. Marcas*' (153–68), on the reasons for the portrayal of violence in the novella; J.-Y. Tadié, 'Balzac ou la mémoire qui tue' (169–75), on his ability to combine or alternate between total recall and sensory memory; J. Noiray, 'Images de la machine et imaginaire de la femme' (177–88), on B.'s rejection of two aspects of the modern world; P. Brunel, 'Balzac de la première d'*Hernani* à la première de *Robert-le-Diable*' (189–200), on his critical reaction to the play and to the opera; A. Vanconini, 'De *Zadig* à *Maître Cornelius*: le récit policier en gestation' (203–16), identifying the novel of 1831 as a predecessor of detective fiction; S. Swahn, 'Poétique des *Paysans*; l'anti-idylle dans un roman de Balzac' (217–27), on his use of a cruel story to distance himself from readers' perceptions of country life; D. Dupuis, 'Dérision du pathétique et pathétique de la dérision' (229–56), on the complexity of B.'s approach to pathos; M. Labouret, '*Madame Firmiani* ou "peindre par le dialogue"' (257–78), on the technique of the 1832 novella; C. Planté, '*Modeste Mignon*: les lettres, la voix, le roman' (279–92), on how an attempt to seek truth while avoiding clichés came to resemble parody; E. Bordas, 'Pratiques balzaciennes de la digression' (293–316), on the development of this feature of B.'s discourse; A.-M. Baron, 'Balzac et l'anagramme' (317–29), on a passion shared with Colleville in *Les Employés*; S. Vachon, ' "Gloire et immortalité balzaciennes"' (333–57), on the development of B.'s literary reputation; A. Compagnon, 'Le Balzac de la IIIe République' (359–74), covering the reception of his work from 1870 to 1914; A. Lascar, 'Frédéric Soulié, lecteur et rival de Balzac' (375–93), on he who was briefly master of the roman-feuilleton, and the consolidation of 19th-c. realism; A. Lorant, 'Proust et Balzac: ultimes scènes de comédie' (395–416), showing how re-reading the later works of *La Comédie humaine* after *À la recherche du temps perdu* enables a clearer perception of tragic events; M. Autrand, 'Rire et humour dans *Le Faiseur*' (429–37), on the originality of the play; J.-C. Yon, 'Balzac et Scribe: "Scenes de la vie théâtrale" ' (439–49), regretting that more attention is not given to the playwright; T. Bodin, 'Esquisse d'une préhistoire de la génétique balzacienne' (463–90), on editions of B. and their approach to MSS and proofs; B. Berthier, 'Regards sur le manuscrit de *Pierrette*' (491–502), on B.'s proof corrections; C. Bustarret, 'Interroger "l'existence matérielle de l'oeuvre" ' (503–27), concerned with the paper on which B. wrote; J.-D. Ebguy, 'Pour un nouveau romanesque: la problématique esthétique du *Bal de Sceaux*' (541–66), showing that social change is reflected in the evolution of B.'s manner of writing; T. Kashiwagi, 'La poétique balzacienne dans *Facino Cane*' (567–74), suggesting that the novel is an allegory of the novelist's beginnings; A. Mura-Brunel, 'Le livre et le lecteur dans *La Muse du département*' (575–92), examining the relationship between B. and the reader. There follow articles on B.'s influence in Hungary, Czechoslovakia, Italy, and Morocco, the representation of his stories in the cartoon strip, his influence on other French authors, views on administrative structures, and style.

Pour Balzac et pour les livres, ed. Thierry Bodin, Klincksieck, 1999, 147 pp., contains the Proceedings of a conference held in June 1996 to pay homage to Roger Pierrot. It includes: M. Ambrière, 'Introduction' (7–10); S. Vachon, 'La bibliographie: pilote, mère et foyer de la recherche (balzacienne)' (11–29), noting B.'s attraction to bibliography, and the fact that the bibliography of his work has been made clearer during the last 90 years; J.-L. Diaz, 'À quoi servent les correspondances? L'exemple de Balzac' (31–40), on the considerable value of B.'s letters, with a plea for a new and complete edition to succeed the five Garnier volumes; T. Bodin, 'Autour de quelques lettres inédites: Balzac et ses procès' (41–61), on letters related to the printing of the *Corps du droit français*, and the publication of the *Physiologie du mariage* and *Le Médecin de campagne*; J. Meyer-Petit, 'Balzac et les estampes: données de la correspondance' (63–70), on letters related to B.'s considerable collection of engravings; R. Chollet, 'Éditer l'autre Balzac' (73–85), referring to the works which do not fall within *La Comédie humaine*, as published in the *Oeuvres diverses*; G. Sagnes, 'Éditer Flaubert aujourd'hui' (87–93), noting the difficulty of doing this in the light of editions of B.'s works; R.-J. Seckel, 'Le bibliothécaire, le bibliographe et l'érudition' (95–101), a librarian's view of a range of cataloguing difficulties; A. Bonnerot, 'Au temps des sessions Lovenjoul à Chantilly' (103–09), on the use of the Spoelberch de Lovenjoul collection before it was moved to Paris; F. Callu, 'Le département des manuscrits: enrichissement et valorisation du patrimoine' (111–14), showing the influence of Pierrot's work in the management of that department; L. Chotard, 'Correspondance et bibliographie: la paix du ménage' (115–24), considering the reproduction of unpublished letters in a biography; R. Pierrot, 'En guise de postface' (125–26), thanking the contributors at the time of publication, yet also regretting the death of two of their number, Guy Sagnes and Loïc Chotard. Danielle and Claude Dufresne, *Balzac et les femmes*, Tallandier, 1999, 318 pp., describes B.'s relationships with Laure de Berny, Laure d'Abrantès, Henriette de Castries, Zulma Carraud, and eventually with Madame Hanska. Martine Gärtner, *Balzac et l'Allemagne*, Paris–Montréal, L'Harmattan, 1999, 192 pp., begins with an account of the 15 years of frequent journeys through Germany to meet Madame Hanska, before dealing with the effect on the novels of B.'s acquaintance with Germans, and his appreciation of German art and culture. Attention is given to characters such as Fritz Brunner, the Graff brothers, Schmucke, and Schwab. Gilbert Gastho, *Honoré de Balzac: un génie européen*, L'Harmattan, 282 pp., is a comparatively brief biography, readable and reasonably thorough. It is questionable whether it covers new territory, and the suggestion that B. was a European, long before Europe became a political entity, could be better exploited.

Jean-Daniel Gollut and Joël Zufferey, *Construire un monde: les phrases initiales de La Comédie humaine*, Lausanne, Delachaux et Niestlé, 149 pp., uses the tools of discourse analysis to examine not only B.'s style but the very nature of his realism. We are shown that, from the very earliest sentences of a novel, B. makes a conscious attempt quickly to establish a credible reality: people, places, times, situations. The schema tends to be constructed through the skilful handling of referents, and analysis of the technique shows it to be an important means for the author to impose his will on the reader. J. Jacob, *Balzac's 'Iliade de la corruption': Säkularisierung des Bösen und 'poésie du mal' im 'cycle Vautrin'*, Heidelberg, Winter, 1999, 418 pp., is concerned with *Le Père Goriot*, *Illusions perdues* and *Splendeur et misères des courtisanes*, the cycle which B. described as the 'colonne vertébrale' of *La Comédie humaine*. Jacob proceeds to examine the novels with attention to style, to sociological history and to ideology, before reaching the conclusion that sociological methods are not appropriate to the study of literary works. An explanation of the phenomenon is offered in a link to the ongoing process of secularization which was taking place in French society as *La Comédie* was being written.

Maison de Balzac, *L'Artiste selon Balzac: entre la toise du savant et le vertige du fou*, Paris–Musées, 1999, 222 pp., was produced in support of the exhibition held from May to September of that year. Following B.'s article, 'Des Artistes', first published in *La Silhouette* in 1830, it contains: J. Meyer-Petit, 'Figures et figure de l'artiste selon Balzac'

(20–30), an introduction to the exhibition; R. Chollet, 'L'homme qui dispose de la pensée' (34–47), on B.'s particular concept of art and his various artist figures in *La Comédie humaine*; M. Ambrière, 'Balzac penseur et voyant' (56–76), starting from Louis Boulanger's portrait and examining B.'s perspective of science and the supernatural; Y. Gagneux, 'Peut-on analyser les dessins de Théophile Bra?' (78–93), on the recently-discovered drawings of a sculptor whom B. admired; D. Morel, 'Palissy, figure tutélaire de Balzac' (94–100), on the Saintonge potter and the influence of his work on descriptions in *La Comédie humaine*; S. Vachon, 'L'écrivain au travail' (118–24), on B.'s proof corrections and how he made them part of the creative process; M. Contensou, 'Fare invenzioni' (136–49), on B. and sculpture, and also on why he never wrote the promised *Les Deux Sculpteurs*; I. L.-J. Lemaistre, 'La sculpture et Balzac' (150–64), on its development during his lifetime and references to it in his writing; T. Bodin, 'Balzac et la musique' (172–88), showing how B.'s limited skills with the violin did not prevent the development of a sublime musical imagination; A. Panchout, 'Gambara et le *Panharmonicon*' (190–98), on moments of creative ecstasy in the novel of that name; B. Léal, 'Ces Balzac de Picasso' (206–20), responding to a text by Michel Leiris with an analysis of the influence of the writer upon the artist.

Maison de Balzac, *Il signor di Balzac: Balzac vu par l'Italie*, Paris-Musées, 110 pp., was in support of an exhibition held from October 2000 to January 2001. It includes: Y. Gagneux, 'Pour introduire "Il signor di Balzac"' (13–17), presenting the exhibition which derived from that held in Rome on the bicentenary of his birth; M. Butor, 'L'Italie phénix' (19–24), describing B.'s five journeys to Italy and his fascination with Italian culture; P. Brunel, 'Dante et Balzac: de la *Divine Comédie* à *La Comédie humaine*' (25–34), showing B.'s acknowledgement of D. in the choice of his title; P. D. Lombardi, 'Les voyages' (35–59), on B.'s journeys to Rome, Turin, Milan, Venice, Genoa, Florence, Bologna, Sardinia, and Naples; R. Pierrot, 'La "Dédicace" des *Parents pauvres*' (60–67), on a MS discovered in the Fondazione Camillo Caetani in Rome, explaining the dedication; P. D. Lombardi, 'Entre le public et la critique: chance et malchance de Balzac en Italie'(69–87), on the diverse fortunes of translations of B. into Italian. Judith Meyer-Petit, *Les Mots de Balzac*, Paris-Musées — Actes Sud, 1999, 127 pp., consists of essays on 60 key words and phrases, each accompanied by an illustration from art in Paris museums. The pictures are interesting, though the text tends to follow well-trodden paths. Girish Mishra, *Balzac, Mirror of Emerging Modern Capitalism*, Delhi, Pragati, 1999, xii + 385 pp., is an interesting reflection on B., apparently undertaken in order to understand the problems of India, and beginning with a comparison between the

French Revolution and the Indian National Movement. As for B. and his ideas on economics and society, it does not really cover new territory. Janell Watson, *Literature and Material Culture from Balzac to Proust*, CUP, 1999, x + 227 pp., considers questions related to collecting, consuming, classifying, and describing, in the work of B. and later writers, following the appearance of the *bibelot* in *Le Cousin Pons*. There are references to Baudrillard, Flaubert, Gautier, Edmond de Goncourt, Huysmans, Nordau, Proust, Simmel, and Zola. Irene Wiegand, *Das Erbe Sades in der Comédie humaine*, Stuttgart–Weimar, Metzler, 1999, viii + 270 pp., takes as a starting point the supposition that B. inherited from Sade the literary tradition of 'vertu malheureuse'. The two differ, not least in their notion of genius, S. following Diderot's principle of exemption from ordinary morals, B. being closer to Helvetius. *La Comédie humaine* is shown to display a modern narrative attitude, contrary viewpoints corresponding to Bakhtin's idea of polyphony. *Écrits sur le roman*, ed. Stéphane Vachon, LP, 350 pp., brings together in a convenient single volume, the various theoretical and critical texts with which B. accompanied his output from 1824 to 1846. The *apparatus criticus* is authoritive, thorough, and detailed.

STENDHAL

X. Bourdenet, 'Représentation du politique, politique de la représentation: les préfets de *Lucien Leuwen*', *Romantisme*, 106:13–26, analyses their performance on cognitive, theatrical, and political levels, concluding that performance is an essential framework for modernity. P. Lécroart, 'Stendhal et Claudel face à la musique du théâtre', *RHT*:127–46, refers to passages in *La Vie de Henry Brulard* concerning S.'s response to music. G. Rannaud, 'Stendhal et la tentation de l'histoire', *Romantisme*, 107:5–22, reveals S.'s continuing interest in history, and his concern that he might not be up to the task of becoming its bard, though only with *Armance* did he find a way of writing the history of his time. Philippe Berthier, *Vie de Henry Brulard de Stendhal*, Gallimard, 242 pp., is a companion to the Folio edition of the work. Although intended as an introduction, it represents an authoritative overview of recent research on the text, and the author takes pains to ensure that what is important is accessible to the reader. *Stendhal et le comique*, ed. Daniel Sangsue, Grenoble, ELLUG, 1999, 312 pp., includes: D. Sangsue, 'Stendhal et le comique' (7–25), an introduction to the papers which originated as a cycle of lectures at the Université Stendhal; P.-L. Rey, 'L'espagnolisme contre le génie comique' (29–42), reminding us of the influence of Cervantes on the young S., though he overcame it by giving characters self-derisory traits; J. Serroy, 'Stendhal et Molière' (43–59), on a profound influence, though he came to prefer Regnard's more innocent laughter; M.-P. Chabanne, '*L'Histoire de la peinture en Italie*: de l'*ekphrasis* à la satire anticléricale' (61–74), showing how the aesthetics of terror, sponsored by the Catholic Church and adopted by Michaelangelo, were transformed by S.'s irony; J. Gallant, 'Stendhal et la caricature' (75–89), on an art form which demonstrated spectacular development under the July Monarchy and which became a thematic motif in S.'s novels; B. Didier, 'Comique, ironie, humour dans les écrits intimes de Stendhal' (93–106), giving particular attention to the *Souvenirs d'égotisme* and to the target and register of comedy; N. Roelens, 'Égotisme et autodérision chez Stendhal: "Je tombe donc je suis"' (107–46), showing that the one implies the other; V. Brombert, '*Henry Brulard*: ironie et continuité' (147–55), suggesting that irony is an indirect way of preserving what is serious; S. Bell, 'La conscience parodique chez Stendhal: le cas d'*Armance*' (159–79), suggesting that, as S. constructed his identity in *La Vie de Henry Brulard* from a parody of texts by Rousseau and Chateaubriand, so in *Armance* the same happens with *La Princesse de Clèves*, *Les Liaisons dangereuses*, *La Nouvelle Héloïse*, and *Le Misanthrope*; M. Reid, ' "Rires" (sur *Lucien Leuwen*)' (181–99), finding that there is more laughter than in *Armance*, mainly through the reversal of the classic comic schema of the son triumphing over the father; B. Vibert, 'Dialogues comiques (À propos de *Lucien Leuwen*)' (201–27), using conversational pragmatics to analyse the function of the comic, irony, and theatricality in dialogues; D. Sangsue, '*La Chartreuse de Parme* ou la comédie du roman' (229–44), showing how far it is an essential part of the novel, yet indissociable from tragedy; C. François-Meynard, 'Un aspect du comique de la province chez Stendhal: le thème des provinciaux à Paris dans *Feder ou le mari d'argent*' (245–65), indicating the reversal of the usual schema of the provincial being considered ridiculous when in Paris; M. Crouzet, '*Lamiel* grotesque' (267–304), examining comic mechanisms linked to the pettiness of Norman society. Dominique Dumas, *Lectures d'une oeuvre*, *La Chartreuse de Parme*, *héros soit qui non y pense*, Temps, 126 pp., guides nervous students past the various stumbling blocks that they may otherwise encounter in the novel, leading them towards a more confident understanding of the author's intention and an appreciation of his modernity.

OTHER WRITERS

ARLINCOURT.　T. J. Hale, 'A forgotten best seller of 1821: *Le Solitaire* by the Vicomte d'Arlincourt and the development of European

horror Romanticism', *GoSt*, 2 : 185–204, identifies this highly successful and much translated novel as the source of the *roman frénétique*, and
also an influence on the English Gothic novel.

DUMAS PÈRE. *Alexandre Dumas, de conférence en conférence*, ed. Claude
Schopp, Centre national du livre — Syndicat Intercommunal de
Monte Cristo, 1999, 373 pp., brings together a series of unpublished
texts of lectures, ten in all, given by D. in Paris, Cherbourg, and
Lyon, to which are added press reviews and other relevant information. He travelled through France from December 1864 to April
1866, giving about 50 talks. *Alexandre Dumas: 1870, l'entrée dans l'éternité*,
ed. Claude Schopp et al., Centre National du Livre — Syndicat
Intercommunal de Monte Cristo, 324 pp., presents documents
relating to the last year of D.'s life and the five years after his death.
Few are by D. himself, as he no longer found it easy to write, but his
final article, 'Le Taureau', shows his narrative skills to be
undiminished.

HUGO. J. Blancart-Cassou, 'Du grotesque hugolien au grotesque
de Ghelderode: influence, rencontres, divergences', *RHLF*,
100 : 1337–50, indicates the considerable influence which H. exerted
on G.'s writing though, whereas for H. the portrayal of the grotesque
was linked to faith in Providence, for G. it was frequently associated
with the idea of evil. F. Chenet-Faugeras, 'Archéologie d'un chapitre
des *Misérables*: "Où on lira deux vers qui sont peut-être du diable" ',
ib., 1527–45, identifies a source of the chapter in the *Histoire de l'abbaye
royale de Jumièges* by C.-A. Deshayes. M. Roman, ' "Ce cri que nous
jetons souvent": le Progrès selon Hugo', *Romantisme*, 108 : 75–90,
finds in the works of exile the aesthetic, political, and philosophical
aspects of H.'s idea of progress. G. F. Imhoff, 'Jeux d'ombre et de
lumière dans *Les Misérables* de Victor Hugo', *NCFS*, 29 : 64–77,
describes the use of light and darkness in the story of Jean Valjean as
a representation of H.'s view of the world as chiaroscuro. James
M. Phillips, *Representational Strategies in Les Misérables and Selected
Drawings by Victor Hugo*, NY, Lang, 1999, 155 pp., is an analysis of the
relationship between text and image, observing that the desire to fuse
reality to fantasy in both media often results in a merger of form and
meaning. Myriam Roman, '*Le Dernier Jour d'un condamné' de Victor
Hugo*, Gallimard, 210 pp., is a companion to the Folio edition of an
influential work. Firstly, it offers a detailed and authoritative analysis
of the text. Secondly, it looks into the broader background,
considering why it was written, and relating it to other works of the
period dealing with capital punishment.

LATOUCHE. C. Torelli, 'Le dialogue avec le lecteur dans les
romans d'Henri de Latouche', *SFr*, 44 : 333–49, examines seven

novels written from 1829 to 1845 and traces the development of a narrative strategy typified by a continuing dialogue with the reader.

MÉRIMÉE. C. Cropper, 'Mérimée's *Colomba* and the July Monarchy', *NCFS*, 29:35–46, proposes a new way of reading M., taking into account the extent to which political and cultural tensions infiltrate his narrative. Id., 'Prosper Mérimée reassessed: the evolution of the French short story', *RoN*, 40:351–60, suggests that M. developed a genre in which action and direct discourse replaced introspection and moral explanations. R. MacKenzie, 'Space, self and the role of the *Matecznik* in Mérimée's *Lokis*', *FMLS*, 36:196–208, explores the themes of duality and division in the self, which are to the fore in one of M.'s last stories. S. Sprenger, 'Consummation as catastrophe: failed union in Prosper Mérimée's *La Venus d'Ille*', *DFS*, 51:26–36, finds that the story continues a long-standing Christian allegorical tradition. K. Vassiler, '*Colomba*: la vengeance entre classicisme et romantisme', *RHLF*, 100:1311–36, suggests that M.'s text breaks established codes and transcends the difference between Classicism and Romanticism. Mario Bois, *La trilogie de Seville: Don Juan, Figaro, Carmen*, Marval, 1999, 203 pp., contains only 17 pages devoted to M.'s Carmen, before moving on to Bizet. The various sources of the story are considered, including M.'s meeting with Manuela de Teba and the story of her brother-in-law's unfortunate affair with a cigarette maker. Clarisse Requena, *Unité et dualité dans l'oeuvre de Prosper Mérimée: mythe et récit*, Champion, 446 pp., starts with the assertion that M. was preoccupied by the idea of unity and duality, and that this was behind his oscillation between comedy and tragedy. His work was not only in literature, but also in history, architecture and archaeology, all three being linked. In addition, he was a polyglot philologist, well aware of Greek and Latin sources. Requena proceeds to trace the mythological element in his writing.

SAND. I. Naginski, 'Préhistoire et filiation: George Sand et le mythe des origines dans *Jeanne*', *Romantisme*, 106:63–71, shows the influence of a treatise by Jean-François Baraillon on a text which questions the origins of the human race and attempts to retrieve a lost feminine psychology. P. Prasad, 'Displaced performances: the erotics of theatrical space', *RoN*, 40:223–33, demonstrates how the theatre animates the erotic life of S.'s characters, yet is the privileged site for the displacement of desire. Pierre de Boisdeffre, *George Sand à Nohant*, Saint-Cyr-sur-Loire, Christian Pirot, 236 pp., is a biography centred on the house where she spent much of her life. It considers her family, her daily life, her loves, her political engagement, her friendship with other writers, and concludes with an examination of her distinct identity and her thought. Marielle Caors, *George Sand et le Berry*, Royer, 1999, 292 pp., is not so much a literary guide to the region as a study of locations in S.'s novels. The development of the 'roman champêtre' is examined carefully, and there is a thorough approach to early serialized editions. The interaction between the location and the narrative is demonstrated, and the present sites are identified. Bernardette Chovelon and Christian Abbadie, *La Chartreuse de Valldemosa: George Sand et Chopin à Majorque*, Payot et Rivages, 1999, 243 pp., is a thorough and accessible account of the well-known story. Françoise Genevray, *George Sand et ses contemporains russes: audience, échos, réécritures*, L'Harmattan, 412 pp., is a detailed examination, supported by a great mass of documentary proof, of the immense influence which S. exerted on Russian writers, and on the development of Russian thought. Her reputation as a feminist, republican, humanitarian socialist enabled her to contribute to the spread of liberal ideas. Belinda Jack, *George Sand: A Woman's Life Writ Large*, London, Chatto and Windus, 1999, xiv + 412 pp., is concerned not only with S.'s biography but particularly with her inner life: feelings and fantasies, ideas and beliefs. It is a convincing explanation of why S. behaved as she did. She has often been misunderstood and misrepresented, not least in different readings of power relations between her and her lovers. Cornelia Personne, *Langage-Narration-Écriture: évolution d'une problématique à travers cinq romans de George Sand*, Heidelberg, Winter, 1999, 332 pp., is concerned with novels written between 1834 and 1871: *André*, *Jeanne*, *La Petite Fadette*, *La Confession d'une jeune fille*, and *Nanon*. Attention is drawn to S.'s sensitivity to language and its importance in narrative.

SEGUR. A. Israel-Pelletier, 'Colonialism and French culture in the Comtesse de Segur', *DFS*, 53:3–11, shows that the imperialist attitudes and the emphasis in an idealized French cultural identity which are evident in the children's stories are symptoms of the unease of one who was born a Russian.

5. DRAMA

P. Berthier, 'Une expérience sans lendemain: le théâtre nautique (1834)', *RHT*: 19–48, describes an attempt to recreate the sea on the Romantic stage.

MUSSET. Michel Maslowski, *Kordian et Lorenzaccio: héros modernes?*, Montpellier, Espaces, 1999, 49 pp., compares M.'s drama with a work by Juliusz Slowacki, a Polish Romantic poet. Both plays are a study of the meaning and results of a heroic act. The comparison reveals the common philosophy of European Romanticism.

SCRIBE. Jean-Claude Yon, *Eugène Scribe, la fortune et la liberté*, Saint-Genouph, Nizet, 390 pp., deals with the author of 425 plays whose influence was particularly profound in Britain. The point is aptly made that his career is representative of the French cultural history of the period. His life and work are traced from his beginnings to the point where he was the most successful playwright in Europe, though his popularity declined after 1848. Above all, this first major work devoted to him goes some way to rescue him from the neglect he has suffered since his death.

6. WRITERS IN OTHER GENRES

BALLANCHE. Alan J. L. Busst, *La Théorie du langage de Pierre-Simon Ballanche*, Lewiston, Mellen, vii + 246 pp., is a careful and convincing analysis, and represents a major contribution to work on the philosopher. Though B. never produced a treatise on his theory, it appears in passages of varying length in most of his works, and was an attempt to reconcile conservative and liberal viewpoints.

FOURIER. Patrick Tacussel, *Charles Fourier: le jeu des passions: actualité d'une pensée utopique*, Desclée de Brouwer, 252 pp., demonstrates the modernity of F.'s social thought which, at the beginning of the 19th c., already brought into question the manner of social and economic development, at the expense of Man's fundamental needs and ecological equilibrium. His ideas on human behaviour can be seen to be close to those of the sociologists of the present day.

GONCOURT. Stéphanie Champeau, *La Notion d'artiste chez les Goncourt*, Champion, 557 pp., is a detailed account of the brothers' ideas on art and artists, with particular reference to the *Journal*. They perceived the artist to be an extraordinarily diverse and complex being who both constructs and destroys himself, but who in so doing is intoxicated by his art and lives in a state of jubilation.

LAMENNAIS. G. Banderier, 'Une lettre inconnue de Lamennais (20 juin [1849])', *FSB*, 76:4–5, is concerned with a document from the collection of Karl Geigy-Hagenbach, now held by the town and university library of Basle.

MAISTRE. Owen Bradley, *A Modern Maistre*, Lincoln–London, Nebraska U.P., 1999, xxi + 273 pp., claims to be the first account of M.'s social and political philosophy, though this is not quite true. It examines closely the basis of his philosophy, concluding that M. belongs as much to the history of the Enlightenment as to that of obscurantism, and is part of the emergence of conservative thought.

MICHELET. P. Petitier, 'Progrès et reprise dans l'histoire de Michelet', *Romantisme*, 108:65–74, describes the evolution of the idea of progress in M.'s work, which was closely linked to his handling of the essay form, not least in his perception of regression as a paradoxical but necessary element.

NAPOLEON.　Andy Martin, *Napoleon the Novelist*, Cambridge, Polity, 191 pp., reminds us that N. had a literary career and suggests that, had circumstances been different, he might have become a writer and man of letters.

SAINTE-BEUVE.　*Romantisme*, 109, is entitled: 'Sainte-Beuve ou l'invention de la critique'. It includes: G. Gengembre, 'Avant Sainte-Beuve: au nom du progrès ou la critique littéraire selon les idéologues' (7–14), showing that the *Idéologues* had laid the foundations on which S.-B. was to construct his particular concepts of genius, taste, and style; S. Travers de Faultrier, 'De l'oeuvre émancipée à la signature intérieure: situation juridique de l'auteur durant le siècle de Sainte-Beuve' (15–22), demonstrating the completion in the 19th c. of a slow evolution in the rights of literary property and the status of the author; A. Ubersfeld, 'Sainte-Beuve dans le *Journal* des Goncourt' (23–31), indicating, despite his physical and moral ugliness, the qualities which stand out; G. Antoine, 'Pour ou contre Sainte-Beuve' (33–44), noting the lively response to recent editions of his works and seeking to revive an old debate between adversaries and supporters; J.-L. Diaz, ' "Aller droit à l'auteur sous le masque du livre": Sainte-Beuve et la biographique' (45–67), on the desire to search for the inner man which lay behind his biographical curiosity; L. Chotard, 'Sainte-Beuve au risque du contemporain' (69–80), on his approach to the contemporary, as defined in *Portraits contemporains*; B. Diaz, ' "Écrire à voix basse": l'écriture féminine selon Sainte-Beuve' (81–97), on his interest in women's writing which he sought to rehabilitate, though he considered it a 'minor' form, in his *Portraits de femmes*; R. M. Verona, ' "Madame Récamier": entre portrait et causerie' (99–106), showing that, while he raised her status to that of a national monument, he remained acutely aware of her 'deficient' relationship with writing.

TALLEYRAND-PÉRIGORD.　Gérard Francoeur, *Talleyrand ou l'art de rouler tout le monde*, Le Cercle, 1999, 128 pp., is an amusing account of T.'s ideas and an explanation of his ability to influence the course of French politics.

THE NINETEENTH CENTURY
(POST-ROMANTIC)
POSTPONED

THE TWENTIETH CENTURY, 1900–1945
POSTPONED

THE TWENTIETH CENTURY SINCE 1945
POSTPONED

FRENCH CANADIAN LITERATURE

By CHRISTOPHER ROLFE, *Senior Lecturer in French, University of Leicester*

1. GENERAL

Robert Lahaise, *Expansion canadienne et repli québécois 1860–1896*, Outremont, Lanctôt, 254 pp., is an important study of the political dimension(s) of French Canadian literature in the 19th century. Antoine Sirois, *Lecture mythocritique du roman québécois*, Montreal, Triptyque, 1999, 136 pp., examines how A. Hébert, J. Ferron, J. Poulin, G. Roy, and Y. Thériault have integrated ancient myths into their works. The final chapter (in what is a somewhat uneven study) is an interesting appraisal of how Roy and Thériault have reworked the Canadian myth of the North. André Belleau, *Le Romancier fictif. Essai sur la représentation de l'écrivain dans le roman québécois*, Quebec, Nota bene, 1999, 232 pp., makes available once again B.'s seminal work. Rosemary Chapman, *Siting the Quebec Novel. The Representation of Space in Francophone Writing in Quebec*, Berne, Lang, 282 pp., tackles, with both perspicacity and perspicuity, a variety of key issues to do with spatiality including gender, 'migrant' writing, and Quebec's place in the wider world. Apart from its comments on more 'obvious' authors, the volume is recommended for its analyses of Madeleine Ouellette-Michalska and Régine Robin. P. Ó Gormaile, 'The representation of Ireland and the Irish in the Québécois novel', *QuS*, 29 : 128–34, usefully returns to a theme that Ó G. has made his own.

P. Rajotte, 'Le récit de voyage au XIXe siècle. Une pratique de l'intime', *Globe*, 3 : 15–37, discusses travel pieces by F.-X. Garneau, F. de Saint-Maurice, and A. Buies, and demonstrates how such pieces were often a favoured vehicle to communicate personal reflection. Maurice Emond, *Le Récit québécois comme fil d'Ariane*, Montreal, Nota bene, 213 pp., is a collection of useful essays on such diverse topics as *le récit fantastique* in Quebec, Franco-Manitoban literature (including pages on Gabrielle Roy), Yves Thériault, and Anne Hébert. Recommended. *QuS*, 28, has an excellent dossier on the contemporary *récit*. R. Gringas, 'Évolution du regard de la critique sur *Né à Québec. Louis Jolliet* d'Alain Grandbois. De l'histoire à la littérature' (121–29) is especially recommended. François Dumont, *La Poésie québécoise*, Montreal, Boréal, 1999, 127 pp., is an engaging overview of the major movements, trends, personalities, and texts that have marked the poetry of Quebec. The political contextualization is particularly effective. **Le Bref et l'instantané: à la rencontre de la littérature québécoise du XXIe siècle*, ed. Guy Poirier and Pierre-Louis Vaillancourt, Orléans (Ontario), David, xv + 236 pp. **Croire à l'écriture: Etudes de littérature* *québécoise en hommage à Jean-Louis Major*, ed. Yvan Lepage and Robert Major, Orléans (Ontario), David, 435 pp. P. Nepveu, 'Writing and reading in the year 2000: a survey of Quebec's mindscape', Molinaro, *Quebec*, 1–14, is a characteristically poised, somewhat melancholic reflection on books in Quebec in the new millennium. Not to be missed. Peter Dickinson, *Here is Queer: Nationalisms, Sexualities and the Literatures of Canada*, Toronto U.P., 1999, 262 pp., brings out how sexuality is yet another social factor in the literary deconstruction of a Canadian nationality/identity. Québécois theatre studies have long posited homosexuality as an integral part of a Quebec nationalist discourse and this ambitious, challenging study explores further those links in the works of M. Tremblay, R.-D. Dubois, and M. M. Bouchard. A. Braz, 'The absent protagonist: Louis Riel in nineteenth-century Canadian literature', *CanL*, 167:45–61, compares and contrasts the response of French and English Canadian writers to R. and brings out how both groups fail to address his national separateness. It includes some interesting pages on P. Le May and L. Fréchette. *Éditions du Blé: 25 ans d'édition*, ed. J. Roger Léveillé, Saint-Boniface, du Blé, 1999, 205 pp., is a celebratory anthology of mostly Manitoban writing and is consequently of value as an introduction to a somewhat neglected aspect of French Canadian literature.

Jean Cléo Godin and Dominique Lafon, *Dramaturgies québécoises des années quatre-vingt*, Montreal, Leméac, 1999, 264 pp., is divided into two parts. The first presents a coherent overview of the theatre of the period. The second presents essays on M. M. Bouchard, N. Chaurette, R.-D. Dubois. Although sensitive and well-informed, the essays are somewhat tame and do not really convey how exciting the plays of Dubois and Chaurette in particular are. *Le Théâtre québécois*, ed. Michel Trépanier and Claude Vaillancourt, Laval, Etudes Vivantes, 90 pp., is aimed at *collégiens* and in its bright but limited way would serve as a useful introduction to the topic. *Les Personnages du théâtre québécois*, ed. Georges Desmeules and Christiane Lahaie, Quebec, L'Instant même, 1999, 133 pp., provides descriptions of more than 70 characters who appear in key plays. A seemingly pointless exercise that might nevertheless provide a short-cut to the study of archetypes etc. *L'Envers du décor. Cahiers de recherche en théâtre*, Montreal, Maxime, 1999, 497 pp., reissues the *Cahiers de la Société du théâtre du Québec* published between September 1990 and June 1992 and constitutes a most useful research tool, presenting as it does often vital material that is no longer readily available. The last two *Cahiers* ('Approches théâtrales: histoire et modernité' and 'Le Vaudeville au Québec, 1900–1920') give an idea of the scope of the material. *LQu*, 97, has a useful little dossier on 'Ecrire le théâtre aujourd'hui' (18–21). *Cahiers de Théâtre. Jeu* remains indispensable to all those interested in aspects of Québécois theatre. In the context of this survey, the following are of particular value: M. Vaïs, 'Jean-Pierre Ronfard', *CTJ*, 93, 1999:135–39, and E. Paventi, 'Redécouvrir l'album de famille. *Tit-Coq* et *Bousille et les Justes*', *ib.*, 95:44–48.

Lori Saint-Martin, *Le Nom de la mère. Mère, filles et écriture dans la littérature québécoise au féminin*, Montreal, Nota bene, 1999, 331 pp. The prolific St.-M. discusses the pivotal mother-daughter relationship in such writers as Jovette Bernier, Gabrielle Roy, Nicole Houde, Anne Hébert, France Théoret, and Elise Turcotte. A clever, subtle, and gratingly polemical study. *Trajectoires au féminin dans la littérature québécoise (1960–1990)*, ed. Lucie Joubert, Montreal, Nota bene, 288 pp., presents the papers given at a conference of the same name held at Queen's University in May 1996. The papers, which seek to respond to the question 'en quoi le féminisme a-t-il ou n'a-t-il pas influencé le travail de nos auteurs durant toutes ces années?' are wide-ranging and often compelling. *Women Writing in Quebec. Essays in honour of Jeanne Kissner*, ed. Paula Ruth Gilbert et al., Plattsburgh, NY State U.P., 151 pp., presents a collection of authoritative articles by widely recognised women scholars. All of the pieces have been previously published but it is good to have them readily available in a volume such as this. *Etres femmes. Poèmes de femmes du Québec et de France*, ed. Claudine Bertrand and Patricia Latour, Trois Rivières, Les Ecrits des Forges, 1999, 172 pp., is an enterprising anthology that unites 16 poems from Quebec and 19 from France that give expression to 'une conscience aigüe de la condition des femmes [. . .] et de la condition humaine'.

L'Année de la science-fiction et du fantastique québécois 1997, ed. Claude Janelle and Jean Pettigrew, Quebec, Alire, 1999, 282 pp., could do with rather more ample articles and analyses but is nevertheless a useful research tool. *Le XIXe siècle fantastique en Amérique française*, Quebec, Alire, 1999, 368 pp., is a *recensement* of some 140 stories published in the 19th century. The volume also includes ten texts, including several which are very well known (by Pamphile Le May and Louis Fréchette, for example) and a very interesting example by Firmin Picard, an Acadian writer. Guy Laflèche, *Bibliographie littéraire de la Nouvelle France*, Laval, Singulier, 251 pp., is an invaluable research tool that covers both 'les textes à l'étude' and 'les études de texte'. Supplementary and complementary material will be added *au fur et à mesure* on <http://tornade.ere.umontreal.ca/~lafleche/nf/>.

2. Individual Authors

AQUIN. J.-F. Hamel, 'De révolutions en circonvolutions. Répétition du récit et temps de l'histoire dans *Prochain épisode*', *VI*, 25:541–62, analyses the many examples of narrative repetition that structure the novel, and sheds light on such issues as collective memory, representations of history, and the experience of the historical present.

BLAIS. K. L. Gould, 'La nostalgie postmoderne? Marie-Claire Blais, Dante et la relecture littéraire dans *Soifs*', *EtLitt*, 31.2, 1999:71–82, presents an analysis of the novel's nostalgic elements evoked by intertextual references, especially to Dante. R. Tremblay, 'Chronotope et sociogramme de la vocation: l'écrivain porte-parole dans *Un Joualonais sa Joualonie* de Marie-Claire Blais', *EtLitt*, 31.3, 1999:139–50, is a dense piece that uses two antithetical concepts to identify the key conflict determining the ideological structure of the novel. S. White, 'The political borders of language in Marie-Claire Blais's *L'Ange de la solitude*', *MLR*, 95:350–61, investigates, in the light of Monique Wittig's ideas on the heterosexual contract, B.'s tragic depiction of the female commune as the inevitable result of the violence of language.

BOSCO. P. R. Gilbert, 'Neurotic disorders: gendered inner violence in selected short stories by Monique Bosco and Hélène Rioux', *QuS*, 29:115–27, is a challenging — and somewhat unsettling — article that examines our role as readers.

BOUCHER. *LQu*, 94, 1999, has a useful dossier on B. (7–15).

CARRIER. Roch Carrier, *La Guerre, yes sir!*, ed. Guy Snaith, Bristol Classical Press, 102 pp., is a more than competent critical edition of this landmark text. The comments (that S. has rehearsed elsewhere) on the carnivalesque elements in the novel are particularly apposite.

CHAURETTE. *VI*, 25.3, has a valuable dossier on C. Alongside essays by such as M.-C. Lesage, P. Riendeau, and S. Nutting, there is an *inédit* by C., a monologue entitled 'Transformations' (431–35).

CHIASSON. F. Paré, 'Herménégilde Chiasson: the uncertain territory of the voice', *Ellipse*, 63:9–17, is a limpid introduction to the Acadian poet who won the Governor General's Award in 1999.

DUCHARME. Brigitte Seyfrid-Bommertz, *La Rhétorique des passions dans les romans d'enfance de Réjean Ducharme*, Sainte-Foy, Laval U.P., 1999, 270 pp., offers a systematic reading of *L'Avalée des avalés*, *Le Nez qui voque* and *L'Océantume*. Inspired by the work of Michel Meyer and Richard Coe, Northrop Frye, and Wolfgang Iser, this seemingly paradoxical study (D. distrusted rhetoric and strove to free himself from it) is a significant addition to D. studies. E. Haghebaert, 'Innovation-rénovation: Ducharme et des retours avant', *EtLitt*, 31.2, 1999:23–37, discusses how innovation in D.'s work is based on strategies which stress nostalgia.

FERRON. *Jacques Ferron: autour des commencements*, ed. Patrick Poirier, Outremont, Lanctôt, 360 pp., is an important collection of essays by such notable F. specialists as M. Biron, J.-P. Boucher, R. Ellenwood,

P. L'Hérault, and P. himself. The volume also contains a significant *inédit* : F.'s *comédie héroïque Les Rats*, with an introduction by Brigitte Faive-Duboz. R. Patry, 'Le vocabulaire francisé dans l'œuvre de Jacques Ferron: le cas du "Farouest"', *QuS*, 29:74–85

GAUVREAU. G. Lapointe, 'La lettre sous le regard du cyclope. La loi du secret dans la correspondance entre Claude Gauvreau et Paul-Emile Borduas', *Globe*, 3:39–63, is a somewhat convoluted piece that sheds light in passing on *Beauté baroque*.

GILL. Charles Gill, *Contes, Chroniques critiques*, ed. Réginald Hamel, Montreal, Guerin, 248 pp., is a vital collection of prose pieces by G. who is generally better known as a poet. The *Chroniques* (which appeared in *Les Débats* and *Le Canada* between 1900 and 1904) illuminate the society of his time but are perhaps especially significant for the insight they provide on the *École littéraire de Montréal*, Albert Lozeau, and Nelligan.

GODBOUT. Yvon Bellemare, *Jacques Godbout: le devoir d'inquiéter*, Brossard, Humanitas, 175 pp., is a lucid presentation of G.'s output, including his films, but offers little that is new or challenging.

GROULX. Juliette Lalonde-Rémillard, *Lionel Groulx. L'homme que j'ai connu*, Montreal, Fides, 59 pp., is the transcript of a talk given to the Société Saint-Jean-Baptiste de Montréal in May 1999, which perhaps says it all. However, L.-R. (G.'s niece) was his secretary for some 30 years and was to set up and direct the Centre de recherche Lionel Groulx in 1978 so the slim volume is not without its value.

HAMELIN. J.-F. Côté and S. Bélanger, 'Le nord-américanité en roman: *Le Soleil des gouffres* de Louis Hamelin', *VI*, 25:525–40, explores how the novel presents a new dimension on the problematic of Americanness in the wake of NAFTA.

HÉBERT. André Brochu, *Anne Hébert. Le secret de vie et de mort*, Ottawa U.P., 284 pp., covers the whole of H.'s output (poetry and theatre as well as the novels) with detailed analysis of the most important texts. A thorough, sensitive study that argues that 'toute l'œuvre est une quête du secret logé dans le cœur charnel, une quête du désir et des risques mortels qu'il fait courir.' L. Bonenfant, 'Loi du nom, loi du genre dans *Kamouraska*', *QuS*, 29:91–103, discusses the function of names as part of an evaluation of the novel's generic *métissage*. D. L. Boudreau. 'Anglophone presence in the early novels of Anne Hébert', *FR*, 74:308–18, examines the role of the English/Englishness in *Kamouraska, Les Enfants du sabbat, Les Fous de Bassan*. *LQu*, 98, has a dossier to mark the passing of H. (5–10).

HÉMON. Mathieu-Robert Sauvé, *Louis Hémon. Le fou du lac*, Montreal, XYZ, 183 pp., a so-called *récit biographique*, is not without interest but needs to be read with caution. C. Mitchell, 'Echoes of antiquity in *Maria Chapdelaine*', *QuS*, 29:54–63, refreshingly analyses the novel from the standpoint of classical mythology and Homeric imagery.

JASMIN.   C. Morgan, 'It's the end of the world as we know it: Quebec's remembered landscapes', *BJCS*, 14, 1999:52–62, is a reading of J.'s little-known road novel *Pleure pas, Germaine* that succeeds in shedding light on a variety of contemporary literary issues.

KOKIS.   E. Figueiredo, 'Représentations du Brésil dans la littérature québécoise contemporaine', *VI*, 25:563–75, concentrates on K.'s three earliest novels beginning with *Le Pavillon des miroirs* (1995).

LABERGE, ALBERT.   J.-P. Boucher, 'Albert Laberge, contestataire avant l'heure', *Globe*, 3:137–57, is a lively appraisal of L.'s short story 'La vocation manquée' (1942) which denounced the power the church had over education. L. appears as a precursor of the changes wrought during the Quiet Revolution. J.-P. Boucher, 'Une nouvelle recueil: *Lorsque revient le printemps* d'Albert Laberge', *QuS*, 29:64–73, confirms F. L. Ingram's contention that L.'s volume of seemingly unconnected tales is rather akin to a 'short story cycle'.

LABERGE, MARIE.   C. D. Rolfe, 'The drama of Quebec past and present: three plays by Marie Laberge', Cardy, *Theatre*, 215–33, discusses three plays by L. that take Quebec as their subject or starting-point. L.'s technique and inventiveness and her use of language are amongst the several facets explored. J. den Toonder, 'Voyages intérieurs dans trois romans contemporains. L'écriture intimiste de Bruno Hébert, Gaétan Soucy et Marie Laberge', *Globe*, 3:65–81, argues that at the end of the 20th c. the Quebec novel is characterized by its intimism. L.'s *Cérémonie des anges* is one of the three novels discussed.

LALONDE.   K. Mezei, '*Le Poème-affiche et la langue d'affichage*: Michèle Lalonde's "Speak White"', Molinaro, *Quebec*, 39–53, is a lively exploration of the poem's different incarnations and as a controversial example of inter-textuality.

LEMAY.   Pamphile Le May, *L'Affaire Sougraine*, Sainte-Foy, ed. Rémi Ferland, Editions de la Huit, 1999, 374 pp., makes available a novel whose value as a social document far outweighs its literary worth. The critical apparatus provided by F. is excellent.

LEMELIN.   Daniel Bertrand, **Roger Lemelin, l'enchanteur*, Montreal, Stanké, 328 pp.

MIRON.   Axel Maugey, *Gaston Miron: une passion québécoise*, Brossard, Humanitas, 1999, 128 pp., is not altogether without interest but does seem stale and even inconsequential.

OUELLETTE-MICHALSKA.   J. LeBlanc, 'Autotextes, avant-textes, intertextes: les journeaux intimes de Madeleine Ouellette-Michalska', *EtLitt*, 31.2, 1999:107–17, analyses some of the discrepancies between O.-M.'s diaries broadcast on Radio-Canada in the 1980s and the published version of *La Tentation de dire*.

PERRAULT. L. Mailhot, 'Pierre Perrault: poetry beyond the pale of literature?', *Ellipse*, 62, 1999:11–24, is a stylish piece that insists that P. 'seeks to restore writing to its source in popular language, the oral, everyday speech'.

POULIN. A.-M. Miraglia, 'Le lecteur-fictif et la lecture critique chez Jacques Poulin: du *Vieux Chagrin* à *Chat Sauvage*', *QuS*, 29:104–14.

ROY. *Le Temps qui m'a manqué: suite de La Détresse et l'enchantement*, ed. F. Ricard, D. Fortier, and J. Everette, Montreal, Boreal, 106 pp.

SAVARD. *Relecture de l'œuvre de Félix-Antoine Savard*, ed. Roger Le Moine and Jules Tessier, Montreal, Fides, 1999, 198 pp., presents an eclectic mix of papers from a conference held at the University of Ottawa in 1996.

THÉRIAULT. Victor-Lévy Beaulieu, *Un Loup nommé Yves Thériault*, Trois-Pistoles, Editions Trois-Pistoles, 1999, 266 pp., is neither a biography nor a literary study and tells us rather more about B. than it does about T. C. Gagnon, 'Orality and narrative: Yves Thériault's radio drama "Le Samaritain" ', Molinaro, *Quebec*, 30–38, is a poised, thoughtful contribution to our understanding of orality in T. and of his writing for radio, an immense body of work that has yet to attract the critical attention it deserves.

TREMBLAY. Michel Tremblay, *Les Belles-sœurs*, ed. Rachel Killick, Bristol Classical Press, 83 pp., is a critical edition that pulls off the difficult trick of introducing a multi-faceted text without spoonfeeding the student. The comments on T.'s use of *joual*, for example, fit the bill exactly. M. Cardy, 'Michel Tremblay: approaches to three plays from the period 1981–1990', Cardy, *Theatre*, 203–14, demonstrates with vigour and clarity that, even if they take second place in critical opinion to his prose fiction, the 'inventiveness and theatrical flair' of the plays T. wrote in the 1980s easily bears comparison with earlier works.

CARIBBEAN LITERATURE

By MARY GALLAGHER, *University College Dublin*

1. GENERAL

Littératures postcoloniales et représentations de l'ailleurs: Afrique, Caraïbe, Canada, ed. Jean Bessière and Jean-Marc Moura, Champion, 1999, 194 pp., includes R. Fonkoua, 'L'espace du "voyageur à l'envers"' (99–124), a typology of travel to Europe from elsewhere, from the 'pittoresque' (African-Americans), to the 'savant' (Africans) and the 'philosophe' (as in Glissant's *Soleil de la conscience*); and F. Simasotchi-Brones, 'Espace et roman antillais: d'un espace problématique à un espace emblématique' (83–98), for whom space is the lynchpin of creole identity: firstly, 'l'espace subi', then 'l'espace accepté et conquis', and finally mythic, poetic, and symbolic space. However, local Caribbean space is studied here to the exclusion of the relational dimension that should, surely, loom large. Sam Haigh, *Mapping a Tradition: Francophone Women's Writing from Guadeloupe* (MHRA Texts and Dissertations, 48), London, MHRA, 234 pp., is informed by a lucid perspective on theoretical positions (in particular Spivak and Irigaray) and gives valuable critical readings of many key texts of this rich tradition. A first chapter probes intersections of the power relations founded on race, gender, and culture in Jaqueline Manicom's *Mon examen de blanc* and Michèle Lacrosil's *Cajou*, while the second shows how Maryse Condé's first two novels highlight the gender bias behind negritude and construct the African connection in relation to issues of gender and origin. The third chapter, on the relation to the past, examines Schwarz-Bart's *Ti-Jean L'Horizon* and Condé's *Les Derniers Rois mages*. Continuing to track the Caribbean quest for its history and identity, subsequent chapters focus on Lacrosil's *Demain Jab-Herma* and Condé's *Traversée de la mangrove*, before locating in two texts (by Condé and Bébel-Gisler) a rewriting of 'dominant historical narratives' and a deployment of a powerful (m)othertongue (Creole, witchcraft, storytelling, etc). Anna Malena, *The Negotiated Self: The Dynamics of Identity in Francophone Caribbean Narrative*, NY, Lang, 192 pp., explores a common concern with issues of identity in Bébel-Gisler's *Léonora*, Condé's *Traversée de la mangrove*, and Ollivier's *Passages*, and as the first and last of these works have been under-analysed, Malena's readings are particularly welcome. Identity is shown to emerge in these works through merging narratives and ongoing dialogic process. In B. Cherubini, 'La créolisation socio-culturelle à l'heure de la mondialisation: interculturalité, créolités, système-monde', *ECre*, 22.1:119–36, interesting comparisons are made between Chamoiseau's *Texaco* and sociological studies of French Caribbean communities. R. and S. Price, 'Shadowboxing in the mangrove: the politics of identity in postcolonial Martinique', pp. 123–62 of *Caribbean Romances: The Politics of Regional Representation*, ed. Belinda J. Edmondson, Charlottesville–London, Virginia U.P., 240 pp., is a cogent critique of the *créolité* movement. The latter's originality is questioned and its insularity and exclusivity are imputed to neglect or ignorance of other New World perspectives on cultural identity. *Postcolonialisme et autobiographie: Albert Memmi, Assia Djebar, Daniel Maximin*, ed. Alfred Hornung and Ernstpeter Ruhe, Amsterdam–Atlanta, Rodopi, 1998, 260 pp., contains M. Praeger, 'Biographie africaine, autoethnographies antillaises' (245–54), as well as C. Chaulet-Achour and D. Maximin, 'Sous le signe du colibri: traces et transferts autobiographiques dans la trilogie de D. Maximin' (203–18), which dialogically elucidates the processes that shape M.'s writing, in particular, intertextuality, dual identity, and dialogism. K. A. Sprouse, 'Lieu de mémoire, lieu de créolité: the Plantation as site of memory', *CRR*, 18:153–61, names the limitations of the notion of 'authentic creole culture' prevalent in *créolité* theory, arguing that it effaces non-European and non-African contributions to creole culture along with the roles of women slaves, house slaves, and *petit marronnage*.

2. INDIVIDUAL AUTHORS

CÉSAIRE. P. De Souza, 'Des cendres de Saint-Pierre au *Cahier* de Césaire', *FS*, 54:177–86, shows how C.'s poetic trajectory and the structure, vocabulary, and imagery of the *Cahier* are modelled on the specifics of Caribbean vulcanism (long latent phases followed by sudden but not completely unpredictable eruptions).

CHAMOISEAU. In Maeve McCusker, 'Entretien avec Patrick Chamoiseau', *FR*, 73:725–33, C. confirms his committment to place and responds to various recent criticisms of his writing and of the *créolité* movement in general. L. Milne, 'From *créolité* to *diversalité*: the postcolonial subject in Patrick Chamoiseau's *Texaco*', pp. 162–80 of *Subject Matters*, ed. Paul Gifford and Johnnie Gratton, Amsterdam, Rodopi, 243 pp., usefully stands back from Chamoiseau's writing to assess the broader value of his 'political-ethical' perspective on identity (based on transcendance of opposition and insistence on 'adaptability and flexibility'), deemed 'fundamental to the sense of self in any culture' and a model 'of the subject in general'. Furthermore, C.'s perspective on identity, founded on Memmi's and Fanon's postcolonial theories and grounded in history and location, is said to be 'not only cultural'.

CONDÉ. P. De Souza, '*Traversée de la Mangrove*: éloge de la créolité, écriture de l'opacité', *FR*, 73:822–33, shows how C.'s novel, set in Guadeloupe, valorizes diversity in a more authentic manner than the creolity pamphlet since its characters relate to the other Caribbean islands and to the American continent, and also because of its polyphonic narrative structure and its construction of gender and class. J. Hayes, 'Looking for roots among the mangroves: *Errances enracinées* and migratory identities', *CRev*, 42, 1998:459–74, studies both the fictionality and the rhetoric of the rootedness evoked in Alex Haley's *Roots*, Simone Schwarz-Bart's *Ti-Jean l'horizon*, as well as Condé's *Traversée de la mangrove* and *Des mangroves en terre haute* by the Congolese writer, P. Ngandu Nkashama, before concluding that the 'essentially queer' articulation of the 'multiple roots of the mangrove disrupt[s] the normativity implied by a notion of "roots" that depends on the family tree'. R. Larrier, 'A roving "I": *errance* and identity in Maryse Condé's *Traversée de la mangrove*', *EsC*, 38.3, 1998:84–94, is a wide-ranging meditation on the imagery of trees, especially roots, and also presents an interesting reading of the name of Condé's anti-hero. D. Licops, 'Expériences diasporiques et migratoires des villes dans *La Vie scélérate* et *Desirada* de Maryse Condé', *NFS*, 39:110–20, studies the alienating and revelatory value of urban space, discerning in the first novel an expanded diasporic logic in which relation to the origin(s) is primary, and in *Désirada* a migratory plot in which access to the origin and to notions of roots and identity is disrupted. In R. Ramsay, 'The nature of hybridity in Maryse Condé's *Traversée de la mangrove*', *NFS*, 39:213–25, the promising notion of hybridity might have been more fully situated.

ÉTIENNE. M.-D. Le Rumeur, 'Le Bon, La Belle, la Bête: *Le Bacoulou* de Gérard Etienne', *ASCALFY*, 4:179–95, shows how this short text crosses generic boundaries to suggest cinematographic references and parallels with fairy-tales, fables, and ideological treatises.

GLISSANT. *Poétiques d'Edouard Glissant*, ed. Jacques Chevrier, Sorbonne U.P., 1999, 369 pp. What is surprising about this volume in comparison with the proceedings of the 1988 Oporto conference (*Horizons d'Edouard Glissant*, Pau, J&D, 1990) is its far narrower range. Since very few articles explore the specifically literary work (novels, plays, poetry) in any depth, the 'poetics' of the title refers principally to the author's essays. Although it features three lively discussions (including one on slavery) and some stimulating studies, the volume would have gained from being more informed by the 1988 'état des lieux', and hence by a sense both of what still needed to be addressed and of Glissant's production in the interval. Significantly, two contributors also involved in the previous project tackle here the delicate question of repetition across Glissant's theoretical works. C. Britton, 'Fictions of identity and identities of fiction in Glissant's *Tout-Monde*', *ASCALFY*, 4:47–59, studies connections made in *Tout-monde* between 'plural, variable, relational personal identity' and the play across boundaries between generic identities, working on movement between text and world, fiction and reality, via the 'indeterminate multiplicity of the *sujets d'énonciation*', including a 'typically rhizomatic movement across different diegetic levels'. L. Moudileno, 'Retrouver la parole perdue', *RR*, 90, 1999:83–91, examines the status of Eudoxie's tale and Hégésippe's construction (or reconstruction) as a 'sujet écrivant, auteur de son propre texte' in *Mahagony*, exploring *entre autres* the relation between writing and oral narrative.

LAFERRIÈRE. A. M. Miraglia, 'Dany Laferrière, l'identité culturelle et l'intertexte afro-américain', *PF*, 56:121–29, situates Laferrière in relation to African-American writers such as Himes and Baldwin, showing how reference to the myths, themes, and clichés of this tradition signals his work as politically motivated and inscribes it in a well-charted 'tradition protestataire'.

LAHENS. K. Gyssels, 'La nouvelle en Haïti, correspondance du Nouveau Monde: les recueils de Yanick Lahens et de Pascale Blanchard-Glass', *PF*, 56:103–20, outlines the role of the short story in Haitian writing, contrasting Lahens's perspective (less emphasis on orality and physical exile and more overtly ideological leanings) with that of her compatriot Blanchard-Glass.

MAXIMIN. K. Gyssels, ' "Capitale de la douleur": Paris dans *L'Isolé Soleil* et *Un Plat de porc aux bananes vertes*', *FR*, 73:1087–99, contrasts the diaries of Siméa and Mayotte and also considers the representation of Paris in other work by Simone Schwarz-Bart and in Gisèle Pineau's writing.

AFRICAN/MAGHREB LITERATURE
POSTPONED

III. OCCITAN STUDIES

LANGUAGE

By KATHRYN KLINGEBIEL, *Professor of French, University of Hawai'i at Mānoa*

1. BIBLIOGRAPHICAL AND GENERAL

C. Bonnet, 'Occitan language', *MLAIntBibl*, 3, 1999 [2000]: 202–04. K. Klingebiel, 'Occitan linguistic bibliography for 1999', *Tenso*, 15: 141–89. M. Westmoreland, 'Current studies in Occitan linguistics [2000]', *CRLN* 49: 48–53. J. Staes, 'Documents concernant la langue gasconne conservés dans les collections de manuscrits des bibliothèques françaises (1)', *RBG*, 1999, no.3: 41–43, presents items located during preparation of the new guide to the Archives of the Pyrénées-Atlantiques. R. Schlösser, **'Der Berliner Beitrag zur Okzitanistik bis 1945', Rieger, *Okzitanistik*, 299–316. B. Cerquiglini and J.-L. Lebrave describe **'Philectre: un projet de recherche pluridisciplinaire en philologie électronique' in *ASNP*, 5, 1998: 233–39.

A. Rieger, **'Zukunftsaussichten und Perspektiven der deutschsprachigen Okzitanistik (mit Diskussionsbeiträgen von T. Meisenburg, J.Rüdiger, T. D. Stegmann, B. Wehr und R. Bauer)', Rieger, *Okzitanistik*, 15–34. A. Rossell, **'Per un projècte interuniversitari per la promocion de la lenga e de la cultura occitana dins l'universitat europèa: L'Arxiu Occità (Arxiu de Llengua, Literatura i Civilització Occitana) de l' Universitat Autònoma de Barcelona e la Ret interuniversitària per la promocion dels estudis occitans', *ib.*, 35–42. C. D. Pusch, **'Das Corpus Occitano-Gascon als Beispiel multimedialer Sprachdatenaufbereitung', *ib.*, 43–56. F. P. Kirsch, **'Okzitania und Frankophonie', *ib.*, 57–69.

La Poésie de langue d'oc des troubadours à Mistral, ed. Suzanne Thiolier-Méjean (*FL*, 129), 1999, 378 pp., contains the proceedings of a conference held at the Sorbonne in December 1998: M. Pfister, 'La lexicographie de l'ancien occitan' (151–60) discusses how exemplary editions of literary and non-literary works can be used to fill lacunae both in *DAO*, I-VII and in *DOM*, I; P. Ricketts, 'Peire Bremon Ricas Novas, problèmes lexicologiques' (161–69), elucidates *covinen* 'accord' and *[mettre en] soan* 'souffrance'; M. Perugi, 'Variantes de tradition et variantes d'auteur dans la chanson XII (BdT 29,8) d'Arnaut Daniel' (115–50), finds two constellations of MSS (*CMSg,Uac*) which may contain authorial variants; S. Häfele, 'L'infini dans les chansons de Raimbaut de Vaqueiras' (325–29), finds the poet placing infinitives in verse-final position, as a type of prosodic instrument; S. Thiolier-Méjean, 'Les études de langue d'oc à la Sorbonne du XIXe s. à nos jours' (39–76), is a valuable retrospective for the modern period; and P. Blanchet, 'Parla Prouvençau encuei: où en sont les pratiques dialectales?' (237–50), maintains his anti-Occitanist stance.

J. Pietri, *OPM*, 93:28, reviews and describes several Occitan institutions of general interest: CIRDOC (Centre Inter-Régional de Développement de l'Occitan), the new Béziers *mediathèque* for Occitania; COL'OC (Centre d'Oralité de la Langue d'Oc, inaugurated Feb. 2000 in Aix-en-Provence), dedicated to capturing spoken usage of Occitan; and CIEL D'OC (Centre International de l'Écrit en Langue d'Oc, in Berre-L'Étang), which aims to record electronically all writings in the languages of *oc*. In *Occitans!*, 95:8–9, L. Castel reviews Gérard Zuchetto's new CD *Trob'Art Concept 1*, with music and songs by many troubadours as well as modern-day composers. Included is a word about the CREMM-Trobar Na Loba, Centre européen des troubadours, in Pennautier (Aude).

2. MEDIEVAL PERIOD (TO 1500)

GENERAL. Maurice Romieu and André Bianchi, *La Lenga del 'trobar': precís de gramatica d'occitan ancian. La Langue du 'trobar': précis de grammaire d'ancien occitan*, Pessac, Bordeaux U.P., 1999, 199 pp., is a bilingual work that will be useful primarily to students.

PHONETICS, PHONOLOGY, MORPHOSYNTAX. P. Bec, 'Encore sur la prononciation du *u* en occitan médiéval: l'apport de l'ancien gascon au problème', *RLaR*, 103, 1999:213–22, brings new arguments to bear on the side of the 'üistes'. K. Dietz, 'Die gotischen Lehnwörter mit *au* im Altprovenzalischen und die Rekonstruktion des gotischen Lautsystems', *Sprachwissenschaft*, 24, 1999:127–56. In Gothic loanwords attested in O Pr, Gothic *au* (< Gmc *au) was taken over as a diphthong rather than as a monophthong. B. Wehr, *'Diathesen im Altokzitanischen (mit einem Exkurs zu den lateinischen Vorläufern des "reflexiven Passivs")', Rieger, *Okzitanistik*, 107–31.

LEXIS AND LEXICOLOGY. N. Hörsch edits Kurt Baldinger's *Dictionnaires onomasiologiques de l'ancien occitan et de l'ancien gascon, Index 1–1185*, Tübingen, Niemeyer, xviii + 251 pp. Provided are convenient alphabetic indexes to currently available *DAO* and *DAG* fascicles, covering sky and atmosphere, earth, and plants. Max Pfister edits Kurt Baldinger's *Dictionnaire onomasiologique de l'ancien occitan. Supplément bibliographique*, Tübingen, Niemeyer, v + 74 pp., with its dual aim to establish a concordance with *DOM*, and to facilitate the unification of the abbreviations used in *DOM* and *DAO/DAG*. To be excluded are Gascon materials (confined to *DAG*); and Occitan attestations after

1600. 49 corrections to *DAG* I–VI are listed by J. Boisgontier, 'Notes
sur le *Dictionnaire onomasiologique de l'ancien gascon*', *RLaR*, 103,
1999:223–27. M. Pfister, *'Überblick über die altokzitanische Lexi-
kologie 1986–1998', Rieger, *Okzitanistik*, 73–96. C. Aslanoff, 'Le
provençal des juifs et l'hébreu en Provence: le dictionnaire *Šar šot ha-
Kesef* de Joseph Caspi', *FL*, 130:41–45. Caspi's inventory of Hebrew
roots contains many glosses that contribute to general knowledge of
13th- and 14th-c. administrative Provençal. R. Cantavella, *'The
meaning of *destral* as 'go-between' in the Catalan Facet and in Old
Occitan', *MAe*, 67, 1998:304–12.

PARTICULAR SEMANTIC FIELDS.   R. M. Medina Granda, 'Sobre el
origen de *pas* en occitano antiguo: algunos nuevos ejemplos', *CILPR*
22, II, 327–35, discusses how *pas*, although not a borrowing in O Pr,
was avoided by the troubadours. A. Comes, 'Nota sull'espressione
provenzale *a tapi*', *CN*, 58, 1998:325–29, argues for 'humbly',
'invisibly' < Lat. *AD TAPINUM. J.-P. Chambon, *'Aocc. *arta* et *gralha*:
encore sur la localisation du manuscrit *Brit. Mus. Add. 17920* (Brunel
MS 13)', *RLaR*, 104:165–68. P. Maurice, *'La Maison et son
ameublement en Gévaudan à la fin du moyen âge', *JS*, 1998:115–58.

ONOMASTICS.   W. Müller, *'Zur vorgeschichtlichen Flussnamen-
landschaft Südfrankreichs', Rieger, *Okzitanistik*, 97–106.

TEXTS.   J. Belmon and F. Vielliard, *'Latin farci et occitan dans
les actes du XIe siècle', *BEC*, 155, 1997:149–83. R. Bòrdas, 'L'Istoria
de Guilhem dau Molin', *PN*, 86:16–17, edits a Latin text dated 1214,
with Occitan commentary and translation. J. Ducos, 'L'écrit scientifique au Moyen Age — langue d'oc et langue d'oïl', *Garona*, 15,
1999:55–71, reviews texts that mix Latin with Occitan, appending a
useful chronology of medieval Occitan scientific texts. J. Taupiac,
'L'occitanitat del gascon administratiu medieval, 3', *Occitans!*, 96:16,
concludes from his reading of 12th- to 18th-c. documents: 'Tot fa
pensar a una unitat del lengatge administratiu del Bearn a la
Provença.' L. Gimeno Betí, *'Català i occità: a l'entorn de la llengua
del *Cançoner dels Masdovelles*', *RLiR* 64:119–65.

H.-I. Radatz, *'Der (wirklich) letzte Trobador: Jordi de Sant Jordi
und die okzitanische Sprache', Rieger, *Okzitanistik*, 133–46.
J. Kabatek, *'Lo Codi und die okzitanischen Texttraditionen im 12.
und 13. Jahrhundert', *ib.*, 147–64. A. Fausel, *'Die Trobadorlyrik
zwischen Mündlichkeit und Schriftlichkeit. Ein Werkstattbericht', *ib.*,
165–76. M. Bernsen, *'Die Minnedichtung Wilhelms von Aquitanien
als Diskurs', *ib.*, 207–16. J. Rüdiger, *'Das Morphem *Frau*. Überlegungen zu einer "Grammatik der Mentalität" im okzitanischen
Mittelalter', *ib.*, 231–48. R. Bauer, *'Wert, Wirkung und Würdigung
der altokzitanistischen Arbeiten von Carl Appel', *ib.*, 317–38.

DIALECTS

GASCON. J.-F. Martin, **Cartulaire de l'abbaye Saint Jean-de-Sorde*, Biarritz, Atlantica, 1999, 358 pp. A. Cauhapé builds a new series around 15th- and 16th-c. texts concerning 'Moulins et meuniers en Béarn', part (A) 'Au commencement est la construction du moulin', *PG*, 190, 1999:5–7, 191, 1999:5–7, 192, 1999:5–7; and part (B) 'De la structure et du fonctionnement d'un moulin à eau', *ib.*, 193, 1999:5–7. I. Shifman edits and translates **A Gascon bill of sale', *CorWPL*, 17, 1999:191–74. F. González Ollé, 'El artículo gascón *et*, *(e)ro, (e)ra* en Aragón y Navarra', *ZRP*, 116:260–78, attributes the trans-Pyrenean presence of these Gascon forms to borrowing and scribal usage.

PROVENÇAL. J.-C. Potteur, 'Une charte en l'an 999', *LSPS*, 137, 1999:4–5, edits the sole charter from the Alpes-Maritimes datable to before AD1000. In connection with the preceding, J.-C. Ranucci, 'Noms de lieux', *ib.*, 16, discusses *rocca, merendol, clemensans, ouart, berra, broch*. F. Rigaud, 'Leis illas de Provènça (*Liber insularum Provinciae*), assai sus la toponimia insulara, sègles XIIen-XVen; (seguida) de l'Illa de Bendor ais illas de Lerins', *EOc*, 23–24, 1998:46–65, continues his studies of small islands off Marseilles and La Ciotat (Bendor, Embiers, Hyères, Lérins).

LIMOUSIN (INCL N. PÉRIGORD). I. Balès edits 'Gaucelm Faidit, "Del Grand gòlfe de mar" ', *ClL*, 123, 1998:1–3, with modernized version, notes, and translation.

AUVERGNAT. P. Olivier, J.-C. Rivière, and J. Vezole, 'Le registre des audiences et des sentences de la justice de Dienne (Cantal), 1425–32', *TLP*, 38:155–251. Another in a series of critical editions of 15th- and 16th-c. Auvergnat texts, this one (Arch. Dép. Cantal, 16 B 469bis, 1425–32, from northeast Cantal) is an important, linguistically complex text, with rich vocabulary covering law, rural life, nature, family, and women. J.-P. Chambon, 'Un document auvergnat du Xe s. passé inaperçu: le testament d'Amblard de Nonette (a.966). Recherches toponymiques et historiques', *MA*, 106:63–99. The 'Campaniago' mentioned in the subtitle of this document is found to be Champagnat (Auvergne) rather than Campagnac (Rouergue); an index of some 45 toponyms is appended. Id., **Un des plus anciens documents linguistiques occitans relatifs à l'Auvergne méridionale', *Lengas*, 48:7–44. J. Vezole, 'Un testament de 1505', *Parlem!*, 52, 1997:7, edits Arch. Dép. Cantal, 3 E 17, f. 187v (12 genièr 1505), and publishes also editions of Arch. Dép. Cantal, 3 E 151 in 'Una quitança del 12 d'agost de 1485', *ib.*, 54, 1997:3; of Arch. Dép. Cantal, 3 E 50, f.101 in 'Una donacion en lenga nòstra (vès 1475–80)', *MO*, 20, 1997:4–5; and translates the will of Astorg de la Tour, Arch.

Dép. Cantal, 3 H 5, no. 8 in 'Un testament de 1375', *Lo Convise*, 27, 1999:15–16).

PROVENÇAL ALPIN. J.-C. Martin, *Documents pour servir à l'histoire de Taulignan*, Taulignan, Assoc. des Onze Tours, 26 pp.

3. POST-MEDIEVAL PERIOD

GENERAL. In an interview with Sébastien Langevin, 'Au début du siècle, les Français étaient tous bilingues', *FMon*, 302, 1999:92–93, Henriette Walter is optimistic about continued appreciation for and use of regional languages, which the French have left behind only in the last century. C. Laux, 'Occitania–Occitan', *L'Occitan*, 138, 1999:11, records that with just under two million speakers, Occitan is the 14th language of the European Union. R. Bistolfi asks 'Les langues régionales de France ont-elles un avenir?', *LSPS*, 138, 1999:34–35, 37, and answers guardedly in the affirmative. *Les Langues régionales de France: un état des lieux à la veille du XXIe siècle*, ed. Philippe Blanchet, Roland Breton, and Harold Schiffman, Louvain, Institut de linguistique générale, 1999, 202 pp. *Langues et cultures régionales de France: état des lieux, enseignement, politiques*, ed. Jean-Baptiste Coyos, Denis Costaouec, and Christos Clairis, Paris–Montréal, L'Harmattan, 1999, 272 pp.

B. Poignant, *Langues et cultures régionales. Rapport au premier ministre*, Collection des rapports officiels, Imprimerie Nationale, 1998, 90 pp., contains the full text (75–90) of the European Charter for Regional or Minority Languages (Charte européenne des langues régionales ou minoritaires). While the report did call for the signing of the Charter, it elicited varying reactions: positive, from B. Giély, *PrA*, 126, 1998:2 and negative, from P. Blanchet'and E. Feraud, *NP*, 68, 1998:12–14. R. Redeker, 'Requiem pour les langues régionales, tombeau pour la République', *TM*, 55:130–35, foresees the eventual mummification of France's regional languages through their very institutionalization. 'Prouvençal lengo d'Europo', *Coumboscuro*, 327–28, 1999:1. France signed the Charter on Regional Languages on 7 May 1999, although later that month the signature was overturned by the Conseil Constitutionnel. It is Italy's turn to ratify, a sentiment echoed in R. Saletta, 'Estre Prouvençal', *ib.*, 333–34, 1999:1, 8. J.-M. Woehrling, 'La France et la charte des langues', *BIO*, 18, 1999:1–2, says that the Conseil Constitutionnel has outlawed France from the rest of Europe by declaring that the French constitution could not be reconciled with its regional languages. 'Los francés per las lengas regionales', *ib.*, 25–26:4, reports on a 1999 survey of some 1000 persons in Alsace, in which 82% favoured ratifying the Charter, 70% favoured amending the French constitution to enable application of this Charter.

Statistics from the 1997 survey in Languedoc-Roussillon are available in *Pratiques et représentations de l'occitan: région Languedoc-Roussillon, janvier 1998*, Castelnau-le-Lez, Média Pluriel Méditerranée, 1998, 52 pp., and summarized in C. Laus, 'Enquèstas lingüisticas', *L'Occitan*, 134, 1998:3. This article also includes the results of the 1997 survey in Aquitaine. In *ib.*, 137, 1998:4, C. Laux publishes results from the Barcelona bulletin *Llengües vives*, 9, 1998, for Occitan in France, Italy, and the Val d'Aran. Unofficially, it is estimated that 10% of the population of the Midi speak Occitan. Official figures are available from neither the French nor the Italian governments. In the Val d'Aran, the 1991 census revealed that 92% understand the Occitan of Aran, 61% speak it, 51% read it, 18% write it.

'Les maires s'organisent pour défendre l'occitan', *BIO*, 19, 1999:1–2. In June 1999, dozens of mayors from across the Midi founded the *Association des maires et des élus occitans*. L. Alexis, 'Front National et langues "régionales"', *EOc*, 23–24, 1998:14–15, describes the new Forum Civique Provençal, created to respond to the threat of extreme right-wing pressures against regional language and culture. J. Petit finds considerable advantages in bilingual education, particulary French-Occitan, *BIO*, 20, 1999:3. 'Une nouvelle circulaire rectorale pour l'occitan en Midi-Pyrénées', *ib.*, 23–24:6, gives the full text outlining the goals of bilingual education, most importantly, the use of either language in all walks of daily life. P. Gardy, **'Escriure, òc. Mai dins la lenga de quau? Devers de mestissatges renovelats'*, *Oc*, 334–35:15–20. Id., 'L'aiguille dans la meule de foin? Le quotidien *Sud Ouest* et l'occitan', *Garona*, 15, 1999:73–93. While Basque figures in this newspaper as a "langue sinon égale, en tout cas comparable au français [. . .], [l'occitan] demeure largement fantomatique". J. Gaudas, 'Oc-TV. Net sur le web', *BIO*, 21–22:3, announces the first digital programming in Occitan, <http://www/oc-tv.net>. Id., 'Oc-TV.net. Oc-TV on the Oeb', *Occitans!*, 91, 1999:11.

M.-L. Gourdon, **'Louis Funel, Antonin Perbosc et Prosper Estieu: une diagonale est-ouest dans la naissance de l'occitanisme'*, *Oc*, 329, 1998:29–42. F. Vergès Bartau, 'Normalisation de l'occitan d'un point de vue aranais,' *BIO*, 23–24:1–2, briefly compares the goals and difficulties of normalization in both languages. L. Fornés, 'Euphemia Llorente i el filòleg Michel Ventura Balanyà', *PdO*, 3, 1999:7–24, describes an ill-fated attempt to produce a pan-Occitan grammar. A. Penella i Ramon, 'Bases per una neokoiné occitano-romànica', *ib.*, 28–33, bases his proposal for a new koiné on the work of Ventura Balanyà and Pompeu Fabra. J. C. Laínez asks 'Ont finís l'Occitania?', *L'Occitan*, 138, 1999:6, and answers: as far south as València; this article follows an earlier piece on 'La nuèit occitana e la vision dels valencians', *ib.*, 135, 1998:7, describing the Occitanism that flourishes in Valencia. M. C. Alén Garabato, 'Percepcion de la lengua occitana (y de los occitanos) entre los estudiantes universitarios gallegos', *CILPR 22*, III, 15–24, discusses how Occitan is seen as a language relegated to the past, of only philological interest for today's students. Looking at the relationship between Occitan and Esperanto are: S. Granier, *'Perque l'occitan en esperantia', *EsperantOC*, 4, 1998:4–6, and Valo, *'Lingvo 'oc' kaj Esperanto', *Kulturaj-Kajeroj*, 2, 1999:9–12.

ORTHOGRAPHY. J. Taupiac, 'L'occitan e las questions de nòrma', *Oc*, 334–35:72–74. In his 1935 *Gramatica occitana*, Alibert complicated things unnecessarily by deciding that verbs would not be spelled according to the same conventions as other vocabulary. S. Granièr, 'La "fatwa" contra los lapins, la refòrma d'Alibèrt e lo *–e* de sosten', *GS*, 33:534–38, reviews the notion of norm in the context of J. Taupiac's campaign against gallicisms in Occitan (*lapin* vs. *conilh*). P. Burgan, 'Istòria meravilhosa de la "fatwa" contra los lapins', *L'Occitan*, 136, 1998:4–5, disagrees vigorously with Taupiac on this point, asking 'Is this the time to create a *complèxe de purisme*?' 'Las novèlas nòrmas' of October 1997 (Conselh de la Lenga Occitana) are listed in *ib.*, 133, 1998:4; some of these 27 sets of spellings have already been implemented in certain journals or by certain presses, e.g. *filosofia* (*-ía)/ *gràcia* (*gracia), *azòt* (*asòt), *realizar* (as against *paralisar*, *precisar* where nouns in *-s* are part of the same family), *linguistic* or *lingüistica* (in free variation). J. Taupiac continues his series 'L'Occitan blos': '*Realizar*', *ib.*, 8; 'Quatre coeréncias graficas', *ib.*, 134, 1998:8 (graphic consistency falls into four types: structural, e.g. use of hyphens in compounds; phonetic; etymological; or pan-Latin); 'La *sal* e lo *cèl*', *ib.*, 135, 1998:8; 'Los mòrts', *ib.*, 137, 1998:8. He finds it reasonable to avoid use of diacritics when the experts are in agreement ('Prudéncia', *ib.*, 138, 1999:8). He also looks at: '*Dimarts*', *ib.*, 139, 1999:8 and 140, 1999:8; 'La *meçorga*', *ib.*, 141, 1999:8; 'Los *beçons*', *ib.*, 142, 1999:8; 'Lo *cinèma* e lo *panorama*', *ib.*, 143, 1999:8; 'Lo *panorama*', *ib.*, 144:8. Many of the same examples are mentioned by the same author in 'Escriure coma cal', in two parts, *Occitans!*, 91, 1999:19, and 92, 1999:20. In the long-running series 'La Vida de la lenga', C. Laux, *L'Occitan*, 133, 1998:7, looks at the spelling of consonant-final paroxytons, e.g. *cònsol*, *vòmit*, *rómec* (and their occasional variants showing stress shifts, e.g. *romèc*). Id., '*L'oroscòp* e *telescòpi*', *ib.*, 134, 1998:7; 'Lo *sindròme*, lo *velodròm*', *ib.*, 136, 1998:7. M. Grosclaude, 'La question du "h" aspiré en onomastique occitane: *La*

Haia/L'Aia, Lo Havre/L'Avre', *PG*, 197:13, recommends maintaining 'h' where appropriate, despite the norms for Languedocien.

PHONETICS AND PHONOLOGY. R. Teulat, 'Vocalas finalas dels mots de manlèu', *Lo Convise*, 28, 1999:18, argues that final vowels restored in the process of normalization must be etymological. J. Taupiac, 'Mangi de pan', *L'Occitan*, 145:8, outlines the three expressions of the Occitan partitive: (north) *mangi del pan*; (central) *mangi de pan*; (gascon) *que mingi pan*.

MORPHOSYNTAX. G. Nariòo, '*Que s'i pòt tostemps saunejar* [on peut toujours rêver]', *PG*, 186, 1998:14, proposes various translations of impersonal *on*. Id., 'Qu'i caben tres cents personas', *ib.*, 193, 1999:12, reviews functions of *càber* 'to contain', 'be contained'. C. Laux, 'Vèrbs de doas conjugasons', *L'Occitan*, 135, 1998:7; a review of verbs (*corrir, morir, dormir, sentir*) that allow either choative or inchoative forms in the different dialects. Id., 'Feminizacion', *ib.*, 139, 1999:7, shows how easily e.g. *ministra, autora, escrivana* are formed.

LEXIS AND LEXICOLOGY. J.-P. Chambon and C. Hérilier, 'Alibert vu d'Auvergne: notes de lexicographie critique en domaine occitan à propos de deux sources aurillacoises du *Dictionnaire occitan-français*', *RLaR*, 104:169–85, find ample cause to use Alibert's dictionary with caution. G. Naro traces 'La lexicographie occitane du XVIIe au XIXe siècle, son apogée et son déclin', *CILPR 22*, IV, 441–47. A. Lagarda, 'Per una lenga imajada', *GS*, 33:169–71, unabashedly demonstrates the superior imagery of the Occitan lexicon, e.g. *èra pus content que si nevava farina*. Catherine Nemausana and Andolfi Coucougnous-Cassade, **Petit dictionnaire des expressions du Midi*, Nîmes, Lacour, 1999, 197 pp. U. Hoinkes, ***Der okzitanische Lehnwortschatz im heutigen Italienisch', Rieger, *Okzitanistik*, 189–204.

PARTICULAR SEMANTIC FIELDS. K. Klingebiel, 'Occ. *aubrada* "arborée, arbre chargé, plein un arbre"', *CILPR 22*, IV, 333–49, tracks the on-going productivity of suffixal *-ada* (units of measure, quantities, recipients), with comparative evidence from French. A. Lagarda, 'Los sèt pecats', *GS*, 33:264–66. Id., 'Lo mistèri de las locucions', *ib.*, 402–4, presents 14 expressions with their histories, e.g. *es lo picar de la dalha* = 'la dificultat màger d'un afar'. R. Chatbèrt, in his series 'Questions de lenga', looks at 'Expressions diversas', *Oc*, 326, 1997: 41–43; 'Encara d'expressions', *ib.*, 327, 1998:35–36; 'Qualques autres mots', *ib.*, 328, 1998:32–35; 'Totjorn d'autras expressions', *ib.*, 329, 1998:21–24; 'Formacions adverbialas amb -s final', *ib.*, 330, 1998:31–34, 'De l'un e de l'autre', *ib.*, 332, 1999:39–41, and *ib.*, 333, 1999:34–37 (i.a., *mai mòrt, en dintrar*). In his series 'L'Occitan blos', J. Taupiac recommends '*Al respècte de*', *L'Occitan*, 147:8, as against the Gallicisms *respèt, respèct*; 'Lo *respècte* e lo *respièch*', *ib.*, 148:8 (*respièch* 'répit, délai'); 'L'*efièch*', *ib.*, 149:8 (*efèit*,

ef(i)èch, efècte are all preferable to *effet*). Id. lists rugby vocabulary in *ib.*,
140, 1999:7 and treats '3 + 2 = 5', *ib.*, 141, 1999:7. Given the tonic
vowel of Lat. GARŬMNA, 'Garona' is preferable to *"Garòna"* (*ib.*,
142, 1999:7). Id., 'Dire l'ora', *ib.*, 143, 1999:7; '*Entre* (preposicion e
prefix)', *ib.*, 147:7; and 'Prefixes *sub-, sos-, sota-, jos-*', *ib.*, 148:7.
C. Rapin, '*Cedar* e *cedir*', *Occitans!*, 84, 1998:19 (*cedir* 'se soumettre').
ONOMASTICS. P. Peyre, 'Toponimia', *AqAq*, 130, 1999:8–9, looks
at 'Natura e cultura' (la nèu, la freg, lo vent); and at 'L'òme e la
natura, de rapòrts conflictuaux [. . .]', *ib.*, 132, 1999:9.
SOCIOLINGUISTICS. F. Cosinièr, 'Comunicar e far de publicitat
per socializar l'occitan', *Occitans!*, 91, 1999:8–10, outlines various
ways to remedy the chronic lack of communication at all levels
(media, marketing, etc.). H. Boyer, *'Regards sur la situation
sociolinguistique de l'espace occitan: fin de substitution?', *Plurilin-
guismes*, 17, 1999:133–55. J.-P. Baldit, 'L'Enquête de "L'enfant
prodigue"', 1806–09', *ClL*, 129, 1999:21–22, sketches a *historique* of
the survey conducted by Coquebert de Montbret, father and son.

4. GASCON AND BÉARNAIS

GENERAL. J. Allières, *'La *Grammaire béarnaise* de Vastin Lespy', Pic,
Lespy, 67–81. G. Bernhard, *'Französisch und Gaskognisch in den
Landes: ein kleiner Einblick in nähesprachliche Kommunikationsge-
wohnheiten', Rieger, *Okzitanistik*, 177–88.
ORTHOGRAPHY. J. Lafitte, *'La graphie du béarnais chez Vastin
Lespy: de la *Grammaire* au *Dictionnaire*', Pic, *Lespy*, 149–73. Id.,
*'Escríver los noms pròpis estrangèrs', *LDGM*, 14:31–33. D. Sumien,
'La question de la "h" dens los noms pròpis estrangèrs', *Reclams*,
777:15; the Conselh de la lenga occitana, scrupulously respecting
Gascon tradition, recommends keeping 'h'. P. Bec, 'Tres punts de
grafia', *PG*, 197:2, proposes minor adjustments for *béarnais*. J. Taupiac, 'Grafia e identitat, ambe d'exemples gascons', *Occitans!*, 94:18,
reviews Occitan graphies for [š]: 'x', '(i)sh', 'ss', as against the
gallicism 'ch'. Id., 'Es que lo gascon fa partida de la lenga occitana?',
ib., 95:19, among other things, argues for retaining 'ish' in *peish/peix*.
PHONETICS AND PHONOLOGY. G. Nariòo, 'Lo men gat gaha de
bèths arrats', *PG*, 192, 1999:17, describes the fricativization of
intervocalic [b], [d], and [g].
MORPHOSYNTAX. Michel Grosclaude and Gilabèrt Narioò, *Répertoire des conjugaisons occitanes de Gascogne*, Orthez, Per Noste — Pau, La
Civada, 1999, 159 pp., present general rules for formation (16–22),
and complete tables of forms. C. D. Pusch, 'L'Énonciatif gascon entre
pragmatique et grammaire: analyse d'un corpus oral', *CILPR 22*, VII,
625–30, approaches *que* as a marker of discourse coherence and of

the boundary between theme and rheme. Id., *'La phrase principale
en gascon: un cas de focalisation figée', pp. 107–19 of *La Thematisation
dans les langues*, Berlin, Lang, 1999, 455 pp. G. Nariòo, 'Quan siam
tots amassa', *PG*, 190, 1999:14, recommends the subjunctive rather
than the future after *quan*. Id., 'Quantes quilòs n'as crompat?', *ib.*,
196:15, reviews adverbs of quantity functioning as indefinite adjectives or pronouns. Id. links '*Lo Patric que se n'a miat lo can*', *ib.*, 197:10,
to *miar-se'n* (not **que s'a enmiat lo can*).

LEXIS AND LEXICOLOGY.   Work on Félix Arnaudin's *Dictionnaire de
la Grande-Lande*, begun by the late Jacques Boisgontier, has been
continued and completed by a team of experts from the Parc Naturel
Régional des Landes de Gascogne. Volume 1, *A–H* (sixth in the series
of complete works by Arnaudin, 1844–1921), is presented by Joël
Miro, in conjunction with the late Jacques Allières, Bordeaux,
Confluences, 680 pp.; the second volume is expected in 2001. Robert
Aymard, **Petit lexique français–gascon*, Uzos, p.p., 1998, 46 pp. M. Belly,
*'Du lexique au dictionnaire, l'art du lexicographe: Vastin Lespy et
Vincent Foix', Pic, *Lespy*, 107–33. P. Salles, *'Aspects du lexique
naturaliste chez Vastin Lespy', *ib.*, 135–48. A. Viaut, 'Le lexique bas-
médoquin de François Conord', *RLaR*, 103, 1999:363–80, presents
the efforts by F. Conord (1882–1973) and a group of his fellow
townspeople to codify the dialect of Lesparre-Médoc.

PARTICULAR SEMANTIC FIELDS.   M. Grosclaude derives *grulh*
('fromage blanc grumeleux, produit en chauffant le petit lait') from
GRANŬCULUM, *PG*, 192, 1999:8. J. Lafita, 'Vocabulari', *LDGM*, 12,
1998:16–19 (*paralisia, paralisi; legidor, legeire, lector; pressa, premsa*).
M. Grosclaude, 'Le *gachassin* n'est pas un gâcheur de plâtre et le *lantar*
n'est pas un fabricant de catafalques!', *PG*, 190, 1999:11–12. In yet
another correction of Palay's dictionary of Gascon, with its occasionally invented words, the proper name *Gachassin* is shown to be a
compound of *Gassie* + *Assin* and *lantà* is corrected to '*lande*', 'village'.
G. Anglada examines *agulha* in *BIO*, 15:3, and *pesolh*, *ib.*, 16:3.

ONOMASTICS.   Marcellin Bérot, *La vie des hommes de la montagne dans
les Pyrénées racontée par la toponymie*, pref. Jean-François Le Nail,
Toulouse, Parc National des Pyrénées and Tarbes, Éditions Milan,
1998, 388 pp. Patrick Épron, **Dictionnaire de l'origine des noms de lieux en
Gironde et en Aquitaine*, Bordeaux, Assoc. de Recherche, de Prospection
et d'Étude, 1998, 244 pp. J. Lafitte, *'Toponymes gascons, I: Béarn',
LDGM, 12, 1998:42–48.

SUBDIALECTS.   Césaire Daugé, *Grammaire élémentaire de la langue
gasconne*, Pau, Princi Néguer, 129 pp., was originally published as
Grammaire gasconne: dialecte d'Aire, in 1905. Yolande Vidal, *Dictionnaire
gascon–français: Le parler du bassin d'Arcachon et de ses environs. D'hier à
aujourd'hui*, Bordeaux, Les Dossiers d'Aquitaine, 1999, 290 pp. 'Pour

baptiser nos maisons', *PGA*, 56, 1998:23–24, and 57, 1998:23–25, covers French and normalized Gascon terms for fauna and flora, with pronunciation in *gascon maritime*.

SOCIOLINGUISTICS.   J.-L. Castéret, 'A quand la parité?', *BIO*, 20, 1999:3, calls for a society in which speakers of *béarnais* can take their rightful place. M. Romieu, 'Il faut avancer vers une socialisation de la langue', *ib.*, 17, 1999:3, outlines general conditions that will favorize the socialization of Occitan.

5.   SOUTHERN OCCITAN

LANGUEDOCIEN (INCLUDING S. PÉRIG.)

MORPHOSYNTAX.   J. Feuillet,'Las questions ligadas a la causida exclusiva de las formas *fach, nuèch, dich* . . . dins una nòrma del lengadocian', *EOc*, 23–24, 1998:66–89, stresses the importance of keeping orthography close to forms as actually pronounced.

LEXIS AND LEXICOLOGY.   A new edition of Christian Laux, **Dictionnaire français-occitan, Languedocien central*, Puylaurens, Section du Tarn de l'IEO, includes an enlarged section of proper names substantially revised by Serge Granier. Laux briefly reviews his own revisions and corrections in *Occitans!*, 94:19. Bernard Vavassori, **Petit précis de parler méridional du Rouergue au Midi toulousain. Régionalismes occitans de la langue française parlée dans le Midi Toulousain et rapprochement avec les langues catalane, espagnole, et italienne*, Portet-sur-Garonne, Loubatières, 1999, 139 pp.

ONOMASTICS.   Paul Fabre, **Dictionnaire des noms de lieux des Cévennes*, Bonneton, 160 pp. Frank R. Hamlin, **Toponymie de l'Hérault*, Millau, Beffroi, 492 pp., is a third edition of his 1983 classic *Les Noms de lieux du département de l'Hérault* and updates some 2,500 entries. L. Balmayer, **'Lignes dialectométriques et isoglosses sur le domaine du Montpelliérain'*, *RLiR*, 64:409–26. **Le Parler palavasien (La lenga dau Grau de Palavas): éléments de grammaire et de lexicographie*, Palavas, Académie palavasienne de Langue d'Oc 'Lus Duzenau', 473 pp.

PAREMIOLOGY.   Christian-Pierre Bedel, **La Barraca Sauvaterra: Bossac, Cambolaset, Castanet, Colombiers, Gramont, Manhac, Moirases, Pradinas*, pref. Denys Jaudon, Rodez, Mission Départementale de la Culture, 1998, 271 pp. Id., **St-Cheli-d'Aubrac: Condom d'Aubrac. St-Chély-d'Aubrac*, Rodez, Mission Départementale de la Culture, 1998, 238 pp. Id., **Sant-Jurveva: Alpueg, La Calm, Cantoenh, Graissac, La Tarrissa, Vitrac*, Rodez, Mission Départementale de la Culture, 255 pp.

PROVENÇAL

LEXIS AND LEXICOLOGY.   Robert Rourret, **Dictionnaire français-occitan provençal*, Nîmes, Lacour, 1999, 487 pp., originally appeared in 1981 and is valuable as it makes Provençal available in normalized 'Occitan' graphy. The second volume of Jean-Claude Rey's *Les Mots de chez nous*, **Fan de chichourlo*, Marseilles, Autres Temps, 1998, 246 pp., provides additional word histories and etymologies. Philippe Blanchet, **Zou, Boulégan: Expressions familières de Marseille et de Provence*, Bonneton, 191 pp. Christian Boucher, **La Flore de Haute-Provence*. Edisud, Aix-en-Provence, 1998, 208 pp. N. Lambert, **'Escouta li besti, regarda lou ceu'*, *PEs*, 6, 1998:5–15.

ONOMASTICS. Chantal Chaibriant and Sylviane Chaumont, **L'Histoire de Pierrevert à travers ses rues*, Manosque, Carnets de Provence, 1998, 60 pp. C. Martel, **'La Nesque à la lumière de la toponymie'*, *ALu*, 127, 1998:46–51. E. Moucadel, **'Escais — noum de vilo, vilage e vilajoun en ribo de Durènço, de Pertus fin qu'au Rose'*, *PEs*, 5, 1998:12–13. A.-M. Corredor Playa, **'Els topònims de les Santes Maries de la Mar: una manera de mantenir vives la llengua i la cultura provençals'*, *SOBI*, 72, 1998:50–56.

SUBDIALECTS. Justin Barroi, Jean Raybaut, Catherine Raybaut, **Lexique français-castillonnais*, Roquebrune, Cercle de Généalogie de Roquebrune et du Mentonnais, 1998, details a *parler* situated 12km. north of Menton, at the very intersection of Provençal and *provençal alpin*. J.-L. Domenge, **'Quelques caractéristiques du parler de Châteaudouble'*, *AVEPB*, 96.2:7. R. Nathiez, 'Echos sur les problèmes de langue', *LSPS*, 138, 1999:37, argues for continued use of *nissart*, whatever its origin. J. Garavagno, 'Expressions et images du nissart', *ib.*, 130, 1998:53. Id., '*Lu bastian countrari*. De l'importance de l'accent tonique', *ib.*, 138, 1999:43, illustrates phonemic word stress in *nissart* with 14 pairs of words. Y. Gilli offers Latin, French and *nissart* terms for 20 types of 'Coquillages des Alpes Maritimes', *ib.*, 134, 1998:27–29.

6. NORTHERN OCCITAN

LIMOUSIN (INCLUDING N. PÉRIG.)

GENERAL. M. Chapduelh, 'Coma èsser lemosin?', *PN*, 85, 1999:8–15, concludes that 'l'occitanitat moderna se definís per la viticultura e l'urbanitat; los lemosins son ruraus e an pas de vinhas ...'. **'Quauquas questions a Robert Savy, president dau conselh regionau dau lemosin'* are published in *Occitans!* 98:4.

LEXIS AND LEXICOLOGY. Jean Roux, *Vocabulari occitan-francés. Lemosin* (*PN*, special no. 84bis), 1999, 40 pp.

ONOMASTICS. E. Théron, 'L'Histoire de Tulle à travers ses fontaines (X), la Fontaine Saint-Pierre', *Lemouzi*, 145, 1998:101–8; 'Les Portes-Chanac et le Fournivoulet', *ib.*, 147, 1998:102–12; 'La 2e Fontaine de la rue de La Barussie à l'entrée de celle-ci, côté ville', *ib.*,

150, 1999:131–35; 'Le Puy-Saint-Clair (fontaine miraculeuse)', *ib.*, 151, 1999:58–64; and 'Le Trech. La fontaine Villeneuve', *ib.*, 154:108–10. Y. Lavalade details 56 bilingual place names from Sadroc (Corrèze) in *ClL*, 129, 1999:4–6. Id. also lists place names for 12 communes of the Creuse in the final issue of *ClL*, 130:23–31.

SUBDIALECTS: Liliane Jagueneau, *Le parlanjhe de Poitou-Charentes-Vendée, nord Gironde, sud Loire Atlantique: la langue poitevine-saintongeaise en 30 questions, La Crèche, Geste, 1999, 63 pp.

AUVERGNAT

GENERAL. J.-P. Chambon and P. Olivier, 'L'Histoire linguistique de l'Auvergne et du Velay: notes pour une synthèse provisoire', *TLP*, 38:83–53. Olivier handles the section on mid-14th- to mid-16th-c. language conflict; Chambon summarizes the as yet incomplete linguistic history of the Auvergne.

MORPHOSYNTAX. J. Fay, 'A prepaus de l'emplèu de *del, dels de la, de las, de (d')*', *La Cabreta*, 151, 1998:15, sketches the history and use of the partitive.

PARTICULAR SEMANTIC FIELDS. J. Fay, 'Barta, bròcas e brancatge', *La Cabreta*, 149, 1998:13–14, lists terms for natural vegetation.

SUBDIALECTS. J.-M. Maurí, 'Biais de dire del nòrd-Chantal', *Lo Convise*, 23, 1998:16–17, presents lexicon and syntactic structures, e.g. alternate contrary-to-fact constructions.

PROVENÇAL ALPIN

GENERAL. André Faure and Pierre Hérisson, 'L'Occitan aupenc', *AqAq*, 126, 1998:7–8, publish a section from their *Aprendre l'occitan aupenc*, IEO Provence – Alpes de Haute-Provence, 1998.

TEXTS. S. Garnero, [Val Mairo] *'La memorio de nosto lengo', *Coumboscuro*, 325–26, 1999:3, offers proverbs and stories, with Italian translations.

LITERATURE

By CATHERINE LÉGLU, *Lecturer in French, University of Bristol*

1. MEDIEVAL PERIOD

Elizabeth W. Poe, *Compilatio: Lyric Texts and Prose Commentaries in Troubadour Manuscript* H *(Vat. Lat. 3207)* (The Edward C. Armstrong Monographs on Medieval Literature, 11), Lexington, Kentucky, French Forum, 307 pp., is a detailed study with edition and commentary of the prose commentary section (ff. 47–49) of this codex. Drawing on codicological analyses of *H*, P. suggests that the codex is mostly the work of one scholarly compiler who had access to many sources owned or composed by Uc de Saint-Circ, and who was pursuing his own private project. Among other insights, P. notes that the famous *trobairitz* collection is framed by parodic and misogynistic texts, that there is a discernable compilation of occasional, satirical *coblas esparsas* by Uc de Saint-Circ, and that the 'commentary collection' is itself a compilation from several other sources. P. points out the connections between MSS *H* and *D*, and the *florilegia* in MSS *J* and *Da*). This study links well with the work of Saverio Guida and William Burgwinkle on the key role played by Uc de Saint-Circ in developing the written troubadour tradition in Italy (see *YWMLS*, 60:204). Catherine Léglu, *Between Sequence and Sirventes: Aspects of Parody in the Troubadour Lyric* (Legenda Research Monographs in French Studies, 8), Oxford, Legenda, x + 147 pp., presents the relationship between a micro-corpus of satirical poems attributed to Marcabru, Peire d'Alvernha, Peire Cardenal, and others, and the paraliturgical Aquitanian corpus, with reference to formal borrowing and social positioning. Claudia Krülls-Hepermann, *Trobador-Liedkunst: Literaturwissenschaft und Musikgeschichte im Kontext,* Frankfurt, Lang, 164 pp., is a detailed and insightful study of the relationship between music and words, with reference to the sometimes divergent development of the disciplines of musicology and philology, and with close readings of poems by Arnaut Daniel, Berenguier de Palazol, and others. *Marcabru: A Critical Edition,* ed. Simon Gaunt et al., Cambridge, Brewer, x + 609 pp., is a complete edition of the poems of Marcabru, with extensive notes, discussions of previous research and editions, and a clear and concise introduction. This is the first complete edition of Marcabru since Dejeanne's in 1909, and shows every sign of providing a definitive corpus. *Sermons de Saint Marçal, s.XII,* ed. Roger Teulat, Aurillac, Lo Convise, 1999, 64 pp., is a new edition of the 18 Occitan sermons in MS Paris BN lat 3548B. Pierre Portet, *Bertrand Boysset, arpenteur arlésien de la fin du XIVe siècle,*

1355–1415 <palissy.humana.univ–nantes.fr/CETE/TXT.boysset/
index.htm>, is an online version of a *thèse de doctorat* presented at
the Université de Toulouse Le Mirail in 1995, and forms an edition
with commentary and detailed study of Boysset's two treatises on
land surveying and measuring boundaries, the *Siensa de destrar* and the
Siensa d'atermenar (both *c.* 1401–1415). The site is intended to include
illustrations from the source MS, Carpentras, Bibliothèque Inguim-
bertine (Bibliothèque municipale), MS 327. Rieger, *Okzitanistik*,
includes H. I. Radatz on the use of Occ. by Jordi de Sant Jordi
(133–45); J. Kabatek on *Lo Codi*, the Occ. translation of the Justinian
Code, and its influence on other vernacular texts (147–63); A. Fausel
on orality and *Schriftlichkeit* in troubadour song from a socio-historical
perspective (165–75); M. Bernsen on Guilhem IX's poetic corpus as
discourse (207–16); K. Städtler and J. Rüdiger both examine *fin'amors*
poetry as praxis, in terms, respectively, of historical anthropology and
linguistic systems (217–30 and 231–47); R. Lug suggests that the
troubadour songs included in the *Chansonnier de Saint-Germain-des-Prés*
are connected to the Waldensian and Cathar communities in Metz
(249–74). *De l'Amour*, ed. Alain Badiou et al. (Collection Champs,
École de la cause freudienne), Flammarion, 1999, 190 pp., publishes
a series of lectures given in 1997–98, concentrating on Lacanian
approaches to desire in French literature with courtly lyric poetry as
paradigm. It includes: J. Roubaud, 'L'amour, la poésie. Hypothèses'
(81–104), which includes discussion of *mezura* and the general
influence of *trobar* on modern expressions of love; R. Dragonetti, 'La
"chose" du plus grand désir dans les chansons du premier troubadour'
(143–76), on Guilhem IX, and the use of myth and fable to describe
love, identified as a (partly) Orphic theme of desire for the Other.
*Sordello da Goito. Atti del Convegno internazionale di Studi (Goito-Mantova,
13–15 novembre 1997)*, is published in 2 volumes as *CN*, 60. In vol. I,
S. Bortolami explores the political context surrounding Sordello's
notorious abduction of Cunniza da Romano (1–43); C. Greco traces
Sordello's last days (c. 1269) as a vassal of Charles I of Anjou (45–58);
A. Radaelli suggests that Uc de Saint-Circ's *danseta*, PC 457, 41, is
part of his cycle of poems about Sordello (59–88); S. Guida finds that
the two *vidas* of Sordello are stylistically typical of others written by
Uc de Saint-Circ (89–123); G. Gouiran finds that Sordello copies
Bertran de Born, but shows singular concern for the threat posed to
ladies' honour by love (125–40); S. Asperti examines the complex
relations between Sordello and his rival patrons, Raimon Berenguer
V and Charles I of Anjou, especially in terms of the works of other
poets, such as Luchetto Gattilusio. He concludes that Sordello was an
esteemed figure around 1260 (141–59); E. Schulze-Busacker presents
an assessment of Sordello's didactic 'period' which she identifies as

the years spent in Provence (c.1233–46), before he moved into the patronage of Raimon Berenguer V. S.-B. traces the use of the *Proverbia Senecae* and *Disticha Catonis* as well as other sources, and concludes that this shows use of the *canso* as much as of didactic material (161–206). In vol. II, A. Solimena examines Sordello's use of metrical structure (207–21); M. Tyssens finds little evidence of strong links with the trouvère lyric, save for one song by Hugues de Berzé (223–31); P. G. Beltrami finds more evidence of links with duecento Italian poetry (232–79); A. Stussi discusses the text and attribution of the 'Sirventese lombardi', 'Poi qe neve ni glaza' (281–310); R. Signorini looks at the mostly Danteian image of Sordello in 15th- and 16th-c. Mantua (311–39); V. Beltran suggests that Sordello's residence in Castile-León, c.1230, may have been short (340–69); finally, E. Gonçalves examines the Galician-Portuguese *tenso* between Johan Soarez Coelho and Picandon, said to have been the *joglar* of Sordello (371–86). S. Spence, 'The topos of discretion in troubadour poetry', *RF*, 112:180–91, notes that *silentia* occurs nowhere, but that muting (the active suppression of speech, expressed in the term *mutz*) is frequent; S. suggests that this treatment of the Ovidian idea of discretion is an innovatory aspect of the troubadour lyric. T. Allen, 'The ambiguous Narcissus figure in *Le Lai de Narcisus* and "Can vei la lauzeta mover" ', *FS*, 54:427–38, reads Bernart de Ventadorn's famous poem and the anonymous *lai* as interpretations of Plotinus's Neoplatonic use of the myth of Narcissus as an allegory of physical love. A. concludes that both texts enact 'a reversal as well as an affirmation' of the Plotinian view that the seductiveness of images may be defeated. M. N. Taylor, 'The *Cansos* of the troubadour Marcabru. Critical texts and a commentary', *Romania*, 118:336–74, presents new editions of 'Contra l'ivern que s'enansa' (PC 293, 14) and 'Lanquan fuelhon li boscatge' (PC 293, 28). T. emphasises that both these songs are *cansos*. G. E. Sansone, 'Per il testo della tenzone fittizia attribuita a Peire Duran', *ib.*, 219–35, is an edition and discussion of 'Una dona ai auzit que s'es clamada' (PC 234, 8), also attributed to Guilhem de Saint-Didier, a comic fictional dialogue between a quarrelling husband and wife. S. resolves the attribution and discusses the metrical structure of the song. P. Gresti, ' "En est son far chansonet'ai noelha" (PC 328,1)', *ZRP*, 116:237–59, gives a new edition of this song attributed variously to Peire de Blai, Peire de Brau, or to Uc Brunenc. F. Gambino, 'L'anonymat dans la tradition manuscrite de la lyrique troubadouresque', *CCMe*, 43:33–90, is a detailed and tabulated exploration of the extant corpus (classified under PC 461) of anonymous songs; G. excludes some texts from the corpus, occasionally without satisfactory explanation. Using Bec's distinction between 'aristocratic' and 'popularizing' genres, she concludes that anonymity is not a question of a generic hierarchy modelled on social rank, but that gender may play a role, in that the names of women poets may have been omitted more frequently. C. Léglu, 'Tearful performance: when troubadours weep', *NMi*, 51 : 495–504, examines selected songs (focusing on Folquet de Marselha) in which tears play a paradoxical role, both as sincere expression (linked to penitential practice) and as conventional display linked to legal petitioning and (aesthetically) to performance. G. Le Vot, *CCMe*, 43 : 326–32, examines the importance of transmitting and editing music in the troubadour lyric. W. D. Paden, 'Why translate?', *Tenso*, 15 : 85–95, considers the question of why scholars are expected to translate cited extracts of Occitan, and (given the woodenness of most renditions into English) whether or not such translations, in editions, should aim at literary effect. P. Uhl, ' "So es devinalh" (PC 461, 226)', *ib.*, 97–117, dicusses the supporting evidence for this putative genre. He finds that the term *devinalh* also refers to slander and calumny, but that short versified riddles did exist, known as *coblas divinativas* and *coblas rescostas* (drawing from Guilhem Molinier's *Leys d'Amor*). U. concludes that the only true example of a *devinalh* would be the anonymous song PC 461, 226. W. Pfeffer, 'Bibliography of Occitan literature for 1998', *Tenso*, 15 : 2–54.

2. AFTER 1500

Daniel Vitaglione, **The Literature of Provence: An Introduction*, Jefferson NC–London, McFarland, 192 pp., is an overview of Provençal literature from Mistral onwards. Fritz Peter Kirsch, **Écrivains au carrefour des cultures. Études de littérature occitane, française et francophone* (collection Saber), Bordeaux U.P., 288 pp., presents an analysis of the role of Occitan literature within France, which establishes parallels with the development of Francophone literature in Québec and Africa. C. Parayre, 'Paysages de *Mirèio*', *NCFS*, 28 : 227–41, explores Mistral's literary treatment of landscape. Id., '*Lo Libre dels grands jorns* de Jean Boudou: poésie des troubadours et revendication culturelle', *Tenso*, 15 : 118–26, looks at how Boudou uses citations from troubadour poems to frame and punctuate a meditation on death and cultural decline. According to P., Boudou's novel of 1964 is intended to be 'the last *alba*' composed in Occitan. M. Glencross, 'Relic and romance: antiquarianism and medievalism in French literary culture, 1780–1830', *MLR*, 95 : 337–49, sets the works of l'abbé Millot (*Histoire littéraire des troubadours*, 1774) and Raynouard (*Choix des poésies originales des troubadours*, 1816–21) in the context of the political and literary debates of their time, especially the question of precedence between northern and southern French poetry. In Rieger,

Okzitanistik, P. Bec examines the reception of troubadour poetry by German Romantics from Herder to Heine, especially Ludwig Uhland (277–98); R. Schlösser gives an overview of Occitan studies in Berlin from 1867 to 1945 (299–315) and R. Bauer discusses the life and career of the philologist Carl Appel (1857–1930)(317–37). M. Décimo, 'Quand Michel Bréal, d'origine juive et berlinoise, alsacien, félibre et citoyen, écrivait à Mistral', *RLaR*, 104:187–218, presents an edition and analysis of the correspondence between Mistral and Bréal (1832–1915), a philologist and grammarian who played a key role in the formation of Third Republic educational policies. D. suggests that Bréal's role in enhancing the academic reputation of the Félibrige was as important as that of Gaston Paris and Paul Meyer. C. Bonnet, 'Le théâtre occitan contemporain: mimésis et identité dans la langue dominée', *RHT*, 51, 1999:274–80, provides an overview of radio and stage plays in Occitan during the 20th c., with extensive discussion of Claude Alranq, *Le Théâtre d'oc contemporain (1939–1993): Les arts de jouer du midi de la France*, Pézenas, Domens, 1995, 256 pp., and Id., *Répertoire du théâtre d'oc contemporain, 1939–1996*, Pézenas, Domens, 1997, 288 pp. On modernist appropriations of troubadour poetry, see the collected volume *Ezra Pound and the Troubadours: Selected Papers from the Ezra Pound Conference, Brantôme, France, 1995*, ed. Philip Grover, Gardonne, Fédérop, 179 pp.

IV. SPANISH STUDIES

LANGUAGE
DIACHRONIC STUDIES

By STEVEN DWORKIN, *University of Michigan*

1. GENERAL

The application of the insights offered by variationist sociolinguistics has led to important advances in the study of language change. Ralph J. Penny, *Variation and Change in Spanish*, CUP, 284 pp., makes use of such concepts as the role of social networks and koineization developed by such specialists as James and Leslie Milroy and Peter Trudgill to account for a large number of phonological and morphological changes documented in Peninsular, New World, and Judeo-Spanish. P. also offers the reader an analysis of the various processes of standardization undergone by Spanish. This important book is essential reading for specialists in the history of Spanish. B. Imhoff, 'Socio-historic network ties and medieval Navarro-Aragonese', *NM*, 101:443–50, exemplifies morphological variation in the simple past tense system of pre-Heredian Navarro-Aragonese using the social network model of diffusion of linguistic change elaborated by the Milroys. Strong Occitanian immigration ties in Navarre account for much of the linguistic variation studied (e.g.,preterite ending in *–ieu*). D. Tuten, 'Linking social change and linguistic change: koineization in Early Castile', Dworkin, *New Approaches*, 97–105, employs Trudgill's koineization model to explain the consolidation in Castilian of the diphthongs /je/ and /we/ and the early loss of preposition + article contractions (*pelo, enno < por+lo, en+lo*).

Roger Wright continues to offer stimulating studies on the relationship of Latin and Romance in the Iberian Peninsula before the 13th century. Within the framework of his hypothesis that the first Romance texts represent a reformed spelling rather than a change of language from Latin to Romance, he analyses in *El Tratado de Cabreros (1206): estudio sociofilológico de una reforma ortográfica*, London, Queen Mary and Westfield College, 130 pp., the orthography found in the two versions of the *Tratado*, the first administrative document written in the new Romance orthography. In Id., 'The assertion of Ibero-Romance', *FMLS* 26:230–40, W. offers historical and cultural background on the struggle in 13th-c. Spain between the Latin and the Romance ways of writing and of the political consequences of the triumph, starting with the Alfonsine period, of the new Romance writing system. Id., 'Las periodizacones del romance hispánico (y sus desventajas)', *CILPR* 22, ii, 481–84, points out that traditional periodization in Spanish language history distorts the realities of linguistic evolution.

Issues concerning the use of Hispano-Romance by Jews, Muslims, and Mozarabs in the context of the complex linguistic mosaic of medieval Spain are discussed by Elaine R. Miller, *Jewish Multiglossia: Hebrew, Arabic, and Castilian in Medieval Spain*, Newark, DE, Juan de la Cuesta, 160 pp. Among the questions surveyed by Miller is the vexed issue of whether the spoken Spanish of the Jews differed from that of their Christian neighbours.

Not all historical work is limited to the medieval language. María de los Angeles Martínez Ortega, *La lengua de los siglos XVI y XVII a través de los textos jurídicos. Los pleitos civiles de la escribanía de Alonso Rodríguez*, Valladolid U.P., 333 pp., discusses various syntactic phenomena as reflected in the texts of four civil suits preserved in the Archive of the Royal Chancellery of Valladolid. F. Lebsanft, 'Geschichte des Neuspanichen als Geschichte der Sprachkuktur', *ZRP*, 116:197–212, discusses methodological issues dealing with the study and recording of the history of modern Spanish raised by his reading of Jenny Brumme, *Spanische Sprache im 19. Jahrhundert. Sprachliches Wissen, Norm und Sprachveränderungen* (Münster, Nodus, 1997).

Two papers in Hernández, *Cid*, examine questions of dating and purpose relevant to the study of the Romance elements in the *Glosas Emilianenses* and *Glosas Silenses*: M. C. Díaz y Díaz, 'A vueltas con las Glosas' (293–95), and C. Hernández Alonso, 'Glosas y glosarios: ¿consultaron un vocabulario los autores de las emilianenses y silenses?' (303–07). The latter gives a negative answer to the question posed in the title of his paper.

2. Diachronic Phonology

The vicissitudes in Hispano-Romance of Latin /f-/ continue to attract the attention of Hispanists. M. Quilis Merín describes the uses and values of <f> and <h> in documents from the Visigothic period to the early 12th c. in her contribution 'El caso de la F- inicial latina y su representación gráfica en el período de orígenes del español', Aleza, *Estudios*, 239–48. In a major contribution C. Pensado, 'Frontera de prefijo, aspiración de "f" y procesos de nasalización en la historia del español', *RPh*, 52:89–112, offers a thorough examination of the development of /f-/ at the prefix/root morpheme boundary. Pensado and J. Méndez Dosuna, 'Sobre la regularidad de ciertas irregularidades en un cambio fonético: *ie* > *i* en castellano medieval', *ALH*, 12–13, 1996–97[1999?]: 125–42, suggest that coarticulation with the following sounds led to shortening of the vowel articulation, producing the change from /je/ to /i/. F. González Ollé, 'Distinción entre *s* estridente y *s* mate propiciada en Sevilla a mediados del siglo XVII', *RFE*, 79, 1999: 5–32, claims that rhyme schemes demonstrate for some speakers a phonetic distinction between orthographic *s* and *z* based on the features *estridente/mate*. D. Hartkemeyer, 'An OT approach to atonic vowel loss patterns in Old French and Old Spanish', Dworkin, *New Approaches*, 65–83, reinterprets vowel syncope in terms of dynamic constraint interactions. This paper illustrates the strengths and weaknesses of the application of Optimality Theory to issues in diachronic phonology.

J. Moreno Bernal, 'Contribución al estudio de la apócope de la vocal final en la *General Estoria IV*', *RFE*, 79, 1999: 261–89, distinguishes carefully between distinct phonetic phenomena traditionally subsumed under the rubric 'apocope'. He notes that some forms of apparent apocope may reflect medieval orthographic practices rather than a phonetic phenomenon. G. Clavería Nadal, 'La variación vocálica en español antiguo', *CILPR 22*, II, 113–22, offers abundant data on wavering between unstressed vowels in Old Spanish.

3. Diachronic Morphology

B. Imhoff, 'Dialect contact and historical linguistic variation: the Old Spanish "*-ie* imperfect" ', *HR*, 68: 381–96, discusses the possible role through dialect contact of the Old Aragonese *-ie* preterite in the rise of the Old Spanish imperfects in *-ie* for *-er* and *-ir* verbs. F. González Ollé, 'Pretérito imperfecto y condicional con desinencia *-ie* en el siglo XVI', *RFE*, 80: 341–77, examines closely 16th c. instances of the survival of *-ie* imperfects. Id., 'El artículo gascón *et* ~ *(e)ro, (e)ra* en Aragón y Navarra', *ZRP*, 116: 260–78, documents and discusses the presence of these forms of the definite article in Medieval Aragon and Navarre. E Ridruejo, 'Apofonía vocálica y cambio de conjugación en español', *CILPR 22*, II, 371–77, explores (without drawing any firm conclusion) a possible link between the presence of vowel apophony and the shift of some Latin –ERE verbs to the *-ir* conjugation in Spanish. K. Anipa, 'A study of the analytic future/conditional in Golden-Age Spanish', *BHS(L)*, 77: 325–37, claims that this construction lasted well into the 17th c. and enjoyed identical status with its synthetic counterpart. The author brings forth examples of this analytical construction with *tener* rather than *haber*. J. A. Pascual 'El enfoque histórico en los procedimientos derivativos del léxico español', *Voces*, 8–9, 1997–98[2000]: 249–64, offers a diachronic focus on modern derivations in *-dero, -dor, -tero*.

4. DIACHRONIC SYNTAX

María Teresa Echenique and Rafael Cano Aguilar have rendered a major service to Spanish historical linguistics by coordinating the publication of Rafael Lapesa, *Estudios de morfosintaxis histórica del español*, M, Gredos, 2 vols, 945 pp. These volumes gather together 31 pieces on various problems of Spanish diachronic morphosyntax, of which one 'Morfosintaxis histórica del verbo español' is published for the first time. In what will be for many readers a controversial book, Angel López García, *Cómo surgió el español. Introducción a la sintáxis histórica del español antiguo*, M, Gredos, 235 pp., seeks the origin of Old Spanish (and Romance) syntax in the language of the Vulgate. Essentially, a syntax based on noun morphology yielded to a syntax based on a semantic word-order type dependent on verbs. The title of this stimulating book is somewhat misleading.

C. J. Pountain, 'Pragmatic factors in the evolution of the Romance reflexive (with special reference to Spanish)', *HRJ*, 1 : 5–25, argues that the historical trajectory of the reflexive follows an evolutionary hierarchy ordered according to semantic and pragmatic criteria. Direct and indirect object functions must be distinguished. In his paper 'Capitalization', *ICHL 12*, 1, 295–309, P. presents the development of *ser* and *estar* as an example of a phenomenon he labels 'capitalization', a process by which an already existing linguistic feature is substantially exploited for wider purposes. Such is the case of the functional/semantic history of *estar*. A. Enrique-Arias, 'Spanish object agreement markers and the typology of object agreement morphology', Dworkin, *New Approaches*, 149–64, seeks to identify the causes in Early Modern Spanish for the obligatory preverbal placement of Spanish clitic object pronouns. He claims that object pronouns had become affixal object markers and were prefixed to the verb since tense, aspect, mood, and subject agreement markers already functioned as suffixes. Similar analyses had been proposed previously by J. Rini and T. Riiho. M. Davies, 'Syntactic diffusion in Spanish and Portuguese infinitival complements', *ib.*, 109–127, evaluates the merits of the Principles and Parameters approach and grammaticalization as a means of explaining syntactic change. The data come from his earlier work on clitic climbing, causal constructions, and subject raising in Spanish and Portuguese. E. Mallén, 'A minimalist perspective on Wackernagel's Law', *ib.*, 199–215, seeks to apply the insights of Chomsky's Minimalist Program to issues of clitic placement in Old Spanish. This paper is accessible only to readers versed in the chosen theoretical framework.

F. J. Herrero Ruiz de Loizaga, 'Sobre la evolución de las oraciones y conjunciones adversativas', *RFE*, 79, 1999:291–328, traces the development of these constructions. Despite its title, R. Pellen, 'Les "temps composés" et l'accord du participe passé avec "haber" dans les *Milagros* de Berceo', *Kock Vol.*, 411–33, also examines choice of auxiliary, order of the elements, and the role of prosodic factors. M. Batllori Dillet, 'La impersonalización en español medieval: recursos formales y semanticos', *CILPR 22*, II, 15–24, surveys various strategies available for impersonal constructions in 13th-c. Spanish. L. Díaz Suárez, 'Las preposiciones *per* y *por* en el asturiano del siglo XIII', *ib.*, 139–47, offers semantically-classified raw data from Asturian documents on the two prepositions at issue. P. Sánchez-Prieto Borja examines locative uses of the preposition *a* in 'La preposición *a* con valor "lugar en donde" en español antiguo', *ib.*, 393–406. Flora Klein-Andreu synthesizes much of her earlier work on clitics in *Variación actual y evolución histórica: los clíticos le/s, la/s, lo/s*, Munich, Lincom Europa, 167 pp. J. García Medina, 'Leísmo no personal y neutro de materia', *RFE*, 80:51–68, describes and documents the use of *le* with reference to inanimate direct objects in the 16th century. This use never occurs in the plural. The author tries to link *leísmo* with inanimate nouns to the presence in North-Central Spain of vestiges of the so-called *neutro de materia*.

5. Lexis

With the publication of fascicle 20, B. Müller's *Diccionario del español medieval* has reached the word *albañal*. Surely it is time to consider making available in electronic format the treasure trove of lexical materials that form the foundation of this valuable research tool. E. Boucher,'Aportación al *Diccionario español de textos médicos antiguos (DETEMA)*', *CLHM*, 23:7–11, offers additions to that major reference work based on her edition of the *Tratado de las fiebres* of Isaac Israeli. T. J. Walsh, 'The etymology of Hispano-Romance *tomar* 'to take', *HR*, 68:243–65, presents semantic and phonetic evidence which he believes supports his claim that *tomar*, a long-standing crux of Spanish etymology, goes back to the family of Lat. DOMARE 'to tame', specifically *ADDOMARE. He presupposes a phonetic devoicing of rare lat –DD- [d:]. X. L. García Arias, 'Los vientos de Isidoro de Sevilla y sus pervivencias en asturiano', *RLiR*, 64:5–15, describes the survival in Asturian of the names of the winds in Isidore of Seville's *Origenes sive Etymologiae*. Dalila Fasla, *Lengua, literatura, música. Contribución al estudio semántico del léxico musical en la lírica castellana de la baja Edad Media al primer Renacimiento*, Logroño, Universidad de la Rioja, 1998, 640 pp., offers lexical vignettes of relevant musical terms found in the early Spanish lyric. This book is a readable combination of diachronic lexicology and musical history.

The title of Consuelo García Gallarín, *Léxico del 98*, M, Complutense, 1998, is somewhat misleading. This book offers a classified
catalogue of those lexical items found in the prose of Valle-Inclán,
Baroja, and Unamuno that were not recorded in the 1984 edition of
the *DRAE*. L. Nieto, 'Vocabulario y glosarios del español de los siglos
XIV al XVI', *RFE*, 80: 155–80, discusses the value for diachronic
research of medieval and early modern lexical compilations involving
Spanish. A. Quilis, 'Las palabras españolas contenidas en el Vocabulario de las *Introductiones Latinae* de Antonio de Nebrija', *ib.*, 181–91,
lists and discusses the Spanish words found in the vocabulary
appended by Nebrija to his *Introductiones Latinae* (1481). T. Bargetto-
Andrés, 'A lexical contribution from a 15th-c. Spanish translation of
the *Divine Comedy*', *RN*, 41: 37–43, studies OSp. *trecha*, *monchón*, and
alborar as used in the version of Enrique de Villena's translation of
Dante's poem as preserved in BNM MS 10186. P. Alvarez de
Miranda explains the circumstances surrounding the inclusion in the
DRAE of selected ghost-words in his essay, 'Palabras y acepciones
fantasma en los diccionarios de la Academia', Chevalier, *Néologie*,
55–73. D. Oliver Pérez, 'Historia del arabismo *alhanía* y del falso
alhamí del diccionario académico', *ALH*, 12–13, 1996–97[1999?]:
147–60, describes the history of OSp. *alhanía* 'alcoba' and the
erroneous creation of *alhamí* in the 19th century. H. N. Urrutibeheity,
'On the meaning of the word *laña* in the *Cantar del* [sic] *Mío Cid*',
Lopez-Grigera Vol., 519–24, claims that *laña* (st. 599) is a variant of *landa*
'grande extensión de tierra llana en que sólo se crían plantas
silvestres'.

6. Spanish in the New World

The last years have witnessed a mini-boom in research into the
history of New World Spanish. Most such studies involve the linguistic
analysis of non-literary archival documents from the colonial period,
investigations which also throw light on Early Modern Spanish in
general. The leading worker in this area is Juan Antonio Frago
Gracia. Much of his insightful work and critical evaluations of
previous research on the contributions of regional varieties of
Peninsular Spanish to the constitution of New World Spanish is
synthesized in his book *Historia del español de América*, M, Gredos, 1999,
350 pp. His 'Fondo lingüístico canario y afinidades americanas (siglos
XVII-XVIII)', *RFE*, 80: 319–40, analyses the linguistic features of
rural documents from Tenerife and discusses the role of the Spanish
of the Canary Islands in the formation of New World varieties.
Methodologically instructive for the editing and linguistic analysis of
archival documents are his essays: 'Criterio filológico y edición de

textos indianos: sobre documentos de la Nueva España', *RPh*, 53, 1999: 119–35, and 'Tradición e innovación ortográfica en manuscritos mexicanos: implicaciones culturales y lingüísticas en el hecho textual', Blecua, *Grafemática*, 96–121. This same volume contains several other studies dealing with the orthography of early New World documents: M. Carrera de la Red, 'Grafías y grafemas representativos de sibilantes en documentos dominicanos de los siglos XVI y XVII' (25–35); A. Elizaicín, M. Malcouri, and M. Coll, 'Grafemática histórica: seseo y yeísmo en el Río de la Plata' (75–82); M. B. Fontanella de Weinberg, 'La variable sexo y las grafías de los hablantes bonaerenses en los siglos XVIII y XIX' (83–95). A useful sample of current work on the history of Spanish in the New World can be found in Vol. 3 of *ALFAL 11*, pp. 1793–2022, and in *ALH*, 12–13, 1996–97[1999?], published as *Homenaje al Dr Germán de Granda*.

The history of Spanish in the US Southwest is examined in two major pieces. G. Bills and N. Vigil, 'Ashes to ashes: the historical basis for dialect variation in New Mexican Spanish', *RPh*, 53, 1999: 43–67, describe the linguistic history of one of the most isolated Spanish colonies in the New World. W. Bright, 'Hispanisms in Southwest Indian Languages', *ib.*, 259–87, exhaustively surveys Spanish loanwords in several Indian languages of the US Southwest, tracing the varying degrees of social contact and linguistic borrowing.

MEDIEVAL LITERATURE
POSTPONED

ALJAMIADO LITERATURE
POSTPONED

LITERATURE, 1490–1700
(PROSE AND POETRY)

By CARMEN PERAITA, *Villanova University*

(This survey covers the years 1998–2000)

1. GENERAL

Francisco Márquez Villanueva, *Menosprecio de Corte y alabanza de aldea (Valladolid, 1539) y el tema áulico en la obra de fray Antonio de Guevara*, Santander, Cantabria U.P., 1999, 176 pp., re-examines the perplexities which reading G. raises, and debates whether *Menosprecio* could be classified as a medieval or Renaissance, erudite or popular text. Jeremy Robbins, *The Challenges of Uncertainty. An Introduction to Seventeenth-Century Spanish Literature*, Lanham, Rowman and Littlefield, 1998, 160 pp., is an interpretative introduction to the inventive, challenging, and powerful works of Baroque imagination, such as Cervantes, Quevedo, Gracián, Lope de Vega, Góngora, Tirso de Molina, Calderón de la Barca, Velázquez, and Murillo. R. examines how Baroque creativity responded to an unprecedented sense of uncertainty fostered by developments across Europe, emphasizing major themes, trends, and ideas that justify viewing the century as a separate period, with a distinct identity. This is primarily due to the crisis in knowledge which was a marked feature of the early modern period; intellectual uncertainties challenged many of the artists and writers to explore the limits of human knowledge. Together with a general culture of uncertainty, R. investigates other social and political factors that shaped the Spanish Baroque, such as the resurgence of religious militancy and the slow decline of Spanish political authority. Jorge Checa, *Experiencia y representación en el Siglo de Oro*, Valladolid, Junta de Castilla y León, 1998, 218 pp., includes chapters on 'Cortés y el espacio de la conquista: la *Segunda Carta de Relación*', 'Experiencia y representación en Santa Teresa de Jesús', 'Gracián y las *cifras* del mundo' and 'Sor Juana Inés de la Cruz: la mirada y el discurso'. C. analyses experience and representation as two poles to access otherness, which can be applied to a variety of disciplines: history, political science, travel books, and mystic texts. From the standpoint that representation is an ideologically mediated textual activity, C. discusses why engaging directly in the experience of things became so important in early modern Europe. No text can include the whole experience, therefore the representation operates rhetorically as a synecdoche, constituting a part of the whole. Semantic irresolutions in the texts are created by the debatable character of what is chosen to be represented. The sphere of the experience is formed in each case by the space (geographical, political, mystic, natural, etc) in which the representation acts. In Cortés's *Second Letter* the otherness that constitutes the experience is identified with the political and cultural space that he tries to appropriate. From the individual sphere of secret communication with God, Teresa de Jesús represents her spiritual writings as a sort of commentary and translation of the experienced otherness, intended to legitimate an individual 'experience' in opposition with the theological science of the *letrados*. C. examines ways in which *Criticón* manifests an epistemological uncertainty stemming from trying to represent and regulate spheres of experience in which human actions are faced with unexpected and contingent factors, and concludes by commenting on several of Sor Juana Inés de la Cruz's poems, dealing with the idea that adequately representing experience causes conflicts that are difficult to resolve.

2. Reading, Libraries, and Printing

READING. *Leer y escribir en tiempos de Cervantes*, ed. Antonio Castillo et al., B, Gedisa, 1999, 360 pp., presents 12 essays on topics such as text production strategies, practices of reading and the social diffusion of the written word. R. Chartier reflects on the relations between author, spoken word, and written text in European 17th-c. drama (243–54); F. M. Gimeno Bley studies the typographic differences in the crowns of Castille and Aragon (193–210); A. Viñao Frago investigates literacy and educational practices (39–84); R. Marquilhas examines uses in Portugal of written texts and letters as magical devices (111–28); F. J. Bouza Álvarez analyses the role played by the book in the creation of modern bureaucracy (85–109); V. M. Mínguez evaluates the functions of images, illustrations and engravings in books (256–83), and J. M. Prieto Bernabé writes on the practice of erudite reading (313–43). M. G. Profeti, 'Estrategias editoriales de Lope de Vega', *Actas* (Madrid), I, 679–85, studies Lope de Vega's complex strategies as a professional writer promoting and publishing his *comedias* and poetry, wishing to enhance his image as a mythical 'Fénix de los ingenios', and therefore paying attention also to external aspects of his book production, such as including his portrait in his printed texts. M. Frenk, 'Más sobre la lectura en el Siglo de Oro: de oralidades y ambigüedades', *ib.*, 516–21, raises the question of the appropriateness of applying the term *oralidad* to a variety of different occurrences. F. comments on Golden Age passages stressing the ambiguities of the terminology concerning the practice of reading; '*ver*' with the meaning of '*leer*' (Pedro de Navarra, 'la escritura se vee, escrita y se oye si es leyda'); '*palabra*' understood as word pronounced, not written (Guevara, 'si un príncipe anciano quisiesse escribir con la péñola; y si no, que nos lo dixesse por palabra qué infortunios ha passado'); 'hablar' as meaning to write, 'hablar en escritos', 'hablar por letras', 'hablar con la pluma'. *Cultura escrita, literatura e historia. Conversaciones con Roger Chartier,* ed. Alberto Cue, Mexico, FCE, 1999, 271 pp., is a series of talks with four Latin-American professors dealing with 'Coacciones transgredidas y libertades transgredidas'; it includes 'La cultura escrita en la perspectiva de larga duración' (19–74); 'Los espacios de la historia del libro' (75–111); 'Literatura y lectura' (113–156); 'Prácticas privadas, espacio público' (157–194); 'La revolución del texto electrónico' (195–226). *El escrito en el Siglo de Oro. Prácticas y representaciones,* ed. Javier Guijarro Ceballos, Salamanca U.P., 1999, 331 pp., gathers essays on the history of the book and the practice of reading, the conception, formation, and uses of libraries, as well as the status and function of the written text; it includes, among others, F. Géal, 'Algunas reflexiones sobre la lectura voraz en el Siglo de Oro' (129–46); P. Cátedra, 'Los escritos y la biblioteca deseados' (43–68); M. Ambrosio Sánchez 'La biblioteca del predicador (en el siglo XVI): renovación y continuidad' (289–304); P. Bravo comments on the use of the *pasquín* in the Aragonese revolt (32–42); and P. Civil examines frontispieces in the first half of the 17th century (69–84).

LIBRARIES. Trevor J. Dadson, *Libros, lectores y lecturas. Estudio sobre bibliotecas particulares españolas del Siglo de Oro,* M, Arco, 1998, 604 pp., studies the diffusion of reading, the book trade, readers, and their readings. D. examines libraries of the nobility (D. Hurtado de Mendoza; Ruy de Silva, prince of Eboli; the third duke of Pastrana's books and paintings, and other noblemen); libraries of professional *letrados* and authors (Alonso de Barros, author of *Proverbios morales,* and the Count of Salinas, among others); the book market, Cristóbal López's (1606) and Miguel Martínez's (1629) *librerías.* D. dedicates five articles to women's libraries and painting collections, those of Brianda de la Cerda y Sarmiento, duquesa de Bejar (1602); the condesa de Puñonrostro (1616); Francisca de Paz Jofre de Loaysa (1626); Antonia de Ulloa, condesa de Salinas (1605), and Isabel Montero (1629). Anthony Hobson, *Renaissance Book Collecting: Jean Grolier and Diego Hurtado de Mendoza, their Books and Bindings,* CUP, 1999, 275 pp., compares two 16th-c. libraries, that of 'the Prince of Bibliophiles' — Grolier — and that of Hurtado de Mendoza, a poet, historian, Greek scholar, and Arabist, ambassador in Venice (1540–46), at the Council of Trent (1545–6) and of the Pope (1547–52). Both bibliophiles held offices in public service, spent time in Italy collecting books, coins, and antiquities, and had careers interrupted by disgrace and imprisonment. H. includes a partial reconstruction of Hurtado de Mendoza's catalogue of books based on a variety of sources, the principal being an incomplete copy of the 1576 inventory made about 1604 by the Hieronymite friar Gabriel de San Jerónimo for Philip IV's chaplain, the abbé Jules Chifflet. It will never be possible to compile a complete list of Don Diego's printed books, since the inventory made in 1576 perished in the Escorial fire of 1671. H. also studies the main binding shops in Venice in the mid-16th century.

PRINTING. Fermín de los Reyes Gómez, *El libro en España y América. Legislación y censura (siglo XV - siglo XVII)*, 2 vols, M, Arco, 767, 708 pp., is an extraordinary, documented study of the evolution of legislation concerning printing, printing practices, ideological control, and censorship of written texts in early modern Spain. R. examines an array of topics such as differences in legislation across the Spanish kingdoms; the function of the Inquisition and *Indices;* Catholic reforms from the Lateran Council of 1515 up to the Council of Trent, and the Trentine influence; negative opinions about books, the burning of books and Bibles; *pleitos* concerning the printing of *bulas*; printing envisaged as business, and other topics. R. also explores systematically the evolution of processes of granting *privilegios de impresión*, and *licencias*; taxes on printing; state interventions concerning printing; and he analyses a variety of questions such as the quality of the printers and the prohibition to print *comedias* or prose fiction in 1635. The second volume provides a chronological legislative appendix (1479–1815) of *pragmáticas, cédulas, autos, privilegios*, council *disposiciones* and other, as well as an appendix of documents related to printing legislation and state and inquisitorial censorship (1480–1805). R. provides further important indexes of laws and documents, as well as an analytical index, which makes this study an indispensable reference tool.

José García Oro and María José Portela Silva, *La monarquía y los libros en el Siglo de Oro*, Alcalá U.P., 1999, 495 pp., is an erudite and detailed analysis, enriched with new documentation, of varied facets of the Spanish kings' role (from the *Reyes Católicos* to Philip II) regarding aspects such as authoring, editing, printing, trading, collecting, and legislating. The study is a key to understanding the circulation and diffusion of humanist texts in the Spanish Golden Age. E. Sánchez García, 'Libros españoles editados en Nápoles', *Actas* (Madrid), 1, 720–28, examines Spanish books printed in Naples in the 17th c., dealing with aspects such as celebrating and panegyric literature, preaching, chronicles of miracles, reports of special news (e.g. the eruption of Vesuvius in 1631), or political advice for kings, such as Alejandro Ros's *Cataluña desengañada* (1646), Giulio Antonio

Brancalasso's *Labirinto de Corte* (1609), or *La libra [. . .] Pesante las ganancias y las perdidas de la monarquía de España en el reynado de Felipe IV el grande*, by Grivilio Vezzalmi (the pseudonym of Virgilio Malvezzi)

BIBLIOGRAPHY. José Manuel Lucía Megías, *Libros de caballerías castellanos en las bibliotecas públicas de París. Catálogo descriptivo*, Alcalá U.P. — Pisa U.P., 1999, 325 pp., is an important reference work which includes an introductory study commenting on the impact of the French Revolution on Paris libraries, G. Naudé's influence in shaping early modern libraries, and the social roles of the library. M. A. Etayo-Piñol, 'Influencia de las ediciones literarias españolas en Lyon en los siglos XVI y XVII', *Actas* (Madrid), I, 495–99, stresses the roles played by French translations of Spanish works between 1526 and 1621, of sentimental and chivalric novels (Diego de San Pedro, Juan de Flores, *Amadis*), and authors such as Guevara and Gracián, in spreading the image of an ideal courtier.

3. HUMANIST THOUGHT AND RHETORIC

HUMANIST THOUGHT. Erika Rummel, *Jiménez de Cisneros: On the Threshold of Spain's Golden Age*, Tempe, ACMRS, 1999, viii + 152 pp., presents a concise and documented account of Cisneros's pivotal role in Spanish history, examining the main aspects of his career as statesman, reformer, missionary, and patron of learning. Cisneros's interest in philology led him to recognize the importance of the newly developed art of printing and to promote textual criticism, which underpinned the transformation from manuscript to print culture. Luis de León, *Escritos sobre América*, ed. and trans. Antonio Moreno Mengíbar and Javier Martos Fernández, M, Tecnos, 1999, 77 pp., provides a selection from León's juridical and theological corpus, centered on the idea of America. Luis de León reads in the light of Old Testament prophecies, following the idea that the discovery of America was announced by the prophets. *Calamvs Renascens*, I, includes: L. De Cañigral Cortés, 'Mistificaciones en Luis Hurtado de Mendoza y Luisa Sigea: Francesco Tanzi, Vincenzo Calmeta y Brantome' (31–52); G. Lazure, 'Perceptions of the Temple, projections of the divine. Royal patronage, biblical scholarship and Jesuit imagery in Spain, 1580–1620' (155–88); M. V. Pérez Custodio, 'Sobre los ingresos de los catedráticos de retórica de Alcalá en la segunda mitad del XVI' (277–98). Juan Gil, *Arias Montano en su entorno (bienes y herederos)*, Mérida, Junta de Extremadura, 1998, 413 pp., presents an exhaustive documentation which helps to contextualize M.'s life and humanistic production. Lu Ann Homza, *Religious Authority in the Spanish Renaissance*, Baltimore–London, Johns Hopkins U.P., xxi + 312 pp., combines erudite perspectives to demonstrate that not all humanists were progressive nor were the scholastics invariably opposed to the methods and aims of humanist scholarship. H.'s sharp-edged critical methodology, sound scholarship, and expanded body of sources challenge some of Bataillon's reflections on the understanding of the complexity of Spanish Renaissance thought.

RHETORIC. *Renaissance Debates on Rhetoric*, ed. and trans. Wayne A. Rebhorn, Ithaca, Cornell U.P., viii + 322 pp., is an anthology of 25 Renaissance texts examining the meaning of rhetoric, as well as the role it played in Renaissance life. R. claims that Renaissance debates about rhetoric are basically debates about the Renaissance itself, and takes on a wide selection of European rhetoricians, starting with Petrarch ('Letter to Tommaso da Messina, concerning the study of eloquence'), and ending with passages from J. F. Le Grand's *A Discourse on French Rhetoric*, paying attention to, among others, Vives (*On the Causes of the Corruption of the Arts* and *On Teaching the Disciplines*), Agrippa (*On the Uncertainty and Vanity of the Arts and Sciences*), J. Amyot (*Epitome of Royal Eloquence*), Ramus (*Logic*), Patrizzi *(Ten dialogues on Rhetoric)* and Juan de Guzmán (*The First Part of Rhetoric*). Ángel Luis Luján Atienza, *Retóricas españolas del siglo* XVI. *El foco de Valencia*, M, CSIC, 1999, 332 pp., is structured in three sections: traditional rhetoric, sacred oratory, and epistolary rhetoric. Special attention is paid to Furió Ceriol and the Ramist influences, as well as to Andrés Sempere and Pedro Juan Nuñez. V. Pineda, 'El arte de traducir en el Renacimiento (La obra de Francisco de Támara)', *Criticón*, 73, 1998:23–35.

VIVES. Juan Luis Vives, *El arte retórica. De ratione dicendi*, ed. and trans. Ana Isabel Camacho, introd. Emilio Hidalgo-Serna, B, Ánthropos, 1999, 343 pp., and Id., *Del arte de hablar*, ed. and trans. José Manuel Rodríguez Peregrina, Granada U.P., 200 pp., fill a major gap in rhetorical studies. Id., *Obras políticas y pacifistas*, ed. Francisco Calero (BAE, 199), M, Atlas, 1999, 334 pp., includes 'Sobre las perturbaciones de Europa', originally addressed to Pope Adrian VI; 'Sobre la captura del Rey de Francia'; 'Sobre el gobierno del reino' and 'sobre la guerra y la paz', both addressed to Henry VIII; 'Sobre las disensiones de Europa y la guerra contra los turcos'; a letter to John, bishop of Lincoln, and the pacifist texts 'Sobre la concordia y la discordia en el género humano', and 'Sobre la pacificación'. *Luis Vives y el humanismo europeo*, ed. F. J. Fernández Nieto et al., Valencia U.P., 1998, 161 pp., includes E. González González, 'La crítica de los humanistas a las universidades. El caso de Vives' (13–40); A. Losada, 'Luis Vives y la polémica entre fray Bartolomé de la Casas y Juan Ginés de Sepúlveda sobre las justas causas de la guerra contra los Indios' (41–54); J. Ijsewijn, 'Lo stato attuale dei testi di J. L. Vives' (55–68); E. V. George, 'Rhetoric in Vives: the testimony of early *Orationes*' (69–96); C. Mattheeussen, 'Vives et la problématique sociale de son temps, son attitude envers la mendicité et le vagabondage' (107–15); C. Vasoli, 'La concezione filosofica in Vives' (117–29); V. del Nero, 'L'educazione in Vives' (131–46) and M. Batllori, 'Juan Luis Vives: comentarista del *De civitate Dei* de san Agustín. Apuntes para una lección en torno a la ortodoxia de Vives' (147–59).

4. CULTURAL STUDIES

Jorge Baéz de Sepúlveda, *Relación verdadera del recibimiento que hizo la ciudad de Segovia a la Magestad de la Reyna Nuestra Señora Anna de Austria, en su felicisimo casamiento que en la dicha ciudad se celebró*, ed. Sagrario López Poza and Begoña Canosa Hermida, Segovia, Fundación Juan de Borbón, 1998, 254 pp. is an exhaustively annotated edition accompanied by L.P.'s erudite introduction (7–39), which analyses the celebrative text published without the author's name in Alcalá by Juan Gracián (1572). The edition includes F. and I. Collar de Cáceres's graphic reconstruction of the *Arcos Triunfales*, and F. Collar de Cáceres's study, 'Arte y arquitectura en la entrada de Anna de Austria en Segovia' (177–254). Juan de Mal Lara, *Recebimiento que hizo la muy noble y muy leal ciudad de Seuilla a la C. R. M. del rey D. Philipe N. S.* (1570), ed. Manuel and Antonio Miguel Bernal, Seville, Fundación El Monte, 1998, 484 pp. Richard L. Kagan, *Urban Images of the Hispanic World, 1493–1793*, New Haven–London, Yale U.P., 235 pp., studies the role played by cities in Spanish and Hispanic-American culture, the peculiar character of Spain's 'empire of towns', and investigates different ways in which artists, map-makers, surveyors, and military engineers viewed the city as source of knowledge and pleasure, and represented them as built structures and human communities. Joaquim Aierdi, *Dietari Notícies de València i son regne, de 1661 a 1664 i de 1667 a 1679*, ed. Vicent Josep Escartí, B, Barcino, 1999, 500 pp., an edition of an important 'written memory' in which observations about 17th c. religious life and public celebrations are predominant.

Fernando Rodríguez de la Flor, *La península metafísica. Arte, literatura y pensamiento en la España de la Contrarreforma*, M, Biblioteca Nueva, 1999, 411 pp., investigates what R. de la F. considers Spanish differences and peculiarities, drawing from the idea of a metaphysical peninsula. The excellent documentation and erudition deserves to be read, even if the style is somewhat irritating. Unfortunately the editors did not include an index nor a bibliography; it includes '*Mundus est fabula*. La lectura de la naturaleza como documento político-moral en la literatura simbólica' (59–84); 'La ciencia del cielo. Representaciones del saber cosmológico' (85–121); 'El jardín del Yahvé. Ideología del espacio eremítico' (123–54); '*Vanitas litterarum*. Representaciones del libro como jeroglífico de un saber contingente' (155–200); 'Las sedes del alma. La figuración del espacio interior en la literatura y en el arte' (201–31); 'La *puella pillosa*. Representaciones de la alteridad femenina (de Sánchez Cotán a José de Ribera, pasando por Sebastián de Covarrubias)' (267–306); 'Eros místico. Visiones e imágenes de la carnalidad lúgubre' (233–66); 'Gasto, derroche y dilapidación del bien cultural. La economía simbólica de la fiesta' (347–62). Manuel José de Lara Ródenas, *La muerte barroca. Ceremonia y sociabilidad en Huelva durante el siglo XVII*, Huelva U.P., 1999, 557 pp., describes social practices organized around dying, resorting to 17th c. wills, devotional literature, hagiographic writings, books on '*artes de bien morir*' — such as Orozco's *Victoria de la muerte* — as well as travel books (Bertaut, Madame D'Aulnoy, Pinheiro, Wynn, and others). The first section reflects on social and spiritual practices ('El cuerpo a la tierra', 'El alma a Dios') and analyses rituals for the dead body ('Las transformaciones de la casa mortuoria y el exhibicionismo del cadáver'; 'La vestidura de los santos. El amortajamiento'; 'Signos de duelo: los lutos'; 'El cortejo de vanidades'; 'Pompa y paradoja: el traslado del cuerpo'). The second part 'El alma a Dios' deals with consciousness of eternity and the functions of the '*sufragios devotos*', '*novenarios*', '*misas*', '*capellanías*'. A much-needed study which contextualizes Golden Age texts dealing with the ubiquitous topic of death.

Thomas S. Acker, *The Baroque Vortex: Velázquez, Calderón, and Gracián under Philip IV*, NY, Lang, 152 pp., compares the use of metaphor and symbol in Gracián and Calderón, particularly in the latter's *autos sacramentales* and the *comedias mitológicas*, with the use of techniques similar to those in Velázquez's paintings. The three artists shared interpretative and philosophical traditions, and their respective works dealt with common religious, historical, and mythological themes. A. examines the intellectual environment, Spanish Habsburg mythology, syncretic naturalism and religious syncretism, and mythological imagery. Javier Portús, *Pintura y pensamiento en la España de Lope de Vega*, Hondarribia, Nerea, 1999, 250 pp., studies the relationships between painters and poets, Lope de Vega's attitudes toward art and artists, and functions of the image in Counter-Reformation Spain. Javier Portús and Jesusa Vega, *La estampa religiosa en la España del Antiguo Regimen*, M, FUE, 1998, 631 pp., fills an important gap on the study of varied facets and uses of religious prints: typology and functions, circulation and trade, legislating and collecting.

Philippe II et l'Espagne, ed. Annie Molinié-Bertrand and Jean-Paul Duviols (Iberica, 11), Paris, Presses de l'Université de Paris-Sorbonne,

264 pp., includes: A. Merle, 'L'image des morisques au temps de Philippe II à travers quelques textes contemporains' (157–74); A. Molinié-Bertrand, 'Philippe II, roi catholique et roi prudent' (7–20); M. Bouyer, 'Philippe II et Le Greco' (35–44); S. Roubaud, 'Les lettres de Philippe II à ses filles' (193–202); C. Sokhn-Baduel, 'Gerónimo Castillo de Bobadilla et le voyage de Philippe II à Guadalajara en 1585' (203–16); P. Nogueira, 'Philippe II d'Espagne: les femmes de sa vie' (217–34). Antonio Feros, *Kingship and Favoritism in the Spain of Philip III, 1598–1621*, CUP, xvi + 299 pp., examines the rise to power of the Duke of Lerma, the first of a series of European favourites and prime ministers with a key influence both in politics and arts in the 17th century. F. contests historians' traditional views of Lerma and Philip III as *fainéant* rulers, mostly interested in personal enrichment, and convincingly demonstrates Lerma's concern and ability to forge a discourse to justify royal power exercized in personal monarchies, and able to conceptualize and legitimate favouritism. F.'s study is essential for contextualizing Lope de Vega's and Quevedo's works. Eleonora Belligni, *Lo Scacco Della Prudenza: Precettistica politica ed esperienza storica in Virgilio Malvezzi*, Florence, Olschki, 1999, 364 pp., is a key study for better understanding Spanish political thought in the 17th c. and the influence of this intellectual and politician *italiano spagnolato*, in search of producing consensus. B. examines the 'anomalies' regarding the paradigm of the reason of state in M's belief in the primacy of justice over *prudenza*. Resorting to extensive historical documentation, B. investigates the underpinning of M.'s political vocation, and analyses the different and heterogeneous facets of M.'s intellectual and political life, his rhetorical, moral, historiographic, and philosophic concerns. The influence of M's laconic style on the Spanish court is interestingly documented.

5. Picaresque and Poverty

Anne J. Cruz, *Discourses of Poverty: Social Reform and the Picaresque Novel in Early Modern Spain*, Toronto U.P., 1999, xvii + 297 pp., analyses the different approaches by which the picaresque genre represented the social realities faced by the subculture of the poor, and the increasingly complex interrelations of the impoverished with other social groups, paying attention to diverse aspects such as rhetoric and the role of the reader in the picaresque, among others. C. studies the evolution and perception of confinement and control of the poor in Spain and analyses charity, poverty, and liminality in the *Lazarillo*. Lazaro is identified with the poor, which in the Middle Ages was an integral part of society, since poverty played a key symbolic role, within the social structure. In the 16th c., when beggars proliferated in urban centres, the poor became less socially accepted. Epistemic changes alter the traditional perception of the poor, who are then considered criminal. The abandonment of the Christian ideal of charity is precisely what is at stake in the *Lazarillo*. C. stresses that the novel deals with the history of poverty itself, the relation between society and poverty, and not only with Lazaro's own poverty. C. also brillantly discusses the key debates on welfare in the 16th c. (Soto versus Robles, Giginta, Pérez de Herrera, and other *arbitristas*). 'The picaresque as *Pharmakos*' examines Alemán's critique of state in *Guzmán de Alfarache*, Gonzales de Cellorigo's *Restauración de Estado*, and the doctrine of free will. 'Textualizing the other's body' studies scatology and the social body in Quevedo's *Buscón*. The feminist reading of *La pícara Justina*, male voice and misogyny, the investigation of the *pícaras* as prostitutes and female enclosure in the female picaresque, are especially insightful. C. dedicates the chapter 'From *Pícaro* to soldier' to the 'other' and the military revolution, and reads soldiers tales — such as *Alonso de Contreras* and *Estebanillo González* — as lives of *pícaros*. César Hernández Alonso and Beatriz Sanz Alonso, *Germanía y sociedad en los Siglos de Oro. La cárcel de Sevilla*, Valladolid U.P., 1999, 525 pp, includes studies on the topography, language, vocabulary, evolution of *germanía*, the gypsies and the *germanía*, Seville in the Golden Age, 'Jaques y bravos', 'Mancebías y prostitutas', a critical edition of *Relación de la cárcel de Sevilla*, as well as an anthology of significant *germanescos* literary texts. Juan Luis Vives, *On Assistance to the Poor*, introd. and trans., Alice Tobriner, SNJM, Toronto U.P., 1999, 62 pp., is a re-edition of one of the first humanist texts to debate the responsability of government for the care of the poor. Miguel de Giginta, *Tratado de remedio de pobres*, ed. Félix Santolaria Sierra, B, Ariel, 207 pp., edits and studies the fascinating '*Memorial*' and '*Diálogo*' which form the *tratado* published in 1578.

6. EMBLEMS

The fascinating area of Spanish emblems is attracting a great deal of interdisciplinary scholarship. Antonio Bernat Visitarini and John T. Cull, *Emblemas españoles ilustrados*, M, Akal, 952 pp., includes a CD-ROM, surveys Spanish illustrated emblem books, and Castilian commentaries published in the 16th and 17th cs, to compile an encyclopedia of 1732 Spanish emblems arranged alphabetically according to the theme in the *pictura* of the emblem. Each entry provides a brief description of the *pictura* or image; the name of the author; the *inscriptio* or motto, and translations into Spanish and English; the emblemist's source; literary antecedent; the *subscriptio*, a commentary based on the *explicatio* or *amplificatio* in prose that normally accompanies the majority of emblems and Spanish *empresas*; thematic keys (for Alciato, B. and C. follow Daly and Callagan's thematic keys). The encyclopedia includes several useful indexes (iconographic themes from the *descriptio* of the *pictura*, mottos, authors and works, Spanish and English glossaries). Peter M. Daly and John Manning, *Aspects of Renaissance and Baroque Symbol Theory, 1500–1700*, NY, AMS Press, 1999, xxii + 283 pp., is a collection of interdisciplinary studies divided into three sections: the first studies terminology and cultural specificity; the many terms for emblematic devices and their historical evolution in the Spanish national setting are examined in P. F. Campa, 'Terms for emblem in the Spanish tradition' (13–26), which illustrates some aspects of theory and practice in the development of the meaning of *emblema, empresa, jeroglífico, mote, pegma, cifra, enigma*, in order to compare past and present emblematic nomenclature. The second section, 'Perceiving, seeing and meaning', addresses the cultural context and presents D. S. Russell, 'Perceiving, seeing and meaning: emblems and some approaches to reading Early Modern culture' (77–92), and J. J. García Arranz, 'Image and meaning: emblems and moral teaching in emblematic animals' (93–108); the third section deals with 'The authority of the sign' and includes D. L. Drysdall, 'Authorities of symbolism in the sixteenth century' (111–24); W. E. Engel, 'Mnemonic emblems and the humanist discourse of knowledge' (125–43); J. D. Loach, 'The influence of the Counter-Reformation defence of images on the contemporary concept of emblem' (155–200). *Emblemata Aurea. La emblemática en el arte y la literatura del Siglo de Oro*, ed. Rafael Zafra and José Javier Ardanza, M, Akal, 1999, 365 pp., includes, among other studies, I. Arellano, 'Emblemas en el *Quijote*' (9–32); A. Bernat Vistarini, 'La emblemática de los jesuitas en España: los libros de Lorenzo Ortíz y Francisco Garau' (57–68); J. Checa, '*El peregrino en su patria* de Lope de Vega y la cultura simbólica del Barroco' (99–110); R. García Mahíques, '*Sedes virtutis quadrata*. Consideraciones sobre la iconografía de los santos penitentes' (209–24); J. M. González de Zárate, 'Imagen y Poder, alegorías en emblemas' (225–34); V. Infantes, 'La primera traducción de Alciato en España: Hernando de Villa Real y su *Emblema o scriptura de la Justicia* (1546)' (235–50); G. Ledda, 'Estrategias y procedimientos comunicativos en la emblemática aplicada (fiestas y celebraciones, siglo XVII)' (251–62); S. López Poza, 'Los libros de emblemas como tesoros de erudición auxiliares de la *inventio*' (263–80); C. Mata Induráin, 'Aspectos emblemáticos de la *Silva curiosa de historias* (1583) de Julián de Medrano' (281–96). *Estudios sobre literatura emblemática española. Trabajos del grupo de investigación 'Literatura emblemática hispánica' (Universidade da*

Coruña), ed. Sagrario López Poza, El Ferrol, Sociedad de Cultura Valle Inclán, 271 pp., includes A. Bernat Vistarini and J. T. Cull, 'Guerra y paz en la emblemática de los jesuitas en España' (9–30); C. García Román, 'Análisis y clasificación tipológica de los motes en los *Emblemas morales* de Horozco y de las *Empresas sacras* de Núñez de Cepeda' (81–154); R. Lamarca Ruiz de Eguílaz, 'Los *exempla* de los reyes míticos. Moralidad para una ausencia en la emblemática política hispana' (175–92); S. López Poza, 'El disimulo como virtud política en los tratados emblemáticos españoles de educación de príncipes' (221–34); and Id., 'Dos libros de emblemas manuscritos en la Biblioteca del Palacio Real de Madrid' (193–220). Diego de Saavedra Fajardo, *Empresas políticas*, ed. Sagrario López Poza, M, Cátedra, 1999, 1077 pp., is a much-needed erudite edition of this famous Spanish book of emblems. L. P.'s exhaustive introductory study sheds new light on Saavedra's text. C. Perugini, 'Las fuentes iconográficas de la Editio Princeps de *La lozana andaluza*', *Salina*, 14:65–72, analyses in detail each illustration included in the first known edition, stressing the links between the text and the iconographic representations.

7. Women's Studies

Juan Luis Vives, *The Education of a Christian Woman: A Sixteenth-Century Manual*, ed. Charles Fantazzi, Chicago U.P., xxx + 343 pp., is a much-needed critical edition with an introductory study that reviews the circumstances surrounding the composition of the treatise, dedicated to Henry VIII's wife, Catherine of Aragon, its sources and cultural background. F. examines V.'s interest in preconizing education for all women as the way to improve virtue, and translates the 1538 Basel edition that was thoroughly revised by V. himself, making it very different from the original version published in 1524, which is the one used by Hyrde, and partialy reproduced by Watson. M. Flynn, 'Taming anger's daughters: new treatment for emotional problems in Renaissance Spain', *RQ*, 51, 1998:864–86, examines the appreciation of physiological dimensions to human behavioural problems in the Renaissance, which does not rely exclusively on ascetic discipline and rational reflection as means to subdue undesirable emotions, but to music, dance, conversation, baths, and meditation on graphic image as mood-altering techniques. F. investigates topics such as the Thomist view on emotional distress, blasphemy, and the 'vice of anger', resorting to Vives, Ciruelo, M. Cano's *Victory over Oneself*, Martín de Azpilcueta's *Confessor's Manual*, Luis de Granada *Sinner's Guide*, and Sabuco's *A Discussion about Self-Understanding*. Luis de León, *A Bilingual Edition of 'La Perfecta Casada'*, ed. John A. Jones and Javier

San José Lera, NY, Mellen, 1999, lxvii + 280 pp., presents a new translation of the Augustinian moral treatise, which provides an exhaustive analysis of its historical and literary context, as well as classical, patristic, and humanist influences and sources.

SANTA TERESA DE JESÚS.   Santa Teresa de Jesús, *Las moradas del castillo interior*, ed. Dámaso Chicharro, M, Biblioteca Nueva, 1999, 470 pp., is an erudite annotated edition with an excellent introductory study. José Antonio Álvarez Vázquez, *Trabajos, dineros y negocios. Teresa de Jesús y la economía del siglo XVI (1526–1582)*, M, Trotta, 310 pp., reconstructs and reinterprets Teresa de Jesús's economic and institutional activity — especially in her last 20 years, an active period of economic activity in her life when she founded several monasteries — resorting to her writings, letters, and economic documentation from the monasteries. From a general background, which takes on the biographical, theological, literary, political, and psychological context, A. examines Teresa de Jesús's economic relationship with the *estamental* society, her relations with *mercaderes*, her family, the nobility, and the Jesuits, as well as the nun's institutional innovations and her knowledge of economics, her ability to solve economic problems, broaching topics such as poverty, alms, income, the buying of houses, and the '*aparejo para fundar*'. E. Rhodes, 'What's in a name: on Teresa of Ávila's books', *Giles Vol.*, 79–106, and J. Ackerman, 'Teresa and her sisters', *ib.*, 107–39.

LUISA DE CARVAJAL.   *This Tight Embrace. Luisa de Carvajal y Mendoza (1566–1614)*, ed. and trans. Elizabeth Rhodes, Milwaukee, Marquette U.P., xiii + 314 pp., provides a selection of poetry and letters, including three letters to Magdalena de San Jerónimo, confidant of the Archduchess Isabel Clara Eugenia, as well as the texts 'Spiritual life story', 'Vows' (poverty, obedience, greater perfection, and matyrdom), and 'Society of the Sovereign Virgin Mary, Our Lady'. E. Rhodes, 'Luisa de Carvajal's Counter-Reformation journey to selfhood (1566–1614)', *RQ*, 51, 1998:887–911. M. Bradburn-Ruster, 'The beautiful dove, the body divine: Luisa de Carvajal y Mendoza's mystical poetics', *Giles Vol.*, 159–68.

Women in the Inquisition. Spain and the New World, ed. Mary E. Giles, Baltimore-London, Johns Hopkins U.P., 1999, ix + 402 pp., presents 14 studies on diverse aspects of women's relationships with the Inquisition in Spain and New Spain; these include: A. Alcalá, 'María de Cazalla, the grievous price of victory' (98–118); E. Rhodes ,'Ana Domenge and the Barcelona Inquisition' (134–70); C. Colahan, 'María Jesús de Agreda, the sweetheart of the Holy Office' (155–70); M. E. Perry, 'The *morisca* visionary Beatriz de Robles' (171–88); G. T. W. Ahlgreen, 'The visionary Francisca de los Apóstoles and Toledo reform in sixteenth-century Toledo' (119–33); K. J.

McKnight, 'An African slave woman before the Mexican Inquisition' (229–53); K. Myers, 'The New Spanish Inquisition and the hagiographic biography of Catarina de San Juan' (270–95); and studies on topics such as blasphemy as resistance, or popular female religiosity in colonial Mexico City and the New Spanish Inquisition. A. Powell, 'Making use of the Holy Office: exploring the contexts and concepts of Sor Juana's references to the Inquisition in the *Respuesta a Sor Filotea*', *Giles Vol.*, 193–216. Magdalena S. Sánchez, *The Empress, the Queen, and the Nun. Women and Power at the Court of Philip III of Spain*, Baltimore–London, Johns Hopkins U.P., 1998, xii + 267 pp., focuses on the behind-the-political-scene works of three main female members of the royal family, Empress Maria (Philip III's grandmother), Philip's wife, Margaret of Austria, and Margaret of the Cross (Philip's aunt), as they try to win favors for the causes of the Austrian Habsburgs. S. stresses the political power wielded by the three women, their approaches to negotiating and working through informal and indirect ways as well as through formal avenues of power, and examines the powerful ways in which women used religious piety, childbearing, illness such as melancholy, and marriage arrangements to sway political decisions. They employed distinct strategies and languages in informal settings such as meals, masquerade celebrations, and religious ceremonies to influence the political scene. Marcia L. Welles, *Persephone's Girdle: Narrative of Rape in Seventeenth-Century Spanish Literature,* Nashville, Vanderbilt U.P., 275 pp., explores the meaning of the tradition of rape narratives in canonical works of secular Spanish literature. W. reinterprets gender relations as central rather than marginal, and articulates the silenced private realm, not so much ignored as subsumed into the clamour of the public world, state interest, and the politics of power. W. studies the various narrative functions of sexual violence, as a prelude to revolution (*Fuenteovejuna*, Rojas Zorrilla's *Lucrecia y Tarquino*), and a corollary to war (*El alcalde de Zalamea*), and class privilege (*Peribáñez y el comendador de Ocaña* and Cervantes's *La fuerza de la sangre*).

MARÍA DE ZAYAS Y SOTOMAYOR. María de Zayas, Leonor de Meneses, and Mariana de Carvajal, *Novela de mujeres en el Barroco. Entre la rueca y la pluma*, ed. Evangelina Rodríguez Cuadros and María Haro Cortés, M, Biblioteca Nueva, 1999, 510 pp., is an anthology of seven *novelas*, prefaced with a study of the literary genre as practised by Golden Age female writers, contextualizing the narrative frameworks, thematic contents, and the characters' rhetorical programmatic configuration. María de Zayas, *Novelas amorosas y ejemplares*, ed. Julián Olivares, M, Cátedra, 562 pp., is a much-needed critical and annotated edition of Zayas's fascinating stories of abuse and cruelty, which explore ambiguously the fictional nature of gender. Margaret

R. Greer, *María de Zayas tells Baroque Tales of Love and the Cruelty of Men*, University Park, Penn State U.P., xii + 468 pp., reads Zayas from the perspective of Lacanian psychoanalytic theory, bringing the theory into dialogue with Kristeva's rereading of Freud and Lacan, as well as other significant feminist contributions to psychoanalytic discourse. G. surveys Zayas's biography, publication history, as well as a theory of the reception of Zayas's texts. She analyses in detail the logic of the feminist apology in her prologue, the frame-tale format, as well as aspects such as Zayas's occasional refusal of masculine dominance, the pattern of maternal absence and presence in relation to her insight into the unconscious roots of sexual desire. Marina S. Brownlee, *The Cultural Labyrinth of María de Zayas*, Philadelphia, Pennsylvania U.P., xvi + 214 pp., explores Zayas's treatment of a variety of discourses (sexuality, gender, socioeconomic status, racial and national identity) and her polyvalence and perspectivism in all its complexity. The labyrinth represents both the writing subject and the reading subject in the Zayesque enterprise. Zayas recalls for her reader the consummately Baroque topos of the deceptive nature of appearances and of epistemological ambiguity. E. H. Friedman, 'Enemy territory: the frontiers of gender in María de Zayas' *El traidor contra su sangre*', *Stagg Vol.*, 41–68.

8. POETRY

Harriet Goldberg, *Motif-Index of Folk Narratives in the Pan-Hispanic Romancero*, Tempe, ACMRS, xliv + 308 pp., proposes a thematic classification system using as a sample corpus Armistead's *Catálogo-Indice*. G. assigns thematic designations to the ballad and to the separable narrative units following Stith Thompson's divisions. *Criticón*, 74, 1998, includes: V. Dumanoir, 'De lo épico a lo lírico: los romances *mudados, contrahechos, trocados* y las prácticas de la reescrituras en el Romancero viejo' (45–64); J. M. Micó, 'Épica y reescritura en Lope de Vega' (93–108); F. B. Pedraza Jiménez, 'Algunos mecanismos y razones de la reescritura en Lope de Vega' (109–24); N. Ly, 'La rescritura del soneto primero de Garcilaso' (9–29). Bienvenido Morros, *Las polémicas literarias en la España del siglo XVI*, B, Quaderns Cremá, 1998, 338 pp., discusses how Herrera's *Anotaciones a Garcilaso* triggered the *Observaciones* of Prete Jacopín (probably an Erasmian follower from Valladolid) and a counter-attack, the anonymous *Respuesta* to Jacopín. M. studies H.'s contribution as well as the general background of Italian and Spanish literary controversies in the mid-16th century. José Lara Garrido, *Los mejores plectros. Teoría y práctica de la épica culta en el Siglo de Oro* (*AMal*, Anejo 23), Málaga U.P., 1999, 454 pp., posits that epic poetry in the Golden Age resulted from an innovative reformulation of the canon in the *Orlando Furioso*, and the multiple dynamics between theory and practice that take place from Ariosto to Tasso's *Discorsi* and *Gerusalemme liberata*. From complementary hermeneutical standpoints, L. re-examines Luis Barahona de Soto's *Las Lágrimas de Angélica*, Lope de Vega's *La hermosura de Angélica* and *Jerusalem conquistada*, and the theory and practice of López Pinciano's reading from the Tassian canon in *Philosophia antigua poética* and *Pelayo*.

9. PROSE

Viaje de Turquía, ed. Marie-Sol Ortolá, M, Castalia, 970 pp., is an excellent edition which fills a major gap, focuses on the innumerable textual problems of the enigmatic text, using a comparison of five manuscripts. O. studies in detail the Turkish vocabulary of the dialogue and includes brilliant notes on the ideological context. *Desatinos y amoríos. Once cuentos españoles del siglo XVI*, ed. Gonzalo Pontón, B, Muchnik, 1999, 245 pp., and *Prodigios y pasiones. Doce cuentos españoles del siglo XVII*, ed. Gonzalo Pontón, B, Muchnik, 1999, 362 pp., present an interesting selection of *novelas* from the 16th and 17th cs. They include canonical authors (Cervantes, Tirso, and Lope de Vega) but also lesser known writers (A. de Eslava, J. Camerino, and B. Mateo Velázquez), who have not been easily accessible to the general reader (J. de Medrano's *Silva curiosa*, L. de Zapata Chaves's *Varia historia*, L. G. Dantisco's *Galateo español*). The characters who actually need to work to earn a living in Alemán's 'Historia de Dorotea y Bonifacio' are conspicuously interesting. A useful glossary complements both selections.

Alonso Fernández de Avellaneda, *El ingenioso hidalgo don Quijote de la Mancha*, ed. Luis Gómez Canseco, M, Biblioteca Nueva, 789 pp., is an excellent annotated edition, preceded by an exhaustive study.

10. INDIVIDUAL AUTHORS

CERVANTES. Miguel de Cervantes, *Don Quijote de la Mancha*, dir. Francisco Rico (Instituto Cervantes), B, Crítica, 1998, 2 vols, cclxxxvi + 1247, 1294 pp. + CD-ROM; in addition to the outstanding *aparato crítico*, this provides a series of studies — Canavaggio, Domínguez Ortíz, S. Roubaud, E. Riley, A. Close, E. M. Anderson. G. Pontón, F. Rico — illustrations, and commentaries ('lecturas') of each chapter by a different scholar. Stanislav Zimic, *Los cuentos y las novelas del Quijote*, M, Iberoamericana, 1998, 349 pp., reflects on *DQ*'s structure, and the functions of the interpolated tales. A parodic design structure in the first part of the interpolated tales is built around the topic of confusion between fiction and daily life. In the second part, the parodic intention no longer structures the interpolated tales. The plot is unified through an interaction of all the characters, and their goal of revelation of significant attitudes via their behaviour. Rosa Rossi, *Tras las huellas de Cervantes. Perfil inédito del autor del Quijote*, trans. Juan Ramón Capella, M, Trotta, 123 pp., comprises a series of short essays which suggest indirect but possible ways in which C.'s visions could have been influenced, such as living with women '*no encerradas en la jaula del matrimonio*', his Algerian experiences, the Valladolid incidents, the final solitude in Madrid. Anthony Close, *Cervantes and the Comic Mind of his Age*, OUP, viii + 375 pp., examines basic values of comedy and satire; the prologue to *DQ* part 1 and its implications, investigates the theory of comedy, the satire of pedantry and its motives; two chapters study 'The truth of the history, relevance and rhetorical pitch'; 'Evolution of Spanish attitudes to comedy (1500–1600)' explores the concept of a collective comic mind and the *mote* tradition; 'Socio-Genesis, ideology, and culture' focuses on courtly manners and humour, social and religious discipline, and academies and academicism; 'The new comic ethos: social and aesthetic premises' deals with López Pinciano's theory of comedy, Hidalgo's *Diálogos de apacible entretenimiento*, and Tirso de Molina's *Cigarrales de Toledo*; 'Cervantes between Guzmán de Alfarache and its heritage' concludes the volume. Carroll B. Johnson, *Cervantes and the Material World*, Urbana, Illinois U.P., 239 pp., investigates the cultural, ideological, economic, legal, and material environment in which C. placed his characters, stressing key aspects such as the clash between two different economic systems, inequality in the distribution of wealth or the ownership of the means of production; it includes 'Feudalism and stillborn capitalism', 'Gender, class, modes of production', which pays attention to Christians, Muslims, aristocrats and gypsies, and 'Ideological antagonism and commerce', which analyses *El amante liberal* and the Ottoman empire, as well as *La española inglesa* and Protestant England. *Stagg Vol.* gathers mostly articles on C.; R. R. Jones on the Baratarian Archipielago; A. Martí Alanis on lust in *DQ*; A. Sánchez, on bibliography; S. Harrison and O. Hegyi, 'Algerian Babel reflected in *Persiles*'; D. Eisenberg on C. in Argel; J. J. Allen, on the transformations of satire; it includes also essays on Spanish Golden Age theatre (D. Fox), Quevedo (R. G. Moore), and the embedded narration in *Guzmán de Alfarache* (H. Mancing). *Para leer a Cervantes. Estudios de literatura española Siglo de Oro*, Vol. 1, ed. Melchora Romanos et al., BA, EUDEBA, 1999, 366 pp., includes, among other studies, A. Close, 'Los episodios del *Quijote*' (25–47); I. Lerner, 'Formas del conocimiento y ficción cervantina' (65–82); M. D. Estremero, '*La fuerza de la sangre*, otra concreción de la profecía de la bruja cervantina' (121–32); A. M. Barrenechea, 'Cervantes y Borges' (281–90); W. Romero, 'La construcción de la imagen de Italia en Cervantes' (343–48).

GÓNGORA. Luis de Góngora, *Epistolario completo*, ed. Antonio Carreira, with concordances by Antonio Lara, Lausanne, Hispania Helvética, 622 pp., edits the 124 extant letters together with concordances. Góngora, *Romances*, ed. Antonio Carreira, B, Quaderns Crema, 4 vols, xxii + 789, 557, 624, 657 pp., a much-needed critical edition. Antonio Carreira, *Gongoremas*, B, Península, 1998, 454 pp., provides a textual criticism of Góngora's corpus and its oral transmission; the controversy on *Las Soledades* includes several of Góngora's letters on the topic; the *Romances* and his posthumous renown and Góngora's reception in the 17th c.; 'Etopeya y entorno' deals with Góngora's years in Madrid and his relation with the Duke of Lerma; C. comments on some of Góngora's poems of dubious authorship. J. M. Micó, 'Un verso de Góngora y las razones de la filología', *Criticón*, 75, 1999:49–68.

GRACIÁN. Baltasar Gracián, *El Criticón*, introd. Emilio Hidalgo-Serna, ed. Elena Cantarino, M, Colección Austral, 1998, 839 pp. J. García Gibert, 'Medios humanos y medios divinos en Baltasar Gracián (La dialéctica ficcional del aforismo 251)', *Criticón*, 73, 1998:61–82. A. Egido, 'La historia de Momo y Baltasar Gracián', Romanos, *Lecturas*, 21–60.

QUEVEDO. Francisco de Quevedo, *Mundo caduco*, ed. Javier Biurrun Lizarazu, Pamplona, EUNSA, 138 pp., is based on the discovery of a new manuscript of *MC*. B. presents the conjecture that the text is finished and not, as is generally thought, fragmented. Francisco de Quevedo, *El chitón de las taravillas*, ed. Manuel Urí Martín, M, Castalia, 1998, 128 pp., edits a pamphlet written by assignment from the Count-Duke (Elliott thinks that both the royal secretary A. Hurtado de Mendoza and the Jesuit confessor of Olivares, H. de Salazar participated in the writing of *El chitón*) to defend the minister from the numerous attacks and criticisms against the failures of his government. F. de Quevedo, *Discurso de las privanzas*, ed. Eva María Díaz Martínez, Pamplona, EUNSA, 283 pp., is a critical edition of the text (the authorship of which until recently was in doubt), together with an exhaustive and erudite analysis of textual sources. Elias L. Rivers, *Quevedo y su poética dedicada a Olivares*, Pamplona, EUNSA, 80 pp., annotates preliminary texts to Q.'s editions of Luis de León's and Francisco de la Torre's poetry, within the context of Olivares's court and the polemic against *gongorismo*. Q. claims stylistic clarity, resorting to the definition of *lexis* in Aristotle's *Poetics*, in order to condemn a style relying on metaphor, latinism, and hyperbaton. Luisa López Grigera, *Anotaciones de Quevedo a la Retórica de Aristóteles*, Salamanca, p.p., 1998, 171 pp., is a general background study and edition of Quevedo's marginalia to Ermolao Barbaro's Latin translation of Aristotle's *Rhetorica* (Lyon, 1547, Theobaldo Pagano), now in the Biblioteca Ménendez Pelayo. *Sentencias político-filosófico-teológicas (en el legado de Antonio Pérez, F. de Quevedo y otros)*. *Del tacitismo al neoestoicismo*, ed. Andrea Herrán and Modesto Santos, B, Ánthropos, li + 233 pp., discusses Q.'s dubious authorship of *Migajas sentenciosas*, and edits the *Sentencias*, establishing a comparison of the manuscripts from the Biblioteca Nacional and the Biblioteca Menéndez Pelayo. The introductory study revises the Erasmian, Tacitist, and neo-Stoic thought in the text, and adds biographical summaries of A. Pérez, Malvezzi, and Quevedo, the main writers from whom the *Sentencias* were compiled. Francisco de Quevedo, *Un Heráclito cristiano, Canta sola a Lisi y otros poemas*, ed. Ignacio Arellano and Lía Schwartz, B, Crítica, 1092 pp., is a profusely annotated edition and erudite study. Santiago Fernández Mosquera, *La poesía amorosa de Quevedo. Disposición y estilo desde Canta sola a Lisi*, M, Gredos, 1999, 419 pp., provides a structural and stylistic study of Quevedo's love poetry comparing it to that of Herrera, Francisco de la Torre, and Lope de Vega. It focuses on the influence of Petrarch in Q.'s love poetry and analyses *Canta sola a Lisi*, providing also a study of the characters in the Quevedian *cancionero* and of *Canta sola a Lisi* as an example of a Petrarchan *canzoniere;* F.M. analyses stylistically diverse tropes such as the *homo viator* and love-prison metaphors as well as animal, vegetable, mineral, astronomical, cosmological, and mythological metaphors; metaphors based on the natural elements; the uses of metonymy, synecdoche, hyperbole, and other tropes. It also examines the poetic *Yo*, the author and characters in the Quevedian *cancionero*, and concludes with a meticulous textual study. *La Perinola. Revista de investigación quevediana*, 1999, 3, includes: H. Ettinghausen, 'Austeridad viril *vs.* Consumismo afeminado: Quevedo ante el final del reinado de Felipe II' (143–55); V. Nider, 'Sobre algunos pasajes bíblicos en la agudeza de Quevedo' (195–207); C. Peraita, 'La *copia* erasmiana y la construcción retórica de la *Política de Dios*' (209–24); F. Plata, 'Contribución al estudio de las fuentes de la poesía satírica de Quevedo: Ateneo, Berni y Owen' (225–47). *La Perinola. Revista de investigación quevediana*, includes: C. Peraita, 'Observaciones preliminares para anotar el *Epítome a la historia de fray Tomás de Villanueva* de Quevedo' (251–66); F. Plata, 'Nuevas versiones manuscritas de la poesía quevediana y nuevos poemas atribuidos: en torno al manuscrito BMP 108' (285–307); A. Rey, 'Las variantes de autor en la obra de Quevedo' (309–44); V. Roncero López, 'Las anotaciones de *El Buscón*' (379–91). Pablo Jauralde Pou, *Francisco de Quevedo (1580–1645)*, M, Castalia, pref. Alonso Zamora Vicente,

1998, 1071 pp., is a ground-breaking biography exhaustively documented. Alessandro Martinengo, *El 'Marco Bruto' de Quevedo. Una unidad en dinámica transformación*, Berne, Lang, 1998, 129 pp., examines Q.'s reworking of classical sources and includes a critical edition of Seneca the Elder's *suasorias*, which are part of the *MB*. M. focuses on studying the text rather than Q.'s position on tyrannicide, the unicity of conception and style that characterizes the three parts of *MB*, in spite of the different textual typology and the different time in which they were written. W. H. Clamurro, 'Leyendo a Quevedo leer'. *Actas* (Madrid), 1, 460–66, presents a suggestive reading of Q.'s *Carta a Fernando el Católico*. *Rostros y máscaras: personajes y temas de Quevedo*, ed. Ignacio Arellano et al., Pamplona, EUNSA, 1999, 218 pp., presents the proceedings of 'Aspectos de Quevedo', a conference which took place at the Casa de Velázquez (Madrid, 1999). The articles study a variety of topics such as Q.'s idea of nobility and war (Rey), his attitude towards Judaism (Riandière), the burlesque transformation of the Danae myth (Martinengo), or animals in Q.'s poetry (Arellano). Victoriano Roncero, *El humanismo de Quevedo: filología e historia*, Pamplona, EUNSA, 178 pp., fills a major gap on the study of *España defendida*. R. presents extended versions of previously published articles: 'La *España defendida* y la ideología quevediana' (13–36); 'Las fuentes humanísticas en la historiografía quevediana: los reyes primitivos en la *España defendida*' (89–120) and 'Los *Grandes anales de quince días*: historia humanista' (121–54); 'El humanismo en la *España defendida*' (37–88) offers an overview of the place of Q.'s historical and philological writings in the European humanist tradition. Romanos, *Lecturas*, includes E. L. Rivers, 'Quevedo y Aristóteles contra el Gongorismo' (289–94); L. Schwartz, 'Catálogo de amores: variaciones de un motivo poético grecolatino' (295–315).

LITERATURE 1490–1700 (DRAMA)
POSTPONED

LITERATURE, 1700–1823

By GABRIEL SÁNCHEZ ESPINOSA, *Lecturer in Hispanic Studies, The Queen's University of Belfast*

1. BIBLIOGRAPHY AND PRINTING

Fermín de los Reyes Gómez, *El libro en España y América: legislación y censura (siglos XV–XVIII)*, 2 vols, M, Arco Libros, 1465 pp., introduces us to the legislative context of the book world (which is taken to include also brochures, periodicals, and posters) in both Spain and Spanish America during the *Ancien régime*. The first volume contains an analysis of the different legislative regulations and their practical consequences. The second volume comprises a complete, chronologically ordered appendix of other legal documents, which is complemented by some highly useful indexes. The fact that this work puts at the reader's disposal in a single source documentation that was previously dispersed, will doubtlessly heighten its utility for those interested in the history of the book and its reception.

2. THOUGHT AND THE ENLIGHTENMENT

We welcome the appearance of *Cuadernos dieciochistas* (*CDi*), an annual, interdisciplinary journal from the *Sociedad Española del Siglo XVIII*, whose first issue, appearing in 2000, is dedicated to the transitional period between the Austrian and Bourbon dynasties. The following contributions stand out from among many: A. Mestre Sanchís, 'Monarca, instituciones e individuos en los orígenes de la Ilustración' (19–37); E. Velasco Moreno, 'Nuevas instituciones de sociabilidad: las academias de finales del siglo XVII y comienzos del siglo XVIII' (39–55); M.-J. Rodríguez Sánchez de León, 'La Guerra de Sucesión española en los pliegos poéticos de la Biblioteca Universitaria de Salamanca' (185–208).

El Conde de Aranda y su tiempo, ed. José Antonio Ferrer Benimeli, 2 vols, Zaragoza, Institución Fernando el Católico, 847, 673 pp., are the proceedings of a conference dedicated to the Aragonese aristocrat and politician, leader of the *partido aragonés*, which took place in Zaragoza in 1998. Articles that merit special attention include: M.-A. Pérez Samper, 'Chocolate, té y café: sociedad, cultura y alimentación en la España del siglo XVIII' (1, 157–221); M. Torrione, 'Felipe V y Farinelli: *Cadmo y Anfión*, alegoría de una fiesta de cumpleaños (1737)' (1, 223–50); C.-M. Trojani, 'Amistad y amistad del país' (1, 691–723); A. Saura, 'Luzán y la *comédie larmoyante*' (1, 777–89); J. Pradells Nadal and J. Rico Giménez, 'Notas sobre un polígrafo de la Ilustración española: Ignacio de Asso (1742–1814)' (I, 804–18); E. Soler Pascual, 'Los Villanueva, una familia aragonesa del Antiguo Régimen' (I, 819–29).

Economía y economistas españoles. Vol. 3: La Ilustración, ed. Enrique Fuentes Quintana, B, Galaxia Gutenberg–Círculo de Lectores, 799 pp., brings together a series of essays by specialists that centre around the principal ideas and economic trends in Enlightenment Spain, all of which are written with great clarity. It is a work that will interest all concerned with the reformist thinking of the leading figures of the Spanish Enlightenment. Individual essays are dedicated to M.-A. de la Gándara, B. Ward, P. Rodríguez Campomanes, P. de Olavide, G.-M. de Jovellanos, F. de Cabarrús, and V. de Foronda.

Federico II de Prusia y los españoles, ed. Hans Joachim Lope, Frankfurt, Lang, 145 pp., collects different approaches to the literary reception — in the form of biographies, *comedias militares,* newspaper articles, and poems — of the myth of the enlightened Prussian despot in Spain during the second half of the 18th century. The myth of Frederick II was politically very useful to the ministerial governments of Charles III and Charles IV in the years leading up to the beginning of the French Revolution.

Joaquín Fernando Quintanilla, *Naturalistas para una Corte ilustrada,* Aranjuez, Doce Calles, 1999, 446 pp., recounts the history of the establishment of the main scientific institutions concerned with natural history in Madrid in the second half of the 18th c., also taking account of their parallel literary production. The thread of continuity in this work is provided by the figures of Pedro Franco Dávila, Director of the Gabinete de Historia Natural, and of Casimiro Gómez Ortega, first Director of the Jardín Botánico del Prado. Considered throughout the work is the intervention in scientific policies by erstwhile cultural spin-doctors and intellectuals such as G. Mayans, B. and T. de Iriarte, J.-B. Muñoz, J. Viera y Clavijo, A.-J. Cavanilles, and many more. Rather than providing a definitive study, this work serves as a useful and enjoyable introduction to the topic.

3. LITERARY HISTORY

GENERAL. F. López, 'La institución de los géneros literarios en la España del siglo XVIII', *BH,* 102:473–517, provides a study of literary criticism in 1737, in which there appeared I. Luzán's *Poética,* G. Mayans' *Vida de Cervantes,* and the *Diario de los Literatos de España,* Spain's first literary review periodical. His distinction between classicists and neo-classicists is of particular interest. According to López, the latter cannot dispense with the notion of a literary genre.

A. Mestre Sanchis, 'Humanismo e ilustración: Cerdá y Rico', *BH*, 102:453–71, reviews the editorial work of the royal librarian F. Cerdá y Rico, especially his interest in the Spanish humanists of the 16th c., which builds on the work done by the Valencian G. Mayans. Mestre does not waste this opportunity to defend the enlightened character of the humanist school of thought of the Spanish Enlightenment in view of the criticism this interpretation has recently received by F. Sánchez Blanco, who emphasized the basically conservative nature of its ideas.

PERIODICAL LITERATURE. M.-E. Arenas Cruz, 'Pedro Estala como *Censor mensual* en el *Diario de Madrid* (1795–1798)', *RLit*, 124:327–46, identifies the Hellenist Pedro Estala as the author of the very interesting and highly critical literary reviews written under the pseudonym *el censor mensual*, rejecting any identification with the Augustinian Juan Fernández de Rojas.

I. Urzainqui, 'La crítica literaria en la prensa del siglo XVIII. Elementos de su discurso teórico', *BH*, 102:519–59, is centred on theatrical criticism, which tended to consist of an evaluation of the literary qualities of each individual work according to the principles of classical poetics.

POETRY. J. Checa Beltrán, 'Una poética inédita del siglo XVIII', *RLit*, 124:317–26, focuses on a hitherto unstudied manuscript from the BN Madrid entitled, *Tratado de la poesía* (1784), which, following fundamentally the ideas of I. Luzán and the article 'poésie' in the *Encyclopédie*, adds some unique analysis on the concept of 'entusiasmo', to which little attention was paid in 18th-c. Spanish poetics (except in that of A. Burriel).

4. INDIVIDUAL AUTHORS

ANDRÉS. Juan Andrés, *Origen, progresos y estado actual de toda literatura*, 5 vols, M, Biblioteca Valenciana–Verbum, 1997–2000, 416, 409, 536, 490, 570 pp., has been edited by Pedro Aullón de Haro and Jesús García Gabaldón, not from the perspective of 18th-c. studies, but with the clear purpose of rehabilitating one of the most outstanding Spanish contributions to the study of comparative literature, one whose example still makes a valid contribution to this discipline and to its practice in Spain. This first comparative history of universal literature was originally written and published in Italian by the expelled Jesuit Juan Andrés. It was originally published in 7 volumes, in Parma, by the renowned G. Bodoni between 1782 and 1799, and was received with great success in Europe. Its Spanish translation, printed in Madrid by A. de Sancha between 1784 and 1806, consisted of some 10 volumes, which were chosen as text book by the chair of literary history in the Reales Estudios de San Isidro. The main difference between the two editions lies in the fact that the previously untranslated final two volumes of the Parma edition have been translated for the first time and will appear in the sixth and final volume of this work. This edition will undoubtedly facilitate the inclusion of this essential work by the *abate* Andrés in studies of literary and aesthetic history of this period, in which it has been more referred to than read, due to the difficulties in accessing his work.

AZARA. A. Alemany Peiró, 'El embajador Azara y los hermanos Mayans', pp. 755–75 of *Disidencias y exilios en la España Moderna*, ed. Antonio Mestre Sanchis and E. Giménez López, Alicante U.P., 1997, 848 pp., edits 25 letters written by Canon J.-A. Mayans to Azara, between October, 1791 and April, 1797, to which, unfortunately, Azara's replies are missing.

CADALSO. J. Álvarez Barrientos, 'El *violeto* de Cadalso como *bel esprit*', *Sebold Vol.*, 43–62, interprets *Los eruditos a la violeta* as a manifestation of the confrontation between the supporters of the new culture, more conversational and social and less bookish, and those defending the superiority of an erudite culture, reverentially respectful of the book. Barrientos identifies the *violeto* with the *bel esprit* of the new salons, that is, with the new intellectual. He sees a greater ambiguity in Cadalso's satire than previously thought; *Los eruditos a la violeta* is seen as revealing the loss of old humanist values and the appearance of new modern values within the Spain of his time.

José de Cadalso, *Cartas marruecas. Noches lúgubres*, ed. Emilio Martínez Mata, B, Crítica, 432 pp., has an introductory essay by N. Glendinning. When studying the history of the manuscripts for the *Cartas marruecas*, the editor considers that the changes to the first version of the text, which took place beginning in June 1778, were a result of the self-censure carried out by J. Cadalso himself within the context of the inquisitorial proceedings against Bernardo and Tomás de Iriarte and Pablo de Olavide.

José de Cadalso, *Cartas marruecas. Noches lúgubres*, ed. Russell P. Sebold, M, Cátedra, 410 pp., admirably situates both works by J. Cadalso in the context of the development of the Romantic and *costumbrista* literary currents. It is a very attractive edition to use in class, because of its stress on the modernity of Cadalso's works and biography.

FERNÁN NÚÑEZ. Francisco Gutiérrez de los Ríos y Córdoba, conde de Fernán Núñez, *El hombre práctico, o discursos varios sobre su conocimiento y enseñanza*, ed. Jesús Pérez Magallón and Russell P. Sebold, Córdoba, Cajasur, 323 pp., recovers a scarcely known text from pre-Enlightenment Spain, in this case a *manual de comportamiento* written by a modern-thinking aristocrat, around 1680, for his own

children's education. After its first edition in 1686 it was re-edited by
J. Ibarra in 1764.

GONZÁLEZ DEL CASTILLO. José Ignacio González del Castillo,
Sainetes, Cádiz, Fundación Municipal de Cultura–Ayuntamiento de
Cádiz, 419 pp., gathers together 15 *sainetes* taken from the not very
extensive body of work — some 44 pieces in total — by this author
from Cadiz, who fell victim to the plague in the year 1800. The *sainetes*
by González del Castillo are to the cosmopolitan and enterprising
Cadiz what the *sainetes* by R. de la Cruz are to a courtly and
governmental Madrid. The edition highlights those aspects that point
to the apparition of Andalusian *costumbrismo*, later to be established as
a genre in the articles by S. Estébanez Calderón.

MAYANS. *Actas del congreso internacional sobre Gregorio Mayans (Valen-
cia-Oliva, 6 al 8 de mayo de 1999)*, ed. Antonio Mestre Sanchis, Valencia,
Ayuntamiento de Oliva, 1999, 711 pp., is a collection of studies that
are of great interest for attaining greater depth in the open debate
that centres on the position held by the Valencian humanist within
the Spanish Enlightenment. The following works stand out: J. Álvarez
Barrientos, 'Gregorio Mayans (1699–1781), hombre de letras'
(239–49), which places the Valencian in the polemic between *antiguos
y modernos* within the *República de las letras*; P. Álvarez de Miranda, 'En
torno al epistolario de Mayans y Martínez Pingarrón' (265–68),
which comments on the different aspects of Mayans's epistolary
practices in his correspondence with the royal librarian, who was his
faithful source of information in Madrid; M. Martínez Gomis, 'Don
Gregorio Mayans y la biografía del duque de Alba: un proyecto
histórico entre el mecenazgo y la independencia intelectual' (363–88),
which sets out Mayans's struggles and difficulties to obtain protection
and help from influential aristocrats in the Court, whilst at the same
time zealously attempting to keep his intellectual independence;
A. Astorgano Abajo, 'La venta de los libros prohibidos de la biblioteca
mayansiana (1801)' (625–59), studies a list, presented to the Inquisition in 1803, of 97 prohibited books that used to belong to the
Mayans brothers, with the intention of obtaining authorization for
the sale in bulk of the brothers' library, sold in 1801 by their
inheritors.

OLAVIDE. G. Dufour, '*El Evangelio en triunfo* en el dispositivo
político del Príncipe de la Paz', *Sebold Vol.*, 159–66, focuses on the
protection given to Olavide by his brother-in-law Luis de Urbina,
Captain General of Valencia, during the time of the publication of
his epistolary novel. Dufour sees the hand of the Príncipe de la Paz
behind Urbina. The *Cartas de Mariano a Antonio* (cartas XXVI-XLI of *El
Evangelio en triunfo*) are the product of the interest paid by M. Godoy,

during these years, to mobilize the parish priests to bolster the new agriculture.

PÉREZ BAYER. Francisco Pérez Bayer, *Viajes literarios*, Valencia, Edicions Alfons el Magnànim, 1998, 674 pp., is an edition of the antiquarian travel journal written by the Valencian Hebraist, well-connected to both Court and government, between April and December of 1782 on his travels between Valencia, Andalusia, and Portugal. Of particular interest are his observations on his various personal contacts and his bibliophile interests. Also included is a fragment of the diary of his journey to Rome, corresponding to the year 1754 (609–74); the rest of this work has been lost.

VIERA Y CLAVIJO. Victoria Galván González, *La obra literaria de José de Viera y Clavijo*, Las Palmas, Cabildo de Gran Canaria, 1999, 612 pp., fails to go into depth despite the lengthy analysis of the work, ideology and personality of this literary figure.

LITERATURE, 1823–1898
POSTPONED

LITERATURE, 1898–1936

By K. M. SIBBALD, *McGill University*

I. GENERAL

BIBLIOGRAPHY. Catching up on material not covered here is worthwhile and useful information may be found in the following: 'Bibliografía', *NRFH*, 48: 105–252, in the section 'Siglo xx' (227–52), with information on Baroja, Guillén, Juan Ramón, Ortega, and Valle-Inclán; and the usual round-up of C. Byrne, 'Review of miscellanies', *BHS(G)*, 77: 539–45, containing items on Salinas and Valle-Inclán. Nicolás Kanellos and Helvetia Martell, *Hispanic Periodicals in the United States, Origins to 1960: A Brief History and Comprehensive Bibliography*, Houston, Arte Público, 359 pp., is of limited value in this context.

LITERARY AND CULTURAL HISTORY. Lily Litvak, *Imágenes y textos. Estudios sobre literatura y pintura, 1849–1936*, Amsterdam–Atlanta, GA, Rodopi, 1998, 187 pp., is a collection of eight essays that show familiarity with a wide range of cultural studies and art history as well as Classical and Renaissance literature, all brought to bear on the various readings of visual and verbal texts. Three essays are noteworthy here: the first, 'Después del arco iris. Espacio y tiempo en el paisaje español de finales del siglo XIX', which examines the effect of scientific thought on the work of painters and writers such as Haes, Amárica, Urgell, Unamuno, Antonio Machado, and Azorín; the fifth of the series, 'El laberinto del amor y pecado. El tema del jardín en la *Sonata de primavera* de Ramón del Valle-Inclán', which starts in the Renaissance and echoes through Borges; and, finally, 'La novela corta erótica de entreguerras, 1920–1936', which deals with the demystification of the female figure in art and literature in the stereotype of the thoroughly modern woman so popular in the magazines of the 1920s. Although Robert Jay Glickman, *Fin de siglo: retrato de Hispano-América en la época modernista*, Toronto, Canadian Academy of the Arts, 1999, 375 pp., does not strictly belong here, much useful background material is provided from the commonality in literature on both sides of the Atlantic, and his 'Revista antológica: 1875–1910' (51–348), deserves our attention.

The 1998 centenary celebrations continue to spill over into print. Francisco J. Romero Salvadó, *Twentieth-Century Spain: Politics and Society in Spain, 1898–1998*, NY, St. Martin's Press, 1999, 242 pp. Making it a double celebration, *Crítica Hispánica*, 21, 1999, examines the coincidences between Mariano José de Larra and the 1898 Generation and later, particularly in J. Álvarez Barrientos, 'Violetas para Larra' (5–13), finding fellow travellers in Cadalso, Azorín, and Cernuda for his literary travelogue; A. Amell, 'Larra y los regeneracionistas: la siembra que no cosechó la generación del 98' (14–26); M. A. Ayala, 'Entre Larra y el 98' (27–38), which remarks on shared visions of society and customs; J. Belmonte-Serrano and P. Guerrero Ruiz, 'Lo que queda de un escritor' (39–50), tracing links with contemporary writers; J. Rubio Jiménez, 'La época de los banquetes: Larra y *Prometeo*' (108–18), which recounts the feast held in Fornós on 24 March 1909, with Gómez de la Serna 'con patillas a lo Larra' holding forth to guests who included Maeztu, Azorín, and Miguel Santos Oliver; A. F. Sherman, Jr., 'Re-reading Unamuno' (119–32), re-reads the 1931 essay not as a jealous and arrogant diatribe but as the intimate portrait of Unamunian thought processes, showing Larra as neither icon nor literary standard, but as the catalyst for new ideas; and, righting the balance, Amparo Hurtado edits with a useful biographical prologue, notes, and necessary onomastic index, Carmen Baroja y Nessi, *Recuerdos de una mujer de la generación del 98*, B, Tusquets, 1998, 245 pp., which recalls for the record the stifling atmosphere of a woman's place in a masculine society, and some devasting comments about heavy-weight *machos* like Pío Baroja, Marañón, and Ortega, made by the younger sister of Pío and Ricardo, the wife of Rafael Caro Raggio, and the mother of Julio and Pío Caro Raggio. G. Pozzi, 'Carmen de Burgos and the war in Morocco', *MLN*, 115:188–204, documents the work of the first female Spanish war correspondent of the *Heraldo de Madrid*, covering the woman's-eye view of hospitals in Málaga and Almería and battlefields in Melilla that provided material for her novel *En la guerra* (1909), in which Burgos rejects the usual hierarchies, the sanctification of culture, and the European monopoly of civilization in all the jingoism of the time. From the opposite end of the country, in a rather different nationalistic discourse, D. Flitter, 'Icons and imperatives in the constitution of Galician identity in the "Xeneración Nós"', *FMLS*, 36:296–309, examines the foremost Galician cultural group of the 1920s and 1930s and, specifically, the contrast between the two principal conceptions of Galicianhood it encompassed.

Terence McMullan, *The American Dream in Spanish Poetry: Some Early Twentieth-Century Visions of the United States*, Maynooth, National University of Ireland, 27 pp., considers five texts composed between 1916 and 1929 that illustrate various major trends, namely, *modernismo* (Juan Ramón Jiménez's prose poem 'Orillas del sueño'), *purismo* (Guillén's 'La Florida'), *creacionismo* (oddly, Alberti's syntactical whodunit, 'Telegrama'), and *surrealismo* (Cernuda's jazz-inspired 'Quisiera estar solo en el mar' and García Lorca's vision of the Great Depression in 'La aurora'), all with America as their pre-text. Interest centres on the avant-garde. *Ínsula*, 642, is devoted to 'La revolución creacionista' and contains: J. L. Bernal, 'El creacionismo como tradición' (3–5); G. Morelli, 'La correspondencia inédita Huidobro-Diego-Larrea: primeras cartas. En busca del inevitable encuentro' (5–8); A. Soria Olmedo, '*Favorables París Poema* y la "joven literatura"' (9–11); H. Wentzlaff-Eggebert, 'El creacionismo puesto en situación: "Espíritu nuevo", "nueva sensibilidad" y "emoción"' (11–15); J. P. Ayuso, 'Insistencia en Juan Larrea' (15); J. M. Díaz de Guereñu, 'Bibliografía creacionista de la última década' (16–19); R. de Costa, 'Gerardo Diego: ultraizado' (19–20); F. J. Díez de Revenga, 'Música y poesía creacionista: Gerardo Diego, últimos años' (21–23); J. Neira, 'Fidelidad creacionista de Gerardo Diego' (23–27); E. Serrano Asenjo, 'Una elegía creacionista de Luis A. Piñer: "La hora más oscura"' (27–31); and J. M. Díaz de Guereñu, '"*Altazor* en descenso": un homenaje de Luis A. Piñer' (32–34). Biruté Ciplijauskaité, *De signos y significaciones. 1. Juegos con la vanguardia: Poetas del 27*, B, Anthropos, 1999, 175 pp., neatly gathers up 12 previously published essays on the 1927 Generation as a whole, and in particular on José Moreno Villa, Salinas, Guillén, Aleixandre, Ernestina de Champourcín, and Concha Méndez, in a useful collection that attests to a lifetime of careful reading. Antonio Sáez Delgado, *Órficos y ultraístas. Portugal y España en el diálogo de las primeras vanguardias literarias (1915–1925)*, Mérida, Editora Regional de Extremadura, 1999, 598 pp., is a welcome comparative study that, first, pays homage to Portugal's early experimentation with vanguard poetics and likens the 'primer modernismo' of Mario Sá-Carneiro, Fernando Pessoa, and José de Almada Negreiros in reviews like *Orpheu, Exílio, Centauro, Portugal Futurista, Contemporânea*, and *Athena*, published between 1915 and 1925, to Spanish *ultraísmo*, with Gómez de la Serna as its guru, over the same period in such publications as *Los Quijotes, Cervantes, Grecia, Cosmópolis, Ultra, Parábola, Alfar, Horizontes*, and others; Part III (325–470), is devoted to Pessoa and relations with fellow poets and translators like Rogelio Buendía, Adriano del Valle, and Isaac del Vando-Villar in a series of excerpts from the gigantic *corpus* of letters written and exchanged that will whet scholarly appetites and provide excellent browsing material for more general readers; the 'Bibliografía' (485–597), is a comprehensive and vital adjunct to further research in this area. Ana Rodríguez Fischer, *Prosa española de vanguardia*, M, Castalia, 1999, 492 pp., is a provocative compilation that combines an introduction (9–75), that focuses on the period and its new sensibilities, a select bibliography (75–82), and some unexpected selections from Rosa Chacel, Antonio Espina, Jorge Guillén, and María Teresa León that complement the more standard entries from Dámaso Alonso, Francisco Ayala, Ramón Gómez de la Serna,

Ernesto Giménez Caballero, José María Hinojosa, Benjamín Jarnés, Juan Larrea, and the like; it may be profitably read together with the postscript comments in *Ínsula*, 646, 'Contra el olvido: las prosas del veintisiete', an unusually good *homenaje* which features: D. Ródenas de Moya, 'Las prosas de la generación del 27' (3–6), a general overview that includes a lengthy bibliographical breakdown of the 'jirones sin cuento' and the burning question of style; J. Pérez Bazo, 'La novela nueva en la época de la vanguardia histórica' (7–10), a revisionist reading that refutes the charge of dehumanization by arguing that this was, indeed, prose concerned with identity and the metadiscourse of creativity and evocation from *modernismo* through *creacionismo* and *ultraísmo* to the authors of the Nova Novarum; V. Fuentes, 'Tendencias y polémicas literarias en la España de los años veinte, con enfoque en la narrativa de avanzada' (10–13), is tendentious and polemical about those writers who took to the streets, not as literary *flâneurs* but as social activists; F. J. Díez de Revenga, 'Tres narradores de vanguardia olvidados (Guillén, Gerardo, Dámaso)' (13–15), rescues forgotten prose pieces like 'El paraguas y el viento' (1926), 'El vendedor de crepúsculos' (1926), and 'Acuario en Virgo' (1927), to revindicate writers better known for their poetry; N. Dennis, 'En torno a la prosa breve en la joven literatura' (15–19), concentrates on Ramón Gómez de la Serna and José Bergamín as specialists in the cultivation of the art of brevity, but also gives the nod to lesser-known contributors to *La Verdad* and *Alfar*; F. Lough, 'Arte, vida y la narrativa de Benjamín Jarnés' (19–21), discusses the role of the reader in *El profesor inútil* and *Locura y muerte de Nadie*; F. M. Soguero, 'Narradores vanguardistas: poetas de la historia' (21–23), comments on the new lease of life for biography found in the work of Antonio Espina, César M. Arconada, and Benjamín Jarnés, as well as that of critics like Enrique Díez-Canedo and Antonio Marichalar; J. Gracia, 'Un experimento prematuro: la revista *Mundo Ibérico* (1927)' (24–25), documents the ten issues, published June to November 1927, of Mario Verdaguer's magazine; while L. Fernández-Cifuentes, 'Cuentos y novelas, periódicos y libros, kioscos y bibliotecas' (26–28), elucidates most intelligently the various functions of the printed word in the consumerism of text as merchandise. R. J. Fasey, 'The presence of Russian revolutionary writing in the literary climate of pre-civil war Spain (1926–36)', *FMLS*, 36:402–11, considers the varying fortunes of *Post-Guerra* (1927–28), *Nueva España* (1930–31), and *Octubre* (1933–34), in a country Bakunin believed to have sufficient spirit for revolutionary action.

The seventh art form is well-served: María Asunción Gómez, **Del escenario a la pantalla: la adaptación cinematográfica del teatro español*, Chapel Hill, North Carolina U.P., 231 pp.; Fernando López Serra, *Figuras y* *sombras: de los teatros de títeres a los salones de cine*, M, Complutense, 1999, 288 pp., which is particularly good on the early beginnings of the kinetoscope in the Sala Edison witnessed by Echegaray and Unamuno among others; *De Baroja a Buñuel. Cuentos de cine*, ed. Rafael Utrera Macías, M, Clan, 1999, 264 pp., is a curious anthology of poetry, theatre, short stories, and periodical writings by the Quinteros, Azorín, García Lorca, Buñuel, and others; while, with specific reference to members of the 1927 Generation and beyond, C. B. Morris, 'La pantalla cinematográfica como espejo en Cernuda, Lorca y Alberti', *BFFGL*, 26:9–33, contributes important details on the relationship between Hollywood stars and the Spanish poets, and how film influenced the latter's discovery and disclosure of self in their poetry, and J. Urrutia, 'Epistemología y metodología de las relaciones del cine con la literatura', *RCEH*, 25:169–82, leaves comparative methodology and semiotics behind to enquire further into the possibilities for language systems in the 'post-cine, literatura, post-literatura' period. Zeroing in on a particular film-maker: Marsha Kinder edits with a comprehensive bibliography, *Luis Buñuel, The Discreet Charm of the Bourgeoisie*, CUP, 1999, x + 224 pp., nine different perspectives on the particular films, using reception theory and feminist criticism to good effect, and highlighting the films' subversive narrative structure with reference to the treatment of surrealism, satire, gender, and sexual issues by this transnational experimentalist; to be read against the specific attempt at reclaiming Buñuel as a *Spanish* phenomenon in the dossier compiled for *CHA*, 603, containing: J. A. Ramírez, 'Buñuel y Dalí en la estación surrealista' (7–12), which makes the good point that the connection here is not confined to the relatively short period spent together at the *Residencia de Estudiantes*, but that Dalí's presence may be traced in *Viridiana*, *Simón del desierto*, and *Los olvidados*, as well as in his critico-paranoic method discernible in all Buñuel's cinema; C. Barbáchano, 'Avatares literarios de un guionista' (13–16), merely points to a contradictory figure with a literary bent and many literary friends and acquaintances; A. Sánchez Vidal, 'El espejo incierto de Luis Buñuel' (17–22), gives an intelligent overview of the films with some personal reminiscing; R. Utrera Macías, 'Retablo nocturno del perro andaluz' (23–32), documents literary relations behind the film scripts with reference to Goya, Huysmans, Gómez de la Serna, and Federico García Lorca; G. Urrero Peña, 'Por un retrato de Luis Buñuel. Entrevista con Carlos Saura y Francisco Rabal' (33–36), is a lively press conference that outlines the fascinating possibilities realized in the triangle formed by Buñuel, Goya, and Saura over the years between 1926 and 1999; J. Bello Lasierra, 'Posdata sentimental' (43–48), is a collection of personal anecdotes about intimacy in the

Residencia with details on the tea-parties, the parodies of the *Tenorio*, Buñuel's (lack of) boxing prowess, *machismo*, and the ups and downs in the relations between Dalí, Buñuel, and García Lorca; while E. McGregor, 'Transterrados en el desierto' (37–42), adds his memories of exiled Spanish actors in the Mexican setting of the Mezquite Valley on the scene set of *Simón del desierto* in 1965.

From a specific point of view: David William Foster edits short entries on *Spanish Writers on Gay and Lesbian Themes: A Bio-Critical Sourcebook*, Westport, CT, Greenwood, 1999, 212 pp., which enquires into the 'gender trouble' of some canonical writers and includes those of professed gay identity, those who have incorporated gay themes into their work, and those who show some type of gay sensibility, although greater research is needed on the definitions as applied. Relevant here are the few pages devoted to Vicente Aleixandre, Pío Baroja, and Ramón J. Sender. On the same theme, the cultural analysis is worth noting in Jaime Manrique, *Eminent maricones: Arenas, Lorca and Me*, Wisconsin U.P., 1999, 116 pp., a series of six inter-related essays in Latino-queer-cultural studies that considers the widely divergent propositions contained in the denominations *maricón*-homosexual-gay, that should alleviate the repetitive homophobia and over-privileging of normative heterosexuality in so much commentary on whether García Lorca was gay and, if so, if it matters. Two articles to be read together are: E. Bejel, 'Positivist contradictions in Hernández Catá's *El ángel de Sodoma*', *ALEC*, 25:63–76, which centres on Hernández Catá as a Spanish writer caught in a positivist web of cultural prejudice woven in the prologue to his novel by Gregorio Marañón and the epilogue by Luis Jiménez de Asúa; and J. C. Galdo, 'Usos y lecciones del discurso ejemplar: a propósito de *El ángel de Sodoma* de Alfonso Hernández Catá', *Chasqui*, 29:19–32, which also also refers to this propagandistic positivist discourse, but points up the Latin American element in the nationality and nationalism debate about 'lo hispano' that hedges this early treatment of homosexuality.

2. POETRY

**Teoría del poema: la enunciación lírica*, ed. Fernando Cabo Aseguinolaza and Germán Gullón, Amsterdam–Atlanta, GA, Rodopi, 1998, includes essays by Ángel Abuín González on irony in modern poetry; Germán Gullón proposing a revisionist look at the Hispanic van-guard; Javier Blasco on Unamuno's 'vinculación simbolista'; and Teresa Vilarino Picos on Dámaso Alonso and Carlos Bousoño and their theories of poetic creation. Silvia Bermúdez, *Las dinámicas del deseo: subjetividad y lenguaje en la poesía española contemporánea*, M, Prodhufi, 1997, 206 pp., uses Lacan to comment upon Juan Ramón and Pedro

Salinas, and of note is her extensive analysis of 'Quería decir un nombre', where desire becomes the language of fullness and plenitude, as well as her exegesis of *jouissance* in 'Dulce nombre' in the play between language and subjectivity. M. A. Márquez, 'El versículo en el verso libre de ritmo endecasilábico', *BHS(G)*, 77:217–34, documents an innovative usage in poetry by Luis Cernuda and Vicente Aleixandre. The specialized collection, *Fragmentos de la modernidad. Antología de la poesía nueva en Aragón (1931–1945)*, ed. Enrique Serrano Asenjo, Huesca, Instituto de Estudios Altoaragoneses, cxx + 129 pp., comes with a long and informed introduction that glosses previous criticism (and much of it in English) on Spanish modernity, always with an eye to how such pointers might elucidate the particular Aragonese manifestation; explicates the importance of Ramón Gómez de la Serna and Benjamín Jarnés as mentors; and documents the history of the vanguard in Northeastern Spain, all rounded off with a functional bibliography and an excellent selection of texts, infrequently cited and often of difficult access, by poets like Tomás Seral y Casas, Ildefonso Manuel Gil, Maruja Falena, Carlos Eugenio Baylín Solanas, and Miguel Labordeta, that certainly opens up the field under scrutiny. E. Izarry, 'Juan Ramón Jiménez, cronista de Puerto Rico', *La Torre*, 13, 1999:527–37, is little more than the travelogue of Jiménez's voyage of discovery of what he baptized as the 'isla de la simpatía'. H. López González Orduña, 'Juan Larrea en el poema "?"', *ALEC*, 25:239–58, chronicles Larrea's rejection of *ultraísmo*. Zeroing in on the turn of the century poet and dramatist now acclaimed beyond just narrow regional success, Vicente Medina, *Antología poética*, ed. Francisco Javier Díez de Revenga, M, Castalia, 1999, 233 pp., concentrates on Medina's 'popular' vein, but provides useful documentation on the circumstances of his emigration to Argentina and his open support for the Popular Front. J. Valender, 'A propósito de las *Poesías completas* de José Moreno Villa', *NRFH*, 47, 1999:385–98, celebrates all the work of a poet usually cited only for the impact of his publication *Garbo* in 1913, and underscores a closeness with Cernuda and an important sense of sacrifice common to both. Francisco Chica, *El poeta lector. La biblioteca de Emilio Prados*, Anstruther, La Sirena, 1999, 255 pp., centres on the poet's intellectual biography, illustrating his 'itinerario de lectura' with emphasis on the discovery of Husserl and Heidegger made in the year Prados spent in Fribourg (1922–23), his contacts with others of the Generation of 1927 through León Sánchez Cuesta and *Litoral*, and the final period in Mexico, all rounded off with a practical bio-bibliography intended primarily for the general reader.

INDIVIDUAL POETS

ALEIXANDRE. Francisco Javier Díez de Revenga, *La poesía de Vicente Aleixandre: testimonio y conciencia*, Málaga, Centro Cultural Generación del 27, 1999, 210 pp., conducts the reader through the various stages of A.'s poetic life, offering up-dated commentary and recent bibliographical references in a most agreeable format. Rosa Fernández Urtasun, *La búsqueda del hombre a través de la belleza*, Kassel, Reichenberger, 1997, 163 pp., is a comparative study of French surrealism and the work of A., which concludes that the Spanish poet goes beyond the French school in his desire to humanize through poetry.

CERNUDA. C.'s experience of exile fascinates the critics: L. Gómez Canseco, 'Cernuda y la lengua poética: una revisión intencionada de la poesía española', *RLit*, 62:185–94, argues that changes in C.'s later work were due not only to his deepening interest in English poetry, but also to the revision of the Spanish tradition that he was forced to undertake as part of his academic preparation for teaching at the University of Glasgow, all of which resulted in C.'s attempts to define a lyrical trajectory from Campoamor onwards into which he might insert his own work; while S. Faber, ' "El norte nos devora": la construcción de un espacio hispánico en el exilio anglosajón de Luis Cernuda', *His(US)*, 83:733–44, draws parallels with the idealistic pan-Hispanism advocated by José Enrique Rodó to elucidate the repetitive mythic patterns of the cultural nationalism closely aligned with Herder's cultural historicism that C. exhibited in England, and from whose inherent ideological contradictions did he escape only in Mexico.

FUERTES. Two studies *in memoriam* complement one another quite neatly: D. K. Benson, 'La voz inconfundible de Gloria Fuertes, 1918–1998: poesía temprana', *His(US)*, 83:210–21, muses on the reasons for the lack of canonizing studies and, for the record, rescues her 'accesibilidad y virtuosismo, coloquialismo, hondo lirismo y anti-lirismo juguetón', but comes up short in producing evidence to support this; while, tackling the problem directly, M. L. Cooks, 'The humanization of poetry: an appraisal of Gloria Fuertes', *ib.*, 428–36, not only concentrates on how she broke with previous norms to create a new canon for the 1950s, but also exemplifies well the shock tactics inherent in the anti-poetical use of colloquial discourse, slang, swear words, and verbal play employed by this trail blazer, literary missionary, and folk poet.

GARCÍA LORCA. Some new editions are now available: Arturo del Hoyo edits and writes a prologue to *La zapatera prodigiosa*, M, Libertarias, 1999, 262 pp; **Bodas de sangre*, ed. Manuel Cifo González, M, Castalia, 1999, 195 pp.; and Mariano de Paco edits with a useful introduction and full editorial apparatus *La casa de Bernarda Alba*, B, Octoedro, 1999, 155 pp. Useful as usual, with particular reference to centenary publications, editions, *homenajes*, and reviews not collected here, is A. A. Anderson, 'Bibliografía lorquiana reciente (1984–2000)', *BFFGL*, 26:127–38. C. Ramos, 'Federico García Lorca en Eden Mills 70 años después', *ib.*, 119–24, records for posterity some unedited details of Philip Cummings's invitation to G.L. to the family summer house and recounts the celebratory visit to the New England town organized by Wellesley College in August 1999. A. A. Anderson, ' "El primer lírico español contemporáneo": Ricardo Baeza, Federico García Lorca y el *El romancero gitano*', *ib.*, 103–18, collects early reviews in which the renowned critic of *El Sol* praises a new generation of poets, naming G.L. and his contemporaries Alberti, Salinas, Guillén, Diego, (perhaps surprisingly) Claudio de la Torre, and Antonio Espina, with Jiménez and (perspicaciously) Gómez de la Serna singled out as mentors, and drops the grain of incense following the long-awaited publication of G.L.'s gypsy ballads, together with the transcription of this 'Marginalia' (109–18) for those interested in how reputations are made. J. Herrero, 'The war of the stars and the birth of the moon: homosexual poetics in the early Lorca', *BHS(L)*, 77:571–84, pores over the juvenile modernist images to discern the conflict and horror in the discovery of the 'tristeza de la fisiología' and finds in the encompassing image of the moon as the pale star that hides a cold heart in idealized beauty a definition that will dominate G.L.'s art for the rest of his life. If K. A. Nance, 'The dynamic of folklore in Lorca's early poetics: opening *Libro de poemas* and unfolding "Pajarita de papel" ', *ALEC*, 25:505–28, laudably tries to advance from earlier influence studies, credibility is stretched rather far in claims to find the Dionysian evocation that will later emerge as *duende* in this particular poem of folkloric origin. Javier Salazar Rincón, '*Rosas y mirtos de luna . . .' Naturaleza y símbolo en la obra de Federico García Lorca*, M, Universidad Nacional de Educación a Distancia, 1999, 476 pp., takes Joseph Zdenek's 1980 study (see *YWMLS*, 42:349) even further in a commentary upon the abundant vegetal symbols that includes a cultural overview of citations in poetry of each plant, discussion of G.L.'s predecessors in vegetable lore, and examples from the complete literary and artistic work, although a concluding chapter might have saved this from reading like another annotated concordance. N. Santiáñez, 'Lorca, poeta neoclásico: la "Oda a Salvador Dalí" ', *ALEC*, 25:587–607, tries, without signal success, to find evidence of Horatian and Pindaric sources of inspiration and then see the way clear to surrealism from G.L.'s classical knowledge. Different perspectives on the poetry freshen

jaded palates, and the following are to be read together as complementary pieces: R. Stone, ' "Quiero llorar": Lorca and the flamenco
tradition in *Poeta en Nueva York*', *BHS(G)*, 77:493–510, highlights
interesting parallels with traditional flamenco verse in how G.L.
assumed the role of *cantaor* in defending the persecuted and the
marginalized in the New York poems; and, envisioning the poet as
'prophet', R. Havard, 'Lorca's mantic poet in New York', *ALEC*,
25:439–77, focuses upon the quite different tradition of 'functional
polysemousness' found in biblical texts to elucidate the ideological
structuring and interactive effect of the same poems; starting from the
coincidental proximity of the deaths, just one month apart in 1934, of
the bull-fighter and the eminent man of science, Santiago Ramón y
Cajal, X. de Ros, 'Science and myth in *Llanto por Ignacio Sánchez
Mejías*', *MLR*, 95:114–26, explores contemporary medicine as modern thaumaturgy and, by teasing out G.L.'s scientific metaphors,
shows how both art and medicine provide some defence against
finitude, although, more flamboyantly, S. Poeta, 'Aproximaciones a
la teatralidad del *Llanto por Ignacio Sánchez Mejías*', *ALEC*, 25:193–216,
concentrates on the experimentalist *par excellence* that was G.L. in his
multiple roles as author, actor, director, musician, singer, orator, and
choreographer. M. T. Pao, 'The poet, the rooster and the painter:
aesthetic theory in "Historia de este gallo" ', *RoQ*, 47:41–54, reads
the playful prose texts of *gallo* (1928) as an artistic manifesto which
reflects G.L.'s aesthetic desiderata and refutes Salvador Dalí's
'asepsia' through the legend of Don Alhambro. N. Dennis, '*Viaje a la
luna*: Federico García Lorca y el problema de la expresión', *RCEH*,
25:137–49, reviews the unlikely itineraries, preceding their publication in final form, of the MSS of the New York cycle comprising the
film script, the drama *El público*, and the edition of *Poeta en Nueva York*,
before tackling G.L.'s ironical treatment of the death of love in sexual
satisfaction that reflects G.L.'s creative impotence, which is the real
problem here. Concentrating on the theatre: G. Edwards, 'Productions of *La casa de Bernarda Alba*', *ALEC*, 25:699–728, documents the
various stagings from that of Margarita Xirgu in Buenos Aires in
1945, through the first Spanish productions by Juan Antonio Bardem
in Saragossa in 1965 and José Carlos Plaza in Madrid in 1984, to a
discussion of what makes, or more likely breaks, versions in English
in the US and the less successful performances in the UK, often
defined by cultural prejudice despite the efforts of such sterling
actresses as Mia Farrow, Glenda Jackson, Joan Plowright, and Helen
Bonham Carter, directors Nuria Espert and Polly Teale, and Tom
Stoppard's theatrical expertise. On a quite different tack, J. Corbin,
'Lorca's *Casa*', *MLR*, 95:712–27, uses anthropological parameters to
explain how, without a connecting street, Bernarda's house does not

form part of the local community, and goes on to probe pre-modern
cultural inconsistencies and ambiguities in this example of Andalusian
ethnography to conclude that, if sex is certainly foregrounded, the
real problem lies in social inequality; C. Jerez-Farrán, 'Towards a
Foucauldian exegesis of Act V of García Lorca's *El público*', *ib.*,
728–43, illustrates well the dialectical tensions inherent in G.L.'s
treatment of homosexuality, while M. Allinson, ' "Una comedia sin
público"; metatheatre, action and reaction in Lorca's *Comedia sin
título*', *ib.*, 1027–37, investigates the potential social and artistic
applications of G.L.'s experimental theatre.

MACHADO, A. C. J. Morales, 'Dos versiones del modernismo: la
conciencia del tiempo en Rubén Darío y Antonio Machado', *RLit*,
62:107–129, deals another death blow to the idea of the mutual
exclusivity between *modernismo* and the Generation of 1898 by
pointing out the common ground between these two almost contemporaneous figures, particularly in their shared perception of time as
an existentialist drama that then led to somewhat different spiritual
and stylistic developments in their individual poetry. N. Dennis,
'Appropriations of Antonio Machado', *FMLS*, 36:310–21, documents the competing strategies in 1940 of both 'Pilgrim Spain' and
the Falangists in power in Spain to claim the veteran poet as their
own, and contrasts José Bergamín's edition, made with the blessing
of brothers José and Joaquín, for Séneca in Mexico, and the truncated
anthology produced by Dionisio Ridruejo for Espasa Calpe and the
Spanish market under the aegis of the other brothers, Manuel and
Francisco.

MACHADO, M. Rafael Alarcón Sierra, *Entre el modernismo y la
modernidad: la poesía de Manuel Machado ('Alma' y 'Caprichos')*, Seville,
Diputación de Sevilla, 1999, contextualizes *Alma* in the Madrid-
Seville-Madrid years between 1883 and 1899 as the 'cetro y símbolo
finesecular' through some very close readings, and then pursues the
Bohemian interlude in Paris, relations with Juan Ramón, and the
socio-literary *tertulias* of 1902 to 1905 in some definitive interpretations
of the poems of *Caprichos*. In the very different auto-analytical satire,
Id., 'Contra Manuel Machado: la deconstrucción de su no-identitidad
en *El mal poema*', *HR*, 68:161–81, finds that M.'s attempts to reconcile
his *alter ego* in art and life fail, but sees in the poetical use of irony
evidence of the proximity of the vanguard.

SALINAS. Carlos Feal Deibe, *Poesía y narrativa de Pedro Salinas*, M,
Gredos, 325 pp., is a new, and very much augmented, version of his
earlier *La poesía de Pedro Salinas* (1965), that now deepens comparisons
with eminent philosophers (Scheler, Ortega, Heidegger, Merleau-
Ponty, and Emmanuel Levinas) and partakes of fashionable psychoanalysis (Erik H. Erikson, Donald W. Winniecott, and Christopher

Bollas), in a commentary that extends beyond the poetry to include the prose writing, both creative and critical, as well as S.'s theatre, in the attempt to illustrate the 'pasión, lucidez, piedad, ironía' of this remarkable humanist. K. M. Sibbald, 'Cástor y Pólux en París: *flâneries* generacionales', Sibbald, *Ciudades*, 349–57, documents the cultural experience lived by both S. and Jorge Guillén as *lectores* at the Sorbonne. L. A. Hernández Pérez de Landazabal, 'Realidad virtual con luz artificial. (Glosa de "El poema de todo más claro" y otros poemas de Pedro Salinas, en el 50 aniversario de su publicación, con apéndice final científico-ficticio)', *RLit*, 62:505–14, is the long-winded title of a close reading that underscores the importance of the Theory of Relativity to a poetical hypothesis that borders on science fiction. (See also GÓMEZ DE LA SERNA below.)

3. PROSE

Walking the fine line between the mundane and the extraordinary, E. Rosales, '*Memorias de Leticia del Valle*: Rosa Chacel o el deletreo de lo inaudito', *His(US)*, 83:222–31, compares Chacel's short story 'Atardecer en Extremadura' with Ana María Matute's 'El niño al que se le murió el amigo' in order to decipher Chacel's narrative strategies in using a child narrator and disallowing other views of reality to maintain the suspense over the seduction without ever naming the act. Two articles deal with misery and death in city life: J. Amezua, 'El tópico de la ciudad decadente en Hoyos y Vinent', Sibbald, *Ciudades*, 27–35, considers both *Mors in vita* (1904) and *El monstruo* (1915), to elucidate turn of the century horror at the price of modernity, while F. A. Pérez Pérez, 'La ciudad vanguardista: *Hermes en la vía pública*', *ib.*, 311–18, finds in this 'última carcajada' before the outbreak of war the parodic reification of the same society, still bent on alienation, disintegration, and ultimate destruction. A. Pego Puigbó, 'El género intermedio de Benjamín Jarnés', *RLit*, 62:411–29, concentrates on *Libro de Esther* and *Eufrosina o la gracia* to discern in the play between transgression and innovation how Jarnés constructs a novel genre. María Teresa León, *Memoria de la melancolía*, ed. Gregorio Torres Nebrera, M, Castalia, 1999, 544 pp., provides the critical apparatus for different levels of reading of this important contribution to Spanish cultural history by highlighting the experience of exile, the writing of testimonial literature, and the revindication of the role of Spanish women throughout history in León's biographical novels. Zeroing in on the most anglophile of the 1898 Generation, J. A. G. Ardila, 'La peculiaridad psicológica del español según Maeztu', *RLit*, 62:486–504, explicates well how images of British culture and references to Great Britain add depth to the Generation's investigations of Don Quixote, Don Juan, and the Celestina as cultural icons. T. Gajic, 'Reason, practice and the promise of a New Spain: Ortega's "Vieja y nueva política" and *Meditaciones del Quijote*', *BHS(G)*, 77:193–215, breaks with some canonical judgements of Ortega's work, refusing to construct a line from the 1930s to José María Aznar's contemporary politics, and, instead, concentrates on a change in Ortega's philosophical paradigms that had effect on both his 'new politics' and the poetics of the novel. L. Arrigoni de Allamand, 'Ramón Pérez de Ayala: ensayo y discurso autobiográfico en la situación de exilio', Genoud de Fourcade, *Estudios*, 1–29, examines the connections between autobiography and literature in, particularly, articles in *La Prensa* and letters to Miguel Rodríguez-Acosta. C. Puebla Isla, 'El determinismo ambiental en la novelística de Alejandro Sawa', Sibbald, *Ciudades*, 319–28, draws attention to the 'novela médico-social' used by López Bago and Sawa to indict society *à la Taine* and set up modern novelists as contemporary historians. *Homenaje a María Zambrano: estudios y correspondencia*, ed. James Valender, Anthony Stanton, Rosa Corral, et al., Mexico, Colegio de México, 1998, 813 pp.

INDIVIDUAL WRITERS

AUB. *Manuscrito cuervo*, ed. José Antonio Pérez Bowie, Alcalá U.P., 1999, 262 pp. E. Nos Aldas, 'Escombros sociales en la narrativa de Max Aub', Sibbald, *Ciudades*, 245–56, centres on cities, as described in *Laberinto mágico*, of the front line during and the oppression after the Spanish Civil War.

AZORÍN. More editions become available: *Castilla*, ed. Gregorio Torres Nebrera, M, Biblioteca Nueva, 141 pp., provides an erudite introduction to this volume in a new series, although *Castilla*, ed. José Manuel Molina, M, Bruño, 1999, 203 pp., is plagued by typographical and other errors, all the more unfortunate in a text designed for student use; while *Diario de un enfermo*, ed. Francisco Martín, Biblioteca Nueva, 260 pp., provides the necessary scholarly apparatus to read this first novel published in 1901 with turn-of-the-century ideas on revolution, nihilism and suicide; and *Los norteamericanos*, ed. Laureano Robles, Alicante, Instituto Gil-Albert, 1999, 170 pp., collects A.'s periodical articles written in the context of World War I as an *aliadófilo* and war correspondent in France, and includes pieces previously collected in book form as *París bombardeado* (1919), *Los norteamericanos*, incorporated into the 1967 edition of the *Obras completas*, and yet others re-edited under the title *Con bandera de Francia* in 1950. Ramón F. Llorens García, *El último Azorín (1936–1967)*, Alicante U.P., 1999,

163 pp., breaks the silence on A.'s return to Spain in the Francoist years. Less polemically, Magdalena Rigual Bonastre, *J. Martínez Ruiz: lector y bibliófilo*, Alicante U.P., 131 pp., explores the dynamic relation between author as reader and writer. A. is remembered for his passionate interest in the cinema in Rafael Utrera's prologue to *El cine y el momento*, M, Biblioteca Nueva, 132 pp. J. Maurice, 'Azorín y *La Andalucía trágica*: ¿una nueva estructura de lo social?', *ECon*, 13:99–107, examines tone and composition to conclude that herein lies further proof of A.'s literary inspiration that softens real reality.

BAROJA. N. Norris, 'César Moncada como protagonista baroji-ano en búsqueda de su identidad', *HisJ*, 20, 1999:119–30, elucidates how B. points up the politics of social reform in Spain through the change of this Schopenhauerian character into a man of action. C. M. Andoni Alonso, 'Técnica y ciencia en la Generación del 98: el caso de Pío Baroja y Ortega', *La Torre*, 11, 1999:1–19, finds in B. a surprisingly contemporary voice showing dissatisfaction with the development of science and technology, and also presses Ortega into the ranks denouncing crass materialism. J. Fernández Mosquera, 'Baroja y la retórica en tono mayor', *ALEC*, 25:217–37, defends B.'s own desire for 'la claridad, la precisión y la elegancia' and his corresponding dislike of 'barbaric' rhetoric full of musical sophistry and literary lies. M. G. Tomsich, 'Los barrios antiguos de Madrid y París en las *Memorias* de Pío Baroja', Sibbald, *Ciudades*, 359–66, meanders through the old cities, musing vaguely upon possible parallels with Tönnies, Durkheim, Simmel, Weber, and urban sociology.

BLASCO IBÁÑEZ. L. Rubio García, 'Las cartas de Blasco Ibáñez al Marqués de Dosfuentes', *RLit*, 124:571–90, reproduces five letters dated between 1924 and 1926 from Hong Kong and Menton, telling of the (unsuccessful) plans for a secret wedding in 1925 and the difficulties inherent in an itinerant friendship. T. R. Franz, '*Cañas y barro*, Sardou's *Tosca*, and Puccini's *Tosca*', *Hispanófila*, 129:15–22, explores the intertextualities between Tosca and Neleta as liberated women, the key role of the criminal, and shared Naturalist ideology.

GANIVET. Editing of the *obras* continues: *La conquista del reino de Maya por el último conquistador español Pío Cid*, ed. Raúl Fernández Alarcos, Granada, Diputación de Granada, 451 pp., whose 'Estudio preliminar' (13–54) gives details on 19th-c. travel literature to contextualize G.'s pessimistic vision of civilization, while Fernando García Lara comments on textual variants in a useful 'Historia del texto' (55–62). *Los trabajos del indefatigable creador Pío Cid*, ed. Germán Gullón, Granada, Diputación de Granada, 691 pp., takes up the theme 'Pío Cid y el desencanto del hombre moderno' in the preliminary study (11–46), and Fernando García Lara contextualizes the present edition (47–51). Luis Álvarez Castro, *El universo femenino de Ángel Ganivet*, Granada, Diputación de Granada, 1999, 319 pp., takes up G.'s tumultuous relationships in real life, documents G.'s views on love, marriage, and women's emancipation, and transcribes the short prose piece 'El secreto' from the MS held in the Biblioteca Nacional (301–06). Id., 'En torno a la ciudad simbolista-modernista: las huellas de Rodenbach en la génesis de *Granada la bella*, de Ángel Ganivet', Sibbald, *Ciudades*, 16–26, pursues the paradigm formed by Bruges, Rodenbach, John Ruskin, and the Greek *polis*. N. Santiáñez, 'Carlyle and Ganivet', *BHS(G)*, 77:329–41, is the English translation of a good but previously published article (see *YWMLS*, 61:275).

GÓMEZ DE LA SERNA. James H. Hoddie, *El contraste en la obra de Ramón Gómez de la Serna*, M, Pliegos, 1999, 267 pp., considers the variety of genres subsumed in the *greguería*, autobiography (*Morbideces* and *Automoribundia*), short biographies of acknowledged predecessors (Nerval, Baudelaire, and Rémy de Goncourt), the long biography (on Edgar Allan Poe), and the new novel (*La viuda en blanco y negro*, *El gran hotel*, and *El torero Caracho*). *Ramón Gómez de la Serna*, ed. Evelyne Martín Hernández, Clermont-Ferrand, Blaise-Pascal U.P., 1999, 309 pp., collects papers from the 1996 conference organized by the *Centre de Recherches sur les Littératures Modernes et Contemporaines*, under four main headings: I. 'La personne, le personnage', containing I. Zlotescu, '*Ramonismo*: entre ficción y realidad' (9–18); J. Heuer, '*Automoribundia*: autojustificación y autocrítica' (19–27); D. Corrado, '*Diario postúmo*: le journal de Ramón Gómez de la Serna' (29–38), a mosaic of different types of writing; G. Mercadier, 'L'autoportrait selon Ramón' (39–51), a ramonian auto-vivisection; C. Nicolle-Robin, 'Gómez de la Serna: *Diario del lector*, miroir de l'histoire ou miroir de soi' (53–60), on commitment and intellectual abstraction in G. de la S.'s column for *La Tribuna* (1914–15); II. 'L'esprit du lieu', comprising: J.-A. Díaz, 'La phénoménologie du *Rastro* par Ramón' (61–76), which reads Ortega along with the prologues to the first (1914) and third (1931) editions; A. Valero, 'Madrid-Paris: itinéraire d'un promeneur de cour' (77–92), concentrating on the 1920s; N. Alba, 'Sobre algunos personnages de *Pombo* y *Automoribundia*' (93–102), zeroing in on Celso Lagar, José Nogales, and Jose Sánchez Rojas; M. Albert, 'Para una estética pombiana' (103–20), identifying *Pombo* as the hothouse of the Spanish vanguard; III. 'Des genres, des formes, une esthétique', encompassing: C. Le Bigot, 'La *greguería*: trope ou genre?' (121–31), which opts for genre by way of rhetoric; C. Herrero Vecino, 'Las pantomimas de Ramón Gómez de la Serna' (133–43), which looks at the spectacles of the Paris of La Polaire and Colette; I. Soldevila Durante, 'Ramón, las primeras narraciones (1905–1913)' (145–56), proving the worth of this self-appointed 'intelectual humanitario'; W. Helmich, 'Le lieu historique du *novelista* ramonien' (157–69), contextualizing the metaliterary tradition in which to insert *El novelista*; L. Alcoba and E. La Vagueresse, 'Une esthétique de l'éclatement' (170–89), two for the price of one title; IV. 'Amitiés, parentés, influences', taking in: A. Montardon, 'Ramón Gómez de la Serna et Jules Renard' (221–32), with coincidences in moon imagery, attention to detail, freedom of language, and humour; B. Mousli, 'Ramón et Valerio' (233–43), documenting relations with Valéry Larbaud begun in Alicante in 1916 (see also R. Duroux, below); C. Boulay, 'Ramón Gómez de la Serna et Paul Morand' (245–58), comparing visions of Madrid and Paris; A. Janquart, 'La greguería est-elle exportable?' (259–67), enquiring into G. de la Serna's influence on Miguel Ángel Asturias; D. Míglos, 'Funambulismes' (269–74), drawing parallels with Rosa Chacel; J.-P. Castellani, 'De Ramón a Paco' (275–82), tracing affinities between G. de la S. and Francisco Umbral; J. Lajarrigue, 'A propos de quelques exemples de greguerías dans la poésie autrichienne des années 50' (283–92), exploring similarities with René Altmann and Hans Carl Artmann; R. Duroux, 'Ramón dans la Thébaïde de Valéry Larbaud' (293–306), documenting G. de la S. in his friend's library holdings (see also B. Mousli, above); E. Baeza, 'El espacio biográfico-autobiográfico en Ramón Gómez de la Serna', Genoud de Fourcade, *Estudios*, 31–75, documents the use of masks in the biographies that led, finally, to *Automoribundia*. C. Herrero Vecino, 'El cosmopolitismo de Ramón Gómez de la Serna: *El novelista*', Sibbald, *Ciudades*, 147–55, establishes the relation between cityscapes and the vanguard novel; and using the same text, R. C. Spires, 'New art, new woman, old constructs: Gómez de la Serna and Pedro Salinas and vanguard fiction', *MLN*, 115:205–23, goes on to compare how both writers perpetrate old gender practices but bear witness to the power of vanguard discourse to change both narrative and social projections.

UNAMUNO. P. E. Badillo, 'Unamuno, Ortega, Zubiri y el ateísmo actual', *La Torre*, 11, 1999:135–46, reasserts a common intellectual formation. C. Pascual Pérez, 'Espacio interior y espacio exterior en la poesía de M. de Unamuno', Sibbald, *Ciudades*, 269–75, posits briefly a teleological and theological slant to all of U.'s poetry. Critiques of the novels range widely. T. R. Franz, 'Augusto's mysterious travel plans in Unamuno's *Niebla*', *HisJ*, 20, 1999:81–95, presses Freud, Bakhtin, and Genette into service to explore systematically the travel motif as connected with sex and death; J. Herrero, 'Imaginación erótica en *Amor y pedagogía*: la planta en el hogar', *BHS(G)*, 77:41–55, turns on the theme of love ignored in previous criticism. Comparative studies include: T. R. Franz, '*Abel Sánchez* y *Le Colonel Chabert*', *RCEH*, 24:408–13, underscores U.'s innovative use of intertextuality in a

curious appropriation from Balzac in Derville's final comments; while
J. Biggane, 'Yet another other: Unamuno's *El otro* and the anxiety of
influence', *BHS(G)*, 77:479–91, tips her hat to other influence studies
ennumerating Dostoievski, Henry James, Pirandello, Calderón,
Rappaport, and Max Aub as possible sources, but decides that this
play is a metatextual commentary on its own literary and performative identity as U. recognized the difficulty in ever staging his theatre.
Feminist studies have their effect: J. P. Gabriele, 'From sex to gender:
towards femino-centric narrative in Unamuno's *La tía Tula* or "Cómo
se hace una novela feminista" ', *HisJ*, 20, 1999:105–17, tries hard to
make the claim that U. achieved a narrative integrity of the female
self within a male authorial frame; T. R. Franz, 'Ibsen's *Hedda Gabler*
and the question of feminist content in Unamuno's *La tía Tula*', *ALEC*,
25:77–98, finds notable similarities in characterization, imagery, and
schema, but plumps for Hedda as the real feminist; while E. Arrington
Bruner Smith, '(S)mothering in Miguel de Unamuno's "Dos madres":
the fatal repercussions of the nineteenth-century idealization of the
mother', *HisJ*, 20, 1999:351–61, illustrates U.'s reasoning that this
exaltation of motherhood not only alienates men from women, but
further hinders the liberation of women in its re-enactment of male
patriarcal domination. (See also VALLE-INCLÁN below.)

VALLE-INCLÁN. Robert Lima, **Ramón del Valle-Inclán: An Annotated
Bibliography*. 1. *The Works of Valle-Inclán*, London, Grant and Cutler,
1999, 293 pp. Rosemary C. Lodato, *Beyond the Glitter: The Language of
Gems in Modernist Writers Rubén Darío and José Asunción Silva*, Lewisburg,
PA, Bucknell U.P., 1999, 213 pp., goes beyond strictly literary matters
into the realm of the plastic arts; of use here is her examination of
modernismo's language of jewellery in V.-I.'s *Sonatas*. J. Gómez-
Montero, 'La lírica de Ramón María del Valle-Inclán ante el discurso
poético de la modernidad', *ALEC*, 25:99–145, elucidates the hermen-
eutics of *Claves líricas*. M. A. Gómez Abalo, 'Nuevas aportaciones a la
recepción crítica de *Farsa y licencia de la reina castiza*, de Valle-Inclán',
ib., 1025–94, traces the line from the original serial publication in *La
Pluma* (1920) to the *estreno* of 1931, with full details about critical
reception in the press. H. Thurston-Griswold, ' "Del sentimiento
trágico de la vida" en dos *Sonatas* de Valle-Inclán', *HisJ*, 20,
1999:97–103, argues that V.-I. should be included in the Generation
of 1898, insisting that his critical depiction of his Don Juan figure as
'esteticista, escéptico y hedonista' reflects a tragic view of life. Catalina
Míguez Vilas, *Valle-Inclán y la novela popular: 'La cara de Dios' (Proceso de
escritura y estrategias genérico-narrativas)*, South Carolina U.P., 1998,
160 pp., brings some fresh air to the high moral tone of the 1970s
debate concerning plagiarism and authorship but, while coincidences
with Arniches and Dosteievski, Poe and Balzac are dealt with, some

will not appreciate the structuralist strait-jacket imposed here; and, from another literary stance, F. de Diego, 'El espacio urbano en *La cara de Dios* de Valle-Inclán', Sibbald, *Ciudades*, 69–77, underlines the downfall of the rural aristocracy, victims of the mercantilism of city life. Dru Dougherty, *Guía para caminantes en Santa Fe de Tierra Firme: estudio sistémico de 'Tirano Banderas'*, V, Pre-Textos, 1999, 316 pp. E. Drumm, 'Ekphrasis in Valle-Inclán's *Comedias bárbaras*', *REH*, 34:391–407, finds in this 'imagetext' not the static representation of a forgotten past but rather a potent polyvalence characteristic of the modern Spanish theatre. A. N. Zahareas, 'A new look at politics and literature', *ALEC*, 25:259–302, reviews at length the achievement of Margarita Santos Zas (see *YWMLS*, 56:400) in this reappraisal of V.-I.'s remarkable career in politics and literature.

4. THEATRE

Critical work on the drama of the period is also noted above under GARCÍA LORCA, SALINAS, UNAMUNO, and VALLE-INCLÁN. Supplementary information on Max Aub, García Lorca, and Valle-Inclán can be found in P. Sheppard, C. Costello and M. Dodaro, 'Modern drama studies: an annual bibliography', *MoD*, 43:59–170, see particularly section E: Hispanic (108–18); details of editions, reviews and doctoral theses not collected here, together with items on Azorín, García Lorca, and Valle-Inclán, are gathered up in a comprehensive and systematic fashion by K. Aggor and C. J. Harris, 'El drama español del siglo xx: bibliografía selecta del año 1998', *Estreno*, 26.1:46–54; while the general round-up by M. F. Vilches de Frutos, 'La temporada teatral español 1997–98', *ALEC*, 25:961–1023, has information relevant here on García Lorca and Valle-Inclán, the staging of *San Juan*, readings from the Generation of 1898, and news of a revival of interest in Pedro Muñoz Seca. On the theatre specifically, *Nuevas perspectivas sobre el 98*, ed. John P. Gabriele, M, Iberoamericana, 1999, 303 pp., contains L. S. Glaze, 'Jacinto Benavente: la re-escritura del concepto de la honra' (195–203); E. J. Doll, 'Arniches en la Segunda República' (205–12); E. Drumm, ' "... To return to the origin": Valle-Inclán's *Comedias bárbaras* and Gaudí's *Sagrada familia*' (213–22); R. L. Bandeira, 'Don Juan en el teatro de Unamuno' (231–37); C. Leonard, 'Gendered spaces in two dramatic works by Valle-Inclán: *Cenizas* and *El yermo de las almas*' (261–69); and Á. G. Loureiro, 'Valle-Inclán: la modernidad como ruina' (293–303). *La renovación teatral española de 1900: manifiestos y otros ensayos*, ed. Jesús Rubio Jiménez, M, Asociación de Directores de Escena de España, 1998, 374 pp., has a useful 'Estudio preliminar' (21–52), that contextualizes the commentaries collected here by, principally,

Jacinto Benavente, Valle-Inclán, Ángel Guerra, Ramón Pérez de Ayala, and Unamuno concerning a period of transition and regeneration of the Spanish theatre. Margot Versteeg, *De fusiladores y morcilleros: el discurso cómico del género chico (1870–1910)*, Amsterdam, Rodopi, 484 pp. J. Maire Bobes, 'La revista madrilena *El teatro por dentro* (1906–1908): la vida cotidiana de actores y actrices', *ALEC*, 25:923–60, documents the 37 issues running from November 1906 until May 1908 that divide into two periods, the first comprised of Antonio Velasco's interviews with the leading lights of the day, and the second, from number 22 onwards, more eclectic in subject matter and written by a variety of hands, all neatly rounded off with useful appendices listing authors and actors mentioned. M. T. García-Abad García, 'Diaghilev en Madrid: un hito de la moderna puesta en escena', *BHS(G)*, 77:57–71, makes good use of contemporary reviews to document the fascination in Madrid with the *Ballets russes*, generated as much by the costumes and 'barbaric' scene sets, as by the vigorous eroticism of the dancing, that made the visit to the Teatro Real in 1916 such a wild success. *La escena moderna. Manifiestos y textos sobre el teatro de la época de vanguardias*, ed. José Antonio Sánchez, M. Akal, 487 pp., is a most useful anthology, sensibly not confined to Spanish sources, wherein comments by Gordon Craig, Isadora Duncan, Vasily Kandinsky, Cocteau, Apollinaire, and Antonin Artaud jibe nicely with texts by Adriá Gual, Pérez de Ayala, Valle-Inclán, Rivas Cherif, García Lorca, and Max Aub. F. Foguat i Boreu, 'El teatro universitario en la Cataluña de la Segunda República (1935–1937)', *ALEC*, 25:821–88, records a piece of theatre history and, of importance here, the visit to Barcelona of *La Barraca* in 1936. J. E. Checa Puerta, '1998–1999: últimas ediciones de textos teatrales españoles en lengua castellano', *ib.*, 673–97, takes a hard look at editorial criteria, market success, and new trends to find that Valle-Inclán, García Lorca (together with Buero Vallejo, Arrabal and Antonio Gala) still top the best-selling lists, while, unsurprisingly, the general public shows little interest in José María Pemán, Torcuato Luca de Tena, and Edgar Neville, is luke-warm about collected works generally, but welcomes the forthcoming *obras* of Miguel Mihura. *ADE Teatro*, 77, 1999, has much general commentary on the modern theatre, including: Á. Montesinos, 'Últimas décadas del teatro musical en Espana' (274–78), documenting the *zarzuela*; commentaries on staging and reviewing in the early part of the century in C. Oliva, 'Comedia española de principios de siglo y puesta en escena' (38–47), E. Pérez-Rasilla, 'La dirección escénica entre 1900 y 1936: un cúmulo de tentativos' (186–203), J. Ruesga, 'Los teatros en España entre 1900 y 1939' (244–50), C. de Vicente Hernando, 'Concepto y tendencias del teatro revolucionario y de agitación social

entre 1900 y 1939' (133–43), and E. Pérez-Rasilla, 'La crítica en
España entre 1900 y 1940. ¿La edad de oro de la crítica?' (279–87);
with more specific details in J. Rubio Jiménez, 'Los nuevos horizontes
de la literatura dramática de 1900 a 1920' (16–26), C. Santolaria
Solano, 'Enrique Díez-Canedo o el ejercicio de una crítica erudita y
honrada' (289–90), M. F. Vieites, 'De *Juan José* a *Tres sombreros de copa*.
Algunas consideraciones previas al estudio de las relaciones entre
creación dramática, espectáculo teatral y educación popular en el
primer tercio del siglo XX' (298–304), F. Onrubia, 'El teatro en
Pamplona entre 1900 y 1939' (96–98), and C. de Vicente Hernando,
'Bibliografía sobre el teatro español entre 1900 y 1939' (331–32).
A. A. Anderson, 'La campaña teatral de Ricardo Baeza e Irene López
Herredia (1927–1928): historia externa e interna de una colaboración', *RLit*, 62 : 133–53, documents well the plan of this new company
to infiltrate rather than confront the theatre-going public in its
tournées in the provinces and stagings in the capital, and, by
recording performances, repertoire, and itinerary, reconstructs the
method of educating public taste by offering a middle option between
elitist experimentation and mere box-office success. C. C. Soufas, Jr.,
'Benavente and the Spanish discourse on theatre', *HR*, 68 : 147–59,
intelligently revindicates *Los intereses creados* (1907) as the first significant contemporary exercise of self-referential criticism of Spanish
stage practices in a meditation on the theatre that invokes the long
history of the European stage to comment upon the wrong interests
governing the theatre values of contemporary Spain. Gregorio
Martínez Sierra, *Teatro de ensueño. La intrusa*, ed. Serge Salaün, M,
Biblioteca Nueva, 1999, 318 pp., contains a useful introduction
(1–144), that contextualizes the following works: *Por el sendero florido*
(145–65), *Pastoral* (167–96), *Saltimbanquis* (197–265), *Cuento de labios en
flor* (267–96), as well as Martínez Sierra's version in Spanish of *La
intrusa*, by Maurice Maeterlinck. A. Fernández Insuela, 'Un drama
didáctico y polémico: *El pueblo dormido* (1917), de Federico Oliver',
ALEC, 25 : 729–63, dismisses the charges of plagiarism of Luis Antón
del Olmet's *El sembrador*, uses the revues of the period to document
relations between *aliadófilos* and *germanófilos* that affected Oliver's
fortunes, but assigns the blame for this box-office flop to heavy-
handed didacticism in presenting Regenerationist and Naturalist
ideals.

LITERATURE, 1936 TO THE PRESENT DAY

By IRENE MIZRAHI, *Boston College*

1. PROSE

GENERAL

M. L. Abellán, 'Determinismos sociales del realismo de medio siglo', *Ojáncano*, 18:24–40, presents mid-century social realism as the result of determinant social and political conditions created by the struggle between power spheres in Francoist society, concluding that 'El único reproche que el ensorbecido crítico literario podía proferir contra las tendencias de la narrativa críticosocial sería el de haber sido producto de su época.'

M. P. Rodríguez, 'Encierros y fugas en la narrativa femenina española de los años cincuenta', *RHM*, 53:121–32, revises the traditional notion of the body as a non-historical and determined biological entity through the study of the physical, textual, and social body in women's novels of the 1950s such as Dolores Medio's *Nosotros los Ribero* and Carmen Martín Gaite's *Entre visillos*, concluding that these novels can be read in terms of a more participatory interpretation of female writers to their social and political environments. D. Odartey-Wellington, 'De las madres perversas y las hadas buenas: una nueva visión sobre la imagen de la mujer en las novelas de Carmen Martín Gaite y Esther Tusquets', *ALEC*, 25:529–56, approaches the question of feminine image through an analysis of the re-elaboration of the fairy tale motif of 'good fairy–malevolent mother' in M.G's *Caperucita en Manhattan* and *La reina de las nieves*, and T.'s *El mismo mar de todos los veranos*, and argues that both writers 'acuden a esta convención de los cuentos de hadas para poner en tela de juicio la imagen femenina construida a base de las expectativas occidentales.'

B. Epps, 'Writing in accessible language: Benet, Goytisolo, Galdós', *REH*, 34:351–87, is an interesting discussion about the accessibility of realist works that begins with 'the critical and creative responses of Benet and Goytisolo to Galdós and realism', moves on to 'a brief look at a passage from *Fortunata* itself', and then concludes by establishing the difference between the inaccessibility inscribed in Pérez Galdós's text and that inscribed in Benet's and Goytisolo's writings. M. E. Altisent, 'Máscaras transsexuales en la escritora femenina española contemporánea', *LF*, 26:193–212, studies contemporary novels by female authors which have male narrators or interlocutors, and argues that these writers' masculine unfolding corresponds to four paradigmatic situations: androgyny, correction of twisted morality, sexualization of field of vision, and fragmented consciousness. Novels such as Olga Guirao's *Mi querido Sebastian*, Ana María Moix's *Walter, ¿por qué te fuiste?*, Cristina Fernández Cubas's *El año de gracia*, Carmen Martín Gaite's *Retahilas* and *El cuarto de atrás*, and Lourdes Ortiz's *Urraca* pertain to the first situation, 'un proyecto andrógino, a nivel actancial, temático o estructural'. Works such as Alicia Giménez Barlett's *Diario de un camionero* belong to the second situation, 'un correctivo implícito a una moral o psíquica distorcionadas', while novels such as Guirao's *Admirables adversarios* fit into the third situation, 'una sexualización del campo de visión obtenida desde la perspectiva contraria'. Finally, creative works such as Elena Quiroga's *La careta*, Ana María Matute's *Fiesta al Noroeste*, Martín Gaite's *Ritmo lento*, Moix's *Walter, ¿por qué te fuiste?*, Ortiz's *Luz de la memoria*, Soledad Puértolas's *Todos mienten*, Rosa Montero's *Amado Amo*, Pilar Nasarre's *El país de nunca jamás*, Guirao's *Mi querido Sebastian*, and Belén Gópegui's *La escala de los mapas* correspond to the last situation, 'un acercamiento o identificación con una perspectiva alienada cuya disociación refleja la de una ideología o sistema cultural opresivos'.

D. Ingenschay, 'Homotextualidad: imágenes homosexuales en la novela española contemporánea', *Antipodas*, 11–12:49–68, after considering general issues such as the present state of gay, lesbian, and queer studies, an approach to gay literature through Barthes and Foucault, and the situation of gay studies in Spain, discusses homosexual images in Spanish novels such as Manuel Vázquez Montalbán's *Los alegres muchachos de Atzavara*, Lluís Todó's *El juego del mentiroso*, Luis Antonio de Villena's *Fuera del mundo*, Terenci Moix's *Garras de astracán*, Juan José Millás's *Letra muerta*, Molina Foix's *La comunicación de los atletas*, Alvaro Pombo's *Los delitos insignificantes*, Mendicutti's *Los novios búlgaros*, Vicente García Cervera's *Saguia-el-Hambra — Tánger*, and José Ángel Mañas's *Historias del Kronen*, and claims both that these images 'no permiten una conclusión definitiva, dado que dentro de los grupos representados se comprueba una constitución bastante dispersa de los "tipos" representados', and that, although these images seem associated with the changes of Spanish society since 1975, and depend on possible discursive realizations, they do not offer 'un reflejo verdadero de la realidad'. S. Fouz-Hernández, '¿Generación X? Spanish urban youth culture at the end of the century in Mañas's and Armendáriz's *Historias del Kronen'*, *RoS*, 18:83–98, examines how the generational characteristics proposed by Douglas Coupland in his 1991 publication *Generation X, Tales for an Accelerated Culture* apply to the youths represented in M.'s novel (1994) and A.'s film adaptation (1995), and claims that it is not appropriate to include the characters of *Kronen* (in its two versions) within the 'X' label, despite some coincidences found between them and the mythical X-ers and 'Global Youths' of the Coupland novels. In the critic's view, although both the novel and the film *Kronen* demonstrate the extent to which the X-ers' global label is a construction, the term 'X' itself works and 'becomes a way of avoiding the labelling of a generation, since it includes all its possible variables in age (a 20-year range), background or origin'.

INDIVIDUAL AUTHORS

CHACEL. C. Janés, 'Rosa Chacel y la libertad', *Salina*, 14:151–58, discusses the theme of freedom as a capacity to preserve open possibilities in C.'s *Estación, Ida y vuelta, Desde el amanecer, La Sinrazón, La confesión, Saturnal, Memorias de Leticia del Valle*, and *Alcancía. Estación termini*. E. Rosales, '*Memorias de Leticia Valle*: Rosa Chacel o el deletreo de lo inaudito', *His(US)*, 83:222–31, claims that the narrative strategy of this novel is based on the relationship it establishes between two meanings of the word 'inaudito': a new meaning, 'lo inaudito por cotidiano, lo que de tanto sonar ya *no se oye* y pasa inadvertido', and a commonly accepted meaning, 'lo inaudito por extraordinario: *lo que nunca se ha oído*'. According to R.: 'Lo impronunciable, lo inconcebible se gesta en el día a día detallado de su protagonista.'

DÍAZ-MAS. M. A. Rey López, '*El sueño de Venecia*, de Paloma Díaz-Mas: reflexiones sobre la historiografía', *LF*, 26:185–92, argues that, through the investigation of the process of narrating a history, this novel incorporates a metadiscursive reflection that at the same time implies a review of the mechanisms and omissions of History.

ESPINOSA. J. I. Moraza, 'La homofobia en el discurso del honor en *Tríbada: Theologiae Tractatus*, de Miguel Espinosa', *Antípodas*, 11–12:143–58, shows how, in this novel, the author agrees with and reproduces certain views and discursive devices of the established power that he himself wanted to condemn in both this novel and a previous one, *La fea burguesía*. In M.'s words, 'A pesar de atacar el orden burgués, su censura de numerosas actitudes se llava a cabo apelando precisamente a un orden basado en valores intemporales, y que, en última instancia, reproduce el discurso religioso-moralizante del franquismo.'

ETXEBARRIA. C. de Urioste, 'Las novelas de Lucía Etxebarria como proyección de sexualidades disidentes en la España democrática', *REH*, 34:123–38, analyses the different sexual practices featured in the two novels written by this author to date: *Amor, curiosidad, prozac y dudas* (1997) and *Beatriz y los cuerpos celestes* (1998).

FALCÓN. I. Velez, 'Luchando contra el olvido: literatura y feminismo en la vida y obra de Lidia Falcón', *BHS(L)*, 77:65–76, is an interview with F. on questions such as the advances of feminism in recent years, the impact, besides that of opening up the canon, of feminist criticism, the idea of a feminist project shared by Latin America and Spain, the support she gets from Spanish universities, the influences on her from female writers in her family, the relationship between being a woman and writing autobiographical texts, the state of mind of her characters in *Postmodernos*, the validity of the interpretations by foreigners of Spanish writings, the creation of a 'feminine language' in Spanish literature, the future of feminist literature in Spain, and her goals if she could participate in the creation of a feminist European party.

FERNÁNDEZ CUBAS. J. A. Folkart, 'Interpretations of gender: performing subjectivity in Cristina Fernández Cubas's *Los altillos de Brumal*', *ALEC*, 25:383–416, argues that, instead of privileging the feminine over the masculine as a paradigm of agency, as some critics suggest, F.C.'s short stories 'blend "masculine" order with "feminine" fluidity, in an alteration of the stakes of power'.

GOYTISOLO. A. Ribeiro de Menezes, 'En el principio de la literatura está el mito': reading Cervantes through Juan Goytisolo's *Reivindicación del Conde don Julián* and *Juan sin tierra*', *BHS(L)*, 77:585–600, in essence contends that, in these novels, 'Goytisolo has established a textual dialogue with Cervantes similar to that which Cervantes conducted with his own literary predecessors'.

JARNÉS. J. J. Lanz, 'La novelística de Benjamín Jarnés en el primer exilio: hacia la novia del viento', *BH*, 102:133–68, tries to rescue from critical oblivion J.'s writings during his exile by opening a way to their examination *via* the detailed analysis of *La novia del viento*, his first novel published during his Mexican exile in 1940, which, so claims L., 'marks an axis between his so-called "dehumanized" writings before the civil war and his exile production, drawing a continous line with the short stories written during the war'.

LANDERO. J. B. Margenot III, 'Musical subtexts and parody in *Caballeros de fortuna*', *Ojáncano*, 18:41–60, offers a reading of this novel based on the premise that the ludic character 'stems from the parodic treatment of inherited texts', and brings into focus music's central role in relation to the novel, concluding that the strategy of an operatic framework, through which the novel reveals how other frames operate, 'creates a greater awareness among readers regarding the manipulation of narrative conventions'.

MARSÉ. J. Belmonte Serrano, '*El embrujo de Shanghai*: regreso de las sombras tabernarias', *Ojáncano*, 18:3–23, studies this work in the context of M.'s development as a novelist, establishing clever parallelisms between *El embrujo* and earlier and later publications such as *El amante bilingüe*, *Ronda del Guinardó*, *Un día volveré*, *Últimas tardes con Teresa*, *Si te dicen que caí*, and *La muchacha de las bragas de oro*.

A. Lee Six, 'Blind woman's buff: optical illusions of feminist progress in Juan Marsé, *El amante bilingüe*', *JILAS*, 6: 29–42, uses a sophisticated theoretical foundation to achieve her goals of showing how this novel (1990) and a previous one by this author, *La oscura historia de la prima Montse* (1970), share the same underlying idea, indicating the key differences that make this single idea have a tragic outcome in the former and a comic resolution in the latter, and analyzing the implications of this change of outcome from a feminist viewpoint.

MARTÍN GAITE. J. Jurado Morales, 'De vida y literatura existencial: *Lo raro es vivir* (1996)', *ECon*, 13 : 37–56, finds an existential approach to narrative elements of this novel such as the treatment of time and space, the themes of dialogues, the titles of the novel and its chapters, and the configuration of the protagonist, and claims that this approach proceeds mainly from the vital inclinations of the author.

MARTÍN SANTOS. E. Fernández, 'La fractura del espacio urbano: el Madrid galdosiano en *Tiempo de silencio*', *AG*, 35 : 53–64, argues that, although both writers use Madrid in the same manner (as a game board in which characters' movements serve to distinguish them), they present a different Madrid: Pérez Galdós offers 'una ciudadela intramuros en continua fase de expansión inclusiva', while Martín Santos proposes a city in which 'el concepto mismo de ciudad se ha fragmentado'.

MOIX. J. Mari, 'La astronomía de la pasión: espectadores y estrellas en *El día que murió Marilyn* de Terenci Moix', *MLN*, 115 : 224–47, shows how movies, their peculiarities and stars, as well as other aspects related to them, are used by this novel's narrators as constant referents in their process of reconstructing a personal and collective history.

MONTERO. A. E. Hardcastle, 'Postmodern fantasy and Montero's *Temblor*: the quest for meaning', *ALEC*, 25 : 417–38, examines this novel as example of an emerging current called 'postmodern fantasy' which includes works that 'combine the conventions of fantasy fiction with the destabilization of reality seen in postmodern texts to create a provocative and entertaining hybrid form'.

MUÑOZ MOLINA. T. R. Franz, 'Jazz specifics and the characterization and structure of *El invierno en Lisboa*', *REH*, 34 : 157–64, aims to discover the artistic effect of the 'limited but extremely insistent specifics' of the jazz atmosphere painted in this novel. E. T. Gurski, 'Antonio Muñoz Molina and Jorge Luis Borges: buried intertextualities in *Beatus Ille*', *BHS(G)*, 77 : 343–57, focuses on themes of this novel (such as the ambiguity and unintelligibility of reality and the erasure of borders between fiction and reality) that also appear in many

Borges stories, and discusses some of the narrative techniques that M.M. employs to develop them.

PRADO. A. Percival, 'Playing games of identity: Benjamín Prado's *Alguien se acerca*', *RoQ*, 47:205–14, argues that this novel, in which 'primacy is given to self-conscious discourse, ludic effects, and the use of metafiction, parody, and intertextuality', can be included in Bonmatí's category of quest novel because it is 'obsessively concerned with identity'.

PUÉRTOLAS. F. H. Blackwell, 'Conventions of detective fiction and their subversion in "A través de las ondas" and *Queda la noche* de Soledad Puértolas', *LF*, 26:171–84, contends that both P.'s poem and novel utilize conventions of detective fiction that cause readers to establish certain expectations, which P. then frustrates, since ' "solving the case" does nothing to bring justice or a fairer social order'.

TORRENTE BALLESTER. D. Knickerbocker, 'Technology, nature, and dehumanisation in Gonzalo Torrente Ballester's *Quizá nos lleve el viento al infinito*', *ALEC*, 25:147–70, explores T.B.'s 'use of characters and conventions taken from Ian Fleming's James Bond novels, his utilization of elements of the science fiction genre [. . .], the presence of several icons of the Hollywood film industry, and the work's intertextual dialogue with its apparent source of inspiration, nineteenth-century French author Philippe-August Villiers de L'Isle-Adam's novel *L'Eve future*', and claims that, through these elements, T.B. 'probes the problematic relationship between nature, human identity, and technology'.

TUSQUETS. I. Pertusa, '*El mismo mar de todos los veranos* y el poder subversivo de la confesión', *Antipodas*, 11–12:125–42, uses the figure of the closet proposed by Eve Kosofsky Sedwick to argue that this novel can be read as an attempt to leave the closed space created by the secret surrounding lesbian relationships. The protagonist uses confession mechanisms — the control tool employed by heterosexual discourse — to weaken the power of social order on lesbian subjects, and thereby debilitate such a discourse.

UMBRAL. C. X. Ardavín Trabanco, '*A la sombra de las muchachas rojas* de Francisco Umbral: memoria simultánea, reescritura y esperpentización de la transición política', *REH*, 34:139–56, points out this novel's affinity with journalism, explaining that it is based on 'simultaneous memory' and constitutes the formal characteristic of U.'s approximation to the transition theme. According to A.T., the 'técnica esperpéntica', a reactualization of the most demystifying Valle-Inclán, is also an important feature of the novel, and 'refuerza la concepción guerracivilista de la historia española en general y de la transición política en particular'. Id., 'Poética de la memoria:

novela, historia y política en Francisco Umbral', *RHM*, 53:153–61, discusses novels such as *A la sombra de las muchachas rojas*, *Los helechos arborescentes*, *Madrid 1940*, *Capital del dolor*, and *Las señoritas de Aviñón*, and argues that, rather than memories of a 'notarial' type, U. cultivates a genre that could be labelled 'memorias *imaginativas*' because the origin of these memories is a historical reality reinvented during the writing process. In the critic's opinion: 'Este fenómeno tiene como resultado un trasvase genérico que desdibuja las fronteras entre novela y memoria, llegando en ocasiones a ser poco menos que idénticas.'

VÁZQUEZ MONTALBÁN. M. Santana, 'Manuel Vázquez Montalbán's *Los mares del Sur* and the incrimination of the Spanish transition', *REH*, 34:535–60, explores the question of the generic and modal nature of Spanish crime fiction (its status as 'realist' detective stories), suggesting that the novels of transition by Montalbán and other writers of the *novela negra* present two fundamental claims: first, that the proper space of the novels is 'a self proclaimed democratic city whose apparent order is to be read with the same suspicions as the old city of the dictatorship' and second, 'that in order to comprehend the extent and limitations of democratic political change it is necessary to investigate both the present and the past'.

ZÚÑIGA. L. B. Almería, 'Las estéticas de Juan Eduardo Zúñiga', *ALEC*, 25:357–88, studies this author's work, with a focus on the aesthetic rather than the historical aspects of his short stories, and suggests that more critical attention should be devoted to his contributions to this genre.

2. POETRY

GENERAL

A. Iravedra, 'Antonio Machado y la "generación poética de 1970"', *Salina*, 14:169–82, argues that the first *novísimos*'s reaction against M.'s poetry, a model for the preceding generation, constitutes only one of the orientations of the diverse 'generación de los 70'. I. reviews the successive phases and different profiles that M.'s reception experienced during this period in poets such as Pere Gimferrer, Guillermo Carnero, José Ángel Valente, Joaquín Marco, José Infante, Antonio Colinas, Augustín Delgado, Luis Mateo Díez, Ángel Fierro, José Antonio Llamas, Diego Jesús Jiménez, Antonio Hernández, Lázaro Santana, Juan Luis Panero, Alfonso López Gradolí, Justo Jorge Padrón, Antonio Martínez Sarrión, Luis Antonio de Villena, Miguel D'Ors, and Antonio Carvajal, and concludes that this generation's initial negation of M.'s model 'fue con el tiempo y por muchos de los propios protagonistas rectificada, denunciada su injusticia y reconocidas las motivaciones extraestéticas de la maniobra negadora'. T. Escaja, 'On angels and androids: Spanish/American women poets facing centuries' end', *Hispanófila*, 130:91–104, analyses poetry by Delmira Agustini, Ana Rossetti, and Silvia Guerra, and proposes that 'by revisiting their traditional role as angels, women writers at the turn of the 19th c. and at the end of the current millennium are ultimately seeking the right not just to be the image, the servile creature, but to impose their gaze, the right to create and to (re)formulate the Word'. Of particular interest here is the section 'On the gender of angels: Ana Rossetti's Devotions' (96–99), in which E. concentrates on R.'s *Devocionario*. M. Jato, 'Exilio interior e identidad nacional: el concepto de *matria* en la poesía de Carmen Conde, Anguela Figuera y Angelina Gatell', *HPR*, 2:35–50, shows that, through an anti-bellicose maternity, these authors' poetry manifests an effort to transform the space of violence and death commonly called 'patria' into a space of peace and fraternity. B. Ciplijauskaité, 'Criatura frente a la creación', *Salina*, 14:159–68, focuses on several poetic modalities such as 'el/la poeta frente a la naturaleza, frente a la creación por el hombre (ciudad, obra de arte) y a su desintegración (la ruina), frente a la nada' to call attention to what seems to be a return to a contemplative and even mystic attitude in some recent poetic works by Antonio Colinas, María Sanz, Guillermo Carnero, Alejandro Duque Amusco, Antonio Enrique, and Concha Zardoya. J. J. Lanz, 'La ruptura poética del 68: la idea de ruptura con la poesía anterior como justificación de las antologías con carácter generacional', *BHS(L)*, 77:239–62, is an enlightening study that defends the idea of its title through the analysis of anthologies such as J. M. Castellet's *Nueve novísimos*, Enrique Martín Pardo's *Antología de la nueva poesía española*, José Luis García Martín's *Treinta años de poesía española*, and J. J. Lanz's *Antología de la poesía española 1960–1975*.

INDIVIDUAL AUTHORS

BIEDMA. J. Mayhew, ' "At last the secret is out" : re-reading Jaime Gil de Biedma', *Antípodas*, 11–12:69–78, is a striking study that uses poems such as 'Pandémica y Celeste' and B.'s translation of Auden's 'At last the secret is out' to show how B.'s poetry addresses 'two audiences simultaneously, offering one message for the putatively heterosexual general public and another for more "specialized" readers who are attuned to the nuances of a specifically gay writing'. According to M., only the latter will know how to read B.'s work as a 'closeted work', as one 'that paradoxically *makes visible* the very act of concealing its homosexuality'.

BRINES. J. Mayhew, 'Francisco Brines and the Humanist closet', *RHM*, 53:140–52, reads this author's poetry as a product of a specifically gay sensibility, and convincingly claims that his existentialist universalism is partial and incomplete since his view of the subject is ultimately defined and limited by his androcentric vision of humanity and by his understanding of sexuality as something at odds with the heterosexual norm. J. Andújar Almansa, 'Una biografía poética: sobre *Poesía Completa* de Francisco Brines', *ALEC*, 25:13–62, offers a standard humanist interpretation that stresses what B. shares with all other human beings — 'alguien a través de cuya vida [. . .] quedan expresadas las experiencias fundamentales de la vida de todos los hombres' — and thefore gets caught in the trap exposed by Mayhew in the preceding article.

CERNUDA. S. Faber, ' "El norte nos devora": La construcción de un espacio hispánico en el exilio anglosajón de Luis Cernuda', *His(US)*, 83:733–44, intelligently argues that a patriotic pride and an imperial nostalgia predominate in C.'s poems about Spain, despite the fact that at first sight the poet seems to maintain an ambivalent attitude towards both the exile environment and the lost land. F. finds in these poems a nationalistic ideology that allows for the construction of an idealized Hispanic space: one governed by the spiritual values of the 'España eterna' with which the poet identifies himself, while preserving, however, some ironic consciousness of 'las contradicciones inherentes a su propia cosmovisión idealista'.

CUENCA. J. J. Lanz, 'En la biblioteca de Babel: algunos aspectos de intertextualidad en la poesía última de Luis Alberto de Cuenca', *RHM*, 53:242–68, discusses several of C.'s books of poetry, in particular the latest *El hacha y la rosa* and *Por fuertes y fronteras*, within the context of the differences between modern intertextual practices, *imitatio*, medieval parody, pastiche, and interdiscoursive practices, and claims that C.'s intertextality, like Magritte's *Elogio de la dialéctica*, 'nos permite percibir, a través del texto, otros textos, que no se anulan mutuamente sino que se integran sintéticamente en una dimensión infinita que nos facilita un viaje eterno, en el que el sistema literario se alimenta a sí mismo y por el que el lector se integra en él, como en un laberinto micénico, sin posibilidad de salida'.

FIGUERA AYMERICH. J. Robbins, 'La mujer en el umbral. La simbología de la madre en la poesía de Ángela Figuera', *ALEC*, 25:557–86, examines the image of the mother and its implications in this author's social poetry.

FUERTES. D. K. Benson, 'La voz inconfundible de Gloria Fuertes, 1918–1998: poesía temprana', *His(US)*, 83:210–21, is a well-documented study that highlights the most original aspects of Fuertes's earlier poems and demonstrates that these creations 'no sólo empleaban la poliglosia, la intertextualidad, lo "irracional" y el conceptismo como su poesía subsiguiente (Browne), sino que consistentemente los combinaba en *un solo texto* con hablantes y propósitos enteramente suyos'. M. L. Cooks, 'The humanization of poetry: an appraisal of Gloria Fuertes', *His(US)*, 83:428–36, considers the author in the context of her relationship to peninsular poets of her generation and the audience that she creates in order to reveal the way in which she achieves her goal of humanizing poetry. In C.'s view, F. puts 'the emotions of ordinary persons at the center of her poetry' and uses 'their everyday language as the mythical vehicle of poetic discourse'.

MORENO. M. Mudrovic, 'La "poesía de la experiencia" rediviva: empatía y juicio, vida y arte en *Cuaderno de campo* de Luis Javier Moreno', *HPR*, 2:7–34, explains the concept of 'poesía de la experiencia' and applies it to two poems of this work: 'Horacio' and 'Fenómeno a observar'.

PACHECO. R. J. Friis, 'The postmodern twist of José Emilio Pacheco's *No me preguntes cómo pasa el tiempo*', *REH*, 34:27–46, argues that this collection of poetry published in 1969 begins a phase of transition for the author who 'carries out a characteristically modern search for origins within a decidedly postmodern context', one that features a blend of new modes such as protest against misguided power, use and abuse of *culteralismo*, allusions to *modernismo*, criticism of imperialism and capitalism, exploration of the limits of translation and kitsch, and some doses of humour, in addition to decentred subjects, intertextuality, and disruption of hierarchies between high and popular art.

RODRÍGUEZ GARCÍA. C. Bousoño, 'Claudio Rodriguez García (1934–1999)', *BRAE*, 279:15–26, does homage to this author, one of the leaders of the 'generación poética de los cincuenta', who has recently passed away, by discussing the originality of his poetry collections *Don de la ebriedad, Conjuros, Alianza y condena*, and *El vuelo de la celebración*.

ROSSETTI. T. Escaja, ' "Muerte de los primogénitos": Ana Rossetti y la estética del SIDA', *RHM*, 53:229–41, studies this poem dedicated to friends of the author, 'Juan y José', both victims of AIDS, in the context of Susan Sontag's *AIDS and its Metaphors* in order to highlight the images of apocalypse and AIDS that denounce the imminence and reality of a fact: 'la muerte de las víctimas del SIDA'. J. Robbins, 'Seduction, simulation, transgression and taboo: eroticism in the work of Ana Rossetti', *Hispanófila*, 128:49–66, visits once again the theme of eroticism in R.'s poetry.

RUBIO. C. Ferradáns, 'Articulaciones urbanas en el discurso poético de Fanny Rubio', *Hispanófila*, 128:37–48, argues that her poetry of the 1980s in the tradition of Gloria Fuertes leans towards popular forms, while *Dresde* (1990), in the modern tradition, has a tendency to cultivated forms, and that 'El hilo conductor del discurso poético de Fanni Rubio es la ciudad como lugar donde confluyen estos elementos dispares, el espacio intermedio entre el yo y el mundo, el sitio donde se construye — se teje — el texto'.

SÁNCHEZ ROBAYNA. L. López Fernández, 'El esencialismo en la poesía de Andrés Sánchez Robayna', *ALEC*, 25:171–92, suggests a parallelism between the essentialism of this author and that of José Ángel Valente, Jaime Siles, and Pere Gimferrer, pointing out that, like them, S.R. meditates on being, language, and the world, although, in S.R., 'esta estructura tripartita se funde en una misma dicción que desemboca en lo insular como experiencia consagrada a los límites, es decir, lo insular deviene espacio de exilio, la escritura se convierte en excritura y cualquier intento de definición de un sujeto poético se disemina en la constante reescritura de cada texto.'

3. DRAMA

GENERAL

M. F. Vilches de Frutos, 'La temporada teatral 1997–1998', *ALEC*, 25:961–1024, again provides an excellent panoramic view, including the performances of Spanish works (from the Classics to the postwar period) and foreign works in the areas of Madrid, Catalonia, and the autonomous communities. J. E. Checa Puerta, '1998–1999: últimas ediciones de textos teatrales españoles en lengua castellana', *ib.*, 673–98, analyses recent editions of dramatic texts, observing the presence of Classics such as Valle-Inclán, García Lorca, Buero Vallejo, Arrabal, and Gala, dramatists who were successful during the 1980s, women playwrights, historical theatre, and sophisticated introductions composed by academics and critics, while finding, at the same time, an unjustifiable absence of complete works by established authors. R. X. Roselló, 'De la ficción teatral a la interacción escénica o qué enseñar para el análisis del teatro', *Gestos*, 29:9–24, is a reflection about the dramatic event divided into three parts. The first part deals with several conceptions of theatre: 'teatro como arte del espectáculo', 'como discurso de ficción', 'como mostración de una historia', 'como discurso sobre el mundo y como metadiscurso'. The second part focuses on stage interaction as a perspective of analysis, the relationship between the public and a representation, and a work's effect on spectators. The last part extends these points to the study of dramatic writings. K. Spang, 'Muérete ¡y verás!: cómo nace una figura dramática', *ib.*, 25–38, studies the manner in which dramatic figures are created. R. Knowles,

'Making meaning in the late-capitalist cultural economy of the international theater festival', *ib.*, 39–55, takes up several questions related to international festivals, among them, 'the question of how, and in what ways, the recontextualizing involved in remounting productions at international festivals that emerged from particular cultural contexts or where designed for specific local audiences changes the cultural work that they perform and the ways in which they are read'. E. Rozik, 'Is the notion of "theatricality" void?', *ib.*, 30 : 11–30, is a theoretical essay that discusses recent approaches to 'theatricality' and suggests a revised one that both 'reconnects it to "theatre"' and leads to a definition that narrows down the meaning of this notion.

M. Huguet-Jerez, 'Entrevista con dos dramaturgas de la Generación Bradomín: Yolanda Pallín e Itziar Pascual. ¡Larga vida al galardón!', *Estreno*, 26.1 : 5–9, explains the term 'Generación Bradomín' as the name given since 1985 to a group of dramatists such as Sergi Belbel, Daniela Fejerman, Margarita Sánchez, Carmen Delgado, Yolanda Pallín, Eva Hibernia, and Itziar Pascual, who won the Marqués de Bradomín theatre prize designated for young writers under the age of 30, and then reproduces an interview with Pallín and Pascual on both the award itself and the personal style of each author. H.J.'s interview is followed by two commentaries on Pascual's theatre by P. Zatlin, *ib.*, 10–14, and one commentary by V. Serrano on Pallín's *Luna de Miel*, *ib.*, 22–23. H. Cazorla, 'La mujer como terrorista en dos dramas de Luis Riaza y Lourdes Ortiz: *La emperatriz de los helados* y *Yudita*', *ib.*, 26.2 : 26–31, after establishing the effort to reveal the motivations of terrorism and urban violence as a characteristic of several works of the 1980s and 1990s such as Buero Vallejo's *Jueces en la noche*, Sastre's *Análisis expectral de un comando al servicio de la revolución proletaria*, Cabal's *Ello dispara*, Pallín's *Lista negra*, Pedrero's *Cachorros de negro mirar*, and del Moral's *Rey negro*, analyses the two plays mentioned in the title and claims that, although they notably coincide in their argument and dramatic structure, they differ in their treatment of the same female figure (a terrorist who experiences interior conflicts when faced with pressures imposed by her terrorist group).

INDIVIDUAL AUTHORS

BUERO VALLEJO.   P. W. O'Connor, 'Buero o la sabiduría bondadosa: reflexiones desde la madurez', *Estreno*, 26.1 : 43–5, is an interview with this influential dramatist on personal rather than professional questions such as his plans and resolutions about the thorny issues he has been investigating both inside and outside the theatre, positive and negative coincidences that made an impact on his life, his moral standards, his dreams of being a painter, his aspiration of achieving a 'stereoscopic effect' in his paintings (an effect similar to the one reached by the protagonist of his latest play, *Misión al pueblo desierto*), his small human pleasures, his imperfections, his wishes for a more complete and moral democracy, his projects for the future, his advice to young playwrights, the professional contributions that make him feel proud, and the works by which he wants to be remembered. L. M. Anson, 'Antonio Buero Vallejo (1916–2000)', *BRAE*, 279:169–75, reflects after his death on this author's life and work.

MARTÍN RECUERDA. R. Lima, 'Homenaje a José Martín Recuerda y memorias de una colaboración a distancia', *Estreno*, 26.2:5–7, reproduces the words about this dramatist and his play *Las arrecogías del beaterio de Santa María Egipciaca* originally pronounced by R.L., the translator of the play into English, in a homage to M.R. celebrated in Granada and other Andalusian cities during the first week of November, 1999.

MAYORGA. J. P. Gabriele, 'Juan Mayorga: una voz del teatro español actual', *Estreno*, 26.2:8–11, is an interview with this author on questions such as mounting a production of *Cartas de amor a Stalin* in Teatro María Guerrero, last year's interruption of *El jardín quemado*'s first performance, the formal function of history and art in plays such as *Cartas de amor a Stalin, Siete hombres buenos, El sueño de Ginebra, El jardín quemado*, and *El hombre de oro*, the issues presupposed by his work in El Astillero, his participation in productions of his plays when others direct them, the influences upon him, the apparent contradiction between the familiar and the magical inherent in plays such as *Siete hombres buenos, El sueño de Ginebra, El jardín quemado*, and *Concierto fatal de la viuda Kolakowski*, the lack of interior contextual logic and exterior linear narrative in plays such as *El traductor de Blumemberg* and *Más ceniza*, the process he adopts when writing a play, the precise definition of his theatre, and his contribution to the theatre of the end of the 20th c. and the beginning of this one, followed by G.'s 'Postmodern rhetoric in three plays by Juan Mayorca', *ib.*, 12–14, in which this critic discusses the postmodern attributes of *Amarillo, Brgs*, and *La Mala imagen*. See also Id., 'Entrevista con Juan Mayorga', *ALEC*, 25:95–104.

NIEVA. K. Aggor, 'Francisco Nieva, postmodern playwright', *HR*, 68:429–52, studies N.'s theatre and dramatic theory in order to establish him as a postmodern dramatist (one who has bridged the gap between avant-gardism and post-modernism) and to redefine, at the same time, the existing historical frontiers of postmodern Spanish theatre. N.'s plays considered in this study are: *El combate de Ópalos y Tasia, El rayo colgado, Nosferatu, El fandango asombroso, Tórtolas, crepúsculo y telón, Caperucita y el otro, El maravilloso catarro de Lord Bashaville, La carroza de plomo candente*, *Coronada y el toro*, *El baile de los ardientes o poderoso cabriconde*, *Pelo de tormenta*, *Te quiero, zorra*, *No es verdad*, and the series of mini-plays collectively entitled *Centón de Teatro*. A. D. Hitchcock, 'The artist through the looking-glass: Francisco Nieva's *Salvator Rosa*', *Estreno*, 26.1 : 38–45, argues that N. engages the concept of mirroring more in this play than in others, 'offering up doubles or foils for most of the characters and championing the notion of reality as subjectively constructed'.

ORTIZ. D. Cavallaro, 'Playing with tradition and transgression: Lourdes Ortiz's *Fedra*', *Estreno*, 26.2 : 21–25, shows how O. makes ironic use of works by Euripides (*Hippolytus* is this play's main reference), Seneca, D'Annunzio, Racine, and Unamuno.

PALLÍN. B. Foley Buedel, 'Defining identity through storytelling and improvisation in Yolanda Pallín's *Los motivos de Anselmo Fuentes*', *Estreno*, 26.1 : 33–7, aims to demonstrate that this piece, with which P. earned the prestigious Calderón de la Barca prize, 'raises complex questions about identity, language, and the difficulty of defining and determining motives', and that 'the recurring motif of jazz with its poetics of improvisation is central to our understanding of the enigmatic protagonist'.

IV. CATALAN STUDIES

LANGUAGE

POSTPONED

MEDIEVAL LITERATURE

By LOLA BADIA, *Professor of Catalan Literature at the Universitat de Girona* and MIRIAM CABRÉ, *Researcher at the Universitat de Girona*

1. GENERAL

BIBLIOGRAPHY AND HISTORICAL BACKGROUND. *BBAHLM*, 13:5–73, provides an annotated list of studies on medieval Catalan in 1999. *Identitat i territori. Textos geogràfics del Renaixement*, ed. A. Alcoberro, Barcelona U.P. — Vic, Eumo, 237 pp., gathers notions on Catalan identity from writers such as Margarit, Pau, and Beuter. D. de Courcelles, 'Ramon Martí, Ramon Llull, Abraham Aboulafia: de Montpellier à Barcelone. Recherche sur l'élaboration des définitions culturelles et la traversée des frontières', Camps, *Languedoc*, 145–59, analyses these three figures, as well as Ramon de Penyafort, as catalysts for the circulation of Jewish, Christian, and Islamic cultures. See also C. Heusch, 'De Lérida a Barcelone. Universités et État en Catalogne à la fin du Moyen Âge', *ib.*, 161–77, on the political agenda behind the foundation of the University of Lleida.

ARCHIVAL RESEARCH AND READERSHIP. Maria Barceló and Gabriel Ensenyat, *Els nous horitzons culturals a Mallorca al final de l'Edat Mitjana*, Palma, Documenta Balear, 224 pp., draw a cultural picture of 15th-c. Majorca based on archival documents about the Valentí family, with a prologue by J. N. Hillgarth. I. Baiges Jardí, 'Els manuscrits de la Catedral de Tortosa en un inventari de 1420', *AEM*, 29, 1999:3–20, analyses the origins of the Tortosa MS holdings. Jesús Alturo Perucho, *El llibre manuscrit a Catalunya, orígens i esplendor*, B, Generalitat de Catalunya, 289 pp., surveys medieval Catalan MS production and provides colour plates. Two studies have been published on King Pere el Cerimoniós: F. M. Gimeno Blay, 'Remarques diplomàtiques al voltant del document de creació de la Biblioteca Reial de Poblet (Poblet, 20 d'agost de 1380)', *AEM*, 29, 1999:335–49, analyses the donation of the king's library to Poblet abbey; and his 'Escribir, leer y reinar. La experiencia gráfico-textual de Pedro IV el Ceremonioso (1336–1387)', *Scrittura e Civiltà*, 21, 1998:119–233, deals with the king's graphic habits. Both J. Hernando, 'El libro, instrumento de cultura y objeto económico.

Pere Sala, escribano real (siglo xv)', *AEM*, 29, 1999:409–29; and L. Cifuentes, 'La promoció intel·lectual i social dels barbers-cirurgians a la Barcelona medieval: l'obrador, la biblioteca i els béns de Joan Vicenç', *ATCA*, 19:429–79, draw conclusions from data contained in wills about education and the production and circulation of books. José García Oro Marín and María José Portela Silva, *La monarquía y los libros en el Siglo de Oro*, Alcalá U.P., 1999, 495 pp., edit and study documents concerning 15th-c. books and libraries.

2. LYRIC AND NARRATIVE VERSE

AUSIÀS MARCH

A.-J. Soberanas and N. Espinàs have produced a revised edition of A. March, *Poesies*, ed. Pere Bohigas (ENC, B.19), 601 pp., with an updated bibliography. Jesús Villalmanzo, *Ausiàs March. Colección documental*, V, Institució Alfons el Magnànim — Diputació de València, 1999, 510 pp., adds some new documents about the M. family. L. Cabré, 'El palau de la poesia abans d'Ausiàs March' (37–44), on M.'s poetic background, is included in the exhibition catalogue *El gust d'Ausiàs March*, ed. Josep A. Gisbert, Gandia, Ajuntament de Gandia — CEIC Alfons el Vell, 1999. Two more collective volumes are wholly dedicated to M.: *Ausiàs March (1400–1459). Premier poète en langue catalane*, ed. Georges Martin et al., Paris, Klincksieck, 411 pp.; and *Ausiàs March y las literaturas de su época*, ed. Lourdes Sánchez Rodrigo and Enrique J. Nogueras Valdivieso, Granada U.P., 165 pp. P. Vila, 'Una religiosa clarissa de Vic, lectora del *Cant espiritual* d'Ausiàs March (1570)', *RCat*, 150:133–41, presents a new witness of M.'s readership. Xavier Dilla, *En passats escrits. Una lectura de la poesia d'Ausiàs March*, B, Empúries, 304 pp., polemically presents M.'s works as deriving from an author songbook. A. Espadaler, 'La recepció d'Ausiàs March a la Renaixença', *Reduccions*, 72:25–43, reviews M.'s reception by 19th-c. intellectuals.

OTHER LYRICAL AND NARRATIVE POETRY

S. Asperti, 'I trovatori e la Corona d'Aragona. Riflessioni per una cronologia di riferimento', *Mot, so, razó*, 1, 1999:12–31, reviews the patronage of troubadours in the Aragonese royal court. A. Espadaler, 'El final del *Jaufré* i, novament, Cerverí de Girona', *BRABLB*, 47:321–34, dates this narrative poem to the final period of King Jaume I's reign; and C. Lee, 'L'elogio del re d'Aragona nel *Jaufre*', *AHLM 8*, 1051–60, confirms King Jaume's court as the context to set the poem. *RIALC, Repertorio informatizzato dell'antica letteratura catalana. La poesia* <www.rialc.unina.it> offers the whole corpus of 14th- and

15th-c. Catalan poetry. *Cançoner Aguiló*, ed. Gabriel Ensenyat et al., Palma, Societat Arqueològica Lul·liana, 503 pp., is a facsimile with edition of one of the main MSS for medieval Catalan poetry. Two articles by V. Beltran deal with compilation of Iberian MSS: 'Tipología y génesis de los cancioneros. La organización de los materiales', Beltran, *Poesía*, 9–54, and 'Tipologia i gènesi dels cançoners. La reordenació de *J* i *K*', *LlLi*, 11 : 355–95, which pays specific attention to two Catalan songbooks. J. Parramon, 'Els apèndixs del cançoner Vega-Aguiló', *BRABLB*, 47 : 383–404, edits five poems from the songbook. On love poetry and debate genres: R. Archer, 'Las coplas "de las calidades de las donas" de Pere Torroella y la tradición lírica catalana', *ib.*, 405–23; R. Cantavella, 'The Catalan medieval *Demandes d'amor*', *HRJ*, 1 : 27–42; and I. de Riquer, 'La "mala cansó", source occitane du maldit catalan', Camps, *Languedoc*, 17–37. C. Di Girolamo and D. Siviero, 'D'Orange a Beniarjó (passant per Florència). Una interpretació dels *estramps* catalans', *RECat*, 2, 1999 : 81–95, suggest Occitan and Italian connections for the *estramps*. A. Fratta, 'Per una rilettura di *Jus lo front* di Jordi de Sant Jordi', *ER*, 22 : 177–95, also attributes Italian debts to Sant Jordi's *estramps*. F. García-Oliver and V. G. Labrado, 'L'entorn familiar de Jordi de Sant Jordi', *Afers*, 35 : 220–29, elaborate on Sant Jordi's Moorish origins, based on a document published in 1998 by Rubio Vela in his *Epistolari de la València Medieval*. R. Lafont, 'Conexion e disjoncion del sentiment literari: l'Afar dels "Jocs Florals" ', Camps, *Languedoc*, 9–15, includes an analysis of the medieval poetic contests in the Crown of Aragon. A. Luttrell, 'Margarida d'Erill Hospitaller of Alguaire (1415–1456)', *AEM*, 28, 1998 : 219–49, gives the historic background to a poetic challenge. C. Tato, 'Pedro de Santa Fe: ¿poeta en catalán?', Beltran, *Poesía*, 113–35, questions Pedro de Santa Fe's authorship of 'Non siau tal pux conexeu'. Joan Bastardas, *Sobre el 'Carmen Campidoctoris'*, B, p.p., 28 pp., proposes a date after 1094 and interprets this Latin poem as a panegyric. Josep Romeu i Figueras, *Corpus d'antiga poesia popular* (ENC, B18), 421 pp., edits and studies a corpus of 437 poems.

3. DOCTRINAL AND RELIGIOUS PROSE

RAMON LLULL AND LULLISM

A. Soler, 'Selecció d'edicions i estudis lul·lians (1996–1998)', *LlLi*, 11 : 477–82, is a critical bibliography of Lullian studies. Harvey J. Hames, *The Art of Conversion. Christianity and Kabbalah in the Thirteenth Century*, Leiden, Brill, 332 pp., explores Kabbalah materials and Trinitarian arguments in L.'s works. A. Soler, 'Il papa angelico nel *Blaquerna* di Ramon Llull', *SM*, 40, 1999 : 857–77, analyses the

adaptation of an eschatological motif by Llull. *SLu*, 39, 1999, contains
J. Gayà, 'Informe Olivi sobre una teoría de las razones reales
esenciales' (3–23), a study on Joan Olivi, a contemporary of L.'s; and
J.-A. Ysern, '*Exempla* i estructures exemplars en el primer llibre del
Fèlix' (24–54), on the sources of L.'s *exempla*. See also Amador Vega,
Passió, meditació i contemplació. Sis assaigs sobre el nihilisme religiós, B,
Empúries, 1999, 182 pp., on L.'s mystical approach. Several studies
deal with L.'s 'new' disciplines: J. Aragüés Aldaz, '*Falses semblances*,
ejemplarismo divino y literatura ejemplar a la luz de Ramón Llull',
AHLM 8, 175–83, on the *Rhetorica nova*; L. Badia, 'Ramon Llull y la
cuadratura del círculo', *Concentus Libri*, 12:300–05, on geometry;
R. Llull, *Lògica nova*, ed. Anthony Bonner (Nova Edició de les Obres
de Ramon Llull, 3) Palma, Patronat Ramon Llull, 1998,
liii + 186 pp., on logic. Three articles on Lullism by J. de Puig-Oliver
have appeared in *ATCA*, 19 (7–296, 297–388, 597–609).

ARNAU DE VILANOVA AND OTHER SCIENTIFIC TEXTS

A. Soler, 'Selecció d'edicions i estudis arnaldians recents', *LlLi*,
11:482–85, is an annotated bibliography on Vilanova. The edition
Tractatus de intentione medicorum, Arnaldi de Villanova Opera Medica Omnia,
5.1, ed. Michael R. McVaugh, B, Fundació Noguera, 222 pp., makes
available an essential work to understand V.'s position, between
Aristotelism and Galenism. A number of scientific and technical
treatises have also been edited: L. Cifuentes and C. Ferragud, 'El
Llibre de la menescalia de Manuel Dies: de espejo de caballeros a manual
de albéitares', *Asclepio*, 51.1, 1999:93–127, studies the work of a
courtier of King Alfons el Magnànim; A. J. Iglesias, 'Un bifoli en
pergamí de la parròquia barcelonina de Vilanova del Vallès: el
testimoni en català més antic del *Llibre de conservació de sanitat* de Joan
de Toledo (s. XIV)', *ATCA*, 19:389–428, sets a new witness of the
treatise in context; G. Martínez Ferrà, 'Una nova versió catalana del
Liber de conservanda sanitate de Johannes de Toleto', *AEM*, 29,
1999:585–99, deals with dietetics.

VICENT FERRER, FRANCESC EIXIMENIS AND OTHER MORAL TEXTS

M. I. Toro Pascua, 'La transmisión impresa de los sermones
castellanos de San Vicente Ferrer', *Actas* (Corunna), 719–30, analyses
16th- and 17th-c. editions of Ferrer. D. Guixeras, 'La tradició textual
del *Regiment de la Cosa Pública* de Francesc Eiximenis: una aproximació', *ib.*, 323–38, offers an approach to the stemma of chapters
357–95 of E.'s *Dotzè*. K. Rivers, 'Memory and medieval preaching:

mnemonic in the *Ars praedicandi* of Francesc Eiximenis', *Viator*, 30, 1999:253–84, is a thoroughly documented study of the only preaching treatise that deals with mnemonic. M. J. Peláez, 'Notas sobre el Derecho Canónico y las fuentes eclesiásticas en el pensamiento de Francesc Eiximenis', *AEM*, 29, 1999:835–42, analyses canon law notions on several of E.'s works. E. Ayensa, 'Un testimoni literari inèdit sobre Elionor d'Aragó, reina de Xipre (circa 1333–1416)', *Anuari del Centre de Recerca Científica*, 26:157–65, edits and analyses a passage of E.'s *Terç*. C. Wittlin, 'Francesc Eiximenis i les seves fonts', *LlLi*, 11:41–107, typifies E.'s sources. D. J. Viera, 'On the king's chancellor: chapter 680 of Fra Francesc Eiximenis *Dotzè del Crestià*', *CatR*, 12.2, 1998:89–97, suggests sources for this episode. A. G. Hauf, 'Corrientes teológicas valencianas, s. xiv-xv: Arnau de Vilanova, Ramon Llull y Francesc Eiximenis', pp. 9–47 of *Teología en Valencia: raíces y retos. Buscando nuestros orígenes, de cara al futuro, Actas del X Simposio de teología histórica (marzo 1999)*, V, 651 pp., analyses the social use of theology, with examples from E., Llull, and Vilanova. M. de Epalza, 'Die Aktualität von Anselm Turmeda in der islamisch-christlichen Polemik in Frankreich und Katalonien', pp. 182–92 of *Religionen im Gespräch*, ed. Reinhard Kirste et al., Nachrodt, Zimmermann, critically reviews the bibliography on Turmeda and the *Tuhfa*. M. A. Sánchez, 'La originalidad y el supuesto origen agustiniano de las *Homilies d'Organyà*', *AHLM 8*, 1611–30, proposes close Latin models for the *Homilies* within the core preaching repertoire. The incunable *Arte de bien morir y Breve confesionario: (Zaragoza, Pablo Horus: c. 1479–1484): según el incunable de la Biblioteca del Monasterio de San Lorenzo de El Escorial; Anónimo; edición y estudio de Francisco Gago Jover; precedido de Las palabras de la muerte, de Enrique Lázaro*, Palma, Olañeta–Illes Balears U.P., 1999, 172 pp., also includes a 15th-c. Catalan confession manual. A. Bover has devoted two articles to the transmission of the *Spill de la vida religiosa*: 'Sobre la difusió germànica del *Spill de la vida religiosa* (Barcelona 1515)', pp. 83–90 of *Ex nobili philologorum officio. Festschrift für Heinrich Bihler zu seinem 80. Geburtstag*, ed. Dietrich Briesemeister and Axel Schönberger, Berlin, Domus, 1998, 999 pp., and 'The *Spill de la Vida Religiosa* (Barcelona, 1515) and its Luso-Hispanic transmission', pp. 57–67 of *Multicultural Iberia: Language, Literature and Music*, ed. D. Dougherty and M. M. Azevedo, Berkeley, California U.P., 1999, 258 pp. J.-A. Ysern has devoted two articles to an *exempla* collection: 'Edició i estudi del *Recull d'exemples morals*, contingut en el MS. S. Cugat 39 de l'Arxiu de la Corona d'Aragó', *BRABLB*, 47:51–126; and 'Els elements meravellosos dins del *Recull d'eximplis*', pp. 387–412 of *Actes de l'Onzè Col·loqui Internacional de Llengua i Literatura Catalanes (Mallorca, 1997)*, II, ed. Joan Mas et al., PAM, 533 pp.

4. HISTORICAL AND ARTISTIC PROSE, NOVEL

HISTORIOGRAPHY

S. M. Cingolani, 'Memòria i estratègies comunicatives al *Libre* del rei Jaume I', *RCat*, 154:111–41, analyses the models and political aims of the *Libre*. V. Orazi, 'L'adaptació de la *Crònica* de Ramon Muntaner al *Llibre de les nobleses dels reis* de Francesc de Barcelona', *AHLM 8*, 1405–22, studies the use of Muntaner as a source. Martí de Riquer, *Llegendes històriques catalanes*, B, Quaderns Crema, 243 pp., and A. Cortadellas, 'Sis llegendes inèdites de la historiografia catalana medieval', *LlLi*, 11:7–39, edit a series of pseudohistorical texts. J. Villanueva, 'Observacions sobre *La fi del comte d'Urgell*: datació, transmissió manuscrita, contingut ideològic', *ATCA*, 19:612–35, interprets the text as literary and dates it to 1470.

BERNAT METGE

L. Badia, 'Entre *Los amores deleitables* petrarquescos y la condenada opinión de Epicuro: en el laberinto de *Lo somni* de Bernat Metge', *AHLM 8*, 257–68, sheds light on M.'s concealed sources and double meanings. J. Butinyà, 'Un altre Metge, si us plau (al voltant de la dissortada mort del rei Joan a Foixà, a propòsit de noves fonts de *Lo somni* i d'una reconsideració sobre la data), *Institut d'Estudis Gironins. Annals*, 51:27–50, offers an interpretation of M.'s figure. S. M. Cingolani, 'Política, societat i literatura. Claus per a una reinterpretació de *Lo somni* de Bernat Metge', *RCat*, 150:106–32, reads *Lo somni* in a political key of monarchic apology. Albert G. Hauf, *L'home que riu: entorn de la paròdia medieval*, Manacor, Patronat de l'Escola Municipal de Mallorquí, 62 pp., analyses several aspects of parody, including the case of M. and Turmeda. R. Alemany, 'Tres reescrituras del mito de Orfeo en las letras catalanas medievales: Bernat Metge, Joan Roís de Corella y Francesc Alegre', *AHLM 8*, 117–27, compares the degree of complexity in dealing with a common theme. V. Fàbrega, 'L'eròtica ovidiana i l'humanisme català: el mite d'Hermafrodit en les *Transformacions* de Francesc Alegre', *RevAl*, 9.9, 1998:257–71, offers a linguistic analysis of Alegre's version of the classical myth.

TIRANT LO BLANC AND *CURIAL E GÜELFA*

J. Pujol, 'Escriptura, imitació i memòria al *Tirant lo Blanc*', *EMarg*, 65, 1999:23–50, categorises *T*'s literary sources. R. M. Mérida, 'Sicilia y la ficción caballeresca catalana en los siglos XIV y XV', pp. 417–29 of *Congresso di Storia della Corona d'Aragona (Sassari-Alghero, 1990)*, ed. M. G. Meloni and O. Schena, V–Cagliari, Univ. of Cagliari, Istituto di

Storia Medievale, 1999, traces back some motifs which appear in *T* and Torroella's *Faula*. G. Sabaté and L. Soriano, 'Martorell i la taula rodona: la matèria de Bretanya al *Tirant lo Blanch*', *AHLM 8*, 1575–85, surveys Arthurian elements in *T*, and the evidence of dilution in its knighthood ideals. José Manuel Lucía Megías, *Imprenta y libros de caballerías*, M, Ollero & Ramos, 646 pp., concerns the circulation of the 1511 edition of *T*. See also G. Sabaté, 'El *Tirant lo Blanc* i la seva traducció castellana del segle xvi', *Actas* (Corunna), 607–20, on the innovations introduced by the Castilian translator.

JOAN ROÍS DE CORELLA

Ludolphus de Saxonia, *Meditationes vitae Christi*. *Lo Quart del Cartoixà aromançat per Johan Roiç de Corella*, Ajuntament de València, 1998, 58 pp., is a facsimile edition of the 1495 incunable. T. Martínez Romero, 'De poesia i lògica corelliana: comentaris a *La mort per amor*', *ER*, 22:197–212, analyses C.'s 'Si en lo mal temps' beside the troubadour and bestiary traditions; and Id., 'Alguns comentaris sobre l'orde de la Garrotera: del *Triümfo de les dones* al *Tirant lo Blanch*', pp. 503–17 of *Las órdenes militares: realidad e imaginario*, ed. María Dolores Burdeus et al., Castelló de la Plana, Universitat Jaume I, 712 pp., studies the diverging concepts of knighthood in the works of C. and Martorell. Arthur Terry, *Three Fifteenth-Century Valencian Poets*, PMHRS, 64 pp, contains essays on C., March, and Jordi de Sant Jordi. J. L. Martos, 'La *Vida de Sancta Barbara* del *Jardinet d'orats*: Joan Roís de Corella o la recepció de la seua obra', *AHLM 8*, 1269–87, edits the text and proposes C.'s authorship.

5. TRANSLATIONS AND OTHER GENRES AND TEXTS

Traducir la Edad Media. La traducción de la literatura medieval románica, Granada U.P., 1999, 466 pp., contains two articles on Ausiàs March: A. Deyermond, 'Ausiàs March en inglés' (267–94), and E. J. Nogueras Valdivieso and L. Sánchez Rodrigo, 'Notas sobre la traducción de la poesía románica medieval: cuatro siglos de Ausiàs March' (167–206). On Boethius's translator into Catalan: J. de Puig-Oliver, 'Alguns documents sobre Antoni Ginebreda, O.P. (1340?–1395)', *ATCA*, 19:511–25. F. Ziino, 'Some vernacular versions of Boethius's *De Consolatione Philosophiae* in medieval Spain: notes on their relationship with the commentary tradition', *Carmina Philosophiae*, 7, 1998:37–65, analyses comparatively Catalan and Castilian versions and accompanying commentaries. P. Quer, 'Andreu Febrer, contemporani d'Ausiàs March', *Reduccions*, 72:81–99, on Febrer's translation and Dante's presence in March's works. G. Avenoza, 'El paper d'Antoni

Canals en la traducció catalana de Valeri Màxim', *BHS(L)*, 77:339–57, detects a source of the Catalan version of Valerius Maximus. R. Recio, 'Puntualizaciones sobre la traducción catalana del *Triunfo de amor* de Petrarca según el manuscrito 534 de la Biblioteca Nacional de París', *Actas* (Madrid), I, 213–20, is concerned with the role of Bernardo Illicino as a source. J. M. Perujo Melgar, 'Prolegòmens per a una edició crítica de la traducció catalana de la *Historia destructionis Troiae* de Guido delle Colonne', *AHLM 8*, 1469–86, enumerates textual witnesses and proposes a stemma. J. Sánchez Martí, 'La *Historia de Amicus y Amelius* en Cataluña: el *Eximpli e miracle dels dos leals amichs Amich e Meliç*', *ib.*, 1603–10, studies the Catalan version of the *Alphabetum narrationum*. On translations of moral and scientific texts: A. Bataller Català, 'Les traduccions castellanes del *Liber de moribus* de Jacobus de Cessolis', *ib.*, 337–52; and L. Cifuentes, 'Tres notes sobre traduccions quirúrgiques medievals al català', *ATCA*, 19:561–609. The edition of Hippocrates, *Aforismes. Traducció catalana medieval*, ed. Antònia Carré and Francesca Llorens, B, Curial–PAM, 102 pp., includes a glossary of technical terms. M. Vilallonga, 'Jeroni Pau en el umbral de un mundo nuevo: Quinto centenario de su muerte', pp. 647–57 of *Acta conventus neo-latini abulensis* (Àvila, 1997), ed. Rhoda Schnur et al., Tempe, Arizona Center for Medieval and Renaissance Studies, 679 pp., updates some aspects of her 1986 study and edition. V. Orazi, 'Die verfolgte Frau: per l'analisi semiologica di un motivo folclorico e delle sue derivazioni medievali (con speciale attenzione all'ambito catalano)', *ER*, 22:101–38, studies a folk motif with special reference to Catalan witnesses; and her edition of '*Història de la filla del rei d'Hungria' e altri racconti catalani tardomedievali, studio folclorico ed edizione critica*, Rome, Mauro Baroni, 1999, 167 pp., focuses on some of these Catalan cases. See also J. Requesens, 'Profecies polítiques del Renaixement o la catacresi com a gènere literari', *BRABLB*, 47:431–51, on prophecy as a genre.

6. DRAMA

J. Romeu i Figueras, 'Joglaria: espectacle i incidència en el teatre a la Catalunya medieval', pp. 21–25 of *El teatre popular a l'Edat Mitjana i al Renaixement. Actes del II Simposi Internacional d'Història del Teatre (Barcelona, 1997)*, B, Institut del Teatre, 1999, 515 pp., analyses medieval performance. L. Martín Pascual, 'Aproximació a l'estudi del text de la Passió catalana de París', *AHLM 8*, 1195–208, focuses her analysis on language and versification. F. Huerta, 'La cançó popular en el teatre nadalenc medieval', pp. 177–90 of *Actes de l'Onzè Col·loqui Internacional de Llengua i Literatura Catalanes (Mallorca, 1997)*, III, ed. Joan

Mas et al., PAM, studies the use of folkloric elements in Christmas plays.

MODERN LITERATURE
POSTPONED

VI. PORTUGUESE STUDIES

LANGUAGE
POSTPONED

MEDIEVAL LITERATURE
POSTPONED

LITERATURE 1500 TO THE PRESENT DAY
POSTPONED

VII. GALICIAN STUDIES

LANGUAGE

POSTPONED

LITERATURE

By Dolores Vilavedra, *Departamento de Filoloxía Galega, Universidade de Santiago de Compostela* and Derek Flitter, *Senior Lecturer in Modern Spanish Language and Literature, University of Birmingham*

1. General

Diccionario da literatura galega. III: Obras, ed. Dolores Vilavedra, Vigo, Galaxia, 512 pp., is the latest volume in an ongoing project, this one detailing a selection, with critical commentary, of the most significant works of Galician literature. D. Flitter, 'Icons and imperatives in the construction of Galician identity: the "Xeración *Nós*"', *FMLS*, 36:296–309, examines the diversity of intellectual sources of Galician nationalism and pinpoints some of the ideological tensions within the *Nós* grouping.

2. Women's Studies

H. González, 'Literatura galega de muller, unha visión sistémica', *AELG*, 1999:41–67, analyses the conflictive position of women's literature within the wider Galician context. Volume VI of the *Breve historia feminista de la literatura española*, ed. Iris Zavala, B, Anthropos, 460 pp., includes several articles on Galician women's writing: K. March, 'Rosalía de Castro: escritora de su tiempo' (161–74), examines Rosalía as a foundational figure; C. Blanco, 'La escritura matrilineal galaica: Luz Pozo Garza habla a Rosalía de Castro' (175–95), considers the poetic dialogue between these authors; 'Las poetas y las poéticas desde la posguerra hasta hoy: "¡Yo también navegar!"' (196–218), is a study of Galicia's post-Civil War women poets; M. Bar, 'Escritoras dramáticas gallegas: dos propuestas subversivas' (219–36), covers the work of two playwrights, Xohana Torres and María Xosé Queizán; C. Noia, 'La narrativa gallega de mujeres' (237–64), furnishes a general survey of prose fiction. P. Pallarés, 'El canon de la poesía escrita por mujeres: diversidad idiomática y escrita', pp. 139–52 of *La poesía escrita por mujeres y el canon: III Encuentro de mujeres poetas*, ed. E. López, n.p., Cabildo Insular de

Lanzarote–Gobierno de Canarias, 1999, reviews the work of the few
Galician women writers traditionally included in the literary canon.
C. Blanco, 'Sumisión, resistencia y subversión en la poesía gallega de
mujeres', Dadson, *Voces subversivas*, 90–10, deals with the evolution of
Galician women's writing in the period after the Civil War.

3. MEDIEVAL LITERATURE

M. O'Neill, 'Oral and literate processes in Galician-Portuguese song',
GalR, 3–4:8–18, stresses the interaction of these processes in the
move from oral to written culture. T. Amado and P. Lorenzo, 'Os
estudos de poesía lírica galego-portuguesa (1978–1998)', *BGL*,
23:7–38, surveys recent work with a view to identifying salient
tendencies in criticism. M. Arbor, 'As gardas de amor na lírica galego-
portuguesa', *Carvalho Vol.*, II, 19–44, provides an analysis of a specific
motif. X. B. Arias, '¿e *u* era? ¿A clave da cantiga de Meendinho?',
BGL, 24:77–82, reviews the several hypotheses and solutions.
M. Brea, '*Levantou-s'a velida*, un exemplo de sincretismo harmónico',
Carvalho Vol., II, 139–52, examines the original elements and the
synthesis of existing traditions in Dom Dinis's *cantiga*. L. Díez, 'Once
de las 427 *Cantigas* de Alfonso X el Sabio son de tema judaico.
¿Fueron obra de un judío converso?', *Losada Vol.*, 324–49, looks at the
question of authorship of this group. E. Fidalgo, 'Cantigas "de amor"
a Santa María', *Carvalho Vol.*, II, 255–66, assesses the employment of
courtly love motifs in the CSM. Y. Frateschi, 'A *soidade/suidade* na
lírica galego-portuguesa', *ib.*, 807–24, studies the presence and
meaning of these terms in the medieval lyric. P. Meneses, 'Fenomenol-
ogia da morte-por-amor: do influxo das teorias médicas antigo-
medievais na actividade poética trovadoresca', *ib.*, 491–506, adopts a
medical perspective on the lover's complaint. J. M. Montero, 'As
legendas das miniaturas das *Cantigas de Santa María* (códices T e F)',
ib., 507–52, supplies a commentary on the texts accompanying these
miniatures. F. Nodar, 'O sistema paralelístico galego-portugués:
sintaxe lóxica e harmónica, rima e selección léxico-semántica', *ib.*,
581–96, approaches some of the structural issues affecting the
medieval lyric via the application of certain metrical paradigms.
J. Paredes, '*Faroneja*: para una interpretación de la cantiga *O que foi
passar a serra* de Alfonso X', *ib.*, 613–18, attempts to uncover the
meaning of a term crucial to the *cantiga*'s interpretation.

Parkinson, *Cobras e son* contains, aside from a summary of round-
table discussion: M.P. Ferreira, 'Andalusian music and the *Cantigas de
Santa María*' (7–19); M. O'Neill, 'Problems of genre definition: the
Cantigas de Santa María in the context of the Romance lyric tradition'
(20–30); D. Wulstan, 'The rhythmic organization of the *Cantigas de*

Santa María' (31–65); A. Domínguez, 'En torno al Arbol de Jesé (siglos XI-XIII): tres ejemplos en las *Cantigas de Santa María'* (70–92); S. Zapke, 'Belleza y *Weltanschauung* en las *Cantigas de Santa María'* (93–105); V. Bertolucci, 'Primo contributo all'analisi delle varianti redazionali nelle *Cantigas de Santa Maria'* (106–18); J. Montoya, 'Algunas precisiones acerca de la puntuación de las *Cantigas de Santa María'* (119–32); S. Parkinson, 'Layout and structure of the Toledo manuscript of the *Cantigas de Santa Maria'* (133–53); D. Wulstan, 'The compilation of the *Cantigas* of Alfonso El Sabio' (154–85); M. E. Schaffer, 'The "evolution" of the *Cantigas de Santa Maria*: the relationships between MSS T, F and E' (186–213).

A. X. Pociña, 'As aventuras de Ulises: algunhas concordancias e discordancias entre as versións da *Odisea*, a *Crónica Troiana* e a *Historia Troyana'*, *BGL*, 24:57–71, compares the respective accounts of Odysseus's journey home. G. Videira, 'Ecos internos na poesia galego-portuguesa: a proto-heteronimia em João Garcia de Guilhade', *Losada Vol.*, 728–33, examines the doubling of voices in this troubadour's songs, contrasting his own with that of his *amiga. A Idade Media*, Corunna, 503 pp., is Vol. 20 of the *Hércules* project, the first of a series of volumes within that collection dedicated to Galician literature.

4. POPULAR LITERATURE

Antropoloxía, Corunna, Hércules de Ediciones, 535 pp., Vol. 18 of the *Hércules* project, includes D. Blanco, 'Literatura popular de tradición oral' (54–85), from a specialist in the field, a study based on history, sociology and genre. J. L. Forneiro, *El romancero tradicional de Galicia: una poesía entre dos lenguas*, Oiartzun, Sendoa, 317 pp., studies the Galician ballad collections within an Hispanic and European perspective, focusing upon their bilingualism. X. R. Mariño, 'Mouros e tesouros', *Grial*, 148:565–74, provides an analysis of two recurrent motifs. C. Rodríguez Fer, 'La larga noche de piedra de la poesía gallega y el rescate del cantar de ciego', Dadson, *Voces subversivas*, 63–74, looks at popular verse forms as a form of protest during and after the Civil War.

5. NARRATIVE

X. González, 'Veinte años de novela gallega (1979–1998)', *CHA*, 599:7–19, provides a critical commentary on two decades of prose fiction. M. Luis, 'A narrativa galega: cara á consolidación dunha nova novela', *BGL*, 24:99–109, surveys the decade of the 1990s. Dolores Vilavedra, *Sobre narrativa galega contemporánea*, Vigo, Galaxia, 177 pp., is a collection of essays and reviews dealing with Galician prose fiction of the last 20 years.

6. POETRY

Identidades multiculturais, ed. A. Bringas and B. Martín, Vigo U.P., 265 pp., includes: I. Cochón, 'Galicia como vontade e representación: a épica posible no discurso poético dos noventa' (93–102), and A. Casas, 'A crítica literaria na revista *Nós*. Pautas de canonicidade sobre a poesía coeva' (153–66), who studies the role of the journal in the creation of a lyrical canon. X. González-Millán, '¿Unha antoloxía de antoloxías ou unha macroantoloxía nacional? Notas para unha análise cuantitativa de *Río de son e vento. Unha antoloxía da poesía galega*', *AELG*, 1999:135–47, uses the anthology of the title to consider the socio-cultural means and aims of such projects. T. López, 'Poesía galega do (pre)rexurdimento. Tres poemas ignorados e esquecidos en homenaxe ao actor Julián Romea', *Carvalho Vol.*, II, 349–62, reproduces with commentary some early examples of modern Galician verse. The same writer's 'Introducción' (7–43) to *Sementeira de ronseis. Cinco poetas da vangarda*, Corunna, Espiral Maior, is a rigorously argued vision of the Galician avant-garde. K. March, 'Xurdimento e natureza das vangardas en Galiza', *Carvalho Vol.*, II, 415–24, looks at the earliest manifestations of the avant-garde in Galicia. L. Rodríguez, 'Casi un cuarto de siglo de poesía gallega', *CHA*, 599:40–51, surveys the Galician lyric since the death of Franco. A. Varela, 'As antoloxías literarias galegas: do Rexurdimento a 1936', *AELG*, 1999:69–102, considers the contribution to Galicia's evolving lyrical tradition made by the various anthologies appearing in this period.

7. THEATRE

Fadamorgana, no. 5, is dedicated to Galician children's theatre. M. J. Martínez, 'El entremés de *La contienda sobre la pesca del río Miño* (1671): un problema de definición genérica', *Carvalho Vol.*, II, 425–44, is a valuable contribution both to the question of the work's genre and to that of Galician links with contemporary Portuguese theatre. N. Pazó and D. Vilavedra, 'El teatro gallego después de 1975', *CHA*, 599:21–37, survey Galician theatre since the death of Franco. D. Vilavedra, 'A recepción do teatro galego postautonómico: unha ollada ás revistas non galegas', *Losada Vol.*, 734–41, considers the reception of Galician theatre in journals outside Galicia since 1985.

8. INDIVIDUAL AUTHORS

ALCALÁ.   A. Basanta, 'Xavier Alcalá, una obra gallega en curso', *Carvalho Vol.*, II, 75–90, reviews the early stages of A.'s writing career.

BORRAZÁS.   I. Otero, *'Criminal'. 'Eu é'. Dúas novelas de Xurxo Borrazás*, SC, Sotelo, 44 pp., is a short narratological study of the two novels.

CABANILLAS.   D. Flitter, ' "Na praia de Rianxo": la simbología galleguista como protesta cultural', Dadson, *Voces subversivas*, 75–89, examines C.'s elegy to Castelao within the context of Galician cultural resistance to *franquismo*, arguing for C.'s inscribing of himself within a discernibly Galician symbolic tradition.

CARBALLO CALERO.   *Escritos sobre teatro*, Corunna, Biblioteca-Arquivo Teatral Francisco Pillado, 252 pp., gathers together C.C.'s ground-breaking studies of Galician theatre. L. Tato, 'Carvalho Calero, poeta, narrador, dramaturgo', *Grial*, 147:441–60, takes a panoramic view of C.C.'s work. The homage volumes published to coincide with the tenth anniversary of C.C.'s death, *Estudios dedicados a Ricardo Carvalho Calero*, 2 vols, SC, Parlamento de Galicia — Universidade de Santiago, 1007, 1044 pp., contain a cluster of articles dedicated to his work: E. Basanta, 'Umha aproximaçom á leitura do *Auto do prisioneiro*' (I, 97–104); C. Blanco, '*O trevo das catro follas*: un poemario popular inédito de Carvalho Calero' (I, 105–40); C. Delgado, 'O proxecto de facer un romance e o tempo da escrita dramaticamente vivido' (I, 141–54), a metafictional reading of the novel *Scórpio*; L. García, '*Scórpio* e Tauro ou o gozo e o sublime: Barthes e Kant com Carvalho' (I, 183–212); D. Villanueva, 'Lectura de *Scórpio*' (I, 327–36); M. C. Porrúa, Breves notas sobre *Auto do prisioneiro*' (I, 263–66), dealing with the play's symbolism; H. Rabunhal, 'Carvalho Calero e o teatro' (I, 281–92); C. Rodríguez, 'A poesía española de Ricardo Carvalho Calero' (I, 293–320).

CASTELAO.   The 50th anniversary of C.'s death has prompted the appearance of a large number of studies. The edition of C.'s complete works in six volumes is accompanied by a collection of essays entitled *Estudios sobre a obra escrita*, Vigo, Galaxia, 454 pp., which includes the following: H. Monteagudo, 'Castelao: a fábula da súa vida' (7–146), a biographical commentary; H. Monteagudo, 'Castelao escritor. O ensaio' (147–64), which considers C.'s contribution to the definition of this genre in Galician literature; M. Rosales, 'A obra narrativa' (165–96), an examination of narratological startegies; M. F. Vieites, 'Daniel R. Castelao, o movemento dramático nacional e o teatro nacional popular' (197–310), an assessment of C.'s contribution to the development of Galician theatre; J. Beramendi and R. Máiz, 'O pensamento político de Castelao' (311–420), an appraisal of C.'s political thought; M. Rosales, 'Aproximación ó estudio da lingua na obra literaria de Castelao' (421–56), analysing C.'s literary language. Henrique Monteagudo, *Castelao: defensa e ilustración do idioma galego*, Vigo, Galaxia, 274 pp., is a collection of essays linked by their linguistic focus and whose attention is centred principally on the processes of composition of *Sempre en Galiza*. *Castelao na Galiza do século XX*, ed. M. Ferreiro and X. R. Freixeiro, Corunna, ASPG — Dpto de Filoloxías Francesa e Galego-Portuguesa da Univ. da Coruña, 269 pp., contains the proceedings of the Corunna Symposium. H. Monteagudo, 'Lingua, literatura e *Volksgeist* en *Sempre en Galiza*' (39–54), is on language and ideology; M. Rosales, 'Literatura e arte en Castelao' (55–64), challenges the perception of C.'s narrative as spontaneously produced and simple in style; M. Lourenzo, 'Sobre as fontes estilísticas de *Os vellos non deben de namorarse*' (65–70), probes the question of sources; X. C. Valle, 'Castelao e a arte galega do seu tempo' (155–80), studies the evolution of C.'s artistic style within the Galician context of its day. The exhibition catalogue *Castelao. Exposición 50 aniversario*, Fundación Caixa Galicia, 428 pp., contains various articles by the writers already cited, plus others on C.'s artistic production and also A. Capelán, 'Castelao articulista' (115–30), which reviews the neglected area of C.'s journalistic work.

L. Fontoira, ' "A Marquesiña" como síntese simbólica de *Cousas*', *Carvalho Vol.*, II, 267–74, examines the tale as a paradigm of C.'s narrative style. C. P. Martínez, 'Da (est)ética dunha síntese artística. Contributos para a avaliación dunha peza "reteatralizada" ', forms pp. 69–100 of *Os vellos non deben de namorarse*, SC, IGAEM, 199 pp., published to coincide with the production of the play by the Centro Dramático Galego. M. F. Vieites, '¿Teatro de arte, teatro de vangarda ou teatro popular? Algunhas reflexións en torno ó ideario teatral de Castelao', *Grial*, 146:189–230, approaches the thorny question of C.'s connections with the avant-garde.

CASTRO. V. Álvarez, 'Documento para a biografía de Rosalía de Castro: testamento de José Martínez Viojo, presbítero', *Grial*, 146:169–78, brings forward new documentary evidence to shed light on Rosalía's life. The same writer's 'R. de Castro, actriz: noticias e documentos', *RER*, 1:11–44, is a source of important information concerning Rosalía's relationship with the stage. A. R. Baptista, 'Rosalía de Castro no horizonte dos saudosistas portugueses', *ib.*, 49–74, examines the influence of Rosalía's work upon the Portuguese poets. J. Dunne, 'Traducir Rosalía ó inglés: algúns problemas', *ib.*, 45–58, recounts some of the practical problems encountered in his translation of *Follas novas*. A. López, 'El sentido de la interioridad en Rosalía de Castro', *Carvalho Vol.*, II, 363–79, applies modern conceptual understanding of the term to Rosalía's verse. H. Losada,

' "Desierto" y "abismo": dos imágenes del romanticismo trágico en Antero de Quental y Rosalía de Castro', *Losada Vol.*, 485–93, considers the employment of two key metaphors in the poets' work. The same writer's 'El héroe y la naturaleza: dos temas del romanticismo trágico en la elegía a Sir John Moore de Rosalía de Castro', *Carvalho Vol.*, II, 405–14, detects Romantic configurations in Rosalía's verse. A. Pociña and A. López, 'Notas sobre a pervivencia e difusión actuais da obra rosaliana. Ediciós e traduccións de Rosalía dende 1991 ata 1998', *ib.*, 619–38, suuplies a broad critical survey. E. Souto, 'Rosa-negro rosaliano', *ib.*, 689–706, analyses the symbolic function of the rose and the colour black in Rosalía's Galician verse.

CORREA CALDERÓN. X. M. González, *Correa Calderón, celta. Os tempos da avanzada (1915–1936)*, Lugo, Fundación Caixa Galicia, 1999, 211 pp., assesses C.C.'s early work. X. Pardo, 'Evaristo Correa Calderón, a consolidación do nacionalismo galego e a introducción do vangardismo poético na literatura galega', *BGL*, 24:23–56, claims that C.C. was the most active mover in the renovation of Galician literature at the beginning of the 20th century.

CUNQUEIRO. J. Closa, 'De Galicia a Avalón: la *lectio* gallega de Merlín', *Losada Vol.*, 286–90, takes a look at the sources for C.'s Merlin. E. González, 'El mundo clásico en la literatura española: de Guevara y Cervantes a Álvaro Cunqueiro', *Moenia*, 6:319–40. C. C. Morám, 'Sobre a imagem do vento que muge como umha vaca, ou o tempo de mugir a vaca do vento', *Carvalho Vol.*, II, 567–80, examines the genealogy of one of C.'s most curious images. R. Rodríguez, 'O galeguismo como préstamo léxico nas autotraduccións ó castelán de Álvaro Cunqueiro', *ib.*, 624–31, evaluates C.'s *galeguismos* in the Castilian versions of his texts. L. Seixo, 'Cunqueiro e os paxaros', *Moenia*, 6:425–30.

CURROS ENRÍQUEZ. A. M. Aguirre, 'A note on Manuel Curros Enríquez and the Galician *Rexurdimento*', *GalR*, 3–4:34–40, broadly contextualizes C.E.'s position within the Galician revival.

DIESTE. X. M. Moo, ' "O neno suicida": cara a unha teoría do fantástico', *BGL*, 23:143–51, analyses the tale's modes of narrative. A. Tarrío, 'Como está feito o relato "A luz en silenzo" de Rafael Dieste', *Carvalho Vol.*, II, 707–724, examines the piece's structural, stylistic and semantic features.

FANDIÑO. The facsimile edition of *A casamenteira*, Ourense, Linteo, 140 pp., is preceded by three specialist studies: X. R. Barreiro, 'A esaxerada vida de Antonio Benito Fandiño' (15–36), the most illuminating work to date on F.'s life, of which little was known hitherto; L. Tato, '*A casamenteira*: contextualización e análise' (37–84), which locates the play in the literary and more specifically theatrical context of its time; C. Blanco, 'Contra casar sen amor: *A casamenteira*,

O Chufón e "Pimpinela" ' (85–106), considering the various instances of marriage for self-interest and ambition in Galician theatre.

FLORES. J. R. Gómez, 'O teatro galego de Ricardo Flores en Buenos Aires', *Carvalho Vol.*, II, 311–28, assesses the dramatic production of one of Galicia's foremost literary emigrés.

GARCÍA-BODAÑO. X. Carro, 'Compostela na construcción do imaxinario poético de Salvador García-Bodaño', *Losada Vol.*, 248–52, examines the symbolic function of the city in G.-B.'s poetry.

GARCÍA LORCA. J. L. Castillo, 'O falante lírico e o retorno á natureza nos *Seis poemas galegos* de Federico García Lorca', *AELG*, 1999:105–17, considers the poems as a unity founded upon G.L.'s all-encompassing vision of man and Nature.

GONZÁLEZ TOSAR. M. Martínez, 'La poética del viaje en *Remol das travesías* de Luís González Tosar', *RLLCGV*, 6:227–42, focuses upon a specific motif in G.T.'s work.

LEIRAS PULPEIRO. C. Noia, 'A dimensión popular da obra de Leiras Pulpeiro', *Carvalho Vol.*, II, 597–612, elucidates the elements of popular culture present in L.P.'s verse.

LÓPEZ CASANOVA. M. González and F. Llorca, 'De *Mesteres* a *Asedio de sombra* de A. López-Casanova', *RLLCGV*, 6:191–213, considers the issue of the evolution of L.C.'s poetry between the two named collections.

LUGRÍS. X. Campos, 'Comentario literario', *A obra narrativa en galego de Manuel Lugrís Freire*, SC, Xunta de Galicia, 272 pp., appraises L.'s narrative style in an introduction to his edition of the collected work.

MANTEIGA. B. Fernández, 'Aproximación á posmodernidade respecto dunha novela galega', *AELG*, 1999:119–34, assesses M.'s work with a view to asking whether it is appropriate to speak of a distinctive Galician postmodernist fiction.

MÉNDEZ FERRÍN. S. González, 'Aproximación a los recursos estilísticos de *Con pólvora e magnolias* de X.L. Méndez Ferrín', *RLLCGV*, 6:181–90, briefly surveys the dominant thematic, stylistic and metrical issues.

MURGUÍA. The literary, as opposed to historical, work of the honorand of the *Día das Letras Galegas*, has received some attention. R. Fonte, 'O polígrafo destemido: pensamiento literario e crítica en Manuel Murguía', *BRAG*, 361:139–62, examines M.'s work as a literary critic. A. B. Fortes, 'O *Diccionario de escritores gallegos*', *ib.*, 163–76, looks at M.'s sources of inspiration. The same writer's *Manuel Murguía e a cultura galega*, SC, Sotelo, 101 pp., with a predominantly literary focus, appraises M.'s indispensable contribution to the Galician cultural revival.

NORIEGA VARELA. X. R. Freixeiro, 'Noriega Varela, poeta lusófilo', *Carvalho Vol.*, II, 275–300, studies N.V.'s connections with Portugal.

OTERO PEDRAYO. R. Bello, 'Celtismo e saudade como repertórios míticos en Otero Pedrayo', *Carvalho Vol.*, II, 91–104, examines the mythical dimension accorded to these concepts in O.P.'s work. C. Fernández and G. Sanmartín, 'O estilo de Ramón Otero Pedrayo', *ib.*, 213–34, probe the stylistic characteristics of O.P.'s production. C. Patterson, 'North and South and *The Decline of the West*: Galicia, Spengler and Otero Pedrayo', *GalR*, 3–4:52–76, in a groundbreaking article, specifies O.P.'s elaboration of Spengler in his creative outlook. M. Fernández Rodríguez, 'Virginia Woolf from Galicia: hyperborean dream and cosmopolitan symphony', *ib.*, 41–51, examines the presence of Woolf in *Devalar* as well as in Claudio Rodríguez Fer's short story 'Mórbida mole'. E. Torres, '*Medicina legal* vs *Medicina legítima*: a estratégia textual ao serviço dum mundo en declínio num conto de Otero Pedrayo', *Carvalho Vol.*, II, 733–58, analyses narrative strategies aimed at codifying social decadence.

PATO. M. C. Rábade, 'A "Síndrome de Stendhal": contra a lírica cruel, poesía do esquezo', *BGL*, 24:83–98, makes a postcolonial reading of P.'s last work.

PONDAL. M. Ferreiro, 'De Anacreonte a Pondal: un novo poema', *Losada Vol.*, 376–86, elucidates the traces of Anacreon in an unpublished Pondalian poem. The same writer's 'Os carballos pondalianos ("Sobre fillo cativo da gandra")', *Carvalho Vol.*, II, 235–54, looks at one of P.'s favourite motifs. L. G. Soto, 'O inacabamento ético en Pondal', *ATO*, 41:13–25, argues for the 'openness' of P.'s work as a consequence of its ethical positioning.

POZO GARZA. M. Velasco, 'Luz Pozo Garza e o *Códice calixtino*', *RLLCGV*, 6:259–72, provides critical commentary on the work.

RIBALTA. M. E. Agrelo, *Obra narrativa en galego de Aurelio Ribalta y Copete*, SC, Xunta de Galicia, 183 pp.

RISCO. *Teoría do nacionalismo galego*, ed. J. Beramendi, SC, Sotelo, 152 pp., contains an informative introductory essay entitled 'O ideosistema singular de Vicente Risco' (7–54). J. Ventura, *O nacionalismo kármico de Vicente Risco*, SC, Laiovento, 122 pp., probes the esoteric sources for some of R.'s nationalist thought. O. Rodríguez, 'O milenarismo no pensamento de Vicente Risco', *Grial*, 145:55–69, traces the presence of this motif in R.'s literary production and ideology. Id., 'Vicente Risco e *La puerta de paja*: unha valiosa contribución á "novela católica" na posguerra española', *RLLCGV*, 6:243–58, examines R.'s novel within the development of a specific genre.

SIGÜENZA. *Obra galega*, SC, Xunta de Galicia, 200 pp., contains J. Beloso's extensive 'Introducción' (1–86).

TRAPERO. A. M. Rodríguez, *Xosé Trapero Pardo. A crónica dun século*, Lugo, Fundación Caixa Galicia, 350 pp., is a broad survey of life and work.

TURNES. X. M. Dobarro, 'Vicente Turnes e a poesía aúlica', *Carvalho Vol.*, II, 205–12, examines the question of authorship of a specific poem.

TORO. A. F. Pedrós, 'Santiago de Compostela: Urbe e identidade na obra de Suso de Toro', *BGL*, 24: 111–23, analyses the iconic role of the city of Santiago in T.'s fiction.

TORRES. T. Bermúdez, '*Adiós, María* como novela feminina galega', *Losada Vol.*, 165–70, argues for T.'s desire to create a feminist narrative in Galician.

VALENTE. There are various articles dedicated to V. in *Moenia*, 6; worthy of special mention are C. Blanco, 'Lugar Alén. Unha verea na que escoitar as *Cantigas de Alén*' (25–39), and M. Lopo, 'A lingua francesa na poesía de José Angel Valente' (41–49).

VARELA BUXÁN. The collective volume *Manuel Varela Buxán*, Lalín, Seminario de Estudios do Deza, 222 pp., includes L. Tato, 'Varela Buxán no teatro galego' (31–37), a contextualization of V.B.'s theatre, and D. Vilavedra, 'Por unha redescoberta do teatro de Varela Buxán' (39–43), which elucidates V.B.'s quest for fresh dramatic potentialities.

VIII. LATIN AMERICAN STUDIES

SPANISH AMERICAN LITERATURE
THE COLONIAL PERIOD
POSTPONED

THE NINETEENTH CENTURY

By ANNELLA MCDERMOTT, *Department of Hispanic, Portuguese and Latin American Studies, University of Bristol*

1. GENERAL

D. Aporte-Ramos, 'Cuando la Pampa se colorea: los negros en la Argentina decimonónica', *RevIb*, 188–89, 1999:733–39, looks at José Hernández, *Martín Fierro;* Juan Bautista Alberdi, *Bases y puntos de partida [. . .],* Estanislao del Campo, *Fausto,* and José Mármol, *Amalia.* R. Demaría, ' "Querido Alberdi", "Mi querido Echevarría", "Sarmiento camina a lo loco": silencio y palabras en las cartas privadas de la Generación del 37', *Hispamérica*, 86:19–30, finds, beneath the supposed consensus within this generation, underlying conflicts not expressed in public, but visible in their private correspondence. B. González Stephan, 'Colecciones y exhibir: la construcción de patrimonios culturales', *ib.,* 3–17, looks at 19th-c. histories of literature in Latin America as part of the process of construction of national identities. **Letras y divisas: ensayos sobre literatura y rosismo,* ed. Cristina Iglesias, BA, EUDEBA, 1998. *La literatura en la formación de los estados hispanoamericanos,* ed. Dieter Janik, M, Iberoamericana — Frankfurt, Vervuert, 1998, 268 pp., brings together papers from a symposium held at the Johannes Gutenberg University in Mainz, 17–19 October 1996. A. Lera, 'Sin "olor a pueblo": la polémica sobre el naturalismo en la literatura argentina', *RevIb*, 190:139–46, pays particular attention to the novels of Eugenio Cambaceres, especially *Pot-Pourri.* E. Segre, 'The development of *costumbrista* iconography and nation-building strategies in Mexican literary periodicals of the mid-nineteenth century', *BHS(L),* 77:77–105, discusses attempts to foster a collective sense of identity in a variety of periodicals which include: the *Revista Mexicana, El Museo Mexicano, El Gabinete de Lectura, La Ilustración Mexicana, El Liceo Mexicano, El Mosaico Mexicano, El Almacén Universal,* the *Revista Científica y Literaria de México, Panorama de las Señoritas,* and *El Daguerreotipo: Revista Enciclopédica Universal.*

INDIVIDUAL AUTHORS

ALTAMIRANO, IGNACIO MANUEL.   E. Segre, 'An italicised ethnicity: memory and renascence in the literary writings of Ignacio Manuel Altamirano', *FMLS*, 36:267–79, argues that in the 1860s and 70s, A. problematized a consensual notion of Mexico's *mestizo* identity by reflecting on his own Indian ethnicity in his poetry, fiction, and literary criticism.

COLL Y TOSTE, CAYETANO.   G. Puleo, 'Historia y literatura en las crónicas boricuas de Cayetano Coll y Toste y Ana Lydia Vega o dos alas de un mismo pájaro', *La Torre*, 13, 1999:571–86, examines how both writers use the genre of stories inspired by episodes of national history to explore the issue of Puerto Rican identity.

DARÍO, RUBÉN.   Alfonso García Morales, **Rubén Darío. Estudios en el centenario de 'Los raros' y 'Prosas profanas'*, Seville U.P., 1998, 239 pp.

GÓMEZ DE AVELLANEDA, GERTRUDIS.   L. T. González-del-Valle, 'Iniquidad oficial y objeción individual en la España decimonónica a través de algunas cartas inéditas de Gertrudis Gómez de Avellaneda', *BHS(G)*, 77:451–78, reproduces and places in context nine letters written by G. de A., in 1852 and 1853, to Antonio María Rubio, private secretary to the Spanish Queen Mother, María Cristina de Nápoles.

GORRITI, JUANA MANUELA.   M. C. Arambel-Guiñazú, 'Decir lo indecible en los relatos fantásticos de Juana Manuela Gorriti', *RHM*, 53:214–27, sees the use of a 'non-canonical genre' (the fantastic tale) by this woman writer as a way of rendering acceptable the radical nature of the ideas she wished to express about the position of women and contemporary politics.

MANZANO, JUAN FRANCISO.   J. Gomáriz, 'La poética de resistencia de Juan Francisco Manzano', *CAm*, 219:115–20, explores expressions of resistance, often subtle, in M.'s writings.

MARTÍ, JOSÉ.   J. Febles, 'Martí frente a dos deportes anglosajones: antagonismo conceptual y traducción hermética en algunas *Escenas norteamericanas*', *Hispania*, 83:19–30, examines M.'s negative views on baseball and American football. L. A. Lomas, 'Imperialism, modernization and the commodification of identity in José Martí's *Great Cattle Exposition*', *JLACS*, 9:193–212, explores the use in this article of imagery relating to cattle as an allegory for racism. R. Mateix, 'Amor y temor de ciudad grande. Notas sobre la poética urbana de José Martí', Rovira, *Ciudad*, 75–91, examines M.'s attitudes to urban living and nature, relating them to his experience of New York.

OBESO, CANDELARIO.   C. Jauregui, 'Candelario Obeso: entre la espada del romanticismo y la pared del proyecto nacional', *RevIb*,

188–89, 1999:567–90, is concerned with the use of local dialect from the Mompox region in *Cantos populares de mi tierra*.

RODÓ, JOSÉ ENRIQUE. G. San Román, 'Political tact in José Enrique Rodó's *Ariel*', *FMLS*, 36:279–95, examines changes from draft to final version of the essay, for the light they throw on the reasons for the relative absence from *Ariel* of references to the specific social and political conditions of Latin America at the time of its composition, all the more surprising since its author was deeply involved in Uruguayan politics, both as a journalist and as a member of parliament.

SARMIENTO, DOMINGO FAUSTINO. C. Gazzeira, 'Estado y comunicación: el modelo sarmientino de *Argirópolis*', *Hispamérica*, 86:31–42, proposes that this text is the most important theoretical work to be produced by the Generation of 37.

SILVA, JOSÉ ASUNCIÓN. L. Rabina, 'The "voz" and the "vocerío": José Asunción Silva faces culture at the foot of Bolívar's statue', *REH*, 34:607–624, argues that S.'s poem *Al pie de la estatua*, with its reflections on the ambiguities of the monument in Bogotá, is struggling to define culture in turn-of-the-century Spanish American.

VILLAVERDE, CIRILO. D. Alvarez-Amell, 'Las dos caras de *Cecilia Valdés*: entre el romanticismo y el nacionalismo cubano', *His(US)*, 83:1–10, lays particular emphasis on the novel's links with Romanticism.

THE TWENTIETH CENTURY

By D. L. SHAW, *Brown-Forman Professor of Spanish American Literature in the University of Virginia*

1. GENERAL

Robert A. Neustadt, **(Con)Fusing Signs and Postmodern Positions: Spanish American Performance, Experimental Writing and the Critique of Political Confusion*, NY, Garland, 1999, 206 pp. J. E. Adoum, 'De la literatura de protesta a la literatura *light*', *Hispamérica*, 86:93–103, a plaintive protest. M. L. Canfield, 'Un siglo de poesía: balance y perspectivas', *ib.*, 85:3–36, forms a chapter of literary history on 20th-c. poetry. William Rowe, **Poets of Contemporary Latin America: History and the Inner Life*, OUP, 384 pp. Harald Wentzlaff-Eggebert, **Naciendo el hombre nuevo . . . . : fundir literatura, artes y vida como práctica de las vanguardias en el mundo ibérico*, Frankfurt, Vervuert, 1999, 297 pp. Gilberto Mendonça Teles and Claus Muller Bergh, *Vanguardia latinoamericana* i. México y América Central, Frankfurt, Vervuert, 356 pp., covers Mexico, Guatemala, El Salvador, Honduras, Nicaragua, Costa Rica, and Panama. Merlin H. Foster, **Las vanguardias literarias en México y la América Central. Bibliografía y antología crítica*, Frankfurt, Vervuert, 380 pp. *RCL*, 55, has three short essays on Walt Whitman in Spanish America: A. Morales, 'Walt Whitman en la poesía chilena del siglo XX' (179–88); T. E. Martínez, 'Borges y Whitman: el otro, el mundo' (189–94), and F. Pérez, 'Walt Whitman leído en el sur: testimonios en la biblioteca personal de Pablo Neruda' (195–200). **The Places of History. Regionalism Revisited in Latin America*, ed. Doris Sommer, Durham, Duke U.P., 1999, 310 pp., has been very favourably reviewed. J. M. Oviedo and M. Vargas Llosa, 'A conversation', *Review*, 61:6–12, is interesting on the Boom. S. Henighan, 'Two paths to the Boom: Carpentier, Asturias and the performance split', *MLR*, 94, 1999:1009–24, postulates a synthesis of 'specificity' and euro-centred fiction. Jerry Hoeg, *Science, Technology and Latin American Narrative in the Twentieth Century and Beyond*, Lehigh U.P., 144 pp., includes Gabriel García Márquez and Isabel Allende. Rebecca Biron, **Murder and Masculinity: Violent Fictions in Twentieth Century Latin America*, Nashville, Vanderbilt U.P., 1999, 192 pp. L. Padura Fuentes, 'Modernidad y postmodernidad: la novela policial en Iberoamérica', *Hispamérica*, 84, 1999:37–50, is a historical survey. Y. Molina Gavilán and others, 'Cronología de CF latinoamericana 1775–1999', *Chasqui*, 29.2:43–72, is a checklist of science fiction writings. Miguel Gutiérrez, **Faulkner en la novela latinoamerica*, Lima, San Marcos U.P., 1999, 322 pp. Eladio Cortés et al., **Dictionary of Latin American Theatre*,

Westport, Greenwood. Osvaldo Pellettieri, *Indagaciones sobre el fin de siglo (teatro iberoamericano y argentino)*, BA, Galerna, 288 pp. *Propuestas escénicas de fin de siglo*, ed. Juan Villegas, Irvine, Gestos, 1999, 215 pp., contains essays based on the plays at the Cadiz International Festival (1998). Beatriz Risk, *Posmodernismo y teatro en América Latina. Teorías y prácticas en el umbral del siglo XXI*, Frankfurt, Vervuert, 340 pp. See also her 'El arte del performance y la subversión de las reglas del juego en el discurso de la mujer', *LATR*, 33.2:93–111, which is too general on sundry women dramatists. *LATR*, 34.1, has 16 survey articles on theatre in different Spanish American countries plus chicano and exile theatre. Amalia Gladhart, *The Leper in Blue: Coercive Performance and the Contemporary Latin American Theatre*, Chapel Hill, North Carolina U.P., 245 pp. Yolanda Flores, *The Drama of Gender: Feminist Theatre by Women of the Americas*, NY, Lang, 144 pp. examines *inter alia* plays by Carmen Boullosa, Josefina López, and Susana Torres Molina. Michael Aronna, *'Pueblos enfermos'. The Discourse of Illness in the Twentieth Century Spanish and Latin American Essay*, Chapel Hill, North Carolina U.P., 195 pp. H. Jaimes, 'La cuestión ideológica del americanismo en el ensayo hispanoamericano', *RevIb*, 192:557–69, is too general on the shift away from the theme. Nicola Miller, *In the Shadow of the State. Intellectuals and the Quest for National Identity in Twentieth Century Spanish America*, NY, Verso, 1999, 342 pp. Vicente Lecuna, *La ciudad letrada en el planeta electrónico. La situación actual del intelectual latinoamericano*, M, Pliegos, 1999, 222 pp., is basically on literary intellectuals. Patricia D'Allemand, *Latin American Cultural Criticism. Reinterpreting a Continent*, Lewiston, Mellen, 208 pp. See also her 'La crítica latinoamericana en el final del siglo: un balance', *Neophilologus*, 84:59–74, which is really on Angel Rama and Alejandro Losada. B. Trigo, 'Thinking subjectivity in Latin American criticism', *REH*, 34:309–29, praises Angel Rama, Ricardo González Echevarría, Silvia Molloy, and Doris Sommer. F. Schmidt, 'Literaturas heterogéneas y alegorías nacionales: ¿Paradigmas para las literaturas poscoloniales?', *RevIb*, 190:175–85, discusses theoretical approaches by Antonio Cornejo Polar and Fredric Jameson.

GENDERED WRITING. Carol Wasserman, *La mujer y su circunstancia en la literatura latinoamericana actual*, M, Pliegos, 222 pp. *Beyond the Border: A New Age in Latin American Women's Fiction*, ed. Nora Erro Peralta and Caridad Silva, Gainesville, Florida U.P., xxxii + 283 pp. Oralia Preble-Niemi, *Afrodita en el trópico, erotismo y construcción del sujeto femenino en obras de autoras centroamericanas*, Potomac, MD, Scripta Humanistica, 1999, 264 pp. S. Lucas Dobrian, 'La textualización del deseo: el amante desconocido en tres novelas femeninas', *RCL*, 55, 1999:155–68, deals with María Luisa Bombal's *La última niebla* (Chile), Inés Malinow's *Entrada libre* (Argentina), and Carmen Martín

Gaite's *El cuarto de atrás* (Spain). T. R. Arrington, 'Hot and spicy: eroticism and food in the writings of Isabel Allende, Fanny Buitrago and Laura Esquivel', *Secolas*, 31, 1999:125–35, is merely descriptive. Leasa Y. Lutes, **Allende, Buitrago, Luiselli: Aproximaciones teóricas al concepto del Bildungsroman femenino*, NY, Lang, 144 pp. Willy O. Muñoz, *Polifonía de la marginalidad: la narrativa de las escritoras latinoamericanas*, Santiago de Chile, Cuarto Propio, 1999, 275 pp., refers to Ana Lydia Vega, Luisa Valenzuela, Isadora Aguirre, Pía Barros, Andrea Maturana and Sara Levi Calderón. Elizabeth Marchant, *Critical Acts: Latin American Women and Cultural Criticism*, Gainesville, Florida U.P., 1999, 144 pp. deals with Lúcia Miguel Pereira, Victoria Ocampo, and Gabriela Mistral and their contradiction. S. Garabano, 'Geanología e identidad en la narrativa de Diamela Eltit y Matilde Sánchez', *Chasqui*, 29.1:88–100, never really gets to the texts.

ON MORE THAN ONE AUTHOR. *RevIb*, 188–89, 1999, is on Afro-Hispanic writing, with useful articles on Nancy Morejón (Cuba), Jorge Artel (Colombia), Enrique López Albujar (Peru), Nelson Estupiñá Bass (Ecuador), and Luz Argentina Chiriboga (Ecuador). M. DeCosta Willis, 'Can(n)on-fodder: afrohispanic literature, heretical texts and the poetics of canon formation', *AfHR*, 19.2:30–39, argues for including Marta Rojas (Cuba), Aida Cartagena Portalatín (Dominican Republic) and Jaime Manrique (Colombia). *RevIb*, 191, is on Jewish literature in Latin America with general articles and specific ones on José Kozer (Cuba), Alberto Gerchunoff (Argentina), Alicia Dujovne Ortiz (Argentina), and Marcos Aguinis (Argentina). **Reading and Writing the Ambiente. Queer Sexualities in Latino, Latin American and Spanish Culture*, Madison, Wisconsin U.P., 376 pp., contains essays by Rosemary Geisdorfer Feal and David William Foster among others. José Quiroga, *Tropics of Desire: Interventions from Queer Latino America*, NY U.P., 224 pp. *Río de la Plata*, 20–21, contains the *Actas* of a conference on writers and intellectuals from the Plate region with (rather superficial) essays on Leopoldo Lugones, Hugo Wast, Jorge Luis Borges, Eduardo Mallea, Macedonio Fernández, Manuel Mujica Lainez, Eduardo Galeano, Augusto Roa Bastos, Griselda Gambaro, Juan J. Saer, Daniel Moyano, and Abel Posse. J. Schwartz, 'De simios y antropófagos. Los monos de Lugones, Vallejo y Kafka', *NTC*, 23–4, 1999:155–68, deals with 'Ysar' by Lugones, 'Las Caynas' by Vallejo, and Kafka's 'Report to an Academy'. *Visión de la narrativa hispánica*, ed. Juan Cruz Mendizábal and Juan Fernández Jiménez, Indiana, Pennsylvania U.P., 1999, 277 pp., has essays on *modernismo*, Miguel Angel Asturias, Carlos Fuentes, Julio Cortázar, Jorge Luis Borges, and others. **1898–1998. Fines de Siglos. Historia y literatura hispanoamericanos*, ed. Jacques Joset and Philippe Raxhon, Geneva, Droz, 190 pp., has items on Alvaro Mutis and José Donoso. O. Hahn, 'Dos cuentistas paralelos: Alfonso Reyes y Jorge Luis Borges', *CAm*, 219:99–105, suggests parallels between 'La cena' and 'El milagro secreto'. D. Meyer, 'Victoria Ocampo and Alfonso Reyes: Ulysses's malady', *STCL*, 24:307–24, is on their views of Latin American identity. María Silvina Persino, **Hacia una poética de la mirada: Mario Vargas Llosa, Juan Marsé, Elena Garro and Juan Goytisolo*, BA, Corregidor, 1999, 189 pp. A. Varderi, 'Manuel Puig and Evelio Rosero Diago. Writings of the Feminine', *Antípodas*, 11–12:221–32, contrasts the Argentine and the Colombian novelist and their views of women. Reinaldo Laddaga, **Literaturas indígenas y placeres bajos. Feliberto Hernández, Virgilio Piñera y Juan Rodolfo Wilcock*, Rosario, Beatriz Viterbo, 159 pp. *Studies in Honor of Myron Lichtblau*, ed. Fernando Burgos, Delaware, Juan de la Cuesta, 362 pp., has articles on Gálvez, Bioy Casares, Fuentes, and many Argentine topics. Gordana Yovanovich, *Play and the Picaresque*, Toronto U.P., 1999, 152 pp., has articles on Julio Cortázar's *Libro de Manuel* and Antonio Skármeta's *Match Ball*.

2. INDIVIDUAL COUNTRIES

ARGENTINA

On sundry women writers: María del Mar López Cabrales, **La pluma y la represión. Escritoras contemporáneas argentinas*, NY, Lang, 189 pp. Luisa Valenzuela, 'Lo que no puede ser dicho', *Quimera*, 195:14–17, draws attention to new *testimonio* novels by Elsa Osorio, Marcela Solá, and Victoria Slavuski. Rita Gardiel, 'Argentine Jewish women short story writers', *Hispanófila*, 129:117–25, introduces Eugenia Calny, Silvia Plager, Alicia Steimberg, and Cecilia Absatz. María Elena Legaz, **Escritoras en la sala. Norah Lange, imagen y memoria*, Cordoba, Alción, 1999, 199 pp. On poetry: M. Guntsche, 'La poesía edénica de Alfredo Bufano', *His(US)*, 83:198–209, recalls this forgotten figure. Cristina Piña, **Poesía y experiencia del límite: leer a Alejandra Pizarnik*, BA, Botella al Mar, 1999, 147 pp. F. Mackintosh, 'The unquenched thirst. An intertextual reading of "las dos poetas hermanas": Alejandra Pizarnik and Elizabeth Azcona Cranwell', *BHS(L)*, 77:263–78, studies key images. M. Nicholson, 'Alejandra Pizarnik, Georges Bataille and the literature of evil', *LALR*, 54, 1999:5–22, reads the former through the latter. E. Crites, 'De militancia política a la expresión del dolor: análisis del cambio en la voz poética de Juan Gelman', *Secolas*, 31, 1999:92–102, is on the shift after his son's death.

On fiction: José Ruano de la Haza, *Estudios sobre literatura argentina in memoriam Rodolfo A. Borello*, Ottowa, Dovehouse, 318 pp., includes essays on Gálvez, Borges, and Sábato among others. Juan José

Barrientos, *Versiones*, Mexico D. F., Dirección General de Publicaciones, 138 pp., contains essays on Cortázar, Borges, Sábato, and others. J. Amícola, 'El hilo de Arachné y la toma de distancia', *RevIb*, 190:163–74, relates Roberto Arlt to Julio Cortázar and Manuel Puig. Jorgelina Corbatta, *Narrativas de la guerra sucia en Argentina (Piglia, Saer, Valenzuela, Puig)*, BA, Corregidor, 1999, 174 pp., is good both on background and analysis of texts. R. Corral, 'Un cuento de Roberto Arlt en la prensa mexicana del treinta', *Hispamérica*, 85:63–75, reprints and comments on 'Fin de cena'. A. Abós, 'Los últimos mil días de Roberto Arlt', *CHA*, 599:107–26, is on his relationship with Elizabeth Shine. Norman Cheadle, *The Ironic Apocalypse in the Novels of Leopoldo Marechal*, London, Tamesis, 192 pp. Graciela Maturo, *Marechal, el camino de la belleza*, BA, Biblos, 1999, 323 pp.

On Borges: B. Matamoro, 'Borges y Arlt; vasos comunicantes', *Hispamérica*, 85:133–38, is impressionistic. Ivonne Bordelois, *Un triángulo crucial. Borges, Güiraldes y Lugones*, BA, Eudeba, 1999, 182 pp. *Variaciones Borges*, 10, has 13 essays, including items on 'Emma Zunz', 'Deutsches Requiem', 'Abenjacán', and 'El libro de arena'. Carlos Cañeque, *Conversaciones sobre Borges*, B, Destino, 1999, 400 pp. Carlos Meneses, *El primer Borges*, Madrid, Fundamentos, 1999, 140 pp. Carlos García, 'Borges en España, Bibliografía 1919–1926', *RIAB*, 49, 1999:3–12, is very useful. Rafael Olea Franco, *Borges, desesperaciones aparentes y consuelos secretos*, Mexico D.F., Colegio de México, 1999, 312 pp. Amelia Barili, *Jorge Luis Borges y Alfonso Reyes. La cuestión de la identidad del escritor latinoamericano*, Mexico D.F., FCE, 1999, 239 pp. Willis Barnstone, *With Borges on an Ordinary Evening in Buenos Aires: A Memoir*, Champaign, Illinois U.P., 208 pp. Rene de Costa, *El humor en Borges*, M, Catedra, 1999, 152 pp. (also in English: *Humor in Borges*, Detroit, Wayne State U.P., 128 pp.). Jacques Morizot, *Sur le problème de Borges: sémiotique, ontologie, signature*, Paris, Sorbonne U.P., 1999, 262 pp. Marcel Legoff, *Jorge Luis Borges, l'univers, la lettre et le secret*, Paris, L'Harmattan, 1999, 370 pp. Eduardo García de Entería, *Fervor de Borges*, M, Trotta, 1999, 145 pp. *El siglo de Borges*, ed. Alfonso and Fernando de Toro, 2 vols, Frankfurt, Vervuert, 1999, 602, 224 pp., presents papers from the Leipzig and Venice conferences. James Woodall, *Jorge Luis Borges, Ein Mann im Spiegel seiner Bücher*, Berlin, Ullstein, 1999, 368 pp. Osvaldo Sabino, *Jorge Luis Borges. Una nueva visión de 'Ulrica'*, M, Huerga y Fierro, 1999, 117 pp., is an update of his 1987 book. *AntiBorges*, ed. Martin Lafforgue, BA, Ediciones B. Argentina, 1999, 383 pp., is reported to have essays by well-known critics. Pilar Bravo and María Paoletti, *Borges verbal*, BA, Emecé, 1999, 196 pp. Daniel Balderston et al., *Borges, una enciclopedia*, BA, Norma, 1999, 372 pp. *Los laberintos del signo, homenaje a Jorge Luis Borges*, ed. Graciela Ricci, Milan, Giuffré, 1999, 160 pp. *Cuadernos del*

Sur, 30 September 1999, is a homage to Borges with around 40 essays. Similarly *Ínsula*, 631–32, 1999, with essays by major critics. Danilo Alberto et al., **Borges en diez miradas*, BA, Fundación El Libro, 1999, 209 pp. *Variaciones Borges*, 9, has 14 essays and a documentary section. Lucila Paglias et al., **Borges y la ciencia*, BA, Eudeba, 1999, 152 pp. María Calvo Montero and Rocco Capozzi, **Relaciones literarias entre Jorge Luis Borges y Umberto Eco*, Cuenca, Castilla la Mancha U.P., 1999, 296 pp. **Borges y México*, ed. Miguel Capistrán, Mexico D.F., Plaza y Janés, 1999, 424 pp., contains about 20 essays. Steven Carter, 'Borges and his precursor', *NCL*, 29.4:7–8, alludes to Nathaniel Hawthorne. María Caballero Wangüemert, **El nacimiento de un clásico. Borges y la crítica*, M, Complutense, 1999, 210 pp. **Enrique Pezzoni, lector de Borges*, BA, Sudamericana, 1999, 213 pp. **Borges en Bruselas*, ed. Robin Lefere, M, Visor, 182 pp. E. Volek, 'Jorge Luis Borges, precursor postcolonial', *CMar*, 164:71–78 and 165:65–70, argues that his work portends postmodernism and postcolonialism. C. Tissera, 'Cosmogonía profética en la poesía última de Jorge Luis Borges', *SELA*, 44.1:60–74, is on his world-view in *Los conjurados*. G. Meo-Zilio, 'Constantes icónicos en el último Borges', *Thesaurus*, 50, 1995[2000]:337–56, analyses the imagery of *La cifra*. J. J. Muñoz Rengel, '¿En qué creía Borges?', *RCL*, 54, 1999:111–21 (and — disgracefully — in *Iberoromania*, 51:91–104), postulates pantheism. E. Pennington, 'Death and denial in Borges's later prose', *NCL*, 29.4, 1999:2–4, uses 'El disco' as his example. Ion T. Agheana, 'El ajedrez y la vindicación de la esperanza en la prosa de Jorge Luis Borges', *JHispP*, 20, 1995–96[2000]:4–18, tries to cover too much ground. Alberto Ribas-Casasayas, 'Signos mágicos de lo absoluto: aproximación a términos y conceptos de filosofía del lenguaje en tres cuentos de Jorge Luis Borges', *Neophilologus*, 84:855–74, is an excellent analysis of usages in 'El espejo de tinta', 'La escritura del dios', and 'La Biblioteca de Babel'. A. MacAdam, 'Machado de Assis and Jorge Luis Borges: immortality and its discontents', *HR*, 68:115–29, is on 'O imortal' and 'El inmortal'.

On other writers: Jaime Alazraki, **Critical Essays on Julio Cortázar*, New York, G. K. Hall, 1999, 202 pp. Elia Eisterer-Barceló, **La inquietante familiaridad. El terror y sus arquetipos en los relatos fantásticos de Julio Cortázar*, Wilhemsfeld, Egert, 1999, 296 pp. *Revista Proa*, 43, 1999, is a miscellany of items on Cortázar, 128 pp. in all, together with a CD. L. M. Martins, 'La vuelta a Julio Cortázar: el anhelo y el fatalismo de la otredad', *Neophilologus*, 84:411–22, has too many generalizations. J. M. Rodríguez García, 'A vueltas con Keats, Cortázar y la antiguedad clásica', *La Torre*, 13, 1999:587–616, is on Cortázar's essays on 'Ode to a Grecian Urn'. L. Kipnis, 'El transporte público como espacio amenazante en tres relatos de Cortázar',

Neophilologus, 84:75–86, deals with 'Omnibus', 'Después del almuerzo', and 'Manuscrito hallado en una botella'. D. Musselwhite, 'Death and the phantasm: a reading of Julio Cortázar's "Babas del diablo" ', *RoS*, 18:57–68, is interesting but unpersuasive. P. Standish, 'El teatro de Julio Cortázar', *His(US)*, 83:437–44, is a survey. *Medio siglo con Ernesto Sábato*, ed. Julia Constenla, BA, Vergara, 1999, 398 pp. Lucio Yudicello, **Ernesto Sábato: el revés de la utopía*, Cordoba, Narvaja, 1999, 138 pp. E. Weitzdörfer, 'Ernesto Sábato. Sus raíces europeas y su recepción en Alemania', *LetD*, 86:161–75, is superficial. Carolina Depetris, **El conflicto entre lo clásico y lo grotesco en Bomarzo de Manuel Mujica Láinez*, Barañain, Navarra U.P., 126 pp. S. Abate, 'Los manuscritos de *Bomarzo* de Mujica Láinez', *CHA*, 598:105–12, has interesting data. L. H. Davies, 'Portrait of a Lady: postmodern readings of Tomás Eloy Martínez's *Santa Evita*', *MLR*, 95:415–23, is on the treatment of historical 'truth'. Graciela Speranza, **Manuel Puig: después del fin de la literatura*, BA, Norma, 238 pp. Suzanne Jill Levine, *Manuel Puig and the Spider Woman: His life and Fictions*, NY, Farrar, Strauss and Giroux — London, Faber, 512 pp., is a superb critical biography. Mario Vargas Llosa, 'Loco por Lana Turner', *LetLi*, 20:26–28, is dismissive of Puig's *The Buenos Aires Affair*. Laura Demaría, **Argentina(s): Ricardo Piglia dialoga con la generación del 37 en la discontinuidad*, BA, Corregidor, 1999, 206 pp. Ana Nuño, 'Por fin Piglia. Entrevista a Ricardo Piglia', *Quimera*, 198:8–16, discusses his work and criticism. J. Premat, 'Juan José Saer y el relato regresivo. Una lectura de *Cicatrices*', *RevIb*, 192:501–09, shows that it illustrates a crisis of representation. P. Dejbord, 'Casas, casas y más casas: arquitectura de la represión en tres novelas de Marta Traba', *Chasqui*, 29.2:14–23, is on lack of private space under dictadorship. R. Dahl Buchanan, 'Visiones apocalípticos en una novela argentina: *La muerte como efecto secundario* de Ana María Shua', *RevIb*, 192:545–55, is on its sordid subject matter. K. Granrose, 'Entrevista: Mempo Giardinelli', *Hispamérica*, 84, 1999:59–69, has interesting remarks. A. Giordano, 'Situación de Héctor Bianciotti: el escritor argentino y la tradición francesa', *ib.*, 3–12, is chiefly on *Sin la misericordia de Cristo* (1987). Adrián Massli, **Héctor Tizón: una escritura desde el margen*, Cordoba, Alción, 1999, 144 pp. E. Castro, 'Identidad lésbica y sujeto femenino: el papel dela escritura en *En breve cárcel* de Silvia Molloy', *LF*, 26.1–2:10–26, is on writing as subversive. P. J. O'Connor, 'César Aira's simple lesbians: passing *La prueba*', *LALR*, 54, 1999:23–38, is chatty on this punk lesbian novel. H. M. Cavalleri, 'Ilusión, realidad e imaginario femenino: la escritura de Liliana Heker', *LF*, 26.1–2:27–40, surveys her presentation of women characters. M. Erdal Jordan, '*Mares del sur* de Noé Jitrik, ejemplo de ironía absoluta', *Hispamérica*, 85:147–55, is on its metafictional technique.

J. Barry, 'La Patagonia en Chicago: los cuentos de Alejandro Ferrer', *RoN*, 40: 295–301, is on his *Cuentos de Patagonia*.

On Theatre: R. Smetan, 'Roberto J. Payró y el teatro argentino de principios del siglo: su bibliografía puesta al día', *LATR*, 33.2: 113–32, is very full and useful. J. López Mozo, 'El teatro de Osvaldo Dragún en España', *CHA*, 591, 1999: 115–18, is an overview. Jean Graham-Jones, *Exorcising History: Argentine Theater Under the Dictatorship*, Lewisburg, Bucknell U.P., 264 pp., covers 1976–85. Saúl Sosnowski, *La cultura de un siglo*, BA, Alianza, 1999, 589 pp., analyses five groups of literary and political magazines in the 20th century.

BOLIVIA

J. Iffland, 'Pedro Shimose en sus *Reflexiones maquiavélicas*', *Hispanófila*, 129: 75–98, relates the poems to his exile.

CHILE

José Jiménez Lozano, **Maestro Huidobro*, B, Anthropos, 1999, 128 pp. J. Aguilar Mora, 'Buscar a Huidobro: poesía y posmodernidad', *Hispamérica*, 84, 1999: 13–22, is superficial on *Altazor* and today. C. Goic, 'Fin del mundo, fin de un mundo: "Ecuatorial" de Vicente Huidobro', *RCL*, 55, 1999: 5–29, is on the poet's ambiguous vision. L. Zemborain, 'Las resonancias de un nombre: Gabriela Mistral', *RevIb*, 190: 147–61, is on her self-manipulation. M. Bruzelius, 'Mother's pain, mother's voice: Gabriela Mistral, Julia Kristeva and the Mater Dolorosa', *TSWL*, 18, 1999: 215–33, is on the theme of maternal suffering. I. Carrasco, '*Poema de Chile*: un texto pedagógico', *RCL*, 56: 117–25, is on Mistral's 'visión intercultural'. Thomas Fischer, **Das Werk Pablo Nerudas im Zeitlichen Wandel*, Frankfurt, Vervuert, 1999, 212 pp. José Miguel Varas, *Nerudario*, Santiago, Planeta, 1999, 248 pp., is anecdotal on his life and friendships. Alain Sicard, **Pablo Neruda: une utopie poétique*, Paris, Messene, 176 pp. Id., 'Des résidences au chant général. La généralité du chant', *LNL*, 315: 5–18, is on Neruda's quest for totality. S. Decante, 'La representación de la escritura en "Alturas de Macchu Picchu" y "Piedra de Sol" ', *ib.*, 314: 43–55, is unscholarly on the poetic word and authenticity. H. Le Corre, ' "La tierra se llama Juan". Vers une poétique de l'énonciation', *ib.*, 315: 19–36, is on canto 8 of *Canto general*. M. Nerlich, 'La rencontre entre Cervantes y Pablo Neruda. Sur le testament en *Canto general*', *ib.*, 79–90, is on the parallel with Don Quixote's last will. M.-C. Zimmermann, 'La construction de la voix dans *Canto general*', *ib.*, 37–54, analyses the poetic voice. D. Nouhaud, 'Les longs cils noirs du pavot', *ib.*, 55–77, wanders, chiefly on Neruda's imagery. **Lectures d'un oeuvre: Residencia en la tierra – Canto general de Pablo Neruda*, ed. Néstor Ponce, Paris, Ed. du Temps, 239 pp. M. Gomes, 'Escatología y antinerudismo en *Diario de muerte* de Enrique Lihn', *REH*, 34:47–69, is on his rejection of Neruda's poetry after the *Residencias*. M. Sepúlveda, '*Vox tatuada*: un recorrido por la estética de la modernidad', *Atenea*, 480, 1999:43–57, is on Humberto Díaz Casanova's critique of referential language. R. Neustadt, 'Entrevista: Raúl Zurita', *Hispamérica*, 85:77–97, has remarks on the famous Colectivo de Acciones de Arte. Kathrin Bergenthal, **Studien zum Mini-Boom der Nueva Narrativa Chilena*, Frankfurt, Lang, 1999, 301 pp. B. Subercaseaux, 'Las mujeres también escriben malas novelas', *RCL*, 56:93–103, is on the work of Inés Echeverría de Larraín (1869–1949).

On fiction: M. Moody, 'Entrevista: Jorge Edwards', *Hispamérica*, 86:71–81, is on his latest work. H. R. Morell, 'Relaciones musicales en *El obsceno pájaro de la noche: Beethoven, Aldous Huxley y José Donoso*', *REH*, 34:71–86, posits a relationship between the novel and Beethoven's 15th quartet. Richard Callan, **Jung, Alchemy and Donoso's Novel El obsceno pájaro de la noche*, Queenstown, Mellen, 184 pp. A. Herrero-Olaizola, 'Consuming aesthetics: Seix Barral and José Donoso in the field of Latin American literary production', *MLN*, 115:323–39, is enlightening on Seix Barral and the Boom and on Donoso's *El jardín de al lado* as a *roman à clef*. S. M. Linker, 'A collision of spiritualism and rationalism in "El hombre de la rosa" de Manuel Rojas. Decoding the signals', *HR*, 68:21–36, is on its masonic and rosicrucian symbolism. Lloyd Davies, *Isabel Allende: La casa de los Espíritus*, London, Tamesis–Grant & Cutler, 109 pp., is a concise and lucid addition to this fine critical guides series. D. J. McGibboney, 'Orality and narration: subverting the pleasure of privilege in Isabel Allende's *Cuentos de Eva Luna*', *Secolas*, 31, 1999:114–24, sets femininity and orality against masculinity and writing. J. Loss, 'Wordly conjunctions and disjunctions: on cosmopolitanism and nomadism in Diamela Eltit's *Por la patria* (1986) and *El padre mío* (1989)', *Chasqui*, 29.2:24–42, is densely theoretical on her concern for the margins of culture. A. M. Sotomayor, 'Tres caricias: una lectura de Luce Irigaray en la narrativa de Diamela Eltit', *MLN*, 115:299–322, is complex on Eltit's later work. L. C. Ojeda, '*El contagio* de Guadalupe Santa Cruz; oralidad, saturación y carencia en el Chile actual', *LF*, 26.1–2:41–61, is on its satire of oppression. D. Plaza Atenas, 'Lemebel o el salto de doble filo', *RCL*, 54, 1999:123–35, is on Pedro Lemebel's themes of homosexuality and otherness. L. Guerra Cunningham, 'Ciudad liberal y los devenires de la neomodernidad en las crónicas urbanas de Pedro Lemebel', *ib.*, 56:71–92, is on his undermining of national icons. D. C. Niebylski, 'Semiologías del deseo en *Signos bajo la piel* de

Pía Barros', *ib.*, 55, 1999:67–83, is on feminine eroticism in her stories. F. Pérez Villalón, 'Luis Oyarzún: una lectura', *ib.*, 101–28, is thematic. D. Palaversich, 'Rebeldes sin causa. Realismo mágico vs realismo virtual', *Hispamérica*, 86:55–70, is on the recent work of Alberto Faguet and Sergio Gómez. T. R. Stojkov, 'Towards a feminist subjectivity. Reminiscencias de una niña judía en Chile de Majorie Agosín', *RoN*, 40:205–11, is digressive on her autobiography. *Resistencia y poder. Teatro en Chile*, ed. Heidrun Adler and George Woodyard, Frankfurt, Vervuert, 192 pp., has essays on drama from 1968 to 1999. E. Thomas, 'Representación y trascendencia de lo absurdo en el teatro chileno contemporáneo', *RCL*, 54, 1999:5–30, examines examples from Jorge Díaz, Juan Radrigán, and Marco Antonio de la Parra. S. Pereira Poza, 'El drama legendario y bíblico de Antonio Acevedo Díaz', *ib.*, 71–88, is on his proposed alternative to realist theatre.

COLOMBIA

A. Nuño, 'Restauración de la palabra: Entrevista a Eduardo Gómez'. *Quimera*, 197:47–50, comments on Colombian literary culture. M. D. Jaramillo, 'Jorge Zalamea y *El gran Burundán-Burundá*', *RevIb*, 192:587–600, is on its innovatory elements. Plinio A. Mendoza, *Aquellos tiempos con Gabo*, Barcelona, Plaza y Janés, 219 pp., is by a friend on less well-known aspects of García Márquez. *Anthropos*, 187, 1999, was a García Márquez number with a dozen essays and other material. M. L. Friedman, 'The corpses in the corpus: dead bodies in García Márquez's fiction', *RoN*, 40:135–43, is on his 'wisdom about death'. A. López-Mejía, 'La letra con sangre entra: los pasquines en *La mala hora*', *BHS(G)*, 77:451–61, is a Lacanian attempt to read more meaning into them. M. Monet-Viera, 'Brujas, putas y madres: el poder de los márgenes en *La Celestina* y *Cien años de soledad*', *ib.*, 127–46, is on Pilar Ternera and Celestina. J. C. Pettey, 'Some implications of yellow and gold in Gabriel García Márquez's *One Hundred Years of Solitude:* color symbolism, onomastics and anti-idyll', *RHM*, 53:162–78. counts 2187 references and relates them to the themes. M. Hardin, 'Greg Suriss's *Grand Avenue*: variations on three themes in Gabriel García Márquez's *One Hundred Years of Solitude*', *NCL*, 29.4, 1999:5–8, indicates incest, storytelling, and cyclic time. M. Dravasa, 'Authority and dependence in García Márquez's *El otoño del patriarca*', *RCEH*, 24:397–407, is on the collective narrator. S. Sirias, 'Bolivar's corporeal etherialness and his lost dream of unification in García Márquez's *El general en su laberinto*', *RHM*, 53:79–91, argues that the dream is still relevant. L. Otis, 'Signs of life: communication in *El amor en los tiempos del cólera*', *REH*, 34:261–87, is on the success and failure of coded messages.

C. Rincón, 'García Márquez con Hawthorne: la re-escritura en *De amor y otros demonios*', *La Torre*, 19, 1999:433–48, seems far-fetched. W. O. Deaver, 'Obsesión, posesión y opresión en *De amor y otros demonios*', *AfHR*, 19.2:80–85, is on García Márquez's alleged privileging of *mestizaje*. L. E. Porto, 'Claroscuros: el mestizaje cromático, telúrico y racial en *Chambacú: corral de negros*', *ib.*, 59–69, is on the ambiguity of Manuel Zapata Olivella's 1990 novel. A. Castillo Granada, 'La ley del pasajero: entrevista a Ricardo Cano Gaviria', *Quimera*, 197:42–46, discusses Roland Barthes, Walter Benjamin, Pedro Gómez Valderrama, and others. H. D. Fernández L'Hoeste, '*La Virgen de los Sicarios* o las visiones dantescas de Fernando Vallejo', *His(US)*, 83:757–67, is on the national problem. Laurence E. Prescott, **Without Hatreds or Fears. Jorge Artel and the Struggle for Black Literary Expression in Colombia*, Detroit, Wayne State U.P., 298 pp.

COSTA RICA

J. Chen Sham, 'La insurrección de la mujer y su estrategia liberadora en Ana Istarú: el poema III de *La estación de fiebre*', *SELA*, 44.2:19–27, is on the degree of her rebelliousness. W. O. Muñoz, 'El lenguaje y la devaluación del cuerpo preñado en "Simbiosis del encuentro" de Carmen Naranjo', *LF*, 26.1–2:99–110, is on its critique of male-female otherness.

CUBA

Janett Reinstädtler and Ottmar Ette, **Todas las islas la isla. Nuevas y novísimas tendencias en la literatura y cultura de Cuba*, M, Iberoamericana — Frankfurt, Vervuert, 218 pp. Raquel Rumeu, **Voces de mujeres en la literatura cubana*, M, Verbum, 200 pp. Gustavo Pérez Firmat, **My own Private Cuba*, Boulder, SSSAS, 1999, 251 pp., contains essays on Nicolás Guillén, Carlos Loveira and others. *Unión* (Cuba), 33, 1998[2000]:2–30, has a short dossier of essays on José Lezama Lima. Remedios Mataix, **Para una teoría de la cultura: La expresión americana de José Lezama Lima*, Alicante, Cuadernos de América Sin Nombre, 60 pp. César A. Salgado, **From Modernism to Neobaroque: Joyce and Lezama Lima*, Lewisburg, Bucknell U.P. V. Rodríguez Nuñez, 'Extrañeza de estar, certidumbre del otro: la poesía temprana de Cintio Vitier', *Hispamérica*, 84, 1999:23–35, is on his 'acto de resistencia'. L. Feracho, 'Arrivals and farewells: the dynamics of Cuban homespace through African mythology in two Eleggua poems by Nancy Morejón', *His(US)*, 83:51–58, looks at 'Los ojos de ellegua' and 'Cuento la despedida'. G. A. Abudu, 'African oral arts in Excilia Saldaña's *Kele Kele*', *AfHR*, 19.2:21–29, is on her transcriptions of Afro-Cuban myths. W. Hernández, 'Ni arte puro ni arte para: Fina

García Marruz y la poesía cubana de los noventa', *RoN*, 40:235–44, is on the collapse of revolutionary poetry. O. B. González, 'El poema autorretrato en Octavio Armand y sus contemporáneos', *His(US)*, 83:31–41, studies examples from the work of Armand, Reinaldo García Ramos, Luis F. González, and Andrés Reinaldo. J. B. Alvarez, 'El homoerotismo en la narrativa cubana del siglo xx', *Antipodas*, 11–12:25–48, is on three generations of gay writers. J. C. Galdo, 'Usos y lecciones del discurso ejemplar: a propósito de *El ángel de Sodoma* de Alfonso Hernández Catá', *Chasqui*, 29.1:19–32, is on its early use of a homosexual theme. R. Veguez, '*Pedro Blanco el negrero*: ¿novela o biografía novelada?', *Symposium*, 54:43–56, tries to re-evaluate this 1933 novel by Lino Novás Calvo. Gabriel María Rubio Navarro, **Música y escritura en Alejo Carpentier*, Alicante U.P., 1999, 247 pp. J. M. Powell, 'The conflict of becoming: cultural hybridity and the representation of focalization in Caribbean literature', *LitP*, 45, 1999:63–91, sees a blend of cultures in Carpentier's *El reino de este mundo*. Mario Vargas Llosa, '¿Lo real maravilloso o artimañas literarias?', *LetLi*, 13:32–36, discusses *El reino de este mundo* as illustrating the latter. L. A. Martínez, 'El mito-máscara en la obra de Severo Sarduy', *RCL*, 54, 1999:43–53, is on his theory of paradigm shift and neo-baroque writing. L. Ulloa and J. C. Ulloa, 'Manifestaciones de la escritura somática en la narrativa de Severo Sarduy', *SELA*, 44.1:15–27, is on the semantics of the body. María Luisa Negrín, **El círculo del exilio y la enajenación en la obra de Reinaldo Arenas*, Lewiston, Mellen, 188 pp. J. Olivares, '¿Por qué llora Arenas?', *MLN*, 115:268–98, is on *Antes que anochezca* and *Viaje a la Habana*. J. I. Gutiérrez, 'Premisas y avatares de la novela testimonio: Miguel Barnet', *RCL*, 56:53–69, is on the hybridity of the testimonial genre. Phyllis Zatlin, **The Novels and Plays of Eduardo Manet: An Adventure in Multiculturalism*, University Park, Pennsylvania State U.P., 1999, 243 pp., is a survey. R. Castells, 'La novela policíaca en la Cuba del período especial: *Pasado perfecto* de Leonardo Padura Fuentes', *SELA*, 43.4:21–35, is on its transgressive documentalism. M. A. González-Abellás, 'Aquella isla: introducción al universo narrativo de Zoé Valdés', *His(US)*, 83:42–50, is on the theme of exile. J. B. Alvarez, 'El cuento cubano de 1959 a 1990. Un movimiento pendular', *SELA*, 43.3:21–36, is on ideology *versus* imagination. L. Linares-Ocanto, 'Los dioses en sí mismos: lo afro-cubano en *Requiem por Yarini* de Carlos Felipe', *LATR*, 33.2:43–52, is on the play's magical and religious dimensions.

DOMINICAN REPUBLIC

F. Valerio-Holguín, 'El trujillato como causa ausente en *Sólo cenizas hallarás, (bolero)* de Pedro Vergés', *RHM*, 53:206–13, is on its strategy as a historical novel. See also Id., 'Jacques Lacan, Lucho Gatica, Pedro Vergés, el imaginario bolerístico', *La Torre*, 11, 1999:109–19.

U. M. Saine, 'Female representation and feminine mystique in Alicia Yañez Cossío's 'La mujer es un mito'', *LF*, 26.1–2:63–79, is on its intriguing contradictions. Kenneth Wishnia, *Twentieth Century Ecuadorian Narrative. New Readings in the Context of the Americas*, Cranbury, NJ, Bucknell U.P., 1999, 202 pp., deals with Pablo Palacio, José de la Cuadra, Demetrio Aguilera Malta, Eliécer Cárdenas, and Alicia Yañez Cossío, and other topics.

R. K. Anderson, 'Manlio Argueta: a committed Third World author', *SELA*, 43.1–2, 1999:38–49, is on *Un día en la vida*.

Stephen Henighan, *Assuming the Light: The Parisian Literary Apprenticeship of Miguel Angel Asturias*, Oxford, Legenda, 1999, 227 pp., goes up to *El Señor Presidente*. *CA*, 83, contains a homage to Asturias with seven essays. J. Ramírez Caro, 'Lo erótico y la subversión de lo político y lo religioso en *El Señor Presidente*', *Sociocriticism*, 14.2:41–50, and Id., 'La impotencia de Dios en el infierno de la dictadura en *El Señor Presidente*', *ib.*, 51–59, are seriously under-researched on the mythic subtext. L. Porto, 'Transporting the sacred on the shoulders of ants: the uneasy exchange of "base matter" for broken wings in Asturias's *Hombres de maíz*', *RHM*, 52, 1999:487–512, is densely argued using George Bataille's theories. G. García, 'El pacto testimonial en *Me llamo Rigoberta Menchú y así me nació la conciencia*', *ib.*, 523–39, criticizes recent criticism of the book. R. Luzárraga, 'Rodrigo Rey Rola', *Quimera*, 187:8–14, records an interview with this new novelist.

J. Pellicer, 'La *Hora de Junio* de Carlos Pellicer: notas, claves, silencios y alteraciones de una crisis', *RevIb*, 192:481–500, analyses some of the sonnets. José Quiroga, **Understanding Octavio Paz*, Columbia, S. Carolina U.P., 1999, xii + 194 pp., in the well-known series. *LetLi*, 4, 1999, has an essay and sundry journalistic pieces on Paz. Jesús Silva-Hertzog Márquez, 'Sílabas enamoradas. El pensamiento político de Octavio Paz', *Nexos*, 265:71–76, is on his liberalism. N. Valis,

'La voz moral de Octavio Paz', *Salina*, 14:143–49, is mainly on his self-distancing from the Left. C. Román-Odio, '*Blanco*, A Western Mandala', *RCEH*, 34:503–16, is ultimately on its decentredness. E. Ruiz-Fornells, 'La India de Octavio Paz: testimonio y pensamiento', *CHA*, 595:79–90, is chiefly on *Vislumbres de India*. A. Estill, '(Micro)scoping the body: Coral Bracho's Green poetics', *Hispanófila*, 129:99–116, is on lack of gendered identity in her poems. Monika Pipping de Serrano, **Mexikanische Identitätszeichen: Studien zum erzählerischen Werk von José Revueltas (1914–1976)*, Frankfurt, Vervuert, 1999, 292 pp. B. E. Jörgensen, 'Speaking from the soapbox: Benita Galeana's *Benita*', *LALR*, 53:46–66, discusses this early early example of *testimonio*. Michaela Peters, **Weibsbilder. Weiblichkeitskonzepte von Rulfo bis Boullosa*, Frankfurt, Vervuert, 1999, 288 pp. C. Hermann Middelanis, **Lichtblicke. Mexikanisch. Photographische Notizen des Dichters Juan Rulfo*, Kassel, Reichenberger, 1999, 244 pp. M. S. Fernández Utrera, '*El gallo de oro* "Argumento para cine" de Juan Rulfo', *ETL*, 27.2, 1998–99:44–69, gives a detailed over-all analysis. Nuala Finnegan, **Projections of Femininity in the Fiction of Mexican Writer Rosario Castellanos*, Lewiston, Mellen, 196 pp. G. Luongo Morales, 'El modelo autobiográfico en "Dos poemas" de Rosario Castellanos', *RCL*, 54, 1999:89–109, contains a close theory-based analysis. P. J. McNab, 'Humor in Castellanos's *El eterno femenino: The Fractured Female Image*', *LATR*, 33.2:79–91, is excellent, chiefly on Act 1. W. Caldwell, 'En busca de un centro femenino nuevo: una desconstrucción de lo "subfemenino" en dos ensayos de Rosario Castellanos', *La Torre*, 14, 1999:651–58, examines 'Lección de cocina' and 'La mujer y su imagen'. R. Biron, 'Joking around with Mexican history: parody in Jorge Ibargüengoitía, Rosario Castellanos and Gustavo Sainz', *REH*, 34:625–44, deals with *Los relámpagos de agosto*, *El eterno femenino*, and *Fantasmas aztecas*. Jorge F. Hernández, **Carlos Fuentes, territorios del tiempo. Antología de entrevistas*, Mexico D.F., FCE, 1999, 310 pp. D. Nouhaud, '*La región más trasparente*. Pequeñas felonías, cobardía usual; el pan nuestro de cada día', *LNL*, 311, 1999:107–25, examines two sequences in the novel. Yves Aguila, 'A propos des personages de *La región más transparente*', *ib.*, 127–44, is on the links among them. C. Giudicelli, 'Perspectivisme et dialogisme dans *La región más transparente*', *ib.*, 145–56, is on the narrative strategy. K. Hada, 'Christ, culture and conscience: Rudolfo Anaya's *Bless me, Ultima* and Carlos Fuentes's *The Good Conscience*', *NCL*, 29.4, 1999:9–10, is on youthful religiosity. R. J. Friis, 'The postmodern twists of José Emilio Pacheco's *No me preguntes cómo pasa el tiempo*', *REH*, 34:27–45, is too descriptive. J. A. Epple, 'De Santa a Mariana: la ciudad de México como utopía traicionada', *RCL*, 54, 1999:31–42, is essentially on José Emilio Pacheco's *Las batallas en el desierto* (1981). F. Degiovanni, 'Fin de siglo,

mar de sangre: José Emilio Pacheco', *Hispamérica*, 85:139–45, is on
the poem's pessimistic vision. Robin W. Fiddian, *The Novels of Fernando
del Paso*, Gainesville, Florida U.P., 184 pp., is perhaps the year's best.
F. places his novels critically in a wide perspective of modern Latin
American fiction. C. Canfield, 'God and Satan: the ephemeral Other
and self-consciousness of Jesusa Palancares in *Hasta no verte Jesús mío*',
RCEH, 24:275–94, is on her view of self and Other in a religious
context. J. B. Pouwels, 'Political bias in readings of two Tlatelolco
novels: Elena Poniatowska's *La noche de Tlatelolco* and an unwelcome
sequel, Luis Spota's *La plaza*', *BHS(L)*, 77:279–90, compares the two
and the criticism. P. Orgambide, 'Conversación con Elena Poniatowska. La princesa rebelde', *CAm*, 218:103–06, is merely anecdotic.
S. Mato, 'Carmen Boullosa's *La milagrosa*: a light detective fiction or a
dense aesthetic work', *LF*, 26.1–2:125–36, is on its hybridity.
Y. Halevy-Wise, 'Simbología en *Como agua para chocolate: las aves y el
fuego*', *RHM*, 52, 1999:513–22, explains these important symbols.
T. Escaja, 'Reinscribiendo a Penélope: mujer e identidad mejicana
en *Como agua para chocolate*', *RevIb*, 192:571–86, adds nothing to
existing criticism. C. Meacham, 'A woman's testimony on the
Mexican crisis: Guadalupe Loaeza's *Sin Cuenta*', *LF*, 26.1–2:111–24,
is on it as testimonial writing. L. J. Beard, 'Navigating the fictional
text: Julieta Campos's *Tiene los cabellos rojizos y se llama Sabina*',
Hispanófila, 129:45–58, is on its de-centredness. A. Cortázar,
'Implicaciones subalternas de un proliferado discurso coloquial en la
obra narrativa de Luis Zapata', *ib.*, 59–74, is on his 'rebellious' style.
A. Herrero-Olaizola, 'Homosexuales en la escena: identidad y
performance en la narrativa de Luis Zapata', *Antipodas*,
11–12:249–61, surveys four novels. D. Palaversich, 'El fenómeno
monstruoso y la crisis del género en *La hermana secreta de Angélica
María*', *ib.*, 233–48, is on Zapata's 1989 novel and hermaphoditism.
M. Beneyto, 'Invitación a la lectura del último Premio Rulfo',
Quimera, 186, 1999:49–55, introduces Sergio Pitol. J. P. Ressot,
'Pastiche et parodie dans les romans de Taibo II', *LNL*, 311,
1999:157–68, is on Paco Taibo's novels 'as if' they were social.
A. Charlon, 'Mexicanos de segunda, escritores de tercera: los héroes
convocados por Paco Taibo II', *ib.*, 169–80, is on the characters'
social class. Guadalupe Cortina, *Invenciones multitudinarias: escritoras
judeomexicanas contemporáneas*, Newark, Juan de la Cuesta, 160 pp.,
covers Margo Glantz, Ethel Krauze, Sara Levi Calderón, and Sara
Sefchovich. I. Vélez, 'Lecturas con sabor a chocolate de cerezas:
conversando con Margo Glantz en Coyacán', *RevIb*, 192:661–76, is
extensive on her life and writings. E. Hind, 'Entrevista con Sabina
Berman', *LATR*, 33.2:133–39, has some very handy declarations.
A. Luiselli, 'La voz en off de Sor Juana: *Tren nocturno a Georgia* y el

teatro mexicano al comienzo del milenio', *ib.*, 5–20, examines sexual relationships and society in this play by María Luisa Medina. B. A. Padrón-León and C. G. Peale, 'Una tarde con Héctor Mendoza', *ib.*, 33.1, 1999: 161–67, has useful remarks by this director.

NICARAGUA

G. R. Barrow, 'Divine praises in Ernesto Cardenal', *Neophilologus*, 83, 1999: 559–75, is on supplication, especially in 'Como en la rueda de un alfarero'. A. Velásquez, 'Entrevista: Claribel Alegría', *Hispamérica*, 86: 85–92, is on her committed poetry and other issues. L. B. Rhodan, 'The quest for the mother in the novels of Gioconda Belli', *LF*, 26.1–2: 81–97, is on the mother-daughter bond. Reynaldo González, 'Reencuentro habanero con Sergio Ramírez', *CAm*, 219: 134–39, contains important declarations.

PANAMA

H. Zoggyie, 'Ubicaciones de la identidad en *Chombo* de Carlos Guillermo Wilson', *AfHR*, 19.2: 53–58 is on the degree of his *afrocentrismo*.

PERU

Maynor Freyre, **Altas voces de la literatura peruana y latinoamericana. Segunda mitad del siglo. Entrevistas, comentarios y reportajes*, Lima, San Marcos U.P., 350 pp. Yazmín López Leuci, **El laboratorio de la vanguarda en el Peru. Revista culturales de los años veinte*, Lima, Horizonte, 1999, 178 pp. Noel Altamirano, **Vallejo, poeta corporal del alma. Una lectura psicoanalítica*, Lima, San Marcos U.P., 1999, 257 pp. André Coyné, **Medio siglo con Vallejo*, Lima, Univ. Pontificia, 1999, 728 pp. Roland Forgues, **Vallejo da forma a su destino*, Lima, Minerva, 1999, 174 pp. Carlos Henderson, **La poética de la poesía póstuma de Vallejo*, Lima, Biblioteca Nacional, 116 pp. G. Geirola, 'César Vallejo: enunciación y teatralidad', *RCL*, 55, 1999: 31–65, is too general on the 'spectacle' aspect of his work. G. Lambie, 'Vallejo's interpretation of Spanish history and culture in the "Himno a los voluntarios de la República"', *BHS(L)*, 76, 1999: 367–84, is mainly on background. E. O'Hara, 'La curva, la gota de agua', *RCL*, 54, 1999: 137–45, is on Raúl Deusta and the Generación del 50. C. Ruiz Barrionuevo, 'Reescritura e invención en las "canciones" de Carlos Germán Belli', *Hispamérica*, 85: 37–50, is on on his link with the *canción* tradition. César Angeles Caballero, **Alberto Valcarcel: poeta entre dos orillas*, Lima, San Marcos U.P., 1999, 256 pp. C. L. Orihuela, 'The poetics of Nicomedes Santa Cruz and its challenge to the canon of Peruvian hegemonic literature', *AfHR*, 19.2:40–44, is on his incorporation into the canon. Miguel Gutiérrez, **Los andes en la novela peruana actual*, Lima, San Marcos U.P., 1999, 253 pp. Cynthia Vich, *Indigenismo de vanguardia en el Peru*, Lima, Univ. Católica, 279 pp., studies the periodical *Boletín Titicaca*. Daniel Mathews, **La paideia retrógrada: novela y escuela de Arguedas*, Huancayo, Sociedad Científica Andina de Folklore, 1999, 112 pp., is on *Los ríos profundos* by José María Arguedas. *Arguedas en familia*, ed. C. María Pinilla, Lima, Univ. Pontificia, 1999, 415 pp., contains letters to relatives and others. A. Lambright, 'Time, space and gender: creating the hybrid intellectual in *Los ríos profundos*', *LALR*, 55:5–26, is on Ernesto's juxtaposition of opposite characteristics. Ricardo Silva Esteban, **Valdelomar por el mismo, cartas, entrevista, testimonios y documentos*, Lima, Congreso, 2 vols. Jesús Rodero, **Los márgenes de la realidad en los cuentos de Julio Ramón Ribeyro*, New Orleans, U.P. of the South, 1999, 172 pp. See also Id., 'Del juego y lo fantástico en algunos relatos de Julio Ramón Ribeyro', *RevIb*, 190:73–91, discussing 'Doblaje', 'Ridder y el pisapapeles', 'La insignia', and 'El carousel'. Miguel Gutiérrez, **Ribeyro en dos ensayos*, Lima, San Marcos U.P., 1999, 283 pp. **Das Literarische Werk von Mario Vargas Llosa*, ed. José Morales Saravia, Frankfurt, Vervuert, 1999, 352 pp., contains the *Actas* of the 1998 Berlin Conference. Braulio Muñoz, **A Storyteller: Mario Vargas Llosa between Civilization and Barbarism*, Lanham, Rowman & Littlefield, 134 pp. Néstor Ponce, **'La ciudad y los perros' de Mario Vargas Llosa*, Paris, Ed. du Temps, 1999, 160 pp. J. Castro Urrioste, 'Mario Vargas Llosa's *El hablador* as a discourse of conquest', *STCL*, 24:241–55, is a debatable interpretation. B. J. Carbajal, 'Love and sex in Mario Vargas Llosa's *¿Quién mató a Palomino Molero?*', *HR*, 68:267–78, is on the novel's exposure of corruption. H. Klüppelholz, 'Der Weite Weg Litumas zum Detektiv bei Mario Vargas Llosa', *Archiv*, 236, 1999:330–43, is on the two Lituma novels. S. Rosell, 'Los rituales funerarios y el espacio erótico en *La Chunga* de Mario Vargas Llosa', *LATR*, 33.2:53–63, deals with context and the limitations imposed on female characters. E. Zorrozúa Eguren, 'Tres fábulas quiliastas de Mario Vargas Llosa', *LetD*, 84, 1999:105–37, is on millenarism in *La guerra del fin del mundo*, *Historia de Mayta*, and *El hablador*. C. Schwalb, '*Historia de Mayta* y el interrogante de la crisis del Peru', *RHM*, 53:192–205, is on the novel's hidden paradoxical theme. D. Cohn, '"Regreso a la barbarie": intertextual paradigms for Peru's descent into chaos in *Lituma en los Andes*', *LALR*, 55:27–45, postulates references to Cervantes, Borges, Euripides, Rivera, and Miguel Angel Asturias. G. Martí-Peña, 'Egon Schiele y *Los cuadernos de don Rigoberto* de Mario Vargas Llosa: iconotextualidad e intermedialidad', *RevIb*, 190:93–111, relates painting to writing. E. Krauze, 'La seducción del poder', *LetLi*, 19:22–26, is an interview with Vargas

Llosa on *La fiesta del chivo*. A. Vargas Llosa, 'Las dictaduras latinoamericanas', *ib*., 21:20–23, is also a conversation about *La fiesta del chivo*.
H. Aguilar Camín, 'Nos mató la ideología. Una entrevista con Mario
Vargas Llosa', *Nexos*, 271:42–55, is long and meaty, also partly on *La
fiesta del chivo*. D. Wood, 'Identity and cultural identity in Alfredo
Bryce Echenique's *Cuadernos de navegación en un sillón voltaire*', *BHS(L)*,
76, 1999:519–32, is on Martín's quest. M. A. Cabañas, ' "Con los
ojos bien abiertos": la picaresca y *Tantas veces Pedro*', *Hispanófila*,
128:91–101, sees the novel as carnivalizing and transforming the
genre. César Ferreira and Ismael P. Máquez, *De lo andino a lo universal.
La obra de Edgardo Rivera Martínez*, Lima, Univ. Pontificia, 1999,
295 pp., presents essays of varying quality on this recent prose writer.

D. Torres, 'El "hombre de papel" en *Invitación al polvo* de Manuel
Ramos Otero', *Chasqui*, 29.1:33–49, is on its presentation of homo-
sexual love. W. Hernández, 'Política homosexual y escritura poética
en Manuel Ramos Otero', *ib*., 29.2:73–95, is also on his use of
homosexual themes. M. A. Pérez-Ortiz, 'Del voyeur al mirón; la
palabra es la técnica objetivante en los textos de Edgardo Rodríguez
Juliá', *RevIb*, 192:511–32, is primarily on his *crónicas*. I. Ruiz Cumba,
'Edgardo Rodríguez Juliá y las paradojas de la (autor)idad narrativa',
La Torre, 12, 1999:449–68, is on authorial authority in his work.
S. Rosell, 'El embarque y el desborde: navegando el Caribe junto a
Mayra Montero y Ana Lydia Vega', *SELA*, 44.1:47–59, is on the
former's *La última noche que pasé contigo* and the latter's *Encarcamblado*.
G. B. Irizarry, 'La cultura nacional popular puertorriqueña en *Balada
de otro tiempo* de José Luis González', *La Torre*, 13, 1999:539–57, is on
his defence of aspects of national culture. G. Puleo, 'Historia y
literatura en las crónicas boricuas de Cayetano Coll y Toste y Ana
Lydia Vega, o dos alas de un mismo pájaro', *ib*., 571–86, is on their
nationalism. M. Gossler Esquilín, 'La transculturación racial y sexual:
¿treta posmoderna de Ana Lydia Vega', *Chasqui*, 29.2:108–21, is in
the end on her story 'Pollito Chicken'. S. M. Palmer, 'Eros y logos
confrontados: reivindicación de la esencia femenina y destitución del
mito de la superioridad masculina en "La muñeca menor" de Rosario
Ferré', *La Torre*, 14, 1999:679–99, is Jungian.

E. Cróquer Pedrón, 'T(r)opologías: el caso Delmira Agustini', *RevIb*,
190:13–24, criticizes the criticism of her. E. Mallen, 'Conciencia
poética y lenguaje en la obra de Eduardo Espina', *REH*, 34:165–87,

is on the link between language and reality in his poetry. B. Natanson,
'De la teoría a la escritura: estrategias narrativas en "Los fabricantes
de carbón" de Horacio Quiroga', *Hispamérica*, 84, 1999:105–15, is a
technical analysis. J. A. Rosario-Andújar, 'Más allá del espejo: la
división del sujeto en la narrativa de Felisberto Hernández', *RevIb*,
190:37–45, is somewhat Freudian on mirror-imaging in characterization. J. Fombona, 'Cuño, cuña, coño: juegos de Felisberto Hernández', *ib.*, 25–36, is on 'Las hortensias'. F. Graziano, 'Entrevista a
María Isabel Hernández Guerra', *ib.*, 63–70, speaks of her father,
Felisberto Hernández. R. Cánovas, 'Volviendo la mirada hacia
Juntacadáveres de Juan Carlos Onetti', *RCL*, 56:33–52, is on its
narrative structure. G. San Román, 'La geografía de Onetti en *El
astillero*', *BHS(L)*, 77:107–121, is very helpful. C. Schwald, 'La
escritura cifrada de "Un sueño realizado" de Juan Carlos Onetti',
Hispanófila, 129:35–44, is Barthesian on the story as metaliterary.
C. Faccini, 'Hacia la configuración de un discurso contrahegemónico
del exilio uruguayo. Mario Benedetti', *La Torre*, 13, 1999:505–25, is
rather theoretical on his poetry. S. Gregory, '"El rostro tras la
página": el periodismo literario de Mario Benedetti 1950–1970',
Hispamérica, 86:43–50, is too uncritical. R. Roffé, 'Entrevista a Mario
Benedetti', *CHA*, 579:99–110, is rather too chatty and general.
C. Henseler, 'Advertizing eroticism: fetishism on display in Cristina
Peri Rossi's *Solitario de amor*', *ALEC*, 25:479–502, is on female
transgressive eroticism. A. Nuño, 'Entrevista a Cristina Peri Rossi',
Quimera, 185, 1999:9–13, answers some interesting questions.
M. Rowinsky, 'La lectura como acto de complicidad amorosa.
(Entrevista con Cristina Peri Rossi)', *RevIb*, 190:49–62, has quotable
remarks. R. Luzárraga, 'La Itaca global: entrevista a Carlos Liscano',
Quimera, 190:6–9, is chiefly on his recent *El camino de Itaca*. B. Castro,
'Viaje a la posthistoria: *El camino de Itaca* de Carlos Liscano',
Hispamérica, 85:51–61, is on the hero's quest for self-discovery.
I. A. D. Stewart, 'Forgetting amnesia: Tomás de Matto's *Bernabé,
Bernabé* and Uruguayan identity', *RCEH*, 24:383–96, is on seeking
national unity via a selective view of history.

VENEZUELA

M. Ramírez Ribes, 'Invitación al silencio: entrevista a Rafael
Cárdenas', *Quimera*, 193.4:21–23. G. Guerrero, 'Uslar Pietri, cronista
del realismo mestizo', *CHA*, 605:53–62, links him with Miguel Angel
Asturias and Alejo Carpentier. L. Azparren Giménez, 'Román
Chalbaud: el realismo crítico en el teatro venezolano de los 60',

LATR, 33.2 : 21–42, is on his break with 'ingenuous' realism. M. Milleret, 'Staging sex and the midlife woman in Mariela Romero's *Esperando al italiano*', *REH*, 34 : 247–60, is on presenting sex in the life of an older woman.

BRAZILIAN LITERATURE

By MARK DINNEEN, *Spanish, Portuguese and Latin American Studies,
University of Southampton*

1. GENERAL

'Tira-dúvidas com Roberto Schwarz: entrevista a Afonso Fáveo, Airton Paschoa, Francisco Mariutti e Marcos Falleiros', *NovE*, 58:53–71, is a wide-ranging discussion on approaches towards Brazilian literature, in which Schwarz debates some of the key ideas underlying his literary criticism. B. Nunes, 'La crítica literaria en el Brasil, antes y ahora', *CHA*, 601–02:53–65, is a thought-provoking review of the major developments that have occurred within Brazilian literary criticism over the last 50 years. Leyla Perrone-Moisés, *Inútil poesia e outros ensaios breves*, SPo, Companhia das Letras, 364 pp., includes essays on Lispector, Guimarães Rosa, and Mário de Andrade in a collection of over 40 short literary studies of writers from around the world. *Literatura e Identidades*, ed. José Luís Jobim, R, UERJ, 1999, 260 pp., is a collection of 14 conference papers which, from a variety of theoretical positions, discuss the relationship between literature and the construction of identities. Among the Brazilian topics included are the work of Joaquim Norberto Sousa Silva, and of Antônio Cândido, and Afro-Brazilian poetry. José Castello, *Inventário das sombras*, R, Record, 1999, 305 pp., is a work of investigative journalism rather than literary criticism. It attempts to provide brief but intimate portraits of such writers as Clarice Lispector, Caio Fernando Abreu, Nelson Rodrigues, and Dalton Trevisan. *Antônio Cândido: pensamento e militância*, ed. Flávio Aguiar, SPo, Fundação Perseu Abramo, 1999, 336 pp., are conference papers by well-known Brazilian literary and cultural critics given in honour of C., discussing all aspects of his life and work. *NTC*, 23–24, 1999, is a special issue dedicated to reassessing Oswald de Andrade's *manifesto antropófago*. In the light of a wide range of theoretical perspectives, numerous critics debate the significance that the manifesto continues to have for Brazilian culture today. *O berço do cânone*, ed. Regina Zilberman and Maria Eunice Moreira, Porto Alegre, Mercado Aberto, 1998, 351 pp., gathers together nine studies of Brazilian literature by 19th-c. scholars, as a record of the first attempts made to define a distinct body of national literature. Manuel da Costa Fontes, *Folklore and Literature: Studies in Portuguese, Brazilian, Cephardic and Hispanic Oral Traditions*, Albany, State Univ. of NY, 288 pp. *Encyclopedia of Contemporary Latin American and Caribbean Cultures*, ed. Daniel Balderston, Mike Gonzalez, and Ana E. López, London, Routledge, 3 vols, 1754 pp., contains brief entries on an extensive number of Brazilian writers and literary topics.

2. COLONIAL

Adelto Gonçalves, *Gonzaga, um poeta do Iluminismo*, R, Nova Fronteira, 538 pp., is the first full biography of G. Well researched and very detailed, the work sets out to clarify the circumstances which shaped both the poet's writing and his political activity. G. Mártires Coelho, 'A pátria do Anticristo: a expulsão do jesuítas do Maranhão e Grão-Pará e o messianismo milenarista do Padre Vieira', *LBR*, 37.1:17–32, focuses on V.'s *Sermão da Epifania*, in a discussion of his reaction to the expulsion of the Jesuits from Maranhão and Grão-Pará in 1661.

3. THE NINETEENTH CENTURY

Lúcia Granja, *Machado de Assis, escritor em formação (à roda dos jornais)*, SPo, Mercado de Letras, 167 pp., is a study of M.'s early journalism, which seeks to identify within it the development of aspects of style and technique that would characterize his later novels. Paulo Venâncio Filho, *Primos entre si: temas em Proust e Machado de Assis*, R, Nova Fronteira, 153 pp., is a comparative study of the two writers which focuses on how love, humour, and memory affect the conduct of characters. J. Andrews, 'Carlos Gomes' *Il Guarany*: the frontiers of miscegenation in nineteenth-century grand opera', *PortSt*, 16:26–42, studies the differences between Alencar's novel *O guarani* and the operatic version produced by Gomes in order to highlight changing views of race relations in Brazil in the latter part of the century. T. V. Zimbrão da Silva, 'Homo Ludens and *Esaú e Jacó*, Homo Economicus and *Hard Times*: literary representations of the nineteenth-century bourgeoisie', *ib.*, 43–51, discusses Machado's depiction of the distinctive characteristics of the Brazilian bourgeoisie in the 19th c. by contrasting it with European literary representations of the same social class, with Dickens used as the example. N. Afolabi, 'Machado de Assis: uma teorização de ambigüedade', *RevIb*, 190:121–38, seeks to show how ambiguity in M.'s work serves to ridicule the limitations of many of the philosophical theories proposed during the author's lifetime. A. P. Durand, 'Quatre mariages et deux enterrements: *Helena* de Machado de Assis', *RoN*, 41:97–104, argues that the novel's qualities, such as its sophistication of structure and the strength of its existential message, have not been given adequate recognition by critics. *CHA*, 598, contains six essays on Machado de Assis: J. Almino, 'El pesimismo como método: comentario sobre Machado de Assis' (11–25), is an overview of M.'s work, highlighting its unique qualities and discussing the different interpretations of it offered by critics. K. D. Jackson, 'La metáfora antropófaga' (27–33), briefly discusses M.'s novels in the light of Oswald de Andrade's theory of *antropofagia*. A. Dimas, 'El espejo irónico de Machado: entrevista con John Gledson' (36–45), is a discussion of Gledson's critical studies of M.'s work. J. A. Barbosa, 'Mágicas parciales de *Dom Casmurro*' (47–52), concentrates on the narrative techniques employed in the novel. C. A. Pasero, 'Machado de Assis, cuentista' (53–66), is an introduction to M.'s short stories which emphasizes their thematic range. I. Soler, 'La lógica del instinto y el azar' (67–72), also discusses M.'s short stories, highlighting the originality of M's approach to the genre. Leonardo Mendes, **O retrato do imperador: negociação, sexualidade e romance naturalista no Brasil*, Porto Alegre, EDIPUCRS, 228 pp. E. A. Marchant, 'Naturalism, race and nationalism in Aluísio Azevedo's *O Mulato*', *His(US)*, 83:445–53, examines how the novel confronts the question of national identity, highlighting A.'s selective use of determinist theories. S. Dennison, 'Pra inglês ver: Joaquim Nabuco and the Brazilian *Belle époque*', *BHS(L)*, 77:433–49, studies the development of N.'s views on Brazilian national identity within their historical context.

4.　THE TWENTIETH CENTURY

POETRY

José L. Suárez and Jack E. Tomlins, *Mário de Andrade: The Creative Works*, Lewisburg, Bucknell U.P., 195 pp., provides a concise and informative introduction to A.'s work, covering both his poetry and prose. The study particularly stresses the relationship between the development of A.'s writing and the social and cultural changes taking place in Brazil during his lifetime. Maria de Lourdes Teodoro, *Modernisme brésilien et négritude antillaise: Mário de Andrade et Aimé Césaire*, Paris, L'Harmattan, 1999, 350 pp., establishes similarities between the two writers in their approach towards racial issues, and in the way those issues shaped their understanding of national culture. Eduardo Jardim de Moraes, **Limites do moderno: o pensamento estético de Mário de Andrade*, R, Relume Dumará, 1999, 137 pp. Teresa Cabañas, *A poética da inversão*, Goiânia, Univ. Federal de Goiás, 151 pp., is a study of concrete poetry. A discussion of changes in the way poetic creation was conceived during the course of the 20th c. is followed by an analysis of the work of Haroldo de Campos, Augusto de Campos, and Décio Pignatari, and the theories underlying it. M. J. Somerlate Barbosa, 'Strategies of poetic language in Afro-Mineiro discourses', *LBR*, 37.1:63–82, is a study of the work of Edimilson de Almeida Pereira, examined within the historical and cultural context of his native Minas Gerais. L. Sá, '*Invencão de Orfeu* e o palimpsesto indígena', *ib.*, 83–92, examines intertextuality within Jorge de Lima's poem, arguing that it enables the poet to produce a penetrating analysis of the colonization process in Brazil. J. A. Barbosa, 'La poesía crítica de João Cabral', *CHA*, 598:77–82, examines Melo Neto's 1982 anthology, *Poesia crítica*, and discusses the significance of the selection of poems made for it by the poet, and of their organization within the work. B. Nunes, 'Poesía brasileña: expresión y forma', *ib.*, 601–02:67–80, seeks to identify the salient characteristics, both thematic and formal, of Brazilian poetry of the last 20 years. V. Camilo, 'Uma poética da indecisão: *Brejo das almas*', *NovE*, 57:37–58, argues that Carlos Drummond de Andrade's indecision about his political position in the early 1930s explains why this second book of poems was significantly different from his previous poetry. C. F. Moisés, 'Geração, gerações. Esboço de introdução à poesia brasileira contemporânea', *RCLL*, 51:155–63, discusses the problems that have arisen through the use of such terms as *geração* to classify writers, using the so-called *geração de 45* as an example.

DRAMA

David J. George, *Flash and Crash Days: Brazilian Theater and the Post Dictatorship Period*, NY, Garland, 177 pp., provides much needed information on recent theatre activity in Brazil, with sections on such topics as the work of Gerald Thomas, women's drama, and the revival of comedy. The study combats the view that Brazilian theatre has suffered from stagnation since the 1970s by arguing that the end of dictatorship and the weakening of the theatre of political protest have permitted greater variation and experimentation. Irã Salomão, **Nelson, feminino e masculino*, R, Sete Letras, 179 pp., deals with the work of Nelson Rodrigues. A. Pereira Bezerra, 'Retorno às origens ou revisão do instrumento: teatralidade, brasilidade e os caminhos poéticos do oriente', *Caravelle*, 75:151–62, discusses the recent interest shown in Brazil for ancient Japanese theatre forms, and considers how they might be adapted for the Brazilian theatre. H. Pontes, 'Louis Jouvet e o nascimento da crítica e do teatro moderno no Brasil', *NovE*, 58:113–29, examines the influence that the work of the French director Jouvet had on the Brazilian theatre in the 1940s.

PROSE

Idelber Avelar, *The Untimely Present: Postdictatorial Latin American Fiction and the Task of Mourning*, Durham, Duke U.P., 1999, 293 pp., includes studies of the work of Silviano Santiago and João Gilberto Noll in a theoretically sophisticated analysis of Latin American fiction produced in recent decades. The main objectives of the study are to examine how such writing looks back upon the traumas of military dictatorship, and how it responds to the erosion in status which literature has experienced since. *O tempo e o vento: 50 anos*, ed. Robson Pereira Gonçalves, Santa Maria, UFSM–EDUSC, 318 pp., contains 18 studies of Veríssimo's best known work, to mark its 50 years of existence. Though varying widely in approach and focus, the central theme is V.'s presentation of the cultural identity and historical development of Rio Grande do Sul in the work. Márcia Ivana de Lima e Silva, *A gênese de Incidente em Atares*, Porto Alegre, EDIPUCRS, 176 pp. deals with a later work by Veríssimo. Marina Pacheco Jordão, *Macunaíma gigando entre contradicões*, SPo, FAPESP–Annablume, 212 pp., is a detailed study of Mário de Andrade's novel, incorporating psychoanalytic analysis of the work and discussion of its historical context. Arnaldo Bloch, *Fernando Sabino: reencontro*, R, Relume Dumará, 132 pp., is a biographical portrait of S. which gives some insight into his approach towards writing. *Fiction in the Portuguese-Speaking World: Essays in Memory of Alexandre Pinheiro Torres*, ed. Charles M. Kelley, Cardiff, Univ. of Wales Press, 268 pp., includes seven articles on Brazilian prose writing: C. Willis, 'The reception of Graciliano Ramos's *Vidas secas* outside Brazil' (139–57), examines the different interpretations of the novel offered by major critics, and discusses the work's enduring popularity. M. Dinneen, 'Change versus continuity: popular culture in the novels of Jorge Amado' (158–75), argues that changes in A.'s use of Brazilian popular culture have been a crucial factor in enabling him to produce best-selling novels whilst maintaining his claim to be an *engagé* writer. H. Owen, 'Clarice Lispector: re-Joycing in *The Dead*', (176–93), uses feminist literary theory to carry out a comparative study of L.'s *A Partida do Trem* and Joyce's *The Dead*. R. Zilberman, 'O tempo e o vento: história, mito, literatura' (194–216), is a detailed examination of Veríssimo's novel, which focuses particularly on the author's view of the history of his native state, Rio Grande do Sul. C. M. Kelley, 'Riobaldo, Eros and the enigma of Diadorim in *Grande Sertão: veredas*' (217–37) attempts to reach an understanding of the relationship between Riobaldo and Diadorim in Guimarães Rosa's novel by examining the protagonist's relations with women in general. J. Gledson, 'Torture in the work of Ivan Ângelo' (238–45), studies A.'s *A festa* and *A casa de vidro* within the context of the intense military oppression in Brazil in the early 1970s. R. J. Oakley, '*Corpo vivo*'s second hero and the age of iron' (246–63), develops an original interpretation of Adonais Filho's novel, using comparisons between that work and Amado's *Terras do sem fim* as a starting point. José Ariovaldo Vidal, *Roteiro para um *narrador: uma leitura dos contos de Rubem Fonseca*, SPo, Ateliê, 213 pp. *Desafiando o cânone: aspectos da literatura de autoria feminina na prosa e na poesia (anos 70/80)*, ed. Helena Parente Cunha, R, Tempo Brasileiro, 1999, 196 pp., is a collection of 13 essays examining the work of women writers who, in the light of the dramatic cultural changes since the 1960s, have challenged the patriarchal canon. Those studied include the prose writers Patrícia Bins, Sônia Coutinho, Márcia Densar, Lya Luft, and Nélida Piñon, and the poets Adélia Prado and Ana Cristina Cesar. E. Oliveira, 'O gosto amargo da festa: literatura e momento político no Brasil, 1960–1990', *LBR*, 37.1:107–17, examines different literary responses to political developments in Brazil in the latter half of the century, with reference to works by Ivan Ângelo, Moacyr Scliar, and Chico Buarque de Holanda. L. E. Pirott-Quintero, 'A centaur in the text: negotiating cultural multiplicity in Moacyr Scliar's novel', *His(US)*, 83:786–778, is a detailed study of S.'s *O centauro no jardim*, highlighting how the novel problematizes the representation of cultural heterogenity in Brazil. R. Igel, 'Escritores judeus brasileiros: um percurso em andamento', *RevIb*, 191:325–38, briefly mentions numerous authors in an overview of 20th-c. Jewish Brazilian writing, and emphasizes the shift that took place from concentration on the experience of immigration to increasing diversification of theme. Vilma Guimarães Rosa, *Relembramentos: João Guimarães Rosa, meu pai*, R, Nova Fronteira, 514 pp., is a revised and extended edition of an earlier biography, incorporating letters, hitherto unpublished documents, and interviews by G.M. Maria Célia Leonel, *Guimarães Rosa: magma e gênese da obra*, SPo, UNESP, 284 pp. Denílson Lopes, *Nós os mortos: melancolia e neo-barroco*, R, Sete Letras, 1999, 185 pp., offers a new reading of novels by Cornélio Penna, Lúcio Cardoso, and Autran Dourado, in the light of concepts of melancholy and the neo-baroque. Teresa Cristina Montero Ferreira, *Eu sou uma pergunta; uma biografia de Clarice Lispector*, R, Rocco, 1999, 303 pp., is a very readable new biography of L. No literary study is included, but it is packed with detailed information, much of it new material, about all aspects of L.'s life, which will help shed further light on the development of her writing career. R. Dalcastagnè, 'Contas a prestar: o intelectual e a massa em *A hora da estrela*', *RCLL*, 51:83–98, focuses on the role of the narrator in L.'s novel in order to examine the issues of social class and the relationship between classes discussed within it. Jeana Laura da Cunha Santos, *A estética da melancolia em Clarice Lispector*, Florianópolis, Univ. Federal de Santa Catarina, 176 pp. Regina Pontieri, *Clarice Lispector: uma poética do olhar*, SPo, Ateliê, 1999, 234 pp., begins with a review of studies to date of L.'s 1949 novel *A cidade sitiada*, and then offers an alternative detailed analysis of the work, focusing on the original treatment within it of the relationship between the subject who sees and the object which is seen. V. Dantas, 'Desmanchando o naturalismo: capítulos obscuríssimos da crítica de Mário e Oswald', *NovE*, 57:9–27, is a study of two newspaper articles written by Mário de Andrade and Oswald de Andrade which attempts to show how both reveal ideas that later became central to the Modernist Movement. Steven V. Hunsaker, *Autobiography and National Identity in the Americas*, Charlottesville, Virginia U.P., 1999, 176 pp., includes reference to Carolina Maria de Jesus in an examination of how, through autobiographical writing, individuals challenge established notions of national identity by creating alternative identities based on a sense of community. *NovE*, 56:9–42, commemorates the centenary of the birth of Gilberto Freyre by reproducing extracts from studies of F.'s work published by international scholars in the 1940s, 50s and 60s. Tânia Pellegrini, *A imagem e a letra: aspectos da ficção brasileira contemporânea*, Campinas, Mercado de Letras, 1999, 240 pp., examines the relationship between literature, the market and the mass media in order to discuss the conditions under which modern fiction is created in Brazil. The writers studied as examples are Jorge Amado, Caio Fernando Abreu, Sérgio Sant'Anna, Rubem Fonseca, and Raduan Nassar. Idelette Muzart Fonseca dos Santos, *Em Demanda da poética popular: Ariano Suassuna e o movimento armorial*, Campinas, Unicamp, 1999, 421 pp.

IX. ITALIAN STUDIES

LANGUAGE

POSTPONED

DUECENTO AND TRECENTO I
DANTE

By CATHERINE M. KEEN, *Lecturer in Italian, University of Leeds*

1. GENERAL

Dante has caught the imagination, in the year 2000, of a public far wider than the academic readership normally addressed in these pages, thanks to the exhibition of Sandro Botticelli's illustrations to the *DC* mounted in Berlin, Rome, and London, and accompanied by a beautifully produced catalogue, *Sandro Botticelli, pittore della Divina Commedia*, ed. Sebastiano Gentile, 2 vols, Mi, Skira, 277, 295 pp. The first volume, dedicated to the contextual part of the exhibition, contains a number of essays on the reading of D. in Quattrocento Florence, and on B.'s artistic culture, techniques, and environment; it also includes a series of images, in the sixth section of visual material ('Dante nel Quattrocento fiorentino', 215–59), that relate directly to the depiction of D., the illustration of the *DC*, and the production of 15th-c. commentaries, that *dantisti* may find particularly absorbing. C. Vasoli, 'Dante e la cultura fiorentina del maturo Quattrocento' (12–25), discusses the 15th-c. debates over D.'s civic, literary, and philosophical status, tracing the evolution from Bruni to Ficino of approaches to the poet and to the *DC*. He reflects on the political as well as philosophical import of Landino's interpretation of the *DC*, and its influence in establishing a Neoplatonist reading of D. massively indebted to the thought of F. The essay notes, however, that the end of the Laurentian period, the shifts in linguistic and philosophical taste of the next generation of intellectuals, and the advent of Savonarola, all challenged this vision of D. as Neoplatonist poet-philosopher: suggesting that B.'s illustrations are oriented towards the new spiritual climate that tended to reject the Platonist allegorizations of Landino or Ficino. S. Gentile, 'Dante, Botticelli e gli umanisti fiorentini: tra manoscritti e studi geografici' (33–43), investigates the relationship between B.'s *DC* illustrations and contemporary geographical and cartographic works, notably those related to Ptolemy's *Geographia*. Noting the enthusiasm of such distinguished *dantisti* as

Ficino, Landino, and Manetti for geographical lore, the article investigates iconographic and conceptual links between the B. drawings and illuminated Ptolemaic MSS, and additionally discusses the relationship of B.'s work to other D. MSS, all of which helps to contextualize the drawings against the practice of MS preparation in contemporary Florence. P. Scapecchi, 'Cristoforo Landino, Niccolò di Lorenzo, e la *Commedia*' (44–47), discusses aspects of the preparation of Niccolò's edn of the Landino Dante, and notably the questions relating to the insertion of illustrative engravings in the text, noting the paucity of images, and discussing why their inclusion should have proved so problematic. G. Morello, 'La veduta dell'*Inferno* di Sandro Botticelli' (48–53), discusses relationships between B.'s minutely detailed chart and existing or lost 14th- and 15th-c. analogues. The essay highlights the fascination that D.'s description of hell exerted over his readers, noting that visual artists and humanists alike were drawn to the attempt to establish the precise forms and dimensions of the Dantean underworld, among which B.'s own drawing is one of the most detailed and visually successful of the surviving examples. The second volume contains the plates of the *DC* cycle itself, alongside which careful notes provide essential information on the themes and content of each canto and on aspects of B.'s illustrations. The introductory essay to this volume, H.-Th. Schultze Altcappenberg, ' "Per essere persona sofisticata": il ciclo botticelliano di illustrazioni per la *Divina Commedia*' (14–35), discusses art-historical issues (dating, provenance, function, technique, etc.) regarding the illustrations and includes some interesting reflections on narrative technique, noting the progressive diminishing of representational elements from the confusion of visual information in *Inf.* to a sparsely populated, geometrically patterned space in *Par.* The article brings out the highly personal quality of B.'s reaction to the text, which involves total identification with the protagonist: it is his story, rather than the layered narratives of individual souls, classical and Biblical reference, or any other of the text's verbal tissue, that engages B.'s imagination and is transformed into a new, entirely visual, reading.

The visual qualities of the *DC* are also of concern in L. Battaglia Ricci, 'Immaginario visivo e tradizione letteraria nell'invenzione dantesca della scena dell'eterno', *LC*, 29:67–103, an absorbing, and beautifully illustrated, discussion of possible visual stimuli to D. himself in many of the descriptions in the poem. The study shows that some details (e.g. the sleeping St John of the earthly paradise pageant) depend entirely on iconographic rather than written tradition, and offers a number of stimulating suggestions regarding other passages which may have been inspired by the representational conventions of the visual arts, the narrative and didactic schemes of which held particular fascination for D. Illustration of D. is also discussed in D. McLellan, ' "Il novo giorno": earthly paradise at Orvieto, 1500', Baker, *Dante Colloquia*, 143–64, an essay accompanied by a number of illustrative plates that highlight the interest of Signorelli's Dantean imagery, often neglected in favour of the more comprehensive contemporary response provided by Botticelli, and in W. Everling, *'Salvador Dalis Sorgfalt. Zu seinen Illustrationen der Divina Commedia', DDJ*, 75:67–83.

Steven Bemrose, *A New Life of Dante*, Exeter U.P., xxi + 249 pp., provides an accessible and enjoyable introduction in English to the life of the poet, drawing on up-to-date biographical research. Alongside this information — which reminds us once again of the many tantalizing *lacunae* in our knowledge of the poet's biography — B. provides useful contextual information regarding contemporary political, intellectual, and cultural history. Importantly, chapters or chapter-sections also sketch the form and content of the entire Dantean *oeuvre* (including the *Fiore* and the *Detto* within the canon) in brief but informative summaries designed to assist the new reader to approach the texts with confidence; clear bibliographical references provide guidance towards further critical reading. Similar ground is covered in Enrico Malato, *Dante*, Ro, Salerno, 1999, 420 pp., a lengthy study of many aspects of D.'s life and works. It is clearly designed in part as an introductory text, and provides a clear, careful, yet always enthusiastic presentation of the events of D.'s life, skilfully contextualized into the medieval social, political, and intellectual framework; the book also includes introductions to each of the works. The debates over the authorship and dating of the *Fiore*, the *Epistle to Can Grande*, and the *Quaestio*, are surveyed, providing an accessible yet scholarly insight into the critical discussions. Six of the twenty chapters are devoted to the *DC*, and discuss both factual (publication, structure, etc.) and interpretative (allegory, sacred and profane love, language) matters: taking a less objective approach than Bemrose, M. uses these to present his own vision of the poet on some still controversial questions, especially the evolution of D.'s relationship to the works of Cavalcanti. The volume includes a substantial bibliography, a detailed chronology of D., and a selection of useful maps and diagrams. Data of relevance to the reconstruction of the poet's biography is supplied in G. Indizio, 'Tana Alighieri sorella di Dante', *StD*, 65:169–76, which presents the thesis that Tana was D.'s full, rather than half, sister. The study is based on a detailed examination of documents relating to the careers of T.'s own children (her daughter's marriage and her son's activity as a friar) which suggest that they must have been born around the 1280s: the logic of biology suggests that T.'s own date of birth must be very close to D.'s, hence the suggestion that they probably had the same mother (and additional documents provide further support for this). The discussion reminds us that, whilst the *lacunae* in our knowledge of the poet's biography remain frustrating, even the existing documentation can yield new results on closer scrutiny.

Michele Dell'Aquila, *Sopra 'l verde smalto: studi su Dante e Manzoni*, Fasano, Schena, 1999, 171 pp., is a collection that dedicates the great majority of its essays to D. rather than Manzoni. Most of these studies date from the 1990s, and have been previously published elsewhere: they include *letture* of individual canti from the *DC* (*Inf.* XVI, XXVI, *Purg.* XXVII, *Par.* VIII, IX), and discussions of D.'s scientific interests and poetic technique. Studies of D.'s reception in the 20th-c. include a new essay on 'Gli studi danteschi e manzoniani di Mario Sansone' (113–34).

A volume likely to prove welcome to students and scholars alike is *The Dante Encyclopaedia*, ed. by Richard Lansing, NY, Garland, 1006 pp., a compact reference volume that permits rapid consultation of up-to-date critical opinion on the poet's life, works, and social and intellectual environment. The *DC* is a major focus of attention, and entries provide information not simply on content but on interpretative issues of both long-standing and topical debate, as well as on textual tradition and on commentators and critics. Similar treatment is also given to the *opere minori* and *dubbie*. A large number of illustrations enhance the volume, providing images of the medieval cosmos and the Dantean afterworld, and including reproductions of illustrations to the text of the *DC* by artists from many different periods. Of similar utility, an orientation to contemporary Dante resources in electronic form is provided in M. J. Hemmett, 'Dante.com: a critical guide to Dante resources on the Internet', *DS*, 116, 1998[2000]: 127–40, primarily a descriptive survey of a selection of current sites of scholarly standing. Some interesting questions are raised in the concluding section which addresses the possible effects web-based approaches to D. may have on the broader critical field.

The long trajectory of Dante's progression from lyrical *dicitore per rima*, through vernacular philosopher in the *Cvo*, to *poeta* in the *DC* retains a perennial fascination for scholars, and a number of this year's publications engage with questions relating to both technical and conceptual developments in D.'s authorial activity in the course of his career. Patrick Boyde, *Human Vices and Human Worth in Dante's Comedy*, CUP, x + 323 pp., is a study of ethical concerns in Dante's thought and poetry that makes a substantial contribution to the understanding of Dante's place in medieval intellectual and literary culture. The volume stands independently but also forms part of a trilogy with B.'s 1981 and 1993 volumes, which similarly addressed aspects of the relationship between D.'s engagement with philosophy and his creative activity as poet. The first two of the four main sections into which it is divided play a broadly contextual role, investigating the influence of different individual authorities, modes of investigation (especially the Scholastic system), and systems of values (Aristotelian, Christian, and courtly), on the development of D.'s ideas and interests, all amply illustrated, especially with evidence from the *Cvo* and the *DC*. The third section investigates particular categories of vice and virtue (covetousness, pride, justice), again tracing the development of D.'s thinking on each category, on from earlier works to the *DC*, while the fourth section is dedicated to the figure of Ulisse, investigating how it is that D.'s personal understanding 'de li vizi umani e del valore' brings him to condemn U.'s approach whilst poetically shaping him into a figure of compelling, but fatally flawed, attraction. The book's clarity of language, precision of referencing, and methodical argumentative procedures will render it easily accessible to the student reader, while a scholarly as well as an undergraduate audience will come away with its understanding of D.'s status as an innovative and inspiring *poeta rectitudinis* lucidly enhanced. Simon A. Gilson, *Medieval Optics and Theories of Light in the Works of Dante*, Lampeter, Mellen, xiv + 301 pp., addresses another aspect of D.'s vast range of philosophical and poetic interests, in this case his theories about the nature of light and vision. The study maintains an admirable balance between analysis of evidence from D. himself and the presentation of essential contextual material, taking the reader through the complexities of medieval thought on optics and *perspectiva* and on theological 'light metaphysics', and showing that D.'s knowledge of both these areas need not (as some modern critics have argued) have been based on direct knowledge of advanced technical analyses. The volume is divided into two parts: in the first G. deals with optics and perspective, providing a clear and accessible outline of various medieval theories (well supplemented by careful footnoting and an appendix listing the principal relevant treatises, 261) and investigating D.'s own thinking on these topics in the *Cvo* and the *DC*. The second part engages with questions regarding the 'light metaphysics' tradition, which G. shows to have been more complex and heterogeneous than is commonly thought, and for which he again finds little evidence of D.'s direct knowledge of the relevant contemporary literature. Rather, G. argues that in matters of light and vision (as in so much else) the measure of D.'s innovatory capacities, and of the long-recognized imaginative force of many passages from the *DC*, lies not so much in his mastery of highly specialist academic disciplines, as in his capacity to rework traditional material into original and poetically striking forms. Aspects of D.'s poetic development are of concern in M. Picone, 'Dante, Ovidio e la poesia dell'esilio', *RELI*, 14, 1999: 7–23, an exploration of presences of Ovid in D. that proves particularly rewarding for the *DC*. The essay highlights the critical neglect of the impact of O.'s exile writing — the *Tristia* in particular — on D.'s self-presentation as an historical and authorial exile, and makes a compelling case for a reassessment of D.'s knowledge of the relevant texts and enthusiastic response to them. The essay identifies striking structural parallels between O.'s and D.'s narrations of the actual experience of exile, in D.'s case both in his autobiographical comments and in the *DC* fiction: arduous journeying, unfamiliar places of sojourn, the ever-deferred hope of return, the free movement of the poetic text if not of the poet. D., though, diverges from the Latin model both in his incorporation of a transcendant spiritual dimension to the theme of exile (Adamic, Pauline, and Augustinian) and in his rewriting of the cause of exile where, rather than acknowledging just retribution for fault, Florence is often portrayed more in the colours of O.'s Tomis than his Rome, as a place of hostility and injustice. It is thus a fitting analogue to the Christian exile location of D.'s *Inf.*, as P.'s textual analyses show; equally, the article demonstrates that D.'s 'Rome' of repatriation is no earthly city at all, but rather the Christian paradise. T. Barolini, 'Guittone's "Ora parrà", Dante's "Doglia mi reca", and the *Commedia*'s anatomy of desire', *ItQ*, 143–46: 33–49, starts with a comparative exploration of how the two poets in the lyrics cited draw connections between carnal desire (lust) and material desire (avarice) to challenge courtly assumptions about the ennobling potential of erotic love. Attention then shifts to D. alone: B. identifies a continuous and coherent engagement with such issues in his maturer work, analysing the treatment of desire in the *Cvo* and *DC*, in both of which she identifies a sustained rejection of self-centred desire (typified by Ulysses as much as by Francesca or Ciacco) in favour of the liberating and vivifying form of desire associated with the search for spiritual goods. By the same scholar, 'Dante and Cavalcanti (on making distinctions in matters of love): *Inferno* v in its lyric context', *DS*, 116, 1998[2000]: 31–63, addresses similar concerns, in a study that ranges beyond the form of traditional *lectura* suggested by the title allusion to *Inf.* v. The essay investigates Francesca's view of love in relation not, as traditionally, to Guinizelli, but to Cavalcanti, revealing a D. profoundly and continuously engaged with questions about the nature, and the role, of humanity's powers of love and of reason. As in her *ItQ* article, B. takes ample account of D.'s early lyric production, in which negative assessments of love's tempestuously destructive qualities show the influence of a long tradition, from the Sicilians down to Cavalcanti, but where more positive visions of love also appear, again revealing a debt to established traditions, both classical and vernacular (including Guittone). A short bibliographical note at the end of the essay (60–63) reviews recent debates over the D.-C. relationship and urges the need for philologically grounded, rather than speculative, discussion of the case. If Barolini discusses D.'s place in polemical discussions of doctrines of love, his eagerness to engage in debate over matters of theological and political import is investigated in S. Cristaldi, 'Dante, il profetismo gioachimita e la Donazione di Costantino', *LC*, 29:7–65, a densely-packed investigation of D.'s thinking on the Donation within the context of contemporary debate. The long discussion is divided into three parts. In the first (7–32), C. reviews the attitude of Joachim and his followers — notably Pietro di Giovanni Ulivi — towards issues of hierarchy and ecclesiastical poverty, noting shifts in the thinking of later Joachimites away from the pro-hieratic Abbot. The second section (33–49) examines D.'s approach to the same issues in the *Mon.*, with close analysis of the types of argument used and of the context which informs them. The final discussion of 'L'incidenza dei gioachimiti' (49–65) asks what traces of Joachimite thinking may be identified in D.'s discussion of Papal-Imperial relations and of the validity and the effects of the Donation. This section highlights D.'s personal vision of the Romans as a chosen people, giving a distinctive flavour to his contributions to a debate in which professional theologians recognized only the Jewish and the Christian traditions as divinely chosen.

2. FORTUNE

A number of articles address the early reception of D.'s works. N. Bianchi, 'Le due redazioni delle postille del Tasso al *Convivio*: storia, cronologia e proposte di lettura', *StD*, 65:223–81, examines with close attention T.'s practice in his marginal glosses to two editions of the *Cvo*, and proposes a chronology which places his notation (and probably his acquisition) of the 1531 Sessa edn prior to that of the 1521 da Sabio text. The article provides a detailed analysis of different aspects of the glosses, several of which are carefully reproduced and compared: those of the da Sabio text regularly prove to be more developed and to suggest greater familiarity with the treatise. T.'s interests cover philological, exegetical, comparative (especially with reference to the *DVE*), and linguistic concerns, each of which is separately analysed by B.; her conclusions offer additional reflections on the resonances of T.'s reading of the *Cvo* in his *Dialoghi*. P. Nasti, 'Autorità, topos, modello. Salomone nei commenti trecenteschi alla *Commedia*', *The Italianist*, 19 (1999):5–49, investigates the reception of D.'s Solomon in two commentators in particular, Jacopo della Lana and Guido da Pisa. The article, from its title on, provides a stimulating reminder of the diversity of medieval interpretative strategies, here as applied to the Scriptures and to D. It distinguishes a fairly conventional, occasional, and 'safe' use of Sapiential tradition in Lana, as compared with a much more radical and complex reading of Solomonic presences in D. on the part of Guido, whose interest in the question is highlighted by the frequency of his citations. Concentrating especially on the tradition of S. as *scriba Dei*, N. shows that G.'s interpretation allows him to read D.'s achievement as consecrated both poetically and prophetically through its echoing of S.'s in Scripture. G. Savino, 'La più antica difesa di Dante', *StD*, 65 : 159–67, discusses the defence mounted in the *persona* of D. by Guelfo Taviani in reply to Cecco Angiolieri's verse attack, in a sonnet that offers us the earliest known defence of D.'s poetic and historical reputation, which S. is able to date to c. 1307. M. Seriacopi, 'Notizie su un *Commento* inedito in volgare alla *Commedìa* dantesca di Antonio di Tucci Manetti', *L'Alighieri*, 40 (1999): 77–85, discusses the as yet unedited marginal glosses in the *DC* owned and copied by Manetti, the majority of which appear to be in M.'s own hand. Besides a full description of the MS, and an ample bibliography, the article provides a full transcription of the notes to *Inf.* 1. This illustration of M.'s procedures as commentator shows a predominant concern with dates, and with temporal and astronomical references, but also covers moral precepts, revealing for the first canto at least a fairly conventional, allegorical approach to its various figures and events. D. Wallace, 'Dante in Somerset: ghosts, history, periodization', *NML 3*, 9–38, deals with a highly elusive Dantean reception, reconstructing the existence of a Latin translation of the *DC* — almost certainly Serravalle's — in the cathedral library of Wells, recorded in a 16th-c. catalogue but lost in Protestant dispersals of the collection. The article recalls the involvement of English Bishops (of Salisbury and of Bath and Wells) in the commissioning of S.'s Latin *DC* commentary, and the associated translation of the poem, showing their interest in D. to fit well against the background of a vibrant intellectual culture in contemporary Wells. Interesting points are raised about the respective roles of the vernacular and Latin, on the one hand in the estimation of the northern clerics, anxious about Lollard theological vulgarizations but aware that Latin texts will find a limited, largely clerical readership, and on the other hand in that of S., self-consciously adopting an anachronistically rustic, non-humanistic Latin to transpose and to comment on the illustrious Italian of the original and constructing his commentary along the model of Scriptural exegetic literature. The study uses the example of the putative *DC* translation to investigate a wide range of questions regarding English religious and intellectual culture, contrasting an intellectually curious and international medieval experience at Wells with a later Protestant intolerance and isolationism, in the course of which the MS of D. is symbolically lost. M. Zaggia, 'Il "Prologus" della versione dantesca di Matteo Ronto', *StD*, 65:203–21, also addresses the case of a 14th-c. Latin *DC* translation and commentary, discussing questions regarding R.'s Latinity, and his pronouncements on the act of translation, as reflected not only in his apparatus to the *DC*, but also in a vulgarization of the *Psalms*. The study concludes that R.'s interest (like Serravalle's) is not in producing a humanistically sanitized D., but rather in diffusing the text's religious message beyond the linguistic confines of Italy, finding ample evidence for this in R.'s metrical Prologue to the translation. The Prologue itself is edited in the article, accompanied by an Italian translation, and an ample set of notes (213–21).

Later reception is the subject of several book-length as well as article studies. Daniele Maria Pegorari, *Vocabolario dantesco della lirica italiana del Novecento*, Bari, Palomar, xcv + 585 pp., allows *dantismi* in the work of a range of modern poets to be identified, through a dictionary or concordance-style system of reference. The longest sections are dedicated to Saba, Ungaretti, Montale, Pasolini, and Luzi, but many others are included. In each section, a double-column presentation of D.'s and the modern poet's texts alongside one another allows for ease of reference, while indexes of names and *lemmi* provide fertile ground for cross-referencing. The introductory essay on critical study of 20th-c. receptions of D., and on the definition of methodology and intentions for the dictionary itself, both treat a number of important points regarding modern *dantismo*. Graham Smith, *The Stone of Dante and Later Florentine Celebrations of the Poet*, F, Olschki, x + 70 pp., addresses the cult of memorializing D. in the 19th-c., in particular among English writers and travellers, while also giving considerable space to the Italian writers of the Risorgimento and their politicization of such literary tourism. The two monuments on which he focuses most closely are the so-called *sasso di D.* near the Duomo, and the *ritratto di D.* in the Bargello, though he also discusses the cenotaph and statue at S. Croce. The two essays are illustrated with ample citations, and a selection of photographic plates, which provide a vivid and entertaining insight into the flavour of 19th-c. interest in the poet. A number of essays relating to reception of D. in 19th-c. Britain in particular appear in the *Brand Vol.*: T. G. Griffith, 'Italian nationalism, Welsh liberalism, and the Welsh translation of the *Divina Commedia*', *Brand Vol.*, 32–44, discusses the political motivations that prompted Welsh enthusiasts for the cause of Italian unification, especially in its Mazzinian form, to turn to the task of translating D., and provides a clear analysis of the qualities, and defects, of the translation work of Daniel Rees and Gwynn Jones. J. Lindon, ' "Dante intra Tamisi ed Arno" (and Halle am-Saale): the letters of Seymour Kirkup to H. C. Barlow', *Brand Vol.*, 121–42, investigates the enthusiasm for D. displayed by two mid-Victorian Englishmen of very different character, the eccentric K. and the scholarly B., and the discussion in their correspondence of several matters Dantean, notably the critical theories of Gabriele Rossetti and Karl Witte regarding the historicity of D.'s Beatrice. The account of the divergent views of these two scholars, and of the irregular but warm progress of a D.-centred friendship, evokes the enthusiasm with which D. was read in the 19th c., which even led K. to attempt spiritualist communication with the poet. M. McLaughlin, 'Introduction: the centrality of Dante', *Brand Vol.*, 1–12, whilst providing a general introduction to the essays in the volume, also reflects on the enthusiasm of the British response to D. during the past two centuries, both inside the academy and in the imaginative response of writers and artists to the poet's works and to his biography. J. R. Woodhouse, 'Dante Gabriel Rossetti's translation and illustration of the *Vita nuova*', *Brand Vol.*, 67–86, discusses R.'s very personal engagement with the narrative of the *VN*, revealed both in his translation and in his artistic interpretations of episodes from the text (several of these images are reproduced). W. shows that the story of the love relationship between D. and Beatrice was one to which R. responded with enthusiasm, to the extent of discovering symmetries between the poet's courtly inspiration by the memory of B. and his own sentimental and sensual — as W. terms it, 'uxurious' (82) — devotion to his wife, the model for his depictions of B., and like her the victim of an early death mourned at length by her lover (husband). Fascist 'reception' / exploitation of D. is illustrated in L. Scorrano, *'Il Dante "fascista" '*, *DDJ*, 75:85–123. S. Loewe, *'Le rhythme, la terza rima et le sens. Comment réussir tout celà? Zu neueren französischen Dante Übersetzungen', *ib.*, 41–56. G. Zanotti, 'Paolo Amaducci: carte e biblioteca al "Centro dantesco" di Ravenna', *L'Alighieri*, 40 (1999):99–125.

COMPARATIVE STUDIES. The early reception of D. proves as fertile a ground for exploration as ever. T. Bargetto-Andrés, 'A lexical contribution from a fifteenth-century Spanish translation of the *Divine Comedy*', *RoN*, 14:37–44, dicusses three 'headwords' in the Spanish translation which provide etymological and lexical insights into usage in medieval Spanish, and additionally into the evolutions of such terms towards their often very different meanings in modern Spanish. P. Cerchi, 'Il Veglio di Creta nell'interpretazione del Tostado. Fortuna di Dante e/o Boccaccio nella Spagna del Quattrocento',

L'Alighieri, 40 (1999): 87–98, addresses an apparently unique case of interpretation, rather than translation or imitation, of D. in contemporary Spain, in references by the theologian Tostado to the Veglio. These prove, however, to be based almost certainly not on direct knowledge of the *DC* but on Boccaccio's *Genealogia*: the article's analysis of the structural and linguistic similarities between T. and B. is compelling, and the further genre-related parallels between their two humanistic studies of mythography enhance C.'s case. H. Cooper, 'The four last things in Dante and Chaucer: Ugolino in the House of Rumour', *NML 3*, 39–66, investigates Chaucer's complex, and ironic, engagement with the *DC* in several works. The essay shows how C.'s encounter with the *DC* leads him to reflect on the *métier* of poet and the nature of poetry, leading to a sustained critique of D.'s own attitudes. It argues that C. displays an aversion to D.'s assumption that poets can rely on the evidence of poetry, or even of history, in their statements about the past, which is most, though not exclusively, visible in the *House of Fame*'s treatment of reputation and of rumour. It further stresses C.'s reluctance to permit poetic appropriation of the divine office of judgement: this is illustrated through an investigation of C.'s retelling of the Ugolino story, which shows how C.'s removal of the context of damnation, and interest in the calumnied innocence of U. and his companions, radically changes the nature and the status of the story, and of our assumptions about its teller. E. Curti, 'Dantismi e memoria della *Commedia* nelle *Stanze* del Poliziano', *LItal*, 52:530–68, analyses two types of *dantismi* in P., based on 'memoria testuale' or 'memoria tematica'. For the latter in particular, two types of Dantean allusion are discussed, with a number of telling examples: a 'microtextual' *dantismo*; and a more elaborate type of sustained allusion to longer sections of the *DC*. Unlike earlier *cultori*, who drew most heavily on the *Inf.*, P.'s *Stanze* favour the *Purg.* and manage allusions carefully for maximum enhancement of literary effects. L. Scorrano, ' "Gli ha letto Dante". Occasioni dantesche nella *Vita* di Cellini', *RLettI*, 18.2–3:29–45, examines echoes of the *DC*'s phrasing or imagery in C., and outlines a possible structural parallel between D.'s and C.'s tripartite accounts of fall, rise, and salvation. J. Wasserman and L. O. Purdon, 'Sir Guido and the green light: confession in *Sir Gawain and the Green Knight* and *Inferno* XXVII', *Neophilologus*, 84:647–66, investigates the analogous cases of false confession portrayed in the two texts. Lies and linguistic manipulations are of primary concern to both poets (there are some interesting reflections on Ulisse as well as Guido da Montefeltro), lying at the heart of the verbal-performative nexus that constitutes an effective process of confession. The article reveals how both poets' separate approaches to the question of will, whole or defective, are formulated in the chosen passages with strikingly similar language and imagery.

To move to the modern period, a close reading of comparative passages is offered in M. Baker, 'Reflections cast on *Inferno* XXXI–XXXIV by Primo Levi's account of Auschwitz', Baker, *Dante Colloquia*, 43–52. M. G. Riccobono, 'Reminiscenze dantesche e foscoliane in *Rosso Malpelo*', *RLettI*, 18.1 : 21–49, investigates relationships between Verga's novella and D.'s *Inf.* and Foscolo's *Sepolcri*, in the evocation of a subterranean world whose symbolic qualities as a hell or a sepulchre are substantially enriched by the intertextual allusions. In the case of D., the eighth and ninth circles (*Inf.* XVIII–XXXIII) are shown to be used most heavily, assisting V. to establish his atmosphere of harshness and suffering. L. Scorrano, 'Dantismo "trasversale" di Sereni', *L'Alighieri*, 40, 1999 : 41–76, reveals the numerous occasions of an allusive, but notewothy, Steinerian 'real presence' of D. in Sereni, with ample illustration. H. Teschke, 'Sprachliche Zentrifugal-kräfte: Dante, Mandelstam, Deleuze', *CHLR*, 24 : 381–400, is a comparative study of elements linking the three writers, especially in their understanding of how literary texts engage with, reflect, or transform realities, both political and stylistic.

3. Textual Tradition

A number of contributions to Dantean philology are packed into the physically and intellectually imposing volume: Aldo Rossi, *Da Dante a Leonardo: un percorso di originali*, F, SISMEL–Galluzzo, 1999, lxxxiv + 429 pp. It presents the fruits of lengthy research, bringing together questions of critical and textual debate focused around the central question how (technically speaking) did the early writers of the Italian tradition, with the associated questions regarding vernacu-lar–Latin bilingualism, write? R. brings to the discussion an almost overwhelming breadth of critical expertise, drawing on textual philology, palaeography, and a detailed knowledge of a range of linguistic, textual, and paratextual elements, including notably illus-tration, to investigate the case. Questions pertaining to MS composi-tion and transmission, and the penmanship and practice of authors and copyists, are addressed; particular attention is paid to the identification of authoritative *lezioni* and of autograph texts. The latter's being irrecoverable for D. makes the number of contributions on the former front the more startling: evidence regarding his youthful lyric composition and very substantial critical examinations of the *DVE* and the *Mon.* all provide stimulating material for discussion. The major focus of the Dantean chapters is the Berlin codex containing the two Latin treatises, and R.'s investigation produces a surprising number of variant readings with which to review standard critical editions, and sketches a new *stemma codicum* for the *Mon.* that may also help refine current critical assumptions.

Paolo Trovato, *Il testo della Vita nuova e altra filologia dantesca*, Ro, Salerno, 133 pp., collects together a number of essays (some previously published elsewhere) on philological questions, dealing mostly with the *VN* (and especially with issues raised in the wake of Gorni's 1996 edn), but also touching on the *Cvo* and the *DC*. The studies reveal an enthusiatic response to the questions regarding philology and history of the language reopened with the appearance of G.'s edn, backed by the compelling authority of a scholar immersed in the subject, and extend beyond the textual sphere to explore a number of intriguing intertextual and stylistic issues that give insight into D.'s technical and intellectual formation from his earliest through to his last work.

S. Bertelli, 'Un frammento di rime di Dante', *StD*, 65 : 153–57, is a brief article with the declaredly modest but useful intention of drawing to scholarly attention a four-sheet MS fragment (part of a collection of similar miscellanea) in the BNCF containing copies of three Dantean *canzoni*: the essay successfully identifies its provenance from the MS Ricciardiana 2803.

4. Minor Works

On the *VN*: M. Hardt, 'Beatrice und die *Vita nuova*', *Italienisch*, 22.2 : 2–14, argues that analysis of numerical structures in the sequence of chapter numbers, lyric forms, lines of verse, etc., suggest that D. used the numerological technique of *gematria* to encrypt layers of significance within the forms and ordering of the component texts of the *VN*, especially with regard to the names of himself and of Beatrice, but also for a range of intertextual allusion, whether to vernacular verse or to the Latin Bible. M. Marti, 'Acque agitate per *Donna me prega*', *GSLI*, 177 : 161–67, returns to the debate over the D.– Cavalcanti relationship and over the chronology and intentions of the *VN* and of *Donna me prega*. M. engages energetically with the argument (Fenzi, 1999) that C.'s *canzone* postdates the *VN* and reveals a long-standing rupture with D., to restate his own case regarding the positive relationship with C. portrayed in the *VN* (and emphasizing the cumulative composition of its component texts), and reaffirms that both writers, with their different views of love, are experimenting with a shared Guinizellian legacy, although carrying it to divergent conclusions. The same debate over chronology and polemic in the two works is addressed in S. Sarteschi, '*Donna me prega–Vita nuova*: la direzione di una polemica', *RELI*, 15 : 9–35, and this article likewise refutes the theory that Cavalcanti's *canzone* postdates, and polemicizes with, the *VN*. The author stresses instead the evidence of a long evolution of divergence between the two poets' pronouncements on love, again noting a common engagement with earlier traditions (Guittonian and Guinizellian), and a closeness of relationship that makes D.'s naming of C. as *amico* in the *VN* sincere, even as he refutes the doctrine on love found in *Donna me prega*. The article suggests that the *VN* poems indeed show evidence of a careful intertextual engagement with C.'s canzone, especially in *Li occhi dolenti*, but also in *Donne ch'avete* and in *Oltre la spera*, all of which employ themes and terminology from C., to reverse his conclusions by presenting love as vivifying and compatible with reason, with an intertextual precision that S. urges as proof of the prior composition of C.'s *canzone* to D.'s *libello*.

On the *Rime*, vexed questions of attribution are discussed by F. Alfie, 'For want of a nail: the Guerri–Lanza–Cursietti argument regarding the *Tenzone*', *DS*, 116, 1998[2000]: 141–59, who reviews and challenges the thesis that the *tenzone* is an early 15th-c. forgery. The article is based on a review of the MS most crucial to questions of dating, focusing especially on its contents, rather than physical aspects: the poets chosen, the lyric forms included, the ascriptions, etc. A strong case is made for maintaining an early date for the MS as a whole and hence for the *tenzone* lyrics: urging that while this does not of itself prove Dantean authorship, the undermining of a central argument in the forgery thesis suggests that its other elements should be treated with similar caution. Attribution is also the main concern of M. Chiamenti, 'Attorno alla canzone trilingue *Aï faux ris* finalmente recuperata a Dante', *ib.*, 189–207, which similarly reviews critical debate over the sonnet's authorship and champions its restitution to D.

On the *DVE*: M. S. Lannutti, ' "Ars" e "scientia", "actio" e "passio": per l'interpretazione di alcuni passi del *De vulgari eloquentia*', *SM*, 41 : 1–38, offers a detailed analysis of the *DVE*'s position with regard to late classical and medieval debates over the interrelationship in sung compositions between musical and verbal components, and over the status of music as *ars* or *scientia*. Considerable space is given to D.'s pronouncements on syllable, stanza, rhyme, etc., but beyond this, broader issues about creation and performance form the main substance of the discussion. The essay concludes that D. presents poetry as combining technical or theoretical skills from the *trivium* of *artes* (grammar and rhetoric), with those from the *quadrivium* of *scientiae* (music), alongside instinctive or experiential factors as well. The final success of a canzone is further shown to depend on a blend of active and passive elements, i.e. the artifice of composition (*actio*) and

performative consumption (*passio*), in which the notionally subordinate latter nonetheless proves essential to the appreciation of a lyric's
theoretical achievement. J. Luzzi, 'Literary history and individuality
in the *De vulgari eloquentia*', *DS*, 116, 1998[2000]: 161–88, analyses the
text's presentation of literary history in relation to D.'s own autobiographical self-presentation as author, noting how D. presents post-
Babelic literary activity by writers in vernaculars as well as in
gramaticae as establishing a linguistic stability and continuity that
draws together shared aesthetic concerns, and dedication to an
exacting technical craft, across linguistic and geographical divides. It
goes on to investigate the procedures used in the *DVE* and in the *Purg.*
to move away from the *VN*'s self-presentation of D. as part of a
continuous tradition (one in which Guinizelli and Cavalcanti are
prominent, but which also includes the classical Latin canon), to
place him instead in an individual position in which his own
innovations and achievements receive increasing prominence. The
closing paragraphs note how the famous purgatorial self-naming
episode breaks with the pretended anonymity of D.'s earlier self-
citation or -commentary, thereby underlining his distinctive qualities
as a poet, as he faces the challenge of linguistic representation of the
divine, whilst also raising the cultural stakes of vernacular literature
and literary traditions in general.

On the *Fiore*, it is worth noting the appearance of an English-
language translation that seems likely to open up the study of the text
to an Anglo-Saxon student readership for the first time, with
consequent implications for a wider study of the attribution questions:
*The Fiore and the Detto d'Amore: a Late Thirteenth-Century Italian Translation
of the Roman de la Rose, Attributable to Dante*, Santa Casciani and
Christopher Kleinhenz, Notre Dame U. P., ix + 558 pp.

5. COMEDY

Isabelle Abramé-Battesti, *La citation et la réécriture dans la Divine Comédie
de Dante*, Alessandria, Orso, 1999, 185 pp., offers a sustained application of the tools of intertextual and reader-reception criticism to the
text of the *DC*. The author's careful methodological discussion of D.'s
use of overt and covert allusions to previous texts classifies them
under the two headings of her title, as citations or as rewritings. She
goes on to suggest that the distinction in fact is broken down, as the
poet's claims to testamentary veracity mean that all citation becomes
subsumed as rewriting in the innovative poetics of a writer claiming
direct authorization from the Word of God. Modern critical theory
and medieval interpretative practice are both kept in view, in a
methodical investigation of case-by-case examples.

Dante Balboni, *La divina Commedia, poema 'liturgico' del primo Giubileo*, Vatican City, Libreria Editrice Vaticana, iv + 44 pp., is dedicated primarily to discuss the presence of texts from the liturgy in the *DC*. We are reminded that from the first canto of *Inf.* to the end of the *Par.* shorter and longer citations and paraphrases regularly punctuate the text: a schedule appended to the essay matches each *DC* reference to its place in the liturgical calendar. The temporal implications of this liturgical aspect of the poem are investigated in B.'s remarks on the measurement of time in the *DC*: the essay presents a useful discussion of medieval systems for time measurement, both civil and, more importantly, ecclesiastical, stressing the role of liturgical recitation in the clerical 'hours' of office; more controversially, B. also presents a re-examination of the traditional assumptions about the timing of the entire fictional journey, based on analysis of the astronomical references in the *DC*, which moves it to March/April 1301.

Essays and articles that address themes from across the *DC* include P. Armour, 'Dante's *contrapasso*: contexts and texts', *ISt*, 55:1–20, which engages with the question what exactly is the *contrapasso* cited by Bertran de Born in *Inf.* xxviii, and whether the term denotes his punishment alone or a more general scheme applied throughout the *Inf.* and the *Purg.*, and possibly even into the *Par.* The question leads A. to a detailed examination of the contexts in which the term was used by medieval thinkers on law (civil and Biblical) and on theology. He offers a clear and penetrating sketch of its association with the idea of reciprocity, and of its social character, as a regulating mechanism within the social order (in other words, in contexts opposite to those of *Inf.*). The outcome of this re-examination of a term that has become ubiquitous in D. criticism is to remind us that there is great flexibility in D.'s schemes of retribution, that the term itself is a Dantean *hapax* that may not merit extension to other parts of the poem, and that D.'s notion of the inscrutability of divine justice, represented in his own 'alta fantasia', transcends the formulaic application of any single scheme of distribution of punishment and reward. M. Rutledge, 'Dante's mirrors', Baker, *Dante Colloquia*, 135–42, investigates the evidence, in the *DC*, of D.'s fascination with the qualities of light and perception, with reference especially to episodes where reflection or mirroring occur; unlike Gilson (cited above) she assumes D. to have considerable technical expertise in the theory of optics and perspective. Her reading of the final canti of the *Par.* suggests that D. premises many of the visual phenomena described as the protagonist enters and gazes at the Empyrean on the behaviour of reflections in a convex mirror, imagined as lying at the base of the celestial rose — and making the confrontation with the human face of God a self-confrontation with D.-character's own reflected image. G. Bárberi Squarotti, 'Spiegazione e profezia', *LC*, 29: 105–29, suggests a reappraisal of the nature and intentions of the so-called prophetic passages of the *DC*. The article divides these into two categories, starting with the political passages of *post eventum* predictions made to D.-character regarding events after 1300. These are shown not simply to provide factual information, or to release strong (and sometimes vindictive) emotion, but rather each to convey an element of explanation whereby D. shows his readers not just what happens, but also why. The second category comprises the less numerous Messianic prophecies uttered by Virgil, Beatrice, and St Peter, and closely modelled on Biblical modes of prophecy. Precise interpretations of these passages are urged as futile: B. S. does however emphasize the importance of each speaker's distinctive functions with regard to D.-character, and to the structure of the poem, which help demarcate these quasi-mystical prophetic moments from the explanatory ones, all uttered by relatively undistinguished contemporaries of the poet. D. Hallinan, 'The last word', Baker, *Dante Colloquia*, 124–34, focuses on the term *stelle* that closes each of the *cantiche*, investigating structural patterns in the occurrences of the term throughout the poem.

A. A. Iannucci, 'Dante's theological canon in the *Commedia*', *ItQ*, 37:51–56, provides a survey of current critical thinking on D.'s theological *auctoritates* in the *DC*. He discusses the debates over views of D. as 'Thomist', 'Augustinian', etc., and investigates the contribution of other theologians — notably the *Par*. figures Bonaventure and Bernard — to D.'s own views. A concluding paragraph on D.'s use of theology, and on the vexed issue of allegory in the *DC*, provides a useful reminder that hard-and-fast classifications of idea, source, and influence in D. remain endlessly, and inevitably, debatable.

A broad-based discussion by G. Muresu, 'Tra violenza e lussuria: Dante e la "sodomia"', *L'Alighieri*, 40, 1999:7–17, reviews and energetically combats the suggestion that the difference in detailed classification of homosexual sin between *Inf.* and *Purg.* indicates a change in D.'s own attitude to homosexuality. Reviewing the discussions of love and of generation in the *Cvo* and the *DC*, M. argues that homosexuality was the object of D.'s continuous condemnation: the poet deemed it reparable only by the timely recognition and repentance that provides the precondition for entry to purgatory, a realm where damaged selfhood is cured on a scheme totally different from that used for punishment in hell. Sexuality is an important theme also in L. Warner, 'Dante's Ulysses and the erotics of crusading', *DS*, 116, 1998[2000]:65–93, which ranges well beyond the limits of *Inf.* XXVI in its consideration of sources and structures, giving particular attention to Brunetto Latini and to Cacciaguida,

among others, in the search for intratextual and intertextual illuminations of the episode. The opening part of the essay focuses on echoes
of crusading rhetoric in U.'s *orazione*, emphasizing the preachers'
similar engagements with doubts about the perils of crusading
voyages and the threat they might pose to family and civic obligations.
The greater part of the essay is dedicated to questions of eroticism,
procreation, and genealogy, and draws extensive parallels between
the material of canti xv and xxvi of the *Inf*. In the light of medieval
definitions of Muslim occupation of Jerusalem as 'sodomitic' in its
transgressive penetration of a body politic, W. finds a similar
misplaced eroticism in U.'s unlicensed journey, and cites Ulysses,
Ganymede, and Brunetto (in both their Dantean and their extratex-
tual guises) as examples of voyagers whose misplaced endeavour is
spelled out through association with sexual impropriety. The crusades
are a focus likewise for B. D. Schildgen, 'Dante and the Crusades',
DS, 116, 1998[2000]:95–125, an investigation that marshals a
number of stimulating lines of argument. Informative on the background of crusading activity (from the First Crusade to D.'s day) and
of crusading literature (from *Roland* to Trecento lyrics), she gives a
detailed picture of the different manifestations of and attitudes to the
multifaceted activity of crusading, both in the Holy Land and within
Western Latin Christendom. The essay compellingly suggests that
D.'s interest in crusading, and its theology of martyrdom, is driven
primarily by regards concerning the latter sphere: he sees it as a
means of restoring unity — political, religious, intellectual — within
the territory of the Western Empire. By reading in telling juxtaposition
passages from across the *DC*, S. reminds us that D.'s experience of
schism at home, within Italy, played a crucial role in focusing his
attention on crusading and conversional issues.

INFERNO

Volumes dedicated to the *Inf*. this year include two substantial essay
collections. The *Lectura Dantis Turicensis*, ed. Georges Güntert and
Michelangelo Picone, F, Cesati, 482 pp., is presented as the first
volume in what will eventually form a three-part survey of the whole
poem. Based on a series of *lecturae* organized at the University of
Zurich, it collects studies by a cohort of distinguished scholars. The
volume's two editors contribute an impressive number of essays, with
Güntert covering canti iii, iv, xviii, and xxxiii, and Picone canti ii,
viii, xvi, xxi, and xxvi; two apiece are also provided by Z. G.
Barański (xi, xix), R. Fasani (vi, xxvii), E. Fumagalli (ix, xxiv) and
G. Gorni (i, xvii). The remaining essays extend this international
line-up, with contributions from P. Allegretti (xxviii), G. Bardazzi

(VII), G. Cappello (XXXIV), C. Caruso (XII), M. Ciccuto (XXXI), D. Fachard (XXXII), B. Guthmüller (XXV), G. Orelli (XXIX), V. Panicara (XXII), C. Perrus (XXX), L. Rossi (XV), J. A. Scott (XXIII), A. Stäuble (X), and A. Villa (XIII). Picone's introductory essay, 'Leggere la *Commedia* di Dante' (13–25), stresses the importance to the collection as a whole of the idea of an individual encounter with the poem, fundamental to the notion of a *lettura*, and sketches an outline of current critical concerns regarding the poet, the poem, and the study of medieval literary and intellectual culture in general, that provided some of the rationale for establishing the original university series. The individual essays engage with an impressive range of such issues and, while keeping footnotes and bibliography to an essential minimum, provide a stimulating approach to the first *cantica* that is likely to provide a useful resource to both students and scholars.

The second volume dedicated to *Inf.* takes a more comparative approach. The essays collected in the volume *Dante e il locus inferni: creazione letteraria e tradizione interpretativa*, ed. Simona Foà and Sonia Gentili, Ro, Bulzoni, 227 pp., explore the prehistory and the reception of the underworld depicted by D. Eight full-length essays address different aspects of D.'s conception of hell's physical form, of the nature and significance of the infernal journey's encounters, and of the scope of his literary and linguistic achievement in depicting the underworld, with roughly half addressing issues regarding the reception of D. by medieval and Renaissance commentators; the volume ends with a brief 'Conclusione' (205–07) from F. Mazzoni. Some of the studies address aspects of intertextuality and external reference in D.'s *Inf.*: S. Gentili, 'La necromanzia di Eritone da Lucano a Dante' (13–43), investigates D.'s engagement with the classical and post-classical traditions concerning the underworld deriving from the *Pharsalia* and the *Aeneid*, in his description of a Christian *catabasis* where communion with the dead provides fore-knowledge of the future, raising queries for the believer over the eschatological status of these insights as divine prophecy or as diabolical soothsaying. M. Chiamenti, 'Intertestualità *Liber Scale Machometi–Commedia*?' (45–51), recalls how much debate the question of D.'s possible contact with the Muslim tale of afterworld journeying has produced in the past century and reviews the politicization of much of the discussion by the critics' own 20th-c. concerns. In a survey of five of the principal passages adduced to support a Dantean debt to the *Liber Scale*, C. energetically opposes any direct interdiscour-sivity or intertextuality, emphasizing instead the strong debt of both these narratives to a heritage from the Judaeo-Christian and classical culture common to the whole medieval Mediterranean world. C. Di Fonzo, 'La leggenda del *Purgatorio di S. Patrizio* nella tradizione di

commento trecentesca' (53–72), covers similar ground to the longer
essay contributed to *StD* (below), here confining her comments to the
references to the Irish legend in Benvenuto and Alberico. Further
aspects of the commentary tradition are scrutinized by A. Stefanin,
'Indagini sulla tradizione manoscritta delle chiose anonime all'*Inferno*
pubblicate da Francesco Selmi' (73–134), a substantial essay which
engages with questions about what were the cultural expectations
and concerns of the unknown glossator and his public, representatives
of a popular readership of D. whose reactions to the *DC*'s mythological
and legendary elements are shaped, in the absence of Latin skills, by
vernacular rather than learned traditions. Our picture of this public
is also enhanced by S.'s return to the MSS to correct and extend the
Selmian edition, a process illustrated in the article via a number
of often lengthy citations based on the unpublished versions.
P. Pasquino, 'Benvenuto da Imola: una lettura del viaggio dantesco
in chiave "letteraria"' (135–43), discusses B.'s engagement with the
DC as a literary work, a humanistic attitude that breaks with earlier
commentators' predominantly allegorical concerns, stressing the
attention B. gives to explorations of its intertextual relationship with
the classical accounts of journeys to the underworld in the *Odyssey*, the
Aeneid, and the *Bellum civile*, in which the commentator privileges a
concern with how D. deals, poetically, with his *materia*, rather than
simply with what that *materia* actually is. R. Ruini, 'Bruto e Cassio in
Inf. XXXIV 55–69 e la riflessione political fiorentina quattrocentesca'
(145–78), investigates the discussion of the *Inf.*'s final canto by the
15th-c. Florentine humanists, for whom contemporary attitudes to
tyrannicide make D.'s episode problematic, in Salutati's generation
for political and later for aesthetic reasons, as Bruni's portrait of
Niccoli shows. The essay, whose ample footnotes remind us of the
breadth of scholarship on humanist reactions to D., closes with an
appendix on the example of N. ('Il caso Niccoli', 171–78), giving the
text of B.'s speech, and of a number of humanist replies, supplemented
with a substantial bibliography on the question. S. Foà, 'Il *Dialogo sul
sito, forma, e misure dell'Inferno* di Girolamo Benivieni e un particolare
aspetto dell'esegesi dantesca tra XV e XVI secolo' (179–90), relates
the interest shown in establishing the physical site and measurements
of D.'s hell in the 15th c. to the contemporary developments in
architecture, engineering, and the art of perspective represented by
achievements such as Brunelleschi's construction of the Florentine
cathedral dome, and the establishment of rules for two-dimensional
linear perspective. B.'s *Dialogo*, with its fundamental debt to the
dantista and *brunelleschiano* Antonio Manetti, offers ample illustration
of the intellectual excitement produced by such contemporary

breakthroughs and transferred to the task of calculating and representing the dimensions of D.'s hell, undertaken by a generation who saw themselves as bringing a new scientific exactitude to the imprecisions of the medieval 'dark ages' of Dantean reception. N. Bianchi, 'La selva di Saron e la selva dantesca: echi dell'*Inferno* nel XIII canto della *Liberata*' (191–203), investigates the numerous Dantean presences in the episode, showing the impact on Tasso's language of his reading of the *Inf.*, which leaves echoes in the form of single words, phrases, and full citations, examples of which illustrate the analysis.

A linguistic aspect of the *cantica* is explored in some detail in L. Pertile's '*Qui* in *Inferno*: deittici e cultura popolare', *ItQ*, 37:57–67. The use of *qui* in passages from three canti — x, xx, xxix — proves in P's thoughtful *letture* to be more complex than traditional criticism commonly assumes and to draw on the conventions of drama and popular culture to heighten the effect of individual encounters and descriptions. Id., 'Ulisse, Guido e le sirene', *StD*, 65:101–18, also addresses D.'s response to popular culture, turning to the eighth circle of the *Malebolge*. The two principal speakers of the *bolgia*, U. and G., provide complementary evidence for P.'s compelling analysis of how in this episode D. returns to the question of how humans divinely gifted with an exceptional *altezza d'ingegno* (including, implicitly, himself as author) should use it. Patristic and medieval learned allegorizations of U. focused on the sirens episode, presenting U. as intelligently submissive to restraint in order to achieve salvific repatriation to Ithaca–paradise. In the allegory's popular reception, though, P. notes the re-emergence of the theme of ingenuity: U.'s solution allows him to hear the sirens, flirting with temptation, but still to avoid destruction. D.'s U., in P.'s reading, offers a re-literalization of the popularized allegory, in his attempt to 'salvarsi peccando' (116), to travel physically to the earthly paradise by force of *ingegno* rather than by divine grace. The point is strengthened by investigation of G.'s case, which in turn metaphorizes the literal story of U., in the warrior's conversional 'calar le vele' as he approaches the port of death, hearing the siren-songs of Boniface but imagining himself to be preventively bound by the monastic habit; like the U. of canto xxvi, G.'s brilliant *ingegno* brings him within sight of his port, but he is confounded at the last by divine judgement. The second encounter of the *bolgia* provides a perfect complement to the first, in its deliberate play on the stylistic and thematic concerns raised in the encounter with U. A general theme of the *Inf.* is discussed by J. A. Scott, 'Dante and treachery', Baker, *Dante Colloquia*, 27–42, a substantial study of D.'s treatment of treachery in the *DC* which stresses that this theme is not confined to the ninth circle of hell. In his observations on the closing canti, S. notes the intertextual allusions that enrich the sequence (encompassing texts from *Genesis* to the *Chanson de Roland* to D.'s own *Cvo*) and stresses D.'s very Florentine concern to make treachery as antiheroic and repulsive as possible. Treachery is also shown to be of issue in *Inf.* XIX and XXVII, where the corrupt church's hostility to the empire, and abuse of its sacramental privileges, betray the functions of the institutions designated by God to preside over human destiny.

For individual cantos the following are to be noted. *Inf.* IV: M. Gialdrone, *'Commenti antichi e moderni alla collocazione del Saladino nel Limbo dantesco', *DDJ*, 75 : 133–47. *Inf.* V: T. Barolini, 'Dante and Francesca da Rimini: *Realpolitik*, romance, gender', *Speculum*, 75 : 1–28, stresses the importance of a return to historical as well as literary issues for a fuller understanding of the canto. The article provides us with a detailed survey of the civil conflicts of medieval Romagna, in which political and genealogical concerns were addressed with a violence that contributed an impressive number of protagonists to D.'s *Inf.* and *Purg.*, stressing that, in the bloody context of Romagnol dynastic *Realpolitik*, the story of Francesca goes virtually unrecorded prior to D. Taking us back to the text, B. reminds us of the paucity of information provided in the *Inf.* (though amply supplemented by commentators — B. is particularly interesting on the content and motives of Boccaccio's version) and stresses the significance of the extent to which the data that we do find are coloured by F.'s adoption of romance conventions. The analysis of the place of women as protagonists in and consumers of romance leads to intriguing conclusions on gender issues, in which the passivity of romance heroines (victims of male courtship, as F. is of dynastic marriage) paradoxically offers F. access to personal agency, as she manipulates her own situation into reception of Paolo's kiss (with all its fatal consequences). Also, A. Pagliaro, ' "E ciò sa 'l tuo dottore"?' Baker, *Dante Colloquia*, 1–7, discusses Francesca's closing speech. For *Inf.* VII: G. Bardazzi, 'Avari e prodighi, iracondi e accidiosi', *StD*, 65 : 1–39, makes wide reference to other parts of the *DC* (notably *Purg.* XVI–XXII) and to the *Cvo* (Book IV in particular) in his discussion of the sins in question. Detailed consideration is given to the questions why D. places these sets of sin in combination and establishes these chosen locations and forms of punishment for them. An impressive range of intertextual reference is marshalled to sustain the investigation, notably from Ovid, Virgil, and Augustine, although including other classical and Christian *auctoritates*, in an analysis that covers issues as varied as the language of Pluto, D.-author's stylistic *asprezza*, the resurrection of the body, and D.'s doctrine of fortune. For *Inf.* VII–IX: W. Hirdt, *'Gerechtigkeit – Gesetzlichkeit. Zum episodischen

Diskurs der Divina Commedia (Inferno VII–IX)', *DDJ*, 75:7–40.
For *Inf.* x: G. Tanturli, 'Dante poeta fiorentino: (su *Inf.* x)', *StD*,
65:41–72, notes a number of intriguing elements in the structure and
content of the canto. Structurally, T. argues that the canto describes
a formal circle, with an interlude of left-to-right movement corrected
back into the normal 'sinister' direction of the infernal journey, and a
symmetrical patterning of the stage presences of two, three, and four
protagonists (D., Virgil, Farinata, Cavalcanti), and then back to three
and two. This mini-journey, T. suggests, finds D. standing back to
engage with the question of his own status as poet: one who uniquely
manages to follow, and so to match, the elevated example of V.,
whilst also displaying distinctively Florentine qualities. A number of
Virgilian resonances are identified in the canto as a whole: most
telling perhaps is the cross-referencing of D.'s *onesto* speech (praised
by F.) with V.'s *parola ornata* and *onesta* of *Inf.* II (praised by Beatrice).
In the presentation of D. as sole *poeta* of modern Florence the latter
canto, in combination with evidence from the *DVE*, recalls the
importance to D. not simply of *altezza d'ingegno* but also of *lungo studio*
in the formation of a truly outstanding writer. T. argues that Guido
Cavalcanti's neglect of Virgil's example marks a failure of the heroic
labor required for such elevated achievement as D.'s own *imitatio Aenei*,
facing the challenge of return from, as well as descent to, the realm of
Dis, in the literal and the poetic footsteps of the classical epic. Also,
D. Hunter, 'Political factionalism in *Inferno* x', Baker, *Dante Colloquia*,
8–15. For *Inf.* XIII: O. Castellani Pollidori, ' "Nessun"/"Neun" (*Inf.*
XIII 3) e il gioco stilistico in Dante', *StIt*, 12.1:5–25, is a study of a
single word that raises far-ranging discussion. She opposes Petrocchi's
reading of *neun* in this line, taking in questions of stylistics, phonology,
textual tradition (including regional issues), and comparative analysis
of D.'s minor works and those of contemporaries, in a series of
detailed arguments for revision of the Petrocchian *hapax* within the
DC text. For *Inf.* XIV: A. Vallone, 'Inferno XIV', *StD*, 65:73–85,
divides the canto into the two halves dedicated to Capaneo and to the
Veglio. The essay investigates the symmetries between the two
sections in their parallel concerns with the distorted beauties of real
and imaginary human figures (C. and the V.) and landscapes (the
blasphemers' desert and Crete). It stresses D.'s concern with the
methods and the aims of poetic representation, which give the
sequence a sense of realism, modernity, and urgency as he maintains
a tension between dramatic literality and a still more effective
allegorical experimentalism. Also, S. Vazzana, 'Appunti sull'eredità
lucanea e staziana del Capaneo dantesco', *RCCM*, 42:297–304,
argues that D.'s echoes and reworkings of the two Latin poets boost
his self-presentation as *continuatore*, rather than mere *imitatore*, of the

classical epic. Lucan's landscape and character descriptions from Statius combine to emphasize the self-consciously literary qualities of the Capaneo episode, while D.'s Christian sensibilities add a new dimension to the portrayal of an epic *magnanimo* as definitively (if compellingly) flawed. For *Inf.* XVII: E. Bigi, 'Realismo e retorica nel canto XVII dell'*Inferno*', *StD*, 65 : 87–99, acknowledges the realism long identified in the encounter with the usurers and in the Gerione episode, and the usefulness of the traditional allegorical interpretations; but suggests the value of a re-examination of the canto in an Auerbachian figural key, exploring the rhetorical devices that structure the episode. He stresses the deliberation with which rhetorical figures commended by the medieval *artes* are deployed in the canto, finding numerous examples of alliteration, anaphora, periphrasis, *descriptio* and *abbreviatio*, and especially a very high number of similes. Of the latter, the mythological examples clearly provide stylistic elevation; the several animal comparisons, focusing on repellent or humorous characteristics, often using *umile* or *aspro* terminology, are often adduced as providing a lower and more realist tone, but B. shows them to be employed with an attention to rhetorical effect that conforms to the more self-consciously literary elements in the sequence, which collectively strengthen the impact of its figural representation of humanity's fearful confrontation of the sins of fraud, conquered by a recourse to guiding, Virgilian, reason. For *Inf.* XXVI: W. Dowd, 'Some structural aspects of *Inferno* XXVI', Baker, *Dante Colloquia*, 16–19. *Inf.* XXVIII: P. G. Beltrami, 'L'epica di Malebolge (ancora su *Inferno* XXVIII)', *StD*, 65 : 119–52, is a *lettura* that offers a minute examination of each of the canto's sinners, investigating what D. might plausibly have known about them historically, and what he chooses to tell us about them poetically. The essay argues that this nexus between the historical and the mythic is what gives the canto (and indeed the poem overall) an epic force, drawing past, present, and future together and naming the flesh-and-blood reality of its protagonists (including the pilgrim-poet himself). For *Inf.* XXXI: G. Carsaniga, 'Nonsense, sense and meaning in *Inferno* XXXI', Baker, *Dante Colloquia*, 20–26, investigating questions of scansion, register, and stylistics in relation to linguistic debates over D.'s intentions in including a line of giantish nonsense-speak in the canto, and its implications for his understanding of the nature and purpose of human linguistic activity in speech and in writing. For *Inf.* XXXIII: L. Cassata, 'La tragedia del "dolore antico" (*Inf.* XXXIII)', *L'Alighieri*, 40, 1999 : 19–31, draws on the substantial literature on the Ugolino episode to evaluate critical reactions in a new *lettura*. The essay concentrates particularly on the tragic qualities of the episode and its allusions to classical texts, noting in particular presences from Statius,

Virgil, Ovid, and Lucan, and suggesting that it provides confirmation of the Leopardian distinction between *dolore antico* and *moderno* (30–31) in its evocation of a total negation of hope and absorption into grief. Also, on a possible Senecan source: A. Heil, *'Ugolino und Andromache. Ein Senecazitat bei Dante?', *DDJ*, 75:57–65.

PURGATORIO

C. Di Fonzo, 'La leggenda del "Purgatorio di S. Patrizio" fino a Dante e ai suoi commentatori trecenteschi', *StD*, 65:177–201, reviews evidence concerning the Irish legends of St Patrick's Purgatory, and the associated pilgrimage cults, in relation to D.'s *Purg*. The article investigates the popularity of the legend, translated into several European languages, including Italian, and circulating in various adaptations. Versions of the tale are cited by two of D.'s early commentators, Alberico da Rosciate and Benvenuto da Imola, in their remarks on canto I. It also notes that at least two of the early Italian versions placed the location of Purgatory on a mountain, with a sevenfold division of areas of purgation for the capital vices, and suggests that there may be some link here with D.'s admittedly more impressive and accomplished vision in *Purg*. A number of essays on aspects of the *Purg*. appear in Baker, *Dante Colloquia*. These include: D. Modesto, 'The rainbow and the griffin' (104–23), an essay returning to the problematic issue of what the griffin and its dual nature symbolize, and concluding that a possible interpretation would take it as the Roman emperor, in his Kantorowiczian 'two bodies', providing a clear analysis of the details that support her thesis; A. Hawkes, 'Links with the earthly city in Antepurgatory' (73–78), investigating questions in the *Purg*.'s opening canti relating to time, prayer, and community, and the connections between these concerns within and between the worlds of the living and of the dead; K. Gott, 'The Sordello episode and Dante's patriotism' (87–94), reading the political elements of the S. sequence in relation to evidence on D.'s political thinking from the *Cvo* and the *Mon.*, as well as from elsewhere in the *DC*; J. O. Ward, 'Realism, rhetoric and revelation: Dante's use of history in the *Purgatorio*' (165–91), engaging with two episodes from *Purg*. that illuminate D.'s historical outlook and interests: the presence of Cato, and the DXV prophecy. W. provides a rich series of reflections on what he urges is D.'s mystical or figural reading of history, investigating intertextual presences from texts as diverse as *Revelations*, the *Pharsalia*, Brunetto Latini's *Tresor*, and D.'s own *Mon*. and *Cvo*.

Single-canto studies include the following. On canto I: B. Bowden, *'Dante's Cato and the Disticha Catonis', DDJ*, 75:125–32. On canto II: G. Muresu, 'L'inno e il canto d'amore (*Purgatorio* II)', *RLI*, 104:5–48, giving a dense *lectura* of the canto, in which a variety of interconnected points are discussed: M.'s analysis ranges from reflection on the theological implications of the canto's opening astrological references, through discussion of the reappearance in the sequence of material from the *Cvo*, to a series of intertextual analyses of the two central musical episodes cited in the article title; engaging critically with many recent studies, by North American scholars in particular, M. argues for a reading of the canto (and especially of its treatment of Virgil, of Cato, and of D.'s own *rime*) in a more positive key than has often been the case. On canto V: D. Glenn, 'Of thieves and salvation victories: *Purgatorio* V, 133', Baker, *Dante Colloquia*, 66–73, uncovering a striking density of allusion in the speech of Pia, which not only carries Virgilian echoes (from the *Aeneid* and from V.'s own epitaph), but also a Christian one, to the Crucifixion plea by the good thief that Christ remember him: the allusion bears rich implications for the context of Antepurgatorial pleas for prayer and expectations of salvation, rescuing the episode from a 'sentimentality conveyed by some critics' (70) which G. deplores. F. Morgante, 'La Pia dantesca', *L'Alighieri*, 40, 1999:33–40, focusing on the closing encounter of *Purg.* V and showing how it connects with, and concludes, themes addressed earlier in the canto: looking particularly at the linguistic evidence, M. reflects on the way that Pia's speech engages with the concerns about bodily existence raised previously and displays an exquisitely but unobtrusively balanced understanding of human corporeality in her references to her own dead, and D.'s living, bodies. On canto VI: M. Dwyer, 'Palinurus: the shadowy presence in Antepurgatory', Baker, *Dante Colloquia*, 53–66, in fact extending outside the bounds of the canto in its consideration of Virgilian presences in the area of Antepurgatory as a whole. On canto VIII: V. McGill, 'The negligent rulers and the *biscia*', *ib.*, 79–86, discussing theatrical structures in the episode. On canto XXXIII: F. Coassin, 'The function of Lethe', *ib.*, 95–102, investigating the nature of the oblivion conferred by the river's waters in D. and in an impressive range of classical authors. C. argues that this is a form of oblivion that does not obliterate memory, but cathartically liberates it to give a clear self-vision. This purifying effect of the river is related to the theme of memory throughout the *Par.*, where D. encounters souls who, when appearing in the planets, remember, and so place past activity into a fuller understanding of selfhood, but in the Empyrean abandon temporality, and hence memory.

PARADISO

S. Rizzardi, 'Dante e l'orologio', *SPCT*, 60:51–70, is an extensive
discussion of D.'s possible knowledge of, and allusions to, mechanical
clocks in the *Par*. Besides the two explicit references in canti x and
xxiv, three further possible allusions are identified; the article's main
concern is to establish that the poem's closing image of the 'rota
ch'igualmente è mossa' (xxxiii, 144) also refers to a clock. The craft,
the terminology, and the theories of medieval clocks, clock-making,
and time-keeping are carefully reviewed, to provide an intriguing
contribution to critical discussion of the *DC*'s closing lines.

The sequence of the Heaven of the Sun continues to receive
considerable scholarly attention. M. O'Rourke Boyle, 'Closure in
Paradise: Dante outsings Aquinas', *MLN*, 115:1–12, argues that the
episode reveals a very specific interest in the non-completion of
Aquinas's master-work, the *Summa theologiae* and the saint's accompanying declaration of its 'chaffy' qualities (1). She argues that this is
contrasted with D.'s implicit self-presentation as an author, placing
unfinished work behind him (the *Cvo* only is mentioned) to focus on
the *DC*'s plenitude of achievement. Metaphors central to the Aquinas
sequence, but which appear throughout D's *œuvre* — notably those of
bread and of navigation — are analysed to support the contention
that D.'s presentation of the saint is ironical, damning with faint
praise an attempt to speak of the divine that lacks the freedom
accorded to poetic composition, which permits D.'s own language to
face the challenge of ineffability and to utter at least something about
the vision of God. B. Porcelli, 'Numeri e nomi nei canti danteschi del
sole', *GSLI*, 177:1–13, appends a sobering footnote to the very title
of the article, noting the poor standing of numerological and
onomastic interpretations of D.'s works: but the body of the article
provides a vigorous apology for a judicious use of these methods of
approach. The analysis of numerological aspects of the heaven of the
sun, in particular its use of binary pairings, is supported with the
reminder that the *Cvo* associates the sun with the art of arithmetic,
while a range of interesting possibilities are opened up by P.'s
reflections on the use of personal and place names in the biographies
of Saints Francis and Dominic.

Two studies of canto xxvii explore different, but equally stimulating, aspects of a particularly rich canto. C. Moevs, 'The *Primo Mobile*
as pot of time: *Paradiso* 27.115–20', *RoN*, 40:247–57, focusing on B.'s
explanation, to D.-character in these lines, of the origin of time in the
universe as they prepare to leave the *Primum mobile* for the Empyrean.
The essay explores B.'s figuring of the *Primum mobile* itself as a pot
('testo'), containing the 'radici' of the plant of time; the movement

and variety it generates are perceived in the other spheres and on earth as the plant's 'fronde' issuing from the original source. M. discusses the sources for D.'s understanding of the *Primum mobile*'s centrality to the notions of time and change, revealing the subtlety and complexity of the tradition. The essay goes on to discuss numerological references in the canto, drawing out a number of points relating to medieval mathematical lore on number combination and division, and suggesting a number of possible levels of allusion to be contained in the references to the numbers two, five, and ten. S. Sarteschi, 'Ancora sui versi 136–38 di *Paradiso* xxvii', *GSLI*, 177:401–21, identifies the *terzina*'s reference to the daughter of the sun with Pasiphae (and Ovid as source) and the blackening of her white skin with the adulterous sin that perversely generated the Minotaur. The metamorphic allusion is shown to draw together themes that pervade the whole canto, with its references to changing skin tones (Peter's indignation reflected in Beatrice's blush), Ovidian myth (Europa and Hercules), and moral metamorphosis from childhood innocence to sins of incontinence, violence, or fraud (S. argues that this infernal scheme provides the framework for lines 127–38). The latter strand also makes connection with the idea of perversion of the marriage bond, literal in the case of Pasiphae, but metaphorical in the other structuring theme of the canto, concerning the conduct of, and relationship between, the Church (the *sponsa Christi*) and the Empire (whose leader D. elsewhere figures as bridegroom of humanity). The blackening of Pasiphae's skin would thus also provide a complex inversion of the figure of the black bride from the *Song of Songs*, so intriguing to medieval thinkers and to D. himself, as Pertile (1998) has recently reminded us.

DUECENTO AND TRECENTO II
(EXCLUDING DANTE)

By ANTONIA ARVEDA, *Vicenza*, and ROBERTA CAPELLI, *Padua*
(This survey covers the years 1998, 1999, and 2000)

I. GENERAL

Dizionario enciclopedico del Medioevo, ed. Claudio Leonardi, 3 vols, Ro, Città Nuova, 1998–99, 2,161 pp., is an Italian version of a French original edited by André Vauchez with the collaboration of Catherine Vincent. Produced over a period of six years and involving some 600 contributors, it gathers the fruits of the last 30 years' research in medieval studies and aims to pass them on to the general reading public. Organized under headwords, it is equipped with a particularly helpful set of indexes. *La Bibbia in italiano tra Medioevo e Rinascimento./ La Bible italienne au Moyen Âge et à la Renaissance. Atti del Convegno Internazionale, Firenze, Certosa del Galluzzo, 8–9 novembre 1996*, ed. Lino Leonardi, Fond. Ezio Franceschini–École Française de Rome, F, SISMEL–Galluzzo, x + 442 pp., presents the results of research into Italian vernacular versions of the Bible from the origins to the 16th c. In *Il genere 'tenzone' nelle letterature romanze delle Origini. Atti del Convegno Internazionale (Losanna 13–15 novembre 1997)*, ed. Matteo Pedroni and Antonio Stäuble, Ravenna, Longo, 1999, 412 pp., the first eight of the 19 contributions concern the Italian sphere in the 13th and 14th c.: M. Picone, 'La tenzone *de amore* fra Iacopo Mostacci, Pier della Vigna e il Notaio' (13–32); A. Menichetti, 'Le tenzoni fittizie di Chiaro Davanzati' (33–46); G. Lindt, 'Analisi comparata della tenzone e del contrasto in base alla semiologia e alla semantica strutturale' (47–72); P. Allegretti, 'Il sonetto dialogato due-trecentesco. L'*intercisio* e le sue origini gallo-romanze' (73–110); L. Rossi, 'I sonetti di Jacopo da Lèona' (111–32); F. Suitner, 'Metamorfosi di motivi comico-giullareschi in Iacopone' (133–46); R. Castagnola, 'Contrasti amorosi in Cecco Angiolieri' (147–58); G. Frasso, 'Minime divagazioni petrarchesche' (159–64). *Storiografia e poesia nella cultura medievale. Atti del colloquio (Roma, 21–23 febbraio 1990)*, Ro, ISIM, 1999. *L'autobiografia nel Medioevo. Atti del XXXIV Convegno storico internazionale (Todi 12–15 ottobre 1997)*, Spoleto, CISAM, 1998, 352 pp., collects 15 contributions which aim at a better understanding of the rise of autobiography in the Middle Ages, by determining its sources, the contexts in which it originated, and the ways in which it developed. *Anima e corpo nella cultura medievale. Atti del V Convegno di studi promosso dalla Società Italiana per lo Studio del Pensiero*

Medievale (Venezia, 25–28 settembre 1995), ed. Carla Casagrande and Silvana Vecchio, SISMEL–Galluzzo, 1999, 332 pp., is a heterogeneous but interesting collection of essays exploring the theme of the title from the philosophical, theological, and literary point of view. *Lo spazio letterario del Medioevo. 2. Il Medioevo volgare.* 1: *La produzione del testo*, ed. Piero Boitani, Mario Mancini, and Alberto Varvaro, Ro, Salerno, 1999, 653 pp., following on from 'Il Medioevo latino' as the first of the two tomes to be devoted to 'Il medioevo volgare', falls into four main sections headed respectively 'Premesse storico-culturali', 'Cultura orale e cultura scritta', 'Le tradizioni culturali', and 'L'autore'. Pio Rajna, *Scritti di filologia e linguistica italiana e romanza*, ed. Guido Lucchini, pref. Francesco Mazzoni, introd. Cesare Segre, 3 vols, Ro, Salerno, 1998, xxxi + 1831 pp., articulates the philologist's collected writings in five sections: Italian literature; history of the Italian language; textual criticism; romance philology; and 'profili filologici'. Cesare Segre, *Ecdotica e comparatistica romanze*, ed. Alberto Conte, Mi–Na, Ricciardi, 1998, lxviii + 300 pp., brings together 21 essays by Segre and a bibliography of his writings down to and including 1998.

Rosa Casapullo, *Il Medioevo, Bo, Il Mulino, 1999, 476 pp. Massimo Oldoni, *Culture del Medioevo. Dotta, popolare, orale*, Ro, Donzelli, 1999, 95 pp., analysing medieval culture in terms of literary history, interprets it as an amalgam of the recovery of antiquity, the influence of Holy Scripture, and of oral culture. R. Esposito di Mambro, 'Tipologia del libro di viaggio nel Medioevo', *CLett*, 28:151–61, surveys the modes of writing in medieval travel literature in search of its distinguishing features and finds them to lie in the composite structure and hybrid character of the genre. B. Stock, '*Lectio divina* e *lectio spiritualis*: la scrittura come pratica contemplativa nel Medioevo', *LItal*, 52:169–83, identifies *lectio spiritualis* as an encouragement to writing as a contemplative practice, examines late medieval changes in reading habits and looks at Petrarch's experience. Giovanni Bárberi Squarotti, *Selvaggia dilettanza. La caccia nella letteratura italiana dalle origini a Marino*, Venice, Marsilio, 382 pp., pursues the theme of the chase and its symbolic transfigurations (the amorous chase, the infernal chase, the white hind, etc.), analysing texts by Dante, Boccaccio, Petrarch, Poliziano, Tasso, and Marino. S. Guida and F. Latella, 'Il mare come dimensione metaforica nella letteratura italiana del Due e Trecento', *Melli Vol.*, 363–85, analyses the use of the sea as an ethical or religious metaphor for the deceits of the world and a troubled existence, charting a course through texts ranging from the classics, to the Fathers of the Church, and to Italian literature of the Due- and Trecento.

2. Duecento and Trecento

Surveying 13th - and 14th-c. studies, J. Petrie, 'Gli studi di italianistica in Inghilterra: Duecento e Trecento', *EL*, 24.2, 1999:91–5, traces an overview of work on Italian medieval authors published in Great Britain and Ireland from 1993 to 1998, highlighting the absolute predominance of interest in Dante; F. Ardolino, 'Gli studi di letteratura italiana in Spagna: ultimi dieci anni. Duecento e Trecento', *ib.*, 23.1, 1998:125–33, looks at the state of medieval Italian studies in Spain in the period 1987–1997, pointing to a prevalence of the comparative approach and to a disproportion between critical and philological output, on the one hand, and popularization and translation on the other. Methodological questions are broached in G. Borriero, 'Sull'antologia lirica del Due e Trecento in volgare italiano. Appunti (minimi) di metodo', *CrT*, 2, 1999:195–219, which looks at the major anthologies of 13th- and 14th-c. vernacular lyric poetry with reference to the relationship between the anthology proper and its material 'support', identifying the formal and ideological criteria on which each collection is organized. R. Antonelli, 'Bifrontismo, pentimento e forma-canzoniere', Peron, *Palinodia*, 35–49, reflects on relations between poetic production, palinody, and the birth of the *canzoniere* form: the deliberately organized corpus of poems is studied with reference to the example of Guittone, Dante, and Petrarch. Giovanni Cappello, *La dimensione macrotestuale. Dante, Boccaccio, Petrarca*, Ravenna, Longo, 1998, 248 pp., as well as Dante's *Vita Nova* and *Rime* (*YWMLS*, 60:381), looks at the *Decameron* and the *Canzoniere* with reference to the notion of macrotext, elaborating the concept of "weak macrotextuality": the founding principle of the two works is said to be not a strict sequence of subject-matter from text to text but the two-way relationship each text maintains with the initial segment, i.e. the first four novelle of the First Day in Boccaccio and the opening sonnet in Petrarca. M. Chiamenti, 'The representation of psyche in Cavalcanti, Dante and Petrarca: the "spiriti"', *Neophilologus*, 82, 1998:71–81, considers the influence of Aristotle's psychological theories on the work of the three great poets. Giorgio Inglese, **L'intelletto e l'amore: studi sulla letteratura italiana del Due e Trecento*, Scandicci, La Nuova Italia, xv + 236 pp. Marco Santagata, *Amate e amanti: figure della lirica amorosa fra Dante e Petrarca*, Bo, Il Mulino, 1999, 246 pp., reviewing the theme of love's sufferings in early Italian literature, fixes the starting point of its treatment in Dante as singer of Beatrice and subverter of the traditional code of courtly love, while Petrarch as singer of Laura initiates the modern love lyric as the vehicle of self-expression. Paolo Orvieto and Lucia Brestolini, *La poesia comico-realistica. Dalle origini al Cinquecento*, Ro, Carocci, 277 pp., is divided into two main sections: the first, ed. Paolo Orvieto, reaches the Quattrocento with Burchiello's total 'nonsense'; the second, ed. Lucia Brestolin, concentrates entirely on the Cinquecento. On the 'comic' in early Italian literature see also C. Kleinhenz, *'Comic strategies in early Italian poetry', *ItQ*, 37:25–32. For Arthurian literature in Italy: Daniela Delcorno Branca, *Tristano e Lancillotto in Italia. Studi di letteratura arturiana*, Ravenna, Longo, 1998, 275 pp.; and *La storia del San Gradale*, ed. Marco Infurna, Padua, Antenore, 1999, xl + 246 pp., which edits (with a commentary), from a hitherto unknown MS in the Florentine State Archive, an anonymous prose translation (early 14th-c. Florentine) of the first Arthurian text of the *Lancelot*.

Franciscan studies are marked by a general tendency to favour a historical approach. Jacques Dalarun, *François d'Assise, ou le pouvoir en question: principes et modalités du gouvernement dans l'ordre des Frères mineurs*, Paris-Bruxelles, De Boeck University, 1999, 153 pp. or (in Italian) Id., *Francesco d'Assisi. Il potere in questione e la questione del potere. Rifiuto del potere e forme di governo nell'Ordine dei Frati Minori*, trans. Paolo Canali, Mi, Biblioteca Francescana, 1999, 170 pp., examines the institutional aspects of the Order, setting fundamental episodes of Francis's biography, such as his rejection of leadership of the Order (1220), in their historical and cultural context. S. J. Hubert, 'Theological and polemical uses of hagiography: a consideration of Bonaventure's *Legenda Maior* of St. Francis', *Comitatus*, 29, 1998:47–61, defines the position of the *Legenda Major* in the thought and literary production of St Bonaventura, noting how it allows him to read the life of St Francis in metaphorical terms as the mystical journey of the soul. J. Hamesse, *'New perspectives for critical editions of Franciscan texts', *FranS*, 56, 1998:169–87, addresses textual and editorial questions. Gino Zanotti, *I francescani a Ravenna dai tempi di Dante a oggi*, Ravenna, Longo. 1999, 169 pp., and N. Mineo, 'Gli spirituali francescani e l'"Apocalisse" di Dante', *RLI*, 102, 1998:26–46, contextualize the life and preaching of the Order at the time of Dante, pointing to possible influences on D.'s literary production. By another Franciscan: Salimbene de Adam, *Cronica*, I: *a. 1168–1249*, ed. Giuseppe Scalia, Turnhout, Brepols, 1998, lxiv + 506 pp., contains the first part of the chronicle, with only a few modifications compared to the Laterza edition of 1966. Paolo Evangelisti, **Fidenzio da Padova e la letteratura crociato-missionaria minoritica: strategie e modelli francescani per il dominio (secc. 13–15)*, Bo, Il Mulino, 1998, lii + 362 pp.

There have been numerous contributions on the literary manifestations of medieval mysticism. Bernard McGinn, *The Presence of God. A History of Western Mysticism*, III: *The Flowering of Mysticism: Men and Women in the New Mysticism, 1200–1350*, NY, Crossroad, 1998, xvi + 526 pp., pays particular attention to female mysticism: along-side St Francis and Franciscanism, interesting pages are devoted to Clare of Assisi, Angela of Foligno (whose mysticism has much in common with that of Iacopone da Todi, which is tellingly analysed), Hadewijch, Mathilde of Magdeburg, and Margaret Porete. C. Delcorno, 'Biografia, agiografia e autoagiografia', *LItal*, 51, 1999: 173–96, after pointing to the novelties of Christian hagiography as compared with classical biography, looks at the specific character-istics of the hagiographical works produced by the Mendicant Orders. The 'Legend of St Francis' holds a special place, but female sacred autobiography also takes on considerable importance, as in the case of Angela of Foligno. P. Palumbo, 'The body of Christ and religion power in Angela of Foligno's *Libro*', *FoI*, 32, 1998: 36–50, in contrast reinterprets the Tertiary Franciscan's mystical experience in political terms, as a kind of revolt against the 'gender relations dominant in her cultural environment' (36). Growing interest for female mysticism also shows itself in the form of editions such as Chiara d'Assisi, *Lettere ad Agnese. La visione dello specchio*, ed. Giovanni Pozzi and Beatrice Rima, Mi, Adelphi, 1999, 258 pp., the saint's correspondence with Agnes of Prague, the King of Bohemia's daughter, who preferred convent life to a royal marriage. The 'Regesto dei fatti retorici e storici', description of the MSS, critical apparatus, and commentary, are the work of Fr G. Pozzi, while the so-called *Visione dello specchio* is ed. B. Rima. St Catherine of Siena's copious correspondence is gathered in **Le Lettere di Santa Caterina da Siena: versione in italiano corrente*, ed. Giuseppe di Ciaccia, 2 vols, Bo, ESD, 1996–98, 623, 627 pp.

Still within the field of religious literature, or literature produced in the religious sphere, by a particularly important figure who became Bishop of Genoa and whose writings have been extensively reassessed and published in recent years is Iacopo da Varazze, *Legenda Aurea*, ed. Giovanni Paolo Maggioni, 2 vols, F, SISMEL–Galluzzo, 1998 [revised ed. 1999], lxvi + 662, 664–1366 pp., an imposing edition that adds important new information on the driving forces behind the work's composition and on its intricate MS tradition, confirming the hypothesis of a double redaction (LA1 and LA2) and of various phases of rewriting and amplification down to the author's death. There have also been contributions on the minor works: Stefania Bertini Guidetti, *I 'Sermones' di Iacopo da Varazze. Il potere delle immagini nel Duecento*, F, SISMEL–Galluzzo, 1998, ix + 173 pp., purges the Dominican's 750 sermons of quotations of *auctoritates* and biblical insertions, identifying their most important thematic veins with a view to giving maximum emphasis to the original characteristics of the author's style and personality. From the same scholar, 'Fonti e tecniche di compilazione nella *Chronica Civitatis Ianuensis* di Jacopo da Varagine', Leonardi, *Umanesimi*, 17–36, analyses the compositional criteria and historical value of the chronicle of Genoa, highlighting the heterogeneousness of its sources, its abundance of quotations and self-quotations, its preference for a compilatory technique, its *reductio ad exempla* tendency in historical episodes, and its attempt to harmonize the classical and Christian worlds.

The hagiographical genres are closely related to preaching, as is underlined in C. Delcorno, 'Il "parlato" dei predicatori. Osservazioni sulla sintassi di Giordano da Pisa', *LItal*, 52:3–50, which looks at the style of Giordano da Pisa's sermons, identifying a constant tension between application of the rhetorical elements codified in the medieval *ars praedicandi* and a pursuit of syntactic structures and lexical solutions typical of speech. Giordano da Pisa, *Prediche sul secondo capitolo del Genesi*, ed. Serena Grattarola, Ro, Istituto Storico Domenicano, 1999, 226 pp., edits sermons from the acephalous and mutilated Codice C. Cecilia Iannella, *Giordano da Pisa. Etica urbana e forme della società*, Pisa, ETS, 1999, 254 pp., draws on testimony and data from Giordano da Pisa's writings to portray 14th-c. urban reality. A fundamental contribution in this field of research, aimed at the creation of a general repertory of published and unpublished vernacular sermons, is G. Auzzas and C. Delcorno, 'Inventario dei manoscritti di prediche volgari inedite (Biblioteche dell'Italia Centro-Settentrionale)', *LItal*, 51, 1999:602–17, presenting a list of the MSS in the libraries of central and northern Italy containing unpublished material.

A special place in Italian literature is held by the poets who, under the influence of Occitan literature, wrote verse in the *lingua d'oc. CN*, 60, vi + 392 pp., is devoted to the *acta* of a conference on Sordello of Goito: *Atti del Convegno Internazionale di Studi (Goito–Mantova, 13–15 novembre 1997)*, ed. Stefano Asperti and Maria Careri, comprising 15 contributions which analyse the life and work of the Italian troubadour in relation to the cultural, historical, and literary setting of his time. Straddling Provençal and Italian literature, M. Signorini, 'Riflessioni paleografiche sui canzonieri provenzali veneti', *CrT*, 2, 1999:837–59, presents two examples of the usefulness of the palaeographical method when applied to problems of romance philology: an examination of the decoration of 13th-c. MSS in the A, I, and K areas of the Veneto, and an analysis of the corrections to the 14th-c. *canzoniere* Vat. Lat. 3206.

A study of undoubtedly major importance is: A. Stussi, 'Versi d'amore in volgare tra la fine del secolo XII e l'inizio del XIII', *CN*, 59, 1999:1–69, which brings to light two fragments of poetry (copied on the *verso* of parchment 11518 ter. now in the Archivio Storico

Arcivescovile at Ravenna) already mentioned 50 years ago by G. Muzzioli and A. Campana: text A, 'Quando eu stava in le tu' catene', a love canzone comprising five strophes of decasyllables rhyming ABABABCCCZ, and text B, a single strophe of five hendasyllables. A palaeographic analysis of text A carried out by A. Ciaralli and A. Petrucci suggests dating the fragment between 1180 and 1210 and is in accord with the conclusion reached by C. Gallico after studying the musical notation accompanying the canzone. Stussi's minute linguistic analysis brings him to the conclusion that the texts were composed in the Po area, but later copied by median hands. He rightly claims the exceptional interest of the documents, which are almost half a century earlier than any previously known specimens of Italian verse.

The poetry of the so-called Sicilian school continues to pose new critical and philological questions and to stimulate attempts at new overall interpretations. This is shown by the distinguished contributions gathered in *Lingua, rima, codici per una nuova edizione della poesia della scuola siciliana. Atti della giornata di studio (Bologna, 24 giugno 1997)*, ed. Andrea Fassò and Luciano Formisano, published in *QFRB*, 12–13, 1999:9–102. The debate, in which Roberto Antonelli, Furio Brugnolo, and Giuseppina Brunetti took part, centred on G. Sanga's thesis that in the 13th c. an archaic form of 'trivocalic' rhyme, inherited from middle-Latin rhythmics, was already current, whereby –e- rhyming with –i- and –o- rhyming with –u- could be accepted. *Dai Siciliani ai Siculo-toscani. Lingua, metro e stile per la definizione del canone. Atti del Convegno, Lecce, 21–23 aprile 1998*, ed. Rosario Coluccia and Riccardo Gualdo, Galatina, Congedo, 1999, 240 pp., gathers 11 papers exploring the conference theme from the editorial, historical, philological, linguistic, and prosodic points of view: R. Antonelli, 'La tradizione manoscritta e la formazione del canone' (7–28); S. Orlando, 'La poesia dei Siciliani e la lezione dei Memoriali bolognesi' (29–38); R. Coluccia, 'Storia editoriale e formazione del canone' (39–59); G. Brunetti, 'Il libro di Giacomino e i canzonieri individuali: diffusione delle forme e tradizione della Scuola poetica siciliana' (61–92); F. Brugnolo, 'Ancora sulla genesi del sonetto' (93–106); M. Spampinato Beretta, 'Tra "Siciliani" e "Siculo-toscani": casi-limite di incerta collocazione' (107–19); R. Gualdo, 'I sonetti anonimi del Chigiano: questioni di collocazione e di cronologia' (121–53); F. Beggiato, 'Percorso di un vettore tematico' (155–66); C. Di Girolamo and A. Fratta, 'I decenari con rima interna e la metrica dei Siciliani' (167–86); P. G. Beltrami, 'Osservazioni sulla metrica dei Siciliani e dei Siculo-toscani' (187–216); S. Lubello, 'Schede sui Siculo-toscani: i rimatori fiorentini' (217–31).

The circulation of Provençal and Old French poetic models in the Middle Ages, with particular reference to the influence they may have exerted on the poetry of the Sicilian school, is set in context in Luciano Formisano, 'Troubadours, Trouvères, Siciliens', *AIEO 1995*, 109–24. Affording further food for thought, Wilhelm Pötters, *Nascita del sonetto. Metrica e matematica al tempo di Federico II*, Ravenna, Longo, 1998, 185 pp., formulates the novel theory whereby the fixed metrical structure of the sonnet, built around the numbers 11 and 14 (the number of syllables per line and the total number of lines) is the poetic transposition of the geometrical figures and measurements used in the Middle Ages to work out the area of a circle and to define the golden section. From the signatory of the foreword to Pötters' volume: Furio Brugnolo, 'I siciliani e l'arte dell'imitazione: Giacomo da Lentini, Rinaldo d'Aquino e Iacopo Mostacci "traduttori" dal provenzale', *PaT*, 3, 1999:45–74, compares four Sicilian school poems with their Provençal sources and shows, through precise intertextual and metrical convergences, that the poets at the court of Frederick II carried out 'art translations' of the models they chose. The two poems by Giacomo da Lentini, 'Madonna, dir vo voglio' and 'Troppo son dimorato', are to be set in relation, respectively, to the canzone 'A vos, midontç, voill rettrair'en cantan' by Folquet of Marseille and the canzone 'Trop ai estat' by Perdigon; the canzone 'Poi li piace c'avanzi suo valore' by Rinaldo d'Aquino derives from 'Chantan volgra mon fin cor descobrir' by Folquet of Marseille; and lastly, the canzone 'Umile core e fino e amoroso' by Iacopo Mostacci is modelled on 'Longa sazon ai estat vas amor' of uncertain attribution. The correspondences between the Rinaldo d'Aquino canzone and the one by Folquet are also discussed in A. M. Ramazzina, ' "Chantan volgra mon fin cor descobrir" e "Poi li piace c'avanzi suo valore": due testi a confronto', *MedRom*, 22, 1998:352–72. F. Carapezza, 'Un "genere" cantato della Scuola poetica siciliana?', *NRLI*, 22, 1999:321–54, picks out signs of 'vocality' in the corpus of texts available and indicates the so-called *canzonetta* as a possible example of a poetic (sub-)genre that could be set to music.

There is no shortage of articles narrower in range and more specialized in approach: S. Bianchini, 'Per il v. 40 di "Audite forte cosa che m'avene" di Inghilfredi da Lucca', *AION(SR)*, 40, 1998:375–85, which proposes restoring the final line (which is incomplete in the MSS) of Inghilfredi's canzone with l. 11, 'como la spene – che fiorisc' e ingrana', of the sonnet 'Angelica figura e comprobata' by Giacomo da Lentini; G. Giannini, 'Qualità dei gallicismi e fenomeni di attrazione del significante presso i poeti federiciani', *QFRB*, 12–13, 1999:327–49, examining significant cases of Gallicisms which entered the language of the Sicilian school poets not by automatic and generic absorption of foreign words (typical of any early poetic text), but as a result of a conscious process of borrowing, re-elaboration, and insertion of the chosen term into a context that is quite different from its original one. The observations of G. Goebel, 'Giacomo da Lentini und die Ordnung des Sonettes', *Italienisch*, 43:87–91, centre on the guide-figure, Giacomo, as does the research of R. Coluccia and R. Gualdo, 'Sondaggi sull'eredità del Notaro', *SLI*, 26:3–51, who analyse the influence exerted by the Notary on the poetry of the Sicilians and the 'Siculo-toscani' and also provide new evidence of the precocious and still little-known diffusion of texts from Sicily to the southern mainland.

The literary output of Frederick II of Swabia and the evidence of his Court's cultural vivacity deserve a separate paragraph. A general account of great precision and completeness is offered by Salvatore Tramontana, *Il regno di Sicilia: uomo e natura dall'XI al XIII secolo*, T, Einaudi, 1999, xiii + 488 pp. F.'s treatise on falconry is published for the first time in *De arte venandi cum avibus / L'arte di cacciare con gli uccelli*, ed. Anna Laura Trombetti Budriesi, Ro–Bari, Laterza, cxlviii + 1294 pp. + 60 colour illus. The editor comes back to its historical vicissitudes, MS tradition, and content in 'Per un'edizione critica del *De arte venandi cum avibus* di Federico II di Svevia', *Melli Vol.*, 811–27. On F.'s poetic *oeuvre*, R. Pelosini, 'La "noia" di Re Federigo', *CrT*, 2, 1999:809–17, proposes not to emend the repetition of the rhyme-word 'noia' in l. 8 of the canzone 'Dolze meo drudo, e!, va' ·te ·ne!', attributed to 'Re Federigo', in MS Vaticano Latino 3793.

The literary situation of 13th-c. Sicily is illustrated through studies of particular phenomena or of individual personalities of importance. Dorothea Walz, 'Prospettive nuove sull'*Historia destructionis Troiae* di Guido delle Colonne', Leonardi, *Umanesimi*, 817–26, analyses Guido delle Colonne's work with reference to its chief source, the *Roman de Troie* by Benoît de Sainte-Maure and to the political and cultural context in which it was produced, i.e. the Swabian court in Sicily, whereas J. Simpson, 'The other book of Troy: Guido delle Colonne's *Historia destructionis Troiae* in fourteenth- and fifteenth-century England', *Speculum*, 73, 1998:397–423, investigates the reasons for the success of G.'s Latin prose work in England. Giovanni R. Ricci, *L'interpretazione rimossa. I primi due versi del 'Contrasto' di Cielo d'Alcamo*, F, Gazebo, 1999, 57 pp., rejecting earlier interpretations of the two opening lines, proposes that it be read as referring to a situation of female bisexuality. Moving to the aulic register, F. Delle Donne, 'Una disputa sulla nobiltà alla corte di Federico II di Svevia', *MedRom*, 23, 1999:3–20, analyses the characteristics and scope of discussions on the theme of nobility at F.'s court, looking in particular at the *Contentio de nobilitate generis et probitate animi* and providing a complete edition of the text in an appendix.

Iacopone da Todi, who occupies an autonomous position in Duecento poetry, has attracted numerous contributions. Franco Suitner, *Iacopone da Todi. Poesia, mistica, rivolta nell'Italia del medioevo*, Ro, Donzelli, 1999, viii + 277 pp., reconstructs the major events of the poet's life (his conversion, his years of penance, his entry into the Franciscan Order, his imprisonment), setting them in relation to the crucial events of his time (the Franciscans' intestine struggles between 'Conventuals' and 'Spirituals', and the papacy of Celestine V and of Boniface VIII). Z. L. Verlato, 'Notizia su un laudario iacoponico (cod. 151 della Biblioteca del Seminario vescovile di Padova)', *Il Santo*, 40:231–99, announces the discovery of a sylloge of poems by I. in MS 151 at the Paduan Biblioteca del Seminario vescovile. The mutilated fragment (initialled Pd) contains 14 *laude* securely attributable to I. and four of doubtful authorship, which are published in a diplomatic transcription and furnished with a linguistic commentary. L. Tomasin, 'Aspetti della sintassi iacoponica', *Italianistica*, 29:93–112, analyses the more interesting aspects of I.'s syntax, looking particularly at phenomena of dislocation of complements and the use of polyvalent 'che', and stressing the way in which his *Laude* present very marked 'spoken' features. E. Salvaneschi, 'Gita a Cariddi: ordine o disordine?', *IR*, 7, 1998:1–38, devotes the first part of the article (1–8) to the definition of the antithesis order–disorder in I. and Dante. M. Boccignone, 'Un albero piantato nel cuore (Iacopone e Petrarca)', *LItal*, 52:225–64, looks at the *topos* with reference to the medieval allegorical tradition and identifies I.'s output as a probable source of the image in the Petrarch sonnet *RVF*, ccxxviii. G. Jori, ' "Sentenze maravigliose e dolci affetti". Iacopone tra Cinque e Seicento', *ib.*, 50, 1998:506–27, focuses on the reception and *fortuna* of I.'s *oeuvre*, identifying St Philip Neri as an enthusiastic reader. A. Guastella, 'Il futuro della tradizione. Ungaretti e Iacopone', *ON*, 22.3, 1998:91–129, develops in detail and with precise chronology numerous observations already made on intertextual references to I. in Ungaretti.

Guittone d'Arezzo's complex *œuvre* is a field that constantly stimulates new critical and philological observations. Antonello Borra, *Guittone d'Arezzo e le maschere del poeta: la lirica cortese tra ironia e palinodia*, Ravenna, Longo, 111 pp., devoting particolar attention to the arrangement of G.'s poems as they figure in the MSS in which they have come down to us, purports to show that behind the division of the corpus into poems by 'Guittone d'Arezzo' and poems by 'Frate Guittone' lies hidden a precise *intentio auctoris*. G.'s design is well explained in C. Calenda, ' "Palinodie" guittoniane', Peron, *Palinodia*,

51–60, with the observation that the Aretine poet's much flaunted conversion is a widespread literary topos and has, before all else, a rhetorical value, justifying negatively the morally censurable poetics of his youth. A. Poli, 'Una scheda provenzale per Guittone. Le canzoni XX, "Ahi lasso, che li boni e li malvagi", e XLIX, "Altra fiata aggio già, donne, parlato"', *FC*, 25:95–108, identifies a common Provençal source behind G.'s two canzoni: the *sirventese* 'Tant es d'amor honratz sos seignoratges' (BdT 9, 21) by the troubadour Aimeric de Belenoi. E. Gragnani, 'La revisione della produzione guittoniana nelle rime dantesche', *EL*, 24.1, 1999:39–57, shows how the vast repertory of Guittonian suggestions present in D.'s lyric production serves him, on the one hand, to defend his theorization of ennobling love, and on the other, to confirm his detachment from G.'s moral theme.

A number of noteworthy contributions focus on Dante's 'master', Brunetto Latini. On questions of attribution relating to B.'s corpus, I. Hijmans-Tromp, 'La *Sommetta* falsamente attribuita a Brunetto Latini', *CN*, 59, 1999:177–243, refutes the *Sommetta*'s attribution to B. and provides a new edition of it. On the other hand, R. Fasani, 'Il *Fiore* e Brunetto Latini', *SPCT*, 57, 1998:5–36, uses 'external' and 'internal' proof to attribute the *Fiore* to B. Questions of textual criticism and codicology are addressed in M. Longobardi, 'Resti di un volgarizzamento toscano del *Trésor*', *Pluteus*, 8–9, 1990–98:33–65, which announces the discovery of two bifoliate MSS (one at the Bologna State Archive, the other at the Bologna University Library) containing fragments of a Tuscan translation of the *Trésor* which originally belonged to a MS datable to the 14th-c., and in Fr Supino Martini, 'Un "tresor" dei Ventimiglia: il Vat. Reg. lat. 1320', *CrT*, 1, 1998:775–82, which gives a minute description of MS Reginense lat. 1320 of B.'s *Trésor*, reconstructing the story of its various ownership.

On the *Stil novo* there has been a good deal of new work. For convenience it can be divided between lengthy publications concerning the movement and the group's poetics, and work focusing on individual authors. As for the first category, a valuable volume is Claudio Giunta, *La poesia italiana nell'età di Dante. La linea Bonagiunta–Guinizelli*, Bo, Il Mulino, 1998, 390 pp., which, bringing a new orientation to historical interpretation of the early Italian lyric, tends to reduce the division between Bonagiunta and Guinizelli, and indeed to make them both the forerunners of the *Stil novo*. Also interesting is Carlo Paolazzi, *La maniera mutata. Il 'dolce stil novo' tra Scrittura e 'Ars poetica'*, Mi, Vita e Pensiero, 1998, x + 346 pp., which reopens the debate over the possibility or otherwise of considering the *stilnovo* movement an actual 'poetic school'. As proof of the existence of a common, codified poetics P. adduces two new pieces of evidence: the influence of Scripture and of Horace's *Ars poetica*. The study of *stilnovo* names holds some curious discoveries in store: according to B. Porcelli, 'Sui nomi delle donne dello Stil nuovo', *LItal*, 50, 1998:381–86, the names of the women celebrated by the *stilnovo* poets (but the field of enquiry also extends to the comic-realistic poets and to Petrarch), far from being casual, reflect precise phonic and metaphorical criteria. G. E. Sansone, 'Il nome disseminato: Brunetto, Bondie, Dante', *PaT*, 2, 1998:9–20, gives three examples of anagrammatic writing in Duecento Italian poetry: the first two cases are found in Brunetto Latini's canzone 'S'eo son distretto inamoratamente' and in Bondie Dietaiuti's canzone in reply, 'Amor, quando mi membra', where the linear reading of specific phonemes forms the names of these two homosexual lovers. The third case concerns the *sonetto rinterzato* of the *Vita nova*, in which it is possible to trace, between the lines, the anagram of Beatrice, the real addressee of the poem. Deep into the forest of *stilnovo* symbols and metaphors ventures Lucia Lazzerini, in 'L'"allodetta" e il suo archetipo. La rielaborazione di temi mistici nella lirica trobadorica e nello stil novo', *Mazzoni Vol.*, 165–88, reconstructing the dense web of 'sensi ulteriori' (whose ancestry is yet more religious and mystical than troubadoric) concealed behind the metaphor of the skylark in *Par.* xx, 73–75, and behind all the analogous comparisons present in the *stilnovisti*.

There are also more strictly philological contributions. S. Orlando, 'Aggiunte "bolognesi" al corpus delle CLPIO', *SLeI*, 15, 1998:5–20, adds to the *CLPIO* a small set of texts or fragments (to be precise, fragments of *ballate*) which he recently discovered in the *Memoriali bolognesi*. P. Moreno, 'Antiche poesie italiane nel manoscritto Stockholm, Kungliga Biblioteket, Vu 14', *MedRom*, 22, 1998:373–87, publishes, with a metrical and linguistic commentary, the three Italian poems ('Oimè, Amor, perché mi fai morire?', 'Oimè che 'l cuor non ò, anz'è in altru' balia' and 'Chi 'n femina si fida') copied by a probably 14th-c. hand into the last folia of MS Vu 14 of the Royal Library in Stockholm. G. Borriero, 'Nuovi accertamenti sulla struttura fascicolare del canzoniere Vat. Chig. L.VIII.305', *CrT*, 1, 1998:723–50, shows that the displacement of two folia has damaged the original structure of the MS. N. Cannata Salamone, 'L'Antologia e il canone: la Giuntina delle Rime Antiche (Firenze, 1527)', *ib.*, 2, 1999:221–47, traces the chequered editorial history of the *Sonetti e canzoni di diversi antichi autori toscani*, and reflects on the sources and the canonical model of Duecento Italian poetry transmitted by the Giuntina. Giuliano Gasca Queirazza, 'Il serventese romagnolo: una rinnovata lettura', *Melli Vol.*, 353–61, proposes considerable variations in the text and interpretation of the Duecento poem, pointing out the presence in both the *serventese* and the *Commedia* of the very rare rhymes in *–eltro* (respectively, ll. 40–43, *Montefeltro – afeltro – veltro – peltru*, and in *Inf.* I, 101–05) and of the rhymes in *–ido* (respectively, ll. 37 and 39, *nido – Guido*, and *Purg.* XI, 97–99).

Moving on to new work on individual poets: the 'father' of the *Stil novo* is represented by the new edition Guido Guinizelli, *Rime*, ed. Pietro Pelosi, Na, Liguori, 1998, 94 pp. Bonagiunta is the pivot of A. Menichetti, 'La canzone della gioia d'amore di Bonagiunta da Lucca', Picone, *Dante*, 125–37: the scholar gives us a critical edition of the canzone 'Gioia né ben non è sensa conforto', basing it on MS P (BNCF, Banco Rari 217, formerly Palatino 418) and V (Vat. Lat. 3793), and furnishing it with paraphrases and metrical, linguistic, stylistic, and comparative observations. The thought and poetry of Guido Cavalcanti are invested with special critical interest: Enrico Fenzi, *La canzone d'amore di Guido Cavalcanti e i suoi antichi commenti*, Genoa, Il Melangolo, 1999, 300 pp., not only gathers and analyses almost all the commentaries produced on the canzone 'Donna me prega' down to the Cinquecento, but also offers a personal exegetic contribution, siding with the branch of criticism that considers 'Donna me prega' a means of refutation of the positions theorized by Dante in the *Vita Nova*. This position is deemed untenable in M. Marti, 'Acque agitate per *Donna me prega*', *GSLI*, 177:161–67, who reaffirms his own convictions as stated from his review of E. Fenzi's book onwards. Not to be ignored on this subject is N. Pasero, 'Dante in Cavalcanti. Ancora sui rapporti fra *Vita Nuova* e *Donna me prega*', *MedRom*, 22, 1998:388–414, which puts forward fresh elements in favour of the possibility that 'Donna me prega' is a (contrary) reply to Dante's ideas. A compact group of contributions concern influences and reciprocal relations between C. and D.: Danilo Bonanno, *La perdita e il ritorno. Presenze cavalcantiane nell'ultimo Dante*, Pisa, ETS, 1999, 63 pp., explores intertextual links between the *Commedia* and C.'s *canzoniere*, programmatically excluding those passages in which D. refers explicitly to his friend and showing that the presence of Cavalcanti is hidden but constant even in D.'s most 'spiritual' passages. S. Hartung, *'Stilnovismus und Pastourelle bei Cavalcanti. Konfrontation inkompatibler Liebesdiskurse vor Dante', *RJ*, 49, 1998:98–121. A rigorous philological approach distinguishes G. Tanturli, 'Filologia cavalcantiana fra Antonio Manetti e Raccolta Aragonese', *Mazzoni Vol.*, 11–20, centring on the problem of the MS tradition of C.'s *Rime* constituted by the relationship between MS Ca, Cap^2, and Ar. Operating at the level of thematic analysis, D. K. Banerjee, 'The darkening heart and the icon of light: Cavalcanti', *Della Terza Vol.*, 37–46, analyses the relationship Donna–Amore and Amore–Amante and looks particularly at C.'s theory of light. S. Rizzardi, 'Dinamiche intertestuali di un'immagine: il "casser della

mente" cavalcantiano', *SPCT*, 57, 1998:131–57, explains the meaning of the metaphor — peculiarly Cavalcantian and generically
stilnovist — of the 'casser della mente', setting it in relationship with
the rational power and deriving it from the metaphor of the 'arx
capitis' used by Cicero, Augustine, and other middle-Latin authors.
Lusus is the connecting thread of L. Rossi, 'Maestria poetica e *grivoiserie*
nelle tenzoni Orlandi–Cavalcanti', pp. 27–42 of *Studi di filologia e
letteratura italiana in onore di Gianvito Resta*, ed. Vitilio Masiello, 2 vols,
Ro, Salerno, 712, 713–1527 pp., which takes as its example the
tenzoni between Guido Orlandi and Guido C. in order to identify a
double level of expression, the aulic level referring to troubadour
models and the concrete level of obscene double-entendres. There
are also obscene hidden intentions in other C. texts, as is underlined
in M. Cursietti, 'Una beffa parallela alla falsa "Tenzone di Dante con
Forese Donati": la Berta di Cavalcanti cavalcato', *L'Alighieri*, 13,
1999:91–110, and Id., 'I doppi sensi del sonetto "S'e' non ti cagia la
tua santalena" ', *PaT*, 3, 1999:75–83. In this latter case, C. suggests
giving the word 'santalena' the meaning not of 'lucky charm' (Contini
and De Robertis) but of the male sex organ. The author, moreover,
pointing to correspondences of lexis and style between this sonnet
and the sonnets of the contested *Tenzone di Dante con Forese Donati*, finds
new data in support of the possible 15th-c. dating of these burlesque-
obscene compositions and of the MS (Chigiano L. VIII. 305) through
which they have come down to us. Contributions for or against the
authenticity of the *Tenzone di Dante con Forese* constitute a separate
section. The terms of the question are set out in F. Alfie, 'For want of
a nail: the Guerri–Lanza–Cursietti argument regarding the *Tenzone*',
DaSt, 116, 1998:141–59. G. Borriero, 'Considerazioni sulla tradizione manoscritta della *Tenzone* di Dante con Forese', *Antico/Moderno*,
4, 1999:385–405, defends the *Tenzone*'s authenticity on the basis of
an analysis of the MS tradition, but M. Cursietti, 'Dante e Forese alla
taverna del Panìco. Le prove documentarie della falsità della
tenzone', *L'Alighieri*, 16:7–22, demolishes his observations with fresh
evidence — documentary, linguistic and cultural — in favour of the
15-c. forgery thesis. Lastly, C. Keen, 'Images of exile: distance and
memory in the poetry of Cino da Pistoia', *ISt*, 55:21–36, analyses a
group of poems in search of C.'s poetics of exile and shows how
political-autobiographical and amorous-metaphorical interpretations
can be combined in them.

    On Duecento comic-realistic verse, a study of major interest is
G. Marrani, 'I sonetti di Rustico Filippi', *SFI*, 57, 1999:33–199,
minutely analysing the work of the Florentine poet with a view to
reducing the stylistic gap traditionally seen by critics between his
amorous and comic production. F. Alfie, ' "I' son sì magro che quasi

traluco": inspiration and indebtedness among Cecco Angiolieri, Meo dei Tolomei, and Il Burchiello', *ItQ,* 35, 1998:5–28, focuses his attention on the sonnet 'I' son sì magro che quasi traluco', composed by Cecco Angiolieri, taken over by Meo dei Tolomei, and reutilized by Burchiello. A commentary on each of the three versions, accompanied by an analysis of their MS tradition, brings out the points of contact and differences between their respective authors. B. Porcelli, 'Lettura di *Ècci venuto Guido < 'n > Compostello*', *FC*, 23, 1998:11–20, re-examines the burlesque sonnet by Muscia da Siena on Cavalcanti's pilgrimage to Compostella, suggesting a new interpretative key to l. 3, 'Ch' e' va com'oca, e cascàli 'l mantello', and l. 7, 'Ben par che' sappia 'torni del camello'.

Duecento literature also, of course, has prose of notable quality, such as the works of the Milanese Bonvesin de la Riva. M. Cerroni, 'Tipologia dell'allegoria e dinamiche del vero in Giacomino da Verona e Bonvesin de la Riva', *StCrit*, 15:53–74, after identifying allegory as the prime instrument for the expression of relations between *mythos* and *logos*, shows how in Giacomino da Verona's *De Jerusalem celesti et de pulcritudine eius et beatitudine et gaudia sanctorum* and *De Babilonia civitate infernali et eius turpitudine et quantis penis peccatores puniantur incessanter*, and in Bonvesin's eschatological *Libro delle tre Scritture*, the use made of allegory is profoundly different, although directed towards the same didactic ends. G. Domokos, 'Appunti su morfologia e sintassi del milanese di Bonvesin de la Riva', *Aevum*, 72, 1998:619–32, is a purely linguistic discussion of a number of little-studied morphological and syntactic aspects of Bonvesin's language: the first part deals with the conditional, the future, the passive, and the particle 'sì', the second with word order, the position of the clitics with the imperative and constructions with the infinitive, gerund and participle. Id., 'Pronomi personali ed elementi clitici nel volgare milanese antico', *Verbum*, 1:171–81, again starting from his analysis of the *corpus* of Bonvesin's vernacular writings, purports to offer the fullest possible account of the use of the personal pronouns and the various clitic elements in early Milanese.

Another example of Duecento prose is afforded by Marco Polo's *Milione*, and there have been many editions in recent years. Marco Polo, *La description du monde*, ed. Pierre-Yves Badel, Paris, Le Livre de Poche, 1998, 509 pp., is based on a mid 15th-c. MS of the French version *FG*, BNF Fr. 5649, and accompanied by a modern French translation, an apparatus of variants, and notes. In contrast, Marco Polo, *Milione. Redazione latina del manoscritto Z̧*, ed. Alvaro Barbieri, Parma, Fond. Pietro Bembo–Ugo Guanda, 1998, lix + 706 pp., is an edition of draft Z preserved in Latin translation in MS Zelada 49.20 at the Toledo Chapter Archive. In Marco Polo, *Il 'Milione' veneto. Ms.*

CM 211 della Biblioteca Civica di Padova, ed. Alvaro Barbieri and Alvise Andreose, Venice, Marsilio, 1999, 310 pp., an excellent piece of editing, an introduction setting the *Milione* in its literary context, and an analysis of the MS tradition are the work of Barbieri, while Andreose studies the handwriting and language of the MS. Lastly, P. Ménard, 'Le prétendu "remaniement" du *Devisement du monde* de Marco Polo attribué à Grégoire', *MedRom*, 22, 1998 : 332–51, focuses on tricky questions concerning the history and circulation of the work, as well as the attribution (going back to Luigi Foscolo Benedetto's edition of 1928, but here called into question) of the French version of the work to a certain scribe, Grégoire.

The presence of Latin in Duecento life and literature is demonstrated by the texts gathered in Ferruccio Bertini, *Commedie latine del XII e XIII secolo*, Genoa, Genoa University, 1998, 528 pp. As well as Guillaume de Blois, *Alda*, ed. F. Bertini (11–109), Arnolphe d'Orléans (attr.), *Lidia*, ed. I. Gualandri and G. Orlandi (111–318), and *Raptularius II* and *De more medicorum*, ed. P. Gatti (319–78 and 379–427), the volume includes Iacopo da Benevento, *De uxore cerdonis*, ed. F. Bertini (429–503). On this text, A. Bisanti, 'A proposito del *De uxore cerdonis* di Iacopo da Benevento', *FilM*, 6–7 : 295–309, adds to Bertini's edition some observations on the possible sources of the work and on its probable links with other classical and medieval works. Albertini Muxati, *De obsidione domini Canis Grandis de Verona ante civitatem Padovanam*, ed. Giovanna Gianola, Ro–Padua, Antenore, 1999, cxci + 127 pp., taking us into the thick of city-state life and of Paduan prehumanism, is accompanied by a rigorously documented introduction, a description and classification of the MSS, a survey of printed editions, and an analysis of the language and prosody of the opera. Albertano da Brescia, *Liber de doctrina de dicendi et tacendi. La parola del cittadino nell'Italia del Duecento*, ed. Paola Navone, F, SISMEL–Galluzzo, 1998, cxxix + 62 pp., a new edition of another work reflecting the culture and environment of the city republic, is preceded by a detailed introduction providing useful information on the author and his style, the internal organization of the work, and its content.

We note various items exploring the society of the communes and its intense cultural life: Massimo Giansante, *Retorica e politica nel Duecento. I notai bolognesi e l'ideologia comunale*, Ro, ISIM, 1998, 162 pp.; G. Tanturli, 'Continuità dell'Umanesimo civile da Brunetto Latini a Leonardo Bruni', Leonardi, *Umanesimi*, 735–80; G. Zanella, 'Riccobaldo e Seneca', *ib.*, 827–40; L. Ramello, 'Preliminari all'edizione degli antichi volgarizzamenti italiani del *De Senectute*', *Melli Vol.*, 687–713; Pietro Morpurgo, *L'armonia della natura e l'ordine dei governi (secoli XII-XIV)*, F, SISMEL–Galluzzo, 346 pp., explores the close link between *scientia naturalis* and the organization of society in the Middle Ages.

Some works and authors elude the foregoing classification and are mentioned individually here: Garzo, *Opere firmate*, ed. Franco Mancini, Ro, Archivio Guido Izzi, 1999, 261 pp., includes his complete output: the *Proverbi*, the *Storia di S. Caterina*, the *lauda-ballata* on St Clare and eight other *laude* mostly taken from the *laudario cortonese*, are accompanied by painstaking 'exegetic notes', a rhyming dictionary, an essay on 'Strutture rimiche e clausole di *cursus*' (179–92). *Intelligenza. Un poemetto anonimo del secolo XIII*, Parma, Fond. Pietro Bembo–Ugo Guanda, lxv + 687 pp., has an interesting introduction by M. Berisso, who suggests that the work was not in its definitive state when originally circulated. P. Allegretti, 'Modelli provenzali nell'Anonimo Genovese', *MedRom*, 22, 1998:3–15, draws attention to a new Occitan source for the Anonimo Genovese, showing contact-points between text 137, rubricated 'De multis perfectionibus qui posset habere', and the poem 'Ar'agues yeu mil marcx de fin argen' (BdT 372,3) by the troubadour Pistoleta. S. Bertelli, 'Un manoscritto di geomanzia in volgare della fine del secolo XIII', *SFI*, 57, 1999:5–32, announces the discovery of a late 13th-c. MS at the BNCF (Fondo Magliabechiano XX.60) containing a short treatise on geomancy. On the types and diffusion of *litterae textuales*: Fr Supino Martini, 'Orientamenti per la datazione e la localizzazione delle cosiddette *litterae textuales* italiane ed iberiche nei secoli XII-XIII', *Scriptorium*, 54:20–34. C. Giunta, 'Letteratura ed eresia nel Duecento italiano: il caso di Matteo Paterino', *NRLI*, 3:9–98, transcribes and examines the canzone 'Fonte di sapïenza nominato' which refers to problems connected with cathar doctrine: probably addressed to Guittone d'Arezzo, it is attributed to a certain Matteo Paterino in the sole MS in which it has come down to us (Biblioteca Capitolare, Verona, MS 445). P. Chiesa, 'Per un riordino della tradizione manoscritta della *Relatio* di Odorico da Pordenone', *FilM*, 6–7, 1999–2000:295–309, takes up the complex MS tradition of the *Relatio*, the Latin text of which, even today, has never received a real critical edition, and presents a classification of the witnesses 'su base redazionale' (312). On Odorico: we note A. Andreose, *' "Lo libro dele nove e stranie meravioxe cose". Ricerche sui volgarizzamenti italiani dell'Itinerarium del beato Odorico da Pordenone', *Il Santo*, 38, 1998:31–67.

Geographically localized are L. Tomasin, 'Un testo del Duecento relativo a Chioggia', *SMV*, 44, 1998:221–30; P. Fasoli, 'Nota su antichi testi aquilani', *QI*, 19, 1999:93–100; and R. Gualdo, 'Poesie volgari in un codice di testi giuridici (secc. XIII-XIV)', *SLI*, 24,

1998:210–12, which gives a close description of MS Vat. Lat. 1413, containing the Gloss of Accursio and dating from the late 13th or early 14th c., and brings to light four vernacular poems (three sonnets and a *ballata*) copied on f. 11 of the MS.

Half way between linguistic studies and literary-philological analyses: P. G. Beltrami, 'Il *Tesoro della lingua italiana delle Origini* (TLIO) e l'onomastica', *RIOn*, 5, 1999:349–62, while well aware of the lack of a separate word-list for anthroponyms, shows how the *TLIO* database, with its 1,400 literary and documentary texts earlier than 1375, can already do much to facilitate research into onomastics; Id., 'Prima del vocabolario: finalità lessicali di un archivio medievale (tesoro della lingua italiana delle Origini)', Leonardi, *Testi*, 79–95, points to the methodological and practical problems that hamper optimization of *TLIO* (above all, the inconsistent spelling of the texts entered and the problem of selective lemmatization), but he also underlines its considerable merits (it is now possible, for instance, to specify the first attestation of many words with greater reliability); Id., 'La voce "nobiltà" del *Tesoro della Lingua Italiana delle Origini*', pp. 155–80 of *Studi per Umberto Carpi. Un saluto da allievi e colleghi pisani*, ed. di Marco Santagata and Alfredo Stussi, Pisa, ETS, xxv + 710 pp., analyses the term 'nobiltà' in early Italian from the point of view of its meaning and fields of use, and with reference to similar words. An analogous approach is taken in Lino Leonardi, 'Tradizione poetica e dinamica testuale nella lirica italiana del Duecento: funzioni di un ipertesto', Leonardi, *Testi*, 33–54, which illustrates the potential of computer technology when applied to philology, including lexicographical purposes.

LS, 35.4, a special number of the journal devoted to *Linguistica e italiano antico*, ed. Lorenzo Renzi and Antonietta Bisetto, discusses the contribution of the various methodologies to the study of early Italian and gives a good idea of the present state of research, supported by the latest technological aids. G. Salvi, 'Quanto era diverso l'italiano antico?', *Nuova Corvina*, 7:14–21, using a number of examples of word order underlines the considerable, but not immediately perceptible, differences between early and modern Italian. V. Egerland, 'Sulla sintassi delle costruzioni assolute participiali e gerundive nell'italiano antico ed il concetto di "anacoluto"', *RevR*, 34, 1999:181–204, examines editions of 13th and 14–c. Tuscan texts and shows that the term 'anacoluthon' is often inadequate to describe grammatical phenomena so defined by the editors.

On 14th-c. texts and authors: Marina Montesano, '*Fantasima, fantasima che di notte vai*'. *La cultura magica nelle novelle toscane del Trecento*, Ro, Città Nuova, 256 pp., discusses the protagonists of the novelle, the instruments and circumstances of the magic rituals described in them, the superstitions linked to the cult of the saints, and the dreams and apparitions. An appendix contains an extract from Boccaccio's *Filocolo*, novella X,5 of the *Decameron*, and notes on the terminology of the story-tellers' magic. Also on the novella see Anita Simon, *Le novelle e la storia. Toscana e Oriente fra Tre e Quattrocento*, Ro, Salerno, 1999, 159 pp. Sandro Bertelli, 'Il copista del Novellino', *SFI*, 56, 1998:31–45, analyses the five MSS written by the scribe of the *Novellino* and, attempting to reconstruct his identity, puts forward the hypothesis that he was an enthusiast from the Pisa–Lucca area active between the third and sixth decade of the Trecento. R. Baldini, 'Zucchero Bencivenni, "La santà del corpo". Volgarizzamento del *Régime du corps* di Aldobrandino da Siena (1310) nella copia coeva di Neri Corsini (Laur. Pl. LXXIII 47)', *SLinI*, 15, 1998:21–300, publishes an interpretative diplomatic edition of the vernacular version which, being precisely dated, provides important data on the language spoken in Florence in 1310. L. Armstrong, 'The politics of usury in Trecento Florence: the *Questio de monte* of Francesco da Empoli', *MedS*, 61, 1999:1–44, publishes and analyses the Latin text of the *Questio* (1353), the first example of a treatise on the moral and legal problems of the public debt. L. Tanzini, 'Le due redazioni del *Liber de origine civitatis Florentie et eiusdem famosis civibus*. Osservazioni sulla recente edizione', *ASI*, 158:141–59, looks at the crucial aspects and problematic points of Filippo Villani's *Liber*, which represents an important transitional stage between municipal historiography and the new humanistic historiography. L. Azzetta, 'Per la biografia di Andrea Lancia: documenti e autografi (tav.I-IV)', *IMU*, 39, 1996[1999]:121–71, assembles, and sets in order, the documents and autographs that concern the figure of Lancia, a Florentine notary active in the Trecento. On Andrea da Barberino see G. Allaire, 'Un frammento di un romanzo sconosciuto di Andrea da Barberino', *CN*, 58, 1998:101–20, which gives an interpretative-diplomatic transcription of a fragment of an unknown version of the *Storia di Messer Prodesaggio*, analyses its lexis, language, and content, and suggests that it is a late work by Andrea da Barberino; Id., 'Due inediti di Andrea da Barberino nella Biblioteca Palatina di Parma', *Pluteus*, 8–9, 1990–98:19–25, which announces the find of two versions of Andrea da Barberino's *Storie Nerbonesi*, followed by his *Ugone di Alvernia*, in MS Palatino 32 at the Biblioteca Palatina, Parma.

On 14th-c. northern texts and authors: P. Rinoldi, 'Nota al v. 198 della *Morte di Carlomagno*', *MR*, 14:111–18, proposes a new emendation to the 'nonsense' of l. 198 of the Franco-Italian poem, preserved in a MS at the Bodleian Library; M. A. Marogna, 'Un'eco dantesca tra Cremona e Parma negli anni Quaranta del Trecento. La *Rima lombarda*', *Aevum*, 74:539–54, analyses the *Rima lombarda*, a *poemetto* in *terza rima* written between 1343 and 1346, discussing its attribution, language, and points of contact with Dante's *Commedia*. S. Orlando, 'Una pagina preziosa di fine Trecento', *SFI*, 56, 1998:47–55, edits with a linguistic commentary, from a MS (1360) in the Bologna State Archive, a transcription of sonnet 31 of the *Canzoniere*, a passage of Dante, and an as yet unidentified text written in the dialect of Bergamo with traces of Emilian. For particular parts of the north-western area: P. Tomea, 'Per Galvano Fiamma', *IMU*, 39, 1996 [1999]:77–120, provides an updated collection of data on the figure and activity of the Milanese Dominican; and G. Petti Balbi, 'Cultura e potere a Genova: la biblioteca di Raffaele Adorno (1396)', *Aevum*, 72, 1998:427–37, investigates the figure of the Genoese prehumanist Raffaele Adorno, examining his book collection. For the Venice area: L. Bartolucci, 'Appunti sulle redazioni italiane della Lettera del Prete Gianni: la versione del MS Landau-Finaly 13 (Biblioteca Nazionale Centrale di Firenze)', *Melli Vol.*, 45–53, presents a new Italian version of the *Lettera* from the Venice area, further testimony to the success enjoyed by this text in the 14th and 15 c.; Jacopo Gradenigo, *Gli Quatro Evangelii concordati in uno*, ed. Francesca Gambino, Bo, CTLin, 1999, cxxxiv + 408 pp., edits the long poem (upwards of 10,000 lines of *terza rima*), written in 1399, which constitutes one of the most important chapters of the 'biblical current' and is striking evidence of Dante's success in the Veneto; F. Gambino, 'Curiosità lessicali di fine Trecento: i *Quattro Evangelii concordati in uno* di Jacopo Gradenigo', *SLeI*, 15, 1998:301–18, presents a number of lexical notes on the hybrid language of the poem, rich in Latinisms, dialectalisms, neologisms, and solecisms. For central Italy: F. Alfie, 'Immanuel of Rome, alias Manoello Giudeo: the poetics of Jewish identity in fourteenth century Italy', *Italica*, 75, 1998:307–29, presents the figure and writings of Immanuel ben Solomon of Rome, a medieval Jewish poet well-nigh unknown to Italianists, author of four sonnets and a *frottola* in the vernacular.

On the revival of Latin historiography in 14th-c. texts: G. Crevatin, 'Il riuso del *corpus* cesariano nell'Italia del Trecento', *CaH*, 1:119–50, looks at the ways in which Riccobaldo da Ferrara, Petrarch, and Benvenuto da Imola read, interpret, and 'rewrite' the texts of the Caesarian *corpus*. M. Petoletti, '"Nota pro consilio Polistorie mee orationem predictam": Giovanni Cavallini lettore di Livio', *IMU*, 39, 1996 [1999]:47–76, looks at the glosses to the first decad of Livy contained in MS Vat. Lat. 1846 and demonstrates their attribution to Giovanni Cavallini dei Cerroni, author of the *Polistoria de virtutibus et dotibus Romanorum*.

3. BOCCACCIO

The publication of Giovanni Boccaccio, *Tutte le opere*, vols 7–8, Mi, Mondadori, 1998, 2149 pp., completes a project conceived and directed by Vittore Branca and begun in 1964. The whole of B.'s *oeuvre* is now available in reliable *edizioni ragionate*, with an excellent apparatus of introductions, notes, and indexes. The two volumes contain respectively the *Genealogie deorum gentilium*, ed. Vittorio Zaccaria, and the *De montibus, silvis, fontibus [. . .]*, ed. Manlio Pastore Stocchi. Two new monographs devoted to B. have appeared: Lucia Battaglia Ricci, *Boccaccio*, Ro, Salerno, 290 pp., offering an up-to-date outline of recent work which has partially modified B.'s image by pointing to his activity as a textual scholar, cultural intermediary, and thinker; and Francesco Tateo, *Boccaccio*, Ro-Bari, Laterza, 1998, 300 pp., an ample monograph consisting of ten essay-like chapters, in which a good deal of space is given over to analysis of B.'s works.

On B. and the classics: *Gli zibaldoni di Boccaccio: memoria, scrittura, riscrittura. Atti del Seminario internazionale di Firenze–Certaldo, 26–28 aprile 1996*, ed. Michelangelo Picone and Claude Cazalé Bérard, F, Cesati, 1998, 484 pp., comprises 27 contributions on B.'s 'Zibaldoni' (the autograph MSS B.R.50, Laur. 29,8, and Laur. 33,31) grouped in three sections: 'Il sistema del sapere e la biblioteca del B.'; 'Il sistema della scrittura'; 'Il sistema intertestuale e la strategia della scrittura'. E. Filosa and L. Flora, 'Ancora su Seneca (e Giovenale) nel *Decameron*', *GSLI*, 175, 1998:210–19, explores the presence of Seneca's *Epistles to Lucilius* and Juvenal's *Satires* in the *Decameron*, and demonstrates that in his use of sources B. often profoundly modifies remembered data via his imagination, bringing Juvenal's abstract types and Seneca's maxims to life. M. Fiorilla, 'La lettura apuleiana del Boccaccio e le note ai manoscritti laurenziani 29,2 e 54,32', *Aevum*, 73, 1999:635–68, investigates the question as to which MSS B. used in his study of Apuleius, discussing the problem of the authorship of the annotations in MS Laur. 29,2 and publishing all the marginal notes by B. contained in MS Laur. 54,32. Still on B.'s cultural make-up see Antonio Gagliardo, **Giovanni Boccaccio: poeta, filosofo, averroista*, Soveria Mannelli, Rubbettino, 1999, 302 pp.

On the *Decameron*: V. Branca, 'Ancora su una redazione del *Decameron* anteriore a quella autografa e su possibili interventi "singolari" sul testo', *StB*, 26, 1998: 3–97, presents a new list of variants present in the MS tradition of the *Decameron* which confirm that there were two different drafts of the work. On the basis of the variations introduced by rewriting copyists and of a number of *lectiones variae* due to B.'s own extempore interventions, he goes on to propose the hypothesis that other drafts of the *Decameron* must have existed. T. Nocita, 'Per una nuova paragrafatura del testo del *Decameron*. Appunti sulle maiuscole del cod. Hamilton 90 (Berlin, Staatsbibliothek Preußischer Kulturbesitz)', *CrT*, 2, 1999:925–34, considers the narrative's internal divisions as they appear in the autograph of the *Decameron* and argues that it would be appropriate to restore them in a modern edition. F.J. Santa Eugenia, 'L'epicureismo di Pampinea', *BHR*, 62:641–46, explains why B. condemns the hedonistic response of certain Florentines to the tragedy of the plague while justifying the entirely analogous response of the 'lieta brigata': Pampinea's hedonism is said to be legitimized by the dual Epicurean imperatives of avoidance of pain and pursuit of pleasure. P. Marconi, 'Forme dialogiche e metamorfosi dell'identità nel *Decameron*', *FC*, 24, 1999:33–56, examines the dialogue mechanisms used in constructing the identity of the characters, the function of dialogue passages within the novelle, and the mirror-relationship between the implicit author and the narrators. T. Foster Gittes, 'Boccaccio's "Valley of Women": fetishized foreplay in *Decameron* VI', *Italica*, 76, 1999:147–74, examines the sexual implications of the *Valle delle Donne* in the Sixth Day, which is said to represent a kind of self-regulating natural ecosystem, where love is exorcised and exercised at one and the same time. Roberta Bruno Pagnamenta, *Il Decameron. L'ambiguità come strategia narrativa*, Ravenna, Longo, 1999, 162 pp., suggests interpreting the *Decameron* in terms of the ambiguous perspective of literature as play and literature as moral instruction. Marco Veglia, ' *"La vita lieta"*. *Una lettura del Decameron*, Ravenna, Longo, 296 pp., proposes a rereading of the *Decameron* on the basis of its author's cultural-history context: the Epicurean tradition, a reconciliation, via Seneca, between moral philosophy and 'spiritual' Franciscanism, the value of courtesy and laughter, and the problem of evil. R. Ferreri, 'Il motivo erotico-osceno nella cornice del *Decameron*', *StB*, 26, 1998:165–78, analyses the story-tellers' comments on the obscene tales, a device whereby the obscene crosses over from the stories to the frame: this lessens the contrast between the aristocratic life of the young story-tellers and the folk setting of the novelle. We also note: J. Levarie Smarr, 'Other races and other places in the *Decameron*', *ib.*, 27, 1999[2000]:113–36; F. Bausi, 'Gli spiriti magni. Filigrane aristoteliche e tomistiche nella decima giornata del *Decameron*', *ib.*, 205–54.

Numerous contributions analyse individual novelle. R. Morosini, '*Bone eloquence* e mondo alla rovescia nel discorso *semblable a la reisun* nella novella di Madonna Filippa (*Decameron* VI.7)', *Italica*, 77:1–13, in a new reading of the novella, highlights its points of contact with the tale of the peasant and the horse in the *Lais* of Marie de France, analyses its rhetorical and narrative procedures, and brings out its role within the Sixth Day, which is devoted to the power of *la bone* *eloquence*. R. Amendolara, 'I luoghi della novella di Andreuccio da Perugia', *CLett*, 26, 1998:23–40, interprets the localities visited by Andreuccio during his Neapolitan adventure as a kind of filigree within which the psychological development of the protagonist, and the evolution from evil to good and from disorder to order, are inscribed. S. Zatti, 'Il dono perverso di Natan (*Decameron* X, 3)', *Intersezioni*, 19, 1999:25–38, puts forward an anthropological analysis of the novella of Nathan and Mithridanes, interpreting it as an ironic version of the paradoxical effects produced when classical liberality, courtly *largesse*, and the Christian vocation to martyrdom are combined. P. Castignoli, 'Boccaccio e Piacenza. La triste fine di un mercante piacentino nella novella nona della seconda giornata del *Decameron*', *BSPia*, 94, 1999:65–74, reads the novella in the context of the political and military struggle between Guelphs and Ghibellines. M. Migiel, 'Beyond seduction: a reading of the tale of Alibech and Rustico (*Decameron* III, 10)', *Italica*, 75, 1998:161–77, analyses the novella in terms of the relationship between language and action. B. Porcelli, 'Alatiel e i dieci padroni', *StB*, 26, 1998:179–86, identifies the pattern 7 + 2 + 1 as the logical criterion underlying the succession of Alatiel's ten masters and lovers, thus significantly reproducing the division of the ten story-tellers in the *Decameron* and, within each Day, the sequence of the ten novelle. G. Allaire, 'The written eloquence of Frate Cipolla (*Decameron*, VI, 10)', *Neophilologus*, 82, 1998:393–402, analyses the function of Frate Cipolla's reference, in his speech to the people of Certaldo, to his act as a copyist. Lastly, we note: R. Beyer, *'Nastagio, Federigo et les notaires', *ChrI*, 15.1:57–61; C. Delcorno, 'La "predica" di Tedaldo', *StB*, 27, 1999[2000]:55–80; C. Del Popolo, 'Un'espressione di Calandrino (*Decameron* IX 3.21, 24; 5.64)', *ib.*, 107–12; S. Marchesi, 'Lisabetta e Didone: una proposta per *Decameron* IV,5', *ib.*, 137–48.

On intertextual links and borrowings from Boccaccio: V. Branca, 'Consacrazioni e dissacrazioni dantesche nel *Decameron*', *Mazzoni Vol.*, 53–63, identifies three essential features in the novella of Lisetta and the friar-brigand Alberto da Imola (*Dec.* IV, 2): a caricaturally heightened Venetian 'expressivism'; a parody of Dante and Guinizzelli; a reversal of, which is also a homage to, the most admired texts of 14th-c. asceticism. J. Finlayson, 'The wife of Bath's *Prologue*, ll. 328–36, and Boccaccio's *Decameron*', *Neophilologus*, 83, 1999:313–16, through close textual analysis, identifies B.'s Madonna Filippa as Chaucer's source and thus convincingly brings fresh confirmation of C.'s familiarity with the *Decameron*. L. Terrusi, 'Ancora sul "cuore mangiato". Riflessioni su *Decameron* IV 9, con una postilla doniana', *PaT*, 2, 1998:49–62, looks at the history of the eaten heart *topos* and points out the novelties introduced by B. in *Decameron* IV 9, before going on to analyse Anton Francesco Doni's parodistic rewriting of the Boccaccio novella in the *Trattato secondo* of the *Libraria*. M. Innocenti, 'Due rifacimenti in ottava rima della novella boccaccesca di Tancredi e Ghismonda (*Dec.* IV, 1)', pp. 51–59 of *Echi di memoria: scritti di varia filologia, critica e linguistica in ricordo di Giorgio Chiarini*, ed. Chiappini, F, Alinea, 1998, 557 pp., is a comparison between Ghismonda's monologue and two 15th-c. *ottava rima* adaptations, the first by Girolamo Benivieni, the second preserved in Florence at the Laurenziana (Cod. Ashburnhamiano 1136). S. Barsella, 'Boccaccio e Cino da Pistoia: critica alla poetica dell'amore nella parodia di *Filostrato* V e *Decameron* III 5, X 7', *Italianistica*, 29:55–73, examines the parodistic textual echoes of Cino da Pistoia in the *Filostrato* and *Decameron*. D. Pirovano, 'Due novelle del Boccaccio (*Dec.* VI 9 e VII 7) tradotte in latino da Francesco Pandolfini', *GSLI*, 175, 1998:556–76, publishes Latin translations of the novelle of Guido Cavalcanti and of Beatrice bolognese which are the work of the Florentine Francesco Pandolfini and can be dated to the last years of the 15th c. D. Pirovano, 'Olimpia Morata e la traduzione latina delle prime due novelle del *Decameron*', *Acme*, 51, 1998:73–109, publishes and analyses a mid-16th-c. Latin translation of the first two novelle of the *Decameron* by Olimpia Fulvia Morata of Ferrara, a daughter of the humanist Fulvio Pellegrino Morato.

StB, 28, comprises: V. Branca, 'Due manoscritti della *Vita di Dante* e del *Corbaccio*' (3–4); M. Cursi, 'Un nuovo autografo del *Decameron*?' (5–34), on the Italian MS 482 in Paris; V. Branca, 'Prime proposte sulla diffusione del testo del *Decameron* redatto nel 1349–51' (35–72), discussing the same MS; P. Squillacioti, 'Tristano risarcito e Folchetto vendicato: tracce di tradizione cortese in *Decameron* II 3 e IV 3' (73–86); M. Canova, 'Bergamino, gli specchi e il "bersaglio mobile"' (87–97), a reading of *Decameron* I, 7; C. Frugoni, 'La coppia infernale di Andrea Orcagna in Santa Croce a Firenze. Proposta per una possibile fonte della novella di Nastagio degli Onesti' (99–104); L. Battaglia Ricci, '"Una novella per esempio". Novellistica, omiletica e trattatistica nel primo Trecento' (105–24); J. Usher, 'Global warming in the sonnet: the Phaethon myth in Boccaccio and Petrarch' (125–83); S. Carrai, 'Esercizi petrarcheschi (con implicazioni cronologiche) del Boccaccio lirico' (185–97); N. Tonelli, 'Petrarca (R.v.f. 2–3), Boccaccio e l'innamoramento nel tempio' (199–219); G. Auzzas, 'Prime osservazioni sul testo dell'epistola al Nelli' (221–58); M. Dallapiazza, 'Boccaccio nella Germania d'oggi. Rassegna di studi' (259–67).

ItQ, 37, is also largely devoted to B.: M. Riva, '*Hereos/eleos*. L'ambivalente terapia del mal d'amore nel libro *chiamato Decameron cognominato prencipe Galeotto*' (69–106), an investigation into the *topos* of love-sickness in the *Decameron* with reference both to the Ovidian model and to medieval culture; M. Papio, ' "Non meno di compassion piena che dilettevole": notes on compassion in Boccaccio' (107–25), an exploration of the theme of suffering and compassion B. was so fond of: clearly fascinated by the thought that compassion, as a natural reaction to suffering, can be stimulated by literature; R. West, 'Decameron II, 2: a dream trip' (127–42), analyses the novella of Rinaldo d'Asti, bringing out the elements of B.'s art as a 'storybuilder'.

On B.'s minor works: Monica Bardi, *Le voci dell'assenza. Una lettura dell'Elegia di madonna Fiammetta*, T, Tirrenia Stampatori, 1998, 117 pp., analyses the text, bringing out its character as a narrative exposition of the canonical *loci* of love literature; G. Padoan, ' "Habent sua fata libelli", II: Dal Gaetano al Boccaccio: il caso del *Filocopo*', *StB*, 27, 1999[2000]: 19–54; R. Morosini, 'La "morte verbale" nel *Filocolo*: il viaggio di Florio dall'"immaginare" al "vero conoscimento" ', *ib.*, 183–204; Marco Veglia, *Il corvo e la sirena. Cultura e poesia del 'Corbaccio'*, Pisa–Ro, IEPI, 1998, 95 pp., explores the structure of the *Corbaccio* and its function as a palinode of courtly love; Eugenio L. Giusti, *Dall'amore cortese alla comprensione. Il viaggio ideologico di Giovanni Boccaccio dalla 'Caccia di Diana' al 'Decameron'*, Mi, LED, 1999, 190 pp., analyses the phases in B.'s ideological evolution through his vernacular writings, from the model of courtly love to its calling into question; Francesca Favaro, *Nel segno di Ovidio. G. Boccaccio, Luca Pulci e Lorenzo il magnifico autori di metamorfosi*, Bari, Ladisa, 1999, 119 pp., in the first chapter examines the *Ninfale fiesolano* and the references to myths of metamorphosis in other works, showing that B. draws his inspiration from Ovid, sometimes adapting himself to the model, at other times diverging from it; P. Rafti, ' "Lumina dictionum". Interpunzione e prosa in Giovanni Boccaccio. III', *StB*, 27, 1999[2000]:81–106, advances editorial proposals for the *Trattatello in laude di Dante*; G. Padoan, 'Alcune riflessioni sul testo critico della *Consolatoria a Pino de' Rossi*', *ib.*, 26, 1998:265–74, analyses the two textual *cruces* corresponding to paragraphs 35 and 169 of the Mondadori edition and maintains that they are due to B.'s own intervention.

On specific philological, stylistic, or thematic questions we note: V. Branca, 'Codici boccacciani segnalati nuovamente', *ib.*, 127–29, which concerns the MSS containing *Ameto*, *Fiammetta*, *Filocolo*, *Vita di Dante*, *Lettera a Pino de' Rossi*, *De casibus*, *De mulieribus*, *Genealogie*; F. Franceschini, 'Notizia di un frammento padano del *Filocolo*', *ib.*, 27, 1999[2000]:1–18; V. Zaccaria, 'La difesa della poesia: dal Petrarca alle *Genealogie* del Boccaccio', *AMAP*, 111, 1998–99:211–29, which examines the Petrarchan ancestry of Books 14 and 15 of the *Genealogie*; and V. Pacca, 'Il numero di Fiammetta', *Italianistica*, 29:45–52, which shows that B., on the model of Dante and Petrarch, associates his lady with a numeral, the number 5, the choice of which is said to have been suggested by the letters of the word Maria, Fiammetta's real name. G. Meloni, 'Il mercante Giovanni Boccaccio a Montpellier e Avignone', *StB*, 26, 1998:99–126, shows that the *Johannem Boccacci, Mercatorem Montispessulani* referred to in the Royal Charter of the Catalan *Cancilleria*, dated 1355 and preserved in the Archivio de la Corona de Aragòn, may be identified as the author of the *Decameron*. S. Volpato, 'Note sul vocabolario dei mercanti-scrittori dal Boccaccio all'Alberti e al Rucellai: nuove letture interpretative', *ib.*, 131–63, analyses the semantic development of the terms *fortuna*, *ragione*, and *prudenza* respectively in the *Decameron*, in the diaries of Paolo da Certaldo (second half of the 14th c.), Giovanni Morelli (1393–1421), and Bonaccorsi Pitti (1412–1429), in the *Libri della famiglia* by Leon Battista Alberti, and in the *Zibaldone quaresimale* of Giovanni Rucellai (second half of the Quattrocento). V. Branca, 'Domenico Caronelli mercatante coneglianese, boccaccista appassionato fra lenguazo veneto e ipercorrettismo toscano', pp. 35–48 of Id., *La sapienza civile. Studi sull'Umanesimo a Venezia*, F, Olschki, 1998, xix + 316 pp., is an essay on Domenico Caronelli from Conegliano, who produced an autograph copy of the *Decameron* dated 1395. Id. 'Il Boccaccio di Ungaretti', *StB*, 27, 1999[2000]:255–81, analyses and publishes the reading- and teaching-notes written by Ungaretti for a course of lectures at the Università of São Paulo, Brazil.

A valuable reprint is Lionello Sozzi, *Boccaccio in Francia nel Cinquecento*, Geneva, Slatkine, 1999, 156 pp., which documents B.'s vast *fortuna* (not limited to the *Decameron*) in 16th-c. France, examining in particular the *Heptaméron* of Marguerite de Navarre (1558) and the *Apologie pour Hérodote* of Henri Estienne (1566). Finally, on B.'s presence in the history of art, *Boccaccio visualizzato. Narrare per parole e per immagini fra Medioevo e Rinascimento*: I, *Saggi generali con una prospettiva dal barocco a oggi*; II, *Opere d'arte d'origine italiana*; III, *Opere d'arte d'origine francese, fiamminga, inglese, spagnola, tedesca*, ed. Vittore Branca, 3 vols, T, Einaudi, 1999, xvi + 261, 383, 366 pp.

4. PETRARCH

Two monographs have come out: Vinicio Pacca, *Petrarca*, Ro–Bari, Laterza, 1998, 322 pp., is a chronologically ordered survey of P.'s life and output in six chapters; Marco Ariani, *Petrarca*, Ro, Salerno, 1999, 397 pp., analitically reconstructs P.'s human, civil, and literary career and takes stock of achievements in P. studies over the last 30 years.

A portrait of P. *par lui-même* is to be found in Luigi de Vendittis, *Petrarca, accorto demiurgo del proprio mito. Ricognizione fra le pagine autobiografiche*, Alessandria, Orso, 1999, 158 pp., which retraces the author's statements about himself and his passions, about time and memory, and about his love of solitude. E. M. Duso, 'Petrarca e i rimatori veneti del Trecento', *AMAP*, 111, 1998–99:181–210, explores relations between P. and contemporary lyric poets, in particular Giovanni Quirini and Giovanni Dondi.

Numerous essays on P. are brought together in the volumes: Pier Giorgio Ricci, *Miscellanea petrarchesca*, ed. Monica Berté, Ro, Storia e Letteratura, 1999, xiv + 246 pp., which gathers a series of valuable philological studies on P. published between 1942 and 1976, and testifies to the progress of the scholar's research in parallel to the development of P. studies; and Rosanna Bettarini, *Lacrime e inchiostro nel Canzoniere di Petrarca*, Bo, CLUEB, 1998, 194 pp., which arranges nine contributions in a unitary discourse ranging from questions of theme and style to the *Canzoniere*'s relationship with the classics and medieval culture, and to actual textual readings.

On MSS and incunables: Erwin Rauner, *Petrarca-Handschriften in Tschechien und in der Slowakischen Republik*, Padua, Antenore, 1999, xiv + 678 pp., is a weighty inventory of the P. MSS preserved in the libraries of the Czech and Slovak Republics. C. Dondi, 'Per un censimento di incunaboli e cinquecentine postillati dei *Rerum vulgarium fragmenta* e dei *Triumphi*, VIII. Oxford: Bodleian Library', *Aevum*, 74:675–708, is the inventory of 87 incunables and *cinquecentine* of the *Canzoniere* and the *Triumphi* preserved in the Bodleian Library.

On P.'s role as the founder of modern lyric poetry: Maria Teresa Sapegno, *Petrarca e lo stile della poesia*, Ro, Bagatto Libri, 1999, 103 pp., analyses P.'s observations on the theme of 'style' which, for the first time in the modern sense, he understands as a critical and historical category. Devoted specifically to the *Canzoniere* we note: E. Fenzi, 'Sull'edizione commentata del *Canzoniere* petrarchesco curata da Marco Santagata', *Italianistica*, 27, 1998:455–94, which reviews the Santagata edition with commentary, discussing his editorial criteria, questions of spelling, textual problems, and the reconstruction of the *Canzoniere*'s evolution; Guido Capovilla, **Sì vario stile: studi sul Canzoniere di Petrarca*, Modena, Mucchi, 1998, 233 pp.; Massimo Zenari, *Repertorio metrico dei Rerum vulgarium fragmenta di Francesco Petrarca*, Padua, Antenore, 1999, xlii + 566 pp., which is organized in the following sections: metrical repertory; repertories of syllabic quantities, syllabic formulae and strophic patterns; numerical tabulation of all the data; indexes of first lines, alphabetical lists of rhymes, rhyming dictionary. Carlo Pulsoni, *La tecnica compositiva nei Rerum vulgarium fragmenta. Riuso metrico e lettura autoriale*, Ro, Bagatto Libri, 1998, 319 pp., examines the metrical structures of the *Canzoniere*, their links with Provençal models, in particular Arnaut Daniel, and with the *Stilnovo*, stressing the importance of the tradition deriving from

MS Chigiano L.VIII.305. Natascia Tonelli, *Varietà sintattica e costanti retoriche nei sonetti dei Rerum vulgarium fragmenta*, F, Olschki, 1999, 228 pp., on linguistic foundations describes a number of features of P.'s style in 'sonnet-production': cohesion of the *fronte*, coordination and cohesion, types of subordination, syntax-'story' relationship, syntax of the sentence, and punctuation. In conclusion two appendixes: metrical divisions and syntax in standard sonnets; synoptic tables. Id., 'Il caso dell'*ut inversum* nei sonetti di Petrarca', *LN*, 59, 1998:11–16, analyses consecutive clauses in the *Canzoniere* sonnets and identifies the different forms of inversion and their stylistic function. Francesco Petrarca, *Il codice degli abbozzi. Edizione e storia del manoscritto Vaticano Latino 3196*, ed. Laura Paolino, Mi–Na, Ricciardi, xii + 316 pp., is a monograph on the 'codice degli abbozzi': the first, critical-historical, part recontructs the work's history from P.'s death to the present day, and is followed by an edition of the texts it contains. E. Tognozzi, 'La natura come corrispondente esterno ad una condizione psicologico-sentimentale del *Canzoniere*', *FoI*, 32, 1998:51–62, considers the theme of nature in eight texts from the *Canzoniere* and identifies its different functions, finding the most original characteristic of P.'s lyric poetry to lie in its recourse to nature as the antithesis of the social state.

We note various readings of individual texts. T. Zanato, 'Il sonetto CCCXLIV', *AMAP*, 110, 1997–98:425–46, finds the structure of the sonnet in question to lie in two series of antitheses between past and present, and analyses it in relation to Dante's 'comic' style. B. Bartolomeo, '*Solea da la fontana di mia vita* (*RVF* CCCXXXI) e dintorni', *ib.*, 447–68, is a monographic reading of this *canzone*, placed in relation to the trio of preceding sonnets and the '*canzoni* of the eyes', and an exploration of the theme of yearning for a blessed death in the presence of the beloved. M. L. Doglio, 'Il sonetto CLXVIII', *ib.*, 469–84, demonstrates the sonnet's function as a manifesto or *summa*, centring as it does on the basic themes of the *Canzoniere*. D. De Robertis, 'Il trittico del "T" (*RVF* 315, 316, 317)', *ib.*, 111, 1998–99:167–80, analyses the three sonnets, highlighting the central theme of time. F. J. Jones, 'The hidden calendrical implications behind poem 266 of Petrarch's *Canzoniere*', *ISt*, 54, 1999:34–51, from an analysis of the sonnet's temporal data goes on to posit the presence in the *Canzoniere* of a kind of hidden 'calendar', consisting of personal or historical commemorations. F. Danelon, 'Il sogno e il perdono. Una lettura di *Voi ch'ascoltate in rime sparse il suono* (*Rvf*, I)', *FC*, 24, 1999:101–23, is an in-depth analysis of the structure and themes of the opening sonnet of the *Canzoniere*. S. Giusti, 'La "selce" della "petra". Per una lettura dei sonetti dell'aura', *CLett*, 28:439–58, examines the *aura* sonnets, which constitute a veritable system within the macrosystem of the *Canzoniere*, and demonstrates their thematic and stylistic closeness to Dante's *rime petrose*. Lastly, C. Perrus, **'La sextine LXXX du Canzoniere'*, *ChrI*, 16:5–16.

Individual thematic or stylistic questions are addressed in: M. Vitale, 'Noterella petrarchesca', *Acme*, 51, 1998:245–47, which analyses the form *termino* in l. 13 of sonnet 45 of the *Canzoniere* and argues that it goes back to the copyist, not to P.; L. Marcozzi, '"Felice Automedon, Felice Tiphi": il senso di un'allusione ad Ovidio nel sonetto CCXXV dei *Rerum vulgarium fragmenta'*, *FC*, 24, 1999:124–38, which identifies the allegorical procession of the sonnet as a precedent of the *Trionfi* and interprets the text in the light of the reference to Typhis and Automedon and the passage of Ovid which is its source; Id., 'Numeri in Petrarca: il dodici', *Antico/Moderno*, 1999:105–19, reviewing the occurrences of the number twelve in P.'s works in search of its various symbolic, historical, and erudite meanings or reference.

For P.'s other works see: *I Triumphi di Francesco Petrarca. Gargnano del Garda (1–3 ottobre 1998)*, ed. Claudia Berra (Quaderni di Acme, 40), Bo, Cisalpino, 1999, 534 pp., 21 contributions by distinguished scholars who address the chief interpretative problems of the *Triumphi*: metre, the work's relation to medieval Latin poetry, its style and variants, its reception by humanists and in the Cinquecento; M. Gemin, 'Davide poeta soldato nel *Trionfo della fama'*, *EL*, 25.2:71–77, which examines the figure of David in the *Trionfo della Fama* and analyses P.'s textual choices in the successive drafts of the work; M. Moroni, 'La retorica della solitudine in *De vita solitaria* di Francesco Petrarca', *RStI*, 17.2:20–40, which analyses the work's ethical message. F. Petrarca, *Della mia ignoranza e di quella di molti altri*, ed. Enrico Fenzi, Mi, Mursia, 1999, 541 pp., is a careful piece of editing. P. Trovato, 'Sull'attribuzione di "Di ridere ò gran voglia" (Disperse CCVIII). Con una nuova edizione del testo', *AMAP*, 110, 1997–98:371–424, adduces linguistic and stylistic reasons in refuting the attribution of the *frottola* 'Di ridere ò gran voglia' to P. and points out its close connection with the late-14th-c. Florentine tradition of *frottolismo*. E. Fenzi, 'Per una dispersa attribuibile a Petrarca: la frottola "Di ridere ò gran voglia"', *FC*, 23, 1998:169–205, agrees with Trovato's hypothesis as to the constitution of the text, but reasserts the legitimacy of the *frottola*'s attribution to P. and corroborates it with further observations. M. Berisso, 'Che cos'è e come si dovrebbe pubblicare una frottola', *SFI*, 57, 1999:201–33, looks at the differing metrical aspect given to the *frottola* 'Di rider ò gran voglia' in the various editions and proposes a number of corrections, before going on to analyse the metrical patterns used in Sacchetti's *frottole*, where they become a genre based on rhyme, not metre.

D. Goldin Folena, '*Familiarium rerum liber*. Petrarca e la problematica epistolare', pp. 51–82 of *Alla lettera. Teoria e pratiche epistolari dai Greci al Novecento*, ed. Adriana Chemello, Mi, Guerini, 1998, 516 pp., explores the text-macrotext relationship in the *Familiares*, with reference also to the Ciceronian model, and identifies *familiaritas* as the fundamental quality of P.'s epistolary writing. U. Dotti, 'La figura di Dionigi da Borgo Sansepolcro in Petrarca', *Belfagor*, 45:564–71, looks at the letter *Familiari*, 4.2, addressed to Dionigi, suggesting that it was not actually sent and that the figure of the Augustinian canon is introduced in order to forestall possible censorship of his projected 'resurrection' of essentially secular (humanist) thought, by placing it under the protection of a highly respected religious. Francesco Petrarca, *Senile V 2*, ed. Monica Berté, F, Le Lettere, 1998, 101 pp., is a critical edition and translation of *Senile*, V.2, preceded by an introduction examining the problem of the letter's date, the content and compositional characteristics of the text, sources, and the MS and printed tradition. U. Dotti, 'Il vecchio Petrarca', *GSLI*, 176, 1999:161–73, forms an introduction to the eleventh book of the *Senili*, with a view to publishing a complete edition of P.'s second collection of letters. Dotti points out the book's notable complexity and draws a picture of P.'s last stay at Padua. L. Paolino, 'Visibile narrare: l'edizione in facsimile della *Griselda* di Petrarca', *MR*, 13, 1999:301–08, is a presentation of the elegant volumette published by Edizioni dell'Orso at Alessandria, which reproduces the tiny 14th-c. MS Riccardiano 991 containing P.'s Latin reworking (1373) of the last novella of the *Decameron*. L. C. Rossi, 'In margine alla *Griselda* latina di Petrarca', *Acme*, 53:139–60, traces the compositional history of the text, aimed at 'ennobling' Boccaccio's novella, and points out its contact points with Apuleius's *Psyche*. P. Melandri, 'Lo Scipio, Petrarca e i "nuovi Annales"', *SPCT*, 61:5–27, concerns P.'s use of fragments of Ennius in drafting the *Vita Scipionis* and the *Africa*. Lastly, L. D. Reynolds, 'Petrarch and Cicero's philosophical works', *CaH*, 1:37–52, looks at the annotations, assumed to be by P., contained in the margin of a MS of philosophical works by Cicero in the Madrid national library.

On P.'s *fortuna* and the various aspects of his works' reception: *Petrarca e i suoi lettori*, ed. Vittorio Caratozzolo and Georges Güntert, Ravenna, Longo, 216 pp., gathering nine studies different in their methodology but alike in their common concern with the role played by P.'s readers, from the poets and theorists of the 15th and 16th c. to present-day interpreters; F. Cossutta, 'Il Maestro Queriniano interprete del Petrarca', *CLett*, 26, 1998:419–48, analysing the characteristics of the 'commento per immagini' — minute illustrations of the poems of the *Canzoniere* — contained in an incunable at the Brescia

Library and examining the miniature–poem relationship; Jean-Luc Nardone, *Pétrarque et le pétrarquisme*, Paris, PUF, 1998, 128 pp., investigating how and why P.'s vernacular poetry entered the main European literatures and analysing the various 'Petrarchisms' from Italy to France, and from Portugal to Germany; Cesare Segre, *Le varianti e la storia. Il Canzoniere di Francesco Petrarca (Lezione Sapegno 1999)*, T, Biblioteca Bollati Boringhieri, 1999, 70 pp., reviewing the main chapters in the history of textual study of P., from Bembo to Bernardino Daniello, from Ludovico Beccadelli to Federico Ubaldini, and down to Contini; and lastly, Ljiljana Avirovic, *La traduzione poetica in Croazia: aspetti della traduzione del sonetto: Petrarca e il petrarchismo*, Padua, CLEUP, 1999, 57 pp. Taking P. as their starting point and then ranging through the history of culture: *Qui c'era Roma: da Petrarca a Bembo*, ed. Paolo Guerrini and Concetta Ranieri, Bo, Pàtron, 109 pp., an anthology of texts on the journey to Roma (P., Fazio degli Uberti, Giovanni Rucellai, Bernardo Bembo, and Marin Sanudo), with an introductory essay by C. Ranieri on the theme of travel in the Middle Ages and an analysis by P. Guerrini on the subject of literature, witnesses and *mirabilia*; J. Summit, 'Topography as historiography: Petrarch, Chaucer, and the making of Medieval Rome', *JMEMS*, 30:211–46, looking at the ways in which P. (*Letter to Giovanni Colonna*) and Chaucer (*The Second Nun's Tale*) interpreted the ruins of classical Rome, anticipating the positions of Humanism; V. De Angelis, 'Petrarca, i suoi libri e i commenti medievali ai classici', *Acme*, 51, 1998:49–82, underlining the importance of medieval studies for a correct understanding of Humanism and showing how some of what have hitherto been considered innovations on the part of P. or the humanists have antecedents in medieval Latin writing.

HUMANISM AND THE RENAISSANCE

By PAOLO L. ROSSI, *Senior Lecturer in Italian Studies, Lancaster University*

I. GENERAL

One must regret the decline of the monograph in favour of unfocused edited volumes, put together in many cases to fulfil publication targets regardless of any coherent vision or message. *Studi sul manierismo letterario per Riccardo Scrivano*, ed. Nicola Longo, Ro, Bulzoni, 267 pp., has 11 essays on, *inter alia*, mannerist tendencies in Castiglione (A. Quondam), Anton Francesco Grazzini (G. Ferroni), Anton Francesco Doni (M. Guglielminetti), Giambattista della Porta (P. D. Stewart), Dante and Tasso (D. Della Terza), Tasso (G. Baldassarri, N. Longo), and G. Bruno (L. Bolzoni). *Immaginare l'autore: il ritratto del letterato nella cultura umanistica. Convegno di studi, Firenze, 26–27 marzo 1998*, ed. Giovanna Lazzi and Paolo Viti, F, Polistampa, xxiv + 373 pp. Francesco Tateo, *Letteratura italiana: dalla curia di Federico II alla 'republica' delle lettere*, Bari, B. A. Graphis, 1999, 424 pp., avoids the pitfalls of the Whiggish approach by questioning the categories of *grandi* and *minori* and offers insights by placing cultural producton within a social, political, and religious context. *Le metamorfosi di Orfeo*, ed. Anna Maria Babbi, Verona, Fiorini, 1999, 343 pp., is a wide-ranging collection of 16 essays on the figure of Orpheus. S. Carrai revisits M. Martelli's analysis of the philosophical dimension of Poliziano's *Orfeo*, and suggests that the work has little to do with Ficino's Neoplatonism. *L'Orphée de Boëce au Moyen Âge*, ed. J. Keith Atkinson and Anna Maria Babbi, Verona, Fiorini, 258 pp., has 12 essays and the texts of four Latin commentaries. Laura Alcini, *Storia della traduzione letteraria in Italia, 1: Il tradurre dall'antichità greco-romana al Rinascimento con riferimenti al contesto europeo*, Perugia, Guerra, 1998, 118 pp., is a very useful pedagogical resource set out in four parts which include: 'Tradurre nell'umanesimo' and 'Tradurre nel Rinascimento'. Claudio Scarpati, *Castiglione e Leonardo: una mappa e tre studi*, Mi, Università Cattolica, 1999, 164 pp., has six short essays. The section on Castiglione covers biographical documents, the *Cortegiano*, and 'Scritture poetiche, volgari e latine'; the one on Leonardo deals with Codex A, the anatomical writings, and theories on water and fossils.

Il re Adone, ed. Paolo Cherchi, Palermo, Sellerio, 1999, 90 pp., uses texts by Patrizi, Pontano, B. Aquaviva, G. Maio, A. de Guevara, Guazzo, Garzoni, and Marino to study the relationship between beauty, royalty, and majesty and how these were woven into the 'idealizzazione del principe'. Duccio Balestracci, *The Renaissance in the*

Fields. Family Memoirs of a Fifteenth Century Tuscan Peasant, trans. Paolo Squatriti and Betsy Merideth, University Park, Pennsylvania State U.P., 1999, 146 pp., analyses the impulse to produce, and the contents of, two dictated diaries which evince the importance of a literary culture, and the power of the written word as a weapon.

The Cambridge History of Literary Criticism, III, *The Renaissance*, ed. Glyn P. Norton, CUP, 1999, xxiii + 758 pp., is an indispensable work for both scholars and students. There are eight sections with 61 essays on topics that include Horace in the 16th c., commentators into critics, humanist classification of poetry, Petrarchan poetics, humanist education, Italian epic theory, Renaissance theatre and the theatre of tragedy, dialogue and discussion, the genres of epigram and emblem, humour and satire, theory of prose fiction and poetics, Renaissance printing and the book-trade, the Ciceronian controversy, cosmography and poetics, natural philosophy and the new science, literary critical developments, culture, imperialism, and humanist criticism in the Italian city states. Wayne A. Rebhorn, *Renaissance Debates on Rhetoric*, Ithaca, Cornell U. P., 322 pp., uses texts by Petrarch, Salutati, George of Trebizond, Valla, Pico della Mirandola, Speroni, Patrizi to discuss: rhetoric as a vehicle for political discourse; the debates on the nature, goals, and value of rhetoric; rhetoric as a means of social mobility; the relationship between rhetoric and truth. *The Renaissance Text. Theory, Editing, Textuality*, ed. Andrew Murphy, MUP, 226 pp., has 12 essays. Alison Saunders, *The Seventeenth Century French Emblem: A Study in Diversity*, Geneva, Droz, xiii + 437 pp., has much of relevance to the Italian Renaissance. It points to the influence of Alciato and Ripa, as well as the collections put together by G. Simeoni and Giovio, and the way they were used and adapted. It stresses the multi-language nature of the emblem tradition, traces the tradition of emblems and devices, and assesses the writings of the theorists.

Women's studies continue to yield significant work. *Feminism and Renaissance Studies*, ed. Lorna Hutson, OUP, 1999, 480 pp., contains 17 essays which pose fundamental questions (Did women have a Renaissance? What was the purpose of education for women?) and have elements of both social history and deconstructive analysis. This collection succeeds in giving insight into the notion of women in medicine, the marketing of knowledge, witchcraft and fantasy, gender ideologies and the lyric, pamphlet literature, litigation, and music. Cassandra Fedele, *Letters and Orations*, ed. Diane Robin, Chicago U.P., xxvi + 181 pp., has a discussion of humanist and non-humanist themes in the letters, noted for their elegance and self-consciously gendered voice, which are presented under thematic headings. Armando Maggi, *Uttering the Word. The Mystical Performances of Maria*

Maddalena de' Pazzi, A Renaissance Visionary, New York State U.P., 1998, 201 pp., fits the *Colloqui* into their historical and spiritual context and brings out the uniqueness of her performances, which are seen to lie 'in her understanding that rather than "speaking love" she can only speak about love'. *Maria Maddalena de' Pazzi: Selected Revelations*, ed. Armando Maggi, NY, Paulist Press, 368 pp., investigates the nature of her oral mysticism and the significance of the terminology, especially the use of *verbo* when addressing the divinity. Francesca Brezzi, *Invito alla lettura di Maria Maddalena de' Pazzi*, Mi, San Paolo, 92 pp., is a good introduction to her life and the nature of her religious teaching. Jadranka Bentini et al., *Caterina Sforza. Una donna del Cinquecento*, Imola, Mandragora, 222 pp., has 20 essays that investigate: the texts of the chronicles of Forlì; the figure of Caterina in humanist culture and in Machiavelli; a link between Caterina and Leonardo; Caterina's recipes and book of *experimenti* which have an autobiographical dimension. Sister Bartolomea Riccoboni, *Life and Death in a Venetian Convent. The Chronicle and Necrology of Corpus Domini 1355–1436*, ed. and trans. Daniel Bornstein, Chicago U.P., xxvii + 115 pp., describes the lives and deaths of unexceptional women and their complex relationship with the outside world. M. Catto, 'Creazione e trasformazione di un modello tardo-rinascimentale: Irene da Spilimbergo tra fonti letterarie e documentarie', *The Italianist*, 19, 1999:50–76, investigates the importance of her grandfather and the origins and reasons for the literary myth of Irene, and its transformations in the 18th century.

Everson, *Italy in Crisis*, comprises eight essays including A. Brown on the coincidence of the French invasion with political and economic crisis in Florence, and R. Catani on the importance of astrology within the socio-political and religious life of late 15th-c. Florence. Other essays investigate the cultural response, with M. Davie on Pulci, Poliziano, and Boiardo, P. Brand on Boiardo's *Timone*, M. Dorigatti on the link (Ruggiero) between the 1516 *Orlando Furioso* and Boiardo, M. McLaughlin on Poliziano's position vis-à-vis the classical tradition and analogies to our relationship to Modernism and the Western literary canon, L. Panizza on Pico della Mirandola's 1485 parody of scholastic 'barbarians', D. V. Reidy on why Antonio Panizzi chose to study Boiardo.

Patricia Fumerton and Simon Hunt, *Renaissance Culture and the Everyday*, Philadelphia, Pennsylvania U. P., 1999, 366 pp., represents the techniques of new social historicism with anecdotalism linked to materiality and cultural anthropology. Rudolph M. Bell, *How to do it. Guides to Good Living for Renaissance Italians*, Chicago U.P., 1999, xiii + 375 pp., is at one and the same time an entertaining and scholarly study, with chapters on conception, pregnancy, childbirth, raising your child, adolescence, and marital relations. Data is gleaned from a wide range of advice manuals and popular books, and it gives an insight into both popular and learned culture, and the printing industry. *Art, Memory, and Family in Renaissance Florence*, ed. Giovanni Ciappelli and Patricia Lee Rubin, CUP, xix + 316 pp., is a coherent collection of 16 essays which brings different disciplines and methodologies to bear on one theme. Of particular interest are: P. Geary on approaches to memory and memory structures; G. Ciappelli on the popularity and function of family record books (*ricordanze*) in Florence; N. Rubinstein on the historiographical aspects of *ricordanze* in B. Pitti, D. Velluti, and F. Guicciardini; L. Martines on poetry as a condensed memory, a reflection of public conscience, as well as a fomenter of passions; P. L. Rubin on the importance of style as 'a model of presentation or representation [. . .] and how fixing appearances was a means of conditioning memories'; A. Wright and G. B. Johnson on the features of portraiture; A. Molho on the political dimension of family names.

This year sees a number of useful historical surveys and collections on methodology. John Hale, *Renaissance Europe 1480–1520*, Oxford, Blackwell, xiv + 280 pp., has an added preface by M. Mallett. *Early Modern Europe. An Oxford History*, ed. Euan Cameron, OUP, 1999, xxxi + 402, has nine essays including 'The power of the word: Renaissance and Reformation' (E. Cameron), which sees the early Renaissance as a heroic period of promise, potential, and propaganda. Henry Kamen, *Early Modern European Society*, London, Routledge, 281 pp., is a broad-based survey that successfully tackles the task of providing a general view while respecting regional differences. Id., *Who's Who in Europe 1450–1750*, London, Routledge, 321 pp., is an authoritative collection of biographies which will be welcome for its accuracy and breadth of coverage. *The Future of the Middle Ages and the Renaissance: Problems, Trends, and Opportunities for Research*, ed. Roger Dahood, Turnhout, Brepols, 1998, xvi + 194 pp., among its 12 essays includes a detailed study by P. M. Soergel on monstrous birth which investigates the belief systems that made such phenomena plausible and how they were manipulated. *Contextualizing the Renaissance: Returns to History*, ed. Albert H. Tricomi, Turnhout, Brepols, 1998, 238 pp., has ten essays organized in three sections: 'Literature and history as critical practices'; 'Rehistoricizing through the visual arts'; 'New historicism and representation'. The studies challenge traditional historiographical practice. *Reinventing the Middle Ages and the Renaissance. Constructions of the Medieval and Early Modern Periods*, ed. William F. Gentrup, Turnhout, Brepols, 1998, xx + 243 pp., comprising 14 essays historicist in approach, includes an important essay by K. J. E.

Graham which analyses how reformers constructed the notion of discipline.

There are a number of studies on travel. Antonio Pigafetta, *Relazione del primo viaggio attorno al mondo*, ed. Andrea Canova, Padua, Antenore, xiii + 403 pp., comprises a critical text and commentary. John Block Friedman and Kristen Mossler Figg, *Trade, Travel, and Exploration in the Middle Ages: an Encyclopedia*, NY, Garland, xxxix + 715 pp., contains much of interest for students of the Renaissance with entries on such figures as F. Rosselli, M. Sanudo, and P. dal Pozzo Toscanelli, and covers cartographers, geographical terms, concepts and methodologies, learning, marvels and wonders, mythical beings and places, natural history, places of study, and travel writers. *Christopher Columbus and his Family: The Genoese and Ligurian Documents* (Repertorium Columbianum, 4), ed. John Dotson and Aldo Agosto, Turnhout, Brepols, 1998, 484 pp., covers the period 1429–1531 and helps to flesh out the economic, social, and cultural context of his life. *Synoptic Edition of the Log of Columbus's First Voyage* (Repertorium Columbianum, 6), ed. Francesca Lardicci et al., Turnhout, Brepols, 1999, 684 pp., is Las Casas's copy of the original Columbus log, together with the Italian version of the *Historie* of Fernando Colon and Bartolomé de Las Casas's *Historia de Las Indias*. There is a full critical apparatus and a scholarly discussion of the textual tradition and the relationship between the texts. *Las Casas on Columbus: Background and the Second and Fourth Voyages* (Repertorium Columbianum, 7), ed. Nigel Griffin and Anthony Pagden, Turnhout, Brepols, 1999, 350 pp., gives extracts from Las Casas' texts to link Columbus's activities in chronological sequence and show how his voyages were presented as providential in justification of Castilian claims and in order to construct a narrative about the New World and an apologia for Columbus. *Testimonies from the Columbian Lawsuits* (Repertorium Columbianum, 8), ed. Mark D. Johnston, Anne Marie Wolf, and William D. Philips Jr, Turnhout, Brepols, 522 pp., gives the depositions of the participants in, and witnesses to, the voyages of exploration during the series of lawsuits between Columbus and the Spanish Crown. Francesco Ingoli, *Relazioni delle quattro parti del mondo*, ed. Fabio Tosi, Ro, Urbania U.P., 1999, xli + 350 pp., examines the stages of writing of a text based on letters from missionaries and reports from travellers to all parts of the known world. It highlights the author's preoccupation with sources, with Rome as the centre of an information network, and discusses the various themes and the language of the *Relazioni*. R. Norbedo, 'Per l'edizione dell'Itinerario in Spagna di Andrea Navagero', *LItal*, 52:58–73. T. Picquet, 'Voyages d'un florentin: Giovanni da Verrazzano (1485–1528)', *Rinascimento*, 39, 1999:431–65.

The links across cultural and political boundaries have been attracting considerable attention. *Cultural Links between Portugal and Italy in the Renaissance*, ed. K. J. P. Lowe, CUP, xviii + 329 pp. + 32 pls, is a contribution to the study of national and extra-national cultural formation. There are 14 essays arranged in three sections: 'Social and Institutional Relations', with D. S. Chambers on the Venetian perception of Portugal and Lunardo Masser's *relazione* on Portugal; 'Art and Literature', with studies on the influence of Italian architecture (J. B. Bury), the effect of humanism and the influence of Italian painting (D. Rodriguez), the Roman humanist A. Colocci, the *questione della lingua* and his collection of Galician lyrics (J. Lawrence); 'Patronage and Collecting', Portuguese patrons of the Florentine book trade (A. de la Mare), the complex relationship between Queen Leonor and the Benedictine convent of the Murate in Florence, where she received intellectual and spiritual benefits and the Convent material goods. *Islam and the Italian Renaissance*, ed. Charles Burnett and Anna Contadini, London, Warburg Institute, 1999, viii + 239 pp., has ten essays that make a significant contribution to our understanding of the cross-fertilization between two distinct cultures and the influence of Byzantium. Of particular note are essays by: C. Burnett, who assesses Renaissance Latin editions of Arabic texts, and A. M. Piemontese, who uses the Arabic inscriptions of the *Poliphilus* to examine the interest in semitic languages via collections of MSS, books, and the figures of B. Mignanelli, A. Averlino, and B. Scala. Jonathan Woolfson, *Padua and the Tudors. English students in Italy 1485–1603*, Cambridge, James Clarke, 1998, 322 pp., is a scholarly study that investigates the reasons why so many Englishmen went to study at Padua. The study, however, branches out into the complex field of cultural and intellectual interaction and transformation. If Padua encouraged the humanistic disciplines, particularly in respect of Aristotelianism, it was itself reinvigorated by students from the North. Lisa Jardine and Jerry Brotton, *Global Interests. Renaissance Art between East and West*, Ithaca, Cornell U.P., 223 pp., expands our understanding and establishes new approaches for assessing cultural heritage. There are studies of portrait medals, tapestries, sculpture, and equestrian paintings. It succeeds in breaking down the perceived barriers and points to the rich cross-fertilization of ideas, images, and symbols. Bert W. Meijer et al., *Italy and the Low Countries. Artistic relations: the fifteenth century*, F, Centro Di, 1999, 108 pp., adding to our understanding of the longstanding social and economic links, consists of six essays which include a well-documented assessment of the influence of early Netherlandish painting in Florentine art (M. Rohlmann), and studies of the activites and social advancement of Flemish weavers in Siena (H. Smit), and of the art market and cultural exchange (E. Parma). *L'Europa e Roma nelle terre padane e adriatiche: le vie del Giubileo*, ed. Walter Baricchi, Cinisello Balsamo, Silvana, 319 pp., has a chapter by W. Baricchi and P. Foschi examining the movements of writers, scholars, and artists between the Northern courts, the courts as cultural centres, and the significance of the studiolo. The importance of local traditions and the effects of styles imported into the north of Italy are explored in Marco Carminati et al., *Pittura in Lombardia: il Medioevo e il Rinascimento*, Mi, Electa, 1998, 246 pp.

The symbiotic relationship between learning, writing, and the visual arts is the focus of the following studies. Jodi Cranston, *The Poetics of Portraiture in the Italian Renaissance*, CUP, xiii + 258 pp., suggests with reference to texts by Alberti, Aretino, Ariosto, Castiglione, Dante, Danti, Ficino, Leonardo, Petrarch, and P. Pino that 'Renaissance culture perceived and received portraiture as a kind of dialogue, as parallel to language, as analogous to forms of written discourse, including epistolary rhetoric, narration, and description'. Mary Bergstein, *The Sculpture of Nanni di Banco*, Princeton U.P., 230 p., is an excellent study set within the framework of the social history of art which takes Vasari's life of Nanni to task and gives a sensitive reading of Manetti's *Grasso* novella. It emphasizes the importance of the civic nature of his production and sees the new humanism in Nanni's vision of antiquity in representing corporate republican ideals. It examines his interaction with literary and cultural circles where Graeco-Roman civilization was widely discussed, and his synthetic, inclusive attitude to ancient models as opposed to a strictly archeological or historicist approach. Carmen C. Bambach, *Drawing and Painting in the Italian Renaissance Workshop. Theory and Practice, 1300–1600*, CUP, 1999, xxvii + 548 pp., breaks new ground as it makes use of the writings of Alberti, G. B. Armenini, D. Barbaro, Bisagno, Borghini, Cellini, Cennini, Leonardo, and Vasari to investigate the meaning and practice of drawing and its relationship to the finished work. A sensitive analysis of treatises, dictionaries, and letters indicates that drawing was regarded as art of the highest order. This study casts new light on both cultural paradigms and humanist rhetoric.

H.-T. Schulze Altcappenberg et al., *Sandro Botticelli. The Drawings for the Divine Comedy*, London, Royal Academy of Arts, 352 pp., is a splendid catalogue with excellent notes and studies on the themes, images, and techniques. Two essays of particular note are: H. Bredekamp on Vasari's treatment of Botticelli, pointing to a complex relationship between Botticelli and the Medici and to how the images in his paintings reflect tensions within the Medici family; D. Dombrowski on Botticelli's creative capacity and the desire to create a *natura altera*. Diane H. Bodart, *Tiziano e Federico II Gonzaga. Storia di un rapporto di committenza*, Ro, Bulzoni, 1998, 400 pp. + 49 pls, points to how Gonzaga patronage followed that of the Este family, and to how the changing patterns of patronage, and the language adopted to express them, were instrumental in persuading Titian to Mantua. There are three extensive appendixes of documents. James Beck, *Three Worlds of Michelangelo*, NY, Norton, 1999, xvii + 269 pp., sees three men as crucial to M.'s personal development and career during the period 1475–1512: Lorenzo de' Medici, his intellectual father, who introduced him to philosophy and poetry; his real father Lodovico, representing close family ties, whom he had to impress; and Pope Julius II, the patron with whom he had a tempestuous relationship. Ascanio Condivi, *The Life of Michelangelo*, ed. Hellmut Wohl, trans. Alice Sedgwick Wohl, University Park, Pennsylvania State U.P., 1999, xxii + 154 pp., is a second edition of a work first published in 1976, including corrections and revisions and incorporating the marginal notes to the first printing, which represent Michelangelo's judgements on corrections, misinterpretations, and omissions. Karen-Edis Barzman, *The Florentine Academy and the Early Modern State: the Discipline of Disegno*, CUP, 377 pp., is a fundamental study that addresses the question of why the Medici institutionalized the discipline in a formal school, incorporating it first as a confraternity and then as a guild. It sets out the importance of Medici cultural politics, and investigates the place of the Academy in the history of institutions and practices. *Gli statuti dell'Accademia del Disegno*, ed. Francesco Adorno and Luigi Zangheri, F, Olschki, 1998, 208 pp., has a preface that reproduces the text of the 1563 statute on the formation and setting up of the Accademia by Cosimo I and reviews the changes from 1563 to 1978.

There are a number of useful reference works. Stella Fletcher, *The Longman Companion to Renaissance Europe 1390–1530*, Harlow, Longman, xiii + 337 pp., has a miscellany of data from numerous chronologies, plans of buildings, and maps, to lists of heads of state and popes. Francesco Maspero and Aldo Granata, *Bestiario Medievale*, Casale Monferrato, Piemme, 1999, 461 pp., has two essays 'L'animale in epoca medievale', and 'La letteratura dei bestiari', followed by an alphabetical list of animals with their attributes and meanings. The interpretations are still valid for the 15th and 16th c. H. David Brumble, *Classical Myths and Legends in the Middle Ages and Renaissance. A Dictionary of Allegorical Meanings*, London, Fitzroy Dearborn, 1998, xxvi + 421 pp., deals primarily with gods, goddesses, heroes, heroines, and the places of classical mythology, as well as legendary aspects of figures such as Virgil and Aristotle. The introduction lists and describes the different kinds of allegory, and is followed by an alphabetical listing.

BIBLIOGRAPHY, PRINTING AND PUBLISHING

Sergio Rossetti, *Rome: A Bibliography from the Invention of Printing through 1899*, 1: *The Guide Books*, F, Olschki, xxxi + 275 pp., is the first volume of a mammoth project to itemize academies, ephemera, statutes, views, and guidebooks. This volume lists 2,457 items and has excellent indexes which allow interrogation via authors, titles, place of printing, and printers. A useful source for research into the organization of cultural activity is Elizabeth E. Gardner, *A Bibliographical Repertory of Italian Private Collections*, 1: *Abaco-Cutolo*, Vicenza, Neri Pozza, 1999, xvi + 439 pp., which gives excellent references to artists, patrons, collectors, collections, dealers, historians, buildings, and their contents. Given the intellectual cross-fertilization across national boundaries Laurence Grove and Daniel Russell, *The French Emblem. Bibliography of Secondary Sources*, Geneva, Droz, xx + 239 pp., is an excellent resource. It is divided into five sections: 'Research tools' covers dictionaries, special publications, catalogues, exhibitions, bibliographies; 'General studies' word and image theory, emblem and device, parallel forms, *topoi*, printers; 'Precursors' the Middle Ages, the 16th c., Alciato in French; 'French emblem writers' printed works and MSS; 'Applied emblematics' literature, art, and music, and history and politics. *Tesori di una biblioteca francescana. Libri e manoscritti del Convento di San Nicolò in Carpi sec. XV-XIX*, ed. Anna Prandi, Modena, Mucchi, 274 pp., includes seven essays covering the organization of the library, the 15th-c. scriptorium of Johannes Coppo de Prusia and his illuminators, the cultural and religious significance of individual volumes, and the growth of the collection. The catalogue of MSS, incunables, and 16th-c. books comprises 14 illuminated MSS of choral works, 37 MSS of secular works, and 929 books. Saturnino Loggi, *I codici della Libreria di S. Giacomo della Marca*, Monteprandone, Regione Marche, 162 pp., is part of series describing the libraries of the Marche. It has full critical apparatus, describing the mostly 15th-c. MSS, and gives a history of the collection. Anastasia Stouraiti, *La Grecia nelle raccolte della Fondazione Querini Stampalia*, Venice, Fond. Querini Stampalia, 301 pp., is an exhibition catalogue that traces the links between Venice and Greece with a preponderance of bibliographical data. S. Mancuso, 'Biblioteche del clero a Lodi nel secondo Cinquecento', *Archivio Storico Lodigiano*, 115, 1996[1998]: 117–37. Silvia Sbordone, *Gaetano Amalfi (1855–1928) e la sua collezione di libri. Studio analitico dei tipografi e degli editori e comparazione cronologica dei settori disciplinari*, Na, Giannini, 1999, 109 pp., analyses the volumes now in the Biblioteca Nazionale, Naples, though it is of limited value as the titles and authors are not specified. C. Pulsoni, 'Per la ricostruzione della biblioteca bembiana: I. I libri di Dante', *CrT*, 2, 1999:735–49. As a supplement to *Le edizioni italiane del XVI secolo. Per una bibliografia musicale: testi, trattati, spartiti*, Ro, ICCU, 1999, 248 pp., lists 3,470 titles of books published in Italy and works in Italian published elswhere. This is an important resource for assessing patterns of publishing and editorial activity. *Dalla collezione savonaroliana dell'Ariostea: la Bibbia di S. Maria degli Angeli, i codici, le edizioni più preziose*, ed. Luisa Pagnoni, F, SISMEL–Galluzzo, 1998, 129 pp., provides a history of the collection and a full description of the Savonarola Bible (L. Pagnoni), followed by a description of MSS (M. Bonazza) and of the printed texts (A. Ghinato), all with critical apparatus.

Martin Lowry, *Il mondo di Aldo Manuzio. Affari e cultura nella Venezia del Rinascimento*, Ro, Veltro, 461 pp., is a translation of the English edition (1979) with a new chapter which assesses recent biographical contributions, new perspectives on printers as scholars, Manuzio as a publicist, the debate on Greek typography, Manuzio and Venetian intellectual life, the Poliphilus controversy, Manuzio as a grammarian, the price of books, the influence of Manutius on European culture, the progress made in cataloguing Manutius's printed works. Salvatore Bongi, *Annali di Gabriel Giolito de' Ferrari da Trino di Monferrato, stampatore in Venezia*, Mansfield Centre, Martino Publishing, cxiii + 511, 541 pp., provides a facsimile reprint of the 1890 and 1895 editions. Massimo Ceresa, *Una stamperia nella Roma del primo Seicento. Annali tipografici di Guglielmo Facciotti ed eredi (1592–1640)*, Ro, Bulzoni, 328 pp., traces the history of the Facciotti family and the setting up of the printing press, and uses inventories and extant editions to extrapolate the number of works published per year, the relationship with authors, and patronage. There is an analysis of the categories of books published, and of designs for incipits and typographical images, and an appendix of documents followed by an index of 612 works with critical apparatus. The importance of watermarks is studied in Federica Formiga, *Le filigrane nelle edizioni di Bartolomeo Merlo e Angelo Tamo (1600–1630) presso la Biblioteca Civica di Verona*, Verona, La Grafica, 1998, 183 pp., which traces the history of printing in Verona from the pastoral activites of Gian Matteo Giberti in 1529 and sets out the activities of Tamo and Merlo. It lists 264 works with critical apparatus followed by illustrations of the watermarks. D. L. Gants, 'The application of digital image processing to the analysis of watermarked paper and printers' ornament usage in early printed books', pp. 133–47 of *New Ways of Looking at Old Texts*, II, ed. W. Speed Hill, MRTS, 1998, 173 pp.

Bibliofilia, 101, 1999, contains the proceedings of the conference 'Cento anni di Bibliofilia' with studies by C. Fahy and P. Scapecchi on bibliology and incunables, G. Tamiani on the bibliography of Hebrew books, F. Petrucci Nardelli on binding, D. Zancani on the importance of philology, A. Rosenthal on music, and A. Tura on early Florentine incunables. *Bibliofilia,* 102, has a number of studies: D. Fattori, 'Incunaboli sconosciuti e incunaboli semiconosciuti dell'Archivio di Stato di Venezia' (253–64); C. Fahy, 'Ancora sulla stampa musicale del Rinascimento: appunti su tre recenti pubblicazioni' (309–23); U. Rozzo, 'A proposito del Thesaurus de la littérature interdite au XVIe siècle' (325–37); F. Quarto, 'Uno sconosciuto editore del XVI secolo a Napoli: Giovanni Alberto Borgominerio da Trino' (178–205); M. Conway, 'The early career of Lorenzo de Alopa (1–10), which uses the diaries of the printing press of San Jacopo di Ripoli to reconstruct the activities 1477–84; and J. Mosley, 'Sources for Italian typefounding' (47–102). *Le livre illustré au XVIe siècle,* ed. Michel Plaisance, Paris, Klincksieck–Presses de la Sorbonne Nouvelle, 1999, 316 pp., comprises 13 essays on topics that include: the connection between text and image in religious and humanist MSS in the library of the Aragonese Kings of Naples (G. Toscano); the pyramid of the *Hypnerotomachia Poliphili* (M. Gabriele); *Libri delle sorti* by P. Danza and G. Parabosco (M.-C. van Hasselt); text and image in the 1544 edition of the *Divine Comedy* (S. Fabrizio-Costa and F. la Brasca); Venetian printing and the re-use of images in A. F. Doni's *Marmi* (M. Plaisance); illustration, translation, and gloss in L. Dolce's *Trasformationi* (1553) and the link to Ovid's *Metamorphoses* (F. Glénisson-Delannée); images in books and memory images: L. Dolce's *L'Achille* and D. Valades' *Rhetorica christiana* (L. Bolzoni); maps and the literary text in the 1556 *Orlando Furioso* (A. Doroszlai); the significance and changing role of figure illustrations in V. Cartari's *Imagini de i Dei de gli antichi* (F. Decroisette); illustrations to identify specific themes in D. Barbaro's *Vitruvius* of 1556 (L. Miotto); iconography and alchemy in G. B. Nazari's *Della tramutatione metallica sogni tre* (A. Perifano); the complex significance of the frontispiece of R. Gualterotti's *Polemidoro,* 1600 (M. Rossi).

Brian Richardson, *Printing, Writers, and Readers in Renaissance Italy,* CUP, 1999, xii + 220 pp., is more than the modest broad survey claimed by the author, raising as it does fundamental issues by treating such topics as authorial strategies, the financing and selling of books, opportunities for study and advancement, innovations in printing, and the changes in reading patterns due to social, cultural, and religious changes. C. De Frede, 'Un letterato del tardo Cinquecento e i suoi libri (Sertorio Quattromani, 1541–1603)', *AAPN,* 46, 1997[1998]: 119–30. Craig Kallendorf, *Virgil and the Myth of Venice.*

Books and Readers in the Italian Renaissance, OUP, 1999, 249 pp., examines the editions of Virgil, 132 in Latin and 64 in Italian, published between 1470 and 1600. It puts forward the convincing argument that Virgil's poetry was popular 'because it sometimes challenged, but more often confirmed, the specific moral, religious, and social values that those readers brought with them to their books'. *La civiltà del libro e la stampa a Venezia. Testi sacri, cristiani, islamici dal Quattrocento al Settecento*, ed. Simonetta Pelusi, Padua, Il Poligrafo, 175 pp., is a beautifully produced volume with 10 essays that cover: religious publishing in Venice (M. Zorzi); Venetian books in Hebrew (G. Tamani); bibliographical methodology and religious literature (A. Scarsella); the early printing of works in Arabic (G. Vercellin); the printing of Turkish and Ottoman books using Greek type (M. Kappler); the origins of the polyglot Bible (P. Scapecchi); and the format and decoration of choral works in the Marciana (S. Marcon). It includes a catalogue of volumes from an exhibition in the Sansoviniana.

2. HUMANISM

Renaissance Civic Humanism, ed. James Hankins, CUP, 314 pp., has ten essays which seek to reanimate debate and discussion on civic humanism by entering the lists, at times with each other, to assess past and present views, and to point to new methodologies and approaches. Essays include: a re-evaluation of the medieval heritage (J. Blythe); Cicero and diversity in the republican tradition (C. J. Nederman); reasons for early humanist writing (J. M. Najemy, M. Hornquist, and J. Hankins); and a number of contributions on Machiavelli: W. J. Connell on Machiavelli and humanism, innovations in Machiavelli's approach (H. C. Mansfield, P. A. Rahe), Machiavelli, Guicciardini and human nature (A. Moulakis, A. Brown). **Umanesimo e culture nazionali europee*, ed. Francesco Tateo, Palermo, Palumbo, 304 pp.

Alberti continues to stimulate research. Leon Battista Alberti, *Descriptio urbis Romae. Édition critique, traduction et commentaire*, ed. Martine Furno and Mario Carpo, Geneva, Droz, 196 pp., is notable for its critical apparatus and for the extensive commentary that offers a new interpretation of the text. The essays 'Écphrasis géographique et culture visuelle' (M. Carpo) and 'La *Descriptio urbis Romae* dans l'histoire du latin et de la culture humaniste' (M. Furno) point to the important rhetorical nature of a work not written to a practical end but as 'plutôt une sorte de jeu, ou de moyen d'arbitrage d'un débat intellectuel'. *Leon Battista Alberti*, 2 vols, ed. Francesco Furlan, T, Aragno — Paris, Vrin, 587, 1123 pp., is a massive collection of 58 essays grouped in six sections: 'Biographie, autobiographie, contexte historique', has essays which link A. to the Pandolfini, assess his place in humanist debate and cultural politics, reflect on the themes of friendship and crisis in the Alberti family business, and examine family *topoi* in the *Della Famiglia*; 'Lectures, sources et culture', covers the formation of A.'s philosophy, the cultural connotations behind the winged eye, humanist preoccupations, women in A.'s works, a reconsideration of A.'s humanism, and his argumentation in a late treatise; 'Les dialogues et les ludi' investigates Alberti's debt to Apuleius in the *Intercenales* and *Momus*, conception and genesis in the *Della Famiglia*, power and madness in *Momus*, the morality, political themes, and therapeutic dimension of the *Intercenales*, classical sources, allegory, and the moral nature of the *Aruli*, Michael Baxandall and the *De pictura*, and Alberti, Mantegna, and the grotesque; 'Art et traités techniques', covers the role of drawing, the question of perspective relating to landscape, morality, the colossus, and history in the *De pictura*, theory and practical considerations in the *Ludi*, the classification of science and arts, a translation of *De componendis cifris*; 'Architecture et urbanisme: théorie et pratique'; 'Influence et fortune', investigates Poliziano's many allusions to and quotations from A., and the influence of A. on L. de' Medici. Anthony Grafton, *Leon Battista Alberti*, London, Penguin, 417 pp., is an excellent scholarly overview of A.'s humanist erudition, activities, and accomplishments. Particularly fine chapters are 'From new technologies to fine art', 'On painting', and 'Alberti the antiquary', which point to his ever-changing interests and the methodologies he adopted and adapted. A. Bisanti, 'A proposito degli *Apologhi centum* di Leon Battista Alberti', *CLett*, 28:237–62. M. Frati, 'Dal discorso narrativo al discorso proverbiale: i *Convelata* di Leon Battista Alberti ed Erasmo da Rotterdam', *SUm*, 13.2, 1999:55–78. Franco Borsi et al., *Leon Battista Alberti. Architettura e cultura*, F, Olschki, 1999, 386 pp., offers 23 essays and a feast of scholarship. F. Borsi challenges some basic assumptions, A. Bruschi points to the lack of rigidity in his methodology, C. Thoenes tackles the problem of individuality and responsibility, H. Gunthor traces the humanists' and A.'s differing attitudes to Vitruvius with particular reference to learning, A. Tonnesman examines A., Donatello, and the humanist debate on artistic licence and decorum, M. Aronberg Lavin and M. Trachtenberg reflect on A.'s relationship with antiquity, M. Martelli, A. Tenenti, and I. Bonomi grapple with A.'s literary output, C. Vasoli examines the humanistic and philosophical themes in the *Theogenio*, P. Castelli elucidates A.'s stance with regard to motion, L. Zanoncelli revisits the interpretations of proportions, G. Federici Vescovini assesses A.'s technical vocabulary, C. Cieri Via compares A.'s philosophical and cultural reflections on art objects.

Vespasiano da Bisticci, *Il libro delle lodi delle donne*, ed. Giuseppe Lombardi, Manziana, Vecchiarelli — Ro, Roma nel Rinascimento, 1999, cxii + 214 pp. Leonardo Bruni, *Laudatio florentine urbis*, ed. Stefano U. Baldassarri, F, SISMEL–Galluzzo, c + 48 pp., has an exemplary critical apparatus with full consideration of all the MSS. The introduction rightly points to the humanist rhetoric at the service of the expansionist policies of the Florentine oligarchy, sets out Bruni's sources and methodology, and assesses the fortune and influence of the text. Poggio Bracciolini, *L'infelicità dei principi*, ed. Davide Canfora, Palermo, Sellerio, 1999, 130 pp., has an analysis of the dialogue composed early in 1440, which takes as its theme the link between power and unhappiness due to the tendency of the former to corrupt and its attendant cares and worries. The translation is based on the critical edition of the Latin text established by D. Canfora (Ro, 1998). Marco Laffranchi, *Dialettica e filosofia in Lorenzo Valla*, Mi, Vita e Pensiero, 1999, xxii + 354 pp., sees Valla as using rhetoric based on Cicero and Quintilian in order to enter into a dialogue with Aristotelian doctrines and arrive at different conclusions. It offers a new interpretation of what Valla meant by dialectic and the part it played in his philosophy. W. Scott Blanchard, 'The negative dialectic of Lorenzo Valla: a study in the pathology of opposites', *RenS*, 14:149–271, concludes that Valla preferred to define himself against existing doctrines rather than fashion new ones. *Roma parte del cielo. Confronto tra l'antica e la nuova Roma di Manuele Crisolora*, ed. Guido Cortassa, T, UTET, 111 pp., has an introduction by E. V. Maltese that places the work firmly within the context of humanist writing on antiquity and traces the reactions of other humanists to the text. It points to the two main themes that Rome's urban fabric has vitality and is ever changing, and that its beauty lies in the parts rather than the whole. There follows a translation of the *Synkrisis* based on the Laurenziana MS. Romano Ruggeri, *Polidoro Virgili, un umanista europeo*, Bergamo, Moretti & Vitali, 143 pp., is a long overdue reassessment of the humanist's life and works. It investigates: the methodology and critical approach acquired in his editorial activity on N. Perotti's *Cornucopiae*; the didactic use of classical literature to a religious end; his participation in the European religious debate and criticism of traditional theology and of the Church as an institution; his sources and adaptation to a particularly English love of story-telling in the *Anglica historia*; his contribution to the debate on natural and supernatural phenomena; an assessment of the popularity of, and audience for, his works. Maurilio Pérez Gonzalez, *G. Manetti y la traduccion en el siglo XV: edicion critica del*

Apologeticus, Libro V, Leon U.P., 1999, 151 pp., has an introduction that assesses the humanist influence and Biblical sources, and discusses the MS tradition and the textual variants, and is followed by a critical edition with facing Spanish translation. Jacobi Curli, *Bellum civile et Gallicum*, ed. Giuseppe Germano, Na, Università Federico II, 1999, 161 pp., is a humanist work in prose commemorating the victory of Paolo Fregoso in 1461 written by a copyist in the service of Alfonso I of Aragon. The introduction gives the historical background, examines the chequered fate of the MS tradition, traces the echoes of Pliny the Younger, and indicates the humanist circle from which the work emanated. There is an analysis of the language and style, followed by a critical edition of the Latin text with Italian translation. L. Chines, 'Filologia e arcana sapienza: l'umanista Achille Bocchi commentatore e esegeta', *SPCT*, 60:70–80, examines the elements of Bocchi's innovative approach to Cicero and to his teacher G. B. Pio. L. Monti Sabia, D. D'Alessandro, and A. Iacono, 'Alfonso il Magnanimo nel ricordo di Giovanni Pontano', *AAPN*, 47, 1998[1999]:274–95.

Kurt Barstow, *The Gualenghi–d'Este Hours. Art and Devotion in Renaissance Ferrara*, Los Angeles, Paul Getty Museum, 269 pp. + 27 pls, is a beautifully produced and printed volume dealing with a prayerbook made for Andrea Gualengo and Orsina d'Este. The study highlights the relationship between art and religion, and gives a detailed analysis of the illuminations by Taddeo Crivelli and Guglielmo Giraldi within the context of stylistic concerns and humanist discussions in Ferrara. It points to the interest in innovative spatial experiments and traces the links between Crivelli and the humanist Angelo Decembrio. The emotional expressions are shown to refer to Ciceronian rhetoric and to be perhaps related to works by Ficino, Guarino, and B. Facio. Giuseppe Lombardi, *Galiane in rivolta. Una polemica umanistica sugli ornamenti femminili nella Viterbo del Quattrocento*, 2 vols, Manziana, Vecchiarelli, 1998, cclxxvii + 381 pp., deals with three orations emanating from Viterbo and addressed to N. Perotti, two in defence of, and one against, women. The study considers the connotations of the term *specchio* and its use in writings dealing with women, brings out humanistic, moral, and pedagogic themes, points to imitation with regard to Livy, the classical and Christian sources, and the models in N. Sanuti, M. Bosso, and Guarino. The orations were aimed at changes to the city's sumptuary laws and show the need for critical editions of statutes for an understanding of cultural activity. L. Cellauro, 'Daniele Barbaro and his Venetian edition of Vitruvius of 1556 and 1567', *SV*, 40:87–134, is a wide-ranging study touching on family history, Barbaro's humanistic and classical scholarship, and his contribution to the study of Vitruvius, debt to

Fra Giocondo and importance for Palladio. That antiquity and Vitruvius did not hold universal sway is set out in Bruno Adorni, *Alessio Tramello*, Mi, Electa, 1998, 171 pp., which points to the initial impact of Venice and the importance of the local Lombard tradition, a cultural view which must also have been shared by his patrons. Francesco Capolei and Piero Sartogo, *Brunelleschi anticlassico*, T, Testo e Immagine, 1999, 93 pp., reassesses B.'s methodology and original plans which show his anti-classical stance with regard to the manipulation and presentation of space.

PHILOSOPHY AND HISTORY OF IDEAS. *Humanism and Early Modern Philosophy*, ed. Jill Kraye and M. W. F. Stone, London, Routledge, xiii + 270 pp., assembles 12 essays whose aim is 'to demonstrate that a distinctive element of philosophy and intellectual culture of this period is very relevant to our understanding of the practice and development of philosophy in the early modern era'. They cover theology in Valla, dialogue in the Renaissance, casuistry and Aristotelian moral philosophy, Galileo, and Ficino and Renaissance Platonism. Philip Beitchman, *Alchemy of the Word. Cabala of the Renaissance*, New York State U.P., 1998, 364 pp., identifies the existence of three different but interrelated strains of Cabala: Jewish, Christian, and demiurgic Neopagan. Its impact on literature and philosophy is then assessed by examining how it was read, interpreted, and modified by, *inter alios*, Pico della Mirandola, L. Lazzarelli, and Egidius of Viterbo. Gian Luca Ercolani and Donato Loscalzo, *La dieta ermetica. L'alimentazione nel Rinascimento*, Lugano, Todaro, 1999, 203 pp., relates hermetic theories and astrology to the human body and the medical benefits of certain foods and beverages. Flavio Caroli, *L'anima e il volto. Ritratto e fisiognomica da Leonardo a Bacon*, Mi, Electa, 1998, 689 pp., has two sections dealing with the Renaissance: 'I moti dell'animo' and 'Il volto magico'. The former analyses the theories behind Leonardo's portraiture as a starting point for investigating physiognomy; the latter looks to Lorenzo Lotto and the beginnings of psychological portraiture. It considers 16th-c. treatises on physiognomy, the influences of P. Gaurico's *De sculptura*, A. Achillini's *De Chyromantie*, and assesses the theme of melancholia in the writings of Cardano. Roger French, *Dissection and Vivisection in the European Renaissance*, Aldershot, Ashgate, 1999, 289 pp., gives a scholarly evaluation of the extant evidence to propose that the study of anatomy was not done primarily for use in medicine, but was linked to very different concerns (theological, legal), and particularly to showing one's learning in order to attract patients and students. It demonstrates how the accepted classical canons were given different interpretations and highlights the importance of experiment and public displays. Timo Joutsivuo, *Scholastic Tradition and Humanistic Innovation. The*

Concept of Neutrum in Renaissance Medicine, Helsinki, Finnish Academy of Science and Letters, 1999, 288 pp., examines the changes brought about by humanists to the concept of neutral bodies, neither healthy nor ill, which had been a feature of Galenic medicine. The study identifies elements of continuity and divergence, pointing to the ambiguity of attitudes to Galen and Aristotle and the strategies used to deal with inconsistencies. *Memoria e memorie*, ed. Lina Bolzoni, Vittorio Erlindo, and Marcello Morelli, F, Olschki, 1998, 221 pp., gathers 14 essays including L. Bolzoni on the theatre of memory in Della Porta, and an excellent study by M. Rossi on Tommaso Porcacchi's plan for a memory system related to a publishing project. The importance of Claire Fanger, *Conjuring Spirits. Texts and Traditions of Medieval Ritual Magic*, University Park, Pennsylvania State U.P., 1998, xviii + 284 pp., lies in the fact that the texts under consideration in the nine essays circulated widely during the period. The collection gives an insight into the different kinds of magic (demonic, angelic), the sources, and the social, religious, and intellectual context. R. Catani, 'The danger of demons: the astrology of Marsilio Ficino', *ISt*, 55:37–52, proposes a methodology to clarify Ficino's inconsistency on the question of astrology, based on comprehending 'a mentality formed through the confluence of persuasions, discoveries, and pressures. A. Carlini, 'Marsilio Ficino e il testo di Platone', *Rinascimento*, 39, 1999:3–36, investigates the importance of MS Laur. 85.9 and assesses Ficino's real contribution to Plato studies. E. Vitale, 'Sul concetto di materia nella *Theologia Platonica* di Marsilio Ficino', *ib.*, 337–69. *The History of Science and Religion in the Western tradition: an Encyclopedia*, ed. Gary B. Ferngren, NY, Garland, xxi + 586 pp., is organized under chronological sections rather than alphabetically, with individual essays on such topics as views of nature, God and nature, science, Galileo, the conflict of science and religion, and secular humanism. The section on 'Occult Science' has essays on astrology (L. A. Smoller), magic and the occult (W. Eamon), alchemy, numbers, and cabala (P. G. Sobol). The essays are by established scholars who successfully piece together the interactions between philosophy, cosmology, and religion.

Sciences et Religions de Copernic à Galilée (1540–1610), ed. Catherine Brice and Antonella Romano, Ro, École Française de Rome, 1999, 550 pp., gathers 25 essays covering: the importance of science in Renaissance culture; the effect, due to religious and political turmoil, of the curtailment of international scientific collaboration; the relationship between metaphysics and geometrical qualities; the attitudes of the Roman and Protestant Churches with regard to dissection; the condemnation of heliocentricity; thunder, lightning, and natural phenomena as supernatural signs; the Accademia dei

Lincei as a mediator, a centre for scientific inquiry, and as a patron; Neapolitan Jesuits, mathematics, and orthodoxy; religion and scientific inquiry in Messina; the Neoplatonism of Palingenius's *Zodiacus Vitae* and the crisis of Aristotelianism; nature and scientific knowledge in M. A. Severino; Galileo, Federico Cesi, and G. B. Agucchi on *pluralità* and the corruptibility of the heavens; reflections on historiographical approaches and the resulting distortions.

BRUNO. Giordano Bruno, *Œuvres complètes*, ed. Yves Hersant and Nuccio Ordine; *Édition critique des œuvres italiennes*, ed. Giovanni Aquilecchia, Paris, Les Belles Lettres, 1993–99, has been completed with vols 5 and 7: *L'Expulsion de la bête triomphante*, ed. J. Balsamo and N. Ordine, 1999, ccxxxviii + 614 pp.; and *Des fureurs héroïques*, ed. M. A. Granada, P. H. Michel, and Y. Hersant, 1999, cxi + 632 pp. Mondadori marked the fourth centenary of B.'s death by publishing the edition Giordano Bruno, *Dialoghi filosofici italiani*, ed. Michele Ciliberto, Mi, Mondadori, cxiv + 1540 pp., on whose relation to G. Aquilecchia's critical edition of the texts see Id., 'I dialoghi bruniani "a cura" (o sinecura) di Michele Ciliberto', *GSLI*, 177:422–39. Hilary Gatti, *Giordano Bruno and Renaissance Science*, Ithaca, Cornell U.P., 1999, x + 257 pp., is an excellent work that shows critical acumen, precise scholarship, and clarity. It gives an assessment of past and present B. scholarship on fundamental questions and a balanced account of the evolution of B.'s ideas within the context of his own time, and relates B.'s dilemma as a philosopher of science to the epistemological status of modern science. A. Bonher-Vallon, 'Giordano Bruno e la matematica', *Rinascimento*, 39, 1999:67–93, is in three parts: it compares B.'s ideas on the infinite and finite to those of Cusanus and underscores the importance of the concept of *minimo* and the part it played in his atomism; it sets out his unusual critical stance vis-à-vis the various mathematical traditions; it explores his search for a mathematics to express theories which could not be resolved in the Platonic-Aristotelian tradition. Aniello Montano, *La mente e la mano. Aspetti della storicità del sapere e del primato del fare in Giordano Bruno*, Na, Città del Sole, 166 pp., combines erudition with clarity in a study of B.'s activity as an historian of philosophy: of his view as to what constitutes human knowledge and how this has contributed to order, progress, and civilization. There is also a study of parody, polemics, and pre-Platonic philosophy in the *Candelaio*. Tristan Dagron, *Unité de l'être et dialectique. L'idée de philosophie naturelle chez Giordano Bruno*, Paris, Vrin, 1999, 417 pp., is a challenging study that concentrates on *De la causa, principio et uno* as a point of departure for examining his philosophical journey as an 'activité de figuration'. Giovanni Aquilecchia, *Bruno nel suo tempo*, Na, Città del Sole, 22 pp., is much more than a modest introduction for schools as the biographical account has textual analysis embedded in it. Shaw, *Reflexivity Vol.*, includes two essays on Bruno: D. Knox traces the links between Alessandro Citolini and Giordano Bruno to show that they shared intellectual interests, and offers an explanation for the changes concerning Alessandro in the two versions of the *Cena delle Ceneri*; G. Aquilecchia examines Bruno's 'poetics' in the *Eroici furori* whereby a poem can be taken as the artistic and expressive equivalent of a picture, this being a literal reading of Horace's *ut pictura poesis*. *Dialoghi piani di Fra' Agnello Mancin su Gli eroici furori di Giordano Bruno. Interlocutore Franco Manganelli*, Na, Guida, 221 pp., discusses within a contrived dialogic framework (really a monologue) the work's female figures, spatial dimension, and theme of the *summum bonum*. Matteo d'Amico, *Giordano Bruno: avventure e misteri del gran mago nell'Europa del Cinquecento*, Casale Monferrato, Piemme, 464 pp., sees B. as the representative of a 'Rinascimento caldo' in which knowledge is fused with being and action, and where in philosophy there predominates a qualitative vision whereby all things come together in a final synthesis. Giorgio Bárberi Squarotti, *Parodia e pensiero: Giordano Bruno*, Mi, Greco & Greco, 1998, 220 pp.

BrC, 5, 1999, includes: S. Otto, 'Gli occhi e il cuore. Il pensiero filosofico in base alle "regole" e alle "leggi" della sua presentazione figurale negli *Eroici furori*' (13–24); L. Albanese, 'Bruno Ficino e la trinità di Zoroastro' (157–64); M. A. Granada, ' "Esser spogliato dall'umana perfezione e giustizia". Nueva evidencia de la presencia de Averroes en la obra y en el proceso de Giordano Bruno' (305–32); D. Knox, 'Ficino, Copernicus and Bruno on the motion of the earth' (333–66); P. Sabbatino, ' "Scuoprir quel ch'è ascosto sotto questi Sileni". La forma dialogica degli *Eroici furori*' (367–80); D. Tessicini, "Attoniti . . . quia sic Stagyrita docebat'. Bruno in polemica con Digges' (521–26). *BrC*, 6.1 has A. Maggi, 'The language of the visible: the *Eroici furori* and the Renaissance philosophy of *imprese*' (115–42); L. Catana, 'Bruno's *Spaccio* and Hyginus' *Poetica astronomica*' (57–78); and D. Giovannozzi, ' "Porphyrius, Plotinus et alii Platonici". Echi neoplatonici nella demonologia bruniana' (79–104). M. A. Granada, 'La imaginación y la construcción del universo infinito en Giordano Bruno', *NRLett*, 19.2, 1999:39–62. Giordano Bruno, *Le deposizioni davanti al tribunale dell'Inquisizione*, Na, Città del Sole, 75 pp., gives the text of the seven depositions. Enzo Mazzi, *Giordano Bruno: attualità di un'eresia*, Ro, Manifestolibri, 109 pp., sees the Bruno affair as having direct relevance today. The preface by G. Franzoni reviews writings by and on Bruno. Antonio Castronuovo, *Giordano Bruno: il processo e la condanna*, Viterbo, Nuovi Equilibri, 1999, 126 pp., is a collection of documents. *Atti del processo di Giordano Bruno*, ed. David Dei, Palermo, Sellerio, 231 pp., though not giving the full documentation, makes a significant contribution by translating the Latin material. The scholarly introduction surveys B.'s career and the evolution of his ideas.

The fourth centenary of Bruno's execution has been marked worldwide. In September 1999 Beijing's University of Foreign Languages hosted a conference organized by the Chinese Association for the Study of Italian Literature with the support of the Centro Internazionale di Studi Bruniani and the Istituto Italiano per gli Studi Filosofici. The bilingual *acta*: *XI Convegno di Studi sulla Letteratura Italiana: Per Giordano Bruno*, ed. Carlo Laurenti, Beijing, 1999, 274 pp., comprise (with Chinese names rendered *all'italiana*): G. Aquilecchia, 'Filosofia, teatro e poesia nell'opera di Giordano Bruno' (3–24); N. Ordine, 'Vita civile, tolleranza e unità dei saperi in Giordano Bruno' (25–54); Y. Jiehou, 'Un grande precursore del razionalismo scientifico moderno' (55–71); A. Nuzzo 'La contemplazione del filosofo nel divenire dell'universo bruniano: l'uomo e l'"eterna vicissitudine delle cose"' (72–105); P. Cherchi 'Perché celebriamo Giordano Bruno' (106–14); C. Jingang, 'L'amore per la verità *De gli eroici furori*' (115–27); F. Mignini, 'Giordano Bruno: il lessico dell'infinito' (128–57); L. Tongliu, 'Accostarsi alla figura di Giordano Bruno' (158–69); and Y. Lin, 'La nascita del pensiero di Bruno' (243–63). For other papers, marking the presentation of *Il candelaio* in Chinese, the first volume of a projected complete edition of Bruno's works in Chinese translation, to be published by the Chinese Academy of Social Sciences, are noted in section 4, THEATRE, below.

CAMPANELLA. Thomae Campanellae, *De conservatione et gubernatione rerum. Inediti. Theologicorum liber*, ed. Maria Muccillo, Ro, CEDAM, 136 pp., is a critical edition with notes and an Italian translation. Tommaso Campanella, *Metafisica. Universalis philosophiae seu metaphysicarum rerum iuxta propria dogmata, Liber XIV*, ed. Teresa Rinaldi, Bari, Levante, xxii + 207 pp., has an introduction analysing Campanella's concept of metaphysics to reveal his singularly modern stance, particularly in his treatment of man, and followed by the Latin text and an Italian translation and notes. Tommaso Campanella, *Lettere 1595–1638*, ed. Germana Ernst, Pisa–Ro, IEPI, 171 pp., gives the text of 38 letters followed by a list of extant and lost writings not included in the Spampanato edition (1927). The variety of themes illustrates the range of C.'s learning and his standing as an international figure. Vito Angiuli, *Ragione moderna e verità del cristianesimo. La Atheismus triumphatus di Tommaso Campanella*, Bari, Levante, 281 pp., is a scholarly analysis of the philosophical and theological climate in which Campanella consistently revised this work for over 20 years because of problems of censorship. A chapter on the critical reception of the work after publication lays bare the many accusations

(Pelagianism, atheism, libertinism, naturalism) and interpretations. Enzo A. Baldini, *Luigi Firpo e Campanella: cinquant'anni di ricerche e di pubblicazioni*, Pisa–Ro, IEPI, 63 pp., is a highly enjoyable portrait of the deceased scholar and bibliophile followed by a bibliography of his publications and the text of his 'Tommaso Campanella e la sua Calabria'. G. Ciglioni, 'Immaginazione, spiriti, generazione. La teoria del concepimento nella *Philosophia sensibus demonstrata* di Campanella', *BrC*, 4, 1998:37–58.

CARDANO. Anthony Grafton, *Cardano's Cosmos: the Worlds and Works of a Renaissance Astrologer*, Cambridge, Mass., Harvard U.P., 1999, 284 pp., is an important study which allows us to journey further into a rich corpus of texts. Grafton's approach is to chart the evolution of Cardano's thought by placing the texts within their biographical and socio-cultural context, as well as assessing the reactions of his contemporaries. The resulting picture illuminates not only Cardano as an astrologer and man, but the place of astrology within early-modern culture. Girolamo Cardano, *Le opere, le fonti, la vita*, ed. Marialuisa Baldi and Guido Canziani, Mi, Franco Angeli, 1999, 589 pp., consists of 25 essays in two sections. This is a wide-ranging collection with a high standard of scholarship that offers much new material. It includes studies of individual works: *De libris propriis* (I. MacLean); *De consolatione* (M. Baldi); *De sapientia, De immortalitate animorum* (A. Ingegno); *De utilitate* (G. Canziani, M. Baldi); *Praecepta ad filios* (F. Socas); *Dialectia* (I. Schutze); *De subtilitate* (P. Pirzio); *Liber de ludo aleae* (M. Tamborini); *Practica arithmetica* (V. Gavagna); *Carcer* (E. di Rienzo and S. Fazzo); *Pronostico* (G. Ernst). Other essays explore philosophy and religion (M. Bracali), dreams (J.-Y. Boriaud), the soul (G. Giglioni), medicine (N. G. Siriasi), the circulation of MSS (M. Baldi and G. Canziani), and printing history (C. Fahy). D. Giorgio, 'Il *De propria vita liber* di Gerolamo Cardano', *CLett*, 26, 1998:525–52.

FRACASTORO. Girolamo Fracastoro, *L'anima*, ed. Enrico Peruzzi, F, Le Lettere, 1999, 215 pp., discusses Fracastoro's difficulties in writing and preparing his dialogues for publication, and the development of his philosophical ideas with regard to his stance towards Pomponazzi. There follows a critical edition with full notes.

LANDO. Ortensio Lando, *Paradossi*, Pisa–Ro, IEPI, 1999, xviii + 230 pp., has an introduction by E. Canone and G. Ernst that stresses the reformist slant of L.'s writings and his contribution to contemporary cultural, religious, and social debates. The text is a facsimile of the *editio princeps* (Lyon, 1543).

STIGLIOLA. Massimo Rinaldi, *L'audacia di Pythio. Filosofia, scienza e architettura in Colantonio Stigliola*, Bo, Il Mulino, 1999, xiv + 130 pp., traces the teaching of mathematics and astronomy in Naples, the interest in theories of the natural world, and the link to the Lincei. In all of Stigliola's activities Rinaldi discerns a fundamental preoccupation with the *ars aedificatoria*. This theme was to have been the subject of his incomplete *Enciclopedia Pythagorea* which was to encompass the totality of human knowledge. The study analyses the relationship between theory and experience, and the way in which architecture lies at the heart of his philosophical ideas.

RELIGIOUS THOUGHT AND THE CHURCH. Christopher S. Celenza, *Renaissance Humanism and the Papal Curia. Lapo da Castiglionchio the Younger's De Curiae Commodis*, Ann Arbour, Michigan U.P., 1999, 244 pp., gives a critical edition with translation and an excellent introduction that offers a new reading of the text. An analysis of Lapo's position on the virtues points to his role as a subtle critic of the Roman Curia. It sets out his use of humanist historical methodology in his discussion of wealth, and the strategies used for attracting patronage. Giuseppe L. Coluccia, *Niccolò V umanista: papa, e riformatore. Renovatio politica e morale*, Venice, Marsilio, 1998, xix + 415 pp. + 22 pls, sees Nicholas as a transitional figure between the Middle Ages and new humanist ideals, who encompasses both continuity and renewal. It highlights his political, religious, and intellectual achievements, and his activities to promote the *renovatio Romae*, and assesses the humanists and scholars he gathered round him. Alberto Aubert, *Paolo IV. Politica, inquisizione e storiografia*, F, Le Lettere, 1999, 245 pp., places historical events within the context of contemporary judgements. It gives a full account of the political and religious considerations that led to the execution of Carlo and Giovanni Carafa, and of the way the pope was portrayed in the writings of the Veronese historian Onofrio Panvinio, the *pasquinate* of Niccolò Franco, the *Apologia* of Antonio Carafa, and the *Vita* by Antonio Caracciolo. *Tradizioni patristiche nell'Umanesimo*, ed. Mariarosa Cortesi and Claudio Leonardi, F, SISMEL–Galluzzo, xii + 425 pp., is a collection of 14 essays which include a reappraisal of humanist attitudes towards the Church fathers (G. Crevatin) and cover: the differing attitudes to Saint Basil in L. Bruni, who had a personal agenda, and A. Traversari, who was a faithful transmitter (P. Viti); the importance of Saint Augustine in the writings of C. Salutati and the role of Petrarch as a mediating influence (F. B. Gianni); the collection of books of N. Niccoli in the library of San Marco, related to A. Traversari's attempt to recreate a patristic collection, and the annotations of Pico della Mirandola and Ficino (S. Gentile); Zanobi Acciaioli's activities as a translator from Greek to Latin and as librarian at San Marco (M. C. Vicario); the importance of patristic research into the Platonist revival and the direct appeal to biblical sources in Savonarola (G. C. Garfagnini); humanists' use of patristic studies to effect reform

(C. Caby); N. Cusanus as reader and collecter of the Church Fathers
and the problem of the conciliation of Plato and Aristotle (F. Santi);
Valla, Erasmus, and St. Jerome (P. Larder); the genesis and nature of
G. Torelli's involvement with patristic literature and a critical edition
of the homily on Psalm 50 (M. Cortesi); translations of Augustine
from the Greek (G. Rigetti); the textual tradition behind A. Pacini's
translation of Gregorio Nazianzeno's *De virtute* (C. Crimi); and
patristic MSS in Greek from the fall of the Byzantine empire to 1470
(G. de Gregorio). Giorgio Picasso, *Tra umanesimo e devotio. Studi di storia
monastica*, Mi, Vita e Pensiero, 1999, xxvi + 228 pp., is a collection of
14 essays on monastic reform divided into three sections. The first
centres on the reforming activities of Ludovico Barbo who rejected
part of his humanist training to concentrate on biblical and patristic
studies. The second section has a series of studies on Bernardo
Thomei and the Olivetani, while the last section is devoted to
Catherine of Siena. *Verso Savonarola. Misticismo, profezia, empiti riformi-
stici tra Medioevo ed età moderna*, ed. Gian Carlo Garfagnini, F, SISMEL–
Galluzzo, 1999, xx + 152 pp., stresses the medieval antecedents to
Savonarola with an introduction that sees aspects of his life and
teaching as part of a tradition which encompasses Caterina of Siena
and Giovanni Domenici. There follow five essays covering medieval
Christianity and prophecy in Savonarola (C. Leonardi), prophecy
and politics in Brigit of Sweden (A. Valerio), the *libro d'amor di charità*
of Giovanni Domenici. G. Cadoni, 'Savonarola, Machiavelli, Guicciardini in una recente ipotesi interpretativa', *La Cultura*, 37,
1999:493–96. Rita Librandi and Adriana Valerio, *I sermoni di
Domenica da Paradiso: studi e testo critico*, F, SISMEL–Galluzzo, 1999,
clxxix + 170 pp., is an edition of the texts preceded by an excellent
analysis of the political and religious tensions in Florentine and
Christian humanism, and of the way in which Church reform and
individual spiritual renewal are resolved in Domenica's sermons. It
discusses her close links with the Dominicans of San Marco and the
influence of Savonarola and Domenico Benivieni, and considers the
theological ban on women preachers. Caterina da Genova, *Dialogo
spirituale tra anima e capo. Trattato del Purgatorio*, ed. Palmina Trovato,
Casale Monferrato, Piemme, 1999, 147 pp., is a disappointing edition
with barely adequate notes. Roberto Bellarmino, *Autobiografia (1613)*,
ed. Gustavo Galeota, Brescia, Morcelliana, 1999, 99 pp., has an
introduction that discusses the origin and nature of the work, the
textual tradition of its 48 paragraphs, and its fate linked to the Jesuit
fall from grace. *The Jesuit Ratio Studiorum: 400th Anniversary Perspectives*,
ed. Vincent J. Duminuco, NY, Fordham U.P., xii + 307 pp., comprises seven essays including studies by J. W. O'Malley on the Jesuits'
early involvement in education (with particular reference to the

opening of the first school in Messina) and by J. W. Padberg on the development of the *Ratio studiorum* up to the definitive version of 1599. John W. O'Malley et al., *The Jesuits: Cultures, Sciences, and the Arts, 1540–1773*, Toronto U.P., xx + 772 pp., gathers 35 contributions. Part one, 'Jesuit history', covers historiography (J. W. O'Malley), the Jesuit *modus operandi* of accommodation and assimilation rather than a *noster modus* (G. A. Bailey), the importance of rhetoric to Jesuit teaching and learning (M. Fumaroli), and studies of the link between Jesuit intellectual discourse, institutional setting, and the wider political context. Part two, 'Rome', has essays by C. Robertson, L. Rice, M. J. Gorman, M. Murata on: negotiations and compromise in the design of the 'Gesù'; the complex cultural themes aimed at patrons and benefactors in the printed texts of theses; the relationship between scientific activities and theatrical display; Athanasius Kircher's *Musurgia universalis*. Part three, 'Overseas missions', covers the contribution made to scientific knowledge and the processes of adaptation and acculturation. Part four, 'Jesuit adaptability', reflects on the contribution of Italian humanism to the Society's openness to alien customs, on the remarkable flexibility of Jesuit strategies and on how 'shared' appreciation of culture could mask fundamental differences. Part five, 'Tradition, innovation, accomodation', investigates the tensions in education, where Aristotle was used to defend theological positions, censorship, and openness to educational innovation, and shows how accomodation could run perilously close to assimilation. Part six considers architecture, interior decoration, and public performance as a means to effect a transformation or confirmation of faith.

INDIVIDUAL CENTRES. *1570 Porto di mare 1670. Pittori e pittura a Palermo tra memoria e recupero*, ed. Vincenzo Abbate, Na, Electa, 1999, 288 pp., has an essay, 'La città aperta' (V. Abbate), which takes as its starting point the Horatian concept *ut pictura poesis* to examine the theorists and *letterati* involved in the debate on sacred images, the cultural initiatives of the Jesuits, and Palermo's links with Genoa. *Atti del XVI Convegno Internazionale di storia della Corona d'Aragona*, ed. Guido D'Agostino and Giulia Buffardi, 2 vols, Na, Paparo, xxix + 1011, 1012–1910 pp., assembles 104 contributions and three sections devoted to culture, which cover: B. Facio and historiography at the court of Alfonso the Magnanimous; the Italian Renaissance and Spain; the teaching of Greek in Southern Italy; Alfonso and the university; the Catalan language and Naples; the *volgare napoletano* as a literary language in Masuccio Salernitano and Loise de Rosa; Lullism in Italy; images of Alfonso in the writings of Pontano and other humanists; Beccadelli and the siting of a new library; a reassessment of poetic genres and influences at Alfonso's court; Bruni and the translation of Aristotle's *Politics*; Benet Garret (Cariteo) and Jacopo Sannazaro; family history in the bucolic poetry of Sannazaro; translations of Seneca's letters. Other essays deal with patronage, artistic currents, and humanism and the triumphal entry of Alfonso into Naples (1443). G. Albanese and D. Pietragalla, '*In honorem regis edit.* Lo scrittoio di Bartolomeo Facio alla corte napoletana di Alfonso il Magnanimo', *Rinascimento*, 39, 1999:293–336. *Rome the Pilgrim's Dream*, ed. Gloria Fossi, F, Giunti, 1998, 286 pp., has 15 essays which include those of: G. Fossi on pilgrims, scholars, and antiquity, which traces the changing attitude to the traditional mirabilia; S. Maddalo on images of Rome; A. Esch on the preparations of Sixtus IV for the Jubilee of 1475 and the contribution to the *renovatio urbis*; M. Panetta on the changing nature of devotional literature, printing, and the reading public. A. Reynolds, 'Francesco Berni, Gian Matteo Giberti, and Pietro Bembo: criticism and rivalry in Rome in the 1520s', *Italica*, 77:301–10, traces Berni's antipathies towards Bembo and Bembo's complaints when his expectations of patronage from Giberti did not materialize. A. E. Baldini, 'Tre inediti di Francesco Pucci al Cardinal nepote e a Gregorio XIV alla vigilia del suo "rientro" a Roma', *Rinascimento*, 39, 1999:157–223. *Medieval and Renaissance Venice*, ed. Ellen E. Kittell and Thomas F. Madden, Urbana, Illinois U.P., 1999, 345 pp., is dedicated to Donald E. Queller and comprises an appreciation of his contribution to Venetian studies followed by 13 essays including: G. Ruggiero, 'The abbot's concubine: lies, literature, and power at end of the Renaissance' (166–80); R. C. Davis, 'The spectacle almost fit for a king, Venice's *Guerra de' canne* of 26 July 1574' (181–212); R. Finlay, 'The myth of Venice in Guicciardini's *History of Italy*: senate orations on princes and the Republic' (294–326). Stanley Chojnacki, *Women and Men in Renaissance Venice. Twelve Essays on Patrician Society*, Baltimore, Johns Hopkins U.P., x + 370 pp., examines the 'relationship that gave coherence to the ruling class of Venice' and the 'shifting boundaries between the private realm of the family and the state's expanding efforts to set down rules for social relations'.

3. Poetry

Raffaele Girardi, *Modelli e maniere: esperienze poetiche del Cinquecento meridionale*, Bari, Palomar, 1999, 319 pp., is a collection of already published essays. Enrica Benini Clementi, *Riforma religiosa e poesia popolare a Venezia nel Cinquecento: Alessandro Caravia*, F, Olschki, ix + 315 pp. Stefano Carrai, *I precetti di Parnaso. Metrica e generi poetici nel Rinascimento italiano*, Ro, Bulzoni, 1999, 216 pp., focuses on the transformation of poetic genres in response to specific circumstances.

There are five sections: 'Lirica cortigiana' comprises essays on 15th-c. metrical experimentation and L. B. Alberti, the sonnet correspondence of F. Feliciano and G. Testa Cillenio, and metre in Boiardo's madrigals; 'Poesia d'intrattenimento' covers Poliziano's 'Ben venga maggio', courtly implications in the *Orfeo*, and Grazzini on the origins of the *canto carnascialesco*; 'Poesia pastorale' deals with the bucolic poetry of Lorenzo de' Medici and of Luigi, Luca, and Bernardo Pulci, scholarship, patronage, and the genesis of Boiardo's *pastoralia* and *pastorale*, Ariosto and the eclogue; 'Esperienze del classicismo' considers Machiavelli and the satirical epitaph, Latin and vernacular classicism in the poetry of Minturno, Marino and Horace. *Ricerche sulle selve rinascimentali*, ed. Paolo Cherchi, Ravenna, Longo, 1999, 173 pp., after an opening analysis of the genre tracing its classical antecedents and surveying its Renaissance exponents (P. Cherchi), covers: the extent of *riscrittura* (L. L. Westwater); the subject-matter and sources of a work by T. Porcacchi (S. Hill); A. Danti's rejection of classical sources, his use of Boccaccio and his reworking of the genre (S. Magnanini); the structure and scientific dimension of T. Tomai's *L'idea del giardino del mondo* (D. Pastina); the references to seven troubadors in L. Contarini's *Il vago e dilettevole giardino* (M. Ray); the link between D. da Fano and T. Garzoni (D. Papotti); the development of memory theatres and technique (L. Bolzoni). Elio Mosele, *Riflessioni teoriche e trattati di poetica tra Francia e Italia nel Cinquecento*, Fasano, Schena, 1999, 153 pp., comprises 16 essays grouped in five sections with a final *tavola rotonda*. The section 'Tra retorica e poetica', has essays by S. D'Amico on changing attitudes to Homer in the 16th c. and on how humanist theoreticians viewed him at a distance; 'Dall'epopea al romanzo' has G. Giorgi's analysis of G. B. Giraldi and G. B. Pigna on heroic narrative, leading to a wider discussion of the development of epic theory in Italy and France; and 'Tra tragedia e commedia' has P. de Capitani on the theories (combining entertainment with instruction) set out in the prefaces of plays.

Antonio Corsaro, *La regola e la licenza. Studi sulla poesia satirica e burlesca fra Cinque e Seicento*, Manziana, Vecchiarelli, 1999, 220 pp., has six well-researched detailed studies on: the complex classical and literary topoi in Ariosto's satires; the 16th-c. debate on satire and E. Bentivoglio; the *poesia burlesca* of Della Casa, which revisits the textual tradition and sets it within the context of 16th-c. comic verse; comic melancholy and the topos of self-portraiture in Michelangelo; F. Bolognetti's literary career and MSS, which assesses his themes within their social, political, and religious context; and the theory, writing, and the diffusion of satire in the early 17th c. Paolo Orvieto and Lucia Brestolini, *La poesia comico-realistica dalle origini al Cinquecento*, Ro, Carocci, 277 pp., for the 15th c. looks at the *ballata*, the *canto carnascialesco*, the *frottola* and Burchiello, while the section on the 16th c. centres on Berni and his circle with a discussion of misogynist verse, *pasquinate*, and the literary feud between Berni and Aretino. Folengo, C. Scroffa, and parody and satire on pedantry are also covered. G. Forni, 'Rassegna di studi sulla lirica del Cinquecento (1989–1999). Dal Bembo al Casa', *LItal*, 52:100–140, provides a sensitive survey of recent criticism. *Poets and Teachers: Latin Didactic Poetry and the Didactic Authority of the Latin Poet from the Renaissance to the Present*, ed. Yasmin Haskell and Philip Hardie, Bari, Levante, 1999, 211 pp., gathers 11 essays including: an introductory survey by Haskell of recent scholarship; I. Pantin on 16th-c. poetic theory and classical models for cosmological poetry; A. Nüssel on the invocation to the Muses and how in A. Paleario it is linked to discussion of the immortality of the soul; Z. Von Martels on the allegorical interpretation of G. Aurelio Augurello's *Chrysopoeia*, which should be seen as a didactic poem on the reality of alchemy; Y. Haskell on the relationship between truth and fiction in G. Fracastoro, M. Palingenio, and E. di Valvasone; G. Eatough on Fracastoro's inspiration for the *Syphilis* in Peter Martyr's *De orbe novo* and the possibility of a Neoplatonic interpretation; A. Coroleu on the uses of Poliziano's Latin poetry in the 16th-c. curriculum. Marco Villoresi, *La letteratura cavalleresca dai cicli medievali all'Ariosto*, Ro, Carocci, 231 pp., traces the development of chivalric writing through 15-c. prose and poetry and down to Luca and Luigi Pulci, Boiardo, and Ariosto. *Cantari fiabeschi arturiani*, ed. Daniela Delcorno Branca, Mi, Luni, 1999, 194 pp. *Epic Traditions in the Contemporary World. The Poetics of Community*, ed. Margaret Beissinger, Jane Tylus, and Susanne Wofford, Berkeley, California U.P., 1999, 314 pp., groups 14 essays in the sections 'On the margins of the scribal', 'From oral epic to text', 'Epic and authority', 'The boundaries of the epic performance', and 'Epic and lament; epic and pedagogy'. The volume seeks to 'provide an interdisciplinary dialogue between verbal art genres that have rarely been in dialogue: literary and epic'. The essay by J. Tylus on 'Tasso's trees' explores the link between Tasso and Virgil and the problems of universality. *Renaissance Transactions: Ariosto and Tasso*, ed. Valeria Finucci, Durham, NC, Duke U.P., 1999, 328 pp., has ten essays representing the approaches of modern critical schools to issues and controversies raised by Ariosto and Tasso concerning the nature and purpose of literature. Themes include identity, performative representation, genre and gender, social and legal anthropology, and subversive strategies.

M. Rinaldi, 'Il *Parere in difesa di Ludovico Ariosto* di Francesco Patrizi', *SPCT*, 60:81–94, examines P.'s contribution to the Ariosto–Tasso debate written in response to C. Pellegrino's *Carrafa*, setting it within the context of other works, and pointing to P.'s innovative, and anti-Aristotelian, stance. Zsuzsanna Rozsnyoi, *Dopo Ariosto. Tecniche narrative e discorsive nei poemi postariosteschi*, Ravenna, Longo, 157 pp., examines innovation and experimentation in epic poetry, and the accompanying critical debates, with reference to Alamanni's *Girone il cortese*, Giraldi Cinzio's *Ercole*, and Bernardo Tasso's *Amadigi*.

ARIOSTO. Giorgio Bárberi Squarotti and Sergio Zatti, *Ludovico Ariosto. Torquato Tasso*, Ro, Marzorati–Editalia, 302 pp., belongs to the series Letteratura Marzorati–Editalia which follows an approach combining historical and theoretical perspectives and also offering an assessment of the critical fortunes. The section on Ariosto (Bárberi Squarotti) examines the humanist elements in the *Carmina, Rime, Satire*, and comedies, and gives an analysis of the themes of the *Furioso*. Zatti on Tasso, among other things, draws on letters for biography, sees the *Rinaldo* as an engagement with Ariosto and with a previous tradition, highlights the 'musical' dimension of the *Aminta*, investigates the contemporary backdrop to the *Gerusalemme*, and gives an account of Tasso's contribution to critical theory. Julia M. Kisacky, *Magic in Boiardo and Ariosto*, NY, Peter Lang, 189 pp., points to the link between magic, *virtù*, and *fortuna*, and the different part magic plays in both poems. It is seen as less negative in Boiardo, whereas it is contrasted to the positive concepts of order, reason, and harmony in Ariosto. A more extensive analysis of contemporary beliefs in popular and learned magic would have embedded the study in the real world. The assertion that Ariosto denied the existence of magic does little to elucidate the world picture of his audience. Alexandre Doroszlai, *Ptolémée et l'hippogriffe. La géographie de l'Arioste soumise à l'épreuve des cartes*, Alessandria, Orso, 1998, 270 pp., conducts a fascinating exploration of the available cartographic resources for A.'s locations — the East, the land of Prester John, France, Paris, Europe, Hungary, the cosmos — and also investigates links with A. da Barberino. Deanna Shemek, *Ladies Errant: Wayward Women and Social Order in Early Modern Italy*, Durham, NC, Duke U.P., 1998, xii + 258 pp., consists of five case-studies which include: an assessment of the figure of Angelica, object of desire and woman with her own desires, and thus a 'precarious foundation for masculine or cultural identity'; the appropriateness of both male and female roles for Bradamante; Ariosto's position on the nature of gender identity; the intimate structural and thematic relation to Ariosto in the response of Laura Terracina in her *Discorsi sopra tutti i primi canti d'Orlando Furioso*. J. Bernard, ' "Ch'io nol lasci ne la penna": Ariosto's discourses of desire', *Italica*, 76, 1999:291–313. Franco Picchio, *Ariosto e Bacco. I codici del sacro nell'Orlando Furioso*, T, Paravia, 1999, 174 pp., offers a symbolism steeped in Neoplatonism, evangelism, Hermeticism, and heresy, centred on the figure of Bacchus and Egyptian sun worship. D. Delcorno Banca, 'L'inchiesta autunnale di Orlando', *LItal*, 52:379–99, charts the changes, with particular reference to the seasonal import, in the 1516, 1521, and 1532 versions, of cantos IX-XII of the *Furioso*. G. Sasso, 'Croce e Ariosto. L'armonia come contenuto e come forma', *La Cultura*, 37, 1999:367–410.

BATTIFERRI AMMANNATI. Laura Battiferri Ammannati, *Il primo libro delle opere toscane*, ed. Enrico Maria Guidi, Urbino, Accademia Raffaello, 183 pp.

BERNI. *Francesco Berni*, Ro, IPZS, 1999, xiv + 1229 pp., is an anthology edited and introduced by Raffaele Nigro.

BOIARDO. *Fortune and Romance: Boiardo in America*, ed. JoAnn Cavallo and Charles Ross, MRTS, 1998, 371 pp., groups 17 essays in five sections: fortune; romance; humanism and literacy; the arts in Ferrara; B.'s minor works. It offers perspectives from diverse disciplines and theoretical approaches. The section on literacy has studies of B. and Boccaccio (J. McMichaels), B.'s readers (R. F. Sorrentino), literacy (M. Sherberg), and B. and Pico della Mirandola (K. Crozier Egan). Fabio Cossutta, *Itinerarium mundi ac salutis: gli 'Amorum libri' di Matteo Maria Boiardo*, Ro, Bulzoni, 1999, 311 pp., traces B.'s stylistic development, exposing the complex process of assimilation, reflection, and reworking, and with it the work's precise structure. A detailed textual analysis shows the influence of Virgil and Dante, and the fundamental importance of Petrarch, not just for the style but for the values expressed.

BRONZINO Deborah Parker, *Bronzino: Renaissance Painter as Poet*, CUP, 233 pp., shows how the different genres in B.'s poetry (lyric and burlesque) and the disparate elements in his painting (elegance, whimsy and the bizarre, and wit) are mutually enlightening. It points to B.'s highly coded language and to his very personal voice which is different from that of contemporary artist-poets.

BRUNO. G. Aquilecchia, 'Aspetti della "poetica" bruniana', *NRLett*, 18.2, 1998:7–20.

BURCHIELLO. *I sonetti del Burchiello*, ed. Michelangelo Zaccarello, Bo, CTLin, cxxxii + 344 pp., is a critical edition of the 15th-c. vulgate.

CARITEO. Beatrice Barbiellini Amidei, *Alla luna: saggio sulla poesia del Cariteo*, F, La Nuova Italia, 1999, xv + 257 pp.

CELLINI. M. Gallucci, 'A new look at Benvenuto Cellini's poetry', *FoI*, 34:343–71, makes an important contribution to our understanding not only of C.'s anti-Petrarchan stylistic features — parody, personification, caricature, the grotesque — but also of his sexual and anti-social proclivities and of the nature of 16th-c. literacy and learning.

DELLA CASA. John B. Van Sickle, *Giovanni della Casa's Poem Book. Joannis Casae Carminum Liber, Florence 1564*, MRTS, 1999, 156 pp., provides the Latin text, a translation, a commentary, and an analysis of the collection's structure. It gives an account of his models (Propertius, Catullus, Horace) and his innovatory reworking of traditional themes, and presents Della Casa as a humanist writing in a Petrarchan mode. S. Marchesi, 'Una reminiscenza dantesca nella canzone XLVI di Giovanni della Casa', *SUm*, 13.1, 1999:67–80.

FOLENGO. Alessandro Capata, *Semper truffare paratus. Genere e ideologia nel Baldus di Folengo*, Ro, Bulzoni, 722 pp., takes a fresh approach by looking at the following themes: the link with the Spanish picaresque novel; the attitude towards the 'mondo conta-dino'; the erotic dimension; alchemy, cosmology, and astrology; and the relationship between *fantasia-follia* and *fantasia-imitazione*. *Quaderni folenghiani*, 2, 1997–1998, the proceedings of the conference 'Teofilo Folengo e la cultura Siciliana della Rinascenza', assembles 15 studies that cover religion, dialect and *lingua*, sacred and secular plays, music and the oral tradition, the publishing history of the *Hagiomachia*, and comic strategies. Salvatore Davì, *Teofilo Folengo alle Ciambre di Borgetto*, Palermo, Ila Palma, 125 pp., is a cultural biography and psychological appraisal which considers F.'s stay at the Abbey of Ciambre (1538–43) where he wrote *Palermitana, Atto della Pinta, Hagiomachia*, and *Macheronee*.

FONTE. S. Kolsky, 'Moderata Fonte's *Tredici canti del Floridoro*: women in man's genre', *RStI*, 17, 1999:165–84.

FRANCO. Veronica Franco, *Poems and Selected Letters*, ed. Ann Rosalind Jones and Margaret F. Rosenthal, Chicago U.P., 1998, 300 pp., has an introduction which links biography to the poems and letters, and discusses the sources of the *capitoli* and the project of the Venier circle to translate, and write commentaries on, Latin love poetry. The complex nature of the epistolary production is set out, and the letters and poems are critically analysed.

GUARINI. Battista Guarini, *Il pastor fido*, ed. Elisabetta Selmi, Venice, Marsilio, 1999, 475 pp., has an excellent commentary and an introduction by G. Baldassarri that discusses 16th-c. literary theories.

MEDICI. Lorenzo de' Medici, *Rime spirituali; La rappresentazione di San Giovanni e Paolo*, ed. Bernard Toscani, Ro, Storia e Letteratura, ciii + 84 pp.

MOLZA. Francesco Maria Molza, *Elegiae et alia*, ed. Rossana Sodano, T, Res, 1999, 202 pp., gives the Latin texts of established and attributed poems, based on the Codex Borgiano in the Vatican, listing the variants of previous editions. The critical notes list the echoes of Virgil, Tibullus, Propertius, Martial, Ovid, Horace, Pontano, and Poliziano.

MORRA. Isabella Morra, *Rime*, ed. Maria Antonietta Grignani, Ro, Salerno, 111 pp.

POLIZIANO. E. Curti, 'Dantismi e memoria della *Commedia* nelle *Stanze* del Poliziano', *LItal*, 52:530–68, gives a thorough textual analysis of Poliziano's debt and of how he transformed the language of Dante. G. Mazzotta, 'Neoplatonismo e politica nell'*Orfeo* di Poliziano', *ItQ*, 143–46:151–64, sees the themes of chaos and death as a reflection of the political instability of late 15th-c. Florence. G. Morelli, 'Per la cronologia degli *Adnotamenta* del Merula ai *Miscellanea* del Poliziano', *SPCT*, 60:21–49, conducts a detailed analysis of the extant documents and earlier historiography in order to date the original writing of the *Adnotamenta* and their subsequent reworking and publication.

PULCI. *Luigi Pulci e i quattordici cantari*, ed. and introd. Ermanno Cavazzati, ann. Daniela Marcheschi, Ro, IPZS, xxx + 1182 pp.

ROTA. Bernardino Rota, *Rime*, ed. Luca Milite, Parma, Guanda, lxxxvii + 857 pp., is an exemplary critical edition with an introduction that assesses R.'s position in the development of Petrarchism. It points to his debt to the 15th c. in terms of structure, language, and form, and to the importance of humanism (especially Pontano) and the work of his contemporaries Bembo, Della Casa, Ariosto, and Di Costanzo.

SANNAZARO. Iacopo Sannazaro, *Lo gliommero napoletano: Licinio, se 'l mio inzegno*, Na, Libreria Dante & Descartes, 1999, 43 pp.

TASSO. *Torquato Tasso e la cultura estense*, 3 vols, ed. Gianni Venturi, F, Olschki, 1999, 358, 361–857, 861–1460 pp., groups 75 essays in 11 sections: 'La *Liberata* e la nuova forma epica', with studies on the nature of epic poetry, war and heroes, women as magi, fiction and reality, castles and deserts, and repetitions and ambiguity; 'I dialoghi tassiani e la forma del dialogo', with studies on ethics, dialectic and poetry, and formal analysis; 'L'universo delle *Rime* tassiane', reviewing recent scholarship and including studies on a critical edition of the *Rime stravaganti* and the *Rime della crisi*; 'La prosa del Tasso e l'universo del sapere', covering Bembo and T., T. and Lucrezia Marinella, T. and Della Casa, T., the Counter-Reformation and classicism, and T. and Trissino; 'La corte e la città all'epoca del Tasso'; 'Tasso e le arti figurative del suo tempo', with studies on colour in T. and the iconography of Clorinda; 'L'esperienza architettonica al tempo del Tasso'; 'Il teatro del Tasso', with essays on the *Aminta* and 16th-c. pastoral, on the production of *Aminta* on the island of the Belvedere in 1573, and on funereal topoi in T.; 'Musica e parola'; 'I modi della spiritualità'.

Torquato Tasso, *Giudicio sovra la Gerusalemme riformata*, ed. Claudio Gigante, Ro, Salerno, lii + 249 pp. Claudio Vinti, *L'Amyntas de Pinô:*

le Tasse en France, Na, ESI, 1997, 178 pp. Franco Fortini, *Dialoghi col Tasso*, T, Bollati Boringhieri, 1999, 189 pp., has four essays: 'La *Gerusalemme liberata*' reviews T.'s lifelong obsession with the poem, its changing versions, its language, and T.'s psychological make-up; 'L'arme pietose' examines his allusions to the writings of Livy and Machiavelli; 'Tasso epico' looks at narrative structure, T.'s concern to please his audience, the psychological make-up of his characters, and the poem's language and critical fortunes; 'Lettura radiofonica della *Gerusalemme liberata*' is the text of a broadcast. Luigi Montella, *Seguendo d'amor le tracce. Studi di letteratura italiana dal Cinquecento all'Ottocento*, Salerno, Edisud, 1999, 191 pp., includes a study of poetic theory, and of syntactical, lexical, and metrical structures, in Bernardo T.'s *Amadigi* and Torquato T.'s *Rinaldo*, showing how Torquato's vision and aims differed from his father's. Torquato Tasso, *Jerusalem Delivered — Gerusalemme liberata*, ed. and trans. Anthony M. Esolen, Baltimore, Johns Hopkins U.P., offers a thorough introduction tackling T.'s relationship to Ariosto, his struggle with the problems of truth, authority, and religion, and notes on the characters. Andrea Gareffi, *L'Aminta di Torquato Tasso difeso e illustrato a Giusto Fontanini*, Manziana, Vecchiarelli, cxliii + 391 pp., is a facsimile of the 1730 Venice edition, a work of great erudition and the first commentary on the *Aminta* to address the theatrical nature of the work. Gareffi provides a scholarly introduction and a useful bio-bibliographical supplement to Fontanini's index. D. Gibbons, 'Tasso petroso: beyond Petrarchan and Dantean metaphor in the *Gerusalemme Liberata*', *ISt*, 55 : 83–98, concludes that in the *petroso* style, and in 'Così nel mio parlar' in particular, T. seems to have found a practical and acceptable lyric model of *asprezza*, the quality he felt most suitable for the epic. F. D'Alessandro, 'Dall'*Amadigi* al *Floridante*: le tracce di Torquato Tasso nell'opera del padre', *RIL*, 131, 1997[1999]:345–93. S. Miano, 'Le postille di Torquato Tasso alle *Annotazioni* di Alessandro Piccolomini alla *Poetica* di Aristotele', *Aevum*, 74:721–50. M. Corradini, 'Torquato Tasso e il dibattito di metà Cinquecento sul poema epico', *Testo*, 40:159–70. M. L. Doglio, 'Tasso "architetto" dell'"epica poesia" nel *Dialogo* di Camillo Pellegrino', *GSLI*, 176, 1999:481–502. C. Gigante, 'La *Vita di Torquato Tasso* di Giovan Pietro d'Alessandro', *ib.*, 177:59–70. N. Bianchi, 'Tasso lettore di Dante: teoresi retorica e prassi poetica', *MR*, 12, 1998[1999]:223–48.

TORELLI.   Pomponio Torelli, *La Merope*, ed. Vincenzo Guercio, Ro, Bulzoni, 1999, 364 pp., is a critical edition with full apparatus and commentary. The introduction looks at the fable of Merope in the 16th c., notes the distinctive nature of T.'s version, when compared to those of A. Cavallerino and G. Liviera, and brings out its striking political and religious dimension with reference to Seneca and Machiavelli.

4. THEATRE

Agostino Beccari, Alberto Lollio, and Agostino Argenti, *Favole*, ed. Fulvio Pevere, T, Res, 1999, xxxii + 350 pp., has a scholarly introduction that takes as its starting point Guarini's judgement that Beccari's play gave birth to a new theatrical genre, the *tragicommedia*, and that the pastoral fable was directly descended from the eclogue. It then points to more complex lines of transmission and to the way the three fables *Sacrificio*, *Aretusa*, and *Lo Sfortunato* exemplify essential features of the new tradition. *Storia del teatro moderno e contemporaneo*, ed. Roberto Alonge and Guido Davico Bonino, 1: *La nascita del teatro moderno: Cinquecento – Seicento*, T, Einaudi, xxv + 1346 pp., is the first of four projected volumes. Gloria Martellucci, *I luoghi del teatro*, Palermo, Sellerio, 1999, 231 pp., makes a valuable contribution to our understanding of the space for staging spectacles and theatrical productions. It shows that the concern for spectacle was closely linked to urban development and the part played by theatre and spectacle in public life from classical times into the Renaissance. It traces spectacle as a rite, from public display of power under the Normans to the development of a new concept linked to the city under Frederick II, and shows how the rich tradition of religious and humanist spectacle spilled over into town planning. It investigates the first civic theatre in the 16th c. and the urban renewal of Palermo along mythological themes. Giovanni Isgrò, *La forma siciliana del teatro*, Palermo, Ila Palma, 190 pp., points to the late development of a distinctive Sicilian theatre in the late 16th c. and to the influences of elite culture and theatrical entrepreneurs in Palermo. It analyses the urban setting and Sicilian representations in Folengo's *Atto della Pinta* and the specifically Sicilian character of T. Aversa's *La notti di Palermu*. There is an assessment of Jesuit theatre, popular theatre for feast days and festivals, and the tradition of puppet theatre. *Teatri barocchi. Tragedie, commedie, pastorali nella drammaturgia europea fra '500 e '600*, ed. Silvia Carandini, Ro, Bulzoni, xxx + 602 pp., has 26 essays in three sections: 'Il piacere obliquo: esperienze del tragico nel teatro barocco', with essays by P. C. Rivoltella on the theory of *piacere obliquo* and sacrifice in tragedy with particular reference to Castelvetro and R. Tessari on the religious connotations in Della Valle's *Iudit*; 'Filosofia in commedia, Giordano Bruno e il teatro Barocco', with G. Aquilecchia on the many aspects of the *commedia regolare* in Bruno's London dialogues, M. Plaisance on the esoteric characters in Bruno's *Candelaio* and Della Porta's *Lo astrologo*, R. Camerlengo on a link between Bruno and Marlowe, and H. Gatti on Bruno's *Candelaio* and Ben Jonson's *Alchemist*, D. Dalla Valle on the success of the *Candelaio* in French 16th-c. theatre, and A. Gareffi on Bruno's dedication in the *Candelaio*; and 'La ninfa e il bosco: ambienti pastorali nel teatro barocco'.

BRUNO. M. Canova, 'Il caos come metamorfosi nel *Candelaio* di Giordano Bruno', *IR*, 7, 1999:57–78, sheds new light on the allegories of the text, identifying themes already present in the *De umbris idearum*. G. Aquilecchia, 'Componenti teatrali nei dialoghi italiani di Giordano Bruno', *BrC*, 5, 1999:265–76. Four papers on the *Candelaio* were read at the presentation of He Lea Liang's Chinese translation of the play, during the 1999 Beijing Bruno conference, and are published in the *acta Per Giordano Bruno* (see section 1, GENERAL, above): N. Ordine, 'Introduzione alla traduzione cinese del *Candelaio*' (170–95); H. L. Liang, '"Una candela che chiarisce certe ombre dell'idee": discussione su temi e struttura del *Candelaio*' (196–216); L. Xianggan, 'Giordano Bruno e lo spirito del *Candelaio*' (217–31); and R. Zhenming, 'Dalle tenebre dell'ignoranza ai lumi della ragione: la lezione di Giordano Bruno e del suo *Candelaio* per i cinesi di oggi' (232–42).

POLIZIANO. Antonia Tissoni Benvenuti, *L'Orfeo del Poliziano, con il testo critico dell'originale e delle successive forme teatrali*, Padua, Antenore, xiii + 223 pp., a revised edition of a work published in 1986, has the *Fabula de Orpheo* as an appendix.

RUZANTE. Ronnie Ferguson, *The Theatre of Angelo Beolco (Ruzante). Text, Context, and Performance*, Ravenna, Longo, 249 pp., is a thorough study which gives a full list of MSS and 16th-c. editions with notes on the textual tradition and a critical exposition of the play. There follow chapters on reception, genre, language, stagecraft, and the ethics of the natural. M. Canova, 'Lettura antropologica della "Lettera all'Alvarotto" di Ruzante', *REI*, 45, 1999:85–94.

MACHIAVELLI. J. Tylus, 'Theater and its social uses: Machiavelli's *Mandragola* and the spectacle of infamy', *RQ*, 53:656–86, is a challenging study that brings together the story of the Sabines, Ovid's interpretation, Quattrocento concepts of theatre, and the play as a rejection of humanist idealization.

5. PROSE

Maria Luisa Doglio, *L'arte delle lettere. Idea e pratica della scrittura epistolare tra Quattro e Seicento*, Bo, Il Mulino, 236 pp., is a collection of ten studies which do much to clarify the different genres (the letter as novella, as manifesto) and the reasons for writing. It examines the epistolary language of humanists and bureaucrats, as well as the *lettera publica / lettera privata* in Machiavelli. Nicola Longo, *Letteratura e lettere. Indagine nell'epistolografia cinquecentesca*, Ro, Bulzoni, 1999, 146 pp., has five essays which contribute much to our understanding of this literary genre by pointing to rules, influences, and the way in which, and why, letters were prized, collected, and published. The topics covered include: rhetoric and writing in a letter of P. Cortese; the literary system in the *Lettere famigliari* of G. Parabosco; word and body in the letters of S. Guazzo; *scrittura famigliare* in S. Guazzo; and letter-writing in the 16th c. B. Figliuolo, 'Tre lettere inedite di Feo Belcari a Ottone Niccolini', *LItal*, 52:265–71, gives the text of letters that reflect Belcari's narrative style and add to the scant biographical data in our possession.

N. Marcelli, 'Favole, parabole, istorie. Le forme della scrittura novellistica dal Medioevo al Rinascimento', *ASI*, 157, 1999:593–604. M. Cottino Jones, 'Princesses, kings, and the fantastic: a re-vision of the language of representation in the Renaissance', *ItQ*, 143–46:173–84, examines Straparola's description of his stories as *favole* rather than *novelle* and sees them as 'focused on constructing a middle-class, popular imaginary world inspired by the instinctual and the fantastic, rather than by the rational or the logical'.

ALTIERI. Marco Antonio Altieri, *Li baccanali*, ed. Laura Onofri, Ro, Istituto Storico Italiano per il Medio Evo, lii + 416 pp., is an important source for the history of Rome in the period 1510–17, charting the gradual centralization of papal power over that of the civic authorities. This is a scholarly edition, with full critical apparatus, following the MSS in the Rome's Biblioteca Nazionale and Vatican Library, of a collection of letters, short stories, and orations (organized as an *epistolario*) with an appendix of Latin documents.

ARETINO. Pietro Aretino, *Lettere*, ed. Gian Mario Anselmi, Ro, Carocci, 244 pp., is a selection organized under the themes: 'amore'; 'amicizia'; 'arte e letteratura'; 'politica'; 'costumi'; 'liberalità'. The introduction examines A.'s epistolary activity, assesses critical reception, and looks at the editions, with a commentary by E. Menetti and F. Tomasi. Pietro Aretino, *Lettere*, ed. Paolo Procaccioli, Ro, Salerno, 535 pp., is the fourth vol. of the seven-vol. 'Edizione Nazionale' of A.'s correspondence. L'Arétin, *Ragionamenti*, ed. Giovanni Aquilecchia, 2 vols, Paris, Les Belles Lettres, 1998, cix + 212, xv + 317 pp., has a philological essay by Aquilecchia, reviewing the textual tradition and offering some new corrections, and this is followed by the Italian text and French translations, with useful notes by P. Larivaille, and a postface by Nuccio Ordine.

BENCIVENNI. *Il trattato de la Spera volgarizzato da Zucchero Bencivenni*, ed. Gabriella Ronchi, F, Accademia della Crusca, 1999, 213 pp., is a

critical edition of a translation of Sacrobosco's *De Sphaera*, a work
reprinted many times during the Renaissance and which became part
of the canon quoted by the *Vocabolario della Crusca*.

BERNARDINO DA SIENA. Bernardino da Siena, *Favole: lettura in
linguaggio corrente delle prediche a sfondo pedagogico-didattico tenute a Siena
nell'estate del 1427*, ed. Cinzia Bei, Massarosa, Del Bucchia, 1999,
123 pp., includes an appendix containing the original vernacular text.

CASTIGLIONE. Amedeo Quondam, *'Questo povero cortegiano'. Castiglione, il libro, la storia*, Ro, Bulzoni, 647 pp., is difficult to come to grips
with, given its fragmentary structure, but it provides a great deal of
documentary material which allows us to track the genesis, development, corrections, radical reworkings, and publishing vicissitudes of
the *Cortegiano*. J. Cavallo, 'Joking matters: politics and dissimulation
in Castiglione's *Book of the Courtier'*, *RQ*, 53:402–24, explores the
themes of tension and animosity by examining the role of joke-telling
within the context of different regional and political affiliations.
S. Kolsky, 'Learning virtue, teaching politics. Some notes on Book
Four of the *Cortegiano'*, *FoI*, 34:5–29, examines the themes of love,
moral virtues, and princely power in relation to the previous three
books and tests their internal coherence and significance, whilst
pointing to discontinuities and gaps. D. Quint, 'Courtier, prince,
lady: the design of the *Book of the Courtier'*, *ItQ*, 143–46:185–95, points
to Castiglione's assessment of women as a civilizing influence.

CORTESE. Giulio Cortese, *Prose*, ed. Maurice Slawinski, T, Res,
xxxvi + 138 pp., gives the texts of *Dell'imitazione e dell'invenzione, Delle
figure, Avertimenti nel poetare, Regole per fuggire i vizi dell'elocuzione, Lettera
dell'uso delle vocali, Regole per formare epitafi, Dell'ingratitudine*. The
introduction discusses the intense critical debate on the relationship
between the poet and writings on poetry at the end of the 16th c., to
which Cortese made a significant and original contribution.

DE GUEVARA. Antonio de Guevara, *Avviso de' favoriti e dottrina di
cortigiani*, ed. Eduardo Creus Visiers, Alessandria, Orso, 1999,
265 pp., reproduces Vicenso Bondi's translation from the Spanish
(Venice, 1544) which, when compared to Castiglione's *Cortegiano*, is
remarkable for differences rather than similarities.

EQUICOLA. *La redazione manoscritta del 'Libro de natura de amore' di
Mario Equicola*, ed. Laura Ricci, Ro, Bulzoni, 1999, 635 pp., gives a
full description of the MS and publishing tradition, an analysis of the
literary and philosophical issues, and an assessment of Equicola and
the *lingua cortigiana romana*. The linguistic, syntactic, and stylistic issues
are treated with full critical apparatus, and there is a glossary of
difficult terms.

FORTUNIO. Giovanni Francesco Fortunio, *Regole grammaticali della
volgar lingua*, ed. Claudio Marazzini and Simone Fornara, Pordenone,

Accademia San Marco, 1999, 201 pp., is a facsimile of the *editio princeps* (1516) of a very rare work. The introduction discusses the work's links with classical and scholastic grammars, and its methodology, with its particular use of examples in the Tuscan vernacular. There are full references to the sources, especially Dante, Petrarch, Boccaccio, and Bembo.

GIOVIO. Paolo Giovio, *Ritratti degli uomini illustri*, ed. Carlo Caruso, Palermo, Sellerio, 1999, 249 pp., is a well-produced volume that presents 20 *ritratti* with the Latin text taken from the *editio princeps*. The excellent scholarly introduction reviews G.'s life and literary production and gives a critical assessment of the 1972 edition of R. Meregazzi.

GUICCIARDINI. Francesco Guicciardini, *Compendio della Cronica di Froissart*, ed. Paola Moreno, Bo, CTLin, 1999, lxxxix + 166 pp., is a scrupulously researched critical edition that gives the text of the MS *Cronica del Froxarte* (with autograph corrections) in the Archivio Guicciardini. There is a full apparatus that includes the identification of the sources, an account of the approaches to history in G. and Froissart, and an analysis of the language and rhetoric. The text, with full notes, is followed by a comparative table of the *Chroniques* and the G. text. Athanasios Moulakis, *Republican Realism in Renaissance Florence. Francesco Guicciardini's Discorso di Logrogno*, Lanham, Rowman and Littlefield, 1998, 171 pp., followed by a translation of the *Discorso*, points to G.'s innovative political stance as a move away from medieval rather than humanist standpoints and asserts that the *Discorso* is a 'vivid expression of Florentine realist constitution'.

LEONARDO. Laura Gioppo and Paola Redemagni, *Il codice Atlantico di Leonardo da Vinci nell'edizione Hoepli 1894–1904 curata dall'Accademia dei Lincei*, Mi, Anthelios, 207 pp., investigates the Hoepli text before the Codex's restoration in the 1960s and has three sections: the first on the history of the Codex, which reconstructs Pompeo Leoni's intervention on the text; the second on Leonardo's methodology and scientific interests; the third a biographical study of Leonardo.

MACHIAVELLI. Niccolò Machiavelli, *Il Principe, con un saggio su Machiavelli politico di Luigi Firpo*, T, Tallone, 1998, 171 pp., is a beautifully printed volume which follows the text established by F. Chabod (1924) and includes the *Descrizione del modo tenuto dal duca Valentino*, following the Casella text (1929). Firpo's essay emphasizes the precise nature of Machiavelli's methodology in searching for examples and the reasons why some were chosen deliberately from the pre-Christian era. It examines his anti-religious observations and sees him as rejecting the world of intellectual *letterati* for that of the socially committed *volgare*. He is seen as belonging to a mercantile society where risk and experimentation were essential elements and where *arte* had precise connotations. It also gives an account of the stances of Croce and Gramsci and discusses the reception of the *Principe* after 1532. Niccolò Machiavelli, *Ritratti e rapporti diplomatici*, ed. Corrado Vivanti, Ro, Editori Riuniti, 126 pp., discusses the nature of the ambassador and the development of a new genre, the diplomatic report, within the context of the changing political, social, and cultural interests of governments and states. There follows an analysis of M.'s diplomatic missions and the particular importance of his experience of, and reflections on, Cesare Borgia. Francesco Nitti, *Leone X e la sua politica*, ed. Stefano Palmieri, Na, Istituto Italiano per gli Studi Storici, 1998, reprints the edition of 1892 together with the 1893 article on the same theme, the review by Croce and the obituary by O. Tommasini. *Benedetto Croce, Prima del Machiavelli. Una difesa di Re Ferrante I di Napoli per il violato trattato di pace del 1486 col Papa*, Na, Istituto Italiano per gli Studi Storici, 81 pp., is a facsimile of the 1944 Laterza edition. Lucio Villari, *Niccolò Machiavelli*, Casale Monferrato, Piemme, 240 pp., is a biography with no critical apparatus. Emanuela Scarpa, *Intorno a Machiavelli*, Verona, Fiorini, 274 pp., consists of ten scholarly studies which contribute to our understanding of M. and the reception of his ideas. Topics include: M.'s attitude to Petrarch; M.'s poetry; M. and Erasmus; a detailed analysis of the MS tradition of the first *Decennale*; an epigram attributed to M.; the presence of M. 'comico' in Doni's *Marmi*; M. in a legal dialogue of F. Sansovino; the importance of M. in the Veneto assessed through the writings, annotations, and books of Tomaso di Marcantonio Contarini; plagiarism of M. in a dialogue of G. M. Memmo; and M.'s first political writings. Hanna Fenichel Pitkin, *Fortune is a Woman. Gender and Politics in the Thought of Niccolò Machiavelli*, Chicago U. P., 1999, 374 pp., has a new afterthought to the text of the 1984 edition in which the author reflects on the critical reception of her original work and offers further ideas on the images of fortune and the interpretations of A. J. Panel, R. D. Masters, and W. Brown. Eugenio Ballabio, *Machiavelli e la penitenza: la duplice personalità del segretario fiorentino*, Massarosa, Del Bucchia, 59 pp., includes the text of his *Exhortatione alla penitenza*. J. L. Hairston, 'Skirting the issue: Machiavelli's Caterina Sforza', *RQ*, 53:687–712, examines the skirt-lifting episode in contemporary writings to uncover two quite different traditions. It demonstrates, by examining the *Historie fiorentine* and *Discorsi*, how such an act made good theatre but had little political sense. M. C. Figorilli, ' "Odio" e "rovina" in Machiavelli: una lettura del II libro delle *Istorie fiorentine*', *RLI*, 104:373–87, examines M.'s methodology with respect to his source materials and the way he adopts a strategy 'con cui veicolare la sua visione storiografica di natura politico-antropologica'.

MASUCCIO SALERNITANO. Luigi Reina, *Masuccio Salernitano: letteratura e società nel Novellino*, Salerno, Edisud, 2000, 237 pp., is an updated edition of a work first published in 1979.

MERICI. Angela Merici, *Lettere del segretario 1540–1546*, ed. Elisa Tarolli, Mi, Ancora, 160 pp., represent transcriptions from MSS, and Italian versions, of letters written by Gabriele Cozzano, the former secretary of Merici, founder of the Order of S. Orsola, which give an insight into her preoccupation with religious and social issues.

MIARI. Clemente Miari, *Cronaca bellunese dal 1382 al 1412*, ed. Paolo Doglioni, Istituto Bellunese di Ricerche Sociali e Culturali, 1999, 213 pp., was written by a canon of Belluno cathedral who had studied at Padua. The subject-matter ranges from social and domestic events, or the purchase of reliquaries and MSS, to the carrying out of horrific death penalties, and journeys.

MOROSINI. *The Morosini Codex. Vol. 1: to the Death of Andrea Dandolo (1354)*, ed. Michele Pietro Ghezzo, John R. Melville-Jones, and Andrea Rizzi, Padua, Unipress, 1999, xxi + 151 pp., gives the original text with facing English translation of a work written by Antonio Morosini in the first part of the 15th c. As it is part chronicle, part journal / diary, and thus belongs to more than one genre, it should be of interest to scholars of literature, language, and history.

MUZIO. Girolamo Muzio, *Lettere*, ed. Anna Maria Negri, Alessandria, Orso, lxxii + 360 pp., has an excellent detailed commentary and indexes. The introduction addresses the question of the first edition seen through the press by Muzio and the Riccardiana MS 2115, and the censorship of the posthumous edition of Sermartelli (1590). The introduction examines the structure, organized according to theme, the links to Cicero, the humanist influences, and the tradition of letters in the *volgare*.

PASQUALI ALIDOSI. Giovanni Nicolò Pasquali Alidosi, *Istruttione delle cose notabili della città di Bologna*, Bo, Forni, 1999, xxiii, 228 pp., is a facsimile of the 1621 edition printed by Tebaldini.

SANNAZARO. Carlo Vecce, *Gli zibaldoni di Jacopo Sannazaro*, Messina, Sicania, 1998, 225 pp., is a valuable study of humanist methodology, which not only indicates, with attentive scholarship, the impact made by the discovery of new texts and translations from the Greek, but also evokes the spirit that moved such endeavours: the personal engagement to understand the past in order to produce something new for the future.

SASSETTI. Filippo Sassetti, *Vita di Francesco Ferrucci*, ed. Vanni Bramante, T, Res, 71 pp., assesses the Renaissance vogue of biography and discussions on the subject in the Accademia degli Alterati, and sets out the literary strategies and techniques of the genre. It offers an explanation for the metamorphoses of Ferrucci as a heroic symbol after his death in terms of the political ramifications of the affair vis-à-vis Medici power and domination.

SEVERINO. *Felice et divoto ad terrasancta viagio facto per Roberto de Sancto Severino (1458–1459)*, ed. Maria Cavaglià and Alda Rossebastiano, Alessandria, Orso, 1999, 353 pp., gives the text, with glossary, of this lively account by a noble Milanese mercenary from MS 1723 in Bologna University library. The introduction gives a full description of the MS tradition with a discussion of the language.

SIMLER. Iosia Simler, *Commentario delle Alpi*, ed. Carlo Carena, Locarno, Dadò, 1998, 158 pp., gives the text of a work first published in 1574 as *De alpibus commentarium*, which makes use of classical authors and humanistic learning to structure the material. The extensive introduction by M. Milanesi analyses Simler's cultural background and learning and sets out the methodology adopted.

STRAPAROLA. Giovanfrancesco Straparola, *Le piacevoli notti*, ed. Donato Pirovano, 2 vols, Ro, Salerno, lxix + 877 pp.

TAPIA. Carlo Tapia, *Trattato dell'abondanza*, ed. Gaetano Sabatini, Lanciano, Rocco Carabba, 1998, viii + 107 pp., has an introduction that includes a biography, reviews T.'s writings, and gives an analysis of the *trattato*, written in 1594, which discusses natural and supernatural phenomena that affect the availability of food, and man's need of recourse to God.

TASSO. Torquato Tasso, *Il forno, overo della nobiltà. Il forno secondo, overo della nobiltà*, ed. Stefano Prandi, F, Le Lettere, 1999, 277 pp., has full critical apparatus with a commentary and introduction that sets out the distinctive features of the different versions of T.'s major rewriting and restructuring of the text with an assessment of T.'s theories on the Renaissance debate on nobility, especially relating to the topoi of the patron, fate and ability.

SEICENTO

By LETIZIA PANIZZA, *Royal Holloway College, London*, and DOMENICO
CHIODO, *University of Turin*
(This survey covers the years 1999 and 2000)

I. GENERAL

Andrea Battistini, *Il barocco*, Ro, Salerno, 330 pp., surveys the main
aspects of high culture of the Baroque in Italy: from painting to
sculpture, theatre to rhetoric, and architecture to music. The author
argues that contemporary scholars can appreciate more than those of
earlier generations characteristic features of the Baroque such as love
of contradiction and paradox, of hyperbole and the grotesque, and
the acceptance of uncertainty. The emergence of the collector on a
grand scale and the encyclopaedist are also considered, as well as
themes such as the world as theatre, the search for nature's secrets,
and the obsession with death. Stefania Buccini, *Sentimento della morte
dal barocco al declino dei lumi*, Ravenna, Longo, 211 pp., carries forward
into the 17th, 18th and early 19th c. the earlier study of Alberto
Tenenti on the 'sentimento della morte' in the Renaissance, though
here there is no corresponding 'amore della vita'. The pervasiveness
of macabre themes is a distinguishing feature of erotic poetry,
religious/devotional texts, and libertine narratives, not to mention
high art and more lowly emblem-books. In medicine, one often finds
a scientific study of death as in the dissection of the cadaver, rather
than a study of illness, counterbalanced, however, by a proliferation
of illustrated treatises on the *ars moriendi*, with their advice from the
clergy on diminishing anxieties about the afterlife. In art, B. argues,
preoccupation with death results in greater realism, such as that
found in Caravaggio; while the libertine Accademia degli Incogniti is
represented in B.'s study by Cesare Cremonini, Francesco Pona,
Francesco Carmeni, Giovan Francesco Loredan, and above all,
Ferrante Pallavicino, who describes his own imprisonment in Avignon
as a kind of death.

L. Borean, 'Appunti per una storia del collezionismo a Venezia nel
Seicento: la pinacoteca di Lorenzo Delfin', *SV*, 38, 1999:259–91,
documents the interest in the Seicento in forming collections of
paintings, sculpture, and other *objets d'art* by studying the gallery of
this wealthy Venetian senator. A facsimile reproduction of Francesco
Pona, *Sileno, overo delle bellezze del luogo*, with notes by Sergio Marinelli
and Ennio Sandal, Verona, Cierre Edizioni, 1999, 83 pp., gives us
another facet of this Venetian physician, satirical novelist, and
member of the Accademia degli Incogniti. Here, in dialogue, he

provides a description of the gardens, villa architecture, and *objets d'art* of a famous collector, Count Giacomo Giusti, as they were in 1620. The interlocutors reveal the taste of the period in their comments. A. Colantuono, 'Poussin's *Osservazioni sopra la pittura:* notes or aphorisms?', *StSec*, 41:285–312, challenges the orthodoxy laid down by Anthony Blunt that these fragments were not the original precepts but merely notes from his reading. The author returns to the words of P.'s biographer, G. P. Bellori, that Poussin in Rome was writing a theoretical work in Italian — abandoned around 1650 — and argues from other evidence that P. was explicitly following the style of Leonardo da Vinci's aphorisms.

Figure à l'italienne. Métaphores, équivoques et pointes dans la littérature maniériste et baroque, ed. Danielle Boillet and Alain Godard, Paris, Université Paris III Sorbonne Nouvelle, 1999, x + 348 pp., is an impressive collection of eight essays from the Centre Interuniversitaire de Recherche sur la Renaissance Italienne, showing the rich fruits a tough application of literary analysis based on close textual readings can yield. The authors and their texts are: A. Godard (Torquato Tasso's dialogue, 'Il Conte, overo de le imprese'), B. Concolino Mancini (Girolamo Bargagli's *La pellegrina*), F. Decroisette (Giambattista Basile, *Il cunto de li cunti*), S. Fabrizio-Costa (sacred and secular oratory as theatre), E. Ardissino (Matteo Peregrini, *Delle acutezze*), P. A. Frare (Emanuele Tesauro's *Idea dell'arguta et ingegnosa elocuzione*, and the relationship between equivocation and lying).

M. Cottino-Jones, 'Literary-critical developments in sixteenth and seventeenth-century Italy', pp. 566–77 of *The Cambridge History of Literary Criticism*, III, *The Renaissance*, ed. Glyn P. Norton, CUP, 1999, briefly surveys developments in the 'questione della lingua' and debates on Aristotle's *Poetics*: the former involve overturning the grip of classicism on contemporary culture, while the latter see the rise of the *meraviglioso* (Tasso and Marino) together with *concettismo* as the most representative baroque poetics. P. B. Diffley, ' "Uncouth words in disarray": a reassessment of Paolo Beni's critique of the Vocabolario della Crusca', *StSec*, 40, 1999:31–56, presents Beni as a 'modernizer' in conflict with an archaizing Accademia della Crusca bent on limiting literary vocabulary to Trecento practice and Florentine authors. Beni was aware of linguistic developments, which he saw as positive, and also wished to resist the cultural hegemony of Tuscany implied in the Crusca's choices.

Quinto Marini, *Frati barocchi*, Modena, Mucchi, 301 pp., focuses on a distinguishing feature of Counter-Reformation cultural life: the presence of learned, prolific members of religious orders positioned at centres of power and intellectual influence like the court, academies, schools, universities, and publishing houses. They exercised most known genres with consummate rhetorical skills in the dissemination of Catholic, or at least moralistic, ideology. Marini considers: Anton Giulio Brignole Sale (19–62 and 63–112), who late in life became a Jesuit famed for sacred oratory after writing novels, dialogues, pamphlets, and comedies, some of which explore the need for role-playing and dissimulation in social and court life (his most famous novel is a religious romance about Mary Magdalen); the priest Giovanni Ambrosio Marini (113–51) who wrote the most popular novel of the century, *Calloandro fedele*, to which Marini applies the expression 'inviluppati laberinti' to describe the inextricable mixture of romance, adventure, intrigue, epic, and comedy that fortunately ends in matrimony; Angelico Aprosio da Ventimiglia (153–79), Augustinian, famed bibliophile, and literary polemicist, who spent twenty years implacably arguing against the poetry of Marino (a bitter misogynist, he also crossed swords with Arcangela Tarabotti over her rebuttal of attacks on women's fashion, and may have left Venice after she succeeded in persuading the censors to forbid the publication of his diatribes against her); Francesco Fulvio Frugoni (181–217), Minim friar of S. Francesco da Paola, who kept close to the Grimaldi court at Monaco, where his admiration for the widowed aristocrat Aurelia Spinola inspired novels of romantic intrigue extolling, Marini believes, her heroic virtues, and who also revived political and social satire to bite the vices of the age in his *Cane di Diogene*, and even more successfully, in his *Ritratti critici*, modelled on Theophrastus; for the Jesuit Paolo Segneri (219–64), finally, M. offers a fine study of the development of his biography which, in the interests of the Order in Italy, transformed him into an ideal missionary and saint.

Gregory Hanlon, *Early Modern Italy 1550–1800*, Houndmills, Macmillan, 444 pp., challenges the usual periodization by centuries, and for the Seicento makes a division at 1620. He defines a political and cultural 'high summer', from 1550–1620, and places a broad and long decline from 1620 to 1730. The book deals with all aspects of social and cultural life, and affords a new slant to viewing literary production. Periodization within the Seicento in the specific case of Genoa is addressed in E. Graziosi, 'Cesura per il secolo dei Genovesi: Anton Giulio Brignole Sale', *StSec* 41 : 27–87, which argues with great aplomb that there are two contrasting phases and that Brignole Sale was a leading force in both. In the first, Genoa was the Italian capital where the new literary tastes typifying the baroque developed and whence they spread to other Italian centres; Brignole Sale brought cohesion and direction to the lay, aristocratic community, set up publishing projects, and was an indefatigable writer of satire and comedy. The break came with a catastrophic plague bringing death to 40,000 inhabitants, and with the Jesuits (whom Brignole Sale joined in 1649) assuming cultural and, to an increasing degree, political leadership. Brignole Sale's asceticism now led to the censorship and destruction of books and an undermining of the continuity of the former ruling families. 'L'antica capitale si era trasformata in una provincia', as G. comments.

GENDER STUDIES. *Women in Italian Renaissance Culture and Society*, ed. Letizia Panizza, EHRC, xxi + 523 pp., contains three articles relevant to the 17th c.: F. Medioli, 'To take or not to take the veil: selected Italian case histories, the Renaissance and after' (122–27), which finds evidence for some nuns successfully abandoning the convent for life outside; D. De Bellis, 'Attacking sumptuary laws in Renaissance Venice: Arcangela Tarabotti' (227–42), examining Tarabotti's attack on male fashion and adornment that created a furore lasting beyond her death; A. Chemello, 'The rhetoric of eulogy in Lucrezia Marinella's *La nobiltà et l'eccellenza delle donne*' (463–77), exploring the expert use of rhetorical strategies in Marinella's defence of women. *A History of Women's Writing in Italy*, ed. Letizia Panizza and Sharon Wood, CUP, xvi + 361 pp., discusses a number of genres appropriated by women in the period up to 1650. Maria Luisa Doglio (13–24) deals with letter-writing as the most persistent of women's genres; Giovanna Rabitti (37–51) traces the growing autonomy of women's lyric poetry; Virginia Cox (52–64) shows that women writers of fiction — pastoral, chivalric poetry and epic — flourish especially from 1580 to 1650; Letizia Panizza (65–78) finds in women's prose polemics repeated pleas for independent life, a claiming of liberty and equality, and a search for friendship in marriage to replace subordination; and Gabriella Zarri (79–91) brings to light a wealth of forgotten religious and devotional writing. *Donne, filosofia e cultura nel Seicento*, ed. Pina Totaro, Ro, CNR, 1999, 460 pp., contains several articles on the Italian 17th c. A. Bettini, 'Il teatro e la memoria. Letteratura e filosofia nell'*Inferno monacale* di Arcangela Tarabotti' (51–59), examines Tarabotti's metaphor of the religious life as mere theatre, devoid of substance; M. Fintoni, 'L'ingegno negato. L'immaginario antifemminile tra XVI e XVII secolo' (86–108), shows the persistence of Aristotelian commonplaces on woman's irrationality, and consequent inferiority to men, despite equally persistent challenging and overturning of them in writings of men and women; M. Conforti, 'Libri a stampa di antichità romane nella biblioteca di Cristina di Svezia' (264–85), reveals the extent of the library of the famous Italophile who abdicated her throne and converted to Catholicism and to life in Rome; A. Mirto, 'Il ruolo delle donne nel campo dell'editoria tra Cinque e Seicento' (286–92), brings together studies on women and the press to illustrate the extent to which they contributed to editing and publishing; D. Zardin, 'Libri e biblioteche negli ambienti monastici dell'Italia del primo Seicento' (346–83), reveals the range of books in convent libraries which often went beyond spiritual texts to include poetry, drama, and history; M. De Luca, 'L'Autoritratto femminile tra XVI e XVII secolo' (387–92), finds that in the main only daughters of painters were likely to become painters themselves, Artemisia Gentileschi being the most famous Italian example; G. Salvatori, finally, in 'La sindrome delle Muse. Motivi, problemi e orientamenti della critica sulle donne artiste del Seicento europeo' (393–434), notes the idealization of the exceptional woman-artist to the role of 'muse' and provides ample illustrations of paintings to support her point. Lucrezia Marinella, *The Nobility and Excellence of Women, and the Defects and Vices of Men*, ed. and trans. Anne Dunhill, introd. Letizia Panizza, Chicago U.P., 1999, 200 pp., includes the main chapters of Marinella's unrivalled polemic against age-old philosophical and literary arguments, very much alive in her time, which sought to deprive women of their rationality and moral autonomy. Her dismantling of her arch-enemy Giuseppe Passi, author of *I donneschi difetti*, and of celebrated near-contemporaries such as Sperone Speroni and Torquato Tasso are impressive. The vast spectrum of Marinella's sources are indicated by the accompanying notes; and the introduction sets her in a cultural and literary context. The translation is based on the 1601 edition, which considerably expanded the 1600 *editio princeps*. As there is still no modern Italian edition of this feminist classic, the translation with scholarly apparatus is all the more to be valued in disseminating a main stage in the Italian *querelle des femmes*.

BIBLIOGRAPHY. R. Bruni, 'Edizioni fiorentine del Seicento: la Biblioteca Marucelliana', *StSec*, 40, 1999:217–323, is a chapter of Bruni's cataloguing of all Florentine libraries for editions published in Florence between 1601 and 1699. Founded by the abbot Francesco Marucelli (1625–1703), the Marucelliana was contributed to first by other members of the family, and then by private donors. On the basis of various inventories, B. lists 797 editions and composes several indexes to make this catalogue a truly user-friendly research tool. U. Motta, 'La biblioteca di Antonio Querenghi, 1546–1633', *ib.*, 41:177–284, offers a model of how to write a description and analysis of an early-modern library. In the opinion of his contemporary Sforza Pallavicino, Q. was one of the most erudite men of his age: he lived as an ecclesiastic at Rome, wrote Latin and Italian poetry, and was a lifelong bibliophile. M.'s reconstruction is based on a partial inventory in the Ambrosiana, Milan (MS S 77 sup.) of 1,700 books on law, theology, medicine, and science, to which Motta has added an equal number in Latin, Greek, and Italian literature and history, based on other evidence. A. Battistini, 'Un'attiva scuola di studi sul tardo Rinascimento e il Barocco', *ib.*, 431–54, is an illuminating historiographical article, partly celebratory, on the state of Seicento studies in Italy. It singles out a group formed at the Catholic University of Milan under the direction of Claudio Scarpati, and follows their moves to other universities, and their accomplishments. Anyone engaged in research on the Seicento will profit from this account.

2. POETRY

Giovanni Getto, *Il barocco letterario in Italia*, ed. Marziano Guglielminetti, Mi, Mondadori, xi + 480 pp., comprising 'La polemica sul barocco' (1960) and 'Barocco in prosa e in poesia' (1969), is a welcome republication, by one of Getto's first pupils, of texts that were milestones in 17th-c. studies in Italy. From the same department of Turin University comes the collection of papers *Politica e cultura nell'età di Carlo Emanuele I. Torino, Parigi, Madrid. Convegno internazionale di studi, Torino 21–24 febbraio 1995*, ed. Mariarosa Masoero, Sergio Mamino, and Claudio Rosso, F, Olschki, 1999, v + 625 pp. Those relevant to the present survey are: M. Masoero, 'Agostino Bucci e l'epica sabauda' (105–22); C. Peirone, 'Un genere di "confine": le piscatorie' (141–54); A. M. Luisetti, '*Le trasformazioni di Millefonti* di Ludovico San Martino d'Agliè' (155–64); M. L. Doglio, 'Il "teatro poetico" del principe: rime inedite di Carlo Emanuele I di Savoia' (presenting a selection of unpublished poems) (165–89); and M. Guglielminetti, 'Un "portrait du roi" avant la lettre? Note sul mariniano "Ritratto del Serenissimo Carlo Emanuello duca di Savoia"' (191–214). On this last item, the only one concerning a major writer, see MARINO, below.

The chapter 'Dal "grave" al "culto": ipotesi sull'evoluzione della lirica secentesca in Napoli', pp. 141–82 of Domenico Chiodo, *Suaviter Parthenope canit. Per ripensare la 'geografia e storia' della letteratura italiana*, Soveria Mannelli, Rubbettino, 1999, 202 pp., seeks to transcend the simplistic, one-sided view of 17th-c. poetry deriving from Getto. Four phases are distinguished: the pursuit of solemnity (Pignatelli, Cortese, Quattromani, the *casisti*); affected *dulcedo* (Marino, Macedonio, Errico, Maia Materdona, the early Bruni); the phase of 'decorum' (the mature Bruni, Manso, Fontanella, Basso); the 'learned' style (Battista, Pisani, Casaburi, Lubrano). Domenico Chiodo, *L'idillio barocco e altre bagatelle*, Alessandria, Orso, 204 pp., consists chiefly of a detailed investigation of the idyll over the period from 1607, the date of the *editio princeps* of Marino's *Europa*, to 1625, the date of the final draft of Girolamo Preti's *Salmace*. The success of this literary microgenre is also seen as a publishing phenomenon, and as a matter of fashion, marking a decisive stage in the emergence of baroque taste. Data are identified which are useful for the delineation of 17th-c. literary 'geography', such as the contrast between cities like Bologna and Venice, which were receptive to the experimentation of the new poetry, and cities like Rome and Florence which firmly opposed it. A second section of the volume is devoted entirely to Preti, while a third, 'Bagatelle filologiche e letterarie con qualche saggio di poesia', deals, *inter alia*, with Zinani, Campeggi, Testi, Peregrini, Fontanella, Stigliani, and the genre of vernacular Heroides.

To complement the critical study of the idyll the author offers the miscellany: *Idilli*, ed. Domenico Chiodo, T, Res, 1999, xviii + 183 pp., comprising texts by Zinani, Campeggi, Stradiotti, Gigli, Testi, Bracciolini, Cesare Orsini, Basile, Giovanetti, and Marino, and directly demonstrating the potentialities of the genre, from mythological to sacred subjects, from revisited news items to short-story-like fiction, from parodic ingenuity to pathos and effusion.

ACCIANO. Giulio Acciano, *Poesie, ed. Luigi Montella, Alessandria, Orso, 1998, x + 238 pp., *incredibile dictu*, is already out of print: thanks not to a run on the southern baroque, but to the printing of publicly funded editions in small quantities of copies which are then distributed privately.

BASSO. Antonio Basso, *Poesie*, ed. Salvatore Consoli, introd. Francesco Spera, T, Res, 1999, xxi + 168 pp., invites reappraisal of a poet (also a member of the Accademia degli Oziosi) best known for the tragic end that overtook him during the anti-Spanish revolt of 1647, when he was put to death at Naples by order of the Duc de Guise. The edition falls into three parts, the first consisting of sonnets and structured in four sections (amorous, heroic, sacred, various), the second comprising odes, *canzoni, madrigali, ottave*, plus a brief dramatic text, *Il giudicio di Paride*, intended to be set to music, and the third devoted to B.'s Latin verse. The editor also offers an exhaustive appendix of *Poesie disperse*. B.'s verse is very close in style to that of his influential patron Giovan Battista Manso. The sonnet is by far its most congenial form. The other poems, in particular the many intended for musical setting, are often perplexing.

CAMPANELLA. The Giancotti edition of the *Poesie* (*YWMLS*, 60:433–34) has inevitably drawn attention to them. Giancotti himself returns to the subject in order to amplify points only touched upon in the Einaudi volume: F. Giancotti, 'Postille a una nuova edizione delle *Poesie* di Campanella. 4–6', BrC, 5, 1999:203–11, while he goes on to devote himself to a more complex study, which can be discussed once published in its entirety: Id., 'Tommaso Campanella: le poesie della *Scelta* e la loro disposizione. (I)', StSec, 41:3–25. Tommaso Campanella, *Opere*, ed. Germana Ernst, Ro, IPZS, iv + 1027 pp., is a major anthology of C.'s writings (obviously not limited to the poetry) but in a collection (a 100–volume luxury edition of the classics which may only be bought *en bloc*) the absurdity of which was rightly underlined by the previous author of this section (*YWMLS*, 59:546). G. Ernst, 'Note campanelliane', *BrC*, 5:477–98, identifies Ficino and Ruscelli as sources for two *loci* of the *Poesie*, puts forward proposed datings and textual emendations, and in an appendix brings to light a number of hitherto unpublished documents. L. Vanni, 'La poesia filosofica di Tommaso Campanella. Archetipo dantesco e tradizione biblica', *Aevum*, 73:769–805, seeks to demonstrate both Dante's 'archetypal role' in the elaboration of C.'s *Poetica* and the direct stylistic dependence of the poems of the *Scelta* on the lexical fabric of the *Commedia*, declaring both debts to be founded on the need to assert the identity of philosophical poetry and prophecy.

CAMPEGGI. L. Giachino, ' "Aurea catena che le menti annoda". La poesia lirica di Ridolfo Campeggi', *GSLI*, 177:361–84, registers his somewhat naive impressions on reading Campeggi's *Poesie* (Venice 1620), or rather just the sonnet section of the volume, only to conclude with the simplistic observation that the influence of Marino's lyric verse on the Bolognese poet is 'minimal': 'più evidente è invece quella del Rinaldi'. The article has a useful appendix containing an initial census of C.'s scattered poems. Texts by this author can be read in *Idilli*, ed. D. Chiodo, and also in D. Chiodo, *L'idillio barocco*, where the eight sonnets 'in morte di Adone' are reproduced from the 1608 edn of the *Rime*.

CAPPONI. The lack of modern studies devoted to C., the most neglected of the numerous poets active at Bologna in the first quarter of the century, is in part remedied by G. P. Maragoni, 'Arte del verso e del racconto ne *I Bombici* di Giovanni Capponi', *StSec*, 41:123–36, analysing with customary care and skill the author's masterpiece, the idyll *I bombici*, published for the first time in 1610. The reading, which focuses on a formal analysis, is perhaps open to the objection that too little attention is paid to the work's link with Marco Girolamo Vida's *De bombice*, of which C.'s verse is at times little more than an Italian translation.

CHIGI. Production of Latin verse, still widespread in the Seicento, albeit less so than in the previous century, was an activity particularly cultivated at the court first of Urban VIII and then of Alexander VII. A facsimile has been produced of the latter's nephew's *juvenilia*: Fabio Chigi, *Philomati Musae Juveniles. Des Philomatus Jugendgedichte*, 2 vols, Köln, Böhlau, 1999. The first vol. presents the facsimile text with facing German translation by Hermann Hugenroth, the second the translator's lengthy introduction and commentary. Wolfang Hübner, 'Zur Übersetzung der *Carmina* des Fabio Chigi', *HL*, 48:297–306, raises a considerable number of doubts about the translation as well as the commentary.

CICALA. Also on Latin poetry, Gino Rizzo, *Metodo e intelligenza. Tre episodi dal barocco al verismo*, Galatina, Congedo, 149 pp., devotes two chapters to the *carmina* of Girolamo Cicala, a *literato* from the Salento who lived in the first half of the century. His purpose, which he achieves, is to refute Benedetto Croce who saw only Counter-Reformation propaganda and moral education, devoid of poetic inspiration, in the 17th-c. output of Latin verse. Of special interest here, in C.'s production, are a number of Latin translations of contemporary vernacular poems, from Casoni to Achillini, Marino, and Stigliani.

ELLIO. M. E. Raja (ed.), 'F. Ellio, *La rugiada*', *Lo Stracciafoglio*, 1.1:13–24, proposes an idyll by an unknown Milanese *literato* in which the myth of Adonis is revisited with a number of curious inventions.

FAVORITI. M. Scorsone, 'A. Favoriti, *Cleopatra in hortis Vaticanis*', *ib.*, 37–45, edits with notable sophistication a *silva* devoted to a celebrated antique sculptural group preserved in the Vatican gardens. The work is to be considered the masterpiece of one of the chief protagonists of cultural and political life at the court of Pope Alexander VII.

FONTANELLA. D. Chiodo, *L'idillio barocco*, pp. 189–99, has the section 'Scherzi marittimi' from the collection Girolamo Fontanella, *I nove cieli*, Naples, 1640.

GUALTEROTTI From the Strozzi collection of the Newberry Library, S. Magnanini, 'An early draft of Raffaello Gualterotti's *Il Polemidoro*', *StSec*, 40, 1999:325–48, transcribes 81 largely unpublished octaves of the first draft of the first canto of *L'universo ovvero Il Polemidoro*, whose definitive version was printed at Florence by Cosimo Giunti in 1600.

GUIDI. Alessandro Guidi, *Poesie liriche. Le canzoni*, ed. Chiara Ciampolillo, introd. Luana Salvarani, Parma, Centro Studi Archivio Barocco, 1999, xvi + 133 pp., is an edition of, and commentary on, G.'s early *canzoniere* (1671), gathering the production subsequently repudiated after the author's conversion to Arcadia.

MACEDONIO. G. De Miranda, 'Un silenzio assordante. Marcello Macedonio a Roma per la scelta carmelitana e l'ultimo esercizio poetico (1610–1619)', *Aprosiana*, n.s. 8:73–95, a brief but succulent study, traces the poet's biography in his years of conventual reclusion, from his tormented assent to the publication of his profane *canzoniere*, *Le Nove Muse*, to the composition of his sacred *canzoniere*, *I Nove Cori degli Angioli* (Rome, Facciotti, 1615), and to his premature decease in 1619.

MAGGI.   P. Frare, 'La sincerità degli affetti: sulle *Rime varie* di Carlo Maria Maggi', *Testo*, 36, 1998:45–74, reads the Lombard poet's collected poems (published in 1688) as documenting a spiritual conversion that determines an analogous poetics in the name of a return to Petrarch's example against the excesses of *concettismo*. The expression of 'sincerity of the affects' is the goal pursued even at the risk of composing verse that seems monotonous, unadorned, unrefined; yet, as Frare shows, it is not at all a question of abstention from rhetorical orchestration, but of its adoption in an acceptation different from that of *concettismo*, whereby rhetoric is 'destinata, in un certo senso, a cancellarsi mentre si manifesta, per lasciare il posto ad una impressione di naturalezza, di sincerità' (58). So we pass from profane to sacred love, and also from intellectual stimulus to a stirring of the emotions: but one cannot ignore, and the quotations demonstrate inescapably, the fact that the results achieved by M., however 'sincere' their ethical and religious motivation, are decidedly modest. On Maggi see also *Carlo Maria Maggi e la Milano di fine '600 nelle Commedie e e nelle Rime. Itinerario antologico — detti sentenze, proverbi, fonti — nel III centenario della morte, 1699–1999, introd. Gianfranco Ravasi, Mi, Di Baio, 1999, xxx + 386 pp.

MALVEZZI.   F. Longoni, 'Ancora su Lodovico Malvezzi', *StSec*, 41:137–74, studies the major poetry collection of the son of the more famous historian Virgilio Malvezzi, *I delirii della solitudine*, published 1624 — the 'ancora' referring to his aim of adding 'qualche ulteriore riflessione' to an earlier article by E. Taddeo. While agreeing that M. expressed deep hostility to tyrannical regimes, including the Pope's policy to suppress independent rule in Bologna, and exhibited a large measure of proto-Romantic political consciousness, L. investigates his serious beliefs in astrology, and his rewriting in Italian of several episodes in Ovid.

MARINO.   Francesco Giambonini, *Bibliografia delle opere a stampa di Giambattista Marino*, 2 vols, Firenze, Olschki, 922 pp., a monumental and very useful work, comes to completion in volume form after appearing in instalments in *StSec*. On Marino's *oeuvre*: E. Torchio, 'Marino amante ovidiano', *StSec*, 41:89–122, analyses and comments on two *canzoni* from the third part of *La Lira* (*Trastulli estivi* and *Amore incostante*), which as the poet himself pointed out are free paraphrases of elegies by Ovid, respectively I 5 and II 4; while D. Chiodo, *L'idillio barocco*, 168–70, removes the ugly *ottava rima* piece *L'amante convalescente geloso* from the repertoire of Marino's stray poems and restores them to their real author, Pace Pasini. The two most important Marino contributions are: M. Guglielminetti, 'Un "portrait du roi" avant la lettre? Note sul mariniano "Ritratto del Serenissimo Carlo Emanuello duca di Savoia"', pp. 191–214 of *Politica e cultura*, who centres his analysis of the *sestinas* of the *Ritratto* on the skill with which the poet, by his own work, claims to outdo the painter Ambrogio Figino, charged to execute a portrait of Duke Charles Emmanuel, and to render his work superfluous by the portrait already executed in verse: 'il suggeritore ha sopravanzato l'esecutore; e lo stesso Principe è diventato, nei suoi versi, non tanto l'immagine del potere politico, quanto del potere della parola' (214); and especially M. Slawinski, 'Marino, le streghe, il cardinale', *ISt*, 54 : 52–84, where the cardinal is Desiderio Scaglia, the dedicatee of the first biography of M., an inquisitor and author of demonological treatises which display a judicious use of critical reasoning that led him to be suspected of laxism; the biographical sketch of Scaglia leads into an analysis of the role of the occult in the *Adone* through illuminating parallels with the *Furioso* and the *Liberata*; the ironic disenchantment with which Marino treats the powers of the occult in the poem (Slawinski details it abundantly) is the mark of a new interpretation of the man–nature relationship bent on overturning and transcending religious ortho-doxy by substantially denying the existence not only of demonic powers but of any metaphysical dimension outside the world of phenomena. Lastly, we note G. B. Marino, **La canzone dei baci ed altre poesie*, ed. Davide Dei, F, La Càriti, 1999, 59 pp.

MUSCETTOLA. Antonio Muscettola, *Rime*, ed. Luigi Montella, Alessandria, Orso, 1998, 208 pp., reproduces the unpublished pan-egyric for Clemente IX, *La piramide della vertù*, and only the sonnet section of the collected *Poesie* published by Muscettola in 1659. The editing is very approximate and, in addition to the frequent misprints, there are some real blunders, such as *fu 'l petto* for *su 'l petto* (125). The introduction is lengthy but does little to place M.'s production in its late southern baroque setting. He would seem closer to the mid-century poetic norm than to the extremism of his contemporary Casaburi, whose friend and protector he was.

RICCIO. The discovery of two MS collections of poems datable to the second quarter of the century led to research into their authorship and to the volume: Renata D'Agostino, *Impegno intellettuale e pratica della poesia in Onofrio Riccio*, Na, Libreria Dante & Descartes, 203 pp., where, on the limited data that survive, the biography is reconstructed of Riccio, amateur poet and doctor by profession, and a critical reading of his poetic output put forward. Appendixes usefully index the titles and first lines of the poems present in the two MSS.

STROZZI. Giulio Strozzi, **Poesie per il 'Primo libro de' madrigali' di Barbara Strozzi*, ed. Anna Aurigi, F, Studio Editoriale Fiorentino, 1999, 32 pp.

TASSONI. Maria Cristina Cabani, **La pianella di Scarpinello: Tassoni e la nascita dell'eroicomico*, Lucca, Pacini Fazzi, 1999, 314 pp.

VERALDO. D. Chiodo (ed.), 'Paolo Veraldo: da *Mascarate e capricci dilettevoli*', *Lo Stracciafoglio*, 1.1 : 25–29, is a brief anthological specimen of rather smutty verse by a *literato* known as an author of *commedia dell'arte* scenarios.

3. DRAMA

L. Novelli, 'Il sipario della censura sulla scena della controriforma', *Ariel*, 14.3, 1999 : 43–80, notes that, although the theatre was censured by the Church before the 17th c., a double awareness emerges in the Seicento of the form taken by dramatic works: the published text, 'teatro-in-libro', and the performance, 'teatro-in-spettacolo' — both indispensable ways through which modern theatre was institutionalized and fixed in tradition. The Index and forms of editorial control as they relate to the theatre are also investigated.

OPERA. In the context of the celebrations for the fourth centenary of the birth of Giulio Rospigliosi (Clement IX) D. Romei has promoted the publication of the operatic works that have come down to us in MS Vat. Lat. 13,538, in a decidedly modernizing transcription and in two enjoyable volumes: Giulio Rospigliosi, *Melodrammi profani* and *Melodrammi sacri*, ed. Danilo Romei, F, Studio Editoriale Fiorentino, respectively 1998 and 1999, 229 and 218 pp. Each volume contains three works and has no introductory material or commentary whatsoever and, apart from the texts, only flawless philological *apparati*.

TRAGEDY. Mauro Sarnelli, *'Col discreto pennel d'alta eloquenza'. 'Meraviglioso' e classico nella tragedia (e tragicommedia) italiana del Cinque-Seicento*, Ro, Aracne, 1999, xxxix + 219 pp., puts forward a series of formal and stylistic analyses, which in part have already appeared as articles, of works by Antonio Decio da Orte, Giovan Battista Andreini, Prospero Bonarelli, Francesco Bracciolini, and Giovan Battista Albéri. Devoted to the tragic *oeuvre* of Tesauro, on the other hand, is Pierantonio Frare, *Retorica e verità. Le tragedie di Emanuele Tesauro*, Na, ESI, 1998, 204 pp., which analyses individually the three tragedies, *Ermegildo*, *Edipo*, and *Ippolito* printed by the author in 1661 (to whose repertoire must now be added *Alcesti, o sia L'amor sincero*, ed. Maria Luisa Doglio, Bari, Palomar, 143 pp., a 'tragedia musicale' composed for the second marriage of Duke Charles Emmanuel II of Savoy and preserved in a rare Turin edn of 1665), and he concludes by recognizing a specific cultural project in them: the aim to present tragedy as an interpretative model through which otherwise incomprehensible sorrowful events assume form and meaning, for 'la tragedia mette in scena la verità ricorrendo alle false apparenze dello spettacolo'. Other, less celebrated, tragedies and their respective authors, Bonaventura Morone and Girolamo Pipini, are dealt with in Gino Rizzo, *Metodo e intelligenza*. See CICALA, above.

PLAYERS. T. Megale, 'I padroni di Arlecchino', *MR*, 14:273–82, presents a biographical sketch of the Mantuan actor Tristano Martinelli, 'il primo Arlecchino della storia', to whose activity lengthy reference is made in Claudio Burattelli, *Spettacoli di corte a Mantova tra Cinque e Seicento*, F, Le Lettere, 1999, 278 pp.

SPECTACLE. *Feste a Corte e commedie di principi: teatro e musica in Puglia fra Sei e Settecento*, ed. Maria Aurelia Mastronardi and Trifone Gragano, Fasano, Schena, 1999, 341 pp.

THEATRES. In the context of keen interest for spectacle in Medici Florence, N. Michelassi, 'Il teatro del cocomero di Firenze. Uno stanzone per tre accademie (1651–1665)', *StSec*, 40, 1999:149–86, describes the first two phases of activity at the Teatro del Cocomero, its management by the Accademia degli Immobili (1651–54) and by the Accademia dei Sorgenti (1654–63), proposing to devote a specific study in future to the third phase when it was run by the Infuocati (1664–1700). Based on rigorous archival research, the work has the merit of proving that collaboration between amateur and professional actors was common, whereas this is often denied or at least ignored. Also interesting is Id., 'La *Finta pazza* a Firenze: commedie "spagnole" e "veneziane" nel teatro di Baldracca (1641–1665)', *ib.*, 41:313–53, with reference to which 1645, the year of the performance of Giulio Strozzi's *Finta pazza* is identified as marking the transition from the fashion for prose comedy 'alla spagnola' to a fashion for opera 'alla veneziana'. A contribution to the history of the Neapolitan theatres is M. Brindicci, 'La scena e la città. Il teatro napoletano nell'interpretazione di Franco Carmelo Greco: da Giovan Battista Della Porta ad Andrea Perrucci', *Aprosiana*, n.s. 8:97–110.

4. PROSE

Selva di vario narrare. Schede per lo studio della narrazione breve nel Seicento, ed. Maria Antonietta Cortini and Luisa Mulas, Ro, Bulzoni, 587 pp., gives an introduction followed by a catalogue of 1,059 works of a neglected genre characteristic of the Seicento: the short narration, typified by the proliferation of the novella, no longer tied, however, to Boccaccian norms. The brief narrative includes collections of jokes, proverbs, games, anecdotes, fables, weighty sayings of philosophers, short *vite*, practical manuals of teaching and preaching broken down into sections, and encyclopaedias and other reference works bringing together numerous items. This unusual way of classifying literature brings into profile many works that slip through the gaps if we think according to conventional categories.

BASILE. *La fiaba barocca: studi su Basile e Perrault,* ed. Anna Maria Pedullà, Na, ESI, 1999, 118 pp., brings together a number of rewarding essays that look at B.'s fables from the perspectives of modern narrative, taking as a point of departure that the construction of fables comes about by a merging of the stabilizing qualities of myth with the dynamic, combinative qualities of fiction. The comparison with Perrault, present in most contributions, serves to throw into relief B.'s distinguishing features: N. Morra, 'Il racconto popolare di Basile e la fiaba di corte di Perrault' (7–21); M. V. Botta, ' "Le tre fate" in G. Basile e in C. Perrault. Analisi della fiaba' (23–35); D. Pisano, 'Per un'enciclopedia fantastica: "Lo serpe" di G. B. Basile' (37–67); M. Di Rienzo, 'Malinconia e patologia ne *Lo cunto de li cunti* del Basile. Un confronto con la cultura inglese' (69–106); C. Serra, 'Le favole "Petrosinella" e "L'Ignorante" ne *Lo cunto de li cunti* di Giambattista Basile' (107–14); and T. Piccirillo, ' "Gagliuso" e "Le chat botté" ' (115–18). The collection is accompanied by bibliography and notes. F. Decroisette, 'Du bon usage des figures dans le *Cunto de li cunti* de Giambattista Basile', pp. 181–227 of *Figures à l'italianne* (see GENERAL, above), is an excellent study placing B. in the context of the literary disputes of his age about satire and fiction, and the use of figures of speech. She gives detailed examples of B.'s use of the latter and the purposes they serve.

BOCCALINI. Franco Longoni, 'Alcune note sulla tradizione del testo boccaliniano', *StSec*, 40, 1999: 3–29, follows on from Harold Hendrix's 1995 study, which examined the complex and not always easy-to-follow history of the collection of *ragguagli* in B.'s *Pietra del paragone politico*, beginning with 1614, and turns attention to imitators of Boccalini such as Francesco Prati and Girolamo Briani, who mixed genuine Boccalini material with their own.

BONARELLI. M. Capucci, 'Un romanzo di testa. Le *Fortune d'Erosmando e Floridalba* di Prospero Bonarelli', *ib.*, 97–118, provides minute summaries of the complex plot lines of this novel of intrigue, romance, and adventure published in 1642 at the end of B.'s life, to conclude that 'il romanzo ha molto dell'esercizio a freddo, tutto cerebrale'.

CIAMPOLI. L. S. Varanini, '*Il corriero della sconosciuta Amarilli*: un inedito di Giovanni Ciampoli?', *BrC*, 5, 1999: 95–113, discusses the reasons for attributing this anonymous rediscovered MS to the scientist Monsignor Giovanni Ciampoli (1590–1643). Incongruously, the work praises Barberini Pope Urban VIII, elected in 1623, as well as the scientific discoveries of Galileo, whom the Pope first admired but then turned against. The author surmises that this double adulation, permissible early in Urban VIII's reign, may have impeded its publication later.

CRASSO. C. Serra, 'Gli *Elogi d'huomini letterati (1666)* di Lorenzo Crasso', *EL*, 25.1:47–64, examines this collection of eulogies of famous men by Lorenzo Crasso, member of the Neapolitan Accademia degli Oziosi, to determine to what extent the author is presenting well-researched biographies, drawing on primary sources, or is putting together a mere compilation without rigour. She concludes that it hovers on the borders of historiography, like so many other collections of the 17th c.

LOREDANO. A. Morini, 'Drame de l'imprudence: *Gli amori infelici* di Giovan Francesco Loredano', *StSec*, 40, 1999: 57–81, emphasizes the diverse interpretations of the famous Ovidian tale of tragic young love thwarted by parental and social prohibitions, Pyramus and Thisbe, and contrasts Loredan to his contemporaries Giambattista Marino and Théophile de Viau, pointing out that de Viau is more subversive in defending the lovers' right to pleasure, while Loredan judges them imprudent in going against the social order.

SEGNERI E. Ardissino, 'Intorno a un'*Arte di predicar bene* attribuita a Paolo Segneri', *ib.*, 187–213, advances persuasive reasons for removing a treatise on preaching from the *corpus* of the great Jesuit preacher, the reformer of sacred eloquence in his age. She first demonstrates by a comparative analysis the dependence of the supposed S. treatise on an earlier one of exactly the same title by Paolo Aresi, a friar of the Theatine order, first published in 1611. From an examination of S.'s genuine works, and of his correspondence to and from his contemporaries, it results that he does not mention writing such a treatise or discuss preaching and sacred eloquence in terms similar to the supposed treatise. The reduction of Aresi's text and its inclusion in S.'s works was done, A. argues, by an early 19th-c. editor intent on promoting Jesuit oratory.

5. THOUGHT

G. Cozzi, 'Scoperta dell'Anabattismo: lo stupore ammirato di Gregorio Barbarigo ambasciatore veneto', *SV*, 38, 1999: 55–66, analyses a letter, dated 17 October 1614, from the ambassador (sympathetic to Protestants and in Zurich) to Paolo Sarpi, with an account of a persecuted Anabaptist peasant who refused to leave his native city because the land belonged to God not Zwingli. Barbarigo grasped that what was at stake was freedom of conscience. A. Viterbo, 'Socrate nel Ghetto: lo scetticismo mascherato di Simone Luzzatto', *ib.*, 79–128, examines in great detail a philosophical treatise of a distinguished Jewish rabbi at Padua, who published *Socrate overo dell'humano sapere* in 1651. V. links the work persuasively with a sceptical tradition going back to Cornelius Agrippa's *De incertitudine scientiarum* in the first half of the 16th c. and with the premise that human reason does not yield certainty — a view represented in antiquity by Socrates. E. Taddeo, 'Torcigliani e Delfino, patriarca atomista', *StSec*, 40, 1999:83–95, investigates the correspondence of two students of Epicureanism, concentrating on Delfino, cardinal and aristocrat.

Ettore Lojacono, 'Immagini di Descartes a Napoli: da Valletta a Costantino Grimaldi, parte I^a', *NRLett*, 19.2, 1999:95–128; and Id, 'Immagini di Descartes a Napoli: da Valletta a Costantino Grimaldi, parte II^a', *ib.*, 20.1: 45–67, are both concerned with the reception of Descartes among Neapolitan intellectuals in the late 17th c. at the time of prolonged trials by the Inquisition against new thinkers (1688–97). The swift spread of Cartesian thought was soon distorted and denounced by the Church, which labelled Descartes and his 'school' — Lucretius, Gassendi, Hobbes, Digby, and Boyle — 'atheists' and 'atomists'. A zealous Jesuit, Benedetto Aletino, spearheaded the attack, while the lawyer Francesco d'Andrea, supported by jurists, doctors, and scientists, pleaded on behalf of the *novatores*. For the historian Giuseppe Valletta, indeed, Descartes opened up a new way for Christian philosophers to by-pass scholastic Aristotelianism and link up with early Christian writers like Augustine with his attitudes of doubt. Lojacono shows further stages of the debates, concentrating finally on Grimaldi, even more radical than Valletta in his critique of Aristotle, more thoroughly immersed in Cartesianism, and more emphatic about the importance of innovation in philosophy, especially natural philosophy (and mathematics).

BAGLIVI. Giorgio Baglivi, *Carteggio 1679–1704*, ed. Anna Toscano, F, Olschki (Archivio della corrispondenza degli scienziati italiani, 14), 1999, 371 pp. The letters, which, whether Latin or Italian, are supplied with notes, document B.'s position in the Italian and pan-European scientific community in the second half of the Seicento. B. (1668–1707) stressed the need for observation and experiment in medicine (see his famous *De praxi medicina* of 1696). He was the first to propose that life resided in various organs of the body, and he examined the structure and motion of the muscles minutely for their 'proprietà vitali'.

BRUNO. C. Buccolini, 'Una quaestio inedita di Mersenne contro il *De immenso*', *BrC*, 5, 1999:165–75, examines Marin Mersenne's censures against Bruno, which he places in his 1624 tract against libertines and deists, *L'Impiété des déistes*, and gives the passages where Mersenne is critical — particularly about pantheism and the infinity of worlds.

CAMPANELLA. M. Casubolo, 'Metodi linguistici nella ricerca semiotica: il colore nella *Città del Sole* di Tommaso Campanella', *ib.*,

165–75, applies the semiotic theories of Lotman to C.'s use of colour in fields such as costume and complexion. G. Ernst, 'Ancora sugli ultimi scritti politici di Campanella. I. Gli inediti *Discorsi ai principi* in favore del papato', *ib.*, 131–53, gives the Italian text with notes and introduction to a short address, composed in 1636 against Spanish tyranny, in which C. looks to a union of the Papacy and France for deliverance; and in the sequel, 'Ancora sugli ultimi scritti di Campanella. II. Gli *Avvertimenti a Venezia* del 1636', *ib.*, 447–68, she presents C. striving to reconcile anti-clerical Venice with the Papacy on the grounds that religion is important for the well-being of the State. G. Formichetti, 'L'ottava lettera del fondo Colonna: un inedito campanelliano', *ib.*, 6:189–93, examines the significance of a short letter written to Filippo Colonna (related to Urban VIII's nephew Taddeo) after Urban had freed C. from his Neapolitan prison and brought him to Rome, where he was nevertheless surrounded by enemies. Shortly after writing this letter asking Filippo for protection, C. fled Rome in 1634. L. Guerrini, '*Astrologicorum libri VII.* Considerazioni linguistiche e ricognizioni intorno alla tradizione del testo', *ib.*, 199–209, deems this a work of benign astrology, printed between 1629 and 1630, in which the astrologer uses his art to understand how Divine Providence and the celestial intelligences — not demons — regulate the universe and all natural phenomena. The author considers to what extent the variations in successive editions add to C.'s thoughts on the subject.

M. G. Accietto-Gualtieri, 'La conservazione come concetto metafisico-teologico nel pensiero di Tommaso Campanella', *ib.*, 9–33, regards 'conservazione' as a key concept in C.'s natural philosophy, an expression of his view that, while nature changes, there is underlying permanence. Related concepts such as unity and multiplicity, and cause and effect, are also examined, and shown to counter both the Aristotelian doctrine of the eternity of the world and the Epicurean teaching that nature is a product of chance. S. Serrapica, 'Discussioni campanelliane nella Napoli di fine Seicento', *ib.*, 5, 1999:47–66, gives a straightforward account of the points on which the physician Leonardo di Capua, Giacomo Lavagna, and in the next century Antonio Genovesi agreed and disagreed with C. and with one another. M. Conforti, 'Le antiche stampe campanelliane. I. Biblioteca oratoriana dei Girolamini di Napoli', *ib.*, 469–76, is an exercise in the reception of C. from 1591 to 1709, after which 18th-c. editions of C. are very rare. The library is important both as the oldest public library in Naples and as having been endowed in 1726 with the private library of Giuseppe Valletta, to whom all the C. editions discussed here belonged. M. Palumbo, 'Le edizioni di Bruno e Campanella nella biblioteca privata leibniziana', *ib.*,

499–512, shows the modest interest of Leibniz in the Italian philosophers — only three works out of a collection of about 7,000 volumes. P. Goretti, ' "Inhonesta consuetudo": pianelle per piedi di legno', *ib.*, 6: 195–98, picks up Campanella's condemnation in *City of the Sun* of high-heeled clogs, together with make-up, and traces the history of these 'sinful' shoes from, apparently, their Turkish origins to Seicento Venice. M.-P. Lerner, 'Sur la page de titre du *De sensu rerum et magia* (Francfort 1620)', *ib.*, 105–14, is a piece of erudite iconographic detective work that unravels the meaning of the title-page's emblem of two palm-trees with their top branches intertwined, vines wound around the trunks, and a radiant sun shining above. The themes suggested are fertility, friendship, and mutual support.

DIONIGI DA FANO. *Ricerche sulle selve rinascimentali*, ed. Paolo Cherchi, Ravenna, Longo, 1999, 173 pp., discusses Seicento editions of D. in the wider context of the genre in Cherchi's introductory essay, 'La *selva* rinascimentale: profilo di un genere' (9–41), indicating that it was a miscellany or anthology 'dall'organizzazione capricciosa' of literary, philosophical, and scientific material gathered from a variety of sources; for the Seicento the vol. includes *inter alia* D. Papotti, 'Problemata garzoniani nella *Selva* di Dionigi da Fano' (147–56), refers to D.'s incorporation of items from Tommaso Garzoni's *Serraglio degli stupori del mondo* (1613) into his own *Selva* of 1615, reprinted frequently, even as late as 1668 and 1672. The author shows how the *problemata*, ultimately deriving from an Aristotelian tradition of unsolved questions in natural science, went through chaotic reception history down to D.

GALILEI, G., GALILEI, V. Dava Sobel, *Galileo's Daughter*, London, Fourth Estate, 1999, 429 pp., makes use of the letters of Galileo's elder daughter Virginia, known as Suor Celeste in religious life, to her famous father to give us a moving view of their relationship from the time of her entry into the Poor Clare convent of San Matteo in Arcetri outside Florence in 1613, when she was twelve, to her death in 1634. Though Galileo's letters to his daughter have not survived, S. skilfully interweaves excerpts from his other letters and writings to provide a counter-balancing voice. Through careful reconstruction from primary and secondary sources, S. brings to life the scientific and religious issues of the day that constitute Galileo's biography. A finely crafted study of a father-daughter relationship which grew stronger over the years, it leaves the reader wondering what intelligent and omnicompetent Suor Celeste might have become had she had the opportunity. Andrea Battistini, *Galileo e i Gesuiti. Miti letterari e retorica della scienza*, Mi, Vita e Pensiero, 419 pp., is a major study about the discussion and communication of science in the Seicento, inaugurated by G.'s momentous discoveries. B. finds affinities between modern scientific method and narrative practice of the age: both preferred incomplete, provisional structures with diverse points of view within which to convey their message. A master of rhetoric, G. perfected the art of presenting his discoveries in the most advantageous manner possible and answering his enemies in such a way as to leave them no quarter. B. conducts an outstanding analysis (ch. 3) of the letter to Don Benedetto Castelli, showing how thoroughly G. follows the rhetorical pattern of a speech and organizes his proofs with evidence, arguments, and 'authorities'. Ch. 4 contains further examination of G.'s use of conceits and metaphorical language. As for the Jesuits, they followed suit, embracing the method of empirical observation of nature to reinforce, however, a pious science in which 'The heavens declare the glory of God'.

Galileo Galilei, *Lettera a Cristina di Lorena*, ed. Franco Motta, Genoa, Marietti, 173 pp., has a scholarly introduction by M. Pesce which analyses Galileo's proposal 'per definire autonomi di sapere e nuovi assetti di potere intellettuale nei paesi cattolici'. There are critical notes, and documents relating to the condemnation of the Copernican theory. Stillman Drake, *Essays on Galileo and the History and Philosophy of Science*, 3 vols, Toronto U.P., 1999, xxiii + 473, 380, 392 pp., has 80 essays which cover biography, bibliography, textual studies, scientific methodology, astronomy, motion, mechanics, and the *Discorsi*, the *Dialoghi*, Galileo's instruments, science in the late Middle Ages and the Renaissance, early science and the printed book, Aristotle and Renaissance science, music and experimental science, the philosophy of science. Drake's wide-ranging interests and expertise make this a most valuable collection and a tribute to his contribution to G. scholarship.

MALVEZZI. Eleonora Belligni, *Lo scacco della prudenza: precettistica politica ed esperienza storica in Virgilio Malvezzi*, F, Olschki, 1999, 364 pp., is the first 'studio complessivo' of the Bolognese aristocrat (1595–1654), a major political writer who was forced to fuse his study of Tacitus (in 1622 he published his very popular *Discorsi sopra Cornelio Tacito*) and his fondness for writing political novels with his duties as political adviser to the Count-Duke of Olivares and the Spanish court. M. is seen as a Machiavelli in reverse, the former reluctantly entering public life; the latter wanting nothing else. The author explores the ways 'prudenza' conveys the doctrine of *ragion di stato* for the man in the service of a prince: it was distilled from a reading of the classics of political thought — not from experience in politics as for Machiavelli — and provided authoritative certainties to rulers and ruled. C. Carminati, 'Il carteggio tra Virgilio Malvezzi e Sforza Pallavicino', *StSec*, 41:357–430, publishes the correspondence between these two historians and moralists for the years 1645–54, which ended with M.'s death. Though having much in common intellectually, these two writers were on different sides of the political divide: Pallavicino in the circle around Barberini Pope Urban VIII; Malvezzi favouring Spanish domination in Italy and so incurring the Pope's displeasure — he lost the fief he had appealed to the Pope to protect.

REDI. *Francesco Redi, un protagonista della scienza moderna: documenti, esperimenti, immagini,* ed. Walter Bernardi and Luigi Guerrini, F, Olschki, 1999, xi + 388 pp., is a major contribution to the study of a perhaps lesser-known scientist. The articles cover most aspects of his activities: F. Abbri, 'Problemi di ricerca fisico-chimica nei manoscritti di Redi' (3–12); W. Bernardi, 'Teoria e pratica della sperimentazione biologica nei protocolli sperimentali rediani' (13–30); A. Bonciani, 'Esitazioni metodologiche di un empirista radicale' (31–45); L. Guerrini, 'Contributo critico alla biografia rediana, con uno studio su Stefano Lorenzini e le sue *Osservazioni intorno alle torpedini*' (47–69); D. Bertoloni Meli, 'Francesco Redi e Marcello Malpighi: ricerca anatomica e pratica medica' (73–86); M. Conforti, 'Le "Osservazioni intorno alle gocciole e fili di vetro" di Redi in una lettura napoletana di fine Seicento' (87–95); M. Fazzari, 'Redi, Buonanni e la controversia sulla generazione spontanea: una rilettura' (97–127); S. Gómez López, 'Redi, arbitro tra i galileiani' (129–39); A. Ottaviani, 'Redi e la tradizione naturalistica. Dai Lincei a Paolo Boccone' (141–58); O. Trabucco, 'Critica delle fonti e metodo sperimentale nell'anatomia di Redi' (159–93); G. Bianchini, 'La nostra "commune patria". Redi ed i suoi corrispondenti aretini' (197–210); C. Doni, 'Redi privato nella corrispondenza inedita. Con due consulti medici inediti' (211–24); P. Scapecchi, 'Provenienze dei manoscritti Redi delle biblioteche Fiorentine' (225–30); L. Mangani, 'Tra laboratorio e scrittoio: le fonti testuali scientifiche nelle osservazioni e nelle esperienze di Redi' (231–59); S. Casciu, 'Aggiornamenti e nuove acquisizioni per l'iconografia rediana' (263–74); A. Nocentini, 'Metodo sperimentale e ricerca linguistica nell'opera di Redi' (275–85); M. Rak, 'Favola, menzogna, errore, opinione. Modelli e uso della letteratura e altre arti nell'opera di Redi' (287–304); L. Tongiorgi Tomasi, 'L'"infinitamente piccolo". Immagini al microscopio di Redi e al tempo di Redi' (305–15); A. Tosi, ' "Studietti" e "Gallerie" nella Toscana di Redi' (317–20); G. Baffo, 'Il monolite della vita: Vernadskij interprete di Redi' (323–38).

SARPI. A. Tenenti, 'Libertinismo ed etica politica in Paolo Sarpi', *SV*, 38, 1999:67–77, picks up and pays tribute to the views of Luisa Cozzi, who recently passed away, in the introduction to her 1996 edition of Sarpi's *Pensieri*, where she allied Sarpi with sceptical philosophical currents as formulated in Montaigne and Charron, and by the neo-Stoics of the Settecento. Sarpi, he reiterates, saw religion as 'puramente umano'. M. Catto, 'Le monache di S. Chiara in Udine e Fra Paolo Sarpi: tra consuetudine e ragion di stato nel consulto del 1609', *ib.*, 243–57, relates an intriguing episode in the history of a Friuli convent that received rich aristocratic women who often leaned towards Protestant points of view. Called in to give judgement on nuns petitioning to return to the lay state, S.'s solution to the vexed problem was not to be too strict in enforcing Tridentine rules.

SETTECENTO

POSTPONED

OTTOCENTO

POSTPONED

NOVECENTO

By ROBERTO BERTONI, *Senior Lecturer in Italian, Trinity College Dublin* and
CATHERINE O'BRIEN, *Professor of Italian, National University of Ireland, Galway*

1. GENERAL

Letteratura italiana del Novecento, ed. Alberto Asor Rosa, T, Einaudi,
628 pp., attempts to draw conclusions on a century of literature by
combining interest in specific literary themes and procedures, as well
as their relationship with the other arts, history, and society. The
work is subdivided into four sections. Section 1, 'Le grandi linee di
tendenza', includes A. Asor Rosa, 'Fondamenti epistemologici della
letteratura italiana del Novecento' (5–33), which identifies a 'linea
italiana' in the early 20th c. made up of classicism and positivism, and
later marked by realism and the avant-garde, and also discusses
language and publishing strategies; P. V. Mengaldo, 'I critici'
(34–65); R. Antonelli, 'La "doppia curiosità" della critica moderna'
(66–86); M. Zancan, 'Le autrici. Questioni di scrittura, questioni di
lettura' (87–135), which highlights the theme of female subjectivity
and shows how a reading of women's works casts a new light on 20th-
c. Italian literature; G. Ragone, 'Il consumo e le forme letterarie'
(136–79); V. Spinazzola, 'Le articolazioni del pubblico' (180–202),
and R. Rossanda, 'Note su letteratura e politica' (203–21). Section 2,
'Tradizione e innovazione', includes C. Vicentini, 'Pirandello. La
lingua e il dialetto della scena' (225–44); M. Lavagetto, 'Svevo e la
crisi del romanzo europeo' (245–67); S. Giovanardi, 'Metrica: tra
norma e infrazione' (268–80); G. Gorni, 'Metafore del far poesia
nella poesia del Novecento' (281–305); M. Bevilacqua, 'Guido
Gozzano e la condizione crepuscolare. Dalla Poesia Maiuscola alla
poesia minuscola' (306–17); and F. Bernardini Napoletano, 'Poetiche
e scritture sperimentali' (318–35), which shows how experimental
tendencies influenced literature in the course of the 20th c. in Italy,
starting with Federigo Tozzi and Gian Pietro Lucini, and continuing
throughout the century up to the present day. Section 3, 'Le scritture
del Novecento', includes G. Nava, 'La condizione espressionista:
Rèbora, Sbarbaro, Campana' (339–49); S. Giovanardi, 'Nei dintorni
di una poesia metafisica: Montale *versus* Ungaretti' (350–58); G. Ma-
grini, 'Il sublime non negativo' (359–82), which considers the search
for a non-rhetorical form of sublime in 20th-c. poetry; M. Farnetti,
'Scritture del fantastico' (382–409), focusing on dreamy language
and metalinguistic features; M. Corti, 'Reale e realismi' (410–21);
E. Sanguineti, 'Le linee della ricerca avanguardistica' (422–34);
C. Segre, 'Le tre rivoluzioni di C. E. Gadda' (435–48); A. Asor Rosa,

'Calvino e la narrativa strutturale' (449–72). Section 4, 'La letteratura e le altre lingue', includes F. Brevini, 'La poesia dialettale' (475–501); A. Abruzzese, 'Novecento: secolo della vita quotidiana e del corpo diviso' (502–46), which reflects on the revolution provoked by the mass media in the 20th c.; C. Meldolesi, 'Sguardi teatrali al secolo dei Giganti, nato con la prima guerra mondiale' (547–71); A. Mastropasqua, 'Per una ricerca sui rapporti tra poesia e arti visive' (572–89); and F. Razzi, 'Letteratura e musica: un'esperienza' (589–601). *Storia della letteratura italiana. Il Novecento*, ed. Enrico Malato, Ro, Salerno, 1,535 pp., sees literature against the background of political and cultural history, and offers a socially committed model of interpretation while it highlights the main literary currents and the aesthetic contributions made by individual authors to the Italian (but also European) Novecento in the following chapters: L. M. Migliorini, 'Comunismo, fascismo, democrazia liberale' (5–50); F. Restaino, 'Il travaglio culturale del Novecento' (51–162); Id., 'La cultura italiana fra ritardi e accelerazioni' (163–244); M. A. Grignani, 'Convergenze unificanti e spinte centrifughe nell'uso della lingua' (245–86); E. Ragni, 'Cultura e letteratura dal primo dopoguerra alla seconda guerra mondiale' (286–450); S. Pavarini, 'Saba, Ungaretti, Quasimodo. Poetica dell'ermetismo' (451–544); G. Ioli, 'Montale' (545–610); 'Gadda' (611–88); G. Leonelli, 'Politica e cultura. La letteratura tra impegno e sperimentazione' (688–728); T. Iermano and E. Ragni, 'Prosatori e narratori del primo e del secondo Novecento' (729–882); G. Zaccaria, 'Calvino' (883–924); T. Iermano and E. Ragni, 'Scrittori dell'ultimo Novecento' (925–1156); G. Leonelli, 'La poesia del primo e del secondo Novecento' (1157–244); L. Reina and M. Ravesi, 'Le letterature dialettali' (1245–368); S. Ferrone and T. Megale, 'Il teatro' (1369–466); C. Segre, 'Note per un bilancio del Novecento' (1467–520). Fernando Gioviale, *Scenari del racconto: mutazioni di scrittura nell'Otto-Novecento*, Caltanissetta, Sciascia, 326 pp. L. Russo, 'La letteratura narrativa della nuova Italia', *Belfagor*, 55:381–95, written originally in 1922, considers Italian literature from 1860 to the 1920s, and identifies psychological, social, and moral themes, thus anticipating later analysis both on realism and experimentalism. Massimiliano Capati, *Finimondo: una lettura del Novecento italiano*, Ro, Editori Riuniti, 119 pp. Luigi Baldacci, *Novecento passato remoto. Pagine di critica militante*, Mi, Rizzoli, 520 pp., includes essays of a general nature (where the importance of history and reality for criticism is highlighted) and a number of literary reviews on 20th-c. Italian authors. Rossana Dedola, *La musica dell'uomo solo: saggi su Luigi Pirandello, Primo Levi, Leonardo Sciascia e Giovanni Orelli*, F, Polistampa, 157 pp. Giuseppe Muraca, *Utopisti ed eretici nella letteratura italiana contemporanea*, Soveria

Mannelli, Rubbettino, 161 pp., includes essays on Romano Bilenchi, Franco Fortini, Pier Paolo Pasolini, Roberto Roversi, and Ignazio Silone. Gabriella Sica, *Sia dato credito all'invisibile. Prose e saggi*, Venice, Marsilio, 216 pp., is concerned with sincerity, search for truth, religion, and clarity of language in general, as concisely expressed in the essay 'Sia dato credito all'invisibile (201–03), and in particular in the work of number of writers including Elsa Morante (106–14), Lalla Romano (115–21), and Pier Paolo Pasolini (191–96).

On literary theory: Antonio Bernardelli, *Intertestualità*, F, La Nuova Italia, 182 pp., describes and defines intertextuality from various perspectives, adopting Gérard Genette's theories but also discussing other critics (particularly Maria Corti, Julia Kristeva, Cesare Segre, and Jurj Tynjanov). E. Rossi, 'Percorsi dell'intertestualità fra classico e moderno: dieci categorie di trasformazione testuale', *StCrit*, 15:307–29, classifies intertextuality under the following headings: direct reference, accumulation of various combined models, reference to diverse models by analogy, predominance of a single aspect from the models chosen, expansion of the models used, rejection of some aspects of the models, opposition to the models, addition of new aspects to those included in the models, correction of the models adopted, and heterogeneity and complexity of sources. Stefano Calabrese, *L'idea di letteratura in Italia*, Mi, B. Mondadori, 1999, 306 pp., provides a rapid overview of what he sees as the foundations of Italian poetics, including brief summaries of the aesthetic ideas of some 20th-c. writers, namely Pascoli, Croce, Pirandello, Serra, Debenedetti, Contini, Pasolini, and Calvino. Francesco Muzzioli, *Le teorie letterarie contemporanee*, Ro, Carocci, 240 pp., a sequel to *Le teorie della critica letteraria in Italia* (Ro, Carocci, 1994), discusses literary theories in the 1990s under the headings of ideology (67–101), postmodernism (103–37), the avant-garde (139–72), and the rhetoric of literature (173–203). While conducting an objective analysis M. is in favour of a type of poetics capable of being politicized, as well as based on innovative avant-garde textual strategies in the context of the contradictory situation of contemporary literature, which he considers exposed to the risks of being commercialized but also marginalized. Included among the critics examined by Muzzioli are P. Anderson, P. Bourdieu, L. Bloom, P. Bürger, H. Cixous, J. Derrida, T. Eagleton, L. Hutcheon, F. Jameson, W. Krisinski, J. Kristeva, J. M. Lotman, G. C. Spivak, G. Steiner, and the Italian critics R. Ceserani, F. Curi, G. Ferroni, G. Guglielmi, E. Sanguineti, and C. Segre. A panorama of contemporary debate on literature emerges. Among specific points it is worth mentioning discussion on the difference between postmodernism and the avant-garde, on contemporary myth devoid of the sublime, and on cultural studies. Ugo

Volli, *Manuale di semiotica*, Ro–Bari, Laterza, 382 pp., on various aspects including a chapter (ch. 10) on 'La vita sociale dei testi' and one (ch. 11) on 'Identità, soggettività e genere'. 'Beginnings / endings / beginnings' is the title of a large section (7–457) of *AnI*, 18, a special issue with an introd. by D. S. Cervigni who discusses the five sub-sections: 'Towards a theory of beginnings and endings' (7–141), which includes essays by G. Adamo, R. M. Dainotto, A. Nemesio, J. Smith, M. Riva, and C. Klopp; 'Medieval and Renaissance texts: closure, open-endedness, narrative cycles' (142–253), essays by R. S. Beal, D. S. Cervigni, A. Maggi, and L. Monga; 'Beginnings and endings in modern and postmodern literature' (254–374), essays by N. Bouchard, A. Camps, A. Casadei, C. Mazzoni, O. Pelosi, S. Ross, and C. Ryan-Schetz; R. Campa, 'An intellectual's wanderings at the turn of the millennium' (375–436); 'Hymns to a millenary beginning and ending' (437–57), which presents poems by Mario Baudino, Rosita Copioli, Roberto Carifi, Alessandra Carrera, Giuseppe Conte, Gabriella Galzio, Tomaso Kemeny, Massimo Maggiani, Roberto Mussapi, and Laura Stortoni.

G. Petronio, 'Letteratura e cinema: un rapporto difficile. Introduzione a un percorso', *Problemi*, 114–15, 1999: 108–20, refers briefly to the history of genres, then examines some early aspects of the links between cinema and literature, mentioning, among other things, Renato Serra's views on film and Futurist interest in cinema. On war and literature: Alberto Casadei, *Romanzi di Finisterre, narrazione della guerra e problemi del realismo*, Ro, Carocci, 289 pp.; A. Ghibelli, 'Testimonianze di guerra nel nostro tempo: scrittori e scriventi', *NC*, 47: 183–200, showing how some discrepancies may be found between letters and diaries written from the war fronts and their subsequent re-elaboration. On literature for the young: Orsetta Innocenti, *La letteratura giovanile*, Ro–Bari, Laterza, 96 pp., briefly confronts the canon of youth literature in Italy, then examines a number of authors, including Carlo Collodi, Edmondo De Amicis, Emilio Salgari, Italo Calvino, and Stefano Benni. An aspect of sociology of literature is examined in 'Caffè letterario e dintorni', *Resine*, 86: 5–42, through the following essays: J.-F. Rodriguez, 'Soffici e Severini a Parigi fra simbolismo e avanguardia: dalla Closerie des Lilas alla Brasserie de l'Ermitage (1900–1914)' (5–15); 'Tre poeti al caffè: Sbarbaro, Montale, Caproni' (16–18), with an introd. by S. Verdino and passages by the three poets concerned); U. Silva, 'Due caffè a Genova' (19–22), mentioning, among other things, the Caffè Bardi patronized by Sbarbaro; and memoirs by M. Venturi (23–25), M. Milani (26–29), L. Betocchi (30–32), and M. David (33–42).

Some essays focus on various aspects of the history of criticism. Marino Biondi, **Fedele alla critica: Geno Pampaloni e la letteratura* *contemporanea*, F, Polistampa, 118 pp. A. Casadei, 'Appunti sulla critica letteraria italiana', *Italianistica*, 28, 1999:469–76, highlights G. Mazzacurati's sense of history combined with attention to contemporary issues, G. Guglielmi's analysis of formal and structural aspects of literary texts, and P. V. Mengaldo's militant as well as philological approach to criticism. M. L. D'Oglio, 'Il Barocco nella lezione di Giovanni Getto e nella storia della cultura torinese del Novecento', *LItal*, 51, 1999: 593–601, compares G.'s and L. Anceschi's views on the Baroque and sees these two critics as precursors of some recent literary trends, then concentrates on G.'s own contribution to a rehabilitation of the Baroque in Italian critical debate. G. Ungarelli, 'Gianfranco Contini scrittore di lettere', *Belfagor*, 55:37–54, highlights the importance of C. as a writer of letters, and detects a moral attitude in his correspondence with Italian literati. M. Caesar and A. Hallamore Caesar, *L'onestà sperimentale. Carteggio di Emilio Cecchi e Gianfranco Contini*, ed. Paolo Leoncini, Mi, Adelphi, xxxvi + 180 pp., includes an introd., 'Tra metodo e linguaggio: "la critica onesta e umana"' (ix-xxxvi), in which the following three lines of interpretation are pursued: Contini's admiration for Cecchi's work, the same author's method of 'inoggettivarsi' and his empathy with literary texts, and Cecchi's views on politics and literature. M. Caesar, 'Il Novecento italiano nel Regno Unito e in Irlanda', *EL*, 24.4, 1999:93–108, reviews criticism on 20th-c. poetry, theatre, and narrative from 1993 to 1999. Carlo Dionisotti, *Lettere londinesi (1968–1995)*, ed. Giuseppe Anceschi, F, Olschki, 113 pp., includes Dionisotti's letters to Giuseppe Anceschi, and Anceschi's essay 'Il "preteso" della morte. Un italiano all'estero' (9–29), where Dionisotti's biography, his antifascism and partial debt to Benedetto Croce, and his huge and innovative contribution to Italian criticism are highlighted.

On periodicals: P. Hainsworth, 'Florentine cultural journalism under Fascism: *Il Bargello*', *MLR*, 95, 696–711, reviews *Il Bargello* in the 1930s and 1940s, and argues that even its cultural pages, though they included articles by intellectuals such as Elio Vittorini and Alfonso Gatto (who were later to become antifascist), did not correspond to orthodox Fascist policies, yet neither were they directly anti-Fascist. S. Delli Paoli, 'Una rivista napoletana del primo Novecento', *Problemi*, 114–15, 1999:133–48, is about the journal *La Diana* (publ. 1915–17) and its collaborators, including Giuseppe Ungaretti, Pietro Jahier, Corrado Govoni, and Benedetto Croce. Daniela Fabello, *Coenobium, rivista senza frontiere: i retroscena ticinesi*, Locarno, Dadò, 1999, 259 pp., is about the creation of *Coenobium* (1906) and includes a number of letters (179–216). On publishing: Alberto Cadioli, *L'editore e i suoi lettori*, Bellinzona, Casagrande, 65 pp., is not specifically on publishing but rather on cultural production and book distribution. *L'industria culturale. Tracce e immagini di un privilegio*, ed. Alberto Abruzzese and Davide Borrelli, Ro, Carocci, 267 pp., traces the origins of the cultural industry back to antiquity and the Middle Ages, then examines its 20th-c. forms in greater detail and concludes with chapters on cinema and other mass media.

On women's writing: *Parole scolpite: profili di scrittrici degli anni Novanta*, ed. Adriana Chemello, Padua, Il Poligrafo, 1998, 144 pp., includes essays on narrative writers: Luisa Adorno by R. Ricorda, who underlines her Tuscan and communist origins, and appreciates her concentrated and very readable fiction (75–88); Sandra Petrignani by P. Azzolini (89–100); Clara Sereni by A. Chemello (103–20), examining the unitary mosaic emerging from her interest in fragments, and also her Jewish origins and sense of history; and Lia Levi by G. Gardenal (121–28). Elisabetta Rasy, *Le donne e la letteratura*, Ro, Editori Riuniti, 160 pp., a reprint of a 1984 essay, comprises a new introd. (7–14) where the central position recently acquired by women is highlighted, and genre analyses, as well as autobiography combined with historical themes, are indicated among the recent acquisitions of women's literature in Italy.

On writers and politics. Ugo Dotti, *Storia degli intellettuali in Italia*, III: *Temi e ideologie dagli illuministi a Gramsci*, Ro, Editori Riuniti, 1999, xviii + 334 pp. Giuseppe Iannaccone, *Il fascismo 'sintetico'. Letteratura e ideologia negli anni Trenta*, Mi, Greco & Greco, 1999, 231 pp., shows how the itinerary of intellectuals such as E. Vittorini and R. Bilenchi from Fascism to Communism was not inconsistency but rather a continuous ideological development. Joseph Francese, *Cultura e politica negli anni Cinquanta: Salinari, Pasolini, Calvino*, Ro, Lithos, 147 pp. *Dove sono finiti gli intellettuali?*, 'I forum di *Corriere on line*', Internet: http://www.corriere.it/intellettuali.html, contains a number of articles on political commitment among contemporary intellectuals: G. Belardelli, 'Intellettuali, per favore non parlate di politica', March 25th, questions the ability of intellectuals to interpret political events; P. Di Stefano, 'L'intellettuale? È finito', March 26th, contrasts the committed attitudes of intellectuals such as F. Fortini with the inclination of contemporary intellectuals to avoid controversial debate, and concludes that perhaps, in the age of global communication, 'gli intellettuali non comunicano più: forse hanno perso la parola'; F. Ferrarotti, 'Società intellettuale di mutuo soccorso', March 27th, remarks that the context of firm ideologies and utopias which characterized intellectual debate in past decades has disintegrated: thus contemporary intellectual commitment, though still necessary, is bound to be 'pragmatico, verificabile'; G. Giudici, 'I profeti della rassegnazione', March 28th, maintains that 'l'intellettuale, e specialmente l'intellettuale-scrittore, come possibile soggetto politico, è finito' because of the amoral, political, and economic context which frustrates the function of intellectuals as social witnesses; S. Vassalli, 'Fortini? Era un maestro dell'aria fritta', March 28th, laments that 'non c'è nessuno, oggi in Italia, che pensa (e scrive) fuori del coro'; P. V. Mengaldo, 'Lasciamo pure che Grass parli di politica', March 28th, advocates the right and the duty of intellectuals to discuss political issues; G. Mariotti, 'Io non rimpiango l'epoca d'oro dell'impegno', March 29th, holds the view that the 'golden age' of commitment in Italy was not as important as it was deemed to be until recently; G. Conti, 'Le riviste ci sono e anche le idee', March 30th, highlights the fact that intellectual debate continues both in newspapers and journals; there are also articles by A. Arbasino, L. Simonelli, G. Raboni, and by a number of readers of *Il corriere della sera*. Edoardo Sanguineti, *Il chierico organico: scritture e intellettuali*, Mi, Feltrinelli, 317 pp., includes several essays and articles on cultural politics published from 1975 to 1999. Of particular interest is 'Il chierico organico' (13–21), originally published in 1988 which discusses the importance of organic intellectuals, cosmopolitanism, and class consciousness in modern society.

2.   POETRY

Several studies on, and anthologies of, twentieth century poetry were published in the past year. *Poesia del Novecento in Italia e in Europa*, ed. Edoardo Esposito, 2 vols., Mi, Feltrinelli, xix + 370 pp., xix + 324 pp., considers Italian poetry in a European context while each vol. provides useful biographical and bibliographical information. *La poesia italiana del Novecento*, ed. Raouletta Baroni and Piero Cigada, Mi, Vallardi, 252 pp. *L'Europa dei poeti. Atti del Convegno di studi, Bologna, 27–28 aprile 1998*, ed. Nicola Muschitiello and Vincenzo Bagnoli, Bo, CLUEB, 1999, 252 pp. Sergio Pautasso, *Lirica moderna: un ossimoro ideale*, Settimo Milanese, Marzorati — Ro, Editalia, 1999, 324 pp. *Poesia moderna e contemporanea: il Parnaso europeo*, ed. and introd. Carlo Muscetta, Ro, Pagine, 414 pp., is an anthology of 19th and 20th c. Italian poetry and is the third volume of a new 'Parnaso europeo' series. Vol. 5 of the anthology *L'Altro Novecento* features Vittoriano Esposito, *La poesia centro-meridionale e insulare*, Foggia, Bastogi, 1999, 749 pp. *Annuario di poesia*, 3 (2000), ed. Guido Oldani, Mi, Crocetti, 1999, 161 pp. *Poesia '99*, ed. Giorgio Manacorda, Ro, Castelvecchi, 284 pp., includes *inter alia* some unpublished poetry by Pasolini. Enrico Elli and Giuseppe Langella, *Il canto strozzato. Poesia italiana del Novecento*, Novara, Interlinea, 1997, 614 pp., offers an outline of the language of poetry in the 20th century together with biographical and critical commentaries on the work of selected poets.

Marco Forti, *Tempi della poesia. Il Secondo Novecento da Montale a Porta*, Mi, Mondadori, 1999, 370 pp., traces the path of poetic ideas from Montale to Porta and assesses the work of leading poets at that time. Anna Nozzoli, *Voci di un secolo: da D'Annunzio a Cristina Campo*, Ro, Bulzoni, 415 pp. Natale Tedesco, *La coscienza letteraria del Novecento: Gozzano, Svevo ed altri esemplari*, Palermo, Flaccovio, 1999, 300 pp. *1969–1999: la lettura da Ariosto a Zanzotto*, ed. V. Campo, Mi, Mondadori, 1999, xxvii + 377 pp., contains a final section that deals with 20th-c. poetry. Giorgio Zanetti, *Il Novecento come visione. Dal simbolismo a Campana*, Ro, Carocci, 1999, 255 pp., provides an insightful analysis on the role of symbolism in Italian poetry up to the time of Campana. Arnaldo Pini, *Incontri alle Giubbe rosse: Landolfi, Loffredo, Luzi, Malaparte, Montale, Parronchi, Thomas, Traverso*, F, Polistampa, 143 pp. Giorgio Battaglia, *Tre personalità morali e poetiche: Montale, Quasimodo, Saluzzi. Tre canti di vita e amore*, Modica, Moderna, 1999, 30 pp. Maria Antonietta Grignani, 'Derive dell'identità in poesia', *Allegoria*, 34–35:7–22, considers the 'soggetto enunciatore fortemente centripeto' of the 1930s and 1940s. She contrasts it with diverse motivations and the impact of marginalization or 'invasione' that can be detected in recent Italian poetry and which also impacts on the poet's 'loquacità dell'io'. P. Cataldi, 'Il canone e la critica. La poesia moderna nell'antologia di Segre e Ossola', *ib.*, 258–67, queries the lack of a firm structure in this work and the apparent imbalance in the number of pages dedicated to certain poets. In Nicola Merola, *Un Novecento in piccolo. Saggi sulla letteratura contemporanea*, Soveria Mannelli, Rubbettino, 244 pp., part one offers a number of interesting essays on poetry (and prose) in 20th-c. Italy, together with two chapters on characteristics of, and developments in, recent Italian poetry; part two highlights the work of poets such as Ungaretti, Montale, Luzi, Pierro, Zanzotto, and Giudici. P. Cataldi, 'Appunti su Leopardi e la poesia del Novecento, *Allegoria*, 34–35:155–68, outlines various affinities between L.'s poetry and that of Ungaretti, Saba, Montale, Fortini, Zanzotto, Rebora, and Sbarbaro. Mario Moroni, *La presenza complessa. Identità e soggettività nelle poetiche del Novecento*, Ravenna, Longo, 1998, 162 pp., is a literary and theoretical history of Italian poetry from the turn of the century to the present time. *Cambon Vol.* has a selection of essays on 20th-c. poets (notably Montale), literary movements, and Italian poetry in the USA (see below). Thomas E. Peterson, *The Rose in Contemporary Italian Poetry*, Gainesville, Florida U.P., 342 pp. Ferroni, *Passioni*, has a number of chapters on individual poets (see below). Giacomo Debenedetti, *Poesia italiana del Novecento*, Mi, Garzanti (Gli Elefanti) is a new version of the 1993 edition. It contains a preface by Alfonso Berardinelli and an introd. by Pier Paolo Pasolini with articles on the main movements and personalities of Italian and French poetry of the period. Pier Vincenzo Mengaldo, *La tradizione del Novecento*, T, Bollati Boringhieri, 421 pp., examines the situation of dialect poetry, the language of the *crepuscolari*, and the work of many 20th-c. poets.

W. Binni, *Poetica e poesia. Letture novecentesche*, ed. Francesco and Lanfranco Binni, Mi, Sansoni, 1999, 360 pp., collects for the first time articles (previously published in journals) that examine the concept of *poetica* as applied to poets, writers, and critics in 20th-c. Italian literature. Landolfi, *Il sacro*, contains articles by and on individual poets. Two poets discuss the role of the sacred in poetry: M. Luzi, 'Il sacro nell'epoca della modernità' (11–12), and F. Loi, 'La poesia, il sacro' (25–29). Roberto Pasanisi, *Le muse 'bendate': la poesia del Novecento contro la modernità*, Pisa–Ro, IEPI, 170 pp. *'Poesia nonostante tutto'*, ed. Franco Musarra and Bart Van der Bossche, Leuven U.P. — F, Cesati, 1999, 117 pp., records conversations with Rodolfo Di Biasio, Mario Luzi, Leonardo Mancino, Umberto Piersanti, Roberto Sanesi, and Maria Luisa Spaziani. J. Picchione, 'Poetry and the human sciences in Italy (the 1970s and the 1980s)', *FoI*, 33, 1999:263–72. '"La via italiana alla poesia", con interventi di Marco Forti, Pier Vincenzo Mengaldo, e Mario Luzi', ed. Renzo Ricchi, *NA*, 135.2:5–20.

Of particular interest are publications that examine specific literary movements. Giuseppe Farinella, *'Vent'anni o poco più'. Storia e poesia del movimento crepuscolare*, Mi, Otto/Novecento, 1998, 645 pp. Angela Ida Villa, **Neoidealismo e rinascenza latina tra Otto e Novecento. La cerchia di Sergio Corazzini. Poeti dimenticati e riviste del crepuscolarismo romano (1903–1907)*, Mi, LED, 1999, 852 pp. Marco Manotta, 'La scrittura futurista', *Il Verri*, 1999, 10–11:114–29. Antonio Saccone, *Futurismo, Ro, Marzorati Editalia, 109 pp. Id., **La trincea avanzata e la città dei conquistatori. Futurismo e modernità*, Na, Liguori, 172 pp. G. Langella, 'Passaporto per *La Ronda*', *ON*, 24.1:89–104, argues that this journal had a broader, more European dimension than the narrow one usually attributed to it. M. Gazich, 'Trent'anni di studi sull'ermetismo', *Testo*, 39:137–47; R. Marchi, 'Le riviste di poesia oggi in Italia (II)', *ib.*, 149–54, is the sequel to a first part publ. in *ib.*, 37:167–75. M. Guiney, 'The birth of the avant-garde', *Cambon Vol.*, 273–82. E. N. Girardi, 'Politica e poesia. A proposito di mitomodernismo e altro', *Testo*, 39:5–33. P. Valesio, 'I fuochi incrociati delle tribù. Poeti italiani tra Vecchio e Nuovo Mondo', *Cambon Vol.*, 305–40, offers an incisive analysis of the work of poets born in Italy who now write and live in the USA. A. J. Tamburri, 'Studi novecenteschi nordamericani', *EL*, 25.3–4:263–76, evaluates the work of Italians writing in the USA in the 20th c.

Significant too is the attention paid to the work of women poets. M. Bettarini, 'Donne e poesia. Voci *del* Sud, *dal* Sud', *Poesia*, 139:59–76, is the sixth and final part of her analysis of women and poetry in contemporary Italy where she considers the work of 17 poets who work and live in various regions of southern Italy. They include Franca Alaimo, Maria Attanasio, Rossella Cerniglia, Maria Consolo, Assunta Finiguerra, Rosa Maria Fusco, Anna Maria Giancarli, Giuseppina Luongo Bartolini, Giovanna Markus, Biagia Marniti, Marisa Papa Ruggiero, Miriam Pierri, Marisa Righetti, Gianna Sallustio, Anna Santoliquido, Myriam Scasseddu, Matilde Tortora. The increasing interest in dialect poetry is reflected in the number of publications dealing with this topic. A. De Simone, 'Il continente sommerso della poesia in dialetto', *ib.*, 136:68–73, cites an interview with Franco Brevini who outlines his interest in the earliest tradition of Italian dialect literature and the manner in which it impacts on 20th-c. dialect writing in Italy. F. Loi, 'Del dialetto e altro', *ib.*, 74–75, offers an interesting evaluation of Franco Brevini's work and also singles out aspects such as the emphasis on tradition and customs as being particularly helpful in providing a better understanding of both oral and choral dimensions of dialect poetry in Italy. G. Fagiani, 'Alfonso Fagiani and the tradition of the poeta-artigiano in Abruzzo', *FoI*, 34:173–90, delineates the 'poeta-artigiano' model of the Abruzzo region and shows how it influenced thematic choices and literary sensibilities. Particular attention is paid to the work of Fagiani (1862–1935) who wrote in Abruzzese. L. Bonaffini, 'Italian dialects from common speech to literary languages', *Cambon Vol.*, 289–304, defines the elevated status now held by dialect poetry. M. Bordin, 'Fra editi e inediti di due poeti veneti recentemente scomparsi: Tiziano Rizzo e Luisa Zille', *QVen*, 30, 1999:175–302, examines much of the work of these poets and reproduces several of their published and unpublished poems. The following prize-winning thesis looked at poetry in Turin: Maria Paola Biglia, *Indagine sulla poesia a Torino, 1983–96*, Cavalmaggiore, Centro Stampa Cavalmaggiore, 1998, x + 88 pp.

G. Sasso, 'La teoria intralinguistica del testo poetico', *StCrit*, 92:1–51, outlines the correlation between mechanical and neuro-physical reactions that combine to produce anagrams in poetry. I. Travi, 'L'aspetto orale della poesia', *Testuale*, 26–27, 1999:64–70. A. Di Benedetto, *Poesia e critica del Novecento*, Na, Liguori, 1999, 269 pp. *Autografo*, 41, includes many tributes to Vanni Scheiwiller, the publisher who did so much for poetry in Italy and who died in 2000. Luigi Baldacci, *Novecento passato remoto. Pagine di critica militante*, Mi,

Rizzoli, 1999, 519 pp., is a critical overview of the main literary figures in 20th-c. literary criticism.

3. NARRATIVE, THEATRE

Essays on narrative are as follows. 'Il romanzo tra scienza e filosofia', *Nuova civiltà delle macchine*, 18:5–108, introd. V. Marchis (5–8), includes C. Magris, 'Romanzo e conoscenza: appunti per una introduzione' (9–16), where the novel is seen as a form of knowledge of reality; U. Eco, 'Livelli di lettura' (17–28), an analysis of narrative based on the concept of 'double coding' with examples drawn mainly from E.'s own novel *Il pendolo di Foucault*; R. Bodei, 'Vite parallele. Etica e romanzo' (35–42), which argues that the novel today is an intermediate world between reality and imagination; A. Casadei, 'Il romanzo del Novecento e i problemi del realismo' (99–108), arguing that the concept of verisimilitude in the second half of the 20th c. has changed in relation to the development of cinema and television up to the present day, when the novel can be authentically realistic if it tells of what is exceptional (99–108). It also includes essays by writers Marc Augé and John Banville, and critics G. Boniolo, S. Givone, G. O. Longo, G. Morra, and R. Pierantoni. Filippo La Porta, *Narratori di un sud disperso*, Na, L'Ancora, 120 pp., sees the identity of the south of Italy in the context of the larger identity of the southern hemisphere, and discusses works by a number of writers including G. Tomasi di Lampedusa, and L. Sciascia, and contemporary authors such as R. Alajmo, G. Calaciura, and G. Montesano. W. Sahlfeld, 'Literarische Milieus im italienischen Roman vom späten 19. Jahrhundert bis zur Nachkriegszeit', *ItStudien*, 21:213–31.

On narrative genres. Stefano Lazzarin, *Il modo fantastico*, Ro–Bari, Laterza, 88 pp., following in the tracks of Tzvetan Todorov and Remo Ceserani, defines the fantastic as a genre rather than a mode. He sees fantastic texts as creating conflict between daily and extraordinary events, and then examines some foreign and Italian examples including texts by Alfredo Boito and Antonio Tabucchi. On science fiction: E. Corti, 'Il simulacro e lo spettacolare: due aspetti della postmodernità', *ConLet*, 16, 1999:35–65, argues that in science fiction we find two types of story, viz., stories where future developments of contemporary science can be detected and, secondly, stories based on fantasy. He notes that the so-called 'cyberpunk' stories exhibit postmodern features such as advanced computer technology, the reduction of the lives of individuals to mere show business, and a pervasive social Darwinism. Giuseppe Petronio, *Sulle tracce del giallo*, Ro, Gamberetti, 193 pp., illustrates the sociology, style, and functions of detective fiction.

'La narrativa del Novecento *sub specie* culinaria', pp. 233–495 of *Soavi sapori della cultura italiana*, ed. Bart Van den Bossche, Michel Bastiaensen, and Corinna Salvadori Lonergan, F, Cesati, 510 pp., includes B. Van den Bossche, 'Il cibo nella narrativa del Novecento: appunti per una tipologia' (483–95), a general definition of the 'realistic' and 'narrative' functions of food in 20th-c. Italian literature; I. Lanslots, 'Un assaggio della narrativa italiana contemporanea: il sapore di chiusura' (367–82), on some intellectual and psychological aspects of food in Italian 20th-c. fiction; R. Gennaro (317–30) and L. Pavan (429–42) on food in Futurism; and a number of contributions on food in the work of individual authors: M. Actis-Grosso on Giorgio Bassani (235–47), J. Beverly on Isabella Bossi Fedrigotti (247–56), C. Carotenuto on Libero Bigiaretti (257–72), K. Du Pont on Emilio Lussu (273–89), M. Fabrizi on Paolo Volponi (289–306), W. Geerts on Vincenzo Consolo (307–16), G. Giacomazzi on Luigi Malerba (331–44), M. Giuliodori on Mario Puccini (345–54), G. Guidotti on Carlo Emilio Gadda (355–66), D. Mangano (383–96) and I. Van Ackere (471–82) on Italo Svevo, M. Meschini on Antonio Tabucchi (397–404), S. Nemmert on Alessandra Berardi (405–12), C. Nocentini on Italo Calvino (413–28), and H. Salaets on Giuseppe Bonaviri (443–56).

Some essays are about Italian fiction in the 1980s and 1990s. General overviews are Fabio Pierangeli, *Ultima narrativa italiana: 1983–2000*, Ro, Studium, 203 pp., and, more in detail on the late 1990s, Giuseppe Amoroso, *Il notaio della via lattea. Narrativa italiana 1996–1998*, Caltanissetta, Sciascia, 519 pp. *Tirature 2000*, ed. Vittorio Spinazzola, Mi, Il Saggiatore–Fondazione Mondadori, 272 pp., contains a number of essays on genres in the Italian novel in the 1990s including: M. S. Petruzzi on romance (40–49), L. De Federicis on the historical novel (54–60), B. Falcetto on science fiction (61–67), and G. Canova on the detective novel (90–96). Dacia Maraini, *Amata scrittura. Laboratorio di analisi, letture, proposte, conversazioni*, Mi, Rizzoli, 320 pp., based on a television programme conducted by M., includes her views but also several statements on reading and style by living writers (among them Vincenzo Consolo, Maria Corti, and Claudio Magris). Renato Barilli, *È arrivata la terza ondata. Dalla neo alla neo-neoavanguardia*, T, Testo & Immagine, 180 pp., sees some of the writers who emerged in the 1980s and 1990s as members of a new wave of the avant-garde. He particularly values Ermanno Cavazzoni and Gianni Celati for their irony and their distance from consumerism, Roberto Pazzi because he combines the fantastic (or the *romance*) with realism (or the *novel*), Silvia Ballestra, Enrico Brizzi, Aldo Busi, Giuseppe Caliceti, and Giuseppe Culicchia because they express alienated urban environments in a colloquial and vibrant language,

Tommaso Ottonieri for his experimental language, and a number of other writers who have contributed to the renewal of style in the last two decades in Italy. Tommaso Ottonieri, *La plastica della lingua. Stili in fuga in una età postrema*, T, Bollati Boringhieri, 240 pp., appears to see some of the literature of the last two decades as a result of, and a build-up on, the critical ideals of the 1977 movement. He discusses pulp fiction, expressionistic experiments with language and some poetry, and analyses some of the work of authors such as Nanni Balestrini, Silvia Ballestra, Aldo Busi, Aldo Nove, and Tiziano Scarpa. F. Senardi, 'Di alcuni caratteri della più recente narrativa italiana', *Problemi*, 114–15, 1999:166–90, looks mainly at works by best-selling authors, including Andrea Baricco's stories based on literary artifice, the dense plot of Luigi Malerba's novel *La superficie di Eliane*, the pessimism of Sebastiano Vassalli's historical novels, the reasons for the success of Andrea Camilleri's fiction, and other topics. R. Bertoni, 'Aspetti del fantastico in alcuni romanzi italiani degli anni '80–'90', *Italia & Italy*, 2.7:3–7, examines some aspects of the fantastic in relation to the poetics of late modernity in a number of novels by S. Benni, A. Canobbio, E. F. Carabba, and E. Cavazzoni, compares these novels to some of their modernist predecessors', and concludes that even though the modernist and late modern types of the fantastic may be different from each other, some contemporary authors retain both the committed and non-canonical aims of the modern fantastic tradition.

General information on the theatrical season in Italy is given in *Teatro in Italia, '98: cifre, dati, novità della stagione di prosa 1997–98*, Ro, SIAE, 1999, xxvi + 358 pp. *I fuoriscena: esperienze e riflessioni sulla drammaturgia nel sociale*, ed. Claudio Bernardi, Benvenuto Cuminetti, and Sisto Dalla Palma, Mi, Euresis, 358 pp, examines some social uses of theatre. Paolo Puppa, *Parola di scena: teatro italiano tra '800 e '900*, Ro, Bulzoni, 1999, 300 pp., includes a rich crop of short essays on 20th-c. dramatists, from Gino Rocca and Bontempelli to Svevo, Pirandello, and Fabbri, on such actor-dramatists as Giacinta Pezzana, Eduardo De Filippo, and Dario Fo, and also on various theatre critics.

4. Individual Authors

ALERAMO. Sibilla Aleramo and Dino Campana, *Un viaggio chiamato amore. Lettere 1916–1918*, ed. Bruna Conti, Mi, Feltrinelli, 134 pp., documents the exchange of letters which marked their relationship in those years, adding some previously unpublished material to the 1987 Editori Riuniti edition. C. C. Gallucci, 'The body and the letter: Sibilla Aleramo in the Interwar Years', *FoI*, 33, 1999:363–91, argues that *Una donna* portrays an 'evolutionary selfhood' but complicates traditional autobiography because her protagonist is not only individual but also 'communal or choral'. He also states that in later Fascist years A.'s autobiographical work, even though somehow autonomous from politics, occupies a 'transgressive space' both as a literary genre and with respect to predominant cultural and anthropological models. U. Fanning, 'Sibilla Aleramo's *Una donna*: a case study in women's autobiographical fiction', *The Italianist*, 19, 1999: 164–77.

ANEDDA. R. Galaverni, 'Antonella e Amelia', *NArg*, 10: 279–300, suggests various ways of interpreting Anedda's 'Per un nuovo inverno' written after the death of the poet Amelia Rosselli.

BANTI. T. E. Peterson, 'Of the barony: Anna Banti and the time of decision', *MLN*, 114, 1999: 126–42, adopts A. Gargani's concept of 'voce femminile' for an examination of B.'s novels *Il bastardo* (1953) and *Un grido lacerante* (1981).

BERTO. C. Della Colletta, 'Gli anti-*Promessi sposi* di Giuseppe Berto, ovvero il processo ai padri', *MLN*, 115: 94–119, detects echoes of Manzoni in B.'s *Il cielo è rosso*, and shows how, while appropriating his model, B. contradicts it on a number of levels including a lack of historical redemption.

BERTOLUCCI. S. Ramat, 'Attilio Bertolucci. Con l'equilibrio di un classico', *Poesia*, 141: 28–30, is a warm tribute to the poet regarded as 'il patriarca della poesia italiana' who died in June 2000. *NA*, 11, has an entire section devoted to Bertolucci: G. Contini, 'Caro Bertolucci' (54–55); G. Palli Baroni, 'Capricci Invernali: Tenero rifiuto' (58–65), which assesses B.'s 'lati deboli' in his poetry; T. De Meis and V. Volpe, 'I luoghi della *Camera da letto*' (67–85), which has a photographic record of the places referred to in these poems; P. Lagazzi, 'Bertolucci "in campo" '(86–109), evaluating B.'s place in 20th-c. Italian literature; R. Manica, 'Preistoria di Bertolucci: un omaggio' (110–21); D. Maraini, 'Ricordo' (122–23); A. Gibellini, 'In memoriam' (124–25); P. Bertolani, 'Come quando de nòte i tage "a luse" ' (126–27). Attilio Bertolucci, **Ho rubato due versi a Baudelaire: prose e divagazioni*, ed. Gabriella Palli Baroni, Mi, Mondadori, 502 pp.

BETOCCHI. L. Kibler, 'Carlo Betocchi and Paul Verlaine: poetic affinities', *Italiana*, 9: 157–67. S. Ramat, ' "Qualcosa che sa di leggenda". La madre (e il figlio) nella poesia di Betocchi', pp. 57–71 of *Il sacro nella poesia contemporanea*, ed. Giuliano Landolfi and Marco Merlin, Novara, Interlinea, 100 pp. Nino Agnello, **La poesia di Carlo Betocchi: tra relativo e assoluto*, Foggia, Bastogi, 95 pp.

BIAMONTI. G. Cavallini, 'Trittico per Biamonti', on pp. 141–90 of Giorgio Cavallini, *Verga Tozzi Biamonti: tre trittici con una premessa comune*, Ro, Bulzoni, 1998[2000], 194 pp., identifies three key symbols, or 'parole-immagine', in B.'s work: 'vento', 'mare' and 'luce', and analyses other linguistic features of his fiction, in particular the verbal and conceptual aspects of the acts of 'gazing' and 'seeing' ('guardare' and 'vedere').

BIANCHINI. P. Carù, 'L'esperienza dell'altrove in *Capo d'Europa* di Angela Bianchini', *Gradiva*, 18:66–77, illustrates the anonymous protagonist's rite of passage from adolescence to adulthood, psychological itinerary of self-discovery, historical awareness of Fascism and anti-Semitism, and experience of 'deterritorializzazione' through exile, followed by a symbolic 'riterritorializzazione' in a landscape of the mind.

BIANCIARDI. Giancarlo Ferretti, *La morte irridente. Ritratto critico di Luciano Bianciardi uomo, giornalista, traduttore, scrittore*, Lecce, Manni, 120 pp., highlights B.'s antifascism, his collaboration with journals such as *Belfagor*, his political commitment, and his non-conformist personality.

BIANCONI. Marking the hundredth birthday of a noted Ticinese writer, 'Nel centenario della nascita di Piero Bianconi', *Cenobio*, 49:3–50, the *acta* of a 'pomeriggio di studio' held at the Locarno Biblioteca Cantonale, include: D. Isella, 'Ricordo di Piero Bianconi' (7–11); R. Martinoni, 'Dal *Frontespizio* a Roberto Longhi: i carteggi bianconiani' (13–19), and 'Nell'officina di *Albero genealogico*. Alcune pagine inedite' (43–50); S. Geiser Foglia, 'Le lettere con il pittore Emilio Maria Beretta' (21–31); M. Agliati, 'Piero Bianconi negli anni della seconda guerra mondiale' (33–41).

BIGIARETTI. **Libero Bigiaretti: la storia, le storie, la scrittura. Atti del Convegno di Matelica 21–22 marzo 1998*, ed. Alfredo Luzi, Fossombrone (Pesaro), Metauro, 282 pp.

BIGONGIARI. M. C. Papini, 'La poesia pensa: riflessione teorica e prassi poetica nell'ultimo Bigongiari', *RLI*, 103, 1999:449–53, argues that poetic thought is at the basis of all lyricism in B.'s work.

BILENCHI. Ferdinando Banchini, *Bilenchi*, Mi, Laboratorio delle Arti, 1999, 460 pp., gives a balanced analysis of the work of Bilenchi — journalist, novelist, poet, and critic — together with a survey of writers who influenced what he wrote.

BONTEMPELLI. U. Piscopo, ' "Les trahisons", o l'impegno intellettuale di Massimo Bontempelli', *Il Ponte*, 56.10:117–35, investigates B.'s dissociation from Fascism in the 1930s culminating in 1938 with his expulsion from the Accademia d'Italia, and attempts to read his intellectual biography, partly at least, as characterized by Utopian ideals independent of Fascist ideology ever since the 1920s.

BORGESE. L. Parisi, 'Gli scritti politici di Giuseppe Antonio Borgese', *EL*, 24.4, 1999:53–69, illustrates how B.'s initially nationalist views changed subsequently to democratic convictions, while he maintained a position of intellectual superiority .

BRANCATI. G. Ferroni, 'Vitaliano Brancati e le illusioni di un secolo "superbo e sciocco"', *Belfagor*, 55:655–66, argues in favour of B.'s irony and intellectual honesty combined with his rejection of delusive ideology.

BUFALINO. P. Bisciari, 'Gesualdo Bufalino: *L'uomo invaso* come metafora', *LetP*, 106, 1999:25–29, argues that B.'s 'narrativa lirica' compels his readers to free themselves from their sense of reality and daily life in order to meditate on the existential dimension of being, the literary dimension of the fantastic, and the psychological dimension of the impossibility of completely recapturing past memories, combined with memory's attempt to triumph over oblivion and consequently death.

BUZZATI. A. Colombo, 'Contini lettore di Buzzati', *RLettI*, 17.1, 1999:87–105, argues that, even though Contini ignored B. in his *Italia magica*, he read B.'s work, as is shown by two of B.'s works (*Il grande ritratto* and *Il poema a fumetti*) signed by their author and found in Contini's library.

Founded in 1996 and directed by Nella Giannetto, the annual journal of the Centro Studi Buzzati at Feltre now has four weighty volumes to its credit. *Studi buzzatiani*, 3, 1998, contains the following 'essays and notes': M. Farnetti, 'Leggere il mondo per dimostrare i libri. Il personaggio-scrittore nell'opera di Buzzati' (7–26); S. Lazzarin, 'Tra retorica e semantica. Costanti accumulativo-evocative della prosa buzzatiana' (27–51); F. Siddell, 'Surveillance in *Il buttafuoco*' (52–63); R. Carnero, 'Il bestiario di Dino Buzzati: animali reali e fantastici nei racconti e negli articoli: parte prima' (64–94); P. Donazzolo, 'Regolamento e sublime' (95–112); T. Bertoldin, '*Il segreto del Bosco Vecchio*: un'ipotesi di lettura attenta alla psicologia del profondo' (113–32); S. Dal Mas and S. Endrizzi, 'La "Spiegazione" de *I miracoli di Val Morel* come racconto di un viaggio all'altro mondo' (133–42); M. Polesana, 'Incunaboli della narrativa buzzatiana: "Temporale sul fiume"' (143–48). *Studi buzzatiani*, 4, 1999[2000], includes: V. Caratozzolo, '"E forse io mento anche adesso": "Il grande ritratto" di Dino Buzzati, o dell'inattingibilità del senso' (7–33); B. Mellarini, 'Dalle *Lettere a Brambilla* al *Bàrnabo delle montagne*: una proposta di lettura' (34–50); R. Carnero, 'Il bestiario di Dino Buzzati: seconda parte' (51–77); A. Bala Balandard, 'Di Buzzati et le *Désert des Tartares* en Pologne et en polonais' (78–90); R. Zucco, 'Per una lettura di *Paura alla Scala*: testo e contesto' (91–124); C. De Vecchis, 'Il "sottile dialogare". Appunti per un'analisi del dialogo in Buzzati' (125–53).

CALVINO. *Lettere: 1940–1985*, ed. Luca Baranelli, Mi, Mondadori, lxxxvi + 1624 pp., has an introd. by Claudio Milanini (ix-xli) drawing on the letters to reconstruct C.'s poetics, while highlighting the publishing novelty of those from the 1940s. Essays of a general character include: P. Antonello, 'Le forme dell'albero. Su Italo Calvino', *NC*, 46:343–71, which, via theoretical reference to M. Serres's essays, examines the biological and anthropological configurations of the image of the 'tree' in C.'s work and then relates them to C.'s combinatory narrative based on 'trees' of a linguistic nature; R. Rushing, 'The horizon of literature: epistemic closure in Calvino's *I nostri antenati*', *FoI*, 33, 1999:213–33, arguing that 'for C. the beginning of a text is, ironically, a moment of closure': his closures were of a traditional kind in the neo-realist phase but became self-referential in the trilogy, and even more so in *Marcovaldo*, where a comparison between the whiteness of the snow (which symbolizes the real world) and the whiteness of the page after the end of the story seems to indicate a merging of the text with reality beyond the space and time of the fictional dimension; and P. Napoli, 'Italo Calvino attraverso Italo Calvino: "Saremo come Omero"', *FAM*, 17, 1999:81–93, discussing a 1948 article which anticipates a number of important developments in C.'s poetics: choice of style, the function of literature, authorial and biographical selves, and the relationship with the literary tradition. On intertextuality: J. Burns, 'Telling tales about *impegno*: commitment and hindsight in Vittorini and Calvino', *MLR*, 95:992–1006, compares Vittorini's *Diario in pubblico* and C.'s preface to *Una pietra sopra* in that both of them are revisions of juvenilia where the author acts as his own critic, guiding and intruding into a re-interpretation of his own past. M. McLaughlin, 'Dr Calvino and Mr Stevenson', *Italia & Italy*, 1.2, 1999:12–15, ascertains R. L. Stevenson's influence on C.'s work in terms of some similar themes (e.g. the double), of textual analogies, and of C.'s interest in Stevenson's stories and in some of his critical and psychological concerns. On language: N. Scaffai, 'Calvino e la questione della lingua', *NA*, 2216:215–31, examines a number of C.'s essays on language and concludes that he balances out language functionality and density as well as simplicity and precision.

For individual texts: C. A. Calzolari, '*Se una notte d'inverno un viaggiatore*: romanzo della forma', *Gradiva*, 18:51–55, argues that 'la forma è la vera anima' of C.'s novel because it is through form that its content is expressed. L. Pocci, 'Il Signor Palomar, artigiano della meditazione', *RStI*, 17.1, 1999:286–307, examines the 'dissidio interiore', the dialectical opposition, between Palomar's self and his gazing, his combined attempt to be both an exile from the world and attentive to it, and concludes that it is Palomar's paradoxically subjective denial of his subjectivity at the end of the book that resolves his 'dissidio' by bringing together meditation and description, the two textual dimensions which characterize the work in various ways. K. Becker, 'Spiel, Komik und Experiment bei Raymond Queneau und Italo Calvino: Ansätze zu einer "fröhlichen Literaturwissenschaft" ', *ItStudien*, 21 : 15–33, compares *Zazie dans le métro* and *Il cavaliere inesistente*.

CAMILLERI. *La testa ci fa dire. Dialogo con Andrea Camilleri*, ed. Marcello Sorgi, Palermo, Sellerio, 163 pp., is an interview in which C. talks about his life and expresses his views on literary and political commitment (in constructive polemic with Vincenzo Consolo) and on a number of other topics. R. Frattarolo, 'Per una lettura di Andrea Camilleri', *EL*, 24.3, 1999:95–98, offers some samples of C.'s expressionistic vocabulary.

CAMON. R. Liucci, 'Ferdinando Camon', *Belfagor*, 55:545–60, provides an overview of C.'s work from the 1970s, and sees him as a not easily classified author who describes the tensions and contradictions of his native Veneto region, and combines documentary and human concerns in order to depict the situation of the lower classes.

CAMPANA. *Dino Campana alla fine del secolo*, ed. Anna Rosa Gentilini, Bo, Il Mulino, 1999, 203 pp., has the following articles: E. Raimondi, 'Premessa' (7–10); A. Asor Rosa, 'Premesse a Campana' (11–20); S. Ramat, 'Qualche nota per *La Chimera*' (21–38); F. Bandini, 'Note sulla lingua poetica di Dino Campana' (39–50); E. Sanguineti, 'Testimonianza di un lettore' (51–62); V. Colletti, 'Dalla lingua al testo: note linguistiche sui *Canti Orfici*' (63–79); M. A. Bazzocchi, 'Mitobiografia?' (81–107); C. Marabini, 'Luoghi e itinerari campaniani' (109–19); A. Bertoni, 'Appunti sul metro degli *Orfici*' (121–33); G. Zanetti, 'Campana e il mondo delle immagini' (135–68); M. A. Grignani, 'Momenti della ricezione di Campana' (169–87); N. Lorenzini and F. Curi, 'Conclusioni' (189–95). The book ends with a transcript of the 'Dibattito' (197–203) that marked the end of this 1997 conference at Faenza. Carlo D'Alessio, *Il poema necessario: poesia e orfismo in Dino Campana e Arturo Onofri*, Ro, Bulzoni, 1999, 241 pp. S. Ramat, 'Leggende e verità su Dino Campana', *Poesia*, 143 : 16–18, outlines what is fact and fiction in Campana's poetry. A. Di Nicola, 'La musica nella poesia di Campana', *ib.*, 18–20. Dino Campana and Carmelo Bene, *Canti Orfici. Stralci e varianti*, Mi, Bompiani, 1999, 64 pp., also has a 60-minute CD-Rom. The book and CD contain extracts chosen by Bene from Campana's original notebooks and are a fine addition to Campana studies by one of Italy's outstanding actors. A. Francini, ' "La Verna" di Dino Campana: riscontri danteschi', *FoI*, 34:157–61, identifies an analogy between C.'s description of an ascent to La Verna (a prose passage included in the *Canti Orfici*) and Dante's climb to the summit of Mount Purgatory. Giorgio Zanetti, **Dal simbolismo a Campana*, Ro, Carocci, 1999, 255 pp. **Dino Campana sperso per il mondo: autografi sparsi, 1906–1918*, ed. Gabriel Cacho Millet, F, Olschki, xviii + 241 pp. See also ALERAMO, above.

CAMPANILE. Barbara Silvia Anglani, *Giri di parole. Le Italie del giornalista Achille Campanile (1922–1948)*, Lecce, Manni, 216 pp., is a study of C.'s journalism and its influence on his fiction.

CAMPO. M. Ghilardi, 'Una fiaba per Cristina Campo', *AnVi*, 16–17:116–20. G. Fozzer, 'Tre lettere di Andrea Emo a Cristina Campo', *CV*, 55:205–18, details the philosopher Emo's fascination with *Il flauto e il tappeto*, Campo's 1971 volume of essays. They are also a valuable document as Emo kept a copy of all his correspondence whereas Campo's papers were not preserved after her death. Cristina Campo, *Lettere a Mita*, ed. Margherita Pieracci Harwell, Mi, Adelphi, 1999, 404 pp., offers an edited edition of 240 letters written by Campo between 1956 and 1975, the year of her death.

CAPRONI. M. Marrucci, 'Giorgio Caproni è un classico del Novecento?', *Allegoria*, 34–35:268–73. Given the recent profusion of new editions of C.'s work and the quasi unanimous label of greatness accorded to his poetry by the critics over the last two decades ('Caproni è il maggior poeta del secondo Novecento' or 'Caproni è un classico'), the author asks if this has not come about too quickly. He suggests that time may offer a more balanced evaluation of C.'s undoubtedly significant place in 20th-c. poetry. M. Frigerio, 'Il crinale poetico di Giorgio Caproni', *Lingua e letteratura* (Univ. of Feltre) 29, 1998:77–98, examines the centrality of 'Congedo del viaggiatore cerimonioso e altre prosopopee' (1965) to C.'s poetry. For Luigi Surdich, *Le idee e la poesia. Montale e Caproni*, Genoa, Il Melangolo, 267 pp., see MONTALE. C. Caracchini, 'Il linguaggio poetico nell'opera di Giorgio Caproni: a caccia di significato', *StCrit*, 92:151–65. E. Salibra, 'Caproni e Pascoli', *Paragone*, 50, 1999:232–35, explores the intertextual links between C. and Pascoli. G. Ferroni, 'La caccia e la preda', Ferroni, *Passioni*, 111–21. Pietro Benzoni, *Da Céline a Caproni: la versione italiana di Mort à crédit*, Venice, IV, ix + 221 pp.

CARDARELLI. Annamaria Albertini, *Lettere e poesie a una giovane donna: un amore di Vincenzo Cardarelli*, Chieti, Noubs, 1999, 89 pp. S. Jansen, 'Coesione e coerenza in una poesia di Cardarelli. Analisi letteraria e linguistico testuale', *RevR*, 34, 1999:87–116.

CARIFI. R. Bartoli, 'La tragica religiosità di Roberto Carifi', *Poesia*, 137:45–48, looks at the manner in which C. draws comfort from previously feared aspects of life in his recent poetry collection *Europa*.

CATTAFI. *AnVi*, 14, 1999, has the following articles on Cattafi: L. Baldacci, 'Cattafi e Caproni' (49–54); S. Ramat, 'Qualcosa di preciso' (55–60); P. Cudini, 'Tracciare i segni del vuoto e del silenzio.

Appunti per una lettura' (61–69); M. Forti, 'Bartolo Cattafi: altri ventiquattro "Inediti"' (81–87).

CELATI. Rebecca West, *Gianni Celati: The Craft of Everyday Storytelling*, Toronto U.P., 340 pp., examines C.'s work from its experimental beginnings to the present, and includes intertextual reference to Calvino and other writers.

CONSOLO. R. Nisticò, 'La contraddizione della prosa: *Lo spasimo di Palermo* di Vincenzo Consolo', *FAM*, 17, 1999:95–104, argues that, rather than being a poetic break from the style of the novels prior to *Le pietre di Pantalica*, C.'s latest novel shows continuity with the language, structure, and political commitment of his early work.

CORAZZINI. Sergio Corazzini, *Opere. Poesie e Prose*, ed. Angela Ida Villa, Pisa–Ro, IEPI, 1999, 313 pp., offers a series of prose and poetic texts together with an introduction, biographical notes, and a critical bibliography of C.'s work.

CORTI. B. Zecchi, 'Né Penelope né Elettra. Il canto di Maria Corti', *RStI*, 17.1, 1999:308–27, analyses C.'s novel *Il canto delle sirene*, considers whether it belongs to 'scrittura femminile', and concludes that C. writes from a privileged intellectual angle; but her insistence on the theme of hysteria breaks the traditional male-based literary norms and inscribes the author in the field of women's writing.

CRISTINI. E. N. Girardi, 'Ancora su letteratura e religione: l'opera poetica di Giovanni Cristini', *Testo*, 37, 1999:3–36, examines the fundamental religious dimension to the work of this Lombard poet who died in 1995.

D'ARZO. R. Carnero, 'Settecento arcadico su diabolico filo. *All'insegna del Buon Corsiero* di Silvio D'Arzo', *CLett*, 28:547–69. Id., 'La produzione saggistica di Silvio D'Arzo', *Poetiche*, 2, 281–99.

DE ANDRÉ. *Poesie e canzoni. Come un'anomalia. Tutte le canzoni*. T, Einaudi, 1999, 312 pp., considers the poetry and lyrics of this Genoese 'cantautore'.

DE FILIPPO. A. Placella, ' "Come lavorava Eduardo" alla rielaborazione delle commedie della *Cantata dei giorni pari*', *RLettI*, 17.1, 1999:51–86, highlights changes made by D. in 'didascalie' and language (changes from dialect to Italian) in the various versions of the plays included in *Cantata dei giorni pari*, and concludes that such changes prove his increasing 'presenza sul palcoscenico' as well as his intention to achieve a higher degree of literalness. *Eduardo: l'arte del teatro in televisione*, ed. Antonella Ottai, Ro, ERI, 207 pp.

DE GIOVANNI. Luciano De Giovanni, *Il muro che ci separa: carteggio di poeti liguri*, ed. Paola Mallone, Genoa, De Ferrari, 258 pp., details correspondence with other Ligurian poets such as Betocchi, Barile, and Sbarbaro.

DE SIGNORIBUS.   A. Cortellessa, 'Eugenio De Signoribus. Il popolo futuro', *Poesia*, 143 : 69–71, outlines the positive dimension to De S.'s most recent collection *Principio del giorno*.

DURANTI.   M. Spunta, 'A balanced language: spoken and dialogic style in the narrative of Francesca Duranti', *MLR*, 95 : 374–88, highlights D.'s postmodern 'pluridiscursivity' based mainly on a dialogic language and a mixture of literary and spoken registers. The same scholar focuses again on D.'s spoken and dialogic style in 'The language of tolerance: dialogism and orality in Francesca Duranti's *Sogni mancati*', *MLN*, 115 : 120–36.

ERBA.   S. Ramat, 'Luciano Erba. Un poeta nella "terra di mezzo" ', *Poesia*, 144 : 13–16, analyses Erba's most recent work, *Nella terra di mezzo*, and shows how his lyrical gift can focus on the average and ordinary and give it a poetic dimension.

FENOGLIO.   A. Casadei, 'Epica inutile e morte dell'eroe: *Il partigiano Johnny*', *AnVi*, 15, 1999 : 75–92, examines epic aspects, everyday life, and autobiography in F.'s novel.

FO.   *Teatro*, ed. Franca Rame, T, Einaudi, viii + 800 pp.

FONTANELLA.   Luigi Fontanella, *The Transparent Life and other poems*, NY, Gradiva, 84 pp., is a bilingual edn — the originals with Michael Palma's translation — offering a variety of poems touching registers that have both a personal and general dimension in the work of this 'uprooted' Italian who lives and works in the USA. A. Malinconico, 'Nota critica su Fontanella poeta', *CJIS*, 22, 1999 : 77–78. Luigi Fontanella, *Terra del tempo e altri poemetti*, Bo, Book Editore, 99 pp., is dominated by the theme of return which concentrates on the present (New York where the poet now lives) and the past (Mediterranean landscapes recalling his native country). B. Carle, ' "Stanziare le distanze": on the poetry of Luigi Fontanella', *RStI*, 17 : 242–68.

FORTINI.   Franco Fortini, *Le rose dell'abisso. Dialoghi sui classici italiani*, ed. Donatello Santarone, T, Bollati Boringhieri, 128 pp., includes the text of five radio interviews given by F. to Santarone on Dante, Tasso, Leopardi, Manzoni, and Pascoli. F. reiterates the importance of classic authors in his own work and looks at them from original angles. In his introd., 'La prospettiva interculturale nel metodo critico di Franco Fortini' (7–14), Santarone underlines F.'s historical reading of Italian classics, and his eclectic approach to writers from different cultural backgrounds, especially Marxist authors, Eastern writers, and Western classics. Franco Fortini, *Il dolore della verità. Maggiani incontra Fortini*, Lecce, Manni, 61 pp., includes a preface by Maurizio Maggiani (7) and an introd. by Erminio Risso (9–17) where the origins of this book are revealed to be a conversation between Maggiani and F. in 1983. It is followed by a larger section (19–59) where Fortini sees the language of prose as a 'scrittura vincolata', necessarily communicative and relatively simple, whereas the language of poetry is subjective and more difficult. He interprets the language of literature on the whole in a political way as a weapon that can be used by or against vested power. G. Ferroni, 'La guerra vana dell'intellettuale', Ferroni, *Passioni*, 137–51, discusses the idea of the futility of life, so pervasive in Fortini's work.

GADDA. M. Argento, 'Geometria e scrittura combinatoria in C. E. Gadda', *Intersezioni*, 20:143–51, looks into G.'s 'geometrismo' as a substantial aspect of his 'affresco espressionistico' and as an ethical dimension used in order to write about political power and the irrational and erotic impulses. M. G. Bajoni, 'Giorgio Pasquali e Gadda "filologo"', *GSLI*, 116, 1999:396–407, looks at G.'s attitude to Pasquali's philology and at his parody of classics such as Cicero and Catullus. Giancarlo Leucadi, *Il naso e l'anima. Saggio su Carlo Emilio Gadda*, Bo, Il Mulino, 262 pp., is about satire, the sense of smell, and other aspects of G.'s fiction. G. Ungarelli, 'Carlo Emilio Gadda e la vispa Teresa', *Belfagor*, 55:273–77. M. A. Grignani, 'L'Argentina di Gadda fra biografia e straniamento', *ConLet*, 15, 1998:57–73.

GAGLI. Galileo Gagli, *La baccheide: poema eroicomico in ottava rima. La rivolta contro la guerra delle donne di Greve in Chianti, 1 maggio 1917*, ed. Carlo Baldini, Greve in Chianti, 1998, 96 pp.

GALLI. M. Biondi, 'Il rumore della vita in tre poesie di Walter Galli', *LetP*, 31.1:87–90.

GASPARINI. R. Tavoli, 'Conversazione con Gianni Gasparini e dintorni', *CV*, 3, 281–92, describes Gasparini's views on poetry, memory, and what he considers to be the 'destino salvifico' of poetry itself.

GATTO. *Catalogo delle lettere ad Alfonso Gatto, 1942–1970*, ed. Gianfranca Lavezzi et al., pref. Graziana Pentich, Pavia, Pavia University, xxix + 296 pp.

GINZBURG. T. C. Riviello, 'From silence to universality in *Le piccole virtù* by Natalia Ginzburg', *FoI*, 33, 1999:185–99, discusses various themes of the stories included in *Le piccole virtù*.

GIUDICI. M. Forti, 'Giudici e l'*Eresia della sera*', *NA*, 135:217–38, provides an acute analysis of Giudici's third poetry collection, which dates from the 1990s. A. Bertoni, '"Nell'orma di una fuga il rotto filo". La poesia dell'ultimo Giudici', *FC*, 24, 1999:472–85, examines the themes and language used by Giudici in his 1996 collection *Empie stelle*. G. Ferroni, 'Io invento questo inizio al mio finire', Ferroni, *Passioni*, 217–32, relates the ordinary to the sublime in G.'s work. Giovanni Giudici, *I versi della vita*, ed. Rodolfo Zucco, introd. Carlo Ossola, Mi, Mondadori, c + 1880 pp., is a new addition to the 'Meridiano' series.

GOVONI.   Corrado Govoni, *Poesie (1903–1958)*, ed. Gino Tellini, Mi, Mondadori, xlviii + 387 pp.

GOZZANO.   M. Raso, 'Gozzano e Petrarca', *Avanguardia*, 13:27–46, considers how Gozzano, as well as the verbal echoes and citations of Petrarch, uses and often parodies the main Petrarchan themes of love, youth, woman, and interior and exterior landscapes in his poetry. Pier Massimo Prosio, *Da palazzo Madama al Valentino: Torino e Gozzano. Studi sulla letteratura del primo Novecento in Piemonte*, T, Centro Studi Piemontesi, 259 pp. This work also deals with Giovanni Camerana and Cesare Pavese.

GUIDACCI.   A. Frattini, 'Margherita Guidacci: realtà, trascendenza, mistero nel cuore della poesia', *Il Veltro*, 43, 1999:603–11, outlines the manner in which G. treats the themes of reality, transcendency, and spiritual mystery in her poetry. G. Mazzanti, 'Tra pienezza e declino. L'esperienza poetica e religiosa di Margherita Guidacci', Landolfi, *Il sacro*, 91–100. Margherita Guidacci, *Le poesie*, ed. Maura Del Serra, F, Le Lettere, 1999, 567 pp., has an exhaustive introd. to G.'s poetry (1–45) together with the first complete edn of G.'s collected poems.

JACOBBI.   Antonio Piromalli, *L'attività letteraria di Ruggero Jacobbi*, Na, ESI, 162 pp.

LANDOLFI.   L. Anninskij, 'Esistenza–non esistenza di Tommaso Landolfi', *La scrittura*, 4.10, 1999:40–47, examines L.'s writing on the border between chaos and order, reality and surrealism, life and death, and existential intensity and aloofness from historical events. L. Bardelli, 'Fra Pico Farnese e Firenze: il primo Landolfi', *Il Ponte*, 56.2:133–41, illustrates the role played by biographical elements (esp. the house of his birth at Pico Farnese) and by his early reading, especially the works of Dostoyevsky.

LEVI, P.   An untitled section, devoted to L., of *La scrittura*, 4.10, 1999:4–21, contains the following essays: O. Guidi, 'Sul Levi fantascientifico' (4–6); M. C. Mannocchi, 'Un'idea della Palestina' (7–11); R. Simone, 'L'"arte di raccontare" e d'ascoltare: *La chiave a stella* di Primo Levi' (12–16); and L. Ceccarelli, 'Tra Lilit e Laura' (17–21). In Fabio Moliterni, Roberto Ciccarelli, and Alessandro Lattanzio, *Primo Levi. L'a-topia letteraria. Il pensiero narrativo. La scrittura e l'assurdo*, Na, Liguori, 156 pp., Moliterni (3–61) defines L.'s literariness in terms of its non-categorized belonging both in literary tradition and innovation, and argues that with respect to literary genres L.'s work is situated at intermediate locations such as the crossing points between the documentary and the fictional, the oral and the written mediums, and individual and collective memory; Ciccarelli (63–110) examining the relationship between autobiography and narration, observes that in the 1970s, through his literary

Utopia, i.e. his obstinate search for truth, L. reacts against revisionist history and loss of authentic memory of the Holocaust; Lattanzio (111–51) notes conflict between reason and the absurd, and between order and chaos, in L.'s work, where a rational tension towards knowledge of reality prevails and effectively constitutes one of the main meanings of his texts. F. Sossi, 'L'oblio del ricordo. La scrittura sognata di Primo Levi', *NC*, 47:227–44, confronts mainly the ways in which memory re-elaborates past events.

LODOLI.   Anna Nelli, *Marco Lodoli*, Fiesole, Cadmo, 141 pp.

LUSSU.   **Il cavaliere dei Rossomori: vita di Emilio Lussu*, T, Einaudi, x + 395 pp., is a new edition of this work, first published in 1985.

LUZI.   Mario Luzi, *Tutte le poesie*, Mi, Garzanti, 1998, 2 vols, 1244 pp., is the fifth, enlarged edition of L.'s poetry. Giorgio Cavallini, *La vita nasce alla vita. Saggio sulla poesia di Mario Luzi*, Ro, Studium, 119 pp. Gloria Manghetti, *Sul primo Luzi*, Mi, Scheiwiller, 228 pp., concentrates on the style and poetics used by L. in his early work. M. Luzi, 'Dante mio contemporaneo', *NA*, 134, 1999:147–54, is an interview given to Maria Sabrina Titone which records the influence of Dante on L.'s work. M. Merlin, 'Oltre il varco. Il viaggio di Luzi verso il "celestiale appuntamento"', Landolfi, *Il sacro*, 73–83, details the increasingly apparent religious dimension in Luzi's most recent poetry. L. Gattamorta, 'Luzi e Dante: figure e trame di una intertestualità', *StCrit*, 15:193–217, explores the intertextual links that bind L. to Dante, a subject much neglected until now. L. Baffoni Licata, '*Per il battesimo dei nostri frammenti*: l'itinerario del dicibile nella poesia di Mario Luzi', *Italica*, 77:105–25, considers the strong dialogue L. creates with his reader in this collection which highlights both the fragmentary nature of life and the baptism, purification, regeneration, or catharsis that occurs when the reader measures up to the essentials of life as detailed by the poet. L. Crocetti, 'L'"Opera poetica" di Mario Luzi', *AnVi*, 14, 1999: 121–23. *Mario Luzi, 'Prima semina'. Articoli, saggi e studi (1933–1946)*, ed. Marco Zulberti, Mi, Mursia, 1999, 272 pp., contains articles written by Luzi between 1933 and 1946 together with a valuable index of his work as an essayist. *La poesia: 'un debito col mondo'*, Ro, Leonardo da Vinci, 63 pp., includes essays on Luzi by F. Livi and G. Petrocchi and two interviews with him: 'Dove comincia e dove finisce la poesia. (Conversazione con Laura Toppan)' (33–34); and 'Dante ed Eliot: 'un debito col mondo'. (Conversazione con Lorenza Gattamorta)' (36–61). *Resine*, 80, 1999, opens with 'Omaggio a Mario Luzi' comprising M. Luzi, 'Poesie inedite' (5–8); L. Gattamorta (ed.), 'Le vie del ritorno a Dante. Colloquio con Mario Luzi' (9–20); L. Fenga, 'L'opera di Luzi' (21–22); F. Bianchi, 'Il libro di Ipazia: Mario Luzi e il dramma di una crisi epocale' (24–36); and A. Sansa, 'Spazio, stelle, voce' (50–61).

Taccuino di viaggio in India e altri inediti di Mario Luzi, F, Polistampa, 1998, 56 pp. G. Pianigiani, 'Luzi, un classico conteso. L'edizione dei Meridiani', *Allegoria*, 33, 1999: 189–91, criticizes the omission of vital references to L.'s theatrical compositions, which are central to his later writings, in the Mondadori edition of his poetry. L. Cattanei, 'Mario Luzi in Sud-America', *Cenobio*, 49: 157–63.

LUZZI. G. Isella, 'Il *predario* poetico di Giorgio Luzzi', *FoI*, 34: 191–97, analyses the style and themes of L.'s 1997 collection *Predario*.

MAGRELLI. E. Golino, 'Magrelli, il giornale in versi', *AnVi*, 15, 1999: 120–25.

MAGRIS. L. Governatori, *Claudio Magris. L'opera saggistica e narrativa*, Trieste, Lint, 1999, 124 pp.

MALAPARTE. W. Hope, 'The rise of a folk hero: the fulfilment of writer and reader in Malaparte's *Avventure di un capitano di sventura*', *Italica*, 76, 1999: 355–70, examines M.'s 'invention of himself' in the context of Strapaese.

MALERBA. M. Di Gesù, 'Malerba, lo sperimentalismo e il postmoderno', *Allegoria*, 33, 1999: 220–30, analyses narrative procedures in *Salto mortale* in relation to other novels by M. and shows how his adoption of the detective novel as a genre, his setting of the story in a strange Rome, his use of an idiosyncratic language, and his protagonist's disturbed psychology are all postmodern features; yet M.'s ideology questions postmodern mass conformity to conventional social values. A. Rossini, '*Il fuoco greco*: la via di Luigi Malerba al romanzo storico postmoderno', *RStI*, 17.1, 1999: 328–47, argues that M.'s fiction is postmodern, not only on structural grounds but also because it deals with events which might have happened even though they differ from official history: it quotes a number of different sources in an unusual way and provides an interpretation of contemporary events through the framework of ancient history.

MANGANELLI. Giorgio Manganelli, *Cerimonie e artifici. Scritti di teatro e di spettacolo*, ed. Luca Scarlini, Salerno, Oedipus, 102 pp., includes a number of essays by M., originating as theatre reviews (especially on Shakespeare) or newspaper articles (on various topics including television and Arbasino) but containing some of M.'s ideas on literature (e.g. his poetics of the double and art as artifice). *Le foglie messaggere: scritti in onore di Giorgio Manganelli*, ed. Viola Papetti, Ro, Editori Riuniti, 266 pp., includes texts of a biographical nature (by G. Bompiani, L. Manganelli, G. Niccolai, G. Sandri, S. Nigro, and G. Terranova); some essays on intertextuality (A. Cortelessa, 'La "filologia fantastica" di Manganelli', where reference is made to the influence of Henry James on M. (229–59); V. Papetti, 'Manganelli e gli inglesi' (184–92); and A. Vollenweider, 'Il mondo tedesco fra sogno e esperienza' (193–98). It presents two essays on the theme of travel: G. Menechella, 'Manganelli e la geocritica' (131–44) and R. Manica, 'Col Bartoli, in Cina, per esempio' (145–56); it also includes a number of essays on general and particular aspects of M.'s work: G. Agamben identifies M.'s political concerns (37–45); A. Giuliani highlights Junghian archetypes (15–19); M. Mari sees M.'s fiction as situated at the intersection between psychological anxiety and cultural interests (20–33); also included are essays by M. Belpoliti, M. Bricchi, M. Cavadini, R. Deidier, M. C. Papini, E. Trevi, and A. Trocchi. G. Pulce, 'In rissa con la trama: le digressioni di *Hilarotragoedia* di Manganelli', *Allegoria*, 33, 1999: 213–19, shows how, thanks mainly to its digressions, the novel cannot be ascribed to any specific literary genre.

MARAINI.   *The Pleasure of Writing. Critical Essays on Dacia Maraini*, ed. Rodica Diaconescu-Blumenfeld and Ada Testaferri, West Lafayette (Indiana), Purdue U.P., 277 pp.

MARINETTI.   L. Somigli, 'On the threshold: space and modernity in Marinetti's early manifestoes and *Tavole parolibere*', *RStI*, 17.1, 1999: 250–73, argues that the predominance of the concept of space over the notion of time in the early manifestoes is somehow related to Nietzsche's 'capacity of "feeling unhistorical" ', but the article then dwells on a 'threshold' which involves evading history ideologically while admitting the historical nature of art products.

MARNITI.   *Loneliness Two Thousand: Selected Poems of Biagia Marniti*, ed. Catherine O'Brien, NY, Gradiva, 105 pp., contains an introductory essay to M.'s poetry followed by a selection of poems in parallel-text translation. Biagia Marniti, *L'azzurra distanza*, Ro, Empiria, 101 pp., contains a useful critique by Tommaso Debenedetti of M.'s recent poetry collection.

MELDINI.   C. Marabini, 'Piero Meldini', *NA*, 135: 185–87, focuses on M.'s literary representation of evil as a metaphysical entity embodied by his characters.

MERINI.   B. Urbani, 'Folie d'amour … aimer à la folie dans le monde d'Alda Merini', *Italies*, 3, 1999: 40–67, discusses the border between love, sanity, and insanity in M.s work.

MICHELSTAEDTER.   T. Harrison, 'The Michelstaedter enigma', *Differentia*, 8–9, 1999: 125–41. G. Guglielmi, 'La poetica di Michelstaedter', *il verri*, 12: 61–77. A. Perli, 'Michelstaedter e il *Leonardo*', *RLettI*, 17, 1999: 169–86, outlines the links between M.'s work and early 20th-c. writing in *Il Leonardo* during M.'s years at the Istituto di Studi Superiori in Florence.

MONTALE.   A number of useful critical texts on Montale appeared during the year. They include: *Insegnare Montale. Atti del Seminario di studi diretto da Romano Luperini, Forte dei Marmi, 18, 19, 20 aprile 1997*, ed. Valeria Nicodemi, Palermo, Palumbo, 1999, 118 pp. Enrico Testa, *Montale*, T, Einaudi, 121 pp., provides a general outline of M.'s development as a poet and includes the video 'Montale racconta Montale' by Gabriella Sica. Of particular interest is *Montale Readings*, ed. Eanna Ó Ceallacháin and Federica Pedriali, Glasgow U.P., x + 200 pp., which contains eight essays presenting a range of current critical views on M.'s work in both verse and prose: E. Ó Ceallacháin, 'Introduction' (v-x); C. Nocentini, 'Montale read and revisited by Calvino' (1–15); F. Pedriali, 'Resisting Clizia: a narrative for *Le occasioni*' (17–51); M. A. Grignani, ' "Se t'hanno assomigliato" e altro' (53–75); R. Riccobono, ' "Il sogno del prigioniero": heteroglossia as a sign of disaggregation' (77–102); R. Castellana, ' "L'alluvione ha sommerso il pack dei mobili" (*Xenia* II, 14)' (103–25); E. Ó Ceallacháin, 'Readings from *Satura*: public poetry and echoes of prose' (127–48); G. Talbot, 'Montale, Malvolio and the question of sincerity' (149–78); S. Ramat, ' "Tornerà la musica" (*Diario postumo*)' (179–91). A further significant publication, particularly for English-speaking students of Montale is Eugenio Montale, *Selected Poems*, ed. George Talbot, Dublin, UCD Foundation for Italian Studies, 280 pp. This book comes with an introduction, biographical notes, information on the language used by Montale, together with a wide range of poems from M.'s main collections accompanied by useful explanatory notes. L. Rebay, 'Montale testimone del Novecento', *ItQ*, 37 : 281–84, views M.'s work as a mirror of the 20th c. and suggests that readers can find a reflection of what is good and bad in that mirror.

G. Genco, 'Il leopardismo di Montale', *Testo*, 37, 1999: 105–33, details the most salient influence of Leopardi on Montale's intellectual formation and on the thematic and stylistic aspects of his poetry. Luigi Surdich, *Le idee e la poesia. Montale e Caproni*, Genoa, Il Melangolo, 1998, 267 pp. explores thematic links and intertextual connections between the two poets. Particular attention is paid to the impact the War had on their person and poetics. T. De Rogatis, '*Eupalinos* e gli *Ossi di seppia*: tra Valéry e Montale', *Allegoria* 34–35 : 93–126, assesses the impact that Valéry's 1921 dialogue had on expression and language in Montale's *Ossi*. P. Piovanelli and C. Zamagni, 'Abimelec in visita da Eusebio. Eugenio Montale lettore di un frammento dei *Paralipomeni di Geremia*', *SPCT*, 61 : 157–88, refer to the impact this apocryphal Greek text had on Montale. Arcangelo Leone de Castris, *Gli Ossi di Montale*, Lecce, Manni, 71 pp., argues the centrality of this collection in M.'s work.

ChrI, 16, is a special issue on 'Autour de Montale' that includes: M. Colin and M. P. De Paulis-Dalembert, 'Avant-propos' (5–8); J. C. Larrat, 'La tentation du portrait dans la poésie d'Eugenio Montale' (9–20); P. Briganti, ' "Si paga a caro prezzo / un'anima moderna". I segni della modernità nella poesia di Montale' (21–41); M. J. Tramuta, 'Montale le contrebandier ou le fil de la métaphore' (43–53). Two articles look at features of particular texts: F. De Rosa, 'Introduction à *Satura*' (55–77), and M. Fusco, 'Montale entre chronique et poésie: brèves réflections sur *Farfalla di Dinard*' (79–86). Others outline M.'s relationship with the critic Giacomo Debenedetti: V. Agostini-Ouafi, '*Ossi di seppia* lu, réécrit et commenté par Giacomo Debenedetti' (87–107); A. Debenedetti, 'Eugenio Montale e Giacomo Debenedetti: storia di un'amicizia' (109–18). The following comment on the reception accorded to Montale's work in France: M. P. De Paulis-Dalembert, 'L'oeuvre de Montale en France: aperçu sur sa réception critique' (119–43), and 'Répertoire bibliographique des traductions et des études critiques sur Montale en France' (145–71).

A. Benevento, 'Il "parapiglia" del Montale postumo', *RLettI*, 18, 113–24, discusses the literary debate that erupted in the summer of 1997 over the authenticity of M.'s *Diario postumo* (see *YWMLS*, 61:515). V. Pacca, 'Fonti narrative dei *Madrigali privati*', *NRLI*, 2, 1999:397–422, provides narrative sources for some of the poems written by M. for Maria Luisa Spaziani in the sixth section of *La bufera e altro*. Another stimulating series of articles is to be found in *Cambon Vol.*: E. Livorni, '*In limine*. Per una summa di *Ossi di seppia*' (367–88); S. Ramat, 'Appunti sulla trama dei *Mottetti*' (389–404); W. Zampieri, 'Le lettere di Eugenio Montale a Glauco Cambon' (405–12); E. Montale, 'Lettere a Glauco Cambon', ed. W. Zampieri, (413–24). G. Landolfi, 'Eugenio Montale, il prodigio fallito', Landolfi, *Il sacro*, 45–56. Angelo Marchese, *Montale: la ricerca dell'altro*, Padua, Messaggero, 367 pp., also details the search for a spiritual dimension in M.'s poetry.

MORAVIA. Alberto Moravia, *Opere*, ed. Francesca Serra, Mi, Bompiani, xxxiv + 1,730 pp. 'Moravia vicino e lontano', *NArg*, 12:60–147, contains the answers of a number of writers (including Marcello Fois, Tim Parks, Elisabetta Rasy, and Francesca Sanvitale) to questions such as what aspects of M.'s work were still considered valid and what other aspects set him apart from us, whether the interviewees felt any affinity for M., and what characters or episodes from his fiction were most distinctive.

MORETTI. G. Manghetti, 'Gli itinerari europei di Marino Moretti', *AnVi*, 15, 1999, 112–15. *Marino Moretti – Aldo Palazzeschi, Carteggio*, I: *1904–1925*, ed. Simone Magherini, Ro, Storia e Letteratura, 1999, 537 pp., is the first of a four-part series that highlights the affinity between the two men. It also offers an authentic mirror of cultural and existential reality in Italy in the early 20th c. G. Farinella, ' "Le poverazze": scelte per l'addio dell'ultimo Moretti', *ON*,

24.1:79–88, examines two forms of expression in M.'s work: the 'a-iconici' which underline the purely referential structure of language and the 'iconici' which make conventional reference to the multiplicity of individual experiences.

MORI. F. Bettini, T. Follieri, and M. Lunetta, 'Massimo Mori e *Il circuito della poesia*', *Testuale*, 26–27, 1999:40–48, provides three different reactions to this 1997 critical essay by the multi-media poet Mori. It outlines the position of poetry in Florence in the 1980s and makes particular reference to the international experience and to research on poetry and the arts by the 'Ottovolante' group.

MORINA. M. and N. Morina (ed.), 'Omaggio al poeta siciliano Emilio Morina (1888–1981)', *NEeuropa*, 28:93–107, is devoted to the Sicilian dialect poet Emilio Morina and includes the following: E. Fasano, 'Intervista a Emilio Morina' (93–97); F. Pasqualino, 'Prefazione della raccolta *Chiù dugnu – chiù sugnu*' (98–99); G. Prezzolini, 'Lettera di G. Prezzolini a E. Morina' (100); S. Camilleri, 'Introduzione della raccolta *Chiù dugnu – chiù sugnu* di Emilio Morina' (101–04); and D. M. Morina, 'Quando la morte sa attendere' (105–07).

MUSSAPI. D. Bisagno, 'Lo sguardo e "l'umbra": sulla poesia di Roberto Mussapi', *ON*, 24.2:105–60.

NESSI. F. Soldini, 'La lirica di Alberto Nessi: Proposta di lettura', *Versants*, 36, 1999:145–51, suggests ways of interpreting the 1998 collection of poems by this Italo-Swiss poet.

ONOFRI. M. Maggiari, 'Metafisica e inconscio nella poesia di Arturo Onofri', *RStI*, 17, 1999:242–49. See also CAMPANA, above.

ORELLI. P. De Marchi, 'Sul *Quaderno di traduzioni* di Giorgio Orelli', *Testo*, 40:107–30.

ORTESE. C. Della Colletta, 'Scrittura come utopia: *La lente scura* di Anna Maria Ortese', *Italica*, 76, 1999:371–88, argues that Utopia is a category that attempts to define O.'s fiction as tension towards a 'totalità perduta', mystical implications, social concerns, and an unconventional style.

PALAZZESCHI. La *'difficile musa' di Aldo Palazzeschi: indagini, accertamenti testuali, carte inedite*, ed. Gino Tellini, Fiesole, Cadmo, 1999, 339 pp., is a monographic issue of *Studi italiani* to mark the twentieth anniversary of Palazzeschi's death. Articles include: F. Curi, 'Dal "saltimbanco" all'"umorista". Per un'interpretazione storica di "E lasciatemi divertire"' (9–17); M. Guglielminetti, 'Il re scoronato' (19–30), which looks at P.'s prose; G. Tellini, 'Lo scrittore e il suo interprete. Il carteggio di Palazzeschi con Giuseppe De Robertis' (31–80); A. J. Tamburri, 'La poesia ossimorica di Palazzeschi' (81–101), looking at opaqueness of meaning and oxymoron in P.;

G. Guglielmi, 'Gli imperi mancati di Palazzeschi' (103–11); A. Nozzoli, 'Eusebio, Aldino e la Mosca' (113–50), examining the relationship between Montale and Palazzeschi as deduced from letters and cards exchanged from 1928 to 1962; E. Pellegrini, '"La morte euforica" di Palazzeschi' (295–314), examining death as an invisible protagonist in P.'s work; S. Magherini, 'Bibliografia palazzeschiana (1978–1999)' (315–39), a very useful compilation. Other essays include: M. Biondi on *Sorelle Materassi* (151–74); M. Marchi on *Interrogatorio della Contessa Maria* (213–37); R. Stefanini on parodies and displacement of the family (261–75); F. Sessa on the theme of old women in P.'s work (277–93); and A. Dei on autobiographical details (239–59). G. Saviane, 'L'incontro con Palazzeschi', *NA*, 135:214–16, recounts S.'s first encounter with Palazzeschi when he praised S.'s first novel. M. Mascia Galateria, 'La scrittura epistolare "astratta" di Palazzeschi', *Avanguardia*, 14, 133–48, details P.'s correspondence with Moretti, Marinetti, and Rasi, together with Moretti's letter to Palazzeschi.

PAPINI. S. Ramat, 'Papini e Soffici: una grande inquieta amicizia', *Poesia*, 138, 11–17, charts the friendship of the two writers and publishes poems and letters exchanged in their lifetime. *Giovanni Papini – Ardengo Soffici. Carteggio*, II: *1909–1915. Da 'La Voce' a 'Lacerba'*, ed. Mario Richter, Ro, Storia e Letteratura, 1999, 457 pp., the second of a four-volume collection, outlines the centrality of Florence in the lives of these men together with their personal and cultural friendship during the period immediately preceding the Great War.

PARRONCHI. Alessandro Parronchi, *Le poesie*, 2 vols, F, Polistampa, lix + 791 pp., includes some new material and Enrico Ghidetti, 'Alessandro Parronchi: appunti per un ritratto'. **72 missive di Giorgio Morandi ad Alessandro Parronchi*, ed. A. Parronchi, F, Polistampa, 109 pp., publishes personal details for the first time.

PASOLINI. A. Carrera, 'Pro e contro Pasolini. Per farla finita con l'"umile Italia"', *Poesia*, 145:73–6, discusses the extreme and contrasting sides of Pasolini's character which still provoke impassioned discussion twenty-five years after his death. F. Ricci, 'Tra poeti: il caso Pasolini–Montale', *SPCT*, 61:143–55, gives details of the 'confronto–scontro' between P. and M. in the early 1970s following their different interpretation of the social function of the individual and the man of letters at that time. *Pasolini e Bologna*, ed. Davide Ferrari and Gianni Scalia, Bo, Pendragon, 1998, 239 pp., details P.'s contact with people and places in Bologna as outlined in the 1995 conference proceedings organized by the Istituto Gramsci. Franca Angelini, *Pasolini e lo spettacolo*, Ro, Bulzoni, 245 pp., explores a number of relevant themes in P.'s plays and his theory of cinema, and analyses his texts for theatre and film. C. M. Ryan, 'Salvaging the sacred: female subjectivity in Pasolini's *Medea*', *Italica*, 76, 1999:193–204.

PAVESE. On the 50th anniversary of P.'s death, a number of essays attempt a critical reappraisal of his work. Monica Lanzillotta, *Bibliografia pavesiana*, Rende, Centro Editoriale e Librario dell'Università degli Studi della Calabria, 212 pp., includes both a bibliography of criticism of P.'s works and an essay in which the traditional interpretation of P. as a politically committed writer is replaced by an analysis of his open concept of literature and of his moral concerns. Paolo Sanna, *Un 'misfatto' non solo letterario*, Sassari, Delfino, 142 pp., discusses P.'s life in the light of his uncomfortable position in relation to the literary and political establishment, and attempts to relaunch him in contemporary literary discussion. *EL*, 25, 3–4:3–246, includes essays on P. by G. Bárberi Squarotti, P. Dal Bon, C. Di Biase, E. Gioanola, M. Guglielminetti and S. Savioli, G. Isotti Rosowski, P. Laroche, A. M. Mutterle, M. Pietrolunga, M. Santoro, A. Sichera, and G. Venturi. Though diverse, these essays rediscuss P.'s role in Italian literature and evaluate his intellectual function positively as a stimulus for modern readers and writers. F. Billiani, 'Cesare Pavese in Gran Bretagna e Irlanda: 1949–2000', *ib.*, 163–80, details publications on P. in the UK and Ireland during the stated time span.

Testo, 40:6–75, also in part devoted to P., includes E. N. Girardi, 'Attualità e inattualità di Pavese' (5–13), identifying developments in P.'s poetics from a first phase, or poetics of instinct, to a second phase characterized by moral concerns, and a third phase of 'rievocazione nostalgica di un mondo permeato di sacralità'; A. M. Mutterle, 'L'ultimo *Lavorare stanca*' (15–36), on textual and thematic changes in the 1936 and 1943 editions of *Lavorare stanca*; E. Gioanola, 'Da *Feria d'agosto*: "Il mare"' (37–52), a symbolic reading of 'Il mare'; B. Van den Bossche, 'Rassegna della critica pavesiana 1980–2000' (53–75). E. Borsari, 'Cesare Pavese. Critica ai "miti della critica"', *StCrit*, 15:427–61, highlights P.'s mythical, rather than realist, side and also underlines his rational interpretation of myth in contrast to the psychological and biographical approach to his work common to many Italian critics. N. Borsellino, 'Pavese dalle *Lettere*. Il mestiere di morire', *NA*, 2216:188–97. Sergio Pautasso, *Cesare Pavese oltre il mito. Il mestiere di scrivere come mestiere di vivere*, Genoa, Marietti, 232 pp., explores a number of themes, including memory, death, and myth. On P.'s late poetry: H. Hudde, '*Verrà la morte* — Paveses späte Gedichte', *Italienisch*, 44, 84–90, examines the passage from Italian into German of selected *Verrà la morte* poems, translated into German by Christine Fischer in 1991.

PENNA. F. Bernardini Napoletano, 'Il gambo del fiore. Sandro Penna e la poesia del Novecento', *Avanguardia*, 13, 47–85, outlines P.'s relationship with major poets of the time and assesses their impact on his work.

PICCOLI. G. Galeotto, 'Orfeo nella poesia di Piccoli', *Bollettino della società letteraria*, 1998–99:83–86.

PIOVENE. A. M. Hempl, 'Die Konstruktion räumlicher Fremde im Amerikabericht von Guido Piovene', *ItStudien*, 21:81–97.

PIRANDELLO. **Pirandello e le avanguardie*, ed. Enzo Lauretta, Agrigento, Centro Nazionale Studi Pirandelliani, 1999, 313 pp. E. Licastro, 'Pirandello e Jung: il risveglio dell'autocoscienza nelle novelle pirandelliane', *FoI*, 33, 1999:131–46, deals with self-awareness in P.'s characters' existential choices, and includes discussion of some of those who show fear of personal freedom. M. Maggi, 'Pirandello e il fratello oscuro', *EL*, 25.2:33–45, is about the nocturnal side of P.'s poetics. U. Mariani, ' "A will to believe": religion in Pirandello's late plays', *FoI*, 33, 1999:393–401. W. Moretti, ' "Pena di vivere così" di Luigi Pirandello fra angoscia e prosa ritmata', *EL*, 24.1, 1999:3–18, illustrates the rational aspects of theme and structure in P.'s short story. J. Reich, 'Foucault, Pirandello and subject formation in the modern age', *FoI*, 33, 1999:147–60, shows how Vitangelo Moscarda 'de-subjectifies himself' in *Uno, nessuno e centomila*, so that his 'self-formation is self-annihilation' or else the price paid by the 'autonomous subject' in order to become an authentic 'social subject'.

PITIGRILLI. Enzo Magrì, *Un italiano vero: Pitigrilli*, Mi, Baldini & Castoldi, 246 pp., is a biography of Dino Segre (or Pitigrilli) both as best-selling author and spy.

POMILIO. Mario Pomilio, *Emblemi: poesie 1949–1953*, ed. Tommaso Pomilio, Na, Cronopio, 79 pp., includes poems partly published for the first time.

PONTIGGIA. C. Nesi, 'L'etico squilibrio di Giuseppe Pontiggia', *StCrit*, 15:111–31.

PORTA. Antonio Porta, *Poemetto con la madre e altri versi*, ed. Niva Lorenzini, Bo, Book, 64 pp., is an important presentation of two of Porta's poetic compositions unpublished at the time of his death. Lorenzini examines P.'s deliberate linking of birth and death in his *Poemetto con la madre* and *Posizione fetale*.

POZZI. G. De Marco, 'Antonia Pozzi: dal portico della morte al destino delle *Parole* come vita', *Testo*, 39:89–111.

RABONI. Giovanni Raboni, *Tutte le poesie (1951–1998)*, Mi, Garzanti, Gli Elefanti, 472 pp., an enlarged version of the 1997 edition, contains all R.'s poetry to date, together with an anthology of criticism.

REBORA. A. Bettinzoli, 'La coscienza spietata: Rebora, Tolstoj e *I canti anonimi*', *LItal*, 52:184–224, discusses how Rebora's familiarity with Tolstoy's work — he translated 'Family Happiness' into Italian in 1919 — is reflected in this 1920 collection of poetry published before his conversion to Catholicism. *Le prose di Clemente Rebora*, ed. Gualtiero De Santi and Enrico Grandesso, Venice, Marsilio, 1999, 151 pp., is the first of a five-volume series that plans to focus on aspects of R.'s work not yet systematically dealt with by critics. F. Finotti, 'Itinerario di Rebora: dai *Frammenti lirici* ai *Canti anonimi*', Landolfi, *Il sacro*, 31–43. *Omaggio a Clemente Rebora*, Stresa, s.n., 1999, 396 pp.

RÉPACI.   Leonida Répaci, *Poesie*, ed. Dante Maffia, Soveria Man-nelli, Rubbettino, 1999, 220 pp., offers a comprehensive introduction to R.'s poetry (5–33) together with a substantial selection of poems drawn from *La parola attiva* (1975), *Mamma Leonessa* (1984), and the posthumous *Poesia aperta* (1986).

RICCHI.   C. Mezzasalma, 'Le frontiere della notte: musica e poesia per Renzo Ricchi', *RStI*, 17.1, 1999:348–76, illustrates the link between certain poems and specific musical settings. Renzo Ricchi, *Selected Poems*, ed. Catherine O'Brien, introd. Mario Luzi, NY, Gradiva, 67 pp.

ROSSELLI.   T. E. Peterson, '*Il soggiorno in inferno* and related works by Amelia Rosselli', *RStI*, 17.1, 1999:275–85, demonstrates the parallel between linguistic rupture, loss of meaning, and the emotional loss that is a constant in R.'s poetry following her reading of Rimbaud's *Nuit de l'Enfer*. G. Ferroni, 'Un'"altra" vita perduta', Ferroni, *Passioni*, 165–73, highlights the sense of loss in R.'s writings. On similar ground, E. Tandello, 'Amelia Rosselli, o la geometria della passione', pp. 7–18 of 'Amelia Rosselli, un'apolide alla ricerca del linguaggio universale', ed. Stefano Giovannuzzi, *Quaderni del Centro Rosselli*, 17, 1999, concludes (17) that 'geometria della passione ... e passione di ragione ci sembrano gli inevitabili, tronfanti ossimori nei quali questa poesia trova la propria dimensione ideale'. See also ANEDDA, above.

SABA.   A. Girardi, 'Il lessico del primo *Canzoniere* sabiano', *LN*, 61:25–31.

SALVAGO RAGGI.   'Omaggio a Camilla Salvago Raggi', *Resine*, 81–82, 1999: 1–117, includes essays by various authors as well as a bibliography of S. R.'s work and criticism on it.

SANESI.   M. Merlin, 'Lo sguardo interno della scrittura. Avvicina-mento alla poesia di Roberto Sanesi', *Testuale*, 26–27, 1999:25–39.

SANGUINETI.   R. Cavalluzzi, 'Corollari di Sanguineti', *CLett*, 28:571–75, provides a critical analysis of S.'s 1997 poetry collection *Corollario*.

SAVINIO.   Filippo Secchieri, *Dove comincia la realtà e dove finisce. Studi su Alberto Savinio*, F, Le Lettere, 1998, 196 pp., characterizes S.'s writing: his literary forms are described as 'uno spettacolo che è lo spettacolo del senso', where the unexpected is the only recognizable pattern and the paradoxical a compositional principle. F. Amigoni, 'Putting ghosts to good use: Savinio, Bontempelli, Landolfi', *Italica*, 77:69–80. Maria Elena Gutiérrez, 'Alberto Savinio. Lo psichismo delle forme', Fiesole, Cadmo, 208 pp., follows the development of S.'s work and seeks to shed light on certain aspects that still remain unclear. *AnVi*, 16–17, has an entire section, 'Le muse di Alberto Savinio', of papers presented at a conference on Savinio which took place in November 1999 at the Gabinetto Vieusseux: F. Sanvitale, 'Prolusione per Alberto Savinio' (61–69); A. Debenedetti, 'Il signor Betti' (71–77); P. Italia, 'Sul dorso del centauro' (79–102); M. Sabbatini, 'Ermafroditismo linguistico. Gli esordi di Savinio scrittore' (103–11); A. Tinterri, 'L'avventura colorata di Alberto Savinio' (113–18); M. Bucci, 'Alberto Savinio scenografo da Milano a Firenze' (119–34); M. De Santis, 'Savinio compositore per la radio' (135–52).

SBARBARO. P. Guaragnella, *Il matto e il povero. Temi e figure in Pirandello, Sbarbaro, Vittorini*, Bari, Dedalo, 240 pp., contains an essay on Sbarbaro's early work which places particular emphasis on the visual in his poetry.

SCIASCIA. Domenico Ribatti, *Leonardo Sciascia: un ritratto a tutto tondo (con 12 disegni di Bruno Caruso)*, Fasano, Schena, 1997, 95 pp. G. De Donato, 'La coscienza divisa tra "sogno della vita" e "mondo della verità" nell'opera di Sciascia', *Problemi*, 114–15, 1999:149–65. P. Moreno, 'Verità e metodo nella scrittura di Sciascia', *EL*, 24.4, 1999:71–81, adopts S.'s 'paradigma indiziario' in order to analyse not only his detective stories but his fiction in general. G. Traina, 'Sciascia: il nome del pittore, il mistero della pittura', *Il Ponte*, 56.6:128–37, highlights S.'s interest in painting (especially paintings by Fabrizio Clerici) and its influence on his work.

SERENI, C. D. Del Principe, 'Consuming women and animals in Clara Sereni's *Casalinghitudine*', *Italica*, 1999:205–19, interprets S.'s text in relation to 'gender and ecofeminist analysis' and 'gender determinations' in the semantic field of food.

SERENI, V. L. Baffoni Licata, 'Affinità williamsiane nella poesia di Vittorio Sereni. Sereni traduttore di Williams, ovvero quando traduzione è poesia', *Cambon Vol.*, 251–57. M. Forti, 'Ferretti per Sereni editore, e altro', *NA*, 135:209–31, discusses Gian Carlo Ferretti's 1999 book on Sereni's work as an editor. F. D'Alessandro, 'Sul "rovescio" delle due ultime raccolte poetiche di Vittorio Sereni', *RLettI*, 18:191–224. Stefano Raimondi, *La Frontiera di Vittorio Sereni: una vicenda poetica, 1935–1941*, Mi, UNICOPLI, 152 pp.

SERRA M. E. Debenedetti, 'Natura morale di Renato Serra', *EL*, 25.1:65–85 illustrates S.'s tormented search for a coherent variety of ethics.

SILONE. Dario Biocca e Mario Canali, *L'informatore: Silone, i comunisti, la polizia*, Mi, Luni, pp. 275, provides documentation and commentary as regards S.'s reports to the police officer Guido Bellone from 1919 to 1930. Giovanni Casoli, **L'incontro di due uomini liberi: Don Orione e Silone (con lettere inedite)*, Mi, Jaca Book, 170 pp. E. Leake, 'Past imperfect: Ignazio Silone's traumatic self-revision', *FoI*, 33, 1999:403–31. C. Ó Cuilleanáin, 'The Silone centenary: unfinished business', *Italia & Italy*, 2.7:10, reviews a conference on S. held in Edinburgh and highlights the very mixed results achieved in English translations of his work.

SOFFICI. See PAPINI, above.

SPAGNOLETTI. P. Perilli, 'Per gli ottant'anni di Giacinto Spagnoletti', *Poesia*, 138:29–39, documents the fine contribution made by Spagnoletti to Italian literature both as poet and critic.

SPAZIANI. S. Ramat, 'Maria Luisa Spaziani. Un *Oscar* per sette libri', *Poesia*, 142:15–17, marks the publication of an Oscar Mondadori edition of poems drawn from seven collections written by S. between 1954 and 1996. Ramat details the special qualities inherent in her poetry, and also includes an interview with S. who considers the edition to be her poetic autobiography.

SVEVO. P. Rambelli, 'Il principio formale della senilità nell'opera narrativa di Svevo', *Moderna*, 2:109–41. F. Mehltretter, 'Die Wahrheit über Zeno Cosini. Svevos erzählerischer Dialog mit Freud', *ItStudien*, 21:161–200.

TABUCCHI. B. Ferraro, 'Antonio Tabucchi's "returned gaze": art, fiction and reality in "Una bella menzogna"', pp. 31–44 of *Zur italienischen Erzählliteratur der Gegenwart*, ed. Hans Felten and David Nelting, Frankfurt, Lang, 216 pp., analyses the interplay between iconographic sources of inspiration and narrative in a selection of T.'s literary production, with particular emphasis on Velazquez's 'Las meninas' in relation to *Il gioco del rovescio* (1981), and Bosch's 'The temptations of Saint Anthony' in relation to *Requiem* (1991). L. Greco, 'I giochi del *rovescio* di Antonio Tabucchi', *FoI*, 33, 1999:225–37, reads T.'s story 'Il gioco del rovescio' as an interpretation of Velazquez's painting *Las meninas*, and sees T.'s imagery of mirrors and his reverted dimensions as a form of commitment. M. Meschini, 'Between surrealism and postmodernism: notes towards an analysis of the fantastic', *ib.*, 353–62, adopts Tzvetan Todorov's definition of the fantastic as hesitation caused by the absence of definite answers to our doubts, and detects this type of hesitation in T.'s imagery and philosophy.

TAMARO. N. Di Ciolla McGowen, ' "Anima parvuli": a child's destiny according to Susanna Tamaro', *FoI*, 33, 1999:459–84, examines adult ethical self-analysis and the representation of children as the sacrificial victims of society's brutality in T.'s narrative.

TESTORI. F. Crescentini, 'Testori e Moravia. Un dialogo manzoniano inedito', *FC*, 24, 1999:427–52, details the points made by T. and M., on the bicentenary of Manzoni's birth in 1984, concerning the relationship between *I promessi sposi* and history, and between God and the novel's protagonists. Davide Dall'Ombra and Fabio Pierangeli, *Giovanni Testori: biografia per immagini,* introd. Giovanni Raboni, Cavallermaggiore, Gribaudo, 186 pp.

TOMA. S. Agosti, 'La poesia di Salvatore Toma', *Autografo,* 40:9–22, evaluates a recently published anthology of T.'s work.

TOMIZZA. N. Dupré, 'L'autobiografismo oltre frontiera di Fulvio Tomizza', *RLettI,* 18:225–46, includes an interview with T.

TOZZI. A. Barilani, 'Tozzi lettore', *Gradiva,* 18:19–33, argues that T.'s work is not naive but based on meticulous study of language (in particular vocabulary) and on preparatory reading, especially of works by Proudhon, Büchner, Ardigò, and Lombroso consulted by T. in the National Library in Rome from 1904 to 1906. G. Cavallini, 'Trittico per Tozzi', pp. 75–140 of Giorgio Cavallini, *Verga Tozzi Biamonti: tre trittici con una premessa comune,* Ro, Bulzoni, 1998[2000], 194 pp., highlights the importance of style and psychological motifs in T.'s poetics, and underlines his modernity. M. Codebò, 'Straniamento ed epifania in "Pigionali" di Federico Tozzi', *MLN,* 114, 1999:157–71, is a close reading of the title story. E. Saccone, 'L'identità disfatta. Su alcuni motivi dell'ultimo Tozzi', *ib.,* 115:80–93, shows how subjective identity and a sense of a solid world disintegrate in 'Gli egoisti' and other stories by Tozzi. V. Scampati, 'Tozzi tra socialismo e letteratura (con quattro scritti ritrovati)', *AnVi,* 15, 1999:41–60, examines socialist ideals in four early articles by T. (publ. 1901–10). A. Vaccaro, 'Sul teatro di Federico Tozzi', *ib.,* 61–74, shows how relevant, among other ingredients, symbolism and interiorization are to T.'s writing for the theatre.

TUROLDO. Gianfranco Ravasi, *Invito alla lettura di David Maria Turoldo,* Cinisello Balsamo, 93 pp., includes an anthology of poems selected by Marco Ballarini.

UNGARETTI. The comparative and the intertextual, influences and reception, loom large among recent publications. Daniela Baroncini, *Ungaretti e il sentimento del classico,* Bo, Il Mulino, 1999, 288 pp., assesses in particular the impact of Petrarch and Leopardi on U.'s work. R. Gennaro, 'La poetica di Ungaretti e il pensiero di Bergson. Continuità di un rapporto', *RLI,* 103, 1999:429–48, considers the marked influence of Bergson on the themes of time, memory, reverie, absence, emptiness, 'panismo', and language on U.'s poetry throughout his life. M. A. Terzoli, 'Déracinement et nostalgie d'appartenance: le choix d'une identité culturelle chez Foscolo et Ungaretti', *ChrI*, 61 : 147–73, links the search for cultural identity with the themes of being devoid of roots and possessing a strong feeling of nostalgia in the work of Foscolo and Ungaretti. G. di Stefano, 'Triplice eco. Ungaretti nelle versioni di Ingeborg Bachmann, Paul Celan e Hilde Domin', *Testo a fronte*, 21, 1999, 129–61, looks at the manner in which the three writers translate Ungaretti's poem 'Cantetto senza parole'. L. Rebay, 'Ungaretti e Marguerite Audoux', *Cambon Vol.*, 283–88. F. Bernardini Napoletano, 'G. Ungaretti: cartoline a *La Diana*', *Avanguardia*, 14 : 3–56, reproduces from originals in the 'Fondo La Diana', La Sapienza, unpublished postcards sent by U. from the war front to Gherardo Marone. They are accompanied by explanatory notes, biographical abbreviations, and a comprehensive outline of U.'s contacts with cultural circles at the time. A. Mastropasqua, 'Caro Max Jacob', *ib.*, 57–62, presents an Italian translation of a letter written by U. probably in the winter of 1948–49. Id., 'Ungaretti e Max Jacob', *ib.*, 63–72, analyses U.'s link with Jacob and the Parisian avant-garde.

The 30th anniversary of U.'s death was marked by the publication of the following articles in *Poesia*, 141: A. Cortellessa, 'Giuseppe Ungaretti: il teatro naturale' (2–3); A. Zanzotto, 'Ungaretti: *Terra promessa*' (4–5); F. Loi, 'Guardando alcune foto' (6–7); M. Luzi, 'Ungaretti e la tradizione' (8–10); S. Ramat, 'Il naufrago e il nomade' (10). Sereni's 1970 tribute to U. was also republished. *Il verri*, 13–14, is largely devoted to Ungaretti: G. Guglielmi, 'L'invenzione del frammento' (5–6); H. de Campos, 'Ungaretti: l'effetto di frattura abissale' (7–15); S. Agosti, 'Lettura di Ungaretti' (16–45); G. Frasca, 'L'autunno nella vita di un uomo' (46–60); V. Magrelli, ' "Un sillabato tiptologico": fra Apollinaire e Ungaretti' (61–65); M. Manganelli, 'Da Govoni a Ungaretti' (66–76); F. Bernardini Napoletano, 'Cartoline inedite di Ungaretti dal fronte a Gherardo Marone' (77–82); N. Lorenzini, 'D'Annunzio e il "sentimento del tempo" ' (83–102); 'Lettere di Giuseppe Ungaretti a Luciano Anceschi', ed. Enzo Colombo (103–30); P. Montefoschi (ed.), 'Lettere di Giuseppe Ungaretti a don Giuseppe De Luca' (131–39). L. Paglia, 'Il grido e l'ultragrido. Note sulla semantica e sulla stilistica del *Dolore* ungarettiana', *RLettI*, 18 : 359–66. E. Giachery, 'Ungaretti e il sacro', Landolfi, *Il sacro*, 85–89, discusses the spiritual dimension in U.'s poetry. Mario Barenghi, *Ungaretti*, Modena, Mucchi, 1999, 211 pp., provides a biographical analysis together with five essays on Ungaretti.

G. Ungaretti, *Vita di un uomo: viaggi e lezioni*, ed. Paola Montefoschi, Mi, Mondadori, cii + 1647 pp., completes the four-volume Meridiano edition that began to appear in 1969. Andrea Cortellessa,

Ungaretti, T, Einaudi, 151 pp., gives a broad outline of U.'s development as a poet and also includes the video 'Ungaretti racconta
Ungaretti' by Gabriella Sica. Giuseppe Ungaretti, **Nouveau cahier du
route: Giuseppe Ungaretti, inediti, aggiornamenti, prospettive. Atti del Seminario
internazionale di studi, Fondazione La Sapienza–Giuseppe Ungaretti, Roma,
7–8 maggio 1998*, ed. A. Zingone, F, Passigli, 167 pp. Emerico and
Noemi Giachery, **Ungaretti "verticale"*, Ro, Bulzoni, 168 pp.

VILLAROEL. E. Candela, 'La lirica di Giuseppe Villaroel', *ON*,
24.2:85–104, examines the work of the Sicilian poet.

VITTORINI. Demetrio Vittorini, *Un padre e un figlio: biografia famigliare di Elio Vittorini*, Bellinzona, Salvioni, 183 pp. See also CALVINO,
above.

VOGHERA. R. Lunzer, ' "Allergisch gegen das Universum". In
memoriam Giorgio Voghera', *ItStudien*, 21 : 153–60.

VOLPONI. F. Scrivano, 'Individuo, società e territorio nei romanzi
di Paolo Volponi. Le soluzioni narrative di *Memoriale* e *La strada per
Roma*', *EL*, 25.1:87–104, discusses, among other things, the sense of
belonging, estrangement, and the concept of time in V.'s novels.
G. Angelini, 'Aggredire la realtà con le parole: le mosche del capitale
di Paolo Volponi', *ItStudien*, 21 : 3–13.

ZANECCHIA. *Finalmente incerti*, ed. Loredano Matteo Lorenzetti
and Giuseppe Aldo Zanecchia, pref. Giuliana Boccardi, Mi, Franco
Angeli, 117 pp., includes some 45 pages of poems by Zanecchia.

ZANZOTTO. U. Motta, 'Le letture di Zanzotto. Alcune ipotesi per
le *IX Ecloghe*', *Versants*, 36, 1999, 121–43, outlines the influence of
Balzac and Swedenborg on ideas and images used by Zanzotto in the
poems in question. M. Bordin, 'Due autografi dialettali di Zanzotto:
un inedito in margine al Premio Commisso 1980 e la poesia per
Pasolini "tu ti magnéa la tó ciòpa de pan" ', *Autografo*, 40: 55–77,
considers poems given by Z. to Maria Corti and now preserved at
Pavia University. S. Ramat, 'Andrea Zanzotto. "Sulla discarica un
fiore" ', *Poesia*, 135:3–4, offers a critical analysis of the 900 pages
devoted to Z.'s poetry in the 1999 Meridiano edition of his collected
works. A. Cortellessa, 'Andrea Zanzotto, la scrittura, il paesaggio',
Poesia, 136:5–10, looks at the role assigned to landscape in Z.'s
poetry. P. Pellini, 'Paradossi di Zanzotto', *Il Ponte*, 56.4:137–40.
J. Johnson, 'The problem of theory in the poetics of Andrea Zanzotto',
MLR, 95:92–106.

NC, 125, has an entire section devoted to Z. which includes:
M. David, 'Zanzotto e la psicanalisi' (15–32), an interview that
records the role of psychoanalysis in Z.'s formation; A. Prete,
'Margini per Zanzotto' (33–41), looking at the representation of
substance, form ('poiesis'), and word structures in Z.'s poetry;
G. Luzzi, 'Interruzioni di senso nel *Galateo in Bosco* di Zanzotto'

(43–55); S. Verdino, 'Il bel sembiante' (57–67), outlines the 'rilievo segnico ed iconologico' that forms an integral part of Z.'s work; C. Viviani, 'Il coro della materia. (Appunti sul dopo *Meteo*)' (69–72), marking the oscillations of the concrete and abstract in Z.'s later poetry. C. Pezzin, **Andrea Zanzotto. Saggi critici*, Verona, Cierre, 1999, 94 pp. G. Ferroni, 'Il poeta come critico del Novecento', Ferroni, *Passioni*, 193–201. Pierluigi Fabbri, **Andrea Zanzotto: itinerario critico per una poesia possibile*, F, Firenze Atheneum, 109 pp.

ROMANIAN STUDIES*

LANGUAGE

By MARTIN MAIDEN, *Professor of the Romance Languages, University of Oxford*

1. GENERAL

Mioara Avram and Marius Sala, *May We Introduce the Romanian Language to You?*, Romanian Cultural Foundation, 207 pp., is an excellent (but in places poorly translated) brief introduction to the language and its history, of the kind one might recommend to students of general Romance linguistics. Ion Toma, *Limba română contemporană. Fonetică-fonologie, lexicologie*, România de Mâine, 215 pp., is a general descriptive work, apparently aimed at students. K. Rogers, *'Romanian as a pluricentric language', Language and Communication in the New Century*, ed. Jesse Levitt, Leonard Ashley, and Wayne Finke, NY, Cummings and Hathaway, 1998, 179–86.

Appreciations of the lives and works of scholars of Romanian linguistics are: I. Söhrman, 'Alf Lombard — a Swedish linguist, Romanian in his heart', *Biography and Romanian Studies*, ed. Kurt Treptow, Iaşi, Centre for Romanian Studies, 1998, 374–87; also H. Hoffmann, 'Alf Lombard', *Dacoromania*, 2, 1996–1997[1998]: 17–37. P. Ţugui, 'Emil Petrovici şi unele probleme ale lingvisticii româneşti contemporane (II)', *LiL*, 44.2, 1999: 75–84; M. Sala, 'Ion Coteanu: amintiri neşterse', *LiR*, 47, 1998: 3–5. M. Avram, 'Un istoric brănean implicat în cultivarea limbii acum nouăzeci de ani', *ib.*, 111–15, discusses the activities of Ioan Clinciu. L. Renzi, 'Ancora sugli umanisti italiani e la lingua rumena', *RF*, 112: 1–38, dedicated to the sorely missed Marian Papahagi, is a fascinating and richly detailed analysis of the discovery of the Roman origins of the Romanians and their language — not only in the well-known writings of the Italian humanists Poggio Bracciolini, Biondo Flavio, and Enea Silvio Piccolomini, but also in passages from Paolo Pompilio and Martino Segono. As Renzi stresses, the realization that Romanian originated and evolved from Latin was a major intellectual innovation. M. Borcilă, 'Şcoala lingvistică clujeană în perspectivă istorică', *Dacoromania*, 1, 1994–1995[1998]: 15–20.

Institutul de lingvistică "Iorgu Iordan". 50 de ani de existenţă (1949–1999), ed. Mioara Avram, Marius Sala, and Ioana Vintilă, Univers Enciclopedic, 1999, 370 pp., contains numerous articles detailing the history,

---

* The place of publication of books is Bucharest unless otherwise stated.

activities, and personalities of the Institute, including Avram's chilling textual documentation of the ideological repression of Bucharest linguistics under the totalitarian regime. A victim of political disapproval was the journal *Dacoromania*, a major vehicle for Romanian linguistic studies, which ceased publication in Romania in 1948. E. Lüder, ' "Dacoromania" în exil', *Dacoromania*, 1, 1994–1995 [1998]: 21–27, discusses the political, and other, difficulties of the refounding, abroad, of the journal. We can only welcome the reappearance of the new series of this journal in Romania, published in Cluj.

The politics of language in Moldova is the subject of Klaus Heitmann, *Limbă şi politică în Republica Moldova. Culegere de studii*, Chişinău, Editura ARC 1998, 192 pp. The question of the supposed 'autonomy' of the Moldavian language takes centre place in G. Mihăilă, *Unitatea şi specificul limbii române în concepţia lui R. A. Budagov*, Editura Academiei Române, 31 pp., which deals with a Soviet Romance linguist amongst whose merits were the then politically risky recognition of the unity of Romanian and Moldavian. T. Priestly, 'Linguistic propaganda against perceived irredentism', *IJAL*, 9, 1999: 37–75, includes discussion of Moldavian Romanian.

2. HISTORY OF THE LANGUAGE

A. Niculescu, 'Latinitate, romanitate, românitate', *Dacoromania*, 1, 1994–1995[1998]: 69–86, emphasizes the role played by Romanian in the maintenance of 'romanitate' in south-east Europe. Id., 'Tra la romanità e la rumenità. La romanità rumena', *Melli Vol.*, II, 583–93, argues that the distinctive identity of the Romanian language developed only after the division of the empire at the end of the fourth century, and indeed only after the arrival of the Slavs. Constantin Frâncu, *Geneza limbii române şi etnogeneza românilor*, Iaşi, Demiurg, 1999, 155 pp. N. Saramandu, 'Romanitatea răsăriteană în lumina comparaţiei interdialectale', *Dacoromania*, 2, 1996–1997[1998]: 177–82, considers lexical evidence for the original distribution of 'eastern Romanceness' over a wide area both north and south of the Danube. Gheorghe Chivu, *Limba română de la primele texte până la sfârşitul secolului al XVIII-lea*, 156 pp., Univers Enciclopedic, deals with stylistic variation in the earliest texts, distinguishing particularly literary, juridical-administrative and scientific-technological styles. Valeria Guţu Romalo, *Obiectiv şi subiectiv în evoluţia limbii române*, Editura Academiei Române, 1999, 16 pp., examines the role of speakers' subjective perceptions in the evolution of literary Romanian.

Rodney Sampson, *Nasal Vowel Evolution in Romance*, OUP, 1999, vx + 413 pp., dedicates a chapter (298–338) to the development of nasalization in Romanian, giving a thorough and helpful overview of the rather intricate phonological contexts for nasalization and raising in the history of the language. Id., 'Diphthongization and nasalization of /E/ in Romanian proparoxytones', *RP*, 1999:113–31, hypothesizes multiple, linguistic, and sociolinguistic, causation to account for the problematic relationship between these sound changes.

D.-M. Zamfir, 'Iotacizarea verbelor cu radical în sonantă dentală în dacoromâna secolului al XVI-lea (II)', *FD*, 17, 1998:219–28, deals with verbs in root-final /r/. Sergiu Drincu, **Derivarea cu prefixe de la latină la română*, Timişoara, Amphora, 1998, 130 pp.

J. Lindstedt, 'On the Balkan linguistic type', *SSFin*, 15, 1998:91–103, compares Romanian syntax and morphology with those of other 'Balkan' languages, proposing that the class of features which define the Balkan type are not random but of a kind particularly attributable to the contact situation. M. Iliescu, 'Der Einfluss des österreichischen Deutsch auf das Rumänische', Ohnheiser, *Sprachen*, 1–76.

3. TEXTS

A valuable research tool created by a group of researchers in Cluj is described by S. Cherata, T. Vuşcan, E. Tămâianu, '*SILEX* — un sistem lexico–morfologic computerizat pentru analiza textelor româneşti', *Dacoromania*, 1, 1994–1995[1998]:201–12, and '*SILEX* — funcţiile de lematizare şi de generare a paradigmelor', *ib.*, 2, 1996–1997[1998]:273–85.

E. Pavel, 'Ştefan Paşca şi vechiul scris românesc', *ib.*, 1, 1994–1995[1998]:321–31, discusses the Cluj philologist's views on the emergence of writing in Romanian. A. Mareş, 'Note despre un vechi copist bihorean: popa Pătru din Tinăud', *LiR*, 47, 1998:43–51, and L. Agache, 'Jitia sfintei Margareta (Marina), într-o copie de la sfârşitul secolului al XVII-lea', *ib.*, 49–59, both contain remarks of linguistic interest. L. Renzi, 'Cele mai vechi versiuni ale *Mioriţei*', *Dacoromania*, 1, 1994–1995[1998]:87–102, includes linguistic observations on dialectalisms. E. Comşulea, 'Câteva corespondenţe lexicale în vechi versiuni ale *Bibliei*', *ib.*, 213–23. F. Şerban, 'Din lexicul scrierilor lui Dosoftei', *ib.*, 1, 333–51. S. Teiuş, 'Învechit şi regional în *Vat. Rum., 6*', *ib.*, 363–70, deals with the language of one of the early-18th-c. Romanian texts found by I. Dumitriu Snagov in the Vatican Library.

4. ORTHOGRAPHY AND PHONOLOGY

Liliane Tasmowski-De Ryck, *Trăsături neașteptate ale limbii române*, Editura Academiei Române, 15 pp., focuses on differences between French and Romanian in the phonological structure of words. A. Avram, *FD*, 17, 1998:5–19, 'Alternanțe fonologice în legătură cu sonoritatea consoanelor în derivatele românești cu prefixe', discusses voicing variation in prefix-final consonants, and its conditioning (phonological or, in some cases, lexical). Id., 'La semi-consonne yode postconsonantique et initiale de syllabe en roumain', *RRL*, 42, 1997[1999]:31–37. M. Mărdărescu, 'Analiza acustică a consoanelor nazale românești în poziție medială preconsonantică', *FD*, 17, 1998:157–72.

5. MORPHOLOGY AND SYNTAX

A ponderous descriptive work is Corneliu Dimitru, *Tratat de gramatică a limbii române. Morfologia*, Iași, Institutul european, 1999, 852 pp. In fact, the volume also deals with agreement phenomena, adverbs, conjunctions, and prepositions, and includes an annexe on orthographical problems — but surprisingly seems to have little on derivational morphology, and sorely wants an index. Thomas Cychnerski, *Fleksja werbalna w języku rumuńskim*: I, *Podstawy fleksji werbalnej*; II, *II Modele koiniugacyjne*, Poznań, Wydawnictwo Naukowe UAM, 1999, 2 vols, 299 and 257 pp., is a comprehensive and minutely detailed description of the Romanian conjugational system (with text in Polish, Romanian, and English), including information about the phonology and phonetics of the verbal inflectional paradigm, and taking into account the effects of the 1993 spelling reforms. Vol. 1 is a structural survey which will provide a handy reference tool to those who take a theoretical interest in the structure of Romanian verb morphology, dealing as it does with such things as morphophonemic alternation types, inflectional morphemes, auxiliaries, conjugation classes, patterns of syncretism (it also contains a useful bibliography); vol. 2 contains a list of fully conjugated model verbs and an alphabetical index of Romanian verbs enabling the reader to identify conjugation patterns. Adriana Ionescu and Maria Steriu, **Verbul românesc: dicționar sintactic*, Editura Universității București, 480 pp. R. Feldstein, 'Accentul verbului în limba română', *Dacoromania*, 1, 1994–1995[1998]:229–49, believes that much of the complexity of Romanian verb morphology can be reduced to three basic morphophonemic types: unstressed themes, polysyllabic stressed themes and monosyllabic stressed themes. Sergiu Drincu, **Cumpunerea și prefixarea: repere teoretice în lingvistica românească*, Timișoara, Amphora,

1999, 152 pp. E. Vasiliu, 'Context-free alternations', *RRL*, 42, 1997[1999]:413, observes that loss of voiceless final -i has led in Daco-Romanian to a situation in which the corresponding consonantal alternation functions to distinguish morphological classes. Actually, far from being 'context-free' the alternations in question are simply 'morphologized'. A. Merlan, 'Sobre as chamadas "perifrases verbais paratácticas" do tipo "pregar e V" nas línguas románicas (com referência especial ao português e ao romeno)', *LLP*, 16, 1999:159–205, deals with the morphosyntax and semantics of highly grammaticalized constructions of the Romanian type *a lua şi* + verb, *a se apuca şi* + verb, *a se pune şi* + verb. R. Timoc-Brady, 'Pluralité et catégorisation : les substantifs ambigènes du roumain', *FLa*, 14, 1999:207–15.

Virginia Motapanyane, *Comparative Studies in Romanian Syntax*, Amsterdam, Elsevier, 341 pp. The same scholar, 'C/T Merge locations for Focus', *Linguistica Atlantica*, 20, 1998:109–22, examines within a Minimalist framework the relation between Focus and Wh-movement. P. Monachesi, 'The syntactic structure of Romanian auxiliary (and modal) verbs', pp. 101–17 of *Constraints and Resources in Natural Language Syntax and Semantics*, ed. Gosse Bouma, Erhard Hinrichs, Geert-Jan Kruijff, and Richard Oehrle, Stanford, Center for the Study of Language and Information, 1999, xx + 338 pp., takes an HPSG approach to the syntax of auxiliary verbs, making comparison with French and Italian. Larisa Avram, *Auxiliaries and the Structure of Language*, Editura Universităţii Bucureşti, 1999, 263 pp. P. Kempchinsky, 'Mood phrase, case checking and obviation', *LSRL*, 27, 143–54.

G. Alboiu, '(De)-focusing and object raising in Romanian', *CanJL*, 44, 1999: 1–22. A. Cornilescu, 'Aspects of nominalizations: the case of Romanian', pp. 211–36 of *Crossing Boundaries: Advances in the Theory of Central and Eastern European Languages*, ed. István Kenesei, Amsterdam, Benjamins, 1999, 301 pp., refines Grimshaw's distinction between verb bases that indicate complex-events and those that indicate results, showing that projection of the object is obligatory only in [+ telic] nominalizations of transitive verbs. Beyond its theoretical interest, this article throws light on the semantic distinction between -*re* infinitive and supine nominalizations in Romanian, the infinitive emerging as [+ telic], and the supine as unmarked for telicity. L.-S. Florea, 'Optativul — mod sau modalitate? Tipuri de enunţ optativ în franceză şi română', *Dacoromania*, 1, 1994–1995 [1998]:263–76.

R. Dragan and I. Baciu, *Transitive nominalizations in English and Romance languages', *ib.*, 222–29. M. Dimitrova-Vulchanova and G. Giusti, 'Fragments of Balkan nominal structure', pp. 333–60 of *Possessors, Predicates and Movement in the Determiner Phrase*, ed. Artemis Alexiadou and Chris Wilder, Amsterdam, Benjamins, 1998, vi + 386 pp., compares Albanian with Romanian and Bulgarian.

C. Dobrovie-Sorin: 'Clitics across categories: the case of Romanian', Riemsdijk, *Clitics*, 515–42, sets out to show that the two linear orders of clitics characteristic of simple and complex tenses need not be stipulated; rather, they rely on the same underlying hierarchical configuration, their difference being due to the rule of Move-Infl. D.-S. also develops the hypothesis that obligatory phonological cliticization in Romanian is an effect of syntactic Merging. Obligatory phonological modifications of clitics play a central role in A. Popescu, 'The morphophonology of the Romanian clitic sequence', *Lingua*, 110:773–99, which argues that the apparently idiosyncratic morphophonology of Romanian pronominal clitics reflects a unique underlying form whose surface variants depend on the different environments in which they appear and their morphological properties. P. further claims that an Optimality Theoretic ranking of constraints can account for the surface realization of the clitics: a sceptical reader might conclude, however, that they 'explain' nothing — but do provide a handy descriptive tool! The interaction between clitics and verb-final vowels in imperatives and gerunds perhaps deserved further exploration. M. Avram, 'Conséquences grammaticales de la contiguïté des homophones en roumain', *RRL*, 42, 1997[1999]:333–40, discusses the constraints against sequences of identical adverb, conjunction, and clitic forms. M. Cvasnîi Cătănescu, 'L'anaphore pronominale dans le langage populaire' *ib.*, 357–63, examines contexts that contribute to 'oscillation' in pronominal agreement. A. Niculescu, 'Sur la position de l'article défini en roumain', *Dacoromania*, 2, 1996–1997[1998]:253–66, draws attention to the abundant presence of *proclitic* definite articles in Romanian varieties.

D. Draşoveanu, '*Cât, ca, şi decât* într-un microsistem', *ib.*, 1, 1994–1995[1998]:225–27.

6. Lexicon, phraseology and onomastics

The fourteenth volume of *Dicţionarul limbii române*, ed. Mariana Fota, vi + 409 pp., Editura Academiei Române, comprises all words beginning with 'Z' (although the end is not yet nigh: six more volumes are still to come). An earlier volume is the basis of I. Mării, 'Corrigenda et addenda la *Dicţionarul limbii române*, litera S: slab - sponghios', *Dacoromania*, 1, 1994–1995[1998]:297–312.

Lăzar Şăineanu, *Încercare asupra semasiologiei limbei române*, ed. and introd. Livia Vasiluţă, Timişoara, Editura de Vest, 1999, lii + 468 pp.

Luminiţa Hoarţă Lăzărescu, *Sinonimie şi omonimie gramaticală în limba română*, Iaşi, Cermi, 1999, 224 pp. C. Moroianu, 'Omonimia în sfera lexicului', *LiL*, 44.2, 1999:23–33. Sandra Reinheimer Rîpeanu, *Lexicul limbii române actuale în perspectiva romanică*, Editura Academiei Române, 1998, 19 pp., compares the Romanian lexicon inherited from Latin with the inherited lexicon of other Romance languages.

The period under review has seen a number of contributions in the series *Etymologica*, published under the aegis of 'Instititul de lingvistică "Iorgu Iordan"' in Bucharest. Marius Sala, *Introducere în etimologia limbii române*, Univers Enciclopedic, 1999, 254 pp., considers in particular the different etymological 'strata' of Romanian, against the background of an excellent overview of etymology in Romance languages in general; Andrei Avram, *Probleme de etimologie*, Univers Enciclopedic, 203 pp., is the result of 30 years of research in the domain of Romanian etymology. It includes consideration of certain phonological phenomena, such as nasalization, which are best understood with reference to particular lexemes. It also offers reflections on 37 items which according to *Dicţionarul limbii române* are of 'unknown etymology'. Virgil Nestorescu, *Cercetări etimologice*, Univers Enciclopedic, 1999, 179 pp., concentrates particularly on the correct identification of the Slav element in Romanian vocabulary, and on supposed loans from Bulgarian which are actually Romanian loans *to* Bulgarian. Also considered are theoretical issues to do with the creation of *Dicţionarul etimologic al limbii române*, and etymological aspects of the terminology of chess. Vasile Frăţilă, *Etimologii. Istoria unor cuvinte*, Univers Enciclopedic, 185 pp., gathers together and re-presents the author's extensive etymological work of many years, sometimes revised with new notes and updated bibliography. The first part deals with rare, regional, terms, many of them hitherto unattested; the second is a series of six mini-monographs on particularly problematic words (including some toponyms), such as *păcură* and *padeş*. Zamfira Mihail, *Etimologia în perspectiva etnolingvistică*, Univers Enciclopedic, 141 pp., emphasizes the importance of ethno-linguistic knowledge in etymological research. It deals particularly with ethnolinguistics in linguistic geography, the Romanian elements in Bulgarian, and ethnolinguistics and onomasiological fields.

La terminologie en Roumanie et en République Moldova, ed. Marius Sala, et. al., Cluj, Uniunea Latină, 87 pp. (+ disk 'Références biblio-graphiques et factographiques'), contains numerous short articles by experts (including the editors) on aspects of terminological standardization in the general domain of electronic and computational matters. Ioana Vintilă-Rădulescu, *Terminologia şi problemele ei actuale*, Editura Academiei Române, 28 pp., contains a section dedicated to terminological activity in Romania.

Maria Purdela Sitaru, *Etnomedicina lingvistică*, Timişoara, Amarcord, 1999, 238 pp., brings up to date in a single volume the author's work on Romanian popular medical terminology, discussing phonological as well as morphosemantic features of this part of the lexicon. M. Dobre, 'Aspecte ale derivării în cadrul terminologiei populare', *LiR*, 47, 1998 : 128–33, presents a series of derived forms absent from dictionaries and glossaries. Liviu Onu, *Terminologia creştină şi istoria limbii române*, Editura Academiei Române, 20 pp., includes discussion of that old etymological chestnut 'crăciun' ('Christmas') — ascribed here to a Thracian substrate. Ivan Evseev, **Componenta mitologică a vocabularului românesc*, Editura Academiei Române, 1999, 20 pp. C. Mihail, 'Modificări semantice în lexicul latin al României sub influenţa mediului militar (II)', *Dacoromania*, 1, 1994–1995[1998] : 313–19, includes an interesting discussion of the word 'ţară'; Id., 'Modificări semantice în lexicul latin al românei sub influenţa mediului militar (III), *ib.*, 2, 1996–1997[1998] : 325–32.

Constanţa Bărboi, **Onomastică şi istorie: comuna Rucăr — Judeţul Argeş, Rucăr — Făgăraş, Soveja, Rucureni — Dragosloveni*, 1999, 248 pp., Univers Enciclopedic, 1999, 248 pp. Remus Creţan, **Toponimie geografică*, Timişoara, Mirton, 130 pp. I. Toma, 'Particularită[ţile demersului etimologic în toponimie', *Dacoromania*, 1, 1994–1995 [1998] : 371–84, offers methodological considerations. Teodor Oancă, **Geografie antroponimică românească*, Craiova, Editura de Sud, 1998, 244 pp. A. Rezeanu and F. Modoran, 'Enclave toponimice rurale în urbanonimie', *LiR*, 47, 1998 : 72–77. A. Rezeanu, 'Aspecte ale raportului antroponim/toponim în urbanonimie', *ib.*, 123–28. V. Goicu, 'Nume de familie ale românilor din Ungaria', *ib.*, 61–71. A surprisingly rich vein is tapped in Domniţa Tomescu, *Influenţa italiană asupra antroponimiei româneşti medievale*, Editura Academiei Române, 1999, 20 pp.

A. Avram presents etymological notes on 'ţambele', 'ţanc', 'ţâbârcă', 'ţacher', 'ţâhuş', 'ţârfoli', 'ţepchin', 'ţestrai', 'ţigăriş', 'ţipa' in *LiR*, 47, 1998 : 7–17. E. Vrabie offers 'Alte şase etimologii: alamán, cóşcov, culíc, mănăstioară, trivolon, voi', 'Câteva clasificări în etimologia cuvântului 'boboc', and 'Etimologia a doi termeni din domeniul pescuitului fluvial' (dealing with 'sacovişte' and 'splau'), *ib.*, 17–23; V. Ioniţă, 'Un reflex al lui *sebişte* — *şezişte*', *ib.*, 23–26; I. Ştefan, 'Un calc lingvistic: *naigaţiune*', and '*A pinge* şi *a depinge* "a picta" ', *ib.*, 26–30; E. Tănase, '*Cap - ranţă*', *ib.*, 30–31, explores the etymology of the latter term, meaning the 'tails' side of a coin. T. Teaha, 'Descendenţi ai lat. *CATINUM* în română şi în alte limbi romanice', *FD*, 17, 1998 : 235–39. I. Mărgărit, 'Miteluţ, miticuţ, mâţicuţ', *ib.*, 229–34, investigates these words, characteristic of

Moldovan and Ukrainian Romanian. V. Nestorescu, 'Note etimologice', *LiR*, 47, 1998:118–21, refines our understanding of the
etymology of 'bârcâi', 'colnic', 'nebun' (the chess piece) and 'straşnic'
(the plant). I. Ştefan, *Regia* "palat" la I. Heliade Rădulescu', *ib.*, 117.
I. Anghel, 'Note lexicale şi etimologice', *Dacoromania*, 1,
1994–1995[1998]:173–77, deals with 'a-şi da odăjdiile', 'sul, usúl',
'ţăţână (la uşă)'. S. Giosu, 'A (SE) NAŞTE "naître"', *ib.*, 2,
1996–1997[1998]:311–24, is a historical and dialectological survey
of the semantics of this verb.

T. Hristea, *LiL*, 44.2, 1999:5–16, 'Structura şi evoluţia semantică
a subst. "dor". (Un caz de "pletora semantică")'. G. Tohăneanu, *ib.*,
17–22, 'Dihanii, dobitoace, nămăi', looks at the semantic distinctions
between terms for 'animal' in literary texts. Mariana Neţ, *Cărţile de
bucate româneşti. Un studiu de mentalităţii*, Editura Academiei Române,
1998, 13 pp., contains information on the history of culinary terminology. J. Brumme, ' "Inginer şi femeie de serviciu" — Die rumänische
Sprache zwischen patriarchalischer Tradition und postkommunis-
tischen Sexismus', pp. 63–101 of *Sprache und Geschichte in der Romania*,
ed. Wolfgang Dahmen *et al.*, Tübingen, Narr, deals with sexism in
language, and includes a useful survey of nouns denoting professions.
M. Zdrenghea, 'Elemente populare în versiunea românească din
Gramatica limbii latine a lui Gheorghe Şincai', *Dacoromania*, 1,
1994–1995[1998]:167–72. F. Dimitrescu, 'A propos des éléments
italiens récents en roumain', *RRL*, 42, 1997[1999]:379–94.

8. DISCOURSE ANALYSIS, STYLISTICS, AND PRAGMATICS

L. Schippel, 'Limba română vorbită', *LiL*, 44.2, 1999:34–56, highlights the lack of research on spoken Romanian and the paucity of
suitable corpora. Georgeta Ghica, **Elemente fatice ale comunicării în
romána vorbită*, Alcriş-M94, 1999, 248 pp. By the same author is
'Elemente fatice ale comunicării în vorbirea populară', *FD*, 17,
1998:39–68, based on a corpus of dialect dialogues and analyses the
role of 'phatic elements' in speech, combining Malinowskian and
Jakobsonian perspectives. M. Ciolac, *'Competenţa comunicativă* în
perspectiva sociolingvistică', *ib.*, is largely based on Romanian and
offers a multicomponential analysis of communicative competence
distinguishing, among other things, hearer's and speaker's competence. B. Marinescu, 'Observaţii asupra repertoriului lingvistic pe
baza datelor din ALR I', *Dacoromania*, 2, 1996–1997[1998]:111–20,
throws light on the differences in linguistic repertoire between 'limbă
cultă' and 'limbă populară'.

M. Manoliu, 'From *Deixis ad oculos* to discourse markers via *Deixis
ad phantasma*', *ICHL* 12, 243–60, examines uses of 'amu / acmu /

acum(a)' in Romanian texts from the 16th to 18th centuries. M. explores the development of discourse markers from proximal temporal adverbials (where an adverbial phrase anchors text-events in the time-interval of uttering) through 'deixis ad phantasma' (where the adverbial points to a time created by the world within the text), on to discourse markers marking discourse discontinuity. Id., 'Interrogative utterances as non-questions. Romanian markers of talk interaction', *RomGG*, 6, 55–68, is based on conversations represented particularly in the plays of Caragiale and provides data on Romanian interrogative utterances as 'back-channelling' devices expressing a request that the main speaker continue his/her turn, or as devices used by the main speaker to enlist the listener's cooperation. L. Dascălu Jinga, 'Some notes on back channel signals', *RRL*, 42, 1997[1999]: 365–77, offers a typology of conversational back channel devices, illustrated largely from Romanian. Id., 'Rejective repetitions', *ib.*, 47–59, studies the functions of such repetitions, with their characteristic intonation, in Romanian. A. Cehan, 'Two conversational routines: *how are you* and *ce mai faci?*', *RSBA*, 4, 1999:202–08. M. Teleaga, 'Negative connotations in English and Romanian "verba dicendi"', *ib.*, 177–85. I. Vântu, 'L'expression de la cohérence dans les interviews-portraits', *RRL*, 42, 1997[1999]:91–98.

9. DIALECTS

P. Neiescu, 'Câteva probleme privind studiul graiurilor şi al dialectelor româneşti', *Dacoromania*, 2, 1996–1997[1998]:137–51, critically surveys modern Romanian dialectology, lamenting the (often politically motivated) lack of major dialect monographs and complete atlases since the Second World War and calling for the foundation of a society for Romanian dialectology. V. Pavel, 'Atlasul lingvistic român pe regiuni — Basarabia, Bucovina de Nord, Transnistria. Reconsiderări, sarcini, modalităţi de cartografiere', *ib.*, 159–67. Further methodological considerations are raised in T. Teaha, 'Geolingvistică românească în perspectiva elaborării *ALiR*', *ib.*, 183–91, in I. Vântu, 'Ancheta de tip arhivă fonogramică: dialog sau comunicare dirijată', *ib.*, 193–99, and in D. Grecu, 'Probleme comune în chestionarele ALR I şi ALR II', *ib.*, 79–84. I. Mării, 'ALR — Din însemnările unui redactor (VII): documentarea lexicală terminologică şi semsasiologică', *ib.*, 121–31.

Aspects of the history of dialectological interests in Romania are illustrated by V. Iancu, 'Preocupări de dialectologie în săptămânalul *Gutinul* (1889–1890)', *ib.*, 85–89, R. Popescu, 'Dialectologia în paginile revistei *Arhivele Olteniei* (seria veche)', *ib.*, 169–75, and V. Ioniţă, 'Observaţii pe marginea unui glosar dialectal', *ib.*, 91–95, which deals with a manuscript glossary of the dialect of Ilidia (judeţ of Caraş–Severin) by Prof. I. Moise-Aldan. D. Negomireanu, 'Cuvinte regionale şi populare în vocabularul operei lui T. Arghezi', *ib.*, 133–35.

Teodor Oancă, **Onomastică şi dialectologie*, Fundaţia "Scrisul românesc", 1999, 140 pp. I. Florea, ' "Moldovenesc", "românesc", "rusesc" în comentările lingvistice ale subiectelor ALM', *Dacoromania*, 2, 1996–1997[1998]:69–77, deals with etymological judgements by informants of *Atlasul lingvistic românesc*. M. Manu Magda, 'Aspecte ale compartamentului lingvistic al vorbitorilor de limbă română (pe baza textelor dialectale)', *ib.*, 97–104, discusses the use of phraseological units in the identification of dialect boundaries. G. Rusu, 'În legătură cu unele probleme privitoare la "palatalizarea labialelor" în graiurile dacoromâne', *ib.*, 1, 1994–1995[1998]:157–66, attempts to find a consensus among the various scholarly positions on the nature and description of this phonological phenomenon.

Constantin Ţibrian, *Structura morfologică a verbului în graiul muntenesc şi oltenesc (timpurile trecute ale modului indicativ)*, Piteşti, Editura Universităţii din Piteşti, 1999, 103 pp. T. Ferro, 'Din morfologia verbului în *Conciones* de Silvestro Amelio', *Dacoromania*, 1, 1994–1995[1998]: 251–61, shows the importance of verb-forms in the text for Romanian historical dialectology. Much attention is paid in vol. 17 of *FD* to the 'eastern' Romanian varieties of Moldova and Ukraine, including a major contribution to descriptive Romanian dialect studies in M. Marin, I. Mărgărit, and V. Neagoe, 'Graiuri româneşti din Ucraina şi Republica Moldova', *FD*, 17, 1998:69–155, which examines in detail phonology, morphology, syntax, word-formation, and lexicon of the four major dialect groups involved. V. Pavel, 'Graiuri româneşti în medii aloglote. Consideraţii sociolingvistice', *ib.*, 173–84, examines the sociolinguistic situation of easternmost outposts of Romanian in relation to Slav languages, and sees particular cause for concern in the fate of Caucasian, S.E. Ukrainian and River Bug Romanian varieties. Written in the 1940s and only recently rediscovered is D. Şandru, 'Graiul românesc de peste Nistru', *ib.*, 185–200, which surveys the phonology, morphology, and lexicon of several Romanian-speaking localities east of the Dniestr, noting considerable Russian penetration into the lexicon. C.-I. Mladin, 'Consideraţii privind elementele lingvistice comune în graiurile din Banat şi Oltenia', *Dacoromania*, 1, 1994–1995[1998]:133–44. I. Calotă, 'Elemente sud-dunărene în graiul rudarilor din Oltenia', *ib.*, 47–51. I. Nuţă, 'Observaţii asupra graiului unei localităţi anchetate pentru ALR II şi NALR', *ib.*, 153–58, concerns the dialect of Crişteşti (in the judeţ of Botoşani).

A. Ulivi, 'Observații asupra structurii fonetice a conjuncțiilor în graiurile dacoromâne', *ib.*, 207–17. E. Beltechi, 'Perfectul simplu în graiurile bănățene actuale', *ib.*, 103–15, which interprets the simple perfect as a kind of foregrounding variant of the past tense. M. Marin, 'Un mijloc de realizare a actualizării acțiunii verbale in graiurile de tip nord-vestic', *ib.*, 2, 1996–97[1998]: 105–10. N. Mocanu, 'Forme de gerunziu întâlnite în atlasele lingvistice românești', *ib.*, 1, 1994–1995[1998]: 145–55. D. Grecu, ' "Cerbice" și "gușă" la bou. Note pe marginea unor răspunsuri la *chestionarele* ALR I și II', *ib.*, 117–20, discusses semasiological aspects of the dialect lexicon. M. Vulpe, 'Note de semantică dialectală: *dr. BĂNUȚ*, *ib.*, 2, 1996–1997[1998]: 201–05. S. Dănilă, 'Reflexe ale genitivului dialectal în onomastica bănățeană', *ib.*, 61–68.

P. Ionescu, 'Variedades lingüísticas rumanas en la Península Balcánica: arrumano, meglenorrumano e istrorrumano', *RFR*, 16, 1999: 29–58, presents a general survey of the distribution and historical origins of the Sub-Danubian dialects. August Kovačec, *Istroromunjsko-hrvatski rječnik*, Pula, Verba Moritura 1, 1998, 378 pp., is an Istro-Romanian — Croatian dictionary accompanied by a grammatical survey and a selection of texts (partly in phonetic transcription). Dialectal variations between villages are taken into account. The dictionary is based on the dialect material gathered by the author in the 1960s which, alas, never emerged in the form of the more detailed dictionary which he had intended. Elena Scărlătoiu, *Istroromânii și istroromâna. Relații lingvistice cu slavii de sud*, Staff, 1998, 364 pp., argues for a polycentric geographical origin for the Istro-Romanians.

G. Caragiani, 'Notizie e studi pubblicati in Italia sull'aromeno: 1945–1995 (I)', *RRL*, 42, 1997[1999]: 341–56, draws particular attention to the insufficiently known book by T. Ferro on this subject. N. Saramandu, 'Le dictionnaire aroumain (*Dicționar aromân*) de Matilda Caragiu Marioțeanu. Sens et signification', *ib.*, 409–12, is an appreciation of the dictionary, the first volume of which appeared in 1997. M. Bara, 'Categoria gramaticală a determinării în aromână (articularea hotărâtă a adjectivului calificativ)', *Dacoromania*, 2, 1996–1997[1998]: 39–46.

L. Ionescu-Ruxăndoiu, 'Codeswitching and borrowing: remarks on the Aromanian dialect spoken in Greece', *RRL*, 42, 1997[1999]: 403–08, deals with the dialect of Néa-Zoi. M. Ciolac, 'Cu privire la bidialectalismul unor vorbitori aromâni din România', *Dacoromania*, 2, 1996–1997[1998]: 53–60, notes the spread of active bilingualism.

I. Mării, 'ALR - Din însemnările unui redactor (V): documentarea "onomasiologică" şi "semasiologică" a gesturilor în ALR II', *ib.*, 1, 1994–1995[1998]: 121–31, draws attention to the neglected paralinguistic domain of gestures.

LITERATURE

By MIRCEA ANGHELESCU, *Professor of Romanian Literature in the
University of Bucharest*

1. WORKS OF REFERENCE AND OF GENERAL INTEREST

Last year's main event in the field of reference literature must be the
publication of: *Dicţionarul esenţial al scriitorilor români*, ed. M. Zaciu,
M. Papahagi, and A. Sasu, Albatros, 920 pp., in collaboration with a
team of 48 authors, mostly well-known academics. Elaborated by the
group which since 1994 has been publishing the still unfinished
Dicţionarul scriitorilor români, the dictionary benefits from first-hand
information: the 332 entries, most of them on modern and contemporary authors, have a short introductory text briefly characterizing the
author, and a brief biography; and each entry ends with a bibliography of the author's work and of its critical reception. Among those
featured in the dictionary, there are 20th-c. writers who began their
career as Romanian authors but then made a name for themselves in
foreign literatures: Fondane, Ionescu, Istrati, Tzara. However, none
of the old literary authors who wrote in other languages — Slavonic,
Latin, or Greek — is included here. Several regional literary or
cultural dictionaries have been published in this period. George
Vulturescu, *Cultură şi literatură în ţinuturile Sătmarului: Dicţionar
1700–2000*, Sătmărean, Muzeului, 297 pp., presents the authors,
periodicals, and literature-oriented institutions of the county of Satu-
Mare, in the Hungarian, Ukrainian, and other languages, as well as
in Romanian, together with biographical and bibliographical data
and short characterizations. The dictionary favours the modern and
contemporary epoch. Ovidiu Dunăreanu, *Scriitori de la Tomis*, Constanţa, Ex Ponto, 152 pp., contains the records of 37 authors living in
or originating from Constanţa county, and writing in Romanian,
Turkish, or Tatar. The entries include biographical and bibliographical data, and also short excerpts from literary critics. Mircea
Oprişiu and Ion Mariş, *Mic dicţionar cu personalităţi care s-au născut, au
trăit şi au creat, ori au avut legături cu meleagurile sibiene*, ii, Biblioteca Astra,
264 pp., covers letters H, I, and J, and contains over two hundred
names of public personalities in Sibiu county (or persons having
relations, sometimes very vague ones, with Sibiu county). Among
those mentioned, some are authors who write in Romanian, German,
or Hungarian. This is only a pre-print, disseminated in a small
number of copies, after which the texts will be revised and the edition
proper printed. Somewhat close to these dictionaries is Alexandru
Firescu and Constantin Gheorghiu, *Istoria Teatrului Naţional din Craiova*.

1850–2000, Craiova, Aius, 595 pp., in which the chronological history of the theatre (in which a number of important writers played a part — Liviu Rebreanu, Emil Gîrleanu, Adolf de Herz, Adrian Maniu, Ion D. Sîrbu — whether as managing directors or literary secretaries) is complemented with a repertory of the theatres from 1842 on, with several indexes of actors, managing directors, stage directors, and so on, among them an index of authors and plays mentioned in the text.

A. M. Brezuleanu et al., *Bibliografia relaţiilor literaturii române cu literaturile străine în periodice (1919–1944)*, III, Saeculum I.O., 320 pp., is the sequel to a work whose first volume (generalities, problems of comparative literature, translation techniques, etc.) was published in 1997, while the second (concerning English-language literatures) came out in 1999. The volume comprises 9,312 annotated bibliographical entries on articles that deal with Germanic literatures, or on translations from Germanic literatures (German, Austrian, Dutch, etc., arranged according to the decimal classification) published in the Romanian press in the specified period; the volume is complete with an index of names.

In direct relation to the lives of writers in the last two-and-a-half centuries stands Adrian Marino, *Cenzura în România*, Craiova, Aius, 94 pp. The authors and their works are the main target of Marino's investigation, against the background of cultural and political history, with special emphasis on the censorship of literary works under the Communist regime. A bibliography of the works — literary, historical and other — censored under the communist rule is *Gîndirea interzisă. Scrieri cenzurate în România 1945–1989*, ed. P. Caravia, pref. V. Cândea, Enciclopedică, 601 pp.; one also finds a list of manuscripts 'apprehended' during arrests, secret police searches, and so on (568–81). This includes writing by, among others, Felix Aderca, Martha Bibescu, Lucian Blaga, Petru Dumitriu, Victor Eftimiu, Paul Goma, Ion Negoiţescu, and Radu Gyr. Alexandru Popescu, *Viena românească. Un ghid sentimental*, Fundaţiei Culturale Române, 312 pp., offers information on the presence and professional activities of Romanians in Vienna down the centuries; many of them were writers and left behind descriptions of Austria's capital city (from Dinicu Golescu to Titu Maiorescu and Eminescu). The information is backed by bibliographical sources. Mariana Neţ, *Literature, Atmosphere and Society. A Semiotic Approach*, Vienna, Österreichischen Gesellschaft für Semiotik, 275 pp., discusses the pragmatics of atmosphere in literary texts as being a projection of character and a means of contextualizing it. Besides foreign authors, the critic discusses books by Romanian writers: *Hanul Ancuţei* by Mihail Sadoveanu, for example.

A chronology of Romanian contacts with, and knowledge of, American culture and literature is: Ioan Comşa, 'Cronologia relaţiilor româno-americane, I: 1630–1830', in *Revista româno-americană*, n.s., 3–4: 53–64.

2. COLLECTED WORKS, LITERARY MONOGRAPHS, AND CRITICISM

OLD ROMANIAN LITERATURE

Cronograf tradus din greceşte de Pătraşco Danovici, ed. (with a glossary) Gabriel Ştrempel, II, Minerva, 1999, 399 pp., is a compilation of Greek chronographs by Matthaeus Cigalas, Dorotheus of Monembasia, *et al.*, translated in the 17th century with the addition of a few personal notes.

The volume *Naratori şi modelare umană în medievalitatea românească*, Iaşi, Junimea, 171 pp., comprises studies in medieval Romanian literature: C. Pricop, 'Literatura medievală şi stabilirea canonului literaturii române' (7–28); E. Sorohan, 'Naşterea textului narativ' (29–41); V. Stanciu, 'Naraţiunea: retorică şi figuri' (42–100); E. Sorohan, 'Dimensiunea pragmatică şi modelajul uman' (101–38), and 'Geneza personajului istoric' (139–70).

Noi cercetări literare, 5, ed. Dan Horia Mazilu as a bulletin of the Old Romanian Literature Department of the University of Bucharest, includes articles on mediaeval literary models such as the prince or the tyrant: D. H. Mazilu, 'Un "Dracula" pe care Occidentul l-a ratat' (5–11); H. Bogdan, 'Actul de cancelarie în vremea lui Ştefan cel Mare, mijloc de impunere a unui model monarhic' (13–44); D. Grigore, 'Modelul voievodal Ştefanin' (59–84), etc.

Andrei Timotin, 'La littérature eschatologique et apocalyptique dans les manuscrits des archives de la Bibliothèque de l'Académie Roumaine', *Archaeus*, 4:367–411. C. Velculescu, '"Physiologus-Bestiarum"-Bilder und die rumänische Volkskultur, *Synthesis*, 25, 1998:67–78.

EIGHTEENTH CENTURY

CANTEMIR. Dimitrie Cantemir, *Sistema şi religia mahomedană. Cartea celor trei religii, partea a treia*, ed., trans., and introd. Anca Irina Ionescu, Universal Dalsi, 331 pp., is an edn of the Bulgarian original with the Romanian translation of the text which the Bulgarian scholar Sofronie Vračanski (d. 1805) compiled and adapted from Cantemir's book of 1722 about 'the system of the Muslim religion'. Gabriel Mihăilescu, 'Istorie, ficţiune şi persuasiune în *Istoria ieroglifică*', pp. 47–53 of *Cercetarea literară azi* (cf. Paul Cornea, below).

MICU. Teodor Pompiliu, *Sub semnul Luminilor: Samuil Micu*, Cluj, Presa Universitară Clujeană, 506 pp., is a monograph on the life and work of one of Romania's most important Enlightenment figures, extending to general issues such as the Romanians and the Counter-Reformation, the unification of Orthodox Romanians to Rome, and the influence of Emperor Joseph II's reformist programme on the Romanian Enlightenment.

NINETEENTH CENTURY

For a general overview of Romanian romantic poetry see: M. Spiridon, 'Two faces of Romanian romantic poetry', in *NTJRS*, 2, 1999:59–71.

ALECSANDRI. M. Anghelescu, 'Dime lo que comes y te diré quién eres. Alimentacion y literatura en los Balcanes', *RFR*, 19, 1999:167–74.

CARAGIALE, I. L. I. L. Caragiale, *Opere*, ed., with a chronology, by Stancu Ilin, Nicolae Bârna, and Constantin Hârlav, pref. E. Simion, 2 vols, Univers enciclopedic, lxviii + 1835, vi + 1270 pp., comprises the 'Literary prose' (vol. 1) and the 'Theatre, writings about theatre, poetry' (vol. 2). On C. Ştefan Cazimir, *Honeste scribere*, Naţional, 339 pp., includes the essays 'Punctul zero al *Scrisorii pierdute*', 'Palinodie', 'Domn Mitică şi CuzaVodă', etc.).

EMINESCU. Mihai Eminescu, *Opere*, ed. D. Vatamaniuc, vols 4 and 5 of a bibliophile ed., Univers enciclopedic, 1845, 1923 pp., comprise the Journalism: articles published between 1876–1880 and articles published between 1881–1889 or left in manuscript; the volume contains an index of all five volumes of the *Opere*. *Dulcea mea Doamnă/Eminul meu iubit. Corespondenţă inedită Mihai Eminescu–Veronica Micle. Scrisori din arhiva familiei Graziella şi Vasile Grigorcea,*. ed., ann., and pref. Christina Zarifopol-Illias, Iaşi, Polirom, 275 pp., also a bibliophile edition, contains a colour reproduction of the MS. *Eminescu. O sută de documente noi*, ed. George Muntean, Eminescu, 257 pp., assembles documents from family and acquaintances concerning the poet and his posthumous fortunes. *Eminescu văzut de armeni*, ed. Fabian Anton, Ararat, 223 pp., comprises texts by A. Acterian, G. Avakian, H. D. Siruni, *et al.* Constantin Amăriuţei, *Eminescu sau lumea ca substanţă poetică*, Jurnalul literar, 207 pp., gives articles published in magazines in Romania or abroad, and also in *Caiete de dor, România: Revista scriitorilor români*, etc., between 1951 and 2000. Alexandru Ciorănescu, *Eminescu sub fiorul timpului*, foreword N. Florescu, postscript A. Ionescu, Jurnalul literar, 95 pp., reproduces the introd. to M. Eminescu, *Poezii alese*, Madrid, 1990, 'Eminescu în traducere spaniolă' and the homage rendered at the poet's statue in Paris in 1989. Gheorghe Glodeanu, *Avatarurile prozei lui Mihai Eminescu*, Libra, 210 pp. Marin Mincu,

Paradigma eminesciană, Constanţa, Pontica, 322 pp., comprises studies on Eminescu's poetic system, archetypal love, *Luceafărul*, old and new specialists in Eminescu studies, etc. Ion Iliescu, *Mihai Eminescu. Crochiuri de bibliografie*, Timişoara, Mirton, 192 pp., concerns verse by Eminescu reproduced in school-books, represented on illustrated postcards and on music, etc. Alexandra Olivia Nedelcea, *Eminescu, economistul*, Craiova, Scrisul românesc, 204 pp. Mariana Neţ, *Eminescu, altfel: limbajul poetic eminescian — o perspectivă semiotică*, Minerva, 183 pp., puts forward criteria for identifying and defining Eminescu's tropes, relying on Speech Act Theory and sentence pragmatics. Ilie Constantin, 'O lectură a *Luceafărului*', pp. 21–47 of *Lecturi împreună*, Libra; Alexandru George, 'Eminescu supus unor observaţii' and 'Viaţa, opera şi isteria Eminescu', pp. 56–61 and 62–75, respectively, of his collected essays *Alte întîlniri*, Cartea românească, 309 pp. Gisèle Vanhese, '*Luceafărul* d'Eminescu et son après-texte. Sur *Malina* d'Ingeborg Bachmann', *NTJRS*, 2, 1999: 146–59. D. Müller, 'Mihai Eminescu zu Identität und Alterität', pp. 113–20 of *Im Dialog: Rumänische Kultur und Literatur* (cited below). A. G. Sahlean, 'Why translate Eminescu? Expectations and reality', *Revista româno-americană*, n.s., 3–4: 24–30. H. Fassel, 'M. Eminescu', *Südostdeutsche Vierteljahrblätter*, 49: 124–31.

GOLESCU. J. J. Ortega Roman, 'El libro de viajes de Dinicu Golescu: retraso balcanico y progreso occidental', *RFR*, 19, 1999: 147–66.

FILIMON. D. Şt. Rădulescu, *Dicţionarul personajelor din 'Ciocoii vechi şi noi' de Nicolae Filimon*, Ramida, 108 pp.

PAPAZOGLU. Dimitrie Papazoglu, *Istoria fondărei oraşului Bucureşti*, ed., pref., ann., and indexed by Marcel Dumitru Ciucă, Minerva, 349 pp.

TWENTIETH CENTURY

Dumitru Micu, *Literatura română în sec. al XX-lea*, Fundaţiei Culturale Române, 383 pp., is a (mostly correct) inventory of 20th-c. writers and works. It contains only rare and inadequate overviews of movements, tendencies, literary groupings and the causes that produced them; it gives scant attention to avant-garde and exiled authors and indeed hardly rises above minimal information. Preliminary research for another history of 20th c. literature is published in Ion Bogdan Lefter, *Recapitularea modernităţii*, Piteşti, Paralela 45, 219 pp., subtitled *Pentru o nouă istorie a literaturii române*, which sets the criterion of modernity at the basis of the critical enterprise, a criterion in which Lefter sees 'the key concept of Romanian literature' between the wars. The period following the Second World War is discussed from the perspective of the postmodern cultural model in Id.,

Postmodernism. Din dosarul unei 'bătălii' culturale, Piteşti, Paralela 45, 282 pp. From the same scholar we also have the first volume (covering letters A to F) of the 'bio-bibliographical' dictionary: Id., *Scriitori români din anii 80–90*, Piteşti, Paralela 45, 266 pp., comprising 127 writers who have made their debut or asserted themselves since 1980. This is a much amplified version of the dictionary published in English, by the same house, in 1999 (cf. *YWMLS*, 61:541). Much material for a history of contemporary Romanian literature is to be found in Anneli Ute Gabanyi, *The Ceauşescu Cult: Propaganda and Power Policy in Communist Romania*, The Romanian Cultural Foundation Publishing House, 432 pp., documenting state manipulation of the cultural patrimony and the support given by certain writers, and the official writers' associations, to the Ceauşescu personality cult, etc.

Several volumes are devoted to studying a literary grouping or a relatively unitary phenomenon. Emil Manu, *Generaţia literară a războiului*, Curtea Veche, 480 pp., presents and discusses the group of writers who made their debut shortly before or during the Second World War: Ion Caraion, D. Stelaru, C. Tonegaru, Marin Preda, P. Chihaia, and others, including the writers and essayists grouped in 'the literary circle' of Sibiu. Devoted to this same group, and to the distinct presence of its members in the literature of the period, is Ovid S. Crohmălniceanu and Klaus Heitmann, *Cercul literar de la Sibiu şi influenţa catalitică a culturii germane*, Universalia, 431 pp., with ample chapters devoted to the resurrection of the ballad in the poetry of the group's young members (Stefan Doinaş, Radu Stanca, Ioanichie Olteanu), to their preoccupations with theatre, to the group's prose writers, especially Ion D. Sîrbu, and so on.

A thematic anthology, Ruxandra Cesereanu, *Deliruri şi delire. O antologie a poeziei onirice româneşti*, Piteşti, Paralela 45, 251 pp., ranges from Eminescu and Macedonski to the contemporary poets Gellu Naum, Simona Popescu, Mircea Cărtărescu.

Concerning Nietzsche's influence on Romanian poets and thinkers between the Wars: Lucia Gorgoi, *Friedrich Nietzsche şi cultura română interbelică*, Cluj, Casa Cărţii de ştiinţă, 296 pp., refers particularly to Eliade, Cioran, and Blaga. Also on the debates of the inter-war years there is C. Pricop, *'Generaţii'*, *AŞUI*, (f), 43–44, 1997–98:87–113.

On the literature of Romanian exile: Mircea Anghelescu, *Cămaşa lui Nessus. Eseuri despre exilul literar*, Cartea românească, 160 pp., with studies on, *inter alia*, Peter Neagoe, Grigore Cugler, Paul Miron, the literary journals of exile, the literature of guilt; Radu Bărbulescu, *Ocrotiţi în străinătate. Scriitori români în München, 1944–2000*, Constanţa, Ex Ponto, 180 pp., which contains data on the institutions of Romanian exile — cultural associations, and publishing houses and journals in Munich — and a short literary anthology; N. Florescu,

Noi, cei din pădure. Reevaluări critice ale literaturii exilului, Jurnalul literar, 245 pp., with studies on M. Eliade, N. I. Herescu, L. Constantinescu, and others; V. Ivanovici, 'Exil şi identitate: identitatea exilului', pp. 90–104 of the volume *Repere în zigzag*, Fundaţiei Culturale Române; Cornel Ungureanu, *La vest de Eden*, II, Timişoara, Amarcord, 145 pp., with studies on, among others, Constantin Virgil Gheorghiu, Paul Miron, and Ion Caraion. Devoted to documenting the political organizations of Romanian exile, especially in the first years after the Second World War, Ion Calafeteanu, *Politică şi exil. Din istoria exilului românesc (1946–1950)*, Enciclopedică, 386 pp., contains important information concerning, among other things, the activity of exiled writers. On the literature of exile in a special sense of the word (i.e. the 'inner' exile) writes Gabriel Coşoveanu, 'Feţe ale exilului', pp. 167–88 of his *Vocile canonului*, Craiova, Scrisul românesc, with reference to Nicolae Balotă, Ion D. Sîrbu, and Mihai Şora.

The reinvigoration of the relationship between poetry and the sacred is the focus of Ana Bantoş, *Dinamica sacrului în poezia basarabeană contemporană*, pref. C. Ciopraga, Fundaţiei Culturale Române, 267 pp. In Ilie Constantin, *Lecturi împreună*, Libra, 307 pp., one poet assembles a volume of commentaries on other, contemporary, poets.

The papers of a 1999 conference organized by the Humboldt-Universität in Berlin on the dialogue, in German and Romanian literature, between the past and the present in the ten years since the fall of the Berlin Wall, were gathered in the volume *Im Dialog: Rumänische Kultur und Literatur*, ed. Mircea Anghelescu and Larisa Schippel, Leipziger Universitätsverlag, 273 pp., which includes among other things: Klaus Bochmann, 'Die Rumänen und die anderen' (49–69); Rodica Zafiu, 'Humor im rumänischen publizistischen Diskurs' (121–32); Elsa Lüder, 'Das Konfessive zwischen Literatur und Geschichte' (213–18); Florin Manolescu, 'Erinnern und Vergessen in der rumänischen Literaturgeschichte' (225–32); Mariana Neţ, 'Erinnerung und Mentalitäten' (261–73).

Numerous volumes of essays, interviews, literary recollections, and memoirs have appeared: Constantin Beldie, *Memorii. Caleidoscopul unei jumătăţi de veac în Bucureşti*, pref. N. Leonăchescu, Albatros, 377 pp., by the editor of the well-known weekly journal *Ideea europeană*, 1919–1928; Pavel Chihaia, *Legendele unei lumi posibile*, Jurnalul literar, 207 pp.; Cornelia Comorovski, *Oameni sub vremi*, Univers, 311 pp.; Sanda Golopenţia, *Vămile grave*, Univers, 230 pp.; Virgil Ierunca, *Trecut-au ani . . . Fragmente de jurnal. Întîmpinări şi accente. Scrisori nepierdute*, Humanitas, 451 pp., Ierunca's diary from the years 1949–1951 and 1960; Paul Miron, *Măsura urmelor*, pref. M. Anghelescu, epilogue by C. Ungureanu, Timişoara, Marineasa, 339 pp.; Romul Munteanu, *O viaţă trăită, o viaţă visată*, Libra, 426 pp.; Petre Pandrea, *Memoriile mandarinului valah*, Albatros, 600 pp., by a well-known lawyer and publicist of the interwar years, brother-in-law to the communist minister L. Pătrăşcanu, arrested in 1949 and later murdered in jail; Arnold Schwefelberg, *Amintirile unui intelectual evreu din România*, ed. and pref. Leon Volovici, Hasefer, 214 pp., by an important member of interwar Romania's Jewish intelligentsia, the father of the poet Veronica Porumbacu; Mircea Sîntimbreanu, *Carnete de editor*, ed. S. Sîntimbreanu and I. N. Anghel, Timişoara, Amarcord, 237 pp.; Horia Stanca, *Fragmentarium berlinez, 1942–1945*, Enciclopedică, 293 pp. On autobiographical discourse in contemporary Romanian literature (with reference to the diaries of M. Eliade, M. Sebastian, Jeny Acterian, and others): Ion Buzera, pp. 147–203 of *Reinventarea lecturii*, Craiova, Aius.

In Iordan Datcu, *Sub semnul Minervei*, Universal Dalsi, 299 pp., illus., one who was an editor with Minerva for the last quarter century traces the history of the Bucharest publishing house, which has always devoted itself mainly to literature, literary history, and the humanities.

INDIVIDUAL AUTHORS

ARGHEZI. Tudor Arghezi, *Opere*, I, ed., with a chronological table and a bibliography, Mitzura Arghezi and Traian Radu, pref. E. Simion, cxi + 841 pp., gathers the volumes of poetry published between 1929 and 1957; *Opere*, II, 1032 pp., the volumes that appeared after 1961, the children's poetry, and the miscellaneous poetry published in periodicals. B. Mazzoni, 'Un caz de variantistică evolutivă: *Rada* de Tudor Arghezi', pp. 111–16 of *Cercetarea literară azi* (see CORNEA, below).

BACOVIA. V. Ivanovici, 'Boemul şi slujbaşul sau despre virtuţile poeziei "minore"', pp. 216–42 of *Repere în zigzag*, quoted above, concerns symbolist poets: the Romanian George Bacovia and the Greek Costas Karyotakis.

BARBU. Id., 'Ion Barbu în tradiţia "rupturii"', pp. 243–74 of *Repere în zigzag*, quoted above.

BĂNULESCU. Monica Spiridon, *Ştefan Bănulescu*, Aula, Braşov, 94 pp.; E. Popeangă, 'Ciudades imaginarias en las puertas de Oriente', *RFR*, 19, 1999:129–46.

BLAGA. *Lucian Blaga: corespondenţă de familie*, text established and ann. Dorli Blaga, Universal Dalsi, 107 pp., contains letters sent and received between 1920 and 1961. Mircea Cenuşă, *Interviurile lui Lucian Blaga*, Alba Iulia, Şcoala Albei, 133 pp.. Florica Diaconu and Mircea Diaconu, *Dicţionar de termeni filosofici ai lui Lucian Blaga*, Univers enciclopedic, 347 pp., containing almost two hundred terms which explain the poet's categorial system, with a concluding bibliography for each term (consisting of the main passages of B.'s works which interpret and define the respective term), as well as a final anthology of excerpts from the authors who commented on Blaga's philosophy. Geo Săvulescu, *Lucian Blaga: filosofia prin metafore*, Focul veşnic viu, 217 pp.; Lucia Gorgoi, *Friedrich Nietzsche şi cultura română interbelică*, quoted above.

BLECHER   M. *Blecher mai puţin cunoscut. Corespondenţă şi receptare critică*, ed. Mădălina Lascu, pref. Ion Pop, Hasefer, 390 pp., contains Max Blecher's correspondence with poet Geo Bogza, painter Lucia Demetriade Bălăcescu (in French), critic Pompiliu Constantinescu, and others, two previously unpublished texts, and an anthology of critical texts from the interwar period dedicated to Blecher, as well as a critical bibliography.

BOTEZ.   Alice Botez, 'O noapte în cimitirul lunei', *Manuscriptum*, 30, 37–42, consists of unpublished prose texts.

CARAGIALE, M.   Roxana Sorescu, 'Gore Pirgu, cherubinul', pp. 30–86 of her *Lumea, repovestită*, Eminescu, contains an analysis of the system of symbolic relationships among the four characters of C.'s short novel *Craii de Curtea-Veche*.

CIORAN.   Matei Călinescu, 'Reflections on Cioran: tears, saints, history', pp. 105–10 of *Cercetarea literară azi* (quoted under CORNEA, below). Eugen Simion, 'Tînărul Cioran', pp. 26–123 of *Fragmente critice*, IV, Univers enciclopedic. Ilie Gyurcsik, 'Mantia megasilogismului', pp. 213–62 of *Paradigme moderne. Autori, texte, arlechini*, Timişoara, Amarcord.

CORNEA.   *Cercetarea literară azi: studii dedicate profesorului Paul Cornea (cu ocazia împlinirii a 70 ani)*, ed. Liviu Papadima and Mircea Vasilescu, Iaşi, Polirom, 360 pp., in the memoirs section, has texts by Nicolae Manolescu, Leon Volovici, Ion Bogdan Lefter, and others. The volume is rounded off (343–60) with a complete bibliography of the celebrated author.

COTRUŞ.   Aron Cotruş, *Opere*, ed., pref., and ann. A. Ruja, I, Minerva, 248 pp., illus. Ion Iliescu, *Poetul Aron Cotruş. Întregiri pentru viaţă şi operă*, Timişoara, Mirton, 1999, 178 pp.

CRAINIC.   Laura Bădescu, *Retorica poeziei religioase la Nichifor Crainic*, Minerva, 160 pp.

CROHMĂLNICEANU.   *Crohmălniceanu: un om pentru toate dialogurile*, coordinated by Geo Şerban, Universal Dalsi, 181 pp., is a memorial booklet marking the death of the Romanian critic established in Germany, with contributions by Eugen Simion, Mircea Cărtărescu, Paul Cornea, Mariana Şora, Ion Ianoşi, Radu Cosaşu, and others, and a previously unpublished letter by Crohmălniceanu.

ELIADE.   Mircea Eliade, *Dubla existenţă a lui Spiridon Vădastra*, ed. and pref. M. Handoca, Jurnalul literar, 171 pp., is a previously unpublished novel, abandoned by the author in 1944. Some of its pages were eventually incorporated into the novel *Noaptea de Sînziene*. Mircea Handoca, *Viaţa lui Mircea Eliade*, Cluj-Napoca, Dacia, 284 pp., resumes and enriches with new documents and episodes a book published in 1992. Eugen Simion, 'Eliade şi existenţialismul rom-ânesc', pp. 15–25 of his *Fragmente critice*, IV, Univers enciclopedic. Ioan Petru Culianu, 'Secretul doctorului Eliade', pp. 211–395 of his *Studii româneşti*, I, Nemira, paraphrasing the title of a well-known short story by Eliade, gather studies on his literary work and critical posterity. Mircea Handoca, *Pro Mircea Eliade*, Cluj-Napoca, Dacia, 230 pp., brings together several studies of mostly documentary value, such as 'Teoreticianul romanului', 'Folcloristul', 'Luminile rampei', 'Mircea Eliade despre Transilvania', and a set of polemical papers. *Dosarul Eliade (1937–1944)*, ed. and pref. by M. Handoca, Curtea Veche, 292 pp., comprises documentary materials (reviews, articles, press polemics, and excerpts from private letters) relating to books published by Eliade between 1937 and 1944, i.e. *Yoga, Domnişoara Christina, Şarpele, Insula lui Euthanasius*, and others. B. P. Hasdeu, *Esploratori del pensiero umano: G. Dumézil e Mircea Eliade*, ed. Julien Ries and Natale Spineto, Milan, Jaca Book, 431 pp., contains several studies including: N. Spineto, 'M. Eliade: materiali per un bilancio storiografico'; T. Baconsky, 'M. Eliade, il sognatore maltrattato'; R. Scagno, 'Alcuni punti fermi nell'impegno politico di M. Eliade'; M. Handoca, 'La ricezione dell'opera di M. Eliade in Romania'; Mac Linscott Ricketts, 'La risposta americana all'opera letteraria di M. Eliade'. The papers delivered in a section devoted to Eliade at the annual gathering of the German Society of Romance Languages in 1997 and published in *Balkan-Archiv. Neue Folge*, 24–25 (1999–2000), ed. Wolfgang Dahmen and Johannes Kramer, include: D. Petrescu, 'M. Eliade: quelques aventures de la réception' (37–46); E. Behring, 'M. Eliades Persönlichkeitsideal und das Modell des Bildungsromans' (47–58); I. Gregori, 'Fantasticul în proza lui M. Eliade' (69–88); H. W. Mühlroth, 'M. Eliades Konzeption einer "Archaischen Orient"' (89–101), etc. Mac Linscott Ricketts, 'The tangled tale of Eliade's writing of *Traité d'histoire des religions*', *Archaeus: études d'histoire des religions*, 4.4:51–77. M. Timuş and E. Ciurtin, 'The unpublished correspondence between M. Eliade and Stig Wikander (1948–1977)', *ib.*, 4.3:157–85, and 4.4:179–209.

FONDANE. R. I. Petrescu, *'Simboluri alchimice în poezia lui Benjamin Fundoianu', *AŞUI*, 43–44, 1997–98:5–13.

GALACTION. Gala Galaction, *Opere*, V, ed. and ann. T. Vârgolici, Minerva, 405 pp., includes, among other things, his 1903 theology degree thesis on 'the miracle on the road to Damascus', the pamphlet

Sionismul la prieteni printed in 1919, and the short biography of Eminescu (1914).

ISTRATI. D. Popa-Lisseanu, 'Lo real y lo magico en el mundo balcanico de Panait Istrati', *RFR*, 19, 1999:175–88. L. Schippel, 'Panait Istratis Kyra Kyralina — eine übersetzungswissenschaftliche Dreiecksgeschichte', *NIJRS*, 2.1–2, 1999:44–58.

LOVINESCU. Florin Mihăilescu, 'Portret de critic la maturitate', 'E. Lovinescu şi contemporanii lui', etc., pp. 7–30 of his *Critice şi metacritice*, Viaţa românească, 1999. E. Lovinescu, *Sburătorul. Agende literare*, IV, ed. Monica Lovinescu and Gabriela Omăt, ann. A. George, M. Feraru, and G. Omăt, Minerva, 595 pp., includes the entries in the critic's daily notebook between 1933 and 1936. The volume contains a rich set of notes, occupying more than half the volume, and an index of names.

NANDRIŞ. *O radiografie a exilului românesc: corespondenţă emisă şi primită de Grigore Nandriş, 1946–1967*, ed. and pref. I. Oprişan, Vestala, 460 pp., concerns the well-known linguist (d. 1968) who taught at the University of London and who also published literature and memoirs in Romanian exile journals. The volume includes letters sent by (among others) Alexandru Busuioceanu, Aron Cotruş, Mircea Eliade, Vintilă Horia, Basil Munteanu, Emil Turdeanu.

NAUM. Simona Popescu, *Salvarea speciei. Despre suprarealism şi Gellu Naum*, Fundaţiei Culturale Române, 262 pp.

PETRESCU. Radu Petrescu, *Locul revelaţiei*, ed. Adela Petrescu, pref. G. Crăciun, 236 pp., gathers interviews, articles, and chronicles of art from the sixties for the first time in volume form.

PILLAT, D. Carmen Brăgaru, *Dinu Pillat, un destin împlinit*, DU Style, 332 pp., complete with photographs and a genealogical tree, is the first monograph devoted to the critic and novelist Dinu Pillat, son of the poet Ion Pillat. Originally a Ph.D. thesis, it has annexed several documents concerning P.'s arrest, unpublished texts from his early years, etc.

PILLAT, I. Alexandru Cistelecan, *Celălalt Pillat*, Fundaţiei Culturale Române, 363 pp., attempts a positive reappraisal of P.'s traditionalist poetry.

SEBASTIAN. *Sebastian sub vremi. Singurătatea şi vulnerabilitatea martorului*, ed. Geo Şerban, Universal Dalsi, 484 pp., includes contributions by G. Liiceanu, Michael Finkenthal, Eugen Simion, Roxana Sorescu, Nicolae Manolescu, Zigu Ornea, Andrei Corbea, Leon Volovici, Norman Manea, Dorin Tudoran, and Ion Pop. M. Mattusch, 'Identitätskonstruktion gestern und heute – Lektüregeschichten zu M. Sebastians Roman *De două mii de ani*', pp. 233–46 of *Im Dialog: Rumanische Kultur und Literatur* (quoted above).

STANCA. A. S. Ene, *'Imagini obsedante în lirica lui Radu Stanca', *AŞUI*, 43–44, 1997–98: 115–29.

STĂNESCU. R. Stanceva, 'Le symbole de l'œuf comme sujet intertextuel: un dialogue interne de la littérature roumaine moderne', *NTJRS*, 2.1–2, 1999, 72–82, concerns Nichita Stănescu.

STEINHARDT. George Ardeleanu, *Nicolae Steinhardt*, Braşov, Aula, 110 pp.

VOICULESCU. Florentin Popescu, *Detenţia şi sfîrşitul lui V. Voiculescu*, Vestala, 159 pp., brings to light documentary materials on the detention and last years of the writer.

XI. RHETO-ROMANCE STUDIES

By INGMAR SÖHRMAN, *Gothenburg University*

1. BIBLIOGRAPHICAL AND GENERAL

A. Argemí, 'Lingue e culture nell'Europa del nuovo millenio', *Sot la nape*, 52.2:7–20. J. Grzega, 'Das Rätoromanische im Lichte des keltischen Reliktwortschatzes', *ASR*, 113:85–105, argues that the Celtic vocabulary substrate in the Rheto-Romance varieties indicates an old linguistic bond that clearly differentiates them from the Italian varieties. J. Kramer, 'Il problema storico-linguistico del ladino', *Ce fastu?*, 76:49–65, hypothesizes that the notion 'ladino' originated in the Engadine and was later extended to the Dolomites, where it has become the main denomination. The article is a continuation of Id., 'Latinus–ladino, nome di lingua parlata in Italia e nelle Alpi', *Mes Alpes à moi*, 165–74 (cf. *YWMLS*, 61:549).

2. FRIULAN

PHONOLOGY AND MORPHOLOGY. R. Maschi, 'Morfologia storica del friulano: l'evoluzione del sistema verbale dal XIV al XVIII secolo', *Ce fastu?*, 76:197–228, gives a good description of the origin of the Friulan verb system and of how this developed during the first centuries of written language. L. Vanelli, 'À propos de quelques hypothèses sur le frioulan prélittéraire', *RLiR*, 63, 1999: 215–33, polemicizes with Giorgio Cadorini on the originality of the old Friulan two-case declension, and in the same volume (235–39) Cadorini is given the chance to answer.

MORPHOSYNTAX. F. Vicario, 'Primi documenti per una storia linguistica del friulano', pp. 259–74 of *ad Gredine forestum 999–1999*, ed. Emma Comploi et al., San Martin de Tor, Istituto Cultural Ladin 'Micurà de Rü', shows the importance of recently edited medieval documents for the establishment of the development and originality of the Friulan language.

ONOMASTICS AND LEXIS. Pier Paolo Begotti, *Toponomastica storica di Spilimbergo* (Quaderni Spilimberghesi, 5), Spilimbergo, 1999, is a meticulously detailed description of the region west of Udine. The author has collected evidence from published and also archive material, which makes this book a valuable piece of historical linguistics. W. Chiesa, 'Il Borgo di San Rocco nei suoi toponimi friulani', *Borc San Rocco*, 1999, 30 pp. (offprint), consists of a fairly thorough description of 70 toponyms. G. Frau, 'Elementi tedeschi nel friulano', *Sot la nape*, 52.3–4:17–21, argues that the German influence from the Middle Ages has always been present but has never taken over and Germanized Friulan. C. C. Desinan, 'Toponomi di "guerra" in Friuli', *ib.*, 52.1:89–94, albeit brief, gives a fairly detailed description of the remaining onomastics based on the word *guerra*. Id., 'Toponomi friulani derivati da colori', *ib.*, 52.3–4:51–60, is a broad survey of toponyms based on colour names in Friulan and of influences from neighbouring languages like Slavic and German as compared with the Latin origin of most colour names. A Friulan study of a popular linguistic topic. Id., '*Dunum* gallico in Friuli', *RIOn*, 6.1:89–94, shows that in Friuli *dunum* and its derivates always mean 'hill' and never 'town'/*oppidum*. Aldo Gallas, **Toponomi e micro-toponomi della campagna e del Colle di Medea — Vie e piazze del paese*, Medea, Pro Loco di Medea, 1999, fills a gap in street names and other onomastics relating to the immediate vicinity of Colle di Medea. G. Pillinini, 'Lingua, stile e versificazione in Ermes de Colloredo', *Ce fastu?*, 76:67–76, describes the writer's way of mixing archaic forms with innovations. Robert Moscjon, *Là cu gjavà il piçul. Toponomastiche di S. Marie la Lungje. Meret di Cjapitul, Romejetis, Roncjis di Cjapitul*, S. Marie la Lungje, Comune, 1999, 240 pp., a rather extensive book, is a detailed onomastic description of a Friulan region. T. Venuti, 'Riflessioni storico-toponomastiche sull'origine di Povoletto e salt', *Ce fastu?*, 76:285–91.

SOCIOLINGUISTICS AND LANGUAGES IN CONTACT. W. Cisilino, 'La legge di tutela della minoranza linguistica friulana', *ib.*, 293–304, is a critical analysis of the present linguistic situation. A. Hönigsperger, 'La base legale della situazione attuale in Friuli', *ib.*, 137–47, gives a critical view of the effects of the language law from 1996 (1997 in Friuli) and its effects on education and the promotion of the language.

3. LADIN

BIBLIOGRAPHICAL AND GENERAL. H. Goebl, 'Gröden und seine Sprache. Ein wissenschaftshistorischer Rück-, Über- und Ausblick zur "Questione ladina"', *ad Gredine forestum 999–1999*, 127–68. Whether there is a Rheto-Romance unity or not has been discussed ever since Ascoli's days, often with nationalistic interpretations, and Goebl gives a balanced description of this history and presents strong dialectometric evidence for this unity, using material from Jaberg/ Jud's linguistic atlas. The last volume of the Etymological Dictionary of Ladin was finished in 1999: this is discussed in J. Kramer, 'Riflessioni in occasione della conclusione dell'EWD', *ASR*, 113:185–96, where with due respect to the finished work he insists that there is now room for more etymological work based on what is presented in the dictionary. **Le minoranze del Veneto: ladini, cimbri e* *germanofoni di Sappada*, ed. Luciana Palla, n.p., Regione Veneto, 1998, 215 pp., are the *acta* of a conference held at Arabba in 1997. P. Videsott, 'Dolomitenladinische linguistische Bibliographie 1996–1997–1998', *Ladinia*, 22, 1998[2000]:351–63, is an updated continuation of the Ladin part of the Rheto-Romance bibliography that Videsott and Siller Runggaldier published in 1998. In an article that describes research and publications at Innsbruck University during the last decade, P. Videsott, 'Ein Jahrzehnt Rätoromanisch in Forschung und Lehre an der Universität Innsbruck (1988–1999)', *ASR*, 113:161–80, discusses the two main topics dealt with in *Studies on Ladin and Ladin Onomastics at Innsbruck University*. The article also includes a bibliography of the Innsbruck publications in the field. M. Vögeli, 'Qualität und Wert — Dolomitenladinische Lexikographie 1994–1999', *ib.*, 197–220, gives a good view of recent Ladin dictionaries.

MORPHOSYNTAX. V. Pallabazzer, 'Uso di ciasa/cesa al plurale con il valore di singolare. Annotazione ladino-dantesca', *Ladinia*, 21, 1997[1999]:191–92.

ONOMASTICS AND LEXIS. L. Craffonara offers various contributions: 'Die geographische Bezeichnung "Gader": Ursprüngliche Lokalisierung und etymologische Deutung', *ib.*, 153–78; 'Val Muræia: Die alte Bezeichnung für einen Tal des oberen Gadertals', *ib.*, 179–90; '*Vicus — villa* und *curtis* im Gadertal mit Ausblicken auf die angrenzenden Täler. Neue Aspekte der Besiedlungsgeschichte', *ib.*, 22, 1998[2000]:63–162, which is a detailed article on some important onomastic elements; and 'Die Grenze der Urkunde con 1002/1004 im heutigen Ladinien', *ib.*, 163–259, a thorough article on early documents concerning the Norital and Pustrissa counties where Ladin place names and geographical references are given, as the author clearly shows. J. Grzega, 'Zu einigen lexicologischen und semantischen Problemen bei der Ausbreitung des Ladin Dolomitan', *ZRP*, 116:577–90. O. Gsell, 'Galloromanische Worttypen im ladinisch-padanischen Raum', *Ladinia*, 21, 1997[1999]:135–51. Giovanni Mischì, *Wörterbuch Deutsch–Gadertaler mit einem ladinischen Wörterverzeichnis*, San Martin de Tor, Istituto Cultural Ladin 'Micurà de Rü', 926 pp., an extensive dictionary (36,000 German entries and 78,000 correspondent Ladin translations), is intended for administrative and other practical purposes in Val Badia. It includes an introduction to standardized orthography and also gives in the last 130 pages the correct spelling of some 16,000 Ladin words. The grammatical information is reduced to what the Ladin speaker needs in order to find the correct words. The author has also included a great number of neologisms in order to assist in the production of official documents and also to promote the official status (established in 1988 and 1994) of Ladin. SOCIOLINGUISTICS AND LANGUAGES IN CONTACT. W. Cicilino, 'Lenghe e dirit', *Sot la nape*, 52.3–4: 105–08, concerns the teaching of Ladin in the Ladin-speaking provinces of Italy. H. Goebl, 'Die Neoladinitätsdiskurs in der Provinz Belluno', *Ladinia*, 21, 1997[1999]: 5–57. *Ladin, ulà vaste pa? Poscibeltés de svilup dl ladin dles Dolomites*, Bolzano, 1998, are the *acta* of a conference on the situation of Ladin held in Bolzano in 1995. H. Siller Runggaldier, 'Das Grödnerische: Sprache zwischen Idiom, Talvariante und dem Projekt des Ladin dolomitan', *ad Gredine forestum 999–1999*, 169–96, deals with the complicated classification of a peculiar dialect like Gardenese and its close co-dialects at a time when a unified written variety is being created. P. Weber, *Ergibnisse einer Umfrage zum Sprachgebrauch der Ladiner im Gadertal, Gröden, Buchenstein und Ampezzo', *Ladinia*, 21, 1997[1999]: 73–88.

4. Swiss Romansh

BIBLIOGRAPHICAL AND GENERAL. R. Liver, 'Zur Entstehung bündnerromanischer Schriftsprachen (Engadin und Surselva)', *ASR*, 113: 253–66, discusses the first written documents in Romansh and how they are related to a socio-cultural situation in which the Reformation played a strong role; but although there is much Latin, German, and Italian influence, strong evidence also exists for an older, influential, Romansh popular poetry tradition that still has to be explored. MORPHOSYNTAX. M. Grünert, 'Der Konjunktiv als Zitierzeichen und die surselvische Modussyntax', *ib.*, 143–58, discusses Surselvan peculiarities in the use of the subjunctive with personal verb forms and shows fairly convincingly that this is an autochthonous development and does not coincide with German, which has often been seen as the reason for this usage. M. E. Viaro, 'Cumparaziun tranter varsaquantas construcziuns verb + adverb en rumantsch ed en portugais', *ib.*, 281–89, maintains that a certain syntactic parallelism between these two languages proves that the German influence on the verb–adverb construction is less strong than has been thought hitherto: as Portuguese and Romansh have had little contact, parallel development indicates a Romance structural bond which may have been reinforced by German influence, but this did not create the construction. ONOMASTICS AND LEXIS. A. Collenberg, 'LIR, Lexicon istoric retic: Cabbiolo-Cuira, II', *ib.*, 293–335, is a continuation of the etymological onomastic dictionary the first part of which was presented in 1999. Felix Giger et al., *Dicziunari Rumantsch Grischun*, CXXXVII: *lantschetta-laschar*, Chur, Societad retorumantscha, 1999. In J. Kuhn, 'Romanische Orts- und Flurnamen im Raum Mols/St Gallen', *ASR*, 113, 43–68, the presentation of 23 examples of place names of Rheto-Romance origin shows what remains of the former Rheto-Romance domination. G. A. Plangg, 'Namensgeschichten in Vadans (Montafon)', *ib.*, 69–84, discusses other onomastic evidence of lost Rheto-Romance territory.

SOCIOLINGUISTICS AND LANGUAGES IN CONTACT. J. C. Arquint, *'Stationen der Standardisierung', pp. 24–67 of *Die viersprachige Schweiz*, ed. Robert Schläpfer et al., Aarau. W. Cicilino, 'Lenghe e dirit', *Sot la nape*, 52.3–4: 105–08, as well as Ladin in Ladin-speaking areas of Italy, concerns the teaching of Romansh in the Romansh-speaking villages of the Grisons. A pertinent review of technical terminology and its elaboration in Romansh is G. Darms, 'Fachsprachen im Bündnerromanischen des 20. Jahrhunderts und ihre Forschung. Eine Übersicht', pp. 1527–32 of *Fachsprachen: Ein internationales Handbuch zur Fachsprachenforschung und Terminologiewissenschaft*, ed. Lothar Hoffmann and Hartwig Kalverkämper, Berlin, de Gruyter, 1999. A clear description of ongoing work on the elaboration of standard Romansch and on related publishing activities (including the new data bank at the Lia Rumantscha) is given in: A.-A. Dazzi-Gross, 'Actualitads dal project rumantsch grischun da la Lia rumantscha', *ASR*, 113: 223–40. The article also includes an outline of Romansh linguistic politics in Switzerland. G. Gorenko, 'Las perscrutaziuns dil romontsch ella tradiziun filologica russa', *ib.*, 241–49, presents a sociolinguistic analysis of the Romansh varieties and their use in a theoretical framework elaborated by Russian linguists. G. Hilty, 'Das Zurückweichen des Rätoromanischen vom Bodensee bis Sargans (7.–14. Jahrhundert)', *ib.*, 29–42, describes the territorial reduction of a once more widespread Romansh region. F. Jodl, 'Churrätien und das Frankenreich in sprachlicher Hinsicht: Das Zusammenspiel ausser- und innersprachlicher Faktoren und mögliche Folgen für die Herausbildung des Bündnerromanischen', *ib.*, 109–42. C. Solèr, '1938: ina data (be) istorica avant 60 onns?', *Ladinia*, 22, 1998[2000]: 341–48, discusses the almost 60 years it took from the recognition of Romansh as a national language to its present position as a 'partly official' language in 1996.

3

CELTIC LANGUAGES

I. WELSH STUDIES

LANGUAGE

By DAVID THORNE, *Professor of Welsh Language and Literature, University of Wales, Lampeter*

1. GENERAL

Caryl Davies, *Adfeilion Babel: Agweddau ar Syniadaeth Ieithyddol y Ddeunawfed Ganrif,* Cardiff, Univ. of Wales Press, 350 pp., is an important contribution to the discussion of ideas about the origin of language and the relationship between languages as perceived in 18th-c. Wales. The status of key figures such as Dr John Davies, Edward Lhuyd, Rowland Jones, William Owen Pughe and Sir William Jones is explored in detail; Davies also shows how Welsh scholars made contact with their continental counterparts in order to design a platform for the scientific study of the Celtic languages. Price, *Language,* is a concise and valuable discussion of the languages that are spoken at present, or were spoken at some time in the past, in Britain, Ireland, the Isle of Man and the Channel Islands. M. J. Aldhouse Green and M. E. Raybould, 'Deities with Gallo-British names recorded in inscriptions from Roman Britain', *SC*, 33:91–135, investigates religious inscriptions to British and Gaulish deities in the epigraphy of Roman Britain, considering whether the dedications provide a largely Romanized view of the cults or whether they suggest that a substantial number of the votaries were Britons who retained their native traditions and culture but adopted the Roman habit of making literary dedications.

2. GRAMMER

P. Schrijver, 'Spirantization and nasalization in British', *SC*, 33:1–19, explores various aspects of the history of spirantization and nasalization in British and includes useful references to earlier disussions in this and related areas. A. Shisha-Halvey, 'Structural sketches of Middle Welsh syntax (II) *ib.*, 155–234, continues with his study of noun predication and presentative patterns. David Thorne, *Gafael mewn Gramadeg,* Llandysul, Gomer, xii + 252 pp., is an informative discussion of contemporary Welsh. D. W. E. Willis, 'On the distribution of resumptive pronouns and wh- trace in Welsh', *JL*, 36:351–73, contributes to discussions on the analysis of the relative clause in Welsh.

3. ETYMOLOGY AND LEXICOGRAPHY

Parts 54 and 55 of GPC, (ed. G. A. Bevan) cover STREIC – TACMONIAID, TACHMONIAID – TEITH, respectively. *The Pocket Modern Welsh Dictionary*, ed. Gareth King, OUP, is a useful compilation and includes a guide to pronunciation and brief summary of the grammar of the contemporary language in addition to a Welsh-English, English-Welsh dictionary. There are surprising and glaring omissions: the only forms listed, for example, between *allan* and *allwedd* are two derivatives of *allan*. A. Falileyev, *SC*, 33 : 353 has notes on OW *cihun(n)* and *fonn*.

4. SOCIOLINGUISTICS

Glyn Williams and Delyth Morris, *Language Planning and Language Use: Welsh in a Global Age*, Cardiff, Univ. of Wales Press, xxxvi + 268 pp., is a comprehensive survey of current patterns of Welsh language use together with a discussion of public attitudes towards the language. There is also a sound analysis of political and policy issues relating to language planning and discussion of minority languages in the context of global development. H. Williams and D. Thorne, 'The value of teletext subtitling as a medium for language learning', *System*, 28:217–28, describes a pilot study which aimed at gaining insights into how language learners benefit from training in interlingual subtitling. The study showed that students' competence in both L1 and L2 improved while they simultaneously mastered transferable skills. The authors argue that more practically based and vocationally orientated courses, similar to subtitling, would be of benefit to language undergraduates and would contribute to increase motivation in second language acquisition. John Aitchison and Harold Carter, *Language, Economy and Society: The Changing Fortunes of the Welsh Language in the Twentieth Century*, Cardiff, Univ. of Wales Press, 171 pp., is an important thought-provoking study in cultural geography which seeks to re-evaluate prospects for the language at the start of the 21st c. through detailed analyses of spatial distributions. *The Welsh Language and its Social Domains 1801–1911*, ed. Geraint H. Jenkins, Cardiff, Univ. of Wales Press, 629 pp., is the English language version of Jenkins, *Gwnewch Bopeth* (see *YMLS*, 61:555). *Let's Do our Best for the Ancient Tongue: The Welsh Language in the Twentieth Century*, ed. Geraint

H. Jenkins and Mari A. Williams, Cardiff, Univ. of Wales Press, xvi + 700 pp., is a collection of essays examining the social history of the Welsh language in the 20th c. An introduction outlines the problems including the eroding affect of the English media on Welsh. Some of the contributions have appeared in another form in other recent publications, but there is a very interesting chapter comparing the history of Welsh in the present century with that of other minority European languages such as Slovene, Slovak and Czech. Another worthwhile contribution examines Welsh national identity through land and landscape and shows how language emerged as a central feature of nationalist geographical imagination. *Language Revitalization: Policy and Planning in Wales*, ed. Colin H. Williams, Cardiff, Univ. of Wales Press, xv + 388 pp., deals with a frustrating issue both in contemporary Wales and further afield. Essays trace the growth of the Welsh language movement and explore the sources which inform policy decisions. *Cyflwyno'r Gymraeg: Llawlyfr i Diwtoriaid Iaith*, ed. Christine Jones, Llandysul, Gomer, 183pp., is a collection of substantial essays by experienced practitioners reviewing the whole field of teaching Welsh to adults —from immersion teaching to the e-learning experience. Thomas, *Minority Languages*, has a number of papers relevant to this section in the fields of mobility, planning, education, attitudes, identity, variation and technology; many of these contributions have already been published elsewhere.

5. DIALECTOLOGY

The Welsh Dialect Survey, ed. Alan R. Thomas et al. Cardiff, Univ. of Wales Press, xxlv + 741 pp., is the result of the collective enthusiasm of five academic editors on a dialect project initiated by the Board of Celtic Studies in 1991. The work has succeeded in eliciting material from the Anglicised areas of south and mid-Wales but the characteristics of the border counties are less well documented. Informants were older generation speakers and the structured field questionnaire consisted of 726 target items with the aim of producing 'a survey of the principal features of segmental phonology . . . with some morphophonology and morphology, and a few miscellaneous items of historical and other interest'. G. M. Awbrey, 'Y dystiolaeth dafodieithol', *LlC*, 23:136–46, seeks to establish the provenance of the only surviving copy of a 17th-c. elegy to Charles I by an unknown poet discovered amongst the parish records of Tre-gaer, near Rhaglan, by examining the linguistic evidence. She concludes that the work was originally composed in eastern Powys. Huw Evans and Marian Davies, *Fyl'na Weden i: Blas ar Dafodiaith Canol Ceredigion*, Llanrwst,

Carreg Gwalch, 195 pp., is a popular introduction to the Welsh dialect of mid Ceredigion. Glyn E. Jones, *Iaith Lafar Brycheiniog: Astudiaeth o'i Ffonoleg a'i Morffoleg*, Cardiff, Univ. of Wales Press, viii + 170pp., is a valuable study of the phonology and morphology of the Welsh dialects of Breconshire and the dynamic patterning of those dialects within the main dialect regions.

EARLY AND MEDIEVAL LITERATURE

By JANE CARTWRIGHT, *Lecturer in Welsh, University of Wales, Lampeter*

A further four volumes of poetry have appeared this year in the UWCASWC series, *Cyfres Beirdd yr Uchelwyr*, under the general editorship of Anne Parry Owen. *Gwaith Gruffudd Llwyd a'r Llygliwiaid Eraill*, ed. Rhiannon Ifans, Aberystwyth, UWCASWC, xxii + 355 pp., edits eighteen poems attributed to Gruffudd Llwyd including two important praise poems to Owain Glyndŵr which were composed prior to the Glyndŵr uprising. Also included in the volume is an *awdl* by Gruffudd Llwyd's uncle, Hywel ab Einion Lygliw, and poetry attributed to other members of his family. *Gwaith Hywel Swrdwal a'i Deulu*, ed. Dylan Foster Evans, Aberystwyth, UWCASWC, xx + 244 pp., edits the work of Hywel Swrdwal and his two sons, Ieuan and Dafydd. The majority are elegies and formal praise poems to the Welsh nobility, many of which highlight the family's sympathy with the Yorkist cause. Included in the volume is the unusual Middle English poem, written in Welsh orthography, in praise of the Virgin Mary. Religious poetry features greatly in *Gwaith Ieuan Brydydd Hir*, ed. M. Paul Bryant-Quinn, Aberystwyth, UWCASWC, xx + 209 pp., which includes editions of thirteen poems attributed to Ieuan Brydydd Hir, two poems of uncertain authorship and three *cywyddau ymryson* addressed to Ieuan by Tudur Penllyn. *Gwaith Prydydd Breuan, Rhys ap Dafydd ab Einion, Hywel Ystorm a Cherddi Dienw o Lyfr Coch Hergest*, ed. Huw Meirion Edwards, Aberystwyth, UWCASWC, xvii + 152 pp., provides editions of the work of some of the 14th-c. satirical poets whose poetry is preserved in the Red Book of Hergest. All of the volumes in this series are accompanied by brief introductions to the work of each poet and useful notes. Modern Welsh translations of the 14th-c. poems are provided, whereas the 15th-c. poetry is accompanied only by lists of vocabulary. N. Jacobs, ' "Englynion" y Misoedd: testun B neu fersiwn Llanstephan 117 a Pheniarth 155', *Dwned* 6: 9–24, edits four verses of poetry associated with four months of the year and discusses the relationship between the various manuscripts in which they are extant.

R. M. Jones, *Mawl a'i Gyfeillion*, Llandybïe, Cyhoeddiadau Barddas, 258 pp., is a detailed analysis of the nature of praise poetry in Welsh tradition. The study considers both secular and religious praise poetry and focuses primarily on medieval poetry: the *Cynfeirdd* and *Gogynfeirdd*, Dafydd ap Gwilym and the poets of the gentry, but also encompasses the Renaissance and the work of William Williams Pantycelyn. P. MacCana, 'Iwerddon a Chymru yn yr Oesoedd

Canol', *Cof Cenedl* 14:3–36, synthesizes a wide range of literary sources as he considers points of contact between Ireland and Wales from the 7th c. to the 17th c. N. Jacobs, 'Red, brown, and grey cuckoos: a problem in poetic ornithology', *CMCS* 40: 27–33, discusses the semantic development of the term *rhudd* and various interpretations of the line *Rud cogeu goleu ewyn* in 'Cân yr Henwr'. L. W. Lloyd, 'Beth yw perthyn? Pedwar term teuluol ym marddoniaeth yr Oesoedd Canol', *Dwned*, 6: 25–53, traces the semantic development of the four familial terms *teulu*, *tylwyth*, *cenedl* and *câr* and examines their meanings and uses in Middle Welsh poetry. D. Johnston, ' "Ceidwaid yr hen iaith"? Beirdd yr Uchelwyr a'r iaith Saesneg', *Y Traethodydd* 150:16–24, demonstrates that the poets of the gentry frequently used English loan-words in their poetry for both artistic and pragmatic reasons, and thus demolishes the myth that medieval poets helped conserve an ancient pure form of Welsh untainted by English influences. Id., ' "Propaganda'r prydydd": gwleidyddiaeth Beirdd yr Uchelwyr', *Cof Cenedl* 14:39–67, highlights many of the pitfalls that can be encountered when attempting to interpret political poetry from 14th and 15th-c. Wales, and warns against lifting sections of poetry from their literary and historical contexts. P. L. Williams, ' "Ar ganghennau'r gynghanedd": agweddau ar y goedwig yn llenyddiaeth yr Oesoedd Canol', *Dwned* 6: 55–76, surveys references to carpentry, trees and forests in Middle Welsh poetry and highlights the relationship between the forest and the otherworld in medieval Welsh literature. Id., 'Tirlun a thirwedd Cymru: golwg ar lenyddiaeth yr Oesoedd Canol', Univ. of Wales Aberystwyth, occasional series 2, 29 pp., elucidates references to landscape in medieval Welsh poetry and prose, and demonstrates that although a sense of place was extremely important to medieval authors, they were not particularly concerned with the aesthetics of landscape. Id., 'Cywydd "Y Carw" Dafydd ap Gwilym: rhai ystyriaethau', *Y Traethodydd* 155:80–92, considers what inspired Dafydd ap Gwilym to choose a deer as a love messenger in his *cywydd* 'Y Carw'. Marged Haycock, ' "Where cider ends, there ale begins to reign": drink in medieval Welsh poetry', H. M. Chadwick Memorial Lectures 10, Dep. of Anglo-Saxon, Norse and Celtic, Cambridge, 29 pp., discusses references to alcoholic beverages in medieval Welsh poetry. A. Breeze, 'The Blessed Virgin and the sunbeam through glass', *Celtica* 23:19–29, discusses references in medieval poetry to the image of the sunbeam shining through glass and its metaphorical associations with Christ's incarnation and Mary's virginity. The discussion traces the origins and development of the topos and considers six examples from medieval Welsh poetry. O. Thomas, 'Dafydd Epynt: bardd llythrennog o Frycheiniog', *Dwned* 6: 77–94, sheds new lights on the poetic career of Dafydd Epynt, a

15th-c poet from Breconshire who has previously attracted very little attention. Thomas demonstrates that although Dafydd Epynt cannot be considered as one of the most important poets in 15th-c. century Wales, he is nevertheless significant because some of his poetry is recorded in his own hand. J. Walford Davies, ' "Hybu'r galon rhwng yr esgyrn crin": cywydd 'Cysur Henaint' Guto'r Glyn', *Dwned* 6: 95–127, is a detailed critical analysis of Guto'r Glyn's *cywydd* 'Cysur Henaint'. H. M. Edwards, 'Dwyn marwnadau adref', *LlC* 23:21–38, continues his work on elegiac poetry by considering when and where the elegies were performed. G. A. Williams, 'Adolygu'r canon: cywydd arall gan Iolo Goch i Owain Glyndŵr', *LlC* 23:39–73, argues convincingly that 'Cywydd i Owain Glyndŵr pan oedd fwyaf ei rwysg' should be reinstated in the Iolo Goch canon. This fascinating piece of research has major implications for the study of both Welsh literature and Welsh history, since it implies that Iolo Goch was still alive at the time of the Glyndŵr uprising; that the poem was composed *c.* 1403 and is, therefore, a unique witness to the Glyndŵr rebellion. It had previously been assumed that all of the poetry composed for Owain Glyndŵr was written prior to the revolt and that Iolo Goch died *c.* 1397/8. Appended to the article is an edition of the poem. Id., 'Beirdd Cymru a'r goron', *Cof Cenedl* 15:31–68, discusses attitudes towards the English crown in Welsh poetry from the Middle Ages onwards. B. O. Huws, 'Ieuan Gethin, Owain Glyndŵr a stori Iolo Morganwg', *Y Traethodydd* 155:137–47, carefully examines each of the elements in a story about Ieuan Gethin recounted by Iolo Morganwg. Having considered other literary and historical references, Huws comes to the conclusion that the nucleus of the story is true and that Ieuan probably was pardoned by Henry V after going into hiding on Anglesey following the Glyndŵr rebellion. Glanmor Williams, *Cymru a'r Gorffennol: Côr o Leisiau*, Llandysul, Gomer, 229 pp., is a useful collection of essays on Welsh history which includes two articles relevant to this section: 'Proffwydoliaeth, prydyddiaeth a pholitics yn yr Oesoedd Canol' (31–40), previously published in *Taliesin* (1968), looks at the political significance of prophetic poetry in medieval Wales and 'Harri Tudur: Mab Darogan' (41–53), examines attitudes towards Henry Tudor and the way in which Welsh poets depicted Henry VII as the Prophesied Son, descendant of Cadwaladr, who would free the Welsh from tyranny. R. White, 'Caernarfon and the origins of the Kingdom of Gwynedd', *CHST* 61:23–39, is an historical article which draws on a number of literary texts. T. Hallam, 'Ysgrife(nu) Lewys Glyn Cothi', *LlC* 23:74–94, considers the relationship between orality and the written medium in the work of Lewys Glyn Cothi.

The Welsh King and his Court, ed. T. M. Charles-Edwards, Morfydd
E. Owen and Paul Russell, Cardiff, Univ. of Wales Press,
ix + 603 pp., is a detailed and authoritive account of the organization
and operation of the Welsh royal court prior to the Edwardian
conquest. The study provides a thorough analysis of the Laws of
Court, editions of primary texts and English translations and includes
the following articles which are relevant to this section: D. Jenkins,
'*Bardd teulu* and *pencerdd*' (142–66), carefully examines the roles of the
pencerdd and *bardd teulu* and demonstrates that whilst *pencerdd* names a
status in the independent bardic organization, *bardd teulu* names an
office in the state organization. P. I. Lynch, 'Court poetry, power and
politics' (167–90), also examines the status of court poets and their
relation to both court and state, but focuses primarily on the political
aims of their poetry. T. M. Charles-Edwards and N. A. Jones,
'*Breintiau Gŵyr Powys*: the liberties of the men of Powys' (191–23),
analyse an unusual poem by Cynddelw Brydydd Mawr which
champions the liberties of the men of Powys and demonstrates that
Madog ap Maredudd's *pencerdd* was capable of expressing views
contrary to the interests of the rulers of Powys. M. E. Owen, 'Royal
propaganda: stories from the law texts' (224–54), discusses a series of
stories and anecdotes recorded in the Welsh law texts and considers
the purpose of these stories. Editions of the Middle Welsh texts and
English translation are provided in an appendix. P. Russell, '*Canu i
Swyddogion Llys y Brenin*', (552–60), comments on a series of verses to
the officers of the court and offers an edition based on John Jones of
Gellilfdy's transcription. H. Pryce, 'The context and purpose of the
earliest Welsh lawbooks', *CMCS* 39:39–63, demonstrates that the
earliest Welsh lawbooks were written for a variety of different reasons
and that they reflect 'a wider affirmation of Welsh culture and identity
stimulated by the threat of English conquest and settlement'.
J. Goering and H. Pryce, 'The *De modo confitendi* of Cadwgan, Bishop
of Bangor', *MedS* 62: 1–27, outlines the life and writings of Cadwgan,
Bishop of Bangor from 1215 to 1235/6, and provides an edition of
his treatise concerning the confession of sins.

Daniel Huws, *Medieval Welsh Manuscripts*, Cardiff, Univ. of Wales
Press, xvi + 352 pp. + 36 pls, is the most significant study of medieval
Welsh manuscripts since J. Gwenogvryn Evans, *Report on Manuscripts
in the Welsh Language* (1889–1910). Although the majority of the
articles have previously been published elsewhere and the rather
modest Preface suggests that the study is 'offering nothing new', this
superb collection is an invaluable introduction to the Welsh manuscript tradition and draws together some of the most lucid and
detailed analyses of important Welsh manuscripts such as *Liber
Landavensis*, the Hendragadredd Manuscript, the White Book of

Rhydderch and the Hengwrt-Peniarth and Mostyn collections. Issues relating to palaeography, dating, patronage and scribal practice are all addressed and the list of all manuscripts in Welsh up to 1540 is an indispensable aid for anyone studying medieval Welsh literature. Articles on Welsh vernacular books 1250–1400 and the Hendragedredd Manuscript (one of the most important sources for *Gogynfeirdd* poetry) are here translated into English for the first time. *The Cambridge Juvencus Manuscript Glossed in Latin, Old Welsh, and Old Irish*, ed. Helen McKee, 2 vols, Aberystwyth, CMCS Publications, x + 594 pp., provides a complete edition and facsimile of Cambridge, University Library, MS Ff.4.42 (1285). Originally copied in 9th-c. Wales, the manuscript contains a number of additions and annotations in OW and OI which include twelve *englynion* believed to be the oldest surviving poetry in OW. Id., 'Scribes and glosses from Dark Age Wales', *CMCS* 39 : 1–22, further scrutinizes the manuscript's vernacular glosses and notes that the scribe responsible for the OW *englynion* was one of the first to add material to the Cambridge Juvencus. McKee tentatively suggests that the manuscript may have been produced at Llanilltud Fawr or Llancarfan.

Math Uab Mathonwy Pedwaredd Gainc y Mabinogi, ed. Ian Hughes, Aberystwyth, Dep. of Welsh, Univ. of Wales, Aberystwyth, xli + 114 pp., provides a new edition of *Math Uab Mathonwy*, the fourth branch of PKM. His edition is based on the White Book of Rhydderch, but also lists the most significant variant readings found in the Red Book of Hergest. A useful introduction is provided which includes information on the manuscripts, previous editions of the text, translations, dating, structure, authorship and characterisation as well as two maps relating to the legend. The eleven tales known collectively as the *Mabinogion* have been translated into Portuguese and a translation of *Ystorya Taliesin* is included in an appendix: *O Mabinogion*, trans. José Domingos Morais, Lisbon, Assírio & Alvim, 443 pp. A second German translation has also appeared: **Das Sagenbuch der walisischen Kelten: Die Vier des Mabinogi*, trans. Bernhard Maier, München. *The Mabinogion*, trans. Lady Charlotte Guest, London, Harper Collins, x + 355 pp., republishes Lady Charlotte Guest's English translation of the *Mabinogion*, which first appeared in three volumes in 1846. This beautifully illustrated volume also includes Guest's notes on the tales, a brief introduction by Alan Lee, the illustrator, and facsimile reproductions of the wood engravings which originally appeared in the 1877 reprint. *The Mabinogion*, trans. Gwyn Jones and Thomas Jones, London, Everyman, xliii + 259 pp., is a revised edition of the classic Jones and Jones translation with the addition of a Preface by John Updike and some erroneous information printed on the dust jacket.

Gwyn Thomas, 'Yn rhith anifeiliaid' (1–20) in *Gair am Air. Ystyriaethau am Faterion Llenyddol*, Cardiff, Univ. of Wales Press, vii + 194 pp. + 6 pls, assumes that many of the characters of the *Mabinogion* are associated with Celtic gods and goddesses, and considers rather tenuous links between images of animals on pre-Christian archaeological artefacts and the role of animals in medieval Welsh legends, such as PKM and *Culhwch ac Olwen*. 'Annwn, y byd arall' (21–39) in *ib.*, discusses the portrayal of the otherworld in Welsh legends and concludes that it combines both pagan and Christian elements; 'Siôn Cent a noethni'r enaid', (40–57) in *ib.*, compares and contrasts the work of Siôn Cent (*c.* 1400–30/45) with that of late 14th-c. Welsh poets, focussing in particular on his preoccupation with sin and death. E. P. Hamp, '*Mabinogi* and archaism', *Celtica* 23:96–110, assesses Ifor Williams's and Charles-Edwards's phonological arguments concerning the dating of PKM and examines the title *Mabinogi*. Sioned Davies, *O'r Pair i'r Sosban*, Y Ddarlith Lenyddol, Eisteddfod Genedlaethol Llanelli a'r Cylch, 22 pp., traces references to cauldrons in medieval Welsh literature and comments on authorship and the relationship between orality and literacy in the *Mabinogion*. I. Daniel, '*Ymborth yr Enaid* a'r chwedlau brodorol', *LlC* 23:1–20, compares the language and style of *Ymborth yr Enaid* and the *Mabinogion* and proposes that the Dominican author of *Ymborth yr Enaid* was also responsible for six of the *Mabinogion* legends. Having reiterated his view that Cnepyn Gwerthrynion was possibly responsible for *Ymborth* and *Gramadegau'r Penceirddiaid*, he tentatively suggests that some of the *Mabinogion* legends may have been composed at a Dominican house in North Wales, possibly at Bangor or Rhuddlan. R. M. Jones, 'Macsen Wledig a'i berthynas â'r genedl', *Cof Cenedl* 15:3–28, examines the character of Macsen Wledig (Magnus Maximus) and the ways in which Welsh literature and Welsh scholars have depicted him as the founding father of the Welsh nation. C. Lloyd-Morgan, 'La violence contre les femmes dans la littérature galloise du Moyen Âge', in *Violence et société en Bretagne et dans les pays celtiques*, Brest, Centre de Recherche Bretonne et Celtique, 339–47, discusses episodes in Middle Welsh literature where women are subjected to violence, focusing in particular on the female characters of the *Mabinogion*. Although the majority of the texts in question are generally assumed to be of male authorship, Gwerful Mechain's poetry provides a unique glimpse of a female author's attitude towards violence, sexuality and life in general.

Canhwyll Marchogyon Cyd-destunoli Peredur, ed. Sioned Davies and Peter Wynn Thomas, Cardiff, Univ. of Wales Press, x + 162 pp., provides a detailed and thorough analysis of the Middle Welsh Arthurian legend *Peredur*. The study suggests that the earliest written versions of the legend derive from North Wales and may be associated with the royal court at Gwynedd. D. Huws, 'Y pedair llawysgrif ganoloesol' (1–9), is a brief discussion of the four medieval manuscripts which preserve the legend. Huws focuses primarily on the earliest extant manuscripts, Peniarth 7 and Peniarth 14ii; P. W. Thomas, 'Cydberthynas y pedair fersiwn ganoloesol' (10–49), discusses the complex relationship between the four medieval versions of *Peredur*, and suggests that the earliest written text (*c.* 1275–1325) contains dialectal features associated with North Wales; S. Davies, 'Cynnydd Peredur Vab Efrawc' (65–90), compares and contrasts structural and stylistic features from three different versions of *Peredur*, and traces the development of the written legend from its less sophisticated, formulaic beginnings in Peniarth 7 to its more polished expression and extended narrative structure in Peniarth 4; B. F. Roberts, 'Y cysyniad o destun' (50–64), also focuses on the textual development of *Peredur* and the transition from 'fluidity' and variance to a more standardized, authoritive text. Trends in editorial methods and literary criticism are also considered; M. E. Owen, ' "Arbennic milwyr a blodeu marchogyon": cymdeithas *Peredur*' (91–112), places *Peredur* in its social context and highlights the importance of chivalry in this particular Arthurian legend. The discussion focuses on the development of Peredur's military prowess, as he becomes a knight, and demonstrates that the social milieu and personnel of *Peredur* betray Anglo-Norman influence; C. Lloyd-Morgan, 'Y cyd-destun Ewropeaidd' (113–27), places the legend in its European context, focusing primarily on the relationship between the Welsh and French texts; S. Knight, 'Resemblance and menace: a post-colonial reading of *Peredur*' (128–47), offers a post-colonial reading of *Peredur* and concludes that '*Peredur* can and should be read as a complex representation of and negotiation with the real conditions of its sociopolitical context'.

O. J. Padel, *Arthur in Medieval Welsh Literature*, Cardiff, Univ. of Wales Press, Writers of Wales series, 139 pp., is a succinct, reliable survey of Arthurian literature in medieval Wales, from the 9th-c. Welsh-Latin *Historia Brittonum*, through the early poetry and *Culhwch ac Olwen* to the post-Geoffrey romances and references in 16th-c. Welsh poetry. C. Lloyd-Morgan, 'The Celtic tradition', in *The Arthur of the English. The Arthurian Legend in Medieval English Life and Literature*, ed. W. R. J. Barron, Cardiff, Univ. of Wales Press, 395 pp. (1–9), briefly surveys 'Celtic' sources for Arthurian literature and focuses on the development of Arthurian tradition in Wales proposing that the seeds of later continental and Arthurian tradition were implicit in the earliest Welsh sources, although Arthurian tradition in England developed autonomously. J. C. Crick, 'The British past and the Welsh future: Gerald of Wales, Geoffrey of Monmouth and Arthur of Britain', *Celtica* 23:60–75, reassesses Gerald de Barri's criticisms of Geoffrey of Monmouth's *Historia regum Britannie* and demonstrates that whilst both authors can be viewed as counterparts because of the way in which they exploited their sources and viewed the British past, they differed considerably in their visions of the British future. Crick argues that Gerald actively sought to discredit Geoffrey's vision of a unified kingship of Britain.

T. D. Breverton, *The Book of Welsh Saints*, 606 pp., is a popular publication published by the author's own press. Despite its rather naïve, non-academic introduction to the 'Age of the Saints', it provides a considerable amount of information on the traditions associated with Welsh saints. It draws on a number of hagiographical sources and summarizes relevant legendary material, although it does not list its sources and should be used with care. Karen Jankulak, *The Medieval Cult of St Pedroc*, Woodbridge, Boydell, xi + 261 pp., is a detailed and thorough analysis of the medieval cult of St Petroc and its related hagiography. The study pays particular attention to Brittany and Cornwall, but also examines Welsh hagiographic material including *Vita Cadoci*, the Welsh triads and poetry by Dafydd Nanmor. The Welsh triads claim St Pedrog as one of the 'three just knights' of Arthur's court and Dafydd Nanmor refers to the tradition that Pedrog dedicated himself to the religious life following the battle of Camlan and was later buried at Y Ferwig. *Two Mediaeval Lives of Saint Winefride*, ed. Ronald Pepin and Hugh Feiss, Toronto, Peregrina, 126 pp., provides English translations of the two 12th-c. Latin Lives of St Winefride (Gwenfrewi) of Holywell: the brief anonymous Life and the more detailed *vita* by Robert, Prior of Shrewsbury, which includes an account of the translation of her relics from Gwytherin to Shrewsbury. *Gogoneddus Arglwydd, Henffych Well: Detholiad o Ryddiaith a Barddoniaeth Gristnogol Gymraeg drwy'r Canrifoedd*, ed. Gwynn ap Gwilym, xliv + 325 pp., brings together a selection of religious poems and sections of prose. The first part covers the period up to 1499 and contains twenty-eight texts chosen by J. E. Caerwyn Williams, including anonymous early poetry, poetry of the *Gogynfeirdd* and *Cywyddwyr* and short sections of prose such as *Mabinogi Iesu Grist*, *Efengyl Nicodemus* and *Gwyrthiau y Wynfydedig Fair*. *Gesta Romanorum*, ed. Patricia Williams, Cardiff, Univ. of Wales Press, lxvi + 201 pp., highlights the importance of this previously neglected collection of moral tales which were translated from Latin into Welsh *c.* 1600. Williams edits the Welsh text, extant in only one manuscript, and considers the text's authorship, dating, orthography, linguistic characteristics, main themes and images, as well as its relationship to the Latin manuscripts and Wynkyn de Worde's English edition.

LITERATURE SINCE 1500

By A. CYNFAEL LAKE, *Lecturer in Welsh, University of Wales Swansea*

D. M. Smith, 'Y Marchog Crwydrad a'r alegori yn yr Oesoedd Canol', *Dwned*, 6:129–42, comments on the Welsh version of 'The Voyage of the Wandering Knight', its background, audience (with specific reference to Glamorganshire's recusant community), and structure. A. Ll. Hughes, 'Y cerddi i'r "Barwn Owain" o Ddolgellau', *JMHRS*, 13:286–95, brings together eight poems addressed to Lewys ab Owain of Dolgellau, murdered in 1555. *Y Canu Mawl i Deulu'r Fron-Deg*, ed. Dafydd Wyn Wiliam, Llangefni, p.p., 32 pp., contains thirteen pieces by eight poets to Lewys ab Owain (c. 1509–91), his family and home in Newborough parish, Anglesey. Ceri Davies, 'Cerddi rhagymadroddol Lladin a llyfrau'r Dyneiddwyr Cymreig', *LlC*, 23:95–108, refers to dedications in verse in volumes published by Welsh Humanists, and reveals intriguing links between authors and dedicants. A. Breeze, 'Dr Siôn Dafydd Rhys and Chinese printing', *THSC*, 1999[2000], 9–13, considers the significance of one passing reference in Rhys's introduction to his grammar of 1592. Jerry Hunter, *Soffestri'r Saeson*, Cardiff, Univ. of Wales Press, 147 pp., focuses on paradoxical strands in the historical writings of Elis Gruffydd. Although influenced by renaissance historiography's scientific approach, he nevertheless valued traditional prophetic material and attempted to justify its study. L. M. Davies and G. M. Awbery, 'Cofnod o archifdy Gwent: cerdd am ddienyddiad Siarl I', *LlC*, 23:109–46, discuss a free-metre poem concerning the execution of Charles I, possibly composed prior to the Restoration in 1660. For an English version, see L. M. Davies, 'The Tregaer manuscript: an elegy for Charles I', *NLWJ*, 31:243–70 and G. Awbery, 'The origin of the Tregaer elegy for Charles I', *ib.*, 271–82. Maredudd ap Huw, 'Hynt a helynt llyfrgell yr Hen Ficer', *Y Casglwr*, 68:5, draws attention to two sermons by Rhys Prichard, one in print, the second in MS at Jesus College Oxford. Gwyn Thomas, 'John Griffith, Llanddyfnan, bardd o'r ail ganrif ar bymtheg', *THSC*, 1999[2000], 14–37, introduces a relatively unknown figure, and shows that his compositions fairly typify 17th-c. Welsh poetry, in form and content.

The publication of *A Guide to Welsh Literature c. 1700–1800*, ed. Branwen Jarvis, 342 pp., and *A Guide to Welsh Literature c. 1800–1900*, ed. Hywel Teifi Edwards, 247 pp., both Cardiff, Univ. of Wales Press, completes the *Guide* series launched in 1976. Whereas the former presents a comprehensive introduction to the 18th c., the latter presents the 19th c., noted for its voluminousness, through studies of a relatively small but outstanding group of contributors in poetry, prose and letters. A. Jones, 'Traethiadau Lewis Morris', *Taliesin*, 108:64–83, discusses seven satirical prose pieces by Lewis Morris. A. Cynfael Lake, *Anterliwtiau Huw Jones o Langwm*, Caernarfon, Barddas, 277 pp., offers an edited version of three interludes probably written between 1762–1770. Although 18th-c. interludes were disjointed by nature, Huw Jones meticulously structured his own compositions. Id., 'Y Methodistiaid trwy lygaid dau o anterliwtwyr y ddeunawfed ganrif', *Y Traethodydd*, 155:25–42, looks at the way in which the Methodists were portrayed in two 18th-c. interludes, and shows that the venom which characterises William Roberts's diatribe, *Ffrewyll y Methodistiaid*, is largely absent in Huw Jones's *Protestant a Neilltuwr*. S. Rosser, 'Cip ar faledi Jonathan Hughes', *Canu Gwerin*, 23:25–45, outlines the central themes in Hughes's ballads. C. Evans, 'Y faled a therfysgoedd Beca yn ne orllewin Cymru, 1839–43', *JPHS*, 9:21–38, deals with a ballad by Levi Gibbon concerning the Becca revolt. K. Jenkins, 'Pantycelyn's Women Fact and Fiction: an assessment', *JWRH*, 7:77–94, describes the role and experiences of Methodist women and the contrasting image presented by Pantycelyn in his elegies, long poems, and prose works. E. W. James, 'Ann Griffiths, y cefndir barddol', *LlC*, 23:147–70, describes the social and cultural background in north east Wales at the turn of the 18th c., and considers Ann's literary inheritance. B. F. Roberts, 'Robert Jones, Rotherhithe', *NLWJ*, 31:135–47, assesses Jones's contribution to the Cymmrodorion Society, his work on Goronwy Owen and his extraordinary library. S. Davies, 'Perfformio o'r pulpud: rhagarweiniad i'r maes', *Y Traethodydd*, 155:256–80, describes the stage skills of 19th-c. nonconformist preachers, and draws some of her evidence from contemporary novels and biographies. Robert Rhys, *Daniel Owen*, Cardiff, Univ. of Wales Press, 227 pp., offers a stimulating biographical study of Wales's foremost novelist together with a penetrating critical assessment where own and other commentators's viewpoints are skilfully balanced. Owen's treatment of hypocrisy, especially in religious circles, is highlighted, but evidence of the concern of contemporaries at the decline in religious life is also provided. The society and characters depicted in the novels are shown to closely mirror Owen's native Mold. G. Thomas, 'Profedigaethau Enoc Huws', *Gair am Air*, Cardiff, Univ. of Wales Press, 58–81, focuses on the theme of hypocrisy in Daniel Owen's *Enoc Huws*. Tecwyn Ellis, *Dewi Glan Peryddon a'i Nofel Fer*, Y Bala, p.p., 41 pp., outlines the career of the author of the short novel *Ceinwen Morgan y Rian Dwylledig*.

R. Gerallt Jones, 'Llenyddiaeth Gymraeg oddi ar 1914', Jenkins, *Eu Hiaith*, 381–404, in his survey of 20th-c. literature reiterates the view that the First World War represents a crucial watershed. He also outlines the importance of the literature-supportive agencies which developed during the second half of the century. M. W. Thomas, 'Keeping the Rhondda for Wales: the case of J. Kitchener Davies', *THSC*, 1999[2000], 119–34, questions the myth associated with Davies and promoted by Rhydwen Williams and Gwenallt. His reading of 'Sŵn y gwynt sy'n chwythu' suggests a complex spiritual and psychoanalytical quest. Alan Llwyd, '"Atgof" Prosser Rhys', *Barddas*, 256:4–8, *ib.*, 257:4–7, *ib.*, 258:4–10, links the poem 'Atgof' with the birth of modernism, analyses its themes and describes the outrage which accompanied its publication. B. G. Owens annotates poems by Waldo Williams in *Barddas*, 257:22–23, *ib.*, 258:34–36. Gwyn Thomas, 'Yr Haf a'r Gaeaf: Golwg ar waith R. Williams Parry', *Gair am Air*, Cardiff, Univ. of Wales Press, 81–128, analyses the main themes in Williams Parry's two volumes of poems and contrasts the romanticism of 'Yr Haf' with the sombre tone of 'Cerddi'r Gaeaf'. J. W. Davies, '"Gwisga'r awen liwiau hynod": 'Y Llwynog' R. Williams Parry', *LlC*, 23:171–91, offers a new analysis of Williams Parry's renowned sonnet, 'Y Llwynog'. Donald Allchin et al., *Sensuous Glory*, Norwich, Canterbury Press, xi + 154 pp., contains translations of 35 poems by Gwenallt and two essays which focus on the poet's spiritual pilgrimage and the way he 'brings before us a memorable picture of the Wales of his time as he experienced it; a land of stark contrasts, with its ugliness and beauty'. A. Price, 'Chwarae geiriau fel gwyddbwyll: barddoniaeth Gymraeg Gwyneth Lewis', *Taliesin*, 110:113–25, identifies three strands connected with one central theme in Lewis's poems. A. L. Evans, 'Y bardd yn ei gynefin', *Barddas*, 256:32–39, *ib.*, 257:14–18, sheds light on his own compositions, and the importance of boundaries in his life and works.

Dramâu Saunders Lewis: Y Casgliad Cyflawn Cyfrol II, ed. Ioan M. Williams, Cardiff, Univ. of Wales Press, 1005 pp., the second volume of collected plays by Saunders Lewis, contains works written between 1958 and 1989 together with sketches of four other plays found amongst Lewis's papers. As in the first volume (published 1996), all plays are accompanied by a valuable introduction and notes. B. Jarvis, 'Saunders Lewis: a Welsh Catholic view of women?', *JWRH*, 7:119–35, commences with Lewis's conversion to Catholicism and proceeds to study Catholic-related themes in his novel, *Monica*, and plays, and the attributes and conduct of his heroines. G. Miles, 'Oes aur y ddrama Gymraeg', *Barn*, 448:48–49, *ib.*, 453:56–62, outlines the philosophy behind early 20th-c. dramatic works which were so abhorrent to Saunders Lewis. W. R. Lewis, *LlC*, 23:192–207, 'Areithiau hirion dramâu John Gwilym Jones: "Diofal ym Dim"', considers linguistic devices used by Ibsen and Synge and seeks parallels in Jones's plays. Francesca Rhydderch, ' "They do not breed de Beauvoirs here": Kate Roberts's early political journalism', *WWE*, 6:21–44, discovers manifestations of Roberts's feminism in her contributions to *Y Ddraig Goch* during the years 1926–29, and contrasts the conservative tone of her later journalism with the probing analysis of her central character in *Tywyll Heno*. Jeni Williams, 'The place of fantasy: Children and narratives in two short stories by Kate Roberts and Dylan Thomas', *ib.*, 45–66, reveals a significant gender and cultural divide between the authors of 'Nadolig y Cerdyn' ('Christmas Journey') and 'A Story'. Mihangel Morgan, *Caradog Prichard*, Caernarfon, Pantycelyn, 65 pp., argues that the central theme of insanity binds together Prichard's novel and *eisteddfod* poems. The ambiguity, both thematic and structural, prevalent in *Un Nos Ola Leuad* is explored in detail. T. Robin Chapman, *Islwyn Ffowc Elis*, Cardiff, Univ. of Wales Press, 90 pp., considers Elis's mission as a writer and argues that his most important works were written between 1952–61. *Y Sêr yn eu Graddau*, ed. John Rowlands, Cardiff, Univ. of Wales Press, 264 pp., contains essays on eleven contemporary novelists, Alun Jones, William Owen Roberts, Aled Islwyn, Dafydd Huws, Gareth Miles, Angharad Tomos, Eirug Wyn, Robat Gruffudd, Robin Llywelyn, Mihangel Morgan and Manon Rhys. Angharad Price, *Robin Llywelyn*, Caernarfon, Pantycelyn, 63 pp., contemplates the cultural significance of *Seren Wen ar Gefndir Gwyn*, and the relationship between author and reader. L. Davies, 'Mwy na *Darn o Dir*? Cymru a Chymreictod yn nofelau Emyr Humphreys', *Efrydiau Athronyddol*, 63:96–113, justifies her claim that Wales and Welshness are not mere trimmings but central elements in Humphrey's novels. H. T. Edwards and I. Williams, 'Dai Culpitt ac Ifor Kelly', Edwards, *Cwm Gwendraeth*, 143–60, see the influence of Gwendraeth's industrial environment on the works of Culpitt and Kelly. The same region is depicted in two compositions by Bernard Evans, as R. Rhys, 'Cyfarwydd Cawre: Bernard Evans, mapiwr cynefin', *ib.*, 171–84, shows.

S. Rh. Williams, 'Llwydlas, Gwenynen Gwent a dadeni diwyllian-nol y bedwaredd ganrif ar bymtheg', *Cof Cenedl*, 15:97–128, outlines Lady Elizabeth Coffin Greenly's involvement with the Abergavenny *eisteddfodau* and the Welsh Manuscripts Society, and her possible influence on Lady Augusta Hall. Rh. A. Williams, 'Y Gymraeg yn Eisteddfodau Cenedlaethol Llanelli', Edwards, *Cwm Gwendraeth*, 225–45, considers several issues connected with the four *eisteddfodau* held at Llanelli, but draws particular attention to contrasting views regarding the Welsh language, its role and future. Vivian Parry Williams, *Owen Gethin Jones, ei Fywyd a'i Feiau*, Llanrwst, Gwasg Carreg Gwalch, 149 pp., offers a lively portrayal of the builder and bridge constructor who was also renowned for his poetic interests and involvement in local *eisteddfod* and *gorsedd* activities. David Griffith, *Right Man, Right Time*, Bradford on Avon, 192 pp., contains interesting biographical details of Clwydfardd, the first archdruid.

Rh. Llwyd, 'Meirionnydd a'r fasnach lyfrau Gymraeg', *JMHRS*, 13:227–42, traces the publication of the works of Edmwnd Prys, John Davies of Mallwyd, Rowland Vaughan, Caergai, and Morgan Llwyd. Huw Walters, 'Darganfod y *Morgrugyn Coll*', *NLWJ*, 31:125–27, describes the one remaining copy of a taster journal which appeared in November 1845. Glanmor Williams, 'Printers, publishers and book-lovers in Merthyr Tydfil', *MerH*, 11:1–12, traces publications connected with Merthyr from 1801 onwards, and shows how the Welsh-medium items, predominant in the early decades, were gradually replaced by mainly English works.

II. BRETON AND CORNISH STUDIES

By Humphrey Lloyd Humphreys, formerly *School of Modern Languages,
University of Wales, Lampeter*
This report covers publications for the years 1999, 2000.

1. Breton

Owing to the number of items arising from the postponement of last
year's report, it has been found convenient to group together those
appearing in the same publication rather than to redistribute
thematically.

There is a wide variety of articles in *Breizh ha pobloù Europa / Bretagne
et peuples d'Europe, mélanges en l'honneur de Per Denez*, ed. H. ar Bihan,
Rennes, Hor Yezh-Klask-PUR, 738 pp. Some are concerned with
social aspects of Breton: P.-Y. Belan, juridical (57–78); J.-M.
Rousseau, economic (561–566); G. ar [Le] Menn, 17th–19th-c.
official texts (469–81); L. Kergoat, identity symbol (415–26). Literature is represented by J. Cünnen and H. L. C. Tristram, comparing
Añjela Duval and the German Sarah Kirsch (99–126); G. Denez on
F. Elies-Abeozen's *Darbarer Sant Pêr* (151–55); A. Renault discusses
post-*Gwalarn*, women writers (541–46). F. Favereau, analyses popular
journalistic texts from *Ar Bobl* (223–38), while F. Elégoat,
pp. 185–200, provides an ethnotext. Lexical questions are covered in
J. E. Caerwyn Williams, Middle Welsh, Middle Breton, *gan(t)* OIr. *la*,
(711–18), P.-Y. Lambert, Old Breton, *morbran(n)* (441–44); M. Me-
nard, Breton names of the Milky Way (457–67). J.-Y. Urien, returns
to the problematic verbal particles (645–75), while J. Stephens
examines the language of young *néo-bretonnants* (581–605). E. Vallerie,
analyses a sample from a 400 pp. diary (1910–20) of a native of
Sulniac (677–98); G. Guillaume, though rambling, is an interesting
link between dialectological work in both linguistic subdivisions of
Brittany (339–67). A. Botrel, considers the role of huntsmen,
magicians and pupils in *Buhez Santez Nonn* (79–80); G. an Dug [Le
Duc], presents critical notes by G. Milin on published texts of his
time (157–68); B. F. Roberts, notes some Breton library collections in
Wales (547–60).

Grammatical material of general nature is mainly represented by a
substantial classified corpus of syntactical examples being produced
by R. Le Gléau, *Etudes syntaxiques bretonnes*, Brest, pp., vol. 1, 'Les
volitives', 1999, 192 pp.; vol. 2, 'Les subordonnées énonciatives
complétives', 1999, 196 pp., vol. 3, 'Les subordonnées énonciatives
circonstantielles', 2000, 264 pp.; vol. 4, 'Les subordonnées énonciatives circonstantielles (suite) et les relatives', 2000, pp. 271–501 [*sic*].

The basically traditional analysis deals with written examples, generally by native speakers; the metalinguistic commentary is concise and although details may be quibbled with, this will prove a useful reference work. D. Costaouec, 'A propos des "mutations consonantiques" du breton', *La Linguistique*, 34, 1998:87–106, advocates the alignment of Celtic with generalist usage in the restriction of 'mutation' to the diachronic scene and stressing that it refers to morphological alternations. V. Favé, *Notennou yezadur*, Brest, Emgleo Breiz, 1998, 145 pp. and J.-Y. Plourin, *Initiation au breton familier et argotique*, Crozon, Armeline, 230 pp. defend native Br. *Sprachgefühl* against a rising tide of gallicizing idiom. L. A. Timm, '*Brezhoneg-beleg*: priests' Breton', *Studia Celtica Japonica*, 8, 1996:27–46, is a well-structured and thoughtful presentation of the language most abundantly found in devotional works, but also in official translations of 1789–93. Particular attention is given to the massive presence of Fr. lexemes (firmly established in Middle Breton and not necessarily technical) and the *pehini* relative construction.

In dialect studies two posthumous works must be mentioned: A. Sinou, *Le Breton de Léchiagat – quelques aspects du système phonologique du parler breton de Léchiagat (Finistère)*, n.pl., Hor Yezh, 1999, 104 pp., contains interesting and stimulating discussion, even if the false economy of denying phonological status to semi-vowels leads to rather unmanageable transcriptions; Id., *Brezhoneg Lechiagad – geriaoueg*, n.pl., Hor Yezh, 140 pp., is a summary glossary of about 2000 items from the same dialect, with established spellings preceding phonetic transcriptions and Fr. glosses. E. Le Pipec, *Le Breton de Malguénac: quelques aspects*, Lesneven, Mouladurioù Hor Yezh, 132 pp., concentrates on vowels and stress in a NE Vannetais dialect and examines the relationship between the sung and the spoken language. P. Le Besco, *Joseph Loth: Le Breton de l'Ile-aux-Moines*, Brest, Ar Skol Vrezoneg, 1999, 84 pp., is a reworking, with phonological analysis, of Loth's articles in *Annales de Bretagne* (1895–99) on this extinct dialect. Id., *Le Breton de Belle-Ile-en-Mer*, Brest, Emgleo Breiz, 1998, is a handy and slightly modified, though not fully corrected edition of recent articles in *EC*. A more technical contribution is I. Kanellos et al. 'Assistance informatique à l'interprétation des données en cartographie linguistique – informatisation anthropocentrée du *Nouvel Atlas linguistique de la Basse-Bretagne (ALBB)*', *Géolinguistique*, [Grenoble], 8, 1999: 181–96.

Onomastics accounts for a number of publications. A. Deshayes, *Dictionnaire des noms de lieux bretons*, Douarnenez, Le Chasse-Marée-ArMen, 1999, 605 pp., is a substantial volume, generally sound, semantically classifying elements found in hamlet names. The absence of a bibliography is surprising and the origin of elements is not always specified even when the etymology is known; the introduction and index are very useful though far from exhaustive. Id., *Dictionnaire des prénoms celtiques*, Douarnenez, Le Chasse-Marée-ArMen, 208 pp., is less scholarly in intent, but quite useful despite some slips. M. Madeg, *Anoiou parreziou Bro Leon hag o distagadur*, Brest, Emgleo Breiz-Ar Skol Vrezoneg, 229 pp., is an excellent inventory of the Breton pronunciation(s), local and not so local, of the 116 parish-names of Léon, with full commentary. M. Madeg and P. Pondaven, *Renabl anoiou lehiou arvor Bro Bagan: Brignogan, Plouneour-Trêz, Goulhen, 3 – Etre Enez Kerlouan hag an Aod Veur*, Brest Emgleo Breiz-Ar Skol Vrezoneg, 183 pp., continues an important inventory of the names of coastal features. M. Priziac, *Dictionnaire toponymique du Centre-Ouest-Bretagne*, Grâces-Guingamp, Patrimoines Buissonniers, I, 349 pp., II, 254 pp., is only mentioned to draw attention to its gross inaccuracies and shoddiness – this also applies to other works with less pretentious titles published by the author in 1995, 1997, 1999.

E. Vetter, *Plus de breton? Conflit linguistique en Bretagne rurale*, 254 pp., Le Relecq-Kerhuon, An Here, 1999, (transl. of *Nicht mehr Bretonisch? Sprachkonflikt in der ländliche Bretagne*, Frankfurt, Peter Lang, 1997), has some hard information on the situation in Ploumoguer and more discussion, affirming the conflictual nature of the situation; more concision and precision was appropriate here. M. C. Jones, *Language Obsolescence and Revitalisation: Linguistic Change in Two Sociolinguistically Contrasting Welsh Communities*, OUP, vii + 452 pp., contains substantial sections on Breton (295–333) and Cornish (334–49). Breton is generally dealt with in a satisfactory way and the important point is made that many aspects of standardization have been counterproductive, alienating native speakers; traditional Cornish only permits more general inferences, while the observations on revivalist activities deserve more solid attention. R. Calvez, *La Radio en langue bretonne – Roparz Hemon et Pierre-Jakez Hélias: deux rêves de la Bretagne*, CRBC-PUR, Brest-Rennes, 330 pp., is an extremely well-documented study of two contrasting pioneers of a medium which could have had a real impact on the status of Breton had it been developed from its early days as a substantial service of a functional nature. P. Denez, *Yezh ha bro*, Lesneven, Hor Yezh, 1998, 163 pp., is a collection of mainly militant articles, which are a useful contribution to the history of Breton language activism. M. Simon, *Bleun-Brug: expression d'un idéal breton*, Landevennec, Musée de l'ancienne abbaye, 1998, 122 pp., is a brief, abundantly illustrated history of J.-M. Perrot's popular, pro-Breton, Catholic movement founded in 1905. E. Evenou, *La Langue bretonne en quête de légitimité dans l'éducation et la vie publique*, Spézet, Keltia Graphic, 112 pp., is a thoughtful and well-documented essay by the former inspector with responsibility for the teaching of Breton in state

schools. F. Broudic, *Qui parle breton aujourd'hui? Qui le parlera demain?*,
Brest, Brud Nevez, 1999, 150 pp., is a good combination of dense
and sound documentation with extreme concision. A. Quéré, *Les
Bretons et la langue bretonne – ce qu'ils en disent*, Brest, Brud Nevez,
104 pp., is a well-structured, interview-based report, illuminated by
parallel fieldwork on Martinique creole. In *Langues et cultures régionales
de France – Etat des lieux, enseignement, politiques*, ed. D. Clairis et al.
Paris-Montréal, L'Harmattan, 1999, 272 pp., Y. Le Berre and J. Le
Dû, 'Le qui pro quo des langues régionales: sauver la langue ou
éduquer l'enfant' (71–83), discuss the minute impact of immersion
teaching and suggest that generalized teaching with lower aims might
be more useful, if more costly; F. Broudic, 'Entre histoire et
prospective' (125–32), discusses the significance of the signing of the
European charter; J.-D. Robin, 'Brezhoneg, ur yezh evit an dazont/
Le breton un outil pour construire l'avenir' (215–27), provides a
militant view of the scene; D. Costaouec, 'Encore du travail pour les
linguistes et les enseignants' (249–52), is a closing statement centred
on Breton, stressing the necessity of far deeper study of the
complexities of both linguistic and social aspects and suggesting the
desirability of building bridges between local and more standard
varieties.

Two articles by G. Le Menn on hymns appear, 'Notes sur les
chants en langue bretonne (X^e au XVIIIe siècles)', pp. 403–08 of ed.
A. Croix, A. Lespagnol and G. Provost, *Eglises, éducation, lumières . . .
Histoires culturelles de la France (1500–1830)*, 507pp. + 35pls., Rennes,
PUR, 1999; and 'Les premiers cantiques bretons', pp. 173–82, in
Chrétientés de Basse-Bretagne et d'ailleurs – les archives au risque de l'histoire,
(Mélanges Jean-Louis Le Floc'h), Quimper, Soc. Archéologique du
Finistère, 1998. F. Morvannou, *Kanennoù ar Feiz – Bretagne – Les chants
de la Foi*, Paris, Ed. du Layeur, 1998, 48 pp., contains fifteen 18th and
19th-c. hymns, with introduction, individual commentaries and CD.

Bulletin de la Société Archéologique du Finistère, 1997 126, contains a
number of items dealing with Breton. P.-Y. Lambert, 'Etymologie du
nom Corentin' (259–60); B. Tanguy, 'Du lieu habité à l'espace
communautaire: VILLIER/GWILER, GWILAR dans la toponymie bretonne' (261–65); A.-Y. Bourgès, 'A propos de *Gousperoù ar raned*'
(269–71); J.-C. Cassard, 'Un témoignage indirect sur le breton de
Guérande' (271–73); E. Vallerie, 'Le journal d'un paysan bretonnant
aux confins de la Basse-Bretagne' (274–80); F. Broudic, 'Nouvelle
toponymie bretonne' (280–84), P. Helloco, 'Entre Ellé et Isole:
l'Inam ou le Ster-Laer? Une quête d'identité incontestable'
(285–302); A. Tanguy, 'A propos du théâtre populaire breton de
Kerjean: lettres inédites d'Anatole Le Braz, Jean-Marie Perrot et
Louis Dujardin' (302–06).

The distant past is most strikingly represented by A. Chédeville, H. Guillotel and B. Tanguy, *Cartulaire de l'abbaye Saint-Sauveur de Redon*, Rennes, Association des Amis des archives historiques du diocèse de Rennes, Dol et Saint-Malo, 78 pp. + 185 plates, contains explanatory articles by A. C. (society, economy), H. G. (MS., chronology) and B. T. (onomastics), and full colour reproductions of all the sheets of the 11th-c. copy of a 9th-c. original. This is the most important corpus of early onomastic material in Breton. In other fields we have L. Fleuriot, 'Les sources littéraires non bretonnes sur les migrations bretonnes et la date de celles-ci.', *Annales de Bretagne et des Pays de l'Ouest*, 107.4 : 7–13; and P. Schrijver, 'Spirantization and nasalization in British', *SC*, 33, 1999 : 1–19, is a detailed exposition, but seems to have missed the important point that, between Quimper and Quimperlé, *an/am* are still the only forms of the definite article.

Hor Yezh, here abbreviated as *HY*, contains an interesting range of material (dates of numbers are given here to avoid repetition: vols 217–220, 1999; 221–223, 2000). P. Herbert continues his corpus of bird-names, *HY*, 217:5–16, 220:5–12 and H. ar Bihan continues and concludes his glossary of words associated with children, *HY*, 217:17–51, 218:5–25, 219:5–35. N. Davalan, *HY*, 218:31–35, gives a further word-list from Plounévez-Quintin. Notes covering a variety of mainly lexical and toponymic matters and often quite substantial, occupy more room; here it seems more useful to identify the points covered than the individual authors. *HY*, 217:53–58, (24. *muenn*, 25. *kehela(ñ)*). *HY*, 218:37–46, (26. *a-rafoll*; 27. *raouiell*; 28. *sifoc'h(ell)*); 29. Fr. *campagnol*; 30. *chifronell*; 31. Fr. *britto/bretophone?*; 32. Plouézoc'h; 33. *Lez* + parish-name). *HY*, 219:49–59, (34. *peur-*; 35. *Lancolvett*, *Lan(n)* < *nant*; 36. *soulas*; 37. *divi(j)añ*; 38. Plouézoc'h; 39. *Lez-*; 40. *-eg*; 41. *Roaz(h)on*. *HY* 221:59–68, (42. *mantokiñ*; 43. *logodenn benndoull*; 44. *didalvedegezh*; 45. *merak*. *HY*, 223:47–49, (46. *demat*; 47. *morvarc'h*; 48. *logodenn min doull*). An unannotated dramatic piece on the resurrection is reprinted from H. de La Villemarqué's 1865 edition, *Le Grand mystère de Jésus*, (1530), *HY*, 221:5–41, while G. ar [Le] Menn presents R. Hemon's copy of *Ar Resurrection* (1728), completed by G. an Dug [Le Duc], *HY*, 222:9–44, 223:17–45. D. Gervella [Kervella] proposes as standard generally not too delocalized pronunciations for commune names in Léon and Trégor, *HY*, 220:43–47 and various aspects of personal names are discussed by A. K., *HY*, 219:37–47 and J. Konan, *HY*, 222:5–8, 223:5–7. G. ar [Le] Menn, *HY*, 221:43–57, presents an 1839 bilingual petition to a government minister, with detailed linguistic analysis. A. Botrel, *HY*, 220:13–18, analyses R. Hemon's use of internal rhymes; H. ar Bihan, *HY*, 220:19–41, discusses the impact of Santiago de Compostela on both written and oral literature.

G. Le Menn's important *Bibliothèque bretonne*, Skol, Saint-Brieuc, continues with reprints, texts and bibliographical material. N° 4: L. Fleuriot, *Notes lexicographiques et philologiques*, 1998, 240 pp., are reprints with an index from *EC*, (1962–87). N° 5: *Tragedien sacr par Jan Cadec – premier texte trégorois (1651?)*, ed. G. Le Menn, 239 pp., 1999, contains two versions of a religious verse text of 54 quatrains, together with the devotional prose texts which precede it; full textual and bibliographical information is provided, as well as analysis of the versification, while the word index runs to 115 pp.; the texts are accompanied by a modernized Br. version and a Fr. translation N° 6: R. Hemon (ed.), *Ar Varn diwezhañ/Le Jugement dernier*, Vol. 1:1–476; Vol. 2:483–865, prepared for publication by G. Le Duc et G. Le Menn, 1998; the 5647-line verse drama from a 1793 Trégor MS. is accompanied by a modernized Breton version and Fr. translation. In addition to detailed discussion of MS., themes and action, there is a very full section (97–194) analyzing the language and relating it to both Middle Breton and modern dialect. N° 7: E. Ernault, *Glossaire cryptologique breton*, 1999, 400 pp., reprints, with introduction and notes, a collection of sexual and scatological material published (1883–1911) in the rare and surreptitious *Kryptadia*. N° 8: G. Bailloud, *L'Imprimerie Lédan à Morlaix (1805–80) et ses impressions en langue bretonne*, 1999, 205 pp., has a preface on the activities of this popular publisher; half the 420 titles listed are concerned with edification, generally religious. To these must be added Y. Le Berre *et al. Buez Santez Nonn – Mystère breton – Vie de sainte Nonne*, Brest-Treflevenez, CRBC-Minihi-Levenez, 1999, 199 pp., the transcription and translation of this later 16th-c. MS. is preceded by a socially oriented general presentation including a synoptic guide to the text. B. Tanguy discusses toponymic aspects of the cult of Nonn and Divi, Y.-P. Castel its iconography.

La Bretagne et la littérature orale en Europe, ed. D. Laurent and F. Postic 293 pp., Brest-Mellac CRBC-CIRCTO, 1999, contains six papers delivered at the Quimperlé colloquium of 1995 marking the centenary of the death of Théodore Hersart de La Villemarqué. D. Laurent, 'La Villemarqué et les premiers collecteurs en Bretagne' (153–67), provides a concise and authoritative presentation of the *Barzaz-Breiz* controversy; Y.-B. Piriou, 'De François-Marie Luzel à Anatole Le Braz' (170–76), M. Oiry, 'L'école vannetaise (1825–1916) et les collectes d'Yves Le Diberder' pp. 177–89, F. Postic, 'De François-Marie Luzel à Paul Sébillot: l'invention de la littérature orale' (191–99), are concerned with later collectors, the last mainly with a *Gallo* who, inspired by material collected in Breton-speaking Brittany, pioneered the study of oral literature in Romance-speaking France. M. Nassiet, 'La littérature orale bretonne et l'histoire' (201–27), is a carefully structured examination of the possibilities such material offers the historian, while J.-M. Guilcher, 'Le chant dans la danse' (229–40), discusses one of the most striking uses of oral texts as the musical accompaniment to dancing. Also in the field of oral literature are Vannetais texts collected by Iwan an Diberder, *A liù el loér hag er stéred/Couleur de lune et d'étoiles*, with a preface by M. Oiry, Brest-Rennes, CRBC-PUR, 426 pp. D. Giraudon, *Traditions populaires de Bretagne. Du coq a l'âne*, Douarnenez, Le Chasse-Marée-Ar Men, 360 pp., is a very well-documented exploration of oral microtexts and beliefs concerning animals. G. Le Menn, 'Les femmes dans les dictons et proverbes en langue bretonne', *Mémoires de la Soc. d'histoire et d'archéologie de la Bretagne*, 78:311–35, explores the treatment of another theme by the same genre.

Die Deutsche Keltologie und ihre Berliner Gelehrten bis 1945, ed. S. Heinz, Frankfurt am Main, Peter Lang, 292 pp., contains the proceedings of a 1998 Berlin colloquium on Celtic studies in Nazi Germany. In it a number of controversial questions are examined. R. Calvez, 'Le réenchantement d'un monde. Mouvement breton, nazisme et émissions de radio en breton' (101–137), is a closely argued antihagiography very fully illustrated from original texts with translation, emphasizing the all-pervasive nature of R. Hemon's political stance. G. N. Sven-Myer, 'The response of the Breton journal *Gwalarn* to the Second World War' (139–146), far more condensed, claims that the political content of Hemon's literary bi-monthly was minimal. Different aspects of Weisgerber's ideas and role in occupied Brittany are the subject of N. Blanchard, ' "Volk", "Muttersprache" und "Bretonentum" bei Weisgerber' (147–154), and J. Cünnen and H. L. C. Tristram, 'Weisgerber und *Oral History*: zwei Fallstudien aus der Bretagne' (155–166).

Violence et société en Bretagne et dans les pays celtiques, (*Kreiz* 13), ed. J.-Y. Carluer, Brest, CRBC, 557 pp., has a number of articles discussing the theme mainly in oral and popular literature. D. Laurent, 'Chanter la violence. Le témoignage des *gwerziou*.' (137–49); D. Giraudon, 'Complaintes criminelles sur feuilles volantes au XIXe siècle en Basse-Bretagne', (169–98), P. Combot, 'Jean Conan (1765–1834): réponse d'un homme du peuple à quelques formes de violence' (405–09); R. Calvez, 'Violence et Pangée. Du bon usage de la violence écrite dans la presse en langue bretonne, 1940–44' (411–28), examines the nationalist press.

2. Cornish

P. Payton, 'The Cornish language', pp. 109–19 of Price, *Languages*, is an excellent general presentation of the external history of the language, its final quarter dealing with the revival scene. For M. C.

Jones, *Language Obsolescence* . . ., see above under Breton. *Cornish Studies* 6 and 7 (but not 8) contain a number of relevant articles, which are listed for convenience in order of appearance.

Cornish Studies, 6, 1998: M. Spriggs, 'Rev. Joseph Sherwood: A Cornish Language Will o' the Wisp' (46–61), presents the author of a lost MS. of 1680 containing Cornish sermons; E. Mitchell, 'The myth of objectivity: the Cornish language and 18th-c. antiquaries' (62–80), discusses academic attitudes to Cornish; R. R. M. Gendall, 'The verbs *cowas*, *cafas* and *cafel* in late Modern Cornish' (163–71) is full of useful observations and examples, though W. *canfod* does not belong here; N. [J. A.] Williams, 'Indirect statements in Cornish and Breton' (172–82), usefully compares the subordinating conjunction *fatel/del* with Breton *penaos*. Two review articles, G. Price, 'Modern Cornish in context' (on R. R. M. Gendall, *A Practical Dictionary of Modern Cornish*, I) (187–93), and A. P. Grant, 'Defending Kernewek Kemmyn' (on P. Dunbar and K. George, *Kernewek Kemmyn: Cornish for the XXIst Century*) (194–99), contribute to our understanding of recent controversies.

Cornish Studies, 7, 1999: J. Hall, 'Maximilla, the Cornish Montanist: the final scenes of *Origo Mundi* (165–92), relates these passages to their sociocultural and historical context; J. Mills, 'Reconstructive phonology and contrastive lexicology: problems with the *Gerlyver Kernewek Kemmyn*' (193–218), is a closely argued criticism of K. George's work, claiming among other things that it is flawed by not taking into account all spellings attested in texts; M. Everson, ' "An event of great significance" [sic]: a review of George's *Geriadur Kres*' (242–53), provides detailed criticism of another of George's dictionaries. N. J. A. Williams, '*Saint* in Cornish' (219–41), referring to Welsh, Breton and Irish usage, consider the prefix *synt/sen(t)* to be late and to be more readily attached to foreign than to native saints. J. Mills, 'A comparison of the semantic values of Middle Cornish *luf* and *dorn* with Modern English *hand* and *fist*' *LSc*, 18 : 1–2, 1996 : 71–86.

In A. M. Kent and T. Saunders, *Looking at the Mermaid. A Reader in Cornish Literature, 900–1900*, London, Francis Boutle, 366 pp., virtually all extant traditional Cornish texts are represented, the longer ones by selections, accompanied by an English translation. A quarter of this important volume contains a selection of writings about Cornwall, which make particular comments on its cultural and linguistic specificity. Dates, sources and circumstances are given in concise commentaries. B. Murdoch, 'Legends of the Holy Rood in Cornish drama', *Studia Celtica Japonica*, 9 1996 : 19–34, emphasises the originality of the treatment of the theme and its European significance. C. Penglase, 'La Bible en moyen-cornique', *EC*, 33 : 233–43, points out that biblical passages quoted in the *Homilies*, make frequent use of simple tenses whereas periphrastic forms are used almost exclusively in Tregear's part of the text. These archaisms suggest Middle Cornish composition of course, but the suggestion that a complete Bible existed overstretches the evidence. N. J. A. Williams, *English-Cornish Dictionary/Gerlyver Sawsnek-Kernowek*, Redruth Dublin, Agan Tavas-Everson Gunn Teoranta, 510 pp., with 25,000 headwords, is aimed at the Neo-Cornish market, for others, it is unfortunate that there is no indication regarding pre-revival attestations.

III. IRISH STUDIES

EARLY IRISH

By Kevin Murray, *Department of Early and Medieval Irish, University College, Cork*

1. Language

M. Cahill, 'The Turin glosses on Mark: towards a cultural profile of the glossator', *Peritia*, 13:173–93, believes that these glosses were written on the continent, probably at 'Auxerre in the latter half of the ninth century'. A. Garrett, 'On the prosodic phonology of Ogam Irish', *Ériu*, 50:139–60, argues from the Ogam record that Primitive Irish apocope 'usually stated as a single change, was in fact a complex set of developments'. If this position is accepted, the 'conditioning of lenition and nasalization in early Old Irish' may need to be re-examined. L. Mac Mathúna, 'Irish perceptions of the cosmos', *Celtica*, 23:174–87, contends 'that close analysis of textual extracts containing *nem – talam – muir* helps to provide a referential framework for wider areas of the lexicon describing the physical world'. P. McQuillan, 'Complementation and the subjunctive in Early Irish', *Ériu*, 50:87–131, extends his own work (particularly on modality) in this lengthy study to argue that 'the use of the subjunctive in complementation in Early Irish provides useful evidence of its non-arbitrariness as a category'. P. Schrijver, *ib.*, 133–7 has a short note on vowel rounding by Primitive Irish labiovelars; D. Testen, *ib.*, 161–4 considers Celtic terms for 'pig'; J. Carey, *ib.*, 165–8 discusses the term *ferp cluche*; F. O. Lindeman, *ib.*, 179–81, 183–4 examines *doe, dae* 'human being' a possible Middle Irish cognate of Germanic **dewz-á-* 'a living being' and the origin of the Celto-Germanic etymon **nent-*; K. Murray, *ib.*, 185–7 discusses the forms *at(t)ba/éc at(t)bai*. M. Ní Dhonnchadha, 'The semantics of *banscál*', *Éigse*, 31:31–5, shows how the secondary meaning of *banscál* 'laywoman' displaced the primary meaning 'female warrior' because 'women's active role in warfare was in reality extremely limited'. F. O. Lindeman, *Celtica*, 23:155–6 has a note on *inne* and G. Mac Eoin, *ib.*, 169–73 discusses *briugu* and related words. A. Macdonald, *Peritia*, 13:259–75, examines the use of the word *reiclés* in the Irish annals before 1200 AD.

2. Literature

J. Borsje, 'Omens, ordeals and oracles: on demons and weapons in early Irish texts', *Peritia*, 13:224–48, argues that the religious and literary background of certain demons present in medieval Irish literature is 'formed by certain types of supernatural creature, especially the Irish war goddesses'. J. Carey, 'Transmutations of immortality in "The Lament of the Old Woman of Beare"', *Celtica*, 23 : 30–7, shows how the Old Woman of the title is 'associated on the one hand with catastrophic floods in the distant past; on the other with periodic rejuvenation, and the miraculous recovery of youth and beauty', while noting that the 'Lament' is amenable to numerous different interpretations. T. Charles-Edwards, 'Geis, prophecy, omen and oath', *ib.*, 38–59, focuses primarily on *Togail bruidne Da Derga* and argues that 'the story teller could assume in his audience an interest in the unavoidable connexions between events and the impotence of men to escape their fates', an approach prefigured by the title of the article. B. Hillers, 'Ulysses and the judge of truth: sources and meanings in the Irish *Odyssey*', *Peritia*, 13 : 194–223, explores among other things the classical background of *Merugud Uilix meic Leirtis*, the Irish adaptation of the *Odyssey*. B. Jaski, 'Cú Chulainn, *gormac* and *dalta* of the Ulstermen', *CMCS*, 37 : 1–31, presents an assessment of the crucial relationship between Cú Chulainn and his maternal uncle, Conchobor, building on (and to some extent disagreeing with) T. Ó Cathasaigh's portrayal of this legal bond in *Peritia*, 5 : 128–60.

B. Lambkin, 'Blathmac and the Céili Dé: a reappraisal', *Celtica*, 23 : 132–54, re-examines the context in which Blathmac son of Cú Brettan produced his famous corpus of poetry and argues that 'he may yet come to be recognised as an even greater poet than his re-discoverer and editor would allow'. J. Lowe, 'Kicking over the traces: the instability of Cú Chulainn', *SC*, 34 : 119–30, paints a picture of Cú Chulainn as a very unstable character within the Ulster Cycle and he analyses 'the threat Cú Chulainn poses to order on both an individual and a social level' in order to better understand 'his role in early Irish literature'. J.P. Mackey, 'Mythical past and political present: a case-study of the Irish myth of the sovereignty', *ZCP*, 51 : 66–84, presents a study of 'the persistent influence of myth in human society', as represented by the sovereignty myth in Irish sources.

K. McCone, *Echtrae Chonnlai and the Beginnings of Vernacular Narrative Writing in Ireland*, Maynooth, Maynooth Medieval Irish Texts, iv + 222 pp., represents a detailed study of the Old Irish tale *Echtrae Chonnlai*, a critical edition of same (with notes, vocabulary etc.) along with an in-depth examination of the various contexts within which the story may be approached with profit. There is a great deal of analysis here for such a short text (comprising only 2.5pp. of the book in total), with the author addressing previous written opinions on the genesis of the text and the vexed question of the nature of its relationship with *Immram Brain*. His own conclusion on this latter issue is that 'it looks as though the shorter *Echtrae Chonnlai* was to all intents and purposes composed first . . . followed at no great remove by the longer *Immram Brain* . . . [and that] . . . it seems likely enough that a diptych was planned from the beginning either by a single author or by two writers working in close collaboration'.

K. Muhr, 'Water imagery in Early Irish', *Celtica*, 23 : 193–210, examines the utilisation of water imagery in early Irish poetry, the *dindshenchas* and medieval Irish religious literature (among other sources) to demonstrate its effects on this body of literature. N. Ní Shéaghdha, 'The poems of Blathmac: the "fragmentary quatrains" ', *ib.*, 227–30, presents a diplomatic edition of the fragmentary quatrains (nos 260–303) of the poems of Blathmac and also suggests that NLI G 50 may have been written by an Ó Luinín scribe. R. Ó hUiginn, 'Rúraíocht agus románsaíocht: ceisteanna faoi f horás an traidisiúin', *Éigse*, 32 : 77–87 (from the Gerard Murphy Commemorative Conference), discusses various possible interpretations of parts of the corpus of early Irish literature and the many uses to which this material was put. A.M. O'Leary, 'The identities of the poet(s) mac Coisi: a reinvestigation', *CMCS*, 38 : 53–71, revisits the thorny issue of how many poets named mac Coisi were at work in medieval Ireland and argues that Iorard mac Coisi may have had no historical existence. P. Ó Néill, 'The Latin colophon to the *Táin bó Cúailnge* in the Book of Leinster: a critical view of Old Irish literature', *Celtica*, 23 : 269–75, argues that the colophon 'betrays a new, critical, attitude towards native Irish literature, one which presages the end of the compact between the two learned classes of native *filid* and monastic *literati*'. E. Poppe, 'Reconstructing medieval Irish literary theory: the lesson of *Airec menman Uraird maic Coise*', *CMCS*, 37 : 33–54, (building particularly on work by M. Herbert) argues that texts such as *Airec menman Uraird maic Coise* were intended to be understood 'by some sections of their audiences as allegories for the present'. E. Poppe, 'Cormac's metrical testament: "Mithig techt tar mo thimna" ', *Celtica*, 23 : 300–11, is an edition of a Middle Irish poem put into the mouth of Cormac mac Cuilennáin, one of a group of 'retrospective speech poems attributed to a saint which are intended as a means to define certain aspects of the status and affiliation of a church or monastery within a specific historical context'. G. Toner, 'Reconstructing the earliest Irish tale lists', *Éigse*, 32 : 88–120, makes the first detailed survey of the growth of the Irish tales lists since P. Mac Cana, *The Learned Tales of Medieval Ireland* (Dublin, 1980) and argues that 'List A and part of List B go back to a common ancestor, X, which was compiled some time before the appearance of List A in the Book of Leinster in the latter half of the twelfth century'. In another essay

concerned with classification and interpretation of our native literature, G. Toner, 'The Ulster cycle: historiography or fiction?', *CMCS*,
40 : 1–20, argues that medieval redactors of the Ulster cycle believed
in the historicity of much of their material, a view which has
implications for the way in which we approach our analysis. H. L. C.
Tristram, 'The "cattle-raid of Cuailnge" between the oral and the
written: a research report (SFB 321, Projekt A 5, 1989–1996)', *ZCP*,
51 : 125–9, briefly summarises the findings of the research group on
the oral and written elements in *Táin bó Cúailnge*. M. West, 'The
genesis of *Togail bruidne Da Derga*: a reappraisal of the 'two-source'
theory', *Celtica*, 23 : 413–35, re-examines the argument that the
inconsistencies in the tale happened as a result of the fusion of two
distinct versions but concludes that to propose these strictures 'is to
impose a rigidity of structure which all the evidence within the tale
denies'.

3.　Onomastics

S. Arbuthnot, 'Short cuts to etymology : placenames in *Cóir anmann*',
Ériu, 50 : 79–86, extends the work of R. Baumgarten to establish 'how
the names of place . . . in *Cóir anmann* . . . are analysed for meaning';
she shows how 'an unetymologized name, even a placename, was an
unwelcome anomaly' in this Middle Irish tract. P. McKay, *A Dictionary
of Ulster Place-names*, Belfast, The Institute of Irish Studies, 1999,
xiv + 159 pp., part of the ongoing work of the Northern Ireland place
name project, is a reliable, modern publication dealing primarily
with the place names of Ulster listed in the Ordnance Survey's
Gasaitéar na hÉireann Dublin, 1989. In *Ptolemy: Towards a Linguistic Atlas
of the Earliest Celtic Place-names of Europe*, ed. D. N. Parsons and P. Sims-
Williams, CMCS, Aberystwyth, ix + 188 pp., Irish place names are
the focus in G. Toner, 'Identifying Ptolemy's Irish places and tribes'
(73–82), and P. de Bernardo Stempel, 'Ptolemy's Celtic Italy and
Ireland: a linguistic analysis' (83–112).

　　D. Ó Murchadha, 'The formation of Gaelic surnames in Ireland:
choosing the eponym', *Nomina*, 22 : 25–44, demonstrates that *Mac*-
type surnames are generally (*c.* 150 years) later than *Ua*-type ones,
whose emergence he would date to the mid-tenth c. He notes that
'once *Mac* had become established, however, it came to be used for
almost all new surnames after the eleventh century'. D. Ó Corráin,
Peritia, 13 : 310–11, rejects the derivation of the place name Sceillec
as a borrowing from Old Norse. D. Ó Murchadha, 'Where was Ráith
Breasail', *Tipperary Historical Journal* (1999) 151–61, identifies the
location of this important medieval synod in the modern townlands
of Kilvilcorris and Clonbrassil, in the barony of Eliogarty, county

Tipperary. In an extended article, G. Toner, 'Settlement and settlement-terms in medieval Ireland: *ráth* and *lios*', *Ainm*, 8:1–40, shows that the term *ráth* 'had largely ceased to be productive in place-names in Ulster and much of Leinster as early as the tenth century' though it continued to be used in the south and west for a long period afterwards while *lios*-names (usually later in date than *ráth*-names) 'were becoming more common in most parts of the country as early as the twelfth or thirteenth century'. D. Ó Murchadha, 'A reconsideration of some place-names from *Fragmentary annals of Ireland*', *ib.*, 41–51 continues his re-assessment of annalistic place names and he further suggests ('Ainm Gaeilge ar an *Great Saltee*', *ib.*, 60–4) that *Éininis*, 'bird island', was the pre-Viking name of the Great Saltee Island, co. Wexford. M. B. Ó Mainnín, 'Marrassit: a corrupted townland name in county Armagh', *ib.*, 52–5, postulates an original Irish form of this place name as *Ma(i)gh Rámhaid / Rámhada* 'The plain of the main route', while T. G. Ó Canann, 'A postscript on medieval Gleann Néimhthinne', *ib.*, 56–9, further supplements his research on an important early territory. A. Ó Maolfabhail, 'Ar lorg na Breatnaise in Éirinn', *ib.*, 76–92, utilises place name elements to analyse 'possible traces of Welsh influence in Ireland'.

4. OTHER

P. Ó Riain, 'Rawlinson B 502 alias Lebar Glinne Dá Locha: a restatement of the case', *ZCP*, 51:130–47, counters the arguments raised by C. Breatnach in *Éigse*, 30:109–32 and reasserts his belief that Rawlinson B 502 and the Book of Glendalough are 'different names for the same manuscript'. P.A. Breatnach, 'More on Ware's *Psalter Narann*', *ib.*, 31:133–4, contributes a short piece to this ongoing debate. W. O'Sullivan, 'The book of Domhnall Ó Duibhdábhoire-ann, provenance and codicology', *Celtica* 23:276–99, presents us with an in-depth study of Eg. 88 in the context of an overview of other important legal manuscripts.

J. Carey, *A Single Ray of the Sun: Religious Speculation in Early Ireland*, Andover – Aberystwyth, Celtic Studies Publications, 1999, ix + 123 pp., is a collection of three essays on 'some of the more distinct manifestations of early Irish religious thought'. The author emphasises that 'however interesting the peculiarities of early Irish theology may be, they were supplemental to a faith which was in all essentials that of the rest of Christendom'.

C. Ireland, *Old Irish Wisdom Attributed to Aldfrith of Northumbria: An Edition of Bríathra Flainn Fhína maic Ossu*, Tempe, Arizona Center for Medieval and Renaissence Studies, 1999, xiv + 244 pp., presents a detailed introduction to Old Irish wisdom literature, a critical edition of the maxims attributed to King Aldfrith of Northumbria (†705) along with diplomatic editions of the best witnesses to the three different recensions, *N*, *Y* and *L*, in-depth linguistic notes and a full bibliography of previous work on this genre of material.

In *Akten des zweiten deutschen Keltologen-Symposiums*, ed. S. Zimmer, R. Ködderitzsch and A. Wigger, Tübingen, Max Neimeyer Verlag 1999, viii + 333 pp., P.S. Hellmuth analyses the version of *Aided Chon Roí* from the Yellow Book of Lecan ('*Aided Chon Roí* im Gelben Buch von Lecan: die Gesichte eines Todes als Lebensretter', 65–76); G. R. Isaac makes a contribution on metrics of the period 700–1100 ('Zur frühen keltischen Metrik', 77–95); U. Mac Gearailt examines the Irish literary language of the eleventh century ('Zur literarischen Sprache des 11. Jahrhunderts', 105–20); M. Ní Úrdail examines the use of *ogham órdha* in 18th and 19th-c. manuscripts ('*Ogham órdha* in den späteren irisch-gälischen Handschriften', 149–62). A. Ó Corráin treats of the impersonal construction in Irish ('Über unpersönliche Konstruktionen im Irischen', 163–73) and E. Veselinović looks at aspects of two important Old Irish verbs, *ad-cí* and *ro-cluinethar* ('Zu den formalen und funktionalen Gemeinsamkeiten von *ad-cí* und *ro-cluinethar* innerhalb der irischen Sprachentwicklung', 305–13). In *Breis faoinár ndúchas spioradálta*, ed. R. Ó hUiginn, *LCC*, 30, 146 pp., Maynooth, An Sagart, M. Herbert examines aspects of Irish hagiography in the pre-Viking period ('Gnéithe den naomhsheanchas in Éirinn sa tréimhse réamh-Lochlannach', 65–74) and shows how productions from this time reflect a society which had long reached a real accommodation between native and Christian, while J. Carey looks at magical texts in Ireland in the early Middle Ages ('Téacsanna draíochta in Éirinn sa mheánaois luath', 98–117), where in the appendix he provides text and translation of a number of the pieces under discussion.

Celtic Connections: Proceedings of the Tenth International Congress of Celtic Studies, vol. 1, ed. R. Black, W. Gillies and R. Ó Maolalaigh, Tuckwell, Edinburgh, 1999, xxiv + 568pp, focuses on the areas of language, literature, history and culture. Therein P. K. Ford, 'Blackbirds, cuckoos, and infixed pronouns: another context for early Irish nature poetry' (162–70), analyses the famous Old Irish poem *Dom-fharcai fidbaide fál* and argues that the immediate context of the poem is best understood by reference to the manuscript. The quatrains are found as marginalia to a discussion of pronouns in Priscian and the author argues that the five infixed pronouns in the poem (in eight lines of verse) are a contribution to this section of the grammar; M. Herbert, 'Literary sea-voyages and early Munster hagiography' (182–9), focuses on two sections in the life of Ailbe to show how they 'enhance our view of the ideological and formal significance of the Irish literary *topos* of sea-journeying'; J. Carey, 'Cú Chulainn as ailing hero' (190–8), notes some possible parallels between shamanism in other cultures and the presentation of Cú Chulainn in stories such as *Serglige Con Culainn* and argues that 'Cú Chulainn served as the champion of his people, even – or especially – when incapacitated or entranced'.

Fled Bricrenn: Reassessments, ed. P. Ó Riain, Irish Texts Society, London, 2000, ix + 114pp., the result of a one-day conference on the subject, contains five new studies of this important Irish text: B. Maier, 'Comparing *Fled Bricrenn* with classical descriptions of continental Celts: parallels, problems and pitfalls' (1–14), J.T. Koch, '*Fled Bricrenn*'s significance within the broader Celtic context' (15–39), N. Jacobs, '*Fled Bricrenn* and *Sir Gawain and the Green Knight*' (40–55), P. S. Hellmuth, 'The role of Cú Roí in '*Fled Bricrenn*' (56–69) and P. Mac Cana, 'Notes on structure and syntax in *Fled Bricrenn*' (70–91).

Seanchas: Studies in Early and Medieval Irish Archaeology, History and Literature in Honour of Francis J. Byrne, ed. A. F. Smyth, Dublin, Four Courts, 2000, xxiii + 478pp., contains many articles in the disciplines of archaeology and history. Other contributions include: D. Ó hAodha, 'Rechtgal úa Síadail, a famous poet of the Old Irish period' (192–8), P. Mac Cana, 'The motif of trivial causes' (205–11) and M. Ní Dhonnchadha, 'On Gormfhlaith daughter of Flann Sinna and the lure of the sovereignty goddess' (225–37), which includes an edition of *Éirigh a ingen an rígh*.

In *Übersetzung, Adaptation und Akkulturation im insularen Mittelalter*, ed. E. Poppe and H. L. C. Tristram, Münster, Nodus, 1999, 346 pp., K. H. Schmidt, 'Haustiernamen und Sprachwandel im älteren Irischen' (37–45) investigates the etymologies of domestic animal names and associated terminology while H. L. C. Tristram, 'Bedas *Historia ecclesiastica gentis anglorum* im Altenglischen und Altirischen: Ein Vergleich' (51–72) compares the treatment of Bede's *Ecclesiastical History* in Old English and Old Irish. N. Müller, 'Kodewechsel in der irischen Übersetzungsliteratur: *Exempla et disiderata*' (73–86) looks at examples of 'code-switching' in medieval Irish translation literature, C. J. Hyland, 'Crecha und Tána: Rinderraubzüge in der Geschichte und Literatur Irlands' (105–22) compares the historical *crecha* with the literary *tána bó* and P. Ó Riain, 'Die Bibliothek des Verfassers des kommentierten *Félire Óengusso*' (87–104) examines the nature of the works that the compiler of the commentary to the Martyrology of Óengus had access to, which makes possible a dating of the commentary to 1170–74. Other adaptations into Irish examined in this collection of essays include U. Mac Gearailt, *Togail Troí* (123–29); B. Hillers, *Sgél in Mínaduir* (131–44); B. Smelik, *Eachtra an Mhadra*

Mhaoil (145–59) while M. Ní Úrdail (319–36) looks at some translations from other languages into Irish in manuscripts from Cork. *The Otherworld Voyage in Early Irish Literature*, ed. J. M. Wooding, Dublin, Four Courts, 2000, xxviii + 290pp., reprints many of the more important articles on the medieval Irish voyage tales (the Latin *Navigatio Brendani* and the Irish *immrama*). Along with a general introduction to the material by the editor, the book contains three new articles: K. Murray, 'The role of the *cuilebad* in *Immram Snédgusa ocus Maic Riagla*' (187–93); T. O. Clancy, 'Subversion at sea: structure, style and intent in the *immrama*' (194–225) and J. M. Wooding, 'Monastic voyaging and the *Nauigatio*' (226–45). K. Jankulak provides a translation of the Latin passages from M. Esposito's important article in an appendix (246–50) while J. M. Wooding and K. Jankulak have compiled an extremely useful and thorough bibliography of Irish voyage literature (251–77).

MODERN IRISH

POSTPONED

IV. SCOTTISH GAELIC STUDIES

By SHEILA M. KIDD, *Lecturer in Celtic, University of Glasgow*

Richard A. V. Cox, *The Languages of the Ogam Inscriptions of Scotland*, Aberdeen, University of Aberdeen, Department of Celtic, 1999, xvi + 187 pp., is a study of 17 Ogam inscriptions of Scottish provenance and two non-Ogam which argues that linguistically Scotland's Ogam inscriptions are derived from Old Norse. R. Ó Maolalaigh, 'Transition zones, hyperdialectisms and historical change: the case of final unstressed -igh/ich and -idh in Scottish Gaelic', *SGS*, 19, 1999:195–233, draws on data from the *Survey of the Gaelic Dialects of Scotland* (1995–97) and discusses these phonological developments based upon grammatical category and demonstrates that these changes have been more rapid when endings bear grammatical meaning. Attention is focused on the Gaelic of southern Islay as a transitional dialect. Seumas Grannd, *The Gaelic of Islay: A Comparative Study*, Aberdeen, University of Aberdeen, Department of Celtic, 147 pp., offers a comparison between the Gaelic of Islay and that of other dialects in Argyll and Arran, incorporating some eighty maps which indicate the geographical distribution of individual words and expressions and also the distribution of variant pronunciations of certain words or word types. S. Watson, 'Aspects of some Nova Scotian Gaelic dialects', *ICCS 10*, 1:347–59 considers progressive features of Inverness County dialects. J. Shaw, 'The ethnography of speaking and verbal taxonomies: some applications to Gaelic', *ib.*, 309–23 examines the relationship between aspects of Gaelic speech and the cultural and social values held by Gaelic society by considering the semantic range of words such as *beul* and *cainnt*.

C. Ó Baoill, 'Moving in Gaelic musical circles: the root *lu*-in music terminology', *SGS*, 19, 1999:172–94 considers the various forms in Scottish Gaelic derived from Early Gaelic *luïd*. A. Breeze, 'Gaelic etymologies for Scots *pippane* 'lace', *ron* 'seal', *trachle*, 'bedraggle', *ib.*, 246–52, offers explanations for the derivation of these three forms, the first two of which were in use in the Scottish court early in the 16th c. Id., 'Some Celtic place-names of Scotland', *ScL*, 18, 1999:34–51, traces the origins of a number of names including Dalriada, Kincarden, Abercorn, Coldingham and Girvan. R. A. V. Cox, 'Leumaragh-Leumrabhagh', *SGS*, 19, 1999:253–56, explores the possible derivations of these two forms of the Lewis village name. W. MacLeod, 'Galldachd, Gàidhealtachd, Garbhchrìochan', *ib.*, 1–20, discusses the origins and developments of these three terms. Drawing on evidence from the 14th c. to the 20th, he demonstrates that while *Galldachd* and *Gàidhealtachd* are used to refer to both people and places, *Garbhchrìochan* is a purely geographical term, initially for the Highlands as a whole and now for a more limited part of the Highlands. W. Lamb, 'A diachronic account of Gaelic news-speak: the development and expansion of a register', *ib.*, 141–71, studies the linguistic features of BBC news-scripts since 1959, considering aspects of lexicon, morphology, orthography, syntax, dialect and prosody, and also discusses the factors which influenced this evolving register. W. MacLeod, 'Official Gaelic: problems in the translation of public documents', *ScL*, 19:100–16, highlights some of the variations, inconsistencies and omissions which are a feature of the translation currently carried out on an *ad hoc* basis. W. Gillies, 'Scottish Gaelic', pp. 181–84 of *The Oxford Guide to Literature in English Translation*, ed. Peter France, OUP, xxii + 656 pp., traces the origins of translations from Gaelic to English since the mid-18th c. and the influence of James MacPherson's *Ossian*, with its resultant stimulation of collecting, translating and publishing oral material in the 19th c. The 20th c. is characterised by the Scottish Gaelic Texts Society editions of poetry and by the translation of modern poetry by Sorley MacLean and George Campbell Hay among others. K. MacKinnon, 'Scottish Gaelic', Price, *Languages*, 44–57, gives a general sociolinguistic account of the decline of Gaelic over the centuries and focuses on the position of Gaelic today and the various influences affecting it. On a similar theme is D. S. Thomson, 'Scottish Minorities', 635–44 of *Breizh ha poblou Europa: pennadou en enor da Per Denez*, Rennes U.P., 1999, 738 pp., in a survey which is both retrospective and prospective compares and contrasts the fates of Gaelic and Scots, placing the languages in a European context. With the focus on Gaelic he considers a range of factors affecting its future such as government provision for the language and the rising number of learners. F. Macintosh, 'The Prospects for Gaelic', *ICCS 10*, 1:457–69 is in the same vein in its discussion of the contradictory signs of resurgence and decline currently affecting Gaelic.

  Collected Poems and Songs of George Campbell Hay (*Deòrsa Mac Iain Dheòrsa*), ed. Michel Byrne, 2 vols, EUP, xxii + 459, xiv + 251 pp., is a landmark edition being the first publication to bring together all the poems of this major 20th-c. poet, not just those in Gaelic, but his work in Scots, English, French, Italian and Norwegian. Volume 1 presents all the poems chronologically from those composed in 1932 through to the last ones from 1983. Unusually for a Gaelic publication, the English translations are placed unobtrusively at the foot of each page. Volume 2 encompasses an extensive biography, an assessment of form and theme in Hay's work and commentary on each poem. *An Tuil*, ed. Ronald I. M. Black, Edinburgh, Polygon,

1999, lxx + 825 pp., is another notable publication. This massive anthology which includes 351 Gaelic poems, with parallel translations, spans the entire 20th c. and brings together in one volume both traditional poets composing for local audiences and poets of international stature such as Sorley MacLean and Iain Crichton Smith. Black's introduction traces the development of Gaelic poetry in the course of the century and explores some of the tensions during the century such as that between those who favoured traditional verse and those who were more innovative. The inclusion of extensive biographical details about each poet, along with notes relating to each poem, is invaluable.

Orain Dhòmhnaill Ailein Dhòmhnaill na Bainich: the Songs of John Allan MacDonald, 1906–1992, ed. John Angus Macdonald, Muir of Aird, Comuinn Eachdraidh nan Eilean mu Dheas, 1999, xxiii + 317 pp., is an edition of thirty-five songs by this South Uist poet, collected by the editor from the poet himself and from local oral tradition. The poet's place in both Gaelic and local tradition is examined as are the processes of composition and transmission. The work of another traditional poet from South Uist, Dòmhnall Aonghais Bhàin (Donald MacDonald) has been gathered together and published in *Smuaintean fo Éiseabhal: Thoughts under Eiseaval*, ed. Ronald Black, Edinburgh, Birlinn, xxix + 115 pp. *Scottish Religious Poetry from the Sixth Century to the Present: an Anthology*, ed. Meg Bateman, Robert Crawford and James McGonigal, Edinburgh, Saint Andrew Press, xxviii + 330 pp., spans 15 centuries from St Columba to the present day. There is a significant amount of Gaelic verse with parallel translation and includes verse by Muireadhach Albanach, Sìleas na Ceapaich, Dùghall Bochanan, Somhairle Mac'Illeathain and Fearghas MacFhionnlaigh. N. McGuire, 'Amy Murray's Eriskay Collection', *SGS* 19, 1999:83–92 offers a brief discussion of this American musician and collector's work in the early 20th c. and includes a listing of over 100 songs collected by her which have recently come to light. D. Ní Suaird, 'Jacobite Rhetoric and Terminology in the Political Poems of the Fernaig MS (1688–1693)', *ib.*, 93–140 categorises examples in poetry of the theory of the divine and hereditary right of kingship and also the various terminology used to legitimise the Jacobites' claim and to undermine that of the Williamites. D. P. McLean, 'The Songs of William Smith', *TGSI* 60, 1997–98[2000]:125–47, provides some biographical details of this late 18th-c. Badenoch poet and includes his 14 extant compositions. D. MacAulay, 'The Poetry of Seonaidh Phadraig (John Smith) the Earshader bàrd', *ib.*, 1–16, offers a valuable discussion of this 19th-c. poet, drawing on Iain N. MacLeòd's *Bàrdachd Leòdhais* (1916) and on a recently discovered manuscript version of his poems. The poet is

placed in his literary and historical context with particular attention
being given to his condemnation in verse within Christian parameters
of 19th-c. Highland landlordism. J. MacDonald, 'Aimhreit an
Fhearainn agus Bàrdachd Leòdhais', *ib.*, 92–107 outlines the response
of Lewis poets to the events of the Land Agitation years, and traces
the development from nostalgia through to more confident and
critical verse in the later 19th and early 20th c. K. Cardell and
C. Cumming, 'Gaelic voices from Australia Part I', *SGS* 19,
1999:21–58 draws attention to the Gaelic sources, including letters,
poems and prose, which tell of the experiences of emigrant Gaels in
Australia in the 19th c. In this, the first in an intended series on the
subject, attention is given to the propaganda which attracted
emigrants to Australia in the first place and to some accounts of the
voyage to Australia. H. Cheape, 'Etymologies and traditions: A
Lochaber minister's notebook, 1858–1864', *ib.*, 66–82, concerns the
Rev. Dr Archibald Clerk of Kilmallie who was one of the many
Gaelic-speaking ministers who engaged in scholarly activities in the
19th c. He recorded words and phrases, local historical anecdotes,
proverbial material and weather lore in his notebook and these are
reproduced in the second part of this essay. J. Macinnes, 'Gaelic song
and the dance' *TGSI* 60, 1997–98[2000]:56–73, explores the connection between *òrain-luaidh* and dance, beginning with 19th and 20th-c.
theories that the ballad in various European countries is derived from
dance-songs and going on to consider the possibility of French
influence on Gaelic song through Highland kindreds of French stock.
He also draws on historical evidence for the existence of native
traditions of dance and on more recent evidence from Cape Breton
of singing while moving. D. S. Thomson, 'Gaelic renaissance
c. 1900–1930', *ib.*, 283–301, studies the range of factors which
contributed to this renaissance, noting in particular the link between
politics and literature dating from the Land Agitation years and the
increasing importance of new urban Gaelic communities. Among the
various developments considered is the influence of Ruaraidh Erskine
of Mar who is credited with the transformation of written Gaelic by
his use of the language as a medium for the discussion of nationalistic
politics in his various periodicals. M. NicLeòid, '"Smuaintean an
Eilthirich": Leòdhas agus Fànas ann am Bàrdachd Ruaraidh Mhic-
Thòmais', *SGS* 19, 1999:59–65 considers MacThòmais's often
conflicting attitudes to his native island and traces the development
in his relationship with the island over his first three collections of
poetry.

Women's poetry has been the subject of a number of articles
recently. A. C. Frater, 'Women of the Gàidhealtachd and their Songs
to 1750', pp. 67–79 of *Women in Scotland, c.1100–c.1750*, ed. Elizabeth

Ewan and Maureen M. Meikle, East Linton, Tuckwell, xxx + 272 pp., examines the way in which Gaelic poetry underlines the position of women in society over the centuries and discusses how they used it as a means of breaking the taboos of contemporary society and accessing the world of men, as for instance in political verse. D. U. Stiùbhart, 'Women and gender in the early modern western Gàidhealtachd', *ib.*, 233–49, provides an overview of women's social history in the 17th and early 18th centuries by drawing on literature and oral tradition and concludes by discussing the spread of new cultural mores from the south by the end of the period. R. L. Reddington-Wilde, 'Violent and damning words: women's lament in Scottish Gaelic Poetry', *ICCS 10*, 1:265–86, suggests that female poets enjoyed more freedom to offer criticism of the clan than male poets whose relationship with the aristocracy tended to constrain them. D. S. Thomson, 'Scottish Gaelic traditional songs from the 16th to the 18th century', *PBS*, 105:93–114, gives some attention to the songs of women in his consideration of the variety of extant Gaelic song from this period. *The Church in the Highlands*, ed. James Kirk, Edinburgh, Scottish Church History Society, 1998, vii + 176 pp., contains six essays covering the late medieval period to the present day. M. MacGregor, 'Church and culture in the late medieval Highlands', *ib.*, 1–36, explores the interaction between secular and sacred, and demonstrates that the fact that members of the clergy were drawn from the learned orders strengthened the relationship with secular culture, and goes on to discuss both the clergy's dependence on lay patrons and its own role as a patron. D. Meek, 'The Reformation and Gaelic culture: perspectives on patronage, language and literature in John Carswell's translation of "The Book of Common Order"', *ib.*, 37–62, considers the way in which Gaelic culture was deployed by Carswell in his 'translation' to meet the requirements of the Reformation and offers parallels with contemporary Wales and Ireland, R. Black, 'Later additions in Gaelic: transcription, translation and commentary', pp. 336–45 of John Higgitt, *The Murthly Hours: Devotion, Literacy and Luxury in Paris, England and the Gaelic West*, London, The British Library — Toronto U.P., xxii + 362 pp., discusses the late Gaelic texts which were added to this Book of Hours *c.* 1370–*c.* 1430. It is suggested that in terms of scribal and orthographic conventions the texts are similar to those of the Book of the Dean of Lismore, with a Scots-based script and orthography being used. The texts are transcribed, with alternative readings and commentary provided and it is concluded that these texts are to be understood in the context of charms and the belief in the healing power of written charms. Donald E. Meek, *The Quest for Celtic Christianity*, Boat of Garten, The Handsel

Press, vii + 273 pp., offers a critical overview of the phenomenon of
Celtic Christianity, dealing with both historical and modern aspects
of Christianity in the British Isles. Karen Ralls-MacLeod, *Music and
the Celtic Otherworld: from Ireland to Iona*, Edinburgh, Polygon,
xi + 211 pp., draws on a wide range of sources from early Celtic tales
to saints' lives, poetry and proverbs in her exploration of the
supernatural or spiritual dimension of music.

4

GERMANIC LANGUAGES

I. GERMAN STUDIES

LANGUAGE

By CHARLES V. J. RUSS, *Reader in the Department of Language and Linguistic Science, University of York*

1. GENERAL

SURVEYS, COLLECTIONS, BIBLIOGRAPHIES. A fascinating insight into the German linguistic soul is provided by G. Stickel and N. Volz, *Meinungen und Einstellungen zur deutschen Sprache. Ergebnisse einer bundesweiten Repräsentativerhebung* (Amades, 20), Mannheim, Institut für Deutsche Sprache, 1999, 55 pp., which tracks the answers to 54 questions by 2,025 speakers on subjects such as the development of modern German, regional variation in German, the relationship betwen East and West, German and other languages, in particular the relationship between German and other languages in the European Union. Predictably, English loans come in for some criticism, although only about 40% of respondents were interested in language matters. This is a very valuable study. A bibliography from the same institute is M. W. Hellmann, *Wende-Bibliographie. Literatur und Nachschlagewerke zu Sprache und Kommunikation im geteilten und vereinigten Deutschland ab Januar 1990* (Amades, 1), Mannheim, Institut für Deutsche Sprache, 1999, 94 pp., which lists videos as well as books. The volume consists of contributions of a scientific and popular nature as well as those from the press and radio/TV, dictionaries, and reference works, as well as works of a documentary nature and then secondary literature from related areas. It will be of interest not only to linguists but anyone interested in Germany of that period. The **Wortatlas der deutschen Umgangssprachen*, ed. J. Eichhoff, vol. 4, Munich, Saur, 56 pp. + 79 maps, is now complete. Also noted on a general theme are C. Földes, 'Was ist die deutsche Sprache wert? Fakten und Potenzen', *WW*, 50 : 369–96, and **Nation und Sprache. Die Diskussion ihres Verhältnisses in Geschichte und Gegenwart*, ed. A. Gardt, Berlin, de Gruyter, vi + 924 pp.

The growing use of corpora in linguistic studies and increasingly for German is reflected in the contributions to *Working with German Corpora*, ed. W. Dodd, Birmingham U.P., 299 pp. This work contains:

W. Dodd, 'The relevance of corpora to German studies (1–39); Id., 'When Ost meets West: a corpus-based study of binomial and other expressions before and during German unification' (69–95); G. J. A. Burgess, 'Corpus analysis in the service of literary criticism: Goethe's *Die Wahlverwandtschaften* as a model case' (40–68); P. Gupta, 'German *be-* verbs revisited: using corpus evidence to investigate valency' (96–115); R. L. Jones, 'A corpus-based study of German accusative/dative prepositions' (116–42); D. Kenny, 'Translators at play: exploitations of collocational norms in German-English translation' (143–60); A. Lawson, '"Die schöne Geschichte": a corpus-based analysis of Thomas Mann's *Joseph und seine Brüder*' (161–80); A. Mackeson, 'Towards a corpus-based comparison of two journals in the field of business and management German' (181–98); P. Roe, 'The ASTCOVEA German Grammar in conText Project' (199–216); J. West, 'An electronic corpus of Early New High German' (217–44); A. Wichmann and J. Nielsen, 'Rights snd obligations in legal contracts' (245–66); and N. Witton, 'Inflected and periphrastic subjunctive forms in German newspaper texts of the 1960s and 1990s' (267–96).

GERMAN IN OTHER COUNTRIES. A full-scale study is M. M. Glauninger, *Untersuchungen zur Lexik des Deutschen in Österreich* (Schriften zur deutschen Sprache in Österreich, 28), Frankfurt, Lang, 246 pp., whereas a critical review article is P. Wiesinger, 'Zum "Österreichischen Wörterbuch"', *ZGL*, 28 : 41–64; Also noted: J. Grzega, 'Österreichische Nachrichtensprache: Paradigmatische und syntagmatische Divergenzen zwischen österreichischer und bundesdeutscher Distanzsprache', *ZDL*, 67 : 53–66. The language of former East Germany is in evidence as a background feature as is illustrated by B. Wolf, **Sprache in der DDR. Ein Wörterbuch*, Berlin, de Gruyter, 320 pp.; H. Hausendorf, **Zugehörigkeit durch Sprache. Eine linguistische Studie am Beispiel der deutschen Wiedervereinigung* (RGL, 215), xxi + 645 pp.; **Kommunikation in gesellschaftlichen Umbruchsituationen. Mikroanalytische Aspekte des sprachlichen und gesellschaftlichen Wandels in den Neuen Bundesländern*, ed. P. Auer and H. Hausendorf (RGL, 219), ix + 325 pp., and U. Fix et al., **Sprachbiographien. Sprache und Sprachgebrauch vor und nach der Wende von 1989 im Erinnern und Erleben von Zeitzeugen aus der DDR. Inhalte und Analysen narrativ-diskursiver Interviews* (Leipziger Arbeiten zur Sprach- und Kommunikationsgeschichte, 7), Frankfurt, Lang, 719 pp.

German in other parts of the world features in E. M. Müller, **Sprachwahl im spanisch-deutschen Sprachkontakt in Südchile. Ergebnisse einer sprachsoziologischen Untersuchung unter Nachfahren deutscher Einwanderer*, Berne, Lang, xii + 347 pp. The language of Jews from pre-war Germany is treated in **Sprachbewahrung nach der Emigration. Das Deutsch* *der zwanziger Jahre in Israel.* II. *Analysen und Dokumente,* ed. A. Betten and M. Du-Nour, Tübingen, Niemeyer, 500 pp., and H. P. Althaus, 'Relikte des Jüdischen in der Sprache deutscher Juden', *Fest. Munske,* 225–49. A century is an important landmark and U. Engel, 'Jean Fourquet — 100 Jahre alt', *DSp,* 27, 1999 : 287–91, and M. Philipp, 'Zum hundertsten Geburtstag von Jean Fourquet', *ZDL,* 67 : 1–5, ensure that Jean Fourquet's achievement is celebrated in a proper way. The history of *Germanistik* is the subject of **Fritz Mauthner — Sprache, Literatur, Kritik. Festakt und Symposium zu seinem 150. Geburtstag,* ed. H. Henne and C. Kaiser (RGL, 224), 200 pp.; H. J. Heringer, ' "Through permanent interplay to a common end" — Hermann Paul als Vorreiter der sprachlichen Evolution', *Fest. Eroms,* 235–44, and **Germanistische Linguistik in Erlangen. Eine Bilanz nach 50 Jahren,* ed. H. Munske and M. Habermann, Erlangen, Palm & Enke, viii + 167 pp.

INTERDISCIPLINES. Publications on literature and language include: **Reflexionen über Sprache aus literatur- und sprachwissenschaftlicher Sicht,* ed. A. Gellhaus and H. Sitta (RGL, 218), ix + 14 pp.; A. Betten, 'Thomas Bernhards Syntax: keine Wiederholung des immer Gleichen', *Fest. Eroms,* 169–90; and **Übertragung, Annäherung, Angleichung. Sieben Beiträge zu Theorie und Praxis des Übersetzens,* ed. C. Fabricius-Hansen and J. Østbø (Osloer Beiträge zur Germanistik, 25), Frankfurt, Lang, 149 pp.

On specialist language: M. G. Ditlevsen, 'Die Verständlichkeit von deutschen Fachtexten am Beispiel der Substantivphrase', *DaF,* 37 : 82–86; F. Kostrzewa, 'Probleme der Vermittlung von Fachsprachen an der Universität', *ib.,* 104–08; **Hermetik und Manipulation in den Fachsprachen,* ed. K. Morgenroth (FF, 55), 350 pp.; **Sprachen im Beruf. Stand — Probleme — Perspektiven,* ed. K.-D. Baumann (FF, 38), 328 pp.; R. Gardner and S. Luchtenberg, 'Reference, image, text in German and Australian advertising posters', *JP,* 32 : 1807–21; and C. Dürscheid, 'Sprachliche Merkmale von Webseiten', *DSp,* 28 : 60–73.

Children's language is the subject of: P. Gretsch, **Fokale Ellipsen in Erwachsenen- und Kindersprache* (LA, 427), xi + 237 pp.; C. Kauschke, **Der Erwerb des frühkindlichen Lexikons. Eine empirische Studie zur Entwicklung des Wortschatzes im Deutschen* (Language Development, 27), Tübingen, Narr, 320 pp.; M. Schecker et al., **Defizite der Sprachverarbeitung und gestörtes Gesprächsverhalten bei psychisch kranken Kindern* (Cognitio, 5), Tübingen, Narr, 142 pp.; and C. Knoblich, ' "Künstlich natürlich!" Spracherwerb und Sprachwandel', *DUS,* 52 : 17–27.

Second language acquisition of German features in the following: K. Müller, **Zum dialogischen Erwerb des Deutschen bei türkischen und italienischen Kindern* (TBL, 445), viii + 286 pp.; M. Chavez, 'Teacher and student gender and peer group gender composition in German foreign language classroom discourse: an exploratory study', *JP*, 32 : 1019–58; R. S. Baur, 'Schulischer Zweitsprachenerwerb bei Migrantenschülern — Theorie und Empirie', *DaF*, 37 : 131–35; J. Roche, 'Lerntechnologie und Spracherwerb. Grundrisse einer medienadäquaten, interkulturellen Sprachdidaktik', *ib.*, 136–43; I. Thonhauser-Jusnick, 'Wozu Schreiben im Fremdsprachenunterricht? Eine Analyse neuerer DaF-Lehrwerke', *ib.*, 195–98; M. Gwenzadse, 'Kommunikativ-grammatische Paradigmen gesprochener Sprache und ihre Bedeutung für DaF', *ib.*, 217–20; H. Blühdorn, 'DaF und die Grammatik des Deutschen. Über die Fruchtbarkeit des neuen Blickes', *ib.*, 221–27; M. Carroll et al., 'The relevance of information organization to second language acquisition studies: the descriptive discourse of advanced adult learners of German', *Studies in Second Language Acquisition*, 22 : 441–66; and V. Wenzel, ' "Ich sag allebei": Strategien beim frühen Erwerb einer verwandten Zweitsprache', *IRAL*, 38 : 247–60.

Medical matters are examined in M. Schecker et al., **Sprache, Denken, Gedächtnis bei Alzheimer-Demenz* (Cognitio, 6), Tübingen, Narr, 180 pp.; G. Kochendörfer, **Simulation neuronaler Strukturen der Sprache. Eine Einführung mit CD-ROM* (Cognitio, 10), Tübingen, Narr, 161 pp.

Feminist matters are the concern of D. Nübling, 'Warum können schwedische Männer *Krankenschwestern* (*sjuksköterskor*) werden, deutsche aber nur *Krankenpfleger*? Zum Einfluß sprachinterner und sprachexterner Faktoren im Deutschen und im Schwedischen', *LBer*, 182 : 199–230.

GENERAL LINGUISTICS, PRAGMATICS, AND TEXTLINGUISTICS. General items include T. Ickler, 'Wirkliche Zeichen', *Fest. Munske*, 199–223; K. Braunmüller, 'Direkter Transfer und strukturelle Adaption. Überlegungen zum Sprachwandel und zur Mehrsprachigkeit', *ib.*, 315–32; F. Debus, 'Variation oder Paradigmenwechsel? Betrachtungen zur Geschichte der Sprachwissenschaft', *Fest. Löffler*, 53–70; N. Dittmar and M. Glier, 'Zur Wissenschaftsgeschichte der Soziolinguistik im deutschsprachigen Raum', *ib.*, 71–86; T. Diegritz et al., 'Der Aufbau von Sprachbegleitbewußtsein bei Grundschülerinnen durch Reflexion über die Sprache', *WW*, 50 : 67–99; and K.-H. Siehr, 'Sprachkritik und Muttersprachunterricht. Anmerkungen aus linguistischer Sicht', Thieroff, *Grammatik*, 287–97.

Spoken language and discourse are examined in G. Brünner, **Wirtschaftskommunikation. Linguistische Analyse ihrer mündlichen Formen* (RGL, 213), ix + 331 pp.; A. Golato, 'An innovative German quotative for reporting on embodied action: *Und ich so/und er so — 'and I'm like/and he's like*", *JP*, 32 : 29–54; S. Habscheid, ' "Medium" in der Pragmatik. Eine kritische Bestandsaufnahme', *DSp*, 28 : 126–41;

U. Bredel, '*Ach so* — Eine Rekonstruktion aus funktionalpragmatischer Perspektive', *LBer*, 184 : 401–21; S. Günther, *Vorwurfsaktivitäten in der Alltagsinteraktion.* *Grammatische, prosodische, rhetorisch-stilistische und interaktive Verfahren bei der Konstitution kommunikativer Muster und Gattungen* (RGL, 221), ix + 404 pp.; S. Günther, 'Zwischen direkter und indirekter Rede', *ZGL*, 28 : 1–22; K. Adamzik, 'Dialogerträge. Vorschläge für eine mehrperspektivische Gesprächsanalyse', *ib.*, 185–206; B. Sandig, 'Zu einer Gesprächs-Grammatik: prototypische elliptische Strukturen und ihre Funktionen in mündlichem Erzählen', *ib.*, 291–318; F. C. Dörge, 'Grundbegriffe zur Analyse illokutionärer Akte', *LBer*, 183 : 309–23; S. Kowal and D. C. O'Connell, 'Psycholinguistische Aspekte der Transkription: zur Notation von Pausen in Gesprächstranskripten', *ib.*, 353–78; R. Stibbard, 'Is discourse intonation applicable to German? Evidence from politicians' speeches in the Bundestag and from a television news broadcast', *IRAL*, 38 : 125–46, and B. Ahrenholtz, 'Modality and referential movement in instructional discourse: comparing the production of Italian learners of German with native German and native Italian production', *Studies in Second Language Acquisition*, 22 : 337–68. Spoken language is also covered in the following articles in *SpLit*, 85: D. Tophinke, 'Autonome Aspekte gesprochener und geschriebener Sprache' (3–22); R. Fiehler, 'Über zwei Probleme bei der Untersuchung gesprochener Sprache' (23–42); P. Auer, 'On-line-Syntax — oder: was es bedeuten könnte, die Zeitlichkeit der mündlichen Sprache ernst zu nehmen' (43–56); S. Günther, 'Grammatik im Gespräch: zur Verwendung von "wobei" im gesprochenen Deutsch' (57–74); R. Weinert, 'Satzbegriff, Einheiten und Verbindungen in gesprochener Sprache. Syntax oder Diskurs' (75–96); L. Springer, 'Mediale und interaktive Erklärungsansätze für die Variabilität agrammatischer Sprachäußerungen' (97–116).

Text analysis is the subject of H. Kniffka, 'Anonymous authorship analysis without comparison data? A case study with methodological implications', *LBer*, 182 : 179–98; E. Strassner, **Journalistische Texte* (Grundlagen der Medienkommunikation, 10), Tübingen, Niemeyer, vi + 106 pp.; F. Wagner, **Implizite sprachliche Diskriminierung als Sprechakt. Lexikalische Indikatoren impliziter Diskrimierung in Medientexten* (SDSp, 20), 180 pp.; A. Linke, 'Informalisierung. Ent-Distanzierung? Familisierung?', *DUS*, 52 : 66–77; M. Nickl, **Gebrauchsanleitungen. Ein Beitrag zur Textsortengeschichte seit 1950 aus der Perspektive der Verständlichkeitsforschung* (FF, 52), 350 pp.; I. Mummert and G. Pommerin, 'Über die allmähliche Verfertigung von Texten (II)', *DaF*, 37 : 3–9; I. Thonhauser-Jursnick, 'Textmuster und Textproduktion im DaF-Unterricht. Kurstagebücher', *ib.*, 93–96; C. F. G. Schendra, 'Die Erforschung der Verständlichkeit von normativen Texten. Eine kritische Darstellung von Modellen, Methoden und Ergebnissen', *ZS*, 19 : 3–33; K. Brinker, 'Aspekte der Textkohärenz am Beispiel einer Rundfunkpredigt', *Fest. Eroms*, 191–202; U. Fix, 'Wie wir mit Textensorten umgehen und sie ändern — Die Textsorte als ordnender Zugriff auf die Welt', *DUS*, 52 : 54–65; E. Felder, 'Nachhaltiges Erinnern durch sprachliches Handeln am Beispiel von Gedenkreden', *DSp*, 28 : 254–77; and S. Stein and C. Baldauf, 'Feste sprachliche Einheiten in Erpresserbriefen. Empirische Analysen und Überlegungen zu ihrer Relevanz für die forensische Textanalyse', *ZGL*, 28 : 377–403.

Language and violence is discussed in U. Fix, 'Die Macht der Sprache über den Einzelnen und die Gewalt des Einzelnen über die Sprache', Corbineau-Hoffmann, *Gewalt*, 19–35; and A. Mieth, ' "Gewalt" durch Lehrersprache?', *ib.*, 37–54.

2. HISTORY OF LANGUAGE

Two general publications on historical development are: T. Roelcke, 'Drift? Die Strömungstheorie im Licht der deutschen Sprachgeschichte', *ZGL*, 28 : 167–84; and G. Zimmermann, 'Sprachvielfalt — Sprachmischung — Sprachspiel. Historische und fiktionale Aspekte nationaler und dialektaler Mehrsprachigkeit', *ZDL*, 67 : 317–36. *Regionale Sprachgeschichte*, ed. W. Besch and H. J. Solms(*ZDP*, Sonderheft), Berlin, Schmidt, 1998, 208 pp., contains contributions dealing with specific regions: J. Gut and W. Haas, 'Zur regionalen Sprachgeschichte der Eidgenossenschaft. Zwei Fallbeispiele' (4–19), concentrates on two different personalities, one using a regional variety and the other, albeit a foreigner, proposing a supraregional form of German; P. Gilles, 'Die Emanzipation des Lëtzebuergeschen aus dem Gefüge der deutschen Mundarten' (20–35), traces the rise of the Luxembourg *koiné* through different developments in Luxembourg and Moselle Franconian whereby the political border has become a stronger language border; H. Eickmans, 'Zur regionalen Sprachgeschichte des nördlichen Rheinlands' (36–49), shows how the complicated territorial development makes a treatment of space, time, form, and function in a linguistic history of the region difficult; J. Macha, 'Schreibvariation und ihr regional-kultureller Hintergrund: Rheinland und Westfalen im 17. Jahrhundert' (50–66), illustrates his theme from witchcraft trials, and shows how some variation is not important but that one should note the transposition of statements into High German with hypercorrections; interestingly, there are also some Bavarian features which are accepted as related to the Counter-Reformation; G. Kettmann, 'Das mittelelbische Wörterbuch als Quelle für die Traditionsforschung (Auswertungsmöglichkeiten eines

Mundartenwörterbuches)' (67–81), shows how a dialect dictionary can evidence the retreat of Low German lexis and local customs; J. Gessinger and C. Fischer, 'Schriftlichkeit und Mündlichkeit in Brandenburg-Berlin' (82–107), take a dynamic view of the concept of region. The change from Low German to High German is regionally different and in the 19th c. we see the formation of *Berlinisch*; R. Peters, 'Zur Sprachgeschichte des niederdeutschen Raumes' (108–27), is a detailed yet succint account which covers a large geographical area. One of his main points is that Middle Low German shows much more variation than linguists realise; P. Wiesinger, 'Probleme einer regionalen Sprachgeschichte Österreichs' (128–43), emphasizes how linguistic development in Austria was bound up with that of Bavaria until the Early NHG period, when Austria developed a more independent role; K. J. Mattheier, 'Gibt es eine regionale Sprachge-schichte der Rheinlande?' (144–51), treats general problems, pointing out that the Rhineland is a recent creation; W. Hoffmann, 'Das Projekt eines historischen rheinischen Wörterbuchs und seine Kon-zeption als historisches Regionalwörterbuch' (152–62), shows that not many dialect dictionaries have a historical dimension and lays out plans for one covering the Rhineland; J. E. Schmidt, 'Moderne Dialektologie und regionale Sprachgeschichte' (163–79), maintains that different regions show different stages of development but that there is a lack of empirical studies; D. Breuer, 'Raumbildungen in der deutschen Literaturgeschichte der frühen Neuzeit als Folge der Konfessionalisierung' (180–92), points out how emphasis has been laid on Protestant east-central German works, and Catholic works from the area have been overlooked despite the presence of Catholic Upper German preachers working in North Germany; A. Gardt, 'Begriffsgeschichte als Methode der Sprachgeschichtsschreibung' (192–204), traces the development of words and concepts for describing the history of German as part of the history of the language itself; and J. P. Hoffmann, 'Forschungsprojekt "Robert Bruch". Analytische Kulturraumforschung (205–08), describes a project using a psycholinguistic approach to *Kulturraum*. This volume reflects the fact that German has developed differently in different areas. There are no contributions on Swabia, Alsace, East Franconia, nor even Bavaria. As well the case studies there are a number of contributions on general principles, including the basic question of what a region is. This is a very stimulating book.

A fascinating volume in honour of Hartmut Schmidt is *Amades* 2, which contains contributions concentrating on different aspect of linguistic history. It contains: G. Harras, '(Sprach)Geschichte er-zählen' (21–32), discusses how linguistic history could be told; M. Bierwisch, 'Sprachgeschichte in der Wende' (33–41), is an account of the linguistic and political changes over the years and B.'s growing friendship for Hartmut Schmidt; W. U. Wurzel, 'Verläuft Sprachwandel gezielt?' (43–56), is an objective discussion of the principles of natural change showing how often there are several possibilities, and he comes to the conclusion that we do not know as much about the phenomenon as we might to like to think; U. Hass-Zumkehr, ' "Moderne Linguistik" versus "traditionelle Sprachwissenschaft" — Wörter, die Geschichte machen' (57–70), examines the collocation of these two adjectives and the use of the phrases in introductory books on linguistics. They have largely become slogans and what is needed is a fresh history of linguistics in the 20th c.; J. Dückert, '*Abenteuer*. Zur Neubearbeitung des Deutschen Wörterbuchs (= ²DWB)' (71–84), starts with H. Schmidt's entry for *Abenteuer* and gives a detailed account of the revision of the *Deutsches Wörterbuch*, especially during the *Wende* and beyond; J. Schildt, 'Entwicklungstendenzen im verbalen Bereich bei der Herausbildung der neuhochdeutschen Standardsprache' (85–90), exemplifies, using *brechen*, a trend for the different meanings of simple verbs to be replaced by prefixed forms; O. Vietze, 'Die sprachliche Leistung historischer Gartenbau-Texte' (91–110); H. Kämper, 'Europa-Formeln der frühen Nachkriegszeit' (111–22), examines the importance and continuity of collocations for discourse on national identity; K.-D. Ludwig, 'Archaisierung und Archaismenlexicographie' (123–36), argues for a dictionary of archaisms; while G. Stickel, 'Englisch-Amerikanisches in der heutigen deutschen Lexik und was die Leute davon halten' (137–49), examines the present-day attitude to English loans by lay people who are often critical of them, and urges linguists to tackle these, sometimes difficult, issues. Also noted: A. Mihm, 'Zur Deutung der graphematischen Variation in historischen Texten', *Fest. Löffler*, 367–88; W. Hoffmann, 'Inschriften und Sprachgeschichte: Anwendungsperspektive der "deutschen Inschriften" ', *ZDP*, 119 : 1–29.

On general Germanic matters: R. Schmidt-Wiegand, 'Harmscara. Missetat und Strafe in der germanischen Rechtssprachgeographie', *Fest. Munske*, 1–8, suggests that these terms were borrowed into the language of the Carolingian court and then obtained their specifically legal meaning; T. Vennemann, 'Germania Semitica: + plôg-/ + pleg-, + furh-/ + farh-, + folk-/ + flokk-, + felh-/ + folg-', *Fest. Eroms*, 245–62; A. Lahiri and B. E. Dresher, 'Open syllable lengthening in West Germanic', *Language*, 75, 1999 : 678–719; B. R. Page, 'The Germanic *Verschärfung* and prosodic change', *Diachronica*, 16, 1999 : 297–334; A. Bammesberger, 'Zur Etymologie von westgermanisch *beur-a-*', *Sprachwissenschaft*, 25 : 229–31; *Theodisca. Die Stellung althochdeutscher und altniederdeutscher Sprache und Literatur in der Kultur des frühen Mittelalters*, ed. F. Haubrichs et al., (Reallexikon der Germanischen Altertumskunde. Ergänzungsbände, 22), Berlin, de Gruyter, ix + 440 pp.

On Gothic: D. Fertig, 'Null subjects in Gothic', *AJGLL*, 12 : 3–21; G. W. Davis, 'Notes on the etymologies of English *big* and Gothic *ga-*', *ib.*, 41–52; P. M. Vogel, 'Persönliches und unpersönliches Passiv im Gotischen', *Fest. Munske*, 9–26, claims that the passive in Gothic tends to be promotional with accusative, dative, and genitive objects being promoted as well as having few true intransitive passives; N. B. Pimenova, 'Die semantische Distribution der gotischen Abstrakta auf *-ei* und *-itha*', *BGDSL*, 122 : 3–22.

On Old Saxon: C. M. Stephens, 'The derivational suffixes and suffixoids of Old Saxon: a panchronic approach to a linguistic category', *AJGLL*, 12 : 53–79; C. Arnett, 'A cognitive approach to the Old Saxon processual passive', *ib.*, 81–99.

On OHG: G. W. Davis, 'Rounding the corner: progress in Old High German linguistics at the turn of the century', *Diachronica*, 16, 1999 : 335–55. On OHG syntax: R. Lühr, 'Verallgemeinernde Relativsätze im Althochdeutschen', *Fest. Eroms*, 263–82; K. Donhauser, 'Negationssyntax im Althochdeutschen. Ein sprachhistorisches Rätsel und der Weg zu seiner Lösung', *ib.*, 283–98; F. Simmler, 'Makrostrukturen in der lateinisch-althochdeutschen Tatianbilingue', *ib.*, 299–336; J. Schwerdt, 'Zur Funktion der Parenthese bei Otfrid und im Heliand. Ein Beitrag zur historischen Syntax', *Fest. Mettke*, 317–54; P. Suchsland, '. . . *ibu dû mî ênan sagês, ik mî dê ôdre uuêt.* Zur Syntax des *Hildebrandliedes*: eine Fallstudie', *ib.*, 355–80; A. Bammesberger, 'Der Vokalismus von altenglisch *fersc* und althochdeutsch *frisk*', *Sprachwissenschaft*, 25 : 113–15.

On MLG: *Mittelniederdeutsches Wörterbuch*, vol. 2, fasc. 28, *prêdikanten-solt — quât*, cols 1665–1792.

On Middle High German and later: S. Weigelt, 'Die städtische Eisenacher Kanzlei um 1400 und die autographen Urkunden des Johannes Rothe', *Fest. Mettke*, 409–28; H.-P. Prell, 'Die Stellung des attributiven Genitivs im Mittelhochdeutschen. Zur Notwendigkeit einer Syntax mittelhochdeutscher Prosa', *BGDSL*, 122 : 23–39; C. Grolimund, ' "als ir uns verschriben hand": zur Kommunkationsform Brief am Beispiel der Basler Ratsbriefe im Spätmittelalter', *Fest. Löffler*, 279–98; I. Reiffenstein and H. Scheutz, 'Kausatives *tun* in mittelfränkischen Urkunden', *Fest. Eroms*, 337–50.

On Early NHG: *Besch Vol.* includes: G. Bellmann, 'Das "Exercitium puerorum grammaticale" (1485–1505)' (9–31); R. Bentzinger, 'Zur Erfurter Stadtsprache des Spätmittelalters. Vorüberlegungen zur Edition der Erfurter Historienbibeln des 15. Jahrhundert' (33–41); N. Berend, 'Konrad von Megenbergs "Buch der Natur" (1350):

schriftsprachliche Varianten im Deutsch des 14. Jahrhunderts als Ausdruck für regionales Sprachbewußtsein und dessen Reflexion' (43–58); R. Bergmann, 'Zur Herausbildung der deutschen Substantivgroßschreibung. Ergebnisse des Bamberg-Rostocker Projekts' (59–79); W. Besch, 'Zur sprachgeschichtlichen Rolle Luthers' (81–95); S. Grosse, 'Zum Deutschunterricht in den Sächsischen Fürsten- und Landesschulen' (97–109); W. Haas, 'Zweitsprachenerwerb und Herausbildung der Gemeinsprache — Petrus Canisius und das Deutsche seiner Zeit' (111–33); K. J. Mattheier, 'Siedlung oder Bildung? Überlegungen zu zwei Prinzipien im Prozeß der Entstehung des Neuhochdeutschen' (135–46); H. Nitta, Variantenreichtum und Polysemie — Konditionale Konjunktionen im Frühneuhochdeutschen' (147–59); R. Peters, 'Die Rolle des Niederdeutschen bei der Entstehung des Neuhochdeutschen' (161–73); S. Sonderegger, 'Die Vielschichtigkeit des Sprachbewußtseins in frühneuhochdeutscher Zeit' (175–208); C. Wells, 'Nicht-Lutherisches in der Orthographie der nach-Lutherschen Bibel- und Psalmenausgaben des 16. Jahrhunderts' (209–40); P. Wiesinger, 'Zur bairisch-oberdeutschen Schriftsprache des 16. und frühen 17. Jahrhunderts in Österreich unter dem Einfluß von Reformation und Gegenreformation' (241–73); and N. R. Wolf, 'Wort- und Begriffsbildung und ihre Rolle in der Ausbildung der deutschen Standardsprache' (275–86).

Another extensive volume on Early NHG is *Gesellschaft, Kommunikation und Sprache in der frühen Neuzeit*, ed. K. J. Mattheier et al., Munich, Iudicium, 1997, 316 pp., a result of European, chiefly German, and Japanese cooperation, with the following contributions: E. Skála, 'Zentrum und Peripherie in der Graphie der Lutherzeit' (11–22), which shows that 'Luther' forms are present in South German in the 13th and 14th cs; W. Besch, 'Wortschatzwandel in deutschen Bibeldrucken der frühen Neuzeit' (23–39), which examines the glossaries to Luther Bibles in the 17th c. and later; H. Nitta, 'Versuch einer textlinguistisch-pragmatischen Erforschung der Wortstellung des Frühneuhochdeutschen' (41–53), which examines the word order in 14th c. sermons that show many cases of paratactic constructions which may be due to the influence of the spoken language; Y. Kudo, ' "Du woltest kommen, vnd deine Hand auff sie legen." Zum Konjunktivischen Gebrauch von "wollen", "sollen" und "werden" in der Lutherbibel' (55–66), which uses the whole of the New Testament as a corpus and comes to the conclusion that Luther's language should be seen as the mid-point of a process of change, the use of *wollen* showing the most changes; M. Shigeto, 'Komplexe Verbformen in "Der Ackermann aus Böhmen" ' (67–82), wants to include functional verbs in his definition; K. Nakajima, 'Zum zweigliedrigen Verbalkomplex im eingeleiteten Nebensatz. Eine textsortenbezogene statistische Untersuchung der frühneuhochdeutschen Quellen' (83–99), which investigates Bavarian usage but concludes that it is difficult to be precise about trends; A. Fujii, 'Zur Augsburger Druckersprache im 15. Jahrhundert — Bericht über ein Projekt' (101–48), which flags up differences within the city, within printing firms, and within texts, using the works of two printing offices, G. Zainer and J. Bämler; Y. Kawasaki, 'Untersuchungen zur Entwicklung der Dentale im Niederdeutschen — Eine graphematische und phonematische Studie' (149–71), which concludes that it is not clear if there was final devoicing in Old Low German; R. Peters, 'Regionale Schreibsprachen oder normierte Hansesprache? Das Projekt "Atlas frühmittelniederdeutscher Schreibsprachen"' (173–86), which uncovers the myth of a uniform Hansa language; the atlas uses 57 localities and is building up a corpus of forms from documents of the 14th and 15th c. which he illustrates here from five localities; I. Rösler, 'Niederdeutsche Interferenzen und Alteranzen in hochdeutschen Verhörsprotokollen. Zum Problem des Erschließens gesprochener Sprache aus schriftlich überlieferten Texten' (187–202), which uses texts from Mecklenburg in the 16th and 17th cs; the new division of the legal process into investigation and trial led to more detailed written records; Low German was transposed into indirect speech in High German with some code-switching and interference; H. Takada, 'Grammatische Änderungen in den Drucken der Lutherbibel des 17. Jahrhunderts. Eine Pilotstudie' (203–24), which uses a wide range of Luther editions, tracing phonological and morphological developments, giving tables which show chronological development, mostly after the middle of the century; M. Papsonová, 'Zum Wortschatz deutschsprachiger Rechtsquellen aus dem Gebiet der Slowakei' (225–41), which uses legal sources to show how changes led to better comprehensibility; M. Ono, 'Zur Textstruktur der Trnavaer Testamente des Bürgertums aus der ersten Hälfte des 16. Jahrhunderts' (243–62), which examines 23 wills showing a similar seven-part structure; R. Metzler, 'Argumentative Strukturen in Chroniken des 16. Jahrhunderts' (263–78), which sees a rise in argumentative structures expressed through coordination and subordination; Y. Nishimoto, 'Zum Begriff "endannemung" in der Grammatik von Ch. Gueintz' (279–86), which expounds the meaning of this seemingly vague and opaque form which has a wide-ranging semantic application; N. Babenko, 'Vorreden des XVI. Jahrhunderts in soziokultureller und sprachgeschichtlicher Sicht' (287–99), which comes to the conclusion that these are a mixed type of text; and N. N. Semenjuk, 'Zur Sprache der ältesten deutschen Zeitungen aus dem XVII. Jahrhundert. Stilistische und lokale Schichtung im Wortschatz'

(301–16), which exemplifies the lexis as being dominated by nouns, especially loans, and characterized by features of both bookish and spoken language. A very wide-ranging book, although some of the contributions lack clear conclusions.

Also noted: T. Roelcke, 'Die frühneuhochdeutsche Brücke. Überlegungen zur sprachtypologischen Periodisierung der deutschen Sprachgeschichte', *ZDP*, 119 : 369–96; O. Ludwig, 'Valentin Ickelsamers Beitrag zum Deutschunterricht', *ZGL*, 28 : 23–40; N. Langer, 'Zur Verbreitung der *tun*-Periphrase im Frühneuhochdeutschen', *ZDL*, 67 : 287–316; A. Greule, 'Frühneuhochdeutsch in der Oberpfalz. Die Sprache des Gebenbacher Pfarrbuchs von 1418–1437', *Fest. Eroms*, 381–88; T. Fritz, 'Textstrukturen eines Briefes von Sebastian Brant an den Straßburger Rat', *ib.*, 369–80; G. Kettmann, 'Studien zur amtlichen Schriftlichkeit der Universität Wittenberg in der Reformationszeit (Annotationen zum Thema Universität und deutsche Sprache in der ersten Hälfte des 16. Jahrhunderts)', *Fest. Mettke*, 209–18; A. Lötscher, 'Verbendstellung im Hauptsatz in der deutschen Prosa des 15. und 16. Jahrhunderts', *Sprachwissenschaft*, 25 : 153–191.

On Luther: H. Wolf, 'Luthers spielerischer Umgang mit Spracheigenheiten anderer', *ZDL*, 67 : 148–67; T. A. Francis, 'The linguistic influence of Luther and the German language on the earliest complete Lutheran Bibles in Low German, Dutch, Danish, and Swedish', *SN*, 72 : 75–94. W. Besch, ' "[. . .] im Hochdeutschen veraltet, im gemeinen Leben noch jetzt üblich." Veraltender Wortschatz in der Lutherbibel', *Fest. Munske*, 27–42, studies five words, all of which are eventually replaced in revised editions, probably because they are regional and dialectal.

On the 17th c.: L. M. Eichinger, ' "Als ich aber im besten Thun war" — Verwendungsweisen des Verbs *tun* in H. J. Ch. von Grimmelshausens "Simplicius Simplicissimus" ', *Fest. Eroms*, 351–68; and M. Hundt, **'Spracharbeit' im 17. Jahrhundert, Studien zu Georg Philipp Harsdörffer, Justus Georg Schottelius und Christian Gueintz* (SLG, 57), xii + 499 pp.

On the 18th c.: J. Herrgen, **Die Sprache der Mainzer Republik (1792/93). Historisch-semantische Untersuchungen zur politischen Kommunikation* (RGL, 216), xv + 315 pp.; K.-P. Wegera, ' "Gen, oder wie Herr Gottsched will, chen." Zur Geschichte eines Diminutivsuffixes', *Fest. Munske*, 43–58, shows how *-gen* was gradually given up; H. Scheuringer, ' "Paßau, im Jäner" — Deutsche Wortgeschichte in lokaler Ausprägung', *Fest. Eroms*, 389–98; and K. Jakob, 'Zwischen Alltag und Institution. Antrags- und Beschwerdeschreiben am Ende des 19. Jahrhunderts', *Fest. Löffler*, 299–310.

Das 20. Jahrhundert. Sprachgeschichte — Zeitgeschichte, ed. H. Kämper and H. Schmidt, 1998, Berlin, de Gruyter, vi + 446 pp., contains the following: P. von Polenz, 'Vom Sprachimperialismus zum gebremsten Sprachstolz. Das 20. Jahrhundert in der sprachenpolitischen Geschichte der deutschsprachigen Länder' (9–26); J. Hörisch, ' "Seekrankheit auf festem Lande" — Zur Krise der Literatursprache' (27–42); S. Grosse, 'Lyrik und Linguistik' (43–58); D. Cherubim, 'Kontinuität und Diskontinuität in der deutschen Sprache des 20. Jahrhunderts' (59–85); H. Schmidt, 'Traditionen des Formulierens: Apposition, Triade, Alliteration, Variation' (86–117); F. Grucza, 'Aspekte des Deutschen aus polnischer Sicht' (118–36); V. Hinnenkamp, 'Mehrsprachigkeit in Deutschland und deutsche Mehrsprachigkeit. Szenarien einer migrationsbedingten Nischenkultur der Mehrsprachigkeit' (137–62); E. M. Jacobs and U. Püschel, 'Von der Duckstraße auf den Datenhighway' (163–87); W. Teubert, '*Eigentum, Arbeit, Naturrecht*. Schlüsselwörter der Soziallehre im Wandel' (188–224); U. Hass-Zumkehr, 'Die Weimarer Reichsverfassung — Tradition, Funktion, Rezeption' (225–49); G. Stötzel, 'Geschichtliche Selbstinterpretation im öffentlichen Sprachgebrauch seit 1945. Der Befreiungsdiskurs zum 8. Mai' (250–74); K. Ehlich, ' "...,LTI, LQI, ..." Von der Unschuld der Sprache und der Schuld der Sprechenden' (275–303); H. Kämper, 'Entnazifizierung — Sprachliche Existenzformen eines ethischen Konzepts' (304–29); and D. Herberg, 'Schlüsselwörter — Schlüssel zur Wendezeit' (330–44). Also noted: C. Schmitz-Berning, *Vokabular des Nationalsozialismus*, Berlin, de Gruyter, xlii + 710 pp.; H. Kämper, 'Sprachgeschichte — Zeitgeschichte. Die Tagebücher Victor Klemperers', *DSp*, 28 : 25–41; G. Stötzel, 'Zur Sprachgeschichte der letzten 50 Jahre', *Fest. Munske*, 375–90.

3. Orthography

This year sees the publication of the 22nd edition of *Duden 1. Die deutsche Rechtschreibung*, Mannheim, Dudenverlag, 1152 pp. which is also available on CD-ROM. As well as the 120,000 entries the volume contains instructions on using the dictionary, juxtaposition of old and new spellings, instructions on using e-mail, and numerous spelling rules. After the main body of the entries there is a full copy of the official spelling rules and as a tit-bit on the back inside cover there is a list of *Wörter* (from 1977) *und Unwörter* (1991) *des Jahres* to the present. Having it on CD-ROM also means that groups of words, e.g. those marked as English loans or Helvetecisms etc., can be produced at the touch of a button. There is no sign that the spelling reform has had an adverse effect on Duden. Also noted: A. M. Lasselsberger, **Die*

Kodifizierung der Orthographie im Rechtschreibwörterbuch. Eine Untersuchung zur Rechtschreibung im "Duden" und im "Österreichischen Wörterbuch" (RGL, 217), ix + 318 pp.; W. Scholze-Stubenrecht, 'Das morphematische Prinzip in der Umsetzung der Reform. Lexikographische Erfahrungen bei der Anwendung der neuen Rechtschreibregeln', *Sprachwissenschaft*, 25 : 143–51; W. Abraham, 'Deutsche Rechtschreibreform auf sprachwissenschaftlicher Grundlage? Zu sprachwissenschaftlich nicht legitimierten Teilen der Reform', *MGS*, 24, 1999 : 1–7; B. Primus, 'Suprasegmentale Graphemik und Phonologie: die Dehnungszeichen im Deutschen', *LBer*, 181 : 9–34; W. Sternefeld, 'Schreibgeminaten im Deutschen: ein Fall für die Optimalitätstheorie', *ib.*, 35–54; H.-W. Eroms, 'Die Neuregelung der *s*-Schreibung und die Prinzipien der deutschen Orthographie', *Fest. Munske*, 357–73, suggests that several principles overlap in this reform which will be greeted positively by foreign learners of German; however, is still undecided whether it will lead to easier writing; C. F. Földes, 'Die Neuregelung der deutschen Rechtschreibung im Kontext von Deutsch als Fremdsprache', *DaF*, 37 : 199–209; H. Ortner, **Schreiben und Denken* (RGL, 214), vii + 636 pp.; A. Schübel, 'Mit der Silbe besser rechtschreiben?', Thieroff, *Grammatik*, 13–28, argues that any additional help in the armoury of teaching orthography is welcome; C. Kustusch and B. Hufeisen, ' "Ich hätte gerne doppelt so lange Schreibunterricht . . .". Bericht über einen DSH-Schreibkurs am Computer', *DaF*, 37 : 144–48; and R. Faistauer, 'Schreiben in Gruppen — den Schreibprozess sichtbar machen. Ein Experiment aus der Lehrerfortbildung', *ib.*, 149–54.

On historical aspects of orthography: P. Eisenberg, ' "Ohne Beinkleider zu gehen, soll Leuten sehr dienlich sein, die sich verändern wollen." Georg Christoph Lichtenberg und die neue Ortokrafi', *Fest. Munske*, 59–68, shows how some of the discussion on orthographic reform reflects 18th c. discussions; D. Nerius, 'Rudolf von Raumer und die I. Orthographische Konferenz von 1876', *ib.*, 69–78, shows how von R. played an important role; Id., 'Die Bedeutung der II. orthographischen Konferenz (1901) in der Geschichte der deutschen Rechtschreibung', *ZDP*, 119 : 30–45; H. Günther, ' ". . . und hält den Verstand an" — Eine Etüde zur Entwicklung der deutschen Interpunktion 1522–1961', Thieroff, *Grammatik*, 275–86, using Bible extracts shows that punctuation was always determined by grammatical factors.

4. PHONOLOGY

Familar territory is covered in J. Schwerdt, **Die 2. Lautverschiebung* (Jenaer germanistische Forschungen, n.F., 8), Heidelberg, Winter,

396 pp. T. B. Klein, *"Umlaut" in Optimality Theory. A Comparative Analysis of German and Chamorro* (LA, 416), vii + 152 pp.; R. Smith, 'Testing compensatory theories of umlaut', *LB*, 88, 1999 : 133–51. Contrastive studies are: T. Berg and J. Niemi, 'Syllabification in Finnish and German. Onset filling vs. onset maximization', *JPh*, 28 : 187–216; R. Bannert and J. Schwitalla, 'Äußerungssegmentierung in der deutschen und schwedischen gesprochenen Sprache', *DSp*, 27, 1999 : 314–35; and U. Gut, **Bilingual Acquisition of Intonation. A Study of Children Speaking German and English* (LA, 424), x + 180 pp. Intonation is the subject of E. Stock, 'Zur Intonation des Schweizerhochdeutschen', *Fest. Munske*, 299–314, whose chief concern is the typical *Tonhöhenverlauf* which is a cliché but which seems to depend on the situational use of language; M. Selting, 'Berlinische Intonationskonturen: der Springton', *DSp*, 28 : 193–231. Also noted: K. Reinke, 'Ein Babylon der Emotionen? Das Problem der kultur- und sprachenübergreifenden Erforschung der phonetischen Emotionssignale', *DaF*, 37 : 67–72; R. Regina, 'Selbst gesteuerter Ausspracheerwerb via Multimedia. Lerntheoretische und fertigkeitsbezogene Anforderungen an multimediale Lernumgebungen', *ib.*, 73–81; W. König, 'Wenn sich Theorien ihre Wirklichkeit selbst schaffen: zu einigen Normen deutscher Aussprachewörterbücher', *Fest. Löffler*, 87–98; G. Zimmermann, 'Idealistische und naturalistische Bühnensprechstile im Zeitraum von Goethe bis Reinhardt', *ZGL*, 28 : 207–22; B. Höhle and J. Weissenborn, 'Lauter Laute? Lautsegmente und Silben in der Sprachperzeption und im Spracherwerb', *Thieroff, Grammatik*, 1–11, discuss how children perceive primarily rhythmic units and not sounds; not until an alphabet is learned do they distinguish between sound segments; G. Klasmeyer, **Akustische Korrelate des stimmlich emotionalen Ausdrucks in der Lautsprache* (Forum Phoneticum, 67), Frankfurt, Hector, 1999, x + 238 pp.

5. Morphology

The concept of the word is examined by W. U. Wurzel, 'Was ist ein Wort?', *Thieroff, Grammatik*, 29–42, who devises a scale whereby one can distinguish words, semi-words, and phrases; R. Raffelsiefen, 'Evidence for word-internal phonological words in German', *ib.*, 43–56, uses prosodic arguments to support the claim that a word can consist of several phonological words; and G. Smith, 'Word remnants and coordination', *ib.*, 57–68, examines when they can be grammatically relevant.

Inflectional morphology in its historical aspect finds coverage in D. Fertig, *Morphological change up close* (LA, 422), ix + 179 pp. F. examines texts from Nuremberg between 1356 and 1619. After a discussion of theoretical issues of morphology and analogy he proceeds to the quantitative analysis of variation and change in inflectional endings, stem-vowel alternations, inflectional class transfer and the prefix *ge-*. F. is concerned to try and correlate variation where possible with extralinguistic features. In many cases he has to draw a blank but one important variable is education. There is in some instances a distinction between the usages of Chancery scribes and other male administrators on the one hand and women writers on the other. There are a wide range of examples whose analysis makes interesting reading but the picture that emerges is that linguistic change is extremely complex and often unclear. For instance in one period *gewesen* predominates, then in the next *gewest* and later again *gewesen*. In other cases, a change, e.g. of *eu* (MHG *iu*) to *ie*, seems governed by individual verb forms. There is an alphabetical verb frequency list as well as samples of the coding of the verbs in the corpus. In general this is an interesting and stimulating book.

Derivational morphology has been extensively written about this year. B. Naumann, *_Einführung in die Wortbildungslehre des Deutschen_, 2nd edn, Tübingen, Niemeyer, ix + 90 pp., is a new edition of a work on word formation; while a completely new work is L. M. Eichinger, *_Deutsche Wortbildung_, Tübingen, Narr, 260 pp. Also noted: W. U. Dressler and M. Ladányi, 'Productivity in word formation (WF): a morphological approach', *ALH*, 47 : 103–44; W. U. Wurzel, 'Morphological properties in the lexicon: diachronic evidence', *ib.*, 345–56; R. Sadzinski, 'Generierungsoffene Verarbeitung deutscher Nominalkomposita als lexikographische Aufgabe', *Fest. Eroms*, 215–22; R. Hinderling, '"Huckepackformen" in der deutschen Gegenwartssprache', *ib.*, 223–33; S. Vandermeeren, 'Semantische Analyse deutscher Substantivkomposita. Drei Untersuchungsmethoden im Vergleich', *LB*, 88, 1999 : 69–94; N. Fuhrhop, 'Zeigen Fugenelemente die Morphologisierung von Komposita an?', Thieroff, *Grammatik*, 201–13, claims that linking elements are a sign in the re-analysis of syntactic elements of the general tendency to morphologize compounds.

Fest. Munske contains the following contributions on word formation: M. Habermann, 'Fremde Wortbildungselemente in deutschen Grammatiken des 17. bis 19. Jahrhunderts' (79–102); R. Bergmann, 'Zum Problem der Produktivität europäischer Wortbildung im Deutschen' (103–14); P. O. Müller, 'Deutsche Fremdwortbildung. Probleme der Analyse und der Kategorisierung' (115–34); H. Schmidt, 'Hochkomplexe Lexeme: Wortbildung und Traditionen des Formulierens' (135–58), deals with the fashionable stringing together of several elements; N. R. Wolf, 'Motion im (Kon-)Text' (159–70), treats some of the difficulties of designating female beings;

J. Erben, '*Befindlichkeit* — Bemerkungen zur Wortbildung, Semantik und pragmatischen Sprachgeschichte' (171–79), outlines the context of the rise of this fashionable word. The contributions on the foreign element in German word formation in this volume are especially to be welcomed. Also noted on inflectional morphology: D. Nübling, **Prinzipien der Irregularisierung. Eine kontrastive Analyse von zehn Verben in zehn germanischen Sprachen* (LA, 415), xi + 338 pp.; and D. Fertig, 'Analogical "leveling" from outside the paradigm: stem-vowel changes in the German modals', *Diachronica*, 16, 199 : 233–60.

Praxis- in Inegrationsfelder der Wortbildungsforschung, ed. I. Barz et al. (Sprache — Literatur und Geschichte, 18), Heidelberg, Winter, 350 pp., is dedicated entirely to word formation and includes: G. Augst, 'Die Mächtigkeit der Wortfamilien — Quantitative Auswertungen zum "Wortfamilienwörterbuch der deutschen Gegenwartssprache"' (1–18); H. Bergenholtz, 'Lexikographie und Wortbildungsforschung' (19–30); I. Hyvärin, 'Zur Wortbildung in einem deutsch-finnischen Großwörterbuch im Werden — Probleme der Lemmatisierung von Wortbildungselementen' (31–54); L. Kolehmainen, 'Deutsche Präfixe bzw. Partikelverben und finnischdeutsche Lexikographie' (55–90); M. Schröder, 'Kurzwörter im Wörterbuch. Lexikographische Aspekte der Kurzwortbildung' (91–105); J. Splett, 'Wortgeschichte und Wortstrukturgeschichte' (107–30); S. Bračič, 'Fremdsprachendidaktische Aspekte der Wortbildungs und des Wortgebrauchs im Text' (131–43); L. M. Eichinger, 'Verstehen und Spaß haben. Wortbildung im literarischen Text' (145–58); J. Erben, 'Wortbildungsstrukturen und Textverständlichkeit' (159–66); U. Fix, 'Urteile über Wörter. Kriterien für die Bewertung von Wortbildungsprodukten in Stilistiken und Stillehren' (167–86); E. Hallsteinsdóttir, 'Aspekte des Verstehens okkasioneller Wortbildungsprodukte in der Fremdsprache Deutsch' (187–97); H. Poethe, 'Fachsprachliche Aspekte der Wortbildung. Die Leistung der Wortbildung für Fachsprache und Fachtext' (199–218); M. Thurmair, 'Vergleich in der Wortbildung' (219–38); C. Playten, '*Köpi, Kelts* und *Knusperone* — Morpheme in den Zeiten der Marktwirtschaft' (239–51); G. Schuppener, 'Entlehnung deutscher Maßbezeichnungen ins Tschechische' (253–67); A. Simečka, 'Akzeptanzbedingungen für fremde Wortbildungselemente und -strukturen in den Sprachen. Am Material des Deutschen und des Tschechischen' (269–80); H. Wellmann, 'Deutsche Wortbildung in europäischen Bezügen — Auswertung einer Bibliographie zur historischen Wortbildung' (281–98); I. Barz, 'Zum heutigen Erkenntnisinteresse germanistischer Wortbildungsforschung. Ein exemplarischer Bericht' (299–316); and Id. and M. Schröder, 'Bibliographie zur Wortbildung der deutschen Gegenwartssprache (1990–2000)' (317–50). This volume covers a number of separate themes, including how word formation can be covered in dictionaries, in actual textual usage as well as in teaching German as a foreign language. To a lesser extent borrowing also figures. The bibliographical contributions are very valuable. All in all an excellent book for all fans of word formation.

Also noted: V. D. Kaliuscenko, **Typologie denominaler Verben* (LA, 419), xi + 255 pp.; E. Donalies, 'Das Konfix. Zur Definition einer zentralen Einheit der deutschen Wortbildung', *DSp*, 28 : 144–59; M. Kinne, **Die Präfixe post, prä- und neo-. Beiträge zur Lehn-Wortbildung* (SDSp, 18), xiv + 391 pp.; I. Nortmeyer, **Die Präfixe inter- und trans-. Beiträge zur Lehn-Wortbildung* (SDSp, 19), 456 pp.; O. Siebold, **Wort — Genre — Text. Wortneubildungen in der Science Fiction*, Tübingen, Narr, 300 pp.; A. Steinhauer, **Sprachökonomie durch Kurzwörter. Bildung und Verwendung in der Fachkommunikation* (FF, 56), 380 pp., and R. Bergmann, 'Historische Wortbildungslehre und historische Lexikographie. Beobachtungen zu den *er-* Verben anhand der Neubearbeitung des "Deutschen Wörterbuch"', *Fest. Eroms*, 399–410.

S. Strecker, *Substantivbildung durch Suffixableitung um 1800. Untersucht an Personenbezeichnungen in der Sprache Goethes* (Germanistische Bibliothek, 6), Heidelberg, Winter, x + 714 pp. + CD-ROM, is a major work which presents just a small fraction of an enormous corpus. S. outlines the state of research on historical word formation, not extensive in recent years but growing, then presents a detailed account of the corpus. Goethe rivals Luther in the volume of relevant examples that he produced. S. next outlines and clarifies her terminology, particularly for loan formations, for that is an area where Goethe shows a clear difference from earlier writers. The corpus is then analysed from two points of view: the morphological-semantic aspect, and the onomasiological-functional aspect. Both of these could be abbreviated to form and meaning. Goethe uses 31 suffixes which designate people of which about 20 are foreign but only 12 of them occur in 50 lexemes or more. Finally the results are compared with those from previous periods of the language and their productivity examined. The order of frequency of suffixes is very similar to that in NHG, with *-er* being the most frequent. There are plenty of clear tables and diagrams to illustrate the processes which make this a book that is easy to consult. This has set a high benchmark for studies in historical word formation.

6. SYNTAX

A number of articles on syntax are contained in *Fest. Eroms*: J.-M. Zemb, 'Von einem Grammatiker, der auszog, das Definieren zu lernen' (2–20); J.-F. Marillier, '"sein/haben + P2": Morphologie oder Syntax? Oder: das deutsche Perfekt revidiert' (21–34); W. Abraham and A. Fischer, 'Das grammatische Optimalisierungsszenario von *tun* als Hilfsverb' (35–48);J. O. Askedal, 'Satzmustervariation und Hilfsverbproblematik beim deutschen Verb *scheinen*' (49–74); M. van de Velde, 'Nominales Subjekt und pronominales Objekt im Mittelfeld' (75–92); N. R. Wolf, 'Metakommunikative Nebensätze im Vorfeld' (93–100); and G. Helbig, 'Plädoyer für Satzarten' (121–36). Thieroff, *Grammatik*, includes the following: H. Wegener, '*Da, denn* und *weil* — der Kampf der Konjunktionen. Zur Grammatikalisierung im kausalen Bereich' (68–81); C. Fabricius-Hansen, 'Die Geheimnisse der deutschen *würde*-Konstruktion' (83–96); O. Leirbukt, 'Passivähnliche Bildungen mit *haben/wissen/sehen* + Partizip II in modalen Kontexten' (97–109); L. Gunkel, 'Selektion verbaler Komplemente. Zur Syntax der Halbmodal- und Phasenverben' (111–21); A. Ijbema and W. Abraham, 'Die syntaktische Funktion des infinitivischen *zu*' (123–37); B. Wiese, 'Warum Flexionsklassen? Über die deutsche Substantivdeklination' (139–53); K.-M. Köpcke, 'Starkes, Schwaches und Gemischtes in der Substantivflexion des Deutschen. Was weiß der Sprecher über Deklinationsparadigmen? (155–70); O. Teuber, 'Gibt es zwei Genitive im Deutschen?' (171–83); H. Vater, '"Pronomantien" — oder: Pronomina sind Determinantien' (185–99); M. Reis, 'Anmerkungen zu Verb-erst-Satz-Typen im Deutschen' (215–27); E. König and P. Siemund, 'Zur Rolle der Intensifikatoren in einer Grammatik des Deutschen' (229–45); W. Dieckmann et al., '"Satzarten" in Gebrauchsgrammatiken des Deutschen' (247–61); and D. Rösler, 'Zur Beschreibung und Vermittlung erweiterter Partizipialattribute' (263–74). The volume has a nice spread in the contributions on syntax between the verb, noun, and sentence, and is very well produced with clear diagrams and tables.

Also noted: E. Diehl et al., *Grammatikunterricht: Alles für der Katz? Untersuchungen zum Zweitsprachenerwerb Deutsch* (RGL, 220), xx + 412 pp.

Word classes are the subject of M. Hundt, '*Deutschlands meiste Kreditkarte* — Probleme der Wortartenklassifikation', *DSp*, 28 : 1–24; G. Rauh, 'Wi(e)der die Wortarten! Zum Problem linguistischer Kategorisierung', *LBer*, 184 : 485–507. Minor word classes are treated in: M. T. Rolland, 'Die Konjunktionen im Deutschen', *WW*, 50 : 109–18; Id., 'Die Präpositionen im Deutschen. Flexionsbezug und Wortart', *ib.*, 297–302; G. Zifonun, '"Man lebt nur einmal." Morphosyntax und Semantik des Pronomens *man*', *DSp*, 28 : 232–53; and G. Helbig, 'Zur Binnengliederung der Fügewörter im Deutschen', *DaF*, 37 : 210–16.

The noun phrase and its members are treated in: E. Leiss, **Artikel und Aspekt. Die grammatischen Muster von Definitheit* (SLG, 55), viii + 309 pp.; B. Sandberg, 'Zur Distribution *Friede — Frieden* nach semanto-syntaktischen Variablen', *Sprachwissenschaft*, 25 : 119–142; A. Rowley, '*Eine Bier, die Herz* und *das Wurm*. Scheinbare Genusabweichung in gesprochener Alltagssprache, *Muttersprache*, 109, 1999 : 331–38; G. Helbig, 'Die Kasus — gestern und heute', *DaF*, 37 : 10–21; D. Hole and G. Klumpp, 'Definite type and indefinite token: the article *son* in colloquial German', *LBer*, 182 : 231–44. Valency is covered in V. Ágel, **Theorien der Valenz: Überblick, Orientierung, Entwicklung*, Tübingen, Narr, 300 pp.; S. Engelberg, *Verben, Ereignisse und das Lexikon* (LA, 413), viii + 360 pp.; and I. Hyvärin, 'Valency and Konstruktion', *NMi*, 101 : 185–207. Facets of the verb are the subject of M. Hennig, *Tempus und Temporalität in geschriebenen und gesprochenen Texten* (LA, 421), ix + 211 pp.; L. M. Eichinger, 'Eine Welt aus Wörtern', *Fest. Munske*, 181–98; G. Diewald, '*Scheinen* als Faktizitätsmarker', *ib.*, 333–55; R. Kozmová, 'Zur Darstellung des deutschen Tempussystems für Deutsch als Fremdsprache', *DaF*, 37 : 87–92; W. Klein, 'An analysis of the German Perfekt', *Language*, 76 : 358–82; M. Kammerer, **Lemmazeichentypen für deutsche Verben* (Lexicographica Series Maior, 104), Tübingen, Niemeyer, 420 pp.; W. Abraham, 'Das Perfektpartizip seine angebliche Passivbedeutung im Deutschen', *ZGL*, 28 : 141–66; and M. Wratil, 'Die Syntax des Imperativs', *LBer*, 181 : 71–118.

Other word classes feature in W. Timmermann, 'Zeitadverbiale — Vielfalt mit System', *DaF*, 37 : 155–62; G. Müller, 'Das Pronominaladverb als Reparaturphänomen', *LBer*, 182 : 139–78; M. Bader et al., 'Syntaktische Funktions-Ambiguitäten im Deutschen — Ein Überblick', *ZS*, 19 : 34–102; K.-E. Sommerfeldt, 'Zum Problem der Modalwörter im Deutschen', *WW*, 50 : 100–08.

Also noted: T. Oya, 'Er bettelt sich durchs Land — Eine *one's way*-Konstruktion im Deutschen', *DSp*, 27, 1999 : 356–69; G. Diewald, 'Grammatikalisierung: hier entsteht die Grammatik?', *DUS*, 52 : 28–40; H. W. Eroms, 'Kurzer und langer Satz', *DUS*, 52 : 29–37; W. Köller, 'Konjunktionen und konjunktionale Verkettungen von Aussagen', *ib.*, 38–47; I. Paul, '"Satzarten" im Lernbereich: Reflexion über Sprache', *ib.*, 48–57; R. Funke, 'Wann ist grammatisches Wissen in Funktion?', *ib.*, 56–68; T. Schmid, 'Die Ersatzinfinitivkonstruktion im Deutschen', *LBer*, 183 : 325–51; F. Heck, 'Tiefenoptimierung: deutsche Wortstellung als wettbewerbgesteuerte Basisgenerisierung', *ib.*, 184 : 441–68; N. Frank, 'Probleme lexikalischer Selektion und abhängige Verbzweitsätze', *ib.*, 469–83; and J. O. Askedal, 'Satzarten-Differenzierung und Sprecherwechsel in "berichteter Rede"', *SN*, 72 : 181–89.

Language   583

Contrastive studies include: J.-K. Cho, 'Vergleichende Analyse der Infinitivkonstruktionen und verwandter Ausdrucksformen im Deutschen und im Koreanischen', *DSp*, 28 : 160–90; and H. Blühdorn, 'Zur Verwendung einiger Transportverben im Deutschen und im brasilianischen Portugiesisch', *IRAL*, 38 : 261–78. U. Demske, *Merkmale und Relationen. Diachrone Studien zur Nominalphrase im Deutschen* (SLG, 56), 352 pp. *Fest. Valentin* is dedicated to synchronic and diachronic studies on the noun phrase: J. O. Askedal, 'Periodenumfang und Nominalisierungshäufigkeit in älterer und neuerer deutscher philosophischer Sprache' (9–26); J. Riecke, 'Beobachtungen zur Syntax und Semantik der Nominalgruppe in mittelalterlichen medizinischen Texten' (27–39); H. U. Schmid, '*baldlîhho sprehhan* > *baldlîhhiu wort.* Adjektive auf *-lîh* in abgeleiteten Nominalgruppen im Althochdeutschen' (41–51); R. Lühr, 'Zur Wortstellung in der althochdeutschen komplexen Nominalgruppe: Die Stellung von Quantoren' (53–69); M. Krause, 'Binnenstruktur temporaler Nominalgruppen im Akkusativ und Genitiv' (71–97); F. Simmler, 'Zur morphologischen Struktur der prä- und postnuklearen Adjektivattribute und ihrer Funktionalität in der Geschichte der deutschen Sprache vom 16. bis 18. Jahrhundert' (99–177); J. Haudry, 'Zur Vorgeschichte der Artikel in den germanischen Sprachen' (179–85); E. Glaser, 'Zur Verwendung des Artikels in den althochdeutschen Glossen' (187–212); Y. Desportes, 'Artikel im Mittelhochdeutschen: lässt sich Paul Valentins Modell des Artikelsystems im heutigen Deutsch auf das Mittelhochdeutsche übertragen?' (213–53); E. Oubozar, 'Zur Entwicklung von ein in der Nominalgruppe des Althochdeutschen' (255–68), and O. Schneider-Mizony, 'Erweitertes Attribut versus Relativsatz in der zweiten Hälfte des 15. Jahrhunderts' (269–79). The contributions are characterized by judicious use of text corpora for the historical studies. Other historical studies include: J. Sabel, 'Das Verbstellungsproblem im Deutschen: Synchronie und Diachronie', *DSp*, 28 : 74–99; M. L. Kotin, 'Das Partizip II in hochdeutschen periphrastischen Verbalfügingen im 9.–15. Jh. Zur Ausbildung des analytischen Sprachbaus', *ZGL*, 28 : 319–46; H. U. Schmid, 'Die Ausbildung des *werden*-Futurs. Überlegungen auf der Grundlage mittelalterlicher Endzeitprophezeiungen', *ZDL*, 67 : 6–27.

7. SEMANTICS

General semantic considerations are discussed in G. Harras, 'Jenseits von semantischen Konventionen — zum Beispiel: tautologische Äußerungen', *ZGL*, 27, 1999 : 1–12; A. D. Oguy, 'Probleme der experimentellen Erforschung der Wortbedeutung. Überblick über

Polysemieuntersuchungen', *Sprachwissenschaft*, 22, 1998 : 113–40; A. Kertész, 'Kognitive Semantik als naturalisierte Wissenschaftstheorie', *PapL*, 59, 1998 : 107–36; I. Warncke, 'Wortartenübergreifende lexikalische Kategorien — Prototypensemantik vs. Merkmalsemantik', *Spillmann Vol.*, 223–40; *Räumliche *Konzepte und sprachliche Strukturen*, ed. C. Habel and C. von Stutterheim (LA, 417), vii + 282 pp.; B. Löbach, **Semantikerwerb. Ein Beitrag zu einer empiristisch-naturalistischen Bedeutungstheorie* (LA, 423), vii + 217 pp.; G. Kurtz, 'Zur Vermittlung des sprachlichen Ausdrucks logischer Beziehungen', *DaF*, 37 : 97–103; C. Maienborn, 'Zustände — Stadien — stative Ausdrücke: zur Semantik und Pragmatik von Kopula-Prädikativ-Konstruktionen', *LBer*, 183 : 271–307; E. Lavric, *'folgender, obiger, letzter, besagter, fraglicher, selbiger, ebendieser*. Referenzsemantische Verschrobenheiten', *DSp*, 27, 1999 : 69–94; A. D. Oguy, 'Approximativ-quantitative Charakteristika der Polysemie', *Sprachwissenschaft*, 24, 1999 : 75–103; and J. Chur, 'Inclusive opposition und lückenhafte Wortfelder', *Fest. Vater*, 353–66.

On phraseology: H. Bürger, **Phraseologie. Eine Einführung am Beispiel des Deutschen* (Grundlagen der Germanistik, 36), Berlin, Schmidt, 1998, 224 pp.; M.-A., Cheon, **Zur Konzeption eines phraseologischen Wörterbuchs für den Fremdsprachenunterricht. Am Beispiel Deutsch-Koreanisch* (Lexicographica. Series Maior, 89), Tübingen, Niemeyer, 1998, ix + 180 pp.; G. Gréciano, 'Fachphraseologie', *Fest. Faucher*, 183–95; **Phraseologismen in Text und Kontext. Phrasemata I*, ed. J. Wirrer (Bielefelder Schriften zu Linguistik und Literaturwissenschaft, 11), Bielefeld, Aisthesis, 1998, 253 pp.; H. Burger, 'Konzepte von "Variation" in der Phraseologie', *Fest. Löffler*, 35–52; H.-U. Dietz, **Rhetorik in der Phraseologie. Zur Bedeutung rhetorischer Stilelemente im idiomatischen Wortschatz des Deutschen* (RGL, 205), 1999, xi + 422 pp.

A big event of 1999 was the publication of the third edition of *Duden Das große Wörterbuch der deutschen Sprache*, Mannheim, Dudenverlag, 10 vols, 4800 pp. In addition to the vast word-hoard and usual instructions for use there are some additional features, including the following articles: H. Heckmann, 'Sprechen wir in der Zunkunft noch Deutsch?', I, 9–13 (H. also gives at the end of vol. 10 the rules of German spelling); J. A. Bär, 'Die Geschichte der deutschen Sprache. Ein Abriss', and finally a short word history of 30 'words of the century', from *Autobahn* to *Urknall*. All in all a feast for philologists.

Lexicographical studies also include: **Wörterbücher in der Diskussion* IV. Vorträge aus dem Heidelberger Lexikographischen Kolloquium, ed. H. E. Wiegand (Lexicographica Series Maior, 100), Tübingen, Niemeyer, vi + 372 pp.; M. Schwarz, **Indirekte Anaphern in Texten. Studien zur domänengebundenen Referenz und Kohärenz im Deutschen* (LA,

413), ix + 175 pp.; W. Müller, *Das Gegenwort-Wörterbuch. Ein Kontrastwörterbuch mit Gebrauchshinweisen*, Berlin, de Gruyter, xxxviii + 580 pp.; M. Schulz, 'Zur Eignung von älteren Wörterbüchern und Wörterbuchvergleichen für eine Analyse von Wortschatz und dessen Wandel', *Sprachwissenschaft*, 25 : 63–75; K. Casemir, 'Zur Digitalisierung des Deutschen Wörterbuches von Jacob und Wilhelm Grimm, *ib.*, 77–102; W. Teubert, 'Korpuslinguistik und Lexikographie', *DSp*, 27, 1999 : 292–313; C. Földes and P. Uzonyi, 'Großwörterbücher mit Deutsch als Ausgangs- bzw. Zielsprache: zur Problemlage in der Relation Deutsch-Ungarisch und Ungarisch-Deutsch', *ib.*, 336–355; K. Steyer, 'Usuelle Wortverbindungen des Deutschen. Linguistisches Konzept und lexikographische Möglichkeiten', *ib.*, 28 : 101–25; A. Abel, 'Das lexikographische Beispiel in der L2–Lexikographie (am Beispiel eines L2–Kontext- und Grundwortschatzwörterbuches)', *DaF*, 37 : 163–69; H. Kämper, 'Wörterbuch und Literatur. Fragen und Gedanken (nicht nur) zur Neubarbeitung des "Großen Wörterbuchs der deutschen Sprache in acht Bänden" ', *Muttersprache*, 109, 1999 : 24–42; A. Neudeck, 'Spuren der Wortschatzentwicklung im Rechtschreibduden. Eine Betrachtung getilgter Lemmata', *ib.*, 157–74; U. Hass-Zumkehr, **Deutsche Wörterbücher — Brennpunkt von Sprach- und Kulturgeschichte*, Berlin, de Gruyter, 256 pp.; M. Schlaefer, 'Zur Darstellung wortgeschichtlicher Zusammenhänge des 17. bis 20. Jahrhunderts in historischen Wörterbüchern', *Sprachwissenschaft*, 25, 1999 : 195–220; R. Bergmann, '*Projekt* und *Projektmacher*. Ein Beispiel für lexikographische Benutzerinteressen und lexikographische Befunde', *ib.*, 337–60; M. Schulz, 'Der lexikographische Informationsgehalt in älteren Bedeutungswörtbüchern. Zugleich Überlegungen zum Nutzen einer Retrodigitalisierung älterer Wörterbücher', *ib.*, 24, 1998 : 47–73; C. Fraas and U. Hass-Zumkehr, 'Vom Wörterbuch zum lexikalischen Informationssystem LEXXIS — ein neues Projekt des Instituts für deutsche Sprache', *DSp*, 27, 1999 : 289–303.

An excellent bilingual dictionary is *Duden Oxford. Großwörterbuch Englisch. Deutsch-Englisch, Englisch-Deutsch*, 2nd edn, Mannheim, Dudenverlag, 1999, 1740 pp., which sets out every word and its meaning(s) very clearly. Technical language is well represented.

The thinking and influences behind Friedrich Kluge's approach to etymology are treated in R. K. Bloomer, 'Rudolf Hildebrand's impression on Friedrich Kluge', *AJGLL*, 12 : 23–39.

On borrowing: A. Topalova, 'Die Germanismen in der bulgarischen Sprache', *Muttersprache*, 109, 1999 : 54–59; G. Hentschel, 'Zur Komplexität deutsch-"jüdisch"-slavischer Lehnkontakte. Über eine deutsches oder auch nicht-deutsches ("jüdisches") Lehnwort im Polnischen und Russischen: *blat'*, *Fest. Szulc*, 87–117. The concept of internationalisms is the chief subject of P. Eisenberg, 'Stirbt das Deutsche an den Internationalismen? Zur Integration von Computerwörtern', *DUS*, 3, 1999 : 17–24; M. Habermann, 'Latein — "Muttersprache Europas". Zum Einfluss des Lateinischen auf den Wortschatz europäischer Sprachen', *ib.*, 25–37; B. Schaeder, 'Internationalismen im Bereich der Fachsprache der Grammatik — am Beispiel der Wortarten', *ib.*, 38–49; and I. Philipper, ' "Ist Pizza eigentlich ein Internationalismus?" Internationalismen in den Lebensbereichen Mode, Musik, neue Medien', *ib.*, 72–80. Loan words are included in *Deutsches Fremdwörterbuch*, 2nd edn, ed. G. Strauss et al., vol. 3, *Baby* — *Cutter*, Berlin, de Gruyter, 1997, xiii + 852 pp.; vol. 4, *da capo* — *Dynastie*, 1999, xii + 971 pp.; K. Dietz, 'Sind engl. *beer* und dt. *Bier* Erb- oder Lehnwörter?', *Sprachwissenschaft*, 25 : 103–11; U. Schröter, 'Akademie und seine Wortverbindungen'. Zur Etymologie eines Internationalismus und zur Geschichte seiner Semantik sowie seiner Syntagmen speziell im Deutschen', *LB*, 88, 1999 : 113–31; G. Zifonun, 'Grammatische Integration jugendsprachlicher Anglizismen' *DUS*, 52 : 69–79; H. Boková and H. Lukásová, 'Die Widerspiegelung älterer deutscher Sprachperioden im tschechischen Wortschatz', *Fest. Mettke*, 39–48; W. J. Jones, **German Lexicography in the European Context. A Descriptive Bibliography of Printed Dictionaries and Word Lists Containing German language (1600–1700)* (SLG, 58), lx + 754 pp.

Contrastive studies include: C. Di Meola, 'Der Besitzwechsel als metaphorisches Modell der Zustandsveränderung. Deutsche und italienische Beispiele', *Fest. Vater*, 367–86.

Studies on individual words and phrases include: J. Goossens, 'Mandel', *Fest. Stellmacher*, 317–21; H. Fleischer, 'Suggestivkraft einer Formel: *der real existierende Sozialismus*', *Muttersprache*, 109, 1999 : 148–55; R. Métrich and G. Courdier, 'Die Zukunft des Menschen *aber* ist immer so lang wie seine Vergangenheit', *Fest. Faucher*, 275–97; A. Rousseau, '*Als* und *wie*: semantische Operatoren in den Nominalgruppen. Ein Beitrag zur "natürlichen" Logik', *ib.*, 315–35: H. Scheuer, ' "Sozialaristokratie" — Zur politischen Semantik eines Begriffs im "Kulturkampf" der 1890er Jahre', *Spillmann Vol.*, 211–22; S. Tanaka, 'Wir waren auch dabei. — Wir waren nur dabei?: *auch* als Topikpartikel', *Sprachwissenschaft*, 25 : 1–19, and I. Rapp and A. von Stechow, '*Fast* "almost" and the visibility parameter for functional adverbs', *JSem*, 16, 1999 : 149–204.

Also noted: J. Meibauer, 'Raum und Zeit am Rand und bei', *Fest. Vater*, 413–26; G. Radden, 'Metaphorisierte Zeit', *ib.*, 427–42.

On semantic learning: R. Freudenberg-Findeisen, 'Feldergrammatik als inhaltlich orientierte. (Lerner)Grammatik — dargestellt am Feld des Wünschens', *DaF*, 37 : 22–29; P. Ecke and C. J. Hall,

'Lexikalische Fehler in Deutsch als Drittsprache. Translexikalischer Einfluss auf drei Ebenen der mentalen Repräsentation', *ib.*, 30–36; I. Hyvärinen, 'Zur leitmotivischen Lexik in Günter Grass' Erzählung "Unkenrufe" und der finnischen Übersetzung "Kellosammakon huuto"', *Fest. Eroms*, 303–14. Also noted: R. Keller and I. Kirschbaum, 'Bedeutungswandel', *DUS*, 52 : 41–53.

8. DIALECTS

M. Gerritsen, 'Divergence of dialects in a linguistic laboratory near the Belgian-Dutch-German border. Similar dialects under the influence of different standard languages', *LVC*, 11, 1999 : 43–65. R. Berthele, **Sprache in der Klasse. Eine dialektologisch-soziolinguistische Untersuchung* (RGL, 212), xxi + 310 pp. H. Klausmann, 'Changes of dialect, code-switching, and new kinds of usage: the divergence of dialects along the border between Germany and France in and around the region of the Oberrhein', *IJSL*, 145 : 109–30.

H. Spiekermann, *Silbenschnitt in deutschen Dialekten* (LA, 425), viii + 239 pp., is a detailed phonetic and phonological work. S.'s survey covers a good network of dialects, including some from East Prussia and the Sudentenland. He uses recordings from the *Lautbibliothek der deutschen Mundarten* from 1957–64. Dialects in Switzerland and Austria are not treated. S. attempts to show that there are acoustic correlates for *Silbenschnitt*, namely measurements of energy curve. If the curve is highest relatively far back in the syllable, this is short, whereas if the highest point is relatively far forward then the syllable is long. The dialects in the north show most clearly the feature of *Silbenschnitt*. This work is at times not easy reading and will certainly not be the last word on this complex subject.

Fest. Löffler contains items on dialectal and other kinds of variation: G. Hilty, 'System — Diasystem — Variation' (27–43); E. Werlen, 'Variation in der Feldforschung: Triangulation' (99–110); H. Bickel, 'Das Internet als Quelle für die Variationslinguistik' (111–24); B. Henn-Memmesheimer and E. Eggers, 'Berechnung und Darstellung der Streuung spezifischer sprachlicher Muster' (125–38); L. Hofer, 'Sprachliche Ähnlichkeit und Gruppen von Sprecherinnen und Sprechern in der Basler Sprachgemeinschaft' (139–58); P. Leuenberger, 'Ortsloyalität und Variationsverhalten' (159–72); A. Häcki Buhofer, 'Psycholinguistische Aspekte der Variation: das Sprachbewusstsein in der Variationstheorie' (173–86); W. Besch, 'Variantentyp Hyperkorrektion' (187–94); J. Macha, 'Ein deutsches Kriegstagebuch aus dem US-Bürgerkrieg: Beobachtungen zur Schreibvariation' (195–211); R. Schmidlin, 'Erzähllerner in der

Deutschschweizerdiaglossie' (211–26); M. Gyger, 'Das Diglossie-Dilemma: jugendliche Migranten im Spannungsfeld zwischen Mundart und Standardsprache' (227–44); H. Christen, 'Standardsprachliche Varianten als stilistische Dialektvarianten?' (245–60); W. Kallmeyer, 'Sprachvariation und Soziostilistik' (261–78); I. Werlen, 'Variation im gesprochenen Hochdeutsch in der deutschen Schweiz — am Beispiel der Nachrichten von Radio DRS 1 und Radio DRS 3' (311–28); G. Kolde, 'Zur Varianz in der Anrede und in Bezugnahme auf Dritte' (329–42); V. Schupp, 'Variation und Bildmuster' (343–54); and H. Steger, 'Funktionale Sprachvarietäten und Semantik' (355–66).

A major work on vocabulary is H. Stern, *Wörterbuch zum jiddischen Lehnwortschatz in der deutschen Dialekten* (Lexicographica Series Maior, 102), Tübingen, Niemeyer, vii + 245 pp. S. notes the study of Yiddish only got under way in the 1960s. She has a theoretical introduction to the dictionary, covering terminology, history of Yiddish-German linguistic contact, the semitic languages, the dictionaries she uses, and the structure of the dictionary entries. Yiddish-German language contact has taken place since the 15th c. Many of the oldest words have come from horse dealers and *Rotwelsch*, while many came into the language through urban colloquial contact in the 19th and 20th cs in towns such as Frankfurt, Berlin, and Vienna. The dialect areas where there was most contact are West Central German and Alemannic. Most words are of Hebrew origin and have already been changed in Yiddish to make them more Germanic. S. has combed all the dialect dictionaries and modern, e.g. post 1970, standard dictionaries, for her collection. A notable exception among 19th-c. dictionaries is that of D. Sanders. Although the study emphasizes German dialects the standard language is just as important. This is a unique and very important collection. The Yiddish component in German vocabulary, both dialectal and standard, has been underestimated. This volume will set that balance right. Also noted on Yiddish: A. Klepsch, 'Die Überreste des Westjiddischen in Mittelfranken', *Fest. Munske*, 251–82.

On Bavarian: *Vom Sturz der Diphthonge. Beiträge zur 7. Arbeitstagung für bayerisch-österreichische Dialektologie in Regensburg, September 1998*, ed. A. Greule et al. (TBL, 450), 250 pp.; R. Harnisch and R. Hinderling, '*Das schönes Haus* — Zur Bedeutung des starken Adjektivs nach bestimmtem Artikel in der deutschen Sprachgeschichte und im Bairischen der Gegenwart', *Fest. Mettke*, 201–08; H. J. Simon, ' "KinnanS Eahne fei heid gfrein" — Über einen Typ von Verb-Erst-Aussagesätzen im Bairischen', *Fest. Eroms*, 137–54; E. Glaser, ' "Fai schoo Guade-àà!" — Position und Funktion der Partikel *auch* im Bairischen', *ib.*, 155–68.

The following dialect atlases have appeared: *Sprachatlas von Bayerisch-Schwaben, 4. Lautgegographie* II. Qualität der mhd. Kurzvokale, ed. W. König and H. Heidenreich, Heidelberg, Winter, 1999, xxvi + 602 pp., contains 165 maps, each illustrating the development of the reflex of words with a particular MHG sound. There are *Kombinationskarten* with a number of words and *Einzelkarten* where only one word is illustrated. In addition there are *Kommentarkarten* which deal with phonetic features such as rounding, nasalization etc. Particularly interesting in this volume are the different maps on umlaut vowels, e.g. umlaut before *s* and *sch*. One feature lacking is a systematic treatment of phonological oppositions, e.g. MHG *ë* vs. *e* (from Gmc. *a*). This can be seen, but only by implication in comparing different maps. This volume treats some well known developments such as the loss of *n* before fricatives, e.g. in *fünf* etc., and the lack of umlaut in some dialects in words with velars such as *drücken, Küche*. The Lech forms quite a strong dialect boundary again and again. This volume helps to complete our detailed knowledge of the dialects in this area.

Sprachatlas von Bayerisch-Schwaben, 8. Wortgeographie II, ed. W. König and M. Renn, Heidelberg, Winter, xviii + 441 pp., contains 108 onomasiological maps as well as a small number of semasiological maps. The lexical areas covered are mainly rural, the farm house, buildings and furnishings, the weather, wild animals, insects, plants, fruit and vegetables, and cider-pressing. In contrast to the first volume on word geography the maps and the text are mixed together. Each map is a symbol map with the main forms normalized. There is, however, always a complete list of forms from each locality as well. Different dialect dictionaries are used to create non-standard head forms. Where available there is a discussion of the etymology of the forms. What comes across is the amazing variety of dialect forms in this one area. As with the phonetic maps, the Lech shows itself as a strong boundary. This is a really important resource for the study of this area.

Also noted: **Kleiner Deutscher Sprachatlas*, vol. 2, *Vokalismus, Teil 2, Langvokale, Diphthonge, Kombinationskarten*, ed. W. H. Veith, Tübingen, Niemeyer, 1999, ix + maps, 338–462 pp.

Alemannic and Swabian feature in the contributions to *Bausteine zur Sprachgeschichte: Referate der 13. Arbeitstagung zur Alemannischen Dialektologie in Augsburg (29.9. bis 3.10.1999)*, ed. E. Funk (Sprache — Literatur und Geschichte, 19), Heidelberg, Winter, 376 pp., which contains: R. Berthele, 'Vom Mississipi an den Oberrhein. 100 Jahre Nigger-Jim-Problem und seine vorläufige Lösung durch einen Alemannen' (13–28), on different translations of *Huckleberry Finn*; H. Bickel, 'Dialekt — lokale Schreibsprache in Basel am Ende des

16. Jahrhunderts' (29–43), describing the language competence of one writer in Basle; H. Christen, 'Von Mamme zu Mammi, von Baba zu Papi — diachrone und diatopische Aspekte verwandtschaftlicher Anredeformen' (43–61), which uses a sample of death notices to outline trends in familial address, whereby *Vati* and *Mutti* have been ousted by *Papi* and *Mammi*; D. Crévenat-Werner, 'Französische Lexeme in der Straßburger Mundart in historischer Perspektive' (63–85), showing how French loans have amounted to about 10% and come in waves over the years. In the past they have nearly always had German synonyms but not so much in recent years; P. Gilles and R. Schrambke, 'Divergenz in den Intonationssystemen rechts und links des Rheins. Die Sprachgrenze zwischen Breisach (Baden) und Neuf-Brisach (Elsass)' (87–98), describing similar dialects but different intonation patterns; H. Graser, 'Augsburg und die deutsche Sprachgeschichte' (99–120), illustrating language use in 17th-c. Augsburg from a range of texts, showing the printed language to be the most innovative; J. Gut, 'Die "begird der erkantnuß frömbder sprachen". Zu den Sprachforschungen des Luzerner Stadtschreibers Renward Cysat (1545–1614)' (121–35), showing how C. produced, only in manuscript form, a polyglot dictionary, based on local language and a list of names, all for his own interest as a Humanist scholar, but which is now of great interest to others; V. Harm, 'Regionale Varietäten in der Neubearbeitung des Deutschen Wörterbuchs' (137–49), finding that regional forms have been reduced since the 1960s and that there is no distinction in stylistic level used in describing their provenance. The notion of the written language that is used is very much of the 19th c. What is needed is a new dictionary from the 17th c. to the present; L. Hofer, 'Aktuelle Veränderungsprozesse in der Basler Stadtmundart im Lichte der Sprachgeschichte' (151–64), describing Basle's unique position, which is exemplified by changes such as [k] > [x] which only occur in a few older words; S. Krämer-Neubert, 'Alemannisches in Unterfranken?' (165–79), which reviews the evidence, linguistic and otherwise, and answers 'no', the similar features being due to common *Elbgermanisch* origins; K. Kunze, 'Familiennamen-Geographie und Sprachgeschichte — Beispiele aus dem Alemannischen' (181–98), which exemplifies how regional name types show older areal distribution, e.g. *ai* in *Maier*; A. Lötscher, 'Verbstellungsprobleme in der schweizerischen Schreibsprache des 16. Jahrhunderts: die Abfolge der Elemente in zweiteiligen Verbalkomplexen' (199–215), which discovers great variability, but the change of V1V2 to V2V1 is evidenced the higher the stylistic level of the text and the more formal the register. There is also evidence from outside in the shape of the incipient supraregional trends to normalization. Some of the internal differences between

texts are reflexes of probable dialect differences in Swiss German; D. Nübling, 'Entwicklungen im Flexionsklassen- und Ablautsystem des Alemannischen' (217–29), dealing with the loss of the preterite in a pangermanic context. The ablaut system is still stable and has a strong influence which attracts new verbs. Through reduction of syllables even the potentially long bracketing constructions are quite short; A. Rowley, 'Augsburger Wortschatz von Mertens (1789) bis heute' (231–40), reviewing older dictionaries of the Augsburg dialect. M. contains several Swabian words which are now only used in the country; H. Ruef, 'Germanisch -n(k)- im Südalemannischen. Überlegungen aus kognitiv-linguistischer Sicht' (241–48), which treats an area with both [nkx] and [x] forms. The informants understand the variant forms within a frame of their linguistic experience; H. U. Schmid, ' "IN DEM NAMEN GOTTES ALS MAN ZALT . . ." ' Epigraphische Texte des nordalemannischen Raumes als sprachhistorische Quellen' (249–59), which illustrates the use of inscriptions on grave stones, houses etc., exemplifying three grammatical instances. The form of the language of these rather public sources tends to be free from local influences; C. Schmutz, 'Behandlung von Sprachgeschichte im Senslerdeutschen Wörterbuch' (261–70), which exemplifies how diachronic development can be portrayed in a dialect dictionary, with a scale of obsolescence; B. Siebenhaar, 'Strukturierung von Variation und Sprachwandel in einer dialektologischen Labilitätszone' (271–87), showing how change goes in different directions in phonology and morphology and that the older generation lead the change in pronunciation; B. Stör, 'Mit der Trambahn ins Schwäbische — Alemannisch-ostschwäbische Lautformen in der westlichen Region Münchens' (289–320), which maintains with detailed exemplification how Swabian forms are nearer to those of Munich than one might expect, especially among the younger generation; J. Szabó, 'Deutsch-ungarische Interferenz am Beispiel der Winzerterminologie und des Atlasses der rumämenungarischen Dialekte' (321–29); R. Trüb, 'Dialektgeographie als Sprachgeschichte' (331–40); R. Hildebrandt, 'Wortgeschichtliche Mutmassungen anhand des SDS' (343–48); I. Hove, 'Tuufed euer Oore!' (349–52); B. Kelle, 'Wo wird Alemannisch gesprochen? — Einschätzungen von Besuchern des Wissenschaftsmarktes 1997' (353–55); J. Menyhárt, 'Deutsche Lehnwörter in der Mundart von Nyékvárkony' (357–69); T. Steiner, 'Vordeutsche Relikte in Ostallgäuer Flurnamen' (361–65); K. Wild, 'Syntaxwandel in der schwäbisch-alemannischen Inselmundart von Nagyárpád in Südungarn?' (367–71); and L. Zehetner, 'Grüß Gott — ein keltisches Sprachfossil im Oberdeutschen?' (373–76).

Also noted: B. Siebenhaar, *Sprachvariation, Sprachwandel und Einstellung. Der Dialekt der Stadt Aarau in der Labilitätszone zwischen Zürcher und*

Berner Mundartraum (ZDL, Beiheft, 108), iv + 281 pp. M. Schnabel, **Der Dialekt des Weingarts. Eine phonologische und morphologische Untersuchung* (Schriften zum Bayerischen Sprachatlas, 2), Heidelberg, Winter, xii + 341 pp.

On Central German: K.-H. Bausch, *Wandel im gesprochenen Deutsch. Zum diachronen Vergleich von Korpora gesprochener Sprache am Beispiel des Rhein-Neckar-Raums* (Amades, 3), Mannheim, Institut für Deutsche Sprache, 152 pp., is a pilot study, comparing the speech of 11 informants in the Rhine-Neckar area with recordings of themselves in E. Zwirner's archive. Three variables were studied, *w/b* fricativisation, *r/d* rhotacism, and the endings of the past participles of strong verbs. An increase in the use of *w* was found, while *r/d* remained stable. The ending -*e* was found to be the main past participle ending. Some interesting findings were that younger people used a more conservative variety and that some forms were used in a functional way, i.e. to signal new information or the end of a topic. B.'s main conclusion is that an increase in competence in High German need not be coupled with a loss of dialect competence. This is a very stimulating book. H. Girnth, *Untersuchungen zur Theorie der Grammatikalisierung am Beispiel des Westmitteldeutschen* (RGL, 223), 250 pp., contains a detailed discussion of the concept and terms used in grammaticalization. Perhaps there are rather a number of long words, *Obligatorifizierung* (!) and not very familiar terms, *Grammem*. G. uses the maps from ther *Mittelrheinischer Sprachatlas* to illustrate his approach: the use of *brauchen* as a modal, the passive with *geben*, the double particles *hinein-*, *herein-*, the relative clause marker *der wo*, the inflection of conjunctions such as *wenn*, and the plural markers. There is a heavy reliance on V. Schirmunski, and G. gives a detailed description of changes in progress. There are plenty of maps. A stimulating volume, even if the first part is not always clear. Also noted: W. V. Davies, 'Linguistic norms at school: a survey of secondary school teachers in a Central German dialect area', *ZDL*, 67 : 129–47; G. Drenda, **Zentralisierung. Probleme der Vokalentwicklung im Westmitteldeutschen* (Mainzer Studien zur Sprach- und Volksforschung, 23), Stuttgart, Steiner, vii + 203 pp.; L. Gillesen, **Mundart im Heinsberger Land. Dremmener Wörterbuch* (Rheinische Mundarten. Beiträge zur Volkssprache aus den rheinischen Landschaften, 11), Bonn, Habelt, 1999, 410 pp.

On Low German: U. Möller, *Das Wörterbuch des Jakob von Melle. Untersuchungen zur niederdeutschen Lexikographie im frühen 18. Jahrhundert*, Heidelberg, Winter, 219 pp. The dictionary in question is only extant in manuscript form and was only handed back to Germany in 1990. M. reviews the history of LG lexicography. Although v.M.'s life is well studied, his dictionary has been neglected. M. gives a detailed description of the dictionary. It is alphabetical, deals with orthographic doublets, but where did he get his orthographic tradition from? There are 40% nouns and 30% verbs, with the individual word forms of the verbs being listed. The meaning of the words is given by reference to Latin and High German. There are plenty of prefixed verbs and compound nouns. Three areas of vocabulary receive detailed treatment: names, clothing, and professions, of which he lists over 500. It is not an idioticon but lists everyday words. Most of the words are local and have had no influence on later LG dictionaries. M.'s style is repetitive in parts but the volume is extremely well structured and very informative. Also noted D. Willkommen, **Nordstrander Platt. Phonologie des Nordstrander Platt. Niederdeutsch in multilingualer Region* (Forschungen zum Niederdeutschen, 2), Neumünster, Wachholtz, 1999, 225 pp; E. Piirainen, **Phraseologie der westmünsterländischen Mundart. Teil I: Semantische, kulturelle und pragmatische Aspekte dialektaler Phraseologismen. Teil 2 : Lexikon der Redensarten*, Baltmannweiler, Schneider Vlg Hohengehren, 535, 464 pp.

On speech islands: S. Dal Negro, 'Altertümlichkeit, Sprachwandel und Sprachtod. Das Gleichnis vom "Verlorenen Sohn" in zwei piemontischen Walserdialekten', *ZDL*, 67 : 28–52; A. Kopp, **The Phonology of Pennsylvania German English as Evidence of Language Maintenance and Shift*. Selinsgrove, Susquehanna U.P., 1999, 345 pp.; **Wörterbuch der donauschwäbischen Baugewerbe*, ed. H. Gehl (Schriftenreihe des Instituts für donauschwäbische Geschichte und Landeskunde, 7), Stuttgart, Thorbecke, 1009 cols.

An important dictionary for the Fribourg area in Switzerland is *Senslerdeutsches Wörterbuch*, ed. C. Schmutz and W. Haas, Fribourg, Paulusverlag, 728 pp., which has a detailed introduction. One of its innovations is the use of maps to show how words are known to older and younger generations, showing a picture of lexical change. The following dialect dictionaries have appeared: *Preußisches Wörterbuch*, vol. 6, fasc. 5, *Wahrsager-welschen*, Neumünster, Wachholtz, cols 513–640, vol. 6, fasc. 6, *Welschling-Wollust*, cols 641–768; *Schweizerisches Idiotikon*, vol. 15, fasc. 202, *Walt-wult, Waltsch-wultsch, Walzwulz, Wam(m)-wumm(m)*, Frauenfeld, Huber, 1999, cols 1165–1768; vol. 16, fasc. 203, *Wan-wun (wân-wêndig)*, cols 1–128; *Wörterbuch der bairischen Mundarten in Österreich*, vol. 5, fasc. 1, *deu-törren*, Vienna, Österreichischen Akademie der Wissenschaften, cols 1–192,; *Badisches Wörterbuch*, fasc. 57, vol. 4, 1–32, *N-narri(ch)t*, Lahr, Moritz Schauenburg, 1999; *Hamburgisches Wörterbuch*, fasc. 17, *Kiephoot-Knööpnadel*, Neumünster, Wachholtz, 1999, cols 1025–1152; *Brandenburg-Berlinisches Wörterbuch*, vol. 4, fasc. 3, *steinalt-tappen*, Berlin, Akademie, 1996, cols 257–384; *Niedersächsisches Wörterbuch*, fascs 41–43,

Haubön-Himmel, Neumünster, Wachholtz, 1999, cols 1–384; **Ober-harzer Wörterbuch*, ed. K.-H. Weidemeier, Clausthal-Zellerfeld, Ober-harzer Geschichts- und Museumsverein, 1999, vol. 4, *K-M*, 381 pp.

9. ONOMASTICS

A. Bishkenowa, 'Zum Problem der Entstehung von Gattungswörtern auf der Grundlage von Eigennamen im gegenwärtigen Deutsch', *Sprachwissenschaft*, 25 : 21–62; I. Kühn, 'Objektnamengebung als Zeitgeistreflexion', *BNF*, 35 : 1–14; K. O. Sauerbeck, 'Die Funktion von Eigennamen in der Dichtung', *ib.*, 15–39; D. Nübling, 'Auf der Suche nach dem idealen Eigennamen', *ib.*, 275–302; K. Hohensinner, 'Zum Morphem *-in* in der Namenbildung', *ib.*, 393–410; W. Seibicke, *Historisches Deutsches Vornamenbuch. 3: L–Sa. In Verbindung mit der Gesellschaft für deutsche Sprache*, Berlin–New York, de Gruyter, xv + 725 pp.; L. Jacob, *Das neue FALKEN Buch der Vornamen. Im Auftrag der Gesellschaft für deutsche Sprache*, ed. G. Müller, Niedernhausen, Falken, 239 pp. R. Möller, **Niedersächsische Siedlungsnamen und Flurna-men mit k-Suffix und s-Suffix in Zeugnissen vor dem Jahre 1200* (Studien zur Namenforschung), Heidelberg, Winter, 80 pp.; H. Weinacht, 'Jüdi-sche Gebäudenamen in der fränkischen Mikrotoponymie', *Fest. Munske*, 283–97; W. Laur, 'Frauennamen und Bezeichnungen für Frauennamen in Ortsnamen', *BNF*, 35 : 303–14.

A volume which combines contributions on personal and place names is **Personenname und Ortsname. Basler Symposion, 6. und 7. Oktober 1997*, ed. H. Tiefenbach and H. Löffler (Studien zur Namenfor-schung), Heidelberg, Winter, 387 pp.; W. Haubrichs, 'Das *palatium* von Thionville/Diedenhofen und sein Umland im Spiegel frühmittel-alterlicher Siedlungsnamen und Siedlungsgeschichte', *Fest. Mettke*, 171–90; M. Pümpel-Mader, '*Tirol* im Text. Über einen Eigennamen und die Verbalisierung von Konzeptwissen im Text', *DSp*, 28 : 42–59; W.-H. Petershagen, **Die Wahrheit über Deppenhausen. Kuriose Ortsnamen in Baden-Württemberg*, Stuttgart, Theiss, 1999, 189 pp.; B. Grossenba-cher Künzler, **Die Namenlandschaft des Wasseramtes. Namenschwund und Namenwechsel in einer veränderten Landschaft* (Solothurnisches Orts- und Flurnamenbuch, Beiheft, 3), Solothurn, Vogt-Schild–Habegger Medien, 1999, 516 pp.; R. W. L. Puhl, **Die Gaue und Grafschaften des frühen Mittelalters im Saar-Mosel-Raum. Philologisch-onomastische Studien zur frühmittelalterlichen Raumorganisation anhand der Raumnamen und der mit ihnen spezifizierten Ortsnamen* (Beiträge zur Sprache im Saar-Mosel-Raum, 13), Saarbrücken, Saarbrücker Druckerei und Vlg, 1999, xvii + 609 pp.; **Rheinhessische Flurnamen aus dem onomasiologischen Feld 'Hügel, Anhöhe, kleine Bodenerhebung'. Jahrespreis 1998 der Hennig-Kaufmann-Stiftung*, ed. F. Debus, Stuttgart, Steiner, 1999, 37 pp.;

Geographische Namen in ihrer Bedeutung für die landeskundliche Forschung und Darstellung. Referate des 8. Arbeitsstreffens des Arbeitskreises Landeskundliche Institute und Forschungsstellen in der Deutschen Akademie für Landeskunde, Trier 21.–23. Mai 1998, Trier, Dokumentationszentrum für deutsche Landeskunde, Universität Trier, 1999, 270 pp.; P. Gusenberger et al., *Die Orts- und Flurnamen von Spiss*, Innsbruck, Wagner, 1999, 46 pp.; and L. Reichardt, *Ortsnamenbuch des Ostelbkreises. Teil 1: M-Z* (Veröffentlichungen der Kommission für Geschichtliche Landeskunde in Baden-Württemberg, Reihe B, 140), Stuttgart, Kohlhammer, v + 402 pp.

Germanic names are the subject of three studies by N. Wagner: 'Clisekka und Isanclis', *BNF*, 35 : 315–18; 'Der Name des Herulers *Phanitheos* und ähnliche', *ib.*, 379–84; and 'Aufgaben bei der Erforschung der Langobardennamen', *ib.*, 141–69.

MEDIEVAL LITERATURE

By NIGEL W. HARRIS, *University of Birmingham*

1. GENERAL

The two-volume *Encyclopaedia of German Literature*, ed. Matthias
Konzett, Chicago–London, Fitzroy Dearborn, xxii + 1136 pp.,
includes up-to-date articles, with select bibliographies, on the follow-
ing medieval authors: Sebastian Brant (N. Harris), Gottfried von
Strassburg (W. McConnell), Hartmann von Aue (F. G. Gentry),
Heinrich von Veldeke (R. Fisher), Hildegard von Bingen (A. Classen),
Hrosvitha von Gandersheim (H. W. Kraft), Konrad von Regens-
burg/Pfaffe Konrad (S. Calomino), Mechthild von Magdeburg (E. A.
Andersen), Meister Eckhart (B. Morgan), Neidhart (G. Ehrstine),
Oswald von Wolkenstein (N. Harris), Otfrid von Weissenburg
(L. Archibald), Rudolf von Ems (S. Coxon), Walther von der
Vogelweide (R. Fisher) and Wolfram von Eschenbach (M. E. Gibbs).
Anonymous works dealt with are the *Annolied* (G. Dunphy), *Ezzolied*
(R. E. Walker), *Heliand* (W. Hempel), *Hildebrandslied* (R. E. Walker),
König Rother (S. Calomino), *Ludwigslied* and *Merseburger Zaubersprüche*
(both B. Murdoch), and the *Nibelungenlied* (W. McConnell). There are
also entries on Arthurian romance (E. A. Andersen), biblical drama
and *Minnesang* (both M. Chinca), *Meistersang* (J. L. Flood), mystery
plays (J. E. Tailby) and *Sangspruchdichtung* (G. Dunphy); and separate
articles are allotted to OHG and MHG (L. Archibald and W. Whobrey), the Carolingian period (B. Murdoch), court culture (J. Ashcroft),
humanism (M. Reinhart), medieval manuscripts (W. Whobrey),
mysticism (A. Classen), and indeed religion and literature (L. Archibald). Inevitably there are some puzzling omissions (Johannes von
Tepl, Konrad von Würzburg, Der Stricker, *Kudrun*), but the value of
this massive encyclopaedia to the undergraduate and general reader
is clear.

   Die deutsche Literatur des Mittelalters. Verfasserlexikon, ed. Kurt Ruh et
al., reached the end of the alphabet in 1999, but has already spawned
the first fascicle of a supplementary 11th volume (Berlin, de Gruyter,
320 cols). Many completely new articles are planned, along with
corrected and updated versions of existing ones. The first fascicle
stretches from *Abbas* to *Christina*, and includes important new author
entries on Aesop (G. Dicke) and Avianus (M. Baldzuhn), as well as on
Albert of Saxony (H. Berger), Georg Alt (H. Kugler) and Alexander
de Villa Dei (C. Wulf). Other new entries deal with the (relatively)
recently discovered *Budapester Liederhandschrift* (G. Kornrumpf),
almanacs (F. Eisermann), breviaries (A. Häussling), legends of St

Anne (F. Roolfs) and the *Benediktbeurer Spiele* (H. Linke). The achievement of the *Verfasserlexikon* as a whole is evaluated by K. Stackmann, *ZDA*, 129:378–87. There is also a new edition of DTV's three-volume history of medieval German literature (see *YWMLS*, 52:595f.): Dieter Kartschoke, *Geschichte der deutschen Literatur im frühen Mittelalter* (DTV, 30777), 412 pp.; Joachim Bumke, *Geschichte der deutschen Literatur im hohen Mittelalter* (DTV, 30778), 448 pp.; Thomas Cramer, *Geschichte der deutschen Literatur im späten Mittelalter* (DTV, 30779), 450 pp. In each case, however, the only new material included is of a bibliographical nature.

The *Katalog der deutschsprachigen illustrierten Handschriften des Mittelalters*, vol. III, fasc. 3, ed. Norbert H. Ott and Ulrike Bodemann, continues its survey of illustrated manuscripts and incunabula of vernacular chronicles. The latest fascicle covers chronicles about Augsburg (by Sigismund Meisterlin), Bavaria (Andreas von Regensburg, Ulrich Füetrer, Veit Arnpeck), the territory of the Teutonic Order (Nikolaus von Jeroschin), Frankenberg (Wigand Gerstenberg), Cologne (Heinrich von Beeck's *Agrippina*), Constance (Gebhard Dacher), Magdeburg (the *Magdeburger Schöppenchronik*), Mecklenburg (Ernst von Kirchberg, Nikolaus Marschalk) and Lower Saxony (Hermann Bote's *Niedersächsische Weltchroniken*). U. Peters, *ZDP*, 119:321–68, assesses the function of the portraits of authors which appear in German manuscripts of the 13th to 15th cs, paying particular attention to pictures of Rudolf von Ems. C. Bertelsmeier-Kierst, *Wolfram-Studien*, 16:157–74, analyses the quantity and contents of vernacular German manuscripts in the 12th c., demonstrating that these remained relatively few in number and continued to transmit primarily religious works. C. Glassner, *ZDA*, 129:202–09, introduces the invaluable website *Österreichische Handschriften im Internet*, maintained by the Austrian Academy of Sciences. Appropriately, her article can also be accessed online, at <http://www.oeaw.ac.at/varia/zfda2000.htm>. B. Salzmann, *BW*, 33:59–102, discusses issues concerning the reproduction of medieval manuscripts in facsimile books, on microfiche and on CD-ROM. T. Burch, J. Fournier, and K. Gärtner, *Editio*, 14:117–29, describe a project which will make available on CD-ROM a closely interlinked compound of the four most important MHG dictionaries. A version of this is already available online at <http://gaer27.uni-trier.de/MWV-online/MWV-online.html>.

W. Williams-Krapp, *IASL*, 25.2:1–21, surveys and evaluates the achievements of the so-called *überlieferungsgeschichtlich* approach to editing and studying medieval texts, and points to similarities and differences between it and 'New Philology'. M. E. Dorninger and M. Springeth, *Editio*, 14:207–20, provide an annotated bibliography of publications on the editing of medieval German texts from between 1993 and 1996. A few such items are also listed in S. Seifert's bibliography in the same volume (187–206), which encompasses German literature as a whole and covers the years 1997 and 1998. The *Encyclopaedia of Literary Translation into English*, ed. Olive Classe, London–Chicago, Fitzroy Dearborn, 2 vols, xxxvii + 1714 pp., contains entries on English translations of *Das Narrenschiff*, *Das Nibelungenlied*, and *Parzival* (all by N.Harris), as well as of *Reynke de vos* (J. L. Flood). U. Müller, *Editio*, 14:11–28, discusses the importance of translation in the origin and development of medieval German literature, and then lists and comments on several recent translations from MHG into modern German. An appendix by S. Heimann-Seelbach reflects on the use of both bilingual and monolingual editions in university teaching. T. Bein, *Editio*, 14:29–40, also assesses recent translations from MHG, focusing on their widely differing types and purposes; and V. Bok, *Fest. Mettke*, 25–38, comments on 19th-c. and 20th-c. translations of OHG and MHG works into Czech.

An extensive, undergraduate-friendly anthology of women's writing in medieval Germany has long been an urgent desideratum. This gap is now largely filled by Albrecht Classen, *Frauen in der deutschen Literaturgeschichte. Die ersten 800 Jahre. Ein Lesebuch* (Women in German Literature, 4), Berne, Lang, xx + 337 pp. C. includes short texts and/or excerpts from longer works by Hrosvitha von Gandersheim, Frau Ava, Hildegard von Bingen, Die Winsbeckin, Mechthild von Magdeburg, Helene Kottannerin, Margareta von Schwangau and Maria von Wolkenstein, and Elisabeth von Nassau-Saarbrücken, as well as a number of 16th-c. and 17th-c. authors. Regrettably, perhaps, the medieval texts are presented solely in modern German translation; and the choice of works is inevitably controversial (one questions, for example, Classen's inclusion of some *Minnelieder* which probably were not written by women, and his exclusion of all mystics apart from Hildegard and Mechthild). Nevertheless his volume is most welcome. We also now have an expert and judicious summary in English of women's writing in the medieval Empire: M. Ives and A. Suerbaum, Catling, *Women's Writing*, 13–26. Laudably, I. and S. discuss female scribes and patrons, as well as authors.

Petra Hörner, *Zweisträngige Tradition der Evangelienharmonie. Harmonisierung durch den Tatian und Entharmonisierung durch Georg Kreckwitz u.a.* (GTS, 67), 381 pp., traces the development of the Gospel harmony from the OHG *Tatian* through to the later 16th c. H. argues that Tatian's approach of harmonizing the Gospels by merging them into one continuous, contradiction-free narrative gradually gave way to 'harmonies' which juxtaposed several versions of the same story and also included authorial comments or other additions. She identifies as the most important representative of this later form the unpublished harmony of the Silesian Georg Kreckwitz (†1422).

A. Classen, Classen, *Voices*, 7–42, argues that medieval studies not only have nothing to fear from a broad, 'cultural studies'-based approach to Germanics, but can perform a paradigmatic function within it. In the same volume, B. Martin (155–63) stresses the value of medieval studies in enabling students to develop a positive and creative sense of alterity; R. T. Morewedge (81–106) outlines the pedagogical and epistemological value of courses in medieval wisdom literature; and D. F. Tinsley (123–44) suggests that medieval German religious literature might be regarded as a paradigm for Gender Studies. K. Kellermann, *Das Mittelalter*, 5:123–39, seeks to demonstrate the value of applying interdisciplinary cultural studies to medieval topics by examining aspects of the representation of kings. R. Schnell, *AKG*, 82:227–37, reflects upon and deplores recent tendencies to regard medieval and early modern studies as discrete entities.

W. Haug, Huber, *Geistliches*, 195–212, suggests that, in the High Middle Ages, mystical thinkers and authors of secular love lyrics moved in parallel away from a neo-Platonic concept of love for an elevated supreme being, and towards one which stressed mutuality and personal experience. In *Wolfram-Studien*, 16:70–83, Haug identifies in 12th-c. vernacular works a new relationship between literature and experience, which he characterizes as a discovery of fictionality. D. H. Green, *Fest. Johnson*, 161–74, reacts to recent research on the interplay between orality and literacy in medieval literature; and D. Kartschoke, *ZGer*, 10:477–92, discusses time as a narrative phenomenon in medieval and early modern literature. A. Classen, *NMi*:415–28, considers the role of wealth and money in medieval German literature, and observes an awareness of their importance and dangers which increases with time. N. Largier, Huber, *Geistliches*, 291–304, surveys the anecdotes concerning Diogenes the Cynic in ancient, medieval and Renaissance literature; and J. Strothmann, Baumbach, *Tradita*, 59–72, discusses medieval perceptions of Julius Caesar and Augustus.

OTHER WORKS

The New Cambridge Medieval History. VI. *C. 1300–c. 1415*, ed. Michael Jones, CUP, xxx + 1110 pp., adopts, like other volumes in the new series (see *YWMLS*, 60:575–76, 61:597f.) a significantly different approach from its venerable predecessor. Above all, it covers in depth a far wider geographical area, and is less heavily dependent on a traditional narrative framework. It is divided into four sections. The first of these, 'General Themes', includes an introduction by the editor (3–16), followed by chapters on the theory and practice of government in Western Europe (A. Rigaudière, 17–41), currents of religious thought and expression (J. Catto, 42–65: Eckhart is discussed briefly), the universities (J. Verger, 66–81), rural society (P. Freedman, 82–101), urban life (J.-P. Leguay, 102–23), plague and family life (C. Klapisch-Zuber, 124–54), trade (P. Spufford, 155–208), chivalry and the aristocracy (M. Keen, 209–21), court patronage and international Gothic (P. Binski, 222–33), architecture (P. Crossley, 234–56), and literature in Italian, French, and English — though sadly not German (N. Havely, 257–70). Section II deals with the 'states of the West'; the chapter on the Empire is divided between P. Herde's discussion of the period 1292–1347 (514–50) and I. Hlaváček's of the reigns of the Luxemburgs and Rupert of the Palatine (551–69). The latter contains two pages on art and literature. A third section is devoted to the Church, treating the Avignon Papacy (P. N. R. Zutschi, 653–73) and the Great Schism (H. Kaminsky, 674–96); and a fourth offers a pleasingly detailed treatment of Northern and Eastern Europe. It is no doubt otiose to remark that this volume is a major work of reference for all who study the 14th century.

Deutsche Geschichte in Quellen und Darstellung. II. *Spätmittelalter, 1250–1495*, ed. Jean-Marie Moeglin and Rainer A. Müller (UB, 17002), 503 pp., is another volume of fundamental importance, albeit in a different way. It provides texts (translated or modernized as appropriate) of over 80 key documents of late-medieval German history, linked and elucidated by brief commentaries. It also offers a substantial introduction, which begins by distancing itself from traditional perceptions of the period in question as one of decline, and proceeds to give a cogent account of the principal political issues of the epoch. Both introduction and documents arguably focus unduly on aristocratic (especially Imperial) politics, rather than on broader social issues; but, taken as a whole, the book is an outstanding resource for students of history and literature alike.

Two monographs on Emperor Frederick II appeared in 2000. Wolfgang Stürner, *Friedrich II*. II. *Der Kaiser 1220–1250*, Darmstadt, Primus, xiv + 659 pp., is the long-awaited second volume of a work whose first instalment appeared in 1992 (see *YWMLS*, 54:657). Like its predecessor, this volume is a model of clarity, thoroughness and balanced judgment. It contains a substantial chapter (pp. 342–457) on Frederick's aesthetic and scientific interests and those of the many artists and scholars he supported. S. speculates that these may have included not only Walther von der Vogelweide, but also Reinmar von Zweter, Bruder Hermann, and Der Hardegger; he studies in detail the contribution of Michael Scotus to the intellectual vibrancy and fame of Frederick's court; and he offers a detailed and persuasive analysis of the Emperor's own *De arte venandi cum avibus*. Ekkehart Rotter, *Friedrich II von Hohenstaufen* (DTV, 31040), 159 pp., is a slighter and more popular work, attractively presented with many colour illustrations. It provides a sound and readable account, arranged chronologically, of Frederick's career; perhaps inevitably, however, it devotes only two pages to cultural and intellectual matters. Also noted: Ferdinand Seibt, *Karl IV. Ein Kaiser für Europa. 1346 bis 1378* (DTV, 30767), 484 pp. (a reprint of the 1978 and 1994 editions).

Rösener, *Erinnerungskulturen*, contains papers dealing with numerous aspects of the culture of memory in both aristocratic and urban bourgeois contexts in the medieval and early modern periods. Studies of aristocratic forms of *memoria* include R.'s own essay on the importance of memory in the *Codex Falkensteinensis* (35–56), S. Krieb's examination of the relationship between memory, literacy and knightly identity in the 15th-c. writings of the Franconian Herren von Eyb (79–96), and S. Jaek's analysis of the use of swords as symbols of and memorials to chivalric attributes in (amongst other contexts) the *Rolandslied* and *Eckenlied* (57–78). *Memoria* as understood and cultivated in urban contexts is examined, on the basis of chronicles and other written sources, by T. Zotz in respect of Nuremberg (145–61), B. Mauer of Augsburg (163–76), and S. Dzeja of Frankfurt (177–90). Two contributions focus on the relationship between city and country in the later Middle Ages: R. Sprandel (21–33) sketches several aspects of the multi-faceted and ambivalent relationship between rural aristocrats and neighbouring urban patricians (21–33), and K. Graf (191–204) points to an increasing polarization and hostility which is suggested by retrospective accounts of the *Städtekrieg* of 1449–50.

Late-medieval Constance continues to represent an important focus for cultural-historical research. Peter Schuster, *Eine Stadt vor Gericht. Recht und Alltag im spätmittelalterlichen Konstanz*, Paderborn, Schöningh, 353 pp., is a detailed and sophisticated study of criminality and legal processes in the town, which contains many fascinating discoveries — not least the fact that very few convicted criminals actually served the sentences imposed on them. Thomas Rathmann, *Geschehen und Geschichten des Konstanzer Konzils. Chroniken, Briefe, Lieder und Sprüche als Konstituenten eines Ereignisses* (FGÄDL, 20), 303 pp., is perhaps more consistently of interest to students of literature. R. presents the Council as an inherently 'open', discursive event, dominated and shaped by texts of many kinds. His analysis of a wide range of these texts rejects the conventional divide between historical 'documents' on the one hand and fictionalized accounts on the other, and as such seeks to disclose not only the historical veracity of any given text, but also its rhetorical and literary qualities. R. devotes particular attention to the Latin *Gesta Concilii* of Guillaume Fillastre and to the German *Konzilschronik* of Ulrich Richental; but poets such as Muskatblüt and Oswald von Wolkenstein are also accorded appropriate coverage.

A further study by Schuster appears in Blauert, *Kriminalitätsgeschichte* (359–78), in which he discusses the frequent appearances of socially powerful citizens before the Constance courts. Other contributions to this distinguished volume include: K. Graf's survey (245–88) of the 'black books' kept in late-medieval towns; G. Signori's detailed and fascinating examination (289–314) of a case in 15th-c. Basel which suggests that legal documents must also be read at times as works of imaginative literature; and S. Wernicke's paper (379–404) dealing with the contents and implications of 15th-c. oaths of truce from Regensburg.

P. Dinzelbacher, Dinzelbacher, *Mensch und Tier*, 181–292, provides a characteristically magisterial but readable account of the multifarious relationships between people and animals in the Middle Ages, covering the role of animals in nutrition, hunting, warfare, entertainment (including menageries), theology, literature, art, science and a variety of other contexts, and ending with a fascinating discussion of the extent to which medieval people can be said to have felt love for animals.

Manfred Gerwing, *Theologie im Mittelalter. Personen und Stationen theologisch-spiritueller Suchbewegungen im mittelalterlichen Deutschland*, Paderborn, Schöningh, 279 pp., is a thoroughly useful volume aimed at the non-specialist. G. gives a concise and lucid account of the most important theologians active in the German-speaking lands between Alcuin and Nicolaus Cusanus, laying particular emphasis on the relationship between their doctrine, biography, and historical circumstances. Arnold Angenendt's superlative *Geschichte der Religiosität im Mittelalter*, Darmstadt, Primus, xiv + 986 pp. (see *YWMLS*, 59:667–68) has already appeared in a second edition. This differs from the first, however, only in respect of relatively minor details.

2. GERMANIC AND OLD HIGH GERMAN

A. Quak, *ABÄG*, 53:33–39, returns to the runic inscription on the Bergakker scabbard mount (see *YWMLS*, 61:599), suggesting that it conveys a Germanic phrase meaning 'ich gönne dem Wählenden des Schwertes'. Two studies by E. Seebold are to be noted: in *BGDSL*, 122:40–56, he re-assesses the evidence concerning the origins of the Franks; and in Haubrichs, *Theodisca*, 10–37, he sets the appearance of runes in 8th-c. Latin manuscripts in the context of other contemporary examples of interest in 'foreign' scripts and languages on the part of Irish scholars.

Hendrik Davids, *Studien zu den substantivischen Bibelglossen des Clm 19440 aus Tegernsee. Ein Beitrag zur Erforschung der Bibelglossatur M* (SA, 40), 459 pp., is a primarily philological study of the OHG nouns which gloss Latin ones in this 11th-c. manuscript. D.'s painstaking analysis encompasses some 1750 nouns in all, and enables him both to suggest numerous emendations to Steinmeyer and Sievers's edition of OHG glosses and to establish that the manuscript was probably used for instruction at the Tegernsee monastic school. *Regula Benedicti des Cod.915 der Stiftsbibliothek von St. Gallen. Die Korrekturvorlage der lateinisch-althochdeutschen Benediktinerregel*, ed. Achim Masser (SA, 37), 120 pp., is the first of two volumes intended to accompany M.'s 1997 edition of the Latin text of the Rule of St Benedict with OHG interlinear glosses (*YWMLS*, 59:674–75); the second will be a philological commentary. Here M. provides the first edition of the Latin manuscript of the Rule which was used to correct the glossed manuscript. It is a careful diplomatic transcript which preserves the page, paragraph and line divisions of the manuscript, its punctuation, and its use of abbreviations, initials and capitals. In *Fest. Mettke*, 239–58, Masser justifies his editorial methods, this time with reference to the OHG *Tatian*. Other work on glosses includes: the detailed description and analysis by C. Cigni, *AION(FG)*, n.s., 6, 1996:29–64, of the OHG glosses found in a Tegernsee manuscript (now in Augsburg) of an *Excerptum a computo* attributed to the Venerable Bede; the attempt by R. Bergmann, Haubrichs, *Theodisca*, 77–104, to establish a preliminary typology of OHG glosses on the basis of their varying forms of manuscript transmission; N. Henkel's discussion, in the same volume (387–413), of the complex functions of both Latin and OHG glosses in the study of Latin literature; and K. Riedel's article, in *Fest. Mettke*, 295–315, on the manuscripts of the OHG glosses to the prologue of Aldhelm of Malmesbury's *Carmen de virginitate*.

Evelyn Scherabon-Firchow, *Notker der Deutsche von St. Gallen (950–1022). Ausführliche Bibliographie* (SA, 38), 123 pp., expands and updates the author's two earlier Notker bibliographies (see *YWMLS*, 45:632). Sonja Glauch devotes a major two-volume study to Notker's German version of the *De nuptiis Philologiae et Mercuriae* of Martianus Capella: *Die Martianus-Capella-Bearbeitung Notkers des Deutschen* (MTU, 116, 117), 2 vols, x + 655 pp. The core of what G. herself calls a 'commentary on a commentary' is the second volume, in which she provides a parallel NHG translation of Book I of Notker's adaptation and of the corresponding part of Martianus's original, and appends to each chapter of it a detailed line-by-line commentary. This deals particularly with linguistic questions, Notker's techniques of translation and adaptation, and issues raised in earlier secondary literature. The clarity and effectiveness of the volume is reduced by the absence of the original Latin and OHG texts; but G. brings many new insights to bear, as she does also in her first volume, which consists of a series of analytical chapters focusing on the careers of both Martianus and Notker, on Notker's sources and intellectual context, and on various formal and thematic aspects of his translation. A. A. Grotans, Haubrichs, *Theodisca*, 260–75, argues that the system of accents found in Notker manuscripts facilitates the reconstruction of the OHG spoken in the St Gall classroom, as well as indicating the importance of German, alongside Latin, as both medium and subject of instruction. W. Wunderlich, *JIG*, 31, 1999:30–44, discusses Notker Balbulus's *Gesta Karoli Magni*, with particular reference to his account of Charlemagne's just treatment of an avaricious bishop.

Bettina Heinrich, *Frühmittelalterliche Bibeldichtung und die Bibel. Ein Vergleich zwischen den altenglischen, althochdeutschen und altsächsischen Bibelparaphrasen und ihren Vorlagen in der Vulgata* (EH, 1, 1769), xii + 369 pp., is a careful and productive comparison of eight vernacular biblical paraphrases with the texts of the Latin Vulgate. The OHG works considered are Otfrid's *Evangelienbuch, Psalm 138*, and *Christus und die Samariterin* ; OS is represented by the *Heliand* and the *Genesis* paraphrase. H.'s approach enables her to distinguish more clearly than some earlier critics the individual qualities of the works she discusses, and leads in particular to a reassessment of the *Evangelienbuch* as a work of exceptional learning and exegetical sophistication intended to accompany, rather than substitute for, the reading of the Vulgate. Karin Pivernetz, *Otfrid von Weißenburg. Das 'Evangelienbuch' in der Überlieferung der Freisinger Handschrift (Bayerische Staatsbibliothek München, Cgm 14). Edition und Untersuchungen*, 2 vols (GAG, 671), vol. 1 unpaginated, vol. 2 141 pp., contains, in vol. 1, the text of the only one of the three principal Otfrid manuscripts which has not previously been published. The edition is as conservative as is practically possible. Vol. 2 deals with the history of Cgm 14, its linguistic features, its relationship to the other manuscripts (it was manifestly copied from Otfrid's own manuscript V), the working practices of its scribe Sigihart and, not least, the intellectual context in which it was copied. W. Milde, *Fest. Mettke*, 285–93, examines the so-called *Gebet des Sigihard* which follows the *Evangelienbuch* in Cgm 14, and concludes that it was written by a different scribe from the one who copied Otfrid's work. Meanwhile the importance for the reconstruction of Otfrid's language of the some 3,500 corrections he himself made in V is highlighted by W. Kleiber, Haubrichs, *Theodisca*,

118–42; and J. Schwerdt, *Fest. Mettke*, 317–54, discusses his use of parenthesis. M. E. Antstätter, *ABÄG*, 53:87–121, examines poetic techniques and structures in the OS *Genesis*, with particular reference to those which facilitate oral transmission.

Old Saxon forms the subject of a special issue of *ABÄG*, 52, 1999, which consists of a collection of essays, ed. Arend Quak, entitled *Speculum Saxonum. Studien zu den kleineren altsächsischen Sprachdenkmälern*. Its publication was designed to coincide with the centenary of the appearance of Elis Wadstein's collection of short OS texts. Alongside contributions of a purely philological nature, several essays raise literary and broader cultural questions. M. Elsakkers (29–53) examines conceptions of abduction and rape in the *Leges Saxonum*; L. de Grauwe (55–62) sees in the term *sunufatarungo[s]* found in the *Hildebrandslied* echoes of the early Christian Arian controversy; and E. Hellgardt (63–96) comments on the text of the *Freckenhorster Heberolle* and pleads for a new edition of it. T. Hofstra (105–15) discusses the so-called *Altsächsische Homilie Bedas*; E. Langbroek (117–54) studies the OS glosses found in a 10th-c. Oxford manuscript of Virgil's *Georgics*; and G. Lerchner (155–67) investigates Wadstein's corpus for the evidence it provides of a gradual shift from an oral to a written literary culture. A. Quak (197–206) examines the Latin text on which the fragmentary *Lubliner Psalmen* are based; and H. Tiefenbach (227–38) gives details of two manuscript fragments, in Copenhagen and Dresden, transmitting OS glosses which were unknown to Wadstein.

Haubrichs, *Theodisca*, contains a number of papers dealing with the position of German language and literature in early medieval culture. M. Richter (1–9) discusses the implications of three Latin accounts of encounters between clerical culture and oral vernacular literature; T. Klein (38–59) analyses the language of the OHG *Pariser Gespräche*; K. Gärtner (105–17) discusses the difficulties encountered by philologists wanting to distinguish between texts in OHG and those in MHG; and C. Staiti (143–88) examines the equivalents of *superbia* and related Latin concepts in OHG and OS. More specifically literary studies include C. Edwards's discussion (189–206) of the surviving OHG examples of love poetry, which he sees as having been composed in monastic contexts and as having been the object of considerable censorship; U. Schwab's examination (207–59) of Christ's changes of clothes on the Cross and other Crucifixion motifs, as presented in *Tatian*, the *Heliand* and in OE sources such as the *Ruthwell Cross* and the *Dream of the Rood*; W. Haubrichs's characterization (330–63) of Dietrich von Bern as an 'all-purpose' hero, whose presentation varies considerably from narrative to narrative; and S. Müller's analysis (364–86) of the conception and reception of material from heroic sagas in the *Quedlinburger Annalen*. Additionally H.-W. Goetz (290–312) discusses the implications of the terms *gentes* and *linguae* in the OHG period; D. Geuenich (313–29) disputes the appropriateness of referring to Charlemagne's grandson as Louis 'the German'; and K. Ridder and J. Wolf (414–47) assess the techniques, purposes and principles of translation into OHG in the light of recent research.

W. Beck, *ASNS*, 237:338–49, discusses the textual crux *heraduoder* in the first *Merseburger Zauberspruch*, concluding that it means 'Heereszüge' and as such confirms the reading of the text as a pagan charm for the release of prisoners; and M. Schumacher, *Fest. Weber*, 201–15, re-evaluates the relationship between the two arguably distinct parts of the two *Zaubersprüche*.

On the *Hildebrandslied*, R. Evans, *Will Vol.*, 1–12, interprets what he terms Hadubrand's 'Frageversäumnis'; P. Suchsland, *Fest. Mettke*, 355–79, studies syntactical features of the work in the light of later developments in German syntax; and U. Schwab, *Neophilologus*, 84:575–607, points in particular to the relevance for an understanding of the *Hildebrandslied* of Procopios of Caesarea's *History of the Wars of Justinian*.

In *Fest. Mettke*, H. Endermann (61–82) edits and discusses the *Tatian* fragments found in Paris, BN, MS f. lat. 7461; M. Gebhardt (111–36) re-examines the problematic phrase *enteo ni uuento* found in line 6 of the *Wessobrunner Hymnus*; and R. Lühr (219–37) studies the use of abstract nouns and of alliterative rhyme in the *Heliand*. S. Müller, *ZDP*, 119:98–102, interprets the four apparently German words which appear in the 9th-c. Latin *Visio Caroli Magni*. J. M. Jeep, *AJGLL*, 8, 1996:33–67, lists and evaluates alliterating word-pairs in OHG texts; and in *Medieval Feminist Newsletter*, 23, 1997:37–47, he discusses women as characters in, and producers and disseminators of, OHG literature.

3. Middle High German

GENERAL. Fritz Peter Knapp, *Die Literatur des Spätmittelalters in den Ländern Österreich, Steiermark, Kärnten, Salzburg und Tirol von 1273 bis 1439. I. Halbband. Die Literatur in der Zeit der frühen Habsburger bis zum Tod Albrechts II. 1358 (Geschichte der Literatur in Österreich, II/1)*, ADEVA, 1999, 567 pp., is an outstanding and important achievement. Knapp covers an enormous range of Latin, German and indeed Hebrew texts, many unpublished, composed in the Austrian lands between the years in question. Not least because of the relative obscurity of many of the works discussed, he is often able to contribute new findings and perspectives, rather than merely summarizing previous research. His decision to present his material duchy by duchy, rather than, say, genre by genre, whilst thoroughly defensible in historical terms, arguably militates against user-friendliness for those primarily concerned to trace literary developments; but it nevertheless becomes clear that there was a specifically Austrian literary culture in the later Middle Ages, one in which secular lyric and narrative played a relatively insignificant role, and in which the huge mass of theological, catechetical and moral-didactic literature remained largely unaffected by contemporary mystical currents.

J. Schulz-Grobert, *Wolfram-Studien*, 16:175–91, discusses the importance of literary patrons in 12th-c. Germany, with particular reference the archiepiscopal court at Cologne; and in *ZDA*, 129:275–95, he interprets references to clamp irons in courtly literature from c. 1200 as evidence of an interest in realistic architectural details. S. Philipowski, *BGDSL*, 122:455–77, discusses the presentation of gestures in various MHG narratives, dealing in particular with their intentionality, comprehensibility and reliability as conveyors of truth; and in *LiLi*, 17:118–27, she examines ways in which medieval courtly authors (and their characters) think antithetically rather than synthetically. W. Achnitz, *ZDA*, 129:249–74, analyses triple and quadruple rhymes within narratives related generally in rhyming couplets, pointing to the various functions they perform especially in works intended for oral performance. U. Müller, *Fest. Tervooren*, 57–71, stresses and illustrates the intrinsic link between editorial decisions and literary interpretation in MHG literature.

EARLY MIDDLE HIGH GERMAN

James A. Schultz, *Sovereignty and Salvation in the Vernacular, 1050–1150* (Medieval German Texts in Bilingual Editions, 1), Medieval Inst. Publ., Kalamazoo, xii + 164 pp., is the first in a welcome new series under the general editorship of Michael Curschmann, whose commendable aim is to make more widely accessible a variety of lesser known texts from the mid-11th to the end of the 15th century. The texts presented here are the *Ezzolied*, the *Annolied*, lines 247–667 of the *Kaiserchronik*, *Das Lob Salomons*, *Die drei Jünglinge im Feuerofen* and the *Ältere Judith*. S. provides eminently sound MHG editions and English translations of these works, along with a clear and helpful introduction and some perhaps disappointingly thin textual notes. In *Wolfram-Studien*, 16, A. Suerbaum (235–55) examines elements of dialogue and dialogicity in the *Kaiserchronik*; and W. Freytag (192–234) demonstrates that *Drei Jünglinge im Feuerofen* and the *Ältere Judith* reveal to a perhaps surprising degree the influence of Latin rhetorical and allegorical traditions.

608 *German Studies*

Christoph Mackert, *Die Alexandergeschichte in der Version des 'Pfaffen'*
Lambrecht. Die frühmittelhochdeutsche Bearbeitung der Alexanderdichtung des
Alberich von Bisinzo und die Anfänge weltlicher Schriftepik in deutscher Sprache
(Beihefte zu *Poetica*, 23), Munich, Fink, 1999, 367 pp., is an important
new study of the *Vorauer Alexander*. Basing his conclusions initially on a
comparison between the relevant portion of Lambrecht's work and
the surviving fragment of his French source, and then reinforcing
them through close textual analysis of the German work, M. rejects
categorically the conventional picture of the *Vorauer Alexander* as a
clumsy attempt to spiritualize a poetically sophisticated French
source. Rather, he points to the considerable skill with which
Lambrecht re-orders and reflects upon his material, and argues that
he problematizes the figure of Alexander as a paragon of wisdom and
valour who on occasion causes destruction by failing to master his
aggression. As such M. presents the work, at times perhaps too
unequivocally, as a narrative which, both in its techniques of
adaptation and in its affirmative but critical appraisal of the values of
the secular aristocracy, anticipates the courtly romances of the
Blütezeit. This view is implicitly seconded by J. Schulz-Grobert, *Fest.*
Johnson, 321–34, who couples Lambrecht with Wolfram as innovative
exponents of literary portraiture. Elsewhere U. Mölk, *BGDSL*,
122:74–75, examines the term *stuzel* used in lines 1034, 1043 and
1111 of the *Vorauer Alexander*; and A. Classen, *OL*, 55:317–39, argues
that the *Straßburger Alexander* presents reading and writing as central to
the acquisition of knowledge and truth.

König Rother, ed. Peter K. Stein and Ingrid Bennewitz (UB, 18047),
485 pp., is a very welcome new edition, which offers the most reliable
text of the work (based on manuscript H) which has yet appeared,
along with a scholarly NHG translation, introduction and commentary which will be of particular value to students. The volume fills a
major gap, and is a fitting memorial to Stein. Meanwhile E. C. Lutz,
Huber, *Geistliches*, 89–104, argues that the *Rolandslied* has in common
with Chrétien's (though not Hartmann's) *Erec* a profoundly religious
concept of worldly kingship; and J. Bumke, *ZDP*, 119:410–15,
comments on the manuscript tradition of the various versions of
Herzog Ernst.

L. Moulinier, *Sudhoffs Archiv*, 83, 1999:224–38, publishes and
evaluates two fragments from Hildegard von Bingen's *Physica* copied
in the 15th c. by Gerhard von Hohenkirchen; and R. Hildebrant,
Haubrichs, *Theodisca*, 276–89, shows that the pragmatic use of both
Latin and German was an original feature of the *Physica* which was to
some degree obscured by the Latinizing attentions of later adapters.
E. R. Hintz, Classen, *Voices*, 43–60, uses Bakhtinian theories of
multivocality to illuminate the writings of Frau Ava; and J. M. Jeep,

WGT, 14, 1998: 1–18, scrutinizes the literary evidence for friendship between women in medieval religious communities, with particular reference to the *St. Trudperter Hohelied.* E. Brüggen, Huber, *Geistliches*, 27–50, examines ways in which secular culture and temporal concerns are reflected in Der Arme Hartmann's *Rede vom Glauben* and in Heinrich von Melk's *Von des todes gehugde.* K. Gantert, *Poetica*, 31, 1999: 381–414, discusses the relationship between clerical tradition and the 'Brautwerbungsschema' in the *Wiener Oswald* and *Die Hochzeit.*

MIDDLE HIGH GERMAN HEROIC LITERATURE

Das Nibelungenlied nach der Handschrift n, ed. Jürgen Vorderstemann (ATB, 114), xxxvi + 161 pp., is the long-awaited ATB edition of the text of the *Nl.* transmitted in Darmstadt, LB, MS 4257 — the discovery of which was reported by V. as long ago as 1976 (see *TWMLS*, 38: 587). This manuscript, which is dated 1449 and probably originated in Hessen, summarizes the first part of the epic in a mere 19 strophes, before recounting the story of the Burgundians' fateful visit to Etzel's land in a version which is especially obviously indebted to redaction *C, but also reveals parallels with redaction *B, manuscript k, and certain Norse versions of the material. V.'s introduction, critical apparatus and appendix are particularly strong in helping the reader to unravel this complex web of influence and contamination. U. Hennig, *BGDSL*, 122: 427–31, draws attention to the importance for the genesis of the version transmitted by MS n of the manuscript group *Jdh*; and J. Heinzle, *Fest. Johnson*, 207–20, enters a plea for version *C, emphasizing its literary qualities and, above all, its widespread transmission in the Middle Ages. J. Haustein and S. Zimmermann, *Fest. Mettke*, 191–208, describe a 19th-c. manuscript (copied from a print) of the *C-text of the *Nl.* and *Klage.*

Das Nibelungenlied. Eine Auswahl, ed. and trans. Bernhard Sowinski (UB, 18081), 108 pp., offers a new prose translation of salient sections of the epic, linked by summaries. The text is based on U. Hennig's edition of manuscript C. Both S.'s translation and his concise afterword are thoroughly scholarly, and his volume as a whole will provide a reliable introduction to the *Nibelungenlied* for the non-specialist; but given the ready availability of bilingual paperback editions of the whole work, one wonders whether its publication was strictly necessary. Sabine B. Sattel's volume *Das 'Nibelungenlied' in der wissenschaftlichen Literatur zwischen 1945 und 1985. Ein Beitrag zur Geschichte der Nibelungenforschung* (EH, 1, 1739), 535 pp., does, however, make an unequivocally valuable contribution to scholarship. S. surveys research on the *Nl.* published between her chosen dates in four main sections, dealing in turn with work on its precursors, its own origins, its form and (by far the longest section) its literary and thematic content. Her assessment of the work of earlier scholars is at times critical to the point of dismissiveness, and it is regrettable (if understandable) that she discusses no material published after 1985, and pays almost no attention to editorial questions, translations, or studies of reception. Nevertheless this is the first really thorough survey we have had of post-war *Nl.* research, and it is a well-informed and generally judicious one. L. Auteri, *AION(FG)*, n.s.,7, 1998:41–60, discusses animal imagery in the *Nl.* and its relationship to death; and A. Robertshaw, *Fest. Johnson*, 221–29, focuses on the verbal exchanges involving Siegfried and Hagen.

Die Nibelungenklage, ed. and trans. Elisabeth Lienert (SME, 5), 472 pp., combines impressive scholarship with a high degree of user-friendliness. L.'s decision to re-use Bartsch's somewhat hoary edition of the MHG text is perhaps questionable, though she clearly documents his conjectures and other editorial procedures; but her translation is accurate and approachable, and her introduction and commentary provide, concisely and authoritatively, just the kind of information students and others will need as they grapple with the text for the first time. W. Haubrichs, *Fest. Johnson*, 175–206, traces the origins and meanings of the 'Sigi'-names which pervade the various versions of the Nibelung saga.

Karl Bartsch's edition of *Kudrun*, which has been out of print for some years, makes a welcome re-appearance (ATB, 115, xxx + 362 pp.). This printing incorporates the emendations made by K. Stackmann in 1965, and has an entirely new introduction by Stackmann, which however limits itself to codicological and editorial matters. G. Vollmann-Profe, *Fest. Johnson*, 231–44, discusses the presentation of the heroine in *Kudrun*. A. Classen, *ABÄG*, 53:123–43, argues, controversially, that epics such as the *Nl.*, the *Klage*, and *Kudrun* seek to promote the peaceful resolution of conflict, and hence implicitly criticize the violent feuding which underlies the heroic ethos.

Tatjana Rollnik-Manke, *Personenkonstellationen in mittelhochdeutschen Heldenepen. Untersuchungen zum 'Nibelungenlied', zur 'Kudrun' und zu den historischen Dietrich-Epen* (EH, 1, 1764), x + 248 pp., examines techniques of characterization in the works listed in her title (the Dietrich epics discussed are *Dietrichs Flucht* and the *Rabenschlacht*), with particular reference to the changing relationships between characters and the effects these have on the events narrated. As such R.-M. steers a middle course between those studies which have tended to present epic characters as individuals developing in isolation, and those which have perceived them as figures whose actions depend wholly on the circumstances in which they are placed. Her approach is often productive, especially perhaps in the case of the *Nibelungenlied*, which unsurprisingly emerges as the most sophisticated of the works studied in terms of its depiction of the interplay between personal relationships, events, and character. Paying particular attention to the *Eckenlied*, H. Bleumer, *ZDA*, 129: 125–53, discusses the difficulties of generic classification caused by the combination of historical and fictional elements which characterizes 'Dietrichepik'; and S. Kerth, *ZDA*, 129: 154–75, examines the treatment of motifs from 'non-epic' literature in later heroic poetry, as exemplified by *Dietrichs Flucht*, the *Rabenschlacht*, and *Alpharts Tod*. V. Millet, *Wolfram-Studien*, 16: 256–81, speculates on the reasons why heroic epic appears to have been transmitted exclusively orally in the 12th c.

Der deutsche Malagis nach den Heidelberger Handschriften Cpg 340 und Cpg 315, ed. Annegret Haase et al. (DTM, 82), lxxxii + 635 pp., is a monumental first edition, building on the work of numerous scholars over several decades, of a 14th-c. heroic epic from the so-called *barons revoltés* tradition. The German (more accurately, Rhenish-Franconian) *Malagis* is found only in two Heidelberg manuscripts from the second half of the 15th c., and is an extremely close translation of an earlier Middle Dutch text, which has survived only in fragmentary form. Given that the fragments of the Dutch *Madelgijs* are in turn indebted to the French *Maugis d'Aigremont*, this impressively scholarly edition represents a significant step forward for interdisciplinary and comparative *chanson de geste* studies.

THE COURTLY ROMANCE

Jackson, *Arthur*, is an outstanding and and handsomely produced work of reference, whose levels of both scholarship and readability are consistently high. It provides authoritative introductions to all the principal German Arthurian romances (canonical and less well known, including both the *Tristan* and the *Titurel* material), and sets them in their historical-cultural and literary contexts. An introductory chapter by the editors (1–18) evaluates the evidence suggesting a lost Dutch/North West German Arthurian tradition, before introducing issues such as the embeddedness of Arthurian literature in aristocratic culture, the importance of patronage and manuscript transmission, and the differences between the surviving German and Dutch material. Thereafter the work is divided into five parts. The first of these centres on the German verse romances prior to 1300, beginning with I. Kasten's account of the Latin and French background (21–37). Then there are chapters on Hartmann von Aue and Ulrich von Zatzikhoven (S. Ranawake, 38–53); Wolfram's *Parzival* (T. McFarland, 54–68); Wolfram's and Albrecht's *Titurel* romances (M. Gibbs,

69–80); Heinrich von dem Türlin, Der Stricker and Der Pleier (R. E. Wallbank, 81–97); and *Wigamur, Gauriel, Lohengrin* and the fragmentary romances (M. Meyer, 98–114). Part II then treats Tristan narratives (M. Chinca and V. Mertens, 117–41); the Wigalois tradition (V. Honemann, 142–54); the *Prosa-Lancelot* (E. A. Andersen, 155–65); the *Rappoltsteiner Parzifal* and Füetrer's *Buch der Abenteuer* (B. Bastert, 166–80); and *Lorengel* and the *Spruch von den Tafelrundern* (W. H. Jackson, 181–83). Part III is devoted to the Dutch Arthurian material (B. Besamusca, 187–228); and Part IV considers manifestations of Arthurian culture in medieval Bohemia (A. Thomas, 249–56), as well in as such contexts as German heroic poetry (J. L. Flood, 231–41), drama and *Meisterlieder* (J. E. Tailby, 242–48), pictorial art (J. A. Rushing, 257–79) and phenomena such as names, 'round-table' role-playing and a variety of aristocratic pastimes (W. H. Jackson, 280–92). Finally, Part V studies aspects of the Arthurian legacy, such as early printed editions of romances (J. L. Flood, 295–302) and the modern reception of Arthurian legends (U. Müller and W. Wunderlich, 303–23). Krueger, *Romance*, regrettably allots only one chapter to German material (183–202), in which A. M. Rasmussen has to survey the entire tradition from Veldeke to Füetrer. She does this skilfully, though her decision to devote some two pages to the Schmalkalden, Rodenegg, and Runkelstein frescoes is perhaps questionable under the circumstances.

Anja Russ, *Kindheit und Adoleszenz in den deutschen Parzival- und Lancelot-Romanen. Hohes und spätes Mittelalter*, Stuttgart, Hirzel, 405 pp., is an exhaustive and illuminating study of the presentation of *infantia*, *pueritia*, and *adolescentia* in the MHG *Parzival* and *Lancelot* traditions. R. discusses not only Wolfram von Eschenbach and Ulrich von Zatzikhoven, but the *Prosa-Lancelot* and Ulrich Füetrer's *Buch der Abenteuer* and *Lannzilet*; and she also points to parallels in the *Tristan* tradition. Her careful textual analysis bears considerable fruit: she establishes, for example, that the concept of childhood as prefiguring, preparing for and helping to explain adult behaviour which characterizes the romances written around 1200 is lost in later adaptations; that this holds true for subsidiary as well as principal characters; that, at least in MHG romances, the presentation of childhood owes little to Raglan and de Vries's 'hero pattern'; and that the motif of love between children is presented in a much more varied and differentiated way than has often been assumed.

Ute Drecoll, *Tod in der Liebe — Liebe im Tod. Untersuchungen zu Wolframs 'Titurel' und Gottfrieds 'Tristan' in Wort und Bild*, Berne, Lang, 444 pp., is a comparative study of *Tristan* and *Titurel* which centres on their divergent conceptions of the relationship between love and death. In D.'s view, Gottfried perceives death as an intrinsic part of a love which is capable of fulfilment on earth, whereas, for Wolfram, love can only truly be fulfilled after death. She bases her conclusions largely on images found in illustrated manuscripts (not only of *Tristan and Titurel*), as well as on what she calls the 'typologische und ikonographische Bezüge' found in the texts themselves. It is good to have a study of *Titurel* which does not see it primarily in the light of *Parzival*, and D.'s interpretations are often stimulating; but they can also be eccentric and somewhat opaquely expressed.

Achim Jaeger, *Ein jüdischer Artusritter. Studien zum jüdisch-deutschen 'Widuwilt' ('Artushof') und zum 'Wigalois' des Wirnt von Gravenberc* (CJ, 32), x + 465 pp., is a fascinating investigation of two-way influence between German and Jewish-German literature. The works in question lend themselves very well to such a study, in that the late-medieval Jewish-German *Widuwilt* not only used Wirnt's romance as its source but also, in the form of an adaptation known as the *Artushof*, was itself highly influential in German literary circles of the later 17th and 18th cs. J.'s book is centred around a detailed study of the *Widuwilt* author's techniques of adaptation: he shortens Wirnt's work (especially its moralizing passages), recasts its ending and, above all, changes aspects of its cultural and religious content to make it more appealing to a Jewish audience.

R. Hahn, *ASNS*, 237:242–66, examines the (in his view only partly authorial) epilogue of Veldeke's *Eneit*, and re-assesses the contribution of the court of Hermann von Thüringen to the origins and development of courtly literature in German. A. Krass, *Wolfram-Studien*, 16:282–304, shows, with reference to *Eneit, Erec* and *Iwein*, the increasing importance of compassion in the characterization of the hero in 12th-c. romance. In the same volume, G. Althoff (102–20) demonstrates how the rules governing medieval social interaction are portrayed as being obeyed, broken and played with in *Iwein*, Wittenwiler's *Ring* and, especially, *Parzival*; and W. Haubrichs (121–56) examines concepts of confession and their effect on behaviour in a variety of contexts, including *Gregorius, Parzival* and *Reinhart Fuchs*. Meanwhile J. Theisen, Huber, *Geistliches*, 153–69, considers the role of God in relation both to the protagonists and to the narrators in *Der arme Heinrich, Erec, Iwein, Parzival*, and *Tristan*. Also noted: Frank Ringeler, *Zur Konzeption der Protagonistenidentität im deutschen Artusroman um 1200. Aspekte einer Gattungspoetik* (EH, 1, 1752), xii + 326 pp.

HARTMANN VON AUE

There are several new studies of *Erec*. W. Haug, *Fest. Johnson*, 271–90, comments in detail on the *Joie de la curt* episode; M. H. Jones, in the same volume (291–307), examines the interplay between empathy, pretence and narrative perspective; H. Galloway, *FMLS*, 36:33–48, sees in the work reflections of contemporary penitential practice and interprets these as indications of Hartmann's strong interest in his characters' 'inner lives'; and W. C. McDonald, *ColGer*, 33:317–32, argues that he replaces, and re-evaluates, Chrétien's climactic Arthurian coronation by having Erec figuratively crowned at various stages of his career. L. Okken, *ABÄG*, 53:167–86, furnishes a large number of suggested revisions to the 'standard' ATB text of *Erec*, along with a brief excerpt from his own forthcoming edition; W. Achnitz, *Editio*, 14:130–43, reflects on the implications for the work's textual history of the triple and quadruple rhymes in the Wolfenbüttel fragments which do not appear in that 'standard' text; and M. G. Scholz, Huber, *Geistliches*, 135–151, points out that *der hövesche got* (l.3461) and *der saelden wec* (l.8521) are conjectures of early editors, which have arguably led to significant misunderstandings of Hartmann's concept of God. Finally J. Mühlemann, *BGDSL*, 122:76–102, documents a remarkable example of the reception of *Erec*: a cycle of images depicting scenes from the early part of the romance on a crown which forms part of the mid-13th-c. *Krakauer Kronenkreuz*.

Two articles by B. Murdoch compare Hartmann's 'courtly legends' with works of ME literature. In *Fest. Johnson*, 309–20, he discusses the nature of sin in *Gregorius* in the light of the *Incestuous Daughter*, the *Trentalle Sancti Gregorii* and *Sir Eglamour of Artois*; and in *ABÄG*, 53:145–66, he seeks to enhance our understanding of Heinrich's *gemahel* and her concept of salvation by dint of comparisons with *Pearl*. P. Strohschneider, Huber, *Geistliches*, 105–33, essays a new interpretation of *Gregorius* which focuses on its mythic structures and traces Gregorius's development in terms as much of his relationship to the world as of his relationship with God. On *Der arme Heinrich*, C. Kottmann, *LB*, 88, 1999:305–22, interprets the maiden's desire to sacrifice herself as a form of *superbia*, from which she is healed by marriage to Heinrich; K. Gärtner, *Fest. Mettke*, 103–10, discusses the work's manuscript tradition; C. Roth, *BGDSL*, 122:259–62, comments on line 391; and S. Grosse, *Blank Vol.*, 51–59, discusses the position of verbs in subordinate clauses. In *Fest. Mettke*, 429–37, N. R. Wolf examines the significance of the terms *vreude* and *vreuen* in *Iwein*.

WOLFRAM VON ESCHENBACH

Simon Julian Gilmour, *'daz sint noch ungelogeniu wort'. A Literary and Linguistic Commentary on the Gurnemanz Episode in Book III of Wolfram's 'Parzival' (161,9–179,12)* (GB,7), xviii + 376 pp., builds on work by D. N. Yeandle (*YWMLS*, 47:661–62) and B. Eichholz (*YWMLS*,

49:636) by providing a detailed and reliable commentary of what amounts to the last third of Book III of *Parzival*. G.'s approach is not dissimilar to, and in certain respects indeed is consciously modelled on, those of his two predecessors. It combines thorough and clear-headed discussion of textual and linguistic problems with admirably full bibliographical material, and with appropriate references to other literary texts and to relevant historical-cultural matters. The volume is very easy to use, not least thanks to the thoughtful insertion of five leaves of 'fold-out' text, which enable one to follow the Lachmann edition of *Parzival* whilst simultaneously consulting G.

There are two new monographs which take as their point of departure the prologue of *Parzival*; but neither is free from eccentricity. Michela Fabrizia Cessari, *Der Erwählte, das Licht und der Teufel. Eine literarhistorisch-philosophische Studie zur Lichtmetaphorik in Wolframs Parzival* (FBG, 32), xvi + 265 pp., presents the magpie metaphor as a programmatic symbol of Parzival's profound but often misunderstood exceptionality, in which radiant whiteness of both appearance and character is combined with the only apparently black *tumpheit* of a 'pure fool'. This almost wholly positive view of the hero, whose presentation C. regards as owing more to Classical than to Christian models, is not always easy to reconcile with the text; and it inevitably results in some contorted and unconvincing interpretations, especially of Books V and IX. Heinrich Hüning, *Würfelwörter und Rätselbilder im Parzivalprolog Wolframs von Eschenbachs* (EH, 1, 1767), 259 pp., is a quite extraordinary book, loosely constructed and at times self-indulgently written, which combines some interesting interpretations of aspects of the prologue with ideas which are either wilful or simply untenable. H. Brackert, *Fest. Johnson*, 335–47, discusses the opening lines of *Parzival*, focusing especially on the concept of *zwîvel*, which he translates as 'Zwiespalt', 'Schwanken' or 'Uneinssein', and sees as anticipating Wolfram's presentation of a new kind of hero. T. Rausch, *ZDP*, 119:46–74, examines the prologue, *Selbstverteidigung* and *Minne* excursuses, arguing that Wolfram uses them to thematize the relationship between reality and fiction, ultimately rejecting the autonomy of the latter. H. Kästner and B. Schirok, *Blank Vol.*, 61–152, also use the *Selbstverteidigung* as the point of departure for their analysis both of the tension between the narrator's protestations of illiteracy and his obvious dependence on book learning, and of reactions to this tension on the part of medieval, early modern, and 20th-c. readers. B. S. Dieterich, *LJb*, 41:9–65, studies in detail the allusions to Venus in Wolfram's characterization of Orgeluse, which she considers more subtle and playful than Chrétien's. C. J. Steppich, *ABÄG*, 53:187–230, re-examines Wolfram's comparison of Antikonie with the 'Markgräfin auf Burg Haidstein'(403,21–404,10), suggesting that the lady alluded to is indeed his near-contemporary Elisabeth von Vohburg. E. Nellmann, *ZDP*, 119:416–20, lists the notoriously diverse manuscript readings of 467,9, before expressing a preference for the reading of D, G and G^k, *lapsit exillis*. B. Nitsche, *Euphorion*, 94:245–70, discusses the literary significance of eating and drinking in *Parzival*; M. Möhren, *Blank Vol.*, 153–61, examines the narrative technique of the 'Blutstropfenszene'; and B. D. Haage, *Blank Vol.*, 163–68, interprets 489,22–490,30 in the light of 12th-c. knowledge about the pathology of the humours. Meanwhile H. Puff, *ZDA*, 129:70–83, edits and evaluates the single page of handwritten notes found in a copy (from St.Florian, now in Chicago) of Mentelin's 1477 print of *Parzival* and *Titurel*.

Christopher Young, *Narrativische Perspektiven in Wolframs 'Willehalm'* (UDL, 104), viii + 203 pp., makes a sophisticated contribution to the current debates about narrative perspective and characterization in *Willehalm*. Applying theories such as Mieke Bal's notion of focalization, Y. reads the work as a dynamic construct in which both the characters and the narrator develop through interaction with each other and with the events related. This enables both to achieve a degree of multi-dimensionality which is rare in medieval literature, but is arguably in line with the complexity and modernity of Wolfram's world view. Martin Przybilski, *'sippe' und 'geslehte'. Verwandtschaft als Deutungsmuster im 'Willehalm' Wolframs von Eschenbach* (Imagines Medii Aevi, 4), Wiesbaden, Reichert, x + 320 pp., is the second study in recent years to have focused on family relationships in *Willehalm*. In contrast to S. Stevens, however (see *YWMLS*, 59:687–88), P. suggests that the Christians and heathen conceive of and organize their families in significantly different ways: the heathen according to the broad but loosely organized concept of the *sippe*, the Christians in smaller and more tightly controlled units typically denoted by the term *geslehte*. He goes on to argue that the fundamental distinctions between Christian and heathen which these divergent family structures imply are presented as ultimately unbridgeable, even by those characters who have a foot in both cultures.

D. A. Wells, *SM*, 41:591–664, examines the theology of *Willehalm* in the light of the traditions of religious dialogue and apologetic (especially those influenced by Anselm's *Cur deus homo*) to which Wolfram is indebted. F. P. Knapp, *ZDA*, 129:296–302, revisits the vexed question of whether Wolfram (or, more precisely, Giburc) regards the heathen as children of God. D. O. Neville, *Manuscripta*, 1996:96–114, discusses the nature of the tolerance towards the heathen propounded in *Willehalm*, and sees it, and in particular the concept of Giburc as mediatrix, reflected also in the illuminations of MS Hz. A. Gerok-Reiter, Huber, *Geistliches*, 171–94, considers the relationship between religious motivations and values and worldly ones in *Willehalm*; L. Miklautsch, *ZGer*, 10:245–57, analyses Wolfram's use of tears as gestures of mourning; T. Ehlen, *Blank Vol.*, 169–94, discusses the natural images he uses to depict warfare; and N. Harris, *Will Vol.*, 13–24, examines the relationship between the hero and his horse in *Willehalm* and in its source, the *Bataille d'Aliscans*. *Fest. Johnson* has the following articles on *Willehalm*: E. Schmid (349–62) examines the meanings and implications of *snîden* and its derivatives; U. Wyss (363–82) comments on the aesthetic and thematic implications of Wolfram's use of *Fremdwörter*; and S. M. Johnson (383–94) assesses his understanding of genetics.

GOTTFRIED VON STRASSBURG

Christoph Huber, *Gottfried von Strassburg: Tristan* (Klassiker-Lektüren, 3), Berlin, Schmidt, 157 pp., is a revised and updated version of H.'s 1986 Artemis volume (see *YWMLS*, 48:694). As in that work, its various chapters go through the romance section-by-section; unlike it, however, each chapter now has its own annotated bibliography. Walter Haug, *Der Tristanroman im Horizont der erotischen Diskurse des Mittelalters und der frühen Neuzeit* (Wolfgang Stammler Gastprofessur für Germanische Philologie, Vorträge, 10), Fribourg U.P., 48 pp., uses *Tristan* as the prime example of courtly poetry being enabled by its conscious fictionality to develop a concept of erotic love which has freed itself from, but still plays with, other discourses on love current in the Middle Ages. E. Meineke, *Fest. Mettke*, 259–83, and N. Zotz, *GRM*, 50:1–19, consider the nature and implications of Tristan-love with reference to the Carlisle fragment of Thomas's *Tristran*. A. Stevens, *Fest. Johnson*, 409–26, discusses Thomas's and Gottfried's complex treatment of material from Geoffrey of Monmouth and Wace; and A. Classen, *Arcadia*, 35:225–53, postulates an intertextual relationship between *Tristan* and Abelard's *Historia calamitatum* and letters to Heloïse. H. Haferland, *BGDSL*, 122:230–58, interprets the action, characterization and thematic content of *Tristan* as being based on a principle of contrast, which may reveal the at least indirect influence of Augustinian thought; and R.-H. Steinmetz, *ZDA*, 129:388–408, observes links between such *hapax legomena* as *erbeminne* and *erbesmerze* and the Augustinian tradition of inherited sin. T. Dembeck, *ZGer*, 10:493–507, attributes *Tristan*'s arguable opacity at least in part to its having been composed at a time of transition from oral to written culture. M. Kern, *OGS*, 29:1–30, examines Gottfried's allusions to Classical mythology. V. Schupp, *Blank Vol.*, 195–215, studies the Runkelstein Tristan frescoes in the light of Gottfried's romance. J. L. Flood, *Fest. Johnson*, 395–407, surveys the use of laurel as a mark of distinction for poets in Classical, medieval and Renaissance literature, concluding that Gottfried's use of it to honour Hartmann reveals a knowledge of ancient literature unusual for his time. A. Ebenbauer, *Fest. Johnson*, 245–69, discusses various literary presentations of lovers being discovered *flagrante delicto*, but with special reference to *Tristan*.

OTHER ROMANCES AND SHORTER NARRATIVES

Nicola McLelland, *Ulrich von Zatzikoven's 'Lanzelet'. Narrative Style and Entertainment* (Arthurian Studies, 46), Cambridge, Brewer, xii + 260 pp., is a rare monograph on Ulrich, and the first of any real substance in English. It is welcome not just for this reason, but also for its independent, well argued and generally persuasive re-appraisal of the work. For all its indebtedness to its French source, use of traditional Arthurian motifs and affinities with 'post-classical' romances, *Lanzelet* (here dated to 1200–03) is presented by McL. as an original and innovative text — with regard to its stylistic variations, the primacy Ulrich attaches to courage (*manheit*), and his consistent and successful desire to entertain rather than edify.

Heinrich von dem Türlin, *Die Krone (Verse 1–12281). Nach der Handschrift 2779 der Österreichischen Nationalbibliothek Wien*, ed. Fritz Peter Knapp and Manuela Niesner (ATB, 112), xxxii + 381 pp., is the first instalment of what is intended to be the first edition of the entire work since G. H. F. Scholl's in 1852. It follows closely the readings of its base manuscript (V), which offers a reliable text, but one which unfortunately expires in mid-sentence nearly halfway through the work (hence the limitation to the first 12281 lines). The second volume will be based, inevitably, on the later and less reliable manuscript P. The present edition is a thoroughly modern one, conservative but readable, with erroneous readings of V and the variants of P placed in a separate column alongside the main text, and a second apparatus at the foot of the page recording the conjectures of previous editors. There are also, remarkably, two new monographs on *Die Crône*. Peter Stein, *Integration — Variation — Destruktion. 'Die Crône' Heinrichs von dem Türlin* (DLA, 32), 315 pp., is a stimulating and often persuasive study which begins with an analysis of Heinrich's treatment of material from earlier courtly romances. S. courts controversy by suggesting that the only such works manifestly known to Heinrich were *Erec*, *Iwein*, *Lanzelet* and the first six books of *Parzival*, and that *Die Crône* is therefore likely to have been composed some time earlier than its generally accepted date of *c.* 1230. On the basis of detailed comparisons with this block of source material, he proceeds to argue that, through his presentation of combat, love, minor characters and, perhaps most significantly, his hero's integrity and ability to control his own destiny, Heinrich not only playfully varies central features of Arthurian romance but actually undermines them — to the extent that no consistent authorial message can be discerned. Whilst Stein's study emphasizes intertextuality, Thomas Gutwald, *Schwank und Artushof. Komik unter den Bedingungen höfischer Interaktion in der 'Crône' des Heinrich von dem Türlin* (Mikrokosmos, 55), Frankfurt, Lang, 371 pp., takes an avowedly intratextual approach, albeit one which owes much to Niklas Luhmann's theory of social systems. It is a sophisticated if not always readable study of comedy in *Die Crône*. G. accepts the conventional view that many of its comic episodes are indebted to the *Schwank* tradition, but argues that they operate on a wider variety of levels than has often been allowed. In particular, he stresses that *Die Crône*'s comedy is fundamentally dependent on social interaction — between the characters of the romance, between author and audience, and indeed between author and scribe. Also on *Die Crône*, N. Thomas, *MLR*, 95:744–63, highlights Heinrich's imaginative re-casting of Arthurian material, especially his presentation of Arthur himself as an inexperienced king whose affairs are rescued by Gawein; and A. Classen, *MGS*, 24, 1998:113–28, discusses ways in which the work can be seen as foreshadowing postmodernism.

Armin Schulz, *Poetik des Hybriden. Schema, Variation und intertextuelle Kombinatorik in der Minne- und Aventiureepik* (PSQ, 161), 251 pp., breaks new ground by essaying a systematic study of the 'bricolage' approach to narrative technique used in many later medieval romances. Using both insights from post-structuralist textual theories and techniques of close reading, S. analyses three such works which have in common the depiction of an initially illicit love which is eventually legitimized in social terms: Rudolf von Ems's *Willehalm von Orlens* (which he places at the head of this tradition), Konrad von Würzburg's *Partonopier und Meliur*, and Johann von Würzburg's *Wilhelm von Österreich*. He also compares and contrasts their narrative structure with that of a representative work from the 16th c., Veit Warbeck's *Die schöne Magelone*. S.'s study identifies considerable continuity between the works investigated, but shows also that they are all 'hybrid' narratives, which incorporate motifs and structures from other traditions in a variety of ways, and as such create their own unique narrative texture and thematic purport.

Franziska Wenzel, *Situationen höfischer Kommunikation. Studien zu Rudolfs von Ems 'Willehalm von Orlens'* (Mikrokosmos, 57), Frankfurt, Lang, 289 pp., reads Rudolf's romance as a study of inter-personal communication — communication which may be private or public, verbal or non-verbal, oral or written, practised by characters or by the narrator. W. considers in particular the forms of communication which enable the secret love of Willehalm and Amelie to be integrated into courtly society, and the various communicative strategies employed by the narrator in his dealings with his characters, his audience and the literary tradition within which he works. The readability of the study is at times impaired by an over-liberal use of *Fachjargon*, but W. nevertheless offers an intriguing approach to this still underrated work. W. H. Jackson, *Fest. Johnson*, 427–43, examines the diverse uses of chivalric vocabulary in Rudolf's narratives; N. von Merveldt, *Euphorion*, 94:293–317, analyses his presentation of donations and patronage in *Der guote Gerhart*; and A. Classen, *Fabula*, 41:203–28, discerns the influence of Buddhist thought on *Barlaam und Josaphat* (and on other medieval works).

Rüdiger Brandt, *Konrad von Würzburg. Kleinere epische Werke* (Klassiker-Lektüren, 2), Berlin, Schmidt, 158 pp., is, as befits a volume aimed primarily at students, clearly structured and approachably written. B. begins with a summary of Konrad's life and works, then deals with relevant aspects of their historical-cultural and literary context, with Konrad's conception(s) of art, and with references to and reception of his works by later vernacular authors. A brief survey of the main contours of previous research leads into more detailed discussion of four 'kleinere epische Werke': *Das Herzmaere, Heinrich von Kempten, Der Welt Lohn*, and *Engelhard*. B.'s choice of texts is of course debatable, but seems to have been determined above all by their ready availability in bilingual editions and/or translations. It is good to see Konrad being accorded the status of a 'Klassiker', and good also that the task of introducing him to a wider audience has been entrusted to such competent and sensitive hands. A. Koch, *ColGer*, 32, 1999:201–22, comments on the various forms of *triuwe* thematized in *Engelhard*; M. Schnyder, *BGDSL*, 122:263–78, reads *Die halbe Birne* primarily as a study of relationships between the sexes; and B. Quast, *ZDA*, 129:303–20, reflects on the often ambivalent relationship between the material and the symbolic in medieval culture, taking particular account of *Das Herzmaere*.

There are two new editions of what has hitherto been called, for no very good reason, *Moriz von Craûn. Mauricius von Craûn*, ed. and trans. Dorothea Klein (UB, 8796), 1999, 244 pp., is an excellent volume for student use, containing a well-judged introduction and commentary, and a lucid modern German translation. K. is also wise enough to use Edward Schröder's edition of the MHG text, rather than the notoriously interventionist one by Ulrich Pretzel; and she performs the valuable service of providing a text and translation of the related French poem *Du chevalier qui recovra l'amor de sa dame*. The purely editorial part of K.'s book has, however, already been superseded by

Mauritius von Craûn, ed. Heimo Reinitzer (ATB, 113), xxxiv + 112 pp. R.'s edition is an entirely new one. Commendably, his text adheres more closely than that of any previous editor to the only manuscript of the work, the *Ambraser Heldenbuch*, whilst remaining generally easy to read. He also includes a concise and up-to-date introduction, the variant readings of all previous editions, an eight-page partial facsimile of the manuscript and, again, the French *fabliau* (with translation). R.'s profound knowledge of *Mauritius* is evident also in his extensive commentary to the work: *Mauritius von Craûn. Ein Kommentar* (*ZDA* Beihefte, 2), Stuttgart, Steiner, 1999, 246 pp. This goes far beyond offering justifications for his editorial decisions, and includes discussion of linguistic problems, secondary literature, and various thematic questions. It is particularly strong in referring to, and where desirable quoting from, other primary texts.

Der Stricker, *Verserzählungen I*, ed. Hanns Fischer (ATB, 53), xxxii + 160 pp., is a tried-and-tested edition, now reprinted for the fourth time with its bibliography updated by Johannes Janota. A particularly helpful feature is Janota's provision of specific bibliographical references for each of the thirteen stories included in the volume. Also on Der Stricker, H. Dworschak, Michel, *Symbole*, 181–94, interprets Vienna, CPV 2705, the so-called 'Stricker Leithandschrift', as a macrotext which symbolizes the moral evaluation of sexuality; E. Ukena-Best, *LB*, 89:327–62, offers a detailed analysis of *Karl der Große*, considering in particular matters of structure and characterization, and drawing perhaps surprising parallels to the *Ludwigslied*; R. Hartge and J. Heinzle, *ZDA*, 129:176–78, describe a newly discovered fragment of *Der Richter und der Teufel*; and H. Brall, *Euphorion*, 94:319–34, sees the origins of 13th-c. *Schwankdichtung*, as exemplified especially in *Pfaffe Amîs*, in a new and often ambiguous conception of evil.

Amongst studies of other narratives, W. Wegner, *Euphorion*, 94:271–92, argues that Albrecht's *Jüngerer Titurel* communicates its moral teaching not least by deploying techniques of poetic visualization which would be effective in oral performance. S. Leonardi, *SM*, 41:119–49, reads Heinrich's *Reinhart Fuchs* as a complex work set in a topsy-turvy world, in which Reinhart is presented both as a *figura diaboli* and as an exemplary figure; and R. Schlusemann, *FCS*, 25, 1999:331–44, discusses the presentation of violence in the text and illustrations of *Reynke de vos* and of its indirect source, the so-called *Reynaert III* fragments. C. Brinker-von der Heyde, *DUS*, 2000.6:7–19, uses passages from *Helmbrecht* to illustrate the presentation of just and unjust violence in medieval literature. A. Schulz, *BGDSL*, 122:432–54, essays an anthropological and poetological reading of *Der Busant*, a central theme of which is shown to be the tension between nature and culture. T. Weber, *GermL*, 153:75–93, argues for greater appreciation of the works of the 'Schweizer Anonymus', and discusses in particular their thematization of revenge. A. Schnyder, *GermL*, 153:49–73, examines comic elements in the *Mären* of Heinrich Kaufringer; and V. Millet, Huber, *Geistliches*, 273–90, discusses the relationship between the religious epimythia and the often decidedly worldly content of *Mären* such as *Die treue Magd, Drei Mönche zu Kolmar*, and Kaufringer's *Die unschuldige Mörderin*.

LYRIC POETRY

Helmut Tervooren, *'Schoeniu wort mit süezeme sange'*. *Philologische Schriften*, ed. Susanne Fritsch and Johannes Spicker (PSQ, 159), 238 pp., unites some 15 of T.'s publications from between 1968 and 1994. They accurately reflect his main research interests: the literature of the Lower Rhineland, editorial methodology and, above all, the MHG lyric. Harald Haferland, *Hohe Minne. Zur Beschreibung der Minnekanzone* (*ZDP* Beihefte, 10), Berlin, Schmidt, 412 pp., is a stimulating book which reacts against both early biographical approaches to the study of *Minnelieder* and more recent studies which, H. argues, have tended to employ techniques more applicable to modern poetry. H. stresses that 12th-c and 13th-c. *Minnelieder* were typically wooing songs composed for performance in an aristocratic context in which the object of the poet's adulation may have been present or at least known; and he reconstructs a cultural environment for their performance in which (due not least to the pragmatic rigours of contemporary marriage) the public expression of individual emotion was expected and prized. Other general studies: O. Sayce, *Fest. Johnson*, 3–28, lists and assesses exemplary comparisons to named figures in the medieval German (and Romance) lyric; S. Ranawake, *FMLS*, 36:49–63, discusses representations of travel in the works of MHG professional poets; U. Müller, *GermL*, 153:29–48, uses examples from medieval and modern poetry in a study of the comedic effect of lists of proper names; and V. Mertens, *Fest. Johnson*, 141–58, discusses problems associated with the translation of MHG lyrics into modern German, and presents some examples of 'creative' verse translations from a Berlin seminar. In *Fest. Tervooren*, S. Fritsch (103–13) points to some of the gender discourses which can be found in *Minnesang*, stressing the potential value for their interpretation of a Gender Studies paradigm; and J. Spicker (115–34) discusses descriptions of the female body in the late-medieval love lyric. In *ZDP*, 119, *Sonderheft*, H. Brunner and H. Tervooren (1–9) assess the current state of research into *Sangspruchdichtung*; S. Obermaier (59–72) examines the presentation of the relationship between poet and artisan in lyrics by Konrad von Würzburg, Frauenlob, Michel Beheim and Hans Sachs; C. März (73–84) examines the topos of the counting of syllables in 14th- and 15th-c. poetry; S. Kerth (85–98) investigates the functions of adynata in *Sangspruchdichtung* and *Minnesang*; and M. Baldzuhn (252–77) studies aspects of the gradual development from single-stanza *Sangsprüche* to longer *Meisterlieder*.

J. Haustein, *Fest. Tervooren*, 21–31, traces the history of the section headed 'namenlose Lieder' (MF 3,1–6,31) in the various editions of *Minnesangs Frühling*, and suggests ways in which this section might be presented in any future revision. In the same volume (33–43), H. Brunner enters a plea for just such a new edition, again with suggestions as to its contents and format.

Reinhard Bleck, *Mittelhochdeutsche Bittlieder. 1. Die Lieder Hergers, Spervogels und des Jungen Spervogel/Jungen Stolle* (GAG, 688), vi + 157 pp., argues, as his title suggests, that the stanzas transmitted under the names of the poets in question, far from being independent lyrics, in fact constitute lengthy continuous songs. Especially in the case of Spervogel, B. is able to do this only by disregarding almost entirely the order of stanzas in the surviving manuscripts. His conclusions about the thematic material of the songs and, especially, about the extent to which the biographies of the poets can be constructed from them, are frequently bold but unconvincing. K. Brem, *ZDP*, 119, *Sonderheft*: 10–37, examines the complex role of the first person narrator/singer in the lyrics of Herger and Spervogel.

T. Bein, *Fest. Tervooren*, 45–56, outlines the principles and format of a planned textual critical commentary to C. Cormeau's edition of Walther von der Vogelweide's songs (see *YWMLS*, 58:743), and demonstrates these using the example of L.69,1. M. Chinca, *Fest. Johnson*, 101–22, uses the manuscript tradition of L.69,1 to discuss the role of writing in promoting both variability and invariance in medieval texts. Other studies of Walther in *Fest. Johnson*: E. Nellmann (53–65) re-interprets the final three lines of L.19,5; J. Ashcroft (67–86) analyses the poet's self-reflexions in L.62,6 and 66,21; and H. Brunner (123–39) discusses 19th-c. and 20th-c. perceptions of Walther, with special reference to those conveyed in public lectures by Würzburg professors. Elsewhere, M. Schumacher, *WW*, 50:169–88, interprets and translates L.100,24.

C. Bertelsmeier-Kierst, *Fest. Johnson*, 87–99, examines the 13th-c. manuscript transmission of Walther's lyrics, stressing that it differs significantly from that in the Codex Manesse. She also suggests that the mutual influence of Walther and the poems of the Codex Buranus might imply that the latter originated at the court of the Patriarch of Aquileia. Also on the Codex Buranus, U. Kühne, *BGDSL*, 122:57–73, re-examines the relationship between its Latin and German stanzas;

and S. de Laude, *Paragone*, 598, 1999:94–106, comments on CB 82 and CB 88 (which she relates to the *De amore* of Andreas Capellanus).

E. and H. Wenzel, *Fest. Tervooren*, 87–102, establish that each of the surviving Neidhart manuscripts conveys a different profile of the author, and discuss the implications of this for an understanding of the whole corpus. L. Voetz, *Fest. Mettke*, 381–408, essays a partial reconstruction of the missing sections of the Neidhart corpus in the Codex Manesse on the basis of notes written *c.* 1600 by Melchior Goldast von Haiminsfeld, whom V. believes was responsible for removing the pages in the first place. D. Klein, *ZDA*, 129: 1–30, offers an interpretation of Neidhart's 'Sommerlied 11', focusing on its manuscript transmission, intertextual relationships, and possible programmatic intention. With special reference to Neidhart, I. Bennewitz, *Fest. Tervooren*, 73–85, explores the use of bird imagery to illuminate the roles and performance practices of *Minnesänger*.

Sangsprüche in Tönen Frauenlobs. Supplement zur Göttinger Frauenlob-Ausgabe, ed. Jens Haustein and Karl Stackmann (AAWG, 232), 2 vols, 740 pp., is an important and long-awaited addition to the so-called 'Göttingen edition' of the lyrics of Frauenlob. It edits some 500 strophes composed in melodies attributed to Frauenlob which are transmitted more than once in surviving manuscripts, but which were not regarded as genuine by the earlier editor, Helmuth Thomas. Especially given its extremely high philological standards, this new book provides us with a far more reliable basis than we have had hitherto for forming judgements as to the actual extent of Frauenlob's *œuvre*, as well as constituting a valuable anthology of late-medieval *Sangspruchdichtung*. S. Köbele, Huber, *Geistliches*, 213–35, discusses the almost symbiotic relationship between religious and secular discourse in Frauenlob's *Lieder*; and S. Fritsch, *ZDP*, 119, *Sonderheft*: 222–36, examines Frauenlob's presentation of the Eucharist in stanzas in his 'Langer Ton' and 'Grüner Ton'.

Margarete Payer, *Das religiöse Weltbild des Mönchs von Salzburg in den geistlichen Liedern G 33, G 34, G 37 und G 46* (GAG, 669), viii + 221 pp., complements recent research on the Monk's secular songs (see *YWMLS*, 61:621–22) by focusing attention again on his religious lyrics. On the basis of essentially circumstantial evidence, P. suggests that the Monk may have been an Austin Canon who studied in Avignon, and that his religious songs are marked by a strong desire to communicate fundamental Christian truths to a lay audience. The songs she studies in detail ascribe particular importance to the Trinity (especially the Holy Spirit) and relatively little to the saints; and she draws several parallels with the *Summa Theologica* of Thomas Aquinas and the *Legenda Aurea* of Jacobus a Voragine. Both the choice of poems studied and that of other material with which they are compared do, however, seem somewhat arbitrary.

Mittelhochdeutsche Minnereden und Minneallegorien der Prager Handschrift R VI Fc 26. 1. *'Standhaftigkeit in der Liebesqual'*, ed. Michael Mareiner (EH, I, 1650) is a conscientious edition, with parallel modern German translation, of a discourse on love found (immediately after a copy of *Iwein*) in a Prague manuscript variously dated 1464, 1467 and 1472. It is preceded by an immensely detailed account of the text's phonetic and orthographical features. One would like to know more about the role played by this work in the development of its genre; but for answers to literary questions such as this we will have to await the appearance of a forthcoming second volume.

Articles on other poets: C. Young, *Fest. Johnson*, 29–51, explores the interaction between vision and discourse in Morungen's songs MF 145,1, 133,13 and 127,1; R. Fisher, *AUMLA*, 93:1–16, interprets the differing manuscript versions of Hartmann's *Wê, war umbe trûren wir* as records of different performances of the song; M. Niesner, *ZDA*, 129:38–69, discusses the presentation of the Jews in the works of Heinrich der Teichner; and F. Niemeyer, *Blank Vol.*, 305–30, assesses the originality of the references to sirens in those of Michel Beheim. M. Schiendorfer, *Fest. Tervooren*, 135–57, discusses some of the little known poems composed in the context of the Devotio Moderna; G. Kornrumpf, *Fest. Tervooren*, 159–90, examines the two versions of the 14th-c. Latin and German Christmas song *In dulci iubilo*, along with their 16th-c. reception; and J. Knape, *ZDA*, 129:321–26, edits and discusses a 15th-c. love song from an Einsiedeln manuscript. In *ZDP*, 119, *Sonderheft*, L. Lieb (38–47) investigates the relationship between *Sangspruchdichtung* and *Minnesang* in the œuvre of Heinrich von Veldeke; F. V. Spechtler and H. Waechter (50–58) suggest that Bruder Wernher (and perhaps other poets) borrowed musical techniques from medieval psalmody; M. J. Schubert (99–111) studies ways in which Reinmar von Zweter plays with and undermines generic conventions; R. Hahn (112–29) examines the references to the legend of St Brendan in the *Wartburgkrieg*, arguing that some of them derive from *Parzival*; P. Kern (130–42) edits and analyses Rumelant von Sachsen's *Got in vier elementen sich erscheinet*; W. Layher (143–66) studies the evidence of literary contact between Northern Germany and Scandinavia in the late 13th c., with particular reference to Rumelant von Sachsen; N. Miedema (167–82) considers whether poetic units of more than one stanza occur in Konrad von Würzburg's 'Hofton'; M. Schiendorfer (183–96) examines the poems attributed in the Codex Manesse to the shadowy 'Gast'; J. Haustein (197–207) discusses the coherence and literary quality of *Meisterlieder* with reference to a song attributed to Boppe; J. Spicker (208–21) discusses the literary function of lists of geographical names in the Boppe corpus; and M. Egidi (237–51) examines the levels of discourse and the function of the first-person singer in lyrics by Suchensinn. Elsewhere, M. Baldzuhn, *ZDP*, 119:427–33, draws attention to the absence of three leaves from the Codex Manesse which appear originally to have contained lyrics by Suchensinn; H. Schwarz, *ZDP*, 119:397–409, comments on the diminutive *meinel* which occurs only in poems by Tannhäuser; and M. Schiendorfer, *ZDP*, 119:421–26, examines Heinrich Laufenberg's 'Liedercodex' for the light it sheds on the text of his song *Stand vf vnd sih Ihesum vil rein*.

DIDACTIC, DEVOTIONAL AND RELIGIOUS LITERATURE

Maria C. Sherwood-Smith, *Studies in the Reception of the 'Historia scholastica' of Peter Comestor. The 'Schwarzwälder Predigten', the 'Weltchronik' of Rudolf von Ems, the 'Scolastica' of Jacob van Maerlant and the 'Historiebijbel van 1360'* (*MAe* Monographs, n.s., 20), x + 181 pp., is an admirable study of the complex relationships between Comestor's exegetical compendium and the four, very different, German and Dutch works listed in its title. Whilst these relationships vary considerably, S.-S. identifies trends in the vernacular reception of the *Historia* which imply that is was valued as a source of extra-biblical stories, of abridged paraphrases of biblical narratives, of historical and geographical background information to these, and, not least, as a guarantor of truth. It is often extremely difficult to differentiate between material taken from the *Historia* and that garnered from elsewhere, not least given the highly variable nature of the *Historia*'s own textual history (documented by S.-S. in a substantial introduction); but she solves numerous problems arising from this by dint of painstaking and judicious textual analysis. K. Ruh, *ZDA*, 129:35–37, argues that MS Gr of the *Schwarzwälder Predigten* was written by the preacher himself.

Mauritius Wilde, *Das neue Bild vom Gottesbild. Bild und Theologie bei Meister Eckhart* (Dokimion, 24), Fribourg U.P., xvi + 384 pp., is a study by a systematic theologian of the relationship between Eckhart's theory of imagery, his use of specific images (especially the mirror), and the images of God suggested in his writings. On the basis of a comparative study of Eckhart's 'Bildlehre' and those of Augustine, Thomas Aquinas and Dietrich von Freiberg, W. suggests that the concepts of dynamism and dimensionality which inform both the theory and practice of Eckhart's imagery together constitute a key to the understanding of his theology. Cornelia Rizek-Pfister, *Ein Weg zu Meister Eckharts Armutspredigt* (DLA, 30), 465 pp., is, by contrast, the work of a Germanist. Taking Eckhart's 'Armutspredigt' (Quint 52) as a paradigm, R.-P. asks what exactly a 21st-c. reader needs to know in order to arrive at an adequate understanding of his sermons. Her response stresses the importance of, and provides relevant information about, such matters as medieval liturgical and homiletic practice, theological traditions such as 'negative theology', the social and intellectual context (nuns, béguines, heresy, etc.) and, not least, aspects of contemporary mystical language. Overall, she provides a sound and differentiated framework for the interpretation of Eckhart which will be of particular value to students. In a paper in Michel, *Symbole* (99–107), Rizek-Pfister argues that Eckhart's oft-expressed loss of personal identity through union with God is, paradoxically, a powerful assertion of identity. In Haug, *Mystik*, G. Steer (253–81) discusses Eckhart's sermons 'von der êwigen geburt' (Pfeiffer 1–4), which he sees as a coherent cycle datable to around 1303; F. Löser (283–316), examines his theory and practice of prayer; O. Langer (317–46) analyses his concept of self-negation and 'Ich-Theorie', with reference especially to his 'Armutspredigt' and 'Gelassenheitspredigt'(Quint 12); and M. Wehrli-Johns (223–52) raises the fascinating possibility that Eckhart may have been involved in the repression of heresy in both Strasbourg and Cologne before himself being accused of it.

Bardo Weiss, *Ekstase und Liebe. Die Unio mystica bei den deutschen Mystikerinnen des 12. und 13. Jahrhunderts*, Paderborn, Schöningh, x + 987 pp., is a monumental study of the phenomena of ecstasy, love and mystical union as expressed in works written by, in conjunction with, or simply about, over 20 female German and Dutch mystics from between the mid-12th and late 13th cs — including, of course, all the major figures from Helfta and Brabant. W. begins by analysing the various terms, symptoms and experiences associated with ecstasy, and then studies the ways in which mystics experience the 'loss' of self, before tackling the complex question of *unio mystica* itself. This last section, of nearly 600 pages, considers first the imagery of mystic union, and then its essential nature and its consequences for the soul. W. performs the massive task he has set himself in a painstaking, systematic, lucid and balanced way which consistently commands admiration.

Hildegard Elisabeth Keller, *My Secret is Mine. Studies on Religion and Eros in the German Middle Ages* (Studies in Spirituality, Supplements, 4), Leuven, Peeters, x + 297 pp., examines various implications of the eroticized concepts of God and his bride, based not least on allegorical interpretations of the Song of Songs, which informed much medieval religious culture and are reflected in manifold ways in literature. She shows for example how the concept of the bride of Christ came to be appropriated increasingly by female religious, how the relationship between Christ and bride was frequently expressed in terms of current gender stereotypes, and how the realms of spiritual and secular marriage were constantly interlinked in literary discourse. K. bases her investigations on a wide range of predominantly German texts from the 12th to the 17th cs; an entire chapter is devoted to the relatively seldom studied *Christus und die minnende Seele*. Barbara Weber, *Die Funktion der Alltagswirklichkeit in der Metaphorik Mechthilds von Magdeburg* (GAG, 683), iv + 194 pp., explores a wide variety of Mechthild's figures of speech (W.'s definition of a metaphor is a very broad one), drawn from areas such as motherhood, illness, medicine, food and drink, clothing, work, trade and money, the law, and nature. In respect of each of these, the metaphors are first listed (in annoyingly small print), and then analysed with reference to their rhetorical function, their literary sources and (often rather less convincingly) the light they might shed on the actual circumstances of Mechthild's life. Elizabeth A. Andersen, *The Voices of Mechthild of Magdeburg*, Berne, Lang, 255 pp., is an invaluable introductory monograph on Mechthild, the first of its kind in English. A. draws particular attention to the pronounced dialogic nature of *Das fließende Licht der Gottheit*. Following initial sections on the work's literary and theological context, she accordingly divides her material into four chapters dealing with a variety of different 'voices': that of the béguine and nun (involving a discussion of Mechthild's biography and socio-historical environment); that of the author (dealing with issues of authorship, transmission and reception); those of the Psalter and the Song of Songs (presented as seminal texts for the development of Mechthild's thought); and that of the ecstatic visionary (focusing especially on her concepts of time and eternity). Sound judgment and clarity of expression are consistent characteristics of a volume which wears its considerable erudition attractively lightly. Elsewhere, S. S. Poor, *Exemplaria*, 12:417–53, also discusses the question of female authorship in Mechthild's writings; and F. Tobin, *Giles Vol.*, 9–22, examines Mechthild's presentation of the Devil and Antichrist. In Haug, *Mystik*, G. Vollmann-Profe (133–56) compares aspects of *Das fließende Licht* to its Latin translation and draws conclusions about the latter's purpose and methods; B. Hasebrink (157–74) examines Mechthild's use of the mirror metaphor; and B. McGinn (175–94) analyses her claims to quasi-scriptural authority.

Irmtraud Just, *Die Vita Luitgarts von Wittichen. Text des Donaueschinger Codex 118. Mit Einleitung, Kommentar und frömmigkeitsgeschichtlicher Einordnung* (DLA, 31), 301 pp., tells the reader all he is likely to want to know about Berthold von Brombach's hagiographical account of the life of Luitgart (1292–1349), founder of the house of Poor Clares at Wittichen in the Black Forest and a mystic with links (especially via

Gerhart von Rappoltsweiler) to the so-called 'Friends of God'. J. provides an edition of Berthold's text which (perhaps as a reaction against earlier, unduly interventionist editions) favours fidelity to the base manuscript over readability; and she complements this with an excellent commentary, dealing with linguistic, literary, theological and historical questions. Work on other female mystics includes: M. Gsell's discussion (Haug, *Mystik*, 455–82) of the *Offenbarungen* of the Zürich Dominican Elsbeth von Oye, which she classifies as an 'ecstatic' text; S. Bürkle's examination, in the same volume (483–513), of Christine Ebner's *Gnadenvita*, which draws particular attention to its episodic structure and problematic narratorial perspective; and B. Morgan's study, in Davies, *Autobiography*, 35–51, of the spiritual autobiographies of visionary nuns and their Dominican confessors in 14th-c. Germany. Specifically on sorority books, S. Linden, *OGS*, 29:31–76, discusses the presentation of death and dying in the *Engelthaler Schwesternbuch*; W. Schneider-Lastin, Haug, *Mystik*, 515–61, edits and comments on the *vita* of the quondam béguine Adelheit von Freiburg from the *Ötenbacher Schwesternbuch*; B. A. Zimmermann, in the same volume (563–80), sees accounts of nuns' lives in the sorority books as examples of narrative theology; M. Hubrath, Michel, *Symbole*, 83–97, discusses the thematization of eating and fasting in sorority books; and A. Winston-Allen, Classen, *Voices*, 145–53, problematizes notions of gendered authorship when discussing Johannes Meyer's 1482 versions of earlier nuns' *vitae*.

Other articles on mysticism: in Haug, *Mystik*, A. M. Haas (9–29) reflects on the comprehensibility of mystical experience and language; P. Michel (61–92) assesses the extent to which mystical discourse can be based on the Bible and/or its exegesis (he includes passages from the *St. Trudperter Hohelied* and from Eckhart's sermon Quint 71); N. Largier (93–117) problematizes the concepts of 'Dominican mysticism' and 'Frauenmystik', arguing that texts and their inter-relationships, rather than authors and 'schools', should be the principal focus of research; H. E. Keller (195–221) examines the elements of secretiveness and mystery inherent in mysticism; J. F. Hamburger (353–408) surveys the history of the concept of specula-tion, making detailed reference to Seuse's *Exemplar* and Gertrud von Helfta's *Legatus divinae pietatis*; J. Theisen (409–23) discusses the extent to which the argumentative structure of Tauler's (and Eckhart's) sermons is influenced by their liturgical context; H.-J. Schiewer (581–603) establishes that the Dominican convent of St. Katharinen-tal bei Dießenhofen was a major centre of literary activity in the 14th c., and was particularly active in compiling and combining vernacular works, including mystical revelations; and N. F. Palmer (605–52) prints a collection of mystical *Sprüche* and exempla from Reading,

UL, MS 137, one of a group of 15th-c. manuscripts from the Carthusian house at Buxheim near Memmingen which transmit earlier mystical writings (including Eckhart). Both W. Beierwaltes, Haug, *Mystik*, 425–54, and A. M. Haas, *Blank Vol.*, 217–35, discuss mystical elements in the thought of Nicolaus Cusanus. O. Pfefferkorn, *Muttersprache*, 110:214–28, draws parallels between the rhetoric of late-medieval mysticism, 17th-c. didactic literature, and contemporary advertising.

Sabine von Heusinger, *Johannes Mulberg OP (†1414). Ein Leben im Spannungsfeld von Dominikanerobservanz und Beginenstreit* (Quellen und Forschungen zur Geschichte des Dominikanerordens, n.s., 9), Berlin, Akademie, x + 201 pp., is a worthy study of Mulberg, whose life (many details of which are conveyed by Johannes Nider's *Formicarius*) was spent principally in Basel and Colmar. H.'s biography of him contains ample and at times original coverage of the two main public issues in which he was involved, the reform of his order and the béguine controversy in Basel between 1405 and 1411, which was arguably ignited by one of his sermons. The volume also contains editions of Mulberg's Latin *Tractatus contra Beginas et Beghardos*, and of a German letter by Konrad Schletter which records his death *en route* for the Council of Constance in 1414. Helga Haage-Naber, *Drei Basler Predigten Heinrich Kalteisens OP (= Die deutschen Predigten Heinrich Kalteisens OP, II). Edition und Untersuchung* (GAG, 677), 225 pp., builds, as its subtitle suggests, on the edition of three of Kalteisen's German sermons published by B.D. Haage in 1983. H.-N. offers texts of three more (V, VII and X) of the ten sermons Kalteisen preached to the sisters of the Dominican convent 'An den Steinen' in Basel in 1434. Her introductory material on Kalteisen's career and the manuscripts and language of his sermons is apposite and concise, and her edition seems reliable — although its user-friendliness is reduced by the listing of textual variants in a series of 2289 endnotes. Other work on sermons: J. Dahmus, *Medieval Sermon Studies*, 44:37–52, compares and contrasts sermons on the Ten Commandments by Berthold von Regensburg and by Johannes Nider; R. Benzinger et al., *Fest. Mettke*, 1–24, edit Berthold's vernacular *Meßerklärung* from a 15th-c. Mainz manuscript; and D. Neuendorff, *NMi*:301–12, shows that the apparently highly personal statements he makes in his German sermons actually constitute sophisticated rhetorical devices. D. L. Stoudt, *Medieval Sermon Studies*, 44:53–67, argues that preaching formed a less important part than has often been assumed of the *cura monalium* practised in 14th-c. Dominican convents; and C. Fasbender, *Fest. Mettke*, 83–101, analyses the late 14th-c. *Leipziger Predigtsammlung* of Dietrich von Gotha.

Using a model developed by Wolfgang Iser, I. de la Cuadra, *ZDP*, 119:75–97, analyses the interplay of the historical and the fictional in the 'Bauernszene' of Hugo von Trimberg's *Renner* and the eighth *Seifried Helbling* poem. K.-E. Geith, *Blank Vol.*, 237–51, postulates that a German version of the legend of Pilate and Veronica was used both by Gundacker von Judenberg in his *Christi hort* and by the so-called 'Österreichischer Bibelübersetzer' in his *Klosterneuburger Evangelienbuch*. K. Klein, *ZDA*, 129:184–86, demonstrates that the 'Melker' and 'Budapester' fragments of the *Väterbuch* originally formed part of the same manuscript. H. Broszinski and H.-H. Steinhoff, *ZDA*, 129:414–19, present fragments of a 14th-c. *Passional* manuscript found in the binding of an early printed book at Fulda; and K. Zimmermann, *ZDA*, 129:179–83, describes a somewhat less extensive *Passional* fragment from Heidelberg. U.-D. Oppitz and K. Klein, *ZDA*, 129:409–13, print and describe a newly discovered fragment of Heinrich von Hesler's *Apokalypse*. C. Fasbender, *OGS*, 28, 1999:1–21, prints and discusses a German translation (from Nuremberg) of an exemplum by Jakob von Paradies describing a demonological experiment. C. Kottmann, *LB*, 89:363–87, examines the German *Contemptus mundi* poem and the *Spiegelbuch*, paying particular attention to their conceptions of the world and of death. H. Beifuss, *Mediaevistik*, 12, 1999:7–40, provides a detailed description and analysis of the contents of Berlin, Staatsbibliothek, MS 242, a late 15th-c. compendium of mystical-ascetic works, probably written in Nuremberg. B. Döring, *Fest. Mettke*, 49–60, discusses the neglected treatise *Die himlische fundtgrub* (c.1490) by Johannes Jeusser von Paltz.

DRAMA

Yumi Dohi, *Das Abendmahl im spätmittelalterlichen Drama. Eine Untersuchung der Darstellungsprinzipien der Abendmahlslehre in den englischen 'Mystery Cycles' und ihren Vorlagen im Vergleich mit den französischen und den deutschsprachigen biblischen Spielen* (EH, XVIII, 95), 399 pp., is an exhaustive comparative study of the presentation of the Last Supper and its sacramental implications in a number of plays, taking into account historical, dramatic, dogmatic and liturgical aspects. D. is primarily interested in the English *N-Town Cycle*, but she draws examples from several German dramas, such as passion plays from St Gall, Heidelberg, Admont, the Tyrol, Alsfeld, Lucerne, Eger, Sterzing, Donaueschingen, Augsburg and Halle, as well as the *Frankfurter Dirigierrolle* and the *Freiburger Fronleichnamsspiel B*. C. Kuné, *Neophilologus*, 84:241–53, investigates the influence of motifs drawn from the visual arts on dramatic presentations of the baptism of Christ in the later medieval and early modern periods; W. de Cubber,

ZDA, 129:420–44, examines the German equivalents of *resurgere* and *resurrectio* in plays from the 13th to 16th cs; S. K. Wright, *Allegorica*, 20, 1999:45–91, edits and translates two German Christmas plays from the *Erlau Playbook*; and J. M. Pastré, *FCS*, 25, 1999:193–203, identifies the continuing presence of techniques from the 15th-c. *Fastnachtspiel* in Jakob Ayrer's *Der uberwunden eifferer*.

SCIENTIFIC AND SPECIALIZED LITERATURE

Sabine Heimann-Seelbach, *Ars und scientia. Genese, Überlieferung und Funktionen der mnemotechnischen Traktatliteratur im 15. Jh. Mit Edition und Untersuchung dreier deutscher Traktate und ihrer lateinischen Vorlagen* (FN, 58), x + 551 pp., is a substantial and impressive study of important but largely neglected 15th-c. treatises devoted to the *ars memorativa*. The first of its three sections summarizes the contents of, and gives codicological and bibliographical information related to, some 100 predominantly Latin works within this genre; the second offers editions of three German translations of Latin treatises (Nicolaus Italicus's *Tractatus de arte memorativa*, the *Tractatus magistri Hainrici* and Johannes Hartlieb's *Gedächtniskunst*) and studies their techniques of adaptation; and the third investigates various features which are typical specifically of 15th-c. mnemonic works.

A monograph of comparable importance is Barbara Gärtner, *Johannes Widmanns 'Behende vnd hubsche Rechenung'. Die Textsorte 'Rechenbuch' in der Frühen Neuzeit* (RGL, 222), xvi + 662 pp. G.'s study of *Rechenbücher* centres around an edition of Widmann's prototype of the genre, which is based very closely on the incunable published by Konrad Kachelofen (Leipzig, 1489); but it also places the work in the context of the history of mathematics, and of such cultural trends as urbanization and commercialization. Particularly welcome are G.'s short analytical introductions to some 27 mathematical works predominantly of the 15th and 16th cs, few of which are available in modern editions.

Grubmüller, *Schulliteratur*, contains a number of excellent studies and editions, which by definition are concerned principally with Latin texts — such as the *Speculum grammaticae* of Hugo and Konrad Spechtshart and the *Flores grammaticae* of Ludolf de Luco. An exception, however, is H. Bleumer's painstakingly researched study of the late-medieval urban *Deutsche Schulen* (77–98); and A. Suerbaum (383–434) mentions some vernacular glosses in her examination of the textual history of Avianus's fable collection. Heinz Meyer, *Die Enzyklopädie des Bartholomäus Anglicus. Untersuchungen zur Überlieferungs- und Rezeptionsgeschichte von 'De proprietatibus rerum'* (MMS, 77), 523 pp., is similarly concerned mainly with Latin texts, namely the various versions of Bartholomaeus' 13th-c. encyclopaedia. M. does, however, include a brief account of the use of material from Bartolomaeus in three vernacular German works: a version of Konrad von Megenberg's *Buch der Natur*, Michael Baumann's *Buch von der natur und eygenschafft der dingk*, and the German translations of Hugo Ripelin von Strassburg's *Compendiae theologicae veritatis*. D. Gottschall, *FZTP*, 47:77–100, examines Megenberg's theoretical reflections on language, with particular reference to the prologue of his *Buch der Natur* (which she prints alongside a modern German translation); and K. Speckenbach, *Blank Vol.*, 261–73, edits and comments on a brief treatise about dreams, excerpted from the *Buch der Natur*, which appears in a late 15th-c. Freiburg manuscript.

A. Sorbello Staub, *AION (FG)*, n.s., 7, 1997:33–52, discusses problems encountered when editing late-medieval technical literature, with particular reference to the set of recipes in Basel, UB, MS D II 30. C. Tenner and G. Keil, *BW*, 33:188–94, introduce their online edition of the *Kopenhagener Wundarznei* in Copenhagen, GHS 3484, a late 15th-c. manuscript from Northern Alsace — see < http://webdoc.sub.gwdg.de/ebook/m/2000/wundarznei.pdf >. Keil, with K. Goehl, *Sudhoffs Archiv*, 84:104–05, also reports on a recently re-discovered manuscript of the astrological-medical compendium known as the *Iatromathematisches Korpus*. N. McDowell, Classen, *Voices*, 107–22, discusses the pronounced contemporary relevance of much medieval medical literature.

OTHER LATER MEDIEVAL LITERATURE

Johannes von Tepl, *Der Ackermann*, ed. and trans. Christian Kiening (UB, 18075), 181 pp., immediately supersedes all previous paperback editions of the work. As his recent *Habilitationsschrift* has demonstrated (see *YWMLS*, 60:610), K.'s knowledge of it is second to none, and this knowledge is very evident in his edition of the original (more interventionist than some, but defensibly so), in his translation, and perhaps above all in his outstandingly useful commentary, which focuses not just on elucidating textual details, but also on situating them within a broader literary and intellectual context.

Ralf-Henning Steinmetz, *Exempel und Auslegung. Studien zu den 'Sieben weisen Meistern'* (Scrinium Friburgense, 14), Fribourg U.P., xiv + 210 pp., builds on his recent studies of the German versions of the Seven Sages by examining the relationship between their common Latin source (the *Historia septem sapientum*, before 1342) and its French source (the *Roman des sept sages de Rome*, c. 1200). Careful textual analysis discloses that the marked discrepancy in the quality of argumentation in the exempla related by the sages as against those offered by the Empress is a feature of the Latin and (after it) the German versions, but not of the French. As such, it constitutes a critique in narrative form of the inappropriate use and interpretation of exempla. D. Roth, *Medieval Sermon Studies*, 44:87–107, considers the original structure of the *Historia septem sapientum* and its transformation in the course of its manuscript transmission.

Bettina Wagner, *Die 'Epistola presbiteri Johannis' lateinisch und deutsch. Überlieferung, Textgeschichte, Rezeption und Übertragungen im Mittelalter* (MTU, 115), xii + 732 pp., is the first really thorough investigation of the Latin and German versions of the letter ascribed to Prester John since those of Friedrich Zarncke. W. offers a detailed account of the Latin manuscripts and prints, and of their history; and she provides texts of the nine Latin versions which have hitherto been edited either inadequately or not at all. She then studies the six vernacular German versions of the letter (including the one found in the *Jüngerer Titurel*), and edits a previously unknown prose version from an early 15th-c. manuscript written in Speyer. For all their diversity, W. shows that most German versions have in common a narrative framework and an emphasis on social criticism. D. Huschenbett, *Chloe*, 31:119–51, surveys late-medieval vernacular prose texts describing pilgrimages to the Holy Land. In the same volume, X. von Ertzdorff (219–62) discusses, with particular reference to narrative technique, the massive Latin *Evagatorium* of the Ulm Dominican Felix Fabri; and in *JIG*, 31, 1999:54–86, she compares this work with Fabri's own 1484 German version of part of it, as well as with the pilgrimage report of Johann Werner von Zimmern. R. Hahn, *Fest. Mettke*, 147–69, examines the manuscript tradition of the 15th-c. Upper German prose version of *Brandans Reise*.

Karina Kellermann, *Abschied vom 'historischen Volkslied'. Studien zu Funktion, Ästhetik und Publizität der Gattung historisch-politische Ereignisdichtung* (*Hermaea*, n.s., 90), Tübingen, Niemeyer, x + 416 pp., clarifies and develops our understanding of those short verse texts, circulating mainly in towns, which discuss (usually trenchantly) contemporary political events. These early examples of journalism with poetic ambitions have generally been misleadingly characterized by the term 'historisches Volkslied', a misnomer which K. wisely suggests replacing with 'historisch-politische Ereignisdichtung'. The contours of the genre are established through the provision of texts, translations and analyses of some 14 pieces dealing with events which took place during the 'Markgrafenkrieg' of 1449–53; and K. adds chapters dealing with the sociology of their production and reception, as well as certain of their aesthetic qualities.

Christine Mittlmeier, *Publizistik im Dienste antijüdischer Polemik. Spätmittelalterliche und frühneuzeitliche Flugschriften und Flugblätter zu*

Hostienschändungen (Mikrokosmos, 56), Frankfurt, Lang, 184 pp., is an exemplary and pioneering study of the baleful contribution made to anti-Semitism by illustrated leaflets and pamphlets from the period around 1500 — a contribution which, as M. reminds us in a chilling conclusion, remains influential even today. She concentrates particularly on publications dealing with alleged desecrations of the host in Passau, Sternberg, and Knobloch. These are interpreted in the light both of the precise (and differing) historical contexts in which they were written and read, and of more general trends — such as contemporary tendencies to portray Jews as spiritually blind murderers of God, the growing use of pictures in the popularization of religious ideas, and the role played by pamphlets in the description and legitimization of increasingly uniform legal practices. The two most recent volumes of *GJ* contain several articles concerning the early years of printing which will be of interest to Germanists. In *GJ*, 74, 1999, K.-M. Sprenger (42–57) publishes and evaluates a letter in which Nicolaus Cusanus appears to request that a letter of indulgence be printed by Gutenberg in Mainz; F. Eisermann (58–74) introduces a new copy of the 31-line letter of indulgence (GW 6556) and other recently unearthed 15th-c. single-leaf prints; and D. Mauss (123) identifies the scribe of the Rostock manuscript of *Iwein* and rubricator of numerous incunabula as one Peter von Urach. In *GJ*, 75, S. Füssel (7–26) surveys the most important 20th-c. contributions to Gutenberg research and provides a list of recent catalogues of incunabula; K. Flasch (27–41) suggests that Gutenberg and other early printers merit an important place in the history of ideas; F. Schanze (42–63) edits and discusses the late-medieval vernacular Sybilline prophecy found in the binding of an early printed book from Mainz; G. Gerritsen-Geywitz (64–72) discusses the early history of the Harvard Gutenberg Bible; L. Hoffmann (73–81) examines aspects of the early book market; H.-J. Martin (82–87) assesses the relationship between Guillaume Fichet and Johannes Heynlin von Stein; M. Embach (132–44) re-evaluates Johannes Trithemius's defence of handwritten books in the print era; and L. Hellinga (152–59) studies the contributions of 15th-c. compositors and editors to the preparation of texts for printing. Perhaps most importantly, F. Eisermann and V. Honemann (88–131) survey the wide range of single-leaf prints published in German between 1454–55 and 1475, basing several of their conclusions on recently discovered items. K. Jensen, *NQ*, 245:1–4, discusses the incunable collection of the Bayerische Staatsbibliothek, with special reference to its new catalogue and to its value for research.

Frey, *Totentänze*, is a handsomely produced exhibition catalogue which contains articles on various examples of the Dance of Death tradition between the 15th and 20th cs. Of particular interest are I. Wilhelm-Schaffer's introductory chapter (9–26), which traces the origins of the tradition, interprets it, and sets it in its religious and cultural context; F. Egger's examination of the surviving textual and pictorial fragments of the late-medieval *Basler Totentanz* (43–56); H. Freytag, B. Schulte and H. Vogeler's presentation of the Dance of Death dating from 1463 in the Marienkirche in Lübeck (83–135); and, not least, Frey's own contribution (61–82), which traces the hierarchical ordering of the participants in the dance back to such sources as Berthold von Regensburg and *Des Teufels Netz*, and attibutes at least part of its popular success to the message that people of all stations should live a life pleasing to God. C. Dietl, *NMi*: 145–58, discusses a now fragmentary Dance of Death friese at the Finnish port of Inkoo, which was plainly at least indirectly based on the Lübeck paintings.

C. Riviello, *RCCM*, 42:241–87, gives a detailed account of the *Gandersheimer Reimchronik*. R. Schmid, Michel, *Symbole*, 159–79, surveys the appearances of the symbolic bear of Berne in literature and in other forms of art between the 14th and 16th cs. S. Weigelt, *Fest. Mettke*, 409–28, discusses the activities of, and the language used in, the Eisenach Chancery *c.* 1400, with particular reference to Johannes Rothe. H. Lähnemann, Huber, *Geistliches*, 305–28, demonstrates how traditional divides between the spiritual and the secular are both upheld and creatively relativized in Erhard Gross's *Witwenbuch*. In the same volume (237–72) C. Kiening discusses the varying relationships between hagiographical and genealogical narrative structures in the 'Maiden without Hands' legend, and edits two German versions of it from a late 15th-c. Stuttgart manuscript. F. J. Worstbrock, *ZDA*, 129:187–201, prints and comments on a letter, based on Italian models, sent by Hermann Schedel to Siegmund Gossembrot on the occasion of the latter's election as Mayor of Augsburg in 1458. H. Puff, *JMEMS*, 30:41–61, edits, translates, and interprets an account of the trial for Lesbian activities undergone in Speyer in 1477 by Katherina Hetzeldorfer of Nuremberg. C. Winter, *BGDSL*, 122:279–91, discusses the rape of Lucretia as related in the *Römische Historie* of Bernhard Schöfferlin and Ivo Wittich. A. Classen, *FCS*, 25, 1999:345–64, assesses the extent to which chapbooks (especially *Melusine* and *Fortunatus*) reflect identifiably early modern perspectives, not least with regard to the past; and W. Röcke, *ZGer*, 10:11–29, discusses the apocalyptic fears and monstrous visions which accompanied the half-millennium in 1500.

THE SIXTEENTH CENTURY

By MARK TAPLIN

1. GENERAL

Europa und die Türken in der Renaissance, ed. Bodo Guthmüller and Wilhelm Kühlmann (FN, 54), vii + 451 pp., investigates the European response to Ottoman expansion during the Early Modern period. Contributors discuss the portrayal of 'the Turk' in the literature of those countries most affected by the Ottoman advance, and the role of this construct as a focus for unity in a confessionally divided Europe. The volume contains several essays that will be of interest to Germanists. They include M. Brecht (9–27), on Luther's attitude towards the Turks and Islam; H. Wiegand (177–92), 'Neulateinische Türkenkriegsepik des deutschen Kulturraums im Reformationsjahrhundert', which considers poems by Balthasar Nusser and the Transylvanian Saxon Christian Schesäus; W. Kühlmann (192–248), 'Der Poet und das Reich — Politische, kontextuelle und ästhetische Dimensionen der humanistischen Türkenlyrik in Deutschland'; and W. Neuber (249–65), 'Grade der Fremdheit: Alteritätskonstruktion und *experientia*-Argumentation in deutschen Turcica der Renaissance'. *Einblattdrucke des 15. und frühen 16. Jahrhunderts: Probleme, Perspektiven, Fallstudien*, ed. Volker Honemann, Sabine Griese, Falk Eisermann, and Marcus Ostermann, Tübingen, Niemeyer, x + 533 pp. This volume, published by the research project 'Textierte Einblattdrucke im Deutschen Reich bis 1500 als Ausdruck pragmatischer Schriftlichkeit', considers questions relating to the production, reception, and interpretation of single page prints from the 15th and early 16th cs. As one would expect given its origins, the work is primarily late medieval in focus, but it includes several contributions of relevance to our period. The most important are F. Schanze (45–122), which questions the usefulness of the traditional distinction between incunabula and post-incunabula in the categorization of early printed texts, listing more than 100 works that have been wrongly dated to before 1500; F. Eisermann (143–77), 'Auflagenhöhen von Einblattdrucken im 15. und frühen 16. Jahrhundert'; N. Henkel (209–45), on illustrated prints as evidence for a laicization of religion predating the Reformation; and J. Hamel and E. Rothenberg, which provides guidance on the dating of printed astronomical tables from this period. V. Riedel, *Antikerezeption in der deutschen Literatur vom Renaissance-Humanismus bis zur Gegenwart: Eine Einführung*, Stuttgart, Metzler, viii + 515 pp., has a useful chapter on the reception of the classics in Germany between 1450 and 1600, covering both vernacular and neo-Latin literature. *Deutsche Frauen der Frühen Neuzeit*, ed. Kerstin Merkel and Heide Wunder, Darmstadt, Primus, 294 pp., contains biographical essays on Caritas Pirckheimer and Elisabeth von Braunschweig-Lüneburg. H. Watanabe-O'Kelly, 'Women's writing in the Early Modern period', Catling, *Women's Writing*, 27–44, focuses mainly on the 17th c. but includes a discussion of the fate of women writers in the Reformation. A. Classen, *GSR*, 23:13–31, reviews recent work on the history of German literature by women up to 1600. Id., 'Frauen als Buchdruckerinnen im deutschen Sprachraum des 16. und 17.Jahrhunderts', *Gutenberg-Jb.*, 75:181–95. Id., 'Jewish-German women writers in sixteenth- and seventeenth-century Germany: a literary mirage or the discovery of a lost tradition?', *GN*, 31:147–57. H.-J. Bachorski, 'Narrengesichter: zur Idiomatik des Lachens im 16. Jahrhundert', *Eulenspiegel-Jb.*, 39, 1999:13–55.

2. Humanism and the Reformation

Humanismus im Norden: Frühneuzeitliche Rezeption antiker Kultur und Literatur an Nord- und Ostee, ed. Thomas Haye (*Chloe*, 32), Amsterdam, Rodopi, x + 384 pp., collects papers presented to a symposium held at the University of Kiel in September 1998. The volume aims to widen the geographical focus of scholarly interest in German humanism to include the Baltic and North Sea coastal 'periphery' alongside such well-known centres of the new learning as Nuremberg, Basle, and Erfurt. Items of interest include W. Ludwig (1–43) and D. Lohmeier (43–61), which highlight Heinrich Rantzau's patronage of humanists in Schleswig-Holstein; T. Haye (63–104), which illustrates the close connection between humanism and the Reformation in Schleswig-Holstein through an examination of Bernhard Vaget's poem written to mark the establishment of the grammar school in Bordesholm; Hermann Wiegand (105–33), which detects the influence of Ulrich von Hutten's *Querelae* in the Latin *carmina* of Johannes Hadeke-Hadelius; J. Leonhardt (135–55), on David Chytraeus's Latin style in his letters; U. Neddermeyer (175–220), 'Klassiker und humanistische Schriften auf dem nord-deutsch-protestantischen Buchmarkt (1465–1650)'; F. Rädle (221–49), 'Zum dramatischen Schaffen des Gulielmus Gnapheus im preussischen Exil', which examines G.'s use of comedy in his play *Morosophos* as a vehicle for the dissemination of his spiritualist religious views; and J. Schilling (341–52), on the Catholic 'humanist' Lütke Namens. E. Rummel, *The Confessionalization of Humanism in Reformation Germany*, OUP, 211 pp., assesses the impact of the Reformation on the development of humanism in Germany during the 1520s and 1530s. R. argues that in the early years of the Reformation humanism and 'Lutheranism' were widely perceived as two aspects of the same movement, on the basis of their shared opposition to scholasticism and support for the reform of religious abuses. This perception was encouraged both by evangelical propagandists and by their conservative opponents, who saw in it an opportunity to discredit the new learning. During the course of the 1520s, however, the alliance between humanists and reformers began to unravel, with many of the former (including erstwhile supporters of Luther such as Eobanus Hessus) coming to suspect that Protestant anti-intellectualism had replaced scholasticism as the chief threat to the *studia humaniora*. The emerging evangelical churches sought to rebut this charge by throwing their weight behind an ambitious programme of educational reform but, as R. notes, the Protestant (and Counter-Reformation Catholic) appropriation of humanist pedagogy was selective: in Protestant and Jesuit schools, the humanist ideal of universal learning rapidly degenerated into an emphasis on 'dogma and languages'. Another casualty of confessional polarization was the humanist tradition of 'Christian scepticism', whose chief exponents R. identifies as Erasmus, Agrippa von Nettesheim, and Sebastian Castellio. Individual humanists responded to the changed intellectual climate in a variety of ways: by withdrawal from public life, by professional reorientation or by dissimulation, termed Nicodemism by Calvin. By the second half of the 16th c. humanism had disappeared as an independent force, surviving only in its 'confessionalised' Protestant and Catholic incarnations. T. Maissen, *Schweizerische Zeitschrift für Geschichte*, 50:515–44, provides a comprehensive survey of recent secondary literature on Swiss humanism. W. P. Klein, 'Die ursprüngliche Einheit der Sprachen in der philologisch-grammatischen Sicht der frühen Neuzeit', pp. 25–56 of *The Language of Adam / Die Sprache Adams*, ed. Allison P. Coudert, Wiesbaden, Harrassowitz, 1999, 304 pp.

Flugschriften gegen die Reformation (1525–1530), ed. Adolf Laube, 2 vols, Berlin, Akademie, 1332 pp., follows on from earlier volumes in this series dedicated to *Flugschriften* of the early Reformation. The edition contains more than 60 works (some abridged) by Catholic writers from the period between the Peasants' War and the Diet of Augsburg. They include a large number of tracts directed against Luther, as well as responses to the Anabaptists and the Swiss reformers. Among the best known are Johannes Cochläus's polemics on the theme of 'seven-headed Luther', which aimed to expose not only the disagreement between the leading reformers but the theological inconsistencies in Luther's own works. Cochläus and the other major Catholic controversialists (Thomas Murner, Hieronymus Emser, Kaspar Schatzgeyer) are well represented in the volumes, but many less well known writers — including Duke George of Saxony, at this time the leading princely opponent of the Reformation — also feature, along with non-German authors (Henry VIII and John Fisher). Some of the works published here relate to specific events and controversies, such as the disputations of Baden and Berne or the 'Packsche Händel', while others tackle the broader doctrinal issues at stake in the Reformation debate (justification, the Mass, papal supremacy, and the relative authority of scripture and tradition). All texts are accompanied by detailed explanatory notes and other critical apparatus. The introduction provides an analysis of each work featured as well as an overview of other Catholic controversial literature of the period. *The Reformation World*, ed. Andrew Pettegree, London, Routledge, xvi + 576 pp., is a wide-ranging introduction to the Reformation, which reassesses its impact on Early Modern Europe in the light of recent scholarship. Of particular interest are the essays contained in part II of the volume, which deal with the Reformation in Germany. *The Bible as Book: The Reformation*, ed. Orlaith O'Sullivan, London, British Library–Oak Knoll, x + 182 pp., adds to the growing body of scholarship concerned with the reception, translation and interpretation of the Bible in 16th-c. Europe. Relevant contributions include W. S. Campbell (103–14), on Luther's exegetical method in his Romans lectures of 1515–16; A. Pettegree (123–35), on the use of the law and the gospel as a theme in Bible title-page illustrations by German and Dutch Protestant printers; and T. C. String, 'Politics and polemics in English and German Bible illustrations' (137–43). W. Simon, ' "Catechismus" im Medium Buchdruck: Mainzer Katechismusdrucke der Reformationszeit', *Gutenberg-Jb.*, 75 : 160–80, links the production of Catholic catechisms in Mainz between 1537 and 1555 to the reformist circle around archbishops Albrecht von Brandenburg and Sebastian von Heusenstamm. C. Brinker-von der Heyde, 'Das 16. Jahrhundert: Ende der Zeit?', *ZG*, n.F., 10 : 30–41, discusses apocalypticism in the writings of the radical reformers Hans Hut, Hans Hergot, Melchior Hoffmann, and Thomas Müntzer. T. Hohenberger, ' "Also bedarff man jetz by vnseren zyten eins anderen sant Pauls": Theologischer Systembruch als Proprium der Lutherrezeption in den frühen reformatorischen Flugschriften', *Luther*, 71 : 67–84. M. Germann, 'Zwischen Konfiskation, Zerstreuung und Zerstörung: Schicksale der Bücher und Bibliotheken in der Reformationszeit in Basel, Bern und Zürich', *Zwingliana*, 27 : 63–77.

3. GENRES

DRAMA AND DIALOGUE

A. Daskarolis, *Die Wiedergeburt des Sophokles aus dem Geist des Humanismus: Studien zur Sophokles-Rezeption in Deutschland vom Beginn des 16. bis zur*

Mitte des 17. Jahrhunderts (FN, 55), x + 394 pp. This impressively researched monograph is divided into three parts. Part 1, 'Aneignung und Kanonisierung', describes the 'rediscovery' of Sophocles by humanist writers (Reuchlin, Hutten, Erasmus, Melanchthon) in the early part of the 16th c. In part 2, 'Die Bedeutung des Sophokles für die Dichtungstheorie zwischen Humanismus und Barock', D. argues that in early humanist poetics Sophocles was valued principally for his exemplary style and rhetorical abilities. Only from around 1550 did writers such as Jakob Micyllus, Georg Fabricius, and Julius Caesar Scaliger begin to appreciate the specifically dramatic qualities of his work. The final part of the book examines the reception of the mythological subject matter of Sophocles's plays in writers as diverse as Sebastian Franck and Joseph Justus Scaliger. This section includes a detailed analysis of Wolfgang Waldung's Christianizing adaptation of the Theban cycle, *Oedipi Tragoedia*. G. Ehrstine, 'Of peasants, women and bears: political agency and the demise of carnival transgression in Bernese Reformation drama', *SCJ*, 31:675–97, compares the carnival plays of Niklaus Manuel with two works performed following the introduction of the Reformation in Berne, *Elsli Tragdenknaben* and Hans von Rüte's *Abgötterei*. E. sees in the later plays an attempt to accommodate the carnival tradition (shorn of its subversive elements) to Protestant ideals and to bolster the religious and secular authority of the Berne council. Id., 'Vom Zeichen zum (leeren) Abbild: Das Drama der Frühen Neuzeit als visuelles Medium', pp. 407–17 of *Künste und Natur in Diskursen der Frühen Neuzeit*, ed. Hartmut Laufhütte (WAB, 35), 2 vols, 1196 pp., examines changing approaches to the staging of Early Modern dramas with reference to three plays: the Lucerne *Osterspiel* (1583), Valten Voith's *Ein schön lieblich Spiel von dem herlichen vrsprung* (1538), and Gryphius's *Catharina von Georgien*. E. attributes the demise of the medieval *Simultanbühne* during the 16th and early 17th c. in part to the influence of Leon Battista Alberti's teaching on perspective.

PROSE AND VERSE

I. Simon, 'Über einige Sprichwortsammlungen des 15. und 16. Jahrhunderts', *NdW*, 31, 1999:429–52, includes a consideration of Heinrich Bebel's *Proverbia Communia*. M. Stern, *Fest. Böschenstein*, 49–62, discusses the reception of Aesop's fable of the wanderer and the satyr by medieval and Early Modern writers, including Hans Sachs, Burchard Waldis, and Erasmus Alberus. *Tübinger Epicedien zum Tod des Reformators Johannes Brenz (1570)*, ed. Wulf Segebrecht (BDL, 24), 262 pp. This facsimile edition of 22 Latin and Greek poems forms part of the wider research project 'Edition von Gelegenheitsge-dichten', which aims to make available to scholars a representative selection of Early Modern occasional verse. The poems, which first appeared as an appendix to Jakob Heerbrand's funeral sermon in honour of the Württemberg reformer Johannes Brenz, include works by Nicodemus Frischlin and his rival Martin Crusius (who most probably prepared the anthology for publication). Here each poem is accompanied by a short commentary, together with biographical information on its author; a transcription of Greek texts is provided. Explanatory materials include a survey of Brenz's life, reforming activities, and theology, to which detailed reference is made in the poems, and a prosopographical analysis of the contributors to the volume. Common elements in the portrayal of Brenz in the poems are highlighted. *Deutsche Frauenlieder des fünfzehnten und sechzehnten Jahrhunderts: Authentische Stimmen in der deutschen Frauenliteratur der Frühneuzeit oder Vertreter einer poetischen Gattung (das "Frauenlied")?*, ed. Albrecht Classen (APSL, 136), 1999, xxxii + 228 pp. In this anthology, C. presents 120 examples of Early Modern *Frauenlieder*, defined as songs in which 'sich eine Frau zu Wort meldet und aus ihrer idiosynkratischen Perspektive einen Eindruck von ihrem Leben als Frau, von ihrer Liebesbeziehung und ihren Empfindungen vermittelt'. The songs reproduced here are drawn principally from five major manuscript and published collections, some of which were themselves compiled by or on the instructions of women. Although the volume contains a few works by named authors (Maria of Hungary, Elisabeth Creutzinger), the vast majority are anonymous. This has made it possible for scholars to dismiss *Frauenlieder* as in most instances the work of male poets choosing to write from behind a 'mask'. C. challenges this position, on the basis that it is more plausible to assume female authorship of texts that are written explicitly from a woman's point of view and that deal with women's experience. The volume makes a compelling case for the need to re-evaluate assumptions about the extent of literary activity by women in Germany during the Late Medieval and Early Modern periods. J. Ammann-Bubenik, 'Kaiserserien und Habsburgergenealogien — Eine poetische Gattung', Baumbach, *Tradita*, 73–89, identifies the Classical models for the Early Modern *Herrscherserie* (Ausonius's *Caesares* and Vergil's *Aeneid*) and makes the case for considering it as a genre in its own right. Id., 'Centonendichtung als Habsburg-Panegyrik', *HL*, 48, 1999:235–50. W. Salmen, 'Literarisch-Musikalische Lustgärten im 16. und 17. Jahrhundert', *Euphorion*, 94:401–22.

4. OTHER WORK

A. Manko-Matysiak, *Das Teufelsmotiv in der schlesischen Wunderzeichenliteratur der frühen Neuzeit* (Schriftenreihe der Kommission für deutsche und osteuropäische Volkskunde in der Deutschen Gesellschaft für Volkskunde, 79), Marburg, Elwert, 1999, 207 pp., is concerned with the treatment of preternatural phenomena (meteorological disasters, monstrous births, instances of demonic possession) in Silesian works of the 16th and 17th c. M.-M. notes the leading role played by Protestant clerics in developing the genre of *Prodigienliteratur*, which served both as an acceptable substitute for the *Mirakelbücher* popular in Catholic areas and as a powerful adjunct to penitential preaching. The startling events described in the *Wunderzeichenbücher* were easily interpreted by their authors as manifestations of the devil's activity in the world and as portents of divine wrath, to be averted only by lasting and genuine repentance. This message continued to find resonance in Silesia as late as 1700, long after the popularity of *Prodigienliteratur* had waned in the rest of Germany. P. M. Soergel, 'The afterlives of monstrous infants in Reformation Germany', pp. 288–309 of *The Place of the Dead: Death and Remembrance in Late Medieval and Early Modern Europe*, ed. Bruce Gordon and Peter Marshall, CUP, xiii + 324 pp., considers printed accounts of prodigious births from the second half of the 16th c., showing how Lutheran pamphleteers used these events to reinforce Protestant teaching on original sin and the depravity of human nature. H. Tesch, *ÖGL*, 44:205–35, examines the portrayal of father-son relationships in late 16th-c. Austrian autobiographies. K. Patz and U. Müller Hofstede, '"Alberti Teutsch": Zur Rezeption rhetorischer Kunstlehre in Deutschland', pp. 809–22 of Laufhütte, *Künste und Natur* (see p. 641 above), includes a discussion of Walther Hermann Ryff's German translation of L. B. Alberti's treatises *De Pictura* and *De Statua*. W. Schmidt-Biggemann, pp. 81–121 of Coudert, *Language of Adam* (see p. 639 above), investigates the use of the Kabbala by Christian writers, including Johannes Reuchlin and Paulus Riccius. G. Kettmann, 'Studien zur amtlichen Schriftlichkeit der Universität Wittenberg in der Reformationszeit (Annotationen zum Thema Universität und deutsche Sprache in der ersten Hälfte des 16. Jahrhunderts)', *Fest. Mettke*, 209–17. S. De Angelis, 'Zur Galen-Rezeption in der Renaissance mit Blick auf die Anthropologie von Juan Luis Vives: Überlegungen zu der Konfiguration einer "Wissenschaft vom Menschen" in der Frühen Neuzeit', Baumbach, *Tradita*, 90–109.

5. Individual Authors

AMERBACH, BONIFACIUS. *Aus der Werkstatt der Amerbach-Edition*, ed. Ueli Dill and Beat Rudolf Jenny (Schriften der Universitätsbibliothek Basel, 2), Basle, Schwabe, 483 pp.

BOTE, HERMANN. H.-L. Worm, *Eulenspiegel-Jb.*, 1, 1999:127–41, examines B.'s portrayal of the mentally and physically disabled in his works.

BULLINGER, HEINRICH. The publication of B.'s correspondence continues with volume 8, *Briefe des Jahres 1538*, ed. H. U. Bächtold and Rainer Henrich, Zurich, Theologischer Vlg. R. Charbon, 'Lucretia Tigurina: Heinrich Bullingers *Spiel von Lucretia und Brutus* (1526)', *Fest. Böschenstein*, 35–47, detects in B.'s play allusions to contemporary political debates in Zurich, notably that concerning mercenary service.

CANISIUS, PETRUS. *Petrus Canisius SJ (1521–1597): Humanist und Europäer*, ed. Rainer Berndt (Erudiri Sapientia, 1), Berlin, Akademie, 500 pp., contains the proceedings of an international symposium held in Frankfurt in September 1997 to mark the 400th anniversary of C.'s death. The volume seeks to illuminate three important aspects of C.'s career: his engagement with humanism, his role within the wider context of the European Catholic Reformation, and his contribution to the Jesuit mission in Germany. Of particular interest are the articles by J. Lössl (121–54), which notes how C.'s 1562 edition of Jerome's letters combines a humanist concern for textual accuracy with criticism of Erasmus and respect for late medieval tradition; F. Rädle (155–68), 'Petrus Canisius als lateinischer Autor in seinem Verhältnis zum Humanismus'; R. Haub (313–46), which interprets C.'s testament as a spiritual autobiography in the tradition of Augustine's *Confessions*; H. Pörnbacher (365–84), on C.'s contribution to the emergence of Baroque literature in southern Germany; and M. Sievernich (399–422), which compares the catechisms of C. and Luther, showing how they are structured around guiding principles of the writers' respective theologies — in C.'s case the distinction between wisdom and justice, in Luther's the antithesis of law and gospel.

DANTISCUS, JOHANNES. M. Mejor, 'Die Reste der Heilsberger Bibliothek von Johannes Dantiscus in den Sammlungen der Warschauer Bibliotheken', *WNB*, 24, 1999:133–40.

EOBANUS HESSUS, HELIUS. K. Enenkel, 'Autobiographisches Ethos und Ovid-Überbietung: Die Dichterautobiographie des Eobanus Hessus', *NJb*, 2:25–38.

ERASMUS, DESIDERIUS. R. Günthart, *Daphnis*, 29:61–80, identifies E. as the author of the preface to a 1518 Basle edition of Aesop's fables on the basis of his links with the bishop of Sion, Matthäus Schiner, to whom reference is made in the work.

EULENSPIEGELBUCH. H.-J. Behr, 'Narrenbilder: Rolle und Funktion des Narren im *Eulenspiegel-* und im *Lalebuch (Schiltbürgerbuch)*', *Eulenspiegel-Jb.*, 39, 1999:59–78. M. Aichmayr, *Eulenspiegel-Jb.*,

40:41–58, investigates the role played by women characters in *Till Eulenspiegel.*

FISCHART, JOHANNES. J. K. Glowa, *Johann Fischart's Geschichtklitterung: A Study of the Narrator and Narrative Strategies,* NY, Lang, 164 pp., reinterprets the *Geschichtklitterung* as a paraphrase, rather than a mere translation, of Rabelais's *Gargantua,* which F. has expanded and manipulated to reflect his own, often very different, artistic concerns. The result, according to G., is a complex and multilayered novel, in which the author self-consciously reveals his artifice through linguistic virtuosity and, above all, his mastery of narrative technique. At the heart of the study is a detailed and illuminating analysis of the preliminary sections of the *Geschichtklitterung,* which, G. claims, F. uses to create a fictional narrator distinct from the author (with whom he is all too often confused). This narrator is 'the real hero of the *Geschichtklitterung*' and its 'unifying centre', as he both participates in and stands outside the fictional events described, mediating them to the reader. Through an exploration of the complex set of relations between author, narrator, text, and reader, G. shows that past criticism of the *Geschichtklitterung* as incoherent and unstructured stems from a failure to appreciate the narrator's central role in the novel and the rhetorical principle of *amplificatio* that informs F.'s work. His study reveals F. as an author of surprising modernity, whose narrative strategies bear comparison with writers such as Joyce and Robbe-Grillet. U. Seelbach, *Ludus lectoris: Studien zum idealen Leser Johann Fischarts,* Heidelberg, Winter, xvii + 510 pp., seeks to establish the 'Bildungsanspruch oder -grad, den der Autor Fischart implizit für das Verständnis seiner Texte voraussetzt'. S. defines his approach in opposition both to traditional 'Quellenforschung' and to the concept of intertextuality, which he subjects to a detailed critique. The study concentrates on three texts — the prefaces to the *Eulenspiegel reimenweis,* the *Catalogus catalogorum* and the *Geschichtklitterung* — which S. regards as making particularly high demands on the reader. By identifying the literary allusions and hidden quotations in these works he is able to build up a profile of their ideal readers, as well as a list of texts that can be assumed to constitute F.'s 'canon' (primarily the classics, but also contemporary Latin and vernacular works, such as Hans Sachs's *Toter Mann* and Heinrich Bebel's *Facetiae*). S.'s research makes clear that the traditional perception of F. as a populist is without foundation, and lends support to the arguments of other recent scholars that he is best viewed as an educated writer whose works are targeted at a learned, although not intellectually exclusive, bourgeoisie. A series of appendices provide detailed information on the works to which F. alludes in the *Geschichtklitterung,* as well as on the works that appear in the *Catalogus*. F. Schlossbauer, **Zur Geschichtlichkeit literarischer Komik am Beispiel Fischarts und Lessings* (Studies in Modern European History, 80), NY, Lang, 1998, vi + 297 pp.

FRANCK, SEBASTIAN. P. G. Bietenholz, 'How Sebastian Franck taught Erasmus to speak with his radical voice', *BHR*, 62 : 233–48, focuses on F.'s portrayal of Erasmus in his *Chronica und Geschichtbibel.* B. shows how, by quoting Erasmus selectively or out of context, F. was able to present him as a supporter of heterodox religious positions.

GERENGEL, SIMON. Simon Gerengel, *Das Johannesspiegel: Die schön euangelisch History von der enthauptung des heiligen Johannis des Tauffers*, ed. Michael Gebhardt, Innsbruck, Institut für Germanistik, 216 pp., presents the first modern edition of G.'s only surviving play, dated 1553. In his introduction, the editor summarizes G.'s career as a Protestant preacher in Lower Austria, Rothenburg, and Burgenland, and explores the relationship between the two surviving printings of the *History* (denoted as A and B), along with its possible sources (most notably Hans Sachs's play on the same theme). Gebhardt argues that G.'s choice of the John the Baptist story as the subject for his drama was influenced not only by his experience of religious persecution in Austria, but by Luther's emphasis on John's theological significance as mediator between the New and Old Testaments. For G. John also represents the model evangelical preacher; a clear parallel is drawn in the play between the corrupt court of Herod and the contemporary Catholic church. The text published here is based on A (identified by Gebhardt as the first edition), with variant readings from B provided in the footnotes.

GRUMBACH, ARGULA VON. A. Classen, 'Die "Querelle des femmes" im 16. Jahrhundert im Kontext des theologischen Gelehrtenstreits: Die literarischen Beiträge von Argula von Grumbach und Anna Ovena Hoyers', *WW*, 50 : 189–213, notes G.'s appeal to biblical precedent (Judith, Deborah) to justify her intervention in the Reformation debate.

HECHLER, HANS. C. Gerhardt, 'Das Exempel "Vom Vater, Sohn und Esel" als Theaterstück: Ein Spiel von Hans Hechler', *Daphnis*, 29 : 81–102, suggests that the text in question originated as a *Fastnachtspiel.*

KRÜGER, BARTHOLOMÄUS. S. Heimann-Seelbach, 'Bartholomäus Krügers "Hans Clauert": Zur moraldidaktischen Stillegung der Eulenspiegelfigur im 16. Jahrhundert', *Fest. Träger*, 536–50.

LALEBUCH. H.-G. Schmitz, 'Die melancholischen Schildbürger: Das *Lale-* oder *Schiltbürgerbuch* im Licht der zeitgenössischen Anthropologie und Medizin', *Eulenspiegel-Jb.*, 39, 1999 : 79–93. U. Seelbach, *ib.*, 95–111, explores the relationship between *Schwank* and *Lügendich-tung* in the *Lalebuch*. O. Becker, 'Die Deutung des *Lalebuchs* aus neostoizistischer Sichtweise', *ib.*, 40:89–108.

LUTHER, MARTIN. R. Kolb, *Martin Luther as Prophet, Teacher and Hero: Images of the Reformer, 1520–1620*, Grand Rapids, Baker Books, 1999, 278 pp. This study by one of the foremost scholars of later 16th-c. Lutheranism examines the uses to which L.'s memory and works were put by his followers between his death and the outbreak of the Thirty Years War. K. argues that early Reformation propaganda produced three predominant images of L. — as an inspired prophet of God, as a pious and learned teacher, and as a German national hero — all of which continued to be cultivated by German Protestants throughout the period covered by the study. According to K., the image of L. as prophet had the strongest resonance during the middle decades of the 16th c., when Gnesio-Lutheran writers such as Cyriakus Spangenberg, Andreas Musculus and Johannes Wigand appealed to the reformer's works as an adjudicatory authority in their doctrinal disputes with Philippists and Crypto-Calvinists. After 1580 this function was assumed by the Formula of Concord and greater emphasis was placed on L.'s role as a teacher of pure doctrine and symbol of heroic resistance to the papacy. K. provides a fascinating survey of the different visual and literary media (woodcuts, medallions, biographies, dramas) which L.'s followers deployed in order to keep his image fresh in the public mind. At the same time, he shows how the reformer's works were repackaged (as florilegia and commonplaces, for example) to reflect the preoccupations of confessional Lutheranism, and how the emphasis of L.'s theology was changed in the process. B. Stolt, *Martin Luthers Rhetorik des Herzens*, Tübingen, Mohr Siebeck, xii + 200 pp., is an accessible summary of the author's work on L.'s rhetoric, and provides a valuable corrective to the popular image of L. as the exponent of a 'volkstümliche Alltagssprache'. S. begins with an examination of L.'s bilingualism, most evident in the 'lateinisch-deutsche Mischsprache' of the *Tischreden* and, to a lesser extent, in the reformer's lectures and correspondence. She argues convincingly that L.'s German cannot be properly understood without taking into account the profound influence of Latin on his syntax and lexis. S. takes issue with those scholars who have dismissed L.'s style as 'formlos', providing examples of his indebtedness to the Augustinian tradition of the *sermo humilis* and to Quintillian's *Institutio oratoria*. In L.'s hands this becomes a 'rhetoric of the heart', closely bound in with his understanding of faith as an affair of the emotions as well as of the intellect. The same conviction informs L.'s approach to translation, which skilfully combines the principles of 'word for word' and 'sense for sense'. As S. shows, L. often prefers a literal rendition of the Bible's original Hebrew or Greek where he judges that to have greater affective force than a more colloquial German expression. Hebraisms may have an additional function, serving to reinforce the reader's awareness of the sacredness of the biblical text. Other subjects discussed in the volume include L.'s use of music as an aid to rhetoric in the *Deutsche Messe* (1526), and the role of humour in his writings. J. Kunze, *Erasmus und Luther: Der Einfluss des Erasmus auf die Kommentierung des Galaterbriefes und der Psalmen durch Luther 1519–1521*, Münster, Lit, 337 pp., offers a fresh perspective on the early relationship between L. and Erasmus. While not seeking to play down L.'s fundamental differences with Erasmus over the issue of free will, K. argues that previous scholarship has tended to neglect the Dutch humanist's contribution to L.'s development as a writer, theologian, and biblical exegete. Erasmus's influence, he suggests, is most apparent in L.'s two early commentaries on Psalms (1519) and Galatians (1521). In part 1 of the study, K. provides a historical overview of the contacts between L. and Erasmus during the period leading up to the publication of these works, in which he demonstrates that L.'s early popularity was due precisely to the fact that contemporaries associated his protest against the sale of indulgences with the biblical humanism of which Erasmus was the foremost exponent. This perception was encouraged, partly for political reasons, by L. and Erasmus themselves; indeed, K. argues, L.'s choice of the commentary (a form favoured by humanist writers) for his works on the Psalms and Galatians was part of a calculated strategy to distance himself from scholasticism and to establish his credentials as a member of the new literary élite. The second part of the study is given over to a detailed analysis of L.'s exegetical method in the commentaries, which is shown to resemble closely that sketched out by Erasmus in his *Ratio seu Methodus compendio perveniendi ad veram theologiam*. According to K., L. shares Erasmus's grammatical-rhetorical approach to the interpretation of biblical texts, his respectful but critical attitude to the Church fathers and, above all, his view of the exegete's task as being to establish the *sensus germanus* of scripture. Despite these similarities in method, L. and Erasmus come to very different theological conclusions, because of their differing understandings of the *scopus* of scripture. For Erasmus this is best summed up in the sermon on the mount, whereas for L. it is expressed rather in the Pauline doctrine of justification by faith. G. J. Miller, 'Luther on the Turks and Islam', *Lutheran Quarterly*, 14:79–97, argues that L. departs from medieval tradition in his understanding of Islam not as a Christian heresy but as a religion of 'works righteousness'. J. Loehr, *AR*, 91:47–86, considers the use by L. and Melanchthon of ancient dramatic theory as an interpretative framework for events at the Diet of Augsburg. W. Besch, *Die Rolle Luthers in der deutschen Sprachgeschichte* (Schriften der Philologisch-historischen Klasse der Heidelberger Akademie der Wissenschaften, 12), Heidelberg, Winter, 1999, 70 pp., reassesses L.'s contribution to the development of a standard German written language. B. disputes the existence of a specific 'Luthersprache', arguing instead that L.'s language is representative of the early 16th c. in its blending of East Middle and East Upper German forms. He contrasts the enduring influence of L.'s Bible translation with the more restricted impact of L.'s other writings, concluding that the Bible, rather than L., was the single most important factor in shaping modern *Hochdeutsch*. H. Wolf, 'Luthers spielerischer Umgang mit Spracheigenheiten anderer', *ZDL*, 67:148–67, provides examples of the interplay between parody and polemic in L.'s writings. A. Lexutt, *Luther*, 71:4–21, considers the role played by humour in the writings of L. and Erasmus. F. Pannen, 'Luther über Johannes Gerson: Eine Untersuchung der Aussagen Luthers über den "Doktor des Trostes"', *ib.*, 117–25. T. A. Francis, 'The linguistic influence of Luther and the German language on the earliest complete Lutheran Bibles in Low German, Dutch, Danish and Swedish', *SN*, 72:75–94.

MANUEL, NIKLAUS. H. R. Schmidt, 'Elsli Tragdenknaben: Niklaus Manuels Ansicht des geistlichen Gerichts', pp. 583–602 of *Kriminalitätsgeschichte: Beiträge zur Sozial- und Kulturgeschichte der Vormoderne*, ed. Andreas Blauert and Gerd Schwerhoff, Konstanz U.P., 920 pp.

MELANCHTHON, PHILIPP. *Melanchthons Briefwechsel: Kritische und kommentierte Gesamtausgabe*, ed. Heinz Scheible, Stuttgart–Bad Cannstatt, Frommann-Holzboog, continues with vol. *T 3: Texte 521–858 (1527–1529)*. *Melanchthon und die Marburger Professoren (1527–1627)*, ed. Barbara Bauer, 2 vols, Marburg, Völker & Ritter, 1999, 956 pp., sheds new light on M.'s role in the development of a Protestant higher education system in Germany. The work catalogues more than 100 titles, arranged according to discipline, that reflect M.'s pedagogical influence on the University of Marburg during the first century of its existence. Particularly relevant to literary scholars are the sections on rhetoric (123–51) and poetry (153–95). Also of interest are the essays in volume two by M. Rener, '*Unica Musarum morientum vita, Philippe* — Philipp Melanchthon im Spiegel der Dichtungen seines Zeitgenossen Helius Eobanus Hessus' (737–56), which considers M.'s support for the *studia humaniora* against the backdrop of humanist unease about the future of the classics under Protestantism, and P. Dilg (849–64), on M.'s relations with Euricius Cordus. *Werk und Rezeption Philipp Melanchthons in Universität und Schule bis ins 18. Jahrhundert: Tagung anläßlich seines 500. Geburtstages an der Universität Leipzig*, ed. Günther Wartenberg, Leipzig, Evangelische

Verlagsanstalt, 1999, 209 pp., assesses the impact of Melanchthonian pedagogy on the teaching of theology, rhetoric, the classics, and law in Early Modern Germany. Relevant items include S. Rhein (53–69), 'Philipp Melanchthon als Gräzist'; R. Kössling (71–81), on M.'s Latin grammar of 1525–26; R. Seidel (99–122), which examines M.'s use of the verse prologue in his editions of Classical plays to defend the pedagogical value of Protestant school drama; A. Sieber (133–46), on the popularization of M.'s teaching on rhetoric and dialectics through vernacular works such as Chaspar Goldwurm's preaching manual *Schemata Rhetorica* (1545), Ortholph Fuchsberger's *Wahre Dialectica* (1533), and Wolfgang Bütner's *Dialectica deutsch* (1576); and G. Wartenberg (179–94), 'Melanchthonbiographien vom 16. bis zum 18. Jahrhundert'. C. P. Arand, *Lutheran Quarterly*, 14:281–308, analyses M.'s defence of the doctrine of justification by faith alone in the *Apology* in the light of his teaching on rhetoric. J. Knape, 'Melanchthon und die Historien', *AR*, 91:111–26, argues that M.'s conception of history, as a 'thesaurus exemplorum', is deeply rooted in medieval tradition. H. Hofmann, *NJb*, 1, 1999:99–128, notes M.'s uncritical approach to the study of Classical texts and compares his achievements in this field unfavourably with those of other humanists.

MOLLERUS, BERNHARDUS. B. Czapla, *NJb*, 1, 1999:21–48, considers M.'s *Rhenus* as an example of an Early Modern *Lehrgedicht*.

MÜNSTER, SEBASTIAN. S. G. Burnett, 'A dialogue of the deaf: Hebrew pedagogy and anti-Jewish polemic in Sebastian Münster's *Messiahs of the Christians and the Jews (1529/39)*', *AR*, 91:168–90, examines M.'s use of Hebrew sources in the *Messiahs*. B. suggests that M.'s main purpose in writing the work was to equip his Christian readers with the linguistic and theological tools to respond effectively to Jewish objections to Christianity.

PIRCKHEIMER, CARITAS. E. Lippe-Weissenfeld Hamer, *Pirckheimer Jb. für Renaissance- und Humanismusforschung*, 14, 1999:121–55, discusses P.'s correspondence with her cousin Sixtus Tucher, her brother Willibald, and Konrad Celtis.

PISCATOR, HERMANNUS. U. Goerlitz, **Humanismus und Geschichtsschreibung am Mittelrhein: Das 'Chronicon urbis et ecclesiae Maguntinensis' des Hermannus Piscator OSB* (FN, 47), 1999, xvii + 525 pp.

PLATTER, THOMAS. **Zehn Blicke auf Thomas Platter*, Visp, Rotten, 1999, 191 pp.

REUCHLIN, JOHANNES. *Reuchlin und Italien*, ed. Gerald Dörner (Pforzheimer Reuchlinschriften, 7), Stuttgart, Thorbecke, 1999, 205 pp., presents papers given to the third international Reuchlin conference, held at Pforzheim in June 1996. The volume highlights the importance of R.'s Italian connections (established during his three visits to Italy in the 1480s and 1490s) for his intellectual development, particularly in the spheres of philology, theology, and law. Consideration is also given to the role of Italy (specifically, the Roman curia) in R.'s protracted struggle with Johannes Pfefferkorn and the Cologne Dominicans, which ended with his condemnation by the papacy in June 1520. Items of interest include M. Dall'Asta (23–43), on R.'s contacts with Italian printers and booksellers, especially Aldus Manutius; C. Förstel (45–56), which suggests possible sources for R.'s *De quattuor Graecae linguae differentiis*; G. Busi (57–67), on R.'s Christian Kabbalism; S. Campanini (69–85), on R.'s relations with his Hebrew teachers Ya'aqov Yehi'el Loans and Ovadyah ben Ya'aqov Sforno; T. Leinkauf (109–32), which assesses the influence of the Florentine Neoplatonists Giovanni Pico della Mirandola and Marsilio Ficino on R.'s thought; G. Dörner (149–79), on R.'s links with the papal chamberlain Jakob Questenberg and their significance for the conduct of his trial; and G.-R. Tewes (181–97), which identifies the prime movers in the condemnations of both R. and Luther as a group of conservative theologians schooled at the universities of Louvain and Cologne.

REICHART, WOLFGANG. W. Ludwig, 'Eine unbekannte humanistische Korrespondenz: Die Briefe zwischen Wolfgangus Rychardus und seinen Sohn Zeno', *NJb*, 1, 1999, 141–9.

SCHÖFFERLIN, BERNHARD. C. Winter, 'Weipplich Brust — Manlich Hertz: Lucretia in der Römischen Historie', *BGDSL*, 122, 279–91, locates S.'s Lucretia in a popular late medieval tradition of exemplary but exceptional masculine women, whose transgression of gender boundaries serves only to reinforce contemporary views of gender difference.

SCHÜTZ ZELL, KATHARINA. E. A. McKee, **Katharina Schütz Zell* (Studies in Medieval and Reformation Thought, 69), 2 vols, Leiden, Brill, xxviii + 506 and xv + 403 pp.

TSCHUDI, AEGIDIUS. The critical edition of T.'s *Chronicon helveticon* concludes with *13. Teil*, ed. Bernhard Stettler (Quellen zur Schweizer Geschichte, n.F., 1, VII.13), Basle, Allgemeine Geschichtsforschende Gesellschaft der Schweiz, 2 vols, 118* + 499 pp. These two volumes present T.'s account of events within the Swiss Confederation between 1450 and 1470, which was based on nearly 150 documents copied or collected by the author during the course of his political and diplomatic career. The introduction provides information on T.'s sources, an assessment of T.'s strengths and weaknesses as a chronicler, and a modern historical analysis of the period covered by this part of the chronicle.

WURSTISEN, CHRISTIAN. M. Lailach, *WRM*, 24:1–19, argues that, despite the lack of any obvious thematic connection between the iconography of the title page to W.'s *Baszler Chronick* and the work itself, the former has an important function: to demonstrate the erudition of the author to his readers.

THE SEVENTEENTH CENTURY

By ANNA CARRDUS, *University of Bristol*

1. GENERAL

J. L. Flood, 'Poets Laureate of the Holy Roman Empire', *Hungarian Journal of English and American Studies*, 3, 1997[1999]: 5–23, surveys ancient traditions for honouring poets that were revived with the laureation of Petrarch in 1341 and persisted within the Empire until 1806–07. Of the more than 600 laureations performed during this time over half took place in the 17th c., mostly in universities, but also within 'Sprachgesellschaften': as heads of such societies, Sigmund von Birken, Johannes Rist, and Philipp von Zesen each crowned a number of poets. F. cites descriptions of specific ceremonies and their participants. He is preparing a bio-bibliographical handbook on poets laureate. Watanabe, *Festivals*, is a bibliography of publications related to European court, civic, and religious festivals and ceremonies (1500–1800) in the holdings of the British Library (London), the British National Art Library (Victoria and Albert Museum, London), the Herzog August Bibliothek (Wolfenbüttel) and the Bibliothèque de l'Arsenal (Bibliothèque Nationale, Paris). As such publications fall into numerous categories and are notoriously hard to trace, even in online catalogues, this bibliography is particularly welcome. It is organised by country of origin (including the Holy Roman Empire and individual territories and cities within it), and contains no less than eight indices. Entries are annotated. H. Watanabe, 'Women's writing in the early modern period', Catling, *Women's Writing*, 27–44, initially considers the social and historical reasons behind the scarcity both of women writers, and of texts by those women who did write in this period. W. then focuses mainly on poetry, which she presents as the most practicable genre for 17th-c. women, taking Hoyers, Sibylle Schwarz (1621–38), Greiffenberg, and Kuntsch as examples, but also looking at the few women — mostly aristocratic — known to have written novels and the even fewer known to have written drama. She cites Sophie Elisabeth, Duchess of Braunschweig-Lüneburg (1613–76), as unusual in writing in all three genres, but stresses that much work remains to be done on retrieving, publishing, and contextualizing 17th-c. writing by women. K. Merkel and H. Wunder, ' "Das eröffnete Cabinet deß gelehrten Frauen = Zimmers." Dichterinnen, Malerinnen und Mäzeninnen im Heiligen Römischen Reich Deutscher Nation', Merkel, *Frauen*, 7–17, introduces a volume of essays on women active between the Reformation and the end of the 18th c. as writers, artists, or patrons of the arts. M. and H. give a succinct historical survey of the social and cultural currents which encouraged these women's work, and which the women themselves contributed to. Essays on 17th-c. women writers are discussed under their individual names. Kurz, *Meditation*, is a collection of essays by Germanists and theologians arising from the colloquium 'Meditation und Erinnerung', held in 1998 under the auspices of the special research project on 'Erinnerungskulturen' at the University of Giessen. Its detailed treatment of 17th-c. devotional practices helps redress the neglect suffered until quite recently by the many meditational manuals that were bestsellers in their time and exerted considerable influence on literature. Apart from contributions discussed below under the names of individual authors, it contains: U. Sträter, ' "Wie bringen wir den Kopff in das Hertz?" Meditation in der Lutherischen Kirche des 17. Jahrhunderts' (11–35), which suggests reasons behind the spread of meditational practices in personal devotions, i.e. those performed at home rather than in church, from about 1570. S. argues against the notion of meditation as primarily consolatory, seeing it rather as a means to the reform urged by many members of the church. Meditation would bring individuals to heartfelt understanding of God's Word (merely 'heard' in sermons) and ultimately aid its fruition in daily life. J. J. Berns, 'Höllenmeditation. Zur meditativen Funktion und mnemotechnischen Struktur barocker Höllenpoesie' (141–73), discusses the meditations on hell which, perhaps surprisingly, formed part of Protestant and of Catholic literature on the 'Vier letzte Dinge' (death, judgement, heaven, hell), analysing Schottel's *Grausame Beschreibung und Vorstellung Der Hölle Und der Höllischen Qual* (1676) to emphasize, in particular, S.'s use of onomatopoeia and *composita* to encourage meditation and create mnemonic devices. Several of the astonishing engravings from S.'s work are reproduced. S. Wodianka, 'Francois de Sales und die "Introduction a la vie devote" — weibliche Meditation für jedermann?' (175–200), discusses a widely-read meditation manual (1609, translated into German by Johann Andreas Gerhard in 1677) which explicitly addresses a female reader. W. examines the author's belief that women's intellectual simplicity amounted to a talent for meditation and at the exercises designed to match this belief, which are milder than those of Ignatius Loyola and thus theoretically accessible to all lay people. G. Kurz, 'Zur Bedeutung der "Betrachtung" in der deutschen Literatur des 17. und 18. Jahrhunderts' (219–50), systematically examines the relationship between meditational practices, exemplified by Loyola's exercises, and literary practices. K. pays particular attention to the activation and focusing of individual memory in 'Betrachtung', a concept which he analyses closely and relates in general to different literary genres (e.g. elegy, aphorism). As examples of 17th-c. literary practices he discusses Gryphius's sonnet 'Vber des Herrn Leiche' (1643), Opitz's prose 'Betrachtung' (1628) on Christ's passion, and a passage from the 'Continuatio' in Grimmelshausen's *Simplicissimus* (1665), where the hermit Simplicius transforms natural aspects of 'his' island into a garden of devotional mementos.

D. Breuer, 'Endzeitliche Ausblicke ins Himmlische Jerusalem bei Johannes Matthäus Meyfart, Angelus Silesius and Martin von Cochem', *Morgenglantz*, 10:67–94, places these three authors in the context of 17th-c. writings on the 'Vier letzte Dinge' and discusses their descriptions of the New Jerusalem (Revelations 21) in order of affective intensity: M., an orthodox Lutheran, refrains from all 'Enthusiasterey' in *Tuba Novissima* (1626); the Catholic convert S. (i.e. Johannes Scheffler) deliberately stimulates readers' imaginations in *Sinnliche Beschreibung der vier letzten Dinge*; the Capuchin C. goes one step further, combining vivid visual imagery with explicit appeals to the emotions in *Nutzlicher Zusatz* (1682). Steiger, *Kantaten*, contains the proceedings of a colloquium on the theme 'Tod und Sterben', held in 1991 at the Herzog August Bibliothek, Wolfenbüttel, in conjunction with the 'Internationale Arbeitsgemeinschaft für theologische Bachforschung'. The publication commemorated the 250th anniversary of Bach's death. Three essays, including two on 'Kirchenlieder' (discussed below under POETRY, OTHER WORK), consider aspects of the literary background to B.'s cantatas. R. Lenz, 'Leichenpredigt und Epitaph in der Frühen Neuzeit' (109–23), discusses literary approaches to a pastor's death, caused in 1683 when he rushed into his burning parsonage to rescue a two-year-old grandchild. L. focuses on how the various parts of the pastor's funeral sermon, and the inscriptions and portraits on his tombstone (illustrated), sought to convince the congregation that his sudden and horrific death was not — as could have been assumed — a sign of divine wrath, but martyrdom in the name of love. A. Linton, 'Der Tod als Brautführer. Bridal imagery in funeral writings', *Daphnis*, 29:281–306, examines the history and theological significance of metaphors based on the notion of the believer's marriage with Christ, then draws on funeral sermons to analyse their use in 17th-c. Germany in consolatory argument addressed usually, though not exclusively, to parents on the death of daughters who had reached marriageable age. She interestingly discusses how such metaphors were amplified, developed and adapted to match individual circumstances.

Klaus Garber, *Imperilled Heritage: Tradition, History, and Utopia in Early Modern German Literature. Selected Essays*, ed. and introd. Max Reinhart (Studies in European Cultural Transmission, 5), Aldershot,

Ashgate, xxx + 268 pp., contains seven characteristically wide-ranging essays by Klaus Garber, previously published in German between 1983 and 1998, and now translated into English by a team of North American scholars for the benefit of non-German speakers. Garber himself contributes the (new) preface and has made additions to certain essays. K. A. Wurst, 'Gender and the aesthetics of display: baroque poetics and sartorial law', *Daphnis*, 29:159–75, links the clothing metaphors used to designate stylistic register in rhetoric and poetics with the hierarchically organized systems of sartorial orna-ment current in the 17th c., and compares the structuring roles of class, rank, and gender in both style and sartorial display.

2. POETRY

INDIVIDUAL AUTHORS

BALDE. W. Kühlmann, 'Alamode-Satire, Kultursemiotik und jesuit-ischer Reichspatriotismus — Zu einem Gedichtzyklus in den *Sylvae* (1643) des Elsässers Jacob Balde SJ', *Simpliciana*, 22:201–26, considers a writer born in Alsace who, though in exile from it for most of his life, constantly refers back to it. The cycle in question, *De moribus veteris ac novae Germaniae*, appeared as the third book of B.'s *Sylvae*; K. concentrates on two odes from it which he appends to the article with modern German translations.

FLEMING. M. Koch, 'Die erinnerte Geliebte. Zu einem Petrarca-Motiv in der deutschen Lyrik des 17. und frühen 18. Jahrhunderts', Kurz, *Meditation*, 328–55, interestingly traces the history of the view that Paul Fleming (1609–40) and Johann Christian Günther (1695–1723) were early practitioners of 'Erlebnislyrik' and forerun-ners of Goethe, and rejects it, arguing rather that the sense of personal individuality which F. so strikingly conveys in his love poetry derives from meditational recourse to stoic self-possession as a remedy for separation from the beloved, and the corresponding shift from the conventions of Petrarchan style to the seemingly colloquial stoic style.

GREIFFENBERG. L. Tatlock, 'Catharina Regina von Greiffenberg (1633–1694)', Merkel, *Frauen*, 93–106, is a concise yet detailed survey of C.'s life and work which emphasizes the intertwining of her personal spiritual practices and her poetic artistry. Emphasis is also placed on the views G. expresses in relation to her sex, on her relationships with women — including her mother, on feminist reception of her work, and on her 36 prose meditations, which have only recently become the focus of research. T. also draws particular attention to G.'s use of alchemical metaphors. B. Thums, 'Zur Topographie der memoria in frühneuzeitlicher Mystik: Catharina

Regina von Greiffenbergs "Geistliche Gedächtnisorte"', Kurz, *Meditation*, 251–72, looks closely at the interdependence of memory, meditation and mysticism in two works by G., *Andächtige Betrachtungen* and *Geistliche Sonnette, Lieder und Gedichte*. The 'geistliche Gedächtnisörte' of the title, G.'s own formulation, refers to the external, everyday activities which normally interfere with meditation but which she converts into mementos of Christ. C. Soboth, ' "Herr/ mein Gedächtniß ist vom Wachs zu deinen lenken" — Formen und Funktionen der memoria in den "Geistlichen Sonnetten, Liedern und Gedichten" von Catharina Regina von Greiffenberg', *ib.*, 273–90, systematically traces the details of G.'s poetics through those poems which give explicit expression to the dynamics of her meditative practices, considering traditional theories of memoria, G.'s relationship to them and use of metaphors from them, and asking which aspects of G.'s poetics can be seen as specifically feminine. K. E. Schöndorf, 'Catharina Regina von Greiffenberg. Ein Beitrag zu ihrem kulturellen Umfeld und dichterischen Schaffen', pp. 173–98 of *Aus dem Schatten treten. Aspekte weiblichen Schreibens zwischen Mittelalter und Romantik*, ed. K. E. Schöndorf et al. (Osloer Beiträge zur Germanistik, 28), Frankfurt, Lang, 266 pp., serves as an introduction to G.'s life and work. S. concentrates on the influence of the literary climate in Nuremberg, but also relates G.'s work to Böhme and Schottel and highlights her links with Harsdörffer and Birken, especially in connection with her expressive use of language. He sees her as the first 'Pietistin' of the 17th c.

GRYPHIUS. J. A. Steiger, *Schule des Sterbens. Die 'Kirchhofgedanken' des Andreas Gryphius (1616–1664) als poetologische Theologie im Vollzug*, Heidelberg, Palatina, 92 pp., prints the text of this important poem by G. and provides a welcome strophe-by-strophe commentary on it which charts its relationship to both mainly theological (Luther, Johann Gerhard, the Bible) and mainly literary influences (Jacob Balde; rhetorical structures). S. shows that G.'s poem, in spite of its debt to Balde, a Jesuit, represents ideas central to Lutheran orthodoxy. C. v. Zimmermann, 'Andreas Gryphius' "Threnen des Vatterlandes/ Anno 1636"', *Daphnis*, 28, 1999:226–44, re-examines this much-discussed sonnet, taking issue in particular with Theodor Verweyen's interpretation (1997) by using the poem as the basis for a demonstration that rhetorical analysis is reductive if it focuses on only one of the three main rhetorical techniques (*inventio, dispositio,* and *elocutio*), instead of taking account of interactions between them. Z. relates this sonnet to both the chria, a school exercise in combining precisely these techniques, and the lament.

HOYERS. C. Niekus Moore, 'Anna Ovena Hoyers (1584–1655)', Merkel, *Frauen*, 65–76, surveys connections between H.'s life and work, discussing her early religious 'Streitschriften', her poem of advice to a child, and her occasional poetry, and emphasizing her exceptional qualities — not only as a middle-class woman who chose to write, but as one who published under her own name during her lifetime and took part in the public arena through her writing, even as a widow. Her collected *Geistliche und Weltliche Poemata*, edited by a member of the Schwenkfeldian sect she defended in poems published earlier, appeared in 1650.

KUNTSCH. A. Carrdus, 'Margaretha Susanna von Kuntsch (1651–1717) und 16 Altenburger Dichterinnen', Merkel, *Frauen*, 123–38, surveys K.'s life and work, published posthumously as *Sämmtliche Geist= und weltliche Gedichte* (1720), and uses them to elucidate the lives and work of 16 almost unknown younger women related to her by either kinship or friendship. C. looks at how these women's writing skills grew out of devotional practices, and how they put them to use in occasional poetry to commemorate close personal ties. K. clearly served as a role model to younger women, while her husband and grandson played differing yet crucial roles in bringing her writing and that of other Altenburg women into print.

OPITZ. W. Ludwig, 'Des Martin Opitz Epicedium auf Erzherzog Karl von Österreich', *Daphnis*, 29:177–96, gives the Latin text of the 1624 funeral poem which led to O.'s laureation in Vienna in the following year. It is accompanied by a modern German prose translation and an interpretation which places it within the literary traditions of lament, consolation, and panegyric. L. presents this study as a foretaste of the edition of O.'s Latin work now in progress.

STIELER. J. P. Aikin, 'Private piety in seventeenth-century Germany and the devotional compilations of Caspar Stieler', *Daphnis*, 29:221–79, focuses on a hitherto neglected aspect of S.'s literary output. A. examines four collections, setting them against a detailed background of the various types of devotional compilations current in 17th-c. Germany, and against the particular spiritual movement with which S. became involved *c.* 1665–86. She pays particular attention to S.'s relationship with Ahasverus Fritsch, and to the love of music and of language which unites his devotional work with earlier comic and erotic works.

ZEIDLER. *Jungferlicher Zeitvertreiber, Das ist allerhand Deudsche Gedichte Bey Häußlicher Arbeit und stiller Einsamkeit verfertiget und zusammen getragen Von Susannen Elisabeth Zeidlerin, Neudruck der Ausgabe von 1686*, ed. Cornelia Niekus Moore, Berne, Lang, xlvi + 140 pp., is a welcome addition to the very few modern editions of 17th-c. women's work at present available. Although little is known of Z. (1657–c. 1706), daughter and wife to Lutheran pastors, the introduction usefully looks at the encouragement she received from male members of her family and places her within the general social and educational context of country pastors' life. Z. apparently stopped writing soon after her marriage in 1685; her work, mainly devotional or occasional, includes notable poems of friendship addressed to women.

H. Grasmück, '"Schaubühne des Todes." Zur Bildlichkeit des protestantischen Kirchenliedes im 16. und 17. Jahrhundert — Der Choral als Kontrafaktur des Todes und die Figur des Todes as "Totes Bild"', Steiger, *Kantaten*, 45–73, looks at how funeral hymns 'stage' death and thus enhance their function as an *ars moriendi* for the living. G. traces elements of this theatrical quality back to pre-Reformation sacred drama, processional hymns, and images of the 'Totentanz', then analyses differing 16th-c. and 17th-c. treatments of it in hymns by Luther, and by Andreas Gryphius, Valerius Herberger, and Michael Franck. I. Drost, 'Das Kirchenlied in der Leichenpredigt', *ib.*, 207–21, cites many instances of the uses of funeral hymns: as *ars moriendi*, as consolation, or as a blend of both for the dying and those gathered round them. D.'s source is the collection of funeral sermons for members of the nobility held by the Herzog August Bibliothek, Wolfenbüttel. The naming or quoting of specific hymns enables D. to establish that while 16th-c. funeral hymns remained popular throughout the 17th c., in its last decades hymns with greater subjectivity, especially those by Paul Gerhardt (1607–76), rose in favour. Thomas Neukirchen, *Inscriptio. Rhetorik und Poetik der Scharfsinnigen Inschrift im Zeitalter des Barock* (SDL, 152), 1999, 298 pp., is a revised doctoral thesis which meticulously analyses this peculiarly 17th-c. poetic form in terms of genre, style, and typography. N. places it in the context of the 'Argutia-Bewegung', sees Harsdörffer and Birken as crucial to its introduction into Germany, and Weise as central to its slightly later theory and practice.

3. PROSE

INDIVIDUAL AUTHORS

ANDREAE. R. Edighoffer, '"Menippus redivivus": Johann Valentin Andreae als Satiriker', *Simpliciana*, 22:189–200, examines *Menippus sive dialogorum satyricorum centuria*, which A. published anonymously and with a fictional place of publication, but which in fact appeared in Strasburg in 1617.

ARNDT. O. Pfefferkorn, 'Predigt, Andachtsbuch und Gebetbuch bei Johann Arndt', *Daphnis*, 28, 1999:347–85, sets out to define the types of text that fall under the huge category of 17th-c. *Erbauungslitera-tur* by conducting a detailed literary analysis of style in three works which were arguably the most widely read within this category: A.'s collection of sermons or postilla (1615–17), his meditation manual *Vier Bücher vom wahren Christentum* (1605–10), and his prayer book *Paradiesgärtlein* (1612). P. finds that these three texts match the traditional stages of meditation, the sermons corresponding with *lectio*, the manual with *meditatio*, and the prayer book with *oratio*, but that none of A.'s texts match the fourth, mystic stage of *contemplatio* — not unexpectedly, as his works aim above all at encouraging an active faith; A.'s style, however, frequently mirrors the central process of meditation, *ruminatio*. This essay valuably complements those in Kurz, *Meditation* discussed under the GENERAL heading, above, and under the names of individual authors, below.

CZEPKO. F. van Ingen, 'Daniel von Czepkos *Consolatio ad Baronis-sam Cziganeam.* Tröstung, Rhetorik, Psychologie', *Daphnis*, 29:197–220, analyses a substantial work written by C. as a young man (c. 1633) on the death of a woman he was attracted to. This is the first literary analysis of a work previously examined by scholarship only as evidence of C.'s mystical beliefs, but found by van Ingen to represent a remarkable new departure within the consolatory genre.

GERHARD. J. A. Steiger, 'Meditatio sacra. Zur theologie-, frömm-igkeits- und rezeptionsgeschichtlichen Relevanz der "Meditationes Sacrae" (1606) Johann Gerhards', Kurz, *Meditation*, 38–56, intro-duces a widely-read work of 17th-c. Lutheran orthodoxy, relating it to traditional and contemporary theological movements, examining G.'s concept of *meditatio* and indicating the influence of the work on literary figures such as Rist, Gryphius, and Quirinus Kuhlmann.

GRIMMELSHAUSEN. D. Breuer, 'Grimmelshausen und Straßburg', *Simpliciana*, 22:313–29, looks not only at passages in *Simplicissimus*, *Springinsfeld*, *Vogelnest*, and *Rathstübel Plutonis* which are set in or comment on Strassburg, but also at G.'s links with other satirists and literary figures connected with the town (Fischart, Moscherosch, the 'Tannengesellschaft'), and at his (unfortunate) relationships with Strassburg publishers and the ruling Fürstbischof Franz Egon von Fürstenberg. J.-M. Valentin, 'Krieg und Frieden bei Grimmel-shausen. Oder die Grenzen der Satire', *ib.*, 331–42, looks in some detail at one particular aspect of G.'s satirical technique — praise as a form of criticism, used in the 'Mummelsee' episode during Simplicius's replies to questions about the human world from the ruler of the sylphs. W. E. Schäfer, 'Georg Andreas Dollhopf(f), ein Straßburger Verleger', *ib.*, 343–61, examines the hitherto neglected life and work of D., focusing on his activities as one of G.'s three publishers (the others being Georg Heinrich Frommann of Leipzig and Wolf Eberhard Felssecker of Nuremberg). S. appends a facsimile extract from D.'s catalogue of publications for 1672–73. T. Strässle, 'The symbolism of salt in Grimmelshausen's *Simplicissimus Teutsch*', *ib.*, 379–95, shows how the religious symbolism of salt fits in with the main theme of G.'s novel, appearing, for example, in crucial early episodes: in the pillage of Simplicius's supposed father's farm and in his meeting with his real father, the hermit. A. Wicke, ' "Eine solche/ wie ihr wisset daß ich bin . . ." ' — Strategien der Selbsterfindung im Simplicianischen Zyklus, untersucht am Beispiel der *Lebensbeschreibung der Landstörtzerin Courasche*', *ib.*, 403–60, investigates the concept of 'self-discovery' in *Courasche*, treating it as an aspect of narrative technique which is related to the mock autobiographical, confessional structuring of the picaresque novel in general, yet which takes on a new function in this particular novel because the central figure so utterly rejects the penitence that traditionally accompanies confession. R. Uhrig, 'Courasche, die Motte? Das Titelkupfer von Grimmelshausens zweitem Roman als Rezeptionsanleitung', *ib.*, 461–85, argues that G. uses a number of techniques to discredit the 'autobiographical' life history of the central figure in this novel, and that such means of guiding readers' responses are largely metatextual — like the frontispiece, which U. analyses in some detail in this light.

HARSDÖRFFER. E. Meier, 'Die Titelkupfer der *Frauenzimmer Gesprächspiele* Harsdörffers', *Morgenglantz*, 10:239–60, 34 illus., demonstrates how the title engravings in H.'s *Gesprächspiele* (1641–8) match his own precepts for relating illustrations to a text, and how some reflect the conversational structure of the work by resembling designs for stage sets. She also shows that engravings illustrating discussion of the theatre in the sixth *Gesprächspiel* are copies from Italian publications on theatrical performances which H. may have seen in Italy, and that this helps to confirm links between the underlying concept of the *Gesprächspiele* and cultural diversions common in Italian academies. B. Bannasch, 'Von der "Tunkelheit" der Bilder. Das Emblem als Gegenstand der Meditation bei Harsdörffer', Kurz, *Meditation*, 307–25, discusses the emblem theory H. presents in the *Frauenzimmer Gesprächspiele* in some detail, concentrating on the function of obscurity in the interplay of image and motto, the two constituent parts of what H. called the 'Sinnbild' (the emblem 'proper' includes an epigram or *subscriptio*), and finding that H. prepared the way for a modern, post-Lessing understanding of the aesthetic / meditative relationship between text and image.

KNORR. I. M. Battafarano, 'Bibel in barocker Bildlichkeit. Massenmord und Endzeit bei Giovan Battista Marino und Christian Knorr von Rosenroth', *Morgenglantz*, 10:37–66, compares M.'s 1632 verse epic on Herod's slaughter of the Holy Innocents (*La strage degli Innocenti*) with K.'s 1670 commentary on Revelations (*Eigentliche Erklärung über die Gesichter der Offenbarung S. Johannis*), analysing the evocative and emotional dynamics of imagery in two very different Bible-based works which both aim to encourage moral living in their readers.

MOSCHEROSCH. J. Schillinger, 'J. M. Moscherosch, Frankreich und die Gallomanie der Deutschen', *Simpliciana*, 22:227–45, re-examines M.'s reputation as a 'nationalist' writer, calling for more cautious interpretation of his anti-foreign stance. S. discusses his reliance on anti-France stereotypes in the 'A la mode Kehrauß' section of the *Gesichte Philanders* (1643), reveals similarities between these and stereotypes applied by earlier French writers to Italy, and cites examples of M.'s positive views of French culture. D. Martin, 'Johann Michael Moscheroschs Aktualität in der nationalen Bewegung des frühen 19. Jahrhunderts', *ib.*, 271–90, shows that although early 19th-c. reception of the *Gesichte Philanders* was selective, focusing only on certain sections of the work, it was nevertheless — contrary to previous opinion — as widespread as the contemporary reception of Grimmelshausen's work. Argument is supported by a tabular diagram. The author bases this essay on the chapter on M. in his recently published volume on the reception of 17th-c. literature in Germany from 1770 to 1830.

SPEE. F. Harzer, ' "Bilde dir für. . ." Meditation und Imagination in Friedrich Spees "Güldenem Tugend = Buch" ', Kurz, *Meditation*, 291–305, explores the theology behind the appeals to the imagination made by S. in this manual, discussing both his debt to and divergence from the Jesuit psychology based on Aristotle, and Loyola's tech-niques involving the evocation of sensory experience. Taking the poetic quality of S.'s images into account, H. nevertheless finds their function to be in accordance with theological systems of prayer. VEIRAS. R. Zeller, 'Heutelia zwischen Reisebeschreibung, Utopie und Satire', *Simpliciana*, 22:291–311, analyses the neglected *Heutelia* (1658), supposedly by Hans Franz Veiras (d. 1672) and taken in the past to be a description of Switzerland. Z. sees it as a fictional travel account, discusses the confessional and political issues it touches upon, and seeks to define its genre.

OTHER WORK

It has only recently been recognized that collections of stories, on the pattern, for example, of Wickram's well-known *Rollwagenbüchlein*, continued to be published in large numbers during the 17th c. *Simpliciana*, 21, 1999, contains the proceedings of the colloquium entitled 'Barocke Erzählsammlungen' which was held in 1999 at the Herzog August Bibliothek, Wolfenbüttel, to initiate scholarly exploration of such collections and their influence on Grimmelshausen and others. They include: I. Timmermann, ' "löbliche Conversation" als "Einübung ins Räsonnement". Das Gespräch als Ziel und Funktion barocker Erzählsammlungen am Beispiel der *Lustigen Schau = Bühne von allerhand Curiositäten* des Erasmus Francisci (1627–1694)' (15–40); J. A. Steiger, 'Exempla fidei. Die Exempelhermeneutik Luthers und die Exempelsammlungen der lutherischen Orthodoxie' (41–66), which discusses L.'s views in connection with numerous types and examples of compendia of edifying stories or 'Predigtmärlein'; R. Zeller, 'Wunderbares, Ingeniöses und Historien. Zu Pedro Mexías *Geschicht- Natur- und Wunderwald*' (67–92), which looks at a work by the Spanish Mexía (1497–1551) that was a late 16th-c. and early 17th-c. bestseller in German-speaking lands and republished there yet again as late as 1668–69, but was also known in various translations throughout Europe; R. Wimmer, 'Bidermanns *Utopia*. Gedanken zu Struktur und Intention frühbarocken Erzählens' (93–103), which discusses a Latin work of 1604 now available in an edition with commentary and a modern German translation (by M. Schuster, 1984); A. Halisch, 'Barocke Kriminalgeschichtensammlungen' (105–24), which examines 17th-c. collections of stories hitherto neglected by literary historians, who tend to place the beginnings of the crime-fiction genre at around 1800; I. M. Battafarano, 'Von Sodomiten und Sirenen in Neapel. Barocke Erzählkunst bei Martin Zeiller und Georg Philipp Harsdörffer' (124–40); R. G. Czapla, 'Mythologische Erzählstoffe im Kontext polyhistorischer Gelehrsamkeit. Zu Peter Laurembergs *Acerra philologica*' (141–59), which discusses a collection that contained 200 stories when first published in 1633, but 700 when republished in 1667, and, like many similar 'expanding' collections, went into several editions in the 17th c. alone; K. Haberkamm, 'Kornmanns "collectanea" *Mons veneris* (1614) und *De Miracvlis Mortvorum* (1610). Kurioses von stoffgeschichtlicher und hermeneutischer Relevanz' (161–76); R. G. Bogner, 'Exempel, Dialoge, Digressionen. Die anonyme Erzählsammlung *Hundstägige Erquickstund* (1650/53)' (177–93); B. Kasties, 'Zwischen Realpolitik und Don Quevedos Visionen. Charakteristika einer barocken Erzählsammlung des "Pseudo-Moscherosch" ' (195–212); É. Knapp und G. Tüskés, 'Das erste Mirakelbuch von Mariatal (1661) und seine Wirkungsgeschichte' (213–32); W. Brückner, 'Die Legendensammlungen des Martin von Cochem. Narrative Popularisierung der katholischen Reform im Zeitalter des Barock' (233–58), which looks at C.'s extraordinarily and lastingly popular yet hitherto little studied collections of stories, such as his *Guldener Himmels-Schlüssel* of 1690, which has been reprinted over 300 times.

V. Meid, 'Höfisch-historischer Barockroman, Absolutismus und Utopie', *Morgenglantz*, 10:133–56, firmly separates the largely theologically motivated tradition of the Utopian novel founded by Thomas More from the more politically motivated courtly-historical novel, then goes on to claim that the latter genre argues for a 'Utopie des Absolutismus', that is, for a form of rulership which secures lasting peace and order for its subjects. As M. points out, the price paid by the individual for such earthly happiness is complete subordination. He draws examples from late 16th- and 17th-c. theoretical writings, both political and literary, and from novels which include John Barclay's *Argenis* (1621), Andreas Heinrich Bucholtz's *Herkules* (1659–60), and Philipp von Zesen's *Assenat* (1670).

4. DRAMA

INDIVIDUAL AUTHORS

BIDERMANN. J. L. Hagens, 'Spielen und Zuschauen in Jakob Bidermanns *Philemon Martyr*. "Theatrum Mundi" als dramatisches und pädagogisches Prinzip des Jesuitentheaters', *Daphnis*, 29:103–57, argues that B.'s school drama of 1618 does not conform to the rigid Jesuit concept of education; its genre as tragicomedy enables it to represent a playful version of pedagogy.

FRIESE. A. Carrdus, 'Friedrich Friese's dialect comedy of 1687: a taste of Altenburg school theatre', *GLL*, 53:303–13, outlines the activities of school theatre in Altenburg 1660–1704, which included performances of plays by Gryphius and Weise as well as of dramas written and produced by teachers at the Altenburg 'Gymnasium' to celebrate the annual school and civic festival, the 'Gregoriusfest'. The unity of F.'s pedagogic and dramatic interests is introduced within this context and the text of his play is given.

GRYPHIUS. *Daphnis*, 28.3–4, 1999, is a tribute to Konrad Gajek on his death in 1999. It takes the highly appropriate form of papers on Gryphius's work which were given in 1996, on Konrad Gajek's own invitation, at the founding conference of the 'Internationale Andreas-Gryphius Gesellschaft'. F. van Ingen, 'Die schlesische Märtyrertragödie im Kontext zeitgenössischer Vorbildliteratur' (481–528), highlights the edifying effects of martyr tragedies on audiences and performers by analysing the neglected genre of the 'Märtyrbuch', of which many examples appeared in Germany in the 16th and 17th c. Their influence is perceptible in dramas by both G. and Hallmann. I. Schleier, 'Die Vollendung des Schausspielers zum Emblem' (529–62), fascinatingly re-examines contemporary illustrations of characters and scenes from 17th-c. dramatic events from the point of view of the 17th-c. performer faced with a space to perform in. An actor on the 'Illusionsbühne' of G.'s time, for example, would have had to regulate movements so as not to disrupt the perspectival foreshortenings of the scenery on which the illusion of reality depended. S. also analyses stage directions and textual references to scenery and props in G.'s work (interestingly, there are more in his tragedies than his comedies). She includes 17 illustrations and suggests that an experimental reconstruction of 17th-c. theatre performance is long overdue. T. Borgstedt, 'Angst, Irrtum und Reue in der Märtyrertragödie. Andreas Gryphius' *Catharina von Georgien* vor dem Hintergrund von Vondels *Maeghden* und Corneilles *Polyeucte Martyr*' (563–94), looks in particular at treatments of Aristotelian concepts such as reversal and protagonists' tragic flaw. R. G. Bogner, 'Die Not der Lüge. Konfessionelle Differenzen in der Bewertung der unwahren Rede am Beispiel von Andreas Gryphius' Trauerspiel *Catharina von Georgien*' (595–611), looks at how the plot is driven by lies and broken promises, and examines such events in the light of Catholic and Protestant doctrines. N. Kaminski, 'Matyrogenese als theatrales Ereignis. Des *Leo Armenius* theaterhermeneutischer Kommentar zu Gryphius' Märtyrerdramen' (613–30), reopens controversy over which of G.'s tragedies are martyr tragedies (and why) by interestingly using *Leo Armenius* — the very play which many critics view as *not* a martyr tragedy — as 'commentary' on *Carolus Stuardus*, *Catharina von Georgien* and *Papinianus*. A. Solbach, 'Amtsethik und lutherischer Gewissensgriff in Andreas Gryphius' *Papinianus*' (631–73), reconsiders the moral background to issues raised by this overtly Christian play in a non-Christian setting. K. Kiesant, 'Andreas Gryphius und Brandenburg — nur eine biographische Episode?' (675–89), questions the strategies of praise in the references made by G.'s earliest biographers to his connections with Brandenburg, and examines their political and confessional implications. H. Loos, '*Catharina von Georgien*: Unio mystica und virtus heroica — Leitbegriffe einer Interpretation' (691–727), looks at the treatment of these concepts by authors contemporary to G., some of whom he had either read or heard preach, and relates them to G.'s play. J.-L. Raffy, 'Die *Civitas Dei* in Gryphius' Trauersspiele' (729–60), sees G.'s concept of the *civitas dei* as blurred by pessimism and teases out its details as it informs what R. refers to as G.'s four political / historical dramas.

LOHENSTEIN. Jane O. Newman, *The Intervention of Philology: Gender, Learning and Power in Lohenstein's Roman Plays* (University of North Carolina Studies in the Germanic Languages and Literatures, 122), Chapel Hill–London, North Carolina U.P., xv + 226 pp., deals with the various roles played by the discipline of philology in the writing, understanding and modern editing (in the 1950s) of L.'s *Sophonisbe* (1669), *Epicharis* (1665), *Agrippina* (1665), and *Cleopatra* (1680). N. stresses the continuing historical and political instability of the texts in terms of their origin in Silesia, their relationship to Rome, and their performance by schoolboys dressed as women in the eponymous roles. Especially interesting is her examination of those texts, both classical and contemporary, which L. drew upon in the plays and discussed in the extensive notes he appended to each. L.'s polymathy lent depth and complexity to issues of power, gender and race which engaged performers, audiences and readers in the 17th c. but still resonate today. H. Esselborn, 'Der Mensch und die Ordnung der Natur. Lohensteins Naturbildlichkeit im Trauerspiel *Sophonisbe*', *Daphnis*, 28, 1999, 245–64, interestingly categorizes the natural images which preponderate in this drama, particularly in descriptions of the central figure, and relates them to emblematic tradition and contemporary scientific knowledge. E. argues that by using these images in a context of acute social and political disorder, L. articulates a belief in the constancy of natural order — to which humans ultimately belong. S. Colvin, ' "Die Wollust ist die Cirz". Daniel Caspar von Lohenstein and the notion of witchcraft', *ib.*, 265–86, draws illuminating parallels between the early modern concept of witchcraft, its manifestation in witchcraft trials, and L.'s representation of the heroines in *Sophonisbe, Epicharis, Agrippina* and *Cleopatra*. C. shows that L.'s legal training under Benedikt Carpzov (1595–1666) and practice as 'Stadtsyndikus' of Breslau familiarised him with the concept in depth, and argues that he draws upon it as a dramatist to promote the triumph of rationality over lust in his schoolboy performers (and in male members of his audiences), and thus, ultimately, to promote stable social and political order.

WEISE. P.-H. Haischer, 'Zur Bedeutung von Parodie und Karneval in Christian Weises *Zittauischem Theatrum*', *Daphnis*, 28, 1999:286–321, deals with the 1682 trilogy consisting, in accordance with traditions of school theatre in Zittau, of a biblical drama (*Von Jacobs doppelter Heirath*), a tragedy (*Masaniello*), and a comedy (*Tobias und der Schwalbe*). H. argues that the interdependence of these plays resides in their parody of specific dramatic forms and texts, and in their reflection of the 'verkehrte Welt' celebrated by carnival (they were performed at Shrovetide); the resulting mix of genres both created a pedagogically effective sense of reality and represented a defence of school drama against purists adhering to Opitz's classically orientated definitions of dramatic genres.

THE CLASSICAL ERA

By JEFFREY MORRISON, *Lecturer in German, National University of Ireland, Maynooth*

1. GENERAL

GENERAL STUDIES AND ESSAY COLLECTIONS. Catling, *Women's Writing* contains a compact and lucid chapter by Leslie Sharpe (pp. 47–67) on women's writing during the Enlightenment. It covers conventional literature as well as correspondences and journal publications and provides evidence of the expansion of female participation in the business of literature by the end of the period, albeit of expansion from a low base.

PERIODS

AUFKLÄRUNG. Uwe Steiner, *Poetische Theodizee: Philosophie und Poesie in der lehrhaften Dichtung im achtzehnten Jahrhundert*, Munich, Fink, 384 pp., approaches the much-debated question of the relationship between philosophy and literary arts during the Enlightenment from an interesting angle and on the basis of an unusual corpus of texts. The starting point is a discussion of the death of the first Prussian Queen in 1705. The sad event was processed poetically in poems by Johann von Besser, Benjamin Neukirch, Christian Reuter, and, most significantly, Gottfried Wilhelm Leibniz. S. investigates the different responses to the death, which range from the politically expedient 'Gelegenheitsgedicht' to the 'philosophisches Lehrgedicht' of Leibniz in which the question of theodicy is central. The philosophical/ educational value of literature, with a particular focus on the question of theodicy, is further investigated in a study of 18th-c. fables and in connection with Voltaire's poem on the Lisbon earthquake. *Disrupted Patterns: On Chaos and Order in the Enlightenment*, ed. Theodore E. D. Braun and John A. McCarthy (Internationale Forschungen zur allgemeinen und vergleichenden Literaturwissenschaft, 43), Amsterdam–Atlanta, Rodopi, xiii + 219 pp., contains a wide range of material on French, English, and German texts. The uniting principle is the attempt to explore the significance of modern chaos theory for literary studies. The three articles which have a direct bearing upon our period are: J. Reahard, 'Motion in form: Goethe's force of nature' (161–74); H. Rowland, 'Goethe's *Hermann und Dorothea* and the chaotic and complex order of history' (175–90); J. M. van der Laan, 'Essayistic orders of chaos' (191–201), which includes discussion of Goethe, Voltaire, and Pope. The section of the text entitled 'Theoretical concerns' (9–49), locates the territory explored by the text in general and many of the other individual articles on (e.g.) Montesquieu or Locke could have implications for the German scholar. Ralph-Rainer Wuthenow, *Die gebändigte Flamme: Zur Wiederentdeckung der Leidenschaften im Zeitalter der Vernunft* (BNL, 178), 151 pp., ranges widely for a short monograph, covering aspects of French and German literature and philosophy. The focus on the German contribution to the 'enlightened' debate on the merits and demerits of emotion is largely confined to section III (pp. 83–132) and deals with Hamann, Herder, Goethe, Lenz, and Heinse and their contribution to the rehabilitation of passion.

Articles on aspects of the period include: R. Bledsoe, 'Harnessing autonomous art: Enlightenment and aesthetic education in Johann Adam Bergk's *Die Kunst, Bücher zu lesen*', *GLL*, 53:470–86; J. S. Librett, 'Stolen goods: cultural identity after the Counterenlightenment in Salomon Maimon's *Autobiography*', *NGC*, 79:36–66; A. Strum, 'What Enlightenment is', *ib.*, 106–36; W. Goetschel, 'Kant and the Christo effect: grounding aesthetics', *ib.*, 137–56.

EMPFINDSAMKEIT, STURM UND DRANG   Ulrich Karthaus, *Sturm und Drang: Epoche — Werk — Wirkung* (Arbeitsbücher zur Literaturgeschichte), Munich, Beck, 280 pp., manages a very clever balancing act. The author, despite an awareness of the huge bibliography on this period and a strong sense of the elusiveness of any useful definition of its essential character, nonetheless manages to produce a very useful introduction to the *Sturm und Drang* which contains treatment of the intellectual/cultural background to the period, discussion of its aesthetics in general terms and treatment of its literary products in the most important genres. The examination of specific texts, whilst necessarily compact, is what makes this text so successful in its own terms and it will become a prized teaching tool. By contrast, Georg W. Bertram, *Philosophie des Sturm und Drang: Eine Konstitution der Moderne*, Munich, Fink, 284 pp., seeks to open up a new perspective on the period in terms of its (post-)modernity. Indeed the text is substantially an investigation of the relationship between the modern and the postmodern, explored in philosophical (rather than narrowly literary) terms with a theoretical framework derived variously from Freud, Foucault, Derrida, and Lyotard. Whilst the text is undoubtedly a heavy read for a non-philosopher, it provides an interesting perspective from which to judge a period which is generally seen as marginal, as an explosive counter-movement in the broad sweep of German literary/intellectual history. Another introduction to the period is offered in Bruce Duncan, *Lovers, Parricides, and Highwaymen: Aspects of Sturm und Drang Drama* (SGLLC), 1999, viii + 267 pp. Whilst the text is clearly aimed in part at the non-specialist (with all quotations presented in English), it manages a very compact introduction to the genesis, literary products, and, most impressively, reception of the period, and will undoubtedly find a very useful place on university bookshelves. Individual articles on these periods include: M. N. Niazi, 'Encountering the Other in general text: an approach to intertext through poetry of the German Sensibility', *CL*, 52 : 97–118 (contains some treatment of the Göttinger Hainbund and Klopstock); M. Willems, 'Wider die Kompensationsthese: zur Funktion der Genieästhetik der Sturm-und-Drang Bewegung', *Euphorion*, 94 : 1–42; F. Breithaupt, 'Anonymous forces of history: the case of infanticide in the *Sturm und Drang*', *NGC*, 79 : 157–76.

CLASSICISM   Articles dealing with the idea of classicism include: P. Bishop, 'Affinities between Weimar Classicism and analytical psychology: Goethe and Jung on the concept of the Self', *FMLS*, 36 : 74–91; A. Köhler, 'Weimar, *London und Paris*: the provincial cultural elite views the big wide world?', *PEGS(NS)*, 69, 1999[2000] : 52–64.

GENRES

Joseph Kohnen, *Lyrik in Königsberg 1749–1799* (RBDSL, 74), 290 pp., provides an interesting survey of the poetry produced in Königsberg, an obvious centre in other disciplines, only to dismiss most of it as mediocre. The question of 'why?', which is perhaps the most interesting one which could have been asked is raised only in the conclusion. The text nonetheless provides exposure to the poetry of (e.g.) Immanuel Kant, the young Herder, Lenz, and Hamann, as well as to many more or less obscure contemporaries. Sarah Colvin, *The Rhetorical Feminine: Gender and Orient on the German Stage 1647–1742*, Oxford, Clarendon, 1999, x + 332 pp., is, as the title suggests, substantially concerned with an earlier period. There is little doubt, however, that some characteristics of the portrayal of women, blacks, and Turks on the German stage were preserved well into the 18th c. The treatment of representatives of any or all of these typically fell into two categories — they were either idealized or, on the other hand, seen as sources of chaos or disorder. As C. indicates in her conclusion, similar tendencies survived much later than her period of study. This volume will provide very valuable background reading for scholars of the earlier part of our period. Individual articles on genres include: E. Trunz, 'Deutsche Abendgedichte von Gryphius bis Rilke', *JWGV*, 100–01, 1996–97[1998] : 93–110.

THEMES

Burkhard Dohm, *Poetische Alchimie: Öffnung zur Sinnlichkeit in der Hohelied- und Bibeldichtung von der protestantischen Barockmystik bis zum*

Pietismus (SDL, 145), vi + 468 pp., is substantially concerned with an earlier period but does contain treatments of Gottfried Arnold, Nikolaus Ludwig von Zinzendorf, and Johann Gottfried Herder in the terms suggested by the title. *Kunst und Wissenschaft um 1800*, ed. Thomas Lange and Harald Neumeyer (Stiftung für Romantikforschung, 13), Würzburg, Königshausen & Neumann, 297 pp., contains a number of articles of direct relevance to scholars of our period rather than of that suggested by the series title. The volume is interdisciplinary and international in its perspective but nonetheless deals with important German literary/literary-theoretical figures. Articles include: K. Lange and H. Niemeyer, 'Kunst und Wissenschaft um 1800' (7–18); M. Bergengreuen, ' "Heißbrennende Hohlspiegel": Wie Jean Paul durch die Optik seine Poetik sichtbar werden läßt' (19–38) (contains a great deal on 18th-c. theories of perception); R. Borgards, 'Die Wissenschaft vom Auge und die Kunst des Sehens: von Descartes zu Soemmerring, von Lessing zu A. W. Schlegel' (39–62); H. Neumeyer, ' "Wir nennen aber jetzt Melancholie" (Adolf Henke). Chateaubriand, Goethe, Tieck und die Medezin um 1800' (63–88); S. Gröf, 'Diagnose: Heimweh — Begriffsgeschichtliche Betrachtung zu einem Phänomen zwischen Wissenschaft und Literatur' (63–88) (contains a discussion of Mignon's homesickness); J. Steigerwald, 'Schwindelgefühle: das literarische Paradigma der "Darstellung" als Anthropologicum (Klopstock, Sulzer, Herz, Hoffmann)' (109–32); J. Fohrmann, 'Subjektivität, Echo, Wissenschaft: eine Konstellation um 1800' (133–50); C. Behle, ' "Allharmonie von Allkraft zum All-Wohl": Jacob Hermann Obereit zwischen Aufklärung, Hermetismus und Idealismus' (151–74); C. Dongowski, 'Winckelmanns *Geschichte der Kunst des Altertums*: "Kunst/Geschichte" als Abfall (von) der Naturgeschichte' (219–236); S. Pott, 'Imbecillitas und Genius: Überlegungen für eine Interpretation der "philosophische(n) Romane" Friedrich Maximilian Klingers vor dem Hintergrund differenzierender Wertungen in der Literaturhistoriographie des 19. (und 20.) Jahrhunderts' (237–58).

Regina Hartmann, *Deutsche Reisende in der Spätaufklärung unterwegs in Skandinavien: Die Verständigung über den 'Norden' im Konstruktionsprozeß ihrer Berichte* (TUGS, 44), 348 pp., will serve a dual purpose for most readers. Firstly, it will introduce the relatively unknown body of German travel and other literature on Scandinavia to a wider public. Secondly, it provides a very interesting examination of the complex construction of images of Scandinavian countries and peoples during the late Enlightenment and of the implications that these images had for the German self-image. The text provides a very lucid account of the ways in which expectations, even clichés, about the region were propagated and mutated by German writers in isolation or combination. *Das achtzehnte Jahrhundert*, 24.2, is a special number devoted to *Abenteuer und Abenteuerer im 18. Jahrhundert*. The volume ranges widely: only three substantial articles have a German focus, namely: A. Rieke-Müller, ' "ein Kerl mit wilden Thieren": zur sozialen Stellung und zum Selbstverständnis von Tierführern im 18. Jahrhundert' (163–74); U. Zeuch, 'Abenteuer als Weg zum *nosce te ipsum*? Umschlagserfahrung und Selbsterkenntnis bei Grimmelshausen und Wieland' (176–90); R. Stach, 'Abenteurliche Biografien: Marginalien zu Robinsonaden des 18. Jahrhunderts' (191–204).

Volker Riedel, *Antikerezeption in der deutschen Literatur vom Renaissance-Humanismus bis zur Gegenwart: Eine Einführung*, Stuttgart, Metzler, viii + 515 pp., contains a substantial section on the reception of antiquity in our period (pp. 109–86) covering the whole of the 18th and early 19th cs. Of necessity the treatment of individual instances of reception is brief (typically 1–5 pages) but does provide a means of orientation appropriate to the introductory nature of the text. Arguably, the coverage of the 20th c. is more novel and useful since the matter of the reception of antiquity in our period is central in many studies, albeit often in reference only to single authors or movements. Baumbach, *Tradita*, contains a number of much more detailed treatments of the mechanics of the reception of antiquity from our period, including: S. M. Schreiner, '*Sedes Pacis Martis Austriaci* — Ein panegyrisch-aitiologisches Gedicht auf Prinz Eugen von Savoyen und das Belvedere' (253–70); H. Müller, 'Wielands fragmentarisches Gedicht *Psyche*' (271–80); S. Elit, 'Übersetzen als internationaler Dichterwettstreit: Klopstocks Übersetzung horazischer Oden als doppelter poetischer Überbietungsversuch' (281–95); A. Müller, ' "Der Marmor ist vom feinsten Korn . . .": Ästhetische Erfahrung am Ende des 18. Jahrhunderts' (297–319); E. K. Wittich, 'Das Einzelne und Ganze — Detail(un)genauigkeit und Wissenschaftsanspruch der Antikerezeption bei Karl Friedrich Schinkel' (339–54). Albrecht Koschorke, *Körperströme und Schriftverkehr: Mediologie des 18. Jahrhunderts*, Munich, Fink, 1999, 507 pp., provides a complex anthropological analysis of two contemporaneous phenomena and their interrelationship. In the first instance it examines the shifting 18th-c. understanding of the operations of the human body and the consequent shift in the sense of self. This is investigated alongside and in fascinating combination with an investigation of the expansion of writing as a medium of communication to overcome distance between (newly-defined) individuals. The self-declared aim of the text is to produce an 'Anthropologie der modernen Schriftkultur' on the basis of an examination of that point in the development of the culture where its shape was most radically changing.

Individual articles on varied themes include: H. F. Weiss, 'Der Mittwochs- und der Professorenklub: zur Geselligkeit in Jena am Ausgang des achtzehnten Jahrhunderts', *JFDH*, 1999:94–120; M. J. Sosulski, 'Trained minds, disciplined bodies: Konrad Ekhof and the reform of the German actor', *LY*, 31, 1999[2000]:131–57; A. Košenina, 'Von "des Jahrhunderts ernstem Ende,/Wo selbst die Wirklichkeit zur Dichtung wird": Literarische Reflexionen der Jahrhundertwende 1800', *ZGer*, 10:61–76; S. Martus, 'Die Entstehung von Tiefsinn im 18. Jahrhundert: zur Temporalisierung der Poesie in der Verbesserungsästhetik bei Hagedorn, Gellert und Wieland', *DVLG*, 74:27–43; D. von Mücke, 'Experience, impartiality, and authenticity in confessional discourse', *NGC*, 79:5–35 (Pietism, Adam Bernd); C. Stockinger, 'Von der Idylle zum "Blutbad": die Vergeschichtlichung der Alpendarstellung in der Literatur des 18.und 19. Jahrhunderts', *ZDP*, 119:161–78; P. Guilbert, 'Welche neuzeitlichen Strategien für die Rettung der antiken Mythologie? Vergleich von drei "Handbüchern zur Götterlehre" um 1790: K. W. Ramler — Ch. G. Heyne/ M. G. Hermann — K. Ph. Moritz', *GY*, 9, 1999:186–221.

2. GOETHE

EDITIONS. *Goethe: Selected Poems*, ed. Terence John Reed, London, Bristol Classical Press, 1999, xxxi + 107 pp., provides a sample of some 50 poems by G. of very differing kinds, with an introduction and helpful notes. It will undoubtedly prove a useful starting point for new readers of G. whom it will encourage to 'work outwards' towards other texts. The publication of Johann Wolfgang Goethe, *Tagebücher: Historisch-kritische Ausgabe*, continues with vols II.1 and II.2, namely *Tagebücher 1790 bis 1800: Text*, ed. Edith Zehm, Stuttgart–Weimar, Metzler, pp. 1–413, and *Tagebücher 1790–1800: Kommentar*, ed. Wolfgang Albrecht and Edith Zehm, Stuttgart–Weimar, Metzler, pp. 414–987. These volumes continue the extraordinary undertaking of reproducing accurately original documents on the basis of manuscripts and recording all subsequent or contemporaneous variants. The edition will on that basis ultimately provide a more reliable, or at least transparent, version of the diaries with exhaustive commentary which will prove invaluable to scholars who are keen to track events, texts, or individuals who have had a bearing upon G. The majority of these volumes is concerned with the diary of the 1797 Swiss journey but the rather thinner contributions on G.'s everyday life will also prove interesting. Overall the two volumes also make clear G.'s rather ambivalent attitude towards diary writing, so variable are the scope and quality of the entries. '*Meine Schatzkammer*

füllt sich täglich . . .': Die Nachlaßstücke zu Goethes 'West-östlichem Divan',
ed. Anke Bosse, 2 vols, Göttingen, Wallstein, 1999, 588,
589–1248 pp., will prove an extremely useful research tool as it
provides for the first time easy access to the unpublished material
produced in connection with G.'s massive *Divan* project. That
material is arranged chronologically, provided with exhaustive
commentary connecting G.'s background work to the published
material, with concordances, bibliography, indeed all of the help that
one could need in approaching the body of material. Particularly
useful features for the non-specialist are the short essays which
introduce the different phases of the *Divan* project. K. Mommsen,
'Aufforderung zur Suche nach einem Goethe-Autograph', *GY*, 9,
1999:343–45.

GENERAL STUDIES AND ESSAY COLLECTIONS. *Von Goethe war die Rede
. . .*, ed. Jattie Enklaar and Hans Ester (*DK*, 49), 1999, 212 pp.,
contains a wide range of articles on aspects of Goethe's work and
reception: P. Delvaux, 'Goethes Leben und Werk in gegenseitiger
Erhellung' (7–19); T. Kramer, 'Thomas Mann: *Lotte in Weimar*'
(20–37); S. Onderdelinden, 'Goethe als avantgardistischer
Dramatiker' (38–55); P. Claessens, 'De roos, de marionet en de
matroesjka: over faustische expansie en Goethesche dynamiek'
(56–76); H. Ester, 'Goethe, das Christentum und Fausts Himmelfahrt'
(77–95); K. Gille, ' "Mich selbst [. . .] auszubilden, das war dunkel
von Jugend auf mein Wunsch": zur Einführung in *Wilhelm Meisters
Lehrjahre*' (96–115); J. Schmidt, 'Planspiele des Schicksals: Goethes
Wahlverwandtschaften' (116–28); J. von der Thuisen, ' "Auch ich war in
Arkadien" — Goethes *Italienische Reise*' (129–40); A. Bosse, ' "Ein
wunderliches Ganze" — zu Goethes *West-östlichem Divan*' (141–64);
E. Verzaal, 'Der Besuch von Frans Hemsterhuis bei Goethe in
Weimar' (165–80); L. Decloedt, ' "Es gibt so viele Goethes wie es
Erdbewohner gibt": niederländische und flämische Reaktionen auf
Goethe im zwanzigsten Jahrhundert' (181–98); H. Ester, 'Goethe
und Rembrandt. eine Ausstellung als Brücke zwischen Amsterdam
und Weimar' (199–200).

Wolfgang Butzlaff, *Goethe — 'Trostlos zu sein ist Liebenden der schönste
Trost': Gesammelte Studien zu Werk und Rezeption* (GTS, 66), 278 pp.,
contains seven articles derived from papers given in Goethe museums
or to Goethe societies; the articles in part still have something of the
tone of lectures. Three of them were previously unpublished, and two
of these have a Goethe connection: ' "Je lirai, je penserai, j'écrirai —
vive la plume!": Goethes französische Briefe' (11–72); ' "Trostlos zu
sein ist Liebenden der schönste Trost": neue Beiträge zur Interpretation der *Marienbader Elegie*' (149–80).

POETRY. Individual articles on poetry include: E. Trunz, 'Goethes Gedicht *Der Spiegel sagt mir . . .*', *JFDH*, 1999: 1–2; C. Perels, 'Irdische Paradiese mit kleinen Mängeln. Zu Goethes Gedicht *Der Park*', *ib.*, 3–13; A. Bohm, 'The tell-tale chalice: *Es war ein König in Thule* and *Orlando Furioso*', *MDLK*, 92: 20–34; E. Boa, 'Hermann und Dorothea: an early example of Heimatliteratur?', *PEGS(NS)*, 69, 1999[2000]: 20–36; I. Wagner, '*Hermann und Dorothea* in the context of Kant and Voss: a question of peace and patriarchy', *GY*, 9, 1999: 166–68; R. E. Dickerson, 'Textual variations among folio editions of Goethe's *Reineke Fuchs* illustrated by Wilhelm von Kaulbach', *ib.*, 1–46; B. Neymeyr, 'Navigation mit *virtus* und *fortuna*: Goethes Gedicht *Seefahrt* und seine stoische Grundkonzeption', *GJb*, 115, 1998[1999]: 29–44; S. Matuschek, 'Was ist ein "Troubador der Erlebnislyrik"? Epochenblick durch ein Goethe-Sonett', *ib.*, 69–76.

DRAMA. Birgit Wiens, '*Grammatik*' *der Schauspielkunst: Die Inszenierung der Geschlechter in Goethes klassischem Theater* (Theatron: Studien zur Geschichte und Theorie der dramatischen Künste, 31), Tübingen, Niemeyer, xii + 248 pp., could usefully be read in conjunction with Sarah Colvin's monograph on earlier German theatre (see above). The narrower focus in Wiens's work is upon the orientation and organization of the genders on the Weimar stage, although it does deal extensively with theatre and broader cultural history as well as contemporary dramatic theory. Indeed the exploration of the context of Goethe's dramas is more extensive than the treatment of the dramas themselves, but this 'background' work is most valuable in giving us a sense of Goethean innovation and his role in constructing a very specific picture of gender roles and gender difference on stage with which some contemporaries felt very ill at ease. G.'s dramas are seen as a first step on the road to an anti-illusionistic drama which culminated in Brecht, although G.'s gender definitions are seen as idealized and 'zugleich de-naturalisiert' and hence they form part of a dramaturgy which 'möglicherweise unfreiwillig bereits ihre eigene Kritik impliziert'. Individual articles on G.'s drama include: F.-J. Deiters, 'Goethes *Iphigenie auf Tauris* als Drama der Grenzüberschreitung oder: die Aneignung des Mythos', *JFDH*, 1999: 14–51; S. Martus, 'Sinn und Form in Goethes *Egmont*', *GJb*, 115, 1998[1999]: 45–62.

FAUST. Individual articles on *Faust* include: M. N. Niazi, 'Faust's violence against the mothers', *GQ*, 72, 1999: 221–31; U. Japp, 'Über Interpretation und Intertextualität: mit Rücksicht auf *Faust* II, 2 ("Klassische Walpurgisnacht")', *DVLG*, 74: 395–412; R. C. Zimmermann, 'Klarheit, Streben, Wiederbringung. Drei Beiträge zum Verständnis Goethes *Faust*', *ib.*, 413–64; J. M. van der Laan, 'Faust's divided self and moral inertia', *MDLK*, 91, 1999: 452–63; M. Bell,

'Sorge, Epicurean psychology and the classical *Faust*', *OGS*, 28, 1999:82–130; S. Matuschek, 'Goethes *Faust*: von der Leichtigkeit der letzten Dinge', *Poetica*, 31, 1999:452–61; P. Bishop, 'Intellectual affinities between Goethe and Jung, with special reference to *Faust*', *PEGS(NS)*, 69, 1999[2000]:1–19; D. C. Reichel, ' "Esprit faustien" — "Esprit chrétien": Goethe's *Faust* and Teilhard de Chardin's *Le Phénomène humain*', *GY*, 9, 1999:318–42; H.-J. Schings, 'Fausts Verzweiflung', *GJb*, 115, 1998[1999]:97–124; R. C. Zimmermann, 'Goethes Humanität und Fausts Apotheose: zur Problematik der religiösen Dimension von Goethes *Faust*', *ib.*, 125–46; Y. Takahashi, 'Reiz und Rätsel des *Faust* für die Japaner', *ib.*, 116:85–95; G. Mahal, 'Goethes *Faust* auf dem deutschen Theater des 20. Jahrhunderts', *ib.*, 144–57; K. Eibl, 'Zur Bedeutung der Wette im *Faust*', *ib.*, 271–80.

NARRATIVE.   Ill-Sun Joo, *Goethes Dilettantismus-Kritik: 'Wilhelm Meisters Lehrjahre' im Lichte einer ästhetischen Kategorie der Moderne* (Heidelberger Beiträge zur deutschen Literatur, 4), Frankfurt, Lang, 1999, xii + 338 pp., would appear from its title to be covering familiar territory. However, whilst the text basis is known, Joo offers a new perspective on the question of dilettantism. Dilettantism is taken, in Joo's (and Goethe's) definition, to refer to a particularly ineffective manner of relating to the external world. In ideal circumstances a given individual develops an active relationship with the external world on the basis of 'wechselseitige Zusammenwirkung' between subject and object. For the most part, however, individuals develop knowledge of the external world without knowing themselves or become absorbed with themselves to the exclusion of the external world. This is the realm of the dilettante who in Goethean terms has an unresolved or 'unreal' sense of self. On this basis, Joo provides highly illuminating analysis of aspects of the *Lehrjahre* and the dangers of subjectivism. There is a strong connection in theme between the above text and Werner Schlick, *Goethe's 'Die Wahlverwandtschaften': A Middle-Class Critique of Aesthetic Aristocratism* (BNL, 172), x + 538 pp. The connection is in the treatment of aesthetic/artistic pretention and dilettantism and the absence of true creativity. Schlick's argument leads, however, in a different direction. The criticism of the aesthetic aspirations is seen as indicative of a negative political attitude towards the class which the central protagonists represent. Schlick does, however, distance himself from those critics who see the text as openly radical, maintaining that the indicators of a critical stance are clear but subtle — subtle enough indeed for most contemporary readers, especially those from the class criticized, to fail to notice it.

Sometimes the title of a text can be off-putting, as for this critic is the case with Gordon A. Burgess, *A Computer-Assisted Analysis of Goethe's 'Die Wahlverwandtschaften': The Enigma of Elective Affinities* (SGLL, 23),

1999, x + 264 pp. The content of the text is, however, much more illuminating that one might expect and provides interesting treatments of leitmotifs, relationships, patterns of direct and indirect speech, and narration. The most fascinating aspect for this reader is the treatment of the narration of the stories within the story and the hesitantly presented conclusion that the voice of the main and manipulative narrator pervades all parts of the text. Interestingly, in another text from the same publisher, a very different case is made for one of the sub-stories in a different text. Laura Martin, *Narrative Feminine Identity and the Appearance of Woman in some of the Shorter Fiction of Goethe, Kleist, Hawthorne, and James* (Women's Studies, 23), Lewiston, Mellen, xv + 212 pp., contains an article entitled 'A tricksy sprite: Johann Wolfgang Goethe's "Die pilgernde Törin" (*Wilhelm Meisters Lehrjahre*)' (25–56), which is precisely concerned to analyse from a feminist perspective the distinctive and deeply ambiguous voice which is introduced through a subsidiary tale. Returning to *Die Wahlverwandtschaften*, Paul Bishop, *The World of Stoical Discourse in Goethe's Novel 'Die Wahlverwandtschaften'* (BGP, 10; SGLL, 25), xvi + 115 pp., explores in a compact form the nature of the influence of stoicism, often mediated through Spinoza, upon this difficult G. text. B. investigates not only human attitudes and world views associated with stoicism and so with characters in G., but also the implications for the form of the novel (see chapter 3: 'Aphoristic form and stoical discourse', 21–28). G. is shown not to produce the grim and didactic text which might be expected but rather a sophisticated and even humorous novel which remains, however, in its basic tenets stoic. The analysis clearly helps in our understanding of the key notion of 'Entsagung' but, as B. makes clear, this does not make this an easy novel particularly as, in a deconstructive impulse, the text questions the value of the aesthetic.

Individual articles on narrative include: U. Hentschel, 'Goethes *Werther* und die Schweiz', *RG*, 29, 1999:15–25; E. Powers, 'The Artist's escape from the idyll: the relation of Werther to Sesenheim', *GY*, 9, 1999:47–76; J. A. Kowalik, 'Pietist grief, *Empfindsamkeit*, and Werther', *ib.*, 77–130; G. Sasse, 'Woran leidet Werther? Zum Zwiespalt zwischen idealistischer Schwärmerei und sinnlichem Begehren', *GJb*, 116, 1999[2000]:245–58; T. Valk, ' "Alles macht einen ewigen Zirkel in mir": Aurelie als Melancholikerin in Goethes *Wilhelm Meister*', *ib.*, 259–70; A. Haverkamp, 'Hamlet Anamorphose: Goethes Meisterstück', *Arcadia*, 35:137–49 (concerns *Wilhelm Meister*); P. Currie, 'Ambiguous figures in *Wilhelm Meisters Lehrjahre*', *OGS*, 29:77–94; G. Bersier, 'Goethe's parody of "Nazarene" iconography: the Joseph story in *Wilhelm Meisters Wanderjahre*', *GY*, 9, 1999:264–78;

S. Keppler, 'Die Heiligung der "sündigen Liebe"': Goethes *Wahlver-wandtschaften* und der Tristanstoff', *ASNS*, 237:64–91; A. Fineron, '"Man halte sich an's fortschreitende Leben"': Goethe's late essays *Wohlgemeinte Erwiderung* and *Ein Wort für junge Dichter?*', *PEGS(NS)*, 69, 1999[2000]:37–51; F. Farina, 'Unterwegs mit Goethe: das Gardasee-Erlebnis als Schlüssel zur *Italienischen Reise*', *GJb*, 115, 1998[1999]:229–30; B. C. Witte, '"In uns selbst liegt Italien!"' Johann Wolfgang von Goethe, Barthold Georg Niebuhr, Friedrich Preller: drei Deutsch-Römer in drei Generationen', *ib.*, 237–44.

THEMES. *Gottes ist der Orient! Gottes ist der Occident! — Goethe und die Religionen der Welt*, ed. Wolfgang Beutin and Thomas Bütow (BBLI, 31), 225 pp., contains articles produced as a result of a conference held at the Evangelische Akademie in Bad Segeberg during 1999, although the contribution by Jost Hermand was presented sub-sequently. The various contributions all attempt to explore aspects of Goethe's 'Weltfrömmigkeit' in the light of organized religions or of a heathen world view. Each of the contributions is individually interesting but, given the different academic backgrounds of the contributors (e.g. as theologians, Germanists, Orientalists) and the scale of the theme, readers would have gained from a stronger editorial hand than that provided by the editors in two brief contributions amounting to some five pages. The substantial contri-butions include: E. Reichert, 'Goethes Verhältnis zu Martin Luther und der Geschichte des Protestantismus' (13–22); H. Beutin, '"Ich bin so frei geboren als ein Mann." — Frauenbild, weibliches Priestertum und Humanität in Goethes Schauspiel *Iphigenie*' (23–50); C. Shareghi, 'Goethes Kenntnisse über den Orient und seine Begegnung mit dem persischen Dichter Hafis' (51–76); W. Beutin, 'Goethes *Faust* als Weltanschauungsdichtung' (77–108); K. Bothe, 'Der junge Goethe und die Natur: zu einigen Parallelen zwischen *Urfaust* und *Werther*' (109–34); J. Dvorák, 'Goethes Weisheit: Bemer-kungen zu Wissenschaft, Kunst und Religion' (135–48); F. Mülder, 'Sinnlichkeit und Heidentum — Als Autor auf den Spuren des Weltanschauungsdichters Johann Wolfgang von Goethe' (149–76); W. Beutin, 'Goethes Weltfrömmigkeit' (177–204); J. Hermand, '"Es ist des Herren eig'ner Geist, in dem die Zeiten sich bespiegeln": der politisch in Dienst genommene Goethe' (205–22). Another perspect-ive on Goethe's work is offered in the fine collection of articles *Über die Grenzen Weimars hinaus: Goethes Werk in europäischem Licht*, ed. Thomas Jung and Birgit Mühlhaus (Osloer Beiträge zur Germanistik, 27), Frankfurt, Lang, 202 pp. This volume, like many others, was produced in the wake of the jubilee year 1999. However, unlike many others, it contains papers of a uniformly high standard. Whilst the range of textual material covered is wide and the European focus of

the volume broad, a combination of factors which can be danger-
ous — and which betrays the genesis of the volume as a product of
guest lectures and symposia — the individual contributions make the
volume most worthwhile. The contributions include: R. Otto,
'Goethe in Weimar — Realitäten, Hoffnungen und Enttäuschungen'
(11–22); R. Steiger, 'Goethes drei Reisen durch die Schweiz' (23–34);
Id., 'Reise nach Italien, ins Land der Wiedergeburt' (35–44); G.-L.
Fink, 'Goethes Dialog mit Frankreich' (45–68); I. Sagmo, 'Goethe
und Skandinavien' (69–80); R. Stephenson, 'Über naïve und senti-
mentalische Rezeption: Goethe und die Briten — eine fruchtbare
interkulturelle Beziehung?' (81–90); J. John, 'Der vereinnahmte und
der geteilte Goethe: zur Goethe-Rezeption in Deutschland nach
1933' (91–114); D. Borchmeyer, 'Goethes Universaltheater'
(115–23); H.-J. Schings, 'Goethes Romane — Wege in die Moderne'
(123–34); G. Neumann, ' "Die höchste Lyrik ist entschieden histor-
isch" — Goethes Werk als Lebens-Werk' (135–72); H. B. Nisbet, 'Die
ethische Grundlage von Goethes Naturwissenschaft' (173–84);
B. Leistner, 'Goethe und (k)ein Ende oder Des Klassikers ernstlich
Späße'(185–98). *Durchgeistete Natur: Ihre Präsenz in Goethes Dichtung,
Wissenschaft und Philosophie*, ed. Alfred Schmidt and Klaus-Jürgen
Grün, Frankfurt, Lang, 321 pp., is interesting not just in its subject-
matter but also through the fact that the contributors come from
different academic spheres including literature, philosophy, natural
sciences, and medicine. The main contributions are: A. Schmidt,
'Die Natur im Dichten und Denken Goethes' (15–28); G. Böhme,
'Goethes Farbenlehre als Paradigma einer Phänomenologie der
Natur' (31–40); F. Siemsen and N. Stützle, 'Goethe und der
Elektromagnetismus: Im Anfang war die Tat' (41–56); W. Singer,
'Goethe — ein Konstruktivist?' (57–66); R.-R. Wuthenow, 'Natur in
Goetheschen Gedichten' (67–80); V. Sarris, 'Goethes Farbenlehre
aus heutiger wahrnehmungpsychologischer Sicht' (81–90); D. Kuhn,
'Die Idee der Morphologie bei Pflanzen und Tieren' (93–100); H.-
W. Korf and G. Storch, 'Goethes Entdeckung des Zwischenkieferkno-
chens und seine Wirbeltheorie des Schädels' (101–14); K.-J. Grün,
'Goethe und Darwin — War Goethe ein Evolutionstheoretiker?'
(115–26); G. Zizka, 'Goethe und die Botanik — Morphologie im
Wandel der Zeit' (127–36); W. Schad, 'Goethes Zeitauffassung und
die heutige Heterochronieforschung' (137–43); G. Kreft, 'Ornament
und Program: zur Ästhetik der Goethe-Zitation bei jüdischen Neu-
rowissenschaftlern in Frankfurt am Main' (144–57); H. Gebelein and
E.-W. Grabner, 'Chemie und Alchemie in Goethes poetischen und
wissenschaftlichen Werken: Versuche zum Anschauen und Begreifen'
(161–76); C.-D. Schönwiese, 'Wolken und Witterung aus der Sicht
Goethes und heute — "Ein Angehäuftes, flockig löst sich's auf" '

(177–86); U. Kienzle, 'Des Menschen Stimme und die Unendlichkeit der Musik: Goethes anthropologische "Tonlehre"' (187–204); J. Villwock, 'Die Weile der Ewigkeit — Goethe und das kosmische Naturverständnis der Griechen' (205–16); M. Trömel, 'Über Goethe hinaus? Goethe und die moderne Naturwissenschaft' (217–21); K. Jeziorkowski, 'Der poetisch-philosophische Naturbegriff Goethes' (225–30); H. Schipperges, 'Goethe und die Kunst zu leben' (231–40); H. Siefert, 'Goethe und die Medizin' (241–50); T. Görnitz, 'Goethe — Künstler, Naturforscher und philosophischer Denker — auch heute ein inspirierender Partner' (251–60); W. G. Saltzer, 'Goethe — Naturwissenschaft, Kunst und Weiterleben komplementär' (261–76).

Sigrid Krines, *Das häusliche Umfeld Goethes* (Helicon: Beiträge zur deutschen Literatur, 26), Frankfurt, Lang, 285 pp., pursues Goethe through his households in Weimar and Jena and examines the choice of home. Within the given home, it examines the spaces which he found preferable on the basis of his letters and other literary hints. The defining principles in his choice of space are identified as simplicity and isolation. Kurt Hübner, *Eule — Rose — Kreuz: Goethes Religiosität zwischen Philosophie und Theologie* (Berichte aus den Sitzungen der Joachim Jungius-Gesellschaft der Wissenschaften, 17.4), Göttingen, Vandenhoeck & Ruprecht, 29 pp., deals with the complex relationship between poetry, philosophy, and religion (in turn rose, owl, and cross) as expressed in the poem *Die Geheimnisse*, *Wilhelm Meisters Wanderjahre* and the finale of *Faust*.

Individual articles on varying themes in G. include: J. Stenzel, 'Symbolische "Scheitholzflöss-Anarchie" oder Meisterschaft und Diletanntismus: zu Goethes Brief an Zelter vom 16.–19. März 1818', *JFDH*, 1999:52–67; H. Jesse, 'König Ludwig I. von Bayern und Johann Wolfgang Goethe', *GJb*, 116, 1999[2000]:300–305; G. Schmid and I. Schmid, 'Goethe der Chef — Beobachtungen zu seiner amtlichen Tätigkeit seit 1788', *ib.*, 306–18; W. von Engelhardt, 'Goethe und die Geologie', *ib.*, 319–30; P. Hofmann, 'Goethes Theologie der Natur', *ib.*, 331–44; E. Trunz, 'Sechs kleine Goethe-Studien', *JWGV*, 100–01, 1996–97[1998]:15–38; E. Trunz, 'Goethes Haus und seine Sammlungen', *ib.*, 39–54; H. Dressler, 'Chladnis Klang- und Seebecks Farbfiguren in Goethes Vergleich und einige Widerspiegelungsaspekte der Farb-Ton-Analogien in der Ästhetik der Goethezeit', *ib.*, 55–68; H. Langer, 'Reconstructing a nation's birth: monotheism, nationalism, and violence in Goethe's reading of the Pentateuch', *ColGer*, 33:103–22; J. Pizer, 'Goethes "World Literature" paradigm and contemporary cultural globalization', *CL*, 52:213–27; D. Bell, 'Goethe's piety', *GLL*, 53:450–69; P. Currie, 'Goethe's mental images', *OGS*, 28, 1999:131–50; M. Vöhler, 'Im Sturm durch die Antike. Anmerkungen zum jungen Goethe', *Poetica*,

31, 1999:437–51; S.-E. Rose, 'Goethe's splitting image: male sexuality and/as writing in *Das Tagebuch* and beyond', *GY*, 9, 1999:131–57; W. Maierhofer, 'Goethe on Emma Hamilton's "Attitudes": Can classicist art be fun?', *ib.*, 222–52; P. Bishop, 'Epistemological problems and aesthetic solutions in Goethe and Jung', *ib.*, 278–317; H. D. Irmscher, 'Prophet und Dichter: über Goethes Versuche, Hamann zu verstehen', *GJb*, 115, 1998[1999]:13–28; A. V. Michajlov, 'Die Natur in Goethes schöpferischem Denken', *ib.*, 147–54; U. Enke and M. Wezel, 'Wißbegierde contra Menschlichkeit — Goethes ambivalentes Verhältnis zur Anatomie in seiner Dichtung und Biographie', *ib.*, 155–70; E. Pielmann, 'Goethes Treppenhäuser', *ib.*, 171–82; K. Mommsen, 'Goethes Morgenlandfahrten', *GJb*, 116, 1999[2000]:281–90.

INFLUENCE. RECEPTION. Wuneng Yang, *Goethe in China (1889–1999)*, Frankfurt, Lang, 185 pp., contains a survey of Goethe-reception in China, a perpective upon Goethe's relationship with the East which has otherwise been little explored. The author ties the pattern of reception into the profound political changes which took place in China during this period. Particularly promising are the last two chapters which concern patterns of reception in modern Chinese literature, particularly in the work of Guo Moruo, and amongst modern individuals, including sportsmen and actors. However, the treatments of the individual cases are very brief or anecdotal and hence rather disappointing. *Deutsche Italomanie in Kunst, Wissenschaft und Politik*, ed. Wolfgang Lange and Norbert Schnitzler, Munich, Fink, 304 pp., contains two articles concerned with Goethe-reception (broadly understood) in connection with the experience of Italy, namely: W. Lange, 'Auf den Spuren Goethes unfreiwillig: Rolf Dieter Brinkmann in Italien' (255–82); C. Noll, 'Rom in Weimar: das Haus am Frauenplan, Goethe, Kafka und in die Ferne führende Folgerungen' (283–302). The former contribution is concerned to highlight the radically different Italian experience of Brinkmann when compared to that of the reborn Goethe, whilst the latter consists of a writer's personal reflections on Goethe. Wolfgang Mieder, *Aphorismen, Sprichwörter, Zitate von Goethe und Schiller bis Viktor Klemperer* (Sprichwörterforschung, 22), Berne, Lang, 362 pp., continues the author's extensive work in this field and contains one article on the bizarre fate of Goethe's words in the hands of the modern media: ' "Edel sei das Zitat": Goethes geflügelte Worte in den Massenmedien' (11–34). *Dauer im Wechsel? Goethe und der Deutschunterricht*, ed. Bodo Lecke (Beiträge zur Geschichte des Deutschunterrichts, 44), Frankfurt, Lang, 512 pp., looks from a variety of angles at the roles that the figure Goethe and his work have been made to play in the context of the German classroom from 1800 to the present day.

Contributions include: B. Lecke, 'Einleitung — Goethe unter den Deutschen: Rezeptionsästhetik / Pädagogik / Literaturdidaktik' (21–79); W. Leppmann, 'Goethe im Stehkragen und Blue Jeans — Goethe im Deutschunterricht' (81–116); W. Seiffert, 'Bildungsidee und Literaturdidaktik bei Goethe' (117–38); J. Schulze-Bergmann, 'Goethe im Lehrplan des Deutschunterrichts im 19. Jahrhundert — Zur Kanonisierung eines Klassikers' (141–62); K. Behr, 'Goethe — ein guter Deutscher? Einige Gedanken zur schulischen Rezeption des Klassikers in der Weimarer Republik und im Dritten Reich im Anschluß an empirisch-statische Befunde' (163–80); C. Kretschmann, ' "Führer" oder "Lügner"? Zum Goethebild im nationalsozialistischen Deutschunterricht' (181–210); K. Lindemann, ' "Zitate und geflügelte Worte aus diesem gigantischen Werk": Goethe im Abitur in und zwischen den Weltkriegen' (211–38); R. Denk, ' "Verteufelt existentiell": Goethes *Iphigenie* in Methodikerhand, oder Anmerkungen zur Behandlung eines Klassikers im Deutschunterricht der fünfziger und sechziger Jahre' (239–62); W. Ingendahl, 'Das Wahre, Schöne und Gute der Germanistik vor dem Hintergrundwissen der Lernenden' (265–90); G. Vitz, 'Von Faust, Gretchen und Co. oder Von der Unauslöschlichkeit "klassischer" Klischees' (291–308); H. Grundmann, 'Klassische Texte als geeignete Medien zur Aufklärung und Reflexion über die moderne Arbeitswelt im Literaturunterricht' (309–32); D. Gwose, 'Sich dem Wahren des Lebens über das Dichterische nähern' (333–54); V. Frederking, 'Goethes *Faust I* — ein rezeptions-, motiv- und mediengeschichtliches Modell in produktiv-kreativer und identitätsorientierter Perspektive' (355–90); A. Wierlacher, 'Ent-Fremdete Fremde — Goethes *Iphigenie auf Tauris* als Drama des Völkerrechts' (393–412); L. Böcker, ' "Und es gewöhnt sich nicht mein Geist hierher" — Reflexionen über Fremdheit: Goethes *Iphigenie auf Tauris* im Deutschunterricht als Chance zum Interkulturellen Lernen' (413–50); N. Mecklenberg, '*Iphigenie* und ihre türkische Verwandtschaft' (451–60); M. Maquardt, 'Zu einigen schul- und hochschuldidaktischen Aspekten des Goethebildes in Frankreich' (461–76); E.-B. Berndt, 'Goethe digital und multimedial oder Vom Nutzen der Klassik-CD-ROMs für den Deutschunterricht' (479–94); H. Jonas, 'Der multimediale *Werther*' (495–512). Other instances of reception are discussed in: W. Butzlaff, ' "Saftfrüchte sollen nicht vermahlen werden": Käthe Kollwitz — ein Leben mit Goethe', *JFDH*, 1999:304–38; G. Maertz, 'Henry Crabb Robinson's 1802–1803 translations of Goethe's lyric poems and epigrams', *JWGV*, 100–01, 1996–97[1998]:69–92; M. Durzak, 'Stefan George und Goethe: poetische Vereinnahmung oder produktive Aneignung und Verwandlung?, *StG*, 37, 1999:205–22; J. Osinski, 'Goethe oder Eichendorff? Literaturmodelle des 19. Jahrhunderts',

GLL, 53:143–61; K. S. Guthke, 'Goethe and George Butler', *GY*, 9, 1999:158–65; G. Brude-Firnau, '*Die Wahlverwandtschaften* als Referenztext in Martin Walsers Erzählwerk', *GJb*, 115, 1998[1999]:183–98; Y. Wuneng, 'Goethe in China. Das Goethe-Jahr 1932 und die neuerliche Goethe-Verehrung', *ib.*, 199–210; K. Mommsen, 'Goethe und unsere Zeit', *ib.*, 116:27–40; J. Simpson, 'Goethe und England', *ib.*, 41–53; G.-L. Fink, 'Goethe, der andere Deutsche? Die französische Goethe-Rezeption zwischen 1870 und 1949', *ib.*, 54–74; J. K. Brown, 'Goethe und die amerikanische Literatur — der Fall Edith Wharton', *ib.*, 75–84; L. Kaufmann, 'Goethe und die Moskauer Universität in der zweiten Hälfte des 19. Jahrhunderts', *ib.*, 96–101; W. Gilmanow, 'Goethe und das "Silberne Zeitalter" der russischen Kultur', *ib.*, 102–12; M. Jaeger, 'Goethe im Widerstreit des liberalen und des radikalen Denkens in der Weimarer Republik', *ib.*, 112–28; D. Kemper, 'Goethes Individualitätsbegriff als Rezeptionshindernis im Nationalsozialismus', *ib.*, 129–43; V. Braun, '"Dem Geyer gleich": Goethe und Kafka in der Natur', *ib.*, 158–67; W. Vosskamp, 'Wilhelm Meisters *Theatralische Sendung* und dessen *Lehrjahre* im 20. Jahrhundert bei Botho Strauß und Thomas Bernhard', *ib.*, 168–77; E. Schmidhäuser, 'Goethes Denken über Recht und Staat — aus der Sicht von gestern und heute', *ib.*, 178–90; C. Günzler, 'Goethe und die Pädagogen: exemplarische Etappen einer wechselhaften Rezeptionsgeschichte', *ib.*, 191–205; D. Borchmeyer, '"Die Genies sind eben eine große Familie . . .": Goethe in Kompositionen von Richard Strauss', *ib.*, 206–23; D. von Engelhardt, 'Goethes Farbenlehre und Morphologie in den Naturwissenschaften des 19. Jahrhunderts', *ib.*, 224–33; I. Müller, 'Goethes Farbenlehre und Morphologie in den Naturwissenschaften des 20. Jahrhunderts', *ib.*, 234–44.

BIOGRAPHY. The extraordinary project which is Nicholas Boyle, *Goethe: The Poet and the Age*, continues with vol. 2 'Revolution and Renunciation, 1790–1803', Oxford, Clarendon, xiv + 939 pp. This volume, like the one which preceded it, manages the extremely difficult task of maintaining multiple and interrelated narratives, dealing with lives, texts, and contexts, and yet against the odds produces an extremely lucid and readable text. This volume covers the period of the French Revolution and key areas of intellectual and personal development in the relationships with Schiller and Christiane Vulpius. B.'s account will undoubtedly represent the backbone of G. scholarship for the foreseeable future. Other biographical contributions include: R. Schillemeit, 'Neues zum Leipziger Goethe: das Stammbuch des Benedict Christian Avenarius und andere Handschriftenfunde', *GJb*, 115, 1998[1999]:211–28; T. Richter, 'Doris Zelters Briefe nach Weimar, 1818–1834. Teil II: "ich weine mich täglich satt" — Die Briefe an Goethes Umkreis', *ib.*, 245–85; G. Niggl, 'Das Problem der morphologischen Lebensdeutung in Goethes *Dichtung und Wahrheit*', *ib.*, 116:291–99.

3. Schiller

LITERARY WORKS. Götz-Lothar Darsow, *Friedrich Schiller* (SM, 330), 261 pp., lives up to the expectations that readers have of this series. The impossible task of providing in less than 300 pages a critical overview of S.'s life, work and reception is undertaken with gusto, and this text, like the others in the series, will provide a very useful starting point for the study of Schiller. David Pugh, *Schiller's Early Dramas: A Critical History* (SGLLC), xxx + 231 pp., deals with critical responses to Schiller from the period of production of his plays to the present day. P. focuses upon the plays *Die Räuber*, *Fiesco*, *Kabale und Liebe*, and *Don Carlos* which he naturally sees as the uneven products of a young writer attempting to establish a direction. The pattern of reception of the texts is revealed as similarly uneven, particularly in more recent times. As P. points out in his compact conclusion, 'the confrontation of such overwrought texts with a scholarly tradition that shared the neuroses and traumas of post-Bismarckian German has led to a strange and distorted critical history.'

Individual articles on Schiller's works include: Christoph E. Schweitzer, 'A defense of Schiller's Wilhelm Tell', *GY*, 9, 1999:253–63; A. Kornbacher, 'August Wilhelm Schlegels Einfluß auf den Aufsatz *Über epische und dramatische Dichtung von Goethe und Schiller* (1797)', *GJb*, 115, 1998[1999]:63–68.

THEMES. Frank Suppanz, *Person und Staat in Schillers Dramenfragmenten: Zur literarischen Rekonstruktion eines problematischen Verhältnis* (Hermaea, n.F., 93), Tübingen, Niemeyer, xi + 405 pp., investigates a familiar series of problems on the basis of a less familiar body of texts. The discussion is taken further than the title might suggest since the question of 'literarische Rekonstruktion' is of primary importance. Whilst there is clearly extensive treatment of Schiller's theoretical/ historical/philosophical/political statements on the matter of the relationship between the individual and the state, much of the material will be familiar. More interesting is the investigation of the irreconcilable demands of theory and dramatic practice; 'reconstruction' of core debates in literary form is revealed as deeply problematic since it demands compromise; it requires either a dilution at the level of theme or a failure at the level of dramatic action. Suppanz is most compelling in his treatment of Schillerian dramatic experiments whether in high tragedy, comedy, or supposedly trivial dramatic genres. On a thematic level Suppanz makes the case that the treatment of both the individual and the state and their respective rights is highly sophisticated but that this means that they cannot be reconciled in theoretical or indeed in dramatic terms. Individual articles on themes in S. include: N. Rossbach, ' "Gewalt ist die beste Beredsamkeit": Sprache und Gewalt in Schillers frühen Dramen', *Der Deutschunterricht*, 52.6: 19–29; F. Bridgham, 'Emancipating amazons: Schiller's Jungfrau, Kleist's Penthesilea, Wagner's Brünnhilde', *FMLS*, 36:64–73; M. Hertl, 'Schillers faule Äpfel', *GJb*, 115, 1998[1999]:231–36.

INFLUENCE, RECEPTION. Mieder, *Aphorismen* (see p. 680 above) contains an article on a unlikely but interesting aspect of Schiller-reception, namely ' "Wo neue Kräfte sinnvoll walten?"': zur Umformung Schillerscher Zitate zu Aphorismen und Graffiti' (35–54). Individual articles on S.'s influence include: C. Louth, 'The question of influence: Hölderlin's dealings with Schiller and Pindar', *MLR*, 95:1038–52.

BIOGRAPHY. Helmut Koopmann, *Schillers Leben in Briefen*, Weimar, Böhlau, vi + 602 pp., provides a lively read but, whilst it divides the letters and hence the life into sensible sections and provides each of these with an introduction, it does not constitute a substantial contribution to our knowledge of S.

4. INDIVIDUAL AUTHORS
(EXCLUDING GOETHE AND SCHILLER)

BODMER. U. Hentschel, 'Der Fall Bodmer: zur Literaturgesellschaft Zürichs im 18. Jahrhundert', *WW*, 50:5–16.

BÜRGER. *Will Vol.* contains D. Hill, 'Bürger and "das schwankende Wort *Volk*" ' (25–36), which focuses upon questions of national identity and democratic sovereignty and investigates the difficult negotiation of the loaded terminology available to describe 'the people'.

FORSTER. *Wahrnehmung — Konstruktion — Text: Bilder des Wirklichen im Werk Georg Forsters*, ed. Jörn Garber (Hallesche Beiträge zur Europäischen Aufklärung, 12), Tübingen, Niemeyer, viii + 233 pp., contains a large number of articles produced in the period since 1993. They have in common the fact that they are not concerned in the first instance with F. as traveller or revolutionary. The articles deal rather with varying treatments by F. of matters of perception, the processing, experiencing, or understanding of reality. The motivating principle is to undermine an assumed German tendency to read Forster's works as novels. The articles included are: J. Garber, 'Statt einer Einleitung: "Sphinx" Forster' (1–19); M. Ewart, 'Literarische Anthropologie: Georg Forsters *Leckereyen*' (20–30); U. Kronauer, 'Georg Forsters

Einleitung zu *Cook der Entdecker:* Forsters Auseinandersetzung mit Rousseau über Fortschritt und Naturzustand' (31–42); L. Uhlig, 'Die Humanität des Künstlers: Georg Forsters Genieästhetik im zeitgenössischen Kontext' (43–59); H. Peitsch, 'Zur Rezeption von Georg Forsters *Die Kunst und das Zeitalter*' (60–76); O. Hochadel, 'Natur — Vorsehung — Schicksal: zur Geschichtsteleologie Georg Forsters' (77–104); H. Peitsch, 'Rhetorik und Gewalt: Herder, Forster und die englische Debatte über die Französische Revolution' (105–27); G. Pickerodt, 'Georg Forsters Briefe aus Frankreich 1793: zehn Thesen mit Erläuterungen' (128–42); M. R. Sanches, 'Vernunft und Revolution: zum Verhältnis von Forsters *Über die Beziehung der Staatskunst auf das Glück der Menschheit* und *Parisische Umrisse*' (143–61); P. Schmitter, 'Georg Forsters "allgemeine Naturgeschichte" und die "allgemeine Sprachkunde" Wilhelm von Humboldts' (162–92); J. Garber, '"So sind also die Hauptbestimmungen des Menschen[...]": Anmerkungen zum Verhältnis von Geographie und Menschheitsgeschichte bei Georg Forster' (193–230). Individual articles on F. include: L. Uhlig, '*Instructio Peregrinatoris*: Georg Forsters Lehrjahre im Schatten seines Vaters', *Euphorion*, 94:43–78; Id., 'Georg Forster und Friedrich Heinrich Jacobi', *GRM*, 50:155–70.

GOTTSCHED.   In many ways Katherine R. Goodman, *Amazons and Apprentices: Women and the German Parnassus in the Early Enlightenment*, Rochester, Camden House, 1999, xiv + 316 pp., does not deserve to be placed in the Gottsched section. However, it is in this context that the value of the text most strongly emerges. It deals explicitly with G.'s *Die vernünftigen Tadlerinnen* and with women writers associated with G., particularly Christiane Mariane von Ziegler and Luise Gottsched. However, its central concern is to investigate contemporary perceptions of the appropriate scope and nature of female intellectual and literary activity and the tensions which existed between women's expectations and that which could be achieved in the prevailing atmosphere. The development of the argument through the first three chapters is highly interesting. An examination in turn of Gottlieb Siegmund Corvinus's *Frauenzimmerlexikon* and Johann Caspar Eberti's *Schlesiens Hoch- und Wohlgelehrtes Frauenzimmer*, as well as G.'s *Tadlerinnen* reveals that definitions of womanhood and of what it means to be a learned woman were deeply problematic at this time. Correspondingly, the products of such women also prove problematic and much more interesting than conventional criticism might lead us to believe. The women were more than just dutiful followers of Gottsched's fashion. Gabriele Ball, *Moralische Küsse: Gottsched als Zeitschriftenherausgeber und literarischer Vermittler* (Das achtzehnte Jahrhundert: Supplementa, 7), Göttingen, Wallstein, 483 pp., is interesting to read alongside Goodman's work. From a different angle we are also asked to investigate G.'s sphere of influence. This exhaustive text, based upon a doctoral thesis, details the means by which influence in matters of taste can make itself felt, either by direct publication or statement or — and this is the focus of the volume — by literary/critical networking and indeed network control. B. details G.'s activities as publisher, literary facilitator and popularizer, reviewer and public figure for the first time in such detail (including investigation of the journal publications themselves and some preparatory correspondence), and reveals how this can be seen as an enlightened enterprise and a matter of management.

HAASE. J. M. Tudor, 'The Baltic fringe: a German clergyman in Swedish territory, and Lutheran culture in late eighteenth-century Germany', *OGS*, 28, 1999:22–81, deals with Johann Georg Haase from Wismar and his MS *Vita*.

HERDER. Ernst-Richard Schwinge, *'Ich bin nicht Goethe': Johann Gottfried Herder und die Antike* (Berichte aus den Sitzungen der Joachim Jungius-Gesellschaft der Wissenschaften, 17.2), Göttingen, Vandenhoeck & Ruprecht, 1999, 62 pp., is concerned to highlight differences in the views of antiquity of H. and G. on the basis that Herder's historical view is complex even to the point of being contradictory at times whereas G.'s is — in H.'s view — simplistic to the point of being childlike. John D. Baildam, *Paradisal Love: Johann Gottfried Herder and the Song of Songs* (Journal for the Study of the Old Testament, Supplement Series, 298), Sheffield, Sheffield Academic Press, 1999, 368 pp., contains extensive treatment of H.'s preoccupation with the Song of Songs, his reception and translation of it; in the latter connections B.'s treatment is comparative, drawing upon the pattern of reception exhibited by important contemporaries (Goethe), by highly influential predecessors (Luther), or whole traditions (Jewish and Christian). Whilst the investigation of the detail is novel the conclusions in many respects confirm expectations that scholars with a more general knowledge of Herder might already have. The investigation by H. of the nature of the songs as primitive poetry and as products of a specific culture might well have been predicted. Less predictable was B.'s presentation of H.'s response to the eroticism of the songs. The understanding of the erotic as pure and paradisal would appear to have more to do with H. himself and the culture he represents than with the source culture; it is in that sense deeply ahistorical. Individual articles on H. include: E. A. Menze, ' "Gang Gottes über die Nationen": the religious roots of Herder's *Auch eine Philosophie* revisited', *MDLK*, 92:10–19; G. Ehrhardt, 'Wahl-Anziehung — Herders Spinoza-Schrift und Goethes *Wahlverwandtschaften*', *GJb*, 115, 1998[1999]:77–96.

LA ROCHE   H. S. Watt, 'Sophie La Roche: von der Glückseligkeit des Reisens zur Schreibseligkeit', *LY*, 31, 1999[2000]: 111–30.

LEISEWITZ   A. Mathäs, 'Narcissism and male desire in *Sturm und Drang*-drama: Johann Anton Leisewitz' *Julius von Tarent*', *LY*, 31, 1999[2000]: 91–110.

LENZ.   Angela Hansen, '*Der Hofmeister*' *von J. M. R. Lenz: Ein Versuch einer Neuinterpretation*, NY, Lang , x + 302 pp., is like many studies of this author in that it focuses upon the 'radical' nature of his material, in this case of his first play. The novelty of this treatment is that it explores Lenz's positive connection to the Enlightenment. The discussion of the figure of Läuffer and his relationship to characters in Lessing and Holberg is most illuminating. The near stock-figure of the would-be cultured 'Deutschfranzose' is transformed in L. Whereas Holberg and Lessing used such figures for satirical purposes, to mark distance from some manifestations of the French Enlightenment, L. has a more subtle purpose, although this does not exclude mocking of the rococo and Frenchifying aspects of contemporary German culture. Läuffer is presented as a psychologically plausible character whose pretentions are perverse expressions of an unresolved relationship with his father and the (theological) order which he represents. He is seen in general as someone who fails to emancipate himself from the prevailing order in any aspect of his being, from his sexual behaviour through his family relations to his employment. H. also draws interesting parallels with Goethe's *Faust* project, comparing Läuffer and Faust and their love affairs. The conventional assumption is that L. and G. were working along the same lines. H. suggests that L. is more productively seen as an alternative to G., a more radical alternative in as far as he engages more profoundly with the emancipatory tendencies of the age. On first glance Jörg Schlieske, *Lenz und die Mimesis: Eine Untersuchung der Nachahmungspolitik bei Jakob Michael Reinhold Lenz (1751–1792)* (EH, I, 1777), 412 pp., would appear to be an investigation of familiar territory, namely of Lenz's assumed attempts to capture something of reality in his writing. The ambitions of the volume are, however, considerably grander. Whilst the text contains extensive treatment of contemporary theories of mimesis, S. indicates that we need to expand our understanding of that term in order to understand aspects of L. which might otherwise seem bewildering. Mimesis is, in Lenz's terms, more than putting life (e.g.) on stage. A complex process is at work which, whilst it contains 'general reference to social reality', also involves the processing of that reality in aesthetic/theatrical terms and, furthermore, the processing of available aesthetic/literary models. S.'s treatment of L.'s reception of Goethe and its ideological implications is most interesting as it reveals an author who is teetering on the brink of aesthetic liberation. 'Imitation' as a means of liberation may sound contradictory but S. makes an interesting case for the consistency of the idea.

LESSING. Gotthold Ephraim Lessing, *Kleinigkeiten: Faksimile des Marbacher Manuskripts*, ed. Jochen Meyer, Göttingen, Wallstein, 238 pp., contains, alongside the facsimile text, a clear transcription of the early and mostly light-hearted poems (pp. 105–57), and extensive notes and discussion of the nature of the text and its textual history (pp. 159–238). Monika Fick, *Lessing Handbuch: Leben — Werk — Wirkung*, Stuttgart–Weimar, Metzler, xii + 517 pp., is an extremely useful volume. Whilst the title might make potential readers assume an encyclopaedic treatment of L., they actually receive something much more detailed, although sensibly the author does not aim at exhaustiveness. The first section of the text aims at locating the phenomenon L. in terms of his biography, reception, and position in the history of ideas and of literature. The second and much larger section comprises individual treatments of literary and theoretical texts, each of which has a very sensible and useful structure. F. deals in turn with the genesis of the given text and its specific context and offers a compact treatment of the state of research in the field. There follows an analysis of the work and a discussion of its reception. Given the nature of the text the individual treatments must be brief but they are not superficial and will allow rapid and effective orientation within L.'s *œuvre* without disguising its complexity. It is difficult in a short notice adequately to summarize the tight arguments of Daniel Müller Nielaba, *Die Wendung zum Bessern: Zur Aufklärung der Toleranz in Gotthold Ephraim Lessings 'Nathan der Weise'*, Würzburg, Königshausen & Neumann, 291 pp. At first glance the text may appear to investigate familiar territory but, whilst the text clearly deals with enlightened debate on the issues of education and tolerance, the discussion of these in general terms is restricted to the introductory sections. N. is concerned to investigate L. largely in his own terms, i.e. to investigate the process by which an individual can come to realize himself in the fullest possible form or 'Genie werden'. This is seen by L. in part as a matter of learning from others but importantly also of growing from within so that one's identity is not a fixed entity. The close textual analysis reveals the linguistic indicators of the process of growth of key characters towards a position of tolerance, towards an under-standing of an employment of a subtle rhetoric of tolerance. Individual articles on Lessing include: I. von Treskow, 'Zur Entste-hung von Lessings Fabelkonzeption. Die Auseinandersetzung mit La Fontaine und seinen Nachfolgern am Beispiel von *Der Rabe und der Fuchs*', *ASNS*, 237:1–23; C. Wild, 'Der theatralische Schleier des Hymens: Lessings bürgerliches Trauerspiel *Emilia Galotti*', *DVLG*,

74:189–220; K. S. Calhoon, 'Blind gestures: Chaplin, Diderot, Lessing', *MLN*, 115:381–402 (deals with mimicry, representation of the supernatural/ghosts); G. Braungart, 'Streitbare Humanität: zur Aktualität Lessings', *LY*, 30, 1998[1999]: 1–4; F. Rädle, 'Lessings *Der junge Gelehrte* auf der Folie des religiösen lateinischen Theaters seiner Zeit', *ib.*, 5–10; S. A. Jørgensen, 'Die "Jungen Gelehrten" von 1750', *ib.*, 11–20; W. Schmidt-Dengler, 'Lessings *Der junge Gelehrte* und Kurz-Bernardonds *Prinzessin Pumphia*: Versuch einer kontrastiven Lektüre', *ib.*, 21–30; A. von Bormann, '*Philotas*-Lektüren: zum Verhältnis von Tragödie und Aufklärung', *ib.*, 31–52; G.-L. Fink, 'Lessings *Philotas* und seine Auseinandersetzung mit dem "Republikanismus" (1757–1760)', *ib.*, 53–72; J. Schröder, '*Ernst und Falk*: Gespräche für Freimaurer — Das sechste Gespräch', *ib.*, 73–80; T. J. Reed, 'Von den Motoren der Menschheitsgeschichte: zu Geschwindigkeitsunterschieden im teleologischen Denken des 18. Jahrhunderts', *ib.*, 81–90; H. Göbel, 'Das große und das kleine Ich. Eine Bemerkung zu Lessings *Erziehung des Menschengeschlechts*', *ib.*, 91–98; A. Schilson, 'Denken als Dialog und "produktive Rezeption": über die Lektüre von Lessings *Erziehung des Menschengeschlechts*', *ib.*, 99–104; J. H. Smith, 'Lessings didaktisch-dialektisches Testament für uns, "die wir itzt leben"; oder: How "Erziehung" makes a difference', *ib.*, 105–16; H. Turk, '*Erziehung des Menschengeschlechts*. Verzögerung oder Beschleunigung?', *ib.*, 117–30; W. Adam, 'Lessings Briefschlüsse', *ib.*, 131–40; G. E. Grimm, 'Botschaften der Einsamkeit — Briefe Lessings aus Wolfenbüttel', *ib.*, 141–50; W. Mauser, '"Billigkeit": zu Lessings Brief an Herzog Karl vom 8. August 1778', *ib.*, 151–60; R. Vierhaus, 'Lessing und Elise Reimarus', *ib.*, 161–70; D. Döring, 'Ein unbekannter Brief G. E. Lessings vom 16. Dezember 1778 an Heinrich Boie', *ib.*, 31:1–10; T. Unger, '"Es ist theatralischer Unsinn." Die *Emilia-Galotti*-Lektüre des Prinzen August von Sachsen-Gotha und Altenburg', *ib.*, 11–39; D. Neiteler and Winfried Woesler, 'Zur Wahl der Textgrundlage einer Neuedition von Lessings *Nathan der Weise*', *ib.*, 39–64; H. B. Nisbet, 'The rationalisation of the Holy Trinity from Lessing to Hegel', *ib.*, 65–90.

MENDELSSOHN. M.'s relationship to various aspects of the Enlightenment is explored in the interesting volume *Moses Mendelssohn im Spannungsfeld der Aufklärung*, ed. Michael Albrecht and Eva J. Engel, Stuttgart–Bad Cannstatt, Frommann-Holzboog, 284 pp., which includes: M. Albrecht, '"Aber ich folge dem Schlechteren": Mendelssohns mathematische Hypothese zum Problem des Handelns wider besseres Wissen' (13–36); C. Buschmann, 'Wie bleibt Metaphysik als Wissenschaft möglich? Moses Mendelssohn und seine Konkurrenten um den Preis der Preußischen Akademie für 1763' (37–50); E. J.

Engel, 'Literaturkritik als Wissenschaft und Kunst' (51–72); G. Gaw-lick, 'Ein vergessener "Anti Phädon" aus dem Jahr 1771' (73–88); R. A. Jacobs, 'A Jewish reading of Moses Mendelssohn's response to Lavater' (89–100); H. Klenner, 'Rechtsphilosophisches zur Kant/Mendelssohn-Kontroverse über das Völkerrecht' (101–18); H. Lausch, 'Moses Mendelssohn und die zeitgenössische Mathematik' (119–36); A. von der Lühe, ' "Catarticon" oder "organon": Kausali-tät und Induktion bei Hume und Mendelssohn' (137–58); L. Lüt-teken, 'Moses Mendelssohn und der musikalische Diskurs der Aufklärung' (159–94); U. Ricken, 'Mendelssohn und die Sprachtheo-rien der Aufklärung' (195–242); D. Sorkin, 'Moses Mendelssohn's biblical exegesis' (243–76).

MORITZ.   A. Gailus, 'The case of individuality: Karl Philipp Moritz and the *Magazine for Empirical Psychology*', *NGC*, 79:67–105.

WINCKELMANN.   E. Décultot, 'Les ambiguïtés du paradigme grec: étude sur les sources de Winckelmann', *RG*, 29, 1999:1–14.

· THE ROMANTIC ERA

By Laura Martin, *Lecturer in German, University of Glasgow*

1. General Studies

Marion Gray, *Productive Men, Reproductive Women. The Agrarian Household and the Emergence of Separate Spheres in the German Enlightenment*, NY, Berghahn, 1999, 369 pp., is a highly important and very interesting study which discusses the 'Haushaltsbücher' used on agrarian estates, and analyses how terms such as 'Haushalt' and 'Wirtschaft' in these and in other writings changed meanings across the centuries, simultaneously bringing about and reflecting changes in the social roles for men and women. Angela Esterhammer, *The Romantic Performative. Language and Action in British and German Romanticism*, Stanford U.P., xix + 357 pp., is an important new interdisciplinary and comparative study of the philosophies of language in Germany and Britain. Well before modern theories existed, Romantic writers could already see that the act of speaking creates a subjective identity, intersubjective relations, and objective reality. Modern speech-act theory and deconstruction are discussed before returning to Scottish Enlightenment and German Idealist writers, then on to Wilhelm von Humboldt, Coleridge, Hölderlin, Kleist, and Godwin.

Barbara Becker-Cantarino, *Schrifstellerinnen der Romantik. Epoche — Werke — Wirkung*, Munich, Beck, 320 pp., is a very welcome new contribution by this leading author on women writers. It gives a thorough background to the problems surrounding women's writing in the period, varying its focus from general issues such as letter-writing and ideas of femininity, and specific studies of particular women (Therese Huber, Dorothea Schlegel, Karoline von Günderrode, and Bettine von Arnim). More specifically political, Mechtilde Vahsen, *Die Politisierung des weiblichen Subjekts. Deutsche Romanautorinnen und die Französische Revolution 1790–1820* (PSQ, 162), 225 pp., studies works by women writers to see how they used ideas from the French Revolution in their depictions of women and of their social role, whereas most earlier works on the subject have concentrated on the changes to social conditions and the possibility of women's writing at all. Authors studied are Sophie von La Roche, Isabella von Wallenrodt, Therese Huber, Sophie Mereau, Caroline de la Motte Fouqué, and Henriette Fröhlich. Another welcome contribution to the study of women's writing is *Sappho in the Shadows. Essays on the Work of German Women Poets of the Age of Goethe (1749–1832)*, ed. Anthony J. Harper and Margaret C. Ives, Berne, Lang, 280 pp., which provides easy introductions to seven women writers. All quotes are translated and there are 5–10 poems, in German and in English translation, at the end of each chapter. This volume is reminiscent of J. Blackwell's *Bitter Healing* (1990: *YWMLS*, 53:736) but more emphasis is placed on the biography and an interpretation of the life rather then on republishing the works, as was the case in Blackwell's volume. B. Keith-Smith, 'Friederike Brun (1765–1835): in tears too there is joy' (145–88), presents an admittedly less than great writer who was, however, quite important in her own time. (See also below under MEREAU, SOPHIE and GÜNDERRODE, KAROLINE VON.) Judith Purver, 'Revolution, Romanticism, Restoration (1789–1830)', Catling, *Women's Writing*, 68–87, provides a brief, readable overview covering the main genres (lyric, drama, letters, the salon, diaries, autobiography, travel-writing). Most helpful is the section on women dramatists, which gives brief accounts of plays still very much unknown.

Romantik and Romance. Cultural Interanimation in European Romanticism, ed. Carol Tully, Glasgow, Univ. of Strathclyde, 148 pp., is not quite as pan-European as the title makes it sound, focusing as it does on the Spanish-German interaction. In her own article in the volume, 'The mysterious Muse: Oriental alterity and the feminine Other in the German Romantic reception of Spain' (7–24), T. gives an interesting analysis of the feminine and the Spanish 'other' which Romantics such as F. Schlegel give voice to, albeit this voice is very much filtered through the perspective of these male, German writers. In the same volume, J. Purver, ' "Das romantische selbst ist eine Übersetzung": Eichendorff's translations from Spanish in their Romantic context' (25–58), first presents an amazingly wide-ranging overview, con-sidering the amount of space allowed to it, of the importance of translation to romantic Germany, before turning to Eichendorff's Spanish translations, which are key to his work as a whole and which point towards the future of German literature, as exemplified in Hugo von Hofmannsthal.

Rereading Romanticism, ed. Martha B. Helfer (*ABNG*, 47), Rodopi, 406 pp., includes many fine essays which will prove important to the field. J. K. Brown, ' "Es singen wohl die Nixen": *Werther* and the Romantic tale' (11–25), reads Goethe's early novel as the missing link between fairy and folk tales on the one hand and Romanticism on the other, finding parallels between this work and Wilhelm Müller's later lyric song cycles; W. Menninghaus, 'Hummingbirds, shells, picture frames: Kant's "Free Beauties" and the Romantic arabesque' (27–46), gives an account of the discourse on the post-1780s arabesque by tying it into the contemporary discourse on aesthetics, and concludes with a discussion of Tieck's *The Seven Wives of Bluebeard*; J. M. Hess, 'Kant's critique of historical judgment: aesthetic auto-nomy and the displacement of politics' (75–102), sees a relationship between the aesthetic and the political, not an escape from the latter through the former; M. Redfield, '*Lucinde*'s obscenity' (101–30), finds in F. Schlegel's novel a description of the performativity of gender which both enables and undermines gender differences; M. Chaouli, 'Critical mass, fission, fusion. Friedrich Schlegel's volatile system' (131–49), investigates the relationship of fragment to system in F. Schlegel. Writing is an ambiguous system of dividing and combining, and it can lead to a breakdown in communication; A. Seyhan, 'Allegorie der Allegorie: romantische Allegorese als kulturelle Erinnerung' (151–67), furthers the rehabilitation of allegory in the face of the 19th-c. preference for the symbol; K. Schutjer, 'A ground of one's own: Hölderlin, *Eigentum*, and *Eigentümlichkeit*' (169–92), argues for the poet a balance between a rootedness on a individual/national level and a more universal sense of belonging; A. Esterhammer, 'Hölderlin and the inter/subjective speech act' (193–226), looks at *Hyperion* and *Der Tod des Empledokles* to see how utterance is both subjective and intersubjective, cognitive, and communicative; F. Breithaupt, 'The ego-effect of money' (227–57), compares and contrasts two concepts of money: money as self-extension (the early Romantics F. Schlegel and Tieck) and money as a neutral medium of exchange which leaves the self untouched (the later Romantics de la Motte Fouqué, Chamisso, and Adam Müller). The modern conception contains both strands; A. Gilleir, ' "Als ob der Gegenstand der Gegenstand wäre." Die Kunstbetrachtungen Wackenroders, Friedrich Schlegels und Ludwig Tiecks' (259–84), argues that the transcendental revelation of the Romantics is in fact grounded in a rational aesthetics; S. Kassouf, 'Textuality and manliness: Heinrich von Kleist's *Michael Kohlhaas* (1810) and the journal *Phöbus*' (301–25), reads the story as the expression of ambivalence towards the ideals of masculinity expressed in the journal; C. Strathausen, 'Eichendorff's *Das Marmorbild* and the demise of Romanticism' (367–87), sets the text on the cusp of Romanticism to Modernity due to its questioning of the authority of human imagination; J. H. Petersen, '*Wilhelm Meisters Wanderjahre* — ein "romantisches Buch" ' (389–406), reads Goethe's last novel as an unwitting exemplification of F. Schlegel's Romantic, 'universal poetry'. Also in this volume: H. Müller-Sievers, 'Tidings of the earth: towards a history of Romantic *Erdkunde*' (47–73); H. J. Schneider, 'Wahllandschaften: Mobilisierung der Natur und das Darstellungsproblem der Moderne in Goethes *Wahlverwandschaften*' (285–300); C. Brodsky Lacour, 'From the pyramids to Romantic poetry: housing the spirit in Hegel' (301–25).

Der Streit um die Romantik (1820–1854), ed. Walter Jaeschke, Hamburg, Meiner, x + 454 pp., represents the fourth in a series of volumes on philosophical and literary disputes about the Romantic era during later Romanticism and the *Vormärz* era. Several primary texts (including ones by F. Schlegel, Hegel, and Eichendorff amongst others) are collected for easy consultation. The volume is a 'Studienausgabe' reprinted from an original publication of 1995 as vols 4 and 4.1 of the *Philosophisch-literarische Streitsachen,* and it includes titles such as H. Bock, 'Vom Ende der "klassischen Kunstperiode". Widersprüche und Streitsachen einer Übergangsgesellschaft' (41–65); V. Hansen, '"Die Reformation der Liebe." Friedrich Schlegel, Schleiermacher und Karl Gutzkow' (121–39); H. Schultz, 'Die letzten Ritter der Romantik im Vormärz. Ludwig Tieck, Joseph von Eichendorff und Bettine von Arnim' (153–71); and M. Schraven, 'Schelling und die Revolution von 1848' (193–206). *Poetologien des Wissens um 1800,* ed. Joseph Vogl, Munich, Fink, 1999, 298 pp., contains articles from various contributors on the topics of 'Sinne, Zeichen, Signale', 'Regierung und Regulation' and 'Text der Geschichte'. *Bild und Schrift in der Romantik,* ed. Gerhard Neumann and Günter Oesterle (Stiftung der Romantikforschung, 6), Würzburg, Königshausen & Neumann, 1999, 468 pp., is likewise a collection of contributions on diverse topics.

THEMES

Bettina Gruber, *Die Seherin von Prevorst. Romantischer Okkultismus als Religion, Wissenschaft und Literatur,* Paderborn, Schöningh, 1999, 306 pp., studies both Justus Kerner's (pseudo)-scientific-religious writings on the mentally disturbed Friederike Hauffe and then expands the study to include admittedly literary treatments of occultism, from Victor Hugo to C. G. Jung and the New Age, in order to see how the various discourses each affect the narratives they produce. Winfried Menninghaus, *In Praise of Nonsense. Kant and Bluebeard,* trans. Henry Pickford, Stanford U.P., 1999, 257 pp., a translation of a 1995 work, discusses Kant's ideas of nonsense and no-sense (*Unsinn, Ohnesinn*) and their association with genius in early German Romanticism, particularly in the fairy tale. Tieck's *The Seven Wives of Bluebeard* is taken as a paradigmatic text of arabesque nonsense. Angelika Corbineau-Hoffmann, *Testament und Totenmaske. Der literarische Mythos des Ludwig van Beethoven* (Berliner Beiträge zur Geistes- und Kulturgeschichte des Mittelalters und der Neuzeit, 17), Hildesheim, Weidmann, 400 pp., alludes mostly to references from the later 19th and early 20th cs, but it nevertheless traces the 'Romantization' of an important figure of the German Romantic Era, and so it seems appropriate to include mention of it here. Beethoven's status as the epitome of the composer has less to do with his compositions and more to do with the mythologizing his name has somehow attracted. S. Elkholy, 'What's gender got to do with it?' A phenomenology of romantic love', *Athenäum*, 9, 1999:121–59, interestingly compares F. Schlegel's *Lucinde* and Isadora Duncan's *My Life* (1927) to show how conceptions of romantic love, unique to the western world and also pervasive in it, affect the ability to express oneself in art positively for men and negatively for women. M. Gamper, ' "daß ich meinen Zweck fast ganz und gar vergesse" — Unentschlossenheit und Laune als ethische und ästhetische Konzepte der Frühromantik', *ib.*, 9–38, investigates the negative aspects of Hamlet-like indecisiveness in Christian Garve, Novalis, F. Schlegel and A. W. Schlegel, Kant, Tieck, and D. Schlegel.

Bettine Menke, *Prosopopoiia. Stimme und Text bei Brentano, Hoffmann, Kleist und Kafka*, Munich, Fink, 854 pp., makes use of deconstruction and media analysis to tie Kafka into German Romanticism, which, she says, he relates to intertextually. Prosopopoiia, or personification, gives a 'voice' to the text, bridging the divide currently said by deconstructionists to be between text and voice. Romantic writers mentioned include the 3 in the title as well as Novalis, Hegel, J. Grimm, Tieck, A. W. Schlegel, F. Schlegel, and others. Idiosyncratic punctuation such as brackets in the text and sudden semi-colons make the text unfortunately very hard to follow.

Pia-Elisabeth Leuschner, *Orphic Song With Daedal Harmony. Die 'Musik' in Texten der englischen und deutschen Romantik* (Stiftung für Romantikforschung, 9), Würzburg, Königshausen & Neumann, 246 pp., is a comparative study which uses Charles Pierce's concept of the sign to explain semiotic similarities. Also on music, Ulrich Tadday, *Das schöne Unendliche. Ästhetik, Kritik, Geschichte der romantischen Musikanschauung*, Stuttgart, Metzler, 1999, 335 pp., seeks to divorce the term 'Romantic' from E. T. A. Hoffmann's earlier term 'absolute Musik', and apply it instead to the varied production of a later generation which had no such simplistic ideas about the nature of music. Special emphasis is placed on Schumann and his use of the term 'romantisch' in musical and other contexts. *Kabbala und die Literatur der Romantik. Zwischen Magie und Trope*, ed. Eveline Goodman-Thau et al. (CJ, 27), 1999, viii + 266 pp., has articles on the Kabbala in the *Frühromantik*, in Novalis, Brentano, E. T. A. Hoffmann, Hölderlin, and in *Volksliteratur. Romantik und Ästhetizismus. Festschrift für Paul Gerhard Klussmann*, ed. Bettina Gruber and Gerhard Plumpe, Würzburg, Königshausen & Neumann, 1999, 343 pp., has a varied selection of contributions on general topics as well as ones on Kleist and E. T. A. Hoffmann.

Also noted: Werner Keil and Charis Goer, **'Seelenaccente'* — *'Ohrenphysiognomik': zur Musikanschauung E.T.A. Hoffmanns, Heinses und*

Wackenroders (Diskordanzen: Studien zur Neueren Musikgeschichte, 8), Hildesheim–NY, Olms, 337 pp.; Michael J. Hofstetter, *The Romantic Idea of the University: England and Germany, 1770–1850*, NY, Palgrave, 162 pp.; Paola Mayer, *Jena Romanticism and its Appropriation of Jakob Böhme: Theosophy, Hagiography, Literature*, Montreal–London, McGill–Queen's U.P., 256 pp.; Irving Massey, *Philo-Semitism in Nineteenth-Century German Literature*, Tübingen, Niemeyer, vi + 199 pp.

GENRES

Das romantische Drama. Produktive Synthese zwischen Tradition und Innovation, ed. Uwe Japp, S. Scherer, and C. Stockinger (UDL, 103), ix + 287 pp., the proceedings of a conference in Karlsruhe in 1999, testifies to the growing interest in Romantic drama. Previous studies used Classical definitions unsuitable for this genre, which values versatility over unity, or they focused too exclusively on issues such as the response to the French Revolution. This volume has articles which give a background to the field as well as ones which concentrate on particular authors of works. G. Schulz, 'Romantische Drama. Befragung eines Begriffes' (1–19), investigates in a clear and perceptive manner the difficulties in using a term like 'Romantic' to describe drama, but concludes that the term does have a useful function in distinguishing the modern from the ancient; M. Cometa, 'Die Theorie des romantischen Dramas bei Friedrich Schlegel' (21–43), scours F. Schlegel's works to cull his pronouncements on drama, which together combine to create an important contribution to the age's concept of it; for J. Brummack, 'Narrenfiguren in der dramatischen Literatur der Romantik' (45–87), Romantic fool-figures have the double duty of criticizing the Gottschedian rules for drama and of bringing about a return to earlier dramatic forms, while special emphasis is placed on explicitly named fools in Tieck and Eichendorff; J. Endres, 'Szenen der "Verwandlung". Novalis und das Drama' (65–87), brings to light Novalis's neglected work 'Poetik des Dramas', in which the author attempted to reconcile Romantic ideas of 'Innerlichkeit' with the externalized representation in drama; L. Stockinger, 'Ludwig Tiecks *Leben und Tod der heiligen Genoveva*. Konzept und Struktur im Kontext des frühromantischen Diskurses' (89–118), places Tieck's drama in the context of the Jena circle and reads it together with Novalis's *Die Christenheit oder Europa* in order to tease out its programme of creating a new mythology that could comment on church and state; J. F. Fetzer, 'Clemens Brentano; Die Schwelle als Schwäche oder Stärke des romantische Dramas?' (119–36), adds another chapter to his work on the 'threshold' in Romantic literature, concentrating in particular on Brentano's *Die*

Gründung Prags; D. Kremer, 'Durch die Wüste. Achim von Armims uferloses Drama *Halle und Jerusalem*' (137–57), approaches an admittedly chauvinistic and anti-Semitic text aesthetically in order to reveal meanings neglected by overly superficial political interpretations; U. Japp, 'Dramaturgie der Vertauschung. Achim von Arnims *Die Päpstin Johanna*' (159–73), finds the named play both the most radical 'universal drama' of the Romantic period and also the epitome of the 'romantisches Buch'; H. J. Kreutzer, 'Zeitgenossichenschaft. Kleists *Amphitryon*, ein romantisches Drama' (227–39), investigates Kleist's uses of sources; V. Nölle, 'Der schizoid Mund. Nachwirkungen von Tiecks *Verkehrter Welt* auf die Produktionsgrammatik späterer Autoren' (241–57), finds echoes of Tieck's play in Keller's *Das verlorene Lachen*, Kleist's *Der zerbrochene Krug*, and Hofmannsthal's libretto *Ariadne auf Naxos*. Also in this volume: S. Scherer, 'Verworrne Doppelschrift. Christlich-nationale Erneuerung und poetische Ambivalenz in Eichenorffs *Ezelin von Romano*' (175–98); R. Simon, 'Romantische Verdoppelungen — komische Verwechslungen. Von der romantischen Reflexionsphilosophie über die Verwechslungskomödie zur Prose und zurück' (259–80).

Theorie der Romantik, ed. Herbert Uerlings, Stuttgart, Reclam, 435 pp., provides a very broad selection of the theory which includes everything from G. F. Schubert to F. Schlegel, Jean Paul to Günderrode, and Wackenroder to Runge. The selections are categorized under the following headings: 'Philosophie und Religion', 'Poetologie', 'Ironie', 'Ältere Poesie und Volksdichtung', 'Märchen', 'Literaturkritik, Lesen, Hermeneutic', 'Malerei und Musik', and 'Geschichtsphilosophie und Politik'. There is also a very helpful 35-page introduction. *Romantic Fairy Tales*, ed. Carol Tully, London, Penguin, xxv + 159 pp., has translations of Goethe's *Märchen*, Tieck's *Der blonde Eckbert*, de la Motte Fouqué's *Undine*, and Brentano's *Die Geschichte des braven Kasperls und schönen Annerls* as well as an introduction.

2. INDIVIDUAL AUTHORS

ARNIM, BETTINE VON. There are two new biographies of B.v.A. this year as interest in women writers continues to grow. Angel Thamm, *Romantische Inszenierung in Briefen. Der Lebenstext der Bettine von Arnim, geboren Brentano* (Berliner Beiträge zur Germanistik), Berlin, St Albin, 367 pp., is not just a biography (though it does have a complete chronology of B.v.A.'s life, including all writings and correspondence) but instead is about the 'Schreibprozess' and foregrounds the therapeutic, self-defining aspects of writing for B.v.A. as well as for her grandmother Sophie von La Roche. The deep-hermeneutics of

Alfred Lorenz are taken as a tool, and the writer's projection of an inner world on the outer are shown to enable her to say things which are never explicitly acknowledged. This study is an unusual one, and it deals with highly current concerns about the nature of writing, the definition of the self through writing and through art (which we have seen in several publications this year). Ulrike Landfester, *Selbstsorge als Staatskunst. Bettine von Arnims politisches Werk* (Stiftung für Romantikforschung, 8), Würzburg, Königshausen & Neumann, 411 pp., has a more traditional outline than Thamm's book, but also focuses on the 'Schreibprozess', even using the same term. Landfester reads all of B.v.A.'s work together in an attempt to come to an understanding of the author, and in particular of her politics. Von Arnim tried to get a concept of mutual 'Selbstsorge' to be accepted by the likes of Goethe and Friedrich Wilhelm IV as well as many other correspondents, thus mixing private and public in a way utterly opposed to the Machiavellian politics of power without ethics. Continuing her work on B.v.A. and politics, U. Landfester, 'Das Schwiegen der Sibylle. Bettine von Arnims Briefe über die Revolution von 1848', *Jb. der Bettina von Arnim-Gesellschaft*, 11–12:121–43, explains the silence of the otherwise prolific political writer on the events of 1848 as coming from family concerns as well as being a futile attempt to keep the dialogue with Friedrich Wilhelm IV open. In the same volume, W. Bunzel, 'Empfänger unbekannt? Adressatenbezug und Wirkungsstratagie der "Polenbroschüre" Bettine von Arnims' (145–59), shows how B.v.A.'s strategies in writing to the King, which included a kind of role-playing for both 'correspondents', became ineffective in the revolutionary period; H. Schultz, ' "Was alt und faul, beherzt zu unterwühlen." Reaktionen auf die Revolution von 1848 bei Joseph von Eichendorff und Bettine von Arnim' (161–77), claims a greater political openness for Eichendorff and shows B.v.A.'s ideas to be not so much political theory as the application of *Frühromantik* ideas. U. Landfester, ' "Die echte Politik muß Erfinderin sein." Überlegungen zum Umgang mit B. v. As politischem Werk', pp. 1–37 of *'Die echte Politik muß Erfinderin sein.' Beiträge eines Wiepersdorfer Kolloquiums zu Bettina von Arnim*, ed Hartwig Schultz, Berlin, St. Albin, 1999, xv + 404 pp., sees in B.v.A.'s political writings a conscious attempt to undermine distinctions between aesthetics and politics, in a dialogic form which remains open-ended. In the same volume U. Püschel, 'Bettine, politisch — Beispiel Polen. Mit zwei briefen Ludwik Mieroslawskis' (39–107), also gives weight to B.v.A.'s political engagement, this time in the so-called *Polenbroschüre*, which have yet to be fully commented upon; H. Schultz, ' "Das freie Bürgertum, was sich immer mehr veredelt." Bettine's Frankfurter Mitgift' (109–30), discusses the ruse of setting *Dieses Buch gehört dem König* in the Frankfurt of about 1800 in order to circumvent the Prussian censors of the 1840s, and shows how B.v.A. lived her ideals practically without creating new political theories; P. A. von Arnim, ' "Der eigentliche Held in dieser Zeit, die einzige wahrhaft freie und starke Stimme." Die jüdischen Aspekte in Leben und Werk Bettina von Arnims als Herausforderung' (163–215), problematizes B.v.A's attitudes towards Jews, but ends with a positive assessment of her contribution to their emancipation in the strongly anti-Semitic times following the 1848 Revolution; B. Becker-Cantarino, 'Zur politischen Romantik. Bettina von Arnim, die "Frauenfrage" und der "Feminismus" ' (217–48), is about the co-opting of B.v.A. as a supposedly feminist thinker by the feminist movement on the 1960s. The context of B.v.A.'s distanced relationship to the younger generation of 'first wave' 19th-c. feminists is presented here clearly and unflinchingly; B. Petzinna, 'Im Spiegel-kabinett. Zum Bild der Romantik im Umkreis der "Konservativen Revolution" ' (249–75), concerns the reception of the Romantic era in the 1920s and 1930s; and K. R. Mandelkow, 'Vom Kaiserreich zur neuen Bundesrepublik. Romantik-Rezeption im Spiegel der Wandlungen von Staat und Gesellschaft in Deutschland' (277–306) is also about the reception of the writer. Also in this volume are several hitherto unpublished letters, in C. Becker, 'Bettine von Arnim und die Revolution von 1848. Sieben bisher unveröffentlichte Briefe an ihre Söhne' (309–60).

U. Landfester, 'Echo schreibt Narziß. Bettine von Arnims Mythopoetik des schöpferischen Dialogs und *Goethes Briefwechsel mit einem Kinde* (1835)', *Athenäum*, 9, 1999:161–91, shows how B.v.A.'s use of the Echo myth, alongside the myths of Demeter, Sibylle, and Psyche, reinforces her defence of women's right to self-expression. Also noted: Lisabeth M. Hock, *Replicas of a Female Prometheus: The Textual Personae of Bettina von Arnim* (NASNCGL, 27), xx + 260 pp.

ARNIM, L.A. VON. The first of two volumes of A.v.A's correspondence has come out this year, *Ludwig Achim von Arnim. Briefwechsel 1788–1801*, ed. Heinz Härtl, vol. 30 of *Werke und Briefe. Historisch-kritische Ausgabe*, ed. Roswitha Burwick et al., Tübingen, Niemeyer, xvi + 682 pp. Letters meant for newspaper publication and official correspondence are included, and everything is in chronological order. There is also a very detailed commentary. Hae-Kyong Lee, *Kulturkonstrative Untersuchungen zu 'Des Knaben Wunderhorn' und zu der koreanischen 'Sammlung der Kasalieder'* (EH, 1, 1773), 266 pp., rehearses old arguments about the viability of comparative literature and remains throughout naively untheoretical. There is no reference to the major players in folklore studies, no mention of J. Zipes, R. Bottigheimer, S. Thompson, nor to any psychoanalytical theory, and yet Lee wishes to find a 'national voice' in the German and Korean texts.

The Arnim-Gesellschaft has produced two volumes of conference proceedings this year, the first being *Universelle Entwürfe — Integration — Rückzug: Arnims Berliner Zeit (1809–1814)*, ed. Ulfert Ricklefs (Wiepersdorfer Kolloquium der Internationalen Arnim-Gesellschaft, 1), Tübingen, Niemeyer, xxi + 304 pp. In this volume: R. Burwick, ' "Der Kreis des Wissens dreht sich wandelnd um." Arnims kulturpolitisches Programm in der Berliner Jahren. Die "Kleinen Schriften" 1809–1814' (1–24), ties A.'s speculations on natural science into his ideas of culture and history. The scientist moves 'systemlos durch Systeme', not allowing any system to become an end in itself, and thus uniting the new with the old; G. Oesterle, 'Der tolle Invalide auf dem Fort Ratonneau. Aufklärischere Anthropologie und romantische Universalpoesie' (25–42), also sees A. as allowing particular viewpoints to exist, thus historicizing perception, blending into the story legend and novella as well as blending a case of 'honour' with a medical case history; B. Fischer, 'Achim von Arnims "Wintergarten" als politischer Kommentar' (43–59), shows how A. writes and studies history from an individual's perspective, rather then from any sort of distanced viewpoint, whilst the uncovering of literary remnants from the past replaces the earlier more ambitions projects of creating a new poetry; B. Knauer, 'Achim von Arnims "Wintergarten" als Arabesquenwerk' (61–72), discovers a close relationship between art and life in the story, which is a critical take on Goethe's 'Unterhaltungen deutscher Ausgewanderten'. The Romantic arabesque is a rewriting and paraphrasing of history enabling the creation of new myths; P. Staengele, 'Achim von Arnim und Kleists *Berliner Abendblätter*' (73–88), throws light on both authors as well as on the social milieu in Berlin in which they worked, and he discusses the problem of ascribing authorship for the journal's contributions; S. Nienhaus, ' "Wo jetzt Volkes Stimmen hören?" Das Wort *Volk* in den Schriften Achim von Arnims von 1805 bis 1813' (89–99), shows how the word *Volk*, which for A. was always cultural and not meant in the sense of political nationhood, runs through A.'s work. Rather than bringing folklore to the upper classes, as Tieck tried to do, A. instead wants to revive the spirit and identity of the folk because, unlike their social superiors, they were capable of development; L. Ehrlich, 'As poetisch-politisches Theaterprojekt und die "Schaubühne" von 1813' (101–15), again sees A. as mixing high and low, change with tradition; J. Barth, ' "Dieses Elend der Gelehrten" — Wissenschaftskritik in Arnims *Die Päpstin Johanna*' (117–32), finds that favouring the lowly over the over-learned is also the topic of this play, where the 'Gelehrtensatire' uses a metaphor on 'light', which includes Lucifer

as well as Prometheus; J. Knaack, 'Achim von Arnim und der
"Preußische Correspondent"' (133–41), is a contribution on A.'s
journalistic output; U. Ricklefs, '"Ahasvers Sohn."' Arnims Städted-
rama *Halle und Jerusalem*' (143–244), investigates the concepts 'Chris-
tian' and 'German' in the play and finds a surprising layer of
freemasonry in the text; J. Barth, 'Arnim-Bibliographie 1925–1995'
(245–300), is the first thorough bibliography since 1925.
The second volume of the journal is *'Frische Jugend, reich an
Hoffen.'Der junge Arnim. Zernikower Kolloquium der Internationaler Arnim-
Gesellschaft,* 2, ed. Roswitha Burwick and Heinz Härtl, Tübingen,
Niemeyer, xi + 244 pp., and includes the following: H. Baumgart,
'Die Große Mutter Caroline von Labes: Das Leben der Großmutter
Arnims 1730–1810' (1–24), gives an account of A.'s maternal
grandmother, her biography, and probable influence on the young
Arnim; H. Härtl, 'Zur geistigen Physiognomie des jungen Arnim
aufgrund seines frühen Briefwechsels' (25–30), traces intellectual
strands through the early correspondence and ends by arguing for
the need for a professionally edited volume of the correspondence;
S. Dickson, 'Arnims Beschreibungen von Reisen in Brandenburg and
Mecklenburg 1794–1795' (31–41), sets A.'s early writings in the
context of his school assignments, then looks more closely at three
travel descriptions written in consecutive years which show his
development into a more independent writer and thinker; M. Simon,
'Arnims lateinischer Schülerarbeiten' (42–48), follows a similar vein.
Three contributions all discuss A.'s scientific endeavours: M. Gerten,
'Die Bedeutung Kants und Baaders für die dynamische Naturphiloso-
phie um 1800' (49–84); F. Moiso, 'Arnims Kraftehre' (85–120); and
R. Burwick, 'Arnims Meteorologie-Projekt' (121–45). J. Sänger,
'Arnims Briefe aus Paris — Paris in Briefen Arnims 1803' (147–63),
investigates A.'s letters to Brentano and de Staël, where he presents a
negative image of the city and shows himself more concerned with
developing himself as a writer than with giving a typical traveller's
account; B. Zscheidrich, 'Ein krakówer Konvolut Arnims mit
Exzerpten, Konzepten und Notizen 1806–1807' (165–80), explains
how A. would transcribe sections of his letters to keep them as a kind
of journal of his ideas before she embarks on a description of a MS
found in Cracow which first came to light in 1996; S. Nienhaus,
'Dichteraussichten: Anmerkungen zu zwei Bildgedichten Arnims'
(181–88), shows that the two poems, inspired by paintings by Jan
Breughel and Carl Maratti, are not the didactic verse Brentano took
them to be, but are instead religiously motivated. Also in this volume:
E. Spoglianti, 'Arnims Plan eines nationalen Volkstheaters' (189–99);
F. Schaible, 'Die Geschichte zur Wahrheit läutern: Arnims "Wieder-
täufer"-Fragment' (201–11), and the concomitant 'Szenenfolge und

Edition einer Szene des Fragments' (212–15); P.-A. von Arnim, 'Die Arnims in Zernoikow' (217–38).

S. Dickson, 'An apology for the conduct of the Gordons: *Dichtung und Wahrheit* in Achim von Arnim's *Mistris Lee*', *ERR*, 11:300–21, reveals the source of A.'s story in the explanation published by a participant in the real events which the story describes. A.'s version makes the Gordon brothers less innocent and Mrs Lee more complex a character than Loudon Gordon's account had done. T. Bulang, 'Tücken des Fragments. Zu zwei neueren Studien über Achim von Arnims *Kronenwächter*', *Jb. der Bettina von Arnim-Gesellschaft*, 11–12:237–46, discusses Roland Hoermann's *Achim von Arnim's 1854 'Kronenwächter' Text. Bettina's Forgery or Bertold's Forerunner — Start of a Sequel or End of an Ur-Kommentar*, Stuttgart, Heinz, 1990, and Helga Halbfass's *Komische Geschichte(n). Der ironische Historismus in Achim von Arnims Roman 'Die Kronenwächter'*, NY, Lang, 1993.

BRENTANO, CLEMENS. Hartwig Schultz, *Schwarzer Schmetterling. Zwanzig Kapitel aus dem Leben der romantischeschen Dichters Clemens Brentano*, Berlin, Berlin Vlg, 538 pp., is a much needed new biography of the author by the eminent C. B. scholar. It is both highly readable and very sensitive. *Geist und Macht. Die Brentanos*, ed. Bernd Heidenreich, Wiesbaden, Westdeutscher Vlg, 287 pp., has chapters on all the famous Brentanos, from Peter Anton B. (1735–97) to Heinrich von B. (1904–64), each chapter written by a different author. Hartwig Schultz has written the contribution on C. B. and Ulrike Landfester the one on Bettina Brentano von Arnim. Also noted: Victor Velarde-Mayol, *On Brentano*, Belmont, Wadsworth, 92 pp.; H. Härtl, 'Wo fand Brentano die blaue Blume der Romantik?' *ZDP*, 119:179–89; D. Arendt, 'Clemens Brentano's speech about philistinism at the end of the Romantic period, or the war against the philistines and its inglorious capitulation', *OL*, 55:81–102.

DE LA MOTTE FOUQUÉ, FRIEDRICH. There is a surprising revival of interest in d.l.M.F. this year: Wolf Gerhard Schmidt, *Friedrich de la Motte Fouqué's Nibelungentrilogie 'Der Held des Nordens'* (SBL, 68), 333 pp., sets the context of saga reception in the early 19th c. before analysing the text, the first in German to rework the saga using the original Old Norse source (not the Middle High German *Nibelungenlied*). De la Motte Fouqué's philosophy and aesthetics and his understanding of Germanic mythology are all discussed. Claudia Stockinger, *Das dramatische Werk Friedrich de la Motte Fouqués. Ein Beitrag zur Geschichte des romantische Dramas* (SDL, 158), vi + 372 pp., is the first systematic study of d.l.M.F.'s dramas, and also contributes to the growing body of work on the much neglected Romantic drama. Stockinger sets out to prove the literariness of d.l.M.F.'s dramas, to put them in their historical context, and to indicate the source materials. Topics include myth, history, the poet as historian, religion, Schiller reception, the Gesamtkunstwerk. Also noted: Irene Krieger, *Undine, die Wasserfee: Friedrich de la Motte Fouqués Märchen aus der Feder der Komponisten* (Reihe Musikwissenschaft, 6), Herbolzheim, Centaurus, 168 pp.

EICHENDORFF, JOSEPH VON. There are two short biographies of E. and a full length one out this year. Helmut Bernsmeier, *Literaturwissen für Schule und Studium, Joseph von Eichendorff*, Stuttgart, Reclam, 151 pp., has a chronology, a brief biography and summaries, and interpretations of seven novels and novellas and six poems. Hermann Korte, *Joseph von Eichendorff*, Reinbek, Rowohlt, 157 pp., has more biographical information than the Reclam edition, including colour pictures and ample material on the general background. Günther Schiwy, *Eichendorff. Eine Biographie*, Munich, Beck, 734 pp., is the first comprehensive biography since Hans Brandenburg's in 1922 and the shorter one by Paul Stöcklein in 1963. It portrays E. as a disappointed soldier and civil servant who nevertheless became a popular Romantic poet, and it takes into account new scholarship which shows E. to be a writer of serious lyric poetry, a strong fighter for what he believed was right, a sharp critic of current affairs, and an ecumenically-minded Catholic ahead of his time — all as opposed to the reactionary conservative he was long taken to be. Footnotes are kept out of the text, making it more easily readable, but there is an extensive bibliography included. Otto Eberhardt, *Es 'Taugenichts'. Quellen und Bedeutungshintergrund. Untersuchungen zum poetischen Verfahren Eichendorffs*, Würzburg, Königshausen & Neumann, 757 pp., has a 17-page table of contents and is at least 10 times longer than the text it is about. Undoubtedly, the tome contains much that is useful (such as the main source-text for the story) but this reader doubts that the weight of this interpretation can be supported by the light fabric of the original text. The *Taugenicht*'s neglect of his garden, for example, is hardly likely to be a metaphor for the Enlightenment's neglect of the *Volkslied* — one of the many glosses Eberhardt gives to each episode of the story. Also noted: David Ferris, *Schumann's Eichendorff Liederkreis and the Genre of the Romantic Cycle*, NY, OUP, 320 pp.; J. Osonski, 'Goethe or Eichendorff? Nineteenth-century Catholic literary models', *GLL*, 53:143–61.

FICHTE. A. La Vopa, 'Fichte's road to Kant', pp. 200–29 of *Representations of the Self from the Renaissance to Romanticism*, ed. Patrik Coleman et al., CUP, 285 pp.; H.-J. Becker, *Fichtes Idee der Nation und das Judentum: den vergessenen Generationen der jüdischen Fichte-Rezeption*, Amsterdam–Atlanta, Rodopi, 417 pp.; Sally Sedgwick, *The Reception of Kant's Critical Philosophy: Fichte, Schelling, and Hegel*, CUP, x + 338 pp.; Wolfgang H. Schrader, *Die Spätphilosophie J. G. Fichtes: Tagung der Internationalen J. G.-Fichte-Gesellschaft (15.–27. September 1997) in Schulpforte in Verbindung mit der Landesschule Pforta und dem Istituto per gli Studi Filosofici (Napoli)* (Fichte-Studien, 17), Amsterdam–Atlanta, Rodopi, viii + 328 pp.; Michael Baur and Frederick Neuhouser, **Fichte: Foundations of Natural Right*, CUP, 358 pp.; Reinhard Weber **Wahrheit und Geschichte: ein kritischer Kommentar zum sechsten Kapitel von J. G. Fichtes 'Anweisung zum seligen Leben' (1806)*, Hamburg, Kovac, vi + 145 pp.; P. R. Sweet, 'Sir Isaiah Berlin, Fichte and German Romanticism', *GSR*, 23:245–56; G. J. Seidel, 'The fate of innate ideas in Fichte', *Idealistic Studies*, 30:79–90; J. E. Andersen, 'The weathering of the ground — Idealistic Romanticism in the work of Fichte and Hölderlin', *LiLi*, 30:144–54.

GRIMM, JACOB AND WILHELM.   Heinz Rölleke, *Die Märchen der Brüder Grimm. Quellen und Studien. Gesammelte Aufsätze* (Schriftenreihe Literaturwissenschaft, 50), Trier, Wissenschaftlicher Vlg, 288 pp., is a collection of 30 of Rölleke's most important articles from 1975 to 1998, most of which were not included in the 1980 and 1985 collections of his works. This will be a handy reference for anyone working on *Märchen*. Also noted: J. Zipes, 'The contamination of the fairy tale, or the changing nature of the Grimms' fairy tales', *Journal of the Fantastic in the Arts*, 11:77–93; C. Goldberg, 'Gretel's duck: the escape from the ogre in AaTh-327', *Fabula*, 41:42–51, studies the Grimms' *Hansel und Gretel* as a traditional ogre tale according the the Aarne/Thompson classification of folktales; S. Carlos, 'Grimms' tales in the Indian narrative situation', *ib.*, 52–75; J. E. Sennewald, ' "Di bist min ich bin din": regarding the original text in KHM-67: "Die zwölf Jäger" ', *ib.*, 119–24; K. Casemir, 'The digitalization of the *Deutsches Wörterbuch* of Jacob and Wilhelm Grimm', *Sprachwissenschaft*, 25:77–102.

GÜNDERRODE, KAROLINE.   M. C. Ives, 'Karoline von Günderrode (1780–1806): the "Tian" legend', pp. 87–111 of *Sappho in the Shadows* (see pp. 691–92 above), is a humane, readable account showing that G. is more complex than the legend. Eight of the writer's poems and their translations into English are included. Also noted: A. Simonis, ' "Das verschleierte Bild." Mythopoetik und Geschlechterrollen bei Karoline von Günderrode', *DVLG*, 74:254–78.

HAUFF, WILHELM .   R. Dusterberg, 'Wilhelm Hauff's "opportunistic" anti-semitism', *ZDP* 119:190–212.

HEGEL.   Otto Pöggeler, *Hegels Kritik der Romantik* (Philosophie an der Jahrtausendwende, 2), Munich, Fink, 1999, 245 pp., discusses the mature H.'s attitudes to what we now call Romantic (and Classical) writers and thinkers. It is a reprint of a thesis originally published in 1955. Also noted: Marion Schmaus, ' "Die Wunden des Geistes heilen." Zur Autobiographie des melancholischen Geistes oder der "Fall Hölderlin" in Hegels *Phänomenologie*', *Athenäum*, 9, 1999:67–99.

HOFFMANN, E. T. A. Ute Klein, *Die produktive Rezeption E. T. A. Hoffmanns in Frankreich* (KSL, 12), 395 pp., sets out to analyse why H. was so much more respected in France than in Germany in the 19th c., as well as to give evidence of his reception, both as a figure in French stories and opera and in the emulation of his narrative techniques and structures of the *contes fantastiques*, which are an imitation of and variation on H.'s idea of the fantastic. Stefan Bergström, *Between Real and Unreal. A Thematic Study of E. T. A. Hoffmann's 'Die Serapionsbrüder'* (STML, 49), vi + 141 pp., is a bit uneven in style, but provides a useful Todorov-informed interpretation in English of fantasy and the fantastic in the *Serapionsbrüder* stories. The study is arranged thematically and concludes that it is, in fact, themes which unite the otherwise disparate narratives of this collection. Jeang-Yean Goak, *Die Ich-Problematik in E. T. A. Hoffmanns 'Die Elixiere des Teufels'. Eine psychoanalytische Untersuchung in Auseinandersetzung mit der deutschen idealistischen Philosophie* (AD, 43), 246 pp., is a Freudian interpretation of the novel with a sidelong glance at the German Idealists and a short section on Lacan. R. Schmidt, 'Klassische, romantische und postmoderne musikästhetische Paradigmen in E. T. A. Hoffmanns *Ritter Gluck*', pp. 11–61 of Keil, *Seelenaccente* (see pp. 695–96 above), is a clearly presented and persuasive argument for reading the Romantic author as belonging to his own time, not our own, highlighting therefore differences from, not similarities to, (post)-modern ways of thinking. The study is interdisciplinary, bringing as it does musical knowedge to the text, and it analyses the text itself as well as the contemporary discourses on music, literature, and aesthetics. Susanne Gröble, *Literaturwissen für Schule und Studium. E. T. A. Hoffmann*, Stuttgart, Reclam, 100 pp., is a handy reference with a brief biography and interpretations of the works. B. Schemmel, '"Bloß das mechanische Schreiben!" Zur Handschrift E. T. A. Hoffmanns', *E. T. A. Hoffmann-Jb.*, 7, 1999:9–28, analyses the handwriting of manuscripts and official and social correspondence to determine nothing more than that the MSS were written in a smaller hand so that the author could judge the quantity of printed material it would produce. In the same volume, M. Klier, 'Kunstsehen: E. T. A. Hoffmanns literarisches Gemälde *Doga und Dogaresse*' (29–49), uses the idea of 'intermediality' to relate the story to the painting by Carl Wilhelm Kolbe, which is a relation, too, of inner to outer worlds; O. Schmidt, '"Die Wundernadel des Meisters" — Zum Bild-Text Verhältnis in E. T. A. Hoffmanns Capriccio *Prinzessin Brambilla*' (50–62), also discusses the relationship of image to text, this time focusing on the subjective meaning given to the painting by the viewer; W. Hoch, 'Das Namenstagsfest in Hoffmanns *Kater Murr*. Fanal einer Festarabeske zwischen barockem

Schein und romantischer Entgrenzung' (63–83), finds three strands of narrative which intertwine in a contrapuntal arabesque during the festivity scene in the novel. Also in this volume: A. Pohsner, 'Berglinger, Kreisler, Lemm ... oder Wieviel Hoffmann ist in Turgenev?' (84–101); J. Petzel, '"... da habe ich mich in E. T. A. Hoffmann eingegraben" oder Ein erster Blick in Franz Fühmanns Arbeitsbibliothek und in seine E. T. A. Hoffmann-Sammlung' (102–06); W. Keil, 'Konzerte mit Ouvertüren und Bühnenmusik' (107–09); and A. Olbrich and A. Pohsner, 'Bibliographie der Sekundärliteratur über E. T. A. Hoffmann 1997–1998 (Mit Nachträgen)' (110–31).

H. F. Weiss, 'Ein neuentdeckter Brief E. T. A. Hoffmanns', *E. T. A. Hoffmann-Jb.*, 8:7–12, has found a letter to Joseph Engelmann dated 10 July 1819 concerning the commission for a story by H. for the *Taschenbuch für deutsche Frauen*; A. Klüglich, 'Aufstieg zu vollendetem Künstlertum. Ein Beitrag zur Kunstauffassung in E. T. A. Hoffmanns Erzählung *Don Juan*', *ib.*, 13–36, interprets the character of the 'reisender Enthusiast' in *Don Juan* as an illustration of H.'s concept of the proper function of art to inspire the viewer/hearer; C. Steinwachs, 'Die Liebeskonzeption in E. T. A. Hoffmanns *Die Elixiere des Teufels*', *ib.*, 37–55, interprets love in the *Elixiere* as an idealizing which necessarily goes awry. The attempt to break the boundaries of selfhood through the love of another fails and instead leads to a hardening of the limits as a self when the beloved (Aurelia) is murdered; P. Meyer, 'Das Unheimliche als Strafe und Warnung. Zu einem Aspekt von E. T. A. Hoffmanns Kritik an der Frühromantik', *ib.*, 56–68, shows the author's use of the *Unheimlich* in the *Serapionsbrüder* stories to undermine not only the rational optimism of the *Aufklärung* but also as the revelatory optimism of the *Frühromantik*; R. Safranski, 'Über E. T. A. Hoffmann und Jacques Offenbach', *ib.*, 69–80, draws parallels between author and composer in their love of an audience; H.-D. Holzhausen, 'Aus den Papieren eines bekannten Hoffmannforschers: Hans von Müller zum 125. Geburtstag am 30.03.2000', *ib.*, 81–105 rehabilitates von Müller's editions of H.'s works and gives a history of his obsession with the author; V. Bendt, '"Wahnsinnige Wissenschaft." E. T. A. Hoffmann, Exil und das Jüdische Museum Berlin,' *ib.*, 106–39, gives the history of the building of the museum in the 1990s and its strange relationship to the so-called E. T. A. Hoffmann-Garten, which is a part of it; A. Jammers, 'Hoffmanniana in der Staatsbibliothek zu Berlin. Ein Bericht aus gegebenem Anlaß', *ib.*, 140–46.

Friedrich Kittler, 'Eine Mathematik der Endlichkeit. Zu E. T. A. Hoffmanns *Jesuiterkirche in G*', *Athenäum*, 9, 1999:101–20, studies the *Nachtstück* via Lacan, the innovations in perspective painting in the

Renaissance and modern computer graphics. H. Steinecke, 'Britisch-deutsche Romanlektüren im frühen neunzehnten Jahrhundert — Hoffmann und Scott zum Beispiel', pp. 103–16 of *The Novel in Anglo-German Context. Cultural Cross-Currents and Affinities*, ed. Susanne Stark (IFAVL, 38), 466 pp., investigates not the personal links between the two authors, but rather shows the development of contrary ideas about the novel in Germany and Britain. Also noted: J. Quack, 'E. T. A. Hoffmanns Verhältnis zum Judentum. Eine Lektüre der "Brautwahl", der "Irrungen" und der "Geheimnisse"', *ZGer*, 10:281–97; B. Röder, ' "Sie ist dahin und das Geheimnis gelöst" — Künstler und Mensch in E. T. A. Hoffmanns *Rat Krespel*', *GLL*, 53:1–16.

HÖLDERLIN, F. H. *Gedichte*, ed. Gerhard Kurz, Stuttgart, Reclam, 666 pp., takes its selection mainly from the *Große Stuttgarter Ausgabe* of 1951 (ed. Friedrich Beissner), though later editions (Jochen Schmidt, Michael Knaupp) have also been consulted, and later commentary has been taken on board. The volume covers all periods of the poet's life, including the final half, in chronological order, and there is an afterword by Bernhard Böschenstein. Heike Bärtel, *'Centaurengesänge'. Friedrich Hölderlins Pindarfragmente* (Ep, 318), 200 pp., is a welcome study of H. from a 'Germanistik' point of view as opposed to the many philosophical works found today. Bärtel presents close readings and commentary on the nine Pindar fragments, relating them to the 'originals' (from which they are often actually very distinct), accessing the texts by means of the dictionary H. used to translate the Greek, and by analysing sound and rhetorical associations as well as sense and meaning. There is not an attempt to give a unified interpretation to these hybrid creations — 'centaurs' — but rather to open the texts to new meanings. This she does in a style of admirable clarity. Harald Weilnböck, *'Was die Wange röthet, kann nicht übel sein.' Die Beziehungsanalyse der Entfremdung bei Hölderlin und Heidegger*, Würzburg, Königshausen & Neumann, 464 pp., studies H.'s poetry and Heidegger's exegesis of it in order to show how habits of perception can change and new interpretations be developed. It uses relational analysis, as opposed to Freudian psychoanalytical theory, to do so. Monika Kasper, *'Das Gesez von allen der König.' Hölderlins Anmerkungen zum Oedipus und zur Antigonä* (Ep, 265), 219 pp., sees the 'Gesetz' as the highest epistemological category in H.'s poetological texts. The emphasis is on the Greek translations, although there is some mention of H.'s lyric output as well.

The Recalcitrant Art. Diotima's Letters to Hölderlin and Related Missives, ed. and trans. Douglas F. Kenney and Sabine Menner-Bettscheid, pref. David Farrell Krell, NY, SUNY, xiv + 255 pp., is a truly amazing book, perhaps more for what it says about modern scholarship than its ostensible subjects, H. and Susette Gontard. The two editors disagreed violently about the form, if any at all, the book should take. They died in a car crash after Kenney had sent the MS to the publisher. The form it now takes has Kenney's introduction (about H.) on the verso, with Menner-Bettscheid's incensed commentary and criticism on the recto (she objects to Gontard's letters being thus co-opted for a book on H. in a manner allegedly objective but which she finds objectionable because it in fact eliminates the woman). In the main text — the translations — Gontard's letters appear in large print, verso, and the recto is reserved for related texts from the 18th and 19th cs and, in smaller print, imaginative productions by Menner-Bettscheid. It is truly a blazingly vivid example of disunity in the conception of modern literary studies and their purpose, and highly to be recommended for that. Kenney remains reserved and reasonable but anodyne; Menner-Bettscheid's contribution is angry, passionate, and compelling. Also noted: Violetta Waibel, *Hölderlin und Fichte 1794–1800*, Paderborn, Schöningh, 384 pp.; Uwe Beyer, *Streit und Frieden hat seine Zeit: Hölderlins Entwicklung seiner Geschichtsphilosophie aus der Anschauung der Gegenwart: fünf Zeitgedichte vor 1800*, Stuttgart, Metzler, xiii + 388 pp.; Georg Mein, *Die Konzeption des Schönen: der ästhetische Diskurs zwischen Aufklärung und Romantik: Kant — Moritz — Hölderlin — Schiller*, Bielefeld, Aisthesis, 224 pp. D. Kadir, 'Heidegger, Hölderlin and the "essence of philosophy": an adversative conversation', *Neohelicon*, 27:69–78; R. Schier, 'The Danube as paradigm of creativity on Wordsworth and Hölderlin', *JEGP*, 99:157–69; S.-M. Weineck, 'The abyss above: philosophy, tragedy and madness in Hölderlin's encounter with Sophocles', *Seminar*, 36:161–81. *Europe — Revue Litteraire Mensuelle*, 78, has a special volume on H. including articles by Jean-Paul Michel, Roger Laporte, Luis Cernuda, Jacques D'Hondt, Jean Ruffet, and François Garrigue.

KLEIST. Maximilian Guiseppe Burkhart, *Dekonstruktive Autopoiesis — Paradoxe Strukturen in Kleists Trauerspiel 'Penthesilea'* (MSLKD, 33), 165 pp., uses deconstruction to highlight the self-reflexive aspects of the work. B. gives a thorough theoretical background before embarking on a close reading of the enigmatic play. There is also a section on aesthetic theories in K.'s time (Kant, Schiller). Less adventurous is Harald Ritter's *Die Dichtung Kleists. Studien zu ihrem episch-dramatischen Spannungsfeld*, Aachen, Shaker, v + 449 pp. This represents yet another 'werkimmanent' interpretation of all the dramas and novellas, including a section on gestures as communication. It is not clear what is particularly new in this study, but it is certainly thorough. Miran Kwak, *Identitätsprobleme in Werken Heinrich von Kleists* (HBG, 28), 293 pp., makes a passionate plea against deconstructionist readings (mainly Bernhard Fischer's). K. is viewed within the context of Romanticism and early 19th-c. nationalism. Four plays and one story are analysed in depth: *Michael Kohlhaas, Die Hermannsschlacht, Prinz Friedrich vom Homburg, Penthesilea,* and *Die Verlobung in St. Domingo.* Hans-Dieter Fronz, *Verfehlte und erfüllte Natur. Variationen über ein Thema im Werk Heinrich von Kleists,* Würzburg, Königshausen & Neumann, 416 pp., is a well-documented study of nature as ideal in K.'s work, focusing on imagery and metaphors in the work and the underlying musical structure. Laura Martin, *Narrative Feminine Identity and the Appearance of Woman in Some of the Shorter Fiction of Goethe, Kleist, Hawthorne and James,* Lewiston, Mellen, xv + 212 pp., has a chapter on K. wherein she attempts to show the distance between author and work in what is said in the text, particularly concerning the gender roles in *Die Marquise von O . . .* C. Hein, 'Von den unabdingbaren Voraussetzungen beim Kleist-Lesen', *BKF,* 13, 1999:7–15, gives a highly personal (and very brief) indication of how he thinks K. should be taught, relating the events in *Prinz Friedrich vom Homburg* and *Michael Kohlhaas* to the recent division of Germany and the activities of the RAF. H.-G. Thalheim, 'Lebensplan, Eingliederungszwang, Selbsterkundung. Kleists Landschafts- und Städtebilder während der Reise nach Würzburg', *ib.,* 17–60, presents a discursive biography of K.'s early years based on the few writings of his which are still extant; V. Nölle, 'Eine "gegenklassische" Verfahrungsweise. Kleists *Penthesilea* und Schillers *Jungfrau von Orleans', ib.,* 158–74, finds K.'s refusal to use monologue (as illustrated in *Penthesilea*) as indicative of his difference from Schiller's classical world view. P. Ensberg, 'Das Gefäss des Inhalts. Zum Verhältnis von Philosophie und Literatur am Beispiel der "Kant-Krise" Heinrich von Kleists', *ib.,* 61–123; H. Häker, 'Fünf Miszellen zu Kleists Leben und Werk', *ib.,* 124–36; S. C. Ho, 'Erkenntnis — Wahrheit — Ich: Kleists *Amphitryon', ib.,* 137–57; H. F. Weiss, 'Verschüttette Spuren zu Heinrich von Kleists Freund Ludwig von Brockes', *ib.,* 175–85.

In *BKF,* 14, A. Wiegel, 'Das imaginäre Theater Heinrich von Kleists. Spiegelungen des zeitgenössischen Theaters im erzählten Dialog *Ueber das Marionettentheater*' (21–114), sets K.'s essay into its immediate social context of 1810 Berlin, examining terms such as 'Oper' and 'Marionettentheater', 'Publicum' and 'Pöbel' in their contemporary meanings, thus assuming that the essay was written expressly for the *Berliner Abendblätter* shortly before publication; M. Beckmann, 'Das Geheimnis der *Marquise von O*' (115–154), presents a reading of the story that is based on some rather far-fetched anagrams of words, names and phrases taken seemingly randomly from the text; M. Bohn, 'Kommunikationsproblematik in

Heinrich von Kleists *Die Verlobung in St. Domingo'* (155–95), brings little new to the discussion of K.'s obsession with the impossibility of communication. The most interesting article in the volume is E. Siebert, ' "Grüner Gläser" und "Gelbsucht". Eine neue Hypothese zu Kleists "Kantkrise" ' (213–24), wherein S. demonstrates convincingly that the likely immediate cause of K.'s crisis and the source of his famous letter to Wilhelmine von Zenge is Sebastian Mutschell's *Versuch einer solchen faßlichen Darstellung der Kantischen Philosophie, daß daraus das Brauchbare und Wichtige derselbe für die Welt erleuchten möge* of 1799. Also in this volume: J. Reich, 'Wo find' ich es, dies Frankfurt?' (9–20); H. F. Weiss, 'Eine unbekannte Fassung der *Germania-Ode* Heinrich von Kleists' (196–212); H. Häker, 'Kleist auf Rügen' (225–34); Id., 'Nachrichten vom Offizierscorps der königlich preussischen Armee von 1806' (235–64); and W. Ort, 'Ein intriquer und unruhiger Geist. Auskunft aus Frankfurt (Oder) und Magdeburg über Heinrich Zschokke' (265–72).

F. Bridgham, 'Kleist's *Familie Schroffenstein* and "Monk" Lewis's *Mistrust*: give and take', pp. 75–101 of *The Novel in Anglo-German Context. Cultural Cross-Currents and Affinities*, ed. Susanne Stark (IFAVL, 38), 466 pp., speculates on possible links between the two authors, especially via C. M. Wieland and his son Ludwig Wieland. K. Rek, ' "Und alle Greul des fessellosen Krieges!" Legitimation und Motivation von Gewalt in Heinrich von Kleists *Hermannschlacht*', Corbineau-Hoffmann, *Gewalt*, 103–31, reads the play as K.'s failure to present a coherent apology for violent action, wherein the failure is precisely what rescues the piece for the modern reader. G. Bonheim, 'Kleists *Gegenwort*', *DVLG*, 74:221–53, uses a term coined by Paul Celan to interpret the dramas of K.

Also noted: F. Bridgham, 'Emancipating amazons: Schiller's Jungfrau, Kleist's Penthesilea, Wagner's Brunhilde', *FMLS*, 36:64–73; Bernhard Greiner, **Kleists Dramen und Erzählungen: Experimente zum 'Fall' der Kunst*, Tübingen, Francke, vii + 460 pp.; Timothy J. Mehigan, **Heinrich von Kleist und die Aufklärung*, Rochester, NY, Camden House, xix + 246 pp.; Christian Paul Berger, **Bewegungsbilder: Kleists Marionettentheater zwischen Poesie und Physik*, Paderborn, Schöningh, xxiii + 361 pp.; Gabriele Kapp, **'Des Gedankens Senkblei': Studien zur Sprachauffassung Heinrich von Kleists 1799–1806*, Stuttgart, Metzler, 447 pp.; Erika Berroth, **Heinrich von Kleist: Geschlecht, Erkenntnis, Wirklichkeit* (STML, 58), 250 pp. S. Engelstein, 'Out on a limb: military medicine, H.v.K., and the disarticulated body', *GSR*, 23:225–44; J. Mieskowski, 'Breaking the laws of language: freedom and history in Kleist's *Prinz Friedrich von Homburg*', *StRom*, 39:111–37; H. J. Schneider, 'Standing and falling in Heinrich von Kleist, *MLN*, 115:502–18.

MEREAU, SOPHIE. A. J. Harper , 'Sophie Mereau (1770–1806): living to love and loving to live', pp. 113–43 of *Sappho in the Shadows* (see pp. 691–92 above), provides a discursive biography of the writer and includes five poems with their translations into English. C. Höhn, ' "Hier siehst du ein Gemälde meiner Welt und meiner Freuden." Zur Identifizierung von zwei unbekannten Texten Sophie Mereaus', *Jb. der Bettina von Arnim-Gesellschaft*, 11–12:227–26, reveals a story (*Der Reisegefährte*) and a poem (*Trennung vom Leben*) published in M.'s journal *Kalathiskos* to be by M. herself, as revealed in the 1997 publication by Katharin von Hammerstein of diary entries, fragments, and sketches.

NOVALIS. Verena Anna Lukas, *Der Dialog im Dialog: Das Inzitament bei Friedrich von Hardenberg* (ZGS, 55), 202 pp., is not seeking to find a unified interpretation, but instead shows how N.'s work incites the reader to a dialogue. Meaning inheres neither in the work nor in the interpretation, but in a community. The two *Dialogues* of N. are given special attention and the connections of N.'s thought with so-called 'Brownianism' are outlined. Marion Schmaus, *Die poetische Konstruktion des Selbst. Grenzgänge zwischen Frühromantik und Moderne: Novalis, Bachmann, Christa Wolf, Foucault* (Hermaea, n. F., 92), Tübingen, Niemeyer, ix + 407 pp., is somewhat hard going. Fichte's philosophy and influence on N. is explained. One chapter is dedicated to N. (mostly *Heinrich von Ofterdingen)* and one each to the other three authors in the title. For all four authors, the creation of a self is a 'Kunstwerk' brought about by the creation of actual art. On the same relationship is Berward Loheide, *Fichte und Novalis. Tranzendentalphilosophisches Denken im romantischen Diskurs* (Fichte-Studien-Supplementa, 13), Amsterdam–Atlanta, Rodopi, 417 pp. Loheide maintains that Fichte's influence on N. has been unjustly ignored. N. knew F. from a very early age, as the latter was patronized first by N.'s uncle then his father, and N.'s poetry can only be understood if its philosophical import, which is highly influenced by Fichte's and at times even anticipates the philosopher's later work, is taken into account. There is a detailed analysis of Fichte then of N., with ample cross-referencing between chapters.

'Blüthenstaub.' Rezeption und Wirkung des Werkes von Novalis, Tübingen, Niemeyer, vi + 432 pp., is the proceedings of the second conference of the Novalis-Gesellschaft and includes discussion notes from the conference. In this R. Martin, 'Heine und Novalis' (43–64), claims a greater influence by N. on Heine than generally thought, and in particular on the latter's idea of a 'Freyheitsreligion'; K. Feilchenfeldt, 'Novalis und die bildende Kunst' (65–98), discusses mostly N.'s influence on the painter Philipp Otto Runge, but also tries to go beyond simple ideas of direct influence; L. Stockinger, 'Novalis und

der Katholizismus' (99–124), examines the reception of N. by the 19th-c. Catholic church; W. A. O'Brien, '"Blüthenstaub": Dekonstruktion der Symbolik' (125–39), finds similarities with modern deconstruction in N.'s work, in that his symbols are never to be pinned down but rather remain in the realm of irony and allegory, the study not being intended to prove that N. was a precursor to Derrida, but rather to use the similarities to make sense of N.'s work; D. F. Mahoney, 'Die Stimme eines Fremden. Zur Novalis-Rezeption in Großbritannien und Amerika' (141–56), traces the reception of N. by T. Carlyle, H. W. Longfellow, and the American Transcendentalists, from the interest in the spiritual writings, through the sparse years of the 20th c., to recent translations into English of *Heinrich von Ofterdingen* and the theoretical writings; G. Schultz, 'Novalis und die Dichterinnen' (157–71), praises Penelope Fitzgerald for her lively portrayal of N.'s youth in *The Blue Flower*, though her account is not always factually accurate. Klara Hofer's 1925 novel *Zur Hochzeit ruft der Tod* is not as appreciated for its more sentimental approach, but Gisela Kraft's story *Prologue zu Novalis* (1990) and Marion Titze's *Unbekannter Verlust* (1994) are deemed to be worthy productions; S. Vietor, 'Novalis und die Anthroposophie' (339–64), gives first an overview of anthroposophy, then traces the similarities between N. and Rudolf Steiner, finally outlining Steiner's actual reception of the poet. Also in this volume: H. Uerlings, 'Novalis und die Moderne. Seghers — Hilbig — Benn — Bachmann' (7–41); L. Zagari, 'Literarische Novalis-Rezeption in Italien' (173–90); S. A. Romaschko, 'Novalis in Rußland. Ein schwieriger und unvollendeter Weg' (215–29); J. Schrier, 'Novalis-Vertonungen. Die musikalische Rezeption der Texte Friedrich von Hardenbergs — Anzeige eines Forschungsdesiderats' (231–66); U. Karthaus, 'Novalis und Musil' (267–87); H. Esselborn, 'Novalis-Rezeption in der deutschen Moderne' (289–310); J. Endres, 'Hofmannsthal und Novalis. Zur Ambivalenz des Erbes' (311–37); J. Egytien, 'Liebe und Tod auf dem Staubfaden Erde. Zu Ernst Meisters Novalis-Lektüre' (365–87); L. Pikulik, 'Romantisierung als Inszenierung. Magisches Welttheater bei Novalis und Botho Strauß' (389–410); and I. Kasperowski, 'Novalis-Zitate in Caribaldis Gesprächen. Zur Novalis-Rezeption in Thomas Bernhards *Die Macht der Gewohnheit*' (411–32).

Also noted: Dirk Winkelmann, *Selbstbeschreibungen der Vormoderne: Theorietypologien und ästhetische Reflexionen gesellschaftlicher Ausdifferenzierung bei Schiller, Novalis, Forster und Marx* (FLK, 68), 294 pp.; Angelika Rauch, *The Hieroglyph of Tradition: Freud, Benjamin, Gadamer, Novalis, Kant*, Madison, Fairleigh Dickinson U.P., 249 pp.; S. Grimm, 'Types of poetries and systemologies of knowledge. The influence of post-Kantian methods for organizing knowledge on the debate between

Novalis and Friedrich Schlegel over poetological genres', *Euphorion*, 94:149–71; H. F. Weiss, 'Ernst Ludwig von Berger and Friedrich Ludwig Lindner — Note on Friedrich von Hardenberg's circle of friends and acquaintances', *ib.*, 113–21; O. Schefer, 'The "Fichte-Studien" of Novalis and *Tathandlung* put to the test of transcendence', *EP*:55–74.

RICHTER, JEAN PAUL.   Jean Paul, *Ideen-Gewimmel. Texte und Aufzeichnungen aus dem Nachlaß*, ed. Thomas Wirtz and Kurt Wölfel, Munich, DTV, 300 pp., is organized according to topic or theme and contains notes, dreams and thoughts, with the length varying from a few words to about a page long. It is a varied and enjoyable read. Rolf Vollmann, *Das Tolle neben dem Schönen. Jean Paul*, Munich, DTV, 263 pp. is an interesting, quite subjective biography of J.P. and will provide a good way to make an initial acquaintance with the author. Dirk Otto, *Der Witz-Begriff Jean Pauls. Überlegungen zur Zeichentheorie Richters*, Munich, Utz, 1999, 196 pp., applies a three-pronged semiotic theory (influenced by Charles Pierce, Friedrich Kittler, and Niklas Luhmann) to J.P. The triadic theory is first set out then J.P.'s own semiotic theory is described; lastly *Das Kampaner Tal* is studied in terms of J.P.'s idea of 'Witz'.

SCHELLING.   Christoph Asmuth et al., *Schelling: zwischen Fichte und Hegel* (Bochumer Studien zur Philosophie, 32), Amsterdam–Philadelphia, Grüner, vii + 423 pp.; Bernhard Rang, *Identität und Indifferenz: Eine Untersuchung zu Schellings Identitätsphilosophie*, Frankfurt, Klostermann, viii + 249 pp.; Temilo van Zantwijk, *Pan-Personalismus: Schellings tranzendentale Hermeneutik der menschlichen Freiheit*, Stuttgart, Frommann-Holzboog, 312 pp.; M. C. Challiol-Gillet, 'The critique of the ontological evidence of the existence of God in Schelling and Kierkegaard', *RMM*:237–45; T. Buchheim, 'Schelling and the metaphysical celebration of evil', *Philosophisches Jb.*, 107:47–60.

SCHLEGEL, FRIEDRICH.   Edith Höltenschmidt, *Die Mittelalter-Rezeption der Brüder Schlegel*, Paderborn, Schöningh, xxii + 900 pp., is the first full study of the topic and concentrates on the influence of medieval literature on Romantic literature and aesthetics. It is a heavy tome, but clearly an indispensable contribution to scholarship for romanticists and medievalists alike. P. Schnyder, 'Politik und Sprache in der Frühromantik. Zu Friedrich Schlegels Rezeption der Französischen Revolution, *Athenäum*, 9, 1999:39–65, looks at the relationship between 'les mots et les choses' in the Revolutionary period to explain the important contribution by the German writers who, however, experienced no political revolution in their own country. The article is a résumé of the third part of Schnyder's 1999 book *Die Magie der Rhetorik* (*YWMLS*, 61:702). Also noted: M. Enders,

'Das romantische Unverständlichkeitsverständnis Friedrich Schlegels', *DVLG*, 74:44–83; A. Arndt, 'The natural laws of human culture — The historical philosophy program of the early Romantic period in the work of Friedrich Schlegel', *Deutsche Zeitschrift für Philosophie*, 48:97–105. Several books out this year have sections on F.S., namely: Jeffrey S. Librett, **The Rhetoric of Cultural Dialogue: Jews and Germans from Moses Mendelssohn to Richard Wagner and Beyond*, Stanford U.P., xxiii + 391 pp.; Götz Pochat and Brigitte Hagenlocher-Wagner, **Kunst/Geschichte; Zwischen historischer Reflexion und aesthetischer Distanz*, Graz, Akademischer Druck- und Verlagsanstalt, 176 pp.; and Michael Clark, **Revenge of the Aesthetic: The Place of Literature in Theory Today*, Berkeley, California U.P., viii + 251 pp.

SCHLEGEL-SCHELLING, CAROLINE. *Romantische Liebe und romantischer Tod. Über den Bamberger Aufenthalt von Caroline Schlegel, Auguste Böhmer, August Wilhelm Schlegel und Friedrich Wilhelm Schelling im Jahre 1800*, ed. Wulf Segebrecht et al. (Fußnoten zur Literatur, 48), Bamberg U.P., 251 pp., takes as its subject the trip to Bamberg where C.S. recovered from an illness and her daughter Auguste contracted and died of dysentery; the beginning of the end of the Jena-Circle had arrived. Short chapters on a variety of topics directly related to the protagonists (how they travelled, where they stayed) as well as about more general topics (for example, on Brownianism, the medical doctrine Schelling vainly tried out on Auguste, and which may have actually killed her) give this 'footnote' a surprisingly wide range and interest.

TIECK, LUDWIG. Ruth Petzoldt, *Albernheit mit Hintersinn. Intertextuelle Spiele in Ludwig Tiecks romantischen Komödien* (Stiftung für Romantikforschung, 7), Würzburg, Königshausen & Neumann, 293 pp., on five of T.'s comedies, is another timely study of the oft-neglected genre of Romantic drama. The 'Albernheit' refers to the childish/childlike playfulness with which Romantic comedy reflects back on itself: like Menninghaus (see p. 692 above), Petzholdt finds the quality of playfulness characteristic of T.'s work.

TIECK, SOPHIE. C. Gerlach, 'Sophie Tieck (1775–1833): Schriftstellerin der Romantik', pp. 163–85 of *Wenn die Geschichte um eine Ecke geht* (see below), provides a mini-biography of the sister of the famous L. Tieck, which in its original form accompanied an exhibition on S.T. in Berlin in 1996.

VARNHAGEN, RAHEL LEVIN. The publication *Wenn die Geschichte um eine Ecke geht. Almanach der Varnhagen Gesellschaft*, ed. Nikolaus Gatter, Berlin, Arno Spitz, 391 pp., covers more than R.V., including as it does her younger husband Karl August Varnhagen von Ense and Ludmilla Assing, her niece, as well as publishing modern poetry which is in some sense inspired by the Varnhagens. Several poems by

R.V. are published here: 'Rahel Varnhagen Gedichte, ausgesucht und zur Veröffentlichung vorbereitet von Irina Hundt' (45–48), and A. Gustas, 'Rahel Varnhagens Wetternotizen' (49–65), illustrated by Kornelia Löhrer, is a selection from R.V.'s letters of remarks she made about the weather, which evidently had a great influence on her life; R. Neumann, 'Nicht mehr lieblich schweigen oder: Weibliche Selbstdarstellung um 1800 am Beispiel der Briefe Rahel Varnhagens' (110–60), is an essay first written in 1977–79 and published here posthumously; N. Gatter, ' "Sie ist vor allen die meine . . ." Die Sammlung Varnhagen bis zu ihrer Katalogisierung' (239–60), gives an account of the Varnhagen collection of MSS, including the troubled history of Karl August Varnhagen von Ense's publication of R.V.'s letters and Ludwig Stein's directorship of the collection in the late 19th c.; and 'Anhang: die Sammlung Varnhagen in Testamenten und Verfügungen' (261–71), publishes R.V.'s will alongside a few letters from her husband and niece. Also noted: Georges Solovieff, *Rahel Varnhagen: Une révoltée féministe a l'époque romantique*, Paris, Harmattan, 165 pp.

WACKENRODER. Roland Bogards and Harald Neumeyer, 'Die Macht, die Kunst macht: Winckelmann und Wackenroder zitieren Raffael', *Athenäum*, 9, 1999:193–225, rehearse the differences between Classical and Romantic aesthetics by comparing Winckelmann's *Gedanken über die Nachahmung der griechischen Malerei und Bildhauerkunst* (1755) and W.'s *Raffael's Erscheinung* (1796), which both quote a letter of Raphael's of 1516. Kevin F. Yee, *Aesthetic Homosociality in Wackenroder and Tieck* (SMGL, 94), 185 pp., refrains from discussing the putative authorship for sections of the *Herzensergießungen* and its sequel the *Phantasien über die Kunst von einem Kunstliebenden Klosterbruder*, but takes these works as collaborative efforts not intended to be thus dissected, despite Tieck's misleading statements to the contrary. Like Tieck and W., characters in the work, especially the Friar and Berglinger, are all men bound by fraternal and paternal bonds which exclude women. Also noted: Alexandra Pontzen, *Künstler ohne Werk: Modelle negativer Produktionästhetik in der Künstlerliteratur von Wackenroder bis Heiner Müller*, Berlin, Schmidt, 430 pp.; A. Beutel, 'Art as the manifestation of infinity: the text of Wilhelm Heinrich Wackenroder's *Outpourings of the Heart* on the function of art in religion from early German Romanticism', *Zeitschrift für Theologie und Kirche*, 97:210–37.

WERNER, ZACHARIAS. *Der Herr und der Cyniker. Ausgesuchte Gedichte*, ed. Leo Kreutzer and Jürgen Peters (Schriftstücke, 6), Hanover, Revonnah, 52 pp., is a welcome collection of some of the difficult to find pieces of an author no longer considered great. There is a short six-page biography and a few pages of notes on the selection of 37 poems.

LITERATURE, 1830–1880

By BOYD MULLAN, *Senior Lecturer in German in the University of St Andrews*

1. GENERAL

REFERENCE WORKS AND GENERAL STUDIES. The third, revised and enlarged edition of the *Quellenlexikon zur deutschen Literaturgeschichte: Personal- und Einzelwerkbibliographien der internationalen Sekundärliteratur 1945–1990 zur deutschen Literatur von den Anfängen bis zur Gegenwart,* ed. Heiner Schmidt et al., has reached the letter R with the appearance of vols 22–25, Duisburg, Vlg für pädagogische Dokumentation, 512 pp. per volume. *Deutsches Theater-Lexikon: Biographisch-bibliographisches Handbuch,* ed. Ingrid Bigler-Marschall (formerly W. Kosch), Band 4, Berne, Saur, 1998, 2209 pp., covers names from Singer to Tzschoppe. The new Goedeke, *Deutsches Schriftsteller-Lexikon 1830–1880: Goedekes Grundriss zur Geschichte der deutschen Dichtung. Fortführung,* has reached the letter G with the addition of vol. 3.1, ed. H. Jacob, Berlin, Akademie, 639 pp. *Encyclopedia of German Literature,* ed. Mathias Konzett, 2 vols, Chicago–London, Fitzroy Deardorn, xxii + 516, xiv + 517–1136 pp., contains articles on themes (Aesthetics, The Holocaust), periods (Biedermeier, *Vormärz*), genres (Epistolary Novel, *Heimatroman*) and a wide range of authors from all periods. Most of the 19th-c. authors included are canonical, but a welcome effort has been made to find space for some less well known figures like Louise Aston and Louise von François. The articles are fairly lengthy (typically upwards of 2,000 words) and include surprisingly extensive bibliographical references. The work is a considerable achievement and will be much appreciated by both scholars and undergraduates. *Metzler Lexikon der deutsch-jüdischen Literatur: Jüdische Autorinnen und Autoren deutscher Sprache von der Aufklärung bis zur Gegenwart,* ed. Andreas B. Kilcher, Stuttgart–Weimar, Metzler, xx + 664 pp. + 255 pls, is the work of an international team of 65 scholars containing articles on 270 authors of Jewish or partly Jewish background who wrote in German. The articles have an average length of between two and four pages, followed by five or ten lines of bibliographical references. Each entry follows the same general pattern, giving a biographical account of the writer, a survey of his or her literary output and an assessment of his or her attitude to Judaism. A deliberate attempt is made to avoid any ideological baggage and to remain strictly factual and neutral. Among the 19th-c. authors treated are Auerbach, Börne, Franzos, Heine, Heyse, Kompert, Lewald,

Lorm, Rodenberg, and Saphir. The volume is rounded off with a full index of names (not merely those of the Jewish writers in question) and a short general bibliography. Thomas Sirges, *Leihbibliothekskataloge aus Hessen-Kassel: Quellen zur populären Lesekultur und Bildungsgeschichte in Deutschland im 18. und 19. Jahrhundert* (STSL, 72), 1999, ix + 193 pp., complements the pioneering work of the author's monograph *Die Bedeutung der Leihbibliothek für die Lesekultur in Hessen-Kassel 1753–1866* (1994). The book is accompanied by a *Beilage* of 17 microfiches listing the contents of many of the popular commercial libraries of the area.

THEMES. Ritchie Robertson, *The 'Jewish Question' in German Literature, 1749–1939: Emancipation and its Discontents*, OUP, 1999, 534 pp., is a work of outstanding thoroughness and scholarship, though more concerned with the wider cultural dimensions of the subject than directly with literature. Of particular interest to Germanists specializing in the period 1830–1880 will be the third chapter on vareties of anti-Semitism and literary images of the Jew, with extended comment on Wagner's *Das Judentum in der Musik*, Raabe's *Der Hungerpastor* and Saar's *Seligmann Hirsch*. Elsewhere there is also some treatment of works by Heine (*Der Rabbi von Bacherach, Die Bäder von Lucca*), Auerbach (*Schwarzwälder Dorfgeschichten, Dichter und Kaufmann, Spinoza*), Lewald (*Jenny*), Franzos (*Die Juden von Barnow, Der Pojaz, Moschko von Parma*), and Ludwig Jacobowski (*Werther, der Jude*). *The German-Jewish Dialogue: An Anthology of Literary Texts 1749–1993*, ed. Ritchie Robertson, OUP, 1999, xli + 382 pp., presents translations of both texts by German-speaking Jews and of texts by Gentiles about Jews. The book includes extracts from the works of Börne, Heine, Franzos, and the complete text of Saar's *Seligmann Hirsch*. *Mythos Don Juan: Zur Karriere eines männlichen Konzepts*, ed. Beatrice Müller-Kampel (Reclam-Bibliothek, 1675), Leipzig, Reclam, 1999, 314 pp., R. Whittle, 'Moments of emancipation: The nineteenth-century heroine in German Literature', *Will Vol.*, 37–50, focuses on Lewald, Hahn-Hahn, and Johanna Kinkel. Catling, *Women's Writing*, has two chapters relevant to our period: P. Howe, 'Women's writing 1830–1890' (88–103); and P. Boden, 'Political writing and women's journals: the 1848 revolutions' (104–08). Christl Griesshaber-Weninger, *Rasse und Geschlecht: Hybride Frauenfiguren in der Literatur um 1900* (Literatur — Kultur — Geschlecht. Große Reihe, 16), Cologne–Weimar, Böhlau, vii + 294 pp., is a 1998 Washington dissertation that discusses texts in which the heroines are of foreign origin and includes Keller and Gabriele Reuter among the authors studied. Jost Hermand, *Formen des Eros in der Kunst*, Vienna, Böhlau, 283 pp., has some discussion of sexual themes in Heine and Platen. *Nationale Identität: Aspekte, Probleme und Kontroverse in der deutschsprachigen Literatur*, ed. Joanna Jabłkowska et al., Lódź U.P., 1998, 509 pp., contains: D. Arendt, 'Heinrich Heine zwischen Patriotismus und Europäismus' (75–93); J. Kałazny, '"Hinterm Berg wohnen auch Leute": einige Bemerkungen zu Theodor Fontanes Reisebüchern *Kriegsgefangen: Erlebtes 1870* und *Aus den Tagen der Okkupation: Eine Osterreise durch Nordfrankreich und Elsass-Lothringen 1871*' (130–39). *National Identität aus germanistischer Perspektive*, ed. Maria K. Lasatowicz et al., Opole U.P., 1998, 337 pp., has: I. Surynt, 'Zur nationalen Differenzierung der literarischen Gestalten im Erzählwerk Marie von Ebner-Eschenbachs' (123–31); J. Joachimsthaler, '"Wucherblumen auf Ruinen": nationalliterarische (Des)Integration bei Paul Heyse' (217–14). *Beiträge zur Rezeption der britischen und irischen Literatur des 19. Jahrhunderts im deutschsprachigen Raum*, ed. Norbert Bachleitner (Internationale Forschungen zur allgemeinen und vergleichenden Literaturwissenschaft, 45), Amsterdam–Atlanta, Rodopi, x + 534 pp., contains four articles that fall into our period: R. West, 'English nineteenth-century novels on the German stage: Birch-Pfeiffer's adaptations of Dickens, Brontë, Eliot and Collins' (293–316); S. Neuhaus, ' "Sechsunddreißig Könige für einen Regenschirm": Heinrich Heines produktive Rezeption britischer Literatur (410–42); A. Ritter, 'Die Bekannten und die beiden "großen Unbekannten"': Scott, der historische Roman und sein Einfluss auf Charles Sealsfield' (443–77); H. V. Geppert, 'Ein Feld von Differenzierungen: zur kritisch-produktiven Scott-Rezeption von Arnim bis Fontane' (479–500). *1848: Literatur, Kunst und Freiheit im europäischen Rahmen*, ed. Harmut Melenk et al., Freiburg, Fillibach, 1998, 220 pp., contains: J. Firges, 'Georg Herwegh, eine Symbolfigur des Vormärz' (63–84); F. Genton, 'Lyoner canuts und *Schlesische Weber*: noch einmal Heine und die Folgen' (119–35); M. Siguan, 'Heine und Spanien' (137–56). *Politics in German Literature: Essays in Memory of Frank G. Ryder*, ed. Beth Bjorklund et al. (SGLLC), 1998, 235 pp., contains: P. M. Lützeler, 'The American European Karl Postl/Charles Sealsfield on the US and Europe in the 1820s' (27–35); R. T. Gray, 'The (mis)fortunes of commerce: economic transformation in Adalbert Stifter's *Bergkristall*' (36–59); M. E. Ward, 'The personal is political — the political becomes personal: Fanny Lewald's early travel literature' (60–82). *History and Literature: Essays in Honor of Karl S. Guthke*, ed. W. C. Donahue et al. (Stauffenburg Festschriften), Tübingen, Stauffenburg, 512 pp. includes articles on Stifter, Fontane, Kürnberger, and Wagner. Volker Riedel, *Antikerezeption in der deutschen Literatur vom Renaissance-Humanismus bis zur Gegenwart: Eine Einführung*, Stuttgart, Metzler, viii + 515 pp., is aimed at both Germanists and Classicists, and contains two chapters dealing with the 19th-c. reception of the ancient world. Among the German authors included are Grillparzer, Heine, Grabbe, Büchner, Immermann, Stifter, Mörike, Hebbel, Heyse, Meyer, and Dahn. It is pleasing to note, too, the attention paid to less well known figures like Geibel and Adolf von Wilbrandt. In a monograph that casts its net as widely as this one it is inevitable that there will be some factual errors, such as the statement that Heyse was awarded the *Schillerpreis* for his early play *Die Sabinerinnen* when he in fact won it for *Alkibiades* and other dramas of the 1880s.

Smith, *Metaphor and Materiality*, explores the relationship between literature and science from the 18th to the 20th c. and includes treatment of Büchner and Stifter: 'Defining the human: Büchner's *Dantons Tod* and *Woyzeck*' (151–200); 'The lawful realm: Stifter's *Bergkristall* and *Kalkstein*' (201–64). Ulrich Kinzel, *Ethische Projekte: Literatur und Selbstgestaltung im Kontext des Regierungsdenkens. Humboldt, Goethe, Stifter und Raabe* (Das Abendland, n.F., 27), Frankfurt, Klostermann, x + 609 pp., is a Hamburg *Habilitationsschrift*. Karl S. Guthke, *Der Blick in die Fremde: Das Ich und das Andere in der Literatur* (Edition Patmos, 3), Tübingen–Basle, Francke, vi + 450 pp., includes Büchner and Nietzsche among the authors discussed.

Hartmut Steinecke, *Unterhaltsamkeit und Artistik: Neue Schreibarten in der deutschen Literatur von Hoffman bis Heine* (PSQ, 149), 1998, 226 pp., is concerned with the process by which in the first half of the 19th c. — for the first time in the history of German literature — the gulf was bridged between popular literature which was written as 'entertainment', and 'artistic' writing. Steinecke sees Hoffmann and Heine as the two authors who contributed most to this breakthrough, and he devotes a complete chapter to each of them. The other three chapters of the book deal with innovations in the genres of the historical novel (Alexis), travel literature (Pückler-Muskau and Sealsfield), and literary criticism (the Young Germans). *Briefkultur im 19. Jahrhundert*, ed. Rainer Baasner, Tübingen, Niemeyer, 1999, vi + 279 pp., is a collection of essays analysing the correspondence of a number of important figures of the 19th c., drawn mainly from the literary world. No newly discovered letters are published, but there is much interesting and revealing comment on the different styles, conventions, preoccupations, and degrees of formality and informality of the various writers, and on the light that their correspondence throws on the high and low points of their careers. An introductory article by the editor deals with the history of letter-writing, bringing out particularly well its important psychological and social function in overcoming the isolation of intellectuals in the fragmented Germany of the 18th and much of the 19th cs. There then follow well-written and informative articles by leading experts on the individual authors. One misses the articles that could have been written on such major figures as Büchner, Hebbel, Storm, or Fontane, but there is much to interest the 19th-c. specialist in the articles on those who are included. For most users of the book the following essays are likely to be of particular value: G. Dürbeck, 'Die Gräfin und der Kardinal: der Briefwechsel Ida Hahn-Hahns mit Kardinal Diepenbrock' (37–54); M. Günter, ' "Dank und Dank: — ich wiederhole mich immer, nicht wahr?"': zum Briefwechsel zwischen Marie von Ebner-Eschenbach und Julius Rodenberg' (5–71); A. Jäger, ' "Ich habe für den Bettel höflich gedankt . . .": Conrad Ferdinand Meyers Briefe an Kollegen' (83–99); K. Koebe, ' ". . . dass eine unbedeutende Fremde es wage": Grillparzerverehrung in Briefen' (101–18); M. Ritzer, ' "Es liegt mein Stil in meinem persönlichen Wesen": Individualitätsbegriff und Kommunikationstheorie im Briefwechsel des Realismus am Beispiel Gottfried Kellers' (183–206); B. Spies, 'Ein bürgerlicher Groß-schriftsteller: Paul Heyses Briefwechsel' (207–38).

Eveline Goodman-Thau, 'Golem, Adam oder Antichrist: kabbalistische Hintergründe der Golemlegende in der jüdischen und deutschen Literatur des 19. Jahrhunderts', pp. 81–134 of *Kabbala und die Literatur der Romantik: Zwischen Magie und Trope* (CJ, 27), 1999, viii + 266 pp. W. Pape, '*Vom Gedächtnissmahl zum gräulichen Festmahl*: Kannibalismus als Metapher und Motiv bei Nestroy, Novalis und Kleist', *Rölleke Vol.*, 145–60. W. Wülfing, ' "Bagatell-Leben — Bagatell-Literatur": politisch-ästhetische Aspekte der deutschen *Provinzialismus*-Diskussion vor allem des 19. Jahrhunderts', *ChrA*, 7, 1998–99:69–75. H. Fischer, ' "Grenzpfahl mit Ordenskreuz": Überlegungen anlässlich unveröffentlichter Dokumente', *SGP*, 24, 1999:67–79. Alfons Huber and Karl Firsching, *Agnes Bernauer im Spiegel der Quellen, Chronisten, Historiker und Literaten vom 15. bis zum 20. Jahrhundert: Ein Quellen- und Lesebuch*, Attenkofer, Straubing, 1999, 223 pp., A. Steidele, 'Von keuschen Weibern und lüsternen Tribaden: der Diskurs über sexuelle Handlungen zwischen Frauen im 18. und 19. Jahrhundert', *FHL*, 35, 1999:5–34. H.-H. Ewers, 'Liebesgeschichten mit Hindernissen: männliche Adoleszenz in Märchendichtungen des ausgehenden und frühen 19. Jahrhunderts (Aufklärung, Romantik, und Biedermeier)', *Rölleke Vol.*, 1–16. A. B. Kilcher, ' "Was ist deutsch-jüdische Literatur?" Eine historische Diskursanalyse', *WB*, 45, 1999:485–517. A. Bunyan, ' "Notwendige Genossenschaft": perceptions of the boundary between fiction and historical writing in nineteenth-century Germany', *Sagarra Vol.*, 41–51. R. Paulin, ' "In so

vielseitiger Wechselwirkung": some problems in nineteenth-century
Anglo-German literary relations', *ib.*, 567–78. Eoin Bourke, ' "Dr
Mond schennt, dr Wabr flennt": German weavers in the poetry and
song of the first half of the nineteenth century', *ib.*, 129–43.
R. Selbmann, 'Unverhofft kommt oft: eine Leiche und die Folgen für
die Literaturgeschichte', *Euphorion*, 94 : 173–204, has some comment
on Hebbel, C. F. Meyer, and the minor Viennese writer Johann
Nepomuk Vogl.

LYRIC. Jürgen Schröder, *Deutschland als Gedicht: Über berühmte und
berüchtigte Gedichte aus fünf Jahrhunderten in fünfzehn Lektionen* (Reihe
Litterae, 74), Freiburg, Rombach, 441 pp., traces the history of what
would once have been called *Vaterlandslieder* from the 16th c. to the
present day. The topic is a fascinating one and Schröder's treatment
of it is masterly. As well as being a mine of interesting information
and a model of scholarly research and good judgement the book is
also hugely entertaining, for Schröder writes with much wit and irony
without ever compromising the fundamental seriousness of his
purpose. An early chapter deals with the composition, interpretation,
and impact of Hoffmann von Fallersleben's *Lied der Deutschen* (1841)
and the (unsuccessful) attempts made to replace it after it was banned
in 1945. The following chapters trace the variegated history of the
patriotic song through the centuries. Four chapters are devoted to
the 19th c., with discussion of — among others — Hölderlin, Arndt,
Körner, Rückert, Geibel, Herwegh, Freiligrath, and Nickolaus
Becker. The later chapters, dealing with the uses to which the genre
was put in the two World Wars, the Third Reich, and the bleak post-
1945 era, make much more chastening reading. Throughout the
book Schröder brings out well the elements of *Kitsch* that bedevil so
many of the songs and result in unconscious humour (in contrast to
the conscious humour of the parodies penned by the likes of Heine).
Attention is also drawn to the frequent admixture of religious ideas
and to the latent masochism and fear of sexual inadequacy. An
extensive bibliography and full indexes of names and titles round off
one of the outstanding publications of the year. Walter Hinck,
*Stationen der deutschen Lyrik: Von Luther bis in die Gegenwart. 100 Gedichte
mit Interpretationen*, Göttingen, Vandenhoek & Ruprecht, 240 pp.
Ballade und Historismus: Die Geschichtsballade des 19. Jahrhunderts, ed.
Winfried Woesler (Beihefte zum *Euphorion*, 38), Heidelberg, Winter,
317 pp., Lorie A. Vanchera, *Political Poetry in Periodicals and the Shaping
of German National Consciousness in the Nineteenth Century* (NASNCGL,
26), x + 290 pp., + CD-ROM, studies the role of political verse in
influencing German public opinion and shaping German national

consciousness during the period from the Rhine crisis of 1840 to the foundation of the Empire in 1871. The searchable CD-ROM makes available 950 poems, most of them otherwise difficult or impossible to obtain, collected from 81 newspapers and journals of the time. Petra Wanner-Meyer, *Quintett der Sinne: Synästhesie in der Lyrik des 19. Jahrhunderts*, Bielefeld, Aisthesis, 1998, 163 pp., is a 1997 Stuttgart dissertation. Peter von Matt, *Die verdächtige Pracht: Über Dichter und Gedichte*, Munich, Hanser, 1998, 338 pp., contains: 'Knalleffekt und Raffinesse' (118–21, on Heine's 'Belsazar'); 'Wünscht Heine sich den Tod? Die Unfassbarkeit des Ichs im lyrischen Text' (202–12, on 'Die Loreley'); 'Das doppelte Gesicht der Annette von Droste-Hülshoff: über das Gedicht "Die Schwestern"' (231–45). J. Schönert, '"Am Himmel fährt ein kalt Gewölk daher!" Zu Anspruch und Krise des Erfahrungs- und Deutungsmodells "Natur" in der deutschsprachigen Lyrik 1850–1890', *Sagarra Vol.*, 171–85. C. Vratz, 'Das Grabmotiv bei Ludwig Uhland und Gottfried Keller in der Tradition der englischen Gräberpoesie', *WW*, 50:17–32.

NARRATIVE. *Deutsche Erzähler des 19. Jahrhunderts: Von Heinrich von Kleist bis Adalbert Stifter*, ed. Rainer Hillenbrand (Bibliothek der Weltliteratur), Zurich, Manesse, 1999, 778 pp., contains among other texts Gotthelf's *Die schwarze Spinne*, Droste-Hülshoff's *Die Judenbuche*, Auerbach's *Toneli mit der gebissenen Wange*, Stifter's *Brigitta*, and Grillparzer's *Der arme Spielmann*. *Deutsche Erzähler des 19. Jahrhunderts: Von Gottfried Keller bis Gerhart Hauptmann*, ed. Christof Laumont (Bibliothek der Weltliteratur), Zurich, Manesse, 753 pp., follows the usual pattern of this attractive series; the texts of 12 Novellen of the second half of the 19th c. are followed by a 24–page *Nachwort*, ten pages of biographical notes on the various authors, and seven pages of explanatory notes on the stories. The laudable aim of the anthology is partly to make available less well known Novellen which are not otherwise readily accessible, though the editor also argues that selected texts are linked by similarities in narrative technique which reveal the increasingly critical attitude of the age. The 12 Novellen in the book are: Keller's *Pankraz der Schmoller*; François's *Die goldene Hochzeit*; Raabe's *Holunderblüte*; Halm's *Die Freundinnen*; Wildenbruch's *Brunhilde*; Meyer's *Die Richterin*; Ebner-Eschenbach's *Er lässt die Hand küssen*; Storm's *Ein Doppelgänger*; Hauptmann's *Bahnwärter Thiel*; Saar's *Schloss Kostenitz*; Isolde Kurz's *Schuster und Schneider*; and Heyse's *Die Nixe*. *Romantheorie: Texte vom Barock bis zur Gegenwart*, ed. Hartmut Steinecke et al. (UB, 18025), 1999, 577 pp., includes short extracts from the theoretical and critical writings of a dozen 19th-c. authors including Alexis, Laube, Prutz, Spielhagen, and Fontane. Matías

Martínez and Michael Scheffel, *Einführung in die Erzähltheorie (C. H. Beck Studium), Munich, Beck, 1999, 198 pp. *Reclams Romanlexikon: Deutschsprachige erzählende Literatur vom Mittelalter bis zur Gegenwart*, ed. Frank R. Max et al., Stuttgart, Reclam, 1183 pp., combines in one handy, bound volume the contents of the previously published set of five paperback volumes. Plot summaries are given of over 1,700 texts, though the meaning of the word *Roman* is stretched to cover 'alles, was nicht Drama und nicht Lyrik ist'. This means that room is found for some unexpected oddities such as Wackenroder/Tieck's *Herzensergießungen* and Nietzsche's *Also sprach Zarathustra*). No attempt is made to introduce any of the authors or place them in any kind of context, nor is any secondary literature listed; usually only the details of first publication of the work in book form are given, with occasional references to initial printings in journals. There is a full index of titles, though the useful indexes of authors which were a feature of the paperback version have gone, presumably because the authors now appear in alphabetical rather than chronological order. The undeniable strength of the book, and the reason why it will certainly be a commercial success, is that it offers at a very affordable price new and reliable plot summaries of a large number of canonical works. Florian Krobb, *Selbstdarstellungen: Untersuchungen zur deutsch-jüdischen Erzählliteratur im neunzehnten Jahrhundert*, Würzburg, Königshausen & Neumann, 206 pp., takes further the author's earlier work on the portrayal of aspects of Jewish life, especially ideas presented in his 1993 monograph *Die schöne Jüdin: Jüdische Frauengestalten in der deutschsprachigen Erzählliteratur vom 17. Jahrhundert zum Ersten Weltkrieg* (see *YWMLS*, 55:882). The book falls into three main parts, of which the first deals with historical novels written by German-speaking Jews in the 19th-c. tradition that owed its origin to the influence of Sir Walter Scott (Auerbach's *Spinoza* and *Dichter und Kaufmann*, Heine's *Der Rabbi von Bacherach*, Salomon Kohn's *Gawriel*). The second part is concerned with humorous and sentimental ghetto tales (Kompert's *Der Dorfgeher*, K. E. Franzos's *Judith Trachtenberg* and *Der Pojaz*). In the third part the focus is on the German-Jewish *Zeitroman* (Ludwig Jacobowski's *Werther, der Jude*, Schnitzler's *Der Weg ins Freie*, Theodor Herzl's *Altneuland*). What all the authors have in common is their preoccupation with the question of Jewish identity and the place of the Jew in German society at a time when assimilation was perceived by many as the way forward. The book is well written and highly readable; an index of names and titles rounds off a most interesting and valuable publication.

Jeffrey L. Sammons, *Ideology, Mimesis, Fantasy: Charles Sealsfield, Friedrich Gerstäcker, Karl May, and Other German Novelists of America* (UNCSGL, 121), 1998. xiv + 342 pp. Jerry Schuchalter, **Narratives of America and the Frontier in Nineteenth-Century German Literature* (NASNCGL, 25), x + 302 pp. *Konzepte der Moderne*, ed. Gerhart von Graevenitz (Germanistische Symposien: Berichtsbände, 20), Stuttgart, Metzler, 1999, vii + 694 pp., includes R. Simon, 'Gespenster des Realismus: Moderne-Konstellationen in den Spätwerken von Raabe, Stifter und C. F. Meyer' (202–33); W. Groddeck, 'Heinrich Heines *Reise von München nach Genua* als Paradigma einer "modernen" nachromantischen Poetologie' (350–66). Gustav Frank, *Krise und Experiment: Komplexe Erzähltexte im literarischen Umbruch des 19. Jahrhunderts*, Wiesbaden, Dt. Univ.-Verl., 1998, x + 590 pp., is a 1996 Passau dissertation which analyses in great detail some ten 'Romane des Nebeneinander' by Immermann, Gutzkow, Alexis, Hackländer, Oppermann, Willkomm, and May. Irving Massey, *Philo-Semitism in Nineteenth-Century German Literature* (CJ, 29), vi + 199 pp., includes discussions of Droste-Hülshoff, Grillparzer, Gutzkow, Hebbel, Freytag, Fontane, Raabe, Sacher-Masoch, Anzengruber, Ebner-Eschenbach, and Saar. Alfred D. White, *The One-Eyed Man: Social Reality in the German Novel 1848–1968* (German Linguistic and Cultural Studies, 5), Oxford–Berne, Lang, 189 pp., has some treatment of Fontane and Raabe, though most of the authors studied belong to the 20th c. Michael Boehringer, **The Telling Tactics of Narrative Strategies in Tieck, Kleist, Stifter and Storm* (NASNCGL, 24), 1999, x + 204 pp. Kerstin Wilhelms, *Literatur und Revolution: Schauplätze und Geschlechterdramaturgie in Romanen der 1848er Revolution* (Literatur — Kultur — Geschlecht. Große Reihe, 17), Cologne–Weimar, Böhlau, vi + 301 pp., is a 1999 Zurich dissertation that deals with a dozen lesser-known authors and texts. *Nation als Stereotyp: Fremdwahrnehmung und Identität in deutscher und französischer Literatur*, ed. Ruth Florack (STSL, 76), vi + 344 pp., publishes the papers given at a 1997 Stuttgart conference and has some treatment of Börne and Heine. Helmut Pfotenhauer, *Sprachbilder: Untersuchungen zur Literatur seit dem achtzehnten Jahrhundert*, Würzburg, Königshausen & Neumann, 260 pp., is a collection of essays that includes some treatment of Stifter, Keller, and Fontane. *The Novel in Anglo-German Context: Cultural Cross-Currents and Affinities. Papers from the Conference at the University of Leeds 15–17 September 1997*, ed. Susanne Stark (Internationale Forschungen zur allgemeinen und vergleichenden Literaturwissenschaft, 38), Amsterdam–Atlanta, Rodopi, x + 466 pp., deals with novels from the 18th to the 20th cs and contains: P. Hasubek, 'Das

Geheimnis des schwarzen Ritters oder Scott und Immermann'
(117–28); C. Ujma, 'England und die Engländer in Fanny Lewalds
Romanen und Reiseberichten' (145–56); S. Stark, 'Dickens in
German guise? Anglo-German cross-currents in the nineteenth-
century reception of Gustav Freytag's *Soll und Haben*' (157–72);
M. Andermatt, ' "Engelland" als Metapher: Walter Scott, Augustin
Thierry und das mittelalterliche England in Conrad Ferdinand
Meyers Novelle *Der Heilige*' (195–211); P. Bridgwater, 'Who's afraid
of Sidonia von Bork?' (213–28, on Wilhelm Meinhold's novel *Sidonie
von Bork, die Klosterhexe* of 1847–48). W. Hinderer, ' "Die Schornsteine
müssen gestürzt werden, denn sie verpesten die Luft": Diskurse über
Industrialisierung und Natur in deutschen Romanen des 19. Jahrhunderts', *Fest. Steinecke*, 99–115, has comment on Immermann, Robert
Prutz, and Spielhagen among others. H. Chambers, 'Humour and
irony in nineteenth-century women's narratives in German', *Sagarra
Vol.*, 389–401, focuses on the humorous treatment of relationships
between the sexes in the work of a range of writers from Ida Hahn-
Hahn to Ricarda Huch. M. Jones, 'Emancipation and Louise: female
perspectives on the events of 1848', *ib.*, 417–42, concentrates mainly
on Louise Aston and Louise Otto-Peters. H. Rasche, ' "Padd weint
und lacht zwar anders als wir [. . .]" ': Ottilie von Goethe, Ferdinand
Kühne und *Die Rebellen von Irland*', *ib.*, 547–57. H. P. Gabriel,
'Prescribing reality: the preface as a device of literary realism in
Auerbach, Keller and Stifter', *ColGer*, 32, 1999 : 325–44. M. Manczyk-
Krygiel, 'Freiheit und Zwang: berufstätige Frauen in der Prosa der
Marie von Ebner-Eschenbach, Bertha von Suttner und Marie
Eugenie delle Grazie', *GeW*, 118 : 223–41.

DRAMA.   Andrea Heinz, *Quantitative Spielplanforschung: Neue Möglichkeiten der Theatergeschichtsschreibung am Beispiel des Hoftheaters zu Coburg
und Gotha (1872–1918)* (Jenaer germanistische Forschungen, n.F., 4),
Heidelberg, Winter, 1999, 466 pp., in a 1996 Erlangen dissertation
analyses over 18,000 (!) performances of over 2,000 works, revealing
the popularity of many writers now forgotten and showing that the
canonical authors became firmly established in the theatre only
towards the end of the 19th c. *Komödientheorie: Texte und Kommentare.
Vom Barock bis zur Gegenwart*, ed. Ulrich Profitlich et al. (Rowohlts
Enzyklopädie, 55574), Hamburg, Rowohlt, 316 pp. Hedwig Meier,
**Die Schaubühne als musikalische Anstalt: Studien zur Geschichte und Theorie
der Schauspielmusik im 18. und 19. Jahrhundert sowie zu ausgewählten 'Faust'-
Kompositionen*, Bielefeld, Aisthesis, 1999, 182 pp., is a 1995 Munich
dissertation. *Die großen Komödien Europas*, ed. Franz N. Mennemeier
(MFDT, 22), 414 pp., contains: D. Kafitz, 'Visuelle Komik in Georg

Büchners *Leonce und Lena* (265–84); and H.-P. Bayerdörfer, 'Komödie und Posse: Johann Nestroy, *Der Zerrissene* (1844)' (285–314). J. Bertschik, ' "Kleider machen Leute" — Gerade auf dem Theater: zu einem vernachlässigten Gegenstand des Volksstücks', *ZDP*, 119:213–44, discusses the role of clothes and fashion in Gottfried Keller's story and in a wide range of dramas from the 19th c. to the present day. Among the authors discussed are Raimund, Nestroy, and Anzengruber.

MOVEMENTS AND PERIODS. *'Emancipation des Fleisches': Erotik und Sexualität in Vormärz*, ed. G. Frank et al. (Forum Vormärz Forschung, 5), Bielefeld, Aisthesis, 1999, 475 pp., contains 16 articles, some of which are concerned with social and historical aspects of the topic or with English literature. Most of them however deal directly with German literature of the 19th c. and break interesting new ground by introducing texts that have so far been little studied: G. Frank, *'Crime and Sex*: zur Vor- und Frühgeschichte der "Sexualität" ' (11–35, with some discussion of Nestroy and Fontane); I. Rippmann, 'Die ersäuften Liebhaber: zu einem Motiv zweier Werke aus dem Jahre 1835' (37–65, on Theodor Mundt's novel *Madonna* and Büchner's *Dantons Tod*); K. Wiedemann, 'Gefangene von Eros und Macht: Sexualität und weibliche Identität in George Sands *Indiana* (1832) und Verarbeitungen bei Ida Hahn-Hahn und Louise Aston (127–40); W. Lukas, ' "Weiblicher" Bürger vs. "männliche" Aristokratin": zum Konflikt der Geschlechter und der Stände in der Erzählliteratur des Vor- und Nachmärz' (223–61); S. Ledanff, ' "Rahel, Bettina, die Stieglitz": drei "Parzen" der jungdeutschen Emanzipationsdiskurse. Zur Problematik einer Theatralik des Unbewussten in weiblichen Textdenkmälern' (261–93, on R. Varnhagen v. Ense, B. v. Arnim, and Charlotte Stieglitz); M. Zens, ' "Siehst du die Maske nun, der ewiglich/Sich zu entkleiden ihr Natur versagt?": Politik und Erotik in Paul Heyses Versnovelle *Urica*' (295–315). S. Bierwirth, 'Die Erotik der "Gesundheitsliebe": Heine und seine Mouche' (317–26); A. Klär, 'Friedrich Hebbel und die Sexualität' (327–40, on *Judith*); S. P. Scheichl, 'Berichte aus einem "dissoluten Leben": Liebesaffären in Holteis Autobiografie' (314–54); M. Podewski, 'Der Gott in unseren Küssen: Anmerkungen zu Heines Konzeptualisierung einer "Emanzipation des Fleisches" in *Seraphine*' (35–67); R. Steegers, 'Eucharistie und Eros: zu Heines Reisebild *Die Stadt Lukka* (1831)' (369–402). *Vormärz — Nachmärz: Bruch oder Kontinuität. Vorträge des Symposions des Forum Vormärz Forschung e. V. vom 19. bis 21. November 1998 an der Universität Paderborn*, ed. Norbert O. Eke et al. (Vormärz-Studien, 5), Bielefeld, Aisthesis, 486 pp., has contributions from the fields of literature, history, theology, and philosophy. Among the articles by Germanists are: M. Hoffmann, 'Götter im Exil im Vor- und Nachmärz: Bruch oder Kontinuität. Zur Entwicklung eines Motivs bei Heinrich Heine' (169–83); J. Ferner, ' "O wer lesen könnte!' ': Heines geschichtsphilosophisches Denken im Kontext von Vor- und Nachmärz' (185–211); R. Werner, 'Flucht in die Geschichte: ästhetischer Historismus in Gedichten von Hermann Lingg, Heinrich Leuthold und Conrad Ferdinand Meyer' (299–330); W. Beutin, ' "Die plattdeutsche Literatur ist plötzlich wieder auf den Markt getreten und sogar mit einigem Lärm' ': zur Renaissance der niederdeutschen Dichtung im Nachmärz (Fritz Reuter — John Brinckmann — Klaus Groth)' (357–95); A. Ritter, 'Von "politischen Katarakten", zur "Windstille in den Köpfen", die Desavouierung "aller wahrhaft liberalen Prämissen" 1848–50 und Charles Sealsfields Publikations- wie Rezeptionsblockade' (397–421); D. Göttsche, 'Der Zeitroman der Revolution von 1848: Strukturmodelle des Erzählens und ihre zeitkritische Darstellungsfunktion im Nachmärz' (423–62). Rolf Parr, **Interdiskursive As-Sociation: Studien zu literarisch-kulturellen Gruppierungen zwischen Vormärz und Weimarer Republik* (STSL, 75), x + 460 pp., is a Dortmund *Habilitationsschrift*. Rainer Warning, **Die Phantasie der Realisten*, Munich, Fink, 1999, 249 pp., has some treatment of Fontane. H. Ridley, 'Vormärz: Systemtheorie und Literaturgeschichtsschreibung', *Sagarra Vol.*, 53–63. J. L. Sammons, 'Der Streit zwischen Ludwig Tieck und dem Jungen Deutschland: verpasste Möglichkeiten in einem Dialog der Tauben', *Fest. Kreutzer*, 343–52. G. Butzer, 'Programmatischer oder poetischer Realismus? Zur Bedeutung der Massenkommunikation für das Verständnis der deutschen Literatur im 19. Jahrhundert', *IASL*, 25:206–17. M. Birk, 'Die deutschsprachige Dramenproduktion am ständischen Theater in Ljubljana (Laibach) im Vormärz', *Sprachkunst*, 30, 1999:213–26.

LITERARY LIFE, JOURNALS, AND SOCIETY. P.-H. Kucher, 'Jacob Kaufmann (1814–1871)', *LK*, no. 337, 1999:103–09, sheds light on this forgotten minor Jewish writer who was for a time a contributor to *Die Grenzboten*. Ludwig Pietsch, *Wie ich Schriftsteller geworden bin: Der wunderliche Roman meines Lebens*, ed. Peter Goldammer, Berlin, Aufbau, 67 pp. Elke Blumenauer, *Journalismus zwischen Pressefreiheit und Zensur: Die Augsburger 'Allgemeine Zeitung' im Karlsbader System (1818–1848)* (Medien in Geschichte und Gegenwart, 14), Cologne–Weimar, Böhlau, vi + 222 pp. Paul Rowe, *A Mirror on the Rhine? The 'Nouvelle revue germanique', Strasbourg 1829–1837* (French Studies of the Eighteenth and Nineteenth Centuries, 2) Oxford–Berne, Lang, 340 pp., investigates the reception and evaluation of German culture in France as found in the *Nouvelle revue germanique* and its predecessors, the *Bibliothèque nationale* and the *Revue germanique*; the book contains a detailed analysis of a French translation of Heine's *Die Harzreise* that appeared in the journal. Johanna Bertsch, *Wider die Journaille: Aspekte der Verbindung von Sprach- und Pressekritik in der deutschsprachigen Literatur seit Mitte des 19. Jahrhunderts* (FLK, 69), 283 pp., in a Siegen dissertation examines the (mostly negative) views of a wide range of German writers to the language of the press; among those discussed are Freytag and Kürnberger. G. Oesterle, ' "Unter dem Strich": Skizze einer Kulturpolitik des Feuilletons im neunzehnten Jahrhundert', *Sagarra Vol.*, 229–50. T. Kindt and H.-H. Müller, 'Dilthey gegen Scherer: Geistesgeschichte contra Positivismus. Zur Revision eines wissenschaftlichen Stereotyps', *DVLG*, 74:685–709.

REGIONAL LITERATURE. *Literarisches Leben in Österreich 1848–1890*, ed. Klaus Amann et al. (Literaturgeschichte in Studien und Quellen, 1), Vienna–Cologne, Böhlau, 918 pp., is a major collection of some 30 articles, grouped thematically, that survey Austrian literature of the years between the 1848 Revolution and the *fin de siècle*, the literature of which has in the editors' opinion tended to overshadow the work of the earlier period. Much attention is paid to the social, historical, and cultural context of the second half of the 19th c. and the way in which it influenced the writers of the time. Particularly interesting here is the contribution of Peter Sprengel, 'Darwin oder Schopenhauer? Fortschrittspessimismus und Pessimismus-Kritik in der österreichischen Literatur (Anzengruber, Kürnberger, Sacher-Masoch, Hamerling)' (60–93). There are several essays on the state of the literary market-place, notably M. G. Hall's ' "Fromme Wünsche": zur Situation österreichischer Autoren und Buchhändler im 19. Jahrhundert' (171–99); and another group on the role of newspapers and the *Feuilleton*. In the group concerned with genres special mention should be made of J. Holzner et al., 'Der historische Roman in Österreich 1848–1890' (455–504), and J. Vogel, 'Das Wolterdrama: Dramaturgie zwischen Phidias und Michelangelo' (525–45, on new style in drama and theatrical performance in Vienna). There are also studies of individual authors including Sealsfield, Hebbel, Saar, Ebner-Eschenbach, and Kompert. An index of names aids access to the contents of this excellent volume. *Major Figures of Nineteenth-Century Austrian Literature*, ed. Donald Daviau, Riverside, Ariadne, 1998, v + 572 pp., contains a 128-page introductory chapter by the editor, followed by 15 chapters of between 25 and 40 pages on individual authors: K. Segar, 'Ludwig Anzengruber' (129–59); C. Steiner, 'Eduard von Bauernfeld' (160–86); F. Krobb,

'Jakob Julius David' (187–220); C. Steiner, 'Karl Emil Franzos' (221–51); R. C. Cowen, 'Franz Grillparzer' (252–77); I. H. Solbrig, 'Joseph von Hammer-Purgstall' (278–308); I. Spörk, 'Ferdinand Kürnberger' (309–30); J. M. Herz, 'Nikolaus Lenau' (331–53); M. L. Caputo-Mayr, 'Johann Nepomuk Nestroy' (354–86); R. Ferrel, 'Betty Paoli' (387–416); B. Becker-Cantarino, 'Caroline Pichler' (417–34); D. James, 'Ferdinand Raimund' (435–71). M. T. O'Pecko, 'Leopold von Sacher-Masoch' (472–94); K. J. R. Arndt, 'Charles Sealsfield' (495–522); G. H. Hertling, 'Adalbert Stifter' (523–61). R. Reichensperger, 'Zur Wiener Stadtsemiotik von Adalbert Stifter bis H. C. Artmann', pp. 159–85 of *Literatur als Text der Kultur*, ed. Moritz Csáky et al., Vienna, Passagen, 1999, 216 pp. T. Namowicz, 'Zur Literatur in Ostpreußen als einem Phänomen der "Grenzraumliteratur"', *SGP*, 24, 1999:81–89. C. Niem, 'Wilhelm Oertel von Horn: ein moralischer Erzähler und Kalendermacher vom Mittelrhein', *ZV*, 44, 1999:143–55. G. Häntzschel, 'Das literarische Helgoland: eine Insel zwischen Utopie und Apologie', *ib.*, 27–40. H. Lengauer, 'Kontinuität und Diskontinuität: zur Hermeneutik einer österreichischen Literaturgeschichte des neunzehnten Jahrhunderts', *ib.*, 65–76. B. Müller-Kampel, 'Gebannte Geschichte: Modelle historischer Selbstidentifikation am Beispiel österreichischer Geschichtsdichtungen aus dem neunzehnten Jahrhundert', *ib.*, 77–88, deals with some minor literary works that treat themes from Tyrolean history.

2. INDIVIDUAL AUTHORS

ALEXIS. *Willibald Alexis (1789–1871): Ein Autor des Vor- und Nachmärz*, ed. Wolfgang Beutin et al. (Vormärz-Studien, 4), Bielefeld, Aisthesis, 405 pp., publishes the papers given at a conference held in Arnstadt in 1998 to mark the bicentenary of A.'s birth. The aims of the conference were to raise the profile of an author whose reputation was high in his lifetime but who has been largely neglected since, to assess his achievement and his reputation, and to identify the main gaps in research. The editors note that a welcome quickening of scholarly interest in A. in the last third of the 20th c. has succeeded in correcting the earlier view of him as a nationalistic *Heimatdichter*. With some 20 articles of generally high quality the book breaks significant new ground in 19th-c. research, its only lack being that of an index. The individual articles are: P. Stein, 'W. A.: ein schwieriger Autor für die Vormärzforschung?' (15–28); G. Frank, 'Chancen und Gefahren eines Literatursystems im Wandel: W. As' literarische Optionen 1830–1840' (29–54); N. Eke, Die Kritiker in der Kritik: W. A., das

Junge Deutschland und As' autobiographische Fragmente *Erinnerungen aus meinem Leben*' (55–80); L. Tatlock, 'W. As' *Märchen aus der neuen Zeit*: poetisierter Alltag im industriellen Zeitalter' (81–98); S. Kramer, 'Darstellung und Funktion der Folter in Tiecks *Hexensabbat* und As' *Urban Grandier*' (99–118); J. Bark, '*Härings-Salat*: A. und Börne im Streit' (119–39); A. Berger, '"Der Häring wird ein Sansküllot"': zum politischen Engagement des Journalisten W. A.' (141–57); J. Hermand, '"Empor, empor! Zur Sonne, mein Adler!"': zur "fritzischen" Gesinnung im *Cabanis*-Roman von W. A.' (159–76); W. Beutin, 'Melpomenes Dolch und Klios noch schärferer Griffel; die brandenburg-preußischen ("vaterländischen") Romane von W. A.' (177–94); B. Potthast, 'Märkische Geschichte als unvollendete Heilsgeschichte: eine neue Interpretation von W. As' historischem Roman *Der falsche Woldemar* (1842)' (195–215); A. Sroka, 'Das Bild der Reformation in As' Roman *Der Werwolf*' (217–31); H.-W. Jäger, 'A. als Reiseschriftsteller: seine *Herbstreise durch Scandinavien*' (233–46); A. Ruiz, 'Das Bild Napoleons in W. As' Jugenderinnerungen und Reiseberichten über Frankreich (bis 1829)' (247–73); J. Hein, '"Wien [. . .] ist wie ein Spinngewebe"': W. As' *Wiener Bilder* (1833)' (275–90); J. Dvořák, 'Poesie und Politik im Vormärz im Spiegel der *Wiener Bilder* des W. A.' (291–312); R. Seegers, 'Bilder, Schattenrisse, Reisebilder: W. As' süddeutsche Reiseschilderungen und das Werk Heinrich Heines' (313–30); M. Zens, '"Seine Verdienste sind nicht genug gewürdigt"': W. A. als Kanonproblem' (331–57); T. Neumann, 'W. A.: nationale Rezeptionsstrategien zu Beginn des 20. Jahrhunderts. Eine Werkausgabe bei Hesse und Becker in Leipzig' (359–69); J. Dittrich, 'W. A. und seine Jahre in Arnstadt (1851–71)' (371–85); M. Gärtner, 'Der W.-A. Bund' (387–97); C. Käsgen and M. N. Lorenz, 'Auswahl-Bibliographie zu W. A.' (399–405). M. Niehaus, 'Vaterländische probleme: W. A.', *ZGer*, 10:521–35, is concerned with the fluid conception of patriotism in A.'s novels.

AUERBACH. H. Ferstenberg, 'German-Jewish creative identity in the age of Lessing and beyond: B. A.'s *Dichter und Kaufmann*', *Focus on Literature*, 5, 1998:1–11. W. Martens, '"Zufriedenheit mit seinem Zustande"': Zu B. As Erzählung *Gellert's letzte Weihnachten* (1857)', *Sagarra Vol.* 117–27.

BACHOFEN. J. Bertschik, 'Marie Luise Kaschnitz' *Elissa* (1937) und J. J. Bachofens *Mutterrecht* (1861): eine Wahlverwandtschaft? Zum Mutterkult im "Dritten Reich"', *Fest. Denkler*, 107–18.

BECHSTEIN, LUDWIG. L. B., *Sämtliche Märchen*, ed. Walter Scherf, Düsseldorf, Artemis & Winkler, 1999, 872 pp., is an annotated edition of the 'Ausgabe letzter Hand' of 1845 with 187 illustrations by Ludwig Richter.

BIRCH-PFEIFFER. Birgit Pargner, '*Zwischen Tränen und Kommerz: Das Rührtheater Charlotte Birch-Pfeiffers (1800–1868) in seiner künstlerischen und kommerziellen Verwertung. Quellenforschung am Handschriften-Nachlass*, Bielefeld, Aisthesis, 1999, 512 pp., is a 1998 Munich dissertation. Pargner is also the author of *Charlotte Birch-Pfeiffer: Eine Frau beherrscht die Bühne. Eine Ausstellung im Deutschen Theater-Museum vom 19. November 1999 bis zum 20. Februar 2000*, Bielefeld, Aisthesis, 1999, 191 pp.

BÖRNE. W. Jaspers, ' "Goethe ist der gereimte Knecht, wie Hegel der ungereimte": die deutschen Mandarine und L. Bs "Judenschmerz" ', *Menora*, 10, 1999:155–84.

BÜCHNER. *Erläuterungen und Dokumente: Georg Büchner, Woyzeck*, ed. Burghard Dedner (UB, 16013), 325 pp. Michael Will, **'Autopsie' und 'reproduktive Phantasie': Quellenstudien zu Georg Büchners Erzählung 'Lenz'*, 2 vols (Ep, 254), 350, 200 pp., is a 1998 Würzburg dissertation. Wendy Wagner, *Georg Büchners Religionsunterricht 1821–1831: Christlich-Protestantische Wurzeln sozialrevolutionären Engagements* (SMGL, 93), 1999, 292 pp., examines the impact of B.'s religious education on his writings, especially *Der Hessische Landbote* and *Lenz*. *Büchner-Jb.*, 9, 1995–99[2000], is extremely long at 800 pp. and contains a number of very abstruse contributions that are likely to be of interest only to committed B. specialists. The articles most likely to interest the majority of readers are: S. Lehmann, 'Christian Garve: eine unbekannte Quelle zu Bs 'Kato'-Rede' (7–32); T. M. Mayer, 'G. Bs Situation im Elternhaus und der Anlass seiner Flucht aus Darmstadt Anfang März 1835' (33–92); T. Teroaka, 'Skepsis und Revolte als Grundzug von *Nero* und *Dantons Tod*: zur thematisch-motivischen Affinität der Dramen Gutzkows und Bs' (155–72); T. M. Mayer, 'Zur Datierung von G. Bs philosophischen Skripten und *Woyzeck* H3,1' (281–329). Huimin Chen, **Inversion of Revolutionary Ideas: A Study of the Tragic Essence of Georg Büchner's 'Dantons Tod', Ernst Toller's 'Masse Mensch', and Bertolt Brecht's 'Die Maßnahme'* (STML, 33), 1998, 113 pp. Elisabetta Niccolini, **Der Spaziergang des Schriftstellers: 'Lenz' von Georg Büchner, 'Der Spaziergang' von Robert Walser, 'Gehen' von Thomas Bernhard* (M & P Schriftenreihe für Wissenschaft und Forschung), Stuttgart–Weimar, Metzler, 242 pp., is a 1999 Berlin dissertation. F. Cercignani, 'G. B., la "conversazione sull'arte" e la prassi poetica', pp. 137–69 of *Studia theodisca*, ed. F. Milano (Critica letteraria), Milan, Minute, 1998, 278 pp. D. Steuer, ' "[...] aber das Mühlrad dreht sich als fort ohne Rast und Ruh": Bs Gegenwortkunst und der Satz von der Erhaltung der Schönheit', *Sagarra Vol.*, 365–76. E. de Angelis,

'Über die Handschriften des *Woyzeck*', *Fest. Kreutzer*, 353–62. D. Müller Niebala, ' "Das Auge [. . .] ruht mit Wohlgefallen auf so schönen Stellen" ': G. Bs Nerven-Lektüren', *WB*, 46:325–45. D. Peyrache-Laborgne, 'L'Éros contre la guillotine? Le langage de la sexualité dans *La Mort de Danton*', *EG*, 55:719–35. M. Hoffmann, 'Das Drama des Verrats: geschichtlicher Auftrag und Eigensinn des Einzelnen bei Heiner Müller und Georg Büchner', *WB*, 46:89–104. D. Martin, 'Woyzeck vor B.: Karl Herlosssohns unbekannte poetische Verarbeitung des historischen Falls', *JDSG*, 44:118–35. G. Rings, 'G. Bs *Leonce und Lena*: ein Exemplum subversiver Kunst in einer spätabsolutistischen Gesellschaft', *GN*, 31:113–34.

BURCKHARDT. Christine Tauber, *Jacob Burckhardts 'Cicerone': Eine Aufgabe zum Genießen* (RVVig, 13), viii + 314 pp., is a 1997 Bonn dissertation which investigates the indebtedness of B.'s aesthetic judgement, and in particular his concept of 'Kunst nach Aufgaben', to his experience of Italy. G. Merlio, 'Burckhardt éducateur', *EG*, 55:203–19, is concerned with B.'s conception of history. J. Grosse, 'Die letzte Stunde: über eine Lebens- und Weltgeschichtsmetapher bei J. B. und Wilhelm Dilthey', *DVLG*, 74:654–84. Id., 'J. B. liest La Rochefoucauld und schreibt Albert Brenner', *WB*, 46:89–104.

BUSCH. Reiner Rühle, *'Böse Kinder': Kommentierte Bibliographie von Struwwelpetriaden und Max-und-Moritziaden mit biographischen Daten zu Verfassern und Illustratoren*, Osnabrück, Wenner, 1999, 735 pp. G. Albus, 'Warum lachen eigentlich die Leutchen?', *Fest. Richter*, 257–64. A. Stillmark, 'W. B.: The reductive satirist', *Sagarra Vol.*, 251–63. E. Sagarra, 'Der neue krumme Teufel der Kulturkampfzeit: der Jesuit *Pater Filucius* von W. B. im Zeitkontext', *ZGB*, Beiheft 5, 1999:119–29. Y. Usami, 'Über *Der Heilige Antonius von Padua* von W. B.', *DB*, Sondernummer 43, 1999:77–105 (Japanese with German summary). C. Aigner, 'Der erste Futurist: W. B.', *Morgen*, 23, 1999:24–26. H. J. Neyer, 'Das Testament von W. B.', *Satire*, 1999:49–50.

DROSTE-HÜLSHOFF. A. v. D.-H., *Historisch-kritische Ausgabe. Werke, Briefwechsel*, ed. Winfried Woesler, Tübingen, Niemeyer, has been completed with the appearance of vol. vi.2, *Dramatische Versuche. Dokumentation*, ed. E. Blakert, vi + 263–730 pp., and vol. xii.2, *Briefe an die Droste 1841–48. Kommentar*, ed. E. Blakert, xvi + 273–1129 pp. W. Salmen, ' "Alte Minnelieder und Volksgesänge" im Werk der A. v. D.-H.', *Fest. Moser*, 435–46. R. Nutt-Kofoth, 'Von Fettflecken und anderen Zufälligkeiten des Manuskriptzustandes: zu einer Ursache der Exzeptionalität von A. v. D.-H.s "Haidebild", "Die Steppe" ', Vliet, *Edition*, 179–89. W. Woesler, 'Die Droste und Langewiesche, der Barmer Verleger des *Malerischen und romantischen Westphalens*', *Rölleke Vol.*, 123–43. R. Robertson, 'Faith and fossils: A. v. D.-H.'s poem "Die Mergelgrube"', *Sagarra Vol.*, 345–54. *WWAG*, 10, 1998, is devoted entirely to D.-H. and contains: H. Kraft, 'Erklärungsbilder, Wunschbilder: über A. v. D.-H.' (5–27); P. Howe, '*Ledwina* und *Bei uns zu Lande auf dem Lande*: two unfinished texts by A. v. D.-H.' (29–59); J. Guthrie, 'From Samaratin to criminal: refractions of Schiller in D.-H.'s ballads' (61–92); S. Colvin, ' "Schade wär's/auch um so manches herrliche Talent": D. H's "dramatische Versuche" ' (93–116). H. Fricke, 'Verschleierung der Struktur und Auflösung der Person: nochmals zu A. v. D.-H.s *Judenbuche*', *ColGer*, 32, 1999:309–24. H. Kraft, 'Erklärungsbilder, Wunschbilder: über A. v. D.-H.', *AUMLA*, 94:19–34, has some (rather thin) comment on the poems and the drama *Perdu*.

EBNER-ESCHENBACH. I. Surynt, **Erzählte Weiblichkeit bei Marie von Ebner-Eschenbach*, Opole U.P., 1998, 222 pp. A. Zsigmond, 'Das Menschenbild in M. v. E.-Es Novellen, *Jb. Der ungarischen Germanistik*, 1998:163–73. D. M. Klostermaier, ' "Not recommended for Catholic libraries": M. v. E.-E. and the turn-of-the-century Catholic revival movement', *GLL*, 53:162–77. C. Anton, 'M. v. E.-E. und die Realismusdebatte: Schreiben als Auseinandersetzung mit den Kunstansichten ihrer Zeit', *MAL*, 33:1–15, focuses primarily on the Novelle *Ein Spätgeborener* of 1874–75.

FONTANE. T. F., *Große Brandenburger Ausgabe*, ed. Gotthard Erler, Berlin, Aufbau, is proceeding apace with *Das erzählerische Werk* and has added vol. 9, *Cécile*, ed. Hans J. Funke et al., 213 pp.; and vol. 11, *Stine*, ed. C. Hehle, 213 pp. T. F., *Der Stechlin: Roman. Kritische Ausgabe* (Edition Text, 1), Frankfurt, Stroemfeld, 1998, 404 pp., reproduces the text of the first book edition of October 1898, authorized by F. himself, and all the variant readings to be found in the two earlier serialized printings that appeared during his lifetime in *Über Land und Meer*. A clear picture thus emerges of the subtle alterations that the text underwent at successive stages. T. F., *Jenseit des Tweed: Bilder und Briefe aus Schottland*, ed. Gotthard Erler et al. (ATV, 5286), 1999, 313 pp. T. F., *Aus den Tagen der Okkupation: Eine Osterreise durch Nordfrankreich und Elsass-Lothringen 1871*, ed. Gotthard Erler (ATV, 5279), 404 pp. T. F., '*Wie man in Berlin so lebt*': *Beobachtngen und Betrachtungen aus der Hauptstadt*, ed. Gotthard Erler, Berlin, Aufbau, 224 pp., prints extracts from F.'s letters, novels, and autobiographical writings.

Fontane-Handbuch, ed. Christian Grawe et al., Tübingen, Kröner, xxiv + 1055 pp., is an impressive work by an international team of

22 leading F.-scholars whose challenging aim is to condense the sum of our present knowledge of F. into the pages of one (albeit hefty) compendium. The book is divided into four main sections dealing with his life and times; his literary and cultural context and his aesthetic principles; his published work in all its aspects (novels, lyric poetry, autobiography, journalism, travel books, war writings, theatre criticism); and his influence and reception in the 20th c. Each of these main sections is in turn helpfully divided into short subsections ('Fs Verlags- und Verlegerbeziehungen', 'F. und Heyse', 'F. und die bildende Kunst') that can be read as free-standing contributions complete in themselves. Many of the subsections are concluded with specialized bibliographical references. Full indexes of names and works provide ready access to the contents of an excellent book that is certain to be an indispensable resource for research on F. for many years to come. *Cultural Codes in Flux: New Approaches to Theodor Fontane*, ed. Marion Doebeling (SGLLC), 1999, xxii + 180 pp., contains a 13–page introduction by the editor, followed by eight essays by different contributors. The general aim of the book is to challenge the alleged 'objectivity' of F.'s Realist portrayal of 19th-c. Prussian society and to uncover the underlying truth which becomes apparent precisely when cultural and social conventions break down. F.'s novels are thus held to function in two ways, both as works of fiction and as documents that interpret aspects of Prussian history. For the present reviewer the most illuminating contributions are: R. Holt, 'History as trauma: the absent ground of meaning in *Irrungen, Wirrungen*' (99–115); and W. Goetschel, 'Causerie: on the function of dialogue in *Der Stechlin*' (116–35). The other articles, all of which offer something worth saying, are: H. Turk, 'The order of appearance and validation: Classicism in F.'s society novel *Schach von Wuthenow*' (1–25); M. Doebeling, 'On the theory of the essay and F.'s England essays as modernist signature' (26–37); E. Hannemann, 'Body and nobility: the interrelationship between social position and bodily condition in *Stine*' (38–50); S. Shostak, 'The trauma of separation: public and private realms in *Effi Briest*' (51–67); T. Lang, '*Cécile*: reading a fatal interpretation' (68–98); S. Cramer, '*Grete Minde*: structures of societal disturbance' (136–59). Peter Hasubek, '. . . *wer am meisten red't, ist der reinste Mensch': Das Gespräch in Theodor Fontanes Roman 'Der Stechlin'* (PSQ, 152), 1998, 240 pp., begins with a lengthy *Forschungsbericht* on the first 100 years' research on the novel (9–60). This is followed by a short theoretical chapter on the poetological problems of dialogue, and a rather longer one on the history of dialogue on the German novel. The heart of the book is the fourth

chapter (103–211) where various aspects of the dialogue in *Der Stechlin* are analysed in detail ('Konversation, Plaudern, Geselligkeit', 'Zur Form und Funktion des Streitgesprächs im *Stechlin*', 'Domestikengespräch und Verwandtes'). Walter Jens, *Wer am besten redet, ist der reinste Mensch: Über Fontane*, Weimar, Hermann Böhlaus Nachfolger, v + 126 pp., is a popularizing book containing four chapters: 'Handwerksmeister und Sprachkünstler: Portrait eines homme de lettres' (1–22); 'Immortal William: über die Wallfahrt Fs zu Shakespeare' (23–50); 'Ein ernster Christenmensch: Predigt über F.' (73–86); 'Wer am meisten red't, ist der reinst Mensch: das hohe Lied der Unterhaltlichkeit' (87–116). Gordon A. Craig, *Theodor Fontane: Literature and History in the Bismarck Reich*, NY, OUP, 1999, xiii + 232 pp. Hiltrud Bontrup, *'. . . auch nur ein Bild': Krankheit und Tod bei Theodor Fontane*, Hamburg–Berlin, Argument, 206 pp., is particularly concerned with *Schach von Wuthenow* and *L'Adultera*.

Theodor Fontane: Am Ende des Jahrhunderts: Internationales Symposium des Theodor-Fontane-Archivs zum 100. Todestag Theodor Fontanes 13.–17. September 1998 in Potsdam, ed. Hanna Delf von Wolzogen et al., 3 vols, Würzburg, Königshausen & Neumann, 324, 261, 322 pp., is one of this year's most important publications. For ease of reference the articles in each volume are grouped thematically under three or four headings (*Der Preuße, Das Natinale, Frau, Großstadt*). Vol. 1 contains: 'G. Konrád, 'Bericht über eine Begegnung von F. und Petöfi' (15–18); H. Fischer, 'Wendepunkte: der politische F. 1848 bis 1888' (21–33); W. Rieck, 'Preußens Königshaus im Urteil Fs' (35–50); H. Ester, 'F. und die preußischen Diener des Herrn: Geistlichkeit und Kirche von *Vor dem Sturm* bis zum *Stechlin*' (51–60); P. Sprengel, ' "Nach Canossa gehen wir nicht!" Kulturkampfmotive in Fs *Cécile*' (61–71); P.-P. Sagave, 'Sozialdemokratisches Gedankengut in Fs späten Romanen' (73–80); W. Wülfing, ' "Wasser auf die Mühlen der Sozialdemokratie": zur politischen Bildlichkeit T. Fs' (81–96); R. Berbig, 'Die Mission des Nordlandsmenschen: T. F. in der "Nord-Süd"-Konstellation Mitte des 19. Jahrhunderts' (97–112); D. Storch, ' ". . . unter chinesischem Drachen . . . Da schlägt man sich jetzt herum": F., der ferne Osten und die Anfänge der deutschen Weltpolitik' (113–28); H. D. Zimmermann, 'Was der Erzähler verschweigt: zur politischen Konzeption von *Der Stechlin*' (129–42); B. Witte, 'Ein preussisches Wintermärchen: T. Fs erster Roman *Vor dem Sturm*' (143–55); W. Benz, 'Anitisemitismus als Zeitströmung am Ende des Jahrhunderts' (157–68); H. O. Horch, 'Von Cohn zu Isidor: jüdische Namen und antijüdische Namenspolitik bei T. F.' (169–81); H. H. Remak, 'F. und der jüdische Kultureinfluss in Deutschland: Symbiose und Kontrabiose' (183–95); B. Balzer, ' "Zugegeben, dass es besser wäre, sie fehlten, oder wären anders, wie sie sind'': der selbstverständliche Antisemitismus Fs' (197–209); R. Parr, ' "Der Deutsche, wenn er nicht besoffen ist, ist ein ungeselliges, langweiliges und furchtbar eingebildetes Biest'': Fs Sicht der europäischen Nationalstereotypen' (211–26); G. Loster-Schneider, ' "Die Ordnung der Dinge ist inzwischen durch keine übergeschäftige Hand gestört worden'': zur Interaktion von National- und Geschlechterstereotypen in T. Fs *Kriegsgefangen*' (227–39); H. Aust, ' ". . . und das lachen verging mir'': T. F. und der Nationalismus' (241–54); M. Ossowski, 'Fragwürdige Identität? Zur national-territorialen Bestimmung der Figuren aus dem deutsch-slawischen Kulturgrenzraum in Fs Spätwerk' (265–67); R. Dieterle, 'F. und Böcklin: eine Recherche' (269–83); P. Paret, 'F. und Liebermann: Versuch eines Vergleichs' (285–92). Vol. 2 contains: B. Naumann, 'Schwatzhaftigkeit: Formen der Rede in späten Romanen Fs' (15–26); E. Czucka, 'Faktizität und Sprachskepsis: Fs *Stechlin* und die Sprachkritik der Jahrhundertwende' (27–39); D. Schmauks, 'Zeichen, die lügen — Zeichen, die ausplaudern: linguistische und semiotische Einsichten im Romanwerk T. Fs' (41–54); L. Grevel, 'Die "sanfte Vergewaltigung" im Wort: der Held im Kräftespiel zwischen Wort und Handlung in Fs Erzählung *Schach von Wuthenow*' (55–67); A. Gnam, 'Die prekäre Wechselbeziehung von Körper und Sprache in den Romanen T. Fs' (69–79); R. Böschenstein, 'Ich-Konzeptionen im Horizont von Sinnsuche: zu Fs späten Prosafragmenten' (81–95); B. Plett, 'Der Platz, an den man gestellt ist: ein Topos Fs und seine bewusstseinsgeschichtliche Topographie' (97–107); K. Briegleb, 'Fs Elementargeist: die Preußin Melanie. Eine Vorstudie zum *Stechlin*' (109–22); U. Dethloff, 'Emma Bovary und Effi Briest: Überlegungen zur Entwicklung des Weiblichkeitsbildes in der Moderne' (123–40); P. Kuhnau, 'Nervöse Männer — Moderne Helden? Zur Symptomatik des Geschlechterwandels bei F.' (135–45); W. Wende, ' "Es gibt . . . viele Leben, die keine sind . . .'': Effi Briest und Baron von Innstetten im Spannungsfeld zwischen gesellschaftlichen Verhaltensmaximen und privatem Glücksanspruch' (147–60); C. Liebrand, 'Geschlechterkonfigurationen in Fs *Unwiederbringlich*' (161–71); E. Ziegler, 'Die Zukunft der Melusinen: Weiblichkeitskonstruktion in Fs Spätwerk' (173–85); M. Masanetz, ' "Die Frauen bestimmen doch schließlich alles'' oder die Vorbildlichkeit des Bienenstaates: vom (un)heimlichen Niedergang männlicher Macht und der Macht der Liebe im *Stechlin*' (187–200); H. Schmiedt, 'Die Ehe im historischen Kontext: zur Erzählweise in *Effi Briest*' (201–08); G. Erler, ' "Die Zuneigung ist etwas Rätselvolles'': der

Fontanesche Ehebriefwechsel' (209–15); G. Wittig-Davis, ' "Von den andren ... hat man doch mehr ..."? Kunst und Wirklichkeit, Weiblichkeit und Fremdsein in T. Fs *Mathilde Möhring* als Roman und Film' (217–36). Vol. 3 contains: S. Thielking, 'Denkmal, Turm, Grab und Gruft: Orte der "Memoria" und des "Kultur-Bildlichen" bei T. F.' (15–27); P. C. Pfeiffer, 'Moltkes Hand: zur Darstellung von Geschichte bei F.' (29–37); M. Ritzer, ' "Je freier der Mensch, desto nötiger der Hokuspokus": Natur und Norm bei F.' (39–56); E. Szabó, ' "Vergessen Sie das Geschehene, vergessen Sie mich": die Unlöschbarkeit der Zeichen in Fs *Effi Briest* (57–64); C. Hehle, 'Unterweltsfahrten: Reisen als Erfahrung des Versagens im Erzählwerk Fs' (65–76); K. Lange, 'Merkwürdige Geschichten: Anekdoten in Fs Kindheitsautobiographie *Meine Kinderjahre*, Geschichten und Geschichte' (77–86); H. Nürnberger, 'Epigrammatik und Spruchpoesie: Grillparzer und F. blicken auf ihr Jahrhundert' (87–103); E. Sagarra, 'Kommunikationsrevolution und Bewusstseinsänderung: zu einem unterschwelligen Thema bei T. F.' (105–18); K. Stüssel, ' "Autodidakten übertreiben immer": autodidaktisches Wissen und Autodidaktenhabitus im Werk T. Fs' (119–35); M. Lowsky, ' "Der Bahnoff ist der Ararat": Abstraktion, Modernität und mathematischer Geist in T. Fs Erzählung *Die Poggenpuhls*' (137–47); W. Hettche, 'Vom Wanderer zum Flaneur: Formen der Großstadt-Darstellung in Fs Prosa' (149–60); K. R. Scherpe, 'Ort oder Raum? Fs literarische Topographie' (161–69); O. Gutjahr, 'Kultur der Ungleichzeitigkeit: T. Fs Berlin-Romane im Kontext der literarischen Moderne' (171–88); M. Andermatt, ' "Es rauscht immer, aber es ist kein richtiges Leben": zur Topographie des Fremden in Fs *Effi Briest* (189–99); S. Ledanff, 'Das Bild der Metropole: Berlin und Paris im Gesellschaftsroman T. Fs und in der *Éducation sentimentale* Gustave Flauberts' (201–13); H. Chambers, 'Großstädter in der Provinz: Topographie bei T. F. und Joseph Roth' (215–25); S. Schönborn, 'Das Erbe der Melusine: der literarische Dialiog zwischen Uwe Johnsons *Jahrestagen* und T. Fs *Schach von Wuthenow*' (227–41); S. Oswalt, ' "Man liebt die Autoren, die einem adäquat sind": Kurt Tucholskys Blick auf T. F.' (243–51); M. Scheffel, ' "Der Weg ins Frei": Figuren der Moderne bei T. F. und Arthur Schnitzler' (254–65); C. Grawe, ' "Une saison en enfer": die erste Saison der Freien Bühne und Fs Kritiken' (267–83); W. A. Niemirowski, 'T. F. und die Zeitschrift *Pan*' (285–96).

Theodorus victor: Theodor Fontane, der Schriftsteller des 20. Jahrhunderts. Eine Sammlung von Beiträgen, ed. Roland Berbig (Literatur–Sprache–Region, 3), Frankfurt–Berlin, Lang, 1999, 275 pp., contains:

P. Wruck, 'Bildungsmisere? Die atypische literarische Sozialisation des Schriftstellers T. F. in ihren bildungsgeschichtlichen Zusammenhängen' (15–29); H. Aust, 'F. Lektürewerk: eine einflussgeschichtliche Skizze' (31–50); G. de Bruyn, 'Märkische Musenhöfe oder Anmerkungen zu einem von F. nicht ausgeführten Kapitel der *Wanderungen durch die Mark Brandenburg*' (51–66); H. Fischer, ' "Ein etablierte[r] deutsche[r] Schriftsteller"? F. in den siebziger Jahren des 19. Jahrhunderts' (67–97); R. Berbig, ' "aber zuletzt — . . . — schreibt man doch sich selber zu Liebe": mediale Textprozesse. T. Fs Romanerstling *Vor dem Sturm*' (99–120); E. Sagarra, 'Vorurteil im Fontaneschen Erzählwerk: zur Frage der falschen Optik in *Cécile*' (121–36); C. Hehle, ' "ich steh und falle mit Gieshübler": die Verführung der Effi Briest' (137–62); K. R. Scherpe, 'Allerlei F.: Erlebnisgesellschaft im F.-Roman' (163–78); N. Mecklenburg, 'Fs Erzählkunst der feinen Unterschiede' (179–201); R. Dieterle, 'Im Banne des Vaters: die Fontanesche Familientragödie' (203–20); C. Graw, ' "Mit 78 man ein unsicherer Passagier": T. Fs letztes Lebensjahr — an der Schwelle zum 20. Jahrhundert' (221–41); G. Erler, ' "Tüchtig gelobt und mäßig gekauft": gibt es noch Neues vom alten F.? Ein editionspraktischer Exkurs' (243–51); H. Nürnberger, ' "Theodorus victor": ein Schriftstellerleben' (253–73).

Theodor Fontane im literarischen Leben: Zeitungen und Zeitschriften, Verlage und Vereine, ed. Roland Berbig et al., Berlin–NY, de Gruyter, xiii + 498 pp., is one of this year's most important publications on F., and — as one would expect from this editor — of exemplary quality. Although it is concerned principally with F.'s relationship with a (surprisingly wide) range of newspapers (*Vossische Zeitung, Berliner Tageblatt*) and journals (*Literatur-Blatt des Deutschen Kunstblattes, Die Gartenlaube, Daheim*), it also has some 70 pages on his dealings with an assortment of publishers and a similar amount of space devoted to his involvement with a variety of literary clubs and institutions (*Tunnel über der Spree*, the Berlin branch of the *Deutsche Schillergesellschaft*). A series of indexes makes it easy to find even the most abstruse material with ease. *Fontane und die Fremde, Fontane und Europa*, ed. Konrad Ehlich, Würzburg, Königshausen & Neumann, 450 pp., Marion Villmar-Doebeling, *Theodor Fontane im Gegenlicht: Ein Beitrag zur Theorie des Essays und des Romans* (Ep, 177), 156 pp. Kirstin Breitenfellner, *Lavaters Schatten: Physiognomie und Charakter bei Ganghofer, Fontane und Döblin. Mit einem Exkurs über den Verbrecher als literarische Gestalt von Schiller bis Böll und einer systematischen Biographie zum Thema 'Physiognomie und Charakter'* (Artes liberales, 5), Dresden U.P., 1999, 275 pp., has comment on

Ganghofer's *Schloss Hubertus* and F.'s *Effi Briest*. Heide Rohse, **Unsichtbare Tränen: 'Effi Brest', 'Oblomow', 'Anton Reiser', 'Passion Christi'*. *Psychoanalytische Literaturinterpretationen zu Theodor Fontane, Iwan A. Gontscharow, Karl Philipp Moritz und zum Neuen Testament*, Würzburg, Königshausen & Neumann, 117 pp. H.-K. Jeong, **Dialogische Offenheit: Eine Studie zum Erzählwerk Theodor Fontanes* (Ep, 315), 256 pp., is a 1999 Wuppertal dissertation that views F. in the light of ideas of Habermas.

Ralf Harslem, *Thomas Mann und Theodor Fontane: Untersuchungen über den Einfluss Theodor Fontanes auf das erzählerische Frühwerk von Thomas Mann* (Heidelberger Beiträge zur deutschen Literatur, 7), Frankfurt–Berlin, Lang, 236 pp., in a 1999 Heidelberg dissertation examines F.'s influence with special reference to *Der kleine Herr Friedemann* and *Buddenbrooks*. *Literarisches Doppelportait Theodor Fontane / Fritz Mauthner*, ed. Uta Kutter (Schriften der Akademie für gesprochenes Wort, 4), Stuttgart, Verein der Freunde der Akad. für Gesprochenes Wort, 201 pp., contains: T. Kopfermann, ' "Aut. Aut. . . . denn was steht fest?" Ein nach-denkendes Vorwort zu einem denkwürdigen Doppelportrait' (5–15); G. de Bruyn, 'Altersbetrachtungen über den alten F.' (19–35); P. Michelsen, 'Nebensächliches: zu T. Fs *Stechlin*' (61–80); H. Nürnberger, 'F. und Mauthner' (81–105). *Erzählstrukturen II: Studien zur Literatur der Jahrhundertwende*, ed. Károly Csúri et al. (Acta Germanica, 10), Szeged, Jate, 1999, 174 pp., contains: M. Scheffel, ' "Der Weg ins Freie": Figuren der Moderne dei T. F. und Arthur Schnitzler' (7–18); E. Sándorfi, 'Memoria und Ekphrasis: die kryptisch-mythische Poetik der späten narrativen Texte von F.' (19–33); C. Hehle, 'Berlin, Borsig, Bismarck: zur Konstitution von Räumen in T. Fs *Stine*' (34–46); E. Szabó, 'In Geschichten verstrickt: zu Fs *Effi Briest* und Goethes *Die Wahlverwandtschaften*' (47–61).

Fontane-Blätter, 69, has: S. Dietzsch and K.-P. Möller, ' "Bitte helfen Sie": unbekannte Briefe T. Fs an Friedrich Wilhelm Holtze und ein Geburtstagsbrief des T. F.-Archivs an Prof. Dr Helmut Nürnberger' (10–38); C. Jantzen, 'Linguistische Betrachtungen zu ausgewählten *Unechten Korrespondenzen*: ein Beitrag zur Diskussion um T. Fs Autorschaft' (44–66); R. Selbmann, 'Trauerarbeit: zum literaturgeschichtlichen Ort von T. Fs Lyrik' (67–80); H. Gravenkamp, ' "Um zu sterben muss sich Hr. F. erst eine andere Krankheit anschaffen": neue Fakten zu Fs Krankheit von 1892' (81–98); P. Paret, 'F. und der nicht gegenwärtige Clausewitz' (124–37); P. Schaefer, ' "Der Dichter Fontane hier, der [. . .] von dem englischen Leben — sehr wenig versteht": eine anonyme Äußerung über F. in London und eine Vermutung zur Autorschaft' (160–62); K.-P. Möller and P. Schaefer, 'Auswahlbibliographie' (166–87). *Fontane-Blätter*, 70, has: C. Hehle,

'Überaus sensible Beziehungen: zehn unbekannte Briefe T. Fs an Carl Müller-Grote aus den Jahren 1885–1887' (10–31); K.-P. Möller, 'Die Verlagsverträge im T.-F.-Archiv: Teil 2' (32–66); Id., 'Rehabilitierung für die Ostrower? Ein unbekannter Brief Fs an H. Fr. Von Ossen (Hermione Schildberger)' (67–69); H. Stroszeck, 'Schwalben: ein Nachtrag zu Fs poetischer Avifauna' (76–92); C. Yun-Young, 'T. F. als Zeitgenosse der Moderne: die Problematik der Repräsentation' (93–107); M. Thuret, 'F. in Frankreich: Geistesverwandtschaft und Rezeption' (108–21); H. Fischer, 'Fs *Storch von Adebar* (miscellanea zoologica)' (142–45, on a novel fragment); G. Wolpert, 'Schwierigkeiten mit der kleinen Schwester: offene Fragen zur zweiten Auflage des Wanderungsbandes *Das Oderland*' (146–54); G. Erler, 'F. Rasierseife und die Nymphenburger Ausgabe' (155–58); W. Rasch, 'T. F. als Ibsen-Prophet' (159–60); K. E. Laage, 'Fs "Husumerei" und Gontscharows "Oblomowerei"' (161–65); P. Schaefer, 'Auswahlbibliographie' (168–80).

M. Thormann, ' "Im Kerker der Fremde": Aspekte von Fremdheit und Fremderfahrung in Fs England-Aufenthalten', *Fest. Richter*, 169–83. R. Finke, ' ". . . der Äquator läuft ihnen über den Bauch": Namen und Geschichten zu Afrika in Fs *Effi Briest* und anderswo', pp. 297–315 of *Romantik und Ästhetizismus: Festschrift für Paul Gerhard Klussmann*, ed. Bettina Gruber et al., Würzburg, Königshausen & Neumann, 1999, 343 pp. B. Plett, ' "Sie . . . mit einer Hinneigung zu Russland, ich zu England": die Russlandbilder T. Fs', pp. 566–98 of *Russen und Russland aus deutscher Sicht. 19./20. Jahrhundert. Von der Bismarckzeit bis zum Ersten Weltkrieg*, ed. Mechthild Keller (West-Östliche Spiegelungen, A 4), Munich, Fink, 1160 pp. B. Losch, 'Die Staatsauffassung T. Fs und seine Einstellung zur staatlichen Kirchenpolitik', pp. 172–98 of *Dem Staate, was des Staates — der Kirche, was der Kirche ist: Fest. für Joseph Listl zum 70. Geburtstag*, ed. Joseph Isensee, Berlin, Duncker & Humblot, 1999, xiv + 1115 pp. G. Erler, 'Der Briefwechsel zwischen Theodor und Emilie Fontane', *Sagarra Vol.*, 267–74. G. Martin, 'Tradition and Innovation: the portrayal of the servant figures in the narrative fiction of T. F.', *ib.*, 275–86. K. S. Guthke, 'Gideon ist nicht besser als Botho: gesellschaftlicher Wandel in Fs *Irrungen, Wirrungen*', *ib.*, 287–99. G. Neumann, 'Das Ritual der Mahlzeit und die realistische Literatur: ein Beitrag zu Fs Romankunst', *ib.*, 301–17, discusses primarily *Cécile*. G. Carr, 'Entgleisung und Dekonstruktion: T. Fs "Die Brück' am Tay" ', *ib.*, 319–33. C. Blod-Reigl, ' ". . . der Stimme meines Herzens rückhaltlos gehorchen . . ." : zum Sinnesdiskurs in T. Fs *Cécile*', *Fest. Walliczek*, 402–31. M. Swales, ' "Altersradikalismus" und Modernität: zur

Bedeutung von Fs Spätwerk', *Fest. Steinecke*, 117–24. G. Loster-Schneider, 'T. Fs *Wanderungen durch die Mark Brandenburg*: interkulturelle Identitätsenwürfe eines "in der Wolle gefärbten Preußen"', *Fest. Storck*, 232–55. Joachim Kaiser, *Von Wagner bis Walser: Neues zu Literatur und Musik*, Zurich, Pendo, 1999, 191 pp., has a chapter on 'Der Schriftsteller als Ehemann: T. und Emilie Fontanes Briefwechsel' (54–64). Philip Gaskell, *Landmarks in European Literature*, Edinburgh U.P., 1999, xii + 251 pp., has some discussion of Fontane. R. Muhs, 'T. F. und die Londoner deutsche Presse: mit einem unbekannten Brief des Dichters', *JDSG*, 44:31–61. C. Hehle, '. . . es ist nicht nötig, das die Stechline weiterleben, aber es lebe *Der Stechlin*': der Schluss von Fs letztem Roman im Spiegel der Handschriften', pp. 21–35 of *Theodor-Fontane-Archiv Potsdam, die Fontane-Sammlung Christian Andree* (Patrimonia, 142), Potsdam, T.-F.-Archiv, 1998, 84 pp., E. Heftrich, 'F. — zum Vergnügen gelesen', *Jb. der Bayerischen Akad. der Schönen Künste*, 12, 1998:211–28. H. V. Geppert, 'T. F., *Der Stechlin*', *Große Werke der Literatur*, 6, 1998–99[2000]:103–15. K. S. Calhoun, 'Alchemies of distraction: James's *Portrait of a Lady* and F.'s *Effi Briest*', *Arcadia*, 34, 1999:90–113. M. E. Brunner, '*Effi Briest* von T. F. als Schule des Sehens', *LiLi*, 29, 1999:143–53. A second article by Brunner on a related theme is 'Sehen und Erkennen in *Effi Briest*: ist Wahrnehmung "ein zu weites Feld"?', *Seminar*, 36:399–417. R. Köhne, 'Der Roman *Effi Briest* in Thomas Manns *Anzeige eines Fontane-Buchs*, '*Thomas-Mann-Jahrbuch*, 13:113–22. J. Kilian, ' "Alles Plauderei?" F's *Stechlin* im Blick der historischen Dialogforschung', *Muttersprache*, 109, 1999:338–57. K. R. Scherpe, 'Luogo o spazio? La topografia letteraria di F.', *Cultura tedesca*, 11, 1999:179–88. B. Losch and K. Kranen, 'Fs Kriminalgeschichten', *Neue juristische Wochenschrift*, 52, 1999:1913–19. I. Schroeder, 'Wagner als Chiffre für Sex bei F.', *Entwürfe für Literatur*, 5, 1999:89–92. J. Kałazny, 'Dichter auf der Reise durch Land und Geschichte: einige Bemerkungen zu Fs *Wanderungen durch das Land Brandenburg* und *Wanderungen durch Frankreich*', *SGP*, 1999:81–91. S. Becker, 'Aufbruch ins 20. Jahrhundert: T. Fs Roman *Mathilde Möhring*. Versuch einer Neubewertung', *ZGer*, n. F., 10:298–315. P. J. Bowman, 'T. F.'s *Cécile*: an allegory of reading', *GLL*, 53:17–36. L. Köhn, ' "Verweile doch": Fs *Der Stechlin* als Entgegnung auf Goethes *Faust*', *TeK*, 21, 1999:275–309. N. Mecklenburg, ' "Ums goldene Kalb sie tanzen und morden": philo- und antisemitische Gedichte des alten F.', *WW*, 50:358–81, argues that the world of *Germanistik* has consistently underestimated the measure of F.'s anti-Semitism. E. Herold, 'Die ersten zehn Jahre — die schwersten in der Ehe von Emilie und T. F.: was Briefe und

Tagebücher berichten', *Berliner Lesezeichen*, 8:11–21. K. Eh, ' "Dies ist das Niederdrückendste": T. F. — Moritz Lazarus. Eine tragisch endende Freundschaft', *ib.*, 22–36. R. Berbig, ' "Ich bedaure dann, dass [. . .] ich Euch nicht genug sein kann": Friedrich Eggers — Kunsthistoriker, Redakteur, Vereinsgründer und ein schwieriger Freund T. Fs', *ib.*, 37–52. G. Erler, 'Das stille Leben eines adligen Fräuleins', *ib.*, 53–62, discusses Mathilde von Rohr. M. Horlitz, 'Eltern, Kinder und Geschwister: wenig Bekanntes aus dem Familienleben der Fontanes', *ib.*, 63–74. J. Kleine, 'Friedrich Fontane: Verleger und Nachlassverwalter seines Vaters', *ib.*, 75–91. D. Ullrich, 'Die Fontanes und die Knochenhauers: Bekannte, Freunde, Helfer in der Not? Sprech- und Spielszenen nach Texten T. und Emilie Fontanes', *ib.*, 92–105. G. Schmidt, 'Auf Fs Spuren: zu Besuch in der Geburtsstadt des Dichters', *ib.*, 119–21. H. Fischer, 'F. und der preussische Adel', *Berliner Hefte zur Geschichte des literarischen Lebens*, 3:144–54. Id., ' "Gedichte — Soldatenlieder — Preußenlieder": wie Fs "Preußische Feldherren" volkstümlich wurden', *Jb. für brandenburgische Landesgeschichte*, 59, 1999:136–68. H. Ester, 'T. F. und der Berliner Roman', *DK*, 50:7–16.

FRANZOS. *Aus Anhalt und Thüringen*, ed. Herbert Weisshuhn (ATV, 6071), 377 pp. K. Wagner, 'Die Modernisierung eines Vorurteils: Assimilation als Mimicry im Zeitalter des Schauspielers. George Eliots *Daniel Deronda* und K. E. Fs *Der Pojaz*', *Sagarra Vol.*, 509–19. A. Glück, 'Der Dichter Galiziens: K. E. F. in einer Wiener Ausstellung', *Aus dem Antiquariat*, 1999:A 33–36. S. P. Scheichl, 'Ein umgekehrtes Toleranzedikt: K. E. Fs' *Juden von Barnow*', *Aschkenas*, 9, 1999:169–87.

FREILIGRATH. V. Giel, 'F. F. und Karl Immermann: Bilanz einer Dichterbeziehung', *Fest. Richter*, 117–40. E. Bourke, ' "Dass die Kunde nicht untergeht!": Pückler-Muskau and F. on the Irish tithe system', pp. 63–70 of *Deutsch-irische Verbindungen: Geschichte, Literatur, Übersetzung. Akten der 1. Limericker Konferenz für Deutsch-Irische Studien, 2.–4. Sept. 1997*, ed. Joachim Fischer et al. (Schriftenreihe Literaturwissenschaft, 42), Trier, WVT, 1998, 165 pp., is concerned with Pückler-Muskau's *Briefe eines Verstorbenen* and F.'s *Die irische Witwe*. K. Roessler, 'F. F. und die rheinischen Lyriker in der Revolution von 1848', pp. 228–30 of *Petitionen und Barrikaden: Rheinische Revolution 1848–49*, ed. Ingeborg Schnelling-Reinicke et al. (Veröffentlichungen der Staatlichen Archive des Landes Nordrhein-Westfalen. Reihe D, Ausstellungskataloge staatlicher Archive, 29), Münster, Asschendorff, 1998, xvi + 512 pp. H.-J. Schrader, ' "Wir sind das Volk": ein F.-Vers als Exempel für subversive Wirkungspotenzen von Poesie', *Fest.*

Denkler, 69–72. F. Vassen, 'Löwenritt und Tigersang: F. Fs und Georg Weerths Exotismus im Vor- und Nachmärz', *IJBAG*, 11–12: 197–223. See also under GRABBE.

FREYTAG. H. Scheible, 'G. F. als Germanist', pp. 241–58 of *Zur Geschichte und Problematik der Nationalphilologen in Europa: 150 Jahre Erste Germanistenversammlung in Frankfurt am Main (1846–1996)*, ed. Frank Fürbeth et al., Tübingen, Niemeyer, 1999, xiv + 997 pp. D. Haberland, 'Das gesuchte Buch: zu einem literarischen Motiv von G. F. bis Christoph Ransmayr', *Philobiblon*, 43, 1999: 107–20.

GLASSBRENNER. F. Wahrenburg, 'Poesie der Freiheit: Lieder des "norddeutschen Poeten" Adolf Glassbrenner', *Fest. Steinecke*, 61–80. G. Kreszynski, 'Ein Klassiker im Vormärz: G. liest Lichtenberg', *Die Horen*, 44, 1999: 179–91.

GOTTHELF. B. Rütte and A. Reber, **Jeremias Gotthelf und das Geld*, Berne, Bubenberg-Gesellschaft, 1998, 46 pp. W. Hahl, 'Götzen unter dem Hammer: J. Gs kulturkämpferische Burleske *Der Geltstag*', Sorg, *Gott*, 117–37.

GRABBE. *Grabbe-Jb.*, 17–18, 1998–99, has: G. von Essen, Übersetzung und Kolonialismus: Germanen- und Römerbild in Gs *Hermannsschlacht* (111–63); W. Struck, 'Die letzte Schlacht: C. D. G., *Die Hermannsschlacht*' (164–78); R. Müller, 'C. D. Gs verschwiegene Übernahme von Gedanken Friedrich Nicolais in die *Shakespearo-Manie*' (179–86); A. Schulze-Weslarn, 'Gs "Kritzeleien"' (187–220), and 'Studien zu *Herzog Gothland* in der Bühnenbildklasse von Professor Kreidel an der Kunstakademie Düsseldorf' (221–30); K. Nellner, 'Ein unbekanntes Stammbuchblatt von G. für Freiligrath' (231–37); W. Habicht, 'Schöner Wahnsinn: zu Freiligraths *Horaz und Shakespeare*' (227–82); K. Nellner, 'G.-Bibliographie' (368–73); Id., 'Freiligrath-Bibliographie' (374–79).

GRILLPARZER. Cristoph Leitgeb and Richard Reichensperger, *Grillparzer und Musil: Studien zu einer Sprachstilgeschichte österreichischer Literatur*, ed. Walter Weiss (Sprach — Literatur und Geschichte, 17), Heidelberg, Winter, ii + 274 pp., contains eight articles of which three are on Musil and the following five on G.: R. Reichensperger, 'Dramentheorie und Stilanalyse: Gs *Die Jüdin von Toledo*' (12–41); C. Leitgeb, 'Schicksal und Lüge. Oder: Biedermeierliche Aufklärung. Kant in Gs *Lustspiel*' (42–77, on *Weh dem, der lügt!*); R. Reichensperger, 'Die doppelte Geschichte: F. Gs *Selbstbiographie*' (78–123); C. Leitgeb, 'Gs "Jugenderinnerungen im Grünen"' (124–42); Id., 'Gs *Kloster bei Sendomir* und Musils *Tonka*' (143–80). The articles are all thorough and of good quality, though the editor's claim that the book represents 'Studien zu einer Sprachstilgeschichte österreichischer Literatur' looks over-ambitious. B. Hoffmann, *Opfer der Humanität: Zur Anthropologie Franz Grillparzers*, Wiesbaden, Deutscher Universitätsvlg, 1999, 220 pp., is a 1997 Copenhagen dissertation. U. Fülleborn, 'Goethe durch Gs Augen gesehen', *Fest. Storck*, 221–31. T. Baltensweiler, 'Zu den politisch-sozialen Verweisen des Rahmens von Gs *Der arme Spielmann*', *ColGer*, 32, 1999:297–307. H. Turk, 'Translatio imperii oder revanche de Dieu? Das Problem kultureller Grenzziehungen in Gs *Goldenem Vliess*', pp. 193–219 of *Kulturelle Grenzziehungen im Spiegel der Literaturen: Nationalismus, Regionalismus, Fundamentalismus*, ed. Horst Turk, Göttingen, Wallstein, 1998, 360 pp. G. M. Rösch, 'Labyrinthische Diskurse: Erzählstrategien in Gs Almanach-Novelle *Das Kloster bei Sendomir*, pp. 243–56 of *Assimilation — Abgrenzung — Austausch: Interkulturalität in Sprache und Literatur*, ed. Maria K. Lasatowicz et al. (Oppelner Beiträge zur Germanistik, 1), Frankfurt–Berlin, Lang, 1999, 400 pp. U. C. Steiner, 'Revolution und Gedächtnis bei G. und Stifter', pp. 267–90 of *Revolution 1848–49: Ereignis — Rekonstruktion — Diskurs*, ed. Gudrun Loster-Schneider (Mannheimer Studien zur Literatur- und Kulturwissenschaft, 21), St Ingbert, Röhrig, 1999, 322 pp. J. Riou, 'The currency of affection in G.'s *Der arme Spielmann*', *Sagarra Vol.*, 377–86. D. Borchmeyer, 'F. G.: schweigender Dichter', *Jb. der Bayerischen Akad. der Schönen Künste*, 12, 1998:187–210. E. Reder, 'Der Schwerlaster von der Kriechspur als Linksüberholer: Gs *Bruderzwist* in revolutionärer Beleuchtung', *Lichtungen*, 20, 1999:133–37. J. Grosse, 'Unzeitgemäßheit und Geschichtskritik bei F. G.', *Historisches Jahrbuch*, 119, 1999:186–208. P. Janke, 'Gescheiterte Authentizität: Anmerkungen zu Gs Frauenfiguren', *Lenau-Jb.*, 26:57–72.

GROTH. *Jahresgabe der K.-G.-Gesellschaft*, 42, contains: H. Detering, 'Melancholie und memoria: K. Gs Gedichte in ihrer Epoche' (11–30); U. Bichel, 'Vor 150 Jahren: K. G. im Jahre 1850' (81–112); J. Kühl, 'Ich habe große Fußtouren dazu umsonst unternommen: K. G. und die Mathematik' (135–54).

GUTZKOW. K. G., *Die Selbsttaufe: Erzählungen und Novellen*, ed. Stephen Landshuter, Passau, Stutz, 1998, 414 pp., reprints the texts of *Der Sadducäer von Amsterdam*, *Die Selbsttaufe*, *Imagina Unruh*, and *Die Nihilisten*. K. G., '*Über Goethe': Im Wendepunkt zweier Jahrhunderte (1836). Eine kritische Verteidigung*, ed. O. Kramer, Tübingen, Klöpfer & Meyer, 1999, 136 pp., is a critical edition of G.'s book on Goethe. *Karl Gutzkow: Liberalismus — Europäertum — Modernität*, ed. Roger Jones et al. (Vormärz-Studien, 6), Bielefeld, Aisthesis, 290 pp., publishes the papers given at a conference held at Keele University in 1997 and has: W. Rasch, 'Unbekanntes, wenig Bekanntes, Verschollenes: bibliographische Streifzüge durch Gs Werk' (25–50); M. Lauster, 'Gs

Modernebegriff als Grundlage seines institutionskritischen Liberalismus' (51–67); T. Spreckelsen, ' "Öffentliche Meinung? Die Parole
ist genehmigt!" K. Gs Lustpiel *Anonym / Die Adjutanten* (1845–51)'
(69–83); W. Wülfing, 'Die telegraphischen Depeschen als "Chronik
des Jahrhunderts": K. Gs "Ahnungen" von einem Medium der
Moderne' (85–106); G. Vonhoff, *'Die Ritter vom Geiste/* "Ein Mädchen
aus dem Volke": wann gelingt ein ästhetisches Panorama?' (107–20);
K. Jauslin, ' "Aber auch zum Lesen gehört Virtuosität": Lesarten des
Panoramatischen in *Die Ritter vom Geiste*' (121–48); D. Horrocks,
'Maskulines Erzählen und feminine Furcht: Gs *Wally die Zweiflerin*'
(149–63); R. Kavanagh, 'G. und die Schauerromantik' (165–79);
R. Jones, 'Gs Dramen: Möglichkeiten und Grenzen der Innovation'
(181–96); P. Hasubek, 'Zwischen Essayismus und Poesie: K. Gs
Erzählungen' (197–215); M. Lauster, 'Physiologien aus der unsicht-
baren Hauptstadt: Gs soziologische Skizzen im europäisch-deutschen
Kontext' (217–54); G. Vonhoff, 'Möglichkeiten einer modernen
kritischen G.-Ausgabe' (255–62). Users of the book will be grateful to
the editors for the inclusion of a full index of names and titles, a
feature that is all too rare in collective volumes. M. Lauster,
'Lucinde's unfinished business: women and religion in G.'s works',
Sagarra Vol., 427–42. M.L., 'Englische "Anatomie" gegen deutsche
"Konstruktion" der Geschichte: Gs Versuch, den Sonderweg zu
korrigieren', *ChrA*, 7, 1998–99:57–68.

HEBBEL. Hargen Thomsen, *Friedrich Hebbel: Lebensbilder und Anek-
doten*, Husum, Husumer Druck- und Verlagsanstalt, 1998, 128 pp.
Andrea Rudolph, *Genreentscheidung und Symbolgehalt im Werk Friedrich
Hebbels* (Oppelner Beiträge zur Germanistik, 3), Frankfurt–Berlin,
Lang vi + 493 pp., sees a close link between H.'s use of such symbolic
motifs as the jewel, the veil, and the ring, and the development of his
work from narrative prose and comedy to tragic-comedy and tragedy.
O. Ehrismann, ' "Denn reine Rechnung erhält die Freundschaft": Hs
Verhandlungen über *Mutter und Kind*; ein Protokoll', *Fest. Moser*,
197–207. K. S. Guthke, 'Hs "Blick in's Weite": Eurozentrik und
Exotik', *Fest. Kreutzer*, 363–73. S. Kiefer, 'Die Genovefa-Legende als
dramatisches Sujet bei Maler Müller, Ludwig Tieck und F. H.',
pp. 39–51 of *Maler Müller zum 250. Geburtstag am 13. Januar 1999*, ed.
Ulrike Leuschner et al., Reilingen, Hirschstrasse, 1998, 196 pp.
Hebbel-Jb., 55, is largely concerned with the theme of Hebbel and
Weimar and has: M. Ritzer, ' "Klassik" versus "Moderne": zur
historischen Rekonstruktion eines Topos' (7–38, on H.'s place in
German literary history); H. Reinhardt, 'Der Rest ist Resignation:
Hs Schiller-Rezeption. Nachfolge mit Schwierigkeiten' (39–64);

H. Kaiser, 'H. und die Metaphysik des Tragischen im 19. Jahrhundert' (65–84); P. Rusterholz, 'Hs Verständnis des Komischen im Spiegel von Friedrich Theodor Vischers *Das Erhabene und das Komische*' (85–101); L. Ehrlich, 'Hebbel und Goethe' (103–17); R.-R. Wuthenow, 'Mit einem Blick auf Weimar? F. Hs autobiographische Aufzeichnungen' (119–34); J. Lehmann, 'Städtebild und Image: die Bedeutung Weimars für die Entstehung eines literarischen Deutschlandbildes in der europäischen Literatur des 19. Jahrhunderts' (135–54); O. Ehrismann, 'Ein Brief von Emil Kuhs Schwester Zerline: Nachtrag zur Wesselburener Brief-Ausgabe' (155); H. Thomsen, 'Theaterbericht' (157–82). I. Oesterle, 'Peripherie und Zentrum — Kunst und Publizistik — Wahrnehmungsgrenzfall "große Stadt": die Aufzeichnungen F. Hs in Paris', *Sagarra Vol.*, 187–206. H. Scheuer, ' "Dein Bruder ist der schlechteste Sohn, werde du bie beste Tochter!" Generationskonflikte in F. Hs "bürgerlichem Trauerspiel" *Maria Magdalena* (1844)', *DUS*, 52 : 27–35. H. Reinhardt, 'Die Rezeption Schopenhauers im Theater des 19. und 20. Jahrhunderts: H. — Dürrenmatt — Bernhard', *LJb*, 42 : 223–46.

HEINE.   Christoph auf der Horst, *Heinrich Heine und die Geschichte Frankreichs* (Heine Studien), Stuttgart, Metzler, xii + 434 pp., is a 1998 Düsseldorf dissertation. *Heinrich Heine: Neue Wege der Forschung*, ed. Christian Liedtke, WBG, 311 pp. Dietmar Goltschnigg, *Die Fackel ins wunde Herz: Kraus über Heine. Eine 'Erledigung'? Texte, Analysen, Kommentar*, Vienna, Passagen, 485 pp. Frank Schwamborn, *Maskenfreiheit: Karnevalisierung und Theatralität bei Heinrich Heine*, Munich, Iudicium, 1998, 244 pp., reveals its origins as a Munich dissertation not least in its heavy footnoting. Schwamborn examines H.'s work in the light of Bakhtin's concept of the 'carnivalization' of literature as developed in the latter's books on Rabelais and Dostoevsky. He argues that the spirit of carnival informs both the content and the style of H.'s writing, manifesting itself in aspects of his work that do not appear at first glance to be closely linked — in, for example, his subversive and witty word-play in the *Reisebilder* and his recurring mockery of political repression. Much in the book is intelligent and ingenious, though the argument can at times seem strained, and readers other than Bakhtin enthusiasts are unlikely to find it easy reading. Susanne Kerschbaumer, *Heines moderne Romantik*, Paderborn, Schöningh, 254 pp., in a 1999 Kiel dissertation explores the links between H.'s Romanticism and the lectures of A. W. Schlegel. Delia F.-G. Nisbet, *Heinrich Heine and Giacomo Leopardi: The Rhetoric of Midrash* (STML, 47), viii + 151 pp. Dietrich Schubert, '*Jetzt wohin?*'

Heinrich Heine in seinen verhinderten und errichteten Denkmälern (Beiträge zur Geschichtskultur, 17), Cologne–Weimar, Böhlau, 1999, vi + 380 pp. Heinrich Lindlar, **Loreley-Report: Heinrich Heine und die Rheinlied-Romantik*, Cologne–Rheinkassel, Dohr, 1999, 175 pp. Ralph Martin, **Die Wiederkehr der Götter Griechenlands: Zur Entstehung des 'Hellenismus'-Gedankens bei Heinrich Heine*, Sigmaringen, Thorbecke, 1999, 232 pp., is a 1996 Erlangen dissertation. Ina Bredel-Perpina, **Heinrich Heine und das Pariser Theater zur Zeit der Julimonarchie*, Bielefeld, Aisthesis, 250 pp., is a 1999 Bamberg dissertation concerned with H.'s French theatre criticism. Rudolf Kreis, **Antisemitismus und Kirche: In den Gedächtnislücken deutscher Geschichte mit Heine, Freud, Kafka und Goldhagen*, Reinbek, Rowohlt, 1999, 328 pp. Wilhelm Grosse, *Literaturwissen für Schule und Studium: Heinrich Heine* (UB, 15223), 173 pp., introduces H.'s life and works and offers interpretations of 20 poems, the *Reisebilder* and *Deutschland. Ein Wintermärchen*.

Heine und die Weltliteratur, ed. T. J. Reed et al., Oxford, Legenda, 232 pp., publishes the papers given at the London Heine Conference in 1997 and contains: J. A. Kruse, ' "In der Literatur wie im Leben hat jeder Sohn einen Vater": H. H. zwischen Bibel und Homer, Cervantes und Shakespeare' (1–23); N. Reeves, 'From battlefield to paradise: a reassessment of H. H.'s tragedy *Almansor*, its sources, and their significance for his later poetry and thought' (24–50); R. Paulin, 'H. and Shakespeare' (51–63); R. Robertson, ' "A world of fine fabling": epic traditions in H.'s *Atta Troll*' (64–76); H. Lengauer, 'Nachgetragene Ironie: Moritz Hartmann und H. H.' (77–103); H. Holler, 'Grillparzer und H.' (104–19); H. Steinecke, 'Jüdische Dichter-Bilder in Hs *Jehuda ben Halevy*' (122–39); P. Branscombe, 'H. and the Lied' (142–49); A. Stillmark, 'H. and the Russian poets from Lermontov to Blok' (150–67); E. Timms, 'Topical poetry and satirical rhyme: Karl Kraus's debt to H.' (168–81); T. J. Reed, 'Hs Körperteile: zur Anatomie des Dichters' (184–201); D. Constantine, 'H.'s Lazarus poems' (202–14); A. Phelan, 'The tribe of Harry: H. and contemporary poetry' (215–32). *Lectures d'une Œuvre: Reisebilder de Heinrich Heine*, ed. René Anglade, Paris, du Temps, 1998, 223 pp., has: J. Bel, 'Le *Reisebild* heinéen: sa place dans l'histoire du récit de voyage' (7–26); M. Werner, ' "Zusammengewürfeltes Lappenwerk" oder "harmonisch verschlungene Fäden?": zum Problem der Komposition von Hs *Reisebildern*' (27–49); R. Anglade, "Napoleon und die Französische Revolution stehen darin in Lebensgröße": l'Allemagne de la Restauration dans le miroir de la Révolution' (51–83); G. Höhn, ' "La force des choses: Geschichtsauffassung und Geschichtsschreibung in Hs *Reisebildern*' (84–102); B. Kortländer, ' ". . . ist nicht alles

wie gemalt?" Naturdarstellungen in Hs *Reisebildern*' (103–15); K. Fingerhut, 'Apoll schindet Marsyas: Satiren in Hs *Reisebildern*' (117–38);
A. Betz, 'Vom "Zauberglanz der Waren": frühe Beobachtungen Hs
in London und Paris' (139–58); L. Calvié, 'H. et Goethe ou: de la
dialectique comme un des beaux-arts' (159–73); M.-S. Benoit, 'Les
poems de la *Nordsee*: un style unique entre le *Buch der Lieder* et les
Reisebilder' (175–94); L. Cassagnau, '"Reisebilder"/"Götterbilder":
nature et mythologie dans les poèmes de la *Nordsee* de H. H.'
(195–214); G. Ruhl-Anglade, 'Hs "Meeresstille": Ironie und Kritik'
(215–20). *Heinrich Heine's Contested Identities: Politics, Religion and
Nationalism in Nineteenth-Century Germany*, ed. Jost Hermand et al. (GLC,
26), 1999, xi + 199 pp., publishes the papers given at a conference
held in Berkeley, California, in 1997 on the theme of H.'s identity
and the formative influences on it of his Jewish origin and the politics
of his time. Individual articles in the volume are: J. L. Sammons,
'Who did H. think he was?' (1–24); C. Hofmann, 'History versus
memory: H. H. and the Jewish past' (25–48); B. Goldstein, 'H.'s
Hebrew Melodies: a politics and poetics of Diaspora' (49–68, on the
Romanzero); R. C. Holub, 'Confession of an apostate: H.'s conversion
and its psychic displacement' (69–88); H. C. Seeba, '"Keine
Systematie": H. in Berlin and the origin of the urban gaze' (89–108);
S. Zantop, 'Columbus, Humboldt, H.: or the rediscovery of Europe'
(109–34); J. Kaczynski, 'The Polish question and H.'s exilic identity'
(135–53); J. Hermand, 'Tribune of the people or aristocrat of the
spirit? H.'s ambivalence towards the masses' (155–73); P. U. Hohendahl, 'H.'s critical intervention: the intellectual as poet' (175–99). *Harry
. . . Henri. . . Heinrich Heine: texts réunis par Erika Tunner*, Paris, Avinus,
1998, 93 pp., has: J. Hermand, 'Amalie oder Germania? Die Frage
der unerwiderten Liebe im *Buch der Lieder*' (10–17); D. Goltschnigg,
'Judentum und Moderne: H. H. und Karl Kraus' (19–34); H. Esselborn, 'H. Hs späte Tiergedichte: Fabeltradition mit Humor' (37–48);
H. Urbahn de Jauregui, 'H. H., un bonapartiste allemand' (50–58);
A. Leduc, '"Distance, miroir et conscience": la distanciation littéraire
dans la poésie de H. H. "Wie der Mond sich leuchtend dränget"'
(60–68); L. Cassagnau, 'Une hétérobiographie moderne: *Aus den
Memoiren des Herren von Schnabelewopski*, de H. H.' (70–78). *Heine
voyageur: texts réunis et présentés par Alain Cozic*, Toulouse, Presses
Universitaires du Mirail, 1999, 234 pp., contains: A. Faure, '*Die
Harzreise*: sur les traces de H. H.' (17–44); J. Kruse, '"Mon cœur
jubile": les voyages de H. au bord de la mer' (45–63); A. Cozic, 'H.,
"citoyen du large"?' (65–79); C. Geitner, 'Au sommet du Brocken: le
voyage en littérature de H. ou pourquoi le poète-narrateur n'assiste

pas au lever du soleil' (81–95); F. Knopper, 'H. et la tradition des chroniques de voyage' (99–111); A.-S. Astrup, 'Le voyage identitaire des *Reisebilder*' (113–27); G. Höhn, '"La meilleure formation, un homme intelligent l'acquiert en voyageant"': les *Reisebilder* de H. et (Ver-)Bildungsreisen' (129–40); G. Krebs, 'H., Göttingen et l'Allemagne: histoire d'une intégration' (141–61); T. Bremer, 'München, "seit kurzem ein neues Athen"': der dritte Teil der *Reisebilder* als Diskussion der Möglichkeiten intellektueller Existenz vor 1830' (165–86); L. Calvié, 'H. et Goethe' (187–201); A. Ruiz, 'Napoléon dans les *Tableaux de voyage* de H. H.: un nouveau "mythe du saveur"'' (203–34).

*Der Weg in den Süden: Reisen durch Tirol von Dürer bis Heine. Eine Ausstellung des Landesmuseums Schloss Tirol 2. 8. 98 — 6. 11. 98, ed. Siegfried de Rachwitz, Merano, Medus, 1998, 349 pp., contains: C. Stöcker, 'H. Hs italienische *Reisebilder: Reise von München nach Genua*' (323–28); G. Cusatelli, 'La filatrice de H.' (329–38, also on *Die Reise von München nach Genua*). *Nahe Ferne: 25 Jahre Heine-Museum in der Bilker Strasse. Eine Ausstellung des Heinrich-Heine-Instituts*, ed. Heidemarie Vahl et al. (Veröffentlichungen des H.-H.-Instituts, Düsseldorf), Düsseldorf, Droste, 1999, 126 pp.

H.-Jb., 39, has: T. Rudtke, 'Die Sehnsucht nach "ewiger Kirmes" und "Mockturteltauben"': Hs *Schnabelewopski*. Eine menippeische Satire' (1–21); G. Kluge, 'Hs Lieblingskarikaturen: Holland, Holländisches und Holländer in den *Memoiren des Herren von Schnabelewopski*' (22–46); A. M. Jäger, 'Große Oper der alten neuen Welt: Überlegungen zu Hs *Vitzliputzli*' (47–68); S. Singh, 'H. H. und die deutsche Literatur des 18. Jahrhunderts' (69–94); A. Pistiak, '"Glaube, wer es geprüft"': Hölderlin — Heine. Beobachtungen. Feststellungen. Fragen' (95–110); T. Schmidt-Beste, 'Felix Mendelssohn Bartholdy und H. H.' (111–34); A. Hölter, '"Un monument manqué"': der Elefant auf der Place de la Bastille' (135–64); G. Weiss, 'Alexander Weills *Sittengemälde aus dem elsässischen Volksleben* (1847): volkskundliche Zeugnisse, literarische Kunstwerke und emanzipatorische Botschaften' (165–83, on a minor writer with whom H. was acquainted in Paris); A. Bauer, 'Die Stellung der Juden in der ersten Hälfte des 19. Jahrhunderts und Hs Übertritt zum Christentum' (184–91); M. W. Asmussen, 'Karen Blixen und H. H.' (192–99); W. Zöller, 'Das H.-Denkmal von Carin Kreuzberg in Berlin' (200–05); O. Han-sin, 'Die neue H.-Stele in Seoul (Hankuk-Univ.): zur H.-Rezeption in Korea' (206–08); C. Bartscherer, 'Der Papst im Poetenkittel: Anmerkungen zu H. Hs "blasphemischer Religiosität"''

(209–14); R. Bergmann, 'Nachdenken über (m)einen H.-Denkmal-Film' (215–19); T.-R. Feuerhake, 'H.-Literatur 1998–99 mit Nachträgen' (270–93). *Fest. Žmegač* contains: D. Borchmeyer, 'H. H. und sein abtrünniger Adept Richard Wagner' (53–71); D. Goltschnigg, 'Die "H.-Affäre": ein politisches und kulturelles Phänomen der Wiener Moderne' (153–73); H. O. Horch, 'Die unheilbar große Brüderkrankheit: zum programmatischen Zeitgedicht "Das neue israelitische Hospital zu Hamburg" von H. H.' (41–52). *Klassiker der deutschen Literatur: Epochen-Signaturen von der Aufklärung bis zur Gegenwart*, ed. Gerhard Rupp, Würzburg, Königshausen & Neumann, 1999, 326 pp., contains: G. Gössmann, 'H. H., *Deutschland. Ein Wintermärchen*: eine literarische Inspektion' (75–97); H.-G. Pott, 'Effi Briest, H. H. und der Teufel: Theodor Fontanes Roman *Effi Briest*' (98–116). W. Wülfing, ' "Der Geist der Revoluzion . . . ist unsterblich": H. H., Theodor Fontane und die Revolution von 1848', pp. 81–109 of *Literatur und Revolution 1848–1918: Dokumentation der Tagung der Kurt Tucholsky Gesellschaft vom 28.–31. 5. 1998 in Weiler*, ed. Michael Hepp, Oldenburg, Bibliotheks- und Informationssytem der Univ. Oldenburg, 1998, 191 pp. A. Destro, 'Miti greci e miti biblici in H.', pp. 407–17 of vol. 2 of *Risonanze classiche nell'Europa romantica*, ed. Annarosa Pole et al. (Dimensioni del viaggio, 9), 2 vols, Moncalieri, Centro Interuniversitario di Ricerche sul 'Viaggio in Italia', 1998, 634 pp. A chapter in Adami, *Pan*, 'Der große Pan ist tot: Panvorstellungen im 19. Jahrhundert. Heinrich Heine' (19–28), discusses the significance of H.'s references to Pan in the *Helgoländer Briefe*. G. Holtz, 'Nobilitierung der Großstadtbajadere: H. Hs *Pomare* im Zusammenhang der Geschichte der Ballade', *Fest. Denkler*, 43–53. P. U. Hohendahl, 'H.-Rezeption um 1900', *Fest. Steinecke*, 125–46. D. Goltschnigg, ' "Die Feinde Goethe und Heine" in der *Fackel* des Ersten Weltkriegs', *ib.*, 147–59. M. Beilein, 'Telos und Utopie in den Geschichtsbildern Hs und Eichendorffs', pp. 119–40 of *Unerledigte Geschichten*, ed. G. v. Essen et al., Göttingen, Wallstein, 505 pp. E. Ribbat, 'Alfred Döblin — H. redivivus: über das Verhältnis von Aktualität und Literatur', pp. 9–16 of *Internationales Alfred-Döblin-Kolloquium, 11, 1997, Leipzig*, ed. Ira Lorf et al. (*JIG*, Reihe A, 46), Berne–Berlin, Lang, 1999, 230 pp. B. Brandl-Risi and C. Risi, ' "Meine kleine maliziös-sentimentale Lieder": H. Hs Lyrik und die Frage der Übersetzbarkeit von Ironie am Beispiel von Carl Loewe und Robert Schumann', pp. 175–210 of *Carl Loewe (1796–1869): Beiträge zu Leben, Werk, Wirkung*, ed. Ekkehard Ochs et al. (Greifswalder Beiträge zur Musikwissenschaft, 6), Frankfurt — Berlin, Lang, 1998, xii + 411 pp.

E.-U. Pinkert, 'Die deutsche Misere und das Himmelreich auf
Erden: Anmerkungen zu Wolf Biermanns Auseinandersetzung mit
H. H.', *ChrA*, 1998–99:125–38. L. Calvié, 'Autour du bicentenaire
de la naissance de H.: de la "misère" heinéenne française à la
récurrente "misère allemande"', *ib.*, 151–65. K. Fingerhut, 'Assimilation und Transformation: Goethe-Reminiszenzen in Hs Werk', *ib.*,
167–90. M. Nutz, 'Verstehen durch Kontextuierung: Lyrikinterpret-
ation als historische Diskursanalyse am Beispiel von Hs *Traumbildern*',
DUS, 50, 1998:98–109. K. Briegleb, '"Trotz dem, dass ich ein
heimlicher Hellene bin": Hs Arbeit an Goethe. Eine Relektüre',
Menora, 10, 1999:111–53. G. Kurz, 'Hirsch-Hyazinth: zu einer
Selbstdeutungsfigur Hs', *Aschkenas*, 8, 1999:501–10. J. Skolnik,
'Kaddish for Spinoza: memory and modernity in Celan and Heine',
NGC, 77, 1999:169–86. C. Urchueguía and R. Lüdeke, 'Der
Doppelgänger: für eine funktionsgeschichtliche Beschreibung von
Schuberts H.-Vertonungen', *DVLG*, 74:279–304. B. Morawe,
'"Pauvre homme": Hs Gedächtnisfeier. Über Armut und Würde im
zwölften Lazarus-Gedicht des *Romanzero*', *GRM*, 50:415–41. C. Rau-
seo, 'Abkehr und Rückkehr: Hs *Heimkehr* und Schuberts *Schwanenges-
ang*', pp. 235–45 of *Abkehr von Schönheit und Ideal in der Liebeslyrik*, ed.
Carolin Fischer et al., Stuttgart, Metzler, 390 pp. A. Corkhill,
'Überlegungen zu Hs Sprachkritik', *Neophilologus*, 84:97–106.
H. Wehrmann, 'Hs Musikanschauung', *Acta Musicologica*, 70,
1998:79–107.

HERWEGH. Ulrich Enzenberger, **Herwegh: Ein Heldenleben*, Frankfurt, Eichborn, 1999, 394 pp. I. Pepperle, 'G. H. und Alex Herzen:
unbekannte Briefe zum Bruch ihrer Beziehungen von Richard
Wagner, François Wille und G. H.', *Fest. Richter*, 141–53.

HEYSE. Nicole Nelhiebel, *Epik im Realismus: Studien zu den Versno-
vellen von Paul Heyse* (Literatur und Medienwissenschaften, 73),
Oldenburg, Igel, 270 pp., is a 1999 Bremen dissertation. The
introductory chapter contains a useful *Forschungsbericht* on the current
state of Heyse scholarship. This is followed by a chapter dealing with
the theoretical views of Heyse and other 19th-c. luminaries (F. T.
Vischer, Julian Schmidt, Rudolf von Gottschall) on the form of the
verse *Novelle*. The main part of the book then consists of five chapters
which provide close analyses of each of the main *Novellen*. As far as
possible they are grouped thematically and deal successively with
power struggles (*Die Brüder, Urica, König und Priester*), the position of
women (*Syritha*), comic themes (*Die Braut von Cypern, Die Hochzeitsreise
an den Walchensee, Das Feenkind, Die Madonna im Ölwald*), and the artist
figure (*Michelangelo Buonarotti, Raffael*). The last main chapter examines

Novellen that belong to no particular thematic group (*Thekla, Der Salamander, Der Traumgott*). The book is carefully researched and clearly planned, and represents a significant contribution to Heyse studies. Dietmar Grieser, 'Unheilbar: P. H. und Margarete Kugler', pp. 191–206 of *Im Rosengarten: Eine literarische Spurensuche in Südtirol* (IT, 2509), 1999, 242 pp. N. Nelhiebel, 'Paul Heyses Versnovelle *Die Braut von Cypern* (1856): Boccaccio übersetzt', *SGGed*, 7, 1999:29–43. R. Füllmann, 'Die symbolischen Wunden: P. Hs Novellen und das weibliche Begehren. Teil 1, Frauengestalten zwischen Fantastik und Exotic', *Veszprémi Egyetem: Studia Germanistica Universitatis Vesprimiensis*, 2, 1998:145–66. Id., 'Die symbolischen Wunden: P. Hs Novellen und das weibliche Begehren. Teil 2, Selbstbewusste Weiblichkeit in literarischen und essayistischen Texten', *Veszprémi Egyetem: Studia Germanistica Universitatis Vesprimiensis*, 3, 1999:37–57.

HOFFMANN VON FALLERSLEBEN. *August Heinrich Hoffmann von Fallersleben, 1798–1998: Festschrift zum 200. Geburtstag*, ed. Hans-Joachim Behr (Braunschweiger Beiträge zur deutschen Sprache und Literatur, 1), Bielefeld, Vlg für Regionalgeschichte, 1999, 283 pp., has: K.-W. v. Wintzingerode-Knorr, 'H. v. F.: ein Leben im 19. Jahrhundert' (11–33); G. Tiggesbäumker, 'H. v. F. als Bibliothekar in Corvey' (35–48); E. Fohse, ' "Das Lied der Deutschen" in seiner politischen, literarischen und literaturwissenschaftlichen Rezeption' (51–100); H. Kämper, 'Schlagwort, Begriff, Leitkonzept: H. v. F. als politischer Dichter' (101–19); K. G. P. Schuster, ' "Poesie des Grimms": wie politisch war der Dichter der *Unpolitischen Lieder*?' (121–39); D. Cherubim, 'H. v. F. in der Geschichte der Germanistik' (143–67); H.-J. Behr, 'Eilige Philologie: H. v. F. als Editor mittelalterlicher Texte' (169–81); O. Holzapfel, 'H. v. F. und der Beginn kritischer Volksliedforschung in Deutschland' (183–98); J. B. Berns, 'H. v. F. und die Niederlande' (199–209); H. Blume, 'V. F., A. H. H. und niederdeutsche Mundart seines Heimatorts' (211–24); H. Brunner, 'H. v. F. und Walther von der Vogelweide' (225–38); D. Merzbacher, 'Barocksforschung ohne Barockbegriff: das 17. Jahrhundert im philologischen und literarischen Werk Hs v. F.' (239–56); E. Poettgens, 'Die Splitternachlässe und die Akten zur Person H. v. F.' (259–73). S. Müller, ' "Altdeutsche Kuckkastenbilder": Moriz Haupt und H. H. v. F. machen sich einen Reim auf die Lage der Germanistik. Text und Kommentar eines ergötzlichen Zittauer Abends des Jahres 1837', *Fest. Walliczek*, 231–57.

IMMERMANN. Tilman Spreckelsen, **Das Herz als Kompass: Androiden im Werk Karl Immermanns*, Freiburg i. B., Rombach, 1999, 214 pp. A newcomer this year is *Immermann-Jahrbuch*, 1, which has: G. Schandera et al., ' "... zum Unterricht für meinen Sohn ...": ein frühes Dokument der I.-Biographie' (9–36); H. Marks, ' "Der schlimmste Trug ist der, wodurch man sich selbst trügt": Tartüffe in Deutschland oder "Die Schule der Frommen" ' (37–60); T. Witt, 'Der philosophische Arzt im Zeitroman: zur Rolle des Arztes in K. Is *Die Epigonen*' (61–81); P. Hasubek, 'Autobiographie oder zeitgeschichtliche Studien? Zur Kunstform von Is Schrift *Düsseldorfer Anfänge: Maskengespräche* (1840)' (83–102); M. Windfuhr, ' "Auf Tod und Leben": Is Verhältnis zu Goethe' (103–20); G. Henkel, 'Produktive Rezeption: Raabe und I.' (121–37). P. Hasubek, ' "La vérité, toute la vérité, rien que la vérité": K. I., ein kritisch-satirischer Dichter aus Magdeburg', pp. 213–31 of *Prolegomena zur Kultur- und Literaturgeschichte des Magdeburger Raumes*, ed. Gunter Schandera et al. (Forschungen zur Kultur- und Literaturgeschichte Sachsen-Anhalts, 1), Magdeburg, Scriptum, 1999, 284 pp. T. Spreckelsen, 'Mumiendasein und Befreiung: K. Is Schauspiel *Ghismonda*', *Grabbe-Jb.*, 17–18, 1998–99:349–57. C. Stockinger, 'Von der Idylle zum "Blutbad": die Vergeschichtlichung der Alpendarstellung in der Literatur des 18. und 19. Jahrhunderts', *ZDP*, 119:161–78, includes some discussion of I.'s drama *Das Trauerspiel im Tirol* (1828) and its later reworking *Andreas Hofer der Sandwirth von Passeyer* (1835).

KELLER. The new HKA of K.'s *Sämtliche Werke*, ed. Walter Morgenthaler, Basle–Frankfurt, Stroemfeld, has added vols 23.1 and 23.2, *Das Sinngedicht. Apparat 1 zu Band 7*, and *Das Sinngedicht. Apparat 2 zu Band 7*, ed. W. Morgenthaler, 1998, 431, 477 pp. G. K., *Sieben Legenden*, ed. Peter Goldammer (ATV, 6073), 119 pp. Winfried G. Sebald, *Logis in einem Landhaus: Über Gottfried Keller, Johann Peter Hebel, Robert Walser und andere*, Munich, Hanser, 1998, 192 pp., contains pen portraits and photographs of Swiss writers of whom K. is one. Caroline Loewenich, *Gottfried Keller: Frauenbild und Frauengestalten im erzählerischen Werk* (Ep, 332), 252 pp., is a 1999 Freiburg dissertation concerned with both the position of K.'s female characters in society and their relationship to his own biography. Anne Brenner, *Leseräume: Untersuchungen zu Lektüreverfahren und Lektürefunktionen in Gottfried Kellers Roman 'Der grüne Heinrich'* (Ep, 336), 172 pp., is a 1998 Göttingen dissertation. I. Roebling, ' "Denn lieb ist Dirs von je/wenn größer die Söhne sind als ihre Mutter": Maria als Medium für Größenphantasien in Texten der Nachaufklärung', pp. 175–92 of *Größenphantasien*, ed. Johannes Cremerius (FLG, 18), 401 pp., is concerned with *Sieben Legenden*. By the same author is ' "Mit Venus und Maria in eine schönere Zukunft": Gottfried Kellers schöpferische Ver-Wertung der Antike', *Fest. Böschenstein*, 225–49. G. Sautermeister,

'G. K.: das Bewusstsein des Unrechts', pp. 58–67 of *Grenzfrevel: Rechtskultur und literarische Kultur*, ed. Hans-Albrecht Koch et al. (AKML, 401), 1998, 276 pp. G. Marci-Boehnke, 'Kleider machen Doppelgänger: Projektion und Opposition in Helmut Käutners Film *Kleider machen Leute* aus dem Dritten Reich', pp. 93–112 of *Doppelgänger: Von endlosen Spielarten eines Phänomens*, ed. Ingrid Fichtner (Facetten der Literatur, 7), Berne, Haupt, 1999, ix + 269 pp. M. Swales, 'Replication, representation, and revalenta: on Flaubert, K. and nineteenth-century realism', *Sagarra Vol.*, 219–27. V. Hoffmann, 'Seldwyla — ein genialisches Todesabwehrsystem: zur anthropologisch-ästhetischen Verknüpfung von Einleitung und erster Erzählung *Pankraz der Schmoller* in G. Ks Zyklus *Die Leute von Seldwyla* (1856)', *Fest. Walliczek*, 271–94. G. R. Kaiser, '"Marienfrau" und verkehrte Männerwelt: G. Ks verkanntes Alterswerk *Martin Salander*', pp. 149–73 of *Der unzeitgemäße Held in der Weltliteratur*, ed. G. R. Kaiser (Jenaer germanistische Forschungen, n. F., 1), Heidelberg, Winter 1998, 335 pp. P. Stocker, 'G. Ks Arbeitsplan *Seldwyla II*: zur genetischen Eigendynamik entstehungsgeschichtlicher Dokumente', *Text*, 1999:63–81. R. C. Cowen, 'Reading K.'s *Die missbrauchten Liebesbriefe*', *PCP*, 34, 1999:72–79. H. Laufhütte, 'Gottfried Keller: zu spat im Rosenhaus. Die beiden Fassungen des Romans *Der grüne Heinrich*', *JASI*, 4, 1997[2000]:45–57. V. Nölle, 'Figurenanordnung und epochenspezifische Darstellungsmuster in G. Ks Erzählungen', *JDSG*, 44:136–53.

KOMPERT. A. Fuchs, 'Mimicry und Assimilation: L. Ks Ghettogeschichte in postkolonialer Perspektive', *Sagarra Vol.*, 497–508, is concerned with K.'s collection of Novellen *Aus dem Ghetto* (1848).

KÜRNBERGER. W. Klimbacher, '"Voll romantischer Winkel": F. K. in Kärnten. Eine Reise im Herbst 1870', *ÖGL*, 42, 1998:368–78. Id., "Wo Chassepot und Krupp reden, haben Roman und Novelle zu schweigen": F. Ks Kriegsfeuilletons', *Neohelicon*, 26, 1999:165–83.

KUGLER, FRANZ. R. Hillenbrand, 'F. K. als Erzähler, *ColGer*, 32, 1999:123–47, examines the almost unknown narrative fiction of an art-historian better remembered as the teacher of Jacob Burckhardt and the father-in-law of Paul Heyse. Id., 'F. Ks politische Dramen aus der Revolutionszeit', *LJb*, 41:89–123.

LAUBE. M. Fendri, 'Emanzipation — Zivilisation — Kolonisation: die Eroberung Algeriens im Urteil der Vormärz-Intelligenz am Beispiel H. Ls', pp. 41–53 of *Reisen, Entdecken, Utopien: Untersuchungen zum Alteritätsdiskurs im Kontext von Kolonialismus und Kulturkritik*, ed. Anil Bhatti et al. (*JIG*, Reihe A, 48), Berne–Berlin, Lang, 1998, 121 pp.

LENAU. *Lenau-Jb.*, 25, 1999, includes: H. Steinecke, 'L. im Kontext der politischen Dichtung um 1848: zur Einführung' (9–16); A. Mádl, '"Meister Niklas [. . .] dein Lied [. . .] als Wahrheit leuchtend steht es da": L. als Vorbild der achtundvierziger Österreichs' (17–33); H. Schuller Anger, 'Selbstfindung in bewegten Zeiten: neue Beiträge zum Bild des siebenbürgischen Vormärzautors Josef Marlin (1834–49)' (35–72); E. Pascu, 'Johann Nepomuk Preyer im Kontext der gesellschaftskritischen Strömungen. Zwischen Romantik und Vormärz' (73–85); H. Arnold, 'Ziska-Dichtungen im Vormärz: Alfred Meissners *Ziska*-Gesänge' (163–79); M. Ritter, 'L.-Bibliographie 1999: Erscheinungen aus den Jahren 1997 und 1998 mit Nachträgen aus früheren Jahren' (189–91); G. Mahal, 'Notizen zu Ls *Faust*: ein Versuch, einige Impressionen kontrolliert darzubieten' (448–63). *Lenau-Jb.*, 26, has: M. Wagner, 'N. L. und der Wein: eine Motivzusammenstellung' (5–41); M. Ritter, 'L.-Bibliographie 2000' (135–36). A Mádl, 'Sprache, Heimat und Frage der Identität bei N. L.', pp. 11–22 of *Schriftsteller zwischen (zwei) Sprachen und Kulturen: Internationales Symposion Veszprém und Budapest 6.–8. November 1995*, ed. Anton Mádl et al. (Veröffentlichungen des Südostdeutschen Kulturwerks, Reihe B, 74), Munich, Südostdeutschen Kulturwerk, 1999, 412 pp. M.-O. Blum, 'Le narrateur comme *actor* et *orator* dans *Savonarola* de L.', *CEtGer*, 38:67–80.

LEWALD. *'Mein gnädigster Herr! Meine gütigste Korrespondentin': Fanny Lewalds Briefwechsel mit Carl Alexander von Sachsen-Weimar 1848–1889*, ed. E. Klessmann, Weimar, Hermann Böhlaus Nachfolger, xxiv + 460 pp., makes available for the first time this interesting and valuable correspondence. The editor has added over 20 pages of informative notes, a time-chart of the lives of both participants, and an index of names.

MEYER. The new 12–volume edition of C. F. M.'s letters, *Briefwechsel: Historische-kritische Ausgabe*, ed. Hans Zeller, Berne, Benteli, has added vol. 2, *Conrad Ferdinand Meyer — François und Eliza Wille: Briefe 1869–1895*, ed. S. Graber, 1999, 495 pp. *Elisabeth Meyer-Ulrich: '. . . das ganze Herz deiner Mutter': Briefe an Betsy und Conrad Ferdinand Meyer 1846–1856*, ed. Dagmar Schifferli et al., Zurich, Pendo, 1998, 457 pp. *Conrad Ferdinand Meyer im Kontext: Beiträge des Kilchberger Kolloquiums*, ed. Rosemarie Zeller (Beihefte zum *Euphorion*, 35), Heidelberg, Winter, viii + 304 pp., publishes the papers given at a conference held in 1998 to commemorate the centenary of M.'s death. Major topics in this important volume are M.'s relationship to 19th-c. Realism and his use of history. The individual articles are: R. Zeller, 'M. im Kontext: Blicke auf die Forschung' (1–26);

K. Pestalozzi, 'Zum zweifachen Schriftsinn von C. F. Ms *Engelberg*' (29–40); W. Lukas, 'Kontingenz vs "Natürlichkeit": zu C. F. Ms *Die Hochzeit des Mönchs*' (41–75); M. Wünsch, 'Die realitätsschaffende Kraft des Wortes: zu C. F. Ms *Die Richterin*' (77–95); M. Titzmann, 'An den Grenzen des späten Realismus: C. F. Ms *Die Versuchung des Pescara*. Mit einem Exkurs zum Begriff "Realismus"' (97–138); P. Sprengel, 'Das Schwert des Poeten: Kampfmotive und Symbolik in C. F. Ms Lyrik' (141–56); C. Laumont, 'Auf Spiegeln und Brechen: Allegorie und Autoreflexion in C. F. Ms Lyrik' (157–73); C. Moos, '"Ich behandle die Geschichte souverän, aber nicht ungetreu": Vergangenheit als Erinnerung bei C. F. M.' (175–88); J. Osborne, 'Zum Geschichtsverständnis C. F. Ms am Beispiel von *Gustav Adolfs Page*' (189–204); M. Fauser, 'Historische Größe: Rekonstruktion und Semantik einer Denkfigur des Historismus' (205–21); D. A. Jackson, 'Tabuisierte politische, religiöse und sexuelle Themen im Werk C. F. Ms' (225–40); M. Bircher, 'Sammler und Dichter: Martin Bodmer und sein Großonkel C. F. M.' (241–67). *Conrad Ferdinand Meyer 1825–1898*, ed. Hans Wysling et al., Zurich, Vlg Neue Zürcher Zeitung, 1998, 480 pp., also produced to commemorate the centenary of M.'s death, does not attempt to break new ground academically but is nevertheless a fascinating publication that offers an extremely detailed and copiously illustrated chronological survey of his life, laying particular emphasis on the links between his biography and his fictional work. P. M. Lützeler, 'Historismus und Zeitkritik: der Dreißigjährige Krieg in C. F. Ms *Jürg Jenatsch*', *Fest. Steinecke*, 81–98. R. Nutt-Kofoth, 'Dokumentierte und gedeutete Befunde: zum Abschluss der historisch-kritischen Ausgabe von C. F. Ms Gedichten mit einem Rück- und Ausblick auf die Entwicklung der Editionsphilologie', *Euphorion*, 94:225–41. H. Fuhrmann, 'Inhalts- und Beziehungsaspekt in fiktionaler Kommunikation: C. F. Ms Novelle *Der Heilige*', pp. 77–97 of *Usus linguae: Der Text im Fokus sprach- und literaturwissenschaftlicher Perspektiven. Hans-Otto Spillmann zum 60. Geburtstag*, ed. Ingo Warnke (GTS, 62), 1999, 270 pp. W. Kofler, 'Poggios Plautus: Poetik und Rezeption in C. F. Ms Novelle *Plautus im Nonnenkloster*', Baumbach, *Traditia*, 429–40. M. Ritzer, 'Die Tatsachen der Wahrnehmung: zur Relation von Naturwissenschaft und Literatur im Realismus am Beispiel von Hermann Helmholz und C. F. M.', pp. 203–25 of *Rhetorische Seh-Reisen: Fallstudien zu Wahrnehmungsformen in Literatur, Kunst und Kultur*, ed. Alfonso de Toro et al. (Leipziger Schriften zu Kultur-, Literatur-, Sprach- und Übersetzungswissenschaft, 9), Frankfurt, Vervuert, 1999, 255 pp. B. Böschenstein, 'Die Bedeutung Stefan Georges und C. F. Ms für Paul Celans Frühwerk', *EG*, 53,

1998:481–92. B. Damerau, 'Novellen gegen das Schicksal: C. F. M. und die Geschichte', *ColGer*, 31, 1998:325–37. T. Zabka, 'Ich wird [*sic*] ein andres: zur Negation der Allegorie in einem Gedicht C. F. Ms', *DVLG*, 74:465–87, is concerned with the poem 'Möwenflug'.

MEYSENBUG. M. v. M., *Ausgewählte Schriften*, ed. Sabine Hering et al. (Edition Klassikerinnen), Königstein, Ulrike Helmer, 276 pp. Martin Reuter, **1848*, *Malwida von Meysenbug und die europäische Demokratiegeschichte: Die Politik einer aristokratischen Demokratin im 19. Jahrhundert*, Kassel Jenior, 1998, 414 pp. M. v. M., *1848*. *Kapitel 17 der 'Memoiren einer Idealistin'*, ed. Michael Vogt, Bielefeld, Aisthesis, 1999, 62 pp.

MÖLLHAUSEN. The reprint edition of M.'s *Ausgewählte Werke*, ed. Andreas Graf, Hildesheim, Olms, has added *Abteilung 1, Erzählungen*, vols 2.1 and 2.2, *Reliquien: Erzählungen und Schilderungen aus dem westlichen Nordamerika* (3 vols in 2), 1999, 236, 228, 224 pp.

MÖRIKE. The Stuttgart edition of M.'s works, ed. H. Arbogast et al., has added vol. 9.2, *Bearbeitung fremder Werke: Kritische Beratungen. Beratung Karl Mayers*, ed. Hans-Ulrich Simon, 1999, 697 pp.; vol. 15, *Briefe 1846–1850*, ed. Albrecht Bergold et al., 929 pp.; and vol. 16, *Briefe 1851–1856*, ed. Bernhard Thurn, 885 pp. *Gedichte von Eduard Mörike*, ed. Mathias Mayer (UB, 17508), 1999, 182 pp., has new interpretations of ten of M.'s best-known poems. B. Leistner, 'Notvolle Selbsterbauung: zu einigen M.-Gedichten der zwanziger Jahre', *Fest. Richter*, 107–16. A. Phipps, 'Über Ms *Die schöne Lau*: ein Beitrag zur xenologischen Literaturforschung aus britischer Sicht', *DaF*, 25, 1999:383–97. L. Martin, 'Über die Lauheit und das Lachen der schönen Lau: zu Ms *Historie* aus psychologischer und feministischer Sicht', *ib.*, 398–408. S. Busch, 'Unzeitgemäße Konjunktionen: Saturn und Psychologie in E. Ms Novelle *Mozart auf der Reise nach Prag*', *GLL*, 53:201–15. J. Endres, 'Im Garten der Zeit: zu einem Landschaftselement bei M.', *LJb*, 41:125–43. T. Sato, 'Zwei Liebesarten und Dichterbilder in der deutschen Elegie: Goethes *Römische Elegien* und Ms "Die schöne Buche"', *Goethe-Jb*. (Tokyo), 40, 1998:35–46.

MÜLLER, KARL (FRANZ VON ELLING). W. Kriegleder, 'Ein deutscher *Martin Chuzzlewit*: Franz von Ellings (i.e. Karl Müllers) Roman *Des Lebens Wandlungen* (1854)', *Fest. Moser*, 283–94.

NESTROY. The HKA of N.'s *Sämtliche Werke*, ed. Jürgen Hein et al., Vienna, Deuticke, has added *Stücke, 2, Der gefühlvolle Kerckermeister oder Adelheid die verfolgte Wittib. Nagerl und Handschuh oder Die Schicksale der Familie Maxenpfutsch*, ed. J. Hein et al., xxii + 583 pp.; *Stücke, 4, Die Zauberreise in die Ritterzeit. Genius Schuster und Marqueur*, ed. H. Aust,

1999, xv + 536 pp.; and *Stücke*, 36, *Tannhäuser*, ed. P. J. Branscombe, xiv + 306 pp. *Nestroyana*, 20, has: U. Helmensdorfer, '*Rechts* und *links* auf der Bühne' (5–22, on stage-directions in N.); R. Reutner, 'Noch einmal eine Quisquilie: über idiolektal bedingte Dialektwörter in den Volksstücken Joachim Perinets (1765–1816)' (23–28); J. Hein, 'Nachtrag zu *Der Affe und der Bräutigam* (*Stücke*, 11)' (29–30); Id., 'Wilhelm Raabe über N.' (31–32); E. Frühe, 'N. im Klassenkampf: aus der Geschichte seiner politischen Vereinnahmung' (33–50); G. Stieg, 'Canetti und N.' (51–64); U. Längle, 'Das Haupt des Titus Jochanaan Feuerfuchs: die biblische Salome-Geschichte im *Talisman*' (86–98); W. E. Yates, '"Ich will hiemit gar nicht gesagt haben, dass Herr N. entlehnt . . .": zu Ns Einfällen und Refrains' (99–112); H. Böhm, 'Zwischen Brünn, Graz und Pressburg: J. Ns Jahre in der österreichischen Theaterprovinz. Aspekte und Probleme einer möglichen N.-Biographie' (113–33); J. Hein, 'Wiedergefundene Handschriften zu Ns *Heimliches Geld, heimliche Liebe* aus der "Sammlung Trau"' (134–44); W. Obermaier, 'Unerwartete Entdeckungen: Bemerkungen zu Ns Briefen' (145–56); D. Zumbusch-Beisteiner, '"Ich ersuche hübsche Musik herauszusuchen . . .": Wirkungsbereich des Kapellmeisters einer Wiener Vorstadtbühne in der ersten Hälfte des 19. Jahrhunderts' (157–71); P. Branscombe, 'Ein wiedergefundener Entwurf zu *Umsonst*: Nachtrag zum Band *Stücke 35* der HKA' (172–76). J. Hein, 'Schreibort "Volkstheater": editorische Überlegungen am Beispiel J. Ns. Mit zwei Brief-Entwürfen', Vliet, *Edition*, 191–202. J. Hein, '"Übersetzen s' aus Frankreich a Stuck . . .": J. N. als übersetzender Bearbeiter', *Editio*, 14:72–87.

NIETZSCHE. The Berlin HKA of N.'s *Werke*, ed. Giorgio Colli et al., de Gruyter, has produced *Abt.* I, vol. 2, *Nachgelassene Aufzeichnungen* (*Herbst 1858–Herbst 1862*), ed. G. Figal et al., x + 528 pp.; and *Abt.* I, vol. 4, *Nachgelassene Aufzeichnungen (Herbst 1864–Frühjahr 1868)*, ed. Günter Figal et al., 1999, xiv + 586 pp. F. N., *Sämtliche Gedichte*, ed. Ralph-Rainer Wuthenow (Manesse Bibliothek der Weltliteratur), Zurich, Manesse, 1999, 258 pp. *Die schönsten Gedichte von Friedrich Nietzsche*, ed. Anton Friedrich (kleine detebe, 70161), Zurich, Diogenes, 103 pp. *Friedrich Nietzsche — Franz und Ida Overbeck: Briefwechsel*, ed. Katrin Meyer et al., Stuttgart–Weimar, Metzler, xxxii + 535 pp. F. N., *Die fröhliche Wissenschaft*, ed. Günter Figal (UB, 7115), 325 pp. F. N., *The Birth of Tragedy*, trans. Douglas Smith (Oxford's World Classics), OUP, 208 pp. '*Stehlen ist oft seliger als nehmen': Nietzsche zum Vergnügen*, ed. Ludger Lütkehaus (UB, 18050), 165 pp. Ralph-Rainer Wuthenow, *Friedrich Nietzsche: Leben, Schriften, Zeugnisse* (IT, 2601), 170 pp. Rüdiger Görner, *Nietzsches Kunst: Philosophie und Leben eines*

Denkkünstlers (IT, 2610), 362 pp. The Stiftung Weimarer Klassik has embarked on a major enterprise with the publication of the *Weimarer Nietzsche-Bibliographie*, vol. 1, *Primärliteratur 1867–1998*, ed. Susanne Jung et al. (Personalbibliographien zur neueren deutschen Literatur, 4), Stuttgart–Weimar, Metzler, xvi + 517 pp. This first volume is concerned solely with the publication history of the primary texts and has over 20,000 entries. Four more volumes dealing with the secondary literature and the reception of N.'s work are planned for 2001. *Widerprüche: Zur frühen Nietzsche-Rezeption*, ed. Andreas Schirmer et al., Weimar, Böhlau, 515 pp., contains 28 articles on N. reception. *Nietzsche-Handbuch: Leben — Werk — Wirkung*, ed. Henning Ottmann, Stuttgart, Metzler, xiii + 561 pp. is the first handbook on N. ever to be published and contains an enormous amount of useful material in readily accessible form. It contains 169 articles which are divided thematically into five sections. ('Zeit und Person; 'Werke in chronologischer Reihenfolge'; 'Begriffe, Theorien, Metaphern'; 'Lektüren, Quellen, Einflüsse'; 'Aspekte der Rezeption und Wirkung'). There are incisive articles on such diverse topics as anti-Semitism, the blond beast, music, tragedy, and the '*Übermensch*'. Raymond Furness, *Zarathustra's Children: A Study of a Lost Generation of German Writers* (SGLLC), ix + 220 pp., in a book that is as entertaining as it is erudite traces the influence of N. on seven less well known writers of the generation that succeeded him. Among the authors studied are Rudolf Pannwitz, Ludwig Klages, and the wonderfully eccentric Alfred Schuler. Eckhard Heftrich, *Nietzsches tragische Größe* (Das Abendland, n. F.), Frankfurt, Klostermann, 226 pp., is a collection of the author's essays on N., all previously published between 1964 and 1999. Rüdiger Safranski, *Nietzsche: Biographie seines Denkens*, Munich — Vienna, Hanser, 398 pp. Bernhard H. F. Taureck, *Nietzsche und der Faschismus: Ein Politikum* (UB, 1687), 304 pp. Lou Andreas-Salomé, *Friedrich Nietzsche in seinen Werken* (IT, 2592), ed. Ernst Pfeiffer, 359 pp., is a reprint of the 1894 original. Andrea Gogröf-Vorhees, *Defining Modernism: Baudelaire and Nietzsche on Romanticism, Modernity, Decadence and Wagner* (Studies in Literary Criticism and Theory, 8), NY–Berne, Lang, 1999, x + 201 pp., examines Baudelaire's and N.'s essays on art and culture and the role played by Wagner in their attempts to define 'modernism'. *Entdecken und Verraten: Zu Leben und Werk Friedrich Nietzsches*, ed. Andreas Schirmer et al., Weimar, Hermann Böhlaus Nachfolger, 1999, 412 pp., is a collective volume containing 30 essays by scholars from a range of disciplines on diverse aspects of N.'s life and work. Articles most likely to be of interest to Germanists are: D. Schelling, 'Zwischen griechischem Altertum und Richard Wagner:

verschlungene Denkwege des frühen N.' (93–110); M. Eger, 'Zum Fall Wagner / N. / Hanslick' (111–31); D. Borchmeyer, 'Passion und Polemik: Ns Wagner-Kritik' (148–68). *Friedrich Nietzsche: Chronik in Bildern und Texten*, ed. Raymond Benders et al. (Stiftung Weimarer Klassik bei Hanser), Munich–Vienna, Hanser, 855 pp. Manfred Riedel, *Nietzsche in Weimar: Ein deutsches Drama* (UB, 1685), 357 pp. Alexander Hogh, **Nietzsches Lebensbegriff: Versuch einer Rekonstruktion* (M & P Schriftenreihe für Wissenschaft und Forschung), Stuttgart, Metzler, 205 pp., is a Berlin dissertation. Georg Bayerle, **Wissen oder Kunst: Nietzsches Poetik des Sinns und die Erkenntnisformen der Moderne*, Cologne–Weimar, Böhlau, 1998, ix + 472 pp., is a 1997 Cologne dissertation. E. Strobel, **Das 'Pathos der Distanz': Nietzsches Entscheidung für den Aphorismenstil* (Nietzsche in der Diskussion), Würzburg, Königshausen & Neumann, 1998, 208 pp., is a 1996 Tübingen dissertation. Anette Horn, **Nietzsches Begriff der 'décadence': Kritik und Analyse der Moderne* (Heidelberger Beiträge zur deutschen Literatur, 5), Frankfurt, Lang, 379 pp., is a 1998 Capetown dissertation. Roger Bauer, *Die schöne Décadence: Geschichte eines literarischen Paradoxons* (Das Abendland, n. F., 28), Frankfurt, Klostermann, 421 pp., has some discussion of Nietzsche. Claus Zittel, **Das ästhetische Kalkül von Friedrich Nietzsches 'Also sprach Zarathustra'* (Nietzsche in der Diskussion), Würzburg, Königshausen & Neumann, 261 pp., is a 1999 Frankfurt dissertation. Erhard Naake, **Nietzsche und Weimar: Werk und Wirkung im 20. Jahrhundert*, Cologne–Weimar, Böhlau, viii + 246 pp.

Nietzsche, Philosophy and the Arts, ed. Salim Kemal et al., (Cambridge Studies in Philosophy and the Arts), CUP, 1998, xv + 351 pp., is a collective volume with 13 articles of generally high quality by an international team of N. scholars. The theme of the book is N.'s belief in the transformative and redemptive power of art, and the moral, social and political implications of his ideas. Unsurprisingly, the texts that attract most of the contributors' attention are *Die Geburt der Tragödie, Also sprach Zarathustra, Jenseits von Gut und Böse, Die Genealogie der Moral* and *Ecce homo*. Some of the contributions are concerned with the practical influence of his ideas on the visual arts (Klimt) and on music (the Dionysian impulse in improvised modern jazz!). The individual articles are: E. Behler, 'N.'s conception of irony' (13–35); M. C. Nussbaum, 'The transfigurations of intoxication: N., Schopenhauer, and Dionysus' (36–69); A. del Caro, 'Nietzschean self-transformation and the transformation of the Dionysian' (70–91); R. Havas, 'Socratism and the question of aesthetic justification' (92–127); A. Ridley, 'What is the meaning of aesthetic ideals?' (128–47, on *Die Genealogie der Moral*); S. Bann, 'The splitting of historical consciousness' (148–61, on the second of the *Unzeitgemäße Betrachtungen*); T. W. Hiles, 'Gustav Klimt's *Beethoven Frieze*, truth, and *The Birth of Tragedy*' (162–86); J. Carvalho, 'Improvisations, on N, on jazz (187–211); F. Jenkins, 'Performative identity: N. on the force of art and language' (212–38); H. Staten, 'Dionysus lost and found: literary genres in the political thought of N. and Lukács' (239–56); S. Kemal, 'N.'s politics of aesthetic genius' (257–86); D. W. Conway, 'Love's labor's lost: the philosopher's *Versucherkunst*' (287–309); C. Crawford, 'N.'s Dionysian arts: dance, song, and silence' (310–41). *Nietzscheforschung: Jahrbuch der Nietzsche-Gesellschaft*, 7, has: J. Salaquarda, 'F. N. und die Bibel unter besonderer Berücksichtigung von *Also sprach Zarathustra*' (323–33); G. Figal, 'Kein Grieche und kein tragischer Gott: Ns *Zarathustra*-Dichtung zwischen Platon und Richard Wagner' (335–41). *Nietzsche-Studien*, 28, 1999, has: B. Spannhake, 'Umwertung einer Quelle: vergleichende Anmerkungen zur Buddhismus-Interpretation des jungen N. in *Die Geburt der Tragödie aus dem Geiste der Musik* und der Studie Carl Friedrich Koeppens über *Die Religion des Buddha und ihre Entstehung*' (156–93); É. Dufour, 'Les Lieder de F. N.' (234–54). *EG*, 55 has one number (2) devoted almost entirely to N.'s view of history and contains: H. Schnädelbach, 'Ns Kritik der historischen Bildung' (169–83); G. Raulet, 'Ns Kritik der Historie: ein zweifelhafter Kampf' (185–202); A. Schober, 'L'art de l'histoire selon N.' (221–33); J.-M. Paul, '*Vom Nutzen und Nachteil der Historie für das Leben*: de l'histoire à la morale' (235–48); V. Gerhardt, 'Das Denken eines Individuums: erneutes Nachdenken über Ns zweite *Unzeitgemäße Betrachtung*' (249–67); G. Figal, 'Heidegger und N. über Geschichte: zu einer unausgetragenen Kontroverse' (269–77); P.-H. Tavoillot, 'La *Généalogie* contre le *Tribunal du monde*: la critique nietzschéenne de la dialectique' (279–90); F. Guery, 'Allégories de N.: leur porteé, leur interprétation' (291–302).

T. Fiedler, 'Zarathustras Kind: zu N., Lou und Rainer im *Florenzer Tagebuch*, *Fest. Storck*, 293–318. D. Large, 'The aristocratic radical and the white revolutionary: N.'s Bismarck' *Sagarra Vol.*, 101–13. H.-J. Schings, 'Aufstieg und Krise des modernen Prometheus: von Percy B. und Mary Shelley bis zu N.', *Fest. Denkler.*, 55–68. R. Speirs, ' "Apollo aber schließlich die Sprache des Dionysus": harmony or hegemony in *Die Geburt der Tragödie*', *Will Vol.*, 51–58, is concerned with the relationship between the Apolline and the Dionysiac in tragedy. R. Görner, 'The end-game of aesthetics: N.'s reading of Schiller's theory of aesthetic education in the light of our experience', *Fest. Reeves*, 31–41. K. Kauffmann, 'Nietzscheanische Funken? Zum Verhältnis zwischen F. Ns und Rudolf Borchardts Kulturdenken', pp. 15–27 of *Jugendstil und Kulturkritik: Zur Literatur und Kunst um 1900*, ed. Andreas Beyer et al. (Jenaer germanistische Forschungen, n. F., 7), Heidelberg, Winter, 1998, 230 pp. B. Spannhake, ' "N. war wie ein Ross edelster Rasse, das aber schlecht eingeritten": vergleichende Anmerkungen zur (naturalistischen) N.-Interpretation Stanisław Przybyszewskis am Beispiel seines essayistischen Frühwerks und der Romantrilogie *Homo Sapiens*', *Orbis linguarum*, 13, 1999:43–89. G. Bayerle, 'Metapher und Gelächter: mediale Bewusstwerdung und ästhetische Mobilisierung in Ns Philosophie', *WB*, 46:17–37. E. Kleinschmidt, 'Abwesende Gegenwärtigkeit: Grenzpositionen der Autorschaft in F. Ns *Ecce homo*', *ib.*, 165–79. M. Stingelin, ' "Unser Schreibwerkzeug arbeitet mit an unseren Gedanken": die poetologische Reflexion der Schreibwerkzeuge bei Lichtenberg und F. N.', *Lichtenberg-Jb.*, 1999:81–98. W. Düsing, 'Ns Abhandlung *Vom Nutzen und Nachteil der Historie für das Leben* und die Politik des Geschichtsdramas', *ZGB*, Beiheft 5, 1999, 73–91. T. Keith, ' "Die Welt als ästhetisches Phänomen": Gottfried Benns N.-Rezeption', *ZGer*, n. F., 10:116–26. R. Gutiérrez Girardot, 'La poesía de N.', *Cuadernos hispanoamericanos*, 601–02:205–21. M. Riedel, 'Zwischen Poesie und Prosa: N. und Leopardi', *GRM*, 50:183–202. C. Simonin, 'Heinrich Mann et N. ou la séduction de l'esthétisme', *Germanica*, 26:57–68. L. Blum, 'Else Lasker-Schüler beim kranken N.: Adnoten zu einer Legende', *WW*, 50:325–28. A. del Caro, 'Andreas Salomé und N.: new perspectives', *Seminar*, 36:79–96. J. E. Mann, 'N., music and the artistic Socrates', *ib.*, 399–417.

OTTO-PETERS, LOUISE. J. Ludwig, 'Dem Reich der Freiheit werb' ich Bürgerinnen: Louise Otto — Lerche des Völkerfrühlings', pp. 70–81 of *1848, lass Recht und Freiheit nicht verderben: Zum 150. Jahrestag der Deutschen Revolution von 1848/49 in Sachsen*, ed. Volker Rodekamp (Veröffentlichungen) des Stadtgeschichtlichen Museums Leipzig), Leipzig, Passage, 1998, 152 pp., is an exhibition catalogue.

POCCI, FRANZ VON. Günter Goepfert, **Franz von Pocci: Vom Zeremonienmeister zum 'Kasperlgrafen'. Lebens- und Schaffensweg eines universellen Talents*, Dachau, Bayerland, 1999, 132 pp.

PÜCKLER-MUSKAU. H. v. P.-M., *Liebesbriefe eines alten Kavaliers: Briefwechsel des Fürsten Pückler-Muskau mit Ada von Treskow 1860–1864*, ed. A. Meiners, Berlin, Berliner Handpresse, 1998, 41 pp. Hans-Joachim Schickedanz, *Ästhetische Rebellion und rebellische Ästheten: Eine kulturgeschichtliche Studie über den europäischen Dandyismus* (FLK, 66), 245 pp., has some discussion of Pückler-Muskau. W. Klausewitz, 'Der Zwist zwischen Fürst P. und Eduard Rüppell', *Natur und Museum*, 129, 1999:133–45.

RAABE. W. R., *Drei Federn*, ed. Hans-Jürgen Schrader, Berlin, Aufbau, 177 pp. Dirk Göttsche, *Zeitreflexion und Zeitkritik im Werk Wilhelm Raabes*, Würzburg, Königshausen & Neumann, 184 pp. M. Masanetz, '"Das Ewig-Weibliche zieht uns hinan"? Lebensbilanz als *Faust*-Travestie'. W. Rs *Akten des Vogelsangs*', *Fest. Richter*, 203–25. G. Biegel, 'Margarethe Raabe: Tochter, Künstlerin und Nachlassverwalterin. Ein Leben im und als Schatten eines berühmten Schriftstellers', *ib.*, 227–47. P. Goldammer, 'Idyllisch-gemütvoller Poet oder Kultur- und Gesellschaftskritiker. W. R. in deutschen Konversationslexika', *ib.*, 249–56. *Raabe-Jb.*, 41, has: W. Frühwald, 'Philisterliebe? Zum Alterswerk W. Rs' (1–15); M. Dierks, '"Das Kind noch dabei": R., Freud und Jensen in Altershausen' (16–30); H. Suhrbier, 'Zitat und Schattenriss: Fritz Reuter im Werk von W. R.' (31–51); I. Chopin, 'Die Topographie des Krieges in Erzählungen W. Rs' (52–73); G. Cremer, 'Gott oder Satan? Negierte Heilsbotschaft und Nihilismus in Rs Erzählung *Else von der Tanne*'(74–95); H. Fischer, '"Was fangen wir mit Horacker an?" Ein unbekannter Brief W. Rs an Carl Schultes' (96–101); M. Kindermann, 'Subjektkonstitution als Entfremdung: impliziertes psychologisches Wissen in W. Rs Roman *Die Akten des Vogelsangs*' (102–21); W. Dittrich, 'R.-Bibliographie 2000' (188–93). F. Krobb, 'Geschichtssinn und Narrativität in W. Rs Erzählung *Die Innerste*', *Sagarra Vol.*, 89–99. L. Tatlock, 'Disease and Communion in W. R.'s *Unruhige Gäste*', *MDLK*, 91, 1999:323–41. E. Heftrich, 'W. R.: geheime Quellen des *Doktor Faustus*?', *Thomas-Mann-Jb.*, 13:123–28. U. Karthaus, '*Doktor Faustus*, die *Akten des Vogelsangs*, die Philologie und die Hermeneutik', *ib.*, 129–32. H. Detering, 'Die Geburt der Tragödie im "alten Eisen": Vermutungen über Rs Nietzsche-Lektüre', *Fest. Denkler*, 19–30. S. Fauth, 'W. Rs *Das Odfeld* und Schopenhauers Metaphysik', *TeK*, 21, 1998:59–93.

RAIMUND. Carl Meisl, *Moiasura's Hexenspruch*, ed. Richard Reutner (*Raimund Almanach*, 1998), Vienna, Lehner, 1998, 119 pp., prints for the first time, with some explanatory notes, the text of Meisl's parody of R.'s *Moiasurs Zauberfluch*. Meisl's parody was first performed, with great success, in the Theater in der Leopoldstadt in November 1827, a few days after the première of R.'s play in the Theater an der Wien. A. Piemonti, 'Il flauto magico e il diamante rosa: considerazioni su quanto intercorre tra *Die Zauberflöte* di Mozart e *Der Diamant des Geisterkönigs* di Raimund', *Prospéro*, 5, 1998:89–113.

REUTER, FRITZ. F. R., *Erlebte und geschriebene Geschichte: Ein bisher unveröffentlichtes Manuskript Fritz Reuters*, ed. Liselotte M. David, Hamburg, Bockel, 1998, 91 pp. Cornelia Nenz, *Auf immer und ewig Dein Fritz Reuter: Aus dem Leben der Luise Reuter*, Rostock, Hinstorff,

1998, 99 pp. *Fritz Reuter in Eisenach*, ed. C. Brunners et al., Hamburg, Bockel, 1998, 243 pp., contains 14 articles on Reuter. *Die Zoologie der Träume: Studien zum Tiermotiv in der Literatur der Moderne*, ed. Dorothee Römhild, Opladen, Westdeutscher Vlg, 1999, 261 pp., has: H. Suhrbier, 'Bauschan auf dem Traualtar: Bemerkungen zu einer Szene in F. R's Roman *Ut mine Stromtid*' (19–24); D. Römhild, 'Der Hund als Falke: zur poetologischen und kulturgeschichtlichen Funktion des "Löwengelben" in Storms Novelle *Waldwinkel*' (25–58).

RÜCKERT. The Schweinfurt edition of R.'d works has added *Gedichte von Rom und andere Texts der Jahre 1817–1818*, ed. Claudia Wiener, Göttingen, Wallstein, 748 pp.

SACHER-MASOCH. K. Wagner, 'S.-M.: ein "Naturdichter" auf Abwegen', *Cultura tedesca*, 11, 1999:64–71. S. Wilke, 'The sexual woman and her struggle for subjectivity: cruel women in Sade, S.-M., and Treut', *WGY*, 14, 1999:245–60.

SCHEFFEL. B. Potthast, 'Zu Signaturen ästhetischer Erinnerung in J. V. v. Ss *Ekkehard* (1885)', *Euphorion*, 94:205–24.

SCHOPENHAUER, JOHANNA. J. S., *Im Wechsel der Zeiten, im Gedränge der Welt: Jugenderinnerngen, Tagebücher, Briefe*, ed. Rolf Weber, Düsseldorf–Zurich, Artemis & Winkler, 488 pp. Anke Gilleir, **Johanna Schopenhauer und die Weimarer Klassik: Betrachtungen über die Selbstpositionierung weiblichen Schreibens* (GTS, 64), xx + 372 pp.

SCHWAB, GUSTAV. W. Mieder, '*Der Reiter über den Bodensee*: von der angeblichen Sage über die Kunstballade zur Redensart', *Fabula*, 40, 1999:195–221.

SEALSFIELD. *Charles Sealsfield: Politischer Erzähler zwischen Europa und Amerika. Perspektiven internationaler Forschung. Symposion Bergamo, Oktober 1994*, ed. Gustav-Adolf Pogatschnigg (Schriftenreihe der C.-S. Gesellschaft, 9), Turin, Zamorani, 1998, 215 pp., is mainly concerned with S.'s view of North America and contains: P.-H. Kucher, ' "... they unquestionably afford the clearest and most animated picture of Austrian life": S.'s *Austria as it is*. Argumentative Strategien und wirkungsgeschichtliche Aspekte' (9–29); N. Dacrema, 'Enrico Misley und die politische Publizistik von C. S.' (30–40); G.-A. Pogatschnigg, 'Die politischen Novellen C. Ss im *Englishman's Magazine* von 1831: Vorüberlegungen zu einer kommentierten Textausgabe' (41–57); A. Destro, 'Österreich wie es ist: S. und Nestroy. Ein Vergleich' (58–70); M. L. Roli, ' "Das Sublime und Ridicule ist dicht nebeneinander": C. Ss emphatische Prosa im Hintergrund der kritischen Rezeption' (71–84); M. Ponzi, 'Von der Wildnis zur Modernität' (85–95); C. Giacobazzi, 'Die Duplizität Karl Postl/C. Ss und die Duplizität der Fremde' (96–105); A. Ritter, 'Ein Bankpräsident ohne

Schattenwurf oder: Ss Schreiben gegen die Krise und seine demontierender Umgang mit dem historischen Roman' (106–19, on the *Cajütenbuch*); F. Schüppen, 'Abendländischer Sinneswandel: von Käpitan Murkys Kajüte zu Uncle Tom's Cabin' (120–38); L.-P. Linke, 'Stillstand und Bewegung: Ss *Cajütenbuch* als "joint venture" von amerikanischer "Frontier"-Ideologie und europäischem Fortschrittsdenken' (139–58); W. Grünzweig, 'Die tänzerische Demokratie: C. Ss französische Louisiana' (159–71); G. Scherer, 'C. Ss *Lebensbilder: Die Farbigen*' (172–81); W. Kriegleder, 'Amerikathematik und Erzählsystem in Ss *Lebensbildern*' (182–95); M. Beller, 'Amerikanische Charakteristiken für deutsche und für englische Leser: Schreibstrategien in C. Sidons' *Die Vereinigten Staaten von Nordamerika* (1827) und in *The United States of North America as they are* (1828)' (196–207, on *Die Vereinigten Staaten von Nordamerika nach ihrem politischen, religiösen und gesellschaftlichen Verhältnisse betrachtet*).

In response to the growing interest in S. the Sealsfield-Gesellschaft has founded a new yearbook with the title *Sealsfield-Studien*. *Sealsfield-Studien*, 1, ed. Alexander Ritter (Schriftenreihe der C.-S.-Gesellschaft, 11), Munich, C.-S.-Gesellschaft, 1998, 208 pp., has: W. Kriegleder, 'Amerika-Idyllik und Euro-Skepsis: zum Verhältnis Amerika-Europa im Werk C. Ss' (11–25); P.-H. Kucher, 'Zur europäischen Sealsfield-Rezeption: eine Projektskizze' (27–38); F. Schüppen, 'Mehrsprachige Spätromantik in Europa und Amerika: zu Gérard de Nervals Transkription eines Textes von C. S.' (39–62, on *Christophorus Bärenhäuter*); A. Ritter, ' "Louisiana — the new Egypt!": a European focus by travelogue on the United States. C. S.'s doubled search for identity and his report on the U.S., the South, and Louisiana in the 1820s' (63–95); K. Hara, 'Zwei Paradiese: Sinngebung und Sinnverschiebung in C. Ss Roman *Der Cajütenbuch* im Vergleich mit einigen ausgewählten Texten von Stifter und Nestroy' (97–124); G. Scherer, 'Die Fremde und ihre Transposition in C. Ss *Süden und Norden*' (125–35); G. K. Friesen, 'Some sources of S.'s *Süden und Norden*' (137–44); L.-P. Linke, 'Gespenstische Aufklärung: Überlegungen zur Erzählung *Die Grabesschuld* als Beispiel für Ss Umgang mit populären Genres' (145–65); J. L. Sammons, 'C. S. (Carl Postl) 3. März 1793–26. Mai 1864' (167–76); A. Ritter, 'C.-S.-Bibliographie 1987–1998' (177–202). *Sealsfield-Studien*, 2, has: A. Ritter, 'Versäumte Nähe "der Küche, des Kaminfeuers": C. S., der historische Roman und die ästhetische Funktionalisierung der Geschichte in amerikanischen Geschichten' (23–32); G. Schnitzler, 'Ss erzählte Landschaft' (33–41); F. Schüppen, 'Poetische Wohnorte der Biedermeierzeit 1841: Wald- und Steppenhäuser bei S. und Stifter' (55–69); G. K.

Friesen, ' "S.'s unrealistic Mexiko": A re-evaluation' (71–80); A. Ritter, 'Grenzübertritt und Schattentausch: der österreichische Priester Carl Postl und seine vage staatsbürgerliche Identität als amerikanischer Literat Charles Sealsfield. Eine Dokumentation' (81–122); J. C. Schöpp, 'Österreich im Lichte Amerikas: C. Ss politische Reiseskizzen' (123–36); M. Bernhard, 'Eine Landschaft von Salvator Rosa und eine Landschaft bei C. S. Über die Anwesenheit von Kunst in der Kunst' (137–62); Charles Sealsfield, '*Early Impressions/Frühe Eindrücke*. Übersetzt von Gerald Frodl' (163–76); A. Ritter, 'S.-Bibliographie 1998–2000' (177–81). W. Kriegleder, 'The American Indian in German novels up to the 1850s', *GLL*, 53:487–98, has comment on S., J. C. Biernatzki, and Kürnberger among others. A. Ritter, 'C. S. — Karl Postl-Bibliographie 1987–1998 (Stand November 1998)', *Sprachkunst*, 29, 1998:402–20.

SPIELHAGEN. K. Roper, '1848 in the early novels of F. S.: the making of a German democrat', *GSR*, 23:427–52.

STIFTER. Helena Ragg-Kirkby, *Adalbert Stifter's Late Prose: The Mania for Moderation* (SGLLC), x + 137 pp., aims to adjust the traditional view of S. as an exemplary man of moderation and an heir to the tradition of German Classicism, seeing him instead as a 'closet modernist, and a trailblazer for Kafka and the Absurd'. Without denying that he consciously strove in his life and work to be 'ein Mann des Maßes', she argues that there is in fact a polarity in him between Classicism and modernism, between 'a comforting faith in divine order and human reason' on the one hand and 'a terrifying vision of infinite emptiness and futility' on the other. *Witiko*, with its omnipresent awareness of the abyss, is seen as his characteristic masterpiece which has been unduly neglected in favour of the 'moderate' works of S.'s early and middle periods. The book is strongly argued without being dogmatic, and its clear and fluent style which is refreshingly free from disfiguring jargon ensures that it is highly readable. Birgit Ehlbeck, **Denken wie der Wald: zur poetologischen Funktionalisierung des Empirismus in den Roman und Erzählungen Adalbert Stifters und Wilhelm Raabes*, Berlin, Philo, 1998, 270 pp., is a 1996 Marburg dissertation. Oliver Fischer, '*Ins Leben geschrieben: Zäsuren und Revisionen. Poetik privater Geschichte bei Adalbert Stifter und Wilhelm Raabe*, Würzburg, Königshausen & Neumann, 1999, 333 pp., is a 1999 Munich dissertation. Beatrice Mall-Grob, **Fiktion des Anfangs: Literarische Kindheitsmodelle bei Jean Paul und Adalbert Stifter*, Stuttgart, 1999, 414 pp., is a 1998 Basle dissertation.

Fest. Frühwald has 16 articles on Stifter: E. Ziegler, 'Im Zirkelodem der Sterne: Über *Die Sonnenfinsterniss am 8. July 1842 in Wien*' (4–19); H. Reinhardt, 'Literarische Trauerarbeit: Ss Novellen *Das alte Siegel* und *Der Hagestolz* als Erzähltragödien' (20–39); K. Feilchenfeldt, '*Brigitte* und andere Chiffren des Lebens bei A. S.' (41–60); H. Laufhütte, 'Das sanfte Gesetz und der Abgrund: zu den Grundlagen der Ss Dichtung "aus dem Geiste der Naturwissenschaft"' (61–74); W. Hettche, '"Dichten" oder "Machen"? A. Ss Arbeit an seinem Roman *Der Nachsommer*' (75–86); G. Häntzschel, 'A. Ss *Nausikaa*' (87–96); J. Lachinger, 'Ss *Nachsommer*: ein singuläres episches Werk' (97–100); U. Landfester, 'Der Autor als S. oder *Die Mappe meines Urgrossvaters*' (101–24); H. Gottwald, 'Beobachtungen zum Motiv des Landschaftsgartens bei S.' (125–45); W. Wiesmüller, 'Das Motiv der Stromfahrt in A. Ss *Witiko*: Versuch einer multiplen Kodierung' (146–62); G. Neumann, '"Zuversicht": A. Ss Schicksalskonzept zwischen Novellistik und Autobiographie' (163–87); S. von Steinsdorff, 'Ss "Seze den 2oiger in die Lotterie": der Spieler S.' (188–201); U. Dittmann, 'Fürsorgliche Zensur: bibliographische Ergänzungen und rezeptionsgeschichtliche Anmerkungen zu S.-Texten' (202–16); J. John, 'A. S. in Erzählungen von Johannes Urdizil' (217–43); A. Doppler, 'A. S. als Briefschreiber' (244–54); P. Greipl, 'Drei bisher ungedruckte S.-Briefe' (255–58). *JASI*, 4, 1997[2000]; has: U. Dittmann, 'Die hermeneutische Relevanz der Journalfassungen von A. Ss *Studien*' (8–15); H. Gottwald, 'Beobachtungen zu Ss Weg von der dritten zur vierten Fassung der *Mappe meines Urgroßvaters*' (16–35); W. Hettche, 'Die Textzeugen zu Ss *Granit* und *Bergmilch*' (36–44); A. Brande, '"Keine Spur von Menschenhand ..."': Ss *Hochwald* vegetationsgeschichtlich betrachtet' (77–93). S. Schmidt, 'Wenn Frauen in die Luft gehen: Aspekte eines Kollektivsymbols bei Jean Paul, August Lafontaine, und A. S.', *Fest. Storck*, 175–200, has some comment on S.'s *Der Condor*. W. Hettche, 'Von der Allmählichkeit: Schreibprozesse und Erzählprozesse in A. Ss Prosa', Vliet, *Edition*, 203–11. G. Fussenegger, 'A. Ss pädagogischer Eros', pp. 409–23 of *Grenzüberschreitungen: Festschrift für Gertrud Fussenegger*, ed. Frank-Lothar Kroll, Munich, Langen Müller, 1998, 494 pp. D. Müller, 'Des Gezähmten Widerspenstigkeit: gegenläufige Deutungsperspektiven in A. Ss Erzählung *Nachkommenschaften*', *Raabe-Jb.*, 42:122–35. P.-H. Kucher, 'Verfremdete — fremde Welten: zu Ss *Abdias* (1842), *ZGB*, Beiheft 5, 1999, 25–39. G. K. Schneider, 'Owê war sint verswunden alliu mîniu jâr: Betrachtungen zum Alter(n), Tod und Generationsbeziehungen bei A. S., Jean Améry und Inge Merkel', *Jura Soyfer*, 8, 1999:17–23. H. Pfotenhauer, 'Bild und

Schrift: zur Funktion von Medienwechseln in der realistischen Literatur. S., Keller', *Sagarra Vol.*, 207–17, discusses the presence of the visual and plastic arts in S.'s stories *Feldblumen* and *Nachkommen-schaften* and in Keller's *Sinngedicht*. H. Ester, 'Sprachbildlichkeit in A. Ss Roman *Der Nachsommer*', pp. 147–59 of *Das Sprach-Bild als textuelle Interaktion*, ed. Gerd Labroisse (ABNG, 45), 1999, 405 pp. K. Matsuoka, 'Das verlorene Licht: das "Erhabene" bei A. S.', *DB*, 104 : 122–30 (Japanese with German summary), is concerned with S.'s view of the sublime in *Die Sonnenfinsternis am 8. Juli 1842* and *Aus dem Bayerischen Walde* of 1867. H. Ragg-Kirkby, ' "Sie geht in ihren großen eigenen Gesetzen fort, die uns in teifen Fernen liegen, [. . .] und wir können nur stehen und bewundern": A. S. and the alienation of man and nature, *GQ*, 72, 1999 : 349–61. In a further article by Ragg-Kirkby, ' "Eine immerwährende Umwandlung der Ansichten": narrators and their perspectives in the works of A. S.', *MLR*, 95 : 127–43, it is argued that S.'s work offers no narrative objectivity because all the information the reader receives is rendered unreliable by the use of a constantly shifting and ambivalent perspective. G. Stieg, 'Von der Hommage zum Verriss: der Austriophobe Arno Schmidt über A. S.', *Austriaca*, 24, 1999 : 93–106. W. Kriegleder, 'Natur und Landschaft in A. Ss *Hochwald*', *Sealsfield-Studien*, 2 : 11–21. F. Schössler, ' "Die düstere Schönheit solcher Oeden": zu Ss Landschaften', *ib.*, 43–54.

STORM. T. S., *Der Herr Etatsrat: Novellen*, ed. Peter Goldammer (ATV, 6077), 275 pp., reprints the text of four *Novellen*, that of the title and also *Carsten Curator, Hans und Heinz Kirch*, and *Bötjer Basch*. Karl Ernst Laage, *Theodor Storm: Biographie*, Heide, Boyens, 1999, 286 pp., is aimed at a general readership. With the aid of numerous illustrations it provides a rounded picture of S.'s personality and career. The material is presented in short sections of 10 or 20 pages ('Storm und die Musik', 'Der Bücherliebhaber', 'Storm und die Juristerei'). Ingrid Schuster, *'Ich habe niemals eine Zeile geschrieben, wenn sie mir fern war': Das Leben der Constanze Storm und vergleichende Studien zum Werk Theodor Storms* (CSGLL, 43), 1998, 227 pp., looks at first glance like a monograph but turns out in fact to be a collection of eight essays on S. by the author, four of which have been published before. The most substantial new material in the volume is the long (and interesting) account of the life of S.'s long-suffering first wife Constanze and her often difficult relationship with her egocentric husband, 'Bis dass der Tod euch scheidet: das Leben der Constanze Storm (1825–1865)' (13–108). The other new articles are: 'Liebe zwischen Hölle und Himmel: literarische Zitate und Spiegelungen'

(109–31, on literary sources of *Späte Rosen*, *Von Jenseit des Meeres*, and *Ein Fest auf Haderslevhuus*); 'Stifters *Waldsteig* und Ss *Schweigen*' (153–64); and 'Ss *Waldwinkel* und Fontanes *Graf Petöfy*' (165–82). Wiebke Strehl, *Theodor Storm's 'Immensee': A Critical Overview* (SGLLC), xi + 127 pp., traces both the popular and the critical reception of S.'s most popular Novelle from 1849 to 1998, bringing out well and clearly the enduring popularity of the work before 1914; the attempts made between 1914 and 1945 to portray S. as a nationalistic *Heimatdichter*; the first serious criticisms of the work made by Marxist critics after 1945; and the new types of critical approach adopted in more recent times. There is also a short chapter on film versions of the story. *Die Storm-Handschriften aus dem Nachlass von Ernst Storm. Mit der Edition des 'Concepts' zur Novelle 'Der Schimmelreiter'*, ed. J. Fischer (Patrimonia, 151), Berlin, Kulturstif-tung der Länder, 1999, 80 pp., contains: K. E. Laage, 'Die Geschichte und Bedeutung des handschriftlichen S.-Nachlasses' (5–8); G. Eversberg, 'T. S., "Der Schimmelreiter": das "Concept" (Sommer bis Weihnachten 1887). Rekonstruktion und Edition des *Schimmelreiter*-Manuskripts aus dem Konvolut *Nachlass Ernst Storm* im S.-Archiv' (13–77).

Theodor Storm: Narrative Strategies and Patriarchy, ed. David Jackson et al. (SGLL, 22), 1999, xiii + 264 pp., publishes the papers given at a symposium on S. held in Cardiff in 1997 and contains: P. Goldammer, 'T. S. im Widerstreit der Ideologien' (1–21); R. Fasold, 'Narzissmus und Formdrang in T. Ss Novelle *Auf dem Staatshof* (1859)' (23–47); M. Swales, 'Symptomatisches oder kreatives Schreiben: zu T. Ss *Auf dem Staatshof*' (49–59); E. Pastor, 'T. Ss Novelle *Von jenseit des Meeres*, oder: Überlegungen zu der Frage, ob "es unmöglich ist, einen Mohren weiss zu waschen"' (61–84); C. Weedon, 'Konstruktionen rassischer Differenz in T. Ss *Von jenseit des* Meeres' (85–105); M. Stein, 'Schattenehe: Verleugnung von Differenz in T. Ss Novelle *Viola tricolor*' (109–37); M. Ward, 'Namen, Rolle, Bilder und Identität: Ss *Viola tricolor*' (139–59); G. Eversberg, 'Die Schuld des Erzählers in T. Ss Novelle *Der Herr Etatsrat*' (161–76); C. Bland, ' "Das sind keine Dinge für die Ohren einer jungen Dame": vom Mythos des familiären Schutzes in Ss *Der Herr Etatsrat*' (177–97); D. Jackson. '*Zur Chronik von Grieshuus*' (199–215); P. Howe, '*Zur Chronik von Grieshuus*' (217–37); H. Peitsch, 'Ein S. aus Blut und Boden? Zur literarhistorischen Biographik aus der Zeit des Faschismus am Beispiel Franz Stuckerts' (239–64). *Stormlektüren: Festschriften für Karl Ernst Laage zum 80. Geburts-tag*, ed. Gerd Eversberg et al., Würzburg, Königshausen & Neumann, 416 pp., contains 22 essays by leading S.-scholars from all over the world: R. Berbig, ' "alle diese guten und schlechten Bücher kann ich

nur naschend einsehen'': T. S. als Leser' (21–32); C. A. Bernd, 'Vom
dänischen Kulturerbe: um ein neues Verständnis für Ss Lyrik bittend'
(33–45); R. Fasold, 'T. Ss Verständnis von "Vererbung" im Kontext
des Darwinismus-Diskurses seiner Zeit' (47–58); L. Gerrekens,
'Funktionen von Intertextualität in *Zur Chronik von Grieshuus* und *Zur
Wald- und Wasserfreude*' (59–78); G. Bollenbeck, 'T. S.: bildungsbürgerliche Lebenslagen und bildungsbürgerliche Kunstsemantik' (79–89);
D. Lohmeier, 'Der Briefwechsel zwischen T. S. und Ferdinand
Tönnies' (91–127, with a reprint of the 38 letters of the correspondence as far as possible in their original form and with annotations);
H. Pätzold, 'Der verunsicherte Bürger: Bemerkungen zum Paradigma
misslingender pluripolar Identität in *Carsten Curator*' (129–41); P. Gol-
dammer, 'Culpa patris? T. Ss Verhältnis zu seinem Sohn Hans und
seine Spiegelung in den Novellen *Carsten Curator* und *Hans und Heinz
Kirch*' (143–50); D. Jackson, 'Von Müttern, Mamas, Marien und
Madonnen: *Viola tricolor*, eine Novelle aus patriarchalischer Zeit'
(151–62); E. Pastor, 'Die männliche Stimme: Überlegungen zum
Stormschen Erzählen anlässlich der Novelle *Renate*' (163–82);
I. Roebling, '"Von Menschentragik und wildem Naturgeheimnis":
die Thematisierung von Natur und Weiblichkeit in *Der Schimmelreiter*'
(183–214); P. Boswell, '"Beginn des Endes": das letzte Ergebnis'
(215–26); B. Coghlan, 'Unterschwellige Gedanken zur Entstehung
von "Geh nicht hinein"' (227–40); W. Freund, 'Eros und Thanatos:
zur Balladendichtung T. Ss' (241–53); M. Wünsch, 'Leben im
Zeichen des Todes: zu T. Ss Lyrik' (255–70); R. J. Danilevski and
G. A. Thieme, 'Das Genre "Storm-Turgenjew" und die russische
lyrische Prosa' (270–79); B. Hinrichs, 'Zur Lyrik-Konzeption T. Ss:
Emanzipation von der rhetorischen Phrase und intertextueller
Dialog' (281–99); J. Royer, 'Detlev von Liliencron über T. S.: aus
einem unveröffentlichten Brief Liliencrons an Michael Georg Conrad' (301–11); A. Cozic, '"Der Gespensterbesen": von der Quelle
zur *Kamin*-Geschichte. Ss Auffassung vom Phantastischen' (313–22);
G. Eversberg, '"Vor der Deichnovelle habe ich einige Furcht": Ss
letzter Schreibprozess im Spiegel der *Schimmelreiter*-Textzeugen'
(322–48); H. Detering, 'Entomologische Verwandlungen: Kafka als
Leser von Ss *Der Herr Etatrat*' (349–61); H. Segeberg, '"S. ver-filmt"?
Veit Harlans Film *Unsterbliche Geliebte* (1951)' (363–85, on the film
based loosely on *Aquis submerses*). *Storm-Essays aus japanischer Perspektive:
Jubiläumsband aus Anlass des 15jährigen Bestehens der Theodor-Storm-
Gesellschaft Japan*, ed. Hiroyuki Tanaka et al., Husum, Husum-Druck-
u. Verlagsgesellschaft, 1999, 124 pp., has: H. and M. Tanaka, 'T.

S. in Japan — beliebt und hochgeschätzt' (9–23); Y. Watanabe, 'S.-Rezeption in der japanischen Kinderliteratur nach dem Zweiten Weltkrieg' (37–45); M. Ishibashi, ' "Lyrische Form": zur Formauffassung Ss' (46–55); S. Fukami, ' "Forever *Immensee*" once again: Versuch einer Analyse Erzählung als einer Initiationsnovelle' (56–68); O. Nakamuru, 'Überlegungen zu T. Ss Novelle *Renate* vor dem Hintergrund seiner Kirchenanschauung' (69–81); Y. Miyauchi, 'Landgewinnung in T. Ss *Der Schimmelreiter* und in Goethes *Faust* II' (82–96); C. Nagai, 'T. S. und die schleswig-holsteinische Frage' (97–108); A. Nohara, 'Über drei Katzen, zwei Männer und den Mond in Ss Werken' (109–22). *STSG*, 49, has: B. Coghlan, ' "T. S. geht ins Oper": Beobachtungen zur "Oper auf Haderslevhuus" ' (9–21, on the potential suitability of the Novelle as the basis for an operatic libretto); J. Harnischfeger, 'Modernisierung und Teufelspakt: die Funktion des Dämonischen in T. Ss *Schimmelreiter*' (23–44); K. E. Laage, 'Die Beziehungen T. Ss zu seinem *Schimmelreiter*-Berater Christian Eckermann und dessen Familie (mit unveröffentlichten Briefen)' (45–63); C. Geffers-Browne, 'Calvinismus oder schlicht Hygiene? Zu einigen Aspekten der Novelle *Renate*' (65–69); P. Goldammer, 'Aus dem Briefwechsel T. Ss mit seinem Bruder Otto' (71–125, with 43 letters, mostly by Theodor, and extensive commentary); G. Eversberg, 'T. S. in den "Neuen Medien" ' (127–35, on S. on CD-ROMS and on the Internet); E. Pastor, 'Arme "Elisabeth"! Von der (unverzeihlichen) Unzulänglichkeit des Übersetzens' (137–40, on some appallingly bad French translations of poems of Storm); E. Jakobsen, 'S.-Bibliographie' (141–52). *Storm-Blätter aus Heiligenstadt*, 1999, has: P. Goldammer, 'Ein lebenslanger Freundschaftsbund: T. S. in den Erinnerungen Ludwig Pietschs' (5–11); R. Fasold, 'Culpa patris aquis submersus? Bilder von Müttern in T. Ss Novellen' (12–31); D. Jackson, 'Constanze Storms Heiligenstädter Jahre' (32–50); G. Jaritz, 'Eine Begegnung von großer Bedeutung: T. Ss Bekanntschaft mit Ludwig Löwe in Heiligenstadt' (51–59).

J.-O. Decker and O. Schwarz, 'Von der Novelle zum Film: T. Ss *Immensee* (1850) und Veit Harlan's Film *Immensee: Ein deutsches Volkslied* (1943)', pp. 31–49 of *Geschichte(n): NS-Film–NS-Spuren heute*, ed. Hans Krah, Kiel, Ludwig, 1999, 224 pp. R. Fasold, 'Culpa patris aquis submersus? Mütter und Tod in T. Ss Novellen', *Fest. Richer*, 185–202 (also printed in *Storm-Blätter aus Heiligenstadt*, 1999, listed above). C. Laumont, 'Todesbilder und Heilsgeschichten: zu T. Ss Transformationen des Idyllischen', *Fest. Böschenstein*, 251–62. U. H. Gerlach, 'Aber"glaube" in Ss *Schimmelreiter*?', *Fest. Žmegač*, 101–17. M. Titzmann, 'Die Verarbeitung von Gottfrieds *Tristan* in Ss *Späte Rosen*: die

Begegnung unvereinbarer Anthropologien', *Fest. Walliczek*, 295–322.
K. E. Laage, 'T. S.: Regionalität und Weltliteratur', *Zeitschrift für Kultur- und Bildungswissenschaft*. *Flensburger Universitätszeitschrift*, 8, 1999:79–87. G. Eversberg, 'Vergiss die Rose nicht! Erotische Symbole in T. Ss früher Erzählung *Hinzelmeier*', *ib.*, 89–99. G. Vaagt, 'Das Ophelia-Motiv bei T. S. und anderen Dichtern', *ib.*, 101–07. I. Schuster, 'Tiere als Begleiter und *alter ego* des Menschen: zu vier Novellen von T. S.', *Seminar*, 36:182–93 (on *Immensee, Ein grünes Blatt, Ein Fest auf Haderslevhuus*, and *Bötjer Basch*). C. Neumann, 'Katermord und Mutterflucht: zu den unbewussten Tiefenstrukturen in Ss Novelle *Der Schimmelreiter*', *LWU*, 32:3–16.

UHLAND. H. Taigel, 'L. U. als Pfleger seiner Neffen: zwölf bisher unveröffentlichte Briefe Us', *JDSG*, 44:15–35.

UNGERN-STERNBERG, ALEXANDER VON. A. v. U.-S., *Die Wachskerze: Verschollene Phantasien*, ed. Robert N. Bloch, Passau, EDFC, 1998, 281 pp.

WAGNER. *Richard Wagner und die Juden*, ed. Dieter Borchmeyer et al., Stuttgart, Metzler, 354 pp. Nike Wagner, *Wagner-Theater* (ST, 3079), 1999, 437 pp., is a critical account of the Wagner family by W.'s own great-granddaughter. Jean-François Candoni, **La Genèse du drame musical wagnérien: mythe, politique et histoire dans les œuvres dramatiques de Richard Wagner* (Contacts, 44), Berne–Berlin, Lang, 1998, xvii + 421 pp. Christine Emig, **Arbeit am Inzest: Richard Wagner und Thomas Mann* (Heidelberger Beiträge zur deutschen Literatur, 1), Frankfurt–Berlin, Lang, 1998, 283 pp. is a 1996 Heidelberg dissertation. Walter Schertz-Parey, **Richard Wagners Dichtkunst: Eine literatur-kritische Betrachtung*, Graz, Österreichische R.-W.-Gesellschaft, 1998, 217 pp. Jeffrey S. Librett, *The Rhetoric of Cultural Dialogue: Jews and Germans from Moses Mendelssohn to Richard Wagner and Beyond*, Stanford U.P., xxiii + 391 pp., includes a chapter on W.'s *Das Judentum in der Musik*. **Das Weib der Zukunft: Frauengestalten und Frauenstimmen bei Wagner. Internationales Symposium zu den Bayreuther Festspielen 9.–11. August 1997*, ed. Susanne Vill (M & P Schriftenreihe für Wissenschaft und Forschung), Stuttgart, Metzler, 243 pp. *Richard Wagner im Dritten Reich: Ein Schloss Elmau-Symposion*, ed. Saul Friedländer et al. (Beck'sche Reihe, 1356), Munich, Beck, 372 pp. P. Jost, 'R. Ws *Tannhäuser*-Bearbeitung für die Pariser Aufführung 1861', Vliet, *Edition*, 213–22. D. Borchmeyer, 'R. W. als literarisches Ereignis der europäischen Frühmoderne: Versuch einer Bilanz, pp. 37–51 of *Die Wirklichkeit der Kunst und das Abenteuer der Interpretation: Festschrift für Horst-Jürgen Gerigk*, ed. Klaus Manger (BNL, 164), 1999, 388 pp. U. Bermbach, '"Ästhetische Weltordnung": zum Verhältnis von

Politik, Kunst und Kunstreligion bei R. W.', Sorg, *Gott*, 221–34. W.-D. Hartwich, 'Religion als Oper? Richard Wagner und Leo Tolstoi über das *"Gesamtkunstwerk"* ', pp. 93–110 of vol. 2 of *Ästhetische und religiöse Erfahrungen der Jahrhundertwenden*, ed. Wolfgang Braungart, Paderborn, Schöningh, 301 pp. K. Karbiener, 'The unexpress'd: Walt Whitman's late thoughts on R. W.', pp. 81–99 of *Comparative Romanticisms: Power, Gender, Subjectivity*, ed. Larry H. Peer (SGLLC), 1998, ix + 243 pp. M. Meier, 'Chöre und Leitmotive in den Bühnenwerken R. Ws: von der griechischen Tragödie zum Musikdrama', Baumbach, *Tradita*, 389–406. P. P. Riedl, 'Demosthenes auf der Festwiese: öffentliche Rede in R. s *Die Meistersinger von Nürnberg*', Fest. *Kreutzer*, 391–403. G. Schulz, 'Liebestod: Gedanken zu einem literarischen Motiv', Fest. *Kreutzer*, 375–89, focuses primarily on W.'s *Tristan und Isolde*. M. Swales, 'Schiller, Verdi, Wagner: opera and the tragic mode in the nineteenth century', Fest. *Reeves*, 25–30. S. Breuer, 'R. Ws Fundamentalismus', *DVLG*, 73, 1999: 643–64. J. Kaiser, 'R. W. und die Juden', *Jb. der Bayerischen Akad. der Schönen Künste*, 13.1, 1999: 81–110. K. A. Zaenker, 'The bedevilled Beckmesser: another look at anti-Semitic stereotypes in *Die Meistersinger von Nürnberg*, *GSR*, 22, 1999: 1–20. O. Viktor, ' "Der Kampf gegen W. ist in Wahrheit ein Kulturkampf": die W.-Rezeption in der Wochenschrift *Die Schaubühne/Die Weltbühne* (1905–1933)', *Archiv für Musikwissenschaft*, 56, 1999: 9–28. O. Marcel, 'Identité culturelle et derive politique: à propos de l'analyse du wagnérisme chez Thomas Mann', *RLC*, 72, 1998: 535–54. L. van Eynde, 'Le temps, l'autre et la fantasmagorie: lecture de *Der fliegende Höllander* de R. W.', *EG*, 55: 39–60. F. Bridgham, 'Emancipation Amazons: Schiller's Jungfrau, Kleist's Penthesilea, W.'s Brünnhlde', *FMLS*, 36: 64–73.

WEERTH. J.-W. Goette, 'G. W. und Ferdinand Freiligrath: Erich Mühsams Gedicht "Der Freie Geist" ', *Grabbe-Jb.*, 17–18, 1998–99[1999]: 29–47. R. Hecker, 'Neues über die Überlieferungsgeschichte des Nachlasses von G. W.', *ib.*, 256–64. B. Balzer, 'Die meisten Schwellen tragen Schienen: Anmerkungen zu G. W., Gustav Freytag und zur "Epochenschwelle" von 1848', Fest. *Denkler*, 3–17.

WICHERT, ERNST. E. W., *Ein Schritt vom Wege: Lustspiel in vier Aufzügen*, ed. Oliver Bruhns, Flensburg, Baltica-Vlg Bruhns, 1999, 97 pp.

LITERATURE, 1880–1945

By D. H. R. JONES, *University of Keele*

1. GENERAL

MOVEMENTS AND PERIODS. Patrick Bridgwater, *Anglo-German Interactions in the Literature of the 1890s*, Oxford, Legenda, 1999, 274 pp., is an erudite and illuminating study of reactions of British writers and critics, such as George Moore, Walter Pater, and Oscar Wilde, to German aesthetics, thought, and philosophy. A. F. Grant, 'Innocence and the language of the body in discourses of the "Jahrhundertwende"', *GLL*, 52:343–64. C. Weedon, 'The struggle for emancipation: German women writers of the *Jahrhundertwende*', Catling, *Women's Writing*, 111–27. D. Ipsen, 'Der verstellte Blick: man sieht nur, was man weiß. Antikewahrnehmung in Reiseberichten über Griechenland um 1900', Baumbach, *Tradita*, 459–71. I. Starz, ' "Heiliger Frühling" als Kulturformel der Moderne. Erinnerung und kultureller Raum in der Kunst der Jahrhundertwende', *ib.*, 473–86. Helene Herrmann, *Feinheit der Sprache. Aufsätze zur Literatur aus den Jahren 1903–1937*, Flensburg, Baltica, 1999, 223 pp., includes consideration of Liliencron, Dehmel, Huch, and Rilke. S. Werner-Birkenbach, 'Trends in writing by women, 1910–1933', Catling, *Women's Writing*, 128–145. Erika Fischer-Lichte, *Theater im Prozeß der Zivilisation*, Tübingen, Francke, 342 pp., has a section on Max Reinhardt's Berlin productions of Classical Greek drama and of Shakespeare in the early years of the 20th c. G. Holtz, 'Expressionismuskritik als antifaschistische Publizistik? Die Debatte in der Zeitschrift *Das Wort*', *MDLK*, 92:164–83. Hartmut Vollmer, *Liebes(ver-)lust. Existenzsuche und Beziehungen von Männern und Frauen in deutschsprachigen Romanen der zwanziger Jahre*, Oldenburg, Igel, 1998, 611 pp., is a highly detailed study of relationships between the sexes in Weimar Germany and is based upon reference, not only to works of the well-known figures of the period, but also to now neglected writers such as Heinz Liepmann, Hermann Kesser, Georg Fink, and Joachim Maass. This impressive work is a mine of fascinating information from both a literary and a sociological point of view. Christian Schärf, *Werkbau und Weltspiel. Die Idee der Kunst in der modernen Prosa*, Würzburg, Königshausen & Neumann, 1999, 305 pp. *Aufbruch in die Moderne*, ed. Anton Schwob und Zoltán Szendi, München, Südostdeutsches Kulturwerk, 227 pp. Gisela Dischner, *"Die Mauern stehen sprachlos und kalt." Tragische Erkenntnis in der Moderne*, Bielefeld, Aisthesis, 1999, 156 pp. Andreas Wicke, *Jenseits der Lust. Zum Problem der Ehe in der Literatur der Wiener Moderne*, Siegen, Böschen, 263 pp. C. Groppe,

'Neubeginn durch einen dritten Humanismus? Der preussische Kultusminister C. H. Becker und der George-Kreis in der Weimarer Republik', *CP*, 244–45:41–61. Frank Schirrmacher, *Fünf Dichter — ein Jahrhundert. Über George, Hofmannsthal, Rilke, Trakl und Benn*, Frankfurt, Insel, 1999, 189 pp. *Das Dritte Weimar. Klassik und Kultur im Nationalsozialismus*, ed. Lothar Ehrlich, Köln, Böhlau, 1999, 369 pp. G. Röska, 'Walter Hofmann und der Nationalsozialismus im März 1933. Auseinandersetzung um das Leipziger Volksbüchereiwesen', *Buchhandelsgeschichte*: 172–75. A. Cardinal, 'Women's writing under National Socialism', Catling, *Women's Writing*, 146–56. B. Dodd, ' "Zwischen den Zeilen?" ': the development of Dolf Sternberger's political "Sprachkritik" from the "Wörterbuch der Regierung von Papen" (1932) to "Ein guter Ausdruck" (1937)', *Will Vol.*, 86–98. S. Hilzinger, 'Writing in exile', Catling, *Women's Writing*, 157–166.

AUSTRIA, PRAGUE, AND SWITZERLAND. E. Gombrich, 'Réflexions sur la vie culturelle à Vienne autour de 1900', *Austriaca*, 50:45–61. C. Mondou, 'L'essai Hofmannsthal et son temps (1947–48) de Hermann Broch ou la démythification de la Vienne 1900', *ib.*, 63–78. A. Schwartz, 'Zwischen dem "noch nicht" und "nicht mehr"': Österreichische und ungarische Frauenliteratur der Jahrhundertwende', *MAL*, 33:16–28.

2. POETRY

A. Corbineau-Hoffmann, 'Die Bewaffnung der Worte. Aspekte der Sprachgewalt in moderner Lyrik', Corbineau-Hoffmann, *Gewalt*, 191–227. *Deutsche Gedichte zwischen 1918 und 1933*, ed. Helmut Kreuzer, Stuttgart, Reclam, 1999, 381 pp., is an imaginative and wide-ranging anthology with an excellent 'Nachwort', which places this selection from well over 100 poets of the Weimar period in its social and cultural context. *Lyrik des 20. Jahrhunderts*, ed. Heinz Ludwig Arnold, München, Text und Kritik, 1999, 300 pp., contains the following essays relevant to the period: H. Korte, 'Energie der Brüche. Ein diachroner Blick auf die Lyrik des 20. Jahrhunderts und ihre Zäsuren' (63–106); M. Behre, 'Hölderlin in der Lyrik des 20. Jahrhunderts' (107–24); N. Hummelt, 'Mein Onkel Gottfried Benn' (125–37); K. Schuhmann, ' "Ich brauche keinen Grabstein." Der Lyriker Bertolt Brecht und seine Nachgeborenen' (138–54); H. Göbel, ' "In der Asphaltstadt bin ich daheim." Die große Stadt in der Lyrik des 20. Jahrhunderts' (155–74); U. Heukenkamp, 'Zauberspruch und Sprachkritik. Naturgedicht und Moderne' (175–200); Y. Inauen, 'Verwandelte Körper, verwandeltes Ich. Tanzgedichte von Else-Lasker-Schüler, Gertrud Kolmar, Nelly Sachs und Christine Lavant' (213–30); T. Kling, 'Zu den deutschsprachigen Avantgarden'

(231–45); L. Völker, 'Hilfswerk, Begleitmusik. Dokumente zur Poetik und Poetologie' (265–93). Hartmut Merkt, *Poesie in der Isolation. Deutschsprachige jüdische Dichter in Enklave und Exil am Beispiel von Bukowiner Autoren seit dem 19 Jahrhundert. Zu Gedichten von Rose Ausländer, Paul Celan und Immanuel Weissglas*, Wiesbaden, Harrassowitz, 1999, 278 pp.

3. PROSE

B. Neymeyr, 'Utopie und Experiment. Zur Konzeption des Essays bei Musil und Adorno', *Euphorion*, 94:79–111. As well as two entries below in the Thomas Mann section, Fichtner, *Doppelgänger*, has two further articles relevant to the period: E. Grimm, 'Verschwinden und Wiederkehr des Doppelgängers: mediale Bedingungen eines literarischen Phänomens im Roman der Weimarer Republik' (77–91); and G. Marci-Boehncke, 'Kleider machen Doppelgänger: Projektion und Opposition in Helmut Käutners Film *Kleider machen Leute* aus dem Dritten Reich' (95–112), which refers to Hesse.

4. INDIVIDUAL AUTHORS

BENJAMIN, WALTER. R. Block, 'Selective affinities: Walter Benjamin and Ludwig Klages', *Arcadia*, 35:117–36. D. Darby, 'Photography, narrative and the landscape of memory in Walter Benjamin's Berlin', *GR*, 75:210–25. Irene Pieper, *Modernes Welttheater: Untersuchungen zum Welttheatermotiv zwischen Katastrophenerfahrung und Welt-Anschauungssuche bei Walter Benjamin, Karl Kraus, Hugo von Hofmannsthal und Else Lasker-Schüler*, Berlin, Duncker & Humblot, 194 pp.

BENN, GOTTFRIED. Dorit Beckmann, *Künstlerische Entwicklungsläufe im zwanzigsten Jahrhundert: Gottfried Benn und Bertolt Brecht*, Berlin, Logos, 1999, 154 pp. Alexander D. Daboul, *Die poet(olog)ische Finalisierung des Organischen: Körpertextualisierungen bei Benn und Nietzsche*, Hamburg, Kovac, 446 pp. D. Ostmeier, 'Beastly love: Gottfried Benn/Else Lasker-Schüler', *ColGer*, 33:43–74. D. v. Petersdorff, 'Wie modern ist die ästhetische Moderne? Gottfried Benns Kunst-Vorstellungen in ihrer Entstehung und ihren Folgen', *ZDP*, 118:165–85.

BORCHARDT, RUDOLF. A. Kissler, ' "Die Welt des Wirklichen ist aus Resten gemacht." Individuum und Geschichte in den Reden und Essays Rudolf Borchardts', *WB*, 45:218–239.

BRECHT, BERTOLT. G. Beck, 'Zu Entstehung und Erklärung von Brechts "Baal" ', *ZDP*, 118:110–143. J. Crick, 'Power and powerlessness: Brecht's poems to Carola Neher', *GLL*, 53:314–24. B. Doherty, 'Test and *gestus* in Brecht and Benjamin', *MLN*, 115:442–81. U. Klingmann, 'Lachen, Plattform und Planet: Zur

Deutung von Brechts *Im Dickicht der Städte*', *JIG*, 31:80–101. K.-D. Krabiel, ' "Die Alten und die Jungen." ' Publizistische Kontroversen Bertolt Brechts mit Thomas Mann und Klaus Mann in den zwanziger Jahren. Mit einem unbekannten Text von Brecht', *WW*, 49:63–85. A. Phelan, 'July Days in Skovsbostrand: Brecht, Benjamin and antiquity', *GLL*, 53:373–86. *Brecht's Poetry of Political Exile*, ed. Ronald Spiers, CUP, 257 pp., is the fruit of a series of seminars at Birkbeck College and Birmingham University on the *Svendborger Gedichte*. This, the first comprehensive study of these poems of exile, provides excellent English translations of all German quotations and will therefore appeal to a very wide readership. It contains the following: D. Midgley, 'Svendborg 1938: a historical sketch' (16–28); D. Constantine, 'The usefulness of poetry' (29–46); T. Kuhn, ' "Visit to a banished poet": Brecht's *Svendborg Poems* and the voices of exile' (47–65); K. Hodgson, 'Exile in "Danish Siberia": the Soviet Union in the *Svendborg Poems*' (66–85); T. Davies, 'Brecht, Auden and the "true democratic style" ' (86–99); M. Minden, 'Satire as propaganda: Brecht's "Deutsche Satiren" for the Deutscher Freiheitssender' (100–13); J. Crick, 'The fourth door: difficulties with the truth in the *Svendborg Poems*' (114–34); A. Carrdus, 'The uses of rhetoric in Brecht's *Svendborg Poems*' (135–52); E. Boa, 'Assuaging the anxiety of impotence: poetic authority and power in the *Svendborg Poems*' (153–71); A. Phelan, 'Figures of memory in the "Chroniken" ' (172–89); R. Spiers, 'The poet in time' (190–210); K. Leeder, 'Those born later read Brecht: the reception of "An die Nachgeborenen" ' (211–40). M. Swales, 'Historicity and all that: reflections on Bertolt Brecht's *Die Maßnahme*', *Will Vol.*, 77–85. M. Swales and E. Swales, 'Metonymic cohabitation: on women figures in Brecht', *GLL*, 53:387–93.

BROCH, HERMANN. *Hermann Broch: Psychische Selbstbiographie*, ed. Paul Michael Lützeler, Frankfurt, Suhrkamp, 1999, 214 pp. T. Edelmann, 'Vernunft des Irrationalen oder irrationale Vernunft? Arthur Lieberts Philosophie als Subtext der Wertzerfallessays Hermann Brochs', *ZDP*, 118:186–204. C. Könneker, 'Hermann Brochs Rezeption der modernen Physik. Quantenmechanik und "Unbekannter Größe" ', *ZDP*, 18:205–39.

CELAN, PAUL. Jean Bollack, *Paul Celan. Poetik der Fremdheit*, Darmstadt, Wissenschaftliche Buchgesellschaft, 376 pp. M. Eskin, 'Answerable criticism: reading Celan reading Mandel'shtam', *Arcadia*, 35:66–80. S. Markis, ' "Was das Gedicht spricht." Funktionen der Intertextualität in der Lyrik Paul Celans', *EG*, 55:521–39. C. Ivanovic, 'Eine Sprache der Bilder. Notizen zur immanenten Poetik der Lyrik Paul Celans', ib., 541–59.

DÖBLIN, ALFRED. Simonetta Sanna, *Die Quadratur des Kreises: Stadt und Wahnsinn in "Berlin Alexanderplatz" von Alfred Döblin*, Frankfurt,

Lang, 117 pp. Dietmar Voss, *Ströme und Steine: Studien zur symbolischen Textur des Werkes von Alfred Döblin*, Würzburg, Königshausen und Neumann, 278 pp.

FALLADA, HANS. Deborah Smail, *White Collar Workers, Mass Culture and Neue Sachlichkeit in Weimar Berlin: a Reading of Hans Fallada's 'Kleiner Mann — was nun?', Erich Kästner's 'Fabian' and Irmgard Keun's 'Das kunstseidene Mädchen'*, Berne, Lang, 1999, 235 pp. Reinhard Zachau, *Hans Fallada: eine kritische Untersuchung zur Rezeption seines Werks in den Jahren 1930–1997*, Stuttgart, Heinz, 214 pp.

FREUD, SIGMUND. Graham Frankland, *Freud's Literary Culture* (CSG), 260 pp., approaches F., not through a critique of his psychonanalytical methods and findings, but from the viewpoint of the literary influences on his writings.

GEORGE, STEFAN. Friedrich-Wilhelm von Herrmann, *Die zarte, aber helle Differenz: Heidegger und Stefan George*, Frankfurt, Klostermann, 1999, 328 pp.

HARDT, ERNST. Jaewon Song, *Die Bühnenwerke Ernst Hardts und das neue Drama in der deutschen Literatur um 1900*, Frankfurt, Lang, 173 pp.

HASENCLEVER, WALTER. Christa Spreizer, *From Expressionism to Exile: the works of Walter Hasenclever (1890–1940)*, Columbia SC, Camden House, 1999, 202 pp.

HOFMANNSTHAL, HUGO VON. I. C. Gil, 'Poiesis, Tanz und Repräsen-Tanz: Zu Hugo von Hofmannsthals *Ariadne auf Naxos*', *ColGer*, 33 : 149–62. Nino Nodia, *Das Fremde und das Eigene: Hugo von Hofmannsthal und die russische Kultur*, Frankfurt, Lang, 1999, 212 pp. Sebastian Schmitter, *Basis, Wahrnehmung und Konsequenz: zur literarischen Präsenz des Melancholischen in den Schriften von Hugo von Hofmannsthal und Robert Musil*, Würzburg, Königshausen und Neumann, 321 pp. Robert Vilain, *The poetry of Hugo von Hofmannsthal and French symbolism*, Oxford, Clarendon, 376 pp. P. M. Ward, 'Hofmannsthal, *Elektra* and the representation of women's behaviour through myth', *GLL*, 53 : 37–55. J.-M. Winkler, 'Auto-mythification et auto-dérision. *L'eventail blanc* de Hugo de Hofmannsthal', *Austriaca*, 50 : 109–18. W. Zieger, 'Gewalt der Seele. Zur Spezifik der Gewaltphänomene in Hofmannsthals *Elektra*', Corbineau, *Gewalt*, 173–90.

JÜNGER, ERNST. M. Bullock, 'Beyond 2000: Ernst Jünger's second German century', *MDLK*, 91 : 396–413. Thomas Pekar, *Ernst Jünger und der Orient: Mythos-Lektüre-Reise*, Würzburg, Ergon, 1999, 263 pp. Thomas Rohkrämer, *Eine andere Moderne? Zivilisationskritik, Natur und Technik in Deutschland 1880–1933*, Paderborn, Schöningh, 1999, 404 pp., has a section on Ernst Jünger and technology. I. Stöckmann, ' "Prosa, die von uns gedeutet und beherrscht werden will." Über Ernst Jüngers politische Essayistik', *GR*, 75 : 3–19.

KÄSTNER, ERICH.   Y. Holbeche, 'Goodbye to Berlin: Erich Kästner and Christopher Isherwood', *AUMLA*, 94 : 35–54. S. Neuhaus, 'Erich Kästner und der Nationalsozialismus. Am Beispiel des bisher unbekannten Theaterstücks *Gestern, heute und morgen* (1936) und des Romans *Drei Männer im Schnee* (1934)', *WW*, 49 : 372–87.

KAFKA, FRANZ.   W. Fromm, '*Geschriebene Küsse*. Zur neuen Kafka-Ausgabe', *LiB*, 59 : 28–29. Axel Hecker, *An den Rändern des Lesbaren*. *Dekonstruktive Lektüren zu Franz Kafka*, Wien, Passagen, 1999. P. Priskil, 'Kafkas *Schloß*', *System ubw*, 18 : 50–88. W. H. Sokel, 'Kafka as a Jew', *NLH*, 30 : 837–53. D. Suchoff, 'Kafka and the postmodern divide: Hebrew and German in Aharon Appelfeld's *The Age of Wonders* (Tor Ha-pela'ot)', *GR*, 75 : 149–67. R. Tobias, 'A doctor's odyssey: sickness and health in Kafka's "Ein Landarzt"', *ib.*, 120–31. M. Winkler, 'Kulturkritik in Kafkas "Der Bau"', *ZDP*, 118 : 144–64. J. Zilcosky, 'The traffic of writing: technologies of "Verkehr" in Franz Kafka's *Briefe an Milena*', *GLL*, 52 : 365–81.

KAPP, GOTTFRIED.   H. Eilert and I. M. Battafarano, ' "O, dass die Welt man uns zur Heimat lasse": Gottfried Kapps Erzählsammlung *Wandellose Götter*', *GLL*, 53 : 325–39.

KRAUS, KARL.   P. Reitter, 'Karl Kraus and the soul of form', *GR*, 75 : 99–119. C. Vismann, 'Karl Kraus: Die Stimme des Gesetzes', *DVLG*, 74 : 710–24. Edward Timms, *Karl Kraus, Satiriker der Apokalypse: Leben und Werk 1874–1918*, Frankfurt, Suhrkamp, 1999, 559 pp. *Wörterbuch der Redensarten zu der von Karl Kraus 1899–1936 herausgegebenen Zeitschrift "Die Fackel"*, Wien, Österr. Akad. der Wiss., 1999, 1051 pp.

LASKER-SCHÜLER, ELSE.   M. Klaue, 'Liebesspiele. Zur Liebesmotivik in Else Lasker-Schülers "Mein Herz" ', *ZDP*, 118 : 80–109.

MANN, HEINRICH.   *Heinrich Mann-Jahrbuch*, ed. Helmut Koopmann and Hans Wisskirchen, Lübeck, Schmidt-Römhild, 1999, 260 pp., contains the following: H. Wisskirchen, 'Heinrich Manns Goethe-Bild' (7–27); H. Koopmann, 'Zu Thomas Manns Goethe-Nachfolge. Orientierungsverlust und Imitatio' (29–62); F. Trapp, 'Heinrich Mann: *Der Atem*. Eine Welt ästhetischer Konstrukte' (63–79); A. Bartl, 'Heinrich Manns letzter Roman *Der Atem* zwischen "Greisenavantgardismus" und innovativem Stilexperiment' (81–102); B. Böhm, 'Schopenhauer-Bezüge in Heinrich Manns Romanen *Empfang bei der Welt* und *Der Atem* als Spiegel eines literarische Bruderkonflikts' (103–44). V. Riedel, 'Ein Autor zwischen Herausgebern und Verlegern — Probleme der Heinrich-Mann-Edition', *Berliner Hefte zur Geschichte des literarischen Lebens*, 3 : 174–79.

MANN, THOMAS.   G. Bond, ' "Der Brunnen der Vergangenheit": historical narration in Uwe Johnson's *Heute Neunzig Jahr* and Thomas Mann's *Joseph und seine Brüder*', *GLL*, 52 : 68–84. G. Bridges, 'Sublimation in Thomas Mann's *Doktor Faustus*: love's labor lost', *MDLK*,

91:28–44. E. S. Brinkley, 'Fear of form: Thomas Mann's *Der Tod in Venedig*', *ib.*, 2–27. *Thomas Mann/Käte Hamburger: Briefwechsel 1932–1955*, ed. Hubert Brunträger (*Thomas-Mann-Studien*, 20), Frankfurt, Klostermann, 1999, 201 pp. R. Görner, 'Peinliche Verwandtschaft. Formen der Selbstdiagnose in Thomas Manns Versuch *Bruder Hitler*', Fichtner, *Doppelgänger*, 203–17. Yahya Elsaghe, *Die imaginäre Nation. Thomas Mann und das "Deutsche"*, München, Fink, 429 pp. Id., 'Die "kaufmännischen Und-Zeichen" der "Geschäftsmaschine". Zur Überwindung rassenbiologischer Antisemitismen in Thomas Manns Spätwerk', *ColGer*, 33:349–65. Id., '"Herr und Frau X. Beliebig"? Zur Funktion der Vornamensinitiale bei Thomas Mann', *GLL*, 52:58–67. Ralf Harslem, *Thomas Mann und Theodor Fontane. Untersuchungen über den Einfluss Theodor Fontanes auf das erzählerische Frühwerk von Thomas Mann*, Frankfurt, Lang, 236 pp. Jost Hermand and Wigand Lange, *"Wollt ihr Thomas Mann wiederhaben?" Deutschland und die Emigranten*, Hamburg, Europäische Verlags-Anstalt, 1999, 214 pp. M. Herwig, 'Magic science on the mountain: science and myth in Thomas Mann's *Der Zauberberg*', *GR*, 74:146–56. Harald Höbusch, *Thomas Mann — Kunst, Kritik, Politik 1893–1913*, Tübingen, Francke, 201 pp. S. Kiefer, 'Gesellschaftlicher Umbruch und literarisierte Familiengeschichte. Thomas Manns *Unordnung und frühes Leid* und Klaus Manns *Kindernovelle*', *WW*, 49:355–71. K.-D. Krabiel, '"Die Alten und die Jungen." Publizistische Kontroversen Bertolt Brechts mit Thomas Mann und Klaus Mann in den zwanziger Jahren. Mit einem unbekannten Text von Brecht', *ib.*, 63–85. Hermann Kurzke, *Thomas Mann. Das Leben als Kunstwerk*, München, Beck, 1999, 671 pp., is a consummate biography by one of the leading experts on M. The insights into M.'s life and works and their contextualization within the social and political history of Germany in the first half of the 20th c. are allied to a rare clarity of style and expression. Among the continuous outpouring of publications on M., this biography is of lasting significance. Michael Maar, *Das Blaubartzimmer. Thomas Mann und die Schuld*, Frankfurt, Suhrkamp, 132 pp. William E. MacDonald, *Thomas Mann's 'Joseph and his Brothers'. Writing, Performance, and the Politics of Loyalty*, Rochester NY, Camden House, 1999, 276 pp. Martin Meyer, *Tagebuch und spätes Leid. Über Thomas Mann*, München, Hanser, 1999, 300 pp. Barbara Molinelli-Stein, *Thomas Mann, das Werk als Selbstinszenierung eines problematischen Ichs. Versuch einer psychoexistenziellen Strukturanalyse zu den Romanen "Lotte in Weimar" und "Doktor Faustus"*, Tübingen, Stauffenburg, 1999, 158 pp. H. A. Pausch and D. Spokiene, 'Walter Benjamin, Roland Barthes und die Dialektik der Modesprache im Werk Thomas Manns', *WW*, 49:86–104. A. v. Schirnding, 'Thomas Mann, seine Schwiegereltern Pringsheim und

Richard Wagner', *LiB*, 60:37–45. Wolfgang Schneider, *Lebensfreundlichkeit und Pessimismus. Thomas Manns Figurendarstellung (Thomas-Mann-Studien*, 19), Frankfurt, Klostermann, 1999, 498 pp. C. E. Schwarcz, 'Der Doppelgänger in der Literatur', Fichtner, *Doppelgänger*, 1–14, refers to Thomas Mann and Kafka in her consideration of the double in literature. D. A. Sdwischkow, 'Der einsame Bildungsbürger auf der Suche nach der "Mitte". Rußland im Deutschlandkonzept Thomas Manns', *WB*, 45:180–98. *Doctor Faustus: Archetypal Subtext at the Millenium*, ed. Armand E. Singer and Jürgen Schlank, Morgantown, West Virginia U.P., 1999, 67 pp., contains the following: P. Werres, 'The changing faces of Dr. Faustus' (1–23); J. Campbell, 'Thomas Mann's *Doctor Faustus*: weighing the testimony of Serenus Zeitblom' (25–42); R. Beicken, 'Faust in film: the case of Dr. Caligari' (43–67). D. Turner, 'Balancing the account. Thomas Mann's *Unordnung und frühes Leid*, *GLL*, 52:43–57. P. Werner, ' "Fusel anstelle des Weines des Geistes und der Gesittung." Ein bisher unbekannter Brief Thomas Manns', *GRM*, 50:203–22. R. Whitinger, 'Echoes of Lou Andreas-Salomé in Thomas Mann's *Tonio Kröger*. *Eine Ausschweifung* and its relationship to the *Bildungsroman* tradition', *GR*, 75:21–36.

MUSIL, ROBERT. S. Gödicke, 'Musil et Kraus', *Austriaca*, 50:135–64. P. D. Smith, 'The scientist as spectator: Musil's *Törleß* and the challenge to Mach's neo-positivism' *GR*, 75:37–51. B. Spreitzer, 'Meister Musil. Eckharts deutsche Predigten als zentrale Quelle des Romans "Der Mann ohne Eigenschaften" ', *ZDP*, 18:564–88.

NIETZSCHE, FRIEDRICH. P. Bishop and R. H. Stephenson, 'Nietzsche and Weimar aesthetics', *GLL*, 52:412–29. Michael Hinz, *Verfallsanalyse und Utopie. Nietzsche-Rezeption in Thomas Manns Zauberberg und in Robert Musils Der Mann ohne Eigenschaften*, St. Ingberg, Röhrig, 213 pp.

REUTER, GABRIELE. L. Tatlock, 'Our correspondent in Weimar: G. R. and *The New York Times*, 1923–1939', *GSR*, 22, 1999:369–83, is concerned with the career as a reviewer of German books that was forced upon R. when she lost her savings in the inflation of 1923. A. Kliewer, 'Abgebrochene Aufbrüche: die Enttäuschung an der nächsten Generation in der Frauenbewegung der 20er Jahre. Zu G. Rs Roman *Töchter* (1927)', *Fest. Roebling*, 149–60.

RILKE, RAINER MARIA. *Rainer Maria Rilke. Lyrik und Prosa*, ed. Dieter Lamping, Düsseldorf, Artemis & Winkler, 1999, 874 pp., contains *Neue Gedichte, Duineser Elegien, Die Sonette and Orpheus, Die Aufzeichnungen des Malte Laurids Brigge* and *Die Weise von Liebe und Tod des Cornets Christoph Rilke*, together with early poems, poems in French and poems in Danish, English, Flemish, French, Italian, Latin, Russian, and Swedish translated by Rilke. K. S. Lalhoon, 'The eye of the panther: Rilke and the machine of cinema', *CL*, 52:143–56. *Rilke und die Weltliteratur*, ed. Dieter Lamping and Manfred Engel, Düsseldorf, Artemis & Winkler, 1999, 351 pp. W. Methlagl, 'Rilke, Hammershöj, Cézanne, Kokoschka', *MBA*, 18:8–22. B. Neymeyr, 'Poetische Metamorphosen des Orpheus-Mythos bei Rilke: von seinem Gedicht "Orpheus. Eurydike. Hermes" bis zu den "Sonetten an Orpheus"', *ZDP*, 118:25–59. T. Pettersson, 'Internalization and death: a reinterpretation of Rilke's *Duineser Elegien*', *MLR*, 94:731–43. M. W. Wierschin, 'Zur stilistischen Metamorphose eines Lyrikers: Rilkes Epitaphium und Rosen-Symbol als "reiner Stil"', *GSR*, 22:215–24. *Rilke und die Moderne*, ed. Adrian Stevens and Fred Wagner (PIGS, 74), München, Iudicium, 301 pp.

ROTH, JOSEPH. K. Borck and E. K. Paefgen, 'Leben und Leiden. Hiob, Josef K., Franz Biberkopf und Mendel Singer aus theologischer und literaturwissenschaftlicher Sicht', *WW*, 49:249–72, considers the figure of Job as inspiration for the main characters in *Hiob, Der Proceß*, and *Berlin Alexanderplatz*. J. Hughes, 'Violence, masculinity and self: killing in Joseph Roth's 1920s fiction', *GLL*, 53:216–30. T. Maier, 'Auf der Suche nach dem verlorenen Maß. Beim Lesen von Joseph Roths Erzählung "Das falsche Gewicht"', *LitL*, 23:28–41.

SCHICKELE, RENÉ. Adrien Finck, *René Schickele*, Strasbourg, Salde, 1999, 301 pp. Hans Wagener, *René Schickele: Europäer in neun Monaten*, Gerlingen, Bleicher, 317 pp. Stefan Woltersdorff, *Chronik einer Traumlandschaft: Elsassmodelle in Prosatexten von René Schickele (1899–1932)*, Berne, Lang, 501 pp.

SCHNITZLER, ARTHUR. J.-C. François, 'Didascalies et lutte des classes dans les pieces "viennoises" d'Arthur Schnitzler', *Austriaca*, 50:79–88. A. Koch-Didier, ' "Gegen gewisse, sozusagen mystische Tendenzen." L'oeuvre romanesque d'Arthur Schnitzler', *ib.*, 89–108. M. Rohrwasser, 'Arthur Schnitzlers Erzählung "Die Weissagung". Ästhetizismus, Antisemitismus und Psychoanalyse', *ZDP*, 118:60–79. J. Weinberger, 'A lover's flight: Arthur Schnitzler's "Die Frau des Weisen"', *Neophilologus*, 83:283–90.

SCHWITTERS, KURT. G. Webster, 'Kurt Schwitters and Katherine Dreier', *GL*, 52:443–56.

STADLER, ERNST. R. Sheppard, 'Ernst Stadler in Oxford: addenda, corrigenda and two unpublished letters', *Will Vol.*, 59–76.

TOLLER, ERNST. J. Fotheringham, 'From "Einheitsfront" to "Volksfront": Ernst Toller and the Spanish Civil War', *GLL*, 52:430–42.

TRAKL, GEORG. L. Bluhm, 'Rimbaud — Klammer — Trakl. Eine "palimpsestuöse Lektüre" von Georg Trakls *Winterdämmerung*', *WW*, 49:235–48. W. Braungart, 'Zwischen Protestantismus und Katholizismus. Zu einem poetischen Strukturprinzip der Lyrik Georg Trakls', *ZDP*, 18:545–63. *Gedichte von Georg Trakl*, ed. Hans-Georg Kemper,

Stuttgart, Reclam, 1999, 222 pp. L. A. McLary, 'The incestuous sister or the trouble with Grete', *MAL*, 33:29–65. H. Zwerschina, 'Georg Trakl: *Untergang*. Das Gedicht verstehen: aus der Arbeitsweise Trakls', *MBA*, 18:33–60.

WALSER, ROBERT. I. Denneker, ' "Erzähle ich eine Geschichte, so denke ich ans Essen." Zur kulinarischen Poetologie Robert Walsers', *WW*, 49:46–62. Robert Mächler, *Robert Walser der Unenträtselte. Aufsätze aus vier Jahrzehnten*, Zürich, Pendo, 1999, 234 pp. Sabine Rothemann, *Spazierengehen — verschollengehen. Zum Problem der Wahrnehmung bei Robert Walser und Franz Kafka*, Marburg, Tectum, 221 pp. T. Wägenbaur, 'Robert Walsers Geste des Schreibens und die Komik des "interface" ', *MLN*, 115:482–501.

WEDEKIND, FRANK. M. M. Paddock, 'So ist das Leben: Frank Wedekind's Scharfrichter diary', *MDLK*, 91:342–58. S. Schönborn, ' "Die Königin ohne Kopf." Literarische Initiation und Geschlechtsidentität um die Jahrhundertwende in Frank Wedekinds Kindertragödie *Frühlingserwachen*', *ZDP*, 111, 555–71. Horst Spittler, *Frank Wedekind, Frühlings Erwachen: Interpretation*, München, Oldenbourg, 1999, 120 pp.

WEINHEBER, JOSEF. Albert Berger, *Josef Weinheber (1892–1945) Leben und Werk — Leben im Werk*, Salzburg, Müller, 1999, 367 pp.

ZUCKMAYER, CARL. *Die Briefwechsel mit Carl Jacob Burckhardt und Max Frisch*, ed. Claudia Mertz-Rychner, St. Ingbert, Röhrig, 308 pp. *"Persönlich — wär so unendlich viel zu sagen": der Briefwechsel zwischen Carl Zuckmayer und Annemarie Seidel*, ed. Gunther Nickel, St. Ingbert, Röhrig, 1999, 269 pp.

ZWEIG, STEFAN. Mohammed El-bah, *Frauen- und Männerbilder in den Novellen von Stefan Zweig*, Freiburg, Hochschul-Vlg, 168 pp. *Stefan Zweig lebt: Akten des 2. Internationalen Stefan Zweig Kongresses in Salzburg 1998*, ed. Sigrid Schmid-Bortenschlager, Stuttgart, Heinz, 213 pp.

LITERATURE FROM 1945
TO THE PRESENT DAY

By Owen Evans, *Lecturer in German, University of Wales, Bangor*

1. General

A. Bammer, 'Feminism, *Frauenliteratur*, and women's writing of the 1970s and 1980s', Catling, *Women's Writing*, 216–32. **Literatur und Identität. Deutsch-deutsche Befindlichkeiten und die multikulturelle Gesellschaft*, ed. Ursula E. Beitter, NY, Lang, xi + 339 pp. A. Blioumi, '"Migrationsliteratur", "interkulturelle Literatur" und "Generationen von Schriftstellern". Ein Problemaufriß über umstrittene Begriffe', *WB*, 46:595–602. Elisabeth Boa and Rachel Palfreyman, *Heimat. A German Dream. Regional Loyalties and National Identity in German Culture 1890–1990*, OUP, 234 pp., is a welcome contribution to debates about the nature of 'Heimat' and its significance in shaping identities, regional and national, in Germany. Although the volume adopts an interdisciplinary approach to the discourse of 'Heimat', which means that many elements of the study fall beyond the parameters of this review section, its broad cultural focus proves most stimulating, and it succeeds in laying solid foundations for ongoing investigations into what constitutes German identity. Especially valuable in this regard is the introduction, which delivers an historical and theoretical survey of the notion of 'Heimat', uncovering its myriad uses and meanings and indeed 'mapping the terrain' covered in the chapters that follow. Three factors are adduced to explain the growing importance of 'Heimat' in political debates from the 1970s onwards: the reconsideration of German national identity as the Nazi past grew more distant, the growing importance of environmental issues and the rise of the Green movement, and the impact of *Ostpolitik* and the thawing of the Cold War. Indeed, the text asserts that 'Heimat was clearly "in" in the mid-1980s and can be seen in retrospect as a symptom of the great sea changes bringing the end of the Cold War and German Reunification'. The most provocative section of the introduction explores what it terms the 'socio-psychic connotations and aesthetic contours', which looks closely at the role 'Heimat' plays in identity formation. The definitions offered here will doubtless provoke further debate, touching on aspects such as the spatial and temporal contours, 'Heimat' as image, linked especially with photography, and in the most convincing section, on the deconstructionist notion of 'Heimat' predicated on the existence of its other or negative within it: 'Who must be excluded and who can be integrated are as crucial to the definition of a community as who is from the start included'. This reading seems especially apposite in the light of recent debates about the existence, or not, of a German *Leitkultur*, as well as more general debates about multicultural societies, not just in Germany. This last point is revisited in conjunction with the unification of the two Germanies in the volume's thought-provoking conclusion, by looking at the work of Turkish writers such as Emine Sevgi Özdamar and Feridun Zaimoglu. In those chapters relating to the post-1945 period covered by the current review section, the representation of 'Heimat' in film constitutes a core interest of the study, with a detailed exploration of the post-war *Heimatfilme*, juxtaposed with those productions which sought to subvert the genre, and DEFA productions in East Germany. Quite naturally, there is also an excellent chapter devoted to Edgar Reitz's epic *Heimat*. The chapter which explores *Heimatfilme* includes analysis of Martin Sperr's bleak play *Jagdszenen aus Niederbayern*, the very antithesis of idyllic depictions of 'Heimat', and of Frank Xaver Kroetz's attempt to appropriate the *Volksstück* as a political medium. The exploration of the work of both playwrights forms a striking and effective counterpoint to films such as *Wenn die Heide blüht*. Similar use of contrast is made in the chapter which focuses on the conflict between generations and their different perceptions of 'Heimat', with Siegfried Lenz's *Deutschstunde* considered alongside the work of artist Emil Nolde, who served as the model for Max Ludwig Nansen in Lenz's novel, and Michael Verhoeven's *Das schreckliche Mädchen*, 'which twenty years on takes up the story of young Germans exploring the Nazi past'. It is this comparative approach, teasing out the different ways in which the theme of 'Heimat' underpins German culture, which makes this study such a rewarding read. Lucidly written, it should prove to be a stimulating introduction for under-graduates of different disciplines to a complex, and vexed, topic. E. Boa, 'Writing about women writing in German: postscript and perspectives', Catling, *Women's Writing*, 254–64. K. Bullivant, 'High and low literature and the German reading public', *Will Vol.*, 153–62. **Interkulturelle Literatur in Deutschland. Ein Handbuch*, ed. Carmine Chiellino, Stuttgart, Metzler, x + 536 pp. **Autobiography by Women in German*, ed. Mererid Puw Davies, Beth Linklater, and Gisela Shaw, Berne, Lang, 310 pp. Pascal Fagot, **Mémoires et regards. Le thème de la Pologne dans la prose littéraire allemande (1949–1990)*, Berne, Lang, xvi + 363 pp.

1949/1989. Cultural Perspectives on Division and Unity in East and West, ed. Clare Flanagan and Stuart Taberner, Amsterdam–Atlanta, Rodopi, 297 pp., is a collection of 18 essays, collated from a conference at Bristol in 1998, exploring the two key coordinates in postwar German political and cultural history. The volume includes contributions which take a more general overview of the periods in question alongside analyses of individual texts, theatre, film and socio-political matters. As the preface observes, 'all of the contributions reflect the causal and cultural complexities associated with historical change and point to ongoing discussions in 1990s Germany'. In this respect, the volume will doubtless prove an engaging springboard for research into and debate about the legacy of post-1945 German culture, in the context of discussions about the degrees of change and continuity which can be identified in work now being produced in the 21st century. The opening essay by H. Peitsch challenges existing perceptions of the two German states' attitudes to the Nazi past, comparing 1949 with 1989, and thus forms the cornerstone for the volume as a whole. The next three essays then explore the different perspectives in East and West in the *Stunde Null* period. P. Davies takes Johannes R. Becher as a representative intellectual figure of the GDR's attempt to establish its national identity, while R. Williams concentrates on the issues surrounding the formation and future direction of a specific West German literature, and credits Alfred Andersch for uniting the diverse views of writers in the post-war period, here represented by Arno Schmidt and Hans Werner Richter. C. Flanagan meanwhile explores the apparently passive acceptance amongst intellectuals of the division of Germany in 1949 as an inevitable, if provisional, state of affairs. As a result, discussion of the problem was postponed and an interim solution sought. Flanagan concludes that 'comparisons with unification in 1990 may yield further development of this idea of postponement'. Essays by B. Niven and S. Parker reveal the parallels between 1949 and 1989, with their focus on the issue of responsibility for the past in the post-*Wende* period. Niven's essay in particular offers a provocative interpretation of the role of east Germans in unification, by positing what he dubs the 'self-exclusion theory'. It was on account of their reluctance, or inability, to assume responsibility that former GDR citizens, so used to conforming to required modes of behaviour, were largely circumvented in the revolutionary process they had initiated. Two further essays examine attitudes to the GDR past. B. Miller provides an analysis of the reasons given by those who worked as *inoffizieller Mitarbeiter* for the *Stasi*, while B. Linklater documents material gleaned from interviews with ordinary people from eastern Germany, and uncovers the contours of *Ostalgie*. Interestingly, Linklater attributes some of this nostalgia to the power of story-telling, where oral history has constructed a picture of a safe and successful GDR to counteract the perceived weaknesses of life in the new *Bundesländer*. The issue of *Ostalgie* resurfaces in essays by M. McGowan and M. Kane, with the former exploring the response in eastern German theatre to the *Wende*, and the latter wondering whether Fritz Rudolf Fries's vivacious *Die Nonnen von Bratislava* represents a satirical take on nostalgia or helplessness in the face of rapid socio-political change. M. Uecker explores the attitudes in East and West that emerge in journalistic articles, and questions whether one can truly speak of fundamental differences between the two sides. The remaining contributions all focus specifically on cultural matters, including essays on *Ein weites Feld*, Brigitte Burmeister, post-unification representations of National Socialism, for example in the highly successful *Der Vorleser*, and two fascinating analyses of east German cinema since 1989 with S. Allan looking at depictions of the *Wende* and H. Claus examining Wolfgang Kohlhaase's reappraisal of the 1945–49 period. The volume is rounded off by U. Zitzlsperger's engaging survey of the way the *Wende* has been thematized in international literature which often appears to use Berlin as a synecdoche for broader German concerns. It seems fitting to end this fine volume with such a shift in perspective, as Germany's fate in both 1949 and 1989 was not the sole preserve of the German people. The editors have assembled a broad array of different perspectives on the significance of 1949 and 1989 to questions of German national identity and concede, for this reason, that the volume 'can only ever be provisional'. Be that as it may, it provides exceptionally fertile ground for ongoing discussions and deserves credit for its ambition.

Facing Fascism and Confronting the Past. German Women Writers from Weimar to the Present, ed. Elke P. Frederiksen and Martha Kaarsberg Wallach, Albany, NY State U.P., 320 pp. Hans-Edwin Friedrich, *Deformierte Lebensbilder. Erzählmodelle der Nachkriegsautobiographie (1945–1960)*, Tübingen, Niemeyer, vi + 458 pp. *Postmoderne Literatur in deutscher Sprache: Eine Ästhetik des Widerstands?*, ed. Henk Habers (ABNG, 49), 396 pp. K. Kastberger, 'Dogma. Zu einer Politisierung der postmodernen Literatur', *Wespennest*, 118:104–09. E. Kolinsky, 'Reflections on Jewish culture in Germany since 1945', *Will Vol.*, 163–74. A. K. Kuhn, 'Women's writing in Germany since 1989: new concepts of national identity', Catling, *Women's Writing*, 233–53. M. Littler, 'Restoration and resistance: women's writing 1945–70', *ib.*, 169–89. R. Moritz, 'Das unfähige Leder. Fußball in der deutschsprachigen Literatur', *JFinL*, 31, 1999:30–35. André Müller, * . . . über die Fragen hinaus. Gespräche mit Schriftstellern*, Munich, DTV, 1998, 297 pp. Karoline von Oppen, *The Role of the Writer and the Press in the Unification of Germany, 1989–1990* (GLC, 31), xiv + 277 pp. *Erinnerte und erfundene Erfahrung. Zur Darstellung von Zeitgeschichte in deutschsprachiger Gegenwartsliteratur*, ed. Edgar Platen, Munich, Iudicium, 202 pp. *Jenseits der Grenzen. Die Auseinandersetzung mit dem Fremde in der deutschsprachigen Kultur*, ed. Margaret Stone and Gundula Sharman,

Berne, Lang, 227 pp. U. Vedder, 'Stranger than paradise. Der "locus amoenus" in der Liebesliteratur der Gegenwart', *WB*, 46:547–63. **Mentalitätswandel in der deutschen Literatur zur Einheit 1990–2000*, ed. Volker Wehdeking (PSQ, 165), 248 pp. R. Weninger, 'Literatur als mediales Ereignis. Eine Symptomatik deutscher Literaturdebatten seit 1945', *ColGer*, 31, 1998:205–36. **German-Language Literature Today: International and Popular?*, ed. Arthur Williams, Stuart Parkes, and Julian Preece, Berne, Lang, x + 320 pp. Hans Dieter Zimmermann, **Literaturbetrieb Ost/West. Die Spaltung der deutschen Literatur von 1948–1998*, Stuttgart, Kohlhammer, 216 pp. L. Żylinski, 'Zeitschriftenzeit. Kulturpolitische Zeitschriften der Nachkriegsjahre in Deutschland', *Orbis Linguarum*, 14, 1999:37–50.

WEST GERMANY, AUSTRIA, SWITZERLAND. *Towards the Millennium. Interpreting the Austrian Novel 1971–1996*, ed. Gerald Chapple, Tübingen, Stauffenburg, 300 pp., is a fine and detailed volume which does indeed substantiate the dust jacket's bold claim that rumours of the death of the Austrian novel with Hermann Broch have been much exaggerated. Chapple has gathered together experts on Austrian literature from across North America and Europe, who between them cover most of the leading authors in the period surveyed. Although several writers are unfortunately excluded, such as Frischmuth and Henisch, the editor does offer K. Zeyringer's introductory essay in mitigation, which establishes the literary foundations of the Austrian novel from Aichinger (1948) to Walter Grond (1998) and thereby forms the springboard for the individual studies which follow. As one would expect, there are essays on Bachmann, Bernhard, Jelinek, and Handke, but in many ways the most interesting contributions focus on some of the younger generation of authors, who will carry the Austrian novel into the 21st c. Fittingly in this regard, the final contribution looks at Christoph Ransmayr, arguably the most prominent of contemporary Austrian authors, and his postmodernist *Morbus Kitahara*, which received a mixed critical response after the acclaim which had greeted *Die letzte Welt*. As the editor underlines in his preface, 'the predominant theme in this volume is the persistence of the past in the present' and it is, indeed, striking how the diverse works selected for analysis share this concern. It lends the collection both natural coherence and relevance, when one considers recent political developments in the country. Pleasing, too, is the gender balance of the authors selected for analysis, with eight male and six female writers included, which signals perhaps a significant strength of contemporary Austrian writing. One must not ignore that women's issues have also been the focus of authors such as Handke, and the essay included here examines the moving portrait of his mother in *Wunschloses Unglück*.

Conversely, female authors such as Elfriede Jelinek and Anna Mitgutsch have tackled broader social and political concerns, and not confined themselves solely to feminist concerns. In this respect, the examination of Jelinek's *Oh Wildnis, oh Schutz vor ihr* duly reveals the author's concern for ecological problems, and highlights the direct link made in the text 'zwischen den Unterdrückungsmechanismen, die die Natur zu kapitalistischen Zwecken ausnützen, und denen die Frauen innerhalb einer patriarchalen Gesellschaft dominieren'. Rather disappointingly by contrast, the survey of Mitgutsch's second novel, *Das andere Gesicht*, which was rather overshadowed by her debut, *Die Züchtigung*, simply adopts a feminist approach. The themes of 'Fremdsein' and 'Heimatsuche' in the novel are explored, but the essay remains trapped by its narrow focus and asserts, rather unsatisfactorily, that *Das andere Gesicht* is 'ein ungewöhnlich programmatisches Werk' which embodies a key 'zum allgemeinen Verständnis von Mitgutschs Texten'. In general, however, this volume represents an engaging introduction to recent exponents of the Austrian novel with fine essays on Elisabeth Reichart and Josef Haslinger to name just two. The key to the volume's success is the way in which each contribution places the work in question into the context of the author's canon, which will offer the student and the newcomer to an author an important orientation point. For the expert, on the other hand, the essays offer provocative interpretations designed to stimulate further research.

Herbert Arlt, *Österreichische Literatur. 'Strukturen', Transformationen, Widerspruchsfelder*, St. Ingbert, Röhrig, 1999, 405 pp. F. C. Delius, 'Wie scheintot war die Literatur? Gedanken beim Wiederlesen des *Kursbuch 15*', *Schiller-Jb.*, 43, 1999:573–79. *Schluss mit dem Abendland. Der lange Atem der österreichischen Avantgarde*, ed. Thomas Eder and Klaus Kastberger, Vienna, Zsolnay, 160 pp. C. Hell, 'Leben und Schreiben in zwei Sprachen. Splitter zur slowenischen Literatur in Kärnten', *LK*, 341–42:45–50. Martin Hussong, *Der Nationalsozialismus im österreichischen Roman 1945–1969*, Tübingen, Stauffenburg, 158 pp. J. Joachimsthaler, '"1968" — literarisches Palimpsest und historisches Plagiat', *Orbis Linguarum*, 13, 1999:101–35. *Literature, Markets and Media in Germany and Austria Today*, ed. Arthur Williams, Stuart Parkes, and Julian Preece, Berne, Lang, x + 326 pp.

Domino. Ein Schweizer Literatur-Reigen, ed. Simone Meier, Salzburg, Müller, 1998, 124 pp. B. Eichmann-Leutenegger, '"So steht das Kind allein in der Welt, umgeben von seinen Sternen . . ." Das Kind in der jüngeren Literatur der deutschsprachigen Schweiz', *SchwM*, 80.2:34–38.

EAST GERMANY.   Reinhard Andress, *Protokolliteratur in der DDR. Der dokumentierte Alltag*, NY, Lang, ix + 220 pp. *DDR-Literatur der*

neunziger Jahre, ed. Heinz Ludwig Arnold (TK Sonderband), 218 pp.
Der Lyrikclub Pankow. Literarische Zirkel in der DDR, ed. Roland Berbig,
Berlin, Links, 332 pp. *East Germany: Continuity and Change*, ed. Paul
Cooke and Jonathan Grix, Amsterdam–Atlanta, Rodopi, 185 pp.,
demonstrates, as the preface declares, 'the continuing fascination of
the GDR/Eastern Germany for researchers and, more specifically,
younger researchers'. Based upon a postgraduate colloquium in
Birmingham in 1998, the present volume reveals the broad array of
projects which have been undertaken at British universities in recent
years, and it is pleasing to note that many of the contributors have
become fully fledged lecturers in their own right. The editors have
divided up the collection of essays into five sections, with each one
introduced by a leading academic expert in the relevant field. The
resultant cross-disciplinary examination is highly illuminating and
will make the volume a valuable tool for undergraduate teaching in
particular. There are sections on patterns of behaviour in GDR
society, such as in the churches and the peace movement, on
institutions and parties, on the economy and the role of women, both
before and after reunification, and on the visual arts. Although these
fall outside the scope of this review, by the very nature of the GDR
the analysis of such topics throws useful light upon the socio-political
conditions which were reflected, and in some cases refracted, by the
literature produced by East German authors. The literary surveys
embrace three writers who have made significant, critically acclaimed
contributions to the country's cultural heritage: Wolfgang Hilbig,
Christoph Hein, and Helga Königsdorf. As M. Kane observes in his
introduction, the essays 'not only highlight the complex relationship
between writers and the state [. . .], and give a valuable account of
the adjustments of position brought about by the *Wende*, they also
remind us of the necessity of avoiding the *Pauschalurteil* in our
evaluation of individual east German authors.' Indeed, although only
three authors are in the spotlight here, they do represent a striking
cross-section of experiences, attitudes, and beliefs. In a fascinating
and persuasive essay, P. Cooke explores Hilbig's *Die Weiber*, his first
publication after leaving the GDR in 1985, and the interrelationship
between sexual *Verdrängung* and *Vergangenheitsbewältigung*. In the concluding section, Cooke relates how the narrator of the tale seeks to
attain a sense of identity through his writing, a stock concern of
Hilbig's fiction, but the pornographic fiction he produces might be
read allegorically as documents of his country's inability to deal with
the Nazi past. With the collapse of the GDR, Cooke observes that the
issue of resolving the painful inheritance of the German past has been
exacerbated still further, but Hilbig's continued problematizing of it
serves as a warning against perpetual suppression. The two essays on

Hein which follow similarly reveal an author who has not experienced the events of 1989 as a major hiatus. S. Bevan draws illuminating parallels between the author's *Horns Ende* and *Von allem Anfang an*, teasing out aesthetic and structural differences between the two texts in question but exposing also continuity in theme. Bevan argues persuasively that Hein 'refused to accept the creation of the GDR as a "Stunde Null" ' in *Horns Ende*, and in *Von allem Anfang an* 'insists on a similar appreciation of continuity from the perspective of post-unification Germany'. Thus, the essay dovetails neatly with the results of the survey of Hilbig which precedes it. D. Clarke meanwhile explores Hein's essays from the 1980s and the short story *Die Vergewaltigung* from the perspective of the author's understanding of ideology and its mechanisms. In particular, Clarke is intrigued by the paradox between 'Stabilität und Revolution' which marked the behaviour of GDR citizens in 1989, when a deeply embedded passivity was finally abandoned in favour of a successful physical challenge to the state. The article relates how in his essays Hein asserts the belief that literature can effect change in individuals by exposing the world as it really is and thereby encouraging them to change it. In his fiction, however, Clarke explains that the author shows how the passivity of citizens was quite in keeping with the GDR regime's efforts to impose its flawed ideology on society, by force if necessary, as the aftermath of 17 June 1953 underlines. Clarke's argument is a compelling one, and he concludes with the exhortation to read Hein's work 'as an exploration of the effect of state repression on the capacity of GDR citizens to come to terms with the world as individuals and as members of society'. The final essay in the section on GDR authors examines the way Helga Königsdorf has had to recast her role since the *Wende*, not least as a former Party member. D. Alberghini traces the process of adaptation that the writer was forced to undergo as the GDR crumbled, before redefining her role as that of an intellectual who must warn and encourage her readers. Königsdorf believed more wholeheartedly than Hilbig and Hein in the authors' capacity to educate and shape their readership, but with the *Wende* came the realization that she could no longer function as a spokesperson: the people were finally speaking for themselves. Alberghini argues that, despite such a fundamental reassessment of her role, the author is enthused by the opportunity to engage in open debate about the shape of the new society, but retains 'her lucidity in the frenzy of this period of radical change'. Indeed, Königsdorf's self-critical awareness is presented convincingly as a model to be emulated not just by intellectuals, but by all East Germans at a time when they were having to adapt to a different environment. In conclusion, the entire volume is a provocative and engaging survey of East Germany's legacy, which uncovers the interrelationship between the cultural and socio-political spheres, but which also articulates a warning against a hasty assessment of real and existing German socialism. Hyunseon Lee, *Geständniszwang und 'Wahrheit des Charakters' in der Literatur der DDR. Diskursanalytische Fallstudien*, Weimar, Metzler, 469 pp. Anne Lequy, *'unbehaust'? Die Thematik des Topos in Werken wenig(er) bekannter DDR-Autorinnen der siebziger und achtziger Jahre. Eine feministische Untersuchung*, Frankfurt, Lang, 645 pp. S. Mrozek, 'Der sozialistische Realismus als Instrument der ideologisichen Literaturlenkung', *Orbis Linguarum*, 14, 1999:121–38. R. Schmidt, 'GDR women writers: ways of writing for, within and against Socialism', Catling, *Women's Writing*, 190–99. Petra Stuber, *Spielräume und Grenzen. Studien zum DDR-Theater*, Berlin, Links, 1999, 404 pp. Z. Światlowski, 'Repräsentanten und Tabuverletzer', *Orbis Linguarum*, 14, 1999:75–94. I. Wallace, 'The GDR's cultural activities in Britain', *GLL*, 53:394–408. Karin Wieckhorst, *Die Darstellung des 'antifaschistischen Widerstandes' in der Kinder- und Jugendliteratur der SBZ/DDR*, Frankfurt, Lang, 147 pp.

2. LYRIC POETRY

G.-J. Berendse, 'Das Karnevalprojekt. Chronik eines mißlungenen Lyrik-Experiments 1964–1968', *WW*, 50:248–55. Friedrich Block, *Beobachtung des 'Ich'. Zum Zusammenhang von Subjektivität und Medien am Beispiel experimenteller Poesie*, Bielefeld, Aisthesis, 1999, 346 pp. *Terra di nessuno. La poesia tedesca dopo la caduta del muro di Berlino*, ed. Anna Chiarloni and Gerhard Friedrich, Alessandria, Edizioni dell'Orso, 1999, xvi + 262 pp. K. Leeder, 'Post-1945 women's poetry from East and West', Catling, *Women's Writing*, 200–15. Christoph Meckel, *Dichter und andere Gesellen*, Munich, Hanser, 1998, 189 pp. T. Nolden, ' "Aus der Vergangenheit herausgewandert": Überlegungen zur Lyrik jüdischer Autoren der Gegenwart', *ColGer*, 31, 1998:259–76. Hans Weichelbaum, *Im Namen des Dichters. 45 Jahre Georg-Trakl-Preis für Lyrik — Geschichte und Dokumentation*, Salzburg, Müller, 1998, 144 pp.

3. DRAMA

Hans Amstutz, Ursula Käser-Leisibach and Martin Stern, *Schweizertheater. Drama und Bühne in der Deutschschweiz bis Frisch und Dürrenmatt 1930–1950. Übersicht und Analysen*, Zurich, Chronos, 672 pp. R. Bubner, 'Demokratisierung des Geniekonzepts. Rede über das Theater', *SuF*, 52:683–93. H.-E. Friedrich, ' "Datenschutt" und

"Unsicherheitsrelation": Die ästhetische Konstruktion von Wirklichkeit im Dokumentarliteratur', *ZDP*, 119:268–89.

4. PROSE

Nikolaus Förster, **Die Wiederkehr des Erzählens. Deutschsprachige Prosa der 8oer und 9oer Jahre*, WBG, 1999, x + 261 pp. G. Paiter, ' "Weibliche Körper" im "männlichen" Raum. Zur Interdependenz von Gender und Genre in deutschsprachigen Kriminalromanen von Autorinnen', *WB*, 46:564–81. Chloe E. M. Paver, *Narrative and Fantasy in the Post-War German Novel. A Study of Novels by Johnson, Frisch, Wolf, Becker, and Grass*, Oxford, Clarendon, 1999, 227 pp., provides a detailed dissection of five texts by key authors in the post-war period, investigating the ways in which the first-person narrators in each draw attention to the process of inventing aspects of their narrative. P. neatly terms this device 'overt fictionalization' and her illuminating analysis of the way in which the narrators propose, and then retract, passages represents the first study of this technique. The five texts are: Uwe Johnson's *Das dritte Buch über Achim*, Max Frisch's *Mein Name sei Gantenbein*, Christa Wolf's *Nachdenken über Christa T.*, Jurek Becker's *Jakob der Lügner*, and Günter Grass's *örtlich betäubt*. In order to contextualize her new approach, P. begins her study with an examination of four existing narrative theories and assesses their usefulness as markers for her analysis. Three of them are discarded as rather limited in scope, but Brian McHale's argument in *Postmodernist Fiction* examines some devices, such as erasure, which P. feels correspond to those to be found in the texts under consideration here; P. issues the caveat however, that 'to accept McHale's theoretical framework is not necessarily to accept that the five novels [. . .] are *postmodernist* texts'. It should be stressed that P. herself is not seeking to offer an all-encompassing theory, but simply proposing an analytical tool with which to tackle the novels in question. P.'s detailed close reading of each text in turn identifies the different ways in which the narrators both interweave fiction and fantasy and signal these inventions. Indeed, one could argue that the provisional or qualified nature of each narrative is implied in the titles chosen, but P. maps in convincing detail the contours of these shifting texts. But it is her interpretation of the authors' aims in employing such fickle narrators that impresses. In Johnson's complex text, for example, P. argues that 'overt fictionalization' is used not only to puncture a stereotypical Western view of the GDR, but also to mirror the way in which interpretations of history were prey to manipulation in the GDR. She cites Ulbricht's U-turn in his analysis of the role of the working classes in the rise of Hitler, at first critical of their passivity, but later described as victims: 'Under Ulbricht, then, History was subject to the same kind of revision and cancellation as the story of Achim's life in Johnson's *Das dritte Buch*'. In support of P.'s thesis, one might also add here that the workers' uprising of 17 June 1953 was quite literally expunged from GDR historical records. P. contends that an historical perspective is also at work in Wolf's text, with the suggested and cancelled fictions designed to help the narrator reappraise her friend Christa T. more positively than hitherto. The narrator achieves this re-evaluation by reinventing a past in the present in order to transform her friend's life for the better. P. thus argues convincingly that rather than blurring the image of the eponymous figure, as many critics claim, the narrator is 'working towards a definite "image" of Christa T., and that she is trying to bring this image into focus [. . .] by inventing episodes in Christa's life.' Arguably the best chapter is P.'s analysis of *Jakob der Lügner*. It contains numerous examples of P.'s finely attuned close reading of the text in order to lay bare the subtle devices employed in the narrative. She uncovers similar qualities to those evident in Wolf's text, whereby gaps in the narrative are plugged by tales invented by the narrator, even extending in Becker's novel to the provision of an alternative ending. The narrator's desire to tell a good story, which Becker himself shares, is cited as evidence of the influence of Frisch, and P. explores what is seen to constitute a 'good story' in the context of the novel. She argues that the aims of the narrator are to preserve hope in the face of inhumanity, and proceeds to mount a vigorous defence of Becker's novel from the criticism that it trivializes the Holocaust; a charge, incidentally, that irreparably damaged the performance of the recent Hollywood film adaption of the tale at the box office. P. reiterates, in conclusion, that the narrator's fictions not only reveal his delight at the skill he possesses and operate as a means of dealing with the traumas of the past, but also evince an inherent moral quality: 'His depiction of human folly and frailty, which is gently satirical without ever being censorious or judgemental, promotes tolerance'. This volume is a fine one, written in nicely poised prose which handles a potentially intricate theoretical area with clarity. If there is a disappointment it is in the rather perfunctory conclusion, and at times the intrusion of footnotes into the main body of the text is irritating, but in fairness these are minor quibbles. P. has presented a provocative survey, which boldly opens up new lines of enquiry into five already well-researched novels, and deserves the attention of a wide academic readership. Alfred D. White, *The One-Eyed Man. Social Reality in the German Novel 1848–1968*, Oxford, Lang, 189 pp.

5. INDIVIDUAL AUTHORS

ACHTERNBUSCH, HERBERT. G. Gemünden, 'Gone primitive: the *Indianerphantasien* of H.A.', *GR*, 73, 1998:32–49.

ADLER, H. G. J. Adler, '"Die Macht des Guten im Rachen des Bösen"'. H.G.A., T. W. Adorno und die Darstellung der Shoah', *Merkur*, 54:475–86.

AICHINGER, ILSE. N. Rosenberger, 'Das Prinzip des Ungefügten. Zum geschichtskritischen Potential von I.As Roman *Die größere Hoffnung*', *WB*, 46:121–28.

ANDERSCH, ALFRED. M. E. Brunner, 'Cinemorphe Seh- und Wahrnehmungsweisen in As Roman *Die Rote*', *WB*, 46:602–16. Rüdiger Hessling, **Autobiographie in Erzählungen: Studien und Interpretationen zu den Franz-Kien-Geschichten von A.A.* (EH, 1, 1775), viii + 429 pp. U. Kinzel, 'Das Ende der Reise. Orientierung und Erfahrung in A.As *Hohe Breitengrade*', *Schiller-Jb.*, 43, 1999:403–30. E. Mather, '"Vielleicht ist unter allen Masken, aus denen man wählen kann, das Ich die beste"'. Über die Entstehung einer Legende auf der Grundlage einer Autobiographie: A.As *Die Kirschen der Freiheit*', *Neophilologus*, 84:443–53.

ANDRES, STEFAN. Eric Sigurd Gabe, **Macht und Religion. Analogie zum Dritten Reich in S.As Trilogie 'Die Sintflut'*, Berne, Lang, 326 pp.

ARJOUNI, JAKOB. A. A. Teraoka, 'Detective ethnicity: J.A. and the case of the missing German detective novel', *GQ*, 72, 1999:265–89.

ARTMANN, H. C. D. Horvat, 'Das Märchen-ich-zersetz-dich-Spiel H.C.As', *ZGB*, 5, 1999:393–400.

AUSLÄNDER, ROSE. J. Billen, 'Mutterland Wort. Zur lyrischen Bildwelt R.As', *LitL*, 22:90–108.

BACHMANN, INGEBORG. Hans Höller, **I.B.* (RoM, 50545), 120 pp. S. Kieslechner, 'Dichter in der deutschen Wüste. Was I.B. in Berlin sah und hörte', *SuF*, 52:195–212. Imke Meyer, **Jenseits der Spiegel kein Land. Ich-Fiktionen in Texten von Franz Kafka und I.B.* (Ep, 343), 232 pp. Veronica O'Regan, **'Dieses Spannungsverhältnis, an dem wir wachsen': Growth and Decay in I.B.'s 'Simultan'*, NY, Lang, 150 pp. See also BERNHARD, THOMAS, CELAN, PAUL, and WOLF, CHRISTA.

BECHER, JOHANNES R. P. Davies, 'J.R.B. and the agony of responsibility, 1945–1949', *GLL*, 53:243–60.

BECKER, JUREK. J. Fetscher, 'Mach keine Geschichten. Die Historie und der Trost des Erzählens in J.Bs *Jakob der Lügner*', *Convivium*, 1999:143–62. H.-J. Ortheil, 'Die Furcht des Geschichtenerzählers. Zum Tode von Jurek Becker', *JDASD*, 1997[1998]:193–96.

BERGGRUEN, HEINZ. R. Kudielka, 'Den Fischen läuten. Laudatio auf H.B.', *SuF*, 52:885–87.

BERNHARD, THOMAS.   Oliver Bentz, *T.B. — Dichtung als Skandal* (Ep, 337), 144 pp. P. Bozzi, 'Der Traum als Wiederkehr des Körpers. Zum anderen Diskurs im Werk T.Bs', *SchwM*, 80.9:30–34. *T.B.: Eine Existenz*, ed. Jens Dechering and Mike Wolke, Leipzig, VirtuSens, 85 pp. Karl Hennetmair, *Ein Jahr mit T.B. Das notariell versiegelte Tagebuch 1972*, Vienna, Residenz, 592 pp. Paul Jaeg, *Der Landwiener T.B.*, Scheuring, Black Ink, 132 pp. Horst Jesse, *Die retrospektive Wiederspiegelung der Identitätsentwicklung Jugendlicher anhand autobiographischer Romane von Bernward Vesper, Christa Wolf und T.B.*, Frankfurt, Lang, 314 pp. C. Klein, *'Alte Meister* de T.B. ou "le point aveugle" de l'écriture', *CEtGer*, 38:189–200. *Die Musik, das Leben und der Irrtum. T.B. und die Musik*, ed. Otto Kolleritsch, Vienna, Universal, 249 pp. Kay Link, *Die Welt als Theater. Künstlichkeit und Künstlertum bei T.B.* (SAG, 382), 148 pp. Elisabetta Niccolini, *Der Spaziergang des Schriftstellers. 'Lenz' von Georg Büchner. 'Der Spaziergang' von Robert Walser. 'Gehen' von T.B.*, Stuttgart, Metzler, 242 pp. N. Schumacher, 'Faschismus, Destruktion, Utopie. Die Bedeutung von Ingeborg Bachmanns *Böhmen liegt am Meer* für T.Bs *Auslöschung*', *ZDP*, 118, 1999:572–91.

BEYER, MARCEL.   U. Schönherr, 'Topophony of fascism: on M.B.'s *The Karnau Tapes*', *GR*, 73, 1998:328–48.

BLOCH, ERNST.   Marion Retterath, *Die Metaphysik des moralischen Subjekts bei Emmanuel und E.B.*, Hamburg, Kovac, 220 pp.

BOBROWSKI, JOHANNES.   E. Dzikowska, 'Erinnertes Sarmatien, verlorenes Europa. J.Bs *Levins Mühle* und der polnische Sarmatismus', *Convivium*, 1999:51–63.

BOIE, KIRSTEN.   K. Richter, 'Überlegungen beim Schreiben von Kinderliteratur. Zum Realismus in den Kinderbüchern K.Bs', *DUB*, 51, 1998:282–93.

BÖLL, HEINRICH.   *Interpretationen: H.B. — Romane und Erzählungen*, ed. Werner Bellmann, Stuttgart, Reclam, 300 pp. D. Pruss-Plawska, 'Der Clown als Typus der Narrengestalt in der deutschen Literatur der sechziger Jahre. Eine Studie anhand des Romans *Ansicht eines Clowns* von H.B.', *SGGed*, 7, 1999:97–111. Heinrich Vormweg, *H.B. — Eine Biographie*, Cologne, Kiepenheuer & Witsch, 384 pp.

BRAUN, VOLKER.   K. Botte, 'Schreiben im Niemandsland. Beobachtungen zum Schreibprozeß V.Bs', *WB*, 46:430–53. See also WOLF, CHRISTA.

BRINKMANN, ROLF DIETER.   Christian Kohlross, *Theorie des modernen Naturgedichts. Oskar Loerke, Günter Eich, R.D.B* (Ep, 303), 264 pp.

BROCH, HERMANN.   Robert Halsall, *The Problem of Autonomy in the Work of H.B.* (EH, I, 1778), 260 pp.

DE BRUYN, GÜNTER.   W. Schemmel, 'Diesseits der Kanondebatte: das Thema "Vereinigung". G.d.B.', *Vierzig Jahre*, *DUB*, 50, 1997:585–97.

CANETTI, ELIAS.   A. Christophe, 'Phrasèmes et phrasèmes traduits chez C.: la traduction par analogie', *NCA*, 17, 1999:389–99. S. Ferguson, 'E.C. and multiculturalism', *Poetica*, 29, 1997:532–95. Hildegard Hogen, **Die Modernisierung des Ich. Individualitätskonzepte bei Siegfried Kracauer, Robert Musil und E.C.* (Ep, 323), 184 pp. Ning Wu, **C. und China. Quellen, Materialien, Darstellung und Interpretation* (SAG, 384), 200 pp.

CELAN, PAUL.   **P.C. in den Händen von Experten*, ed. Bernhard Albers, Aachen, Rimbaud, 48 pp. Ulrich Baer, **Remnants of Song: Trauma and the Experience of Modernity in Charles Baudelaire and P.C.*, Stanford U.P., 343 pp. G. Bevilacqua, 'Erotische Metaphorik beim frühen Celan', *EG*, 53, 1998:471–80. Jean Bollack, **P.C. Eine Poetik der Fremdheit*, Vienna, Zsolnay, 384 pp. B. Böschenstein, 'Die Bedeutung Stefan Georges und Conrad Ferdinand Meyer für P.Cs Frühwerk', *EG*, 53, 1998:481–92. Theo Buck, **C.-Studien: IV — Mit entsichertem Herzhirn*, Aachen, Rimbaud, 132 pp. **Zur Lyrik P.Cs*, ed. Peter Buhrmann, Copenhagen–Munich, Fink, 182 pp. Stephanie Dressler, **Giuseppe Ungarettis Werk in deutscher Sprache. Unter besonderer Berücksichtigung der Übersetzungen Ingeborg Bachmanns und P.Cs*, Heidelberg, Winter, 332 pp. John Felstiner, **P.C. Eine Biographie*, Munich, Beck, 432 pp. **Unverloren. Trotz allem. P.C.-Symposion Wien 2000*, ed. Hubert Gaisbauer et al, Vienna, Mandelbaum, 300 pp. Peter Gossens, **P.Cs Ungaretti-Übersetzung. Edition und Kommentar*, Heidelberg, Winter, 381 pp. E. Hünnecke, 'Aspekte der Sprechinstanz in dialogischer Lyrik. P.Cs Gedicht "Allmählich clowngesichtig"', *CEtGer*, 38:37–52. S. Mosès, 'P.C. als Übersetzer Apollinaires. *L'Adieu/ Der Abschied*', *EG*, 53, 1998:493–503. Marko Pajevic, **Zur Poetik P.Cs: Gedicht und Mensch — die Arbeit am Sinn* (BNL, 177), 310 pp. Otto Pöggeler, **Der Stein hinterm Aug. Studien zu Cs Gedichten*, Munich, Fink, 195 pp. Albrecht Schöne, **Dichtung als verborgene Theologie. Versuch einer Exegese von P.Cs Gedicht 'Einer der vor der Tür stand'*, Göttingen, Wallstein, 48 pp. Joachim Seng, **Auf den Kreis-Wegen der Dichtung. Zyklische Komposition bei P.C. in den Gedichtbänden bis 'Sprachgitter'* (BNL, 159), 1998, 321 pp. Margareta Suppan, **Die Lyrik P.Cs*, Gnas, Weishaupt, 96 pp. Jan H. Tück, **Gelobt seist Du, Niemand. P.Cs Dichtung — eine theologische Provokation*, Frankfurt, Knecht, 176 pp. **Paul Celan — Die Goll-Affäre. Dokumente zu einer 'Infamie'*, ed. Barbara Wiedemann, Frankfurt, Suhrkamp, 926 pp.

DODERER, HEIMITO VON.   Su-Jin Lee, **H.v.Ds Roman 'Die Wasserfälle von Slunj'. Eine sprachwissenschaftliche Untersuchung zum österreichischen Deutsch*, Frankfurt, Lang, 311 pp. Lutz W. Wolff, **H.v.D.* (RoM, 557), 120 pp.

DORST, TANKRED.   **T.D.*, ed. Heinz Ludwig Arnold (TK, 145), 99 pp.

DRACH, ALBERT. C. Ruthner, 'Gegen-Pornographie? A.Ds intertextuxtuelle Antwort auf "Josefine Metzenbacher"', *ÖGL*, 44:159–72.

DÜRRENMATT, FRIEDRICH. Gun-Yong Park, *Intertextuelle Analyse zweier Werke von F.D.: 'Mondfinsternis' und 'Der Besuch der alten Dame'*, Bochum U.P., 304 pp. Stefan Riedlinger, *Tradition und Verfremdung. F.D. und der klassische Detektivroman*, Marburg, Tectum, 242 pp. *Die Verwandlung der 'Stoffe' als Stoff der Verwandlung F.Ds Spätwerk*, ed. Peter Rusterholz and Irmgard Wirtz, Berlin, Schmidt, 228 pp.

EICH, GÜNTER. W. Maoping, 'Traum und Identitätswechsel in G.Es Werk', *Literaturstraße*, 1:177–91. *Nach dem Ende der Biographie. G.E. (1907–1972)*, ed. Peter Walther, Berlin, Lukas Vlg für Kunst- und Geistesgeschichte, 112 pp.

ENDLER, ADOLF. C. Jentzsch, 'Lern, Bruder, zuzustechen mit der Silbe. Über A.E.', *StZ*, 153:7–17.

ENZENSBERGER, HANS MAGNUS. Markus Joch, *Brüderkämpfe. Zum Streit um den intellektuellen Habitus in den Fällen Heinrich Heine, Heinrich Mann und H.M.E.*, Heidelberg, Winter, x + 483 pp. Byung-Hee Rim, *H.M.E.* (EH, 1, 1753), x + 189 pp.

FASCHINGER, LILIAN. G. Roethke, 'L.F. im Gespräch', *MAL*, 33:84–103.

FELDMANN, ARTHUR. W. Mieder, '"Der Wolf ist dem Wolf ein Mensch". Zu den sprichwörtlichen Aphorismen von A.F.', *ÖGL*, 44:33–47.

FICHTE, HUBERT. Michael Fisch, *Verwörterung der Welt. Über die Bedeutung des Reisens für Leben und Werk von H.F. Orte — Zeiten — Begriffe*, Aachen, Rimbaud, 288 pp.

FLEISSER, MARIELUISE. *Reflexive Naivität. Zum Werk M.Fs*, ed. Maria E. Müller and Ulrike Vedder, Berlin, Schmidt, 280 pp.

FRIED, ERICH. Christine Dressler, *'Nach dem Landlos greift des Landlosen Hand.' E.F. — ein Exilautor? Eine Untersuchung seines nach 1945 entstandenen Werkes*, Vienna, Praesens, 1998, 236 pp. M. Janka, 'Der Dichter, der Profesor und die "Friedensfrau": Die *Lysistrate*-Bearbeitungen von E.F. (1979/1985) und Walter Jens (1986) in der Tradition der modernen Aristophanesrezeption', Baumbach, *Tradita*, 575–99. W. Pape, 'Papierkorb und Grammophon: Zum politischen Lyrik E.Fs und Wolf Biermanns', *GLL*, 53:351–72. See also BRINK-MANN, ROLF DIETER.

FRISCH, MAX. Urs Bircher, *Mit Ausnahme der Freundschaft. M.F. 1956–1991*, Zurich, Limmat, 300 pp. Jeong-Rin Lee, *Ideologie und Komödie. Zur ideologiekritischen Komödie M.Fs*, Berlin, Logos, 250 pp. Erica Natale, *Rollendasein und verhindertes Erleben. Literatur und literarische Bezüge im Kontext des Stiller von M.F.*, Hannover, Ibidem, 122 pp. Barabar Rowinska-Januszewska, *Zur Freiheitsproblematik im Werk M.Fs*

(EH, I, 1759), 355 pp. Cornelia Steffahn, *Altern, Sterben und Tod im Spätwerk von M.F*, Hamburg, Kovac, 264 pp.

FRISCHMUTH, BARBARA. *B.F. in Contemporary Context*, ed. Renate Posthofen, Riverside, Ariadne, 1999, 346 pp.

FUCHS, GERD. J. Heizmann, 'Interview mit G.F.', *Seminar*, 36:383–98.

FUCHS, JÜRGEN. A. Horn, 'Von keinem Diskurs beherrscht: Das Gedicht "Nicht Alle" von J.F.', *AGJSG*, 26–27, 1998–99:95–106. P. Horn, 'Über die ideologischen und militärischen Schützengräben hinweg: J.Fs "Gedächtnisprotokolle"', *ib.*, 83–93.

FÜHMANN, FRANZ. Margarete Hannsmann, *Protokolle aus der Dämmerung. Begegnungen und Briefwechsel zwischen F.F., Margarete Hannsmann und H. A. P. Grieshaber 1977–1984*, Rostock, Hinstorff, 416 pp.

GOETZ, RAINALD. N. Werber, 'Intensitäten des Politischen. Gestalten souveräner und normalistischer Macht bei R.G.', *WB*, 46:105–20.

GRASS, GÜNTER M. Durzak, 'Grass parodied: notes on the reception of *Die Rättin*', *Will Vol.*, 122–33. W. Hinck, 'G.Gs Hommage an Fontane. Zum Roman *Ein weites Feld*', *SuF*, 52:777–87. C. Hummel, '"Gegen rhetorische Ohnmacht." Die Rezeption politischer Lyrik von G.G. aus den 60er Jahren', *WW*, 50:48–66. Peter Joch, *Zaubern auf weissem Papier. Das graphische Werk von G.G.*, Göttingen, Steidl, 96 pp. A. Krzeminski, 'Symbiosen und unsichtbare Mauern. Rede auf G.G.', *SuF*, 52:291–94. S. Lohr, 'Theo Wuttke alias Fontane. Ein Gespräch mit G.G.', *DUS*, 50.4, 1998:69–73. Sabine Moser, *G.G. Romane und Erzählungen*, Berlin, Schmidt, 215 pp. Julian Preece, *The Life and Work of G.G.: Literature, History, Politics*, Basingstoke, Palgrave, 224 pp. Rainer Scherf, *Das Herz der Blechtrommel und andere Aufsätze zum Werk von G.G.*, Marburg, Tectum, 260 pp. R. Yorioka, 'Der fragwürdige Zeuge G.G. Über die Vielschichtigkeit des Romans *Ein weites Feld*', *DB*, 103, 1999:150–60 (Japanese with German summary).

GRÜNBEIN, DURS. Alexa Hennemann, *Die Zerbrechlichkeit der Körper. Zu den Georg-Büchner-Preisreden von Heiner Müller und D.G.*, Frankfurt, Lang, 130 pp.

HACKL, ERICH. E. Guilhamon, 'Entre fiction et document: *Abschied von Sidonie d'E.H.*', *CEtGer, 38: 147–56*.

HANDKE, PETER. D. Barnett, 'Dramaturgies of *Sprachkritik*: Rainer Werner Fassbinder's *Blut am Hals der Katze* and P.H.'s *Kaspar*', *MLR*, 95:1053–63. N. Jun, 'Das rechte Verhalten in der zivilisierten Zeit. Zu P.Hs dramatischem Gedicht *Über die Dörfer* (1981)', *Literaturstraße*, 1:193–200. T. Karino, 'Das Theater zur Übung des Zuschauens. *Die Stunde, da wir nichts von einander wußten* von P.H.', *DB*, 103, 1999:79–89

(Japanese with German summary). Gerhard Pfister, **Hs Mitspieler. Der literarische Konflikt zu 'Der kurze Brief zum langen Abschied', 'Langsame Rückkehr', 'Das Spiel vom Fragen', 'Versuch über die Müdigkeit'*, Berne, Lang, 368 pp. Ralf Zschachlitz, **'Epiphanie' ou 'illumination profane'? L'oeuvre de P.H. et la théorie esthétique de Walter Benjamin*, Berne, Lang, xx + 475 pp.

HÄRTLING, PETER.   M.-H. Pérennec, 'Polyphonie et stratégies de lecture dans *Das Familienfest* de P.H.', *CEtGer*, 38 : 177–88.

HASLINGER, JOSEF.   R. Acker, 'The question of cultural identity in J.H.'s *Opernball*', *MAL*, 32, 1999 : 100–08. D. L. Colclasure, ' "Die eigene Zukunft ist nur über den Verrat zu erlangen": J.Hs *Opernball*', *ib.*, 109–32.

HAUSHOFER, MARLEN.   Daniela Strigl, **M.H. Die Biographie*, Munich, Claassen, 300 pp. **Die Frau hinter der Wand. Aus dem Nachlass der M.H.*, ed. Liliane Studer, Munich, Claassen, 120 pp.

HEIN, CHRISTOPH.   M. Durzak, 'Die Wunden der deutschen Wende. Zu Kurzgeschichten von C.H., Günter Kunert und Erich Loest', *AGJSG*, 26–27, 1998–99 : 67–81. *C.H.*, ed. Bill Niven and David Clarke, Cardiff, Univ. of Wales Press, xii + 167 pp., is the latest in Swansea's series of monographs on contemporary writers and offers a typically informative insight into one of the most important and successful authors to emerge from the former GDR. The familiar pattern of these studies is adhered to, opening with the text of H.'s speech from 1998 on the influence of Kleist's *Michael Kohlhaas*, followed by an outline biography and a very accessible interview with the volume editors. H. talks candidly about his formative experiences and his perception of the role of literature and authors. Interestingly he asserts that intellectuals have a duty to voice their opinions on political issues, but welcomes nevertheless the removal of pressure on former GDR authors in the post-*Wende* period. A. Drescher's contribution provides a fascinating, and witty, insight into the role of a *Lektor*, with particular emphasis on her role in the creation and publication of *Von allem Anfang an*: she even ventures a wry dismissal of *Germanistik* as an 'unnützes Wissenschaftsfach'. K. Hammer compares the nature of H.'s prose and drama, and highlights the change in technique required of the playwright in order to convey the emotions and thought processes of the characters. Hammer notes for example how H. exploits anachronisms in *Cromwell* in order to interweave past and present, whereas in his fiction the author achieves this by less theatrical, or crude, means. The essay successfully demonstrates H.'s remarkable range as a writer, whilst simultaneously acknowledging that since *Randow*, 'ein sarkastisches Stück', his plays have been performed less and less. There follows then an exploration of the theme of rape in H.'s *oeuvre*, in which

B. Linklater, concentrating primarily on *Der fremde Freund* and the short story 'Die Vergewaltigung', appears somewhat unconvinced about the author's depiction of sexual violence against women. She nevertheless acknowledges the problems inherent in any attempt to portray rape in literature, and welcomes H.'s willingness to tackle such a complex topic. D. Clarke offers a corrective reading of H.'s rather negatively received *Das Napoleon-Spiel*, and seeks to provide a more objective approach to its criticism of Western capitalism than hitherto. Similarly, B. Niven attempts to resuscitate interest in *Randow*, by pleading for a more differentiated approach. Niven constructs a convincing argument, suggesting that the play is a pessimistic sequel to *Ritter der Tafelrunde* and that H. has simply turned his attention to the structures of the West: 'For years [H.] measured socialism by its own standards and found it wanting; now he does the same with Western liberalism, and finds its equally wanting'. Niven's detailed analysis of the play, and the different levels upon which it operates, achieves its aim by illustrating how H. is interested in far more than simply criticizing unification and the problems which have followed in its wake. In the final essay, D. Tate examines *Von allem Anfang an*, the first work wholly conceived and written after the *Wende*, and traces the similarities and differences in the biographies of Daniel, the protagonist of the novel, and H. himself. Tate observes that for any reader familiar with H.'s life, it would be easy to approach the text as autobiography, but such a reading is missing the point. The main focus of the novel is 'on the private experience of the onset of puberty, and the reader's confidence in the authenticity of Daniel's account will derive from the coherence and credibility of the text rather than external biographical considerations'. Tate also warns against scouring the text for insights into GDR life in the 1950s, and places it instead in the classical German tradition of treatments of adolescence such as Musil's *Die Verwirrungen des Zöglings Törless*. Viewed in this light, *Von allem Anfang an* emerges as a touching, and frequently humorous, account of growing up in the GDR, which seeks neither to defend nor condemn the socio-political system. Rather, Tate argues, the text sets 'the tone for the more measured reassessment of life in the GDR which can only properly begin as the turbulence of the years of transition begins to subside.' As ever, the volume is rounded off with a detailed bibliography containing a comprehensive list of primary texts, together with secondary materials from the period 1992–99. With its focus principally on the lesser known and more recent of H.'s works, this fine monograph is certain to prove a stimulating addition to the studies already available.

HEYM, STEFAN.   K. E. Attar, 'The archive and the artist: The S.H. archive revisited', *GLL*, 53:73–88. S. Taberner, 'The writer's fascination with power: S.H.'s *Der König-David-Bericht*', *Neophilologus*, 84:271–83. Anja Reuter, **Die Frömmigkeit des Zweifels. Biblisch-messianische Motive und deren sozialikritische Funktionen im Roman 'Ahasver' von S.H.* (EH, 1, 1768), 264 pp.

HILBIG, WOLFGANG.   P. Cooke, '"Das schreiende Amt": the "bourgeois" tradition and the problems of "objectivity" in W.H.'s *Abwesenheit*', *GLL*, 53:261–78.

HILSENRATH, EDGAR.   Agnieszka von Zanthier, **Julian Stryjkowski und E.H.: Zur Identität jüdischer Schriftsteller nach 1945*, Essen, Die Blaue Eule, 254 pp.

HOCHHUTH, ROLF.   Gerald Rauscher, **Kein Zeichen, kein Wunder. R.H. über Schöpfer, Schöpfung und Geschöpf. Mit einem Schriftstellergespräch*, Frankfurt, Lang, 125 pp.

HOCHWÄLDER, FRITZ.   U. H. Gerlach, 'Vergelten, vergeben, vergessen? Zum Wandel eines Motivs in F.Hs Werk', *ÖGL*, 44:21–31.

HÜRLIMANN, THOMAS.   D. Lenz and E. Pütz, 'Gespräch mit T.H.', *SuF*, 52:525–40.

JAHNN, HANS HENNY.   Joachim Gerdes, **Die Schuld-Thematik in H.H.Js 'Fluß ohne Ufer'* (HBG, 32), 304 pp. Jochen Hengst, **Ansätze zu einer Archäologie der Literatur. Mit einem Versuch über Js Prosa*, Stuttgart, Metzler, 522 pp.

JELINEK, ELFRIEDE.   E. Annuss, 'Zwangsleben und Schweigen in E.Js *Wolken. Heim*', *StZ*, 153:32–49. S. Böhmisch, 'Le sujet d'abjection. Étude sur l'instance narrative dans *Die Klavierspielerin* d'E.J.', *CEtGer*, 38:135–45. P. Janka, 'Ver-rückte Blicke auf die Wirklichkeit. E.Js Texte zu Olga Neuwirths Hörstücken und Opern', *Wespennest*, 118:94–102. R. Miwa, 'E.Js Textcollagen. Anhand von zwei Inszenierungen am Hamburger Deutschen Schauspielhaus', *DB*, 103, 1999:90–99 (Japanese with German summary). I. Nagel, 'Lügnerin und Wahr-Sagerin. Laudatio auf E.J', *JDASD*, 1998[1999]:164–69. I. Nagelschmidt, '"Schreiben kann jeder, der denken kann": Der ferne analytische Blick E.Js', Corbineau-Hoffmann, *Gewalt*, 243–63. O. Niethammer, '"Wer ist denn schon zu Hause bei sich, wer ist denn schon sein eigener Herr?": E.Js Diskussion von Gewaltverhältnissen im Kontext der deutschsprachigen Literatur und Öffentlichkeit', *Literaturstraße*, 1:223–40. C. Schmidt, '"Sprechen Sein". E.Js Theater der Sprachflächen', *StZ*, 153:65–74. E. Swales, 'Pathology as metaphor: E.J.'s *Die Klavierspielerin*', *MLR*, 95:437–49. S. Treude, 'Vom Übersetzen zum Verschwiegenen. Einige Überlegungen zum Übersetzungsverfahren in den Texten von E.J. und Martin Heidegger', *StZ*, 153:75–87.

JÜNGER, ERNST. Thomas Pekar, *E.J. und der Orient. Mythos — Lektüre — Reise*, Würzburg, Ergon, 263 pp. I. Stöckmann, ' "... Prosa, die von uns gedeutet und beherrscht werden will." Über E.Js politische Essayistik', *GR*, 75 : 3–19.

KASER, NORBERT C. M. E. Brunner, ' "Schau hin, schau her/nun gibt es keine Fabeln mehr"? Fabeln, (Kinder)Gedichte und Schultexte von N.C.K.', *MBA*, 17, 1998 : 93–106.

KEUN, IRMGARD. Xenia Srebrianski Harwell, *The Female Adolescent in Exile in Works by Irina Odoevtseva, Nina Berberova, I.K., und Ilse Tielsch* (STML, 57), ix + 175 pp.

KIRCHHOFF, BODO. Torsten Pätzold, *Textstrukturen und narrative Welten. Narratologische Untersuchungen zur Multiperspektivität am Beispiel von B.Ks 'Infanta' und Helmut Kraussers 'Melodien'* (EH, 1, 1779), 379 pp.

KIRSTEN, WULF. H. Helbig, '*Fagus sylvatica hybrida*: Landschaft und Dichtung oder Vorbereitung zur Deutung eines Verses von W.K.', *GR*, 75 : 194–209.

KLEMPERER, VICTOR. H. Kämper, 'Sprachgeschichte — Zeitgeschichte. Die Tagebücher V.Ks', *DSp*, 28 : 25–41. R. H. Watt, '*Landsersprache, Heeressprache, Nazisprache*? V.K. and Werner Krauss on the linguistic legacy of the Third Reich', *MLR*, 95 : 424–36.

KLÜGER, RUTH. J. Klöster, 'Autobiographie als literaturdidaktischer Fundus. Literaturerfahrung in R.K., *weiter leben*', *DUB*, 50, 1997 : 574–84.

KOEPPEN, WOLFGANG. T. Fiedler, ' "eine sehr komplizierte Rechtslage wegen der Urheberrechte": zu Jakob Littner und Wolfgang Koeppen', *ColGer*, 32, 1999 : 103–04. M. Holdenried, 'Zur Modernität autobiographischer Formen und zur Konservativität ihrer Rezeption. Am Beispiel von W.Ks *Jugend*', *WB*, 46 : 180–97. E. Platen, 'Bild oder Abbild? Überlegungen zur Frage der "poetischen Wahrheit" in W.Ks *Treibhaus*', *SN*, 71, 1999 : 196–205. R. Ulrich, 'Vom Report zum Roman. Zur Textwelt von W.Ks Roman *Jakob Littners Aufzeichnungen aus einem Erdloch*', *ColGer*, 32, 1999 : 135–50. S. Ward, 'Border negotiations in the works of W.K.', *MLR*, 95 : 763–78. U. S. Weber, 'Aufgabe des Vaterlandes — Suche nach einer neuen Heimat. Zu W.Ks *Tod in Rom*', *AGJSG*, 26–27, 1998–99 : 57–64. V. Wehdeking, 'Ein Nachmittag mit W.K. Erinnerungen an einen Besuch 1987 in München', *LiB*, 58, 1999 : 47–51.

KRONAUER, BRIGITTE. Ina Appel, *Von Lust und Schrecken im Spiel ästhetischer Subjektivität. Über den Zusammenhang von Subjekt, Sprache und Existenz in Prosa von B.K. und Ror Wolf* (Ep, 299), 200 pp.

LASKER-SCHÜLER, ELSE. Ricarda Dirk, *E.L.-S. Schrift, Bild, Schrift.*, Bonn, August Macke, 255 pp. Markus Hallensleben, *E.L.-S. Avantgardismus und Kunstinszenierung*, Tübingen, Francke, 380 pp. Aihong Jiang, *Yi-jing in der Lyrik E.L.-Ss*, Göttingen, Cuvillier, 176 pp.

Marina Krug, *Die Figur als signifikante Spur. Eine dekonstruktive Lektüre zu den Gedichten 'Esther' sowie 'David und Jonathan' aus dem Zyklus 'Hebräische Balladen' von E.L.-S.* (EH, 1, 1771), xii + 275 pp. D. Ostmeier, 'Beastly love: Gottfried Benn/E.L.-S.', *ColGer*, 33:43–74. Irene Pieper, *Modernes Welttheater. Untersuchungen zum Welttheatermotiv zwischen Katastrophenerfahrung und Welt-Anschauungssuche bei Walter Benjamin, Karl Kraus, Hugo von Hofmannsthal und E.L.-S.*, Berlin, Duncker & Humblot, 194 pp.

LENZ, HERMANN. P. Hamm, 'Die große Kunst des Abstandhaltens. Zum Tode von H.L.', *JDASD*, 1998[1999]:189–93.

LENZ, SIEGFRIED. Dorothée Merchiers, *Le réalisme de S.L.* (EH, 1, 1770), xii + 358 pp.

LOEST, ERICH. M. Kane, 'East German literature and the Cold War: the example of E.L.'s *Die Westmark fällt weiter*', *Will Vol.*, 134–43. See also HEIN, CHRISTOPH.

MANN, KLAUS. Armin Strohmeyr, *K.M.*, Munich, DTV, 160 pp.

MAYRÖCKER, FRIEDERIKE. Klaus Kastberger, *Reinschrift des Lebens. F.Ms 'Reise durch die Nacht'. Edition und Analyse*, Vienna, Böhlau, 470 pp.

MENZINGER, STEFANIE. V. Braun, 'Wanderungen durch das Mark. Laudatio auf S.M.', *SuF*, 52:294–98.

MONÍKOVÁ, LIBUŠE. F. C. Delius, 'Rede auf die Fürstin Libuše. Zum Tode von L.M.', *JDASD*, 1998[1999]:183–88. L. Marven, 'Women in wheelchairs: space, performance and hysteria in L.M.'s *Pavane für eine verstorbene Infantin* and Ines Ecke's *Steppenwolfidyllen*', *GLL*, 53:511–28.

MORGNER, IRMTRAUD. H. Rossoll, ' "Thinking in images." The poetic mode as dissidence in I.M.'s writing', *ColGer*, 31, 1998:339–56. Siegrun Wildner, *Experimentum Mundi — Utopie als ästhetisches Prinzip. Zur Funktion utopischer Entwürfe in I.Ms Romanwerk*, St. Ingbert, Röhrig, 229 pp.

MOSER, MILENA. R. Huber, 'Literatur — Littérature: kleiner Unterschied mit großen Folgen. Zur Rezeption von M.Ms Werk im deutschen und französischen Sprachgebiet', *Runa*, 27, 1997–98:257–68.

MÜLLER, HEINER. F. Baillet, 'Quelques remarques marginales sur la fin du monde chez H.M. et Karl Kraus', *Austriaca*, 24, 1999:111–30. M. Hofmann, 'Das Drama des Verrats. Geschichtlicher Auftrag und Eigensinn des Einzelnen bei H.M. und Georg Büchner', *WB*, 46:89–104. M. Ostheimer, ' "Ich Ajax der sein Blut": H.Ms lyrische Inszenierung des Tods der Tragödie', *ZDP*, 119:245–67. N. Pethes, 'Gebrauchen, Kritisieren, Verraten. Poetologische Anmerkungen zu einem Rechtsstreit um die Rolle des Zitats und die Stimme Brechts in H.Ms *Germania 3*', *ZG*, 10:331–48.

Alexandra Pontzen, *Künstler ohne Werk. Modelle negativer Produktionsästhetik in der Künstlerliteratur von Wackenroder bis H.M.* (PSQ, 164), 432 pp. *H.M. Probleme und Perspektiven. Bath-Symposion 1998*, ed. Ian Wallace, Dennis Tate and Gerd Labroisse (ABNG, 48), 531 pp. R. Yotsuya, 'Dramaturgie der Erinnerung. H.M. und Robert Wilson', *DB*, 103, 1999:46–55 (Japanese with German summary). See also GRÜNBEIN, DURS, and WOLF, CHRISTA.

MÜLLER, HERTA.   B. Driver Eddy, 'Testimony and trauma in H.M.'s *Herztier*', *GLL*, 53:56–72.

MUSCHG, ADOLF.   H. Fischer, 'Alter und neuer *Parzivâl*: Wolfram von Eschenbach und A.M.', *SGP*, 25, 1999:59–68.

NOSSACK, HANS ERICH.   G. Häntzschel, 'Untergang und Neuanfang. Zu E.Ns Bericht *Der Untergang*', *ZGB*, 5, 1999:365–76. S. Thabet, ' "Die Kurve des überstandenen Fiebers": zur Problematik des Schreibens bei H.E.N.', *CEtGer*, 38:157–68.

PAUSEWANG, GUDRUN.   H.-D. Heuer, ' "Der Wille des Menschen hat schon viele Kräfte entwickelt . . ." Gespräch mit der Schriftstellerin G.P.', *DUB*, 51, 1998:529–32.

PIONTEK, HEINZ.   Martin Hollender, *Bibliographie H.P.*, Bielefeld, Aisthesis, 450 pp.

PLENZDORF, ULRICH.   I. Hartl, 'Goethe e a RDA nos anos 70 na obra *Die neuen Leiden des jungen W.* de U.P.', *Forum deutsch*, 4:45–57 (in Portuguese).

PLIEVIER, THEODOR.   M. Rohrwasser, 'T.Ps Kriegsbilder', *SuF*, 52:740–46.

POLLAK, FELIX.   R. Grimm, 'F.P. als Selbstübersetzer', *WW*, 50:256–65.

RANSMAYR, CHRISTOPH.   J. Gindele, 'Immer wieder anders und neu — C.Rs Roman *Die letzte Welt* und das Werk Ovids. Ansätze zu einem Vergleich', Baumbach, *Tradita*, 601–14.

RÜHMKORF, PETER.   Frédérique Colombat-Didier, *La situation poétique de P.R.*, Berne, Lang, xx + 605 pp.

SACHS, NELLY.   Veronika Merz, *Das Universum des Unsichtbaren. Kraftquelle und Vision der Dichterin N.S.*, Arbon, Pandora, 118 pp.

SCHALLÜCK, PAUL.   J. Klapper, 'The paradox of simultaneity: "Vergangenheitsbewältigung" in P.S.'s *Engelbert Reineke*', *Will Vol.*, 99–109.

SCHLESINGER, KLAUS.   A. Erb and C. Hamann, ' "Ich rede nicht über eine beliebige Zeit". Erinnerungsdiskurse in K.Ss Roman *Die Sache mit Randow*', *Runa*, 27, 1997–98:227–44.

SCHMIDT, ARNO.   Wolfgang Albrecht, *A.S.* (SM, 312), 1998, 174 pp. *Alles=gewendet!' Zu A.Ss 'Die Schule der Atheisten'*, ed. Horst Denkler and Carsten Würmann, Bielefeld, Aisthesis, 275 pp. *A.Ss 'Seelandschaft mit Pocahontas'. Zettel und andere Materialien*, ed. Susanne

Fischer and Bernd Rauschenbach, Bargfeld–Zurich, Haffman, 212 pp. Heinrich Schwier, *Lore, Grete & Schmidt. Kommentierendes Handbuch zu A.Ss Roman 'Brands Heide'*, Munich, Text und Kritik, 286 pp.

SCHUTTING, JULIAN.   *Critical Essays on J.S.*, ed. Harriet Murphy, Riverside, Ariadne, 211 pp., represents the first critical appreciation of the work of S. to be published in any language. The essays by an array of leading international scholars explore the main body of S.'s work produced between 1973 and 1997, some focusing on individual collections such as *Der Vater* whilst others assume a more general thematic overview of his work. All in all, the essays dovetail neatly to confirm the poet's important position amongst contemporary writers and 'indicate that S.'s literary and intellectual range is ambitious'.

SCHWAB, WERNER.   A. Herzog, 'Volksvernichtung oder meine Sprache ist sinnlos. W.S. und die Gewalt der Sprache in der neuesten österreichischen Literatur', Corbineau-Hoffmann, *Gewalt*, 265–93.

SEGHERS, ANNA   A. Barker, 'A.S., Friedrich Wolf, and the Austrian Civil War of 1934', *MLR*, 95:144–53. Wilhelm Haefs, *Suchen nach dem Blau, an dem mein Herz hängt — A.S.*, Munich, Econ, 150 pp. Sonja Hilzinger, **A.S.*, Stuttgart, Reclam, 239 pp. Anna Lürbke, **Mexikovisionen aus dem deutschen Exil. B. Traven, Gustav Regler, A.S*, Tübingen, Francke, 203 pp. Christiane Zehl Romero, **A.S. Eine Biographie 1900–1947*, Berlin, Aufbau, 560 pp.

SELIGMANN, RAFAEL.   R. Robertson, 'R.F.'s *Rubinsteins Versteigerung*: the German-Jewish family novel before and after the Holocaust', *GR*, 75:179–93.

SKWARAS, ERICH WOLFGANG.   P. Kampits, 'Abschiedlichkeit. Ein Versuch zum Werk E.W.Ss', *ÖGL*, 44:236–41.

SPARSCHUH, JENS.   F. T. Grub, 'Gestürzte Denkmäler — ratlose Helden: Autorenporträt J.S.', *DUS*, 52.1:87–95.

SPERBER, MANES.   **In treuer Ketzer. M.S. Der Schriftsteller als Ideologe*, ed. Wilhelm Hemecker, Vienna, Zsolnay, 144 pp.

STRAUSS, BOTHO.   Andreas Englhart, **Im Labyrinth des unendlichen Textes. B.Ss Theaterstücke 1972–1996*, Tübingen, Niemeyer, xii + 315 pp. Stefan Willer, **B.S. zur Einführung*, Hamburg, Junius, 168 pp. Johannes Windrich, **Das Aus für das Über. 'Wohnen Dämmern Lügen' und 'Ithaka' von B.S. Eine poetologische Lektüre* (Ep, 307), 210 pp.

SZYSZKOWITZ, GERALD.   J. Thünecke, ' "Nur tote Fische schwimmen mit dem Strom": the conflict of art and politics in G.S.'s play *Servus Du oder Mister Stolz Goes to Israel*', *MAL*, 33:66–83.

THELEN, ALBERT VIGOLEIS.   O. Grossegesse, 'Noch ein Strich Senf oder Anmerkungen zu A.V.Ts Übersetzung *Napoleon, Spiegel des Antichrist*', *Runa*, 27, 1997–98:115–24.

WAGNER, BERND. C. Cosentino, 'B.Ws *Paradies*: ironisch-utopische Dimensionen in der Post-Wende-Literatur', *Seminar*, 36:436–51.

WALLRAFF, GÜNTER. R. Burns, 'Authenticity and the "speaking other": G.W.'s *Ganz unten* as an industrial fiction', *Will Vol.*, 110–21.

WALSER, MARTIN. H. A. Doane, ' "Ein gutes Gewissen ist keins": Überlegungen zu M.Ws Roman *Ein springender Brunnen*', *LitL*, 22:109–20. Georg Eggenschwiler, **Vom Schreiben schreiben. Selbstthematisierung in den frühen Romanen M.Ws* (EH, 1, 1751), 204 pp. O. B. Plouffe, 'M.W.'s *Ein fliehendes Pferd*: a pro-narrative writerly text', *Seminar*, 36:343–57. S. Taberner, 'A manifesto for Germany's "New Right"?: M.W., the past, transcendence, aesthetics, and *Ein springender Brunnen*', *GLL*, 53:126–41.

WALTER, OTTO F. I. Siegel, 'Die verlorene Sprache, die wiedergefundene Gewalt, die verdrängte Geschichte — Zu O.F.Ws letzter Erzählung *Die verlorene Geschichte*', Corbineau-Hoffmann, *Gewalt*, 229–42.

WEIL, GRETE. S. Braese, 'G.W.'s America: a self-encounter at the moment of the anti-authoritarian revolt', *GR*, 75:132–48.

WEISS, PETER. Wiebke A. Ankersen, **Ein Querschnitt durch unsere Lage. Die Situation und die schwedische Prosa von P.W.*, St. Ingbert, Röhrig, 225 pp. J. F. Everlein, 'P.W.'s *Fluchtpunkt*: language and the search for authentic being', *Seminar*, 36:211–25. Jost Hermand and Marc Silberman, **Rethinking P.W.* (GLC, 32), ix + 199 pp. Marita Meyer, **Eine Ermittlung. Fragen an P.W. und an die Literatur des Holocaust*, St. Ingbert, Röhrig, 187 pp. Christoph Weiss, **Auschwitz in der geteilten Welt. P.W. und die 'Ermittlung' im Kalten Krieg*, St. Ingbert, Röhrig, 1380 pp.

WELLERSHOFF, DIETER. Werner Jung, **Im Dunkel des gelebten Augenblicks. D.W. — Erzähler, Medienautor, Essayist*, Berlin, Schmidt, 413 pp. U. Reinhold, 'Beobachtungen an Romanen und autobiographischen Texten von D.W. Anläßlich des Erscheinens der Werkausgabe', *WB*, 46:198–215.

WIDMER, URS. P. Arnds, 'Into the heart of darkness: Switzerland, Hitler, Mobutu, and Joseph Conrad in U.W.'s novel *Im Kongo*', *GQ*, 71, 1998:329–42.

WOHMANN, GABRIELE. W. Pi, 'G.W. — eine frühe Vertreterin der neuen Sensibilität. Ws literarische Thematik und Schreibstile', *Literaturstraße*, 1:201–21.

WOLF, CHRISTA. A. Bohm, 'Seeds of doubt: science and politics in C.W.'s "Ein Besuch" ', *Seminar*, 36:326–42. D. Bresson, 'Les "voix" dans *Medea* de C.W.: la fonction des locutions', *CEtGer*, 38:111–23. M. Butler, '*Was bleibt* revisited: C.W. and the fear of transience', *Will*

Vol., 144–52. U. Klingmann, 'Zur Problematik des Gegensatzes zwischen Macht und Leben in C.Ws Roman *Medea. Stimmen*', *AGJSG*, 26–27, 1998–99:117–31. D. Merchier, '*Medea. Stimmen* (C.W.): un oeuvre polyphonique', *ib.*, 97–109. A. Messerschmidt and E. Peters, 'Kein Freispruch für Euripides. Zu den Medea-Romanen von Ursula Haas und C.W.', *WB*, 46:524–46. Heinz P. Preusser, **Mythos als Sinnkonstruktion. Die Antikenprojekte von C.W., Heiner Müller, Stefan Schütz und Volker Braun*, Cologne, Böhlau, viii + 501 pp. Brigitte Rossbacher, **Illusions of Progress. C.W. and the Critique of Science in GDR Women's Literature*, NY, Lang, 224 pp. Marion Schmaus, **Die poetische Konstruktion des Selbst. Grenzgänge zwischen Frühromantik und Moderne: Novalis, Bachmann, C.W., Foucalt*, Tübingen, Niemeyer, ix + 407 pp. See also BERNHARD, THOMAS.

II. DUTCH STUDIES

LANGUAGE

POSTPONED

LITERATURE

By WIM HÜSKEN, *Senior Lecturer in Dutch, University of Auckland*

1. GENERAL

In varying degrees classical mythology has influenced Dutch literature between the Middle Ages and the present. Paul Claes, *De gulden tak: Antieke mythe en moderne literatuur*, Amsterdam, Bezige Bij, 142 pp., studies how it is reflected in the works of, mainly modern, literary authors, Hugo Claus, Harry Mulisch, Ida Gerhardt, H. C. ten Berghe, Hans Favery, and Lucebert in particular. Occasionally Claes also includes observations related to the works of the 17th-c. poet and dramatist Joost van den Vondel and to foreign authors such as John Keats and Rainer Maria Rilke.

In *Schrijvende denkers*, ed. André Klukhuhn and Toef Jaeger, Amsterdam, Arbeiderspers, 243 pp., ten well-known Dutch authors, among them Geerten Meijsing, Rudy Kousbroek, and Désanne van Brederode, reflect on the relationship between philosophy and literature and the difficulties philosophers such as Plato, Schopenhauer, and Heidegger encountered when transforming their thoughts into words on paper. J. Trapman, *Het land van Erasmus*, Amsterdam, Balans, 1999, 191 pp., wonders to what extent Erasmus's cultural versatility and moral tolerance are reflected or, perhaps, contradicted in the works of Dutch philosophers and literary authors coming after him such as Hugo de Groot, Willem Kloos, and Alphons Diepenbrock. Trapman eventually arrives at the conclusion that Erasmus's spirit has lost its vibrancy.

Kunst & Letterkunst: Opstellen voor George Vis, ed. G. J. van Bork and N. Laan, Amsterdam, Aarts, 160 pp., is a Festschrift for a former lecturer at the University of Amsterdam in which the contributors focus on the relationship between 18th-, 19th- and 20th-c. art and literature. Essays in this volume deal with topics ranging from songs in the works of the 19th-c. poet Johannes Kinker and Manet's influence on post-modern writers and artists, to late 19th-c. poetry criticism, F. Bordewijk's novel *De eiken van Dodona* (1946), and the life and works of the poet Jan Hanlo.

The Flemish town of Ghent has been made an object of veneration by many literary celebrities including Lord Byron, Victor Hugo, and Rainer Maria Rilke, and by Dutch authors such as Karel van de Woestijne, Willem Elsschot, Johan Daisne, and Hugo Claus. *Gent, de dubbelzinnige* (Het oog in 't zeil stedenreeks, 7), ed. Marco Daane and Dirk Leyman, [Amsterdam], Lubberhuizen, 285 pp., contains 18 essays describing the relationship between the city and its literary admirers.

2. THE MIDDLE AGES

Medioneerlandistiek: Een inleiding tot de Middelnederlandse letterkunde, ed. Ria Jansen-Sieben, Jozef Janssen, and Frank Willaert (MSB, 69), 345 pp., presents 25 essays in which the authors aim to introduce a wide audience to the study of medieval literature. The contributors pay special attention to its historical context, to languages in the Low Countries, material aspects (manuscripts and *incunabula*), production, themes, genres, reception, reference works, and the relationship with painting. The book does not set out to be a literary history of medieval Dutch literature, but rather illustrates the various ways of looking at it by studying characteristic aspects or examples taken from the wide range of different types of texts that have come down to our own time. One of the most remarkable features of *Medioneerlandistiek* is that it shows how differently, compared to 20 or 30 years ago, today's scholars look at medieval literature, including as most of them do a much wider range of texts than purely literary ones. It is the merit of one scholar of medieval Dutch literature in particular to whom we owe this different way of perception: Wim Gerritsen, emeritus professor of the University of Utrecht. On the occasion of his retirement Gerritsen was presented with a Festschrift entitled *Hoort wonder! Opstellen voor W. P. Gerritsen bij zijn emeritaat*, ed. Bart Besamusca, Frank Brandsma, and Dieuwke van der Poel (MSB, 70), 192 pp. 26 colleagues, many of them former or current doctoral students of Gerritsen's, contributed to the book which aims at presenting the reader with a representative sampling of present-day research of medieval literature with a special emphasis, following Gerritsen's exemplary work, on how it still manages to surprise us. Topics include, among other things, observations on aspects of Dutch Arthurian novels (Van Anrooij, Besamusca, Brandsma, Hogenbirk, Smelik), medieval song culture (Van den Berg, Van Buuren, Van Dongen, Hemmes-Hoogstadt), *Van den Vos Reynaerde* (Van Aelst, Zemel), and Carolingian novels (Van Dijk, Spijker).

Hadewijch, one of Europe's most important mystics of the 13th c., used the word *orewoet* to express her innermost feelings of spiritual longing. The word has attracted a great deal of speculation about what was really meant by it. Rob Faesen, *Begeerte in het werk van Hadewijch* (Antwerpse Studies over Nederlandse Literatuurgeschiedenis, 4), Leuven, Peeters, xvi + 396 pp., attempts to describe the meaning of the word in Hadewijch's works. Longing or *orewoet* is, according to Faesen, essential to the never ending mental process bestowed on individuals who come to experience physically their love for Christ, as a result of which they will eventually unite with Him in total community. Faesen includes in his observations the works of Hadewijch's sources, William of Saint-Thierry, St. Bernard of Clairvaux, and Richard of Saint-Victor in particular. A further element studied in this book is the position of spiritual longing in the writings of other mystic women of her time. Faesen also presented a new edition, including a translation of the text in modern Dutch, of *Beatrijs van Nazareth, Seven manieren van minne*, Kapellen, Pelckmans, 1999, 91 pp., a treatise describing a 13th-c. nun's mystic experiences. Willem Zonneveld, *Van Afflighem en Chaucer: Het Leven van Sinte Lutgart als jambisch gedicht* (Uitgaven Stichting Neerlandistiek VU, 33), Amsterdam, Stichting Neerlandistiek VU — Münster, Nodus, 104 pp., studies metrical aspects of a hagiography of St Lutgardis, written in Flanders in the 13th c. The text was composed in an iambic verse rhythm. Consequently it represents one of the earliest examples of this particular stylistic feature in European literature, about a century prior to when Geoffrey Chaucer introduced it in English.

One of the most influential treatises on the virtues and vices written in the vernacular was the Italian *Fiore di Virtù* (Flowers of Virtue), written by an anonymous author during the first quarter of the 14th c. The text is available in at least 80 MSS and was widely translated. The Dutch adaptation by Dirc Potter, secretary to the counts of Holland and, on more than one occasion, their envoy to Italy and other European countries, dates to about 1415. Sabrina Corbellini, *Italiaanse deugden en ondeugden: Dirc Potters "Blome der doechden" en de Italiaanse "Fiore di Virtù"* (Nederlandse literatuur en cultuur in de Middeleeuwen, 22), Amsterdam, Prometheus, 309 pp., studies the relationship between the treatise's Italian original and its Dutch rendition. In addition to the information Potter gathered from one of the Italian MSS he used for his adaptation, the author also consulted a number of supplementary sources. One of the most prominent among them is a French translation of Albertanus of Brescia's *Liber consolationis et consilii*, in itself a prime source for the *Fiore di Virtù*. Corbellini advances the thesis that Potter's *Blome der doechden* and his *Mellibeus*, written after 1415, are to be seen as a diptych. A more detailed study of Albertanus's influence on northern European literature — Chaucer's *Tale of Melibee* would be inconceivable without

his lead — would be very helpful for a better understanding of the
exchange between late medieval Italian and northern European
culture, Corbellini concludes.

King Arthur in the Medieval Low Countries, ed. Geert H. M. Claassens
and David F. Johnson (Mediaevalia Lovaniensia, Series 1/Studia,
28), Leuven U.P., xiii + 274 pp., contains essays on Dutch Arthurian
romances, 15 examples of which survived in the Low Countries. Most
of them are found in one single early 14th-c. manuscript, the so-
called *Lancelot Compilation*. Five of these romances are not found
elsewhere and can thus be termed uniquely Dutch. Bart Besamusca
(87–96) and Soetje Oppenhuis de Jong (113–24) trace the stories of
certain individual characters in the romances, the ugly damsel of
Montesclare and Perceval's brother Agloval respectively. Frank
Brandsma (69–86) concentrates on narrative techniques employed
by the compiler of the manuscript. Special attention is paid to one
romance in particular, the *Roman van Walewein*. Bart Veldhoen (35–43)
compares this with *Sir Gawain and the Green Knight*, Ludo Jongen
(45–58) concentrates on Walewein as a confessor, showing how far
removed he is from his remorseless counterpart Gauvain in the
French *Queste del Saint Graal*. The intriguing story the romance of
Walewein opens with, a tale of a flying chess-set entering a window at
Arthur's court at Caerleon, is discussed by Karina van Dalen-Oskam
(59–68). Further essays deal with 'The late-medieval German
reception of Dutch Arthurian literature in Heidelberg and Blan-
kenheim' (Rita Schlusemann, 97–111), narration in the romance of
Moriaen (Norris J. Lacy, 125–34), an attempt to rehabilitate the much
neglected *Queeste vanden Grale* (Geert H. M. Claassens, 135–50),
parody and the *Wrake van Ragisel* (Geert Pallemans, 151–61), the
perfection of Walewein as opposed to the haughtiness of Keye in
Walewein ende Keye (Marjolein Hogenbrink, 163–72), and the role of
the narrator in *Lanseloet en het hert met de witte voet* (Geert H. M.
Claassens, 173–85). In an appendix (187–244), detailed summaries
are presented of all 15 Dutch Arthurian romances. In order to make
these romances from the Low Countries better known to the
international scholarly world, David F. Johnson and Geert H. M.
Claassens have started a series of bilingual editions, with translations
into English, of six Arthurian romances. The first two volumes
include *Roman van Walewein* (Dutch Romances, 1), Woodbridge, D. S.
Brewer, 541 pp., and **Ferguut* (Dutch Romances, 2), Woodbridge,
D. S. Brewer, 263 pp.

B. J. P. Salemans, *Building Stemmas with the Computer in a Cladistic,
Neo-Lachmannian, Way: The Case of Fourteen Text Versions of Lanseloet van
Denemerken*, Nijmegen U.P., viii + 351 pp., presents an analytic model
for establishing the relationship between different versions of a text,

taking the late medieval tradition of the play of *Lanseloet van Denemerken* as his starting point. At the end of his book Salemans arrives at the conclusion that it is possible to draw a trustworthy automated stemma of a textual tradition, but specialist philologists still need to judge and interpret the variant material. Even here computers can never replace human beings. The book comes with a CD-ROM containing the complete textual material analysed in the book.

De crumen diet volc niet eten en mochte: Nederlandse beschouwingen over vertalen tot 1550, ed. Bart Besamusca and Gerard Sonnemans (Vertaalhistorie, 6), The Hague, Stichting Bibliographia Neerlandica, 1999, 160 pp., is an anthology of 40 fragments taken from medieval texts; the authors include an explanation of the translation techniques employed.

Mariken Goris, *Boethius in het Nederlands: Studie naar de tekstuitgave van de Gentse Boethius (1485), boek II* (MSB, 72), 431 pp., analyses and presents a fully annotated edition of the second part of Boethius' *De consolatione philosophiae* as it was printed in 1485. In addition to the complete Latin text the Ghent edition also included a Flemish translation and a detailed commentary. Goris compares this version with the German edition printed in 1473 by Anton Koberger and with Colard Mansion's translation into French published in Bruges in 1477.

3. THE RHETORICIANS' PERIOD

During the religious turbulences of the 16th c., 'Rederijkers' occupied a prominent position in the Low Countries. Their impact on public opinion was recognised by the Habsburg rulers as early as 1492 when Archduke Philip the Fair established the Chamber of Rhetoric *Jesus metter balsembloeme* (Jesus with the Balsam Flower), to which all other Chambers in his lands would be subject. It is this religiously inspired political influence which has inspired Gary K. Waite to publish *Reformers on Stage: Popular Drama and Religious Propaganda in the Low Countries of Charles V, 1515–1556*, Toronto U.P., xxiii + 364 pp. The first two chapters present a brief sketch of 'Civic culture and religious reform in the Netherlands' (3–25), and 'Rhetoricians and urban culture' (26–48). The second part of the book deals with 'Vernacular drama and the early urban Reformation' (49–98), concentrating in particular on the situations prevailing in Antwerp and Amsterdam. The final chapters discuss 'Reform themes in Rhetorician drama' (99–201). In his 'Conclusion' (202–08), Waite notes that Rhetoricians 'shared the naivety of Martin Luther, who believed that the ramifications of his new conception of salvation and rejection of the Roman Catholic hierarchy could be contained within strictly spiritual boundaries'. However, until about the mid-1550s most of them did not unconditionally accept Luther or Calvin as their sole spiritual leader but opted instead for a delicate balance between orthodox convictions and their modern interpretation, professed in a reformed Church.

Hessel Miedema has completed his edition of translations of Karel van Mander's biographies of contemporary artists, published in his famous *Schilder-boeck* (1604). Volume 6 of **The Lives of the Illustrious Netherlandish and German Painters*, Doornspijk, Davaco, 1999, xxxiv + 237 + [63] pp., contains descriptions of the lives and works of, among others, Jacques de Gheyn, Abraham Bloemaert, Francesco Badens, and David Vinckeboons. This volume also includes 63 pages of illustrations and an index to the entire set of six volumes.

Wilhelmus en de anderen: Nederlandse liedjes 1500–1700, ed. Marijke Barend-van Haeften et al. (Tekst in Context, 4), 2 vols, Amsterdam U.P., 104 + 32 pp., introduces less experienced readers of texts from the early modern era to its rich culture of song, placing the genre in its social, political, economic, and religious context. Special focal points for the songs are their background related to the lives and adventures of sailors employed by the United East Indies Company (VOC), to religion, love, social protest, and leisure activities. The texts are not only presented in a modern spelling but have also been translated into present-day Dutch. The book comes with a separate *Docentenhandleiding* (teachers' instruction booklet) and a CD with songs performed by the "Camerata Trajectina" consort.

4. THE SEVENTEENTH CENTURY

Annelies de Jeu, '*'t Spoor der dichteressen': Netwerken en publicatiemogelijkheden van schrijvende vrouwen in de Republiek (1600–1750)*, Hilversum, Verloren, 374 pp., discusses the ways women in the early modern Netherlands built their intellectual and artist networks and how they found access to the world of printing to see their works published. De Jeu mainly concentrates on women active in Dordrecht, a town in the province of Holland, and on those living in the north, the provinces of Groningen and Friesland in particular. The role women played in Dordrecht's cultural life was limited and more often than not they could only be heard after they had attracted the attention of an influential male author. Perhaps the most successful amongst them was Klara Ghyben who lived in the first half of the 18th c. But, as in most other cases, her poems were not printed until ten years after her death, in 1747, in one volume, together with works written by her husband. Much more successful were a number of women poets living in the northern parts of the Netherlands. Over the last few years Titia Brongersma and Clara van Sytzama have enjoyed more attention than they have received during the two centuries after their deaths. The second part of the book deals with the spread of poetry written by female authors. Most of their works were available only in MS or as a laudatory contribution to the introductory part of a poetry collection by a male friend. Prior to the mid-17th c. hardly any non-religious poetry by women appeared in print. However, if their work was of a religious nature they seemed to have had much easier access to the presses. *'t Spoor der dichteressen'* also presents an impressively comprehensive bibliography (283–333) of texts published by female authors between 1600 and 1750, supplemented by a list of some 20 collections in MS.

5. THE EIGHTEENTH CENTURY

Pieter Langendijk was the last important author of comedies in the Renaissance and Baroque era in the Netherlands. Kees Smit, *Pieter Langendijk*, Hilversum, Verloren, 382 pp., is a welcome new biography of a man who started as a writer of poetry but acquired fame as a playwright. His first play, *Don Quichot op de bruiloft van Kamacho* (1712), dramatizes the wedding between Quiteria and Bazilius described in the second part of Cervantes' novel. The play became the most frequently performed of all Langendijk's theatrical pieces. In other plays the author presented a satirical picture of a bragging German soldier, offering a caricatured image of an impoverished nobleman who employs all kinds of tricks to find a rich match but ends up being cheated himself. Langendijk also poked fun at those well-to-do merchants who tried to accumulate wealth on the stock market by investing in 'bubbles'. After 1720 his poetic genius fell silent and, back in his native town Haarlem, he returned to his profession of a weaver of linen and damask. In Haarlem's society of well-to-do business men Langendijk's fame increased but in literary circles he lost his leading position, despite the fact that he became the artistic leader of the stately rhetoricians' guild, *Trou moet blijcken*. In his later years he took up his old line of writing plays but instead of being pure comedies they represented a much more serious type of drama that concentrates on social issues. Abroad his name was not unknown, judging by 18th- and early 19th-c. translations of his works into French and German.

Ans J. Veltman-van den Bos, *Petronella Moens (1762–1843): De Vriendin van 't Vaderland*, Nijmegen, Vantilt, 488 pp., studies the life and works of a remarkable woman in Dutch literature who lost her eyesight at the tender age of four. Her phenomenal memory allowed Moens mentally to store details from her father's reading aloud to her of Dutch literary works. After she had published her first poem in 1785 her star rose quickly but critics also found fault with her metaphorical language. In political matters she was a true Patriot, applauding the French Revolution, and she welcomed the French armies when they invaded the Dutch Republic in 1795. Three years later she founded her own periodical, *De Vriendin van 't Vaderland* (The Friend of the Nation), but it lasted only a year. From a religious perspective Moens is seen to have been inspired by a complex of ideals that would later be termed 'Reformed Enlightenment', a Dutch variant of 18th-c. rationalism allowing its advocates sufficient space to include the Christian revelation in their philosophy. In the field of education Moens greatly admired the poetry of Hiëronymus van Alphen. After her death Moens was, from a literary viewpoint not entirely erroneously, soon forgotten; but for our knowledge of late 18th-c. thinking, notably that of women, her works remain valuable, Veltman-van den Bos observes.

Elizabeth Wolff-Bekker, **De onveranderlyke Santhorstsche geloofsbely-denis: In rym gebragt door eene zuster der Santhorstsche gemeente (1772)*, ed. A. J. Hanou (Duivelshoekreeks, 11), Leiden, Astraea, 172 pp., is a new edition of a treatise in which the author defends the rational creed of a group of intellectuals and religious leaders led by the Amsterdam professor of classical studies, Petrus Burmannus. Mankind should be governed by five principles: freedom, one's own country, tolerance, friendship, and the *summum bonum*.

6. THE NINETEENTH CENTURY

W. van den Berg, *Over literatuur, Amsterdam, Vossiuspers–Amsterdam U.P., 34 pp., contains the text of a public farewell lecture given by a former professor of modern Dutch literature at the University of Amsterdam. In it Van den Berg reviews the ways terms such as literature and belles-lettres were defined in 18th- and 19th-c. criticism, both in the Netherlands and in other European countries. In *De mythe terug: Negentiende-eeuwse literatuur als travestie van maatschappe-lijke conflicten*, Amsterdam, Vossiuspers–Amsterdam U.P., 37 pp., Marita Mathijsen advocates a return to original sources to correct the image, introduced in Dutch literary studies by the critics of the 1880s movement, of 19th-c. Dutch literature entirely being the sphere of activity of moralizing vicars and school teachers. On the contrary, it tells a story that is still worth the attention it currently does not receive, says Marita Mathijsen.

By the end of the 1830s, a literary circle was established in the village of Heiloo with J. P. Hasebroek at its centre. Other members were Nicolaas Beets, R. C. Bakhuyzen van den Brink, and E. J.

Potgieter. **Gij moet hier komen!*, ed. Nico Keuning, Heiloo, Reservaat, 1999, 111 pp., presents an edition of their correspondence.

Tom Phijffer, *Het gelijk van Multatuli: Het handelen van Eduard Douwes Dekker in rechtshistorisch perspectief*, Amsterdam, Bas Lubberhuizen, 143 pp., tries to confirm from the point of view of legal history that Eduard Douwes Dekker, assistant resident of the district of Lebak on the island of Java, was merely following the instructions he had received from his superiors when, in 1856, he accused the regent of extortion and abuse of power. Phijffer does acknowledge the fact that *Max Havelaar*, the novel written by Dekker under the pseudonym 'Multatuli' in which he described the case, is fiction rather than a minute rendering of the facts. But, having returned to the official documents and governmental recommendations regarding the way officials are supposed to deal with the indigenous people, he concludes that Dekker's deeds were perfectly in line with the oath he had sworn the day he was inaugurated in his post as assistant resident. The way the man was seen by his admirers and opponents and how his works were received is discussed by Nop Maas, *Multatuli voor iedereen (maar niemand voor Multatuli)*, Nijmegen, Vantilt, 221 pp. In the first chapter Maas scrutinises the reviews that were published shortly after *Max Havelaar*, in 1860, had appeared in print. Next Maas illustrates how and to what extent Multatuli's *Minnebrieven* were deliberately meant to be provocative. Multatuli, among other things, suggested to the readers of this book that he had cheated on his loyal wife Tine by falling for Fancy, who is not to be seen as the personification of his fantasy but a young attractive girl. Once more, reactions by various critics are part and parcel of this essay. Further chapters are devoted to Multatuli's frustrated ambitions; the reception of his works in *Asmodée*, one of the most critical and satirical periodicals of its time; Multatuli's dealings with Antonius van der Linde, a renowned scholar at the time for whom Dekker entertained feelings of friendship as well as contempt; and, finally, the way Multatuli was, well into the 20th c., made into a caricature.

A periodical with a distinct influence on the development of the Flemish Movement in Flanders, despite the fact that most of its contributions were written in French, is *Le Spectateur Belge*, founded by Leo de Foere. R. F. Lissens, *Een lectuur van 'Le Spectateur Belge' (1815–1823) van Leo de Foere: Traditionalisme in actie* (Studies op het gebied van de cultuur in de Nederlanden, 2), Ghent, KANTL, xiv + 182 pp., attempts to rescue the journal and its editor from oblivion. As a priest De Foere's political views were, of course, firmly grounded in religion. In all likelihood, he is the first Flemish author to pose the problem of whether or not to accept the Romantic Movement. In the area of the theatre he preferred Calderon and

Shakespeare to French classical plays. The way he looked at literature in general was inspired by moral values and religion but he combined this with aesthetic ideals as well. In his life and his publications De Foere proves to be a true traditionalist, believing as he did in the great value of continuity and in the traditions which peoples and nations carefully foster over many centuries.

After the many celebrations in 1999 of the centenary of Guido Gezelle's death, the flood of publications related to this most important 19th-c. Flemish poet has by no means stopped. Marcus de Schepper and Linda Lonfeyne, *Gezelle beschreven, 1899–1999: Selectieve bibliografie van een eeuw Gezellestudie* (Literaire tekstedities en bibliografieën, 5), Ghent, KANTL, v + 351 pp., presents an extensive yet not fully comprehensive bibliography of a century of scholarly reception of Gezelle's life and works. Publications in daily or weekly periodicals have not been included. The compilers used the so-called "snowball method" to supplement the material described in the most important bibliographical reference work for the study of Dutch language and literature, the *Bibliografie van de Nederlandse Taal- en Literatuurwetenschap* (BNTL). The result is an impressive list of 2682 titles, followed by two indexes of names of authors and topics. Particularly helpful is the category of essays dedicated to individual poems, alphabetically arranged according to title (243–96).

7.   1880 TO 1945

H. T. M. van Vliet, **Versierde verhalen: De oorspronkelijke boekbanden van Louis Couperus' werk [1884–1925]*, Amsterdam, Veen, 399 pp., presents a comprehensive survey of the 300 book covers designed for one of the leading novelists of his days, Louis Couperus. Famous artists of the Art Nouveau school, such as Jan Toorop, Richard Roland Holst, and Herman Berlage, were invited by Couperus's publisher, L. J. Veen, to create these designs.

**'Het is me niet mogelik een mening juist te vinden, omdat ze aangenaam is': Brieven van Marcellus Emants aan Gonne Loman-van Uildriks, 1904–1909*, ed. Nop Maas (Achter het boek, 35), The Hague, Letterkundig Museum, 129 pp., publishes the letters of Marcellus Emants, author of a number of successful novels, written between 1904 and 1909 to Mrs Loman-van Uildriks, a professional translator. His correspondence reveals interesting views on various topics, varying from the meaning of life and the author's personal circumstances to reflections on art and literature.

Op gezang en vlees belust: Over leven, werk en stad van Jan Engelman, ed. Liesbeth Feikema, Roman Koot, and Edwin Lucas, Utrecht, Kwadraat, 206 pp., is a collection of seven essays on one of the most celebrated poets and literary critics of the interwar period. After World War II his poems were soon forgotten, even though he was awarded, in 1955, one of the most prestigious literary prizes for his complete works. Ton H. M. van Schaik gives a sketch of Engelman's life in 'O minnares en slank gedicht: een levensschets van Jan Engelman (1900–1972)' (13–41), followed by two essays on the poet's love of his native town, Utrecht, by Renger E. de Bruin, 'De geest van gothiek: Het Utrecht van Jan Engelman' (43–65), and Annemarie Timmer, 'Een ontluisterend rijk: Jan Engelman en de stadsvernieuwing in Utrecht' (67–89). A. L. Sötemann, 'Ritmisch, muzikaal bezeten: de dichter Jan Engelman' (91–117), concentrates on the poet's creed; Roman Koot, 'Er zijn vele woningen in het huis der muzen: Jan Engelman over beeldende kunst in het interbellum' (119–41), reviews his critical essays on art, the most important of which were published between 1925 and 1945. His first collection of essays on literature, published in 1931, are studied by Liesbeth Feikema in 'Bezieling en vakmanschap: Jan Engelman over literatuur in de bundel *Parnassus en empyreum*' (143–67). On the basis of a correspondence consisting of hundreds of letters, Edwin Lucas reconstructs Engelman's involvement with some of the leading literary periodicals between 1930 and 1934: 'Kruisvaarder en kunstenaar: Jan Engelman en de literaire tijdschriften, 1930–1934' (169–94). Franklin Paul Okker, *Dirksland tussen de doerians: Een biografie van Willem Walraven*, Amsterdam, Bas Lubberhuizen, [16] + 276 pp., is a biography of a man who, once he had arrived in the Dutch East Indies, did not hide his feelings of hostility towards the colonial regime. Walraven contributed many of his critical articles to *De Indische Courant* and decided in 1931 to become a professional journalist and author of short stories. In 1943 he died of exhaustion in a Japanese prisoner-of-war camp.

Hedwig Speliers, *Als een oude Germaanse eik: Stijn Streuvels en Duitsland*, Antwerp, Manteau, 1999, 610 pp., studies the pro-German feelings of one of Flanders's most important novelists, Stijn Streuvels (pseudonym of Frank Lateur), between 1903, when the first German translation of one of his novels appeared in print, and *c*. 1960. Speliers discusses the topic from a chronological point of view, starting in the years leading up to the Weimar Republic and finishing with the post-War era of repression. Special attention is paid at the way Streuvels responded to the 'Blut und Boden' theory of the Nazi regime, which he, according to Speliers, readily embraced. The author would have returned to a conservative nationalism whose followers did not hesitate to accept the fascist views of their neighbours to the east. However, Speliers refuses to take into account the long tradition of 'Germanic-mindedness' in Flanders (which is not to say that Flemish authors were collaborating with the German Nazi-regime) brought about by the urge to create a distinct Flemish national profile equal to a dominating French language and culture.

In 1946 Willem Elsschot published his short story *Het dwaallicht*, his last literary work. Between 1957 and 1960, the year of Elsschot's death, Jan C. Villerius corresponded with the author. **Elsschot leest voor: De briefwisseling tussen Willem Elsschot en Jan C. Villerius*, ed. Wieneke 't Hoen and Vic van de Reijt, Amsterdam, Querido, 1999, 199 pp., contains an edition of their letters. The book also reprints some of Villerius's essays on the Flemish author and comes with a CD on which Elsschot recites his poem 'Spijt' and reads passages from two of his best-known stories, *Kaas* and *Tsjip*, based on a recording made on 24 April 1957.

H. A. Gomperts, **Een kern van waarheid*, ed. Eep Francken et al., Amsterdam, Van Oorschot, 230 pp., examines the works of one of the most important literary critics of the interwar period, Menno ter Braak, for alleged anti-semitic thoughts and ideas, partly related to his admiration for the works of Friedrich Nietzsche.

Michel van der Plas, *Daarom, mijnheer, noem ik mij katholiek: Biografie van Anton van Duinkerken*, Amsterdam, Anthos — Thielt, Lannoo, 643 pp., describes the tempestuous life of Van Duinkerken (the pseudonym of Willem Asselbergs from 1923 on). The oldest son of a brewer, Willem developed serious plans to become a missionary priest but after a short period of five months as a novice in a monastery near 's-Hertogenbosch he decided to return to his home town, Bergen op Zoom. He continued his training at a major seminary, in 1927 finally abandoning the idea of becoming a priest. His passion for writing poetry proved to be stronger than his clerical ambitions. Shortly after he had bid his fellow-seminarians farewell, Anton van Duinkerken was offered a permanent position in Amsterdam as literary critic of one of the leading Catholic newspapers of the time, *De Tijd*. His articles attracted a great deal of attention among the Dutch Roman Catholics of his day and Van Duinkerken would soon be seen as their most eloquent spokesperson, notably after having published, on 9 December 1935, a poem in which he attacked the leader of the National-Socialist movement in the Netherlands, Anton Mussert. After having worked for *De Tijd* for a quarter of a century, Willem Asselbergs was appointed, in 1952, professor of Dutch Literature at the Catholic University of Nijmegen. During the years of his professorship he spent most of his time researching historical Dutch literature, Vondel's works in particular. In 1968 he died after a short illness. Mariëlle Polman, *De keerzijde van het leven: Anton van Duinkerken als literatuurcriticus bij 'De Tijd' (1927–1952)* (KDC

Bronnen en Studies, 37), Nijmegen, Valkhof Pers, 523 pp., concentrates on the 25 years of his activities as a critic for *De Tijd*. An impressive grand total of about 800 essays on literary, theological, and cultural historical topics have enabled Polman to reconstruct the author's poetical and critical creed. Central to Van Duinkerken's literary ideal was his view that literature has important educational value. Christian moral principles, Roman Catholicism being the norm for the readers he wanted to reach out to, are best taught by studying the Dutch literary classics, 19th-c. poetry and prose in particular, he claimed. His religious position made him hope for a paradisiacal world order very different from the cultural situation man is facing at present. Not surprisingly, Van Duinkerken occupied a polemic place halfway between those, during the interwar period, who advocated the predominance of form in literature ('vorm') as opposed to those who argued for strong personalities ('vent') in literary authors.

Mariëlle Polman, *Trouw aan de muzen: Helene Nolthenius*, The Hague, Biblion, 1999, 52 pp., reviews the works of Helene Nolthenius, an author of historical novels, travel books, and essays on ancient and classical times. Ironically, Nolthenius only acquired fame in a wider circle of readers after writing a few historical crime novels. Polman includes an extensive bibliography of the author's works.

8. 1945 TO THE PRESENT DAY

Martien J. G. de Jong, *Een verre vrouw van taal: Over Gerrit Achterberg, zijn dichterschap, zijn leven en zijn interpreteren* (Studies op het gebied van de moderne Nederlandse literatuur, 2), Ghent, KANTL, 162 pp., tries to establish links between Gerrit Achterberg's poetry, his turbulent life (Achterberg was a sexually obsessed and violent man), and the spiritual ideas he wanted to express in his poems, yet without wanting to see them as purely biographical documents. For many critics there were ample reasons to do so after Achterberg had killed his landlady and badly injured her daughter, both of whom he was in love with, on 15 December 1937. On the other hand, there were many of Achterberg's friends, acclaimed poets in their own right, and relatives of those involved in this tragedy, who did everything they could to camouflage the real situation the poet lived in, being admitted to a psychiatric asylum. De Jong cautiously returns in this book to Achterberg's poetry, trying to understand it by allowing the reality to speak as it reveals itself in his poems, while at the same time identifying motifs (such as the motif of confession) characteristic of his poetry. De Jong's book is also of importance for our knowledge of two of Achterberg's closest friends, the poets and critics Roel

Houwink and Ed. Hoornik. **De tegenwereld in stelling gebracht: Historisch-kritische uitgave van de gedichten van Gerrit Achterberg*, ed. Peter Guido de Bruijn (Monumenta literaria neerlandica, 11), The Hague, Constantijn Huygens Instituut, 3 parts in 4 vols., 627 + 857 + 1388 pp., presents a new edition of Achterberg's poems.

Michel Dupuis, *De psyche in de spiegelkamer: Psychomachie in de hedendaagse roman* (Studies op het gebied van de moderne Nederlandse literatuur, 3), Ghent, KANTL, [iv] + 151 pp., studies the ways in which the innermost conflicts in the main character of a fictional story are reflected in his environment, which consequently assumes the role of his mental sounding board. This narrative technique is the result of a narrowing of the gap between subject and object which, according to Dupuis, became noticeable in fiction by the turn of the 20th c., one of its best known representatives being, of course, Franz Kafka. Central to Dupuis's observations are six novels, written between 1926 and 1976, by J. van Oudshoorn, F. Bordewijk, S. Vestdijk, J. Daisne, Hubert Lampo, and Harry Mulisch, but the author also refers to a large number of other novels in which the phenomenon can be observed. In them we find characters whose psyches are not described and analysed by way of allowing the reader an introspective image of their thoughts but by depicting their exterior worlds which function as extensions to their minds. A situation frequently found in fiction is the combination of a psychomachian and a psychological novel in which the author switches back and forth between the two different modes of narration. As a special type of psychomachian novel Dupuis identifies those stories in which a chimerical secondary person in the main character's environment develops into the sole focus of the latter's actions.

Jos Muyres, *Moderniseren en conformeren: Biografie van een tweeluik: 'De Kapellekensbaan' en 'Zomer te Ter-Muren' van Louis Paul Boon*, Nijmegen, Vantilt, 303 pp., traces the genesis of the two best known novels by the Flemish author Louis Paul Boon. The topic is particularly relevant to the first of the two novels. Muyres shows, however, that the facts about how the novel developed were quite different from what Boon wanted his readers to believe. The second topic Muyres addresses is that the two novels can be interpreted as modernistic in the sense that the author gives a great deal of attention to the way his story develops, constantly switching between narration and commentary, but they can also been seen from a post-modern perspective in that the problematic relationship between fiction and reality and between narrator and personages are central to their intellectual discourse.

Nop Maas, **Kleine bolsjewieken: De kleuterjaren van Karel en Gerard (van het) Reve*, Amsterdam, Veen, 1999, 96 pp., outlines the lives of the toddlers Karel and Gerard (van het) Reve, who, in their later years, became known as highly reputable men of letters. Maas was able to reconstruct their early years with the help of a weekly column, written by the parents of the two children, for the young readers of the communist journal *De tribune*. Johan P. Snapper, **De wegen van Marga Minco*, trans. Maaike Post *et al*., Amsterdam, Bakker, 1999, 349 + [16] pp., is a Dutch translation of his *The Ways of Marga Minco*, *etc*. Snapper analyses Minco's short stories about Jewish families living in the Netherlands set during the German occupation.

Frans A. Janssen and Sonja van Stek, *Het bibliografische universum van Willem Frederik Hermans: Bibliografie van de afzonderlijk verschenen werken*, Amsterdam, De Bezige Bij, 296 pp., is a bibliography of all W. F. Hermans's works published in book form. Hermans was one of the most influential and important novelists of the post-War period, who died in 1995. This bibliography is the first step, on behalf of the Willem Frederik Hermans Instituut, towards the publication of his complete works.

*Vijf 5tigers: Een bloemlezing uit het werk van Remco Campert, Jan Elburg, Gerrit Kouwenaar, Lucebert, Bert Schierbeek, introd. Gerrit Kouwenaar, afterword by Hans Renders, Amsterdam, De Bezige Bij, 100 pp. + *Vijf 5tigers vijftig jaar* (CD). Relevant for students of 1950s experimental poetry is also Hans Renders, **Braak: Een kleine mooie revolutie tussen Cobra en Atonaal: met een facsimile-uitgave van het tijdschrift*, Amsterdam, De Bezige Bij, 427 pp.

Maria Pfirrmann, **Uw naam is met wijn geschreven: Bijbel, liturgie en dichtkunst in het vroege werk van Willem Barnard, Guillaume van der Graft*, trans. from German by Sytze de Vries, Brasschaat, Buitink — Zoetermeer, Boekencentrum, 1999, 262 pp., examines biblical and liturgical themes in the poetry of Van der Graft (pseudonym of W. Barnard) during the second half of the 1950s. Between 28 November 1999 and 30 January 2000 works of art by the poet and artist Jan Elburg, one of the most-talked about representatives of the international *Cobra* movement, were exhibited in Haarlem and Heerlen. **Jan G. Elburg: Echt raak is dodelijk, ook voor de kunst*, ed. Wil Heins, Zwolle, Waanders, 1999, 176 pp., is a catalogue of this exhibition. The book also includes an edition of Elburg's illustrated collection of poems *Winter lijkt het wel* (1988).

Hugo Bousset, *Bevlogen lichtheid: Essays*, Amsterdam, Meulenhoff — Leuven, Kritak, 1999, 158 pp., is a collection of essays in which the very idiosyncratic personal views of the critic are voiced on recent works by modern prose writers. Bousset reflects on work by, among others, Monika van Paemel, Connie Palmen, J. J. Voskuil, Cees Nooteboom, Nicolaas Matsier, Ivo Michiels, and Arnon Grunberg. Equally idiosyncratic are the observations of Patrick Demompere (pseudonym of an as yet unidentified person) related to a similar slice of the most recent literary harvest in *Erg! Iets over de nieuwste literatuur*, Amsterdam: Bakker, 1999, 162 pp.

In 1932, the Commissie voor de Collectieve Propaganda van het Nederlandse Boek decided to organize an annual campaign, to be held during the month of March, to promote the purchasing of Dutch books. When, in 1983, the committee was replaced by a foundation, its first director decided that the focus of the so-called 'Boekenweek' (book week) should be literary. Onno Bloem, *Zolang de voorraad strekt: De literaire boekenweekgeschenken 1984–2000*, Amsterdam, Stichting CPNB, 71 pp., presents a colourful description of 17 years of producing the booklets, written for the occasion by prominent literary authors, given as a present to anyone who, during book week, buys a book. An appendix lists all those which have appeared in print since 1932.

III. DANISH STUDIES

LANGUAGE

POSTPONED

LITERATURE

POSTPONED

IV. NORWEGIAN STUDIES*

LANGUAGE

By ARNE KRUSE, *Lecturer in Norwegian, School of European Languages and Cultures, University of Edinburgh*

1. GENERAL

A general presentation in German of the Norwegian language and current language situation is H. Sandøy's contribution, pp. 865–905 in *Nation und Sprache. Die Diskussion ihres Verhältnisses in Geschichte und Gegenwart*, ed. Andreas Gardt, Berlin, Mouton de Gruyter. Martin Skjekkeland, *Tysk-danske lånord i nynorsk og i bygdemåla. Om ein frisk debatt- og om ei gransking av ordtilfanget i to bygdemål* (Forskningsserien no. 16), Agder College, 1999, 130 pp., contributes to the discussion about German/Danish loan-words in Nynorsk with an investigation into the actual usage of such words in two local dialects. Other contributions to this debate are by G. Akselberg, pp. 25–35 of *7. Møde om Udforskningen af Dansk Sprog*, ed. Peter Widell and Mette Kunøe, Aarhus U.P., 1999, and among others, H. Sandøy, pp. 209–24 of the report *Språkbrukeren — fri til å velge? Artikler om homogen og heterogen språknorm*, ed. Helge Omdal (Research series no. 17), Kristiansand, Agder College, 1999, 234 pp. The entire report focuses on theoretical and practical implications of restrictive vs. liberal norms for written Norwegian, and questions the validity of the claim that the many optional forms in Bokmål and Nynorsk are to the benefit of the user of written Norwegian.

The three following books are published in the series 'Publications of the Ivar Aasen Institute': *Ny-Noreg møter Svensk-Finland*, ed. S. J. Walton, Volda, Volda College, 47 pp., is a compilation of five articles which compare the situations for Nynorsk and Swedish in Finland. Peter J. Burgess, *Ivar Aasen's Logic of Nation: Toward a Philosophy of*

---

* The place of publication of books is Oslo unless otherwise indicated.

Culture, Volda College, 1999, 158 pp., discusses Aasen as a catalyst of Norwegian cultural identity. Stephen J. Walton, *Litt laust, mest fast*, Volda College, 1999, contains seven texts discussing what problems and possibilities there are for Nynorsk in what the author calls a 'new-baroque culture'. *Ord etter ord. Heidersskrift til Oddvar Nes*, ed. G. Akselberg and J. Bondevik, Bergen, Norsk Bokreidingslag, 1998, 280 pp., is a *Festschrift* to Professor Oddvar Nes. The 23 scholars who contribute to the volume reflect Nes's interest in etymology, language history, dialectology, and onomastics. *Muntlig norsk*, ed. Frøydis Hertzberg and Astrid Roe, Tano Aschehoug, 1999, 197 pp., is a compilation of articles addressing the oral use of Norwegian in classroom situations. Finn-Erik Vinje, *Riktig norsk*, Cappelen 1999, is a handbook of practical Norwegian usage, one of several similar books from the same author. A published doctoral dissertation on how young immigrants read Norwegian texts is Lise Iversen Kulbrandstad, *En studie av fire innvandrerungdommers lesing av læreboktekster på norsk* (*Acta Humaniora*, 30), Scandinavian U.P., 1998, 528 pp. *Språkvitskap og vitskapsteori*, ed. R. B. Brodersen and T. Kinn, Larvik, Ariadne, 201 pp., contains ten articles discussing research methodology and theory concerning linguistics and Norwegian.

2.   HISTORY OF THE LANGUAGE AND TEXTUAL STUDIES

Hildegunn Otnes and Bente Aamotsbakken, *Tekst i tid og rom. Norsk språkhistorie*, Samlaget, 1999, 274 pp., is a history of the language with a new approach, where the examples of texts are the starting point for the discussion of changes over time and in social context. The last spelling reform of Bokmål is thoroughly covered in Gro-Renée Rambø, *Bokmålsreformen i 1981. Med særlig vekt på Særutvalgets arbeid* (Research series no. 20), Kristiansand, Agder College, 462 pp. G. Akselberg puts this reform into context when he sums up the tendencies and changes in language policy over the last 20 years in *Norsklæraren*, 23.3, 1999 : 11–15. A doctoral thesis on word formation is Kristin Bakken, *En studie av leksikaliseringsprosessen belyst ved et gammelnorsk diplommateriale fra 1300–tallet* (*Acta Humaniora*, 38), Scandinavian U.P., 1998, 332 pp. In *Datahåndbok for humanister*, Gyldendal, Oslo, 1999, O. E. Haugen (147–71) introduces methods for computerized text analyses. *Målsamlingar 1851–1854 av Ivar Aasen*, ed. J. Bondevik, O. Nes, and T. Aarset (Publications of the Ivar Aasen Society, Series A, Text no. 6), Bergen, Norsk bokreidningslag, 1999, 238 pp., is a compilation of texts by Ivar Aasen from the period 1851–54, including grammatical explorations and collections of vocabulary from various regions of Norway.

3. RUNOLOGY

Karin Fjellhammer Seim's doctoral dissertation on the form and function of the West Scandinavian futhark-inscriptions from the Viking period and the Middle Ages is discussed by the opponent Judith Jesch in *Maal og Minne*, 154–62, and there is a reply by Seim, ib., 163–70. J. R. Hagland, 'Note on two runic inscriptions relating to the christianization of Norway and Sweden', *Scripta Islandica: Isländska sällskapets årsbok 49 for 1998*, 1999, 34–44, discusses the Eik stone from Rogaland, found in 1972. O. Grønvik comments once more on the Eggja inscription in *ANF*, 115:5–22. M. Schulte discusses runic orthography in the transitional period from Proto-Scandinavian to Old Norse in *Maal og Minne:* 113–26. We also note here Birgit Sawyer, *The Viking-Age Rune Stones: Custom and Commemoration in Early Medieval Scandinavia*, OUP, xxii + 269 pp., and Richard A. V. Cox, *The Language of the Ogam Inscriptions of Scotland*, Aberdeen U.P., 1999, 187 pp. The author suggests that the language used in the ogam inscriptions from Scotland is Old Norse — a controversial theory indeed, according to M. Barnes in a review article in *Northern Studies* 34, 1999:129–39.

4. DIALECTOLOGY AND PHONOLOGY

H. Sandøy summarizes current tendencies in the development of modern Norwegian dialects in *Folkmålsstudier* 39:345–84. Olga Brekke and Helge Sandøy, *Salten-dialekten. En grammatikk*, Fauske, Skjerstad og Fauske bygdeboknemnd, 237 pp., is a grammar of the dialect of Salten, Northern Norway. Ingulv Røset, *Selbu-målet. Ord og uttrykk*, Novus, 1999, 265 pp., covers the traditional vocabulary of the dialect of Selbu in Trøndelag. After an introduction, where, among other things, the transcription of the dialect is explained, the main corpus is a dictionary-type set up of the vocabulary with head words written close to the pronounciation in the dialect. There is a long and exceptionally detailed review article of the book by J. Øverby in *Talatrosten (*Archive for Dialectology, Univ. of Oslo*)*, 33, 1999:26–82. *Austlandsmål i endring. Dialektar, nynorsk og språkhaldningar på indre Austlandet*, ed. T. Kleiva, I. Donali, T. Nesset, and H. Øygarden, Samlaget, 1999, 283 pp., addresses the often dramatic changes that have happened to the dialects of south-east Norwegian over the last generation. U. Røyneland in *Årbok for Nord-Østerdalen*, Tynset, 1999, 6–17, debates whether there is something we may call a distinct Tynset dialect; and he asks if we can observe a regionalization of the dialects in Røros and Tynset in pp. 98–120 of *Språkleg variasjon og regionalisering*, vol. 2, ed. G. Akselberg, Alversund, Målbryting, 1998.

G. Kristoffersen, 'Quantity in Norwegian syllable structure' pp. 631–50 of *The Syllable. Views and Facts*, ed. Harry van der Hulst and Nancy Ritter, 1999, Berlin, Mouton de Gruyter. In the series *The Phonology of the World's Languages*, Gjert Kristoffersen has written *The Phonology of Norwegian*, OUP, 378 pp.

Olaf Husby and Marit Helene Kløve, *Andrespråksfonologi. Teori og metodikk*, Gyldendal, 1998, 208 pp., is an introduction to Norwegian phonology for teachers of Norwegian as a second language. The book compares Norwegian to several other languages and suggests practical exercises in the classroom. A similar publication is Ingebjørg Skaug, **Norsk språklydlære med øvelser*, Cappelen, which compares Norwegian phonetics with French, German, and English.

A good source for sociolinguistic research in Norway is H. Sandøy's bibliography in *Sociolinguistica*, 13, 1999 : 355–60.

5. Onomastics

Jan Erik Kristiansen and Jørgen Ouren, *Fornavn i Norge. Navnemoter og motenavn*, Gyldendal, 1999, 159 pp., is a book on personal names written by two non-linguists interested in the statistical evidence for such names in Norway, and with useful documentation on how fashion dictates the use of personal names. The last chapter gives advice on the choice of names and how to avoid the most common and obvious names.

Gudlaug Nedrelid, *'Ender og daa ein Aslaksen eller Bragestad' — Etternamnsskikken på Sør- og Vestlandet. Studiar i folketeljingsmaterialet frå 1801*, 2 vols (Forskningsserien no. 10 and 11), Kristiansand, Agder College, 1998, 361 + 314 pp., is a doctoral thesis on personal names — so far the only one on this subject in Norway. K. Kruken looks at cycles of changes in personal names during the 20th c. in pp. 27–55 of *Seksjon for namnegransking. Årsmelding* 1998, ed. B. Helleland, 1999. There are two Norwegian contributions to *Studia Antroponymica Scandinavica*, 17: K. Bakken (27–49) discusses whether personal names in Middle Norwegian charters and records from Telemark are written in dialect or standard form; and G. Alhaug (67–92) describes how people in Northern Norway with double names (*Anne Pernille*) are most likely to be addressed with their first name only (*Anne*).

A doctoral dissertation on the Scandinavian contribution to the place-names of Normandy is Åse Kari Hansen, *Språkkontakt i gammelt koloniområde: en studie av normannerbosetningens stedsnavn, med særlig vekt på navnegruppa -tuit*, Bergen Univ., Nordisk Institutt, 312 pp. Two more dissertations for the degree of dr. philos. are the following: Inge Særheim, *Namn og gard: studium av busetnadsnamn på -land*, Stavanger College, 1999, 506 pp., a study of the generic *-land*; and Tom

Schmidt, *Norske gårdsnavn på -by og -bø med personnavnforledd* (Acta Humaniora, 87), 2 vols, Oslo U.P., 620 + 146 pp. This is an investigation into the generic *-by/-bø* in place-names with a personal name as a specific. The author suggests that the area Østfold, Norway, and Båhuslän, Sweden, could be where this name type originated. He also draws comparisons with the name type found elsewhere, including Britain. Tom Schmidt is also the editor of Kåre Hoel, *Bustadnavn i Østfold. 3. Våler*, Section for Name Research, Oslo U.P., 1999, 348 pp. This is part of a series that eventually will cover all names of settlements in the county of Østfold. Arne Kruse, *Mål og méd. Målføre og médnamn frå Smøla*, Trondheim, Tapir Akademisk, 305 pp., is a monograph on names of fishing-grounds off the island of Smøla. Åse Wetås, *Namneskiftet Kristiania-Oslo*, Novus, 242 pp., is a study of the process that led to the changing of the name of the Norwegian capital in 1925.

A useful bibliography on the founding father of Norwegian name research is Anders Løøv: *Oluf Rygh 1833–99. En bibliografi. Skrifter av og om Oluf Rygh*, Trondheim, Luejie, 1999, 40 pp. Two publications from a conference in honour of Oluf Rygh are *Oluf Rygh. Artikler om en foregangsmann i humanistisk forskning*, ed. B. Sandnes, J. Sandnes, O. Stemshaug, and L. Stenvik (NORNA-rapporter, 70A), Uppsala, 148 pp., and from the same editors, *Oluf Rygh. Rapport fra symposium på Stiklestad 13.–15. mai 1999* (NORNA-rapporter, 70B), Uppsala, 232 pp. All contributions have summaries in English.

The following articles are noted in the proceedings of international conferences: G. Akselberg, 'Foreign place names in Norwegian atlases and textbooks', pp. 5–6 of *XX Congresso Internacional de Ciencias Onomásticas*, Instituto da Lingua Galega, Santiago de Compostela, 1999; T. Schmidt, 'Norwegian place names in -by/-bø with anthroponymic specifics', pp. 51–63 of *Onomastik. Akten des 18. Internationalen Kongresses für Namenforschung, Trier, 12.–17. April 1993*, IV: *Personennamen und Ortsnamen*, ed. D. Kremer and T. Andersson (Patronymica Romanica, 17), Tübingen, Niemeyer, 1999; G. Nedrelid, 'Norwegische Familiennamen aus Hofnamen im Jahre 1801', *ib.*, 92–100; B. Helleland, 'Ortsnamen als Ursprung von Familiennamen in Norwegen', *ib.*, 159–68; and 'Entstehung der Familiennamen in Norwegen' *ib.*, 327–28. B. Helleland also discusses the name *Hoen* in Buskerud in pp. 107–16 of *I hast hälsar. Festskrift till Göran Hallberg på 60–årsdagen den 7 oktober 1999*, ed. S. Isaksson, E. Nordin, M. Olsson, C. Ringdahl, and M. Saurow (Dialekt- och ortnamnsarkivet i Lund), Lund U.P., 1999, and the same author sums up onomastic research in Norway over the last hundred years in pp. 77–118 of *Den nordiska namnforskningen. I går, i dag, i morgon. Handlingar från NORNA:s 25:e symposium i Uppsala 7–9 februari 1997*, ed. M. Wahlberg, Uppsala,

NORNA-förlaget, 1999, 272 pp. A good source of information on onomastics research in Norway and Scandinavia is *Nytt om namn*, published by the Section for Name Research, Univ. of Oslo.

6. SYNTAX AND MORPHOLOGY

Hans-Olav Enger and Kristian Emil Kristoffersen, *Innføring i norsk grammatikk. Morfologi og syntaks*, LNU–Cappelen Akademisk, 362 pp., is the first university level textbook since Olav Næs's *Norsk grammatikk* to cover both morphology and syntax. The authors present important aspects of leading theories within modern research without committing themselves to only one of them. Jon Erik Hagen, *Norsk grammatikk for andresspråklærere*, Gyldendal, 432 pp., is another grammar which includes both morphology and syntax, but rather aims at teachers of Norwegian as a second language. In *Nordic Journal of Linguistics* we find articles by H. O. Enger and T. Nesset, 'The value of cognitive grammar in typological studies: the case of Norwegian and Russian passive middle and reflexive', 22:27–59; E. Keer, 'Anti -*that-trace effects in Norwegian and Optimality Theory', *ib.*, 183–203; and H. Lodrup, 'Linking and Optimality in the Norwegian presentational focus construction', *ib.*, 205–29. *Nordica Bergensia*, 21 (Scandinavian Studies, University of Bergen), contains 14 articles on various aspects of the important new standard grammar for Norwegian, *Norsk referansegrammatikk*, published in 1997.

The series *Acta Humaniora* is the outlet for the following doctoral dissertations from the Univ. of Oslo: Hans-Olav Enge, *The Classification of Strong Verbs in Norwegian with Special Reference to the Oslo Dialect. A Study in Inflectional Morphology* (Acta Humaniora, 26), Scandinavian U.P., 1998, 302 pp.; Kjell Magne Yri, *My Father Taught me How to Cry, but Now I Have Forgotten. The Semantics of Religious Concepts with an Emphasis on Meaning, Interpretation, and Translatability* (Acta Humaniora, 29), Scandinavian U.P., 1998, 220 pp.; Anne-Line Graedler, *Morphological, Semantic and Functional Aspects of English Lexical Borrowings in Norwegian* (Acta Humaniora, 40), Scandinavian U.P., 1998, 390 pp.

Øystein Nilsen, *The Syntax of Circumstantial Adverbials*, Novus, 1999, 179 pp., is an attempt to outline the behaviour of circumstantial adverbials in Norwegian applying three different theories. **Menneske, språk og fellesskap. Festskrift til Kirsti Koch Christensen*, ed. Ø. Andersen, K. Fløttum, and T. Kinn, Novus, contains 12 invited contributions, among them Øivin Andersen on agentivity and determination, H. J. J. Dyvik on necessay nodes in Norwegian, and T. Fretheim on relative sentences.

7. LEXICOGRAPHY, DICTIONARIES, AND TRANSLATION

Helge Sandøy, *Lånte fjører eller bunad? Om importord i norsk*, Cappelen, 300 pp., presents and explains the background to new borrowings into Norwegian, especially from English. The book is aimed at teachers and students at an upper secondary level. In *Engelsk eller ikke engelsk? That is the question*, ed. N. Davidsen-Nielsen, E. Hansen, and P. Jarvad (Dansk Sprognævns skrifter, 28), Copenhagen, Dansk sprognævn–Gyldendal, H. Sandøy (65–90), outlines various attempts to deal with English loan-words in Norwegian.

Sylfest Lomheim, *Skrifta på skjermen. Korleis skjer teksting av fjernsynsfilm?* (Forskningsserien, 8), Agder College, 1998, 170 pp., outlines the process of translating films for TV and producing sub-titles on the screen. Concerned with translational correspondences between sentences on the one hand and sentence sequences on the other hand is C. Fabricius-Hansen, 'Information packaging and translation: aspects of translational sentence splitting (German – English/Norwegian)', pp. 175–214 of *Sprachspezifische Aspekte der Informationsverteilung*, ed. M. Doherty (Studia Grammatica, 47), Berlin, Akademie. H. Hassel-gård, 'Thematic structure in translation between English and Norwegian', pp. 145–67 of *Corpora and Crosslinguistic Research: Theory, Method, and Case Studies*, ed. S. Johansson and S. Oksefjell, Amsterdam, Rodopi, 1998. The entire issue of *Nordica Bergensia* 20, ed. C. Laurén and J. Myking, Scandinavian Studies, Univ. of Bergen, 1999, 267 pp., is dedicated to terminology and specialized language under the heading, *Treng små språksamfunn fagspråk? Nordiske fagspråkstudiar*. Scholars from various Nordic countries contribute, among them J. Myking with a long article 'Norsk fagspråkforsking. Ein manglande (?) tradisjon' (17–62), in which he sums up research on terminology in Norway, mainly during the last 20 years. He finds a bias towards normative and didactic work, observes a lack of major technolect studies, but sees some promising work on terminology/language planning theory. L. S. Vikør points to problems with the long time aspect we usually face when producing major dictionaries in pp. 395–405 of *Nordiska studier i lexikografi* 4, ed. P. Slotte, P. Westerberg, and E. Orava (Nordiska föreningen för lexikografi), Helsinki, 1999.

As part of the (re-)publication of the works by Ivar Aasen is his Danish-Norwegian dictionary, **Dansk-norsk Ordbog av Ivar Aasen*, ed. J. Bondevik, O. Nes and T. Aarset, Bergen, Norsk Bokreidingslag. Harald Bjorvand and Fredrik Otto Lindeman, *Våre arveord: etymologisk ordbok*, Novus, 1142 pp., is an etymological dictionary covering the native vocabulary of Norwegian. An introduction discusses the methods applied in the book. The book is meant to replace Falk and Torp, *Etymologisk ordbog*, 1903–06 (German ed. 1910–11), as the standard etymological dictionary for Norwegian. Sverre Klouman, *Moro med ord*, Aschehoug, 1999, popularizes etymology and comments on the background to words, names, and expressions.

Pål E. Korsvold and Helle Snellingen, *Norsk-engelsk/engelsk-norsk økonomisk ordbok*, Cappelen, is a new edition of the dictionary of English and Norwegian economic terms, now enlarged with terms from banking; and Egil Schanke, *Norsk-tysk/tysk-norsk økonomisk ordbok*, Cappelen, covers the same subject area for German terms. Åge Lind, *Norsk-engelsk juridisk ordbok. Sivilrett og strafferett*, Cappelen, is a Norwegian/English dictionary of legal terms, including examples of usage and of how legal systems may differ from Norway to England and USA.

Noted is also the yearbook for lexicography *Ord om ord, Årsskrift for leksikografi*, ed. E. Simensen, L. S. Vikør, and B. Wangensteen, Oslo U.P., 1999.

LITERATURE SINCE THE REFORMATION

By ØYSTEIN ROTTEM, *Cand. phil., Copenhagen*

1. GENERAL

Marianne Egeland, *Hvem bestemmer over livet? Biografien som historisk og litterær genre*, Universitetsforlaget, 366 pp., is a critical examination of the methods and devices used in literary biographies. Egeland maintains that writers of biographies tend to identify too much with the author in question and that they blur the limits between life and work. A whole chapter is devoted to the long tradition of biographical works on Wergeland, but also later books on e.g. J. Bjørneboe (by F. Wandrup), S. Christiansen (by T. Boman-Larsen), and Claes Gill (by K. Fløgstad) serve as objects of critical examination. On the whole Egeland seems to be rather sceptical towards biography as a genre, and is at her best when she points out the pitfalls of biographical writing. Ø. Rottem, *Vårt København. Norske forfattere i Kongens by*, Press, 238 pp. Heming Gujord, 'Norske forfattere i historiens tjeneste', *Edda:* 158–70.

2. THE SIXTEENTH TO NINETEENTH CENTURY

GENERAL

Inger Ekrem, *Historieskrivning og -undervisning på latin i Oslo omkring år 1600. Halvard Gunnarssøns Philippiske Carionkrønike Rostock 1596*, 1998, Universitetsforlaget. *Om barocken i Norden. Meddelanden från avdelningen för nordisk litteratur*, ed. K. Malmio, 1999, Helsinki, Nordica. *Mellom europeisk tradisjon og nasjonal selvbevissthet. Det norsk-klassiske drama 1750–1814*, ed. R. Gaasland and H. E. Aarseth, 1999, Spartacus.

INDIVIDUAL AUTHORS

DASS. A. G. Lombnæs, 'Læbers Pligt og Lemmers Facter. Filologisk tilforsikt og retorisk anfektelse hos Petter Dass', *Norsk Litteraturvitenskapelig Tidsskrift*, 2, 1999: 148–56.
HOLBERG. G. Sivertsen, 'An unknown farce or an unread novel? The enigmatic source of Piotr Baryka's *Z chlopa król* and of Ludvig Holberg's *Jeppe paa Bierget*', *Edda:* 99–109. S. Buus, 'A comedy of malapropism: Ludvig Holberg's *Erasmus Montanus*', *ib.*, 334–45.
WESSEL. H. Skaar, '"En Skredder som er Helt, er ikke Skredder meere"' — om mannlighetens uttrykk i Wessels *Kierlighed uden Strømper*', *Edda:* 203–14.

3. The Nineteenth Century

GENERAL

Nordic Letters 1870–1910, ed. M. Robinson and J. Garton, 1999, Norwich, Norwich Press, 422 pp., contains articles on e.g. the correspondence between G. Brandes and M. Thoresen (by Jorunn Hareide), and between A. Kielland and the Drewsen family (by Tor Obrestad). Of special interest for students of Norwegian literature are three articles on Amalie Skram: J. Garton, ' "Why do Norwegians hate Denmark so much? National consciousness in Amalie and Erik Skram's correspondence', *ib.*, 264–80; J. Messick, 'Amalie Skram's talking cure revisited', *ib.*, 281–305; and K. Hanson, 'Amalie Skram and her publishers', *ib.*, 306–34. *Eit ord — ein stein. Studiar i nynorsk skriftliv*, ed. P. Bjørby, A. Dvergsdal, and A. Aarseth, Bergen, Alvheim og Eide.

INDIVIDUAL AUTHORS

ANDERSEN.   E. Søbye, 'Denne skrekkelige tidsånd — Tryggve Andersen 1885–1892, *Agora*, 17.1–2, 1999:274–330.

GARBORG.   E. Bygstad, 'Heilagbròt og alveland: *Haugtussa* av Arne Garborg', *Edda:* 130–46. L. R. Waage, 'Garborgs *Trætte Mænd* — om "mannlighet", sykdom og frelse', *ib.*, 215–26. J. Sjåvik, 'Reading Arne Garborg's irony: *Bondestudentar, Trætte mænd, Fred*', *ScSt*, 72:63–88. Siri Garborg Talle presents in *Kjære Bror! Arne Garborg og slekten*, Aschehoug, 344 pp., quite a lot of new and interesting material about the relationship between her great-uncle Arne and his sisters and brothers, amongst whom five emigrated to America.

HAMSUN.   The articles in *Hamsun 2000. 8 foredrag fra Hamsun-dagene på Hamarøy*, ed. E. Arntzen and N. M. Knutsen, Hamarøy, Hamsun-Selskapet, 183 pp., is of more ordinary value than we are used to in this biannual publication. An article on *Pan* (by Britt Andersen) stands out amongst the others. Worthy to be mentioned are also articles on Hamsun in Bulgaria (by Snezjana Djenkova) and Yugoslavia (by Ljubisa Rajic). J. Dragvoll, 'Hamsun, *Pan* og Schopenhauer', *Edda:* 14–25. Ø. Rottem, 'Hamsuns dead-end? — Ansatser til en helhetsfortolkning av romanen *Siste Kapitel*', *ib.*, 346–60. Id., 'Hamsun og Langfeldt — Instrumentell fornuft vs. guddommelig galskap', *Tidsskrift for norsk psykologiforening*, 37:707–16. B. Andersen, 'Maskulinitetens hjemløshet. Knut Hamsuns romaner *Siste kapitel* og *Ringen sluttet*', *Norsk Litteraturvitenskapelig Tidsskrift*, 3:16–31. R. Gaasland, 'Veien til livets tre. Kronotopisk analyse av Hamsuns novelle "Et spøkelse" ', *Norsklæraren*, no. 1:5–9. A. Skaftun, 'Ironi, dialog og Hamsuns *Børn av Tiden*', *Norsk Litteraturvitenskapelig Tidsskrift*,

3:153–60. Ø. Rottem, 'Førsteopposisjon', Harald Næss, 'Annenopposisjon', 'Svar fra doktoranden', *Norskrift*, 101:37–88, report the discussions at the doctoral disputation in connection with Lars Frode Larsen's doctoral thesis *Den unge Hamsun (1859–1888)*. *En studie i hans personlige og idémessige utvikling*, presented at the University of Oslo in the autumn of 1998. Problems concerning the methods of biographical research were the main issues.

IBSEN. Gudleiv Bø, "*Nasjonale subjekter.*" *Ideer om nasjonalitet i Henrik Ibsens romantiske forfatterskap*, Novus. Kristian Smidt, *Ibsen Translated. A Report on English Versions of Henrik Ibsen's Peer Gynt and A Doll's House*, Solum. Anne Marie Rekdal, *Frihetens dilemma. Ibsen lest med Lacan*, Aschehoug. Rob van der Zalm, *Ibsen op de planken: een ensceneringsgeschiedenis van het werk va Henrik Ibsen in Nederland 1880–1995*, Amsterdam, International Theatre & Film Books, 455 pp. Philip E. Larson, *Ibsen in Skien and Grimstad: His Education, Reading and Early Works*, 1999, Grimstad, Ibsen House–Grimstad Museum. *Readings on A Doll's House*, ed. H. R. Mitchell, San Diego, Greenhaven, 1999, 160 pp. *Ibsen on Screen*, ed. J. E. Holst and A. Sæther, Centre for Ibsen Studies, 98 pp. J. G. Jørgensen, 'Intervariasjon i Henrik Ibsens skrifter', *Edda:* 192–202. E. Østerud, 'Aktaion-komplekset. Blikk, kropp og "rites of passage" i *Hedda Gabler*', *ib.*, 299–319. Jan Sara, ' "Klistret fast med sort på hvitt": the problem of writing in Ibsen's *Rosmersholm* and *Hedda Gabler*', *Scandinavica*, 39:143–70. M. Robinson, 'England's Ibsen, or performing Ibsen's dramas of contemporary life today', *ib.*, 171–90. A. Swanson, 'Ibsen inside and out: the natural world in the twelve major prose plays', *ib.*, 191–205. J. Templeton, 'The Munch-Ibsen connection: exposing a critical myth', *ScSt*, 72:445–62. The very first volume of *Ibsen Studies*, ed. F. Helland and V. Ystad, published at the Centre for Ibsen Studies, University of Oslo, contains the following articles: T. C. Theoharis, ' "After the first death, there is no other": Ibsen's *Brand* and Kierkegaard's *Fear and Trembling*' (9–29), H. Delbrück, 'Falling for the sphinx. The heritage of the Oedipus myth in Henrik Ibsen's *The Master Builder*' (30–53), T. Arthur, 'Female interpreters of Ibsen on Broadway, 1896–1947' (54–67), A. Hoel, 'The role of women in Henrik Ibsen's *The Pretenders*' (68–80). *Anglo-Scandinavian Cross-Currents*, ed. I.-S. Ewbank, O. Lausund, and B. Tysdahl, 1999, Norwich, Norvik, contains a large number of interesting articles about the literary relationships between England and Scandinavia. Two sections are mainly devoted to the study of the reception of Ibsen: O. Lausund, 'Edmund Gosse: Ibsen's first prophet to English readers' (139–58); S. Jan, 'Naturalism in the theatre: Ibsen's *Ghosts* in 1890s England' (159–73); G. Marshall, 'Ibsen and actresses on the English stage' (174–86); K. Shepherd-Barr, ' "Too far from Piccadilly": Ibsen in England and France in the 1890s' (187–202);

G. Marshall, 'Duse and Ibsen in the 1890s' (203–14); T. Rem, '"Cheerfully dark": Punchian parodies of Ibsen in the early 1890s' (215–30); S.-J. Spånberg, 'Constructions of the artist: Dowson, Ibsen and the Fin de Siècle' (231–43); B. Tysdahl, 'Ibsen's stories in Joyce's *Dubliners*' (265–79); R. Brown, 'James Joyce between Ibsen and Bjørnson: *A Portrait of the Artist* and *The Fisher Lass*' (280–96); I.-S. Ewbank, 'Dickens, Ibsen and cross-currents' (297–317). KIELLAND. *Å lesa Kielland. Rapport frå eit jubileumsår*, ed. A. M. Andersen and H. Gujord, Stavanger, Høgskolen i Stavanger, 1999. B. Tysdahl, 'Alexander L. Kielland på ny', *Edda:* 1–13. P. Bache, 'Alexander Kielland — Mennesker og dyr', *Norskrift*, 99:73–88. K. Svortdal, 'Alexander Kiellands *Professoren* og forholdene ved universitetet', *NLÅ:* 43–47. KINCK. D. G. Myhren, 'Studier i Hans E. Kincks diktning', *Edda:* 26–36.

LØLAND. Harald Bache-Wiig, *Frisetting av barndommen. Rasmus Løland som barnebokforfatter. Etableringen av den norske barndommen*, Institutt for nordistikk og litteraturvitenskap, Oslo Univ.

OBSTFELDER. M. Nag, 'Parhestene Obstfelder og Munch', *Bok-vennen*, no. 4:32–37.

SIVLE. Anders Hovden, *Per Sivle. Ei livssoge*, Samlaget, 153 pp.

WELHAVEN. U. Langås, '"I dette Brev skal jeg lægge all min Kunst og mit hele Hjerte:" Welhavens kjærlighetsbrev til Ida Kjerulf', *Norsk Litteraturvitenkapelig Tidsskrift*, 3:106–21.

WINSNES. Hilde Diesen, *Hanna Winsnes. Dagsverk og nattetanker*, Aschehoug, 424 pp., is a well-written and informative biography in which both life and work are treated in a balanced and satisfactory way. Read as a piece of cultural and social history it is also of great value and presents a vivid picture of the way of life of the middle and upper classes at the beginning of the 19th century.

4. THE TWENTIETH CENTURY

GENERAL

Trond Andreassen, *Bok-Norge. En litteratursosiologisk oversikt*, Universitetsforlaget, 518 pp., is the second and revised edition of this very informative book about the literary system of today's Norway. It is a standard work and a 'must' for those who want to be informed about the background for what is going on in Norwegian literature, in which writers, readers, publishing houses, book stores, book clubs, libraries, literary critics, and the cultural politics of the State are taken into account. Nils K. Jacobsen, *En forlegger og hans hus. Harald Grieg og Gyldendal*, Gyldendal, 558 pp., gives a well-balanced picture of this almost mythical figure in the world of Norwegian publishing and sheds new light on the motives and reflections behind the so-called 'hjemkjøpet' of the Norwegian section of the Danish publishing house Gyldendal in 1925. *Saklighet og sanselighet. Norsk prosa-modernisme på 1930–tallet*, ed. S. Furuseth, S. J. Paulson, and P. Aaslestad, Gyldendal Akademisk, contains the following articles: Terje Borgersen, ' " — en epoke som søker sig selv." Haakon Bugge Mahrts *Modernisme*' (13–34); P. Aaslestad, ' "En utpreget modernist." Haakon Bugge Mahrt som skjønnlitterær forfatter' (35–50); B. O. Borgen, 'Drømmer og fabuleringer. Rolf Stenersens *Godnatt da du* sett i lys av surrealismen' (51–64); S. J. Paulson, 'Erotikkens glitrende lunefullhet. Paul Gjesdahls noveller' (65–78); B. Helland, ' "Jeg vil leke spøkelse med mig selv." Subjektets grenser i Emil Boysons *Yngre herre på besøk*' (79–97); A. S. Larsen, 'Saklighet og sanselighet. Om Gunnar Larsens roman *I sommer*' (98–115); A. F. Hansen, ' "Å hederlig tolke tilværelsens komplikasjoner." Ernst Orvils tekstimmanente verdsbilde' (116–34); A. O. Kopreitan, 'I form av et brudd. Aksel Sandemoses *Vi pynter oss med horn*' (135–49); S. Gimnes, 'Fortrolling av tilveret. Romantiske og modernistiske spor i nokre Vesaas-tekstar frå 1930–talet og 1950–talet' (150–69); S. J. Paulson, ' "Modernisme" og "modernitet" ' (182–87). Alf van der Hagen, *Dialoger 3: Stemmeskifter*, Tiden, 247 pp.

INDIVIDUAL AUTHORS

ANKER. Tordis and Jo Ørjasæter, *Nini Roll Anker. En kvinne i tiden*, Aschehoug.

ASKILDSEN. J. Bakken, 'Thomas F — Outsider i en novellistisk verden', *Norskrift*, 99:7–19.

BELSVIK. S. Sletten, 'Smått og stort. Rune Belsviks bøker om Dustefjerten', *NLÅ*: 175–94.

BORGEN. Espen Haavardsholm, *Øst for Eden. En biografi om Johan Borgen*, Gyldendal, 494 pp., presents a vivid and penetrating portrait of B., and sheds new light on periods in his life which hitherto have been rather in shadow. In a convincing way H. demonstrates how crucial these periods have been for the work of B. As a man and a writer B. stands forth as a more complex and 'demonic' figure than he has been seen as before.

DUUN. H. Gujord, 'Vitalistiske drag i Olav Duuns forfatterskap', *NLÅ:* 48–61.

EGNER. Christopher H. Gylseth, *Thorbjørn Egner — Tigergutt kan alt!*, Schibsted.

EIDSLOTT. *Hellig hav*, ed. A. Aarnes and H. Nordahl, Verbum.

ELVESTAD. A. Engelstad, 'The terror from within. The Gothic tradition and Sven Elvestad's *Haunted House*', *Edda:* 243–55.

ESPESETH. E. Rees, 'Sadism, art and healing: re-examining Karo Espeseth's *Sår som ennu blør*', *Edda*: 256–67.

FOSSE. K. Johnsen, 'Nokon kjem til å kome. Noen punktvise nedslag i Jon Fosses teaterspråk', *Vinduet*, no. 2:27–35. O. Karlsen, ' "Ei uro er kommen over meg." Om Jon Fosses *Naustet* (1989) og den repeterende skrivemåten', *Edda:* 268–79. H. Aarflot, 'Å beskrive det ubeskrivelige. Om det vanskelige forholdet mellom språk og virkelighet med utgangspunkt i Jon Fosses fortelling "Lines hår" ', *Norskrift*, 99:20–31.

GJESDAHL. K. Næss, 'Om Katharina Gjesdahl. Forsøk på å lese en glemt forfatter', *Vinduet*, no. 3:49–59.

HAFF. M. Žagar, 'Bergljot Hobæk Haff: *Skammen*. Å tale med og for far', *NLÅ:* 147–59.

HAUGE. Ole Karlsen, *Fansmakt og bergsval dom. En studie i Olav H. Hauges romantiske metapoesi*, Tromsø, Unipub.

HERBJØRNSRUD. G. Uvsløkk, 'Speilbilder. Melankoli og identitet i en novelle av Hans Herbjørnsrud', *Norskrift*, 99:20–31.

HOFMO. Jan Erik Vold, *Mørkets sangerske. En bok om Gunvor Hofmo*, Gyldendal, 726 pp., is an excellent presentation of a poet who has at last been acknowledged as one of Norway's leading post-war poets. The introductions to H.'s poetry are very well balanced and contain a lot of good observations. Vold also presents some sketches of a biography, based on new material. Hitherto unknown letters, poems, diaries, short stories, and sketches by Hofmo are here published for the first time and reveal new and surprising sides of the poet's character.

HØLMEBAKK. T. Skjævesland, 'Sigbjørn Hølmebakk og Finnmark', *Bokvennen*, no. 4:42–49.

JOHANNESEN. E. Skjeveland, 'Er kunsten å leve en svømmeteknikk? Om Georg Johannesens siste diktsamling: *Ars Vivendi*', *Samtiden*, no. 2–3:42–51.

KJÆRSTAD. F. Wagner, 'Norwegian Psycho. Postmoderne Anthropozentri in Jan Kjærstads Roman *Rand*', *Skandinavistik*, 30:127–38.

LØVEID. L. M. Johansen, 'Cecilie Løveids *Sug*. Symbolske trekk i Kjerstis omverden', *NLÅ:* 120–32.

MOE. N. Simonhjell, 'Din urin vil føre deg langt. Utskiljingar (Karin Moe)', *Vinduet*, no. 3:7–10.

NYGARD. E. Vassenden, 'Fortolkningens forpliktelser. Omkring resepsjonen av Olav Nygards dikt "Eg andar hol i kvitan is" ', *NLÅ*: 62–87.

MYKLE. Ø. Rottem, 'Svermeren og hans demon. Estetisk idiosynkrasi i Agnar Mykles noveller', pp. 178–88 of *På tværs. Til Jette Lundbo Levy*, ed. M. Barlyng, K. P. Mortensen, and K. Sanders, Copenhagen, Spring.

SANDE.   Herbjørn Sørebø, *Ein storm frå vest. Jakob Sande — veit eg*, Samlaget, 178 pp.

SANDEL.   Nina Evensen, *En studie av fortidsdimensionens betydning i Cora Sandels Alberte-trilogi*, 1999, Tromsø, Det humanistiske fakultet, Tromsø Univ. E. Rees, 'Escape from the novel: Cora Sandel's *Kranes Konditori*', *ScSt*, 72:181–98. T. Selboe, 'Byvandringens betydning i Cora Sandels Alberte-trilogi', *NLÅ:* 88–104.

SANDEMOSE.   *Sandemoseprosjektet. Hvorfor flygte fra Jante? Aksel Sandemose 1899–1999*, Nyköping, Morsø Folkebibliotek. B. Stokseth, 'På sporet av A. Sandemoses ironi — i *Det svundne er en drøm*', *NLÅ*: 195–214. E. Arntzen, 'Et vindu mot natten? Noen betraktninger rundt Sandemose-året 1999 og Jorunn Hareides *Aksel Sandemose. Diktning som skjebne*', *ib.*, 215–24.

SKJÆRÅSEN.   Magne Skjæråsen, *Einar Skjæråsen. 'Fra drøm til dikt'*, Orion.

SOLSTAD.   *Narrativt begjær. Om Dag Solstads forfatterskap*, ed. T. Kvithyld, LNU–Cappelen Akademiske, 288 pp., confirms the picture of Solstad as one of the most outstanding prose writers in modern Norwegian literature. The contributors cover most works and periods of his writing, and dig deep into the complex thematic structures of the texts. The book includes the following articles: J. Thon, 'Klassiker, romantiker og kyniker: Solstad på 60–tallet' (13–47); A. Krogstad, ' "Se på ham!" ' — Maoismen som konfigurasjon i Dag Solstads *Arild Asnes, 1970*' (48–78); A. Kittang, 'Dag Solstads elegiske realisme. Ei lesing av krigstrilogien' (79–106); T. Kvithyld, 'Romanen i dialog med et tekstunivers. En lesning av *Roman 1987*' (107–72); N. Simonhjell, 'Erindring og fascinasjon i Dag Solstads *Ellevte roman, bok atten*' (173–200); G. Hjorthol, ' "Bipersonens øyeblikk" — ideologi og kjærleik i Dag Solstads *Genanse og verdighet*' (201–37); Y. S. Jacobsen, 'Nattens refleksjoner. Om blikket i *Professor Andersens natt*' (238–51). K. Marstein, J. E. Riley, and M. Øybø, 'Et foreløpig punktum. Samtale om Dag Solstads forfatterskap', *Vinduet*, 3:12–22. M. Žagar, 'Modernism and aesthetic dictatorship: Dag Solstad's journey from the sixties to the seventies', *ScSt*, 72:199–230. W. Mishler, 'Det mimetiske begjæret. Ei lesing av Dag Solstad mot Henrik Ibsen', *NLÅ:* 133–46.

ULVEN.   F. A. Brøndbo, 'Tor Ulvens dikt', *Bokvennen*, no. 4:50–55.

VESAAS.   D. G. Myhren, 'Folkediktning som resonansbunn hos Tarjei Vesaas', *Bokvennen*, no. 3:42–49. B. Aamotsbakken, 'Sirkulære bevegelser i to dikt av Tarjei Vesaas', *NLÅ*: 105–19.

VOLD.   *Jan Erik Vold og Jan Erik Vold*, ed. O. Karlsen, LNU–Cappelen Akademiske, 393 pp., is a collection of lectures presented at a Vold-symposium in Flisa, at which a great variety of topics concerning Vold's activities as a poet, mediator, and editor were discussed. Of most scholarly interest are the following articles: A. G. Lombnæs, 'I språket, i verden. Jan Erik Volds *Bok 1–10*' (41–60); I. Lemhagen, 'I speglarnas sal. Anteckningar kring Jan Erik Volds debut' (61–79); H. H. Wærp, 'Bøkene "fra rom til rom SAD & CRAZY" (1967) og "BusteR brenneR" (1976) — kortprosa eller prosadikt?' (80–104); B. Kleivset, 'Fraværet som gir nævær. Om Jan Erik Volds fjerde bok: *fra rom til rom SAD & CRAZY*' (105–23); B. Höglund, 'Dikten påminner om världen. Om skillingtrycksestetikken i Jan Erik Volds 90-talstexter' (134–52); Ø. Rottem, 'Jan Erik Vold som tidsskriftredaktør: Profil og Vinduet' (242–58); S. Furuseth, 'Historiefremkalling eller historieforfalskning? Jan Erik Vold og modernismedebatten(e)' (259–77); O. Karlsen, 'En sykkeltur gjennom Jan Erik Volds Olav H. Hauge-lesning' (278–98).

wassmo. The fiction of Wassmo is analysed from a great variety of angles in *Født av spindel og jern. Om Herbjørg Wassmos forfatterskap*, ed. R. C. Krogsveen, LNU–Cappelen Akademiske, 159 pp. The articles included are as follows: I. Engelstad, 'Herbjørg Wassmos forfatterskap' (11–15); R. C. Granaas, '"Den kroppen som ikke var hennes." Noen kommentarer til *Huset med den blinde glassveranda*' (16–35); B. Andersen, 'Krenkelsens kunst. Herbjørg Wassmo: *Det stumme rommet*' (36–54); D. Kristjánsdóttir, 'Under en himmel som ingen hud, ingen hender har' (55–70); Ø. Rottem, 'Det tomme rommet. Herbjørg Wassmo og den melodramatiske forestillingsmåte' (71–91); J. Øverland, 'Lille, store Dina' (92–101); S. J. Paulson, 'Gjentakelse i *Lykkens sønn*' (103–25); H. H. Skei, 'Som i et speil? Som i en gåte?' (126–38). S. Mekjan, 'Wassmos verden', *Vinduet*, no. 3:74–80.

V. SWEDISH STUDIES*

LANGUAGE

POSTPONED

LITERATURE

By BIRGITTA THOMPSON, *Lecturer in Swedish, University of Wales, Lampeter*

1. GENERAL

Nordisk kvinnolitteraturhistoria. v. *Liv och verk,* ed. Elisabeth Møller Jensen et al., Malmö, Bra Böcker, 396 pp., is the final volume of this large project (see *YWMLS*, 55:1036, 58:971–72, 59:913–14). It includes brief biographies in alphabetical order of all women writers in vols I–IV, bibliographical references, and indexes. S. H. Rossel, 'Gibt es eine nordische Literatur?', Paul, *Skandinavistik,* 85–98, is a paper given to German-speaking Scandinavianists at a symposium in Norway, 1997; it discusses whether a common literature for the five Nordic countries is at all possible, and suggests an integrated literary project to heighten international awareness of Nordic literature. Stina Hansson, *Från Hercules till Swea. Den litterära textens färändringar* (SLIGU, 39), 162 pp., examines the transformation of what was recognized as 'literary' in analyses of selected texts from c. 1650 to 1850. It focuses on three established literary criteria and their changing roles, namely Classical rhetoric, the inherited cultural/literary repertory, and the relationship between oral and the 'new' focus on writing and printing. Instead of the generally accepted linear process in literary history and its various epochs, it argues that changes in literary texts and forms happen over a long time through the gradual adjustment of prevailing standards. H. von Born, 'Stockholms röster', *TsSk,* 21:41–53, discusses Stockholm in literature from the Eric Chronicle to the modern day. *Parnass,* no. 2, is a special issue devoted to 'Rupture'; spanning 700 years from Petrus de Dacia to Ylva Eggehorn, it deals with a number of diverse authors: Ellen Key, Amelie Posse, and Sonja Åkesson. E. Lagerroth, 'Litteraturen som motpol till vetenskapen', Sjöberg, *Litteraturens makt,* 131–53, warns of the danger inherent in modern literary theory that threatens to make the text secondary, and hence to diminish the power of literature. C.-G. Holmberg, '"Ord ha taggar." Maktkamp mellan författare och journalister', *ib.,* 199–211, considers the treatment of press and

---

* The place of publication of books is Stockholm unless otherwise indicated.

journalists in literary works, with reference to Haquin Spegel, Esaias Tegnér, Strindberg, and others.

2. THE MIDDLE AGES

S. Würth, 'Eufemia: deutsche Auftraggeberin schwedischer Literatur am norwegischen Hof', Paul, *Skandinavistik*, 269–81, considers Queen Eufemia and her involvement in the translation into Swedish of the three texts of the *Eufemiavisor*. W. Layher, 'Origins of the Old Swedish epic *Hertig Fredrik af Normandie*: a Middle Dutch link?', *TsSk*, 21:223–49, discusses the relationship between the 14th-c. Old Swedish text of one of the *Eufemiavisor* and its lost 13th-c. source.

3. FROM THE RENAISSANCE TO THE GUSTAVIAN AGE

A. Swanson, 'Eriks-visan. Disappearances of a song', *ScSt*, 72:49–62, argues that this patriotic song about Sweden's oldest political event originates in a 16th-c. Latin translation by Johannes Magnus of a well-known old song. Joachim Grage, *Chaotischer Abgrund und erhabene Weite. Das Meer in der skandinavischen Dichtung des 17. und 18. Jahrhunderts* (Palaestra, 311), Göttingen, Vandenhoeck & Ruprecht, 331 pp., diss. with a summary in English, examines the presence of the sea in 17th-c. and 18th-c. Scandinavian literature, concluding that it did not play a significant role until well into the 18th c. Reference is made to examples of baroque sea imagery in writers such as Lucidor and Samuel Columbus; analyses of both topographical and sentimental landscape poetry present changes in the sea motif; philosophical didactic verse on seafaring reflects a problem in the age of Enlightenment. The main part of the study deals with the sea as a subject of literary description in didactic poetry, starting with two Scandinavian verse epics on the creation of the world, the Dane Anders Arrebo's *Hexaëmeron* (1661) and Haquin Spegel's *Gudz Werk och Hwila* (1685).

BELLMAN, CARL MICHAEL. Torkel Stålmarck, *Bellman i verkligheten. Familjeliv, sällskapsliv, konstnärsliv*, Norstedts, 211 pp., examines in nine chapters the various circles and milieux B. frequented and their decisive influence on his writing. From his extensive knowledge of the period, Stålmarck gives a lucid introduction to B.'s life and time. A. Dvergsdal 'Den oppbyggelige Bellman? En studie over Bellmans epistler', *Edda*, 110–29, discusses the importance of religion in B.'s drinking songs.

BRENNER, SOPHIA ELISABETH. S. Müller, '"Herren sargar och läker, han slår och hans hand helar." Konfliktbewältigung in den autobiographischen Texten von Marta Hagman (1765), Sophia Elisabeth Brenner (1722) und Christina Regina vom Birchenbaum',

Skandinavistik, 30 : 1–20, integrates psychotherapeutical theories into an essentially philological analysis of three of the earliest autobiographies written by Swedish women.

HOLMSTRÖM, ISRAEL. Israel Holmsträm, *Samlade dikter*. 1. *Kärleksdikter, förnöjsamhetsvisor, sällskapspoesi, dansvisor, burleska dikter, fabler, gåtor, spådomar, epigram*, ed. Bernt Olsson, Barbro Nilsson, and Paula Henrikson (Svenska författare. Ny serie), Svenska Vitterhetssamfundet, 1999, 415 pp., is the first scholarly edition of H.'s collected poems; this first volume will be followed by a second, including his 'heavier' poetry, such as funeral poems and political poetry, a glossary of older terms and a bibliography for both volumes. Most of the poems remain only in transcripts; the editors have chosen to organize them according to genre, since it is impossible to establish their exact chronology, not to mention the meticulous work necessary to attribute them to H.

KELLGREN, JOHAN HENRIC. A. Swanson, 'Kellgren's libretto for *Aeneas i Karthago*', *ScSt*, 72 : 380–410.

LINNAEUS, CARL. Olof Dixelius, *Linnétraditionen i svensk litteratur. En kritisk översikt* (Filologiskt arkiv, 42), Kungl. Vitterhets Historie och Antikvitets Akademien, 64 pp., evaluates L. as a prose writer. As early as the mid-19th c. L. was established as a classic in Swedish literature thanks to his descriptions of Swedish regions. The study also looks at L.'s prose as a model, in so far as it had a generally stimulating effect on Swedish nature and travel descriptions from L.'s own pupils to the present day, including writers such as Strindberg and Harry Martinson.

STIERNHIELM, GEORG. **Stiernhielm 400 år. Föredrag vid internationellt symposium i Tartu 1998*, ed. Stig Örjan Ohlsson and Bernt Olsson (Konferenser, 50), Kungl. Vitterhets Historie och Antikvitets Akademien–Almqvist & Wiksell International, 368 pp., with summaries in Swedish, English, French, and German.

4. ROMANTICISM AND LIBERALISM

A. Olsson, 'Pendeln mellan nihilism och mystik (Stagnelius/Almqvist)', Olsson, *Läsningar*, 44–61, discusses the vacillation between nihilism and mysticism characteristic of modern poetry, and looks at its presence in the romantic writers Stagnelius and Almqvist. The whole volume, Olsson, *Läsningar*, is a comprehensive study that examines the tradition of 'poetic nihilism' in which the two extremes both attract and repulse each other. Stefan Johansson, *En omskriven historia. Svensk historisk roman och novell före 1867* (AUU, Studia Historica Upsaliensia, 193), Uppsala U.P., 226 pp., diss. with a summary in English, examines the Swedish historical novel and short story from

1828 to 1866; this new genre of prose fiction often rewrote history to suit liberal or conservative thinking during the reshaping of the nation in the 19th c. The most popular period is from 1600 onwards; conservative writers focused on medieval times, while the Viking Age was largely ignored. Towards the end of the period more than four out of five historical novels were written by women, now largely forgotten, as are their male counterparts apart from Almqvist and Rydberg. Ingrid Holmquist, *Salongens värld. Om text och kön i romantikens salongskultur*, Eslöv, Symposion, 276 pp., examines the cultural and social significance of the literary salon from a gender perspective; the focus is on the Uppsala salon of Malla Silfverstolpe as a semi-public intellectual and artistic centre frequented by the better-known romantic male and female writers alike. The study discusses the views on gender expressed by the leading male writers Atterbom, Geijer, and Almqvist; the unabridged MS of Silfverstolpe's memoirs gives further insight into the period and the roles of men and women. Petra Söderlund, *Romantik och förnuft. V.F. Palmblads förlag 1810–1830* (Avdelningen för litteratursociologi, SLIUU, 43), Hedemora, Gidlunds, 427 pp., diss. with a summary in English. Hanna Östholm, *Litteraturens uppodling. Läsesällskap och litteraturkritik som politisk strategi vid sekelskiftet 1800*, Hedemora, Gidlunds, 343 pp., diss. with a summary in English.

ALMQVIST, CARL JONAS LOVE. B. Romberg, 'Inledning', pp. vii-xxvi of C. J. L. Almqvist, *Amorina eller Historien om de fyra*, ed. and comm. Bertil Romberg (Samlade Verk, 18), Svenska Vitterhetssam-fundet–Almqvistsällskapet, xxvi + xxviii + 547 pp., the text-critical edition of the *Collected Works* in 51 volumes; the introduction discusses origin, reception and research. The text is based on the original edition of 1822; the *Collected Works* are published on the Internet: < http://svenska.gu.se/vittsam/almqvist.html >. J. Almer, *Variation på götiskt tema. En studie i C. J. L. Almqvists Sviavigamal*, Gothenburg U.P., xiii + 195 pp., diss. with a summary in German, is a study of the most extensive work of Gothic fiction by A.; although he uses the same mythical material from Snorri Sturluson as the romantics, he interprets it in an entirely different and more ironical way, thus criticizing conventional nationalism. The analysis defines A.'s version of Gothicism and explores its aesthetic and ideological implications, also reflected in his theoretical writings at the same time. Id., 'Almqvists *Strountes* — ett fragment med kommentar', *Samlaren*, 120, 1999[2000]:85–93, argues that A.'s fragment is a joke with a serious meaning; it has been linked mainly with Gunnar Ekelöf's collection of poems *Strountes* from 1955; so far, research into A.'s original fragment has been largely non-existent. B. Romberg, 'Gick det an? Kring Det-går-an-debatten och dess följder', Sjöberg, *Litteraturens makt*, 59–78, considers the debate that followed in the wake of the novel *Det går an*, first published in 1839. J. Mjöberg, 'Almqvist och hans profana motstycke till Notre-Dame', Mjöberg, *Arkitektur*, 227–40, discusses similar architectural patterns in Victor Hugo and *Drottningens juvelsmycke*. D. Götsch, 'Gewalt und Begehren in C. J. L. Almqvists Roman *Drottningens juvelsmycke*', Paul, *Skandinavistik*, 315–23. N. Selmer, 'C. J. L. Almqvists *Amorina* und der Umgang mit K/kriminellen und I/irren Texten', *ib.*, 359–65. G. Mose, 'Papirlapperne i lakskrinet — C. J. L. Almqvist og det romantiske fragment', *Edda*, 37–47, on the remarkable text 'Anecdoticon magnum almaquianum' that can be read as the 'Poetica Magna Almaquiana'. J. Staberg, 'Fantasins gränssnitt. C. J. L. Almqvists konstsaga *Guldfågel i paradis*', *TidLit*, 29.1:48–63, discusses A.'s work on the intersection of medial, social, and educational practices of the time.

BREMER, FREDRIKA. Å. Arping, 'Inledning', pp. v-xxvi of Fredrika Bremer, *Famillen H****, ed. and comm. Åsa Arping (Svenska författare. Ny serie), Svenska Vitterhetssamfundet, xxvi + 242 pp., discusses B.'s comments on her first novel, its origin, publication, reception, and research to date; this is the first text-critical edition of the supposedly earliest Swedish middle-class realistic novel, published anonymously in 1830–31. C. and L. Burman, 'Inledning', pp. v-xxxv of Fredrika Bremer, *Grannarne*, ed. and comm. Carina and Lars Burman (Svenska författare. Ny serie), Svenska Vitterhetssamfundet, xxxv + 417 pp., the first text-critical edition of B.'s fourth novel from 1837; the introduction discusses its popularity in Sweden as well as abroad, especially in the English-speaking world, presents a summary of the novel, its origin, publication, reception, and research to date. *Parnass*, no. 3, is devoted to B., and includes: C. Burman, 'Fredrika och det djuriska' (8–11), with comments on *Grannarne*.

FLYGARE-CARLÉN, EMILIE. J. Svedjedal, 'Inledning', pp. v-xxv of Emilie Carlén, *Pål Värning. En skärgårds-ynglings äfventyr*, ed. and comm. Johan Svedjedal (Svenska författare. Ny serie), Svenska Vitterhetssamfundet, xxv + 298 pp., is the first text-critical edition of F.'s tenth novel written in 1844; the introduction discusses her early literary career, the themes of the novel, origin, reception, and research to date. *Parnass*, no. 1, is devoted to F.

GEIJER, ERIK GUSTAF. H. Engdahl, 'Erik Gustaf Geijer', pp. 165–72 of *Svenska Akademiens Handlingar*, 26, 1999[2000], Svenska Akademien–Norstedts, 172 + 57 pp. Anders Lundahl, *Erik Gustaf Geijer — Filosofen*, Hedemora, Nya Doxa, 1999, 283 pp., stresses the originality of G.'s synthesis of aesthetics and religion, and argues in this penetrating study of his philosophical thinking and achievements that G. was primarily a philosopher. Since there are apparently not too many specialist studies of this aspect of G., this book is a useful complement to literary evaluations.

KNORRING, SOPHIE VON. T. Kessler Agdler, 'Inledning', pp. v–xvii of Sophie von Knorring, *Illusionerna*, ed. and comm. Theres Kessler Agdler (Svenska författare. Ny serie), Svenska Vitterhetssamfundet, xvii + 201 pp., is the first text-critical edition of the 1836 novel, considered to be K.'s masterpiece; the introduction follows the same pattern as in other volumes in the series: it presents a summary of the novel, its origin, publication, and reception, and research to date.

RUNEBERG, JOHAN LUDVIG. R. Norrman, 'Varför är Sven Dufva tvehänt?', *Samlaren*, 120, 1999[2000]: 56–72.

RYDBERG, VIKTOR. B. Sjöberg, '"En gestalt insvept i svart kaftan." Viktor Rydbergs kyrkokritik', Sjöberg, *Litteraturens makt*, 95–110, discusses R.'s criticism of dogmatic Lutheran faith in his novel *Fribytaren på Östersjön* (1857).

STAGNELIUS, ERIK JOHAN. C. O. Hultén, 'Stagnelius och Jung-frun', pp. 3–13 of Erik Johan Stagnelius, *Thorsten fiskare*, Lund, Ellerströms–Sällskapet Erik Johan Stagnelii vänner, 72 pp., discusses previous plans for publishing S.'s farcical play in the early 1950s with modernistic illustrations. L. Vinge, 'Thorsten fiskare — ett Adams barn från Öland', *ib.*, 55–71, comments on this surprisingly light-hearted fairy play. P. Henrikson, 'Frukter åt döden. Riddartornet och den tragiska genren hos Stagnelius', *Samlaren*, 120, 1999[2000]: 26–55, discusses one of the four dramas that S. called *sorgspel*.

WALLIN, JOHAN OLOF. Håkan Möller, **Den wallinska dikten. Från informatorsåren till Dödens ängel*, Uppsala, Lunne böcker, 553 pp., diss. with a summary in English.

5. THE LATER NINETEENTH CENTURY

Anna Nordenstam, *Tidskrift för hemmet. Upptakt och lansering* (MLIGU, 25), 67 pp., discusses the launch of the journal *Tidskrift för hemmet* in 1859, the first women's rights journal in Scandinavia; it is still published, being known from 1886–1913 as *Dagny*, and then as *Hertha*. The privately owned correspondence between the first two editors, Sophie Adlersparre (Esselde) and Rosalie Olivecrona, is the principal source of information. Lars Westman, *Den lysande epoken*, Bilda, 162 pp., is a colourful portrayal of writers and artists in the neoromantic period of the 1890s in the provinces of Värmland and Dalarna; it discusses the writings of Gustaf Fröding and Selma Lagerlöf against their home and cultural background, and the works of contemporary painters and sculptors.

BENEDICTSSON, VICTORIA. C. Lindén, 'Mellan man och kvinna. Ernst Ahlgren och fröken Key — en kärlekshistoria', *TidLit*, 29.2:3–28, discusses the novel *Fru Marianne* (1887) in the light of B.'s and Ellen Key's views on male and female sexuality: both man and woman need to develop in order to transcend their traditional gender roles and achieve real love.

ENGSTRÖM, ALBERT. *Årsbok 2000*, ed. Esse Jansson (Albert Engström Sällskapet, 19), Grisslehamn, 157 pp., includes, apart from the usual splendid drawings by E.: R. S. Samuelsson, on a remarkable philological letter from Strindberg to E. (21–30); H. Lång, on E. and Greek and Latin classics (67–79); L. Jansson, on E.'s visit to the Soviet Union in 1923 (87–102).

FRÖDING, GUSTAF. Peter Graves, *Fröding, Burns and Scott*, Edinburgh, Lockharton, 139 pp., is a stimulating read, and a study of F.'s relations with the two Scottish authors. It presents F.'s poems written with Scott in mind, and the 'superb' translations F. made of 15 of Burns's best known songs. In addition to the original texts with complete translations, the volume includes a critical commentary on text and music of the Burns songs and translations.

HEIDENSTAM, VERNER VON. *Parnass*, no. 4, is devoted to H.

KEY, ELLEN. Ingela Bendt, *Ett hem för själen. Ellen Keys Strand*, Bonniers, 158 pp., makes K. come alive in this beautifully produced volume with striking colour photographs by the author; it is a sensitive depiction of how K.'s personality and aesthetic ideals put their stamp of harmony on every little detail in and around the mansion K. built in 1910, her home until her death in 1926. C. Lindén, 'Moderlighetens metaforer', Pettersson, *Litteratur*, 149–59, on K. and Nietzsche. See also BENEDICTSSON, VICTORIA.

KLEVE, STELLA. J. Björklund, '"Raffinerad, abnorm och blaserad." En annorlunda samhällskritik i Stella Kleves *Berta Funcke*', *TidLit*, 29, 3–4:134–44.

LAGERLÖF, SELMA. Lars Wolf, *Att möta sina domare. Selma Lagerlöfs väg till Gösta Berlings saga och bokens mottagande* (Litteratur och samhälle, 34.1), Avdelningen för litteratursociologi, MLIUU, 175 pp., with an abstract in English, discusses the reception of L.'s first book in 28 contemporary reviews on the basis of Pierre Bourdieu's field theory. *NT*, 76.2, was published in cooperation with the L. Society; it presents papers given at the society's colloquium in 1999 on three important Nordic women writers, namely L., Karen Blixen, and Sigrid Undset, and includes U.-B. Lagerroth, 'Nordism i Selma Lagerlöfs liv och författarskap' (129–46). T. Soila, 'Desire disavowed in Victor Sjöström's *The Phantom Carriage*', *Steene Vol.*, 159–75, discusses the 1921 film version of L.'s *Körkarlen*. Margareta Brandby-Cöster, *Vägen mellan himmel och jord. Underströmmar av luthersk livsförståelse i Selma Lagerlöfs författarskap* (Karlstad University Studies, 2000.28), Karlstad U.P., 141 pp., licentiate diss., explores L.'s Lutheran heritage as an integral part of her social background. From a theological viewpoint it argues that L.'s writings and philosophy of life include undercurrents of Lutheran thinking, irrespective of whether she was religious or not.

STRINDBERG, AUGUST. Jan Myrdal, *Johan August Strindberg* (Litterära profiler), Natur och Kultur, 253 pp., argues that S.'s very Swedishness has prevented a truly international breakthrough in genres other than the drama. This personally coloured and no doubt controversial biography rejects the national monument label and depicts instead an in every sense very normal human being, warts and all. It even dares to discuss S.'s antisemitism in the early 1880s, and claims that S.'s new literary orientation in the late 1890s was due mainly to the agony he suffered when his second wife had left him. James Spens, *'I Musernas bidé.' En essä om Strindbergs 'fula' poesi omkring 1883* (AUSt, Stockholm Studies in History of Literature, 44), Almqvist & Wiksell International, 133 pp., together with the commented edition of S.'s *Collected Works*, vol. 15, 1995, diss. with a summary in English, argues that the poems from around 1883 in the 'Sårfeber' section of *Dikter på vers och prosa* and *Sömngångarnätter på vakna dagar, 1–4*, are part of a larger project; it aims to break the hegemony of idealistic poetry and develop a new realistic or 'ugly' poetic form. While the 'Sårfeber' poems do not suggest any new ideals to replace the old, those in *Sömngångarnätter* ask which of the alternatives, old idealism or modern materialism, can provide an answer to the 'enigma of life'; finally S.'s poetical project came to a dead end and was overtaken by later events. *Europe*, 858, is a special issue; 228 of its c. 330 pp. are devoted to S. The wide-ranging essays by French and Swedish scholars mainly stress other aspects of S. than the dramatist, de-theatricalizing S., as the preface suggests. Catharina Söderberg, *Strindberg som trädgårdsmästare*, Bonniers, 144 pp., presents S. the enthusiastic and expert gardener through extracts from his books, letters, and manuscripts, as well as through contemporary gardening advice and splendid photographs. This lavish book is a useful reference work for texts in which S. depicts the countryside throughout the year. *Strindbergiana*, ed. Birgitta Steene (Strindbergssällskapet, 15), Atlantis, 192 pp., recapitulates events in the aftermath of the 150th anniversary celebrations of S.'s birth. It also includes essays on the dramas *Till Damaskus I*, *Toten-Insel*, and *Ett drömspel*, on S. and international law, his children as adults, and the ideal of the new woman linked to his short story 'Nybyggnad' in *Utopier i verkligheten* from 1885. Stig Norrman, **Jag ser din musik. Musik som uttrycksmedel i August Strindbergs prosa* (Studier i musikvetenskap, 10), Stockholm U.P., 238 pp., diss. with a summary in English. K. Dahlbäck, 'Inledning', pp. 5–24 of August Strindberg, *Min eld är den största. Brev 1858–1912*, ed. and comm. Kerstin Dahlbäck, Ordfront, 1999, 298 pp., argues in this commented selection of 272 of his letters that not mere quantity, but also literary quality makes S.'s letters his main genre. S. used his correspondence as a means of developing his literary style, keenly aware not only of its biographical but also of its literary value. R. Shideler, 'Strindberg's struggle', pp. 99–132 of Ross Shideler, *Questioning the Father. From Darwin to Zola, Ibsen, Strindberg, and Hardy*, Stanford U.P., 1999, ix + 226 pp., discusses the struggle for survival of dominant male characters within the book's general context of undermining the patriarchal family. The chapter concentrates on S.'s transformation of late 19th-c. Darwinistic ideas and the growing women's movement into novels and family dramas related to the questioning of the father, the battle of the sexes, and its ravages on the traditional family. After a brief discussion of *The Son of a Servant*, it examines *The Father*, *Miss Julie*, and *The Creditors*, before turning to three later dramas, *The Dance of Death* and two of the 'Chamber Plays', *Stormy Weather* and *The Pelican*, in the final phase of S.'s lifelong preoccupation with husbands and fathers who resist the wiles of liberated women. I.-S. Ewbank, '"Where do I find my homeland?" Ibsen, Strindberg, and exile', *Steene Vol.*, 9–29. K. Naumann-Magnusson, '"Es war Arkadien." August Strindbergs Schweizer Aufenthalte 1884–1886', *Neue Zürcher Zeitung*, no.12:79, is an informative article on S. in Switzerland in the 1880s, published in connection with an exhibition in Zurich. G. Rossholm. 'Axel och Axel — Strindbergs användning av perspektiv i *En dåres försvarstal*', *TsSk*, 21:195–221. P. Bukowski, 'Die Maske des Vaters. Ein Deutungsversuch von August Strindbergs *Fadren*', *Edda*, 320–33. S. Flühmann, 'Von der "chora" gejagt. Das symbolische Verbrechen in August Strindbergs *Inferno*', Paul, *Skandinavistik*, 305–13. A.-C. Gavel Adams, 'Delacroix's murals in Église Saint-Sulpice and Strindberg's *Jacob wrestles* and *To Damascus I*', *Steene Vol.*, 43–61. A.-C. Harvey, 'The theatrical compulsion of Strindberg's *Carl XII*', *ib.*, 63–90. O. Reinert, 'Meaning compounded: Strindberg's *Charles XII* and the question of genre', *ib.*, 91–104. J. Mjöberg, 'Strindbergs *Dödsdansen* och fängelse-symbolen', Mjöberg, *Arkitektur*, 76–80, discusses the importance of this drama for tracing architecture as a symbolic pattern in literary works. M. M. Roy, 'History revisited and rewritten: August Strindberg, Magnus Smek, and Heliga Birgitta', *Steene Vol.*, 105–18, on how S. modified his portrayals of Magnus Eriksson and Saint Birgitta. Conny Svensson, **Strindberg om världshistorien*, Hedemora, Gidlunds, 285 pp. + 8 pls, with a summary in English, discusses S.'s treatment of world history in *Historiska miniatyrer*, 1905, an optimistic experiment that failed; he finally returned to the theme and a pessimistic outlook in the blue books. Hans-Göran Ekman, *Strindberg and the Five Senses. Studies in Strindberg's Chamber Plays*, London–New Brunswick, NJ, Athlone, xii + 202 pp. + 24 pls, is the English translation of the Swedish original, published in 1997 (see *YWMLS*, 59:912). Ekman writes, 'The so-called chamber plays [. . .], of which *The Ghost Sonata* is the most challenging example, belong to those works by Strindberg that have reached beyond the borders of his native country and played an important role in the development of modern international drama.' Terry John Converse, *The Psychology of the Grotesque in August Strindberg's 'The Ghost Sonata'* (Studies in Comparative Literature, 24), Lewiston, NY, Mellen, 1999, 256 pp., applies Jungian psychology in his argument that S.'s dream play conception and grotesque imagery are inextricably linked; together they create 'a very definite, symbolic and thematic coherence', the perfection of S.'s dream play concept. It is hardly reassuring that the most 'recent' of books and articles listed in the bibliography was published back in 1984. Egil Törnqvist, *Strindberg's 'The Ghost Sonata'. From Text to Performance*, Amsterdam U.P., 269 pp., is the first monograph on S.'s play and the most memorable stagings of it; a 'substantial' part of this book has appeared in earlier publications, but all articles/chapters have been thoroughly revised for this book. It analyses the source text, discusses translation problems in English and American target texts, refers to some significant stage productions and to adaptations for radio and television, and includes a rehearsal diary and a transcription of Ingmar Bergman's 1973 production. K. Knape. '*Toten-Insel* — mehr als ein Fragment. Metaphysische Gedanken in August Strindbergs Drama *Toten-Insel*', *TsSk*, 21:165–94. E. Törnqvist, 'Delad livssyn. Ibsen, Strindberg och deras regissörer', Bråkenhielm, *Modernitetens ansikten*, 361–72.

6. The Twentieth Century

Finlands svenska litteraturhistoria. Andra delen: 1900-talet. Uppslagsdel, ed. Clas Zilliacus, Helsinki, Svenska Litteratursällskapet i Finland–Atlantis, 512 pp., the second volume of this two-volume literary history, covers the 20th c. and includes a reference section with brief biographical notes and indexes for the whole work (see *YWMLS*, 61:821). The second volume devotes itself to today's Finland-Swedish minority literature as it developed in the early years of the last century; it discusses present relations with Finnish Finland and Sweden of a literature under threat, yet highly treasured and nurtured. A main aim is to explain why it exists at all, in particular when one bears in mind that Finnish literature had caught up with Swedish in volume and significance towards the end of the 19th

c. The emphasis is on periods, ideas and genres, not least those genres that have been neglected hitherto, such as popular literature and provincial writing. Individual writers are not portrayed in one single chapter, but appear in several main entries under various chapter headings. Johan Lundberg, *En evighet i rummets former gjuten. Dekadenta och symbolistiska inslag i Sven Lidmans, Anders Österlings och Sigfrid Siwertz lyrik 1904–1907*, Eslöv, Symposion, 320 pp., argues that modern literature in the period *c.* 1900 has been marginalized, not least because the writers themselves distanced themselves from their early symbolist, decadent, and seemingly unworldly poetry. The study reveals a largely overlooked central line in Swedish poetry that runs from the early 20th-c. symbolist poets to those of today. There is a chapter on each of the three writers: 'Sven Lidman och den kluvna verkligheten' (54–123); 'Anders Österling och den lyriska hemkomsten' (123–86); 'Sigfrid Siwertz och diktens kristallisering' (187–259). Marta Ronne, *Två världar — ett universitet. Svenska skönlitterära universitetsskildringar 1904–1943. En genusstudie* (Avdelningen för littertursociologi, 44, SLIUU), 333 pp., diss. with a summary in English, is a comparative gender study of the two different worlds in male and female prose fiction 1904–43 about life at the universities of Lund and Uppsala. Reference is made to influential historical and sociological factors in the 19th c., to Shirley Ardener's theory of gender models and power and to Jürgen Habermas's categories of 'public' and 'private'. The most significant difference is, it is argued, that women writers are more concerned than men with the private sphere, while men favour topics that relate to public and official aspects of university life. Bo Svensén, *The Swedish Academy and the Nobel Prize in Literature*, Norstedts–Svenska Akademien, 85 pp., is a brief presentation of the history of the Swedish Academy and its role today, not least in the awarding of the Nobel Prize for literature.

Olle Thörnvall, *En gång i staden*, Lund, Ellerströms, 168 pp., presents five Stockholm writers from the last century, now forgotten: Hans Magnus Nordlindh was accidentally shot and killed by Henning Berger; Sven Löfgren's first successful novel in the early 1930s did not fulfil its promise; Ragnar Bengtsson never became one of the leading 1940s poets; Gösta Pettersson wrote prose in the 1940s and 1950s, and Peter Lindforss's poetry in the 1970s and 1980s. Magdalena Wasilewska-Chmura, *Musik, metafor, modernism. En linje i den svenska modernismens poetologiska reflexion* (AUSt, Stockholm Studies in History of Literature, 41), Almqvist & Wiksell International, 283 pp., diss. with a summary in English, is a meta-interart study that examines the discussion on lyrical modernism in the 1930s and 1940s to create a 'new' poetry through musical terms. With reference to Gunnar Ekelöf and the 1940s' generation of poets, it argues that 'references to music are a metaphor of new formal solutions in modernist poetry'. The musical terminology does not identify poetry with music; it is used merely to describe literary phenomena that had as yet no descriptive formula. A. Olsson, in the sixth major section of his book, 'Negationens linje i modern svensk poesi', Olsson, *Läsningar*, 235–423, discusses negation in six poets: Diktonius, Ekelöf, Södergran, Trotzig, Tuominen, and Vennberg (see individual authors). P. Tenngart, 'Ungdomskravaller och romantisk poesi. Två försök till revolt i det tidiga 1950–talets Sverige', Sjöberg, *Litteraturens makt*, 181–96, discusses the poetry of the 1950s, in particular Paul Andersson. Lena Malmberg, *Från Orfeus till Eurydike. En rörelse i samtida svensk lyrik*, Lund, Ellerströms, 266 pp., diss. with a summary in English, examines contemporary poetry in the period 1974–95, involving the return to the Orphic myth after the retreat in the 1960s, and the new focus on Eurydice as an emblem of the present time. On the basis of close readings, it discusses the treatment of the myth in poems by Katarina Frostenson, Arne Johnsson, Ann Jäderlund, Birgitta Lillpers, Jesper Svenbro, and Bruno K. Öijer; it also considers differences in male and female writers' treatment of the subject.

Ohlsson, *Läst*, discusses how film has influenced novels by Hjalmar Bergman, Stig Dagerman, Per Gunnar Evander, Gösta Gustaf-Jansson, Stig Larsson, and Vilgot Sjöman; they deal with various aspects of film, and the narrative structures are filmlike, 'filmicalized projection' (see individual authors). The introductory section analyses a text in Henning Berger's collection of stories *Films* (1914) as an example. L. Larsson, 'Att ta texten på allvar. Feministisk litteraturkritik och litteraturvetenskaplig förändring', Sjöberg, *Litteraturens makt*, 235–41, advocates a feministic approach as an alternative to the kind of research that looks only at the formal character of the text. Bråkenhielm, *Modernitetens ansikten*, is the result of a three-year Nordic interdisciplinary research project, involving departments of literature and theology across Sweden, Norway, and Finland; it considers how Nordic 20th-c. literature has depicted ideologies against the background of developments and changes in modern society. In addition to introductory essays and those on individual writers, the anthology includes: J. Ingvarsson, 'Doktor Gorks manuskript. Några nedslag i den nordiska prosans förhållande till media 1965–72' (327–42). Pettersson, *Litteratur*, includes papers given at a symposium on conceptual aspects of 20th-c. literature arranged by the Department of Literature and Nordic Languages at the University of Umeå in 1998. Cristine Sarrimo, *När det personliga blev politiskt. 1970–talets kvinnliga bekännelse och självbiografi*, Eslöv, Symposion, 246 pp., diss. with a summary in English, is a study of confessional and autobiographical feminist literature in the 1970s that reflect the political ideology at the time. The self-portraits of the writers concerned — Kerstin Thorvall, Sun Axelsson, Kerstin Strandberg, Kerstin Bergström, and Åsa Nelvin — raise the question of how the individual relates to her background from an existential, ideological, and confessional point of view. *TidLit*, 29.1, is devoted to new approaches to literature through modern media technology. J. Olsson, ' "SLPRLNTHGTÄAÄA." Röst, skrift & medier i den konkreta poesin', *ib.*, 29–47. *TidLit*, 29.3–4, is a special issue on literary scholarship in the 21st c. *ScSt*, 72.3, is devoted to the 20th-c. Swedish novel. *OB*, no. 4–5, is a special issue on Scandinavian prose and criticism.

Ulla Lundqvist, **Kulla-Gulla i slukaråldern* (SSBI, 72), Rabén & Sjögren, 187 pp., with a summary in English, discusses from both a personal and analytical point of view what girls read in the mid-1900s. Maria Nikolajeva, *Bilderbokens pusselbitar*, Lund, Studentlitteratur, 307 pp., is a study of the picture book, along lines similar to the author's earlier study of children's books (see *YWMLS*, 60:843–44); it provides tools for examining and analysing picture books, and is primarily intended as a student handbook on the subject. Carl-Erik af Geijerstam, *Dag för dag. Essäer och minnen*, Bonniers, 184 pp., includes essays on Vilhelm Ekelund's aphorisms, on the correspondence with Werner Aspenström in 1996 shortly before the latter's death, and on writings for both adults and children by Irmelin Sandman Lilius. *Svenska samtidsförfattare*, 2, Lund, Bibliotekstjänst, 154 pp., presents 15 contemporary writers, previously introduced in individual folders in the series 'Författarporträtt' (1997–99). Gabriella Håkansson and Jonas Thente, *20 bästa .doc*, ed. Stephen Farran-Lee (Doc, no. 9), Norstedts, 251 pp., is an anthology of the supposedly 20 best new prose writers of the 1990s. In addition to the selected texts there are brief presentations of each writer. P. E. Ljung, 'Sverige i romanen: svenska storsäljare', Sjöberg, *Litteraturens makt*, 113–27, considers the reasons for the success of a number of recent best-sellers. B. Widegren, 'Romanens kris — men inte läsandets. Svensk litteratur under 1999', *NT*, 76:319–27. G. Widén, 'I skuggan av Kalevala. Finlandssvensk litteratur 1999', *NT*, 76:289–94, argues that the new translation of the *Kalevala* into Swedish by Lars and Mats Huldén is the year's most important event in Finland-Swedish writing. A.-L. Möller, 'Bland ord-alkoholister och -arkitekter. Finlandssvensk poesiöversikt 1999', *FT*, 354–67. C. Sundström, 'Om att skriva, läsa och resa. Finlandssvensk prosaöversikt anno 1999', *ib.*, 368–81. T. Pettersson, 'Expansion och selektion: den finlandssvenska litteraturhistoriens 1900–tal', *ib.*, 382–99. *Scandinavica*, 39.1, is a special film issue and includes: E. Hedling, 'Swedish cinema alters history. *Ingeborg Holm* and the poor laws debate' (47–64), which discusses Victor Sjöström's silent classic from 1913, based on a play by Nils Krok in 1906. M. B. Sandberg, 'Maternal gesture and photography in Victor Sjöström's *Ingeborg Holm*', Steene Vol., 131–57. J. H. Swahn, 'BLM in retrospect', *SBR*, no.1:2–5, on the demise of a Swedish institution; the last editor of *Bonniers Litterära Magasin*, founded in 1932 and closed down at the end of 1999, writes about the journal that was at the centre of literary discussion in Sweden for most of the 20th c. *SBR*, no.2:2–13, includes tributes to Joan Tate, one of the most remarkable and productive English translators of Scandinavian and especially Swedish literature, who died in June 2000. R. Greenwald, *ib.*, 26–34, and E. Dickens, *ib.*, 35–37, discuss why so few English translations are published of Swedish and other Scandinavian books. *SBR*, Supplement, is a special issue on Swedish literary prizes; more than a hundred are awarded annually and listed here with the names of the last three prizewinners in the 20th c. There is also a selection of brief presentations and extracts in translation of their work.

ahlin, lars.   M. Essunger, 'Frihet och fångenskap. Om rörligheten i Lars Ahlins *Natt i marknadstältet* och François Mauriacs *Ormboet*', Bråkenhielm, *Modernitetens ansikten*, 269–89. A. Tyrberg, 'Kropp som text, text som anrop. Lars Ahlins etiska estetik speglad i den bibliska liknelsens form', Pettersson, *Litteratur*, 168–79.

alfons, sven.   P. Wästberg, 'Sven Alfons assemblage', Wästberg, *Essäer*, 195–200, discusses A. the artist.

aspenström, werner.   P. Wästberg, 'Det flyktigas och det sällsammas poet', Wästberg, *Essäer*, 137–70, is a sensitive appreciation of A.'s qualities.

beckman, erik.   M. Haglund, 'Den nervösa staden. Erik Beckman, David Bailey och Londons blandverkligheter', *OB*, no.2–3:32–47, compares Bailey's photographs with B.'s 1965 novel *Hertigens kartonger*. M. Florin, 'Efterord', pp. 69–70, 'Efterefterord', p. 71 of Eric Beckman, *Kvalstervägen. Pjäs i två akter* (Erik Beckman-sällskapet, 4), Borås, 1999, 71 pp., gives advice on how to read the drama, here published for the first time, and comments on why it was never performed in the mid-1980s at the Stockholm Dramatic Theatre. *Till händelser i livet knyter sig inget som helst språk*, ed. Sven Hansell (Erik Beckman-sällskapet, 5), Borås, 102 pp., includes papers given at a symposium in 1999 (others published in *OB*, 1999, no. 6) and later articles: C. Ekholm, 'På tröskeln — Erik Beckmans deklarativa period' (9–38); E. Ström, 'Lekkamrater, kärleksgubbar. Om Erik Beckmans kritik' (46–53); A. Hallberg, 'Herrhultsmysteriet fyra decennier senare — eller: Var börjar Inlandsbanan?' (54–63); S. Hansell, 'Bergslagsaraberna i Lindesberg' (94–101), on the novel *Kameler dricker vatten* (1971).

Literature 855

BENGTSSON, FRANS G. *Frans G. Bengtsson-studier*, IV. *Lyriskt tjugotal i Lund*, ed. Svante Nordin (Frans G. Bengtsson-sällskapet, 12), Lund, 1999, 23 pp, includes papers given at a B. Society colloquium in 1997 on poets of the 1920s in Lund: Gabriel Jönsson, Sigfrid (Tristan) Lindström, Hjalmar Gullberg, Karl Ragnar Gierow, and B. *Frans G. Bengtsson-studier*, V. *Frans G. Bengtsson, Hérédia och vi*, ed. Svante Nordin (Frans G. Bengtsson-sällskapet, 13), Lund, 32 pp., includes L. Strand, on B.'s French model, José-Maria de Hérédia (5–10); S. Fjelner, on B. and music (23–26); S. Nordin, on a hitherto unknown collection of letters by B., now in the Lund University Library (27–29).

BERGMAN, HJALMAR. J. Mjöberg, 'De hemliga rummen hos Hjalmar Bergman och Kerstin Ekman', Mjöberg, *Arkitektur*, 81–94, discusses secret rooms in the novels *Farmor och Vår Herre*, *En stad av ljus*, and *Häxringarna*. A. Ohlsson, '"med ögat, icke med örat." Hjalmar Bergmans *Farmor och Vår Herre*', Ohlsson, *Läst*, 65–101, discusses the influence of film techniques in the novel, particularly noticeable in the narration. **'Ty utan en stark underström av leende, självironiskt lättsinne finns intet dådkraftigt, intet verkligt allvar.' Texter av och om Hjalmar Bergman* (Hjalmar Bergman Samfundet, 13), Örebro, 174 pp.

BEXELL, EVA. P. Grive, 'Farmor säger att farfar är i himlen. En läsning av Eva Bexells författarskap', *Horisont*, 47.1:51–59, argues for a new appraisal of this children's writer.

BJÖRLING, GUNNAR. L. Friberg, '"Röstens ton, ansiktets drag" — etik och politik hos Gunnar Björling', *HLS*, 75:93–133 (SSLF, 624), discusses the poems '1918' in B.'s collection *Korset och löftet* (1925) and 'van der Lubbe' (1934).

BOYE, KARIN. *Karin Boye, Ett verkligt jordiskt liv. Brev*, ed. and comm. Paulina Helgeson, Bonniers, 346 pp., is a collection of B.'s letters, never published before, with the exception of those to Erik Mesterton. Published for the centenary of her birth, the volume includes 259 letters in chronological order from 1914 to April 1941. The title is a reminder of B.'s intensely active life on earth, and the letters testify to her involvement in Swedish cultural life. J. Mattlar, 'Karin Boyes framtidsroman *Kallocain* som politiskt slagträ', *Horisont*, 47.1:17–21. M. Morén, 'Lyrikens underjordiska språk. Om Karin Boyes världsbild', Bråkenhielm, *Modernitetens ansikten*, 255–68.

DAGERMAN, STIG. A. Ohlsson, '"Bio är bra, bättre än böcker." Stig Dagermans *Bränt barn*', Ohlsson, *Läst*, 102–39, argues that the film medium plays an even bigger role in this novel than in Hjalmar Bergman's *Farmor och Vår Herre*.

DANIELSSON, KENT. A.-L. Möller, '"Gälrörelser under min hud." En jungiansk läsning av diktsamlingen *Anna Valderina Ängelfisk*', *FT*,

327–38, examines the Åland poet's second collection of poems of 1997.

DANIELSSON, TAGE. B. Hedén, 'Humorn som vapen. Tage Danielssons monolog om kärnkraft', Sjöberg, *Litteraturens makt*, 157–162, discusses the impact of humour in D.'s 1979 monologue about the Harrisburg nuclear disaster.

DELBLANC, SVEN. Torbjörn Forslid, *Fadern, sonen och berättaren. Minne och narrativitet hos Sven Delblanc*, Nora, Nya Doxa, 260 pp., diss. with a summary in English, is that rare commodity, an eminently readable and enjoyable doctoral thesis. It ranges widely over most of D.'s books to examine the figures of the Father, the Son and the Narrator; D.'s problematic relationship with his despotic father was fully unmasked when the autobiography *Livets ax* was published in 1991. The study considers at length the relationship between memory and narrativity as the theoretical framework for the examination of the father figure, not primarily from a biographical point of view, but more importantly as a symbolically charged concept. D.'s posthumously broadcast television play *Hemresa* (1993) projects a reconciliation in the father conflict. H. Blomqvist, 'Världsfursten och den dolde guden. Ontologier och gudsbilder i Sven Delblancs Samuelsvit', Bråkenhielm, *Modernitetens ansikten*, 200–16. Margareta Karlsson, *Tro, hopp och kärlek hos Sven Delblanc. Speglat i romanerna Kastrater, Speranza och Jerusalems natt* (Scripta Minora, 42), Växjö U.P., 1999, 45 pp., with an abstract in English, examines structural and thematic similarities in the three novels that make up 'Svartsynens trilogi'; it is argued that faith, hope, and charity give a joint thematic meaning to the novels of the trilogy of pessimism. J. Mjöberg, 'Allegoriska alternativ i Sven Delblancs Eremitkräftan', Mjöberg, *Arkitektur*, 58–64, discusses the strong links with architecture in the allegorical composition of the novel.

DIKTONIUS, ELMER. *Gudsöga, djävulstagg. Diktoniusstudier*, ed. Agneta Rahikainen, Marit Lindqvist, and Maria Antas (SSLF, 619), Helsinki, 233 pp., includes papers given at the centenary symposium of D.'s birth in 1996: T. Ritamäki, on D. as a contemporary writer in the 1932 novel *Janne Kubik* (29–41); O. Nordenfors, on D. and music (43–62); A. Olsson, on masking the ego in D.'s poetry (65–83); M. Lindqvist, on D. as a journalist in the 1930s (85–107); J. Larsson, on the rhythm in D.'s verse (109–27); R. Holmström, on D. and Hagar Olsson (129–42); I. Haag, on D.'s early writing (145–58); G. M. Imbur, on translating D., with comparative examples (161–204). A. Olsson, 'Titanens speglingar (Diktonius)', Olsson, *Läsningar*, 269–91.

EDBERG, ROLF. U.-B. Lagerroth, 'Det litterariserade budskapets makt. Reflexioner kring Rolf Edbergs ekosofiska författarskap',

Sjöberg, *Litteraturens makt*, 25–41, discusses E.'s 'ecosophical' writings on the delicate balance between humanity and the environment, and the impact of his three books *Spillran av ett moln* (1966), *Vid trädets fot* (1971), and *Brev till Columbus* (1973).

EDWARDSSON, ÅKE. C. Whittingham, 'Christian ritual and creed in Åke Edwardsson's *Gå ut min själ*, pp. 113–24 of *Crime Scenes. Detective Narratives in European Culture since 1945*, ed. Anne Mullen and Emer O'Beirne, Amsterdam–Atlanta, GA, Rodopi, vi + 325 pp., a collective volume that reflects the current interest in crime fiction; the essays in this collection are based on papers given at a conference in Exeter in 1997 entitled *The European Detective since 1945*. In this context E.'s novel of 1996 is presented, and its fundamental existential, ethical, and religious issues are explored.

EKELÖF, GUNNAR. Anders Mortensen, *Tradition och originalitet hos Gunnar Ekelöf*, Symposion, 488 pp., diss. with a summary in English, is an impressively authoritative discussion on the fundamental concepts of tradition and originality in E.; it argues that these seeming opposites are decisive for the development and full understanding of E.'s work, given his constant wrestling with them. Seven of the ten main chapters (apart from introductory comments and concluding reflections) are based on close readings of carefully selected key poems in chronological order in E.'s collections of poetry from 1932 until the early 1960s. They show not only the successive revision of E.'s attitude to tradition over the years, but also the central importance that the 'values of originality' have for his writing; he upholds and defends fiercely his own individual originality and integrity by both evading and overcoming any influence of his predecessors, and yet simultaneously honours a canon of 'elective affinities'. The concluding three chapters discuss the effects of E.'s problematic relationships with C. J. L. Almqvist, Arthur Rimbaud, and T. S. Eliot. A. Olsson, 'Att sjunga för ingenting (Ekelöf)', Olsson, *Läsningar*, 292–328. C. Kullberg, 'Det är inte detta som är. En komparativ studie av Stéphane Mallarmés "Sonnet en x" och Gunnar Ekelöfs "Absentia animi"', *Edda*, 48–65.

EKMAN, KERSTIN. R. Wright, 'Textual dialogue and the humanistic tradition. Kerstin Ekman's *Gör mig levande igen*', *ScSt*, 72 : 279–300, argues that E.'s concentration on language and form rather than plot allows her to enter a dialogue with Eyvind Johnson's *Krilon* trilogy. K. Ritter, 'Grenzfälle. Kerstin Ekmans *Händelser vid vatten*, Ulf Durlings *Tills döden förenar oss* und Jean Bolinders *Berättelse för herr Hugo* im Kontext der schwedischen Kriminalliteratur', Paul, *Skandinavistik*, 343–51, discusses three books that go beyond the narrow confines of the detective story genre. A. Surmatz, 'Auf-Lösungen: Anne Holts

Blind gudinne und Kerstin Ekmans *Händelser vid vatten'*, *ib.*, 377–95. See also BERGMAN, HJALMAR.

EKSTRÖM, JOHANNA. S. Death, 'Johanna Ekström: explorer in words and pictures', *SBR*, no. 1 : 6–9, introduces a versatile new writer and poet.

ENCKELL, RABBE. Louise Ekelund, *Rabbe Enckell. Gräshoppans och Orfeus diktare*, Ordfront–Svenska Humanistiska Förbundet, 1999, 263 pp., deals with the life and work of the youngest of the four main Finland-Swedish modernists. It follows in the wake of Mikael Enckell's three-volume biography of his father, and Ekelund's earlier books on E. up to 1946. It is the result of several years' study and friendship with E., and is an excellent presentation not only of his poetry, but also of other aspects of E. until his death in 1974, both as a painter and a stubborn outsider in the radical climate of the 1960s.

ENQUIST, PER OLOV. B. Claesson, ' "Det gives alltid något bättre än döden." ' Det rationella, sökande föregripandet och den trosbundna försoningen i Enquists *Musikanternas uttåg*. En teologisk tolkning', Bråkenhielm, *Modernitetens ansikten*, 98–118. Gunnar Syréhn, **Mellan sanningen och lögnen. Studier i Per Olov Enquists dramatik*, Almqvist & Wiksell International, 235 pp. + 16 pls, with a summary in English.

EVANDER, PER GUNNAR. A. Ohlsson, ' "att få inledningsbilden att komma i rörelse." ' Per Gunnar Evanders *Berättelsen om Josef'*, Ohlsson, *Läst*, 178–213, explores E.'s metafictive novel as an example of the film novel genre.

FOGELKLOU, EMILIA. Malin Bergman Andrews, **Emilia Fogelklou, människan och gärningen. En biografi*, Skellefteå, Artos, 1999, 359 pp.

FORSSTRÖM, TUA. H. H. Skei, 'Plumeria acutifolia, i regn. Om Tua Forsströms *Efter att ha tillbringat en natt bland hästar'*, *NLÅ*, 1998 : 9–14, on F.'s collection of poetry from 1997.

FROSTENSON, KATARINA. M. Wennerström Wohrne, 'Språk som murar och besvärjande sång. En jämförelse mellan Katarina Frostensons och Henri Michaux' språksyn', Bråkenhielm, *Modernitetens ansikten*, 290–306.

GRIPE, MARIA. Ying Toijer-Nilsson, **Skuggornas förtrogna. Om Maria Gripe* (SSBI, 71), Bonniers, 255 pp., with a summary in English.

GUSTAF-JANSON, GÖSTA. A. Ohlsson, ' "hur länge ska du filma den här gången?" ' Gösta Gustaf-Jansons . . . *blev jag dödligt kär'*, Ohlsson, *Läst*, 140–77, argues that G.'s book belongs to the film novel genre.

GUSTAFSSON, LARS. C. Oscarson, 'Literary castlings in *Bernard Foys tredje rockad'*, *ScSt*, 72 : 301–30, analyses his novel to elucidate G.'s postmodern aesthetics. Björn Andersson, *Att visa vägen ut. En studie av den estetiska praktiken i Lars Gustafssons Bröderna* (MLIGU, 24), 115 pp., is a study of G.'s third novel, published in 1960; it is part of a dissertation on G.'s early prose 1959–67. The aim of the study is to determine if and how the novel depicts human and social outsidership, and if and how to overcome it. E. Herrmann, 'Der Fall Caldwell — oder das kriminelle Potential der Gedanken. Eine Interpretation von Lars Gustafssons Roman *Historien med hunden*', Paul, *Skandinavistik*, 325–31. P. Wästberg, 'Lars Gustafssons poesi: lönndörrar mot det okända', Wästberg, *Essäer*, 201–09.

GYLLENSTEN, LARS. Lars Gyllensten, *Minnen, bara minnen*, Bonniers, 317 pp., is G.'s memoirs with portraits of writer colleagues, in particular during his years in the Swedish Academy from 1966 to 1989, when G. resigned from the Academy in protest against its stand on the Salman Rushdie affair. H. Bengtsson, 'Förtvivlan och försoning. En analys utifrån Lars Gyllenstens roman *Det himmelska gästabudet*', Bråkenhielm, *Modernitetens ansikten*, 217–37.

GÖRANSSON, LARS. P. Wästberg, 'På spaning efter Lars Göransson', Wästberg, *Essäer*, 171–94, discusses G.'s promising three collections of short stories in 1944–54.

HELLSING, LENNART. Lena Kåreland, *Gränsöverskridande. Carl Sandburg och Lennart Hellsing — författare för barn och vuxna* (Litteratur och Samhälle, 34.2), Avdelningen för litteratursociologi, MLIUU, 110 pp., with an abstract in English, is a comparative study of the American writer Carl Sandburg and his influence on H., against the background of modernism; both have written books for adults as well as for children. The study argues that Sandburg can be seen as a forerunner to H., and also discusses the issue of crosswriting; H. gradually stopped writing for adults, while Sandburg crossed over to children's literature and still remained a mainstream writer.

HERMODSSON, ELISABET. B. Ivarson Bergsten, 'Gränsöverskridandet som livshållning i Elisabet Hermodssons författarskap', Pettersson, *Litteratur*, 206–11.

HIRN, YRJÖ. J.-I. Lindén, 'Estetik för barn och professorer. Reflektioner kring Yrjö Hirn', *HLS*, 75 : 135–49 (SSLF, 624), discusses H., professor of aesthetics and modern literature before the Second World War, who never produced 'creative literature in the strict sense', but was nevertheless 'a man of letters in the best sense'.

HYLINGER, CLAES. O. Wikström, 'Det förbisedda. Om Claes Hylingers hyllande av vanligheten', Bråkenhielm, *Modernitetens ansikten*, 119–35.

ISAKSSON, ULLA. I. Littberger, 'Dikt och bikt: om fiktion och verklighet i Ulla Isakssons *Boken om E*', Pettersson, *Litteratur*, 206–11.

JANSSON, TOVE. Birgit Antonsson, *Det slutna och det öppna rummet. Om Tove Janssons senare författarskap*, Carlssons, 1999, 212 pp., discusses J.'s books for adult readers written after the Moomin books. It is argued that from 1971 the main theme is spiritual imprisonment as opposed to possible freedom and development; the cosy life in the closed room of the Moominvalley is no longer an ideal. Mirja Kivi, *Mumindalen. Figurerna som kom på museum*, Esbo, Schildts, a beautifully illustrated volume, presents the development of J., brief summaries of each of the Moomin books and their world, and the Mumindalen collection in Tammerfors; it also includes: B. Westin, 'Att se in i kungsrubinens hjärta — konstarternas samspel i muminberättelserna' (70–73), which argues that text and picture together are one of the keys to J.'s successful stories. M. Lagerspetz, 'Småtrollen och postmodernismens epistemologiska dilemma', *Horisont*, 47.1 : 32–40.

JERSILD, PER CHRISTIAN. R. Shideler, 'Jersild's Humpty-Dumpty Darwin', *ScSt*, 72 : 261–78, focuses on two book-length essays in order to comment on J.'s personal, moral, and scientific perspective on humanity in his 1998 novel *Sena sagor*.

JOHNSON, EYVIND. Per-Olof Mattsson, **Eyvind Johnson. Bibliografi* (Acta Bibliothecae R. Universitatis Upsaliensis, 36), AUU, Uppsala U.P.–Eyvind Johnson-sällskapet, 287 pp. Birgit Munkhammar, *Hemligskrivaren. En essä om Eyvind Johnson*, Bonniers, 203 pp., is a perceptive study on aspects of the personal and ideological background to the four parts of *Romanen om Olof* from the 1930s; it is argued that this period together with the early 1940s and the *Krilon* series is a creative peak. Munkhammar's research into J., her later articles, and references to the letters between Rudolf Värnlund and J., as yet unpublished, make this critical 'essay' a valuable contribution to J. studies. R.-E. Sjöström, 'Finlandsvännen Eyvind Johnson', *Horisont*, 47.3 : 56–63. Ö. Lindberger, 'Eyvind Johnson och inbillningens värld', *NT*, 76 : 421–27, is a paper given at a symposium on J. and the modernistic novel in memory of the centenary of his birth.

JÄNDEL, RAGNAR. Ragnar Jändel, *En bok om Kristina Jändel. Dikter och prosatexter*, ed. Nils Lind, Jämjö, Jändelsällskapet, 1999, 80 pp., portrays the mother of J. and her life; J. had noted down her memories of her youth in the section 'Mor berättar' (12–28), a valuable contribution to his own background and to paupers' life in Sweden in the 19th c.

KARNSTEDT, TORGNY. M. Sandin, 'Kampen mot språkfattigdomen. Ett samtal med Torgny Karnstedt', *Horisont*, 47.2 : 3–7.

KIHLMAN, CHRISTER. Mårten Westö and Christer Kihlman, *Om hopplöshetens möjligheter. En samtalsbok*, Helsinki, Söderströms, 314 pp., is a 'conversational' book at the suggestion of K. in order to put the record straight about himself. It provides relevant insight into his life, his relationship with other authors, and not least his own writing.

KYRKLUND, WILLY. O. Widhe, 'Jaget och texten. Om minne, samtidighet och glömska i Willy Kyrklunds prosa', *TidLit*, 29.2 : 83–108, focuses the discussion on the 1964 novel *Polyfem förvandlad*.

LAGERCRANTZ, OLOF. S. Andersson, 'Olof Lagercrantz janusansikte. Den kritiska texten som dialektisk spelplats', *Edda*, 147–57, argues that literary criticism is an independent aesthetic activity equal to literature.

LAGERKVIST, PÄR. Piotr Bukowski, *Ordnungsschwund — Ordnungswandel. Pär Lagerkvist und der deutsche Expressionismus* (TUGS, 43), 241 pp., diss., examines the new norms of modernist aesthetics in the second decade of the last century. From a comparative perspective it discusses two early books by L. in relation to select works by German expressionists; firstly, it draws on the theories in L.'s *Ordkonst och bildkonst* (1913) and early theories of Wassily Kandinsky's; secondly, it considers L.'s collection of short stories *Järn och människor* (1915) and German First World War prose, concluding that there are indeed analogies. L. Munk Rösing, 'Min gud, min mor, min angst. Om Pär Lagerkvist: *Gäst hos verkligheten*', *TidLit*, 29.2:63–82.

LARSON, KATE. L. Schenck, 'Kate Larson', *SBR*, no.2:20, introduces L. with a translation of a short story.

LARSSON, STIG. A. Ohlsson, ' "Synen av ett oavbrutet ingenting." Stig Larssons *Autisterna* och *Nyår*', Ohlsson, *Läst*, 250–84, argues that the film medium is thematically integrated into L.'s postmodern novels.

LARSSON, ZENIA. A. Ohlsson, 'Tal och tystnad i förintelselitteraturen. Exemplet Zenia Larsson', *TidLit*, 29.2:29–48, discusses literature and the Holocaust.

LIDMAN, SARA. F. Hale, 'The South African immorality act and Sara Lidman's *Jag och min son*?', *TsSk*, 21:55–80, argues that L. helped to shape a very different literary image of Africa than that which had been prevalent. J. Tate, 'Working with authors: Sara Lidman', *SBR*, Supplement:66–68, is a vivid description of discussions between the author of *Nabots sten* and her English translator, the indomitable late Joan Tate.

LINDGREN, ASTRID. Jørgen Gaare and Øystein Sjaastad, *Pippi og Sokrates. Filosofiske vandringer i Astrid Lindgrens verden*, Oslo, Huitfeldt, 522 pp., traces philosophical thinking in L.'s books and manages to be convincing, not least by admitting that nobody would have suspected that her books were philosophical to such a large extent. Rasmus and Ronja, Mio and Emil, Jonathan and Rusky, all ponder existential problems: they ask about the meaning of words and the essence of things, they wonder at life, are frightened of death, fight evil, and long for love. This book unmasks L., 'the philosopher', in all her popular, humorous, and down-to-earth wisdom. Vivi Edström, *Astrid Lindgren. A Critical Study* (SSBI, 70), Rabén & Sjögren, 328 pp., is a long overdue translation of the author's 1992 study, *Astrid Lindgren — Vildtoring och lägereld*, 'a thematically arranged study that sets out to change the image of L. by emphasizing her literary and linguistic consciousness and demonstrating the intertextual dependency of her books' (*YWMLS*, 54:967).

LINDGREN, TORGNY. L. Sjöberg, 'Kränk mig icke. Intertextualitet och livsåskådning i *Merabs skönhets* ramberättelse', Bråkenhielm, *Modernitetens ansikten*, 307–23.

LO-JOHANSSON, IVAR. A. Williams, '*Kungsgatans* moderna tider', *Samlaren*, 120, 1999[2000]:5–25, discusses L.'s novel of 1935. R. Wright, 'Realism refined and retouched: Alf Sjöberg's *Bara en mor*', *Steene Vol.*, 177–91, examines the 1949 film version of L.'s novel.

LÖWENHJELM, HARRIET. M. Pennlöw, 'Döden blev dikternas förutsättning. Om myten Harriet Löwenhjelm', *TidLit*, 29.3–4:91–113.

MARTINSON, HARRY. Bengt E. Anderson, *Att rannsaka en barndom. Harry Martinsons Nässlorna blomma: Tillkomst och tematik* (SLIGU, 38), 366 pp., diss. with a summary in English, is the first doctoral thesis on the novel published in 1935. It argues that this psychological novel of development that tells the story of unimaginable hardship experienced by one individual child has distinctly universal implications, both positive and negative; although there are similarities with M.'s own childhood, the story has been fictionalized to such an extent that it is no reliable guide to his early years, nor should it be labelled an autobiography. S. Söderblom, 'Domedag över en barndom', pp. 285–323 of Harry Martinson, *Nässlorna blomma*, ed. Stefan Sandelin, Harry Martinson-sällskapet–Bonniers, 333 pp., discusses M.'s most popular book in which the perspective alternates between the boy and the adult writer who is present throughout to comment and reproach; the very title indicates a formula of simultaneousness between the 'then' of the narrative and the 'now' of the writing.

MELIN, ROGER. R.-E. Sjöström, 'Roger Melin — lyriker i norr', *Horisont*, 47.4:14–21, presents M. and his three collections of poetry since 1994.

MOBERG, VILHELM. *Vilhelm Moberg i blickpunkten*, ed. Ingrid Nettervik (Vilhelm Moberg-sällskapet, 11), Växjö, 1999, 229 pp., includes papers given at a symposium in 1998 on Småland writers: A.-K. Carlstoft, 'Etik och retorik. Några nedslag i Vilhelm Mobergs författarskap'(50–69), examines some anti-Establishment texts of the early 1950s; G. Eidevall, 'Några inblickar i Vilhelm Mobergs arbete som romanförfattare' (70–92), on the writing of the novel *Sänkt sedebetyg* and the four parts of the emigrant cycle; P. Holmes, 'Moberg och Bibeln' (93–115), on biblical motifs and the influence of Bible language in the four emigrant novels; I. Kongslien, 'Vilhelm Mobergs emigrantepos: historisk fortolkning og eksistensiell søking' (116–33);

A. Ringblom, 'Vägar genom livet — om Moberg och Lagerkvist' (134–63).

MÅRTENSON, JAN. Jan Mårtenson, *Att kyssa ett träd. Memoarer*, Wahlström & Widstrand, 600 pp., is M.'s captivating memoirs; it includes: 'Johan Kristian Homan, antikhandlare från Gamla stan' (464–78), an account of M.'s anti-hero private detective in his series of novels. Homan certainly did not fit in with the radical trends typical of the early 1970s: his aesthetic choice of interests and hobbies, such as archaeology, fine wines and food, art, antiques, and history, were similar to those of his creator.

MÖRNE, ARVID. A. L. Hållner, 'Om religiöst grubbel hos Arvid Mörne', *NT*, 76:173–84, presents M.'s short stories of 1928.

NILSSON, PER. R. Gaasland, 'Å holde dommedag over seg selv. En analyse av Per Nilssons Hjärtans fröjd', *Edda*, 66–74, discusses N.'s 1992 novel for young people.

OLSSON, HAGAR. R. Holmström, 'Hagar Olsson och konsten att kritisera', *FT*, 434–41, discusses O. as a critic and literary criticism as art.

OSWALD, GÖSTA. Birgitta Trotzig, *Gösta Oswald. Minnesteckning*, Svenska Akademien–Norstedts, 27 pp.; Id. 'Gösta Oswald. Minnesteckning av fru Trotzig', pp. 63–95 of *Svenska Akademiens Handlingar*, 26, 1999[2000], Svenska Akademien–Norstedts, 172 + 57 pp.

PALM, GÖRAN. J. Ingvarsson, 'Göran Palm: fyra steg till verkligheten', Pettersson, *Litteratur*, 180–195.

REGIS, JULIUS. Dag Hedman, *Den skuggomhöljde Julius Regis* (Litteratur och samhälle, 33.2), Avdelningen för litteratursociologi, MLIUU, 113 pp., with abstracts in English and German, attempts to shed some light on the life and person of this once very popular thriller writer of the early 20th c.; most details about him seem to be lost, and today he and his books are largely forgotten. His crime fiction was still an influence on the Martin Beck novels by Sjöwall and Wahlöö.

RYDSTEDT, ANNA. Jan Olov Ullén, *Kära, kära verklighet. En bok om Anna Rydstedt*, Bonniers, 243 pp., a friend's sympathetic biography of 'Anna in the world', is the first monograph on R.'s life and work. It stresses the significance of her roots, the years when she grew up on an Öland farm with the love and support of her single mother, and her studies in Lund. Her poetry is seen as the reflection of a life-long endeavour to achieve balance between the I and the world.

SCHILDT, RUNAR. See SÖDERBERG, HJALMAR.

SCHOULTZ, SOLVEIG VON. C. Envall, ' "Och säg mig Gud, är kärnan där?" Några reflektioner kring jaget i relation till Gud i fem tidiga dikter av Solveig von Schoultz', Bråkenhielm, *Modernitetens ansikten*, 139–62.

SEEBERG, STAFFAN. J. Ingvarsson, '/"Som pappersbitar e vi!"/ Staffan Seeberg och 1960–talets cybernetiska diskurs', *TidLit*, 29.1:5–27, attempts to reveal with the help of cybernetics central aspects of S.'s 1970 novel *Vägen genom Vasaparken*.

SJÖMAN, VILGOT. A. Ohlsson, ' "Skapa, filma, skriv!" Vilgot Sjömans *Linus och Blenda* samt *Linus och vägvisarna*', Ohlsson, *Läst*, 214–49, discusses S.'s novels as examples of the film novel genre.

SONNEVI, GÖRAN. J. Lidström, 'Upplösta röster, upplöst språk. Vi-positionen i Göran Sonnevis poesi', *TidLit*, 29.3–4:114–33.

STIERNSTEDT, MARIKA. Eva Martinsson, *Attentatet på Dramaten. En studie av Alf Sjöbergs uppsättning av Marika Stiernstedts drama*, Harlösa, Martinssons, 224 pp., diss. with a summary in English, discusses the political and censoring ramifications of this production of 1944 in neutral Sweden; both S. and the director Alf Sjöberg were active opponents of Nazism. The focus is on how far the policy of neutrality was able to limit what was said on the national stage. The study shows that even if the text was neutralized and politically acceptable, audio-visual effects in set designs and music still made it clear that the scene was German-occupied Paris.

SUNDMAN, PER OLOF. N. G. Åsling, 'Per Olof Sundman och kulturpolitiken', *NT*, 76:207–20, is a postscript to the late 1990s discussion on S. and Nazism, supporting the view that S., the MP and writer, was always the defender of democratic ideals. J. Lundström, 'Formens betydelse. Reflexioner kring en Sundmanforskares metod-problem', *TidLit*, 29.3–4:65–74.

SÖDERBERG, HJALMAR. Massimo Ciaravolo, *En ungdomsvän från Sverige. Om mottagandet av Hjalmar Söderbergs verk i Finland 1895–1920* (SSLF, 621; Söderbergsällskapet, 11), Helsinki, 270 pp., discusses the reception and literary influence and significance of S. in Finland-Swedish literature during the first two decades of the 20th c. when Swedish language and literature were under threat in Finland; the study examines the circle around the cultural weekly journal *Euterpe*, the *dagdrivare* (the Finland-Swedish term for the *flaneur*) literary grouping, and finally the position and development of Runar Schildt.

SÖDERGRAN, EDITH. Boel Hackman, *Jag kan sjunga hur jag vill. Tankevärld och konstsyn i Edith Södergrans diktning*, Helsinki, Söderströms, 341 pp., diss. with a summary in English, argues that the predominant view of S. is too dependent on biographical and psychological factors; S.'s writing is not simply a reflection of her distinctive personality and tragic life. The study considers S. in relation to male dominant tradition and discusses her dialogue with contemporary literature and ideas, development from symbolism and Schopenhauer to expressionism, Nietzsche, and finally the ideas of Rudolf Steiner. The aim of the study is to place the poetry firmly in its cultural context and thereby open it up. B. Hackman, 'Själens estetik. Begynnande modernism i Edith Södergrans ungdomsdiktning', Bråkenhielm, *Modernitetens ansikten*, 241–54. A. Olsson, 'Transparens, extas, röst (Södergran)', Olsson, *Läsningar*, 235–68,

TROTZIG, BIRGITTA. A. Olsson, 'Världen som ansikte (Trotzig)', Olsson, *Läsningar*, 388–423. S. P. Sondrup, 'Birgitta Trotzig and the language of religious and literary experience', *ScSt*, 72:330–43, examines 'a profoundly religious sensibility and an accute theologically oriented cognitive power' in T.'s novels, and connects her poetry to the tradition of Hölderlin and Celan.

TUNSTRÖM, GÖRAN. Stina Hammar, *Duets torg. Göran Tunström och tankekällorna*, T. Hammar FoU, 1999, 381 pp., discusses the 1983 novel *Juloratoriet*, and how it relates to language, myths, religious concepts and rites, and the creative powers inherent in humanity. E. Johansson, 'Centrum sökes. En analys av Göran Tunströms roman *Juloratoriet* som Livsberättelse', Bråkenhielm, *Modernitetens ansikten*, 181–99.

TUOMINEN, MIRJAM. A. Olsson, 'Ikonoklasm (Tuominen)', Olsson, *Läsningar*, 329–49. S. Illman, ' "Gud är närvarande." Reflektioner över en bok av Mirjam Tuominen', Bråkenhielm, *Modernitetens ansikten*, 163–80.

VENNBERG, KARL. Anders Johansson, *Poesins negativitet. En studie i Karl Vennbergs kritik och lyrik* (AUSt, Stockholm Studies in History of Literature, 43), Almqvist & Wiksell International, 258 pp., diss. with a summary in English, first examines V.'s critical writing and theoretical views on literature, then applies them to close readings of his poetry; V.'s views, including his leaning towards mysticism, remain largely unchanged in the decades after the 1940s. The conclusion that V.'s poetry is based on the same theoretical basis as his critical writing is further argued in the final chapter that deals with poems about poetry. A. Olsson, 'Att släcka en eld med en annan (Vennberg)', Olsson, *Läsningar*, 350–87.

VREESWIJK, CORNELIS. *Skrifter* I–III. I. *Samlade sånger*. II. *Enskilda sånger*. III. *Dikter Prosa Tolkningar*, ed. and comm. Jan Erik Vold, 3 vols, Ordfront, 443, 525, 669 pp., form the collected works including V.'s songs, poetry, prose, and translations; the edition updates and supplements the earlier collections published 1988–90. Vol. I includes all the song-texts of the troubadour's main 17 albums; vol. II other songs: less well-known recordings, songs recorded by other artists, and songs not yet set to music by his death; vol. III miscellaneous remaining texts in verse and prose, and translations. In addition to the editor's informative preface and commentary in each volume, the edition also includes: J. E. Vold, 'Kungahövding vid vattenbrynet', I, 385–402, a critical appreciation of V.'s work; K. Widén, 'En biografisk skiss', III, 561–579, a brief biographical note. Oscar Hedlund, *Cornelis. Scener ur en äventyrares liv*, Bonniers, 499 pp., is a somewhat rambling biography by a journalist friend from the 1960s. It is aptly subtitled 'scenes from the life of an adventurer', and interspersed with family and friends' reminiscences of V.'s both colourful and tragic life.

WÄGNER, ELIN. G. Domellöf, 'Tidevarvsidéer i Elin Wägners roman *Dialogen fortsätter*', Pettersson, *Litteratur*, 160–67. E. Heggestad, '"Män må icke under någon förevändning taga plats i damkupé." Civilisationskritik och utopi i Elin Wägners *Norrtullsligan*', Bråkenhielm, *Modernitetens ansikten*, 43–59. *Bergs prästgård på Elins tid* (Elin Wägner-sällskapet, 11), Växjö, 22 pp., has three essays on childhood stays in vicarages.

ZETTERSTRÖM, MARIANNE (VIOLA). P. Wästberg, 'En impressionist vid Humlegården', Wästberg, *Essäer*, 225–30, depicts the poetic Stockholm columnist.

5

SLAVONIC LANGUAGES

I. CZECH STUDIES

LANGUAGE*

By Marie Nováková and Jana Papcunová,
Ústav pro jazyk český Akademie věd České republiky, Prague
(This survey covers the period 1999–2000.)

1. General and Bibliographical

GENERAL. The 80th birthday of František Daneš, a notable personality of Czech linguistics, has provided the opportunity for the republication of his less available articles on linguistics, grammar, sociolinguistics, and text linguistics in a selective collection *Jazyk a text: Výbor z lingvistického díla Františka Daneše*, ed. Oldřich Uličný, Dagmar Čapková, and Lucie Římalová, 2 vols, Prague, Charles Univ., 1999, 1–245, 249–471 pp. The Czech National Corpus still remains one of the major topics of present-day Czech studies. A monograph *Český národní korpus*, ed. Jan Kocek, Marie Kopřivová, and Karel Kučera, Prague, Charles Univ., 156 pp., dwells on the basic characterization of corpus linguistics and of the Czech National Corpus. J. Šonková, *SaS*, 61:190–202, also discusses the general characterization and compiling of a subcorpus of spoken Czech. Two other monographs are devoted to Czech in general terms: Irena Bogoczová et al., *Tváře češtiny*, Ostrava, Ostravská Univ., 265 pp., includes all aspects of the present-day language, especially the spoken one; Alois Bauer, *Čeština na dlani*, Olomouc, Rubico, 127 pp., is a survey of contemporary Czech. Two essential articles are devoted to the state of Czech at the end of the 20th c.: J. Kraus, *PLS*, 42, 1999:31–35, and O. Uličný, Zybatow, *Slavia*, 141–57. Another significant topic of the contemporary Czech Studies is common Czech. J. Hronek and P. Sgall, *NŘ*, 82, 1999:184–91, comment on the diminution of differences between standard and common Czech; V. Schmiedtová, *JazA*, 36.3–4, 1999:43–46, presents a special view on the dispute between standard and common Czech, which

* This contribution has been written thanks to the support of programme 28, Language Data Processing, Nr. KSK 3083603.

868 Czech Studies

J. Kořenský, *JazA*, 37.1–2:34–38, revises and sets some facts right. Both M. Krčmová, Hladká, *Čeština*, 11, 63–77, and Z. Rusínová, *ib.*, 79–83, also contribute to the comprehension, definition and functioning of common Czech. J. Kraus, *PLS*, 43:51–55, analyses the situation of present Czech and summarizes the development of Czech purism.

BIBLIOGRAPHICAL. A series of personal bibliographies appears: Jana Papcunová and Alena Nejedlá, *František Daneš - 80 let*, Prague, ÚJČ, 1999, 43 pp., cover the period 1948–99; they both also compile a supplement to the bibliography for Ivan Lutterer (covering 1994–99), *Lutterer Vol.*, 15–17; H. Karlíková, *SPFFBU-A*, 47, 1999:189–93, for Eva Havlová; *ib.*, 48:175–84, for Marie Krčmová (covering 1962–99; no author given); J. Vintr has produced a bibliography for František Václav Mareš, pp. 674–705 of *Cyrilometodějská tradice a slavistika*, Prague, Torst, 736 pp. M. Nováková, *Bibliografie české onomastiky 1995–96*, Prague, ÚJČ, 1999, 74 pp. (with an attached bibliography of theses on onomastics from 1986–91); J. Nekvapil, *Sociolinguistica*, 14:263–65, is a list of 39 entries on Czech sociolinguistics.

2. HISTORY OF THE LANGUAGE

N. Bayerová, *JazLin*, 3, 1999:11–16, deals with the Old Czech adverbial locative and analyses its local, temporal, modal, referential and purpose meaning; N. Kvítková, *ib.*, 133–39, submits a quantitative analysis of nouns in the *Staročeská kronika tak řečeného Dalimila*; K. Hádek, *StBo*, 8:139–43, examines dialogic components of contact in the same document; A. M. Perissutti, *SPFFBU-A*, 47, 1999:129–41, refers to the Gothic period and studies the context, which indefinite determiners with modifier *o, ně-* occur in; Czech of the 17th and 18th cs becomes the centre of attention of Bohemicists gradually: a number of contributions from a symposium on this topic have been published in *Východočeská duchovní a slovesná kultura 18. století*, ed. Václav Petrbok, Radek Lunga and Jan Tydlitát, Boskovice, Albert, 1999, 513 pp.: P. Kosek on punctuation in the hymn book *Slaviček rájský*, by Jan Josef Božan (9–22); T. Berger on the use of Czech as the official language in the second half of the 18th c. (43–78); and A. Stich on the verse in the so-called neighbourly plays of the 19th c. (289–94). The collective volume, *K jazyku a stylu českých barokních textů*, ed. Milan David, České Budějovice, Jihočeská Univ., 142 pp., focuses on similar questions: A. Jaklová on the language and style of the Czech sermons of Ondřej František de Waldt (8–41); Z. Holub, analysing the language of two sermons by Jan Klekar (42–61); M. David, analysing the language of a sermon from 1714 (63–77); J. Alexová on the language and literary heritage of Tomáš Jan Pešina z Čechorodu (79–88); B. Junková on the language of baroque spiritual fairy tales (110–16); and M. Janečková on the language of Daniel Vetter in his travel story *Islandia* (1638) (117–27).

J. Hubáček, *NŘ*, 82:192–202, writes on the use of metaphor and on its functions of composition in *Pres boží* by Jan Amos Komenský; Id., *LFil*, 122:49–63, studies syntactic-stylistic devices (chiasmus and parallelism) in his Czech works; and finally, in *ČL*, 47:339–63, he pays attention to synonymic pairs in his prose; T. Vařeková, *SPFFBU-A*, 48:101–15, studies the construction of the Czech humanist period in works of Viktorin Kornel ze Všehrd, Řehoř Hrubý z Jelení, Tadeáš Hájek z Hájku, Daniel Adam z Veleslavína, Karel starší ze Žerotína and others; P. Kosek, *JazLin*, 3, 1999:127–31, follows dialectal expressions in *Slaviček rájský* by Jan Josef Božan; V. Koblížek, *Čeština*, 10:117–23, covers Czech medical terminology in the baroque period; and J. Pleskalová, *AOn*, 40:186–95, is a diachronic view of Czech minor field names. Sylva Stanovská, *Vergleichende stilistische Untersuchungen zum Ackermann aus Böhmen und Tkadlec*, Brno, Masaryk Univ., 1999, 133 pp., is a stylistic comparison of both works. Nancy Smith, *Grammaticae Bohemicae, ad leges naturalis methodi conformatae et notis numerisque illustratae ac distinctae, libris duo*, Ostrava, Ostravská Univ., 1999, 103 pp., edits the 1603 grammar by Vavřinec Benedikt z Nudožer, with an introductory study.

3. PHONETICS AND PHONOLOGY

F. Y. Gladney, *SaS*, submits some comments on the generative phonology and morphonology of Czech; Z. Palková, Čechová, *Jinakost*, 33–37, discusses the acoustic features and characterization of Czech dramatic speech; I. Balkó, *ib.*, 38–44, examines speech tempo and articulation in spontaneous speeches; and M. Krčmová, Jelínek, *Argumentace*, 297–312, focuses on pronunciation in public speeches. L. Hašová, *ČMF*, 82:22–29, follows the interpenetration of Czech and German from the phonetic viewpoint.

4. MORPHOLOGY AND WORD-FORMATION

A remarkable work by Dušan Šlosar, *Česká kompozita diachronně*, Brno, Masaryk Univ., 1999, 124 pp., explores sets of Czech compound words from the oldest texts to the newest expressions. Jana Schwarzová, *Die Kategorie der Weiblichkeit im Tschechischen: Die Verwendung der femininer und maskuliner Personenbennenung für Frauen im Vergleich zum Deutschen*, Prague, Charles Univ., 1999, 135 pp., deals with the formation of feminines from masculines in Czech and compares it to the situation in German. R. Brabcová, *PLS*, 42, 1999:37–45, follows evolutionary trends in Czech morphology, while E. Lotko, *JazLin*, 3, 1999:141–47, analyses inflectional features of Czech and types of word-formation of new naming units; O. Martincová, *HoreckýVol.*, 382–87, concentrates on multiple-word naming units such as *akrobatický lyžař, stavební spoření, sexuální harašení*, etc., and M. Čejka, *SaS*, 60, 1999:117–22, analyses optative functions of Czech imperative. J. Šimandl, *NŘ*, 83:57–76, 113–31, 169–92, 225–42, has written a series of articles discussing morphologic questions in the Czech linguistic consulting centre; B. Vykypěl, *SPFFBU-A*, 48:73–79, comments on the development of Czech declension; and S. Romportl, *ib.*, 81–90, on the development of terminative verbs in Czech (compared to Turkish).

5. SYNTAX AND TEXT

Topic-focus articulation is a domain of E. Hajičová, in *SaS*, 61:161–69, writing on the application of Optimality Theory in Czech (based on dependency syntax); in Hladká, *Čeština*, 1, 47–54, she deals with topic-focus articulation and the construction of discourse, and in *ib.*, II, 123–29, she expounds two different interpretations of presupposition in Czech. P. Karlík, *SaS*, 61:170–189, introduces a modified valency theory hypothesis; U. Junghanns, *LArb*, 74:127–38, investigates the status of Czech reflexive clitics in the sentence; J. Chloupek, *SaS*, 60, 1999:88–91, deals with the stylistic applicability of syntactic synonymy in communicative situations; J. Cvejnová, *SPFFBU-A*, 47, 1999:77–84, analyses comparative utterances and intensifiers of comparative expressions; P. Karlík, Hladká, *Čeština*, 1, 13–27, studies the subordinate clause from the semantic and pragmatic viewpoint; Id., *SPFFBU-A*, 47, 1999:85–94, analyses resultative complex sentences with the conjunctions *(a) proto, (a) tedy, (a) tudíž, (a) tak/takže*; R. Konvalinková, *ib.*, 105–15, discusses those language means expressing spatial relationships, such as *někdo/něco bývá/pobývá/je někde*. Renáta Tomášková, *Dramatický dialog z hlediska textové koheze a koherence*, Ostrava, Ostravská Univ., 1999, 131 pp., is a systematic analysis of textual cohesion and coherence.

6. ORTHOGRAPHY

K. Kučera, *SaS*, 60, 1999:301–03, continues in his quantitative characterizations of the development of Czech orthographic rules from the 13th c. (see *YWMLS*, 60:864); H. Tešnar, *NŘ*, 83:243–52, reports on orthographic polemics in the 19th c. Several studies cover the orthography of proper names: J. Kolařík, *Lutterer Vol.*, 229–31, and I. Svobodová, *NŘ*, 83:17–21, both on use of capital letters in proper names; V. Šaur, 152–56, of *Propria v systému mluvnickém a slovotvorném*, Brno, Masaryk Univ., 1999, 161 pp., on the orthography of multiple-word names; and J. Bartoška, *ib.*, also on the orthography, pronunciation, declension and use of proper names in the mass media. *Pravidla českého pravopisu*, Prague, Fortuna 1999, 383 pp., is a revised edition of orthographic rules, and Radoslava Brabcová, *Novinky pravopisu a tvarosloví*, Dobřichovice, Kava-Pech, 88 pp., has also revised and completed her handbook from 1996. Last but not least, an enjoyable book by Naďa Svozilová, *Jak dnes píšeme / mluvíme a jak hřešíme proti dobré češtině: Jazykové sloupky z Literárních novin 1992–99*, Jinočany, H&H, 171 pp., throws light not only on orthographic questions but also on other issues (language correctness, pronunciation, word formation, word order, etc.) of present-day Czech.

7. Lexicology and Phraseology

Karel Pala and Jan Všianský, *Slovník českých synonym*, Prague, Nakl. Lidové noviny, 479 pp., is a third revised edition of the dictionary. Eva Mrhačová, *Názvy zvířat v české frazeologii a idiomatice*, Ostrava, Ostravská Univ., 1999, 161 pp., has compiled a thematic phraseological dictionary; the authoress with Eva Jandová and Jürgen Hartung, *Česko-německý slovník: Pojmenování zvířat v české a německé frazeologii a idiomatice*, Ostrava, Ostravská Univ., 223 pp., compare Czech and German denotation systems (animal names). Karel Jaroslav Obrátil, *Velký slovník sprostých slov*, ed. Jan Hýsek, Prague, Lege artis, 314 pp., has gathered together standard, colloquial, dialectal, and Old Czech obscene words.

The team of authors led by Jaroslava Pečírková continues to compile *Staročeský slovník*, ed. Igor Němec, Prague, Academia, 1999, part 23: *pronésti sě–provésti*, pp. 113–224; part 24: *provésti–předložený*, pp. 225–336. M. Křístek, Jelínek, *Argumentace*, 269–77, presents a survey of Czech monolingual dictionaries; R. Blatná, *SaS*, 66, 1999:46–52, analyses musical loanwords from Greek, Latin, Italian, English, and German; I. Němec, *SaS*, 61:257–75 focuses on Czech words of resistance, investigating the correlation between specific derivational strategies and speaker's attitudes; J. Hubáček, *JazLin*, 3, 1999:7–10, writes on polysemy based on metaphorical transfer of meaning; E. Lotko, *StBo*, 8:173–76, discusses negative words in a dictionary of neologisms. Two conference proceedings pay particular attention to Czech vocabulary. *Nová slovní zásoba ve výkladových slovnících: Sborník příspěvků z konference Praha, 31.10.–1.11.2000*, ed. Olga Martincová and Jindra Světlá, Prague, ÚJČ, 113 pp., present a number of studies on neologisms in Czech, on their selection and processing in Czech monolingual dictionaries. *Studia etymologica Brunensia 1*, ed. Ilona Janyšková and Helena Karlíková, Prague, Euroslavica, 375 pp., offer a series of interesting etymological studies: H. Karlíková comments on the Old Czech noun *řepice* (117–20); Ž. Šarapatková on semantic development of the word *mnich* (121–22); I. I. Lučyn-Fedarec compares Moravian and Byelorussian lexical parallels (229–34); P. Valčáková on some names of baked goods (261–65); B. Skalka on the etymology of some slang and argotic expressions (271–76).

8. SEMANTICS AND PRAGMATICS

The proceedings of the 3rd conference on communication, Odaloš, *Retrospektívne*, include a great number of representative contributions concerning contemporary Czech pragmatics. In Vol. 1: M. Čechová on the relationship between discourse and text (32–37); J. Hoffmannová on primitivization and dehumanization of some communication types (85–92); H. Brádková (125–27), A. Jaklová (137–42), and M. Hirschová (161–66) analyse educational communication; E. Höflerová investigates the way of expressing the evaluation of attitudes in children's speech (131–36). Vol II is devoted to more concrete questions of language communication: M. Švehlová on speech as an instrument of political power (14–18); M. Javorská on TV advertising (19–22); O. Müllerová (43–49) and M. Hádková (50–53) on doctor-patient communication; E. Demlová on the spoken discourse of young people (68–74); M. Janečková on conversation in families (75–79); H. Srpová (157–60), B. Junková (161–64), and I. Kolářová (170–73) on communication in journalism. Jana Hoffmannová and Olga Müllerová concentrate systematically on pragmatics, with three monographs devoted to this topic: *Dialog v češtině*, Munich, Sagner, 1999, 259 pp., is a collection of their studies previously published in *NŘ*, *SaS*, and other volumes; with Jiří Zeman in *Konverzace v češtině při rodinných a přátelských návštěvách*, Prague, Trizonia, 1999, 256 pp., they analyse the course and main features of conversation during visits of relatives and friends; and in their newest book, *Jak vedeme dialog s institucemi*, Prague, Academia, 188 pp., they study doctor-patient communication, communication in old people's homes, phone calls to the fire-brigade, etc., concentrating on the organization and structure of dialogue. Both authoresses analyse code mixing in marked situations in Zybatow, *Slavia*, 283–303, and in *Horecký Vol.*, 102–11. S. Čmejrková, *ib.*, 124–40, focuses on the model and reality of media dialogues; O. Müllerová, pp. 87–94 of *Świat humoru*, ed. Stanisław Gajda, Opole, Univ. Opolski, 628 pp., distinguishes between positive and negative laughter in communication; B. Junková, *ib.*, 291–96, follows humour in journalistic texts; I. Bogoczová, *SaS*, 61:18–29, analyses the communication in the North Moravian region of Těšín. *Heterogennost v komunikaci, v textu a v jazyce*, ed. Alena Macurová, Prague, Charles Univ., 1999, 150 pp., includes studies on communication between the deaf and within ethnic minorities, and on non-verbal communication. *Argumentace a umění komunikovat*, ed. Milan Jelínek, Brno, Masaryk Univ., 1999, 327 pp., includes articles on argumentation, rhetoric, communication, and stylistics.

F. Daneš, *SaS*, 61:81–92, writes on modalization in Czech scientific texts and follows the specific modal phenomenon of 'hedging'; J. Šlédrová, *ib.*, 122–37, deals with the semantics of Czech adjectives denoting dimensions; I. Nebeská, *SaS*, 60, 1999:92–101, is a semantic analysis of the verbs *předpokládat, předvídat, doufat, obávat se, očekávat*; I. Kolářová, *NŘ*, 83:193–99, comments on some meanings and functions of the word *to;* J. Kyncl, *SPFFBU-A*, 48:61–72, discusses semantics in expressing the time cathegory in Czech.

Světla Čmejrková, *Reklama v češtině: Čeština v reklamě*, Prague, Leda, 258 pp., analyses language and style varieties and psycholinguistic methods in advertising; moreover, she writes a series of articles on this topic: *ČDS*, 8:118–25, discussing advertising in newspapers and magazines; *Stylistyka*, 117–36, on specific strategies of advertising and types of pretext in it; and pp. 113–23 of *Rhetoric and Argumentation,* ed. E. Rigotti, Tübingen, Niemeyer, 1999, 270 pp.

9. SOCIOLINGUISTICS AND DIALECTOLOGY

Jan Balhar et al., *Český jazykový atlas*, Prague, Academia, 1999, 577 pp., covers the following lexical spheres of activity: field and agricultural work, the farm, agricultural tools, livestock, and poultry. Other significant works in this section are: Libuše Čižmárová, *Jazykový atlas jihozápadní Moravy*, Brno, Masaryk Univ., 446 pp., a voluminous study comparing two stages of development of a southwest Moravian dialect (from the 1950s and from 1993); Stanislava Kloferová, *Mluva v severomoravském pohraničí*, Brno, Masaryk Univ., 130 pp., gives results of research into everyday language in rural territories of North Moravia; and Zdeňka Hladká, *Přenesená pojmenování rostlin v českých dialektech: K sémantickému tvoření lexikálních jednotek v nářečích*, Brno, Masaryk Univ., 243 pp., studies onomasiological methods in the vocabulary (names of plants) of Czech dialects. H. Konečná, *NŘ*, 82, 1999:203–08, deals with the hard declension of adjectives in Czech dialects; Z. Holub, Čechová, *Jinakost*, 226–31, investigates the dialect in the region of Doudleby; M. Janečková, *ib.*, 221–25, follows germanisms in South Bohemian dialects; H. Oberreiterová, *SPFFBU-A*, 47, 1999 : 157–64, analyses the dialect of the East Bohemian city of Broumov; L. Čižmárová, *ib.*, 48 : 121–26, follows past participles in Czech dialects; Z. Hlubinková, *ib.*, studies the formation of demonstrative and indefinite pronouns in East Moravian dialects; and J. Vojtová, *ib.*, is on dialectal vocabulary in the region of Haná. J. Nekvapil, 'On non-self-evident relationships between language and ethnicity: how Germans do not speak German and Czechs do not speak Czech', *Multilingua*, 19 : 37–53, proceeds from the linguistic, social, and political situation on the territory of the Czech Republic over the course of the 20th c. and discusses the relation between language and ethnicity; Id., *SaS*, 61 : 30–46, follows language biographies in a German family living in the Czech Republic. J. Hubáček, Hladká, *Čeština*, 1, 101–05, summarizes the basic concepts of social dialectology; A. Jaklová, *SaS*, 60, 1999 : 293–300, comments on the concept of *argot* and on changes in its contents; J. van Leeuwen-Turnovcová, *ZSl*, 45 : 295–317, focuses on argot vocabulary in Czech; M. Grygerková, *JazLin*, 3, 1999 : 63–70, analyses abbreviation in present-day vocabulary of Czech slang; A. Jaklová, Čechová, *Jinakost*, 216–20, deals with loanwords in South Bohemian slang. Antonín Doležal, **Lékařský slang a úsloví*, Prague, Galén, 1999, 87 pp., compiles a vocabulary of slang expressions from the medical practice. Petr Dvorník, Pavel Kopřiva, and Pavel Č. Jelínek, *Velký slovník hantecu: hanteco-český, česko-hantecový*, Brno, FR Records, 228 pp., have compiled a dictionary of Brno argot expressions.

10. STYLISTICS

GENERAL. The whole of *Stylistyka*, 9, is devoted to Czech stylistics and publishes a great number of essays by both Czech and foreign authors: M. Čechová on functions of special professional style (85–91); M. Jelínek on syntactic condensation as a characteristic feature of non-fiction style (93–102); S. Čmejrková (117–36), and H. Srpová (137–46) on language and style of advertising; and J. Hubáček on correlation of sociolects and stylistics (201–08). František Daneš, Světla Čmejrková, and Jindra Světlá, *Jak napsat odborný text*, Prague, Leda, 1999, 255 pp., is a handbook on how to write Czech special texts; the authors compare Czech and international (especially Anglo-Saxon) norms of academic writing. J. Chloupek and M. Krčmová, *JazLin*, 3, 1999 : 89–99, describe transformations of stylistic norms in present-day Czech; M. Jelínek, in Jelínek, *Argumentace*, 197–219, is on the stylistic prerequisites of successfulness in public speech and presents information on conversational, technical, administrative, journalistic, and rhetoric style; Id., *ib.*, 243–67, comments on syntactic features which define the spoken style of today's Czech; Id., Hladká, *Čeština*, 1, 117–25, deals with style of encyclopaedic entries. P. Mareš, *PLS*, 42, 1999:93–98, refers to the stylistic use of non-standard Czech in modern literature. A basic aid for stylistics is a monograph by Alena Debická *O výstavbě stylu a textu: Stylistické analýzy a interpretace*, Ústí nad Labem, Purkyně Univ., 1999, 177 pp., the book includes twelve stylistic analyses and interpretations of concrete texts.

ASPECTS OF THE LANGUAGE OF INDIVIDUAL WRITERS. M. Červenka, *Z večerní školy versologie*, vol. 4, Prague, Ústav pro českou literaturu, 1999, follows the transformations of the Czech dactyl from the 19th c. to the beginning of the 20th c.; Id., *ČL*, 47, 1999:456–60, analyses accented rhythm in trochee and iamb in modern Czech poetry; D. Tureček, *ib.*, 550–54, is on the structure of Mácha's verse and on semantics of the verb *pněti/pníti* in his distichs; J. Hoffmannová, *JazLin*, 3, 1999:71–79, presents a stylistic characterization of enumerations in the correspondence of Karel Čapek; V. Staněk, *NŘ*, 83:77–96, analyses neologisms in works of Karel Čapek; F. Štícha, *ib.*, 253–59, writes on the anaphoric pronoun *ten* in Czech literature of the 19th c., in particular in works of Antal Stašek; and M. Těšitelová, *ib.*, examines contemporary Czech fiction from the word frequency viewpoint; J. Kořenský, *Stylistyka*, 9:33–40, analyses five poems by Vladimír Holan on Karel Hynek Mácha. M. Křístek, pp. 439–45 of *Świat humoru*, Opole, 628 pp., compares the comic side in *Osudy dobrého vojáka Švejka* by Jaroslav Hašek and in its next part by Karel Vaněk; C. Davies, *ib.*, refers to the same work and contrasts its style with *The History of Mr. Polly* by H. G. Wells; A. Jaklová, *ib.*, discusses verbal humour in Karel Čapek's fairy-tales.

11. ONOMASTICS

Libuše Olivová-Nezbedová and Jitka Maleninská, *Slovník pomístních jmen v Čechách: Úvodní svazek*, Prague, Academia, 169 pp., present an introductory volume of the dictionary of Czech minor field names and inform on the method of processing. Jiří Zeman, *Výslovnost a skloňování cizích osobních jmen v češtině: Severská osobní jména: dánština, faerština, finština, islandština, norština, švédština*, vol. 2, Hradec Králové, Gaudeamus, 180 pp., covers pronunciation and declension of personal names this time in Nordic languages (see *YWMLS*, 60:868). J. Maleninská, *AOn*, 39, 1999:22–26, writes on the common noun *čeřeň* and its derivatives in the Czech toponymy; L. Olivová-Nezbedová, *ib.*, 46–54, is on the hierarchy of onomastic terms; S. Pastyřík, *ib.*, 55–58, is on the gender of hypocoristics; M. Vitochová, *ib.*, 59–111, compiles a reverse index of historical names of mountains and forrests (from the book by August Sedláček, *Snůška starých jmen*, 1920). Worthy of mention are M. Knappová, *AOn*, 40:82–88, on nicknames both in the past and today; K. Komárek, *ib.*, 91–96, on personal names in *Bible drážďanská a olomoucká*; M. Nováková, *ib.*, 141–51, on the toponym *Kocanda;* K. Oliva, *ib.*, 152–55, on the theory of chrematonyms; S. Pastyřík, *ib.*, 178–85, on surnames in the Moravian country in the 17th and 18th centuries. *Lutterer Vol.* contains: I. Lutterer on the Czech onomastic school (18–25); M. Harvalík on two types of minor field names *Podles* and *Podlesí* (109–37); J. Maleninská on the common noun *leb* in Czech toponymy (186–93); I. Němec on naming units derived from personal names in the language of resistance (319–26); L. Olivová-Nezbedová on minor field names derived from common nouns applying to the dispensation of justice, such as *Šibenice, Spravedlnost, Čakan*, etc. (355–88); J. Pleskalová on the oldest Czech minor field names from the 10th to the 13th cs (408–11). *Propria v systému mluvnickém a slovotvorném*, ed. Květoslava Klímová and Helena Kneselová, Brno, Masaryk Univ., 1999, 161 pp., also brings a series of interesting studies: M. Knappová on personal names in the Czech grammatical system and specifically on the derivation of feminine forms from masculine nouns (11–15); E. Mrahačová on surnames with negation (29–34); K. Klímová on the surnames *Vítámvás* and *Nejezchleb* and on their word-formative structure (35–39); N. Bayerová on Czech and Russian surnames derived from Slavonic compound words (24–28); M. Janečková on different types of South Bohemian minor place names (77–81); H. Kneselová on unofficial forms of urbanonyms in Brno (94–95); M. Vondráček on the names of asteroids (133–38). L. Olivová-Nezbedová, *NŘ*, 82, 1999:104–07, focuses on the common noun *lipí, lipina* in Czech minor field names; J. Matúšová, *Österreichische Namenforschung*, 27, 1999:75–81, is on the German common noun *Berg* in Czech toponymy. J. Hasil, 'Kauza Česko', *PLS*, 42, 1999:7–30, refers again to the one-word name of the Czech Republic .

12.   LANGUAGE IN CONTACT AND COMPARATIVE STUDIES

F. Čermák, Hladká, *Čeština*, 1, 67–76, studies polysemy, derivation and composition in three types of languages (Czech, English, and Finnish) based on ten nouns; Id., *SaS*, 61:249–56, compares ten nouns in inflexional, agglutinative, and isolating languages from the semantic and morphological points of view; P. Sgall, Hladká, *Čeština*, 1, 39–46, compares dependency grammar and word order in Czech and analytical languages. On Czech-Russian parallels: Stanislav Žaža, *Ruština a čeština v porovnávacím pohledu*, Brno, Masaryk Univ.,

1999, 122 pp., is a revised edition of his monograph; Id., *SPFFBU-A*, 47, 1999:175–83, compares Czech, Russian and Latin on the lexical, word-formational, morphological, and syntactic levels; P. Adamec, *PLS*, 42, 1999:37–73, compares Czech and Russian aspect in verbs of motion; Id., *PLS*, 43:7–14, compares Czech and Russian numerals; and I. Ohnheiser, Zybatow, *Slavia*, 41–63, compares neologisms in Czech, Russian, Polish, Slovak, and Bulgarian. D. Svobodová, *NŘ*, 82, 1999:122–26, focuses on English and hybrid compounds in Czech and on their adaptation there; E. Hajičová, *Horecký Vol.*, 260–68, discusses the opposite of free and fixed word order in Czech, English and German; E. Skála, *PLS*, 43:77–85, informs on Central European language union (based on contact development of Czech and German); S. Kloferová, Hladká, *Čeština*, 11, 47–52, follows Czech and German parallels in dialects; J. Jodas, *JazLin*, 3, 1999:111–16, compares Czech and Austrian German vocabulary; K. El Biltagi, Čechová, *Jinakost*, 72–77, studies the category of time in Czech and Arabian. Karel Kamiš, *Čeština a romština v českých zemích: Překonávání komunikačních bariér v multietnické společnosti*, Ústí nad Labem, Purkyně Univ., 1999, 137 pp., is a contrastive study of Czech and Romani from the acoustic, graphic, lexical, morphological and syntactic viewpoint. Odaloš, *Retrospektívne*, 1, 190–240, contains contributions on this topic by J. Nábělková, K. Musilová, J. Zeman, E. Jandová, Z. Holub, I. Bogoczová, and K. Kamiš.

13. CZECH ABROAD

The results of an international project from 1993 are summarized in *U nás ve Vídni: Vídeňští Češi vzpomínají*, ed. Jan Balhar, Stanislava Kloferová, Jarmila Vojtová, Brno, Masaryk Univ., 1999, 143 pp. The research has concentrated on the language of Viennese Czechs and on their relation to the language (sociolinguistic approach). J. Jančáková, *PFil*, 44, 1999:239–44, compares the language of Czech re-emigrants from Ukraine to the language on an extinct language island of Střelín in Poland; J. Vojtová, *ČDS*, 8:91–95, studies irregularities and interferences in vocabulary and syntax in Austrian Czech.

14. BILINGUAL DICTIONARIES

Though the production of bilingual dictionaries is extremely large, there are only few dictionaries worth mentioning here. The most up-to-date Czech-English dictionary is *Velký česko-anglický slovník*, comp. Josef Fronek, Prague, Leda, 1597 pp. Other valuable works are Karel Hora, *Makedonsko-český slovník s makedonskou gramatikou F. V. Mareše*,

Prague, Euroslavica, 1999, 638 pp., and Nikolaj Savický, Růžena Šišková, and Eva Šlaufová, *Rusko-český a česko-ruský slovník neologizmů,* Prague, Academia, 1999, 133 pp.

LITERATURE
POSTPONED

II. SLOVAK STUDIES

LANGUAGE
POSTPONED

LITERATURE
POSTPONED

III. POLISH STUDIES

LANGUAGE

By NIGEL GOTTERI, *University of Sheffield*

1. BIBLIOGRAPHY AND SURVEYS

J. Garczyńska and I. Winiarska, 'Przegląd polskich prac językoznaw-czych ogłoszonych drukiem w roku 1998', *PJ*, 1999, no.10:19–62; M. Bryja, J. Garczyńska and G. Seroczyński, 'Przegląd polskich prac językoznawczych ogłoszonych drukiem w roku 1999', *PJ*, no.7:41–77. *PJ*, no.1, is devoted to Witold Doroszewski: R. Grzegor-czykowa, 'Współczesne kognitywistyczne ujęcie znaczenia a kon-cepcja języka Witolda Doroszewskiego' (8–13); H. Satkiewicz, 'Teoria kultury języka Witolda Doroszewskiego a współczesne teorie z tego zakresu' (14–17); B. Bartnicka, 'Udział słownictwa XIX-wiecznego w *Słowniku języka polskiego* pod redakcją Witolda Doroszews-kiego' (18–23); J. Siatkowski, 'O leksykografii czeskiej' (24–37), draws comparisons with D.'s work; M. Przybysz-Piwkowa, 'Refleksja na temat terminu *fonem*' (38–42). K. Klimkowa, 'Profesor Maria Karpluk (w 75. rocznicę urodzin)', *JPol*, 80:321–24, refers to a bibliography of over 20 items. A. Maciejewska, 'Profesor dr hab. Józef Wierz-chowski (13.02.1927 — 31.05.1999)', *PJ*, 1999, no.10:1–7, gives bibliographical information in passing. E. Sękowska, 'Nurt antropologiczno-kulturowy we współczesnym polskim języko-znawstwie', *PJ*, no.6:11–20.

Stanisław Borawski, *Wprowadzenie do historii języka polskiego*, PWN, 277 pp., is an introduction to concepts, terms, hypotheses and controversies connected with the historical study of Polish. Marian Kucała, *Polszczyzna dawna i współczesna. Studia i szkice*, Kw, Instytut Języka Polskiego PAN, 539 pp., carries a bibliography of K.'s works from 1993–99 (531–34) including nine items in preparation. The topics covered in the collection are historical grammar and history of the language (7–232), onomastics (235–91), dialectology (295–347), the contemporary language (351–56), correct usage (459–87), lexico-graphy (489–530). Stanisław Rospond, *Gramatyka historyczna języka polskiego z ćwiczeniami*, Wa-Ww, PWN, 224 pp., is an extensively revised edition. Anna Wierzbicka, *Język — umysł — kultura*, ed. Jerzy Bartmiński, Wa, PWN, 1999, 593 pp., contains translations by various scholars of English papers.

2. PHONETICS AND PHONOLOGY

Danuta Ostaszewska and Jolanta Tambor, *Fonetyka i fonologia współczesnego języka polskiego*, Wa, PWN, 142 pp., give valuable phonological transcriptions (123–24) and phonetic transcriptions (98–100), though their version of IPA, based on the 1977 *Słownik wymowy polskiej*, has a period flavour (cf. *YWMLS*, 61:846). L. Dukiewicz, 'Wybór terminów używanych w fonetyce. Definicje, objaśnienia', *Polonica*, 19, 1998:187–204. Liliana Madelska and Małgorzata Witaszek-Samborska, *Zapis fonetyczny. Zbiór ćwiczeń*, Pń, Adam Mickiewicz U.P., 173 pp., is more than its title suggests, as it includes, for example, information on regional differences and some samples of spontaneous speech. Maria Steffen-Batogowa, *Struktura akcentowa języka polskiego*, Wa-Pń, PWN, 328 pp., sets out to establish appropriate accentual segmentations of Polish speech, to compare these with native intuitions, to establish prosodic influences on the structure of utterances, and to investigate stylistic differentiation of stress patterns. P. Rutkowski, 'O strukturze sylaby', *PJ*, no.3:16–26, looks at syllable structure in Spanish, English, and Polish. On punctuation: Edward Łuczyński, *Współczesna interpunkcja polska. Norma a uzus*, Gdańsk U.P., 1999, 208 pp.; *Nowy słownik ortograficzny PWN z zasadami pisowni i interpunkcji polskiej*, ed. Edward Polański, Wa, PWN, 1999, cxl + 942 pp., which includes pronouncements of the Speech Culture Commission from 1992 to 1998.

3. MORPHOLOGY AND WORD-FORMATION

J. Biniewicz, 'Kategoria osoby w tekstach nauk ścisłych', *PJ*, 1999, no.8–9:88–95. A. Dyszak, *Mały słownik rzeczowników osobliwych (o nietypowej odmianie)*, Kw-Wa, TMJP, 1999, 272 pp., makes a particular point of distinguishing singularia and pluralia tantum and various kinds of indeclinable noun (see *YWMLS*, 61:847). R. Huszcza, 'Jeszcze o honoryfikatywności polskich zaimków osobowych', *PJ*, no.6:21–30, pleads for the question of forms of address to be brought out of stylistics and speech culture and placed firmly within grammar; forms of address such as *Jego/Wasza Magnificencja* also form part of the wide-ranging subject matter of Bogusław Kreja, *Mówię, więc jestem. Rozmowy o współczesnej polszczyźnie*, Gdańsk U.P., 221 pp. (163–67). Id., 'Kiedy *dwóch*, kiedy *dwu*?', *JPol*, 80:153–54, takes a historical approach. R. Łobodzińska, 'Odmiana nazwisk obcych w praktyce językowej', *PJ*, 1999, no.8–9:128–34. Z. Saloni, 'W *Pasymiu*', *JPol*, 80:366–73, argues vigorously for soft declension of *Pasym*.

   S. Bąba and M. Szczyszek, '*Drinkowicz*', *JPol*, 80:207–11. M. Białoskórska, 'Wstępna analiza polskich gniazd słowotwórczych z centrum czasownikowym (cz. II)', *PJ*, no.2:38–48. W. Czechowski, 'Ludyczność wartościujących nazw osobowych w wypowiedziach potocznych młodzieży szkolnej', *JPol*, 80:47–51. H. Duda, 'Kilka uwag o językoznawstwie normatywnym (z powodu *archeolożek, socjolożek,* i *teolożek*)', *PJ*, 1999, no.8–9:115. I. Kaproń, 'Wstępne uwagi o derywacji redukcyjnej', *Polonica*, 19, 1998:179–86, examines forms created by truncation e.g. of names. B. Kreja, 'Drobiazgi słowotwórcze. 46. *Rżysko* i problem kategorii 'pole, na którym cos rosło'', *JPol*, 80:212–18. Id., '*Hamburgery* i inne formacje na -*burger(y)*', *ib.*, 152–53, notes that Polish now has a word *burger*, as in *burgery jarskie* 'vegetarian burgers'; Id., 'O *międzyszczycie* (komunikacyjnym)', *ib.*, 398–99, discusses an expression clearly modelled on *w międzyczasie*. M. Mycawka, 'Derywaty z *mega-* we współczesnej polszczyźnie', *ib.*, 15–22. D. Ochmann, 'Złożenia z *cyber-* we współczesnym języku polskim', *ib.*, 23–34. R. Przybylska, 'Uwagi o nowszych potocznych formacjach słowotwórczych', *ib.*, 197–20. R.S. [Sinielnikoff/Sieczkowski?], 'Działanie analogii', *PJ*, 1999, no.10:63–67; Id., '*Gimbus*', *PJ*, 1999, no.8–9:135–39, is prompted by the neologism formed from *gimnazjum* and *autobus* or *mikrobus*, used for example in Marcin Krygier's translation of Edwin Black, *Format c: powieść o końcu tysiąclecia*, Pń, Zysk, 1999, 523 pp. Mirosław Skarżyński, *Powstanie i rozwój polskiego słowotwórstwa opisowego*, Kw, Universitas, 1999, 215 pp.; Id., *Liczebniki w słowotwórstwie współczesnej polszczyzny (Studium gniazd słowotwórczych)*, Kw, Historia Iagellonica, 144 pp., is a painstaking and thorough study. M. Szczyszek, '*Papieżówka*', *JPol*, 80:362–65, dates the origin of the word, on the model of words like *leśniczówka*, to John Paul II's visit to Licheń in June 1999. Maria Witkowska-Gutkowska, *Staropolskie prefiksalne dublety czasownikowe i ich współczesne odpowiedniki*, Łódź U.P., 1999, 184 pp. P. Zbróg, 'O relacji słowotwórczej pomiędzy leksemami typu *pediatra*₁ *pediatra*₂', *Polonica*, 19, 1998:175–78, finds *Pediatry przyszły* systemically conceivable but at present pragmatically unacceptable.

4. SYNTAX

Gramatyka komunikacyjna, ed. Aleksy Awdiejew, Wa-Kw, PWN, 1999, 173 pp., introduces a theoretical approach which has apparently already been applied with success in teaching, but is here presented with little exemplification. B. Chachulska, 'Analiza łączliwości składniowej polskich leksemów *robić* i *czynić*', *Polonica*, 19, 1998:149–60; K. Cyra, 'Jednostka leksykalna *za każdym razem* — próba analizy składniowej i semantycznej', *ib.*, 113–24; and 'Spójnik jako wykładnik relacji stałego współwystępowania', *PJ*, no.6:31–40, continuing the topic of *PJ*, 1998, no.10:15–25. M. Gębka-Wolak, '*Takie nic to nic takiego*', *JPol*, 80:52–55, notes at least two distinct patterns of syntactic behaviour of *nic*. M. Grochowski, 'Funckcja intratekstualna leksemów a ich cechy gramatyczne (analiza wyrażenia *wszelki*)', *PJ*, no.5 : 1–10. Renata Grzegorczykowa, *Wykłady z polskiej składni*, PWN 1999, 159 pp., is a third edition. B. Milewska, 'Wyodrębnienie przyimków wtórnych w ciągach o strukturze przysłówek + przyimek', *JPol*, 80 : 374–78. L. Styrcz-Przebinda, 'O homonimiczności pewnych odmiennych i nieodmiennych form wyrazowych z punktu widzenia składni, słowotwórstwa i fleksji', *Polonica*, 19, 1998 : 139–48. K. Tutak, 'Problemy opisu składniowego współczesnych tekstów literackich i publicystycznych na przykładzie wybranych typów zdań podrzędnych złożonych', *JPol*, 80 : 56–62. T. V. Vernikovskaia, 'Судьба дательного падежа в польском языке', *Slavianovedenie*, 1 : 98–103, sees the dative narrowing, and some of its functions being taken over by *do* or *dla* + genitive. E. Walusiak, 'Mechanizmy organizacji tekstu — nawiązanie i dodawanie', *Polonica*, 19, 1998 : 41–48; P. Żmigrodzki, 'Strukturyzacja analityzmów werbo-nominalnych w modelu gramatyki generatywno-transformacyjnej', *ib.*, 67–74.

5. LEXICOLOGY AND PHRASEOLOGY

M. Borejszo, 'O zestawieniach metaforycznych w potocznym nazewnictwie roślin pokojowych', *JPol*, 80 : 334–40. D. Gold, 'On the etymology of Polish *kiełbasa* (and related words)', *Polonica*, 19, 1998 : 205–09, rejects derivations from *kiełb* 'gudgeon' or from Hebrew *kol-basar* 'all flesh'. F. Hinze, 'Neuhochdeutsch *Popanz*, "Schreckgestalt, Vogelscheuche, willensloser Mensch"': ursl. dial. *popolúdnica* "Mittagsgespenst" und analoge (gemein-)slawische Wortbildungs- und Bedeutungstypen', *ZSl*, 45 : 215–19. W. Lubaś, 'O powstającym słowniku potocyzmów', *JPol*, 80 : 161–75. J. Nalepa, '*Trzebiegost, trzeba* i potrzeba akrybii w badaniach historyczno-językowych', *ib.*, 141–46. A. Piotrowicz and M. Witaszek-Samborska, 'O słownictwie kosmetycznym we współczesnej polszczyźnie', *ib.*, 39–46. B. Sieradzka-Baziur, 'Nowe słowniki' is an addition to the fourth edition of Stanisław Urbańczyk, *Słowniki i encyklopedie. Ich rodzaje i użyteczność*, Kw, TMJP, 130 pp. (67–109 and bibliography 116–22). V. L. Tsymburskii, 'Праславянское **ostrovъ*: к пересмотру этимологии', *Slavianovedenie*, 1999, no.4 : 50–57. H. K. Ulatowska et al., 'Przysłowia jako teksty', *PJ*, no.7 : 22–30, draw on observations of 200 healthy subjects and over 70 aphasia sufferers. Zh. Zh. Varbot, 'О славянском родстве праславянского глагола **skočiti*', *Slavianovedenie*, no.4 : 22–24. R. Wojtak, 'Wpływ ekonomii a współczesne przemiany polszczyzny', *PJ*, 1999, no.10 : 8–18.

Andrzej Bańkowski, *Etymologiczny słownik języka polskiego*, 1. A-K. 2. L-P, 2 vols, Wa, PWN, liii + 873, xii + 977 pp., will on the appearance of the third volume be the first complete post-war etymological dictionary of Polish. A trend to be welcomed in encyclopaedic lexicography is the adaptation for a Polish audience, rather than straight translation, of internationally established works, with entries accordingly removed or added. Examples are Godfrey Vesey and Paul Foulkes, *Collins słownik encyklopedyczny filozofia*, [Wa?], Wyd. RTW, 1997, xi + 369 pp., and **Słownik pojęć współczesnych*, ed. Alan Bullock et al., Katowice, Wyd. "Książnica", 1999, xvi + 720 pp. *Inny słownik języka polskiego*, ed. Mirosław Bańko, Wa, PWN, 2 vols. lxii + 1213, 1423 pp., whose working title in preliminary discussions was *Nowy słownik*, adds significantly to the array of contemporary Polish dictionaries, since it is based on a corpus, whence directly derive its strengths and weaknesses; it includes, for example, *oszołom*, *notebook*, and *komórka* in the sense of 'mobile phone', and good explanations of *absolutnie* and *puzzle*, not to mention *cypryjski*, *żabojad* and *Szwab*, but frustrates by not including *jamajski*, by omitting *morawski* and thus leaving the user wondering exactly what geographical area is covered by *czeski*, or, given the publication year, by not including *dwutysięczny*. The very common photographic term *zoom* is absent, while *flesz* is given only its photographic sense and not the sense of 'news flash'. This dictionary includes an entry for *barbaryzm*, a term rejected in Aldona Skudrzykowa and Krystyna Urban, *Mały słownik terminów z zakresu socjolingwistyki i pragmatyki językowej*, Kw-Wa, TMJP, 169 pp., including bibliography (165–69), who pass over it in favour of *egzotyzm* and *ksenizm*, which turn out not to be the same thing at all. *Nowy słownik poprawnej polszczyzny*, ed. Andrzej Markowski, Wa, PWN, 42 + 1786 pp., acknowledges a colloquial norm alongside the more formal one. This inevitably leads to questions about the ultimate purpose of a colloquial norm; for example, Markowski rejects *rok dwutysięczny pierwszy* outright (179), insisting on *dwa tysiące pierwszy* though the former is widely used by educated speakers. There are large sections devoted to geographical and ethnic names (here one does find *jamajski* and *Morawy*) (1391–1474), personal names (1475–1555), abbreviations (1555–94), word-forming elements (1595–1612) and linguistic issues (1613–1786). Though bound to be much criticized, this is nevertheless a daring and useful reference work.

S. Bąba, '*Mrożek by tego nie wymyślił*', *JPol*, 80:151–52. Jarosław Liberek, **Innowacje frazeologiczne w powojennej fraszce polskiej*, Pń, 1998, 218 pp. T. Piekot, 'Problem analizy frazeologii socjolektalnej (na przykładzie socjolektu kulturystów nieprofesjonalnych)', *PJ*, no.4:50–56.

6. SEMANTICS AND PRAGMATICS

W. Cockiewicz, 'Wieviele Grammeme hat der slawische Verbalaspekt?', *Polonica*, 19, 1998:161–74, proposes four to six grammemes, depending whether + exhaustive (e.g. *najeść się*) and + usual (e.g. *jadać*) are included. I. Czerwińska, 'O strukturze semantycznej przyimka *z upoważnienia* i pokrewnych', *ib.*, 103–12. Stephen M. Dickey, *Parameters of Slavic Aspect: A Cognitive Approach*, Stanford, California, CSLI, xii + 316 pp., divides the Slavonic languages into western (Czech, Slovak, Slovene and Sorbian) and eastern (Russian, Ukrainian, Belorusian and Bulgarian), with Serbo-Croat and Polish in a transitional zone. In the western group, aspect is organized around the concept of totality, directly comparable to the count-mass distinction in nouns; in the eastern group, aspect is organized round the definiteness of a situation in time. E. Kuryło and K. Urban, 'Przejawy normy kulturowej w językowym obrazie interakcji', *PJ*, no.4:31–39. R. Laskowski, 'Semantyka trybu rozkazującego', *Polonica*, 19, 1998:5–29. T. Malec, 'Jeszcze o zwrotach typu *popełnić książkę*', *JPol*, 80:150. Agnieszka Mikołajczuk, **Gniew we współczesnym języku polskim. Analiza semantyczna*. Wa, Energeia, 1998, 256 pp. M. Mycawka, 'Opis semantyczny neologizmu *dyżurny*', *Polonica*, 19, 1998:125–38. W. Pisarek, 'O *nostalgii* dziś', *JPol*, 80:361. Brygida Rudzka-Olsztyn, *Z rozważań nad kategorią przypadku*, trans. and ed. Elżbieta Tabakowska, Kw, Universitas, 273 pp., collects papers taking a cognitive approach to case. A. Ryzza-Woźniak, 'Czy *euro-* jest skrótem od *Europa, europejski*? — zagadka semantyczna', *PJ*, 1999, no.8–9:122–28. M. Rzeszutko, 'Semantyka symboli w dialogu kultur', *PJ*, no.4:1–11. Z. Saloni, 'Projekt artykułu hasłowego BYĆ', *PJ*, no.3:4–15; and similarly, J. Wojtysiak, 'Słowo "być" w języku polskim', *StSem*, 21–22, 1998:101–08. B. Szumińska, 'Opozycja semantyczna jednostek leksykalnych *prawie* i *niemal*', *Polonica*, 19, 1998:93–102. Urszula Wieczorek, *Wartościowanie perswazja język*, Kw, Księgarnia Akademicka, 1999, 134 pp., continues and synthesizes the recent Polish tradition of evaluation studies and Anglo-Saxon approaches to pragmatics. J. Zgrzywa, 'Co znaczy dziś wyraz *nostalgia*?', *JPol*, 80:355–60.

7. SOCIOLINGUISTICS AND DIALECTOLOGY

Marian Bugajski, *Pół wieku kultury języka w Polsce (1945–1995)*, Wa, PWN, 1999, 197 pp., may be read alongside Antoni Furdal, *Polska oda do radości. Język i kultura narodowa we wspólnej Europie*, Ww-Wa-Kw, ZNiO, 204 pp., which contains much of interest, but far less about language than one might expect of the author of Id., *Językoznawstwo otwarte*, Ww-Wa-Kw, ZNiO, 212 pp. For a panoramic snapshot of contemporary Polish, besides *Polszczyzna 2000* (see *YWMLS*, 61 : 854), many recommend *Język w mediach masowych*, ed. Jerzy Bralczyk and Katarzyna Mosiołek-Kłosińska, Wa, Oświata "UN-O", 234 pp., which includes W. Pisarek, 'III Forum Kultury Słowa' (5–7); Id., 'Język w mediach, media w języku' (9–18); S. Gajda, 'Media — tygiel współczesnej polszczyzny' (19–27); H. Satkiewicz 'Językowe przejawy agresji w mediach' (28–33); A. M. Lewicki and P. Nowak, 'Manipulacja językowa w mediach' (34–42); J. Bralczyk and G. Majkowska, 'Język mediów — perspektywa aksjologiczna' (43–50); H. and T. Zgółko, 'Polszczyzna mediów w komunikacji codziennej — ślady naśladownictwa' (51–59); A. Grybosiowa, 'O dystansie, szacunku i tolerancji w mediach' (60–66); T. Smółkowa, 'Nowe słownictwo w prasie' (67–79); J. Miodek, 'Gramatyczne i stylistyczne znaki czasu w mediach', 79–82); W. Lubaś, 'Słownictwo potoczne w mediach' (83–95); A. Markowski, 'Jawne i ukryte nowsze zapożyczenia leksykalne w mediach' (96–111); K. Mosiołek-Kłosińska, 'Wulgaryzacja języka w mediach' (112–19); W. Kajtoch, J. Kołodziej and P. Planeta, 'Język czasopism dla młodzieży: świat, wartość, perswazja' (120–34); J. Podracki, 'Potoczne elementy językowe w polszczyźnie radia i telewizji' (135–42); W. Cockiewicz, 'Konstrukcje analityczne w języku polskiej telewizji w latach siedemdziesiątych i dziś' (143–53); B. Boniecka and J. Panasiuk, 'Audycja radiowa jako tekst' (154–75); W. Godzic, 'Język w Internecie: Czy piszemy to, co myślimy?' (176–85); A. Choduń and M. Zieliński, 'Język dyskusji medialnej nad tworzeniem prawa' (186–99); E. Polański and B. Skowronek, 'Językowe programy edukacyjne' (200–09); Z. Pietrasik, 'Język krytyki artystycznej' (210–15); W. Gruszczyński, 'Edukacja językowa dziennikarzy' (216–22) and a number of contributions from the floor (223–34). Of related interest, *Polska polityka językowa na przełomie tysiącleci*, ed. Jan Mazur, Lublin, UMCS U.P., 1999, 188 pp., and *Polszczyzna w komunikowaniu publicznym*, ed. W. Gruszczyński, J. Bralczyk and G. Majkowska, Wa, Aspra, 1999, 151 pp.

Władysław Chłopicki and Jerzy Świątek, *Angielski w polskiej reklamie*, Wa-Kw, PWN, 629 pp., in a wide-ranging and perceptive study, have to admit that it is often impossible to prove that an advertisement has been modelled on English rather than simply written in inept Polish.

Język a komunikacja 1. Język trzeciego tysiąclecia, ed. Grzegorz Szpila, Kw, Tertium, 543 pp., presents papers given at a conference in Cracow in March 2000, including A. Awdiejew, 'Komunikatywizm — nowe horyzonty badań nad językiem' (13–23), B. Dunaj, 'O stanie współczesnej polszczyzny' (25–34), E. Tabakowska, 'Językoznawstwo kognitywne — nowe czy dawne horyzonty badań nad językiem' (57–68), which links contemporary cognitive linguistics with Wundt and Rozwadowski; P. Chruszczewski, 'Aspekty dyskursu religijnego' (81–94); Marta Dąbrowska, 'Język e-maila jako hybryda mowy i pisma' (95–112); J. Frejman 'Kilka uwag o języku studenckim dwu zielonogórskich uczelni u progu XXI wieku' (113–20); J. Kowalikowa, 'Wulgaryzmy we współczesnej polszczyźnie' (121–30); E. Manasterska, 'Dziecięce definiowanie pojęć (133–44); A. Niżegorodcew, 'Język studentów filologii angielskiej' (145–56); J. and K. Ozga, 'Język podręczników szkolnych (na przykładzie biologii do klasy I gimnazjum)' (157–66); W. Pędich, 'Znaczenie znajomości gwarowych określeń medycznych w kontaktach lekarz-pacjent' (167–72); Z. Sawaniewska-Moch and W. Moch, 'Jakim językiem mówi polski hip hop?' (173–84); W. Chłopicki, 'Język angielski w polskiej reklamie' (187–96); B. Rejakowa, 'Metaforyka świata mody a świat ubrań, materiałów, kolorów, stylów' (197–207); J. Stawnicka, 'Innowacje frazeologiczne we współczesnych nagłówkach prasowych'(207–14); G. Szpila, 'Skamielina czy żywy organizm — przysłowie w prasie polskiej' (215–24); J. Światek, 'Efekty retoryczne w przekazach reklamowych' (225–34); M. Wojtak, 'O przemianach w języku mediów (prasa wyspecjalizowana)' (235–44); K. Buczak-Sawczyńska, 'Definicja jako narzędzie walki politycznej (na materiale debat prezydenckich Wałęsa-Kwaśniewski)' (257–66); A. Gałczyńska, 'Przeproszenia w dialogu polityków' (267–76); E. Laskowska, 'Przejawy poprawności politycznej w wypowiedziach publicznych (na przykładzie tekstów wygłoszonych podczas sesji Rady Miejskiej Bydgoszczy)' (277–84); A. Pięcińska, 'Język medyczny w służbie satyry politycznej' (285–96); E. Klisiewicz, 'Język polskich i ukraińskich nazw miejscowych (na materiale z byłego województwa tarnopolskiego)' (297–302); J. Labocha, 'Ślady niemieckie w mowie Polaków na Śląsku Cieszyńskim w Republice Czeskiej)' (303–10); A. Ryzza-Woźniak, 'Wpływ Unii Europejskiej na polszczyznę końca XX wieku' (311–18); R. Sosnowski, 'Włoski i polski język informatyki' (319–30); A. Tworek, 'Język sportu — próba definicji (analiza języka polskiego i niemieckiego)' (331–40); and papers on language teaching (353–444) and the language of translation (445–516).

J. Biniewicz, 'Kategoria osoby w tekstach nauk ścisłych', *PJ*, 1999, no.8–9:88–85. B. Boniecka, 'Tekst pisany w ustnej realizacji (na przykładzie radiowych audycji dla dzieci i młodzieży)', *PJ*, no.4:12–30. I. Borkowski, 'Teoretyczne podstawy normatywnej oceny języka polityki i ich praktyczne wykorzystanie w językoznawstwie współczesnym', *PJ*, 1999, no.8–9:49–57. M. Choromańska, 'Żywe metafory w języku dzisiejszej prasy (cz. I)', *PJ*, no.2:49–61, and 'Żywe metafory w języku dzisiejszej prasy (cz. II)', *ib.*, no.3:27–37. Z. Darasz, 'Gwara jako kryterium literackiej normy', *JPol*, 80:146–48, arguing with Skarżyński (*JPol*, 79, 1999:120–21), claims that a linguistic norm must be formulated categorically, like a moral principle. *Słownik gwary miejskiej Poznania*, ed. Maria Gruchmanowa and Bogdan Walczak, Wa-Pń, PWN, 1999, 489 pp. A. Grybosiowa, 'Percepcja sygnałów obcości wyrazów w pokoleniu średnim Polaków', *PJ*, no.6:46–49, and her 'O współczesnym stosunku do normy językowej (uwagi dyskusyjne)', *PJ*, 1999, no.8–9:6–13. J. Jagodzińska, 'Uśmiech i śmiech w dyskusjach internetowych — o sposobach zapisu uczuć towarzyszących wypowiedzi', *PJ*, no.3:38–49, covers emoticons, English-based abbreviations like ROTFL ('rolls on the floor laughing') and Polish expressions like *Pośmiać się można*. M. Kawka, 'Dyskurs i tekst w świetle uwarunkowań konsytuacyjnych', *Polonica*, 19, 1998:31–40. J. Kowalikowa, 'O niejednorodności stylowej prac magisterskich z zakresu metodyki nauczania języka polskiego', *PJ*, 1999, no.8–9:64–72. D. Krzyżyk and H. Synowiec, 'O potrzebie badań nad kompetencją językową uczniów nauczycieli', *ib.*, 82–87. B. Kudra, 'Odchylenia od normy w tekstach oficjalnych jako czynnik kreatywny', *ib.*, 38–42. Iu. A. Labyntsev and L. L. Shchabinskaia, 'Литературное "православных поляков"', *Slavianovedenie*, no.3:81–89, includes (86–89) texts found in manuscript in 1999 of a prayer and of a sermon for Polish Independence Day, which serve as examples of the Polish adaptation of Church Slavonic and Russian textual elements. J. Lizak, 'Elementy reklamy w języku dzieci przedszkolnych', *PJ*, 1999, no.8–9:108–14, and 'Nagłówek reklamy prasowej', *JPol*, 80:219–27. A. G. Matveeva, 'Политика правительства Каприви в сфере преподавания польского языка в Познаньской провинции в 1890–1894 годах', *Slavianovedenie*, no.3:71–80. K. Ożóg, 'Moda na potoczność w tekstach oficjalnych', *PJ*, 1999, no.8–9:29–37. I. Pałucka, 'Czy istnieje "język religijny"?', *JPol*, 80:176–84. M. Peisert, 'Literatura tzw postmodernizmu wobec normy językowej', *PJ*, 1999, no.8–9:24–28. T. Piekot, 'Problem analizy frazeologii socjolektalnej (na przykładzie socjolektu kulturystów nieprofesjonalnych)', *PJ*, no.4:50–56. A. Romanowski, 'The year 1905 and the revival of Polish culture between the Neman and the Dnepr', *CanSP*, 41, 1999, no.1:45–68, is not primarily linguistic, but everything presupposes that 'above all, the Polish language regained its right to exist' (48) and 'became loud and bold' (49, quoting Eliza Orzeszkowa). J. Rusiecki, '"Ja mówię po anglo-polsku" — czyli o polszczyźnie przełomu tysiącleci', *Polonistyka*:342–46. M. Rzeszutko, 'Semantyka symboli w dialogu kultur', *PJ*, no.4:1-11. Z. Sawaniewska-Mochowa and W. Moch, *Poradnik językowy. Polskie gadanie*, Ww, Astrum, 184 pp., includes a section on Wilno regionalisms (121–75). J. Smól, 'Wykorzystanie środków pozaleksykalnych w celach perswazyjnych w prasie', *JPol*, 80:233–44. U. Szyszko, 'Gry językowe w sloganach reklamowych', *ib.*, 228–32. M. Zaśko-Zielińska, 'Recenzja i jej norma gatunkowa', *PJ*, 1999, no.8–9:96–107. J. Zimnowoda, 'Normatywistyka wobec zapożyczeń w języku polskim', *ib.*, 14–23. The texts in I. Bogocz and M. Bortliczek, 'Teksty gwarowe 89. Z Mostów lub Jabłonkowa w Republice Czeskiej', *JPol*, 80:70–76, follow a description of the dialect. Feliks Czyżewski and Stefan Warchoł, **Polskie i ukraińskie teksty gwarowe ze wschodniej Lubelszczyzny*, Lublin, UMCS U.P., 1998, lxx + 497 pp. Karol Dejna, **Atlas gwar polskich, Tom 1. Małopolska*, Wa, 1998, 404 pp., includes 170 maps. E. Dzięgiel, 'Zróżnicowanie gwar polskich na środkowej Ukrainie', *PJ*, no.6:50–61. W. Mańczak, 'Praojczyzna Słowian', *JPol*, 80:325–31, and F. Sławski, 'Do artykułu Witolda Mańczaka', *ib.*, 332–33. W. Steffen, 'Wyrazy pochodzenia francuskiego w dialekcie warmińskim', *ib.*, 63–69. J. Waniakowa, 'Propozycja uogólnionego zapisu cytatów gwarowych w Słowniku gwar polskich', *ib.*, 270–74.

8. INDIVIDUALS, INDIVIDUAL WORKS, STYLISTICS

ANON. H. Karaś, 'O polszczyźnie anonimowej gramatyki języka litewskiego z I ćwierci XIX wieku (przez X.D.K.P.S.). Pisownia, fonetyka', *PJ*, no.7:1–21.

BIBLE. R. Marcinkiewicz, 'Polska eponimia biblijna (*Babilon, Babilonia*)', *PJ*, no.2:27–37.

CIUCHCIA. A. Lobos, 'Nazwy własne w czasopiśmie dla dzieci na przykładzie "Ciuchci" ', *JPol*, 80:245–50.

DIALOG. P. Sulikowski, 'O błędnych tłumaczeniach tekstów prasowych. Na przykładach z niemiecko-polskiego czasopisma "Dialog" ', *JPol*, 80:266–69.

KORWIN-MIKKE. J. Litwin, 'Uwagi o formie językowo-stylistycznej felietonów J. Korwin Mikkego', *PJ*, 1999, no.8–9:58–63, examines Janusz Korwin-Mikke's pieces in the weekly *Angora* in 1998.

STYLISTICS AND VERSIFICATION. M. Kita, 'Słownik jako narzędzie stylu', *Polonistyka*:225–28, in an issue of *Polonistyka* (195–254) containing much on style. W. J. Darasz, 'Polski daktyl', *JPol*, 80:257–65.

MICKIEWICZ. K. Lukas, ' "Litwo! Ojczyzno moja!" w dwóch niemieckich przekładach', *Polonistyka*:358–62.

MŁODA POLSKA. E. Bilas, 'Muzyka, poetyka i stylistyka. Nazwy muzyczne w tytułach wierszy młodopolskich i ich wpływ na językową organizację tekstu', *PJ*, no.4:40–49, continued in 'Muzyka, poetyka i stylistyka, Nazwy muzyczne w tytułach wierszy młodopolskich i ich wpływ na językową organizację tekstu (cz. II)', *PJ*, no.5:11–18, and 'Muzyka, poetyka i stylistyka. Nazwy muzyczne w tytułach wierszy młodopolskich i ich wpływ na językową organizację tekstu (dokończenie)', *PJ*, no.6:41–45.

PROBLEMY. M. Górnicz, 'Elementy anglojęzyczne w tekstach medycznych (na podstawie tekstów z dziedziny immunologii opublikowanych w miesięczniku "Problemy")', *PJ*, no.2 : 17–26.

PUSHKIN. M. Rychlewski, 'Tuwim kontra Wążyk, czyli *Oniegin* w służbie socjalizmu', *Polonistyka* : 347–52.

RILKE. K. Kuczyńska-Koschany, 'O jednym wierszu Rainera Marii Rilkego w ośmiu polskich przekładach', *Polonistyka* : 353–57.

STAFF. M. Walicka, '"Wysokie drzewa" inaczej, czyli o grupie leksykalno-semantycznej drzew w tomie poezji Leopolda Staffa', *JPol*, 80 : 251–56, and her 'Mitologiczne nazwy własne w poezji Leopolda Staffa', *Onomastica*, 43, 1998[1999] : 291–308.

VARIOUS. *Polszczyzna stara i nowa*, ed. Łucja Maria Szewczyk, Wyd. Uczelniane Wyższej Szkoły Pedagogicznej w Bydgoszczy, 193 pp., contains M. Wronkowska-Dimitrowa, 'Z rozważań nad osobliwościami leksykalnymi *Biblii Leopolity*' (9–20), A. Paluszak-Bronka, 'Uwagi o fleksji zaimka w kazaniach *O siedmi Sákrámentách* księdza Piotra Skargi' (21–38) and 'Uwagi o fleksji przymiotnika i imiesłowu przymiotnikowego w kazaniach *O siedmi Sákrámentách* księdza Piotra Skargi' (39–52); M. Pająkowska-Kensik, 'Słownictwo kociewskie na tle gwar sąsiednich' (53–62); M. Marszałek, 'Osobliwości fonetyczne, fleksyjne i składniowe w *Przyrodoznawstwie* M. Skatkina i W. Kwietkowskasa (z badań nad polszczyzną podręczników wydawanych na Radzieckiej Litwie)' (63–80); Z. Sawaniewska-Mochowa, W. Moch, '"Oparta na faktach rymonacja" — uwagi o słownictwie hiphopowym' (97–120); J. Mędelska, 'Z problematyki badań nad powojenną składnią północnokresową' (81–96); W. Czechowski, 'Zakłócenia w porozumiewaniu się ludzi (analiza tekstów mówionych)' (123–36); M. Jaracz, 'Z problematyki kształtowaniu się nazwiska historycznego w Kaliszu doby średniopolskiej' (137–46); Ł. M. Szewczyk and A. Ziółkowska, 'Nazwy osobowe w *Kobietach* Zofii Nałkowskiej' (159–80); Ł. M. Szewczyk, 'Nazwiska Niechcic i Ostrzeński w *Nocach i dniach* Marii Dąbrowskiej' (181–93).

WYBICKI. I. Szczepankowska, 'Konceptualizacja pojęcia prawo w dobie oświecenia (na materiale *Listów patriotycznych* Józefa Wybickiego)', *PJ*, no.2 : 3–16.

9. POLISH AND OTHER LANGUAGES

E. Mańczak-Wohlfeld, 'Jeszcze o najnowszych zapożyczeniach angielskich w języku polskim', *PJ*, no.2 : 74–76. K. Szewczyk, 'Jak przekłada się komizm?', *Polonistyka* : 363–69. E. Teodorowicz-Hellman, 'Teoria prototypów a nazwy barw w języku polskim i szwedzkim. Obrazy konceptualne nazw barw a ich eksplikacje językowe', *Polonica*, 19, 1998:75–92. Z. Tęcza, 'Faux-amis im West-slawischen', *ZSl*, 45:404–12, looks at false friends in Polish, Czech and Slovak. I. Vaňková, 'Kognitivně-kulturní inspirace z Polska', *SaS*, 60, 1999:214–24. W. Witkowski, *Słownik zapożyczeń polskich w języku rosyjskim*, Kw, Universitas, 1999, xxii + 225 pp.

Prace Językoznawcze 199 (ZNUJ, 1224), ed. Stanisław Stachowski, Kw, Jagiellonian U.P., 1999, 176 pp., includes M. Dąbrowska, 'A comparison of politeness in English and Polish questions — their function and meaning' (25–36), observing that questions can show a range from negative politeness which respects the freedom and decision of the addressees to strong criticism (bordering on explicit rudeness) carried by certain exclamatory uses of question structures; M. Kałucka-Bieniek, 'Wariantywność fleksyjna polszczyzny mówionej tarnobrzeżan' (47–56); A. Parzniewska, 'En kort översicht av interjektioner i svenskan och polskan med fokus på emotiva interjektioner' (81–91), using material from contemporary Swedish novels and their Polish translations, and paying particular attention to *a!*, seeks a common model for analysing interjections in Swedish and Polish; G. Szpila, 'Tłumaczenie frazeologizmów: przysłowia', (130–37); A. Vogelgesang, 'Der kommunikative Aspekt der Wortfolge im Deutschen und im Polnischen' (139–51); A. Zajda, 'Z historii polskiego słownictwa rzemieślniczego. Nazwy narzędzi stolarkich w kilku tekstach z okresu od początku XVII do XX wieku' (153–71). *Przekładając nieprzekładalne. Materiały z I międzynarodowej konferencji translatorycznej Gdańsk-Elbląg*, ed. Wojciech Kubiński, Ola Kubińska and Tadeusz Z. Wolański, Gdańsk U.P., 584 pp., presents papers covering cognitivism and translation (19–94), linguistic views of translation (96–138), translation of proper names (141–55), translation and culture differences (173–229), bible translation (233–82), translating Shakespeare (285–323), Polish translation of British and American literature (327–415), translation of Polish literature into other languages (419–74), titles (477–89), and other matters (493–579).

10. ONOMASTICS

E. Breza, 'Nazwiska *Bałenda, Tałanda, Tełęda* i podobne', *PJ*, no.3:65–69; Id., 'Zapomniane imię *Kisz* i jego onomastyczna rodzina etymologiczna', *Onomastica*, 43, 1998[1999]:257–66; Id., 'Raz jeszcze o nazwisku *Mudlaff*', *JPol*, 80:316–17. M. Chorośand Ł. Jarczak, 'Wykaz przejściowych nazw miejscowych na Opolszczyźnie w latach 1945–1948', *ib.*, 53–80. P. Ferenc, 'Zakazane *-ji*. Z zagadnień fleksji onomastycznej', *ib.*, 148–50, is concerned with names like *Ziaja*, genitive *Ziai*, a legacy of the orthographical chaos of earlier periods, especially the 19th c., and notes occurrences of <Ziaji, Stryji, Leji>, reflecting the pronunciation [-ji]. K. Heska-Kwaśniewicz, '"Imiona wojenne", czyli pseudonimy szaroszeregowej młodzieży. Rekonesans badawczy', *ib.*, 341–54. M. Jaśkiewicz, 'Imiona współczesnych mieszkańców Łasku', *Onomastica*, 43, 1998[1999]:171–91. D. Kopertowska, 'Topograficzna motywacja nazw miejscowych (na przykładzie Kielecczyzny)', *ib.*, 37–51. C. Kosyl, 'Kynonimy literackie na tle zoonimii uzualnej (część III)', *ib.*, 309–39. B. Kreja, 'Staropolskie imiona typu *Mszczuj* a współczesne nazwiska *Żdżuj//Zdzuj//Zduj*', *JPol*, 80:10–14. W. Makarski, '*Przeworsk*', *Onomastica*, 43, 1998[1999]:81–100; Przeworsk is between Rzeszów, Jarosław and Przemyśl. E. Oronowicz-Kida, 'Fenomen nazewniczy przezwisk', *ib.*, 249–55. J. Parniewska, 'Nazwy zakładów pogrzebowych', *ib.*, 283–89. R. Plichta, 'Imiona chrzestne w księgach metrykalnych katedry łowickiej w latach 1951–1955 oraz 1991–1995', *ib.*, 101–16. M. Rutkiewicz, 'Przydomki i przezwiska we wsi Bolewice koło Nowego Tomyśla oraz ich formy marytonimiczne, patronimiczne i matronimiczne', *ib.*, 141–69, and 'Semantyka nazw poznańskich aptek', *JPol*, 80:185–96. **Polskie nazwy własne. Encyklopedia*, ed. Ewa Rzetelska-Feleszko, Wa-Kw, Towarzystwo Naukowe Warszawskie PAN IJP, 1998, 544 pp., and her 'Obecne nazwy firmowe w Polsce i w Europie', *Onomastica*, 43, 1998[1999]:267–81. M. Sagan, 'Tendencje nazewnicze w plateonimii najstarszej części Przemyśla (XV-XX w.)' (93–110) is concerned with street names, urban toponyms. H. S[atkiewicz], 'O współistnieniu nazw uwag kilka', *PJ*, no.1:52–54, deals with *Jagiełł(on)owie* and *petro-* and *naftochemia*. R. S. '*Aachen — Akwizgran, Budziszyn — Bautzen*', *PJ*, no.6:73–77, while their 'Nazwy miejscowe', *PJ*, no.3:59–64, covers Wąwolnica, Pelplin, Tczew, Płock, Świdnica, Wola, Lgota and Karolówka. Z. Saloni, 'Co lepsze: *kazachski* czy *kazaski*?', *JPol*, 80:35–38, objects to *kazachski* as an orthographical barbarism. K. Zierhoffer, Z. Zierhofferowa, 'Nazewnictwo zachodnioeuropejskie w polszczyźnie drugiej połowy XIX wieku z perspektywy jego stanu w drugiej połowie XVIII wieku', *Onomastica*, 43, 1998[1999]:9–36.

LITERATURE

By JOHN BATES, *University of Glasgow*

1. GENERAL

Grażyna Borkowska, Małgorzata Czermińska, and Ursula Phillips, *Pisarki polskie od średniowiecza do współczesności. Przewodnik*, Gd, słowo/ obraz terytoria, 217 pp., is an invaluable guide to Polish women writers, divided chronologically into five chapters consisting of an overview followed by short sketches of individual authors. *Literatura polska XX wieku. Przewodnik encyklopedyczny*, ed. Artur Hutnikiewicz and Andrzej Lam, PWN: vol. I, xv + 496 pp., covers the letters A-O, while vol. II, 592 pp., deals with P-Z, and contains supplementary material (578–90). *Dictionary of Literary Biography. Twentieth-Century Eastern European Writers. First Series*, vol. 215, ed. Steven Serafin with Jan Čulík, Bogdan Czaykowski et al., Detroit—San Francisco, Gale, 1999, xxi + 479 pp., includes biographical sketches of key Polish writers from the Modernist era to the immediate postwar period, with useful bibliographies. *Leksykon kultury polskiej poza krajem od roku 1939. Tom 1*, ed. Krzysztof Dybciak and Zdzisław Kudelski (Prace Wydziału Historyczno-Filologicznego, 74), KUL, 567 pp. + 8 pp. of illus., whilst not limited to literature, contains, *inter alia*, an entry for M. Pankowski.

Pieniądz w literaturze i teatrze, ed. Jacek Bachórz, Sopot, Pracownia Impuls, 285 pp., presents materials from a symposium at Gdańsk University in January 2000, and addresses the issue of money in Polish and other cultures from Old Testament times to the present. *Ostrożnie z literaturą (przykłady, wykłady oraz inne rady)*, ed. Stanisław Balbus and Włodzimierz Bolecki (Z Dziejów Form Artystycznych w Literaturze Polskiej, 80), IBL, 231 pp., is an even more eclectic volume from this entertaining series than usual, being based on a conference in Krynica in September 1997. The companion volume based on the following year's conference, Balcerzan, *Osoba*, 276 pp., is largely theoretical, but items on individual authors are dealt with below.

Maria Janion's writings on Polish literature have been collected into five volumes entitled *Prace wybrane*, under the general editorship of M. Czermińska, and published by Universitas in Cracow as part of the 'Klasycy współczesnej polskiej myśli humanistycznej' series. Vol. I, *Gorączka romantyczna*, xxv + 568 pp. contains a general introduction by Czermińska, while vol. II gathers various essays under the general heading of *Tragizm, historia, prywatność*, 466 pp. Her *Do Europy — tak, ale razem z naszymi umarłymi*, Wa, Sic!, 269 pp., contains speeches, interviews and articles devoted to anti-Semitism, A. Mickiewicz, S. Pigoń and other issues. Henryk Markiewicz, *Polskie teorie powieści. Od początków do schyłku XX wieku*, PWN, 1998, 208 pp., complements his 1997 tome on such issues outwith Poland, while his *Dopowiedzenia. Rozprawy i szkice z wiedzy o literaturze*, WL, 323 pp., contains essays on scholars and critics such as R. Ingarden, K. Wyka, J. Kleiner, and K. Irzykowski, as well as particular literary works including A. Fredro's *Pan Jowialski* and an account of the reception of A. Mickiewicz's *Pan Tadeusz* in the years 1925–1998.

Romuald Cudak, *Światopełna treść dziwosłów. Szkice o współczesnej poezji polskiej*, Katowice, Śląsk, 1999, 234 pp., discusses interwar poets associated with Skamander, and postwar writers such as W. Iwaniuk, J. M. Rymkiewicz, R. Wojaczak and M. Białoszewski. Gömöri, *Poles*, is a useful collection of comparative essays published over the past 30 years on primarily modern Polish and Hungarian poetry; the chapters on individual Polish authors are listed below. Jan Grzenia, *Język poetycki jako struktura polifoniczna. Na materiale poezji polskiej XX wieku* (Prace Naukowe, 1785), Katowice, wyd. Uniwersytetu Śląskiego, 1999, 154 pp., is a pragmatic and sociolinguistically oriented study. The two generations in Marian Kisiel's *Pamięć, biografia, słowo. Szkice o poetach dwóch generacji*, Katowice, Gnome, 122 pp., are the wartime and immediate postwar debutants Z. Stroiński and T. Różewicz, and the postwar 'Kontynenty' generation based in emigration, including A. Czerniawski and B. Czaykowski. Jolanta Krzysztoforska-Doschak, *Prawosłowiańskie źródła nowszej poezji polskiej*, Kw, Collegium Columbinum, 202 pp., contains pieces on J. B. Ożóg, B. Leśmian, two articles comparing T. Lenartowicz and M. Jasnorzewska-Pawlikowska and M. Konopnicka. Anna Nasiłowska, *Persona lyriczna*, IBL, 304 pp., focuses upon J. Iwaszkiewicz and K. Wierzyński, amongst others. Jerzy Poradecki, *Prorocy i sztukmistrze. Eseje o poezji polskiej XX wieku*, PWN, 1999, 263 pp., discusses the work of the Nobel laureates as well as J. Tuwim, Z. Herbert and T. Różewicz. Dariusz Tomasz, *Marmur i blask. Studia, szkice, artykuły o poezji polskiej od Mickiewicza do Miłosza*, Bydgoszcz, WSP, 547 pp., collects essays written between 1985 and 1999. Anna Węgrzyniakowa, *Egzystencjalne i metafizyczne. Od Leśmiana do Maja*, Katowice, wyd. Uniwersytetu Śląskiego, 1999, 155 pp., discusses eight poets including A. Świrszczyńska, W. Szymborska and S. Barańczak. *Lyrika polska XX wieku. Analizy i interpretacje. Seria druga*, ed. Włodzimierz Wójcik with Danuta Opacka-Walasek (Prace Naukowe, 1836), Katowice, wyd. Uniwersytetu Śląskiego, 209 pp., analyses individual poems by writers from B. Leśmian to A. Zagajewski.

Tematy i pryzmaty. Studia o prozie polskiej XX wieku, ed. Alina Brodzka and Zygmunt Ziątek, Ww, Ossolineum, 200 pp., contains contributions on P. Jasienica, H. Krall and R. Kapuściński, Nałkowska (by

Borkowska) and others by respected Polish scholars. Michał Janusz-kiewicz, *Tropami egzystencjalizmu w literaturze polskiej XX wieku. O prozie Aleksandra Wata, Stanisława Dygata i Edwarda Stachury* (Poznańskie Studia Polonistyczne. Seria Literacka, 11), Pń, ABEDIK, 1998, 218 pp., is an impressive study. Marek Ruszkowski, *O stylu prozy polskiej XX wieku. Zbiór studiów*, Kielce, WSP, 188 pp., after chapters devoted to style and general related issues, examines the language of such writers as M. Kuncewiczowa (*Cudzoziemka*), W. Gombrowicz, G. Herling-Grudziński's *Dziennik pisany nocą*, B. Schulz, A. Brycht in comparison with M. Hłasko and M. Nowakowski as well as J. Morton's *Appassionata*. Elżbieta Rybicka, *Formy labiryntu w prozie polskiej XX wieku*, Kw, Universitas, 193 pp., discusses this question in relation to W. Berent's *Ozimina* and works by B. Schulz and T. Parnicki, as well as M. Gretkowska's *Kabaret metafizyczny*. Leszek Szaruga, *Historia, państwo, literatura. Polska powieść współczesna jako przestrzeń pytań o sens procesów dziejowych* (Rozprawy i studia, 326), Szczecin, Uniwersytet Szczeciński, 1999, 277 pp., discusses major prose works from the late 19th to the late 20th centuries.

Muzy i bestia. Studia dedykowane Profesor Ludwice Śląkowej, ed. Marcin Cieński and Jacek Sokolski, Ww, Wyd. Uniwersytetu Warszawskiego, 1999, 327 pp. *Między polityką a literaturą*, ed. Marceli Kosman, Pń, "Terra", 1999, 211 pp., includes essays on Mickiewicz, H. Sienkiewicz, the reception of S. Żeromski's *Przedwiośnie* in the Włocławek region and Polish Western (i.e. German) thinking in the journalism and novels published between 1945 and 1980. Aleksander Wojciech Mikołajczak, *Łacina w kulturze polskiej* ('A to Polska właśnie . . .'), Ww, wyd. Dolnośląskie, 1998, 342 pp., is a colourful and richly illustrated account of the influence of Latin upon Polish culture from the beginnings to the present. *Lektury polonistyczne. Literatura współczesna T.II*, ed. R. Nycz, Kw, Universitas, 1999, 533 pp., gathers eminent critics' responses to individual works and writers as well as movements up to the 1990s. Jan Pieszczachowicz, *Smutek międzyepoki. Szkice o literature i kulturze* (Biblioteka Stowarzyszenia Autorów Polskich, 17), Kw, Galicyjska Oficyna Wydawnicza, 552 pp., is an enormously varied collection of essays published over the last 30 years on topics such as the New Wave, L. Buczkowski and M. Brandys. *Z problemów literatury i kultury XX wieku. Prace ofiarowane Tadeuszowi Kłakowi*, ed. Stefan Zabierowski, Katowice, Śląsk, 377 pp., has essays on the interwar poetic avantgarde, T. Różewicz and the diaries of Nałkowska and M. Dąbrowska.

Małgorzata Czermińska, *Autobiograficzny trójkąt. Świadectwo, wyznanie i wyzwanie*, Kw, Universitas, 346 pp. Peter Drews, *Deutsch-Polnische Literaturbeziehungen 1800–1850* (398), Munich, Otto Sagner, 296 pp., examines the Polish reception of German works and vice versa for the period, and presents an overall picture of developments. Bolesław Hadaczek, *Kresy w literaturze polskiej. Studia i szkice*, Gorzów Wielkopolski, Wojewódzki Ośrodek Metodyczny, 1999, 300 pp., devotes its third section to specific writers including J. Iwaszkiewicz, M. Hemar, and Z. Haupt. Gerda Hagenau, *Zwischen deutscher und polnischer Literatur. Vorträge, Aufsätze, Interviews, Laudationes* (Slavische Sprachen und Literaturen, 16), Frankfurt am Main, Lang, 392 pp., gathers essays on many aspects of Polish literature from the Renaissance (M. Rej) to the 20th century (M. Dąbrowska). Elżbieta Konończuk, *Literatura i pamięć na pograniczu kultur*, Białystok, Towarzystwo Literackie im. Adama Mickiewicza, Oddział Białostocki, 221 pp. Chone Shmenek, *Legenda o Esterze w literaturze jidysz i polskiej*, Wa, Wydawnictwo Naukowe N, xi + 153 pp., is a translation by Monika Adamczyk-Garbowska of the 1985 Jerusalem edition. *Folklor i pogranicza*, ed. Andrzej Staniszewski and Beata Tarnowska, Olsztyń, WSP, 1998, 297 pp., contains essays on Lithuanian folk elements in A. Mickiewicz's early work, the poetry of K. Brodziński and the views of J. Czapski.

Halina Bursztyńska, *Kraszewski, Orzeszkowa, Sienkiewicz. Studia i szkice* (Prace monograficzne, 253), Kw, WSP, 1998, 184 pp., contains sketches written between 1985 and 1997. Stanisław Eile, *Literature and Nationalism in Partitioned Poland, 1795–1918*, Houndmills, Basingstoke and London, MacMillan, 234 pp., is a standard account of the relations between literature and Polish society under foreign occupation. Jerzy Narbutt, *Od Kraszewskiego do Parnickiego*, Katowice, Unia, 88 pp., examines the historical novel. *Literatura wobec i wojny światowej*, ed. Maria Jolanta Olszewska and Jadwiga Zacharska, Wa, Wydział Polonistyki Uniwersytetu Warszawskiego, 173 pp. *Literatura polska wobec zagłady*, ed. A. Brodzka-Wald, D. Krawczyńska and J. Leociak, Wa, Żydowski Instytut Historyczny Instytut Naukowo-Badawczy, 291 pp.

A. M. Bąbel, 'Garnek i księga — związki tekstu kulinarnego z tekstem literackim w literaturze polskiej XIX wieku', *TD*, no.6:163–81. I. Węgrzyn, 'Czarna legenda "Greckiej bajadery" — Zofii Wittowej-Potockiej w literaturze polskiej dziewiętnastego stulecia', *RuLit*, 40, 1999:439–56, deals with an alleged Russian informer known to Mickiewicz and others.

2. FROM THE MIDDLE AGES UP TO ROMANTICISM

Źródła wiedzy teoretyczno-literackiej w dawnej Polsce. Średniowiecza — Renesans — Barok, ed. Maria Cytowska and Teresa Michałowska, PWN, 1999, 514 pp., is an anthology of texts with a brief introduction. *Seminaria staropolskie. Literatura w kontekstach kulturowych*, ed. Roman

Krzywy, Wa, Wyd. Uniwersytetu Warszawskiego, 1997, 266 pp., has contributions on Marian songs, Polish perceptions of France and the French in the 17th c., and an essay by M. Stryjkowska on the problem of liberty in the poetry of M. Sęp Szarzyński (77–107). *Inspiracje platońskie literatury staropolskiej*, ed. Alina Nowicka-Jeżowa and Paweł Stępień, Wa, Instytut Literatury Polskiej Uniwersytetu Warszawskiego, 315 pp., considers J. Kochanowski, K. Janicki, J. A. Morsztyn's *Lutnia* and S. Szymonowicz's *Żeńcy, inter alia*. *Wątki neostoickie w literaturze polskiego renesansu i baroku*, ed. Piotr Urbański (Materiały, Konferencje, 40), Szczecin, Uniwersytet Szczeciński, 1999, 276 pp., containing articles on M. K. Sarbiewski, S. H. Lubomirski, and Callimachus's portrayal of Grzegorz z Sanoka as well as a number of essays in English on Kochanowski, stems from a session on Neostoicism in October 1997. *Pisarki polskie epok dawnych*, ed. Krystyna Stasiewicz, Olsztyń, WSP, 1998, 211 pp., is a collection of essays divided into two parts: general reflections and specific authors, such as I. Czartoryska and E. Drużbacka. The third volume in the recently established series 'Humanistyka i płeć', *Publiczna przestrzeń kobiet. Obrazy dawne i nowe*, ed. Elżbieta Pakszys and Włodzimierz Heller, UAM, 1999, 336 pp., contains an essay by E. Skibiński, 'Postaci kobiet w kronikach Galla Anonima i mistrza Wincentego' (19–37). Bogdan Hojdis, *O współistnieniu słów i obrazów w kulturze polskiego średniowiecza*, Gniezno-Pń, Gnieźnieńska Firma Wydawnicza, 163 pp. Marek Prejs, *Egzotyka w literaturze staropolskiej. Wybrane problemy*, Wa, Instytut Literatury Polskiej Uniwersytetu Warszawskiego, 1999, 274 pp., examines the theme of geographical exoticism in writings, both literary and non-literary, on the 'East' in general, Constantinople, Asia and Africa. Bernadetta Maria Puchalska, *Obraz dworów zachodnioeuropejskich w polskiej literaturze pamiętnikarskiej XVI i XVII wieku*, Białystok, wyd. Uniwersytetu w Białymstoku, 176 pp., is largely sociological. The fourth chapter of Ludvík Štěpán's *Polʃká epigramatika žánry fraška a epigram ve spektru malých literárních forem*, Brno, Masarykova Univerzita w Brně, 1998, 168 pp., discusses the history of developments in Poland with reference to J. Kochanowski and the Latin Renaissance epigrams. *Polish Literature from the Middle Ages to the End of the Eighteenth Century. A Bilingual Anthology*, selected and trans. Michael J. Mikoš, Wa, Constans, 1999, 684 pp., is based on his three previous anthologies.

PL(W), 91.3, devoted to Old Polish literature, includes the general essays: M. Górska, 'Konieczność śmierci. Refleksja na temat upadku Polski w piśmiennictwie końca XVIII wieku' (117–46), N. Korniłłowicz, 'Narcyz i narcyzm w poezji staropolskiej' (57–68), M. Prejs, '*Pochwała piersi* i problem rokoka na przełomie XVII i XVIII wieku' (191–200), C. K. Święcki, 'Apogeum kultury średniowiecznego

Płocka. Piśmiennictwo XII wieku' (7–33), W. Wojtowicz, 'Marchołt i mnemonika wieków średnich' (35–55); the comparative H. Bogdziewicz, 'Dwie odmiany lyriki osobistej w utworach pijarów doby oświecenia. Marcina Eysymonta *Job z gruntu nieszczęśliwy* i Piotra Celestyna Tyszyńskiego *Duma w starości'* (95–116), and H. Dziechińska 'Kobieta w *Dworzanie* Baldassare'a Castiglione, Luisa Milana i Łukasza Górnickiego' (69–81). J. Pelc, 'Recepcja idei humanizmu i renesansu w Polsce', *PrzH*, 44.3:21–29. Elżbieta Aleksandrowska, *Zabawy Przyjemne i Pożyteczne 1770–1777. Monografia bibliograficzna*, IBL, 1999, xxiv + 243 pp. + 14 pp. of illus. Marcin Cieński, *Pejsaże oświeconych. Sposoby przedstawienia krajobrazu w literaturze polskiej w latach 1770–1830*, WUW, 308 pp., considers landscape in the work of writers from Naruszewicz to K. Brodziński. J. IJ Van der Meer, ' "Bemerkungen über Warschau" als Gegenstück zu Reiseberichten von Vertretern der europäischen Aufklärung über Polen', *ZSl*, 45:220–33; and his 'Comedies and novels in the memoirs of Julian U. Niemcewicz and Adam J. Czartoryski', *ZSP*, 59.1:123–37. M. Skrzypek, 'Lukrecjusz w poezji filozoficznej polskiego oświecenia', *PrzH*, 44.3:1–19.

INDIVIDUAL WRITERS

BOHOMOLEC. J. IJ Van der Meer, 'The Muchowski-letter and the introduction to *Małżeństwo z kalendarza*: on literary production and criticism in the first years of the Stanisław age', *ZSl*, 44, 1999:93–102, argues that the letter was not in fact a genuine audience response, but reflected rather the growing institutionalization of literary criticism in *Monitor*.

CHRÓŚCIŃSKI. M. Krzysztofik, 'Moralny aspect cierpienia w barokowym przewierszowaniu biblijnej *Księgi Hioba — Jobie cierpiącym [. . .]* Wojciecha Stanisława Chróścińskiego', *RuLit*, 40, 1999:457–68.

CZARTORYSKI. J. IJ Van der Meer, 'A. K. Czartoryski's machinations as a critic, or: Programmatic literary criticism and reviews in the Stanisław Age', *WSl*, 45:79–102.

DŁUGOSZ. T. Ulewicz, 'Długoszowe *Dzieje Polski* w przeróbce angielskiej', *RuLit*, 40, 1999:483–86, is a highly useful critique of the 1997 edition of *The Annals of Jan Długosz*.

GALL ANONIM. Czesław Deptuła, *Galla Anonima mit genezy Polski. Studium z historiozofii i hermeneutyki symboli dziejopisarstwa średniowiecznego*, Lublin, Instytut Europy Środkowo-wschodniej, 395 pp.

KOCHANOWSKI. M. Walińska, '*Lyricorum bibellus* i *Pieśni ksi dwoje —* analizy i propozycje', *PrLit*, 37:5–34.

KONARSKI. P. Żbikowski, 'Stanisław Konarski. W trzechsetlecie urodzin', *RuLit*, 41:155–69.

KRASICKI. R. Drowski, 'Relacje komunikacyjne w *Antymonachomachii* Ignacego Krasicki', *ib.*, 40, 1999:141–56. H. Wiśniewska, 'Zachowania grzecznościowe w listach rodzinnych Ignacego Krasickiego', *PL(W)*, 91.3:161–76.

KRZYCKI. J. Wójcicki, '*Glosa Ciciana*: Sarmackie echo renesansowej epigramatyki', *RuLit*, 40, 1999:125–40, deals with K.'s *In laudem musicae*.

LUBOMIRSKI. J. Dąbkowska, 'Problem erudycji w *Rozmowach Artaksesa i Ewandra* Stanisława Herakliusza Lubomirskiego', *PL(W)*, 91.3:83–94.

J. A. MORSZTYN. Alina Nowicka-Jeżowa, *Jan Andrzej Morsztyn i Giambattista Marino. Dialog poetów europejskiego baroku* (VI, 55), Wa, Wyd. Wydziału Polonistyki Uniwersytetu Warszawskiego, 430 pp. *Czytanie Jana Andrzeja Morsztyna*, ed. Dorota Gostyńska and Adam Karpiński, Ww, Ossolineum, 198 pp.

Z. MORSZTYN. J. Sokolski, ' "Jabłko sodomskiej krainy". Glosa do "Votum" Zbigniewa Morsztyna', *PL(W)*, 91.3:187–90.

NARUSZEWICZ. *Czytanie Naruszewicza. Interpretacje*, ed. Tomasz Chachulski, Ww, Ossolineum, 270 pp.

OSTRORÓG. Maria Wichowa, *Pisarstwo Jana Ostroroga 1565–1622*, Łódź, wyd. Uniwersytetu Łódzkiego, 1998, 372 pp., rediscovers an unjustly neglected writer and presents a thorough analysis and account of O.'s literary activity.

SARBIEWSKI. The fifth chapter (174–216) of Andrzej Borowski's *Powrót Europy*, Kw, Księgarnia Akademicka, 1999, 279 pp., is devoted to the poet. M. Łukasiewicz-Chantny, 'Epigramaty Macieja Kazimierza Sarbiewskiego w świetle jego teorii poetyckiej', *PL(W)*, 91.4:7–14.

SĘP SZARZYŃSKI. *Poezje*, ed. J. S. Gruchała, Kw, Universitas, 1997, 149 pp., contains a useful introduction (5–60).

SZYMONOWIC. D. Chemperek, 'Groteska i śmierć: *Nagrobki zbieranej drużyny* Szymona Szymonowicza', *RuLit*, 40, 1999:289–96.

TWARDOWSKI. Renata Ryba, *'Książę Wiśniowiecki Janusz' Samuela Twardowskiego na tle bohaterskiej epiki biograficznej siedemnastego wieku* (Prace Naukowe, 1832), Katowice, wyd. Uniwersytetu Śląskiego, 157 pp., provides a thorough analysis of the poem, placing it in the context of T.'s own work, of the historical situation and of Polish literature as a whole.

ZABŁOCKI. *Dramaty Franciszka Zabłockiego. Interpretacje*, ed. Marcin Cieński and Teresa Kostkiewiczowa, WUW, 200 pp.

3. ROMANTICISM

Marian Ursel, *Romantyzm. Leksykon Literatury polskiej*, Ww, wyd. Dolnośląskie, 304 pp. *Schweizerische Beiträge zum XII. Internationalen*

Slavistenkongress in Krakau, August 1998, ed. Jan Peter Locher (Slavica Helvetica, 60), Frankfurt am Main, Lang, 1998, 506 pp., contains two essays on Romantic issues: J. Bischof, 'Die Komposition von Juliusz Słowackis Poem *W Szwajcarii*' (21–42) and R. Fieguth, 'Zur Poetik der Komposition bei Mickiewicz. Am Beispiel des *Ustęp* der *Dziady III*' (89–127). G. Królikiewicz, 'Towiański i "czas proroków"', *RuLit*, 40, 1999:1–18. B. Oleksowicz, 'Abaddon (Joachim Lelewel w opinii Kajetana Koźmiana)', *ib.*, 73–87. J. Ziabicka, 'Słowacki i Mickiewicz — dwie kwestie krytyczne. *Beniowski* V 179–180 i *Konrad Wallenrod* IV 255–256', *PL(W)*, 90.6:117–27.

INDIVIDUAL WRITERS

FREDRO. M. Ursel, 'Własna biografia jako temat twórczości pozako-mediowej Aleksandra Fredry', *PrLit*, 37:35–55.

KRASIŃSKI. Z. K. Piechocki, 'Wątki gnostyckie w *Listach do Delfiny Potockiej* Zygmunta Krasińskiego', *PrzH*, 44.1–2:137–50.

KRASZEWSKI. Edward Czapiewski, *Między buntem a ugodą. Kształtowanie się poglądów politycznych Józefa Ignacego Kraszewskiego*, WUW, 240 pp. *PL(W)*, 91.2, has two essays on K.: J. A. Kalmożeska, 'Jeszcze o muzie *Starej Baśni*' (175–79) and B. Mazan, 'Ahasverus polski według *Nocy bezsennych* Józefa Ignacego Kraszewskiego' (45–73).

LENARTOWICZ. M. Bojko, 'Korespondencja Teofila Lenartowicza z Teofilem Kwiatkowskim (1858–1882)', *PrzH*, 44.1–2:151–72, is mostly newly discovered correspondence. D. Dąbrowska, 'Wykłady bolońskie Teofila Lenartowicza', *RuLit*, 41:271–84.

MICKIEWICZ. Dora Kacnelson, *Poezja Mickiewicza wśród powstańców wieku XIX*, Kw, Universitas, 1999, 224 pp. + 1 errata, is based on archives in Vilnius, Lviv and Czytaj. Tomasz Łubieński, *M jako Mickiewicz*, Wa, Świat Książki, 1998, 317 pp., is a literary biography. *Mickiewicz. Sen i widzenie*, ed. Zbigniew Majchrowski and Wojciech Owczarski, Gd, słowo/obraz terytoria, 304 pp., continues this eclectic and illuminating series with contributions by S. Chwin, D. Rosiek, and others, on the role and significance of dreams in M.'s creative work.

Pamiętnik Słówiański, 47–48, 1997–98, contains two essays on M.: Zdravko Malić, 'Mickiewicz, czyli Wielkość poezji' (3–41) and T. Pretnar, 'Znaczenie Adama Mickiewicza dla twórczości France Prešerna' (43–52). I. Grudzińska-Gross, 'How Polish is Polishness: about Mickiewicz's *Grażyna*', *East European Politics and Society*, 14.1:1–11. Ks. B. Miek, 'Mickiewicz w Kole Towiańskiego', *PL(L)*, 23, 1998:15–39. L. Zwierzyński, 'Topika morska w poezji Adama Mickiewicza', *PL(W)*, 91.2:157–73. L. Marinelli, 'O "zagadce"

Najświętszej Panny Kwietnej. Przyczynek do Mickiewiczowskiej "mariologii"', *ib.*, 91.3:201–08. A. Szwed, 'Lyriki Mickiewicza w bułgarskich przekładach Iwana Wylewa', *PrzH*, 44.1–2:67–77.

NORWID. Wojciech Kudyba, '*Aby mowę chrześcijańską odtworzyć na nowo* . . .' *Norwida mówienie o Bogu*, KUL, 191 pp. *TD*, 5, contains two essays on N.: A. Okopień-Sławińska, 'Semantyczna strategia poetyckiego zamilczenia (Przypadek *Jak* . . . Cypriana Norwida)' (30–42), and A. Melbechowska-Luty, 'Sztukmistrz. Kilka uwag o symbiozie sztuk w twórczości Cypriana Norwida' (43–57). R. Gadamska-Serafin, 'Refleksja o starości i starcach w twórczości Norwida', *RuLit*, 40, 1999:381–98. R. Zajączkowski, 'Kirche — Nation — Menschheit: Sozial-religiöse Motive im Denken von Cyprian Norwid', *ŻSl*, 44, 1999:434–46.

SŁOWACKI. Andrzej Kotliński, *Mistrz "czerwonego rymu"*. *Słowacki*, IBL, 223 pp. Jan Zieliński, *SzatAnioł. Powikłane życie Juliusza Słowackiego*, Wa, Świat Książki, 277 pp., is a spicy, if methodologically dubious, account of S.'s life. *PrzH*, 44.1–2, contains six essays on S.: S. Makowiecki, 'Wielki nieobecny (Kilka uwag na zakończeniu Roku Słowackiego)' (1–9); B. Faron, 'Pośmiertny powrót Juliusza Słowackiego do kraju' (11–30); K. Biliński, ' "Pośród niesnaków . . ." Juliusza Słowackiego wobec źródeł biblijnych' (31–36); E. Szymanis, 'Genezyjski kontekst wizji pradziejów Polski w *Lilli Wenedzie* Juliusza Słowackiego' (37–45); B. Adamkowicz-Iglińska, 'Juliusza Słowackiego genezyjski ideał człowieka' (47–55); J. Gromadzki, '*Genezis z ducha* a teorie ewolucji przyrodniczej' (57–66). *PL(W)*, 90.4, 1999, has four essays on S.: P. Matywiecki, 'O kościele bez Boga' (5–33); M. Troszyński, 'Poetycka puenta i . . . całkiem prozaiczny epilog (albumowego wiersza Juliusza Słowackiego)' (35–48); M. Saganiak, 'Słowackiego mistyczna koncepcja poznania i twórczości' (49–82); B. Baczyńska, 'Wiersz *Księcia Niezłomnego* Juliusza Słowackiego wobec wersyfikacji *El príncipe constante* Calderona' (83–116). T. Wyrwa, 'Francuzi o Juliuszu Słowackim', *PL(L)*, 24, 1999:8–19, is a survey of French responses up to the end of the 1920s.

4. FROM REALISM TO NEO-REALISM

Lektury Polonistyczne. Pozytywizm — Młoda Polska. Tom I, ed. Stanisław Grzeszczuk, Kw, Universitas, 1998, 404 pp., maintains the high standards of this series. Ewa Ihnatowicz, *Literatura polska drugiej połowy XIX wieku (1864–1914)*, Wa, Trio, 359 pp. *Mieszczaństwo i mieszczańskość w literaturze polskiej drugiej połowy XIX wieku*, ed. Ewa Ihnatowicz, Wa, ELIPSA, 272 pp., contains essays on G. Zapolska, B. Prus, and others. *Przemiany formuły polskości w drugiej połowie XIX wieku*, ed. Janusz Maciejewski, IBL, 1999, 294 pp., deals with *Lalka* and other works and is based on a session in IBL from 1986. *Literatura i czasopiśmiennictwo polskie 1864–1918 wobec tradycji antycznej*, ed. Andrzej Z. Makowiecki, Wa, wyd. Uniwersytetu Warszawskiego, 289 pp., discusses leading Symbolists and Positivists. *Epoka 'ogniem i mieczem' we współczesnych badaniach*, ed. Mirosław Nagielski, Wa, DiG, 180 pp., though largely encompassing the historical background, does contain several essays on Sienkiewicz's novel. Elżbieta Hurnikowa, *W kręgu wiedeńskiej moderny. Z zagadnień polsko-austriackich powinowactw literacko-kulturalnych*, Częstochowa, WSP, 227 pp., considers such issues as Cracow and Vienna's mutual perceptions, the literary and artistic *Jugendstil* and Młoda Polska movements, as well as the role of women in the literature and culture of the time. Wojciech Kaczmarek, *Złamane pieczęcie księgi. Inspiracje biblijne w dramaturgii Młodej Polski*, KUL, 1999, 346 pp., after a general first part, focuses on specific dramatists: L. Rydel, S. Wyspiański, J. Kasprowicz, A. Szandlerowski, and K. H. Rostworowski. It also contains an annex of Polish biblical dramas for the period 1880–1918. Józef Ratajczak, *Umrzeć z miłości. Szkice o romansach młodopolskich*, Ww, 'Wiedza o kulturze', 1999, 203 pp., has S. Przybyszewski as its central hero. *Nowa świadomość płci w modernizmie*, ed. German Ritz, Christa Binswanger and Carmen Scheide, Kw., Universitas, 341 pp. Leszek Szaruga, *Milczenie i krzyk. Pięć esejów z powodu Młodej Polski*, UMCS, 1997, 109 pp. *W kręgu Młodej Polski* (Seria III), ed. Jolanta Sztachelska, Białystok, Wydawnictwo Uniwersytetu w Białymstoku, 1998, 230 pp., contains pieces on W. Reymont, W. Berent's *Żywe kamienia*, B. Ostrowska, Przybyszewski and Leśmian's *Bajki*.

PL(W), 91.2, is devoted mainly to Positivism and, besides articles devoted to individual writers, contains the following: B. Bobrowska, 'Ziarno i nić Ariadny — dwa symbole wyjścia z labiryntu historycznego w kryptopatriotycznych utworach Adama Asnyka i Marii Konopnickiej' (75–90), S. Fita, 'Nieznane listy Marii Konopnickiej i Marii Dulębianki do Stefanii Wekslerowej, 1908–1910' (181–87), and A. Martuszewska, 'Kłopoty z realizmem (nie tylko pozytywistycznym)' (143–56). J. A. Malik, '"Berlin-Kraków, dzień jazdy." Zapomniany list Adolfa Nowaczyńskiego do Stanisława Przybyszewskiego', *PL(W)*, 91.4:187–96. S. Jakowenko, 'Polska i ukraińska wczesnomodernistyczna krytyka. Niektóre paralele', *RuLit*, 40, 1999:331–49.

INDIVIDUAL WRITERS

CHMIELOWSKI. A. Makowski, 'Kategoria autora w krytyce literackiej Piotra Chmielowskiego', Balcerzan, *Osoba*, 233–54.

GAWALEWICZ. Tomasz Sobieraj, *O prozie Mariana Gawalewicza* (Biblioteka literacka 'Poznańskich Studiów Polonistycznych. Seria literacka' 21), Pń, ABEDIK, 1999, 269 pp.

LANGE. J. Włodarczyk, ' "Z tej otchłani mi płyną niewiadome głosy." O "obcych" słowach w poezji Antoniego Langego', *RuLit*, 40, 1999:413–24; M. Mikołajczak, 'O miejscu *Rozmyślań* Antoniego Langego w liryce Młodej Polski', *ib.*, 425–38.

ŁOZIŃSKI. M. Rudkowska, 'Gra w ludzkie i polskie czyli diabeł odwiedza Sarmację (O opowiadaniach historycznych Władysława Łozińskiego)', *ib.*, 297–315.

ORZESZKOWA. A. Mazur, 'Dwie utopie realizmu: *Nad Niemnem* Elizy Orzeszkowej i *Późne lato* Adalberta Stiftera', *PL(W)*, 91.2:5–18.

PRUS. Barbara Bobrowska, *Bolesław Prus — mistrz pozytywistycznej kroniki*, Białystok, Wydawnictwo Uniwersytetu w Białymstoku, 1999, 235 pp., is an analysis of P.'s views and techniques in his chronicles and feuilletons. Wiesław Sonczyk, *Bolesław Prus: publicysta, redactor, teoretyk prasy*, Wa, Elipsa, 410 pp., discusses P.'s journalism under three headings: his path into the profession, his association with *Nowiny* and the views he expressed on the subject in his letters. M. Gloger, 'Determinizm w *Lalce* Bolesława Prusa', *PL(W)*, 91.2:19–44.

PRZYBYSZEWSKI. M. Nowak, 'Stanisława Przybyszewskiego opis "nagich psychologicznych procesów" ', *PrLit*, 37:57–77.

REYMONT. Barbara Koc, *Reymont*, Wa, LSW, 228 pp + 12 pp. of illus., is a revised and supplemented biographical account. *PrzH*, 44.4, contains 3 essays on R.: H. Karnacka, 'Wokół *Ziemi obiecanej*' (33–58); J. Zacharska, 'Kobiety w prozie Reymonta' (59–69); W. I. Occheli, '*Marzyciel* Reymonta — z problematyki genezy' (71–81). B. Utkowska, 'Małe formy epickie W.S. Reymonta (próba opisu bibliograficznego)', *RuLit*, 40, 1999:213–38. R. Löw, 'Z dziejów Reymonta w literaturze hebrajskiej: *Chłopi*', *TD*, nos 1–2:121–29.

RODZIEWICZÓWNA. B. Szargot, 'Awers i rewers. Dwa odczytania *Między ustami a brzegiem pucharu* ... Marii Rodziewiczówny', *PL(W)*, 91.2:91–105.

SIENKIEWICZ. R. Löw, '*Trylogia* w oczach krytyki hebrajskiej', *PL(W)*, 91.4:181–86.

STAFF. P. Wrzesień, 'Liryzm zorganizowany. *Śladem stopy antycznej* Leopolda Staffa', *RuLit*, 40, 1999:157–81.

SYGIETYŃSKI. M. Kowalski, 'Terminologia krytyczna w portretach literackich Antoniego Sygietyńskiego. Na podstawie cyklu *Współczesna powieść we Francji*', *PL(W)*, 91.2:107–41.

WYSPIAŃSKI. M. Sugiera, 'Powroty Homera: *Powrót Odysa* Wyspiańskiego i *Ithaka* Botho Straussa', *RuLit*, 40, 1999:399–411.

ZAPOLSKA. Krystyna Kłosińska, *Ciało, pożądanie, ubranie. O wczesnych powieściach Gabrieli Zapolskiej*, Kw, eFKa, 1999, 327 pp., is an important new study.

ŻEROMSKI. T. Linkner, 'W mitycznym nurcie *Wiernej rzeki*', *RuLit*, 41:171–88.

5. FROM 1918 TO 1945

I. E. Adel'heim, Польская проза межвоенного двадцатилетия: между Западом и Россией. Феномен психологического языка, Mw, Indrik, 199 pp., comprises two parts: man within history and the everyday world, and poetics and psychological language. Joanna Chłosta, *Polskie życie literackie we Lwowie w latach 1939–1941 w świetle oficjalnej prasy polskojęzycznej*, Olsztyn, wyd. Uniwersytetu Warmińsko-Mazurskiego, 206 pp., devotes its greater part to profiles of contemporary writers active in Lviv at the time, such as J. Przyboś, L. Pasternak, J. Borejsza, etc. Danuta Dobrowolska, *Powieść polityczna dwudziestolecia międzywojennego*, Kielce, Szumacher, 186 pp. Ewa Guderian-Czaplińska, *Szara strefa awangardy. Dramat w teatrze, teatr w dramacie*, Ww, 'Wiedza o kulturze', 1998, 172 pp., examines the work of T. Peiper, J. Kurek, J. Brzękowski, and Przyboś. *Lektury Polonistyczne. Dwudziestolecie międzywojenne, II wojna światowa. Tom I*, ed. Ryszard Nycz and Jerzy Jarzębski, Kw, Universitas, 1997, 367 pp., and *Tom II*, ed. Ryszard Nycz, Kw, Universitas, 1999, 494 pp., are useful collections of essays by various hands. Jerzy Święch, *Poeci i wojna*, PWN, 255 pp., focuses on World War II, and contains chapters on Baczyński and Miłosz.

M. Inglot, 'Stanisława Wasylewskiego lwowski scenariusz *Krakowiaków i Górali* (1941). Struktura i geneza koniunkturalnej adaptacji', *PL(W)*, 91.2:189–202. M. Kareński-Tschurl, 'Czy dlatego, że my się *par example* nie kochamy? O erotyce futuristycznej na przykładzie poezji Brunona Jasieńskiego i Anatola Sterna', *TD*, no.6:45–62. E. Kraskowska, 'Nałkowska i Schulz, Schulz i Nałkowska', Balcerzan, *Osoba*, 186–201. K. Myrdek-Rak, 'Porażka awangardy? Klasyczne i romantyczne elementy w programach okresu międzywojennego — prolegomena', *PrLit*, 37:105–11.

INDIVIDUAL WRITERS

BOY-ŻELIŃSKI. Barbara Winklowa, *Nad Wisłą i nad Sekwaną. Biografia Boya-Żelińskiego*, Wa, Iskry, 1998, 234 pp., is a new biography.

DĄBROWSKA. E. Nawrocka, 'Osoba w podróży (O podróżach Marii Dąbrowskiej)', Balcerzan, *Osoba*, 202–25.

GAŁCZYŃSKI. Jan Nagrabiecki, *Czary-Mary Sztukmistrza Ildefonsa*, Podkowa Leśna, AULA, 73 pp.

GOETEL. *Egzotyzm i swojszczyzna w prozie Ferdynanda Goetla z lat 1911–1939*, Kielce, WSP, 279 pp.

GOMBROWICZ. Leszek Nowak, *Gombrowicz. Człowiek wobec ludzi* (Filozofia polska XX wieku), Wa, Prószyński i S-ka, 326 pp. A. M. Dąbrowska, 'Przeciwko śmierci. *Dzienniki* Witolda Gombrowicza', *PrLit*, 37:191–205. M. Głowiński, 'Gombrowiczowska diatryba', *PL(W)*, 91.4:63–81, and his 'Gombrowicz poprawia Dantego', *TD*, no.5:58–67. G. Gömöri, 'The antinomies of Gombrowicz', Gömöri, *Poles*, 25–39. J. Jarzębski, 'Trudno być Bogiem', *ib.*, 68–77.

IŁŁAKOWICZÓWNA. E. S. Kruszewski, 'Listy Kazimiery Iłłakowiczówny', *PL(L)*, 25:73–95, presents letters from 1927–1938 by the poet to a colleague in Sweden.

IRZYKOWSKI. K. Siatkowska-Callebat, 'Trup — marionetki — pałuba (O kategorii postaci w powieści Irzykowskiego)', *PrzH*, 44.3:61–76.

IWASZKIEWICZ. German Ritz, *Jarosław Iwaszkiewicz. Pogranicza nowoczesności*, Kw, Universitas, 1999, 309 pp., is a Polish translation by Andrzej Kopacki of the German edition of 1996. P. Drobniak, 'Światowid z Stawiska. Jarosław Iwaszkiewicz a idea "wspólnej Europy"', *PrLit*, 37:113–39, analyses the poetry and novels.

LEŚMIAN. Marian Pankowski, *Leśmian czyli bunt poety przeciw granicom*, UMCS, 1999, 223 pp., is a translation from the French by A. Krzewicki. *Poezje Bolesława Leśmiana. Interpretacje*, ed. Barbara Stelmaszczyk and Tomasz Cieślak, Kw, Universitas, 175 pp., comes from sessions at Łódź University in December 1998 and April 1999.

PRZYBOŚ. G. Gömöri, 'The organization of lyrical space in Julian Przyboś's poetry', Gömöri, *Poles*, 85–100. A. Ługin, '"Dobrze wychowani mężczyźni" albo "ciąg dalszy przerywisty", czyli awangarda jako przezwyciężenie i odkrycie kobiecości', *TD*, no.6:63–76.

SCHULZ. Marta Bartosik, *Bruno Schulz jako krytyk*, Kw, Universitas, 137 pp.

STERN. P. Majewski, 'O języku (w) poezji Anatola Sterna', *PrzH*, 43, 1999:103–24.

TUWIM. P. Michałowski, 'Prywatne kolekcje w depozycie fikcji: *Kwiaty polskie* Juliana Tuwima', *TD*, no.3:179–95.

WAT. A. Dziadek, '*Poemat bukoliczny* Aleksandra Wata', *ib.*, 168–78. A. Kaliszewski, *Wiersze śródziemnomorskie* Aleksandra Wata a neoklasycyzm', *RuLit*, 41:221–35.

S. I. WITKIEWICZ. Artur Pastuszek, *Metafizyczne grymasy. Czysta forma Witkacego jako kategoria metafizyki*, Toruń, Wyd. Adam Marszalik, 180 pp., examines the philosophical dimensions of W.'s dramatic theory. Marta Skwara, *Motywy szaleństwa w twórczości Witkacego i*

Conrada. Studium porównawcze, WUW, 289 pp. Joanna Trzos, *W poszukiwaniu dziwności istnienia. Rzecz o dramatach Witkacego*, Kw, Wydawnictwo EJB, 138 pp. *Konteksty*, 54.1–4, 'Malinowski Witkacy. Fotografia: Między nauką a sztuką', is partly devoted to W.'s photography during the trip to the South Pacific. T. Bocheński, 'Kompozycje muzyczne Witkacego', *TD*, no.4: 159–66. G. Grochowski, 'Dziwactwa i dzieła. Inspiracje dandysowskie w twórczości Stanisława Ignacego Witkiewicza', Balcerzan, *Osoba*, 132–48.

ZEGADŁOWICZ. S. Stabro, 'Małe ojczyzny w prozie Emila Zegadłowicza', *RuLit*, 40, 1999: 317–30.

6.   1945 TO THE PRESENT DAY

Przemysław Czapliński and Piotr Śliwiński, *Literatura polska 1976–1998. Przewodnik po prozie i poezji*, WL, 1999, 428 pp. Janusz Drzewucki, *Smaki słowa. Szkice o poezji*, Ww, Wydawnictwo Dolnośląskie, 1999, includes essays on Herbert, the New Wave poets, Iwaszkiewicz, Różewicz, Szymborska and others. *Leksykon dzieł polskiej literatury współczesnej*, ed. Krzysztof Krasuski, Kw, Znak, 295 pp., is intended for schools. Lidia Wiśniewska, *Między biegunem i na pograniczu. O 'Białym małżeństwie' Tadeusza Różewicza i poezji Zbigniewa Herberta*, Bydgoszcz, WSP, 1999, 383 pp.

A number of works have been published that deal with the politicization of literature after World War II. Joanna Hobot, *Gra z cenzurą w poezji Nowej Fali (1968–1976)*, WL, 383 pp., is the first substantial study of the censorship of literature in People's Poland. Apart from an analysis of the workings of the censorship office and writers' responses, it includes an appendix comprising interviews with leading New Wave poets about their experience and samples of censorship documents. Covering a similar period is Iwona Hofman, *Dwugłos o Peerelu. Dzienniki Stefana Kisielewskiego i Mariana Brandysa*, UMCS, 338 pp., a straightforward comparison of the two writers' diaries. Useful bibliographies are: *Bez cenzury 1976–1989. Literatura, ruch wydawniczy, teatr. Bibliografia*, ed. Jerzy Kandziora and Zyta Szymańska with Krystyna Tokarzówna, IBL, 1999, 1156 pp., an important survey, which also contains information on film for this period; and *Katalog druków zwartych wydanych w Polsce poza cenzurą w latach 1976–1990 w zbiorach Ośrodka Karta*, no ed., Wa, Karta, 1999, 180 pp. The Stalinist period is the subject of Stanisław Adam Kondek's exemplary *Papierowa rewolucja. Oficjalny obieg książek w Polsce w latach 1948–1955*, Wa, Biblioteka Narodowa, 1999, 232 pp. *TD*, nos 1–2, comprises essays by the usual suspects largely devoted to Socialist Realism in Poland; H. Markiewicz's response, 'Marginalia do *Samoantysockrytyki*', *TD*, no.4: 239–43, contains useful corrections to several of these articles. M. Zawodniak, ' "Żywy Mickiewicz." Socrealistyczny obraz wieszcza (Kilka wstępnych uwag)', Balcerzan, *Osoba*, 177–85.

A. Dziadek, 'Problem *ekphrasis* — dwa *Widoki Delft* (Adam Czerniawski i Adam Zagajewski)', *TD*, no.4:141–51. H. Gosk, 'Wątek poszukiwania tożsamości w emigracyjnej prozie polskiej (Na przykładzie utworów Zygmunta Haupta z tomów *Pierścień z papieru*, *Szpica* oraz Leo Lipskiego *Dzień i noc*, *Piotruś*)', *PrzH*, 44.3:53–60. T. Mizerkiewicz, 'Mitologizacje. O związkach intertekstualnych z mitologią w powieści polskiej po 1956 roku', *PL(W)*, 91.4:83–104. R. Rędziak, 'Opisać powstanie po latach (Miron Białoszewski *Pamiętnik z Powstania Warszawskiego*—Anna Świrszczyńska *Budowałam barykady*', *RuLit*, 41:305–24, concludes that while both give similar accounts, Ś. expresses more of her inner feelings. R. Wasiak-Taylor, 'Pisarze emigracyjni tworzy dla scen ZASP-u za granicą', *PL(L)*, 25:50–72, discusses the work of Z. Nowakowski, J. Bzowski, and others, during World War II.

B. Helbig-Mischewski, 'Weibliche Subjektlosigkeit in der modernen polnischen Frauenprosa von Izabela Filipiak und Olga Tokarczuk', *ŻSl*, 45, 1999:198–208, concerns *Absolutna amnezja* and *E.E.* respectively. M. Miszczak, 'Gry z "tandetą" w prozie polskiej lat dziewięćdziesiątych. Rekonesans', *TD*, no.4:73–83.

INDIVIDUAL WRITERS

BARAŃCZAK. Z. Bauer, '*Podróż zimowa* Stanisława Barańczaka. Kilka sugestii interpretacyjnych', *RuLit*, 40, 1999:51–71.

BIAŁOSZEWSKI. J. Kopciński, 'Niby — ja, niby — on, czyli zbiorowe ustalenie persony Mirona Białoszewskiego jako dalszy ciąg jego pisarskich autokreacji', Balcerzan, *Osoba*, 168–76. J. Trzcińska, 'Autobiograficzny wymiar prozy Mirona Białoszewskiego. Próba analizy *Rozkurzu* w świetle założeń językoznawstwa kognitywnego', *RuLit*, 41:367–80.

BOBKOWSKI. K. Ćwikliński, 'Rozstanie z formą. O *fragmentach z notatnika* i *fragmentach wspomnień* Andrzeja Bobkowskiego', *PL(W)*, 91.4:105–24.

BOROWY. A. Nasiłowska, 'Wacław Borowy i New Criticism', *TD*, no. 5:153–56.

BRANDSTAETTER. A. Mazan, 'Słowo i tekst w kulturze sakralnej. Na materiale *Jezusa z Nazarethu* Romana Brandstaettera', *PL(W)*, 91.3:147–59.

K. BRANDYS. J. Smulski, ' "Wiem, że trochę giędzę". Proza Kazimierza Brandysa — między "retoryką" a "gadaniem" ', Balcerzan, *Osoba*, 226–32.

BUCZKOWSKI. S. Buryla, 'Proza Leopolda Buczkowskiego — niepokoje i obawy krytyków', *RuLit*, 40, 1999 : 31–50. M. Dąbrowski, 'Buczkowski i Borges — modele intertekstualności', *PrzH*, 44.3 : 37–44.

BUGALSKI. M. Rabrzo-Burek, 'Bolesna świadomość formy — inspiracje plastyczne w poezji Dariusza Bugalskiego', *TD*, no.4 : 107–17.

FILIPOWICZ. *Kornel Filipowicz. Szkice do portretu*, ed. Stanisław Burkot, Jerzy S. Ossowski and Jacek Rozmus, WL, 379 pp., is the most extensive collection of essays devoted to the writer, and consists of materials from a conference at the WSP in Cracow in October 1998.

GRYNBERG. D. Krawczyńska, 'Henryk Grynberg. Tożsamość odzyskana', *TD*, no.5 : 157–66.

HAUPT. W. Lipowski, '*Dziś, przedwczoraj, wczoraj, jutro* . . ., czyli o ćwiczeniach pamięci Zygmunta Haupta', *RuLit*, 41 : 288–303.

HERBERT. *TD*, no. 3, contains ten essays on H.'s creative work and reception: B. Carpenter, 'Poezja Zbigniewa Herberta w krytyce anglosaskiej' (7–19), J. Kornhauser, '*Struna światła* — między ocaleniem a niepokojem' (20–27), H. Filipowicz, 'Szklane oczy Hery. Reinterpretacja sztuk Zbigniewa Herberta' (28–46), B. Sienkiewicz, 'Platon Herberta, czyli o rozumie, namiętnościach, pustce i lęku' (47–60), B. Shallcross, 'Zbigniewa Herberta podróż do zachwytu' (61–78), A. Fiut, 'Ukryty dialog' (148–56) on H. and Miłosz, with the somewhat more left-field M. Dzień, 'Bogowie Herberta' (157–67) and M. Zawodniak, 'Herberta próbka kabały' (213–18); and specific interpretations of the poems 'Drugi pokój' (105–31) and 'Pan Cogito opowiada o kuszeniu Spinozy' (132–47) by J. Kopiński and R. Nycz respectively. *PrzH*, 44.4, contains three essays devoted to H.: A. Zieliński, 'Sława Herberta u Włochów' (1–14); W. Sadowski, 'Formy wersu w poezji współczesnej (na przykładzie *Nike która się waha* Zbigniewa Herberta)' (15–23); J. Potkański, 'Rola przerzutni w wierszach Zbigniewa Herberta' (25–32). G. Gömöri, 'The faces of Mr Cogito (Zbigniew Herbert's poetry 1992–93)', Gömöri, *Poles*, 101–14. B. Shallcross, 'The barbarian's garden: Zbigniew Herbert and the folly of history', *East European Politics and Society*, 14.1 : 47–62.

HERLING-GRUDZIŃSKI. U. Schmid, 'Analogie als künstlerisches Verfahren: Gustaw Herling-Grudzińskis *Dziennik pisany nocą*', *ZSP*, 58, 1999 : 125–38.

HŁASKO. Danuta Kalinowska, *Marek Hłasko: Młody gniewny*, Wa, TELBIT, 86 pp., is a brief biographical account.

KONWICKI. L. Zarnowski, 'Creation of strangeness (the writings of Tadeusz Konwicki)', *NZSJ*, 1999 : 319–24, is a brief overview.

KOZIOL. Małgorzata Mikołajczak, *podjąć przerwany dialog. O poezji Urszuli Kozioł*, Kw, Universitas, 281 pp.

LEM. J. Z. Lichański, 'Stanisław Lem — filozof i pisarz (dyskusja z lemologami)', *PrzH*, 44.3 : 45–52.

MIŁOSZ. *Poznawanie Miłosza 2. Cz. I: 1980–1998*, ed. Aleksander Fiut, WL, 421 pp., reprints a selection of essays written by eminent critics within and outwith Poland, from the time of the award of the Nobel prize.

PrLit, 37, contains two essays on M.: E. Tuz, 'Pesymista ekstatyczny. Rozumienie natury w poezji Czesława Miłosza' (141–61) and R. Kordes, 'Religijna bezdomność Czesława Miłosza' (163–73). G. Gömöri, 'Notes on Czesław Miłosz's life writing', Gömöri, *Poles*, 145–50.

MUSIEROWICZ. Krzysztof Biedrzycki, *Małgorzata Musierowicz i Borejkowie*, Kw, Universitas, 1999, 145 pp. Halina Maczunder, *Humor i komizm językowy w wybranych powieściach Małgorzaty Musierowicz*, Wa, Elipsa, 87 pp.

PANKOWSKI. Krystyna Ruta-Rutkowska, *Polak w dwuznacznych sytuacjach*, Wa, IBL, 153 pp., is a series of discussions with P. on his life and work, and her 'Metateatralne gry w dramacie współczesnym. Na przykładzie twórczości Mariana Pankowskiego', *PL(W)*, 91.4 : 125–53.

PARNICKI. *Inspiracje Parnickiego*, Katowice, Gnome, 139 pp., is a collection of essays drawn from a conference held in Katowice in December 1999.

PIASECKI. Krzysztof Polechoński, *Żywot człowieka uzbrojonego. Biografia, twórczość i legenda literacka Sergiusza Piaseckiego*, PWN, 233 pp. K. Polechoński, 'Problem autobiografizmu w powieściach Sergiusza Piaseckiego', *PrLit*, 37 : 175–89.

RÓŻEWICZ. *Światy Różewicza*, ed. Marian Kisiel and Włodzimierz Wójcik (Obrazy literatury XX wieku, 3), Katowice, Gnome, 165 pp., is derived from a conference in Katowice in April 1999. K. Grabowska, 'Przemieniony Rawenną. Różewicza poetycka kontemplacja świata', *TD*, no.4 : 131–40. A. Skołasińska, '*Białe małżeństwo* Tadeusza Różewicza. W poszukiwaniu polskiej inności', *ib.*, no.5 : 27–44. A. Skrendo, 'Sygnatura Tadeusza Różewicza. Dwie interpretacje ze wstępem i *Post Scriptum*', Balcerzan, *Osoba*, 149–67.

SZYMBORSKA. P. Roguski, '"Und die Moral von der Geschicht" . . .?: anmerkungen zur Lyrik von Wisława Szymborska', *ZSl*, 44, 1999 : 447–54.

TRZYNA. B. Helbig-Mischewski, 'Święta, czarownica, nierządnica. Sakralizacja i demonizacja kobiet oraz kultur w powieści Tomka Trzyzny *Panna Nikt*', *TD*, no.6 : 77–93.

TWARDOWSKI. Aleksandra Iwanowska, '*serdecznie niemodny i szczęśliwie zapóźniony.*' *Jan Twardowski w oczach własnych, recenzentów i czytelników*, Pń, Księgarnia Św. Wojciecha, 327 pp.

TYRMAND. Jolanta Pasterska, *Świat według Tyrmanda. Przewodnik po utworach fabularnych*, Rzeszów, FOSZE, 238 pp. + 6 pp. of photographs.

WOJACZEK. M. Bogdanowska, 'Porządkowanie Wojaczka', *RuLit*, 40, 1999: 183–98.

WOJTYŁA. A. Przybylska, '*Portret malarza*', *RuLit*, 40, 1999: 199–212, deals with W.'s *Brat naszego Boga* (1945–50), and her 'O *Renensansowym psałterzu* Karola Wojtyły', *ib.*, 41: 355–65.

ZAGAJEWSKI. C. Cavanagh, 'Lyrical ethics: the poetry of Adam Zagajewski', *SRev*, 59.1: 1–15.

ZAGÓRSKI. S. Stabro, 'Poetyckie mitologie w wileńskiej poezji Jerzego Zagórskiego', *RuLit*, 41: 205–19.

IV. RUSSIAN STUDIES

LANGUAGE
POSTPONED

LITERATURE FROM THE BEGINNING TO 1700
POSTPONED

LITERATURE, 1700–1820
POSTPONED

LITERATURE, 1820–1900
POSTPONED

LITERATURE FROM 1900 TO THE PRESENT DAY

By Boris Lanin, *Professor of Literature, Russian Academy of Education, Moscow*

1. General

Русские писатели 20 века. Биографический словарь, ed. P. A. Nikolaev, Bol′shaia Rossiiskaia encyclopedia, M, Randevu-AM, 808 pp., is one of the most complete reference books on 20th-c. Russian literature, but nevertheless some important entries are missing, for example Alexander Zinov′ev, Vladimir Ufl′iand, Iurii Gal′perin, Tat′iana Bek, Vladlen Bakhnov, Vladimir Vishnevskii, Victor Shenderovich, Mikhail Zhvanetskii, Alexandr Chaianov, Alexandr Genis, Petr Vail′, Boris Vakhtin, Boris Khazanov, Lev Khalif, and some others. N. G. Kornienko, *Проблемы развития русской прозы конца XX века. Часть 1. Литература новой волны*, Voronezh, Voronezhskii gospeduniversitet, 91 pp., is also of some interest. Modern Russian literature on the Internet is described in M. Adamovich, 'Этот виртуальный мир . . . Современная русская проза в Интернете: ее особенности и проблемы', *NovM*, no.4: 193–207. *Путеводитель по фондам отдела рукописей института мировой литературы РАН*, Vol. 1: *Личные фонды*, ed. A. A. Kuteinikova, M, Nasledie, 336 pp., is a useful guide for scholars.

For reflections on Pushkin in modern Russian literature, see V. Desiatov, 'Клон Пушкина, или Русский человек через двести лет', *Zvezda*, no.2:198–202. Essays on 20th-c. Russian literature include V. Rasputin, 'Видимое и невидимое (Два слова в пользу надежды)', *NSo*, no.2:184–90, and B. Khazanov, 'Лефиафан, или Величие советской литературы', *Oktjabr'*, no.1:165–71 (typical features of Soviet literature). G. Chkhartishvili, *Писатель и самоубийство*, M, Novoe Literaturnoe Obozrenie, 324 pp., provides an impressive study of the suicides of writers — the so called 'bestseller for intellectuals'.

L-критика (Литературная критика). Ежегодник Академии русской современной словесности, ed. E. Shklovskii, M, ARSS, includes work by Academy members: Ageev, Anninskii, Arkhangel'-skii, Ar'ev, Bavil'skii, Basinskii, Bakhnov, Vasilevskii, Genis, Eliseev, Ermolin, Zolotonosov, Zorin, N. Ivanova, Kostyrko, Kuritsyn, A. Latynina, Lipovetskii, Marchenko, Nemzer, Novikov, Rodnianskaia, Toporov, Chuprinin, Shklovskii, Epshtein. In the appendix are essays by Iurii Davydov and Iurii Buida. The preface is by Natal'ia Ivanova. Of some interest is V. A. Kanashkin, *Русская литература всегда и теперь: Национально-исторический критерий как феномен развития*, Krasnodar, Sovetskaia Kuban', 220 pp.; in the same nationalistic style is A. Iu. Bol'shakova, *Нация и менталитет: феномен "деревенской прозы" XX века*, M, Komitet po Telekommunikatsiam i sredstvam Massovoi Informatsii Pravitel'stva Moskvy, 132 pp. *XX век: Проза. Поэзия. Критика. Вып. 3*, ed. O. Ivanova et al., M, Dialog-MGU, 93 pp., has chapters on F. Sologub, I. Bunin, Iu. Trifonov. *Русская литература XX века: эволюция художественного сознания. Сб. научных статей*, Krasnodar, izd-vo Kubanskogo universiteta, 153 pp., and *Политика и поэтика: сборник статей*, M, Institut Slavianovedenia RAN, 239 pp., both contain some interesting material.

LITERARY HISTORY. Among the most important works this year are N. A. Bogomolov, *Русская литература начала XX века и оккультизм: исследования и материалы*, M, NLO, 549 pp.; V. B. Kataev, 'Литература «Знания»: теория и практика дестабилизации', *MSUB*, no.6:30–53 (an interesting study of 'Znanie' stories as seeking the enemy in the hypothetical reader); I. Kondakov, '«Где ангелы реют» (Русская литература XX века как единый текст)', *VL*, no.4:3–44; E. Dobrenko, 'Россия, которую мы обрели', *ib.*, 45–80 (on Russian classics and films of the Stalin era). See also V. V. Abashev, *Пермь как текст: Пермь в русской культуре и литературе XX века*, Perm' University PH,

Perm', 404 pp. Mikhail Odesskii and David Fel'dman, 'Литературная стратегия и политическая интрига. "Двенадцать стульев" в советской критике рубежа 1920–1930-х годов', *DN*, no.12:179–95, clearly reconstructs the history of the novel and the political and cultural life in the Soviet Union of the 1920–30s.

On the Silver Age, see O. Lekmanov, 'Концепция «Серебряного века» и акмеизма в записных книжках А.Ахматовой', *NLO*, 46:216–30, the same author's 'Из заметок об акмеизме', *ib.*, 41:213–17, G. Ryl'kova, 'На склоне Серебряного века', *ib.*, 46:231–44, followed by polemical notes by V. V. Nikolaenko (245–47), and L. Pil'd (247–49), and O. Kling, 'Серебряный век — через сто лет («Диффузное состояние» в русской литературе начала XX века)', *VL*, no. 6:83–113 (Russian literature of the beginning of the twentieth century as a 'diffusion' of various poetics). On modernism see N. V. Guzhieva, '«Русские символисты» — литературно-книжный манифест модернизма', *RusL*, no. 2: 64–81.

On the early years of Soviet literature see Roger Cockrell, *Bolshevik Ideology and Literature, 1917–1929*, Lewiston–Queenston–Lampeter, Mellen, xii + 184 pp. There is a pioneering and definitive study: Leona Toker, *Return from the Archipelago: Narratives of Gulag Survivors*, Bloomington and Indianapolis, Indiana U.P., xviii + 335 pp., which concentrates on Solzhenistsyn and Shalamov but also discusses contributions by others with experience of the Gulag (Evgeniia Ginzburg, Zhigulin, Dovlatov).

On the emigration, see *Литературная энциклопедия русского зарубежья (1918–1940), П-Я.*, ed. A. N. Nikoliukin, INION RAN, Vol. 3. *Books*. Part 3, 392 pp., and *Литературная энциклопедия русского зарубежья (1918–1940). Т.2. Периодика и литературные центры*, ed. A. N. Nikoliukin, M, Rosspen, 640 pp. (more than 1000 Russian émigré newspapers and magazines are described here).

Useful publications are: G. Adamovich, *Собрание сочинений. Комментарии*, selected, ed., and commentaries by O. A. Korostylev, StP, Aleteia, 757 pp. This book consists of 83 chapters of the Washington (1967) publication of this book, and 224 papers published in émigré newspapers and journals, and *Евгений Ляцкий: материалы к биографии*, ed. S. I. Mikhal'chenko, Bryansk, BGPU. 182 pp., the first book devoted to the prominent émigré critic. See also *Газданов и мировая культура*, ed. L. V. Syrovatko, Kaliningrad, GP'KGT', 238 pp., P. V. Basinskii and S. R. Fediakin, *Русская литература конца XIX — начала XX века и первой эмиграции*, M, Academia, 2nd rev. edn, 524 pp.

O. A. Buzuev, *Очерки по истории литературы русского зарубежья Дальнего Востока (1917–1945): Монография*, Komsomol'sk-
na-Amure, izdatel'stvo gospeduniversiteta, 125 pp., looks at Russian
émigré writers in Far Eastern countries. T. Gordienko and
S. Berezhkova, 'Пятнадцать современников. Радиопередачи В.
В. Вейдле о писателях русского зарубежья', *VL*, no.4:314–28, is
about Veidlé's 15 essays on Russian émigré writers. These essays were
saved in the 'Radio Liberty' archive. See also Leonid Livak, *MLR*,
95:779–89 (Iurii Fel'zen). See also *Проблемы изучения жизни и
творчества Б. К. Зайцева: Вторые международные Зайцевские
чтения*, Kaluga, Grif, 220 pp.; V. F. Markov, 'Моцарт', *Zvezda*,
no.2:125–39 (the revised publication of former UCLA Professor
Vladimir Markov's essay). Elena Tikhomirova studies post-
modernistic discourse in émigré prose in *Проза русского зарубежья и
России в ситуации постмодерна: Монография*, M, Narodnyi Uchi-
tel', Vol. 1, 171 pp. Other studies include I. Efimov, 'Сергей
Довлатов как зеркало Александра Гениса', *Zvezda*, no.1:214–19;
Tat'iana Chernova, 'Читая Фридриха Горенштейна', *Oktjabr'*,
no.11:146–52, and A. V. Urmanov, *Поэтика прозы Александра
Солженицына: Монография*, M, Prometei, 231 pp.

On Alexander Piatigorskii (see also interviews): V. Krivulin,
'Покушение на стеллерову корову', *NLO*, 43:266–70; I. Kalinin,
'Охота на бабочек или метапозиция наблюдателя', *ib.*, 271–78;
N. Ia. Grigorieva, 'Pyatigorsky-сутра (метафикция как разновид-
ность йогической дискурсивной практики)', *ib.*, 43:279–85.

THE CONTEMPORARY SCENE. Some interesting themes emerge:
V. V. Ogryzko, *Песни афганского похода: историко-литературное
исследование*, M, Kontsern Literaturnaia Rossia, 207 pp.; A. Varla-
mov, 'Убийство: заметки о современной прозе', *DN*,
no.11:184–92 (works by Ekimov, Vishnevetskaia, Borodin, Afana-
s'ev, and others); *Юрий Рытхеу и русская литература: материалы
обл. научно-практической конференции*, Magadan, Kordis, 47 pp.;
and T. Taiganova, 'Роман в рубище. О романе Василенко
«Дурочка»', *DN*, no.6:184–94. Solomon Volkov recalls a conversation with Anatolii Rybakov, *ib.*, no.1:191–206.

There are some interesting interviews and dialogues on modern
literature: M. Berg and N. Grigor'eva, *Zvezda*, no.2:232–36;
E. Degot' and N. Grigor'eva, *ib.*, no.3:223–26; S. Gandlevskii and
A. Gosteva, *VL*, no.4:264–85; L. Libedinskaia and T. Bek, *ib.*,
no.6:253–77; M. Vishnevetskaia and I. Kuznetsova, *ib.*,
no.4:286–313; A. Melikhov and T. Bek, *ib.*, no.6:226–51;
V. Astaf'ev and G. Sapronov, *LitR*, 13 October.

More general surveys include A. Nemzer, 'Замечательное
десятилетие. О русской прозе 90-х годов', *NovM*, no.1:199–219

(the top 30 works of the 1990s); P. Basinskii, '"Как сердцу высказать себя?" О русской прозе 90–х годов', *ib.*, no. 4:185–92; A. Genis, 'Фотография души. В окрестностях филологического романа', *Zvezda*, no.9:183–89. O. Slavnikova, 'Разговор Берлиоза с Иваном Бездомным: Что должен и чего не должен знать писатель', *NLO*, 46:334–43 (factual mistakes in works by Mikhail Butov, Alexander Vernikov, B. Akunin, and others); M. Kononov, 'Богоборец, или Черное пламя', *Zvezda*, no.2:203–12 (Alexander Melikhov); E. Scheglova, 'Куда пошли «грибники»', *DN*, no.5:213–15 (Valerii Popov); R. Karasti, 'Два генерала', *Zvezda*, no.3:211–22 (an interesting comparative study of Vladimov's *Генерал и его армия* and Alexei German's film *Хрусталев, машину!*). *Reconstructing the Canon: Russian Writing in the 1980s*, ed. A. McMillin, Amsterdam, Harwood Academic Publishers, x + 324 pp., contains detailed discussion of figures both major and minor (Lotman, Ol'ga Sedakova, Elena Shvarts, Aizenberg, Zinik, Siniavskii, Zinov'ev, Sokolov, Village Prose, Russian literature and imperialism, Slavkin, urban prose, and Sorokin).

MEMOIRS. A lot of excellent memoirs were published this year: M. L. Gasparov, *Записки и выписки*, M, NLO, 415 pp. A. Bitov, 'Перепуганный талант, или Сказание о победе формы над содержанием', *DN*, no.10:84–88, remembers Gennadii Gor; Vladimir Dudintsev, *Между двумя романами*, StP, Zhurnal 'Neva', 240 pp. (D. recalls the events that happened between two publications: «Не хлебом единым» and «Белые одежды»). P. Gorelik, *Neva*, no.6:175–85, recalls David Samoilov and Boris Slutsky (B. Zakharchenia, *ib.*, 186–90, also recalls Samoilov). Of interest is D. Ustinov, 'Новые материалы о Г. А. Гуковском: К 50–летию со дня смерти', *NLO*, 44:159–92. See also V. Berestov, 'Прелесть милой жизни', *VL*, no.6:290–303; N. M. Gershenzohn-Chegodaeva, *Первые шаги жизненного пути (Воспоминания дочери Михаила Гершензона)*, M, Zakharov, 283 pp. V. Kornilov, 'О поэтах, стихах и мемуарах', *DN*, no.11:155–68, is a study of the memoir genre, and see also M. Adamovich, 'Судеб скрещенье,' *ib.*,168–82 (on memoirs by Marina Tarkovskaia, Mikhail Ardov, Alla Andreeva). N. Liubimov, *Неувядаемый цвет: Книга воспоминаний*, 3 vols, M, Iazyki Russkoi Kul'tury, is an excellent book. E. Babaev, *Воспоминания*, StP, INAPRESS, 331 pp., is mainly about Akhmatova, but also discusses Pasternak, Simonov, A. Tolstoi, Shklovskii, Berestov, and Georgii Efron (Tsvetaeva's son). R. Karasti, *Zvezda*, no.7:217–27, discusses Lidiia Chukovskaia's memoirs of Akhmatova, as well as memoirs by Lidiia Ginzburg and Emma Gershtein.

Other memoirs of interest are: A. Belinkov, 'Из архива', *Zvezda*, no.2:151–55 (publication by N. Belinkova-Iablokova); Iu. Burtin,

'Исповедь шестидесятника', *DN*, no.12:122–34 (on Sholokhov and Abramov); K. Vanshenkin, 'В мое время. Из записей', *Zvezda*, no.5:143–60; N. Valentinov (Vol'skii N.), *Два года с символистами*, (preface and comments by G. Struve), M, XXI Vek - Soglasie, 382 pp; Iu. Libedinskii, 'О Фадееве', *VL*, no.3:236–52; Natal'ia Il'ina, 'Из последней папки: Записи разных лет (1957–1993)', *Oktjabr'*, no.6:110–40; A. Zholkovsky, 'Из мемуарных виньеток', *Zvezda*, no.3:163–84, no.4:190–209. M. Molovstvov, *ib.*, no.2:147–56, recalls Sakharov and Solzhenitsyn (the author is a former political prisoner and now a popular member of the State Duma). Memoirs on the period of samizdat: B. Ivanov, 'Узкая дорога к демократии', *ib.*, no.4:210–21; see also E. Ignatova, 'Оглянувшись ...', *ib.*, 221–26, and N. Eidelman, 'Дневник (1980–1984)', *ib.*, 29–81. 'Преступление и наказание', *ib.*, 13–18, concerns the trial of Margarita Klimova, accused of distributing Roman Gul''s book 'Одвуконь' (publication by I. A. Ber). Other memoirs include I. Dedkov, 'Холодная рука циклопа. Из дневниковых записей 1983 - 1984 годов', *NovM*, no.11:151–70, no.12:157–69; S. Zalygin, 'Стариковские записки', *ib.*, no.11:147–50; M. Chudakova, 'Людская молвь и конский топ. Из записных книжек 1950 - 1990-х годов', *ib.*, no.1:124–36, no.3:134–47; 'Людская молвь и конский топ. На исходе советского времени', *ib.*, no.6:136–47. 'Из архива Евгения Винокурова', *VL*, no.6:265–78 (publication by I. Vinokurova and A. Kolchinskii: V.'s memoir on Il'ia Erenburg, and ten letters to Vinokurov from Anastasia Tsvetaeva (1975–82).

On the epistolary genre, see N. I. Belunova, *Дружеские письма творческой интеллигенции конца XIX - начала XX в. (Жанр и текст писем): Монография*, St Petersburg U.P., 139 pp.; 'Aleksandr Tvardovskii - Aleksandr Fadeev, «*Будем говорить о литературе и о жизни*»', *DN*, no.5:186–205; letters between Vadim and Daniil Andreev, 1927–46, are in *Zvezda*, no.3:125–39; Lilia Brik and Elsa Triole, 'Неизданная переписка (1921–1970)', coll. and pref. V. V. Katanian, M, Ellis Lak, 686 pp. (the first publication of correspondence between two sisters); 'Из истории русской печати в Финляндии. «Журнал Содружества»: начало пути (1933–1934)', ed. A. G. Timofeev, *RusL*, no.1:190–261 (contains letters by B. P. Vysheslavtsev, Z. A. Shakhovskaia, V. S. Bulich, Iu. Terapiano, and others, and poems by V. S. Bulich). L. Ginzburg and N. Il'ina, '"Зеленое окно за письменным столом". Переписка', *Zvezda*, no.3:161–66; Igor' Smirnov and Boris Groys, 'Subject: Prigov (К 60-летию Д. А. Пригова)', *ib.*, no.11:162–68 (see also the interview between Smirnov and Prigov, *ib.*, no.1:230–34); Georges Nivat and Alexander Arkhangel'skii, 'Диалог в открытом пространстве', *ib.*, no.11:173–81. G. Kruzhkov, '«Мы-двух теней скорбящая чета»', *NLO*, 43:235–60, discusses letters by Viacheslav Ivanov and Zinov'eva-Annibal.

On women's literature, see P. Basinskii, 'Постфеминизм: У русской литературы была женская душа', *Oktjabr'*, no.4:176–79; M. Abasheva, 'Магия тени', *DN*, no.5:206–9 (Irina Polianskaia), B. Paramonov, 'Застой как культурная форма', *Zvezda*, no.4:224–38 (Tat'iana Tolstaia), and two studies of Marina Vishnevetskaia's prose: E. Ermolin, 'Улица, фонарь, аптека', *DN*, no.7:211–17, and O. Slavnikova, 'Вышел критик из тумана', *ib.*, 217–21. See also L. Milne, 'Ghosts and dolls: popular urban culture and the supernatural in Liudmila Petrushevskaia's *Songs of the Eastern Slavs* and *The Little Sorceress*', *RusR*, 59:269–84. See also the interview between Nina Sadur and Dmitrii Babich, *Vremia MN*, 17 October.

<h2 style="text-align:center">2. THEORY</h2>

The Annotated Bakhtin Bibliography, ed. Carol Adlam and David Shepherd (MHRA Bibliographies, 1), London, MHRA, xxx + 413 pp., will be of enormous benefit to scholars. Mikhail Berg, 'О статусе литературы', *DN*, no.7:190–210, offers a penetrating study of the social role and status of literature; see also A. Genis, 'Модернизм как стиль XX века', *Zvezda*, no.11:202–09. *Литинститут в творческих семинарах мастеров. Портрет несуществующей теории*, M, Izdatel'stvo Literaturnogo Instituta, 288 pp., is also of some interest. G. Tihanov, *SEER*, 78:44–65, discusses Shklovskii and Lukács in the 1930s.

Works on Russian postmodernism include: I. S. Skoropanova, *Русская постмодернистская литература*, M, Flinta, 2nd rev. edn, 607 pp.; two important works by Michael Epshtein (apart from innumerable internet publications): 'Слово как произведение: о жанре однословия', *NovM*, no.9:204–15, and *Постмодерн в России. Литература и теория*, M, Ruslan Elinin. Also of considerable note is N. Ivanova, 'Жизнь и смерть симулякра в России', *DN*, no.8:187–96.

Two works by Alexandr Galushkin may be useful for scholars who are interested in the history of theoretical concepts and ideas: '«И так, ставши на костях, будем трубить сбор ...»: К истории несостоявшегося возрождения Опояза в 1928–1930 гг.', *NLO*, 44:136–53 (as an appendix it contains the second edition of Viktor Shklovskii's 'Памятник научной ошибке', 154–58), and also 'Над строкой партийного решения: Неизвестное выступление В. В. Маяковского в ЦК РКП (б)', *ib.*, 41:108–30. About this period see also I. Svetlikova, '«Губернатор захваченных территорий»

(Осип Брик в разговорах Виктора Шкловского с Александром Чудаковым)', *ib.*, 99–107. Finally in this section, see K. Barsht, 'Три литературоведения', *Zvezda*, no.3:191–204, which he sees as: morphological criticism (from Potebnia to Lotman); literary-historical criticism; and linguistic criticism.

On genres, see V. Ovchinnikova, *Литературная сказка XX века Мир - герой - автор*, Yuzhno-Sakhalinsk, SakhGU, 102 pp.; also the hugely impressive *Соцреалистический канон. Сборник статей*, ed. H. Günter and E. Dobrenko, StP, Akademicheskii proekt, 1044 pp., what must be the definite study on the contemporary understanding of Socialist Realism. Iu. S. Stepanov, '«Интертекст», «Интернет», «Интерсубъект» (к основаниям сравнительной концептологии)', *ISLIa*, no.1:3–11, describes intertextuality as 'the death of the author', Teilhard de Chardin's concept of 'personality above individuality', and 'conceptology' as a new discipline in humanities. There are several new linguistic approaches: V. P. Belianin, *Основы психолингвистической диагностики: модели мира в литературе*, M, Trivola, 247 pp., and N. A. Kozhevnikova and Z. Iu. Petrova, *Материалы к словарю метафор и сравнений русской литературы XIX-XX вв.*, M, Iazyki Russkoi Kul'tury (Studia Philogica).

SELECTED WORKS BY MODERN CRITICS AND SCHOLARS. Viach. Vs. Ivanov, *Избранные труды по семиотике и истории культуры: Статьи о русской литературе*, M, Iazyki Russkoi Kul'tury, vol. 2, 879 pp.; L. Katsis, *Русская эсхатология и русская литература*, M, OGI, 655 pp.; I. Zolotusskii, *На лестнице у Раскольникова: Эссе последних лет*, M, Fortuna Limited, 318 pp.; S. M. Kaznacheev, *Апология литературоцентризма: Статьи последних лет*, M, Moskovskaia gorodskaia organizatsiia Soiuza Pisatelei Rossii, 210 pp.; O. A. Lekmanov, *Книга об акмеизме и другие работы*, Tomsk, Vodolei, 704 pp. (a selection of Lekmanov's works mostly published in *NLO*).

3. DRAMA

Two interesting monographs: G. Verbitskaia, *Традиции поэтики А. П. Чехова в драматургии Н. Коляды*, Ufa, Ufimskii gos. institut iskusstv, 53 pp.; T. D. Belova, *Драматургия М. Горького 1900-х годов: Проблемы жанрового анализа*, Saratov, Izdatel'stvo Saratovskogo pedinstituta, 105 pp. See also N. Starosel'skaia, 'Драматургия Леонида Андреева: модерн 100 лет спустя', *VL*, no.6:125–48; L. M. Borisova, 'Трагедии Вячеслава Иванова в отношении к символистской теории жизнетворчества', *RusL*, no.1:63–77; S. A. Iezuitov, '«Васса Железнова» М. Горького и театр С. Э.

Радлова', *ib.*, no.2:99–111; E. G. Krasil′nikova, 'Театр абсурда Музы Павловой', *ISLIa*, no.2:56–61 (Muza Pavlova's plays as the development of avant-garde traditions).

4. Poetry

G. S. Smith, *MLR*, 95:xxix-xli, gives a superb overview of the role of the poet in 20th-c. Russia. See also Gerald Janecek, *Sight and Sound Entwined: Studies of the New Russian Poetry*, NY, Berghahn, 130 pp. (consisting of seven chapters, six of which have already appeared as separate essays, on: Anri Volokhonskii, Elizaveta Mnatsakanova, Joseph Brodskii, Genri Khudiakov, Vsevolod Nekrasov, Gennadii Aigi, Reia Nikonova). Other important publications include M. I. Shapir, *Universum versus. Язык — стих — смысл в русской поэзии XVIII-XX*, Vol. 1, 'Iazyki russkoi kul′tury' (Philologica russica et speculative, 1), M, VIII, 669 pp. Valerii Shubinskii, 'Семейный альбом: заметки о советской поэзии классического периода', *Oktjabr′*, no.8:150–68 (notes on Eduard Bagritskii, Alexander Tvardovskii, Pavel Vasil′ev, and Boris Slutskii — 'the last poet of the classical Soviet era'). See also D. Sukharev, 'Введение в субъективную бардистику', *Zvezda*, no.10:183–200, on the modern Russian 'author's song'.

S. Zavialov, 'Русская поэзия начала XXI века', *DN*, no.8:197–203: this controversial paper points to three main issues in contemporary Russian poetry: the changing of technique; joining 'the European mainstream'; the end of 'logocentrism', that is, the poet should be nothing but a poet. Other significant publications include *Творчество М. В. Исаковского, А. Т. Твардовского, Н. И. Рыленкова в контексте русской и мировой культуры: Материалы докладов научной конференции*, ed. G. S. Merkin, Smolensk, Smolenskii University Press, and L. Zubova, *Современная русская поэзия в контексте истории языка* (Nauchnaia biblioteka), M, NLO (the main idea is that poets penetrate various epochs in the history of language, breaking official linguistic norms).

5. Individual Authors

AKHMADULINA. E. Aizenshtein, 'Мгновенья бытия', *Neva*, no.7:193–97.

AKHMATOVA. A. Kushner, 'Анна Андреевна и Анна Аркадьевна', *NovM*, no.2:176–87. K. seemingly paradoxically compares A. to Anna Karenina. The reply from Natal′ia Ivanova, 'Подстановка' was published in *ib.*, no.9:192–203. M. Kralin,

'Неизвестное об Анне Ахматовой', *NSo*, no.3:236–46, is useful, as is the same author's *Победившее смерть слово: Статьи об Ахматовой и воспоминания о ее современниках*, Tomsk, Vodolei, 383 pp. See also N. Goncharova, «*Фаты либелей» Анны Ахматовой*, M–StP, Letnii Sad, Rossiiskaia gosudarstvennaia biblioteka, 676 pp. Mikhail Georgievskii's memoir is in *Neva*, no.6:219–25.

ANDREEV. *Леонид Андреев: материалы и исследования*, M, Nasledie, 412 pp.

BAGRITSKII. Maxim D. Shrayer, *Russian Poet, Soviet Jew: The Legacy of Eduard Bagritskii*, Lanham, MD, Rowman and Littlefield, xv + 163 pp.

BELYI. A new book: Z. Iur'eva, *Творимый космос у Андрея Белого*, StP, Dmitry Bulanin, 114 pp. See also the publication by M. Spivak, 'Последняя осень Андрея Белого: дневник 1933 г.', *NLO*, 46:178–215. O. Burenina, 'Quia absurdum', *WSl*, 45:265–84, analyzes the poetics of the absurd in works by Kharms and Belyi.

BERGGOL'TS. I. Foniakov, 'Испытание на разрыв', *Zvezda*, no.5:231–38, on unknown lyrics by Berggol'ts.

BLOK. Two new books: A. V. Lavrov, *Этюды о Блоке*, StP, Izdatel'stvo Ivana Limbakha, 319 pp.; O. A. Kling, *Александр Блок: структура 'Романа в стихах'. Поэма 'Двенадцать'*, Moscow U.P., 125 pp. See also H. Fink, *SEEJ*, 44:79–91 (a Kierkegaardian reading of 'Незнакомка').

BRODSKII. There are four new books: David MacFadyen, *Joseph Brodsky and the Soviet Muse*, Montreal, McGill-Queen's U.P., 216 pp.; E. Kelebai, *Поэт в доме ребенка: Пролегомены к философии творчества Иосифа Бродского*, Moscow U.P., 335 pp.; S. Volkov, *Диалоги с Иосифом Бродским*, M, Nezavisimaya Gazeta, 325 pp.; V. F. Medvedev, *Творчество Иосифа Бродского в зеркале культурологии*, Tula, Tul'skii Poligrafist, 146 pp. Several publications on B. mark the poet's sixtieth birthday in *Zvezda*, no.5: an interesting critical debut by Denis Akhapkin, '«Прощальная ода»: у истоков жанра «больших стихотворений»' (104–10), and a paradoxical study of B.'s early poetry by Boris Roginskii: '«Это такая моя сверхидея»' (99–103). Lev Losev comments on Solzhenitsyn's letter to B. (93–98). The original Russian text of B.'s 'Размышления об исчадии ада', *NLO*, 45:148–52, is accompanied by several papers on his poetry: L. Losev, 'Примечания с примечаниями' (153–60); O. Lekmanov, '«Рождественская звезда»: текст и подтекст' (162–65); O. Ranchin, '«Я родился и вырос в балтийских болотах, подле ...»: поэзия Иосифа Бродского и «Медный Всадник» Пушкина' (166–81); R. Timenchik, 'Приглашение на танго: поцелуй огня' (181–86); A. Zholkovsky, 'Бродский и инфинитивное письмо. Материалы к теме' (187–98); I. Kiust,

'Плохой поэт Иосиф Бродский: к истории вопроса' (248–55); O. Sedakova, 'Воля к форме' (232–36). See also A. A. Novikov, 'К вопросу о «классичности» поэзии Иосифа Бродского', *MSUB*, no.6:67–74 (B.'s poetry in the context of various concepts of 'classical' literature). For memoirs, see S. Maksudov (A. Babenyshev), 'Командировка в Норинскую', *NLO*, 45:199–208; L. Shtern, 'Главы из книги «Воспоминания о Бродском»', *ib.*, 208–29, and the same author, *Бродский: Ося, Иосиф, Joseph*, M, Nezavisimaia Gazeta, 210 pp; Ye. Solonovich, 'Под чужим именем. История публикации переводов Бродского из Сабы', *NLO*, 45:230–31.

BULGAKOV. New studies include K. Blank, *Slavonica*, 6.2:28–43 (the music of Igor′ Stravinskii in *Мастер и Маргарита*); I. Sukhikh, 'Евангелие от Михаила (1928–1940. *Мастер и Маргарита* M. Булгакова)', *Zvezda*, no.6:213–25; V. Petelin, *Жизнь Булгакова: Дописать раньше, чем умереть*, M, Centropoligraf, 664 pp.; S. Shargorodskii, 'Заметки о Булгакове', *NLO*, 41:218–27. (B. and Esenin); V. B. Petrov, *Аксиология Михаила Булгакова: Монография*, Magnitogorsk U.P., 246 pp.

CHUKOVSKII. M. Lipovetskii, 'Сказковласть: «Тараканище» Сталина', *NLO*, 45:122–36 (the story as an allegory of Stalin); see also memoirs by T. Syryshcheva, 'Корней Иванович. (Мозаика воспоминаний о Корнее Чуковском)', *Zvezda*, no.10:133–37, and G. Kogan, 'Полотняный завод - Переделкино', *ib.*, 138–49.

CHULKOV. R. V. Kaurkin and E. P. Titkov, *Михаил Чулков: творческое наследие: монография*, Arzamas, Arzamasskii gospedinstitut, 105 pp., is the first monograph on Ch.'s works.

DOBYCHIN. B. Paramonov, 'Добычин и Берковский', *Zvezda*, no.10:214–18.

DOVLATOV. Jekaterina Young, 'Dovlatov's *Compromise*: journalism, fiction and documentary', *Slavonica*, 6.2:44–67.

ESENIN. Several new books: A. Lukianov, *Сергей Есенин: тайна жизни*, Rostov, Feniks, 503 pp.; *Есенин в жизни: Систематизированный свод воспоминаний современников*, ed. E. Gusliarov and O. Karpukhin, 2 vols, Kaliningrad, Iantarnyi Skaz, 357, 391 pp.; V. S. Pashinina, *Неизвестный Есенин: Литература факта и документа*, Syktyvkar, OAO Komi, 329 pp.; G. M. Serdobintseva, '*Я разоблачил человека . . .': С. А. Есенин*, Ryazan′, Russkoe Slovo, 94 pp.; and N. F. Bogdanova, *Сергей Есенин. Женщины и друзья*, Ryazan′, Poverennyi, 135 pp.

GORKII. There are several works based on previously unknown materials: V. Baranov, *Максим Горький: подлинный или мнимый*, M, Prosveschenie, 110 pp.; T. V. Marchenko, 'Почему Максиму Горькому не дали Нобелевскую премию (По материалам архива Шведской академии)', *ISLIa*, no.2:3–16; N. N. Primochkina, 'М.Горький и «левые» евразийцы', *ib.*, 17–32 (on G.'s attitude towards Euro-Asianism, and his role in the fates of P. P. Souvtchinsky, D. P. Sviatopolk-Mirsky, and S. Ia. Ephron).

EROFEEV, VENEDIKT. 'Венедикт Ерофеев: последние годы: Из дневников Натальи Шмельковой', *Literaturnaya Gazeta*, October 25. See also N. A. Bogomolov, 'Блоковский пласт в «Москве-Петушках»', *NLO*, 44:126–35.

KUZMIN. S. Iu. Kornienko, *В "Сетях" Михаила Кузмина: семиотические, культурологические и гендерные аспекты*, Novosibirsk GPI, 148 pp.

KHLEBNIKOV. Two works are among the most important books on Kh. ever published: V. P. Grigor'ev, *Будетлянин* (Studia poetica), M, Iazyki Russkoi Kul'tury, 812 pp.; *Мир Велимира Хлебникова: Статьи. Исследования, 1911–1998*, ed. A. E. Parnis, M, Iazyki Russkoi Kul'tury, 880 pp. (contains studies of Kh.'s works from the first review by Nikolai Gumilev to modern studies). See also L. F. Katsis and M. P. Odesskii, 'Идеи «славянской взаимности» в творчестве В. В. Хлебникова и литераторов его круга', *ISLIa*, no.1:22–41 (traditional Slavic images in Kh.'s works, and Vladimir Dal''s 'Vocabulary' as an ideological source for Russian Futurists' 'slavic' texts). R. Vroon, *SEER*, 78:671–87, analyzes 'Отказ'.

KLUEV. N. M. Solntseva, *Странный Эрос: Интимные мотивы поэзии Николая Клюева*, M, Ellis Lak, 126 pp.

KOROLENKO. N. D. Petropavlovskaya, *Как я люблю ее: из жизни В. Г. Короленко*, M, Flinta, Nauka, 150 pp.

LEONOV. Of several interesting studies, the best is N. Leiderman, 'Парадоксы «Русского леса»', *VL*, no.6:29–58 (the main idea is that L. tried to parody the canons of socialist realism, donning the mask of 'true-believer'). See also V. S. Fedorov, 'По мудрым заветам предков: религиозно-философский феномен романа Л. Леонова «Пирамида»', *RusL*, no.4:46–58 (laboured attempt to make L. an Orthodox writer); V. Anikin, 'Лев Толстой и Леонид Леонов', *Moskva*, no.11:163–91 (an interesting memoir written by MSU professor Vladimir Anikin, a former colleague of L.). See also two books: V. I. Khrulev, *Леонид Леонов: магия художника*, Ufa, Bashkirskii U.P., 276 pp., and *Леонид Леонов и русская литература XX века: Материалы юбилейной научной конференции, посвященной 100–летию со дня рождения Л. М. Леонова,* ed. V. P. Muromskii and T. M. Vakhitova, StP, Nauka, 158 pp.

MAIAKOVSKII. A major book: L. F. Katsis, *Владимир Маяковский. Поэт в интеллектуальном контексте эпохи*, M, Iazyki Russkoi Kul'tury, 776 pp., contains some interesting ideas 'decorated' by many minor mistakes and shortcomings.

MANDEL'SHTAM. In Elena Glazov-Corrigan's *Mandel'shtam's Poetics: A Challenge to Postmodernism*, Toronto U.P., xii + 194 pp., M.'s thoughts on poetry and art are analyzed in the context of the major postmodern literary debates. Glazov-Corrigan examines the essays themselves systematically, not allowing herself to be sidetracked by the poetry. Other studies include D. I. Cherashniaia, 'Тема мавзолея в творчестве О. Мандельштама', *ISLIa*, no.4:36–48 (the theme of the mausoleum as constant in M.'s poetry); M. Epshtein, 'Хасид и талмудист', *Zvezda*, no.4:82–96 (comparative study of Pasternak and M.); M. L. Gasparov, 'Мандельштамовское «Мы пойдем другим путем»: о стихотворении «Кому зима - арак и пунш голубоглазый . . .»', *NLO*, 41:88–98; O. A. Lekmanov, 'На подступах к стихотворению О. Мандельштама «Когда б я уголь взял для высшей похвалы . . .»', *ISLIa*, no.1:62–65 (an attempt to clarify the reasons for writing the verse glorifying Stalin); D. Makogonenko, '«Соборы кристаллов сверхжизненных . . .» («Смысловые формулы» в поэзии О. Мандельштама»)', *VL*, no.6:329–36 (a semiotic study of 'Стихи о неизвестном солдате', 'Может быть, это точка безуми . . .'). See also L. Kikhnei, *Осип Мандельштам: Бытие слова*, M, Dialog-MGU, 146 pp. *Сохрани мою речь*, M, RGGU, Vol. 3 (issue 1, 266 pp., issue 2, 277 pp) (Записки Мандельштамовского общества), contains studies by S. Averintsev, Iu. Freidin, L. Katsis, V. Mikushevich, and O. Ronen.

MOZHAEV. I. Borisova, 'Борис Можаев: воля к независимости', *DN*, no.10:182–97; see also M. Shnore's (M.'s widow) memoirs 'На хуторе Уки', *ib.*, 198–215.

NABOKOV. New books include *Torpid Smoke: The Stories of Vladimir Nabokov*, ed. Steven G. Kellman and Irving Matlin, Amsterdam-Atlanta, Rodopi, 246 pp.; Jean Blau, *Набоков*, StP, Russko-Baltiiskii Informcenter Blitz, 239 pp.; *Классик без ретуши: Литературный мир о творчестве Владимира Набокова: Критические отзывы, пародии*, M, Novoe Literaturnoe Obozrenie, 681 pp. Maxim D. Shrayer publishes materials in *DN*, no.11:193–97. There are further publications by Shrayer: 'Почему Набоков не любил писательниц?', *ib.*, 197–204, and *Набоков: темы и вариации*, StP, Akademicheskii proekt, 375 pp. Studies of N.'s poetics include: G. Barabtarlo, 'Троичное начало у Набокова', *Zvezda*, no.5:219–30; A. V. Zlochevskaia, 'Поэтика Владимира Набокова: новации и традиции', *RusL*, no. 1:40–62; N. A. Karpov, '«Приглашение на казнь» и «тюремная» литература эпохи романтизма (к проблеме «Набоков и романтизм»)', *ib.*, no.2:203–10; V. Maramzin, 'Уроки Набокова. Ленинград, 60–е годы', *ib.*, no.7:201–07; B. Paramonov, 'Возвращение Лолиты', *ib.*, no.12:222–25; M. Niqueaux, '«Венецианка» Набокова, или

Чары искусства', *Zvezda*, no.10:201–05. See also Stephen H. Blackwell, *Zina's Paradox: The Figured Reader in Nabokov's 'Gift'*, (Middlebury Studies in Russian Language and Literature, 23), NY, Lang, 215 pp.; B. M. Nosik, *Мир и дар Набокова: Первая русская биография писателя*, StP, Zolotoi Vek, Diamant, 534 pp.

Mark Amusin, 'О несходстве сходного', *Oktjabr'*, no.2:181–86, borrowing the title from Victor Shklovskii's book on Lev Tolstoi, compares N. with Borges; S. Shenderovich and Y. Shvarts, *SEER*, 78:487–509, discuss André Chénier in Nabokov.

NOSOV. A. Solzhenitsyn, 'Из «Литературной коллекции»: Евгений Носов', *NovM*, no.7:195–99.

OLEINIKOV. O. Ronen, 'Персонажи-насекомые у Олейникова и обэриутов', *Zvezda*, no.8:192–200.

PASTERNAK. A first full book edition: *Пожизненная привязанность: переписка с О. М. Фрейденберг*, M, Art-Fleks. N. Ivanova, *Борис Пастернак: участь и предназначение: Биографическое эссе*, StP, Russko-Baltiiskii informatsionyi centre BLITS, 342 pp., is an excellent biography by a prominent Russian critic. See also B. Pasternak, *Биография в письмах*, M, Art-Fleks, 460 pp. Studies include N. A. Bogomolov, 'Еще раз о Брюсове и Пастернаке', *NLO*, 46:123–31 (on Briusov's influence on P.'s poetry in 1922–23); M. L. Gasparov and I. Iu. Podgaetskaia, 'Пастернак в пересказе: сверка понимания', *ib.*, 163–77 (on P.'s *Сестра моя -- жизнь*); N. A. Fateeva, 'О неявной граммматике поэтического текста (на материале поэзии Б.Пастернака)', *WSl*, 45:201–20; Angela Livingstone, *Slavonica*, 6.2:7–27 (P. and the 1st World War). There is also a new book: L. Gorelik, *Ранняя проза Пастернака: Миф о творении*, Smolensk, Smolenskii gospedunivesitet, 171 pp.

PIL'NIAK. John Elsworth, 'Pil'niak and Belyi', in *Slavonica*, 6.1:7–23, sees the main difference in that Belyi (as Symbolist) moved to an understanding of the necessary limitations of social activity of art. P., who represents post-Symbolist avant-garde, perceived art as a tool for reflection of the world as it is, but felt a need to embody cataclysmic change of the world in a new form of art, and exceeded the generic limitations of prose fiction.

PLATONOV. There are two weighty books: *Страна философов Андрея Платонова: проблемы творчества. Вып. 4. По материалам 4 международной конференции, посвященной 100–летию со дня рождения А. П. Платонова*, M, IMLI RAN, Nasledie, 995 pp., and *Творчество Андрея Платонова. Исследования и материалы*, vol. 2, StP, Nauka, Institut russkoi literatury (Pushkinskii Dom), 318 pp. Articles include Anat. Vernitski, 'A spiritual quest in the market: Christian motifs in Platonov's "Reka Potudan"', *ASEES*, 14, nos 1–2:61–74; M. Iu. Mikheev, 'Скупость ума и жадность чувства

(Деформация привычных понятий в поэтике Андрея Платонова)', *ISLIa*, no.1:42–56 (the concepts of 'stinginess', 'avidity', 'mind', and 'sense' in P.'s world). K. Livers, *SRev,* 59:54–82, looks at the 'recovery of the flesh' in *Счастливая Москва*.

REMIZOV. Three very different works: A. M. Gracheva, *Алексей Ремизов и древнерусская литература,* StP, Dmitrii Bulanin, (Studiorum slavicorum monumenta) (a complete study, the result of many years of research); E. Obatnina, '«Эротический символизм» Алексея Ремизова', *NLO*, 43:199–234 (erotic symbols in R.'s work); and N. A. Nagornaia, *Виртуальная реальность сновидения в творчестве А. М. Ремизова: монография,* Barnaul, BGPU, 150 pp.

SAPGIR. In memoriam: 'Автобиография', *NLO*, 41:232–33; V. Krivulin, 'Голос и пауза Генриха Сапгира', *ib.*, 233–41; A. Ranchin, '«Вирши» Генриха Сапгира', *ib.*, 242–57; G. Sapgir, 'Тактильные инструменты', *ib.*, 257–91; B. Kolymagin, 'Благословление навеки. Об одной религиозной интуиции Генриха Сапгира', *Oktjabr',* no.6:180–82.

SHISKOV. V. Red'kin, *Вячеслав Шишков: новый взгляд: очерк творчества В. Я. Шишкова,* Tver', Oblastnoe knizhnoe izdatel'stvo.

SHMELEV. A new book: O. Sorokina, *Московиана: Жизнь и творчество Ивана Шмелева,* M, Moskovskii rabochii, 2nd edn, rev., 404 pp. See also E. G. Rudneva, 'Цветовая гамма в повести И. С. Шмелева «Богомолье»', *MSUB*, no.6:59–66 (two key images: the light of the rising sun, and the light of the Orthodox faith).

SHOLOKHOV. The age-old problem is still on the agenda: A. G. Makarov and S. T. Makarova, *Вокруг "Тихого Дона": от мифотворчества к поиску истины,* M, Probel, 102 pp. (the authors deny Sh.'s authorship). The history of the enigmatic discovery of Sh.'s manuscripts is recounted in L. Kolodnyi, *Как я нашел «Тихий Дон». Хроника поиска,* M, 'Golos', 460 pp., and V. Kozhemiako, *Приватизаторы Шолохова: Как была найдена рукопись «Тихого Дона»,* M, 'Pravda', Kodeks-M. Also worth reading is F. Kuznetsov, 'Шолохов и «Анти-Шолохов»: конец литературной мистификации века', *NSo*, no.5:268–78, no.6:236–58, no. 7:249–64, no.11:258–87, accompanied by Lev Kolodnyi's letter, in which he denies F. Kuznetsov's charges of his attempts to sell Sh.'s manuscripts (no.11:288). Now available in Russian: H. Ermolaev, *Михаил Шолохов и его творчество* (Sovremennaia zapadnaia Rusistika, 32), StP, Akademichesky proekt. See also N. F. Korsunov, *С Шолоховым: Встречи, беседы, переписка,* Orenburg, Orenburzhskoe knizhnoe izdatel'stvo, 191 pp., and I. Sukhikh, 'Одиссея казачьего Гамлета (1925–1940. "Тихий Дон" М. Шолохова)', *Zvezda*, no.10:219–30.

SHUKSHIN. New books include José Antonio Ita Jiménez, *Герой и композиция в рассказах В. М. Шукшина,* Saratov, GPI, 58 pp.;

Шукшинские чтения. Вып.2, Volgograd, Peremena, 141 pp.; *Бийчане о Шукшине*, Biisk, NITs BiGPI, 201 pp.; G. G. Khisamova, *Язык современной художественной прозы: диалог в рассказах В. М. Шукшина*, Ufa, Bashkrskii U.P., 76 pp.; N. P. Zhilina, *Новеллистика В. Шукшина в литературном процессе 60–70-х годов XX века*, Kaliningrad, Kaliningrad U.P., 77 pp. See also A. Kuliapin, 'Три источника и три составных части рассказа В. М. Шукшина «Срезал»', *Zvezda*, no.2 : 192–97 (an intertextual study of Sh.'s famous story). Vasilii Belov publishes a memoir, *NSo*, no.10 : 106–60.

SLADKOV. D. Granin, 'Памяти Николая Сладкова', *Zvezda*, no.1 : 171–72.

SOLOGUB. New books include V. A. Meskin, *Грани русской прозы: Ф. Сологуб, Л. Андреев, И. Бунин*, Iuzhno-Sakhalinsk, Sakhalin U.P., 150 pp., and N. A. Dvoriashina, *Художественный образ детства в творчестве Федора Сологуба*, Surgut, Surgutskii GPI, 154 pp. Articles include A. D. Semkin, 'Евреинов и Сологуб: к истории постановки пьесы «Ванька-ключник и паж Жеан»', *RusL*, no.2 : 112–19, L. Geller, 'Фантазии и утопии Федора Сологуба: замечания по поводу «Творимой легенды»', *ib.*, 119–26, V. Vavere, 'Федор Сологуб в Латвии', *ib.*, 127–35, J. Elsworth, 'О философском осмыслении рассказа Ф. Сологуба «Свет и тени»', *ib.*, 135–38, J. Merrill, 'Тайное признание в инцесте в драмах Сологуба', *ib.*, 138–45.

STRATANOVSKII. N. Eliseev, 'Клерк-соловей', *VL*, no.4 : 81–97.

STRUGATSKII BROTHERS. M. Amusin, 'Стругацкие и фантастика текста', *Zvezda*, no.7 : 208–16.

TSVETAEVA. New books include E. O. Aizenshtein, *Построен на созвучьях мир . . .: Звуковая стихия М. Цветаевой*, StP, Zhurnal 'Neva', Letnii Sad, 287 pp.; Id., *Борису Пастернаку —навстречу! Марина Цветаева: о книге М.Цветаевой "После России"*, StP, Zhurnal 'Neva', Letny Sad, 383 pp.; A. Babakin, *Словарь рифм Марины Цветаевой*, Tiumen', Izdatel'stvo Iu. Mandriki; A. Saakiants, *Жизнь Цветаевой. Бессмертная птица-феникс*, M, Tsentrpoligraf, 826 pp. (the complete biography); N. O. Osipova, *Творчество М. И. Цветаевой в контексте культурной мифологии Серебряного века*, Kirov, Viatskii GPI, 271 pp. Articles include G. S. Smith, *OSP*, 33 : 108–33 (verse form and function in *Царь-Девица*), and A. W. Dinega, *SRev*, 59 : 547–71 (sexual transcendence in Ts.'s poems to Pasternak). See also A. Smirnov, 'За деревьями,' *VL*, no.6 : 59–82 (a traditional analysis of Ts.'s 'Derevia' circle (1922–23)); N. K. Teletova, *RusL*, no.1 : 78–102 (*Молодец* and *Faust*).

TVARDOVSKII. The year saw T.'s ninetieth birthday, and a stream of publications and memoirs: '«Из записной потертой книжки . . .» (Записи А. Т. Твардовского 1944–1945 гг.)', *DN*, no.6: 175–83 (publication by V. A. Tvardovskaia and O. A. Tvardovskaia); A. Tvardovskii, 'Рабочие тетради 60-х годов', *Zvezda*, no.6: 132–77, no.9: 139–89, no.11: 144–74, no.12: 124–47. Also useful is A. Solzhenitsyn, 'Богатырь', *NovM*, no.6: 129–30, part of the second volume of «Угодило зернышко промеж двух жерновов», written in 1982. There are some interesting studies: Iu. Kublanovskii, 'Этюд о Твардовском', *ib.*, 131–35 ('we should not ignore T.'s heritage though he belongs more to the history of poetry than to the present day'); F. A. Uzunkolev, *Твардовский А. Т. : переводчик и переводы*, StP, Nauka, 216 pp.; V. V. Il'in, *Не пряча глаз: Александр Твардовский. Литературное окружение. Творческие связи*, Smolensk, Smiadyn', 388 pp.; I. Sukhikh, 'О смерти, войне, судьбе и родине - русской и советской (1941–1945. "Василий Теркин" А. Твардовского)', *Zvezda*, no.8: 221–30. See also A. Turkov, '"Я не ранен. Я - убит . . .". Из воспоминаний об А. Твардовском', *ib.*, no.1: 161–74.

VAGINOV. A. Anemone, 'Obsessive collectors: fetishizing culture in the novels of Konstantin Vaginov', *RusR*, 59: 252–68, and A. Dmitrenko, 'Когда родился Вагинов?', *NLO*, 41: 228–31.

VOLOSHIN. Two new books: V. P. Kupchenko, *Жизнь Максимилиана Волошина: Документальное повествование*, StP, Izdatel'stvo zhurnala 'Zvezda', 399 pp., and T. Rozental', *Планета Макса Волошина*, M, Vagrius, 238 pp.

VYSOTSKII. An interesting publication is V. Popov, *Письма о Высоцком*, Ekaterinburg, Bank kul'turnoi informatsii, 295 pp. (a documentary novella on Vysotskii).

ZAMIATIN. A hugely impressive achievement: *Творческое наследие Евгения Замятина: взгляд из сегодня: Научные доклады, статьи, очерки, заметки, тезисы. В 10 книгах*, ed. L. V. Poliakova, Tambov GU. See also *Е. И. Замятин. Материалы к библиографии.* *Ч.2.*, ed. L. V. Poliakova, Tambov, TGU. 51 pp.; L. V. Poliakova, *Евгений Замятин в контексте оценок истории русской литературы XX века как литературной эпохи: курс лекций*, Tambov U.P., 283 pp. Other publications include T. T. Davydova, *Творческая эволюция Евгения Замятина в контексте русской литературы первой трети XX века: Монография*, M, MGUP, 363 pp. ('neorealism' in Z.'s works); Philip Cavendish, *Mining for Jewels: Evgenii Zamiatin and the Literary Stylization for Rus'* (MHRA Texts and Dissertations, 51), London, MHRA, xiv + 272 pp., locates Z.'s work within the tradition of Russian ethnographic belles-lettres and oral-based fiction; the author stresses that Z., whilst certainly a modernist, can be analysed also in Eikhenbaum's terms of 'literary populism'). See also V. V. Perkhin, 'П. И. Лебедев-Полянский как цензор,' *RusL*, no.3: 211–21 (an interesting study on Soviet censorship, particular in connection with Z.). On censorship see also M. V. Zelenov, *Аппарат ЦК РКП (б) —ВКП (б), цензура и историческая наука в 1920-е годы*, Nizhnii Novgorod U.P., 349 pp. See also V. A. Tunimanov, *RusL*, no.2 : 81–98 (Z. and Anatole France: irony and utopian motifs).

ZOSHCHENKO. I. Sukhikh, 'Из гоголевской шинели (1923–1930. «Сентиментальные повести» М. Зощенко)', *Zvezda*, no.2 : 218–27 (an analysis of Gogol's traditions in Z.'s stories), and M. Rakov, 'Михаил Зощенко: музыка перевода', *NLO*, no.44 : 111–25.

V. UKRANIAN STUDIES
POSTPONED

VI. BELARUSIAN STUDIES
POSTPONED

VII. SERBO-CROAT STUDIES

LANGUAGE
POSTPONED

LITERATURE
POSTPONED

VIII. BULGARIAN STUDIES
POSTPONED

ABBREVIATIONS

I. ACTA, FESTSCHRIFTEN AND OTHER COLLECTIVE AND GENERAL WORKS

Actas (Corunna): *Edición y anotación de textos. Actas del I Congreso de Jóvenes Filólogos (A Coruña, 25–28 de septiembre de 1996)*, ed. C. Parrilla et al., 2 vols, Corunna U.P., 1999, 350, 381 pp.

Actas (Madrid), I: *Actas del XIII Congreso Internacional de Hispanistas (Madrid 1998). I. Medieval, Siglo XVI, Siglo XVIII*, ed. Florencio Sevilla and Carlos Alvar, xxix + 847 pp.

Adami, *Pan:* Martina Adami, *Der große Pan ist tot!? Studien zur Pan-Rezeption in der Literatur des 19. und 20. Jahrhunderts* (Innsbrucker Beiträge zur Kulturwissenschaft. Germanistische Reihe, 61), Universität Innsbruck, Institut für Germanistik, 261 pp.

AIEO 1995: Le rayonnement des troubadours. Actes du colloque de l'Association International d'Études Occitanes, Amsterdam, 16–18 octobre 1995, ed. Anton Touber (Internationale Forschungen zur Allgemeinen und Vergleichenden Literaturwissenschaft), Amsterdam–Atlanta, Rodopi, 1997, 400 pp.

AHLM 8: Actas del VIII Congreso Internacional de la Asociación Hispánica de Literatura Medieval (Santander, 1999), ed. Margarita Freixas, Silvia Iriso and Laura Fernández, 2 vols, Santander, Consejería de Cultura del Gobierno de Cantabria—Año Jubilar Lebaniego — Asociación Hispánica de Literatura Medieval, 1830 pp.

Alexiadou, *Possessors: Possessors, Predicates and Movement in the Determiner Phrase*, ed. Artemis Alexiadou and Chris Wilder, Amsterdam, Benjamins, 1998, vi + 386 pp.

Aleza, *Estudios: Estudios de historia de la lengua española en América y España*, ed. Milagros Aleza Izquierdo, Valencia, Universitat de Valencia, 1999, 288 pp.

Auroux, *Geschichte: Geschichte der Sprachwissenschaft. Ein internationales Handbuch zur Entwicklung der Sprachforschung von den Angfängen bis zur Gegenwart / History of the Language Sciences. An International Handbook on the Evolution of the Study of Language from the Beginnings to the Present / Histoire des sciences du langage. Manuel international sur l'évolution de l'étude du langage des origines à nos jours*, ed. Sylvain Auroux, E. F. K. Koerner, Hans-Josef Niederehe, and Kees Versteegh (HSK, 18.1–3), Berlin–New York, Walter de Gruyter, vol. I, lx + 1094 pp.

Baker, *Dante: Dante Colloquia in Australia (1982–1999)*, ed. Margaret Baker and Diana Glenn, Adelaide, Australian Humanities Press, xxv + 207 pp.

Balcerzan, *Osoba: Osoba w literaturze i komunikacji literackiej*, ed. Edward Balcerzan and Włodzimierz Bolecki (Z Dziejów Form Artystycznych w Literaturze Polskiej), Warsaw, IBL PAN, 276 pp.

Baumbach, *Tradita: Tradita et Inventa. Beiträge zur Rezeption der Antike*, ed. Manuel Baumbach (Bibliothek der klassischen Altertumswissenschaften, n.F., 2. Reihe, 106), Heidelberg, Winter, xi + 676 pp.

Beltrán, *Poesía: Estudios sobre poesía de cancionero*, ed. V. Beltrán et al., Corunna, Toxos Outos, 1999, 136 pp.

Bély, *Personne: Personne, personnage et transcendance aux XIIe et XIIIe siècles*, ed. M.-E. Bély and J.-R. Valette (Collection XI-XVII Littérature), Lyon U.P., 1999, 261 pp.

Besch Vol.: Das Frühneuhochdeutsche als sprachgeschichtliche Epoche. Werner Besch zum 70. Geburtstag, ed. Walter Hoffmann, Jürgen Macha, Klaus J. Mattheier, Hans-Joachim Solms, and Klaus-Peter Wegera, Frankfurt, Lang, 1999, 294 pp.

Beugnot Vol.: Inventaire, Lecture, Invention. Mélanges de critique et d'histoires littéraires offerts à Bernard Beugnot, ed. Jacinthe Martel and Robert Melançon (Paragraphes, 18), Université de Montréal, 1999, 449 pp.

Blank Vol.: 'als das wissend die meister wol.' Beiträge zur Darstellung und Vermittlung von Wissen in Fachliteratur und Dichtung des Mittelalters und der frühen Neuzeit. Walter Blank zum 65. Geburtstag, ed. Martin Ehrenfeuchter and Thomas Ehlen, Frankfurt, Lang, 395 pp.

Blauert, *Kriminalitätsgeschichte: Kriminalitätsgeschichte. Beiträge zur Sozial- und Kulturgeschichte der Vormoderne*, ed. Andreas Blauert and Gert Schwerhoff (Konflikte und Kultur — historische Perspektiven, 1), Konstanz, UVK Universitätsverlag Konstanz, 920 pp.

Boivin, *Mélusines: Mélusines continentales et insulaires*, ed. J.-M. Boivin and P. MacCana (Nouvelle Bibliothèque du Moyen Age, 49), Paris, Champion, 1999, 350 pp.

Bråkenhielm, *Modernitetens ansikten: Modernitetens ansikten. Livsåskådningar i nordisk 1900–talslitteratur*, ed. Carl Reinhold Bråkenhielm and Torsten Pettersson, Nora, Nya Doxa, 376 pp.

Brand Vol: Britain and Italy from Romanticism to Modernism. A Festschrift for Peter Brand, ed. Martin McLaughlin, Oxford, Legenda — Modern Humanities Research Association, xx + 195 pp.

Brandis Vol.: Scrinium Berolinense. Tilo Brandis zum 65. Geburtstag. ed. Peter Jörg Becker et al., 2 vols., Staatsbibliothek zu Berlin, Preussischer Kulturbesitz, 1200 pp.

Braun, *Disrupted Patterns: Disrupted Patterns: On Chaos and Order in the Enlightenment*, ed. Theodore E. D. Braun and John A. McCarthy (Internationale Forschungen zur allgemeinen und vergleichenden Literaturwissenschaft, 43), Amsterdam, Rodopi, xiii + 219 pp.

Cambon Vol.: The Craft and the Fury. Essays in memory of Glauco Cambon, West Lafayette, IN, Bordighera Press, 424 pp.

Camps, *Languedoc: Languedoc - Roussillon - Catalogne. État, nation, identité culturelle régionale (des origines à 1659), Actes du Colloque, 20–22 mars 1997*, ed. Christian Camps and Carlos Heusch, Montpellier, Université Paul Valéry, 1998, 382 pp.

Cardy, *Theatre: Aspects of Twentieth-Century Theatre in French*, ed. Michael Cardy and Derek Connon, Berne, Lang, 243 pp.

Carvalho Vol.: Estudos dedicados a Ricardo Carvalho Calero, ed. José Luís Rodríguez Fernández, 2 vols, Santiago de Compostela, Universidade–Parlamento de Galicia.

Catling, *Women's Writing: A History of Women's Writing in Germany, Austria and Switzerland*, ed. Jo Catling, Cambridge University Press, xvii + 395 pp.

Cechova, *Jinakost: Jinakost, cizost v jazyce a v literature. Sbornik z mezinarodni konference*, ed. Marie Cechova and Dobrava Moldanova, Usti n. Labem, J. E. Purkyne Univ., 1999, 409 pp.

Chevalier, *Néologie: La Fabrique des mots. La néologie ibérique*, ed. J.-C. Chevalier and M.-F. Delport, Paris, Presses de l'Université de Paris-Sorbonne, 278 pp..

CILPR 22: Actes du XXIIe Congrès International de Linguistique et de Philologie Romanes, Bruxelles, 23–29 juillet 1998, ed. Annick Englebert, Michel Pierrard, Laurence Rosier, and Dan Van Raemdonck, 9 volumes, I: *L'histoire de la linguistique, médiatrice de théories*, II: *Les nouvelles ambitions de la linguistique diachronique*, III: *Vivacité et diversité de la variation linguistique*, IV: *Des mots aux dictionnaires*, V: *Les manuscrits ne brûlent pas*, VI: *De la grammaire des formes à la grammaire du sens*, VII: *Sens et fonctions*, VIII: *Les effets du sens*, IX: *Contacts interlinguistiques*, Tübingen, Niemeyer, xii + 249, xii + 488, xii + 433, xiv + 628, x + 166, xii + 570, xiv + 733, x + 204, xii + 422 pp.

Classen, *Voices: Medieval German Voices in the 21st Century. The Paradigmatic Function of Medieval German Studies for German Studies. A Collection of Essays*, ed. Albrecht Classen (Internationale Forschungen zur Allgemeinen und Vergleichenden Literaturwissenschaft, 46), Amsterdam–Atlanta, Rodopi, 252 pp.

Cook, *Journalisme: Journalisme et fiction au 18e siècle*, ed. Malcolm Cook and Annie Jourdan, Berne, Lang, 1999, 241 pp.

Connon, *Drama: Essays on French Comic Drama from the 1640s to the 1780s*, ed. Derek F. Connon and George Evans (French Studies of the Eighteenth and Nineteenth Centuries, 7), Oxford–New York, Lang, 236 pp.

Corbineau-Hoffmann, *Gewalt: Gewalt der Sprache — Sprache der Gewalt. Beispiele aus philologischer Sicht*, ed. Angelika Corbineau-Hoffmann and Pascal Nicklas, Hildesheim, Olms, vi + 304 pp.

Courcelles, *Femmes: Des Femmes et des livres: France et Espagnes, XIVe–XVIIe siècle*, ed. Dominique de Courcelles and Carmen Val Julián (Études et Rencontres, 4), Paris, École des Chartes, 1999, 175 pp.

Dadson, *Voces subversivas: Voces subversivas: poesía bajo el régimen (1939–1975)*, ed. Trevor J. Dadson and Derek W. Flitter, Birmingham U. P., xii + 142 pp.

Davies, *Autobiography: Autobiography by Women in German*, ed. Mererid Puw Davies, Beth Linklater, and Gisela Shaw, Berne, Lang, 310 pp.

Debaisieux, *Violence: Violence et fiction jusqu'à la Révolution*, ed. Martine Debaisieux and Gabrielle Verdier (ELF, 66), Tübingen, Narr, 1998, 480 pp.

Della Terza Vol.: Studies for Dante: Essays in honor of Dante della Terza, ed. Franco Fido, Rena A. Syska-Lamparska, and Pamela D. Stewart, Fiesole, Cadmo, 1998, 514 pp.

Démoris, *Folies: Folies romanesques au siècle des Lumières*, ed. René Démoris and Henri Lafon, Paris, Desjonquères, 1998, 417 pp.

Dinzelbacher, *Mensch und Tier: Mensch und Tier in der Geschichte Europas*, ed. Peter Dinzelbacher (Kröners Taschenausgabe, 342), Stuttgart, Kröner, xiv + 670 pp.

Durand Vol.: État et société en France aux XVIIe et XVIIIe siècles: Mélanges offerts à Yves Durand, ed. Dominique Dinet and Jean-Pierre Poussou, Paris, Presses de l'Université de Paris-Sorbonne, 548 pp.

Dworkin, *New Approaches: New Approaches to Old Problems. Issues in Romance Historical Linguistics*, ed. Steven N. Dworkin and Dieter Wanner (Current Trends in Linguistics, 210), Amsterdam–Philadelphia, Benjamins, xiv + 235 pp.

Edwards, *Cwm Gwendraeth: Cwm Gwendraeth*, ed. Hywel Teifi Edwards, Llandysul, Gomer, 246 pp.

Everson, *Italy in Crisis: Italy in Crisis, 1494*, ed. Jane Everson and Diego Zancani, Oxford, Legenda, 204 pp.

Ferroni, *Passioni:* Giulio Ferroni, *Passioni del Novecento*, Rome, Donzelli, 1999, 248 pp.

Fest. Böschenstein: Antiquitates Renatae. Deutsche und französische Beiträge zur Wirkung der Antike in der europäischen Literatur. Festschrift für Renate Böschenstein zum 65. Geburtstag, ed. Verena Ehrich-Haefeli, Hans-Jürgen Schrader, and Martin Stern, Würzburg, Königshausen & Neumann, 1998, 383 pp.

Fest. Brunner: Vom Mittelalter zur Neuzeit. Festschrift für Horst Brunner, ed. Dorothea Klein, Elisabeth Lienert, and Johannes Rettelbach, Wiesbaden, Reichert, x + 752 pp.

Fest. Denkler: Produktivität des Gegensätzlichen. Studien zur Literatur des 19. und 20. Jahrhunderts. Festschrift für Horst Denkler zum 65. Geburtstag, ed. Julia Bertschik, Elisabeth Emter, and Johannes Graf, Tübingen, Niemeyer, xii + 314 pp.

Fest. Eroms: Deutsche Grammatik — Thema in Variationen. Festschrift für Hans-Werner Eroms zum 60. Geburtstag, ed. Karin Donhauser and Ludwig M. Eichinger, Heidelberg, Winter, 1998, 427 pp.

Fest. Frühwald: Stifter-Studien. Festgeschenk für Wolfgang Frühwald zum 65. Geburtstag, ed. Walter Hettche, Johannes John, and Sibylle von Steinsdorf, Tübingen, Niemeyer, vi + 258 pp.

Fest. Hinderer: Signaturen der Gegenwartsliteratur. Festschrift für Walter Hinderer, ed. Dieter Borchmeyer, Würzburg, Königshausen & Neumann, 1999, 328 pp.

Fest. Johnson: Blütezeit. Festschrift für L. Peter Johnson zum 70. Geburtstag, ed. Mark Chinca, Joachim Heinzle, and Christopher Young, Tübingen, Niemeyer, ix + 488 pp.

Fest. Kreutzer: Resonanzen. Festschrift für Hans Joachim Kreutzer zum 65. Geburtstag, ed. Sabine Doering, Waltraud Maierhofer, and Peter Philipp Riedl, Würzburg, Königshausen & Neumann, 504 pp.

Fest. Krolop: Brücken nach Prag. Deutschsprachige Literatur im kulturellen Kontext der Donaumonarchie und der Tschechoslowakei. Festschrift für Kurt Krolop zum 70. Geburtstag, ed. Klaas-Hinrich Ehlers, Steffen Höhne, Václav Maidl, and Marek Nekula, Frankfurt, Lang, 505 pp.

Fest. Löffler: Vom Umgang mit sprachlicher Variation. Soziolinguistik, Dialektologie, Methoden und Wissenschaftsgeschichte. Festschrift für Heinrich Löffler zum 60. Geburtstag, ed. Annelies Häcki Buhofer, Lorenz Hofer, Ulrike Marx, Francis Barcelo, and Christina Schläfli, Tübingen–Basel, 390 pp.

Fest. Mettke: Septuaginta quinque. Festschrift für Heinz Mettke, ed. Jens Haustein, Eckhard Meineke, and Norbert Richard Wolf, Heidelberg, Winter, xii + 437 pp.

Fest. Moser: Leitmotive: Kulturgeschichtliche Studien zur Traditionsbildung. Festschrift für Dietz-Rüdiger Moser zum 60. Geburtstag, am 22 März 1999, ed. Marianne Sammer et al., Kallmünz, Lassleben, 1999, 708 pp.

Fest. Munske: Wortschatz und Orthographie in Geschichte und Gegenwart. Festschrift für Horst Haider Munske zum 65. Geburtstag, ed. Mechthild Habermann, Peter O. Müller, and Bernd Naumann, Tübingen, Niemeyer, ix + 407 pp.

Fest. Reeves: Vermittlungen. German Studies at the Turn of the Century. Festschrift für Nigel B.R. Reeves, ed. Rüdiger Görner and Helen Kelly-Holmes, Munich, Iudicium, 1999, 278 pp.

Fest. Richter: Begegnung der Zeiten: Festschrift für Helmut Richter zum 65. Geburtstag, ed. Regina Fasold, Leipzig U.P., 1999, 419 pp.

Fest. Rischbieter: Theater als Ort der Geschichte. Festschrift für Henning Rischbieter, ed. Theo Girshausen and Henry Thorau, Velber, Friedrich, 1998, 400 pp.

Fest. Roebling: Bei Gefahr des Untergangs. Phantasien des Aufbrechens. Festschrift für Irmgard Roebling, ed. Ina Brueckel, Dörte Fuchs, Rita Morrien, and Margarete Sander, Würzburg, Königshausen & Neumann, xi + 457 pp.

Fest. Steinecke: Literatur und Demokratie. Festschrift für Hartmut Steinecke zum 60. Geburtstag, ed. Alo Allkemper and Norbert Otto Eke, Berlin, Schmidt, 343 pp.

Fest. Steinmetz: Interpretation 2000: Positionen und Kontroversen. Festschrift zum 65. Geburtstag von Horst Steinmetz, ed. Henk de Berg and Matthias Prangel, Heidelberg, Winter, 1999, 307 pp.

Fest. Storck: Korrespondenzen. Festschrift für Joachim W. Storck aus Anlaß seines 75. Geburtstages, ed. Rudi Schweikert and Sabine Schmidt (Mannheimer Studien zur Literatur- und Kulturwissenschaft, 20), St. Ingbert, Röhrig, 1999, 719 pp.

Fest. Tervooren: Edition und Interpretation. Neue Forschungsparadigmen zur mittelhochdeutschen Lyrik. Festschrift für Helmut Tervooren, ed. Johannes Spicker, Susanne Fritsch, Gaby Herchert, and Stefan Zeyen, Stuttgart, Hirzel, 190 pp.

Fest. Träger: Kritische Fragen an die Tradition. Festschrift für Claus Träger zum 70 Geburtstag, ed. Marion Marquardt, Uta Störmer-Caysa, and Sabine Heimann-Seelbach (Stuttgarter Arbeiten zur Germanistik, 340), Stuttgart, Heinz, 1997, 618 pp.

Fest. Valentin: Zur Geschichte der Nominalgruppe im älteren Deutsch. Festschrift für Paul Valentin. Akten des Pariser Kolloquiums März 1999, ed. Yvon Desportes, Heidelberg, Winter, 290 pp.

Fest. Walliczek: 'helle döne schöne.' Versammelte Arbeiten zur älteren und neueren deutschen Literatur. Festschrift für Wolfgang Walliczek, ed. Horst Brunner, Claudia Händl, Ernst Hellgardt, and Monika Schulz (Göppinger Arbeiten zur Germanistik, 668), Göppingen, Kümmerle, 1999, v + 453 pp.

Fest. Wuthenow: Das Paradoxe. Literatur zwischen Logik und Rhetorik. Festschrift für Ralph-Rainer Wuthenow zum 70. Geburtstag, ed. Carolina Romahn and Gerold Schipper-Hönicke, Würzburg, Königshausen & Neumann, 1999, 336 pp.

Fest. Žmegač: Literatur im Wandel: Festschrift für Viktor Žmegač zum 70. Geburtstag, ed. Marijan Bobinac (ZGB, Beiheft 5), 1999, 457 pp.

Fichtner, *Doppelgänger: Doppelgänger. Von endlosen Spielarten eines Phänomens*, ed. Ingrid Fichtner (Facetten der Literatur, 7), Berne, Haupt, 1999, ix + 269 pp.

Frey, *Totentänze: 'Ir müßt alle nach meiner Pfeife tanzen.' Totentänze vom 15. bis zum 20. Jahrhundert in den Beständen der Herzog August Bibliothek Wolfenbüttel und der Bibliothek Otto Schäfer Schweinfurt*, ed. Winfried Frey and Hartmut Freytag, Wiesbaden, Harrassowitz, 276 pp.

Gargett, *Ireland: Ireland and the French Enlightenment, 1700–1800*, ed. Graham Gargett and Geraldine Sheridan, Basingstoke, Macmillan, 1999, xvii + 293 pp.

Genoud de Fourcade, *Estudios: Literatura y conocimiento: estudios teórico-críticos sobre narrativa, lírica y teatro*, ed. Mariana Genoud de Fourcade, Mendoza, Argentina, Universidad Nacional de Cuyo, Facultad de Filosofía y Letras, 1998, 301 pp.

Giles Vol.: The Mystical Gesture. Essays on Medieval and Early Modern Spiritual Culture in Honor of Mary E. Giles, ed. Robert Boenig, Aldershot–Burlington, VT, Ashgate, ix + 226 pp.

Gömöri, *Poles:* George Gömöri, *Magnetic Poles: Essays on Modern Polish and Comparative Literature*, London, Polish Cultural Foundation, 163 pp.

Goodden, *Memory:* Angelica Goodden, *The Backward Look: Memory and the Writing Self in France 1580–1920*, Oxford, Legenda, xi + 194 pp.

Grodek, *Ruse: Écriture de la ruse*, ed. Elzbieta Grodek (Faux Titre, 190), Amsterdam, Rodopi, 455 pp.

Grubmüller, *Schulliteratur: Schulliteratur im späten Mittelalter*, ed. Klaus Grubmüller (Münstersche Mittelalter-Schriften, 69), Munich, Fink, 535 pp.

Haubrichs, *Theodisca: Theodisca. Beiträge zur althochdeutschen und altniederdeutschen Sprache und Literatur in der Kultur des frühen Mittelalters. Eine internationale Fachtagung in Schönmühl bei Penzberg vom 13. bis zum 16. März 1997*, ed. Wolfgang Haubrichs, Ernst Hellgardt, Reiner Hildebrandt, Stephan Müller, and Klaus Ridder (Reallexikon der Germanistischen Altertumskunde, Ergänzungsband 22), Berlin, de Gruyter, x + 460 pp.

Haug, *Mystik: Deutsche Mystik im abendländischen Zusammenhang. Neu erschlossene Texte, neue methodische Ansätze, neue theoretische Konzepte. Kolloquium Kloster Fischingen 1998*, ed. Walter Haug and Wolfram Schneider-Lastin, Tübingen, Niemeyer, xii + 815 pp.

Hernández, *Cid: Actas del congreso internacional El Cid, Poema e Historia (12–16 de julio, 1999)*, ed. César Hernández Alonso, Burgos, Ayuntamiento, 421 pp.

Herring, *Parameters: Textual Parameters in Older Languages*, ed. Susan C. Herring, Pieter van Reenen, and Lene Schøsler (Current Issues in Linguistic Theory, 195), Amsterdam, Benjamins, x + 448 pp.

Hladka, *Čeština: Čeština — univerzalia a specifika*, ed. Zdenka Hladka and Petr Karlik, 2 vols, MU, 1999–2000, 130, 192 pp.

Honemann, *Einblattdrucke: Einblattdrucke des 15. und frühen 16. Jahrhunderts. Probleme, Perspektiven, Fallstudien*, ed. Volker Honemann, Sabine Griese, Falk Eisermann, and Martin Ostermann, Tübingen, Niemeyer, x + 533 pp.

Horecký Vol.: Človek a jeho jazyk. 1. Jazyk ako fenomen kultury: Na pocest profesora Jana Horeckeho, Bratislava, Veda, 522 pp.

Huber, *Geistliches: Geistliches in weltlicher und Weltliches in geistlicher Literatur des Mittelalters*, ed. Christoph Huber, Burghart Wachinger, and Hans-Joachim Ziegeler, Tübingen, Niemeyer, vi + 348 pp.

ICHL 12: Historical Linguistics 1995: Selected Papers from the 12th International Conference on Historical Linguistics, Manchester, August 1995, ed. Richard Hogg and Linda van Bergen, 1. *General Issues and Non-Germanic Languages*, ed. John Charles Smith and Delia Bentley, Amsterdam, Benjamins, xi + 438 pp.

Jackson, *Arthur: The Arthur of the Germans. The Arthurian Legend in Medieval German and Dutch Literature*, ed. W. H. Jackson and S. A. Ranawake (Arthurian Literature in the Middle Ages, 3), Cardiff, University of Wales Press, xii + 337 pp.

Jelinek, *Argumentace: Argumentace a umeni komunikovat*, ed. Milan Jelinek, Blazena Svandova et al., Brno, MU, 1999, 327 pp.

Jenkins, *Eu Hiaith: 'Eu Hiaith a Gadwant'?: Y Cymraeg yn yr Ugenfed Ganrif*, ed. Geraint H. Jenkins and Mari A. Williams, Cardiff, University of Wales Press, 685 pp.

Jones Day, *Writers and Heroines: Writers and Heroines: Essays on Women in French Literature*, ed. Shirley Jones Day, Berne–New York, Lang, 1999, 177 pp.

Keller, *Schriftlichkeit: Schriftlichkeit und Lebenspraxis im Mittelalter. Erfassen, Bewahren, Verändern*, ed. Hagen Keller, Christel Meier, and Thomas Scharff (Münstersche Mittelalter-Schriften, 76), Munich, Fink, x + 361 pp.

Kidd and Reynolds, *Contemporary French:* William Kidd and Siân Reynolds, *Contemporary French Cultural Studies*, London, Arnold, xiii + 322 pp.

Kock Vol.: Estudios en honor del Profesor Josse de Kock, ed. N. Delbecque and C. de Paepe, Louvain University Press, 1998, xxxiii + 988 pp.

Krueger, *Romance: The Cambridge Companion to Medieval Romance*, ed. Roberta L. Krueger, CUP, 320 pp.

Kurz, *Meditation: Meditation und Erinnerung in der Frühen Neuzeit*, ed. Gerhard Kurz (Formen der Erinnerung, 2), Göttingen, Vandenhoeck & Ruprecht, 405 pp.

Lacy Vol.: 'Por le soi amisté'. Essays in Honor of Norris J. Lacy, ed. K. Busby and C. M. Jones (Faux Titre, 183), Amsterdam-Atlanta, Rodopi, xxxiv + 552 pp.

Lahiri, *Analogy: Analogy, Levelling, Markedness. Principles of Change in Phonology and Morphology*, ed. Aditi Lahiri (Trends in Linguistics, Studies and Monographs, 127), Berlin–New York, Mouton de Gruyter, viii + 385 pp.

Landolfi, *Il sacro: Il sacro nella poesia contemporanea*, ed. Giuliano Landolfi and Marco Merlin, Novara, Interlinea, 100 pp.

Lebrave, *Genèses: Écrire aux XVIIe et XVIIIe siècles: Genèses de textes littéraires et philosophiques (Textes et Manuscrits)*, ed. Jean-Louis Lebrave and Almuth Grésillon, Paris, CNRS, 240 pp.

Leonardi, *Testi: Testi, manoscritti, ipertesti: compatibilità informatica e letteratura medievale. Atti del Convegno internazionale (Firenze, Certosa del Galluzzo, 31 maggio - 1 giugno 1996)*, ed. Lino Leonardi, Florence, SISMEL - Edizioni del Galluzzo, 1998, vi + 229 pp.

Leonardi, *Umanesimi: Gli Umanesimi Medievali. Atti del II Congresso dell''Internationales Mittellateinerkomitee' (Firenze, Certosa del Galluzzo, 11–15 settembre 1993)*, ed. Lino Leonardi, F, SISMEL–Edizioni del Galluzzo, 1998, viii + 882 pp.

López Grigera Vol.: Estudios de filología y retórica en homenaje a Luisa López Grigera, ed. E. Artaza et al., Bilbao, Universidad de Deusto, 542 pp.

Losada Vol.: Ensinar a pensar con liberdade e risco. Homenatge a Basilio Losada, ed. Helena González Fernández, Isabel de Riquer Permanyer, and Elena Losada Soler (Colecció Homenatges, 18), Universitat de Barcelona, 756 pp.

LSRL 27: Romance Linguistics. Theoretical Perspectives. Selected Papers from the 27th Linguistic Symposium on Romance Languages (LSRL XXVII), Irvine, 20–22 February 1997, ed. Armin Schwegler, Bernard Tranel, and Myriam Uribe-Etxebarria (Current Issues in Linguistic Theory, 160), Amsterdam–Philadelphia, Benjamins, 1998, viii + 349 pp.

Lund, *Langue: La Langue, les signes et les êtres. Actes du colloque organisé par l'Institut d'Études Romanes de l'Université de Copenhague, octobre 1998*, ed. Hans Peter Lund, Copenhagen, Museum Tusculanum, 1999, 207 pp.

Lutterer Vol.: Onomastické práce 4: Sborník rozprav k sedmdesátým narozeninám univ. Prof. PhDr. Ivana Lutterera, CSc., ed. Libuše Olivová-Nezbedová, Rudolf Šrámek, and Milan Harvalík, Prague, ÚJČ, 495 pp.

Mathews, *Decay:* Timothy Mathews, *Literature, Art and the Pursuit of Decay in Twentieth-Century France*, CUP, xi + 232 pp.

Mauzi Vol.: Amicitia scriptor: littérature, histoire des idées, philosophie: mélanges offerts à Robert Mauzi, ed. Annie Becq, Charles Porset, and Alain Mothu, Paris, Champion, 1998, 358 pp.

Mazouer, *Recherches: Recherches des jeunes dix-septièmistes: actes du Ve colloque du Centre International de Rencontres sur le XVIIe siècle, Bordeaux, 28–30 janvier 1999*, ed. Charles Mazouer (Biblio 17, 121), Tübingen, Narr, 339 pp.

Mazzoni Vol.: Sotto il segno di Dante. Scritti in onore di Francesco Mazzoni, ed. Leonella Coglievina and Domenico De Robertis, Florence, Le Lettere, 1998, xlviii + 367 pp.

Meek, *Women: Women in Renaissance and Early Modern Europe*, ed. Christine Meek, Dublin, Four Courts Press, 230 pp.

Melli Vol.: Filologia romanza e cultura medievale. Studi in onore di Elio Melli, ed. Andrea Fassò, Luciano Formisano, and Mario Mancini, 2 vols, Alessandria, Edizioni dell'Orso, 1998, xxi + 449, vii + 451–915 pp.

Merkel, *Frauen: Deutsche Frauen der Frühen Neuzeit. Dichterinnen, Malerinnen, Mäzeninnen*, ed. Kerstin Merkel and Heide Wunder, Darmstadt, Wissenschaftliche Buchgesellschaft, 294 pp.

Michel, *Symbole: Symbole im Dienste der Darstellung von Identität*, ed. Paul Michel (Schriften zur Symbolforschung, 12), Frankfurt, Lang, xxvi + 371 pp.

Mjöberg, *Arkitektur:* Jöran Mjöberg, *Arkitektur i litteratur*, Stockholm, Carlssons, 1999, 264 pp.

Molinaro, *Quebec: Focus on Quebec 2. Further Essays on Québécois Society and Culture*, ed. Ines Molinaro and Christopher Rolfe, Edinburgh, Le GRECF, 88 pp.

Nativel, *Femmes savantes: Femmes savantes, savoirs des femmes, du crépuscule de la Renaissance à l'aube des Lumières. Actes du colloque de Chantilly (22–24 septembre 1995)*, ed. Colette Nativel (TGS, 11), Geneva, Droz, 1999, 268 pp.

Odaloš, *Retrospektivne: Retrospektivne a perspektivne pohlady na jazykovu komunikaciu*, ed. Pavol Odaloš, 2 vols, Banska Bystrica, M. Bel Univ., 1999, 250, 229 pp.

Ohlsson, *Läst:* Anders Ohlsson, *Läst genom kameralinsen. Studier i filmiserad svensk roman*, Nora, Nya Doxa, 1998, 335 pp.

Ohnheiser, *Sprachen: Sprachen in Europa: Sprachsituation und Sprachpolitik in europäischen Ländern*, ed. Ingeborg Ohnheiser, Manfred Kienpointner, and Helmut Kalb, Innsbruck, Institut fur Sprachwissenschaft, 1999, xi + 516 pp.

Olsson, *Läsningar:* Anders Olsson, *Läsningar av Intet*, Stockholm, Bonniers, 457 pp.

Panizza, *Women: Women in Italian Renaissance Culture and Society*, ed. Letizia Panizza, Oxford, Legenda, xxi + 523 pp.

Panizza, *Women's Writing: A History of Women's Writing in Italy*, ed. Letizia Panizza and Sharon Wood, CUP, xvi + 361 pp.

Parkin, *Humour: French Humour*, ed. John Parkin (Faux Titre, 164), Amsterdam, Rodopi, 1999, x + 232 pp.

Parkinson, *Cobras e Son: 'Cobras e Son'. Papers on the Text, Music and Manuscripts of the 'Cantigas de Santa Maria'*, ed. Stephen Parkinson, Oxford, Legenda — Modern Humanities Research Association, xii + 246 pp.

Paul, *Skandinavistik: Arbeiten zur Skandinavistik. 13. Arbeitstagung der deutschsprachigen Skandinavistik, 29.7.–3.8.1997 in Lysebu (Oslo)*, ed. Fritz Paul, Joachim Grage, and Wilhelm Heizmann (TUGS, 45), 599 pp.

Peron, *Palinodia: La palinodia. Atti del XIX Convegno Interuniversitaria (Bressanone, 1991)*, ed. Gianfelice Peron, Padua, Esedra Editrice, 1998, 265 pp.

Pettersson, *Litteratur: Litteratur och verklighetsförståelse. Idémässiga aspekter av 1900–talets litteratur*, ed. Anders Pettersson, Torsten Pettersson, and Anders Tyrberg, Umeå U.P., 1999, 252 pp.

Pic, *Lespy: Vastin Lespy (1817–1897). Actes du colloque de Pau (10–11 octobre 1997)*, ed. François Pic, Pau, Editions Marrimpouey, 1998, 183 pp.

Picone, *Dante: Dante, mito e poesia. Atti del II Seminario dantesco internazionale, Monte Verità, Ascona, 23–27 giugno 1997*, ed. Michelangelo Picone and Tiziana Crivelli, Florence, Cesati, 1999, 460 pp.

Price, *Languages: Languages in Britain and Ireland*, ed. Glanville Price, Oxford, Blackwell, xi + 240 pp.

Repetti, *Phonological Theory: Phonological Theory and the Dialects of Italy*, ed. Lori Repetti (Current Trends in Linguistics, 212), Amsterdam, Benjamins, x + 301 pp.

Rieger, *Okzitanistik: Okzitanistik, Altokzitanistik und Provenzalistik. Geschichte und Auftrag einer europaïscher Philologie*, ed. Angelica Rieger, Frankfurt, Lang, 347 pp.

Riemsdijk, *Clitics: Clitics in the Languages of Europe*, ed. Henk van Riemsdijk (Empirical Approaches to Language Typology; Eurotyp, 20–5), Berlin –New York, Mouton de Gruyter, 1999, xxii + 1026 pp.

Rölleke Vol.: Romantik und Volksliteratur: Beiträge des Wuppertaler Kolloquiums zu Ehren von Heinz Rölleke, ed. Lothar Bluhm and Achim Hölter (Beihefte zum Euphorion, 33), Heidelberg, Winter, 1999, viii + 214 pp.

Romanos, *Lecturas: Lecturas críticas de textos hispánicos. Estudios de literatura española, Siglo de Oro, Vol. II*, ed. M. Romanos and F. Calvo, Buenos Aires, EUDEBA, 429 pp.

Rösener, *Erinnerungskulturen: Adelige und bürgerliche Erinnerungskulturen des Spätmittelalters und der frühen Neuzeit*, ed. Werner Rösener, Göttingen, Vandenhoeck & Ruprecht, 228 pp.

Rovira, *Ciudad: Escrituras de la ciudad*, ed. J. C. Rovira, Madrid, Palas Atenea, 1999, 282 pp.

Sagarra Vol.: Das schwierige neunzehnte Jahrhundert: Germanistische Tagung zum 65. Geburt von Eda Sagarra im August 1998, ed. Jürgen Barkhoff et al., Tübingen, Niemeyer, xi + 587 pp.

Salen, *L'Atomisme: L'Atomisme aux XVIIe et XVIIIe siècles*, ed. Jean Salen, Paris, Publications de la Sorbonne, 1999, 186 pp.

Sebold Vol.: Ideas en sus paisajes: homenaje al profesor Russell P. Sebold, ed. G. Carnero, I.-J. López, and E. Rubio, Alicante U.P., 1999, 417 pp.

Shaw, *Reflexivity: Reflexivity: Critical Themes in the Italian Cultural Tradition. Essays by Members of the Department of Italian at University College London*, ed. Prue Shaw and John Took, Ravenna, Longo, 226 pp.

Sibbald, *Ciudades: Ciudades vivas/ciudades muertas: espacios urbanos en la literatura y el folklore hispánicos*, ed. K. M. Sibbald, R. de la Fuente, and J. Díaz, Valladolid, Universitas Castellae, 377 pp.

Sicard Vol.: *Chemins ouverts: mélanges offerts à Claude Sicard*, ed. Sylvie Vignes (Les Cahiers de littérature), Toulouse, Presses universitaires du Mirail, 1998, 344 pp.

Silver, *Épistolières: Femmes et toutes lettres. Les épistolières du XVIIIe siècle*, ed. Marie-France Silver and Marie-Laure Girou Swiderski (SVEC 2000:04), Oxford, Voltaire Foundation, xiii + 277 pp.

Sjöberg, *Litteraturens makt: Litteraturens makt*, ed. Birthe Sjöberg (Absalon, 18), SLILU, 270 pp.

Smith, *Metaphor and Materiality:* Peter D. Smith, *Metaphor and Materiality: German Literature and the World-View of Science, 1780–1955* (Legenda Studies in Comparative Literature, 4), Oxford, Legenda — British Comparative Literature Association, xii + 372 pp.

Sorg, *Gott: Gott und Götze in der Literatur der Moderne*, ed. Reto Sorg et al., Munich, Fink, 1999, 294 pp.

Stagg Vol.: *Ingeniosa Invención: Essays on Golden Age Literature for Geoffrey L. Stagg in Honor of His Eighty-Fifth Birthday*, ed. E. M. Anderson and A. R. Williamsen, Newark, NJ, Juan de la Cuesta, 1999, 285 pp.

Steene Vol.: *Stage and Screen: Studies in Scandinavian Drama and Film. Essays in Honor of Birgitta Steene*, ed. Ann-Charlotte Gavel Adams and Terje I. Leiren, Seattle, Washington, DreamPlay Press Northwest, xiv + 265 pp.

Steiger, *Kantaten: Johann Sebastian Bachs Kantaten zum Thema Tod und Sterben und ihr literarisches Umfeld*, ed. Renate Steiger (Wolfenbütteler Forschungen, 90), Wiesbaden, Harrassowitz, ix + 323 pp.

Stephens, *Women's Writing: A History of Women's Writing in France*, ed. Sonya Stephens, CUP, ix + 314 pp.

Thieroff, *Grammatik: Deutsche Grammatik in Theorie und Praxis*, ed. Rolf Thieroff, Matthias Tamrat, Nanna Fuhrhop, and Oliver Teuber, Tübingen, Niemeyer, xii + 300 pp.

Thomas, *Minority Languages: Developing Minority Languages. Proceedings of the Fifth International Conference on Minority Languages, July 1993, Cardiff*, ed. Peter Wynn Thomas and Jayne Mathias, Llandysul, Department of Welsh, Cardiff University — Gomer Press, ix + 763 pp.

Uitti Vol.: *Translatio Studii. Essays by his Students in Honor of Karl D. Uitti for his Sixty-Fifth Birthday*, ed. Renate Blumenfeld-Kosinski, Kevin Brownlee, Mary B. Speer, and Lori J. Walters (Faux Titre, 179), Amsterdam–Atlanta, Rodopi, 349 pp.

Varty, *Reynard: Reynard the Fox: Social Engagement and Cultural Metamorphoses in the Beast Epic from the Middle Ages to the Present*, ed. K. Varty (Cultural Diversities and Intersections, 1), New York–Oxford, Berghahn, xxi + 298 pp.

Vliet, *Edition: Produktion und Kontext: Beiträge der Internationalen Fachtagung der Arbeitsgemeinschaft für germanistische Edition im Constantijn Huygens Instituut, Den Haag, 4. bis 7. März 1998*, ed. H. T. M. van Vliet (Beihefte zu *Editio*, 13), Tübingen, Niemeyer, 1999, vii + 348 pp.

Wästberg, *Essäer:* Per Wästberg, *Edith Whartons hemliga trädgård. Essäer*, Stockholm, Wahlström & Widstrand, 340 pp.

Watanabe-O'Kelly, *Festivals:* Helen Watanabe-O'Kelly and Anne Simon, *Festivals and Ceremonies. A Bibliography of Works Relating to Court, Civic and Religious Festivals in Europe 1500–1800*, London–New York, Mansell, xx + 533 pp.

Will Vol.: *The Challenge of German Culture. Essays Presented to Wilfried van der Will*, ed. Michael Butler and Robert Evans, Basingstoke, Palgrave, xi + 218 pp.

Zybatow, *Slavia: Sprachwandel in der Slavia. Die slavischen Sprachen an der Schwelle zum 21. Jahrhundert*, ed. Lew N. Zybatow, 2 vols, Frankfurt, Lang, 1–524, 528–981 pp.

II. GENERAL

abbrev.	abbreviation, abbreviated to
Acad., Akad.	Academy, Academia, etc.
acc.	accusative
ann.	annotated (by)
anon.	anonymous
appx	appendix
Arg.	Argentinian (and foreign equivalents)
Assoc.	Association (and foreign equivalents)
Auv.	Auvergnat
Bel.	Belarusian
BL	British Library
BM	British Museum
BN	Bibliothèque Nationale, Biblioteka Narodowa, etc.
BPtg.	Brazilian Portuguese
bull.	bulletin
c.	century
c.	circa
Cat.	Catalan
ch.	chapter
col.	column
comm.	commentary (by)
comp.	compiler, compiled (by)
Cz.	Czech
diss.	dissertation
ed.	edited (by), editor (and foreign equivalents)
edn	edition
EPtg.	European Portuguese
fac.	facsimile
fasc.	fascicle
Fest.	Festschrift, Festskrift
Fin.	Finnish
Fr.	France, French, Français
Gal.-Ptg.	Galician-Portuguese (and equivalents)
Gasc.	Gascon
Ger.	German(y)
Gk	Greek
Gmc	Germanic
IE	Indo-European
illus.	illustrated, illustration(s)
impr.	impression
incl.	including, include(s)
Inst.	Institute (and foreign equivalents)
introd.	introduction, introduced by, introductory
It.	Italian
izd.	издание
izd-vo	издательство
Jb.	Jahrbuch
Jg	Jahrgang
Jh.	Jahrhundert
Lang.	Languedocien
Lat.	Latin
Lim.	Limousin

lit.	literature
med.	medieval
MHG	Middle High German
Mid. Ir.	Middle Irish
Mil.	Milanese
MS	manuscript
n.d.	no date
n.F.	neue Folge
no.	number (and foreign equivalents)
nom.	nominative
n.p.	no place
n.s.	new series
O Auv.	Old Auvergnat
O Cat.	Old Catalan
Occ.	Occitan
OE	Old English
OF	Old French
O Gasc.	Old Gascon
OHG	Old High German
O Ir.	Old Irish
O Lim.	Old Limousin
O Occ.	Old Occitan
O Pr.	Old Provençal
O Ptg.	Old Portuguese
OS	Old Saxon
OW	Old Welsh
part.	participle
ped.	педагогический, etc.
PIE	Proto-Indo-European
Pied.	Piedmontese
PGmc	Primitive Germanic
pl.	plate
plur.	plural
Pol.	Polish
p.p.	privately published
Pr.	Provençal
pref.	preface (by)
Procs	Proceedings
Ptg.	Portuguese
publ.	publication, published (by)
Ren.	Renaissance
repr.	reprint(ed)
Rev.	Review, Revista, Revue
rev.	revised (by)
Russ.	Russian
s.	siècle
ser.	series
sg.	singular
Slg	Sammlung
Soc.	Society (and foreign equivalents)
Sp.	Spanish
supp.	supplement
Sw.	Swedish
Trans.	Transactions

trans.	translated (by), translation
Ukr.	Ukrainian
Univ.	University (and foreign equivalents)
unpubl.	unpublished
U.P.	University Press (and foreign equivalents)
Vlg	Verlag
vol.	volume
vs	versus
W.	Welsh
wyd.	wydawnictwo

* before a publication signifies that it has not been seen by the contributor.

III. PLACE NAMES

B	Barcelona	NY	New York
BA	Buenos Aires	O	Oporto
Be	Belgrade	Pń	Poznań
Bo	Bologna	R	Rio de Janeiro
C	Coimbra	Ro	Rome
F	Florence	SC	Santiago de Compostela
Gd	Gdańsk	SPo	São Paulo
Kw	Kraków, Cracow	StP	St Petersburg
L	Lisbon	T	Turin
Ld	Leningrad	V	Valencia
M	Madrid	Wa	Warsaw
Mi	Milan	Ww	Wrocław
Mw	Moscow	Z	Zagreb
Na	Naples		

IV. PERIODICALS, INSTITUTIONS, PUBLISHERS

AA, Antike und Abendland

AAA, Ardis Publishers, Ann Arbor, Michigan

AAA, Archivio per l'Alto Adige

AAASS, American Association for the Advancement of Slavic Studies

AABC, Anuari de l'Agrupació Borrianenca de Cultura

AAC, Atti dell'Accademia Clementina

AAL, Atti dell'Accademia dei Lincei

AALP, L'Arvista dl'Academia dla Lenga Piemontèisa

AAM, Association des Amis de Maynard

AAPH, Anais da Academia Portuguesa da História

AAPN, Atti dell'Accademia Pontaniana di Napoli

AAPP, Atti Accademia Peloritana dei Pericolanti. Classe di Lettere Filosofia e Belle Arti

AARA, Atti della Accademia Roveretana degli Agiati

AASB, Atti dell'Accademia delle Scienze dell'Istituto di Bologna

AASF, Annales Academiae Scientiarum Fennicae

AASLAP, Atti dell'Accademia di Scienze, Lettere ed Arti di Palermo

AASLAU, Atti dell'Accademia di Scienze, Lettere e Arti di Udine

AASN, Atti dell'Accademia di Scienze Morali e Politiche di Napoli

AAST, Atti dell'Accademia delle Scienze di Torino

AAVM, Atti e Memorie dell'Accademia Virgiliana di Mantova

AAWG, Abhandlungen der Akademie der Wissenschaften in Göttingen, phil.-hist. Kl., 3rd ser., Göttingen, Vandenhoeck & Ruprecht

AB, Analecta Bollandiana

ABa, L'Année Balzacienne

ABÄG, Amsterdamer Beiträge zur älteren Germanistik

ABB, Archives et Bibliothèques de Belgique — Archief– en Bibliotheekswezen in België

ABC, Annales Benjamin Constant

ABDB, Aus dem Antiquariat. Beiträge zum Börsenblatt für den deutschen Buchhandel

ABDO, Association Bourguignonne de Dialectologie et d'Onomastique, Fontaine lès Dijon

ABHL, Annual Bulletin of Historical Literature

ABI, Accademie e Biblioteche d'Italia

ABN, Anais da Biblioteca Nacional, Rio de Janeiro

ABNG, Amsterdamer Beiträge zur neueren Germanistik, Amsterdam, Rodopi

ABNG, Amsterdamer Beiträge zur neueren Germanistik

ABor, Acta Borussica

ABP, Arquivo de Bibliografia Portuguesa

ABR, American Benedictine Review

ABr, Annales de Bretagne et des Pays de l'Ouest

ABS, Acta Baltico-Slavica

ABSJ, Annual Bulletin of the Société Jersiaise

AC, Analecta Cisterciensa, Rome

ACCT, Agence de Coopération Culturelle et Technique

ACer, Anales Cervantinos, Madrid

ACIS, Association for Contemporary Iberian Studies

ACo, Acta Comeniana, Prague

AColl, Actes et Colloques

Acme, Annali della Facoltà di Filosofia e Lettere dell'Università Statale di Milano

ACP, L'Amitié Charles Péguy

ACUA, Anales del Colegio Universitario de Almería

AD, Analysen und Dokumente. Beiträge zur Neueren Literatur, Berne, Lang

ADEVA, Akademische Druck- und Verlagsanstalt, Graz

AE, Artemis Einführungen, Munich, Artemis

AE, L'Autre Europe

AEA, Anuario de Estudios Atlánticos, Las Palmas

AECI, Agencia Española de Cooperación Internacional

AEd, Arbeiten zur Editionswissenschaft, Frankfurt, Lang

AEF, Anuario de Estudios Filológicos, Cáceres

AEL, Anuario de la Escuela de Letras, Mérida, Venezuela

AELG, Anuario de Literarios Galegos

AEM, Anuario de Estudios Medievales

AF, Anuario de Filología, Barcelona

AFA, Archivo de Filología Aragonesa

AfAf, African Affairs

AfC, Afrique Contemporaine

AFe, L'Armana di Felibre

AFF, Anali Filološkog fakulteta, Belgrade

AFH, Archivum Franciscanum Historicum

AFHis, Anales de Filología Hispánica

AfHR, Afro-Hispanic Review

AfL, L'Afrique Littéraire

AFLE, Annali della Fondazione Luigi Einaudi

AFLFUB, Annali della Facoltà di Lettere e Filosofia dell'Università di Bari

AFLFUC, Annali della Facoltà di Lettere e Filosofia dell'Università di Cagliari

AFLFUG, Annali della Facoltà di Lettere e Filosofia dell'Università degli Studi di Genova

AFLFUM, Annali della Facoltà di Lettere e Filosofia dell'Università di Macerata

AFLFUN, Annali della Facoltà di Lettere e Filosofia dell'Università di Napoli

AFLFUP(SF), Annali della Facoltà di Lettere e Filosofia dell'Università di Perugia. 1. Studi Filosofici

AFLFUP(SLL), Annali della Facoltà di Lettere e Filosofia dell'Università di Perugia. 3. Studi Linguistici-Letterari

AFLFUS, Annali della Facoltà di Lettere e Filosofia dell'Università di Siena

AFLLS, Annali della Facoltà di Lingua e Letterature Straniere di Ca' Foscari, Venice

AFLN, Annales de la Faculté des Lettres et Sciences Humaines de Nice

AFLS, Association for French Language Studies

AFP, Archivum Fratrum Praedicatorum

AFrP, Athlone French Poets, London, The Athlone Press

AG, Anales Galdosianos

AGB, Archiv für Geschichte des Buchwesens

AGF, Anuario Galego de Filoloxia

AGGSA, Acta Germanica. German Studies in Africa

AGI, Archivio Glottologico Italiano

AGP, Archiv für Geschichte der Philosophie

AH, Archivo Hispalense

AHAW, Abhandlungen der Heidelberger Akademie der Wissenschaften, phil.-hist. Kl

AHCP, Arquivos de História de Cultura Portuguesa

AHDLMA, Archives d'Histoire Doctrinale et Littéraire du Moyen Âge

AHF, Archiwum Historii Filozofii i Myśli Społecznej

AHP, Archivum Historiae Pontificae

AHPr, Annales de Haute-Provence, Digne-les-Bains

AHR, American Historical Review

AHRF, Annales Historiques de la Révolution Française

AHRou, Archives historiques du Rouergue

AHSJ, Archivum Historicum Societatis Jesu

AHSS, Annales: Histoire — Science Sociales

AI, Almanacco Italiano

AIB, Annali dell'Istituto Banfi

AIBL, Académie des Inscriptions et Belles-Lettres, Comptes Rendus

AIEM, Anales del Instituto de Estudios Madrileños

AIEO, Association Internationale d'Études Occitanes

AIFMUR, Annali dell'Istituto di Filologia Moderna dell'Università di Roma

AIFUF, Annali dell'Istituto di Filosofia dell'Università di Firenze

AIHI, Archives Internationales d'Histoire des Idées, The Hague, Nijhoff

AIHS, Archives Internationales d'Histoire des Sciences

AIL, Associação Internacional de Lusitanistas

AILLC, Associació Internacional de Llengua i Literatura Catalanes

AISIGT, Annali dell'Istituto Storico Italo-Germanico di Trento

AION(FG), Annali dell'Istituto Universitario Orientale, Naples: Sezione Germanica. Filologia Germanica

AION(SF), Annali dell'Istituto Universitario Orientale, Naples: Studi Filosofici

AION(SL), Annali dell'Istituto Universitario Orientale, Naples: Sezione Linguistica

AION(SR), Annali dell'Istituto Universitario Orientale, Naples: Sezione Romanza

AION(SS), Annali dell'Istituto Universitario Orientale, Naples: Sezione Slava

AION(ST), Annali dell'Istituto Universitario Orientale, Naples: Sezione Germanica. Studi Tedeschi

AIPHS, Annuaire de l'Institut de Philologie et de l'Histoire Orientales et Slaves

AIPS, Annales Instituti Philologiae Slavica Universitatis Debreceniensis de Ludovico Kossuth Nominatae — Slavica

AITCA, Arxiu informatizat de textos catalans antics

AIV, Atti dell'Istituto Veneto

AJ, Alemannisches Jahrbuch

AJCAI, Actas de las Jornadas de Cultura Arabe e Islámica

AJFS, Australian Journal of French Studies

AJGLL, American Journal of Germanic Linguistics and Literatures

AJL, Australian Journal of Linguistics

AJP, American Journal of Philology

AKG, Archiv für Kulturgeschichte

AKML, Abhandlungen zur Kunst-, Musik- und Literaturwissenschaft, Bonn, Bouvier

AL, Anuario de Letras, Mexico

AlAm, Alba de América

ALB, Annales de la Faculté des Lettres de Besançon

ALC, African Languages and Cultures

ALE, Anales de Literatura Española, Alicante

ALEC, Anales de Literatura Española Contemporánea

ALet, Armas y Letras, Universidad de Nuevo León

ALEUA, Anales de Literatura Española de la Universidad de Alicante

ALFL, Actes de Langue Française et de Linguistique

ALH, Acta Linguistica Hungaricae

ALHA, Anales de la Literatura Hispanoamericana

ALHa, Acta Linguistica Hafniensia

ALHisp, Anuario de Lingüística Hispánica

ALHist, Annales: Littérature et Histoire

ALit, Acta Literaria, Chile

ALitH, Acta Litteraria Hungarica

ALLI, Atlante Linguistico dei Laghi Italiani

ALM, Archives des Lettres Modernes

ALMA, Archivum Latinitatis Medii Aevi (Bulletin du Cange)

ALo, Armanac de Louzero

ALP, Atlas linguistique et ethnographique de Provence, CNRS, 1975–86

AlS, Almanac Setòri

ALT, African Literature Today

ALu, Alpes de Lumière, Fourcalquier

ALUB, Annales Littéraires de l'Université de Besançon

AM, Analecta Musicologica

AMAA, Atti e Memorie dell'Accademia d'Arcadia

AMAASLV, Atti e Memorie dell'Accademia di Agricultura, Scienze e Lettere di Verona

Amades, Amades. Arbeitspapiere und Materialien zur deutschen Sprache

AMal, Analecta Malacitana

AMAP, Atti e Memorie dell'Accademia Patavina di Scienze, Lettere ed Arti

AMAPet, Atti e Memorie dell'Accademia Petrarca di Lettere, Arti e Scienze, Arezzo

AMAT, Atti e Memorie dell'Accademia Toscana di Scienze e Lettere, La Colombaria

AMDLS, Arbeiten zur Mittleren Deutschen Literatur und Sprache, Berne, Lang

AMDSPAPM, Atti e Memorie della Deputazione di Storia Patria per le Antiche Province Modenesi

AMGG, Abhandlungen der Marburger Gelehrten Gesellschaft, Munich, Fink

AmH, American Hispanist

AMid, Annales du Midi

AmIn, América Indígena, Mexico

AML, Main Monographien Literaturwissenschaft, Frankfurt, Main

AMSSSP, Atti e Memorie della Società Savonese di Storia Patria

AN, Академия наук

AN, Americana Norvegica

ANABA, Asociación Nacional de Bibliotecarios, Arquiveros y Arqueólogos

AnAlf, Annali Alfieriani

AnEA, Anaquel de Estudios Arabes

ANeo, Acta Neophilologica, Ljubljana

ANF, Arkiv för nordisk filologi

AnI, Annali d'Italianistica

AnL, Anthropological Linguistics

AnM, Anuario Medieval

AnN, Annales de Normandie

AnnM, Annuale Medievale

ANPOLL, Associação Nacional de Pós-graduação e Pesquisa em Letras e Lingüística, São Paulo

ANQ, American Notes and Queries

ANS, Anglo-Norman Studies

ANTS, Anglo-Norman Text Society

AnVi, Antologia Vieusseux

ANZSGLL, Australian and New Zealand Studies in German Language and Literature, Berne, Lang

AO, Almanac occitan, Foix

AÖAW, Anzeiger der Österreichischen Akademie der Wissenschaften

AOn, Acta Onomastica

AP, Aurea Parma

APIFN, Актуальные проблемы истории философии народов СССР.

APK, Aufsätze zur portugiesischen Kulturgeschichte, Görres-Gesellschaft, Münster

ApL, Applied Linguistics

APL, Associação Portuguesa de Linguística

APPP, Abhandlungen zur Philosophie, Psychologie und Pädagogik, Bonn, Bouvier

APr, Analecta Praemonstratensia

AProu, Armana Prouvençau, Marseilles

APS, Acta Philologica Scandinavica

APSL, Amsterdamer Publikationen zur Sprache und Literatur, Amsterdam, Rodopi

APSR, American Political Science Review

APUCF, Association des Publications de la Faculté des Lettres et Sciences Humaines de l'Université de Clermont-Ferrand II, Nouvelle Série

AQ, Arizona Quarterly

AqAq, Aquò d'aquí, Gap

AR, Archiv für Reformationsgeschichte

ARAJ, American Romanian Academy Journal

ARAL, Australian Review of Applied Linguistics

ARCA, ARCA: Papers of the Liverpool Latin Seminar

ArCCP, Arquivos do Centro Cultural Português, Paris

ArEM, Aragón en la Edad Media

ArFil, Archivio di Filosofia

ArI, Arthurian Interpretations

ARI, Архив русской истории

ARL, Athlone Renaissance Library

ArL, Archivum Linguisticum

ArLit, Arthurian Literature

ArP, Археографски прилози

ArSP, Archivio Storico Pugliese

ArSPr, Archivio Storico Pratese

ArSt, Archivi per la Storia

ART, Atelier Reproduction des Thèses, Univ. de Lille III, Paris, Champion

AS, The American Scholar

ASAHM, Annales de la Société d'Art et d'Histoire du Mentonnais, Menton

ASAvS, Annuaire de la Société des Amis du vieux-Strasbourg

ASB, Archivio Storico Bergamasco

ASCALF, Association for the Study of Caribbean and African Literature in French

ASCALFB, ASCALF Bulletin

ASCALFY, ASCALF Yearbook

ASE, Annali di Storia dell'Esegesi

ASEES, Australian Slavonic and East European Studies

ASELGC, 1616. Anuario de la Sociedad Española de Literatura General y Comparada

ASGM, Atti del Sodalizio Glottologico Milanese

ASI, Archivio Storico Italiano

ASJ, Acta Slavonica Japonica

ASL, Archivio Storico Lombardo

ASLSP, Atti della Società Ligure di Storia Patria

ASMC, Annali di Storia Moderna e Contemporanea

ASNP, Annali della Scuola Normale Superiore di Pisa

ASNS, Archiv für das Studium der Neueren Sprachen und Literaturen

ASocRous, Annales de la Société J.-J. Rousseau

ASolP, A Sol Post, Editorial Marfil, Alcoi

ASP, Anzeiger für slavische Philologie

AsP, L'Astrado prouvençalo. Revisto Bilengo de Prouvenco/Revue Bilingue de Provence, Berre L'Etang.

ASPN, Archivio Storico per le Province Napoletane

ASPP, Archivio Storico per le Province Parmensi

ASR, Annalas da la Societad Retorumantscha

ASRSP, Archivio della Società Romana di Storia Patria

ASSO, Archivio Storico per la Sicilia Orientale

ASSUL, Annali del Dipartimento di Scienze Storiche e Sociali dell'Università di Lecce

AST, Analecta Sacra Tarraconensia

ASt, Austrian Studies

ASTic, Archivio Storico Ticinese

AŞUI, (e), (f), Analele Ştiinţifice ale Universităţii 'Al. I. Cuza' din Iaşi, secţ. e, Lingvistică, secţ. f, Literatură

AT, Athenäums Taschenbücher, Frankfurt, Athenäum

ATB, Altdeutsche Textbibliothek, Tübingen, Niemeyer

ATCA, Arxiu de Textos Catalans Antics, IEC, Barcelona

Ate, Nueva Atenea, Universidad de Concepción, Chile

ATO, A Trabe de Ouro

ATS, Arbeiten und Texte zur Slavistik, Munich, Sagner

ATV, Aufbau Taschenbuch Verlag, Berlin, Aufbau

AtV, Ateneo Veneto

AUBLLR, Analele Universităţii Bucureşti, Limba şi literatura română

AUBLLS, Analele Universităţii Bucureşti, Limbi şi literaturi străine

AUC, Anales de la Universidad de Cuenca

AUCP, Acta Universitatis Carolinae Pragensis

AuE, Arbeiten und Editionen zur Mittleren Deutschen Literatur, Stuttgart–Bad Cannstatt, Frommann-Holzboog

AUL, Acta Universitatis Lodziensis

AUL, Annali della Facoltà di Lettere e Filosofia dell'Università di Lecce

AUMCS, Annales Uniwersytetu Marii Curie-Skłodowskiej, Lublin

AUML, Anales de la Universidad de Murcia: Letras

AUMLA, Journal of the Australasian Universities Modern Language Association

AUN, Annali della Facoltà di Lettere e Filosofia dell'Università di Napoli

AUNCFP, Acta Universitatis Nicolai Copernici. Filologia Polska, Toruń

AUPO, Acta Universitatis Palackianae Olomucensis

AUS, American University Studies, Berne — New York, Lang

AUSP, Annali dell'Università per Stranieri di Perugia

AUSt, Acta Universitatis Stockholmiensis

AUTŞF, Analele Universităţii din Timişoara, Ştiinţe Filologice

AUU, Acta Universitatis Upsaliensis

AUW, Acta Universitatis Wratislaviensis

AVen, Archivio Veneto

AVEP, Assouciacien vareso pèr l'ensignamen dòu prouvençou, La Farlède

AVEPB, *Bulletin AVEP*, La Farlède

AvT, L'Avant-Scène Théâtre

AWR, Anglo-Welsh Review

BA, Bollettino d'Arte

BAAA, Bulletin de l'Association des Amis d'Alain

BAAG, Bulletin des Amis d'André Gide

BAAJG, Bulletin de l'Association des Amis de Jean Giono

BAAL, Boletín de la Academia Argentina de Letras

BaB, Bargfelder Bote

BAC, Biblioteca de Autores Cristianos

BACol, Boletín de la Academia Colombiana

BÄDL, Beiträge zur Älteren Deutschen Literaturgeschichte, Berne, Lang

BADLit, Bonner Arbeiten zur deutschen Literatur, Bonn, Bouvier

BAE, Biblioteca de Autores Españoles

BAEO, Boletín de la Asociación Española de Orientalistas

BAFJ, Bulletin de l'Association Francis Jammes

BAG, Boletín de la Academia Gallega

BAIEO, Bulletins de l'Association Internationale d'Études Occitanes

BAJR, Bulletin des Amis de Jules Romains

BAJRAF, Bulletin des Amis de Jacques Rivière et d'Alain-Fournier

BALI, Bollettino dell'Atlante Linguistico Italiano

BALM, Bollettino dell'Atlante Linguistico Mediterraneo

BalS, Balkan Studies, Institute for Balkan Studies, Thessaloniki

BAN, Българска Академия на Науките, София

BAO, Biblioteca Abat Oliva, Publicacions de l'Abadia de Montserrat, Barcelona

BAPC, Bulletin de l'Association Paul Claudel

BAPRLE, Boletín de la Academia Puertorrigueña de la Lengua Española

BAR, Biblioteca dell'Archivum Romanicum

BARLLF, Bulletin de l'Académie Royale de Langues et de Littératures Françaises de Bruxelles

BAWA, Bayerische Akademie der Wissenschaften. Phil.-hist. Kl. Abhandlungen, n.F.

BB, Biblioteca Breve, Lisbon

BB, Bulletin of Bibliography

BBAHLM, Boletín Bibliografico de la Asociación Hispánica de Literatura Medieval

BBB, Berner Beiträge zur Barockgermanistik, Berne, Lang

BBGN, Brünner Beiträge zur Germanistik und Nordistik

BBib, Bulletin du Bibliophile

BBL, Bayreuther Beiträge zur Literaturwissenschaft, Frankfurt, Lang

BBLI, Bremer Beiträge zur Literatur- und Ideengeschichte, Frankfurt, Lang

BBMP, Boletín de la Biblioteca de Menéndez Pelayo

BBN, Bibliotheca Bibliographica Neerlandica, Nieuwkoop, De Graaf

BBNDL, Berliner Beiträge zur neueren deutschen Literaturgeschichte, Berne, Lang

BBSANZ, Bulletin of the Bibliographical Society of Australia and New Zealand

BBSIA, Bulletin Bibliographique de la Société Internationale Arthurienne

BBSMES, Bulletin of the British Society for Middle Eastern Studies

BBUC, Boletim da Biblioteca da Universidade de Coimbra

BC, Bulletin of the 'Comediantes', University of Wisconsin

BCB, Boletín Cultural y Bibliográfico, Bogatá

BCEC, Bwletin Cymdeithas Emynwyr Cymru

BCél, Bulletin Célinien

BCh, Болдинские чтения

BCLSMP, Académie Royale de Belgique: Bulletin de la Classe des Lettres et des Sciences Morales et Politiques

BCMV, Bollettino Civici Musei Veneziani

BCRLT, Bulletin du Centre de Romanistique et de Latinité Tardive

BCS, Bulletin of Canadian Studies

BCSM, Bulletin of the Cantigueiros de Santa Maria

BCSS, Bollettino del Centro di Studi Filologici e Linguistici Siciliani

BCSV, Bollettino del Centro di Studi Vichiani

BCZG, Blätter der Carl Zuckmayer Gesellschaft

BD, Беларуская думка

BDADA, Bulletin de documentation des Archives départementales de l'Aveyron, Rodez

BDB, Börsenblatt für den deutschen Buchhandel

BDBA, Bien Dire et Bien Aprandre

BDL, Beiträge zur Deutschen Literatur, Frankfurt, Lang

BDP, Beiträge zur Deutschen Philologie, Giessen, Schmitz

BEA, Bulletin des Études Africaines

BEC, Bibliothèque de l'École des Chartes

BelE, Беларуская энцыклапедыя

BelL, Беларуская лінгвістыка

BelS, Беларускі сьвет

BEP, Bulletin des Études Portugaises

BEPar, Bulletin des Études Parnassiennes et Symbolistes

BEzLit, Български език и литература

BF, Boletim de Filologia

BFA, Bulletin of Francophone Africa

BFC, Boletín de Filología, Univ. de Chile

BFE, Boletín de Filología Española

BFF, Bulletin Francophone de Finlande

BFFGL, Boletín de la Fundación Federico García Lorca

BFi, Bollettino Filosofico

BFLS, Bulletin de la Faculté des Lettres de Strasbourg

BFo, Biuletyn Fonograficzny

BFPLUL, Bibliothèque de la Faculté de Philosophie et Lettres de l'Université de Liège

BFR, Bibliothèque Française et Romane, Paris, Klincksieck

BFR, Bulletin of the Fondation C.F. Ramuz

BFr, Börsenblatt Frankfurt

BG, Bibliotheca Germanica, Tübingen, Francke

BGB, Bulletin de l'Association Guillaume Budé

BGDSL, Beiträge zur Geschichte der deutschen Sprache und Literatur, Tübingen

BGKT, Беларускае грамадска-культуральнае таварыства

BGL, Boletín Galego de Literatura

BGLKAJ, Beiträge zur Geschichte der Literatur und Kunst des 18. Jahrhunderts, Heidelberg, Winter

BGP, Bristol German Publications, Bristol U.P

BGREC, Bulletin du Groupe de Recherches et d'Études du Clermontais, Clermont-l'Hérault

BGS, Beiträge zur germanistischen Sprachwissenschaft, Hamburg, Buske

BGS, Beiträge zur Geschichte der Sprachwissenschaft

BGT, Blackwell German Texts, Oxford, Blackwell

BH, Bulletin Hispanique

BHR, Bibliothèque d'Humanisme et Renaissance

BHS(G), Bulletin of Hispanic Studies, Glasgow

BHS(L), Bulletin of Hispanic Studies, Liverpool

BI, Bibliographisches Institut, Leipzig

BibAN, Библиотека Академии наук СССР

BIDS, Bulletin of the International Dostoevsky Society, Klagenfurt

BIEA, Boletín del Instituto de Estudios Asturianos

BIHBR, Bulletin de l'Institut Historique Belge de Rome

BIHR, Bulletin of the Institute of Historical Research

BIO, Bulletin de l'Institut Occitan, Pau

BJA, British Journal of Aesthetics

BJCS, British Journal for Canadian Studies

BJECS, The British Journal for Eighteenth-Century Studies

BJHP, British Journal of the History of Philosophy

BJHS, British Journal of the History of Science

BJL, Belgian Journal of Linguistics

BJR, Bulletin of the John Rylands University Library of Manchester

BKF, Beiträge zur Kleist-Forschung

BL, Brain and Language

BLAR, Bulletin of Latin American Research

BLBI, Bulletin des Leo Baeck Instituts

BLe, Börsenblatt Leipzig

BLFCUP, Bibliothèque de Littérature Française Contemporaine de l'Université Paris 7

BLI, Beiträge zur Linguistik und Informationsverarbeitung

BLi, Беларуская літаратура. Міжвузаўскі зборнік

BLJ, British Library Journal

BLL, Beiträge zur Literatur und Literaturwissenschaft des 20. Jahrhunderts, Berne, Lang

BLR, Bibliothèque Littéraire de la Renaissance, Geneva, Slatkine–Paris, Champion

BLR, Bodleian Library Record

BLVS, Bibliothek des Literarischen Vereins, Stuttgart, Hiersemann

BM, Bibliothek Metzier, Stuttgart

BMBP, Bollettino del Museo Bodoniano di Parma

BMCP, Bollettino del Museo Civico di Padova

BML, Беларуская мова і літаратура ў школе

BMo, Беларуская мова. Міжвузаўскі зборнік

BNE, Beiträge zur neueren Epochenforschung, Berne, Lang

BNF, Beiträge zur Namenforschung

BNL, Beiträge zur neueren Literaturgeschichte, 3rd ser., Heidelberg, Winter

BNP, Beiträge zur nordischen Philologie, Basel, Helbing & Lichtenhahn

BO, Biblioteca Orientalis

BOCES, Boletín del Centro de Estudios del Siglo XVIII, Oviedo

BOP, Bradford Occasional Papers

BP, Български писател

BP, Lo Bornat dau Perigòrd

BPTJ, Biuletyn Polskiego Towarzystwa Językoznawczego

BR, Болгарская русистика.

BRA, Bonner Romanistische Arbeiten, Berne, Lang

BRABLB, Boletín de la Real Academia de Buenas Letras de Barcelona

BRAC, Boletín de la Real Academia de Córdoba de Ciencias, Bellas Letras, y Nobles Artes

BRAE, Boletín de la Real Academia Española

BRAG, Boletín de la Real Academia Gallega

BRAH, Boletín de la Real Academia de la Historia

BrC, Bruniana & Campanelliana

BRIES, Bibliothèque Russe de l'Institut d'Études Slaves, Paris, Institut d'Études Slaves

BRJL, Bulletin ruského jazyka a literatury

BrL, La Bretagne Linguistique

BRP, Beiträge zur romanischen Philologie

BS, Biuletyn slawistyczny, Łódź

BSAHH, Bulletin de la Société archéologique et historique des hauts cantons de l'Hérault, Bédarieux

BSAHL, Bulletin de la Société archéologique et historique du Limousin, Limoges

BSAHLSG, Bulletin de la Société Archéologique, Historique, Littéraire et Scientifique du Gers

BSAM, Bulletin de la Société des Amis de Montaigne

BSAMPAC, Bulletin de la Société des Amis de Marcel Proust et des Amis de Combray

BSASLB, Bulletin de la Société Archéologique, Scientifique et Littéraire de Béziers

BSATG, Bulletin de la Société Archéologique de Tarn-et-Garonne

BSBS, Bollettino Storico–
Bibliografico Subalpino
BSCC, Boletín de la Sociedad
Castellonense de Cultura
BSD, Bithell Series of
Dissertations — MHRA Texts
and Dissertations, London,
Modern Humanities Research
Association
BSD, Bulletin de la Société de
Borda, Dax
BSDL, Bochumer Schriften zur
deutschen Literatur, Berne, Lang
BSDSL, Basler Studien zur
deutschen Sprache und Literatur,
Tübingen, Francke
BSE, Галоўная рэдакцыя
Беларускай савеюкай
энцыклапедыі
BSEHA, Bulletin de la Société
d'Études des Hautes-Alpes, Gap
BSEHTD, Bulletin de la Société
d'Études Historiques du texte
dialectal
BSELSAL, Bulletin de la Société des
Études Littéraires, Scientifiques
et Artistiques du Lot
BSF, Bollettino di Storia della
Filosofia
BSG, Berliner Studien zur
Germanistik, Frankfurt, Lang
BSHAP, Bulletin de la Société
Historique et Archéologique du
Périgord, Périgueux
BSHPF, Bulletin de la Société de
l'Histoire du Protestantisme
Français
BSIH, Brill's Studies in Intellectual
History, Leiden, Brill
BSIS, Bulletin of the Society for
Italian Studies
BSLLW, Bulletin de la Société de
Langue et Littérature Wallonnes
BSLP, Bulletin de la Société de
Linguistique de Paris
BSLV, Bollettino della Società
Letteraria di Verona
BSM, Birmingham Slavonic
Monographs, University of
Birmingham
BSOAS, Bulletin of the School of
Oriental and African Studies
BSP, Bollettino Storico Pisano

BSPC, Bulletin de la Société Paul
Claudel
BSPia, Bollettino Storico Piacentino
BSPN, Bollettino Storico per le
Province di Novara
BSPSP, Bollettino della Società
Pavese di Storia Patria
BSR, Bulletin de la Société
Ramond. Bagneres-de-Bigorre
BsR, Beck'sche Reihe, Munich,
Beck
BSRS, Bulletin of the Society for
Renaissance Studies
BSSAAPC, Bollettino della Società
per gli Studi Storici, Archeologici
ed Artistici della Provincia di
Cuneo
BSSCLE, Bulletin of the Society for
the Study of the Crusades and the
Latin East
BSSP, Bullettino Senese di Storia
Patria
BSSPHS, Bulletin of the Society for
Spanish and Portuguese
Historical Studies
BSSPin, Bollettino della Società
Storica Pinerolese, Pinerolo,
Piemonte, Italy.
BSSV, Bollettino della Società
Storica Valtellinese
BSZJPS, Bałtosłowiańskie związki
językowe. Prace Slawistyczne
BT, Богословские труды, Moscow
BTe, Biblioteca Teatrale
BTH, Boletim de Trabalhos
Historicos
BulEz, Български език
BW, Bibliothek und Wissenschaft
BySt, Byzantine Studies

CA, Cuadernos Americanos
CAAM, Cahiers de l'Association Les
Amis de Milosz
CAB, Commentari dell'Ateneo di
Brescia
CAC, Les Cahiers de l'Abbaye de
Créteil
CadL, Cadernos da Lingua
CAFLS, Cahiers AFLS
CAG, Cahiers André Gide
CaH, Les Cahiers de l'Humanisme

CAIEF, Cahiers de l'Association
 Internationale des Études
 Françaises
CalLet, Calabria Letteraria
CAm, Casa de las Américas,
 Havana
CAm, Casa de las Américas, Havana
CanJL, Canadian Journal of
 Linguistics
CanJP, Canadian Journal of
 Philosophy
CanL, Canadian Literature
CanSP, Canadian Slavonic Papers
CanSS, Canadian–American Slavic
 Studies
CarA, Carmarthenshire Antiquary
CARB, Cahiers des Amis de Robert
 Brasillach
CarQ, Caribbean Quarterly
CAT, Cahiers d'Analyse Textuelle,
 Liège, Les Belles Lettres
CatR, Catalan Review
CAVL, Cahiers des Amis de Valery
 Larbaud
CB, Cuadernos Bibliográficos
CC, Comparative Criticism
CCe, Cahiers du Cerf XX
CCend, Continent Cendrars
CCF, Cuadernos de la Cátedra
 Feijoo
CCMe, Cahiers de Civilisation
 Médiévale
CCol, Cahiers Colette
CCU, Cuadernos de la Cátedra M.
 de Unamuno
CD, Cuadernos para el Diálogo
CDA, Christliche deutsche Autoren
 des 20. Jahrhunderts, Berne,
 Lang
CdA, Camp de l'Arpa
CDB, Coleção Documentos
 Brasileiros
CDi, Cuadernos dieciochistas
CDr, Comparative Drama
ČDS, Čeština doma a ve světě
CDs, Cahiers du Dix-septième,
 Athens, Georgia
CDU, Centre de Documentation
 Universitaire
CduC, Cahiers de CERES. Série
 littéraire, Tunis
CE, Cahiers Élisabéthains
CEA, Cahiers d'Études Africaines

CEAL, Centro Editor de América
 Latina
CEC, Conselho Estadual de
 Cultura, Comissão de Literatura,
 São Paulo
CEC, Cahiers d'Études Cathares,
 Narbonne
CECAES, Centre d'Études des
 Cultures d'Aquitaine et d'Europe
 du Sud, Université de Bordeaux
 III
CEcr, Corps Écrit
CEDAM, Casa Editrice Dott. A.
 Milani
CEG, Cuadernos de Estudios
 Gallegos
CEL, Cadernos de Estudos
 Lingüísticos, Campinas, Brazil
CELO, Centre d'Etude de la
 Littérature Occitane, Bordes.
CEM, Cahiers d'Études Médiévales,
 Univ. of Montreal
CEMa, Cahiers d'Études
 Maghrebines, Cologne
CEMed, Cuadernos de Estudios
 Medievales
CEPL, Centre d'Étude et de
 Promotion de la Lecture, Paris
CEPON, Centre per l'estudi e la
 promocion de l'Occitan normat.
CEPONB, CEPON Bulletin
 d'échange.
CER, Cahiers d'Études Romanes
CERCLiD, Cahiers d'Études
 Romanes, Centre de Linguistique
 et de Dialectologie, Toulouse
CEROC, Centre d'Enseignement et
 de Recherche d'Oc, Paris
CERoum, Cahiers d'Études
 Roumaines
CeS, Cultura e Scuola
CESCM, Centre d'Études
 Supérieures de Civilisation
 Médiévale, Poitiers
CET, Centro Editoriale Toscano
CEtGer, Cahiers d'Études
 Germaniques
CF, Les Cahiers de Fontenay
CFC, Contemporary French
 Civilization
CFI, Cuadernos de Filología
 Italiana
CFLA, Cuadernos de Filología.
 Literaturas: Análisis, Valencia

CFM, Cahiers François Mauriac
CFMA, Collection des Classiques
Français du Moyen Âge
CFol, Classical Folia
CFS, Cahiers Ferdinand de Saussure
CFSLH, Cuadernos de Filología:
Studia Linguistica Hispanica
CFTM, Classiques Français des
Temps Modernes, Paris,
Champion
CG, Cahiers de Grammaire
CGD, Cahiers Georges Duhamel
CGFT, Critical Guides to French
Texts, London, Grant & Cutler
CGGT, Critical Guides to German
Texts, London, Grant & Cutler
CGP, Carleton Germanic Papers
CGS, Colloquia Germanica
Stetinensia
CGST, Critical Guides to Spanish
Texts, London, Támesis, Grant &
Cutler
CH, Crítica Hispánica
CHA, Cuadernos Hispano-
Americanos
CHAC, Cuadernos Hispano-
Americanos. Los
complementarios
CHB, Cahiers Henri Bosco
ChC, Chemins Critiques
CHCHMC, Cylchgrawn Hanes
Cymdeithas Hanes y
Methodistiaid Calfinaidd
CHLR, Cahiers d'Histoire des
Littératures Romanes
CHP, Cahiers Henri Pourrat
CHR, Catholic Historical Review
ChR, The Chesterton Review
ChRev, Chaucer Review
ChrA, Chroniques Allemandes
ChrI, Chroniques Italiennes
ChrL, Christianity and Literature
ChrN, Chronica Nova
ChS, Champs du Signe
CHST, Caernarvonshire Historical
Society Transactions
CHum, Computers and the
Humanities
CI, Critical Inquiry
CiD, La Ciudad de Dios
CIDO, Centre International de
Documentation Occitane, Béziers

CIEDS, Centre International
d'Etudes du dix-huitième siècle,
Ferney-Voltaire
CIEL, Centre International de
l'Écrit en Langue d'Òc, Berre
CIEM, Comité International
d'Études Morisques
CIF, Cuadernos de Investigación
Filológica
CIH, Cuadernos de Investigación
Historica
CILF, Conseil International de la
Langue Française
CILH, Cuadernos para
Investigación de la Literatura
Hispanica
CILL, Cahiers de l'Institut de
Linguistique de l'Université de
Louvain
CILT, Centre for Information on
Language Teaching, London
CIMAGL, Cahiers de l'Institut du
Moyen Âge Grec et Latin,
Copenhagen
CIn, Cahiers Intersignes
CIRDOC, Centre Inter-Régional
de Développement de l'Occitan,
Béziers
CIRVI, Centro Interuniversitario di
Ricerche sul 'Viaggio in Italia',
Moncalieri
CISAM, Centro Italiano di Studi
sull'Alto Medioevo
CIt, Carte Italiane
CIUS, Canadian Institute of
Ukrainian Studies Edmonton
CivC, Civiltà Cattolica
CJ, Conditio Judaica, Tübingen,
Niemeyer
CJb, Celan-Jahrbuch
CJC, Cahiers Jacques Chardonne
CJG, Cahiers Jean Giraudoux
CJIS, Canadian Journal of Italian
Studies
ČJL, Český jazyk a literatura
CJNS, Canadian Journal of
Netherlandic Studies
CJP, Cahiers Jean Paulhan
CJR, Cahiers Jules Romains
CL, Cuadernos de Leiden
CL, Comparative Literature
ČL, Česká literatura
CLA, Cahiers du LACITO

CLAJ, College Language Association Journal

CLCC, Cahiers de Littérature Canadienne Comparée

CLCWeb, Comparative Literature and Culture, A WWWeb Journal, <http://www.arts.ualberta.ca/clcwebjournal/>

CLE, Comunicaciones de Literatura Española, Buenos Aires

CLe, Cahiers de Lexicologie

CLEAM, Coleción de Literatura Española Aljamiado–Morisca, Madrid, Gredos

CLESP, Cooperativa Libraria Editrice degli Studenti dell'Università di Padova, Padua

CLett, Critica Letteraria

CLEUP, Cooperativa Libraria Editrice, Università di Padova

CLF, Cahiers de Linguistique Française

CLHM, Cahiers de Linguistique Hispanique Médiévale

CLin, Cercetări de Lingvistica

CLit, Cadernos de Literatura, Coimbra

ClL, La Clau lemosina

CLO, Cahiers Linguistiques d'Ottawa

ClP, Classical Philology

CLS, Comparative Literature Studies

CLSl, Cahiers de Linguistique Slave

CLTA, Cahiers de Linguistique Théorique et Appliquée

CLTL, Cadernos de Lingüística e Teoria da Literatura

CLUEB, Cooperativa Libraria Universitaria Editrice Bologna

CLus, Convergência Lusíada, Rio de Janeiro

CM, Classica et Mediaevalia

CMA, Cahier Marcel Aymé

CMar, Cuadernos de Marcha

CMCS, Cambrian Medieval Celtic Studies

CMERSA, Center for Medieval and Early Renaissance Studies, State University of New York at Binghamton. Acta

ČMF (PhP), Časopis pro moderni filologii: Philologica Pragensia

CMHLB, Cahiers du Monde Hispanique et Luso-Brésilien

CMi, Cultura Milano

CML, Classical and Modern Literature

ČMM, Časopis Matice Moravské

CMon, Communication Monographs

CMP, Cahiers Marcel Proust

CMRS, Cahiers du Monde Russe et Soviétique

CN, Cultura Neolatina

CNat, Les Cahiers Naturalistes

CNCDP, Comissão Nacional para a Comemoração dos Descobrimentos Portugueses, Lisbon

CNor, Los Cuadernos del Norte

CNR, Consiglio Nazionale delle Ricerche

CNRS, Centre National de la Recherche Scientifique

CO, Camera Obscura

CoF, Collectanea Franciscana

COJ, Cambridge Opera Journal

COK, Centralny Ośrodek Kultury, Warsaw

CoL, Compás de Letras

ColA, Colóquio Artes

ColGer, Colloquia Germanica

ColH, Colloquium Helveticum

ColL, Colóquio Letras

ComB, Communications of the International Brecht Society

ComGer, Comunicaciones Germánicas

CompL, Computational Linguistics

ConL, Contrastive Linguistics

ConLet, Il Confronto Letterario

ConLit, Contemporary Literature

ConS, Condorcet Studies

CORDAE, Centre Occitan de Recèrca, de Documentacion e d'Animacion Etnografica, Cordes

CorWPL, Cornell Working Papers in Linguistics

CP, Castrum Peregrini

CPE, Cahiers Prévost d'Exiles, Grenoble

CPL, Cahiers Paul Léautand

CPr, Cahiers de Praxématique

CPR, Chroniques de Port-Royal

CPUC, Cadernos PUC, São Paulo

CQ, Critical Quarterly

CR, Contemporary Review

CRAC, Cahiers Roucher — André Chénier

CRCL, Canadian Review of Comparative Literature

CREL, Cahiers Roumains d'Études Littéraires

CREO, Centre régional d'études occitanes

CRev, Centennial Review

CRI, Cuadernos de Ruedo Ibérico

CRIAR, Cahiers du Centre de Recherches Ibériques et Ibéro-Américains de l'Université de Rouen

CRIN, Cahiers de Recherches des Instituts Néerlandais de Langue et Littérature Françaises

CRLN, Comparative Romance Linguistics Newsletter

CRM, Cahiers de Recherches Médiévales (XIIIe–XVe siècles), Paris, Champion

CRQ, Cahiers Raymond Queneau

CRR, Cincinnati Romance Review

CRRI, Centre de Recherche sur la Renaissance Italienne, Paris

CRRR, Centre de Recherches Révolutionnaires et Romantiques, Université Blaise-Pascal, Clermont-Ferrand.

CrT, Critica del Testo

CS, Cornish Studies

CSAM, Centro di Studi sull'Alto Medioevo, Spoleto

ČSAV, Československá akademie věd

CSDI, Centro di Studio per la Dialettologia Italiana

CSem, Caiete de Semiotică

CSFLS, Centro di Studi Filologici e Linguistici Siciliani, Palermo

CSG, Cambridge Studies in German, Cambridge U.P.

CSGLL, Canadian Studies in German Language and Literature, Berne — New York — Frankfurt, Lang

CSH, Cahiers des Sciences Humaines

CSIC, Consejo Superior de Investigaciones Científicas, Madrid

CSJP, Cahiers Saint-John Perse

CSl, Critica Slovia, Florence

CSLI, Center for the Study of Language and Information, Stanford University

CSM, Les Cahiers de Saint-Martin

ČSp, Československý spisovatel

CSS, California Slavic Studies

CSSH, Comparative Studies in Society and History

CST, Cahiers de Sémiotique Textuelle

CSt, Critica Storica

CT, Christianity Today

CTC, Cuadernos de Teatro Clásico

CTE, Cuadernos de Traducción e Interpretación

CTe, Cuadernos de Teología

CTex, Cahiers Textuels

CTH, Cahiers Tristan l'Hermite

CTh, Ciencia Tomista

CTJ, Cahiers de Théâtre. Jeu

CTL, Current Trends in Linguistics

CTLin, Commissione per i Testi di Lingua, Bologna

CUECM, Cooperativa Universitaria Editrice Catanese Magistero

CUER MA, Centre Universitaire d'Études et de Recherches Médiévales d'Aix, Université de Provence, Aix-en-Provence

CUP, Cambridge University Press

CUUCV, Cultura Universitaria de la Universidad Central de Venezuela

CV, Città di Vita

CWPL, Catalan Working Papers in Linguistics

CWPWL, Cardiff Working Papers in Welsh Linguistics

DAEM, Deutsches Archiv für Erforschung des Mittelalters

DaF, Deutsch als Fremdsprache

DAG, Dictionnaire onomasiologique de l'ancien gascon, Tübingen, Niemeyer

DalR, Dalhousie Review

DanU, Dansk Udsyn

DAO, Dictionnaire onomasiologique de l'ancien occitan, Tübingen, Niemeyer

DaSt, Dante Studies

DB, Дзяржаўная бібліятэка БССР

DB, Doitsu Bungaku

DBl, Driemaandelijkse Bladen

DBO, Deutsche Bibliothek des Ostens, Berlin, Nicolai

DBR, Les Dialectes Belgo-Romans

DBr, Doitsu Bungakoranko

DCFH, Dicenda. Cuadernos de Filología Hispánica

DD, Diskussion Deutsch

DDG, Deutsche Dialektgeographie, Marburg, Elwert

DDJ, Deutsches Dante-Jahrbuch

DegSec, Degré Second

DELTA, Revista de Documentação de Estudos em Lingüística Teórica e Aplicada, Ŝao Paulo

DESB, Delta Epsilon Sigma Bulletin, Dubuque, Iowa

DeutB, Deutsche Bücher

DeutUB, Deutschungarische Beiträge

DFC, Durham French Colloquies

DFS, Dalhousie French Studies

DGF, Dokumentation germanistischer Forschung, Frankfurt, Lang

DgF, Danmarks gamle Folkeviser

DHA, Diálogos Hispánicos de Amsterdam, Rodopi

DHR, Duquesne Hispanic Review

DhS, Dix-huitième Siècle

DI, Deutscher Idealismus, Stuttgart, Klett-Cotta Verlag

DI, Декоративное искусство

DIAS, Dublin Institute for Advanced Studies

DiL, Dictionnairique et Lexicographie

DiS, Dickinson Studies

DisA, Dissertation Abstracts

DisSlSHL, Dissertationes Slavicae: Sectio Historiae Litterarum

DisSlSL, Dissertationes Slavicae: Sectio Linguistica

DK, Duitse Kroniek

DkJb, Deutschkanadisches Jahrbuch

DKV, Deutscher Klassiker Verlag, Frankfurt

DL, Детская литература

DLA, Deutsche Literatur von den Anfängen bis 1700, Berne —

Frankfurt — Paris — New York, Lang

DLit, Discurso Literario

DLM, Deutsche Literatur des Mittelalters (Wissenschaftliche Beiträge der Ernst-Moritz-Arndt-Universität Greifswald)

DLR, Deutsche Literatur in Reprints, Munich, Fink

DLRECL, Diálogo de la Lengua. Revista de Estudio y Creación Literaria, Cuenca

DM, Dirassat Masrahiyyat

DMRPH, De Montfort Research Papers in the Humanities, De Montfort University, Leicester

DMTS, Davis Medieval Texts and Studies, Leiden, Brill

DN, Дружба народов

DNT, De Nieuwe Taalgids

DOLMA, Documenta Onomastica Litteralia Medii Aevi, Hildesheim, Olms

DOM, Dictionnaire de l'occitan médiéval, Tübingen, Niemeyer, 1996–

DosS, Dostoevsky Studies

DoV, Дошкольное воспитание

DPA, Documents pour servir à l'histoire du département des Pyrénées-Atlantiques, Pau

DPL, De Proprietatibus Litterarum, The Hague, Mouton

DpL, День поэзии, Leningrad

DpM, День поэзии, Moscow

DR, Drama Review

DRev, Downside Review

DRLAV, DRLAV, Revue de Linguistique

DS, Diderot Studies

DSEÜ, Deutsche Sprache in Europa und Übersee, Stuttgart, Steiner

DSL, Det danske Sprog- og Litteraturselskab

DSp, Deutsche Sprache

DSRPD, Documenta et Scripta. Rubrica Paleographica et Diplomatica, Barcelona

DSS, XVIIe Siècle

DSt, Deutsche Studien, Meisenheim, Hain

DSt, Danske Studier

DT, Deutsche Texte, Tübingen, Niemeyer

DteolT, Dansk teologisk Tidsskrift

DtL, Die deutsche Literatur

DTM, Deutsche Texte des Mittelalters, Berlin, Akademie

DTV, Deutscher Taschenbuch Verlag, Munich

DUB, Deutschunterricht, East Berlin

DUJ, Durham University Journal (New Series)

DUS, Der Deutschunterricht, Stuttgart

DUSA, Deutschunterricht in Südafrika

DV, Дальний Восток

DVA, Deutsche Verlags-Anstalt, Stuttgart

DVLG, Deutsche Vierteljahresschrift für Literaturwissenschaft und Geistesgeschichte

E, Verlag Enzyklopädie, Leipzig

EAL, Early American Literature

EALS, Europäische Aufklärung in Literatur und Sprache, Frankfurt, Lang

EAS, Europe-Asia Studies

EB, Estudos Brasileiros

EBal, Etudes Balkaniques

EBM, Era Bouts dera mountanho, Aurignac

EBTch, Études Balkaniques Tchécoslovaques

EC, El Escritor y la Crítica, Colección Persiles, Madrid, Taurus

EC, Études Celtiques

ECan, Études Canadiennes

ECar, Espace Caraïbe

ECent, The Eighteenth Century, Lubbock, Texas

ECentF, Eighteenth-Century Fiction

ECF, Écrits du Canada Français

ECI, Eighteenth-Century Ireland

ECIG, Edizioni Culturali Internazionali Genova

ECL, Eighteenth-Century Life

ECla, Les Études Classiques

ECon, España Contemporánea

EconH, Économie et Humanisme

EcR, Echo de Rabastens. Les Veillées Rabastinoises, Rabastens (Tarn)

ECr, Essays in Criticism

ECre, Études Créoles

ECS, Eighteenth Century Studies

EdCat, Ediciones Cátedra, Madrid

EDESA, Ediciones Españolas S.A.

EDHS, Études sur le XVIIIe Siècle

EDIPUCRS, Editora da Pontífica Universidade Católica de Rio Grande do Sul, Porto Alegre

EDL, Études de Lettres

EDT, Edizioni di Torino

EDUSC, Editora da Universidade de Santa Catarina

EE, Erasmus in English

EEM, East European Monographs

EEQ, East European Quarterly

EF, Erträge der Forschung, Darmstadt, Wissenschaftliche Buchgesellschaft

EF, Études Françaises

EFAA, Échanges Franco-Allemands sur l'Afrique

EFE, Estudios de Fonética Experimental

EFF, Ergebnisse der Frauenforschung, Stuttgart, Metzler

EFil, Estudios Filológicos, Valdivia, Chile

EFL, Essays in French Literature, Univ. of Western Australia

EFR, Éditeurs Français Réunis

EG, Études Germaniques

EH, Europäische Hochschulschriften, Berne–Frankfurt, Lang

EH, Estudios Humanísticos

EHF, Estudios Humanísticos. Filología

EHN, Estudios de Historia Novohispana

EHQ, European History Quarterly

EHR, English Historical Review

EHRC, European Humanities Research Centre, University of Oxford

EHS, Estudios de Historia Social

EHT, Exeter Hispanic Texts, Exeter

EIA, Estudos Ibero-Americanos

EIP, Estudos Italianos em Portugal

EJWS, European Journal of Women's Studies
EL, Esperienze Letterarie
El, Elementa, Würzburg, Königshausen & Neumann
–Amsterdam, Rodopi
ELA, Études de Linguistique Appliquée
ELF, Études Littéraires Françaises, Paris, J.-M. Place — Tübingen, Narr
ELH, English Literary History
ELin, Estudos Lingüísticos, São Paulo
ELit, Essays in Literature
ELL, Estudos Lingüísticos e Literários, Bahia
ELLC, Estudis de Llengua i Literatura Catalanes
ELLF, Études de Langue et Littérature Françaises, Tokyo
ELLUG, Éditions littéraires et linguistiques de l'université de Grenoble
ELM, Études littéraires maghrebines
ELR, English Literary Renaissance
EMarg, Els Marges
EMH, Early Music History
EMus, Early Music
ENC, Els Nostres Clàssics, Barcelona, Barcino
ENSJF, École Nationale Supérieure de Jeunes Filles
EO, Edition Orpheus, Tübingen, Francke
EO, Europa Orientalis
EOc, Estudis Occitans
EP, Études Philosophiques
Ep, Epistemata, Würzburg, Königshausen & Neumann
EPESA, Ediciones y Publicaciones Españolas S.A.
EPoet, Essays in Poetics
ER, Estudis Romànics
ERab, Études Rabelaisiennes
ERB, Études Romanes de Brno
ER(BSRLR), Études Romanes (Bulletin de la Société Roumaine de Linguistique Romane)
ERL, Études Romanes de Lund
ErlF, Erlanger Forschungen
ERLIMA, Équipe de recherche sur la littérature d'imagination du

moyen âge, Centre d'Études Supérieures de Civilisation Médiévale/Faculté des Lettres et des Langues, Université de Poitiers.
EROPD, Ежегодник рукописного отдела Пушкинского дома
ERR, European Romantic Review
ES, Erlanger Studien, Erlangen, Palm & Enke
ES, Estudios Segovianos
EsC, L'Esprit Créateur
ESGP, Early Studies in Germanic Philology, Amsterdam, Rodopi
ESI, Edizioni Scientifiche Italiane
ESk, Edition Suhrkamp, Frankfurt, Suhrkamp
ESor, Études sorguaises
EspA, Español Actual
ESt, English Studies
EstE, Estudios Escénicos
EstG, Estudi General
EstH, Estudios Hispánicos
EstL, Estudios de Lingüística, Alicante
EstR, Estudios Románticos
EStud, Essays and Studies
ET, L'Écrit du Temps
ETF, Espacio, Tiempo y Forma, Revista de la Facultad de Geografía e Historia, UNED
EtF, Etudes francophones
EtH, Études sur l'Hérault, Pézenas
EthS, Ethnologia Slavica
ETJ, Educational Theatre Journal
ETL, Explicación de Textos Literarios
EtLitt, Études Littéraires, Quebec
EUDEBA, Editorial Universitaria de Buenos Aires
EUNSA, Ediciones Universidad de Navarra, Pamplona
EUS, European University Studies, Berne, Lang
ExP, Excerpta Philologica
EzLit, Език и литература

FAL, Forum Academicum Literaturwissenschaft, Königstein, Hain
FAM, Filologia Antica e Moderna
FAPESP, Fundação de Amparo à Pesquisa do Estado de São Paulo

FAR, French-American Review
FAS, Frankfurter Abhandlungen zur
  Slavistik, Giessen, Schmitz
FBAN, Фундаментальная
  бібліятэка Акадэміі навук
  БССР
FBG, Frankfurter Beiträge zur
  Germanistik, Heidelberg, Winter
FBS, Franco-British Studies
FC, Filologia e Critica
FCE, Fondo de Cultura Económica,
  Mexico
FCG — CCP, Fondation Calouste
  Gulbenkian — Centre Culturel
  Portugais, Paris
FCS, Fifteenth Century Studies
FD, Fonetic\ă şi Dialectologie
FDL, Facetten deutscher Literatur,
  Berne, Haupt
FEI, Faites entrer l'infini. Journal de
  la Société des Amis de Louis
  Aragon et Elsa Triolet
FEK, Forschungen zur
  europäischen Kultur, Berne,
  Lang
FemSt, Feministische Studien
FF, Forum für
  Fachsprachenforschung,
  Tübingen, Narr
FF, Forma y Función
FFM, French Forum Monographs,
  Lexington, Kentucky
FGÄDL, Forschungen zur
  Geschichte der älteren deutschen
  Literatur, Munich, Fink
FH, Fundamenta Historica,
  Stuttgart-Bad Cannstatt,
  Frommann-Holzboog
FH, Frankfurter Hefte
FHL, Forum Homosexualität und
  Literatur
FHS, French Historical Studies
FIDS, Forschungsberichte des
  Instituts für Deutsche Sprache,
  Tübingen, Narr
FHSJ, Flintshire Historical Society
  Journal
FilM, Filologia Mediolatina
FilMod, Filologia Moderna, Udine
  –Pisa
FilN, Филологические науки
FilR, Filologia Romanza
FilS, Filologické studie
FilZ, Filologija, Zagreb

FiM, Filologia Moderna, Facultad
  de Filosofía y Letras, Madrid
FinS, Fin de Siglo
FIRL, Forum at Iowa on Russian
  Literature
FL, La France Latine
FLa, Faits de Langues
FLG, Freiburger
  literaturpsychologische
  Gespräche
FLin, Folia Linguistica
FLinHist, Folia Linguistica Historica
FLK, Forschungen zur Literatur-
  und Kulturgeschichte. Beiträge
  zur Sprach- und
  Literaturwissenschaft, Berne,
  Lang
FLP, Filologia e linguística
  portuguesa
FLS, French Literature Series
FLV, Fontes Linguae Vasconum
FM, Le Français Moderne
FMADIUR, FM: Annali del
  Dipartimento di Italianistica,
  Università di Roma 'La Sapienza'
FMDA, Forschungen und
  Materialen zur deutschen
  Aufklärung, Stuttgart — Bad
  Cannstatt, Frommann-Holzboog
FMLS, Forum for Modern
  Language Studies
FMon, Le Français dans le Monde
FmSt, Frühmittelalterliche Studien
FMT, Forum Modernes Theater
FN, Frühe Neuzeit, Tübingen,
  Niemeyer
FNDIR, Fédération nationale des
  déportés et internés résistants
FNS, Frühneuzeit-Studien,
  Frankfurt, Lang
FoH, Foro Hispánico, Amsterdam
FNT, Foilseacháin Náisiúnta Tta
FoI, Forum Italicum
FoS, Le Forme e la Storia
FP, Folia Phonetica
FPub, First Publications
FR, French Review
FrA, Le Français Aujourd'hui
FranS, Franciscan Studies
FrCS, French Cultural Studies
FrF, French Forum
FrH, Französisch Heute
FrP Le Français Préclassique
FrSoc, Français et Société

FS, Forum Slavicum, Munich, Fink
FS, French Studies
FSB, French Studies Bulletin
FSlav, Folia Slavica
FSSA, French Studies in Southern
  Africa
FT, Fischer Taschenbuch,
  Frankfurt, Fischer
FT, Finsk Tidskrift
FTCG, 'La Talanquere': Folklore,
  Tradition, Culture Gasconne,
  Nogano
FUE, Fundación Universitaria
  Española
FV, Fortuna Vitrea, Tübingen,
  Niemeyer
FZPT, Freiburger Zeitschrift für
  Philosophie und Theologie

GA, Germanistische Arbeitshefte,
  Tübingen, Niemeyer
GAB, Göppinger Akademische
  Beiträge, Lauterburg, Kümmerle
GAG, Göppinger Arbeiten zur
  Germanistik, Lauterburg,
  Kümmerle
GAKS, Gesammelte Aufsätze zur
  Kulturgeschichte Spaniens
GalR, Galician Review,
  Birmingham
GANDLL, Giessener Arbeiten zur
  neueren deutschen Literatur und
  Literaturwissenschaft, Berne,
  Lang
Garona, Garona. Cahiers du Centre
  d'Etudes des Cultures
  d'Aquitaine et d'Europe du Sud,
  Talence
GAS, German-Australian Studies,
  Berne, Lang
GASK, Germanistische Arbeiten zu
  Sprache und Kulturgeschichte,
  Frankfurt, Lang
GB, Germanistische Bibliothek,
  Heidelberg, Winter
GBA, Gazette des Beaux-Arts
GBE, Germanistik in der Blauen
  Eule
GC, Generalitat de Catalunya
GCFI, Giornale Critico della
  Filosofia Italiana

GEMP, Groupement
  d'Ethnomusicologie en Midi-
  Pyrénées, La Talvèra
GerAb, Germanistische
  Abhandlungen, Stuttgart,
  Metzler
GerLux, Germanistik Luxembourg
GermL, Germanistische Linguistik
GeW, Germanica Wratislaviensia
GF, Giornale di Fisica
GFFNS, Godišnjak Filozofskog
  fakulteta u Novom Sadu
GG, Geschichte und Gesellschaft
GGF, Göteborger Germanistische
  Forschungen, University of
  Gothenburg
GGF, Greifswalder Germanistische
  Forschungen
GGVD, Grundlagen und Gedanken
  zum Verständnis des Dramas,
  Frankfurt, Diesterweg
GGVEL, Grundlagen und
  Gedanken zum Verständnis
  erzählender Literatur, Frankfurt,
  Diesterweg
GIDILOc, Grop d'Iniciativa per un
  Diccionari Informatizat de la
  Lenga Occitana, Montpellier
GIF, Giornale Italiano di Filologia
GIGFL, Glasgow Introductory
  Guides to French Literature
GIGGL, Glasgow Introductory
  Guides to German Literature
GJ, Gutenberg-Jahrbuch
GJb, Goethe Jahrbuch
GJLL, The Georgetown Journal of
  Language and Linguistics
GK, Goldmann Klassiker, Munich,
  Goldmann
GL, Germanistische
  Lehrbuchsammlung, Berlin,
  Weidler
GL, General Linguistics
GLC, German Life and Civilisation,
  Berne, Lang
GLL, German Life and Letters
GLML, The Garland Library of
  Medieval Literature, New York
  –London, Garland
GLR, García Lorca Review
GLS, Grazer Linguistische Studien
Glyph, Glyph: Johns Hopkins
  Textual Studies, Baltimore
GM, Germanistische Mitteilungen

GML, Gothenburg Monographs in
Linguistics
GMon, German Monitor
GN, Germanic Notes and Reviews
GoSt, Gothic Studies
GPB, Гос. публичная библиотека
им. М. Е. Салтыкова-Щедрина
GPI, Государственный
педагогический институт
GPSR, Glossaire des Patois de la
Suisse Romande
GQ, German Quarterly
GR, Germanic Review
GREC, Groupe de Recherches et
d'Études du Clermontais,
Clermont-l'Hérault
GRECF, Groupe de Recherches et
d'Études sur le Canada français,
Edinburgh
GREHAM, Groupe de REcherche
d'Histoire de l'Anthroponymie
Médiévale, Tours, Université
François-Rabelais
GRELCA, Groupe de Recherche
sur les Littératures de la Caraïbe,
Université Laval
GRLH, Garland Reference Library
of the Humanities, New York —
London, Garland
GRLM, Grundriss der romanischen
Literaturen des Mittelalters
GRM, Germanisch-Romanische
Monatsschrift
GrSt, Grundtvig Studier
GS, Lo Gai Saber, Toulouse
GSA, Germanic Studies in
America, Berne–Frankfurt, Lang
GSC, German Studies in Canada,
Frankfurt, Lang
GSI, German Studies in India
GSl, Germano-Slavica, Ontario
GSLI, Giornale Storico della
Letteratura Italiana
GSR, German Studies Review
GSSL, Göttinger Schriften zur
Sprach– und
Literaturwissenschaft, Göttingen,
Herodot
GTN, Gdańskie Towarzystwo
Naukowe
GTS, Germanistische Texte und
Studien, Hildesheim, Olms
GV, Generalitat Valenciana
GY, Goethe Yearbook

H, Hochschulschriften, Cologne,
Pahl-Rugenstein
HAHR, Hispanic American
Historical Review
HB, Horváth Blätter
HBA, Historiografía y Bibliografía
Americanistas, Seville
HBG, Hamburger Beiträge zur
Germanistik, Frankfurt, Lang
HDG, Huis aan de Drie Grachten,
Amsterdam
HEI, History of European Ideas
HEL, Histoire, Epistémologie,
Language
Her(A), Hermes, Århus
HES, Histoire, Économie et Société
HeyJ, Heythrop Journal
HF, Heidelberger Forschungen,
Heidelberg, Winter
HHS, History of the Human
Sciences
HI, Historica Ibérica
HIAR, Hamburger Ibero-
Amerikanische Reihe
HICL, Histoire des Idées et
Critique Littéraire, Geneva, Droz
HIGL, Holland Institute for
Generative Linguistics, Leiden
HisJ, Hispanic Journal, Indiana–
Pennsylvania
HisL, Hispanic Linguistics
HistL, Historiographia Linguistica
HistS, History of Science
His(US), Hispania, Ann Arbor
HJ, Historical Journal
HJb, Heidelberger Jahrbücher
HJBS, Hispanic Journal of
Behavioural Sciences
HKADL, Historisch-kritische
Arbeiten zur deutschen Literatur,
Frankfurt, Lang
HKZMTLG, Handelingen van de
Koninklijke Zuidnederlandse
Maatschappij voor Taalen,
Letterkunde en Geschiedenis
HL, Hochschulschriften
Literaturwissenschaft,
Königstein, Hain
HL, Humanistica Lovaniensia
HLB, Harvard Library Bulletin
HLQ, Huntington Library
Quarterly
HLS, Historiska och
litteraturhistoriska studier

HM, Hommes et Migrations
HMJb, Heinrich Mann Jahrbuch
HP, History of Psychiatry
HPh, Historical Philology
HPos, Hispanica Posnaniensia
HPR, Hispanic Poetry Review
HPS, Hamburger Philologische
Studien, Hamburg, Buske
HPSl, Heidelberger Publikationen
zur Slavistik, Frankfurt, Lang
HPT, History of Political Thought
HR, Hispanic Review
HRef, Historical reflections /
Reflexions historiques
HRel, History of Religions
HRev, Hrvatska revija
HRJ, Hispanic Research Journal
HRSHM, Heresis, revue semestrielle
d'hérésiologie médiévale
HS, Helfant Studien, Stuttgart,
Helfant
HS, Hispania Sacra
HSLA, Hebrew University Studies
in Literature and the Arts
HSlav, Hungaro-Slavica
HSMS, Hispanic Seminary of
Medieval Studies, Madison
HSp, Historische Sprachforschung
(Historical Linguistics)
HSSL, Harvard Studies in Slavic
Linguistics
HSt, Hispanische Studien
HSWSL, Hallesche Studien zur
Wirkung von Sprache und
Literatur
HT, Helfant Texte, Stuttgart,
Helfant
HT, History Today
HTh, History and Theory
HTR, Harvard Theological Review
HUS, Harvard Ukrainian Studies
HY, Herder Yearbook
HZ, Historische Zeitschrift

IÅ, Ibsen-Årbok, Oslo
IAP, Ibero-Americana Pragensia
IAr, Iberoamerikanisches Archiv
IARB, Inter-American Review of
Bibliography
IASL, Internationales Archiv für
Sozialgeschichte der deutschen
Literatur

IASLS, Internationales Archiv für
Sozialgeschichte der deutschen
Literatur: Sonderheft
IB, Insel-Bücherei, Frankfurt, Insel
IBKG, Innsbrucker Beiträge zur
Kulturwissenschaft.
Germanistische Reihe
IBL, Instytut Badań Literackich
PAN, Warsaw
IBLA, Institut des Belles Lettres
Arabes
IBLe, Insel-Bücherei, Leipzig, Insel
IBS, Innsbrücker Beiträge zur
Sprachwissenschaft
IC, Index on Censorship
ICALP, Instituto de Cultura e
Língua Portuguesa, Lisbon
ICALPR, Instituto de Cultura e
Língua Portuguesa. Revista
ICC, Instituto Caro y Cuervo,
Bogotà
ICMA, Instituto de Cooperación
con el Mundo Árabe
ID, Italia Dialettale
IDF, Informationen Deutsch als
Fremdsprache
IDL, Indices zur deutschen
Literatur, Tübingen, Niemeyer
IdLit, Ideologies and Literature
IEC, Institut d'Estudis Catalans
IEI, Istituto dell'Enciclopedia
Italiana
IEO, Institut d'Estudis Occitans
IEPI, Istituti Editoriali e Poligrafici
Internazionali
IES, Institut d'Études Slaves, Paris
IF, Impulse der Forschung,
Darmstadt, Wissenschaftliche
Buchgesellschaft
IF, Indogermanische Forschungen
IFAVL, Internationale Forschungen
zur Allgemeinen und
Vergleichenden
Literaturwissenschaft,
Amsterdam–Atlanta, Rodopi
IFC, Institutión Fernando el
Católico
IFEE, Investigación Franco-
Española. Estudios
IFiS, Instytut Filozofii i Socjologii
PAN, Warsaw
IFOTT, Institut voor Functioneel
Onderzoek naar Taal en
Taalgebruik, Amsterdam

IFR, International Fiction Review
IG, Information grammaticale
IHC, Italian History and Culture
IHE, Índice Histórico Español
IHS, Irish Historical Studies
II, Information und Interpretation, Frankfurt, Lang
IIa, Институт языкознания
IIFV, Institut Interuniversitari de Filologia Valenciana, Valencia
III, Институт истории искусств
IJ, Italian Journal
IJAL, International Journal of American Linguistics
IJBAG, Internationales Jahrbuch der Bettina-von-Arnim Gesellschaft
IJCS, International Journal of Canadian Studies
IJFS, International Journal of Francophone Studies, Leeds
IJHL, Indiana Journal of Hispanic Literatures
IJL, International Journal of Lexicography
IJP, International Journal of Psycholinguistics
IJSL, International Journal for the Sociology of Language
IJSLP, International Journal of Slavic Linguistics and Poetics
IK, Искусство кино
IKU, Institut za književnost i umetnost, Belgrade
IL, L'Information Littéraire
ILASLR, Istituto Lombardo. Accademia di Scienze e Lettere. Rendiconti
ILen, Искусство Ленинграда
ILG, Instituto da Lingua Galega
ILing, Incontri Linguistici
ILTEC, Instituto de Linguistica Teórica e Computacional, Lisbon
IMN, Irisleabhar Mhá Nuad
IMR, International Migration Review
IMU, Italia Medioevale e Umanistica
INCM, Imprensa Nacional, Casa da Moeda, Lisbon
InfD, Informationen und Didaktik
INLF, Institut National de la Langue Française

INIC, Instituto Nacional de Investigação Científica
InL, Иностранная литература
INLE, Instituto Nacional del Libro Español
InstEB, Inst. de Estudos Brasileiros
InstNL, Inst. Nacional do Livro, Brasilia
IO, Italiano e Oltre
IPL, Istituto di Propaganda Libraria
IPZS, Istituto Poligrafico e Zecca dello Stato, Rome
IR, L'Immagine Riflessa
IRAL, International Review of Applied Linguistics
IRIa, Институт русского языка Российской Академии Наук
IrR, The Irish Review
IRSH, International Review of Social History
IRSL, International Review of Slavic Linguistics
ISC, Institut de Sociolingüística Catalana
ISI, Institute for Scientific Information, U.S.A.
ISIEMC, Istituto Storico Italiano per l'Età Moderna e Contemporanea, Rome
ISIM, Istituto Storico Italiano per il Medio Evo
ISLIa, Известия Академии наук СССР. Серия литературы и языка
ISOAN, Известия сибирского отделения АН СССР, Novosibirsk
ISP, International Studies in Philosophy
ISPS, International Studies in the Philosophy of Science
ISS, Irish Slavonic Studies
IsS, Islamic Studies, Islamabad
ISSA, Studi d'Italianistica nell'Africa Australe: Italian Studies in Southern Africa
ISt, Italian Studies
ISV, Informazioni e Studi Vivaldiani
IT, Insel Taschenbuch, Frankfurt, Insel
ItC, Italian Culture

ITL, ITL. Review of Applied
Linguistics, Instituut voor
Toegepaste Linguistiek, Leuven
ItQ, Italian Quarterly
ItStudien, Italienische Studien
IUJF, Internationales Uwe-
Johnson-Forum
IULA, Institut Universitari de
Lingüística Aplicada, Universitat
Pompeu Fabra, Barcelona
IUP, Irish University Press
IUR, Irish University Review
IV, Istituto Veneto di Scienze,
Lettere ed Arti
IVAS, Indices Verborum zum
altdeutschen Schrifttum,
Amsterdam, Rodopi
IVN, Internationale Vereniging
voor Nederlandistiek

JAAC, Journal of Aesthetics and Art
Criticism
JACIS, Journal of the Association
for Contemporary Iberian
Studies
JAE, Journal of Aesthetic Education
JAIS, Journal of Anglo-Italian
Studies, Malta
JAMS, Journal of the American
Musicological Society
JanL, Janua Linguarum, The
Hague, Mouton
JAOS, Journal of the American
Oriental Society
JAPLA, Journal of the Atlantic
Provinces Linguistic Association
JARA, Journal of the American
Romanian Academy of Arts and
Sciences
JAS, The Journal of Algerian
Studies
JASI, Jahrbuch des Adalbert-Stifter-
Instituts
JATI, Association of Teachers of
Italian Journal
JazA, Jazykovědné aktuality
JazLin, Jazykověda: Linguistica,
Ostravska University
JazŠ, Jazykovedné štúdie
JAZU, Jugoslavenska akademija
znanosti i umjetnosti
JBSP, Journal of the British Society
for Phenomenology

JČ, Jazykovedný časopis, Bratislava
JCanS, Journal of Canadian Studies
JCHAS, Journal of the Cork
Historical and Archaeological
Society
JCL, Journal of Child Language
JCLin, Journal of Celtic Linguistics
JCS, Journal of Celtic Studies
JDASD, Deutsche Akademie für
Sprache und Dichtung: Jahrbuch
JDF, Jahrbuch Deutsch als
Fremdsprache
JDSG, Jahrbuch der Deutschen
Schiller-Gesellschaft
JEA, Lou Journalet de
l'Escandihado Aubagnenco
JEGP, Journal of English and
Germanic Philology
JEH, Journal of Ecclesiastical
History
JEL, Journal of English Linguistics
JES, Journal of European Studies
JF, Južnoslovenski filolog
JFDH, Jahrbuch des Freien
Deutschen Hochstifts
JFG, Jahrbuch der Fouqué
Gesellschaft
JFinL, Jahrbuch für finnisch-
deutsche Literaturbeziehungen
JFL, Jahrbuch für fränkische
Landesforschung
JFLS, Journal of French Language
Studies
JFR, Journal of Folklore Research
JG, Jahrbuch für Geschichte,
Berlin, Akademie
JGO, Jahrbücher für die Geschichte
Osteuropas
JHA, Journal for the History of
Astronomy
JHI, Journal of the History of Ideas
JHispP, Journal of Hispanic
Philology
JHP, Journal of the History of
Philosophy
JHR, Journal of Hispanic Research
JHS, Journal of the History of
Sexuality
JIAS, Journal of Inter-American
Studies
JIES, Journal of Indo-European
Studies
JIG, Jahrbuch für Internationale
Germanistik

JIL, Journal of Italian Linguistics

JILAS, Journal of Iberian and Latin American Studies (formerly *Tesserae*)

JILS, Journal of Interdisciplinary Literary Studies

JIPA, Journal of the International Phonetic Association

JIRS, Journal of the Institute of Romance Studies

JJQ, James Joyce Quarterly

JJS, Journal of Jewish Studies

JL, Journal of Linguistics

JLACS, Journal of Latin American Cultural Studies

JLAL, Journal of Latin American Lore

JLAS, Journal of Latin American Studies

JLH, Journal of Library History

JLS, Journal of Literary Semantics

JLSP, Journal of Language and Social Psychology

JMemL, Journal of Memory and Language

JMEMS, Journal of Medieval and Early Modern Studies

JMH, Journal of Medieval History

JMHRS, Journal of the Merioneth Historical and Record Society

JML, Journal of Modern Literature

JMLat, Journal of Medieval Latin

JMMD, Journal of Multilingual and Multicultural Development

JMMLA, Journal of the Midwest Modern Language Association

JModH, Journal of Modern History

JMP, Journal of Medicine and Philosophy

JMRS, Journal of Medieval and Renaissance Studies

JMS, Journal of Maghrebi Studies

JNT, Journal of Narrative Technique

JONVL, Een Jaarboek: Overzicht van de Nederlandse en Vlaamse Literatuur

JOWG, Jahrbuch der Oswald von Wolkenstein Gesellschaft

JP, Journal of Pragmatics

JPC, Journal of Popular Culture

JPCL, Journal of Pidgin and Creole Languages

JPh, Journal of Phonetics

JPHS, The Journal of the Pembrokeshire Historical Society

JPol, Język Polski

JPR, Journal of Psycholinguistic Research

JQ, Jacques e i suoi Quaderni

JRA, Journal of Religion in Africa

JRG, Jahrbücher der Reineke-Gesellschaft

JRH, Journal of Religious History

JRIC, Journal of the Royal Institution of Cornwall

JŘJR, Jazyk a řeč jihočeského regionu. České Budějovice, Pedagogická fakulta Jihočeské univerzity

JRMA, Journal of the Royal Musical Association

JRMMRA, Journal of the Rocky Mountain Medieval and Renaissance Association

JRS, Journal of Romance Studies

JRUL, Journal of the Rutgers University Libraries

JS, Journal des Savants

JSEES, Japanese Slavic and East European Studies

JSem, Journal of Semantics

JSFWUB, Jahrbuch der Schlesischen Friedrich-Wilhelms-Universität zu Breslau

JSH, Jihočeský sborník historický

JSHR, Journal of Speech and Hearing Research

JSL, Journal of Slavic Linguistics

JSoc, Journal of Sociolinguistics

JSS, Journal of Spanish Studies: Twentieth Century

JTS, Journal of Theological Studies

JU, Judentum und Umwelt, Berne, Lang

JUS, Journal of Ukrainian Studies

JV, Jahrbuch für Volkskunde

JVF, Jahrbuch für Volksliedforschung

JVLVB, Journal of Verbal Learning and Verbal Behavior

JWCI, Journal of the Warburg and Courtauld Institutes

JWGV, Jahrbuch des Wiener Goethe-Vereins, Neue Folge

JWH, Journal of World History

JWIL, Journal of West Indian Literature

JWRH, Journal of Welsh Religious History

JZ, Jazykovedný zborník

KANTL, Koninklijke Akademie voor Nederlandse Taal- en Letterkunde

KASL, Kasseler Arbeiten zur Sprache und Literatur, Frankfurt, Lang

KAW, Krajowa Agencja Wydawnicza

KAWLSK, Koninklijke Academie voor Wetenschappen, Letteren en Schone Kunsten van België, Brussels

KB, Književni barok

KBGL, Kopenhagener Beiträge zur germanistischen Linguistik

Kbl, Korrespondenzblatt des Vereins für niederdeutsche Sprachforschung

KDC, Katholiek Documentatiecentrum

KDPM, Kleine deutsche Prosadenkmäler des Mittelalters, Munich, Fink

KGOS, Kultur- und geistesgeschichtliche Ostmitteleuropa-Studien, Marburg, Elwert

KGS, Kölner germanistische Studien, Cologne, Böhlau

KGS, Kairoer germanistische Studien

KH, Komparatistische Hefte

KhL, Художественная литература

KI, Književna istorija

KiW, Książka i Wiedza

KJ, Književnost i jezik

KK, Kirke og Kultur

KJb, Kleist-Jahrbuch

KLWL, Krieg und Literatur: War and Literature

Klage, Klage: Kölner linguistische Arbeiten. Germanistik, Hürth-Efferen, Gabel

KN, Kwartalnik Neofilologiczny

KnK, Kniževna kritika

KO, Университетско издателство 'Климент Охридски'

KO, Книжное обозрение

KP, Книжная палата

KRA, Kölner Romanistische Arbeiten, Geneva, Droz

KS, Kúltura slova

KSDL, Kieler Studien zur deutschen Literaturgeschichte, Neumünster, Wachholtz

KSL, Kölner Studien zur Literaturwissenschaft, Frankfurt, Lang

KSt, Kant Studien

KTA, Kröners Taschenausgabe, Stuttgart, Kröner

KTRM, Klassische Texte des romanischen Mittelalters, Munich, Fink

KU, Konstanzer Universitäts-reden

KUL, Katolicki Uniwersytet Lubelski, Lublin

KuSDL, Kulturwissenschaftliche Studien zur deutschen Literatur, Opladen, Westdeutscher Verlag

KZG, Koreanische Zeitschrift für Germanistik

KZMTLG, Koninklijke Zuidnederlandse Maatschappij voor Taal- en Letterkunde en Geschiedenis, Brussels

KZMTLGH, Koninklijke Zuidnederlandse Maatschaapij voor Taal- en Letterkunde en Geschiedenis. Handelingen

LA, Linguistische Arbeiten, Tübingen, Niemeyer

LA, Linguistic Analysis

LaA, Language Acquisition

LAbs, Linguistics Abstracts

LaF, Langue Française

LAILJ, Latin American Indian Literatures Journal

LaLi, Langues et Linguistique

LALIES, LALIES. Actes des sessions de linguistique et de littérature. Institut d'Etudes linguistiques et phonétiques. Sessions de linguistique. Ecole Normale Supérieure Paris, Sorbonne nouvelle

LALR, Latin-American Literary Review

LaM, Les Langues Modernes
LangH, Le Langage et l'Homme
LArb, Linguistische Arbeitsberichte
LARR, Latin-American Research Review
LaS, Langage et Société
LATR, Latin-American Theatre Review
LatT, Latin Teaching, Shrewsbury
LB, Leuvense Bijdragen
LBer, Linguistische Berichte
LBIYB, Leo Baeck Institute Year Book
LBR, Luso-Brazilian Review
LC, Letture Classensi
LCC, Léachtaí Cholm Cille
LCh, Literatura Chilena
LCP, Language and Cognitive Processes
LCrit, Lavoro Critico
LCUTA, Library Chronicle of the University of Texas at Austin
LD, Libri e Documenti
LdA, Linha d'Agua
LDan, Lectura Dantis
LDanN, Lectura Dantis Newberryana
LDGM, Ligam-DiGaM. Quadèrn de lingüistica e lexicografia gasconas, Fontenay aux Roses
LE, Language and Education
LEA, Lingüística Española Actual
LebS, Lebende Sprachen
LEMIR, Literatura Española Medieval y del Renacimiento, Valencia U.P.; http://www.uv.es/~lemir/Revista.html
Leng(M), Lengas, Montpellier
Leng(T), Lengas, Toulouse
LenP, Ленинградская панорама
LetA, Letterature d'America
LetD, Letras de Deusto
LETHB, Laboratoires d'Études Théâtrales de l'Université de Haute-Bretagne. Études et Documents, Rennes
LetL, Letras e Letras, Departamento de Línguas Estrangeiras Modernas, Universidade Federal de Uberlândia, Brazil
LetLi, Letras Libres, Mexico D.F.
LetMS, Letopis Matice srpske, Novi Sad
LetP, Il Lettore di Provincia

LetS, Letras Soltas
LevT, Levende Talen
Lex(L), Lexique, Lille
LF, Letras Femeninas
LFil, Listy filologické
LFQ, Literature and Film Quarterly
LGF, Lunder Germanistische Forschungen, Stockholm, Almqvist & Wiksell
LGGL, Literatur in der Geschichte, Geschichte in der Literatur, Cologne–Vienna, Böhlau
LGL, Langs Germanistische Lehrbuchsammlung, Berne, Lang
LGP, Leicester German Poets, Leicester U.P.
LGW, Literaturwissenschaft — Gesellschaftswissenschaft, Stuttgart, Klett
LH, Lingüística Hispánica
LHum, Litteraria Humanitas, Brno
LI, Linguistic Inquiry
LIAA, Litteraturvetenskapliga institutionen vid Åbo Akademi, Åbo Akademi U.P.
LiB, Literatur in Bayern
LIC, Letteratura Italiana Contemporanea
LiCC, Lien des chercheurs cévenols
LIE, Lessico Intellettuale Europeo, Rome, Ateneo
LiL, Limbă şi Literatură
LiLi, Zeitschrift für Literaturwissenschaft und Linguistik
LingAk, Linguistik Aktuell, Amsterdam, Benjamins
LingBal, Балканско езикознание – Linguistique Balkanique
LingCon, Lingua e Contesto
LingFil, Linguistica e Filologia, Dipartimento di Linguistica e Letterature Comparate, Bergamo
LingLett, Linguistica e Letteratura
LíngLit, Língua e Literatura, São Paulo
LinLit, Lingüística y Literatura
LINQ, Linq [Literature in North Queensland]
LInv, Linguisticae Investigationes
LiR, Limba Română
LIT, Literature Interpretation Theory
LIt, Lettera dall'Italia

LitAP, Literární archív Památníku národního písemnictví
LItal, Lettere Italiane
LitB, Literatura, Budapest
LitC, Littératures Classiques
LitG, Литературная газета, Moscow
LitH, Literature and History
LItL, Letteratura Italiana Laterza, Bari, Laterza
LitL, Literatur für Leser
LitLing, Literatura y Lingüística
LitM, Literární měsícník
LitMis, Литературна мисъл
LitP, Literature and Psychology
LitR, The Literary Review
LittB, Litteraria, Bratislava
LittK, Litterae, Lauterburg, Kümmerle
LittS, Litteratur og Samfund
LittW, Litteraria, Wrocław
LiU, Літературна Україна
LJb, Literaturwissenschaftliches Jahrbuch der Görres–Gesellschaft
LK, Literatur-Kommentare, Munich, Hanser
LK, Literatur und Kritik
LKol, Loccumer Kolloquium
LL, Langues et Littératures, Rabat
LlA, Lletres Asturianes
LLC, Literary and Linguistic Computing
LlC, Llên Cymru
LlLi, Llengua i Literatura
LLS, Lenguas, Literaturas, Sociedades. Cuadernos Hispánicos
LLSEE, Linguistic and Literary Studies in Eastern Europe, Amsterdam, Benjamins
LM, Le Lingue del Mondo
LN, Lingua Nostra
LNB, Leipziger namenkundliche Beiträge
LNL, Les Langues Néo-Latines
LNouv, Les Lettres Nouvelles
LoP, Loccumer Protokolle
LOS, Literary Onomastic Studies
LP, Le Livre de Poche, Librairie Générale Française
LP, Lingua Posnaniensis
LPen, Letras Peninsulares
LPh, Linguistics and Philosophy

LPLP, Language Problems and Language Planning
LPO, Lenga e Païs d'Oc, Montpellier
LPr, Linguistica Pragensia
LQ, Language Quarterly, University of S. Florida
LQu, Lettres québécoises
LR, Linguistische Reihe, Munich, Hueber
LR, Les Lettres Romanes
LRev, Linguistic Review
LRI, Libri e Riviste d'Italia
LS, Literatur als Sprache, Münster, Aschendorff
LS, Lingua e Stile
LSa, Lusitania Sacra
LSc, Language Sciences
LSil, Linguistica Silesiana
LSNS, Lundastudier i Nordisk Språkvetenskap
LSo, Language in Society
LSp, Language and Speech
LSPS, Lou Sourgentin/La Petite Source. Revue culturelle bilingue nissart-français, Nice
LSty, Language and Style
LSW, Ludowa Spółdzielnia Wydawnicza
LTG, Literaturwissenschaft, Theorie und Geschichte, Frankfurt, Lang
ŁTN, Łódzkie Towarzystwo Naukowe
LTP, Laval Théologique et Philosophique
LU, Literarhistorische Untersuchungen, Berne, Lang
LVC, Language Variation and Change
LW, Literatur und Wirklichkeit, Bonn, Bouvier
LWU, Literatur in Wissenschaft und Unterricht
LY, Lessing Yearbook

MA, Moyen Âge
MAASC, Mémoires de l'Académie des Arts et des Sciences de Carcassonne
MACL, Memórias da Academia de Ciências de Lisboa, Classe de Letras

MAe, Medium Aevum
MAKDDR, Mitteilungen der
  Akademie der Künste der DDR
MAL, Modern Austrian Literature
MaL, Le Maghreb Littéraire –
  Revue Canadienne des
  Littératures Maghrébines,
  Toronto
MaM, Marbacher Magazin
MAPS, Medium Aevum.
  Philologische Studien, Munich,
  Fink
MARPOC, Maison d'animation et
  de recherche populaire occitane,
  Nimes
MAST, Memorie dell'Accademia
  delle Scienze di Torino
MatSl, Matica Slovenská
MBA, Mitteilungen aus dem
  Brenner-Archiv
MBAV, Miscellanea Bibliothecae
  Apostolicae Vaticanae
MBMRF, Münchener Beiträge zur
  Mediävistik und Renaissance-
  Forschung, Bachenhausen, Arbeo
MBRP, Münstersche Beiträge zur
  romanischen Philologie, Münster,
  Kleinheinrich
MBSL, Mannheimer Beiträge zur
  Sprach- und
  Literaturwissenschaft, Tübingen,
  Narr
MC, Misure Critiche
MCV, Mélanges de la Casa de
  Velázquez
MD, Musica Disciplina
MDan, Meddelser fra
  Dansklærerforeningen.
MDG, Mitteilungen des deutschen
  Germanistenverbandes
MDL, Mittlere Deutsche Literatur
  in Neu- und Nachdrucken,
  Berne, Lang
MDLK, Monatshefte für
  deutschsprachige Literatur und
  Kultur
MDr, Momentum Dramaticum
MEC, Ministerio de Educação e
  Cultura, Rio de Janeiro
MedC, La Méditerranée et ses
  Cultures
MedH, Medioevo e Umanesimo
MedLR, Mediterranean Language
  Review

MedP, Medieval Perspectives
MedRom, Medioevo Romanzo
MedS, Medieval Studies
MEFR, Mélanges de l'École
  Française de Rome, Moyen Age
MerH, Merthyr Historian
MerP, Mercurio Peruano
MF, Mercure de France
MFDT, Mainzer Forschungen zu
  Drama und Theater, Tübingen,
  Francke
MFS, Modern Fiction Studies
MG, Молодая гвардия
MG, Молодая гвардия
MGB, Münchner Germanistische
  Beiträge, Munich, Fink
MGG, Mystik in Geschichte und
  Gegenwart, Stuttgart-Bad
  Cannstatt, Frommann-Holzboog
MGS, Marburger Germanistische
  Studien, Frankfurt, Lang
MGS, Michigan Germanic Studies
MGSL, Minas Gerais, Suplemento
  Literário
MH, Medievalia et Humanistica
MHJ, Medieval History Journal
MHLS, Mid-Hudson Language
  Studies
MHRA, Modern Humanities
  Research Association
MichRS, Michigan Romance Studies
MILUS, Meddelanden från
  Institutionen i Lingvistik vid
  Universitetet i Stockholm
MINS, Meddelanden från
  institutionen för nordiska språk
  vid Stockholms universitet,
  Stockholm U.P.
MiscBarc, Miscellanea
  Barcinonensia
MiscEB, Miscel·lània d'Estudis
  Bagencs
MiscP, Miscel·lània Penedesenca
MJ, Mittellateinisches Jahrbuch
MK, Maske und Kothurn
MKH, Deutsche
  Forschungsgemeinschaft:
  Mitteilung der Kommission für
  Humanismusforschung,
  Weinheim, Acta Humaniora
MKNAWL, Mededelingen der
  Koninklijke Nederlandse
  Akademie van Wetenschappen,
  Afd. Letterkunde, Amsterdam

ML, Mediaevalia Lovaniensia, Leuven U.P.

ML, Modern Languages

MLAIntBibl, Modern Language Association International Bibliography

MLIÅA, Meddelanden utgivna av Litteraturvetenskapliga institutionen vid Åbo Akademi, Åbo Akademi U.P.

MLIGU, Meddelanden utgivna av Litteraturvetenskapliga institutionen vid Göteborgs universitet, Gothenburg U.P.

MLit, Мастацкая літаратура

MLit, Miesięcznik Literacki

MLIUU, Meddelanden utgivna av Litteraturvetenskapliga institutionen vid Uppsala universitet, Uppsala U.P.

MLJ, Modern Language Journal

MLN, Modern Language Notes

MLQ, Modern Language Quarterly

MLR, Modern Language Review

MLS, Modern Language Studies

MM, Maal og Minne

MMS, Münstersche Mittelalter-Schriften, Munich, Fink

MN, Man and Nature. L'Homme et la Nature

MNGT, Manchester New German Texts, Manchester U.P.

MO, Monde en Oc. Aurillac (IEO)

ModD, Modern Drama

ModS, Modern Schoolman

MoL, Modellanalysen: Literatur, Paderborn, Schöningh–Munich, Fink

MON, Ministerstwo Obrony Narodowej, Warsaw

MosR, Московский рабочий

MoyFr, Le Moyen Français

MP, Modern Philology

MQ, Mississippi Quarterly

MQR, Michigan Quarterly Review

MR, Die Mainzer Reihe, Mainz, Hase & Koehler

MR, Medioevo e Rinascimento

MRev, Maghreb Review

MRo, Marche Romane

MRS, Medieval and Renaissance Studies

MRTS, Medieval and Renaissance Texts and Studies, Tempe,

Arizona, Arizona State University

MS, Marbacher Schriften, Stuttgart, Cotta

MS, Moderna Språk

MSB, Middeleeuwse Studies en Bronnen, Hilversum, Verloren

MSC, Medjunarodni slavistički centar, Belgrade

MSG, Marburger Studien zur Germanistik, Marburg, Hitzeroth

MSHA, Maison des sciences de l'homme d'Aquitaine

MSISS, Materiali della Società Italiana di Studi sul Secolo XVIII

MSL, Marburger Studien zur Literatur, Marburg, Hitzeroth

MSLKD, Münchener Studien zur literarischen Kultur in Deutschland, Frankfurt, Lang

MSMS, Middeleeuse Studies — Medieval Studies, Johannesburg

MSNH, Mémoires de la Société Néophilologique de Helsinki

MSp, Moderne Sprachen (Zeitschrift des Verbandes der österreichischen Neuphilologen)

MSSp, Münchener Studien zur Sprachwissenschaft, Munich

MSUB, Moscow State University Bulletin, series 9, philology

MTCGT, Methuen's Twentieth-Century German Texts, London, Methuen

MTG, Mitteilungen zur Theatergeschichte der Goethezeit, Bonn, Bouvier

MTNF, Monographien und Texte zur Nietzsche-Forschung, Berlin — New York, de Gruyter

MTU, Münchener Texte und Untersuchungen zur deutschen Literatur des Mittelalters, Tübingen, Niemeyer

MTUB, Mitteilungen der T. U. Braunschweig

MUP, Manchester University Press

MusL, Music and Letters

MusP, Museum Patavinum

MyQ, Mystics Quarterly

NA, Nuova Antologia

NP, Народна просвета
NP, Nouvello de Prouvènço (Li), Avignon, Parlaren Païs d'Avignoun
NQ, Notes and Queries
NR, New Review
NŘ, Naše řeč
NRE, Nuova Rivista Europea
NRe, New Readings, School of European Studies, University of Wales, College of Cardiff
NRF, Nouvelle Revue Française
NRFH, Nueva Revista de Filología Hispánica
NRL, Neue russische Literatur. Almanach, Salzburg
NRLett, Nouvelles de la République des Lettres
NRLI, Nuova Rivista di Letteratura Italiana
NRMI, Nuova Rivista Musicale Italiana
NRO, Nouvelle Revue d'Onomastique
NRP, Nouvelle Revue de Psychanalyse
NRS, Nuova Rivista Storica
NRSS, Nouvelle Revue du Seizième Siècle
NRu, Die Neue Rundschau
NS, Die Neueren Sprachen
NSc, New Scholar
NSh, Начальная школа
NSL, Det Norske Språk- og Litteraturselskap
NSlg, Neue Sammlung
NSo, Наш современник . . . Альманах
NSP, Nuovi Studi Politici
NSS, Nysvenska Studier
NSt, Naše stvaranje
NT, Навука і тэхніка
NT, Nordisk Tidskrift
NTBB, Nordisk Tidskrift för Bok- och Biblioteksväsen
NTC, Nuevo Texto Crítico
NTE, Народна творчість та етнографія
NTg, Nieuwe Taalgids
NTQ, New Theatre Quarterly
NTSh, Наукове товариство ім. Шевченка

NTW, News from the Top of the World: Norwegian Literature Today
NU, Narodna umjetnost
NV, Новое время
NVS, New Vico Studies
NWIG, Niewe West-Indische Gids
NyS, Nydanske Studier/Almen Kommunikationsteori
NYSNDL, New Yorker Studien zur neueren deutschen Literaturgeschichte, Berne, Lang
NYUOS, New York University Ottendorfer Series, Berne, Lang
NZh, Новый журнал
NZh (StP), Новый журнал, St Petersburg
NZJFS, New Zealand Journal of French Studies
NZSJ, New Zealand Slavonic Journal

OA, Отечественные архивы
OB, Ord och Bild
OBS, Osnabrücker Beiträge zur Sprachtheorie, Oldenbourg, OBST
OBTUP, Universitetsforlaget Oslo–Bergen–Tromsø
ÖBV, Österreichischer Bundesverlag, Vienna
OC, Œuvres et Critiques
OcL, Oceanic Linguistics
Oc(N), Oc, Nice
OCP, Orientalia Christiana Periodica, Rome
OCS, Occitan/Catalan Studies
ÖGL, Österreich in Geschichte und Literatur
OGS, Oxford German Studies
OH, Ottawa Hispánica
OIU, Oldenbourg Interpretationen mit Unterrichtshilfen, Munich, Oldenbourg
OL, Orbis Litterarum
OLR, Oxford Literary Review
OLSI, Osservatorio Linguistico della Svizzera italiana
OM, L'Oc Médiéval
ON, Otto/Novecento

PhilP, Philological Papers, West
  Virginia University
PhilR, Philosophy and Rhetoric
PhilRev, Philosophical Review
PhLC, Phréatique, Langage et
  Création
PHol, Le Pauvre Holterling
PhonPr, Phonetica Pragensia
PhP, Philologica Pragensia
PhR, Phoenix Review
PHSL, Proceedings of the Huguenot
  Society of London
PI, педагогический институт
PId, Le Parole e le Idee
PIGS, Publications of the Institute
  of Germanic Studies, University
  of London
PiH, Il Piccolo Hans
PIMA, Proceedings of the Illinois
  Medieval Association
PIMS, Publications of the Institute
  for Medieval Studies, Toronto
PIW, Państwowy Instytut
  Wydawniczy, Warsaw
PJ, Poradnik Językowy
PLing, Papers in Linguistics
PLit, Philosophy and Literature
PLL, Papers on Language and
  Literature
PL(L), Pamiętnik Literacki, London
PLRL, Patio de Letras/La Rosa als
  Llavis
PLS, Přednášky z běhu Letní školy
  slovanských studií
PL(W), Pamiętnik Literacki,
  Warsaw
PM, Pleine Marge
PMH, Portugaliae Monumenta
  Historica
PMHRS, Papers of the Medieval
  Hispanic Research Seminar,
  London, Department of Hispanic
  Studies, Queen Mary and
  Westfield College
PMLA, Publications of the Modern
  Language Association of America
PMPA, Publications of the Missouri
  Philological Association
PN, Paraulas de novelum, Périgueux
PNCIP, Plurilinguismo. Notizario
  del Centro Internazionale sul
  Plurilinguismo
PNR, Poetry and Nation Review

PNUS, Prace Naukowe
  Uniwersytetu Śląskiego,
  Katowice
PoetT, Poetics Today
PolR, Polish Review
PortSt, Portuguese Studies
PP, Prace Polonistyczne
PPNCFL, Proceedings of the Pacific
  Northwest Conference on
  Foreign Languages
PPr, Papers in Pragmatics
PPU, Promociones y Publicaciones
  Universitarias, S.A., Barcelona
PQ, The Philological Quarterly
PR, Podravska Revija
PrA, Prouvenço aro, Marseilles
PraRu, Prace Rusycystyczne
PRev, Poetry Review
PRF, Publications Romanes et
  Françaises, Geneva, Droz
PRH, Pahl-Rugenstein
  Hochschulschriften, Cologne,
  Pahl–Rugenstein
PrH, Provence Historique
PrHlit, Prace Historycznoliterackie
PrHum, Prace Humanistyczne
PRIA, Proceedings of the Royal
  Irish Academy
PrIJP, Prace Instytutu Języka
  Polskiego
Prilozi, Prilozi za književnost, jezik,
  istoriju i folklor, Belgrade
PrilPJ, Prilozi proučavanju jezika
PRIS-MA, Bulletin de liaison de
  l'ERLIMA, Université de Poitiers
PrLit, Prace Literackie
PRom, Papers in Romance
PrRu, Przegląd Rusycystyczny
PrzH, Przegląd Humanistyczny
PrzW, Przegląd Wschodni
PS, Проблеми слов'янознавства
PSCL, Papers and Studies in
  Contrastive Linguistics
PSE, Prague Studies in English
PSGAS, Politics and Society in
  Germany, Austria and
  Switzerland
PSLu, Pagine Storiche Luganesi
PSML, Prague Studies in
  Mathematical Linguistics
PSQ, Philologische Studien und
  Quellen, Berlin, Schmidt
PSR, Portuguese Studies Review

PSRL, Полное собрание русских
   летописей
PSS, Z polskich studiów
   slawistycznych, Warsaw, PWN
PSSLSAA, Procès-verbaux des
   séances de la Société des Lettres,
   Sciences et Arts de l'Aveyron
PSV, Polono-Slavica Varsoviensia
PT, Pamiętnik Teatralny
PUC, Pontifícia Universidade
   Católica, São Paulo
PUCRS, Pontífica Universidade
   Católica de Rio Grande do Sul,
   Porto Alegre
PUE, Publications Universitaires,
   Européennes,
   NY–Berne–Frankfurt, Lang
PUF, Presses Universitaires de
   France, Paris
PUG Pontificia Università
   Gregoriana
PUMRL, Purdue University
   Monographs in Romance
   Languages, Amsterdam —
   Philadelphia, Benjamins
PUStE, Publications de l'Université
   de St Étienne
PW, Poetry Wales
PWN, Państwowe Wydawnictwo
   Naukowe, Warsaw, etc

QA, Quaderni de Archivio
QALT, Quaderni dell'Atlante
   Lessicale Toscano
QASIS, Quaderni di lavoro
   dell'ASIS (Atlante Sintattico
   dell'Italia Settentrionale), Centro
   di Studio per la Dialettologia
   Italiana 'O. Parlangèli',
   Università degli Studi di Padova
QCFLP, Quaderni del Circolo
   Filologico Linguistico Padovano
QDLC, Quaderni del Dipartimento
   di Linguistica, Università della
   Calabria
QDLF, Quaderni del Dipartimento
   di Linguistica, Università degli
   Studi, Firenze
QDLLSMG, Quaderni del
   Dipartimento di Lingue e
   Letterature Straniere Moderne,
   Università di Genova

QDSL, Quellen zur deutschen
   Sprach- und Literaturgeschichte,
   Heidelberg, Winter
QFCC, Quaderni della Fondazione
   Camillo Caetani, Rome
QFESM, Quellen und Forschungen
   zur Erbauungsliteratur des späten
   Mittelalters und der frühen
   Neuzeit, Amsterdam, Rodopi
QFGB, Quaderni di Filologia
   Germanica della Facoltà di
   Lettere e Filosofia dell'Università
   di Bologna
QFIAB, Quellen und Forschungen
   aus italienischen Archiven und
   Bibliotheken
QFLK, Quellen und Forschungen
   zur Literatur- und
   Kulturgeschichte, Berlin, de
   Gruyter
QFLR, Quaderni di Filologia e
   Lingua Romanze, Università di
   Macerata
QFRB, Quaderni di Filologia
   Romanza della Facoltà di Lettere
   e Filosofia dell'Università di
   Bologna
QFSK, Quellen und Forschungen
   zur Sprach- und Kulturge-
   schichte der germanischen
   Völker, Berlin, de Gruyter
QI, Quaderni d'Italianistica
QIA, Quaderni Ibero-Americani
QIGC, Quaderni dell'Istituto di
   Glottologia, Università degli
   Studi 'G. D'Annunzio' di Chieti,
   Facoltà di Lettere e Filosofia
QIICM, Quaderni dell'Istituto
   Italiano de Cultura, Melbourne
QILLSB, Quaderni dell'Istituto di
   Lingue e Letterature Straniere
   della Facoltà di Magistero
   dell'Università degli Studi di Bari
QILUU, Quaderni dell'Istituto di
   Linguistica dell'Università di
   Urbino
QINSRM, Quaderni dell'Istituto
   Nazionale di Studi sul
   Rinascimento Meridionale
QJMFL, A Quarterly Journal in
   Modern Foreign Literatures
QJS, Quarterly Journal of Speech,
   Speech Association of America

QLII, Quaderni di Letterature Iberiche e Iberoamericane

QLL, Quaderni di Lingue e Letterature, Verona

QLLP, Quaderni del Laboratorio di Linguistica, Scuola Normale Superiore, Pisa

QLLSP, Quaderni di Lingua e Letteratura Straniere, Facoltà di Magistero, Università degli Studi di Palermo

QLO, Quasèrns de Lingüistica Occitana

QM, Quaderni Milanesi

QMed, Quaderni Medievali

QP, Quaderns de Ponent

QPet, Quaderni Petrarcheschi

QPL, Quaderni Patavini di Linguistica

QQ, Queen's Quarterly, Kingston, Ontario

QR, Quercy Recherche, Cahors

QRCDLIM, Quaderni di Ricerca, Centro di Dialettologia e Linguistica Italiana di Manchester

QRP, Quaderni di Retorica e Poetica

QS, Quaderni di Semantica

QSF, Quaderni del Seicento Francese

QSGLL, Queensland Studies in German Language and Literature, Berne, Francke

QSt, Quaderni Storici

QStef, Quaderni Stefaniani

QSUP, Quaderni per la Storia dell'Università di Padova

QT, Quaderni di Teatro

QuF, Québec français

QuS, Quebec Studies

QV, Quaderni del Vittoriale

QVen, Quaderni Veneti

QVer, Quaderni Veronesi di Filologia, Lingua e Letteratura Italiana

QVR, Quo vadis Romania?, Vienna

RA, Romanistische Arbeitshefte, Tübingen, Niemeyer

RA, Revista Agustiniana

RAA, Rendiconti dell'Accademia di Archeologia, Lettere e Belle Arti

RABM, Revista de Archivos, Bibliotecas y Museos

RAct, Regards sur l'Actualité

Rad, Rad Jugoslavenske akademije znanosti i umjetnosti

RAE, Real Academia Española

RAfL, Research in African Literatures

RAG, Real Academia Galega

RAL, Revista Argentina de Lingüística

RAN, Regards sur l'Afrique du Nord

RANL, Rendiconti dell'Accademia Nazionale dei Lincei, Classe di scienze morali, storiche e filologiche, serie IX

RANPOLL, Revista ANPOLL, Faculdade de Filosofia, Letras e Ciências Humanas, Univ. de São Paulo.

RAPL, Revista da Academia Paulista de Letras, São Paulo

RAR, Renaissance and Reformation

RAS, Rassegna degli Archivi di Stato

RASoc, Revista de Antropología Social

RB, Revue Bénédictine

RBC, Research Bibliographies and Checklists, London, Grant & Cutler

RBDSL, Regensburger Beiträge zur deutschen Sprach- und Literaturwissenschaft, Frankfurt–Berne, Lang

RBG, Reclams de Bearn et Gasconha

RBGd, Rocznik Biblioteki Gdańskiej PAN (Libri Gedanenses)

RBKr, Rocznik Biblioteki PAN w Krakowie

RBL, Revista Brasileira de Lingüística

RBLL, Revista Brasileira de Lingua e Literatura

RBN, Revista da Biblioteca Nacional

RBPH, Revue Belge de Philologie et d'Histoire

RBS, Rostocker Beiträge zur Sprachwissenschaft

RC, Le Ragioni Critiche

RCat, Revista de Catalunya

RČAV, Rozpravy Československé akademie věd, Prague, ČSAV

RCB, Revista de Cultura Brasileña

RCCM, Rivista di Cultura Classica e Medioevale

RCEH, Revista Canadiense de Estudios Hispánicos

RCEN, Revue Canadienne d'Études Néerlandaises

RCF, Review of Contemporary Fiction

RCL, Revista Chilena de Literatura

RCLL, Revista de Crítica Literaria Latino-Americana

RCo, Revue de Comminges

RCSF, Rivista Critica di Storia della Filosofia

RCVS, Rassegna di Cultura e Vita Scolastica

RD, Revue drômoise: archéologie, histoire, géographie

RDE, Recherches sur Diderot et sur l'"Encyclopédie'

RDM, Revue des Deux Mondes

RDsS, Recherches sur le XVIIe Siècle

RDTP, Revista de Dialectología y Tradiciones Populares

RE, Revista de Espiritualidad

REC, Revista de Estudios del Caribe

RECat, Revue d'Études Catalanes

RedLet, Red Letters

REE, Revista de Estudios Extremeños

REEI, Revista del Instituto Egipcio de Estudios Islámicos, Madrid

REH, Revista de Estudios Hispánicos, Washington University, St Louis

REHisp, Revista de Estudios Hispánicos, Puerto Rico

REI, Revue des Études Italiennes

REJ, Revista de Estudios de Juventud

REJui, Revue des Études Juives, Paris

REL, Revue des Études Latines

RELA, Revista Española de Lingüística Aplicada

RelCL, Religion in Communist Lands

RELI, Rassegna Europea di Letteratura Italiana

RELing, Revista Española de Lingüística, Madrid

RelLit, Religious Literature

ReMS, Renaissance and Modern Studies

RenD, Renaissance Drama

RenP, Renaissance Papers

RenR, Renaissance and Reformation

RenS, Renaissance Studies

RER, Revista de Estudios Rosalianos

RES, Review of English Studies

RESEE, Revue des Études Sud-Est Européennes

RESS, Revue Européenne des Sciences Sociales et Cahiers Vilfredo Pareto

RevA, Revue d'Allemagne

RevAl, Revista de l'Alguer

RevAR, Revue des Amis de Ronsard

RevAuv, Revue d'Auvergne, Clermont-Ferrand

RevEL, Revista de Estudos da Linguagem, Faculdade de Letras, Universidade Federal de Minas Gerais

RevF, Revista de Filología

RevHA, Revue de la Haute-Auvergne

RevG, Revista de Girona

RevIb, Revista Iberoamericana

RevL, Revista Lusitana

RevLM, Revista de Literatura Medieval

RevLR, Revista do Livro

RevO, La Revista occitana, Montpellier

RevP, Revue Parole, Université de Mons-Hainault

RevPF, Revista Portuguesa de Filosofia

RevR, Revue Romane

RF, Romanische Forschungen

RFE, Revista de Filología Española

RFe, Razón y Fe

RFHL, Revue Française d'Histoire du Livre

RFLSJ, Revista de Filosofía y Lingüística de San José, Costa Rica

RFLUL, Revista da Faculdade de Letras da Universidade de Lisboa

RFLUP, Línguas e Literaturas, Revista da Faculdade de Letras, Univ. do Porto

RFN, Rivisti di Filosofia Neoscolastica

RFo, Ricerca Folklorica

RFP, Recherches sur le Français Parlé

RFR, Revista de Filología Románica

RFr, Revue Frontenac

RG, Recherches Germaniques

RGand, Romanica Gandensia

RGCC, Revue du Gévaudan, des Causses et des Cévennes

RGG, Rivista di Grammatica Generativa

RGI, Revue Germanique Internationale

RGL, Reihe Germanistische Linguistik, Tübingen, Niemeyer

RGo, Romanica Gothoburgensia

RGT, Revista Galega de Teatro

RH, Reihe Hanser, Munich, Hanser

RH, Revue Hebdomadaire

RHA, Revista de Historia de America

RHAM, Revue Historique et Archéologique du Maine

RHCS, Rocznik Historii Czasopiśmiennictwa Polskiego

RHDFE, Revue Historique de Droit Français et Étranger

RHE, Revue d'Histoire Ecclésiastique

RHEF, Revue d'Histoire de l'Église de France

RHel, Romanica Helvetica, Tübingen and Basle, Francke

RHFB, Rapports — Het Franse Boek

RHI, Revista da Historia das Ideias

RHis, Revue Historique

RHL, Reihe Hanser Literaturkommentare, Munich, Hanser

RHLF, Revue d'Histoire Littéraire de la France

RHLP, Revista de História Literária de Portugal

RHM, Revista Hispánica Moderna

RHMag, Revue d'Histoire Maghrébine

RHMC, Revue d'Histoire Moderne et Contemporaine

RHPR, Revue d'Histoire et de Philosophie Religieuses

RHR, Réforme, Humanisme, Renaissance

RHRel, Revue de l'Histoire des Religions

RHS, Revue Historique de la Spiritualité

RHSc, Revue d'Histoire des Sciences

RHSt, Ricarda Huch. Studien zu ihrem Leben und Werk

RHT, Revue d'Histoire du Théâtre

RHTe, Revue d'Histoire des Textes

RI, Rassegna Iberistica

RIA, Rivista Italiana di Acustica

RIa, Русский язык

RIAB, Revista Interamericana de Bibliografía

RIaR, Русский язык за рубежом

RICC, Revue Itinéraires et Contacts de Culture

RICP, Revista del Instituto de Cultura Puertorriqueña

RicSl, Ricerche Slavistiche

RID, Rivista Italiana di Dialettologia

RIE, Revista de Ideas Estéticas

RIEB, Revista do Instituto de Estudos Brasileiros

RIL, Rendiconti dell'Istituto Lombardo

RILA, Rassegna Italiana di Linguistica Applicata

RILCE, Revista del Instituto de Lengua y Cultura Españoles

RILP, Revista Internacional da Língua Portuguesa

RIM, Rivista Italiana di Musicologia

RIndM, Revista de Indias

RInv, Revista de Investigación

RIO, Revue Internationale d'Onomastique

RIOn, Rivista Italiana di Onomastica

RIP, Revue Internationale de Philosophie

RIS, Revue de l'Institute de Sociologie, Université Libre, Brussels

RiS, Ricerche Storiche

RITL, Revista de Istorie şi Teorie Literară, Bucharest
RivF, Rivista di Filosofia
RivL, Rivista di Linguistica
RJ, Romanistisches Jahrbuch
RKHlit, Rocznik Komisji Historycznoliterackiej PAN
RKJŁ, Rozprawy Komisji Językowej Łódzkiego Towarzystwa Naukowego
RKJW, Rozprawy Komisji Językowej Wrocławskiego Towarzystwa Naukowego
RLA, Romance Languages Annual
RLaR, Revue des Langues Romanes
RLB, Recueil Linguistique de Bratislava
RLC, Revue de Littérature Comparée
RLD, Revista de Llengua i Dret
RLet, Revista de Letras
RLettI, Rivista di Letteratura Italiana
RLex, Revista de Lexicologia
RLF, Revista de Literatura Fantástica
RLFRU, Recherches de Linguistique Française et Romane d'Utrecht
RLH, Revista de Literatura Hispanoamericana
RLI, Rassegna della Letteratura Italiana
RLib, Rivista dei Libri
RLing, Russian Linguistics
RLiR, Revue de Linguistique Romane
RLit, Revista de Literatura
RLJ, Russian Language Journal
RLLCGV, Revista de Lengua y Literatura Catalana, Gallega y Vasca, Madrid
RLLR, Romance Literature and Linguistics Review
RLM, Revista de Literaturas Modernas, Cuyo
RLMC, Rivista di Letterature Moderne e Comparate
RLMed, Revista de Literatura Medieval
RLMexC, Revista de Literatura Mexicana Contemporánea
RLMod, Revue des Lettres Modernes

RLModCB, Revue des Lettres Modernes. Carnets Bibliographiques
RLSer, Revista de Literatura Ser, Puerto Rico
RLSL, Revista de Lingvisticä şi Ştiinţä Literarä
RLT, Russian Literature Triquarterly
RLTA, Revista de Lingüística Teórica y Aplicada
RLV, Revue des Langues Vivantes
RLVin, Recherches Linguistiques de Vincennes
RM, Romance Monograph Series, University, Mississippi
RM, Remate de Males
RMAL, Revue du Moyen Âge Latin
RMar, Revue Marivaux
RMC, Roma Moderna e Contemporanea
RMEH, Revista Marroquí de Estudios Hispánicos
RMH, Recherches sur le Monde Hispanique au XIXe Siècle
RMM, Revue de Métaphysique et de Morale
RMon, Revue Montesquieu
RMRLL, Rocky Mountain Review of Language and Literature
RMS, Reading Medieval Studies
RMus, Revue de Musicologie
RNC, Revista Nacional de Cultura, Carácas
RNDWSPK, Rocznik Naukowo-Dydaktyczny WSP w Krakowie
RO, Revista de Occidente
RoczH, Roczniki Humanistyczne Katolickiego Uniw. Lubelskiego
RoczSl, Rocznik Slawistyczny
ROl, Rossica Olomucensia
RoM, Rowohlts Monographien, Reinbek, Rowohlt
RomGG, Romanistik in Geschichte und Gegenwart
ROMM, Revue de L'Occident Musulman et de la Méditerranée
RoN, Romance Notes
RoQ, Romance Quarterly
RORD, Research Opportunities in Renaissance Drama
RoS, Romance Studies
RoSl, Роднае слова
RP, Радянський письменник

RP, Revista de Portugal
RPA, Revue de Phonétique Appliquée
RPac, Revue du Pacifique
RPC, Revue Pédagogique et Culturelle de l'AVEP
RPF, Revista Portuguesa de Filologia
RPFE, Revue Philosophique de la France et de l'Étranger
RPh, Romance Philology
RPL, Revue Philosophique de Louvain
RPl, Río de la Plata
RPLit, Res Publica Litterarum
RPM, Revista de Poética Medieval
RPN, Res Publica nowa, Warsaw
RPol, Review of Politics
RPP, Romanticism Past and Present
RPr, Raison Présente
RPS, Revista Paraguaya de Sociologia
RPyr, Recherches pyrénéennes, Toulouse
RQ, Renaissance Quarterly
RQL, Revue Québécoise de Linguistique
RR, Romanic Review
RRe, Русская речь
RRL, Revue Roumaine de Linguistique
RRou, Revue du Rouergue
RRR, Reformation and Renaissance Review
RS, Reihe Siegen, Heidelberg, Winter
RS, Revue de Synthèse
RSBA, Revista de studii britanice și americane
RSC, Rivista di Studi Canadesi
RSCI, Rivista di Storia della Chiesa in Italia
RSEAV, Revue de la Société des enfants et amis de Villeneuve-de-Berg
RSF, Rivista di Storia della Filosofia
RSH, Revue des Sciences Humaines
RSh, Радянська школа
RSI, Rivista Storica Italiana
RSJb, Reinhold Schneider Jahrbuch
RSL, Rusycystyczne Studia Literaturoznawcze
RSl, Revue des Études Slaves

RSLR, Rivista di Storia e Letteratura Religiose
RSPT, Revue des Sciences Philosophiques et Théologiques
RSR, Rassegna Storica del Risorgimento
RSSR, Rivista di Storia Sociale e Religiosa
RST, Rassegna Storica Toscana
RSt, Research Studies
RStI, Rivista di Studi Italiani
RT, Revue du Tarn
RTAM, Recherches de Théologie Ancienne et Médiévale
RTLiM, Rocznik Towarzystwa Literackiego im. Adama Mickiewicza
RTr, Recherches et Travaux, Université de Grenoble
RTUG, Recherches et Travaux de l'Université de Grenoble III
RUB, Revue de l'Université de Bruxelles
RUC, Revista de la Universidad Complutense
RuLit, Ruch Literacki
RUM, Revista de la Universidad de Madrid
RUMex, Revista de la Universidad de México
RUOt, Revue de l'Université d'Ottawa
RUS, Rice University Studies
RusH, Russian History
RusL, Русская литература, ПД, Leningrad
RusM, Русская мысль
RusMed, Russia Medievalis
RusR, Russian Review
RUW, Rozprawy Uniwersytetu Warsawskiego, Warsaw
RVB, Rheinische Vierteljahrsblätter
RVF, Revista Valenciana de Filología
RVi, Revue du Vivarais
RVQ, Romanica Vulgaria Quaderni
RVV, Romanische Versuche und Vorarbeiten, Bonn U.P.
RVVig, Reihe der Villa Vigoni, Tübingen, Niemeyer
RZLG, Romanistische Zeitschrift für Literaturgeschichte
RZSF, Radovi Zavoda za slavensku filologiju

SA, Studien zum Althochdeutschen, Göttingen, Vandenhoeck & Ruprecht
SAB, South Atlantic Bulletin
Sac, Sacris Eruditi
SAG, Stuttgarter Arbeiten zur Germanistik, Stuttgart, Heinz
SAH, Studies in American Humour
SANU, Srpska akademija nauka i umetnosti
SAOB, Svenska Akademiens Ordbok
SAQ, South Atlantic Quarterly
SAR, South Atlantic Review
SAS, Studia Academica Slovaca
SaS, Slovo a slovesnost
SASc, Studia Anthroponymica Scandinavica
SATF, Société des Anciens Textes Français
SAV, Slovenská akadémia vied
SAVL, Studien zur allgemeinen und vergleichenden Literaturwissenschaft, Stuttgart, Metzler
SB, Slavistische Beiträge, Munich, Sagner
SB, Studies in Bibliography
SBAW, Sitzungsberichte der Bayerischen Akad. der Wissenschaften, phil.-hist. Kl., Munich, Beck
SBL, Saarbrücker Beiträge zur Literaturwissenschaft, St. Ingbert, Röhrig
SBL, Старобългарска литература
SBR, Swedish Book Review
SBVS, Saga-Book of the Viking Society
SC, Studia Celtica, The Bulletin of the Board of Celtic Studies
SCB, Skrifter utgivna av Centrum för barnkulturforskning, Stockholm U.P.
SCC, Studies in Comparative Communism
SCen, The Seventeenth Century
SCES, Sixteenth Century Essays and Studies, Kirksville, Missouri, Sixteenth Century Journal
SCFS, Seventeenth-Century French Studies
SchG, Schriftsteller der Gegenwart, Berlin, Volk & Wissen

SchSch, Schlern-Schriften, Innsbruck, Wagner
SchwM, Schweizer Monatshefte
SCJ, Sixteenth Century Journal
SCL, Studii şi Cercetări Lingvistice
SCl, Stendhal Club
ScL, Scottish Language
ScM, Scripta Mediterranea
SCN, Seventeenth Century News
SCO, Studii şi Cercetäri de Onomasticä
ScO, Scriptoralia, Tübingen, Narr
SCR, Studies in Comparative Religion
ScRev, Scandinavian Review
ScSl, Scando-Slavica
ScSt, Scandinavian Studies
SD, Sprache und Dichtung, n.F., Berne, Haupt
SD, Современная драматургия.
SdA, Storia dell'Arte
SDFU, Skrifter utgivna genom Dialekt- och folkminnesarkivet i Uppsala
SDG, Studien zur deutschen Grammatik, Tübingen, Stauffenburg
SDL, Studien zur deutschen Literatur, Tübingen, Niemeyer
SDLNZ, Studien zur deutschen Literatur des 19. und 20. Jahrhunderts, Berne, Lang
SdO, Serra d'Or
SDOFU, Skrifter utgivna av Dialekt-, ortnamns- och folkminnesarkivet i Umeå
SDS, Studien zur Dialektologie in Südwestdeutschland, Marburg, Elwert
SDSp, Studien zur deutschen Sprache, Tübingen, Narr
SDv, Sprache und Datenverarbeitung
SE, Série Esludos Uberaba
SeC, Scrittura e Civiltà
SECC, Studies in Eighteenth-Century Culture
SEDES, Société d'Éditions d'Enseignement Supérieur
SEEA, Slavic and East European Arts
SEEJ, The Slavic and East European Journal

SEER, Slavonic and East European
Review

SEES, Slavic and East European
Studies

SEI, Società Editrice
Internazionale, Turin

SELA, South Eastern Latin
Americanist

SemL, Seminarios de Linguística,
Universidade do Algarve, Faro

SEN, Società Editrice Napoletana,
Naples

SEP, Secretaría de Educación
Pública, Mexico

SeS, Serbian Studies

SEz, Съпоставително
езикознание

SF, Slavistische Forschungen,
Cologne — Vienna, Böhlau

SFAIEO, Section Française de
l'Association Internationale
d'Études Occitanes, Montpellier

SFI, Studi di Filologia Italiana

SFIS, Stanford French and Italian
Studies

SFKG, Schriftenreihe der
Franz–Kafka–Gesellschaft,
Vienna, Braumüller

SFL, Studies in French Literature,
London, Arnold

SFL, Studi di Filologia e Letteratura

SFPS, Studia z Filologii Polskiej i
Słowiańskiej PAN

SFR, Stanford French Review

SFr, Studi Francesi

SFRS, Studia z Filologii Rosyjskiej i
Slowiańskiej, Warsaw

SFS, Swiss-French Studies

SFUŠ, Sborník Filozofickej Fakulty
Univerzity P. J. Šafárika, Prešov

SG, Sprache der Gegenwart,
Düsseldorf, Schwann

SGAK, Studien zu Germanistik,
Anglistik und Komparatistik,
Bonn, Bouvier

SGECRN, Study Group on
Eighteenth-Century Russia
Newsletter

SGEL, Sociedad General Española
de Librería

SGesch, Sprache und Geschichte,
Stuttgart, Klett-Cotta

SGF, Stockholmer Germanistische
Forschungen, Stockholm,
Almqvist & Wiksell

SGG, Studia Germanica Gandensia

SGGed, Studia Germanica
Gedanensia

SGI, Studi di Grammatica Italiana

SGLL, Studies in German
Language and Literature,
Lewiston-Queenston-Lampeter

SGLLC, Studies in German
Literature, Linguistics, and
Culture, Columbia, S.C.,
Camden House, Woodbridge,
Boydell & Brewer

SGP, Studia Germanica
Posnaniensia

SGS, Stanford German Studies,
Berne, Lang

SGS, Scottish Gaelic Studies

SGU, Studia Germanistica
Upsaliensia, Stockholm, Almqvist
& Wiksell

SH, Slavica Helvetica, Berne, Lang

SH, Studia Hibernica

ShAn, Sharq al-Andalus

SHAW, Sitzungsberichte der
Heidelberger Akademie der
Wissenschaften, phil.-hist. Klasse,
Heidelberg, Winter

SHCT, Studies in the History of
Christian Thought, Leiden, Brill

SHPF, Société de l'Histoire du
Protestantisme Français

SHPS, Studies in History and
Philosophy of Science

SHR, The Scottish Historical
Review

SI, Sprache und Information,
Tübingen, Niemeyer

SIAA, Studi di Italianistica
nell'Africa Australe

SiCh, Слово i час

SIDES, Société Internationale de
Diffusion et d'Édition
Scientifiques, Antony

SIDS, Schriften des Instituts für
deutsche Sprache, Berlin, de
Gruyter

Siglo XX, Siglo XX/20th Century

SILTA, Studi Italiani di Linguistica
Teorica ed Applicata

SiN, Sin Nombre

SINSU, Skrifter utgivna av
    institutionen för nordiska språk
    vid Uppsala universitet, Uppsala
    U.P.
SIR, Stanford Italian Review
SISMEL, Società Internazionale
    per lo Studio del Medioevo
    Latino, Edizioni del Galluzzo,
    Florence
SIsp, Studi Ispanici
SISSD, Società Italiana di Studi sul
    Secolo XVIII
SJLŠ, Slovenský jazyk a literatúra v
    škole
SkSt, Skandinavistische Studien
SKZ, Srpska Književna Zadruga,
    Belgrade
SL, Sammlung Luchterhand,
    Darmstadt, Luchterhand
SL, Studia Linguistica
SLÅ, Svensk Lärarföreningens
    Årsskrift
SlaG, Slavica Gandensia
SlaH, Slavica Helsingensia
SlaL, Slavica Lundensia
SlavFil, Славянска филология,
    Sofia
SlavH, Slavica Hierosolymitana
SlavLit, Славянските литератури
    в България
SlavRev, Slavistična revija
SlaW, Slavica Wratislaviensia
SLeg, Studium Legionense
SLeI, Studi di Lessicografia Italiana
SLESPO, Suplemento Literário do
    Estado de São Paulo
SLF, Studi di Letteratura Francese
SLG, Studia Linguistica
    Germanica, Berlin, de Gruyter
SLI, Società di Linguistica Italiana
SLI, Studi Linguistici Italiani
SLIGU, Skrifter utgivna av
    Litteraturvetenskapliga
    institutionen vid Göteborgs
    universitet, Gothenburg U.P.
SLILU, Skrifter utgivna av
    Litteraturvetenskapliga
    institutionen vid Lunds
    universitet, Lund U.P.
SLinI, Studi di Lingua Italiana
SLit, Schriften zur
    Literaturwissenschaft, Berlin,
    Dunckler & Humblot
SLit, Slovenská literatúra

SLitR, Stanford Literature Review
SLIUU, Skrifter utgivna av
    Litteraturvetenskapliga
    institutionen vid Uppsala
    universitet, Uppsala U.P.
SLK, Schwerpunkte Linguistik und
    Kommunikationswissenschaft
SLL, Skrifter utg. genom
    Landsmålsarkivet i Lund
SLM, Studien zur Literatur der
    Moderne, Bonn, Bouvier
SlN, Slovenský národopis
SLO, Slavica Lublinensia et
    Olomucensia
SlO, Slavia Orientalis
SlOc, Slavia Occidentalis
SlOth, Slavica Othinensia
SlPN, Slovenské pedagogické
    nakladateľstvo
SlPoh, Slovenské pohľady
SlPr, Slavica Pragensia
SLPS, Studia Linguistica Polono-
    Slovaca
SLR, Second Language Research
SLRev, Southern Literary Review
SLS, Studies in the Linguistic
    Sciences
SlSb, Slezský sborník
SlSl, Slavica Slovaca
SlSp, Slovenský spisovateľ
SLu, Studia Lulliana
SLWU, Sprach und Literatur in
    Wissenschaft und Unterricht
SM, Sammlung Metzler, Stuttgart,
    Metzler
SM, Studi Medievali
SMC, Studies in Medieval Culture
SME, Schöninghs mediävistische
    Editionen, Paderborn, Schöningh
SMer, Студенческий меридиан
SMGL, Studies in Modern German
    Literature, Berne – Frankfurt –
    New York, Lang
SMLS, Strathclyde Modern
    Language Studies
SMRT, Studies in Medieval and
    Reformation Thought, Leiden,
    Brill
SMS, Sewanee Medieval Studies
SMu, Советский музей
SMV, Studi Mediolatini e Volgari
SN, Studia Neophilologica
SNL, Sveučilišna naklada Liber,
    Zagreb

SNM, Sborník Národního muzea
SNov, Seara Nova
SNTL, Státní nakladatelství technické literatury
SÖAW, Sitzungsberichte der Österreichischen Akademie der Wissenschaften, phil.-hist. Klasse
SOBI, Societat d'Onomastica, Butlleti Interior, Barcelona
SoCR, South Central Review
SOH, Studia Onomastica Helvetica, Arbon, Eurotext: Historisch-Archäologischer Verlag
SoK, Sprog og Kultur
SopL, Sophia Linguistica, Tokyo
SoRA, Southern Review, Adelaide
SoRL, Southern Review, Louisiana
SOU, Skrifter utgivna genom Ortnamnsarkivet i Uppsala
SP, Sammlung Profile, Bonn, Bouvier
SP, Studies in Philology
SPat, Studi Patavini
SpC, Speech Communication
SPCT, Studi e Problemi di Critica Testuale
SPES, Studio per Edizioni Scelte, Florence
SPFB, Sborník Pedagogické fakulty v Brně
SPFFBU, Sborník prací Filosofické fakulty Brněnské Univerzity
SPFFBU-A, Sborník prací Filosofické fakulty Brněnské Univerzity, A - řada jazykovědná
SPGS, Scottish Papers in Germanic Studies, Glasgow
SPh, Studia philologica, Olomouc
SPi, Serie Piper, Munich, Piper
SPIEL, Siegener Periodicum zur Internationalen Empirischen Literaturwissenschaft
SPK, Studia nad polszczyzną kresową, Wrocław
SpLit, Sprache und Literatur
SpMod, Spicilegio Moderno, Pisa
SPN, Státní pedagogické nakladatelství
SPol, Studia Polonistyczne
SPR, Slavistic Printings and Reprintings, The Hague, Mouton
SpR, Spunti e Ricerche

SPRF, Société de Publications Romanes et Françaises, Geneva, Droz
SPS, Specimina Philologiae Slavicae, Munich, Otto Sagner
SPS, Studia Philologica Salmanticensia
SPSO, Studia Polono–Slavica–Orientalia. Acta Litteraria
SpSt, Spanish Studies
SPUAM, Studia Polonistyczna Uniwersytetu Adama Mickiewicza, Poznań
SR, Slovenská reč
SRAZ, Studia Romanica et Anglica Zagrabiensia
SRev, Slavic Review
SRF, Studi e Ricerche Francescane
SRL, Studia Romanica et Linguistica, Frankfurt, Lang
SRLF, Saggi e Ricerche di Letteratura Francese
SRo, Studi Romanzi
SRom, Studi Romeni
SRoP, Studia Romanica Posnaniensia
SRP, Studia Rossica Posnaniensia
SRU, Studia Romanica Upsaliensia
SS, Symbolae Slavicae, Frankfurt–Berne–Cirencester, Lang
SS, Syn og Segn
SSBI, Skrifter utgivna av Svenska barnboksinstitutet
SSB, Strenna Storica Bolognese
SSCJ, Southern Speech Communication Journal
SSDSP, Società Savonese di Storia Patria
SSE, Studi di Storia dell'Educazione
SSF, Studies in Short Fiction
SSFin, Studia Slavica Finlandensia
SSGL, Studies in Slavic and General Linguistics, Amsterdam, Rodopi
SSH, Studia Slavica Academiae Scientiarum Hungaricae
SSL, Studi e Saggi Linguistici
SSLF, Skrifter utgivna av Svenska Litteratursällskapet i Finland
SSLP, Studies in Slavic Literature and Poetics, Amsterdam, Rodopi
SSLS, Studi Storici Luigi Simeoni

SSMP, Stockholm Studies in Modern Philology

SSPHS, Society for Spanish and Portuguese Historical Studies, Millersville

SSS, Stanford Slavic Studies

SSSAS, Society of Spanish and Spanish-American Studies, Boulder, Colorado

SSSlg, Sagners Slavistische Sammlung, Munich, Sagner

SSSN, Skrifter utgivna av Svenska språknämnden

SSSP, Stockholm Studies in Scandinavian Philology

SST, Sprache — System und Tätigkeit, Frankfurt, Lang

SSt, Slavic Studies, Hokkaido

ST, Suhrkamp Taschenbuch, Frankfurt, Suhrkamp

ST, Studi Testuali, Alessandria, Edizioni dell'Orso

StB, Studi sul Boccaccio

StBo, Studia Bohemica

STC, Studies in the Twentieth Century

StCJ, Studia Celtica Japonica

STCL, Studies in Twentieth Century Literature

StCL, Studies in Canadian Literature

STCM, Sciences, techniques et civilisations du moyen âge à l'aube des temps modernes. Paris, Champion

StCrit, Strumenti Critici

StD, Studi Danteschi

StF, Studie Francescani

StFil, Studia Filozoficzne

STFM, Société des Textes Français Modernes

StG, Studi Germanici

StGol, Studi Goldoniani

StH, Studies in the Humanities

StI, Studi Italici, Kyoto

StIt, Studi Italiani

StL, Studium Linguistik

StLa, Studies in Language, Amsterdam

StLI, Studi di Letteratura Ispano-Americana

StLi, Stauffenburg Linguistik, Tübingen, Stauffenburg

StLIt, Studi Latini e Italiani

StLM, Studies in the Literary Imagination

StLo, Studia Logica

STM, Suhrkamp Taschenbuch Materialien, Frankfurt, Suhrkamp

StM, Studies in Medievalism

STML, Studies on Themes and Motifs in Literature, New York, Lang

StMon, Studia Monastica

StMus, Studi Musicali

StMy, Studia Mystica

StN, Studi Novecenteschi

StNF, Studier i Nordisk Filologi

StO, Studium Ovetense

StP, Studi Piemontesi

StPet, Studi Petrarcheschi

StR, Studie o rukopisech

StRLLF, Studi e Ricerche di Letteratura e Linguistica Francese

StRmgn, Studi Romagnoli

StRo, Studi Romani

StRom, Studies in Romanticism

StRu, Studia Russica, Budapest

StS, Studi Storici

StSec, Studi Secenteschi

StSem, Studia Semiotyczne

StSet, Studi Settecenteschi

StSk, Studia Skandinavica

STSL, Studien und Texte zur Sozialgeschichte der Literatur, Tübingen, Niemeyer

StT, Studi Tassiani

STUF, Sprachtypologie und Universalienforschung

StV, Studies on Voltaire and the 18th Century

STW, Suhrkamp Taschenbücher Wissenschaft, Frankfurt, Suhrkamp

StZ, Sprache im technischen Zeitalter

SU, Studi Urbinati

SUBBP, Studia Universitatis Babeş-Bolyai, Philologia, Cluj

SUDAM, Editorial Sudamericana, Buenos Aires

SuF, Sinn und Form

SUm, Schede Umanistiche

SUP, Spisy University J. E. Purkyně, Brno

SupEz, Съпоставително
езикознание, Sofia
SV, Studi Veneziani
SVEC, Studies in Voltaire and the
Eighteenth Century, Oxford,
Voltaire Foundation (formerly
StV)
SZ, Studia Zamorensia

TAL, Travaux d'Archéologie
Limousine, Limoges
TAm, The Americas, Bethesda
TAPS, Transactions of the
American Philosophical Society
TB, Tempo Brasileiro
TBL, Tübinger Beiträge zur
Linguistik, Tübingen, Narr
TC, Texto Critico
TCBS, Transactions of the
Cambridge Bibliographical
Society
TCERFM, Travaux du Centre
d'Études et de Recherches sur
François Mauriac, Bordeaux
TCL, Twentieth-Century Literature
TCLN, Travaux du Cercle
Linguistique de Nice
TCWAAS, Transactions of the
Cumberland and Westmorland
Antiquarian and Archaeological
Society
TD, Teksty Drugie
TDC, Textes et Documents pour la
Classe
TEC, Teresiunum Ephemerides
Carmeliticae
TECC, Textos i Estudis de Cultura
Catalana, Curial — Publicacions
de l'Abadia de Montserrat,
Barcelona
TeK, Text und Kontext
TELK, Trouvaillen — Editionen
zur Literatur- und
Kulturgeschichte, Berne, Lang
TeN, Terminologies Nouvelles
TeSt, Teatro e Storia
TE(XVIII), Textos y Estudios del
Siglo XVIII
TF, Texte zur Forschung,
Darmstadt, Wissenschaftliche
Buchgesellschaft
TFN, Texte der Frühen Neuzeit,
Frankfurt, Keip

TGLSK, Theorie und Geschichte
der Literatur und der Schönen
Künste, Munich, Fink
TGSI, Transactions of the Gaelic
Society of Inverness
THESOC, Thesaurus Occitan
THL, Theory and History of
Literature, Manchester U.P.
THM, Textos Hispánicos
Modernos, Barcelona, Labor
THR, Travaux d'Humanisme et
Renaissance, Geneva, Droz
THSC, Transactions of the
Honourable Society of
Cymmrodorion
TI, Le Texte et l'Idée
TidLit, Tidskrift för
Litteraturvetenskap
TILAS, Travaux de l'Institut
d'Études Latino-Américaines de
l'Université de Strasbourg
TILL, Travaux de l'Institut de
Linguistique de Lund
TJ, Theatre Journal
TK, Text und Kritik, Munich
TKS, Търновска книжевна
школа, Sofia
TL, Theoretical Linguistics
TLF, Textes Littéraires Français,
Geneva, Droz
TLit, Travaux de Littérature
TLP, Travaux de Linguistique et de
Philologie
TLQ, Travaux de Linguistique
Québécoise
TLTL, Teaching Language
Through Literature
TM, Les Temps Modernes
TMJb, Thomas Mann-Jahrbuch
TMo, O Tempo e o Modo
TMS, Thomas-Mann Studien,
Frankfurt, Klostermann
TN, Theatre Notebook
TNA, Tijdschrift voor Nederlands
en Afrikaans
TNT, Towarzystwo Naukowe w
Toruniu
TOc, Tèxtes Occitans, Bordeaux
TODL, Труды Отдела
древнерусской литературы
Института русской
литературы АН СССР
TP, Textual Practice
TPa, Torre de Papel

TPS, Transactions of the Philological Society
TQ, Theatre Quarterly
TR, Телевидение и радиовещание
TravL, Travaux de Linguistique, Luxembourg
TRCTL, Texte-Revue de Critique et de Théorie Littéraire
TRI, Theatre Research International
TRISMM, Tradition — Reform — Innovation. Studien zur Modernität des Mittelalters, Frankfurt, Lang
TrK, Трезвость и культура
TrL, Travaux de Linguistique
TrLit, Translation and Literature
TRS, The Transactions of the Radnorshire Society
TS, Theatre Survey
TSC, Treballs de Sociolingüística Catalana
TSDL, Tübinger Studien zur deutschen Literatur, Frankfurt, Lang
TSJ, Tolstoy Studies Journal
TSL, Trierer Studien zur Literatur, Frankfurt, Lang
TSLL, Texas Studies in Literature and Language
TSM, Texte des späten Mittelalters und der frühen Neuzeit, Berlin, Schmidt
TsNTL, Tijdschrift voor Nederlandse Taal- en Letterkunde
TSRLL, Tulane Studies in Romance Languages and Literature
TsSk, Tijdschrift voor Skandinavistiek
TsSV, Tijdschrift voor de Studie van de Verlichting
TSWL, Tulsa Studies in Women's Literature
TT, Tekst en Tijd, Nijmegen, Alfa
TT, Travail Théâtral
TTAS, Twayne Theatrical Arts Series, Boston–New York
TTG, Texte und Textgeschichte, Tübingen, Niemeyer
TTr, Terminologie et Traduction

TUGS, Texte und Untersuchungen zur Germanistik und Skandinavistik, Frankfurt, Lang
TVS, Theorie und Vermittlung der Sprache, Frankfurt, Lang
TWAS, Twayne's World Authors Series, Boston–New York
TWQ, Third World Quarterly

UAB, Universitat Autònoma de Barcelona
UAC, Universidad de Antioquia, Colombia
UAM, Uniwersytet Adama Mickiewicza, Poznań
UB, Universal-Bibliothek, Stuttgart, Reclam
UBL, Universal-Bibliothek, Leipzig, Reclam
UCLWPL, UCL Working Papers in Linguistics
UCPL, University of California Publications in Linguistics
UCPMP, University of California Publications in Modern Philology
UDL, Untersuchungen zur deutschen Literaturgeschichte, Tübingen, Niemeyer
UDR, University of Dayton Review
UERJ, Universidade Estadual do Rio de Janeiro
UFPB, Universidade Federal da Paraiba
UFRGS, Univ. Federal do Rio Grande do Sul (Brazil)
UFRJ, Universidade Federal do Rio de Janeiro
UFSC, Universidade Federal de Santa Catarina
UFSM, Universidade Federal de Santa Maria
UGE, Union Générale d'Éditions
UGFGP, University of Glasgow French and German Publications
UL, Українське літературознавство, Lvov U.P.
UM, Українська мова і література в школі
UMCS, Uniwersytet Marii Curie-Skłodowskiej, Lublin
UMov, Українське мовознавство
UNAM, Universidad Nacional Autónoma de Mexico

UNC, Univ. of North Carolina

UNCSGL, University of North Carolina Studies in Germanic Languages and Literatures, Chapel Hill

UNED, Universidad Nacional de Enseñanza a Distancia

UNESP, Universidade Estadual de São Paulo

UNMH, University of Nottingham Monographs in the Humanities

UPP, University of Pennsylvania Press, Philadelphia

UQ, Ukrainian Quarterly

UR, Umjetnost riječi

USCFLS, University of South Carolina French Literature Series

USFLQ, University of South Florida Language Quarterly

USH, Umeå Studies in the Humanities, Stockholm, Almqvist & Wiksell International

USLL, Utah Studies in Literature and Linguistics, Berne, Lang

USP, Universidade de São Paulo

UTB, Uni-Taschenbücher

UTET, Unione Tipografico-Editrice Torinese

UTPLF, Università di Torino, Pubblicazioni della Facoltà di Lettere e Filosofia

UTQ, University of Toronto Quarterly

UVAN, Українська Вільна Академія Наук, Winnipeg

UVK, Universitätsverlag Konstanz

UVWPL, University of Venice Working Papers in Linguistics

UWCASWC, The University of Wales Centre for Advanced Studies in Welsh and Celtic

UZLU, Ученые записки Ленинградского университета

VAM, Vergessene Autoren der Moderne, Siegen U.P.

VAS, Vorträge und Abhandlungen zur Slavistik, Giessen, Schmitz

VASSLOI, Veröffentlichungen der Abteilung für Slavische Sprachen und Literaturen des Osteuropa–Instituts (Slavistiches Seminar) an der Freien Universität Berlin

VB, Vestigia Bibliae

VBDU, Веснік Беларускага дзяржаўнага ўніверсітэта імя У. І. Леніна. Серыя IV

VCT, Les Voies de la Création Théâtrale

VDASD, Veröffentlichungen der Deutschen Akademie für Sprache und Dichtung, Darmstadt, Luchterhand

VF, Вопросы философии

VGBIL, Всесоюзная государственная библиотека иностранной литературы

VH, Vida Hispánica, Wolverhampton

VHis, Verba Hispanica

VI, Военно издателство

VI, Voix et Images

VIa, Вопросы языкознания

VIN, Veröffentlichungen des Instituts für niederländische Philologie, Erftstadt, Lukassen

ViSH, Вища школа

VIst, Вопросы истории

Vit, Вітчизна

VKP, Всесоюзная книжная палата

VL, Вопросы литературы

VLet, Voz y Letras

VM, Время и мы, New York — Paris — Jerusalem

VMKA, Verslagen en Mededelingen, Koninklijke Academie voor Nederlandse Taal- en Letterkunde

VMUF, Вестник Московского университета. Серия IX, филология

VMUFil, Вестник Московского университета. Серия VII, философия

VÖAW, Verlag der Österreichischen Akademie der Wissenschaften, Vienna

Voz, Возрождение

VP, Встречи с прошлым, Moscow

VPen, Vita e Pensiero

VR, Vox Romanica

VRKhD, Вестник Русского христианского движения

VRL, Вопросы русской литературы

VRM, Volkskultur am Rhein und Maas

VS, Вопросы семантики

VSAV, Vydavateľstvo Slovenskej akadémie vied

VSh, Вышэйшая школа

VSh, Визвольний шлях

VSPU, Вестник Санкт-Петербургского университета

VSSH, Вечерняя средняя школа

VV, Византийский временник

VVM, Vlastivědný věstník moravský

VVSh, Вестник высшей школы

VWGÖ, Verband der wissenschaftlichen Gesellschaften Österreichs

VySh, Вища школа

VysSh, Высшая школа

VyV, Verdad y Vida

VZ, Vukova zadužbina, Belgrade

WAB, Wolfenbütteler Arbeiten zur Barockforschung, Wiesbaden, Harrassowitz

WADL, Wiener Arbeiten zur deutschen Literatur, Vienna, Braumüller

WAGAPH, Wiener Arbeiten zur germanischen Altertumskunde und Philologie, Berne, Lang

WAiF, Wydawnictwa Artystyczne i Filmowe, Warsaw

WaT, Wagenbachs Taschenbücherei, Berlin, Wagenbach

WB, Weimarer Beiträge

WBDP, Würzburger Beiträge zur deutschen Philologie, Würzburg, Königshausen & Neumann

WBG, Wissenschaftliche Buchgesellschaft, Darmstadt

WBN, Wolfenbütteler Barock-Nachrichten

WF, Wege der Forschung, Darmstadt, Wissenschaftliche Buchgesellschaft

WGCR, West Georgia College Review

WGY, Women in German Yearbook

WHNDL, Würzburger Hochschulschriften zur neueren Deutschen Literaturgeschichte, Frankfurt, Lang

WHR, The Welsh History Review

WIFS, Women in French Studies

WKJb, Wissenschaftskolleg. Institute for Advanced Study, Berlin. Jahrbuch

WL, Wydawnictwo Literackie, Cracow

WŁ, Wydawnictwo Łódzkie

WLub, Wydawnictwo Lubelskie

WLT, World Literature Today

WM, Wissensliteratur im Mittelalter, Wiesbaden, Reichert

WNB, Wolfenbütteler Notizen zur Buchgeschichte

WNT, Wydawnictwa Naukowo-Techniczne

WoB, Wolfenbütteler Beiträge

WoF, Wolfenbütteler Forschungen, Wiesbaden, Harrassowitz

WP, Wiedza Powszechna, Warsaw

WPEL, Working Papers in Educational Linguistics

WPFG, Working Papers in Functional Grammar, Amsterdam U.P.

WRM, Wolfenbütteler Renaissance Mitteilungen

WS, Wort und Sinn

WSA, Wolfenbütteler Studien zur Aufklärung, Tübingen, Niemeyer

WSiP, Wydawnictwa Szkolne i Pedagogiczne, Warsaw

WSJ, Wiener Slavistisches Jahrbuch

WSl, Die Welt der Slaven

WSlA, Wiener Slawistischer Almanach

WSP, Wyższa Szkoła Pedagogiczna

WSp, Word and Spirit

WSPRRNDFP, Wyższa Szkoła Pedagogiczna w Rzeszowie. Rocznik Naukowo-Dydaktyczny. Filologia Polska

WSS, Wiener Studien zur Skandinavistik

WUW, Wydawnictwo Uniwersytetu Wrocławskiego

WuW, Welt und Wort

WW, Wirkendes Wort

WWAG, Woman Writers in the Age of Goethe

WWE, Welsh Writing in English. A Yearbook of Critical Essays

WZHUB, Wissenschaftliche Zeitschrift der Humboldt- Universität, Berlin: gesellschafts- und sprachwissenschaftliche Reihe

WZPHP, Wissenschaftliche Zeitschrift der pädagogischen Hochschule Potsdam. Gesellschafts- und sprachwissenschaftliche Reihe

WZUG, Wissenschaftliche Zeitschrift der Ernst-Moritz- Arndt- Universität Greifswald

WZUH, Wissenschaftliche Zeitschrift der Martin-Luther- Universität Halle-Wittenberg: gesellschafts- und sprachwissenschaftliche Reihe

WZUJ, Wissenschaftliche Zeitschrift der Friedrich-Schiller- Universität Jena / Thüringen: gesellschafts-und sprachwissenschaftliche Reihe

WZUL, Wissenschaftliche Zeitschrift der Karl Marx Universität Leipzig: gesellschafts- und sprachwissenschaftliche Reihe

WZUR, Wissenschaftliche Zeitschrift der Universität Rostock: gesellschafts- und sprachwissenschaftliche Reihe

YaIS, Yale Italian Studies
YB, Ysgrifau Beirniadol
YCC, Yearbook of Comparative Criticism
YCGL, Yearbook of Comparative and General Literature
YDAMEIS, Yearbook of the Dutch Association for Middle Eastern and Islamic Studies
YEEP, Yale Russian and East European Publications, New Haven, Yale Center for International and Area Studies
YES, Yearbook of English Studies
YFS, Yale French Studies
YIP, Yale Italian Poetry
YIS, Yearbook of Italian Studies
YJC, Yale Journal of Criticism
YM, Yearbook of Morphology

YPL, York Papers in Linguistics
YR, Yale Review
YSGP, Yearbook. Seminar for Germanic Philology
YSPS, The Yearbook of the Society of Pirandello Studies
YWMLS, The Year's Work in Modern Language Studies

ZÄAK, Zeitschrift für Ästhetik und allgemeine Kunstwissenschaft
ZB, Zeitschrift für Balkanologie
ZBL, Zeitschrift für bayerische Landesgeschichte
ZbS, Zbornik za slavistiku
ZCP, Zeitschrift für celtische Philologie
ZD, Zielsprache Deutsch
ZDA, Zeitschrift für deutsches Altertum und deutsche Literatur
ZDL, Zeitschrift für Dialektologie und Linguistik
ZDNÖL, Zirkular. Dokumentationsstelle für neuere österreichische Literatur
ZDP, Zeitschrift für deutsche Philologie
ZFKPhil, Zborník Filozofickej fakulty Univerzity Komenského. Philologica
ZFL, Zbornik za filologiju i lingvistiku
ZFSL, Zeitschrift für französische Sprache und Literatur
ZGB, Zagreber germanistische Beiträge
ZGer, Zeitschrift für Germanistik
ZGKS, Zeitschrift der Gesellschaft für Kanada-Studien
ZGL, Zeitschrift für germanistische Linguistik
ZGS, Zürcher germanistische Studien, Berne, Lang
ZK, Zeitschrift für Katalanistik
ZL, Zeszyty Literackie, Paris
ZMS(FL), Zbornik Matice srpske za filologiju i lingvistiku
ZMS(KJ), Zbornik Matice srpske za književnost i jezik
ZMS(Sl), Zbornik Matice srpske za slavistiku

ZNiO, Zakład Narodowy im. Ossolińskich, Wrocław

ZnS, Знание — сила

ZNTSh, Записки Наукового товариства ім. Шевченка

ZNUG, Zeszyty Naukowe Uniw. Gdańskiego, Gdańsk

ZNUJ, Zeszyty Naukowe Uniw. Jagiellońskiego, Cracow

ZNWHFR, Zeszyty Naukowe Wydziału Humanistycznego. Filologia Rosyjska

ZNWSPO, Zeszyty Naukowe Wyższej Szkoły Pedagogicznej w Opolu

ZO, Zeitschrift für Ostforschung

ZPŠSlav, Zborník Pedagogickej fakulty v Prešove Univerzity Pavla Jozefa Šafárika v Košiciach-Slavistika, Bratislava

ZR, Zadarska revija

ZRAG, Записки русской академической группы в США

ZRBI, Зборник радова бизантолошког института, Belgrade

ZRL, Zagadnienia Rodzajów Literackich

ZRP, Zeitschrift für romanische Philologie

ZS, Zeitschrift für Sprachwissenschaft

ZSJ, Zápisnik slovenského jazykovedca

ZSK, Ze Skarbca Kultury

ZSL, Zeitschrift für siebenbürgische Landeskunde

ZSl, Zeitschrift für Slawistik

ZSP, Zeitschrift für slavische Philologie

ZSVS, Zborník Spolku vojvodinských slovakistov, Novi Sad

ZT, Здесь и теперь

ZV, Zeitschrift für Volkskunde

ZvV, Звезда востока

ZWL, Zeitschrift für württembergische Landesgeschichte

NAME INDEX